What's New in 2013

Standard Deduction. The standard deduction amounts for 2013 are $12,200 for married individuals filing jointly and surviving spouses, $8,950 for heads of households, and $6,100 for unmarried individuals and married individuals filing separately.

Itemized Deductions. The amount of itemized deductions claimed in 2013 is subject to phaseout for higher income taxpayers. The threshold phase-out amount for joint and surviving spouse filers is $300,000, for head of household filers is $275,000, for unmarried filers is $250,000, and for married separate filers is $150,000.

Exemptions. The amount of a personal exemption, and of each dependency exemption, claimed in 2013 is $3,900. The exemption deduction is also subject to phase out in 2013 for higher-income taxpayers. The threshold phase-out amounts are the same as for the phase out of itemized deductions.

Standard Mileage Rates. The standard mileage rate for business miles driven in 2013 is 56.5 cents per mile.

Earned Income Credit. The maximum earned income credit amount for 2013 for taxpayers with no children is $487; with one child is $3,250, with two children is $5,372, and with three or more children is $6,044. The earned income credit is not available to taxpayers with investment income exceeding $3,300.

Net Investment Income (NII) Tax. Taxpayers with modified adjusted gross income (MAGI) in excess of $250,000 if filing jointly or as a surviving spouse ($125,000 if married filing separately; $200,000 for all others) will pay an additional 3.8 percent tax on their net investment income. The amount subject to the tax is the lesser of their net investment income or the amount by which their MAGI exceeds the threshold amount for their filing status.

Additional Medicare Tax. An additional 0.9-percent additional Medicare tax is assessed against earned income in excess of the threshold amount for the taxpayer's filing status beginning in 2013. The threshold amounts are $250,000 for joint and surviving spouse filers, $125,000 for married filing separate filers, and $200,000 for all others.

D1302875

Section at a Glance

Tax Preparer's Checklist

☐ Ensure that all Form W-2s and 1099s are available. Be sure to compare these current forms and amounts to those reported on prior year tax returns.

☐ Ensure that the Social Security number is correct on all Form W-2s and 1099s.

☐ Be sure to request paperwork for the purchase of any stock sold appearing on Form 1099-B.

Relevant IRS Publications

☐ IRS Publication 3, *Armed Forces' Tax Guide*

☐ IRS Publication 17, *Your Federal Income Tax*

☐ IRS Publication 501, *Exemptions, Standard Deduction, and Filing Information*

☐ IRS Publication 504, *Divorced or Separated Individuals*

☐ IRS Publication 519, *U.S. Tax Guide for Aliens*

☐ IRS Publication 521, *Moving Expenses*

☐ IRS Publication 525, *Taxable and Nontaxable Income*

2013 Tax Brackets by Filing Status

Tax Rate*	Single	MFJ or SS	MFS	HOH
10%	$ 0 – 8,925	$ 0 – 17,850	$ 0 – 8,925	$ 0 – 12,750
15%	8,926 – 36,250	17,851 – 72,500	8,926 – 36,250	12,751 – 48,600
25%	36,251 – 87,850	72,501 – 146,400	36,251 – 73,200	48,601 – 125,450
28%	87,851 – 183,250	146,401 – 223,050	73,201 – 111,525	125,451 – 203,150
33%	183,251 – 398,350	223,051 – 398,350	111,526 – 199,175	203,151 – 398,350
35%	398,351 - 400,000	398,351 - 450,000	199,176 - 225,000	398,351 - 425,000
39.6%	Over $400,000	Over $450,000	Over $225,000	Over $425,000

* See Tab 17 for tax tables.

Taxpayer Information

Form 1040 is the principal form for use by individual taxpayers. Even if a taxpayer is eligible to file Form 1040A or Form 1040EZ, Form 1040 may still be used. See MTG ¶105 for requirements to be eligible to file Form 1040A or Form 1040EZ.

Who Must File Form 1040

Individuals who are U.S. citizens or resident aliens, and whose gross income exceeds the amount shown in the following table for their filing status and age, must file an income tax return for 2013. However, even if gross income is less than the amount shown, an individual must still file a return if he or she:

- had net earnings from self-employment of at least $400; or
- had wages of $108.28 or more from a church or qualified religious organization that is exempt from employer Social Security and Medicare taxes.

In addition, any taxpayer who owes any of the following special taxes must file a return:

- Social Security and Medicare taxes on tips not reported to an employer;
- uncollected Social Security, Medicare, or railroad retirement tax on tips reported to an employer;
- the alternative minimum tax;
- household employment taxes;
- additional tax on a qualified retirement plan, including an IRA calculated on Form 5329;
- additional tax on a health savings account (HSA), Archer MSA, Coverdell education savings account (ESA) or qualified tuition program calculated on Form 5329; or
- recapture of certain tax credits and other benefits as reported on line 44 (see page 1-35) and line 60 (see page 1-38), such as the education credit, investment credit, and the credit for alternative fuel vehicle refueling property.

If a taxpayer must file a return only due to the additional tax owed on a qualified retirement plan or IRA, then Form 5329 may be filed by itself. Similarly, if the taxpayer is filing a return only because household employment taxes are due, then Schedule H may be filed by itself. If an individual had income from a U.S. possession, then see IRS Publication 570.

Who Must File a Return in 2013

Filing Status	Age	Gross Income of at Least
Single	Under 65	$ 10,000
	65 or older	11,500
Married Filing Jointly[1]	Under 65 (both spouses)	20,000
	65 or older (one spouse)	21,200
	65 or older (both spouses)	22,400
Qualifying Widow(er) with dependent child	Under 65	16,100
	65 or older	17,300
Married Filing Separately	Any age	3,900
Head of Household	Under 65	12,850
	65 or older	14,350
Single, if may be claimed as a dependent on another return	Under 65	Greater of $1,000 or earned income (up to $5,750) + $350[2]
	65 or older or blind	Greater of $2,500 or earned income (up to $5,750) + $1,850[3]
	65 or older and blind	Greater of $4,000 or earned income (up to $5,750) + $3,350[4]
Married, if may be claimed as a dependent on another return[5]	Under 65	Greater of $1,000 or earned income (up to $5,750) + $350[2]
	65 or older or blind	Greater of $2,200 or earned income (up to $5,750) + $1,550[6]
	65 or older and blind	Greater of $3,400 or earned income (up to $5,750) + $2,750[7]

[1] If spouses lived apart at the end of 2013, Married Filing Separately floor applies.
[2] Taxpayer must also file if unearned income is over $1,000 or earned income is over $6,100.
[3] Taxpayer must also file if unearned income is over $2,500 or earned income is over $7,600.
[4] Taxpayer must also file if unearned income is over $4,000 or earned income is over $9,100.
[5] Taxpayer must also file if income is greater than $5 and spouse itemizes deductions on a separate return.
[6] Taxpayer must also file if unearned income is over $2,200 or earned income is over $7,300.
[7] Taxpayer must also file if unearned income is over $3,400 or earned income is over $8,500.

Special Filing Requirements

Children. If a child is required to file a return, then the investment income of the child may be taxed at the parents' highest marginal rate. This is referred to as the "kiddie tax" and is discussed at Tab 13 and  MTG ¶103. However, the child's parents may elect to report the child's income on their return if the child had only interest and dividend income of more than $1,000 and less than $10,000, had no federal income tax withheld, and made no estimated tax payments. The parents make the election on Form 8814 which must be filed with their return. If the election is made, the child does not need to file a separate return.

 Planning Tip. The election to report a child's income on a parent's return has consequences for the parent's adjusted gross income dependent deductions (for example, medical expenses). Thus, it is best to determine the tax consequences of the election prior to deciding whether to make the election or not.

Resident and Nonresident Aliens. A resident alien is subject to the same filing requirements that apply to U.S. citizens. A nonresident alien, on the other hand, is taxed only on U.S.-source income and must use Form 1040NR to file a tax return if the individual has more than $3,900 in gross income for 2013 or was engaged in a trade or business in the United States during the year. Students, teachers, or trainees under F, J, M, or Q visas are required to file Form 1040NR only if they have taxable income.

For this purpose, an individual (other than a U.S. citizen) is considered a resident alien if he or she:

- is a lawful permanent resident of the United States during the tax year (has a "green card"); or
- was present in the United States for 31 days in the current tax year and a total of 183 days during the current and two proceeding calendar years (all of the days of physical presence in the United States during the current year count as one full day, while each day in the proceeding year counts as one-third of a day, and each day in the second proceeding year counts as one-sixth of a day).

Any alien individual that fails to meet either of these requirements will be considered a nonresident alien. However, even if the substantial presence test is met, an individual can still be treated as a nonresident alien if they can establish (using Form 8840) that during the tax year they:

- were present in the United States for less than 183 days,
- had a tax home in a foreign country, and
- had a closer connection to a foreign country in which they had the tax home.

See MTG ¶2409.

A nonresident alien may elect to be treated as a resident alien for the entire tax year if he or she is married to a U.S. citizen or resident alien on the last day of the tax year. Both spouses must join in the election and the couple must file a joint tax return. The election is effective for the current tax year and all subsequent tax years.

A nonresident alien may also elect resident status for the current calendar year if he or she was a nonresident alien for the entire preceding year. The election can only be made if the individual was present for at least 31 consecutive days during the year and 75 percent of the days in the year beginning with the first day of the 31-day period through the end of the year. See MTG ¶2410.

 Caution. Practitioners should always consult the applicable tax treaty and protocols, if any, prior to preparing an income tax return of a nonresident alien.

Expatriates. U.S. citizens who have relinquished their citizenship and long-term residents whose residency has been terminated may be subject to special rules following their expatriation from the United States. If an individual expatriates, he or she will be subject to a mark-to-market tax regime under which he or she is considered to have sold all of his or her property on the date before expatriation. See MTG ¶2412.

Personal Information and SSN

The taxpayer must include his or her name, address, and Social Security number (SSN) on Form 1040 in the space provided. If filing a joint return, then the names of both spouses must be provided and the SSNs of both spouses must be provided in the same order as the couple's names. If a taxpayer changed his or her name because of marriage, divorce, etc., then the change should be reported to the Social Security Administration before filing the tax return.

 **Planning Tip.** For married taxpayers filing jointly, the same order of the couple's names and SSNs should be used on all forms and documents submitted to the IRS as on Form 1040 for the current tax year and all subsequent tax years to avoid any problems.

ITINs. The IRS will issue an individual taxpayer identification number (ITIN) to any resident or nonresident alien who does not have and is not eligible to get an SSN. Form W-7 is used to apply for an ITIN. This number is used on a tax return wherever an SSN is requested.

Taxpayer's Address. Taxpayers whose address changes from the address shown on their last return may use Form 8822 to notify the IRS. The IRS also uses the U.S. Post Office's database to update taxpayer addresses.

Presidential Election Campaign Contribution

Each taxpayer, who is required to file an income tax return, may elect to designate $3 to the presidential election campaign fund. In the case of joint filers, each spouse may make their own designation. The amount of refund or tax owed is unaffected by this choice.

Filing Status, Lines 1-5

There are five categories of filing status that apply to individual taxpayers to determine tax rates, standard deduction, and eligibility for certain deductions. Filing status for the 2013 tax year is determined as of December 31, 2013. If more than one filing status applies to a taxpayer, choose the one that results in the lowest tax.

Filing Tip. Tax return preparers must be sure that the taxpayer provides all information relevant to determining filing status. See sample interview in Tab 16.

Single/Unmarried

A taxpayer may file as single if he or she was never married during the tax year, or was divorced or legally separated as of December 31, 2013, or was widowed before January 1, 2013, and did not remarry during the year. However, a single taxpayer may file as a head of household (see page 1-6) or qualifying widow(er) (see page 1-7) if certain requirements are met.

Caution. The U.S. Supreme Court ruled that section 3 of the Defense of Marriage Act (DOMA), defining marriage as between a man and woman only, to be unconstitutional in the case of *E.S. Windsor*, SCt. 2013-2 USTC ¶50,400. This ruling would apparently allow legally married same-sex couples in the District of Columbia and the thirteen states that recognize same-sex marriages to file a joint federal income tax return. The Supreme Court opinion specifically stated, however, that they were not ruling on the constitutionality of section 2 of DOMA, which allows the states to determine whether the state will recognize same-sex marriages. Also, the issue of treatement of registared domestic partners and civil unions in certain states that have granted these couples the same rights as a married couple is unresolved. For the latest information, visit CCHGroup.com/TaxUpdates.

Married Filing Jointly

Couples who are married and not legally separated as of December 31, 2013, may elect to file a joint return for the year, even if the couple lived apart at the end of the year. See MTG ¶152. This includes common-law and same-sex marriages recognized by the state in which the union was created.

Planning Tip. The IRS issued Rev. Rul. 2013-17 providing filing status guidance for same-sex married couples (SSMC) following the U.S. Supreme Court decision in *E.S. Windsor* (2013-2 USTC ¶50,400) holding that section 3 of the Defense of Marriage Act (P.L. 104-199), which stated only a man and a woman can be considered married for federal purposes, is unconstitiutional. The revenue ruling states that, effective as of September 16, 2013, same-sex couples married in a state that recognizes same-sex marriages must file as either married filing joint or married filing separate. This guidance is applicable to all open tax years for those taxpayers that elect to amend returns for earlier tax years. The IRS made this an elective choice and is not requiring same-sex married couples to amend prior-year returns. At the time of publication, the District of Columbia, California, Connecticut, Delaware, Iowa, Maine, Maryland. Massachusetts, Minnesota, New Hampshire, New Jersey, New York, Rhode Island, Vermont, and Washingtion are the only jurisdictions recognizing same-sex marriages.

Caution. The IRS will not allow registered domestic partners, civil unions or any other similar relationships to use married filing joint or separate filing status even if state law extends all the same rights and privileges to them as if they were married.

 Gray Area. The IRS also announced that additional guidance would be forthcoming to deal with other issues arising from this change in policy. For the latest information, go to CCHGroup.com/TaxUpdates, and click on the link to 1040 Express Answers.

Generally, a joint return may not be filed if either spouse is a nonresident alien during the year. However, if a nonresident alien or dual-status alien is married to a U.S. citizen or resident at the end of the year, the nonresident may elect to be treated as a resident alien in order for the couple to file a joint return (see page 1-3).

 Caution. Annulment is treated differently than divorce. Since an annulment means the couple was never legally married, any tax returns that were filed as married filing separately or married filing jointly must be amended if the tax year is still open.

If a couple files a joint return, then both spouses are generally responsible for the tax and any interest and penalties due on the return. For this reason, both spouses must generally sign the return (see page 1-44). Once a joint return is filed, the couple cannot choose to file separate returns for that year if the due date for the return has passed. However, the executor of a deceased spouse may disaffirm a joint return and file a separate return within one year of the return due date including extensions.

Surviving Spouse. If a married taxpayer dies during the year, the surviving spouse may elect to file a joint return with the deceased spouse provided the surviving spouse did not remarry during the year. For the next two years, the taxpayer may then be able to file as a qualifying widow(er) provided there is a qualifying child dependent who resides with him or her in his or her principal residence (see page 1-7). In the case of a spouse of a member of the Armed Forces serving in a combat zone and listed as missing, a joint return may be filed for up to two years following the termination of combat activities. The return is valid even if it is later determined that the missing spouse died before the year covered in the return. See MTG ¶175.

Married Filing Separately

Married individuals who do not elect to file a joint return usually have to file as married filing separately. Married filing separately status generally results in higher tax liability than filing a joint return. However, in some cases, filing separate returns may result in a lower tax liability (such as when one spouse has deductions that are subject to an AGI limitation). See the table on page 1-6 and MTG ¶156 for information related to the decision to file jointly or separately.

If a married individual lives apart from his or her spouse at the end of the tax year, then the individual may elect head-of-household filing status if certain conditions are met (see below). However, a married couple must file separately when one spouse is a nonresident alien, unless the election to be treated as a resident alien is made (see page 1-3).

 Caution. When one spouse uses the married filing separately status, the other spouse must also use that filing status unless they qualify for head-of-household filing status. Tax preparers should request that their client make every effort to ascertain the filing status of the other spouse and whether they are going to itemize their deductions. This is because, if one spouse itemizes deductions, then the other must also itemize unless he or she qualifies for head-of-household filing status. A good practice is to always explain thoroughly the consequences of the married filing separately status to clients. Be sure to note on the file that you had this discussion or have the client sign a statement to the effect that you have explained the consequences.

How To File. If a couple files as married filing separately, each spouse must report only his or her own income, exemptions, deductions, and credits on his or her return. In most states, income is allocated to the spouse who earned it. Interest is allocated to the spouse who owned the property or account that earned the interest. Expenses paid from separate funds are treated as paid by the spouse who owned the funds. Expenses paid from joint funds are treated as though each spouse paid half unless otherwise proven.

If the couple resides in a community property state, then income is considered community income, and half is allocable to each spouse regardless of who earned it. See MTG ¶710 and ¶711, and IRS Publication 555. Community property states are Arizona, California, Idaho, Louisiana, Nevada, New Mexico, Texas, Washington, and Wisconsin.

Head of Household

An unmarried person who provides a home for a qualifying person(s) may file as head of household, entitling the individual to a lower tax rate and higher standard deduction than allowed for single individuals or married individuals filing separately. See MTG ¶173. A taxpayer may file as head of household only if:

- he/she is a U.S. citizen or resident alien for the entire tax year;
- he/she is unmarried or "considered unmarried" on the last day of the year;
- he/she paid more than half the cost of keeping up a home in which he or she lives for the year; and
- the taxpayer's household is the principal place of abode for a "qualifying person" for more than half of the year.

Considered Unmarried. To qualify for head-of-household status, an individual must actually be unmarried or "considered unmarried" on the last day of the tax year. An individual is considered unmarried if:

Choosing Married Filing Separately Filing Status

Advantages

- No joint liability. Married taxpayers who file separate returns are not liable for the accuracy of their spouse's returns or for the payment of their spouse's tax.
- If one spouse owes child support or federal debts for which a tax refund may be offset, the other spouse's refund is not at risk.
- Some couples pay less tax. If one spouse has large itemized deductions subject to AGI limits (medical expenses or employee expenses), these deductions may result in a lower tax when the spouses file separately.

Disadvantages

- Tax rate is generally higher than on a joint return.
- The standard deduction is half the amount allowed on a joint return.
- If one spouse itemizes deductions, the other cannot claim the standard deduction.
- Exemption amount for figuring the AMT is half of that allowed on a joint return.
- Capital loss deduction limit is $1,500 (instead of the $3,000 limit for a joint return).
- Amount excluded from income under an employer's dependent care assistance program is limited to $2,500 (instead of the $5,000 limit for a joint return).

Deductions and credits reduced at lower income levels:
- Deduction for personal exemptions
- Itemized deductions
- Child tax credit
- Retirement savings contributions credit

Ineligible for:
- Credit for child and dependent care expenses, in most cases
- Earned income credit
- Exclusion or credit for adoption expenses, in most cases
- Education credits (American Opportunity (modified Hope scholarship) and lifetime learning) and the deduction for student loan interest
- Cannot exclude any interest income from qualified U.S. savings bonds that was used for higher education expenses

If spouses lived together at any time during the tax year:
- Ineligible for credit for the elderly or the disabled
- Must include in income up to 85% of Social Security benefits or equivalent railroad retirement benefits
- Cannot roll over amounts from a traditional IRA into a Roth IRA

- he/she files a separate return;
- he/she paid more than half the cost of keeping up his or her home for the tax year;
- his/her spouse did not live in the home during the last six months of the tax year;
- his/her home was the principal place of abode of their child, stepchild, adopted child, or foster child for more than half of the tax year; *and*
- he/she can claim the child as a dependent (unless the child's other parent can claim the child under the rules for divorced or separate parents, see page 1-11).

If an individual's spouse was a nonresident alien at any time during the year, then the taxpayer will be considered unmarried and eligible for head-of-household filing status unless the election is made to treat the nonresident alien spouse as a resident alien (see page 1-3). However, the nonresident alien spouse is not a qualifying person for head-of-household purposes. In addition, the taxpayer will still be considered married for purposes of the earned income credit.

 Caution. A taxpayer must actually be unmarried (as opposed to being "considered unmarried") to claim any person other than his or her child as a qualifying person for head-of-household status. Thus, a married taxpayer who claims someone other than his or her child as the qualifying person (parent, niece, nephew, etc.) does not qualify for head-of-household status, even if all of the other head-of-household requirements are met.

Keeping Up a Home. To qualify for head-of-household status, an individual must have paid more than half of the cost of keeping up his or her home during the tax year. For this purpose, the cost of keeping up a home includes rent, property tax, mortgage interest, utilities, repairs, food consumed on the premises, and other household expenses. It does not include the costs for education, medical treatment, life insurance, transportation, clothing, or payments received under any public assistance program to pay part of the cost of keeping up a home (for example, Temporary Assistance for Needy Families (TANF)).

Qualifying Person. For purposes of head-of-household filing status, a qualifying person with whom the taxpayer must live includes:

- any qualifying child of the taxpayer (see page 1-8) if:
  - the child is single (whether or not the taxpayer can claim an exemption for the child) or
  - the child is married and the taxpayer can claim an exemption for the child;

- the taxpayer's parent for whom he or she can claim an exemption; or
- any qualifying relative of the taxpayer other than a parent (see page 1-10) who lived with the taxpayer for more than half of the tax year, is related to the taxpayer, and for whom an exemption can be claimed.

A person cannot be a qualifying person for more than one taxpayer for the tax year for purposes of head-of-household filing status. Also, if an exemption can be claimed for a person only because of a multiple support agreement (see page 1-11), that person cannot be a qualifying person.

Example. Jonathan is an unmarried individual. His sister Margaret lived in a home for the developmentally disabled for all of 2013. Margaret had no income during the year and Jonathan provided all of her support. Jonathan can claim Margaret as a dependent on his tax return since she is a qualifying relative under the definitions for a dependent. Margaret, however, is not a qualifying person for Jonathan for purposes of head-of-household filing status since she did not live with him for more than half the year. Jonathan must file as a single individual.

A taxpayer and a qualifying person are considered to live together even when one or both are temporarily absent from the home due to illness, education, business, vacation, or military service, so long as the home is continuously maintained during the absence. Also, a taxpayer may still file as head of household if the qualifying person is born or dies during the year, so long as the taxpayer kept up the home that was the qualifying person's main home for more than half the time the qualifying person was alive.

Qualifying Widow(er)

An individual may file as a qualifying widow(er) in 2013 if all of the following apply:

- the taxpayer's spouse died in 2011 or 2012 and the taxpayer did not remarry as of December 31, 2013;
- the taxpayer was entitled to file a joint return with the deceased spouse for the year in which the spouse died (it does not matter whether a joint return was actually filed); and
- the taxpayer paid over half of the cost of maintaining his or her home during 2013, and the home was the principal residence of the taxpayer's child or stepchild for whom the taxpayer may claim an exemption (foster children do not qualify).

Exemptions, Lines 6a-6d

A taxpayer can deduct $3,900 for each personal and dependency exemption claimed in 2013. The exemption amount is not reduced in the event of the death of the taxpayer, spouse, or dependent during the year. See MTG ¶149.

Personal Exemptions

A taxpayer can claim a personal exemption if he or she cannot be claimed as a dependent by anyone else. On a joint return, a personal exemption can be claimed for each spouse. If married individuals file separate returns, each spouse claims his or her own personal exemption. However, one spouse may claim the personal exemption of the other spouse on a separate return if the other spouse has no gross income, is not filing a return, and is not a dependent of another taxpayer. If one spouse dies during the year, then the surviving spouse may still claim the personal exemption of the deceased spouse on either a joint or separate return, but only if the surviving spouse does not remarry during the year.

 Caution. A taxpayer (or his or her spouse) who *may* be claimed as a dependent on another person's return may not claim his or her own personal exemption (or spouse's personal exemption) even if the exemption is not actually claimed on the other person's return. This is particularly important to remember in the case of college students living at home. See Tab 13.

Dependency Exemption

A taxpayer is allowed to claim an exemption for each person he or she can claim as a dependent. A person can be claimed as a dependent only if he or she is a "qualifying child" or a "qualifying relative" of the taxpayer. However, even if a person is a qualifying child or qualifying relative of a taxpayer, a dependency exemption can only be claimed for the individual if:

- the taxpayer (or spouse, if filing a joint return) may not be claimed as a dependent by another person;
- the qualifying child or qualifying relative is a U.S. citizen, U.S. national, resident alien, or a resident of Canada or Mexico, for part of the year (however, an exception exists for a child legally adopted by a U.S. citizen or U.S. national if the child is a member of the taxpayer's household for the entire year);
- the qualifying child or qualifying relative is not married filing a joint return for the tax year (unless the joint return was only filed as a claim for refund and there is no tax liability for either spouse on separate returns).

A Social Security number (SSN) must be reported by the taxpayer for each person he or she claims as a dependent. If the dependent does not have a SSN or cannot get one as in the case of a resident or nonresident alien, as well as an adoptee, then the taxpayer must provide the dependent's taxpayer identification number (ITIN) or adoption taxpayer identification number (ATIN) in the case of a domestic adoption still pending.

If a child was born and died during the tax year and no SSN was obtained, then enter "DIED" in column (2) of line 6c next to the child's name and attach a copy of the child's birth certificate, death certificate, or hospital records. A child born alive during the year may be claimed as an exemption for the entire year, even if he or she dies during the year. However, a stillborn child may not be claimed.

 Caution. The dependency exemption amount is denied to claimants who fail to provide the dependent's correct SSN or ITIN on the return. The exemption may also be denied if the SSN or ITIN fails to match the name on file with the Social Security Administration (SSA).

Qualifying Child. There are five requirements for an individual to be considered a qualifying child of a taxpayer.

 Filing Tip. An individual who is not a "qualifying child" of the taxpayer because of failure to meet any one of these requirements may still be claimed as a dependent by the taxpayer if the individual meets the requirements for being a "qualifying relative" of the taxpayer (see page 1-10).

1. *Relationship.* In order to be a qualifying child, an individual must be the taxpayer's:

- child, stepchild, adopted child, foster child, or a descendant of any of them; or
- brother, sister, step-brother, step-sister, half-brother, half-sister, or a descendant of any of them (for example, niece or nephew).

An adopted child includes any child lawfully placed with the taxpayer for legal adoption. A foster child is any child placed with the taxpayer by an authorized placement agency or by a judgment or decree issued by a court.

2. *Residency.* The individual must have resided with the taxpayer for more than one-half of the year in the same principal place of abode to be a qualifying child. Temporary absences for illness, education, business, vacation, or military service may count as time lived with the taxpayer. Special rules apply in the case of children of divorced or separated parents (see page 1-11). In addition, a child who is born or dies during the tax year will be considered as living with the taxpayer for the entire year if the taxpayer's home was the child's home for the entire time he or she was alive.

If a child is presumed by law enforcement authorities to have been kidnapped by someone who is not a member of the family of the child or the taxpayer, and the child shared the same principal place of abode as the taxpayer for more than half of the portion of the year preceding the kidnapping, then the child satisfies the residency test for all tax years ending during the period in which the child is missing. A missing child ceases to satisfy the residency test in the taxpayer's first tax year beginning after the calendar year in which the child is determined to be dead or, if earlier, in which the child would have attained the age of 18.

3. *Age Requirement.* A qualifying child is an individual who is:

- under the age of 19 at the end of the calendar year;
- under the age of 24 at the end of the calendar year and a full-time student for at least five calendar months during the year; or
- permanently and totally disabled at any time during the calendar year, regardless of age.

To meet the age test, an individual who is not permanently and totally disabled must be younger than the taxpayer or spouse if married filing jointly; the individual does not have to be younger than both, only one of the married taxpayers. For example, a taxpayer's older brother or sister could not be the taxpayer's qualifying child unless the taxpayer's spouse is older than the sibling.

4. *Support.* The individual must **not** provide over one-half his or her own support during the year to be a qualifying child. For this purpose, a scholarship received by a child who is a full-time student is not considered. This test is different from the support test to be a qualifying relative or to be eligible for head-of-household filing status (see page 1-6).

Example. Jasmine is 19 years old and a full-time student. She lives with her father but only receives one-third of her support from him. The remaining two-thirds of her support comes from a trust set up by her grandmother. As a result, Jasmine is not a qualifying child of her father. The trust income is attributable to Jasmine and she therefore provides more than half of her own support.

5. *Joint Return.* An individual cannot be a qualifying child of another taxpayer if he or she files a joint tax return with his or her spouse for the year unless the joint return is filed *solely* as a claim for refund (for example, a refund of taxes withheld from wages).

Caution. A taxpayer is already prohibited from claiming a dependency exemption for an individual who files a joint tax return for the year. Thus, the separate return requirement does not affect who is a qualifying child for the purposes of claiming a dependency exemption. However, because the definition of a qualifying child is used for claiming other tax benefits, the separate return requirement applies to claiming those benefits (see below).

Qualifying Child of More Than One Person. An individual may meet the requirements to be a qualifying child of more than one taxpayer. However, only one taxpayer can claim the person as a qualifying child for purposes of the following tax benefits (unless the special rule for children of divorced or separated parents applies, see page 1-11):

- dependency exemption;
- child tax credit;
- head-of-household filing status;
- dependent care credit;
- exclusion of dependent care benefits; and
- earned income tax credit.

If two taxpayers have the same qualifying child, they cannot agree to divide these tax benefits between themselves. Instead, they can only decide who will treat the child as a qualifying child for purposes of all of the tax benefits. However, if the taxpayers cannot agree and more than one tax return is filed claiming the same child as a qualifying child, then the IRS will disallow all but one of the claims based on the following ordering rules:

- if only one of the taxpayers is the child's parent, then the child is the qualifying child of the parent;

- if child's parents do not file a joint return, then the child is the qualifying child of the parent with whom the child lived with the longest during the year;
- if the child resided with both parents equally during the year and the parents do not file a joint return, then the child is the qualifying child of the parent with the highest adjusted gross income;
- if none of the taxpayers claiming the child are the child's parent, then the child is the qualifying child of the person with the highest AGI; or
- if the parents may claim the child as a qualifying child, but do not actually do so, then the child may be the qualifying child of any other taxpayer but only if his or her AGI is higher than the AGI of either parent.

Special rules apply in determining how a noncustodial parent may claim a child as a qualified child (see page 1-11).

Qualifying Relative(s). There are four requirements for a person to be considered a qualifying relative of a taxpayer for purposes of the dependency exemption.

1. *Not a Qualifying Child.* A person is not a qualifying relative of a taxpayer if that person meets the requirements for being a qualifying child of any other taxpayer. However, if the other taxpayer is not required to file a return for the year or files a return *solely* as a claim for refund, then the child is not a qualifying child of the other taxpayer.

> **Example.** Mary and her infant son from another relationship move in with her boyfriend Jeff in 2013. Mary has $8,500 of earned income in 2013 from which income taxes were withheld. Even though she is not required to file a return for the year, she files one anyway to obtain a refund of the withheld taxes and to claim the earned income tax credit. If Mary and Jeff remain unmarried to each other during the year, the child is the qualifying child of Mary. The child cannot be the qualifying relative of Jeff even if all other requirements are met because Mary did not file her return solely as a claim for refund.

2. *Relationship or Member of Household Test.* To be a qualifying relative of a taxpayer, a person must have either lived in the taxpayer's home all year as a member of the household or be related to the taxpayer (or spouse, if filing a joint return) by one of these relationships:

- child, stepchild, adopted child, foster child, or a descendant of any of them;
- brother, sister, half-brother, half-sister, step-brother, or step-sister;

- parent, grandparent, or other direct ancestor (other than foster parent), as well as any step-parent;
- brother or sister of the taxpayer's parent (aunt or uncle), as well as any son or daughter of the taxpayer's brother or sister (niece or nephew); or
- father-in-law, mother-in-law, son-in-law, daughter-in-law, brother-in-law, or sister-in-law.

A person is considered to live in the taxpayer's home as a member of the household even if he or she (or the taxpayer) is temporarily absent due to vacation, education, business, illness, or military service. A person who died during the tax year, but lived in the taxpayer's home as a member of household until death also qualifies. Likewise, a dependent born during the year who becomes a member of the household immediately after birth is considered a household member for the entire year.

3. *Gross Income Test.* To be a qualifying relative of a taxpayer, a dependent's gross income for 2013 must be less than $3,900. Gross income includes all income in the form of money, property, and services that is not exempt from tax, such as receipts from rental property, a partner's share of gross partnership income, taxable unemployment compensation, and taxable scholarship and fellowship grants. Gross income does not include income received by a disabled individual for services performed at a sheltered workshop, if the availability of medical services is the primary reason for participation. See MTG ¶143.

4. *Support Test.* In order for a person to be a qualifying relative, the taxpayer must have provided over half of the person's total support during the calendar year. Thus, it is the taxpayer's responsibility to prove not only the support he or she provided to the person, but also the total support the person received during the year, including tax-exempt interest, savings, and borrowed amounts. See MTG ¶147.

"Total support" includes amounts spent to provide food, shelter, clothing, education, medical and dental care, transportation, and similar necessities. Expenses that are not directly related to any one member of a household must be divided among members of the household.

Items **not** included in total support include:

- the person's own funds that are not actually spent for support;
- federal, state, and local income taxes paid by persons from their own income;
- Social Security and Medicare taxes paid by persons from their own income;
- life insurance premiums;
- funeral expenses;

- scholarships received by a taxpayer's child if the child is a full-time student; and
- Survivors' and Dependents' Educational Assistance and Aid to Families with Dependent Children (AFDC) payments used for support of the child who receives them.

> **Example.** Grace lives with her son David and his two children during the year. She had $4,400 in Social Security income during the year, which she used to pay $1,200 in life insurance premiums and $2,200 in medical expenses. The fair rental value of the lodging provided to Grace is $2,400 for the year. David paid all of his mother's other expenses, including an additional $1,200 in medical expenses and $1,000 for other items such as clothing, transportation, and entertainment. He also spent $5,200 in total food expenses for the household. Grace's total support for the year was $7,900. The support David provides to his mother is more than half of her total support ($2,400 lodging + $1,200 medical expenses + $1,300 share of food + $1,000 miscellaneous items).

In most cases, a child of divorced or separated parents will be the qualifying child of one of the parents. However, if the child does not meet the requirements to be a qualifying child of either parent, the child may be a qualifying relative of one of the parents. In this case, the parent who has custody of the child for the greater part of the year as determined under the most recent divorce decree or separate maintenance agreement is generally treated as providing more than half of the child's support for the year, regardless of whether they did or not.

> **Example.** Dana and Casey, a divorced couple, jointly provided for all of their child's total support for 2013. Dana provided 25 percent of the support and Casey provided 75 percent. For the first eight months of the year, Dana had custody of the child under the couple's 2006 divorce decree. On August 31, 2013, a new custody decree granted custody to Casey. Since Dana had custody for the greater part of the year, she is considered to have provided more than half of the child's support during the year.

For special rules on how a noncustodial parent may claim a child as a qualified child or qualified relative, see the discussion at *"Children of Divorced or Separated Parents,"* following.

Multiple Support Agreements. Sometimes no one taxpayer provides more than half of the support of a dependent in order to be a qualifying relative. Instead, two or more persons, each of whom would be able to take the exemption except for the support test, together may provide more than half of the person's support.

When this happens, the taxpayers who provide more than 10 percent of the dependent's support during the year can agree that any one of them may claim the exemption. Each of the other taxpayers must sign a statement agreeing not to claim the exemption for that year. The person who claims the exemption must keep these statements with his or her tax records. A multiple support declaration identifying each of the others who agreed not to claim the exemption must also be attached to the return of the taxpayer claiming the exemption. Form 2120 is used for this purpose.

> **Example.** Three children provided the entire support for their mother for the tax year. Alice provided 55 percent, Bob provided 35 percent and Cliff provided 10 percent. Provided the other requirements for the qualifying relative test are met, either Alice or Bob may claim a dependency exemption for their mother, so long as the other one signs a statement agreeing not to take the exemption. Since Cliff did not provide more than 10 percent of the support, he cannot claim the exemption and Alice or Bob do not have to get a signed statement from him to claim the exemption.

> **Planning Tip.** Several things should be taken into consideration in determining which taxpayer will claim a dependent under a multiple support agreement.
> First, low-income taxpayers do not receive as large a tax advantage in the claiming the exemption because their tax rate is lower. For example, it is generally more advantageous for a taxpayer in the 15 percent tax bracket to relinquish the exemption to a taxpayer in the 28 percent tax bracket.
> Second, medical expenses paid by a taxpayer for someone who is claimed as a dependent by another taxpayer under a multiple support agreement are not deductible. Only the taxpayer claiming the exemption is entitled to deduct medical expenses paid on behalf of the dependent.

Children of Divorced or Separated Parents. Generally, a child of divorced or separated parents is the qualifying child or qualifying relative of the parent who has primary custody of the child during the year. However, a child may be treated as the qualifying child or qualifying relative of the noncustodial parent if:

- the parents are divorced, legally separated, separated under a written separation agreement, or lived apart at all times during the last six months of the calendar year;
- one or both parents provide more than half of the child's total support for the calendar year (determined without regard to any multiple support agreement);
- one or both parents have custody of the child for more than half of the calendar year; and
- the custodial parent makes a written declaration that he or she will not claim the exemption and the noncustodial parent attaches the declaration to his or her tax return for each year the exemption is claimed.

For this purpose, the custodial parent is the parent with whom the child resides for the greater number of nights during the calendar year. Temporary absences count toward the parent the child would have resided with for the night (for example, sleepover at a friend's home or nights on vacation). If the child resides with each parent for an equal number of nights during the year, then the parent with the highest AGI is the custodial parent.

 Caution. A State court order or divorce decree will not apply to allocate the dependency exemption between divorced or separated parents. The rules discussed above are the sole means for determining which parent may claim the exemption.

Form 8332 must be used by the custodial parent to make a written declaration to release the dependency exemption to the noncustodial parent. The release must be signed by the custodial parent and specify the year or years for which it is effective. If it specifies that it applies to all future years, then it is effective the first tax year after the year it is executed. The release must not be conditioned on the noncustodial parent meeting some obligation such as the payment of child support or alimony. The custodial parent may revoke the release for future tax years by providing a written notice of the revocation to the noncustodial parent. A copy of the revocation must be attached to the custodial parent's return for any year he or she claims the exemption as a result of the revocation.

 Planning Tip. The noncustodial parent must attach the signed Form 8332 to his or her return to claim the dependency exemption for the child. If the exemption is released for more than one year, then the original release must be attached to the return for the first year, and a copy must be attached for each later year. The dependency exemption cannot be claimed by a noncustodial parent who merely attaches pages from a divorce decree or separation agreement to his or her return, instead of to Form 8332.

 Filing Tip. Taxpayers filing their returns electronically, must file Form 8332 with Form 8453.

If all of the above requirements are met, the noncustodial parent may only claim a child as a qualifying child for purposes of the dependency exemption, the child tax credit, and any education credits attributable to education expenses paid for the child by the noncustodial parent. The custodial parent may still claim the child as a qualifying child for purpose of head-of-household filing status, dependent care credit, the exclusion of dependent care benefits, and the earned income credit, even if the dependency exemption is released.

However, the child may be treated as a dependent by both parents for purposes of deducting and excluding certain medical and fringe benefits from gross income regardless of whether or not the custodial parent releases the dependency exemption. This includes:

- itemized medical deductions of the taxpayer's child;
- employer medical reimbursements for medical care of an employee's child;
- employer-provided health insurance on behalf of the employee's children;
- fringe benefits for no-additional-cost services or qualified employee discounts due to use by an employee's child; and
- distributions from HSAs and Archer MSAs used to pay qualified medical expenses of the account beneficiary's child.

Overview of the Rules for Claiming an Exemption for a Dependent

- If the taxpayer, or the taxpayer's spouse if filing a joint return, can be claimed as a dependent by another taxpayer, then the taxpayer cannot claim any dependent.

- The taxpayer cannot claim a married person who files a joint return as a dependent unless that joint return is only a claim for refund and there would be no tax liability for either spouse on separate returns.

- The taxpayer cannot claim a person as a dependent unless that person is a U.S. citizen, U.S. national, resident alien, or a resident of Canada or Mexico, for some part of the year.[1]

- The taxpayer cannot claim a person as a dependent unless that person is a qualifying child or qualifying relative.

Tests to Be a Qualifying Child	Tests to Be a Qualifying Relative
1. The child must be the taxpayer's son, daughter, stepchild, eligible foster child, brother, sister, half-brother, half-sister, step-brother, step-sister, or descendant of any of them.	1. The person cannot be the qualifying child of any other taxpayer unless the other taxpayer is not required to file a return for the year or files solely as a claim for refund.
2. The child must be (a) under age 19 at the end of the calendar year and younger than either the taxpayer or the taxpayer's spouse (if filing jointly), (b) under age 24 at the end of the calendar year, a full-time student, and younger than either the taxpayer or the taxpayer's spouse (if filing jointly), or (c) any age if permanently and totally disabled.	2. The person must either (a) live with the taxpayer the entire year as a member of the taxpayer's household,[2] or (b) be related to the taxpayer (or spouse, if filing a joint return) as their child or descendant of a child, sibling, parent, grandparent, step-parent, aunt, uncle, niece, nephew, or in-law.
3. The child must have lived with the taxpayer for more than half of the year.[2]	3. The person's gross income for the year must be less than $3,900.[3]
4. The child must not have provided more than half of his or her own support for the year.	4. The taxpayer must provide more than half of the person's total support for the tax year.[4]
5. If the child meets the rules to be a qualifying child of more than one taxpayer, only one of them may claim the child as a qualifying child for the dependency exemption and other tax benefits.	

[1]   There is an exception for certain adopted children.
[2]   There are exceptions for temporary absences, children who were born or died during the year, children of divorced or separated parents, and kidnapped children.
[3]   There is an exception if the person is disabled and has income from a sheltered workshop.
[4]   There is an exception for multiple support agreements.

Income, Lines 7-22

Generally, all income from whatever source except those items specifically exempted is taxable. Note that some types of income may not be reported to the taxpayer. Not all payers are required to provide an information return (e.g., Form W-2 or 1099) to the recipient. This does not excuse the taxpayer from reporting these unreported amounts as income. See the chart beginning on page 1-23 of common gross income inclusions and exclusions, and where to report includible income.

Line 7, Wages, Salaries, Tips, Etc.

Report on line 7, the taxpayer's (and spouse's, if filing a joint return) wages, salaries, fees, and other compensation earned for personal services performed during the year, including taxable fringe benefits, employee bonuses or awards, employer reimbursements, etc. (see MTG ¶713). For most people, the amount to enter is reported in box 1 of Form W-2. However, other amounts to report on line 7 include:

- wages earned as a household employee for which the employer was not required to issue a Form W-2 because the amount was less than $1,800 in 2013 (enter "HSH" and the amount not reported on Form W-2 on the dotted line next to line 7);
- taxable dependent care benefits (box 10 of Form W-2 and Form 2441);
- taxable adoption assistance provided by an employer (box 12 of Form W-2, code T, and Form 8839);
- strike and lockout benefits provided by a union;
- elective salary deferrals and designated Roth contributions (box 12 of Form W-2, Codes D through H, S, Y, AA, or BB) to the extent they exceed the excludable amount for the year (see Tab 9); or
- disability pensions received before retirement age (Form 1099-R).

Filing Tip. If the "statutory employee" box on Form W-2 is checked, do not enter the amount from box 1 on Form 1040, line 7. Instead, enter the amount on Schedule C, line 1. For a discussion of statutory employees see Tab 3 and MTG ¶941B.

Missing or Incorrect Form W-2. Employers are required to report wages and other earnings paid to an employee in 2013 on Form W-2 by January 31, 2014. A taxpayer who does not receive the form by that date, or receives an incorrect form, should always first contact the employer. If the taxpayer has not received a Form W-2 or corrected Form W-2 by February 15, 2014, then the taxpayer should contact the IRS.

If the taxpayer does not receive a Form W-2 or corrected Form W-2 from the employer by April 15, 2014, then Form 4852 should be used as a substitute for Form W-2 to estimate wages and earnings for the year, as well as taxes withheld from wages. The substitute can usually be created from the taxpayer's last paycheck received from the employer for 2013. The taxpayer should also check his or her Social Security Statement received after the end of the tax year.

 Filing Tip. If the taxpayer receives a Form W-2 from the employer after his or her tax return is filed, and the information differs from that reported on Form 4852, then the taxpayer must file an amended return to match the information reported on Form W-2.

If the taxpayer is convinced that amounts reported to him or her by an employer as self-employment income on Form 1099 are actually wages, then Form 8919 should be used to calculate the taxpayer's unreported Social Security and Medicare taxes from the income. This occurs if the employer misclassifies the taxpayer as an independent contractor, rather than an employee. The income the taxpayer receive should be reported as wages on line 7 and the taxes are included on line 57 (see page 1-37).

 Filing Tip. If the taxpayer is convinced that income he or she receives is from wages and not self-employment, Form SS-8 should also be submitted to request a determination from the IRS of the taxpayer's status for purposes of federal employment taxes and income tax withholding. Submission of Form SS-8, however, does not relieve the taxpayer from timely filing and paying any income and employment taxes due.

Tips. All tips received by the taxpayer are income subject to tax including tips paid by cash, check, debit or credit card, or received in noncash items such as tickets or passes. If the taxpayer received $20 or more of tips in a month, then the tips must be reported to the taxpayer's employer on Form 4070 by the 10th day of the following month. If the taxpayer worked for more than one employer in any month, then the $20 rule applies separately to the tips received while working for each employer and not the total received. The taxpayer may use Form 4070A (found in IRS Publication 1244) to maintain a daily record of tips received.

Tips reported to an employer are included in box 1 of Form W-2 and reported on line 7 of Form 1040. The taxpayer must also include on line 7, all tips not reported to the employer on Form 4070. In addition, the taxpayer's employer may allocate tips to employees under a tip-splitting or tip-pooling arrangement. Allocated tips are reported separately in box 8 of Form W-2 and must be included as wages on line 7, unless the taxpayer can prove a lesser amount was received. See IRS Publication 531 for more information.

Example. John Allen began working at the Diamond Restaurant (his only employer for the year) on June 30 and received $10,000 in wages during the year. John kept a daily tip record showing that his tips for June were $18 and his tips for the rest of the year totaled $7,000. He was not required to report his June tips to his employer, but he reported all of the rest of his tips to his employer as required. John's Form W-2 from Diamond Restaurant shows $17,000 ($10,000 in wages plus $7,000 in reported tips) in box 1. He adds the $18 in unreported tips to that amount and reports $17,018 on line 7 of his tax return.

If the taxpayer received $20 or more in tips in a month from any one job and did not report all of those tips to his or her employer, then Social Security and Medicare taxes on the unreported tips must be paid. The taxpayer must also pay Social Security and Medicare taxes on all allocated tips reported on line 8 of Form W-2. Form 4137 is used to figure these taxes. They are then reported on line 57 of Form 1040. In addition, if an employer cannot collect all the Social Security and Medicare taxes the taxpayer owes on tips reported for the tax year, then the uncollected taxes will be shown in box 12 of Form W-2 (Codes A and B). Those taxes must also be reported on line 57 of Form 1040 (see page 1-37).

Scholarships and Fellowship Grants. A taxpayer who is a candidate for a degree can exclude from income amounts received as a scholarship or fellowship grant that is used for tuition to attend school or fees, books, supplies and equipment required for his or her studies. Any amount used for other expenses, such as room and board, is taxable and must be included on line 7 (enter "SCH" and the taxable amount next to line 7). See Tab 13 and MTG ¶879.

Military Personnel. Generally, any payment a taxpayer receives as a member of the U.S. Armed Forces is treated as wages and reported in box 1 of Form W-2 and on line 7 of Form 1040. However, certain items are excluded from income including retirement pay (which is taxed as a pension), certain allowances (living, moving, traveling, family, death), and combat zone pay (see MTG ¶895). In addition, the taxpayer may elect to treat excludable combat pay as earned income for purposes of determining the earned income credit, the refundable portion of the child tax credit (see Tab 10) and deductible contributions to an IRA (see page 1-31).

Planning Tip. Differential wage payments made by an employer to an active member of the U.S. uniformed services will be reported as wages in box 1 of Form W-2 for income tax withholding purposes. However, the wages will not be subject to FICA or FUTA taxes.

Workers' Compensation. Amounts received as workers' compensation for an occupational sickness or injury are fully exempt from tax if they are paid under a workers' compensation act or similar statute. The exemption also applies to survivors. The exemption, however, does not apply to retirement plan benefits received based on age, length of service, or prior contributions to the plan, even if retirement was due to an occupational sickness or injury. In addition, if part of the workers' compensation reduces Social Security or equivalent railroad retirement benefits, that part is considered Social Security benefits and may be taxable. For more information, see MTG ¶851 and IRS Publication 915.

Filing Tip. Sick pay received by an employee is generally taxable regardless of whether paid directly by an employer or through an insurance company. Sick pay generally means any amount paid under a plan because of an employee's temporary absence from work due to injury, sickness, or disability. However, it does not include disability retirement pay, workers' compensation, medical expense payments, or any other payments unrelated to absence from work.

Lines 8a and 8b, Interest

Interest income is generally reported to the taxpayer on Form 1099-INT (or Form 1099-OID), or on Schedule K-1 of Form 1065 or Form 1120S. The taxpayer's total taxable interest is reported on line 8a. However, the taxpayer must also complete Schedule B of Form 1040 if he or she:

- received more than $1,500 of taxable interest or ordinary dividends during the year;
- is claiming the edcuational expense exclusion from gross income of interest from Series EE or I U.S. savings bonds;
- has accrued interest on a bond between interest payment dates;
- received interest from a seller-financed mortgage and the buyer used the property as a personal residence;
- received interest or ordinary dividends as a nominee;
- is reporting original issue discount interest less than the amount shown on Form 1099-OID;
- is reducing the interest income on a bond by the amount of the amortizable premiums; or
- has a foreign bank account or received a distribution from a foreign trust, was the grantor of a foreign trust, or transferred property to a foreign trust (see Tab 2 for more information).

Tax-exempt interest is reported on line 8b, such as interest from a municipal bond or exempt-interest dividends from a mutual fund.

Caution. Do not include interest earned in an IRA, health savings account (HSA), Archer or Medicare Advantage MSA, or Coverdell education savings account on line 8a or line 8b.

Original Issue Discount (OID). Original issue discount (OID) is reported to the taxpayer in box 1 of Form 1099-OID. For a more detailed discussion of treatment of OID interest, see Tab 2 and MTG ¶1952-¶1956.

Lines 9a and 9b, Dividends

Dividends are distributions of money, stock, or other property paid by a corporation on stock or received through a partnership, an estate, a trust, or an association that is taxed as a corporation. Dividend income is generally reported to the taxpayer on Form 1099-DIV, or on Schedule K-1 of Form 1065 or Form 1120S. There are two types of dividends.

Ordinary Dividends. Ordinary dividends are reported in box 1a of Form 1099-DIV and are fully includible in gross income. A taxpayer reports his or her total ordinary dividends on line 9a of Form

1040. However, the taxpayer must also complete Schedule B if the total amount of ordinary dividends received during the year is over $1,500 or the ordinary dividends were received as a nominee. See Tab 2 and MTG ¶733.

 Caution. Some distributions that a taxpayer receives are called dividends but are actually interest income that must be reported on line 8a (for example, dividends on deposits in credit unions, mutual savings banks). Similarly, other distributions that may be called dividends should be reported as other income on line 21 (patronage dividends of cooperatives, Alaska Permanent Fund dividends, see page 1-21).

 Filing Tip. Some distributions with respect to corporate stock are a return of the taxpayer's cost and reduce the taxpayer's basis in the stock (box 3 of Form 1099-DIV). Once such basis is recovered, the distribution may be considered capital gains and the taxpayer will be required to file Schedule D of Form 1040. See Tab 4 and MTG ¶1736.

Qualified Dividends. Certain qualified dividends are eligible to be taxed at the lower capital gains rates, rather than tax rates that apply to ordinary income. A taxpayer's qualified dividends are shown in box 1b of Form 1099-DIV and reported on line 9b of Form 1040. Qualified dividends are either subject to a 15-percent tax rate or not taxed at all depending on the ordinary income rate that would otherwise apply. The worksheet in the 1040 instructions is used to calculate the tax on qualified dividends and capital gains. See also Tab 4.

To qualify for the reduced tax rate, the dividends must have been paid by a U.S. corporation or a qualified foreign corporation. In addition, the taxpayer must have held the stock for at least 60 days during the 121-day period that begins 60 days before the ex-dividend date (the first date following the declaration of a dividend on which the seller, not the buyer, of a stock will receive the next dividend payment). When counting the number of days the stock was held, include the day the stock was disposed of, but not the day it was acquired.

 Example. Joshua bought 10,000 shares of ABC Mutual Fund common stock on July 1, 2013. ABC Mutual Fund paid a cash dividend of 10 cents a share. The ex-dividend date was July 9, 2013. The ABC Mutual Fund advises Joshua that the portion of the dividend eligible to be treated as qualified dividends equals two cents per share. His Form 1099-DIV from ABC Mutual Fund shows total ordinary dividends of $800 and qualified dividends of $200. However, Joshua sold the 10,000 shares on August 4, 2013. He therefore has no qualified dividends from ABC Mutual Fund because he held the ABC Mutual Fund stock for less than 60 days.

 Caution. In the case of preferred stock with dividends attributable to periods totaling more than 366 days, the stock must be held for at least 90 days during the 181-day period that begins 90 days before the ex-dividend date.

For this purpose, the following dividends will not be considered qualified dividends even if they are shown in box 1b of Form 1099-DIV:

- capital gain distributions (see line 13 on page 1-17 and Tab 4);
- dividends paid on deposits with mutual savings banks, cooperative banks, credit unions, U.S. building and loan associations, federal savings and loan associations, and similar financial institutions (see line 8b on page 1-15);
- dividends from a corporation that is a tax-exempt organization or farmer's cooperative during the corporation's tax year in which the dividends were paid or during the corporation's previous tax year;
- dividends paid by a corporation on employer securities that are held on the date of record by an employee stock ownership plan (ESOP) maintained by that corporation;
- dividends on any share of stock to the extent that the taxpayer is obligated (whether under a short sale or otherwise) to make related payments for positions in substantially similar or related property;
- payment in lieu of dividends, if the taxpayer knows or has reason to know that the payments are not qualified dividends; and
- payments shown on box 1b of Form-DIV from a foreign corporation to the extent the taxpayer knows or has reason to know are not a qualified dividend.

Dividends Received in January. If a mutual fund or real estate investment trust (REIT) declares a dividend (including any interest-exempt dividend or capital gain distribution) in October, November, or December payable to shareholders of record on a date in one of those months but actually pays the dividend during January of the next calendar year, the taxpayer is considered to have received the payments in the year in which they were announced.

Line 10, Taxable Refunds, Credits, or Offsets of State and Local Income Taxes

If the taxpayer received a refund, credit or offset of state or local *income* taxes in 2013, then a portion may be includible in gross income if the taxpayer deducted the taxes for 2012. Generally, the taxpayer should receive Form 1099-G indicating the amount of any refund in box 2.

The worksheet found in the Form 1040 instructions is used to calculate the taxable portion of a taxpayer's refund and the result is entered on line 10 of Form 1040. However, the taxpayer must treat the refund the same as the recovery of any other itemized deduction (see page 1-21) and report it as "Other Income" on line 21 if any of the following applies:

- the refund is for a tax year other than 2012;
- the refund is for state or local general sales tax, real property taxes, or motor vehicle taxes;
- the amount on line 42 (the total of personal and dependent exemptions) of the taxpayer's 2012 Form 1040, is more than the amount on line 41 (adjusted gross income less either the standard or itemized deduction) of the 2012 Form 1040;
- the refund of 2012 state and local income taxes was more than the amount deducted in 2012 by the taxpayer (less the amount of 2012 state and general sales taxes that the taxpayer could have deducted);
- the taxpayer's last payment of 2012 estimated state or local income taxes was made in 2013;
- the taxpayer owed alternative minimum tax in 2012;
- the taxpayer could not deduct the full amount of credits he or she was entitled to in 2012; or
- the taxpayer could be claimed as a dependent by someone else in 2012.

Line 11, Alimony Received

Alimony (also called spousal support, separate maintenance, or maintenance and support) is taxable income of the spouse who receives the payment (and deductible by the spouse who makes the payment on line 31a, see page 1-30). Child support is not alimony and is not taxable to the recipient. The recipient of alimony is required to provide his or her SSN to the payer. For a discussion of the requirements for alimony to be reported on line 11, see Tab 13 and MTG ¶771-¶778.

Line 12, Business Income or Loss

Income from a trade or business is calculated on Schedule C or C-EZ and reported on line 12. See Tab 3 for more information.

 Caution. If an activity is engaged in for profit, it is treated as a business and Schedule C is required. Other proceeds, such as hobby income, are reported on line 21. The IRS may apply strict tests to determine whether an activity is a business or a hobby.

Line 13, Capital Gain or Loss

Schedule D is required to be completed for any capital gain or loss realized during the year, including any capital gain distributions or capital loss carryover from 2012, unless both of the following apply:

- the taxpayer received only capital gain distributions shown in box 2a of Form(s) 1099-DIV or substitute statements, and
- none of the Forms 1099-DIV or substitute statements received by the taxpayer have an amount in box 2b (unrecaptured Section 1250 gain), box 2c (Section 1202 gain), or box 2d (collectibles gain).

If both of the requirements apply, the taxpayer is not required to file Schedule D, but instead enters his or her total capital gain distributions received other than as a nominee (from box 2a of Form(s) 1099-DIV) on line 13 and by checking the box. The taxpayer may then use the Qualified Dividends and Capital Gain Tax Worksheet in the Form 1040 instructions to figure his or her tax. See also Tab 4 for instructions for filling out Schedule D.

Line 14, Other Gains or Losses

Include on line 14 other gains and losses recognized from the sale or exchange of property used in a trade or business and calculated on Form 4797. See Tab 4 for more information.

Lines 15a and 15b, IRA Distributions

Generally, distributions from a taxpayer's IRA are included in income including distributions from a traditional IRA, Roth IRA, simplified employee pension (SEP) IRA, and savings incentive match plan for employees (SIMPLE IRA). The amount of the distribution is reported to the taxpayer on Form 1099-R. The total amount of the distribution should be entered on line 15(b) and line 15(a) should be left blank, unless the distribution meets one of the following exceptions. See Tab 9 and MTG ¶2153G.

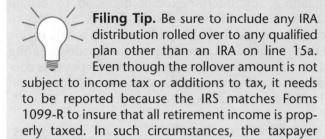

Filing Tip. If more than one exception applies, a statement should be attached to the taxpayer's return showing the amount of each exception, instead of making a separate entry next to line 15b. In addition, if the taxpayer (or spouse if filing jointly) received more than one distribution, then figure the taxable amount of each distribution and enter the total on line 15b.

Caution. If the distribution is made before the taxpayer is age 59½, then a 10-percent additional tax will generally apply (25-percent for SIMPLE IRAs). In addition, if the amount received from a traditional, SEP, or SIMPLE IRA by a taxpayer who is at least age 70½ is less than his or her required minimum distribution, then an additional 50-percent additional tax would also generally apply. The additional taxes are reported on Line 58 (see page 1-37 and Tab 9 for more information).

Rollovers. A qualified IRA distribution is not taxable if it is rolled over: from one IRA to another IRA of the same type (for example, from one traditional IRA to another traditional IRA); from a SEP or SIMPLE IRA to a traditional IRA; or from an IRA to a qualified plan other than an IRA. If the total distribution was rolled over, then enter the total amount distributed on line 15a, write -0- on line 15b, and write "Rollover" next to line 15b. However, if only a portion of a distribution was rolled over, then enter the amount rolled over on line 15a and the amount not rolled over on 15b (unless the exception for nondeductible contributions or for returned or recharacterized contributions applies to the part not rolled over).

Generally, a qualified rollover must be made within 60 days from when the distribution is received by the taxpayer. In addition, the taxpayer cannot roll over any later distribution from the same IRA within one year. For this purpose, a direct transfer from the IRA to another IRA is not considered a distribution and therefore is not a rollover and not subject to the one-year limit. On the other hand, required minimum distributions are not eligible to be rolled over (see Tab 9).

Filing Tip. Be sure to include any IRA distribution rolled over to any qualified plan other than an IRA on line 15a. Even though the rollover amount is not subject to income tax or additions to tax, it needs to be reported because the IRS matches Forms 1099-R to insure that all retirement income is properly taxed. In such circumstances, the taxpayer should attach a statement to his or her return explaining what he or she did.

Conversions. A taxpayer can convert amounts distributed from a traditional, SEP, or SIMPLE IRA to a Roth IRA. While the conversion is considered a rollover contribution to the Roth IRA, it is not an exception to the rule that distributions from a traditional IRA are taxable. The taxpayer must include in income in the year of conversion the distribution from the traditional IRA that would have had to be included in income had it not be converted or contributed to the Roth IRA. The amount to include on line 15b is calculated on Form 8606.

Nondeductible Contributions. Distributions received by the taxpayer from an IRA (other than a Roth IRA) that relate to nondeductible contributions are not taxable. Thus, if the taxpayer made nondeductible contributions to the IRA, then the total amount of any distribution should be reported on line 15a and Form 8606 should be used to calculate the taxable portion to report on line 15b. If a distribution is received from a Roth IRA, Form 8606 does not have to be used and -0- should be entered on line 15b if box 7 of Form 1099-R indicates that the distribution is a qualified Roth IRA distribution (code Q) or the distribution is otherwise not taxable (code T).

Planning Tip. A record should be kept by the taxpayer of nondeductible contributions to an IRA and of deductible contributions to a Roth IRA to determine if a distribution from the Roth IRA meets the five-year holding period and to determine how much, if any, of the distribution is taxable (see Tab 9 for more information).

Return or Recharacterization of Contributions. Report on line 15a the amount of any excess contributions returned to the taxpayer (including any earnings or less any loss) prior to the due date (including extensions) for filing the return for the year. The taxpayer should also include on line 15a any distribution related to the recharacterization of a contribution to a Roth or traditional IRA. Form 8606 should be used to report taxable portions of such distributions.

Caution. Absent further legislation, the direct charitable distribution from an IRA for taxpayers age 70½ or older of up to $100,000 without income recognition is no longer available after December 31, 2013.

HSA Transfers. A taxpayer is allowed to make a one-time rollover of a distribution from an IRA (other than a SEP or SIMPLE IRA) to his or her health savings account (HSA). The amount of the distribution must be included in the total amount of IRA distributions reported on line 15a. It may be excluded from the taxable amount reported on line 15b, but only up to the HSA contribution limit for the year or the amount that would otherwise be taxable (unless another exception excludes it from income). Write "HFD" next to line 15b when excluding any portion of a HSA rollover. If the taxpayer made nondeductible contributions to the IRA, then any rollover of a distribution to an HSA is first considered paid out of otherwise taxable income.

 Caution. An IRA distribution is eligible to be rolled over to HSA only if it is made directly from the IRA trustee to the HSA trustee. The taxpayer can only make one such transfer during his or her lifetime. The amount rolled over reduces the amount that the taxpayer can contribute to the HSA for the year. If the taxpayer fails to maintain eligibility for the HSA for the 12 months following the rollover, then the amount rolled over will be includible in gross income and subject to an additional 10-percent tax. See Form 8889.

Lines 16a and 16b, Pensions and Annuities

Form 1099-R indicates the amount of pension and annuity payments received by the taxpayer including distributions from a qualified retirement plan such as a 401(k), 403(b), or governmental 457(b) plan. Pension and annuity payments are fully taxable (including military retirement pay) and entered on line 16b if the taxpayer did not pay any part of the cost or the taxpayer received the entire cost back before 2013. Line 16a should be left blank in such cases.

 **Filing Tip.** A corrective distribution (including earnings) of excess salary deferrals or contributions to a retirement plan, as well as a disability pension received before minimum retirement age, are considered wages and reported on line 7 of Form 1040. Similarly, railroad retirement benefits reported to the taxpayer on Form RRB-1099 may be taxed as Social Security benefits or as a pension or annuity benefit. See MTG ¶716 and ¶839, as well as IRS Publication 915.

Partly Taxable Payments. If the taxpayer did pay part of the cost of the pension or annuity, then part of the payment received represents a return of the cost. If the Form 1099-R does not show the taxable amount, then the taxpayer must use either the Simplified Method or the General Rule to figure the taxable and nontaxable portions of the annuity payment. See Tab 9 and MTG ¶817 for a discussion of these methods, as well as a worksheet that must be completed if the Simplified Method is used (see page 1-49). The total distribution is entered on line 16a and the taxable part on line 16b.

A taxpayer who is a retired public safety officer (police, firefighter, emergency responder), can elect to exclude from gross income distributions made from a qualified retirement plan to pay accident and health insurance premiums (as well as for long-term care insurance) for themselves, their spouse, or dependents. The exclusion is limited to the lesser of the amount of the premiums or $3,000. The amount reported in box 2a of Form 1099-R may not reflect the exclusion. Thus, the taxpayer must report his or her total distributions on line 16a and the taxable amount on line 16b with "PSO" next to line 16b.

 Filing Tip. If the taxpayer is retired on disability and reporting disability income on line 7, then include only the taxable amount on line 7 and enter "PSO" and the excluded amount on the dotted line next to line 7.

Rollovers. A distribution from a qualified retirement plan that is rolled over to another qualified plan (including an IRA or SEP, but not a Roth IRA) is generally not taxable. If the taxpayer receives the distribution from the plan directly, then it must be rolled over within 60 days in order to be tax-free. Certain distributions, however, may not be rolled over including required minimum distributions, hardship distributions, and a distribution under a series of substantially equal period payments paid at least once a year over the participant's life expectancy or over a period of 10 years or more.

In the case of a rollover to a plan (other than a Roth IRA or designated Roth account), report on line 16a the total amount of the distribution as indicated in box 1 of Form 1099-R. From that subtract the amount rolled over and any after-tax contributions made by the taxpayer (box 5 of Form 1099-R). Enter the remaining amount, even if zero (-0-) on line 16b and write "Rollover" next to line 16b.

In the case of a rollover to a Roth IRA other than from a designated Roth account, follow the same procedures as above. However, in the case of rollover to a Roth IRA or designated Roth account from a designated Roth account, report on line 16a the total amount of the distribution before income tax or other deductions are withheld. From that amount subtract the amount of the qualified rollover distribution. Enter the remaining amount, even if zero (-0-) on line 16b and write "Rollover" next to line 16b.

 Planning Tip. A taxpayer planning on rolling over a distribution from an employer's plan should elect a direct rollover to another plan or IRA (trustee to trustee transfer). A rollover distribution that is directly paid to the taxpayer is generally subject to a 20-percent withholding rate and may also be subject to the additional tax on early distributions.

Lump-Sum Distributions. If the taxpayer received a lump-sum distribution from a retirement plan, then the box 2b "Total Distribution" should be checked on Form 1099-R. Enter the total distribution on line 16a and the taxable part on line 16b. Generally, taxable lump-sum distributions are treated as ordinary income and taxed at ordinary income tax rates. However, certain older taxpayers may be eligible for tax on a portion of their distributions to be at capital gains tax rates and may employ a 10-year averaging option on the portion of the distribution not taxed at capital gains rates. This optional method is available only to taxpayers born before January 2, 1936. Use Form 4972 to figure the tax using the optional method. The tax figured on Form 4972 is added to any other amounts on line 44 (see page 1-35).

Loans from Qualified Retirement Plans. Loans of less than $50,000 or 50 percent of the taxpayer's vested account balance are not taxable if certain requirements are met. The portion of loans in excess of this limit is treated as a taxable distribution. See Tab 9 for more information.

Line 17, Rental Real Estate, Royalties, Partnerships, S Corporations, Trusts, Etc.

Calculate rental and royalty income, as well as gains and losses from partnerships, S corporations, estates, and trusts on Schedule E and report on line 17. See Tab 5.

Line 18, Farm Income or Loss

Calculate income from farming activities on Schedule F and report on line 18. See Tab 3 and MTG ¶767.

Line 19, Unemployment Compensation

A taxpayer should receive a Form 1099-G if he or she received any unemployment compensation during the tax year. Unemployment compensation is taxable and reported on line 19 except to the extent that any overpayment received was repaid during the year. Do not include any unemployment compensation repaid in 2013. Instead, enter "Repaid" and the nontaxable amount on the dotted line next to line 19.

If the taxpayer repaid unemployment compensation in 2013 that was included in gross income in an earlier year, then the amount repaid may be deducted as an itemized deduction on Schedule A (see Tab 2). However, if the repayment was more than $3,000, the taxpayer may choose to either claim the repayment as an itemized deduction or claim a tax credit for the difference in tax that would have resulted had the income not been claimed in the earlier year. Claim the credit on line 71 and enter "I.R.C. 1341" in the column to the right.

Employer and Private Benefits. Employer payments of supplemental unemployment benefits and guaranteed wages paid under a union agreement are treated as taxable wages and reported on line 7. Unemployment benefits paid to union members from regular union dues are reported as income on line 21. However, benefits received from a special union fund for unemployment is reported as income on line 21 only to the extent they exceed any deductible contributions made by the taxpayer.

Lines 20a and 20b, Social Security Benefits

Social Security and Railroad Retirement benefits paid to the taxpayer during the year are reported in box 3 of Form SSA-1099 and Form RRB-1099, respectively. The total amount must be reported on line 20a. The worksheet reproduced on page 1-50 is generally used to calculate the portion of the benefits that is taxable and reported on line 20b. In the case of IRA deductions, repayment of benefits and lump-sum distributions, special rules apply to determine the taxable amount reported on line 20b. See Tab 9 and MTG ¶716 for more information.

 Filing Tip. If the taxpayer is married, filing separately and lived apart from his or her spouse for all of 2013, he or she must enter "D" next to "benefits" reported on line 20a. If the taxpayer lived with his or her spouse during the tax year, then up to 85 percent of Social Security benefits received must be included in gross income.

Planning Tip. If the taxpayer excludes any of the following from gross income, then Worksheet 1 in IRS Publication 915 must be used to calculate the taxable portion of Social Security or Railroad Retirement benefits received:

- employer-provided adoption benefits;
- interest from Series EE or I U.S. Savings Bonds;
- foreign earned income; or
- income from sources within Puerto Rico or American Samoa.

IRA Deduction. If the taxpayer (or the taxpayer's spouse) received Social Security benefits, contributed to a traditional IRA and is covered by an employer-sponsored retirement plan, then the taxable portion of Social Security benefits is computed using a three-step process. First, figure the taxable portion of the Social Security benefits as if no IRA deduction is taken. Second, calculate the IRA deduction on line 32 (see page 1-31) using the taxable Social Security amount determined in step 1. Finally, recompute the taxable portion of the Social Security benefits using the IRA deduction calculated in step 2. See IRS Publication 590.

Repayments. If the taxpayer repaid any Social Security benefits during the year (box 4) and the total amount of repayments exceeds the total benefits received in the year (box 3), then none of the benefits are taxable (enter -0- on line 20b). The excess can be used to offset any net benefits of the taxpayer's spouse (box 5) if a joint return is filed. If any more excess remains, the taxpayer can claim a deduction similar to the deduction for the repayment of unemployment compensation (see above).

Lump-Sum Payments. If the taxpayer received a lump-sum payment of Social Security benefits in 2013 that includes benefits for an earlier tax year, then the taxpayer may elect to calculate the taxable portion of the payment for the earlier year separately (using the income for the earlier year) if it would lower the amount of taxable benefits. See IRS Pub. 915 on how to use the lump-sum election method.

Line 21, Other Income

All taxable income not included on lines 7 through 20 (and related schedules) is reported on line 21. List the type and amount of income included (attach a statement if necessary). The following are examples of the more common types of income reported on line 21 (see also the chart beginning on page 1-23 for common gross income inclusions and exclusions and where they are reported).

 Filing Tip. A taxpayer does not report on line 21 any income from self-employment, nonemployee compensation reported on Form 1099-MISC, or fees received as a notary public. Instead, such income must be reported on Schedule C, C-EZ, or F, even if the taxpayer does not have any business expenses.

Cancelled Debts. Generally, any debt of the taxpayer that is canceled or forgiven will be considered income, unless it is a gift. A debt includes any indebtedness for which the taxpayer is personally liable or that attaches to property he or she holds. See IRS Publication 4681. Income from the cancellation of debt is reported in box 2 of Form 1099-C and should be included on line 21 of Form 1040 if it is a nonbusiness debt. If it is a business debt, report the income on Schedule C or F, as appropriate.

If interest is forgiven with the debt (box 3), then the net amount of the debt (box 2 less box 3) is reported on line 21 but only if the interest would otherwise be deductible by the taxpayer. If the interest would not otherwise be deductible by the taxpayer, then the total amount of cancelled debt cannot be offset by the interest cancelled or forgiven.

 Filing Tip. A discount provided for the early payment on a mortgage is considered cancelled debt and must be included on line 21. On the other hand, if a corporation cancels a shareholder's debt, the amount canceled is a constructive dividend and reported as dividend income on line 9a.

The discharge of a mortgage when the taxpayer disposes of his or her property (including by foreclosure or repossession) will generally result in cancellation of debt income to the extent the mortgage discharge exceeds the fair market value of the property. However, a taxpayer may exclude from gross income up to $2 million ($1 million for a married taxpayer filing a separate return) of any income realized from the cancellation or discharge of qualified principal residence indebtedness. The taxpayer must reduce his or her basis in the home by the amount excluded.

 Caution. Absent further legislation, the principal residence mortgage indebtedness exclusion will no longer be available for indebtedness cancelled or discharged after December 31, 2013.

A qualified principal residence indebtedness is a mortgage personally incurred by the taxpayer to acquire, construct, or substantially improve his or her principal residence that is not more than the cost of the home (plus improvements). It also includes the cost to refinance a qualified mortgage.

 Caution. The exclusion is only available if the taxpayer is personally liable for the mortgage (recourse debt). If the taxpayer is not personally liable for the mortgage (nonrecourse debt), the amount of the mortgage that is discharged when the taxpayer disposes of his or her property (including by foreclosure or repossession) is included in the amount realized on the sale of the property.

 Filing Tip. The discharge of a qualified mortgage is not eligible for the exclusion if it is as a result of service performed by the taxpayer for the lender or other factors unrelated to the financial condition of the taxpayer or decline in value in the property. It is also not available if the taxpayer is in Chapter 11 bankruptcy or insolvent.

There are several other exceptions to the inclusion of canceled debt in income. These include:

- student loans if the discharge is contingent on the taxpayer working for a specified period of time for certain employers such as the government or educational institutions;
- debt cancelled in a Chapter 11 bankruptcy or if the taxpayer is insolvent; or
- qualified farm debt or qualified real property business debt. See MTG ¶885 and IRS Publications 225 and 334.

Recoveries. The taxpayer must include on line 21 refunds, recoveries, and rebates of amounts deducted or claimed as a credit in an earlier tax year. Interest earned on the recovery must be reported as interest income in the year received on line 8a. If the recovery and expense occur in the same tax year, the recovery reduces the deduction or credit and is not reported as income. If the recovery is for amounts paid in more than one prior year, then the recovered amount must be allocated between years.

The most common recoveries are refunds, reimbursements and rebates of itemized deductions from Schedule A. Generally, the full amount of the recovery must be included in income in the year received if the taxpayer itemizes deductions in the current year. State and local income tax refunds are generally reported on line 10 (see page 1-17), and the total of all other recoveries is reported on line 21. A taxpayer may be able to exclude a portion of a recovery from income in the following circumstances:

- only itemized deductions that exceed the standard deduction for the earlier year are subject to recovery; thus, the amount included in income is the smaller of the recovery or the amount by which the taxpayer's itemized deductions for the earlier year exceeded the standard deduction;
- if the taxpayer had negative taxable income in the earlier year, the amount of the recovery included in income is reduced by the negative amount;
- the amount recovered cannot exceed the taxpayer's deduction in the earlier year; thus, the amount included in income is the smaller of the recovery or the amount deducted on Schedule A in the earlier year;
- if the taxpayer's itemized deductions in the earlier tax year were subject to the AGI limits, then the amount recovered that must be included in income is the difference between the amount of itemized deductions actually allowed in the earlier year and the deductions (standard or itemized) that would have been claimed had the taxpayer paid the proper amount in the earlier year; and
- if the taxpayer had any unused tax credits or was subject to the alternative minimum tax in the earlier tax year, then his or her tax liability for the earlier year must be recomputed by adding the recovered amount to taxable income; if the recomputed tax liability is increased, then the recovery is included in income in the current tax year up to the amount of the deduction that reduced the tax in the earlier year.

 Example. Martin incurred $3,000 in medical expenses in 2012. However, due to the 7.5-percent AGI threshold, he was only eligible to claim $500 as an itemized deduction. If Martin receives $2,000 in 2013 as a reimbursement for his prior-year medical expenses, then he must include $500 in income on line 21 on his 2013 return (assuming he itemizes deductions).

 Filing Tip. If a taxpayer is not required to include all of his or her recoveries in income, and he or she has both a recovery of state and local income taxes and other itemized deductions, then the total amount recovered for the year must be allocated for reporting purposes. Recoveries of state and local income taxes are generally reported on line 10 (see page 1-17). Recoveries of other itemized deductions are reported as other income on line 21 of Form 1040.

Barter Income. A taxpayer should report on line 21 the fair market value of any property or services received in a barter transaction to the extent not reportable on another schedule (for example, Schedule C or E). Taxpayers who receive goods or services through a barter exchange should receive a Form 1099-B by February 17, 2014, that shows the value of goods and services received through the exchange during the year. This includes barter exchanges conducted through the internet (for example, eBay sellers with PayPal barter exchanges). The IRS will also receive a copy of Form 1099-B.

Disaster Payments. Do not include in income on line 21 any amount received that is a qualified disaster relief payment or disaster grant. A payment is excluded if it is paid to reimburse or pay reasonable and necessary personal, family, living or funeral expenses that result from a federally declared disaster. See MTG ¶897.

Foreign Earned Income. A qualifying individual may elect to exclude a limited amount of foreign earned income and employer-provided housing expenses from gross income. The amount of the exclusions is calculated on Form 2555 and reported in parentheses on line 21 and subtracted from the taxpayer's income to arrive at the total income on line 22 (enter "Form 2555" in the space provided). See MTG ¶2402.

Other Examples. Additional items of other income to report on line 21 include:

- income from an activity not engaged in for profit (hobby income);
- prizes, awards, and gambling winnings including lump-sum payments received from the sale of future lottery payments;
- taxable distributions from an HSA or Archer MSA, as well as amounts deemed to be income from an HSA because the taxpayer did not remain eligible to contribute during a testing period;
- taxable distributions from a qualified tuition program or Coverdell ESA (see Tab 13);
- rental income from the lease of personal property if the taxpayer was not in the business of renting such property (see also line 36 on page 1-34);
- net operating loss (NOL) carryforward (enter as negative amount and attach statement about NOL);
- loss on a corrective distribution of an excess deferral distributed to the taxpayer (include the loss as a negative amount and identify it as "Loss on Excess Deferral Distribution");
- recapture of a charitable contribution deduction of a fractional interest in tangible personal property (see also line 60 on page 1-38) or the charitable organization disposes of the property within three years (see Tab 2);
- dividends on insurance policies to the extent they exceed net premiums paid;
- alternative trade adjustment assistance payments (box 5 of Form 1099-G);
- Alaska Permanent Fund dividends; and
- jury duty pay (if jury duty pay is surrendered to an employer in exchange for regular compensation, then it is included in income on line 21, but deducted on line 36, see page 1-34).

Common Gross Income Inclusions and Exclusions

Type of Income	Taxable	Nontaxable	How Reported to Taxpayer	Where Taxpayer Reports Income
Advance payments	• All commissions or earnings received during tax year if taxpayer uses cash method of accounting	• Some advanced commissions or earnings received for taxpayers who use the accrual method of accounting	Form W-2, box 1	Form 1040, line 7
Alimony	• Full amount received that is not child support, noncash property settlement, and payment of spouse's part of community income. Alimony is deductible by the payor.	• Amounts received for child support, noncash property settlements, and payment of spouse's part of community income	No IRS form is used to report alimony	Recipient: Form 1040, line 11 Payor: Form 1040, line 31a
Barter	• Fair market value of property or services received	• Portion that is a gift	Form 1099-B, box 3	Schedule C, E, or F, depending on the services provided

Common Gross Income Inclusions and Exclusions (Continued)

Type of Income	Taxable	Nontaxable	How Reported to Taxpayer	Where Taxpayer Reports Income
Bond interest	• Generally, full amount accrued or received during the tax year depending on the taxpayer's method of accounting	• Interest from municipal bonds • Interest from Series EE or I U.S. Education Savings Bonds	Form 1099-INT	Schedule B, generally Form 8815: Education Saving Bond Interest Exclusion
Bonuses and awards	• Full amount received except for certain noncash employee achievement awards	• Achievement awards of tangible personal property of up to $1,600 annually or $400 for qualified plan awards. • Token goodwill bonuses	Employee award: Form W-2, box 1 Nonemployee award: Form 1099, box 3 or 7	Employee award: Form 1040, line 7 Nonemployee award: Schedule C or F
Canceled debt	• Entire amount of debt forgiven, including interest that would not be deductible by the taxpayer • Discount for prepayment of mortgage loans	• Amount for which the taxpayer was not personally liable (non-recourse), that was a gift, or that was forgiven due to bankruptcy or insolvency • Qualified principal residence indebtedness or qualified mortgage (see page 1-21) • Student loans forgiven for performance of certain work • Amount that was qualified farm indebtedness or qualified real property business indebtedness • Canceled debt that would have been deductible	Form 1099-C, box 2, generally; box 3, interest	Form 1040, line 21, for nonbusiness debt Schedule C or F of Form 1040 for business- or farm-related debt
Disability benefits and pensions	• Amounts of disability pension received under health plan that were paid for by the taxpayer's employer	• Amounts of disability pension received under health plan paid for the taxpayer • Military and government disability pensions such as VA disability benefits or benefits received as a result of active service in the Armed Forces • Compensation for permanent loss of a part or function of the body or its use, calculated without regard to period of absence from work or lost wages • Benefit payments from a public welfare trust, including payments received under a worker's compensation or similar law • Compensatory (but not punitive damages) for physical injury or sickness, as well as compensation for permanent loss or loss of use of part or function of body, or permanent disfigurement • Benefits receive under a "no-fault" car insurance policy for loss of income or earning capacity	Taxable amounts: Form W-2, box 1 or Form 1099-R Nontaxable amounts: Form W-2, box 12, code J or Form 1099-MISC, box 3	Disability pension received before retirement, Form 1040, line 7 Disability pension received after retirement, Form 1040, line 16a and 16b

Common Gross Income Inclusions and Exclusions (Continued)

Type of Income	Taxable	Nontaxable	How Reported to Taxpayer	Where Taxpayer Reports Income
Employee and nonemployee compensation	• Amount of cash payments, including wages, salaries, fees, commissions, and tips received for personal services performed – Offerings and fees received by member of the clergy unless earned as agent of religious order – Reimbursement, allowance, or advance paid under employer's nonaccountable plan • FMV of any property or services received in return for services performed, including any restricted property (see ¶MTG 713) • Incentive stock options (taxed when stock is sold, see ¶MTG 1925) • Nonstatutory stock options (taxed when granted if is has ascertainable FMV, see ¶MTG 1923)	• Reimbursement, allowance, or advance paid under employer's accountable plan • Military retirement pay (taxed as a pension) or veterans benefits • Member of the clergy's housing or parsonage allowance (nontaxable for income tax purposes only)	Employee compensation, generally: W-2, box 1 Nonemployee compensation, generally: 1099-MISC, box 7 Member of the clergy's housing allowance: W-2, box 14	Form 1040, line 7 Schedule C or F for business- or farm-related services
Employer-paid benefits	• Adoption benefits in excess of $12,970 (subject to phaseout) • Death benefits, not part of pension or retirement plan • Dependent care benefits in excess of $5,000 ($2,500 for married individuals filing separately) • Disability benefits • Educational assistance payments in excess of $5,250 • Financial counseling fees • Fringe benefits (unless fair market value is paid by taxpayer) • Group-term life insurance cost in excess of $50,000 in coverage • Sickness and injury benefits (including disability) received through an accident or health plan due to employer's contributions	• Accident and health plan coverage provided by employer, including contributions to HSAs, MSAs, health FSAs, HRAs, and long-term care coverage • *De minimis* (minimal) benefits (for example, food discounts, holiday gifts, company picnics) • Employee discounts (for example, reduced sales prices on products or services sold by the employer) • Meals and lodging furnished on employer's premises and for its convenience • Military base realignment and closure benefit payments • Moving expense reimbursement (see page 1-29) • No-additional-cost services (services offered to customers in ordinary course of work provided by employer) • Retirement plan contributions (qualified plan) and retirement planning services • Transportation fringe benefits – $245 per month for commuter vehicles, transit passes, and parking – $20 per month for bicycle commuting • Working condition fringe benefits (for example, use of company car for business purposes)	Taxable amounts, generally: Form W-2, box 1 Adoption: Form W-2, box 12, code T Death: Form 1099-R, box 1, 2a and 7, code 4 Dependent care: Form W-2, box 10 Education: Form W-2, box 14 Fringe benefits, Form W-2, box 1 and 14 Group-term life insurance, Form W-2, box 12, code C Insurance premiums, generally: Form W-2, box 14 Insurance premiums, retirement: Form 1099-R, box 1 and 2a MSA: Form W-2, box 12, code R	Taxable amounts, generally: Form W-2, line 7 Adoption: Form 8839, line 16 Dependent care: Form 2441, line 12 MSA and long-term care insurance: Form 8853

Common Gross Income Inclusions and Exclusions (Continued)

Type of Income	Taxable	Nontaxable	How Reported to Taxpayer	Where Taxpayer Reports Income
Foreign-source income	• All foreign earned income (wages, salaries, etc.), as well as unearned income (interest, dividends, rents, capital gains, etc.) unless exempted by U.S. law or tax treaty	• Up to $97,600 of foreign earned income, as well as certain amount of foreign housing expenses	Form W-2 or Form 1099, if used by the foreign payer, otherwise no IRS form is generally used	Excluded amounts, Form 1040, line 21 (negative), and Form 2555 or Form 2555-EZ
Foster care payments	• Full amount of payments received for the care of more than five individuals age 19 or older • Full amount of difficultly-of-care payments received for the care of more than five individuals age 19 or older, or more than 10 individuals under age 19	Full amount, if received from a state or government agency or qualified foster care placement agency for care in taxpayer's home	Taxable amounts: Form 1099-MISC	Schedule C
Gambling winnings, prizes and award	• Full amount of gambling winnings, including winnings from lotteries and raffles • Prizes and awards received in goods or services other than as an employee (fair market value) • Scholarship prizes if taxpayer is not required to use for education	• Prize for accomplishment in religious, charitable, scientific, education, literary or civic field if taxpayer is not required to perform substantial future services and the prize is directly transferred to a tax-exempt organization	Gambling: Form W-2G, box 1 Prizes and awards: Form 1099-MISC, box 3	Form 1040, line 21
Gifts and inheritance	• Income in respect of decedent that would have been taxable if received by the decedent prior to death	• Property received as a gift, bequest, or inheritance, unless a pension or IRA is inherited, interest in an expected inheritance from a living person is sold, or bequest is for services performed while the decedent was alive	None	Taxable amounts, Form 1040, line 21
Life insurance	• Life insurance proceeds from a policy transferred for valuable consideration prior to the death of the insured • Proceeds from an endowment contract paid in lump-sum at maturity if exceeds the cost of the policy • Cash proceeds from surrender of life insurance policy if exceeds the cost of the policy • Benefits received under a credit card disability or unemployment insurance plan if exceeds premiums paid during the tax year	• Life insurance proceeds paid as a result of the death of the insured unless the policy was transferred for valuable consideration prior to the death of the insured • Accelerated death benefits if the insured is terminally or chronically ill	Life insurance, annuity, and endowment contracts: Form 1099-R Long-term care and accelerated death benefits: Form 1099-LTC	Generally: Form 1040, line 21 Accelerated death benefits: Form 8853
Scholarships, fellowships, and educational grants	• Full amount received if not a degree candidate • Amount used for room, board, travel, or other expenses not required for enrollment • Amount received as payment for services (for example, teaching, research) • Amount received as a prize if not required to use for educational purposes	• Amount received if a degree candidate and used for tuition, fees, books, and other course related expenses • Reduced tuition received by an undergraduate because the student or parent is an employee of the institution, if the tuition program does not favor highly paid employees, and reduced tuition received by graduate students that is not payment for services	Received as payment for services: Form W-2, box 1 Other taxable payments: Not required to be reported	Generally, Form 1040, line 7 (write "SCH" and taxable amount on the dotted line next to line 7) Prizes, Form 1040, line 21 (whether or not used for educational purposes)

Common Gross Income Inclusions and Exclusions (Continued)

Type of Income	Taxable	Nontaxable	How Reported to Taxpayer	Where Taxpayer Reports Income
Tips and gratuities	• Full amount, including allocated tips (see page 1-13)	• Allocated tips when taxpayer can prove less was actually received	Form W-2, box 1 or box 8	Form 1040, line 7
Unemployment compensation	• Amounts paid under a governmental program including state unemployment benefits, railroad unemployment benefits, disability payments under a government program paid as a substitute for unemployment compensation, trade readjustment allowances, and disaster unemployment payments (see page 1-20) • Unemployment benefits paid from union fund, unless contributions to the fund were not deductible • Benefits paid from a private fund (nonunion) to the extent they exceed voluntary contributions made by the taxpayer • Benefits received from an employer-financed fund (to which employees did not contribute)	• Workers' compensation paid to an injured worker or survivors • Railroad sick pay for an injury that is job-related	Form 1099-G, box 1	Form 1040, line 19
Welfare and public assistance	• Welfare payments received as compensation for services or that are obtained by fraud • Full amount of work training program benefits if the amount received exceeds welfare benefits that would otherwise have been paid • Alternative trade adjustment assistance (ATAA) payments	• Public assistance or welfare payments that are based on need • Medicare benefits, Parts A and B • Disaster relief payments received as a result of a federally declared disaster or terrorist/military act • Disaster relief grants	Taxable, generally: Form W-2, box 1 ATAA payments: Form 1099-G	Generally: Form 1040, line 7 ATAA payments: Form 1040, line 21
Workers' compensation	• Salary payments received for performing light duties as a result of an occupational sickness or injury	• Amounts received for an occupational sickness or injury if paid under a workers' compensation or similar law	Salary for light duty work: Form W-2, box 1	Form 1040, line 7

Adjusted Gross Income, Lines 23-37

Amounts deductible against gross income in arriving at adjusted gross income (AGI) are called "above-the-line" deductions. Since these deductions reduce AGI, they may also affect other items with AGI-related thresholds, such as the deduction for medical expenses, casualty losses, and miscellaneous itemized deductions. See Tab 2.

Line 23, Teachers' Classroom Expenses

 Caution. Absent further legislation, the deduction for eligible educator expenses is not available for tax years beginning after December 31, 2013.

Eligible educators may deduct up to $250 of qualified expenses paid or incurred during the year as an adjustment to gross income, rather than as a miscellaneous itemized deduction. In the case of married taxpayers filing a joint return, if both spouses are eligible educators, the maximum deduction is $500 but neither spouse can deduct more than $250 of his or her qualified expenses. Qualified expenses incurred in excess of the limits may be deducted as unreimbursed employee expenses on line 21 of Schedule A.

A taxpayer is eligible to claim the deduction if for at least 900 hours during a school year, the individual was a kindergarten through grade 12 teacher, instructor, counselor, principal or aide in a school that provides elementary or secondary education as determined under state law. Qualified expenses include ordinary and necessary expenses paid for books, supplies, equipment (including computer equipment, software and services), and other materials used in the classroom. Expenses for home schooling and nonathletic supplies for courses in health or physical education do not qualify. In addition, qualified expenses must be reduced by:

- any reimbursements received for the expenses that were not reported on Form W-2;
- excludable series EE and I U.S. savings bonds interest from Form 8815;
- nontaxable earnings from a qualified state tuition program; and
- nontaxable earnings from Coverdell ESAs.

Line 24, Certain Business Expenses of Reservists, Performing Artists, and Fee-Based Government Officials

The performance of services as an employee is considered to be a trade or business and expenses related to that business are generally deductible as miscellaneous itemized deductions (after completing Form 2106). Special rules, however, permit certain taxpayers to deduct expenses as an adjustment to gross income. Such individuals must still complete Form 2106.

Armed Forces Reservists. Reserve members of the Armed Forces of the United States, including the National Guard, who periodically travel (typically one weekend per month and two weeks in the summer) for duty may incur significant travel expenses. To the extent the individual is not reimbursed by the military, he or she may deduct the travel expenses associated with such duty if they travel more than 100 miles from the taxpayer's home. Deductible expenses include meals, lodging and incidentals up to the federal per diem rate for the applicable locality and the standard mileage rate for car expenses (plus any parking fees, ferry fees or tolls). See MTG ¶941E.

Qualified Performing Artists. The business expenses of a qualified performing artist are deductible as an adjustment against gross income if the taxpayer:

- receives wages from at least two employers of at least $200 from each during the tax year in exchange for services in the performing arts;
- has total business expense deductions attributable to the performance of those services exceeding 10 percent of the income received from those services; and
- has an AGI of $16,000 or less (determined before deducting the expenses) from all sources.

If the performing artist is married, the couple must file a joint return in order to deduct the performer's business expense against gross income. If both spouses are performing artists, their expenses and income from performing services are computed separately, but the $16,000 AGI limitation applies to the couple's combined income. See MTG ¶941A.

Fee-Based Public Officials. Expenses paid or incurred with respect to services performed by an official as an employee of a state or local government are deductible, provided that the official is compensated in whole or in part on a fee basis. These expenses are also deductible for alternative minimum tax purposes. See MTG ¶941D.

Line 25, Health Savings Account Deduction

Health Savings Accounts (HSAs) are a type of medical savings account set up to pay for qualified medical expenses of individuals and their families covered by a high-deductible health plan (HDHP). A taxpayer may be able to claim a deduction for his or her contributions (and contributions made by any other person other than the taxpayer's employer) to an HSA.

The maximum deductible contribution that can be made to a taxpayer's HSA for calendar year 2013 is $3,250 for an individual with self-only coverage and $6,450 for an individual with family coverage. If the taxpayer is age 55 or older at the end of the year, then the limit is increased by $1,000. In the case of married taxpayers, if either spouse has family coverage, then both are considered as having family coverage and the limit is split equally between them (unless they agree to a different division). If both spouses are age 55 or older, then each spouse's limit is increased by the additional contribution (thus, a total contribution limit of $8,450 for 2013). If a taxpayer has more than one HSA, then contributions to all HSAs cannot be more than the limits described.

The contribution limits will be reduced by any employer contributions to the taxpayer's HSA, any contributions made to the taxpayer's Archer MSA (including employer contributions), and any qualified HSA funding distributions from a traditional or Roth IRA (see page 1-19). In addition, the limit will be reduced if the taxpayer was not considered eligible to contribute to the HSA for the entire year. Rollover contributions from Archer MSAs and other HSAs will not reduce the contribution limits. However, beginning with the first month the taxpayer is enrolled in Medicare, the contribution limit is zero. Form 8889 is used to compute the taxpayer's contribution limit for the tax year and the amount of the deduction that is reported on line 25.

For this purpose, contributions through a salary-reduction plan (cafeteria plan) are treated as employer contributions. On the other hand, contributions by a partnership to a partner's HSA, or by an S corporation to a two-percent shareholder-employee's HSA, for services rendered are treated as guaranteed payments and may be deducted by the partner or shareholder. In addition, general contributions by a partnership are not employer contributions but instead are treated as a distribution of money and not included in the partner's gross income.

 Planning Tip. Excess contributions to an HSA are not deductible and will be subject to a six-percent excise tax reported on line 58 (see page 1-37). Excess employer contributions not included in the taxpayer's income on Form W-2 should be reported as "Other Income" on line 21. The taxpayer may avoid the excise tax if he or she withdraws the excess contributions by the due date of the return (including extensions) for the year contributions are made and any income earned on the contributions is included on line 21.

Line 26, Moving Expenses

A taxpayer may deduct certain expenses of moving to a new home because of a changed job location or to start a new job if a distance and time test are met. Form 3903 is used to calculate the deduction. If a taxpayer is reimbursed by his or her employer for moving expenses, then use the chart on page 1-30 to determine how to report the expenses. See MTG ¶1073.

 Filing Tip. Members of the Armed Forces do not have to meet the distance and time tests if the move is due to a permanent change of duty station.

Deductible moving expenses include the reasonable cost of moving household goods and personal effects of the taxpayer and members of his or her household. This includes the cost of storing and insuring goods for up to 30 consecutive days during the move. It also may include the cost of traveling (including lodging but not meals) from the old home to the new home. Travel expenses are limited to one trip per person but not all of the members of the household must travel together or at the same time. If the taxpayer uses his or her own car to travel, then a standard mileage rate (plus parking and tolls) may be used to calculate the travel expenses incurred in 2013.

  Planning Tip. The standard mileage rate for moving to a new home is 24 cents per mile for all of 2013.

 Caution. In order to deduct moving expenses, they must generally be incurred within one year from the date the taxpayer first reported to work at the new location.

Distance Test. Moving expenses are deductible only if the taxpayer's new principal workplace is at least 50 miles farther from his or her old home than his or her old workplace was. For example, if the old workplace was three miles from the taxpayer's former home, then the new workplace must be at least 53 miles from the former home.

Time Test. If the taxpayer is an employee, then he or she must work full-time in the general area of the new workplace for at least 39 weeks during the 12 months after the move in order for moving expenses to be deductible. A self-employed person must work full-time in the general area of the new workplace for at least 78 weeks during the 24 months right after the move. The time test does not have to met if:

- the taxpayer's job was transferred for the employer's benefit;
- the taxpayer's job ends because of death or disability;
- the taxpayer is laid off or discharged for a reason other than willful misconduct; or
- the taxpayer is a retiree or survivor living outside the United States.

Filing Tip. Moving expenses can be deducted in the year of the move if the taxpayer expects to meet the time test. If the taxpayer later discovers that he or she did not meet the time test, then an amended return must be filed for the year the deduction was claimed or the taxpayer may report as income the amount of moving expense deduction claimed in the year of the move.

Reporting Your Moving Expenses and Reimbursements

IF your Form W-2 shows...	AND you have . . .	THEN . . .
your reimbursement reported only in box 12 with code P	moving expenses greater than the amount in box 12	file Form 3903 showing all allowable expenses and reimbursements
your reimbursement reported only in box 12 with code P	moving expenses equal to the amount in box 12	do not file Form 3903
your reimbursement divided between box 12 and box 1	moving expenses greater than the amount in box 12	file Form 3903 showing all allowable expenses but only the reimbursements reported in box 12
your entire reimbursement reported as wages in box 1	moving expenses	file Form 3903 showing all allowable expenses, but no reimbursements
no reimbursement	moving expenses	file Form 3903 showing all allowable expenses

Line 27, Deductible Part of Self-Employment Tax

A self-employed taxpayer who files Schedule SE may deduct a portion of the self-employment taxes paid for the tax year (Schedule SE, line 6). See Tab 3 for more information.

Line 28, Self-Employed SEP, SIMPLE, and Qualified Plans

A self-employed taxpayer (including partner in a partnership) who makes contributions to his or her own SEP, SIMPLE, or other qualified retirement plan may claim a deduction for such contributions. The deduction is calculated using the worksheets in IRS Publication 560 See Tab 9 for more information.

Line 29, Self-Employed Health Insurance Deduction

Self-employed taxpayers may deduct amounts paid for health insurance (including qualified long-term care insurance) for themselves, their spouses, and their dependents if they are:

- self-employed with a net profit reported on Schedule C or F;
- a partner with net earnings from self-employment (box 14, Code A, Schedule K-1 of Form 1065); or
- a shareholder owning more than two percent of an S corporation who receives wages from the corporation.

The insurance plan must be established under the taxpayer's business. This means the policy can be in the name of the individual or the business. However, in the case of a partner or more-than-two-percent shareholder, the partnership or S corporation must either pay the premiums or reimburse the taxpayer for payment of the premiums. The amount paid or reimbursed by a partnership will be reported to the taxpayer as guaranteed payments on Schedule K-1 of

Form 1065. The amounts paid or reimbursed by an S corporation will be reported to the taxpayer as wages in box 1 of Form W-2.

The deduction for health insurance is not permitted for any month in which the self-employed person was eligible to participate in any subsidized health plan provided by an employer of the taxpayer or the taxpayer's spouse. Amounts paid for health insurance coverage from retirement plan distributions for retired public safety officers also cannot be used to figure the deduction (see page 1-19).

Generally, a worksheet in the Form 1040 instructions is used to calculate the amount of the deduction. However, if the taxpayer is a trade adjustment assistance (TAA) or Pension Benefit Guaranty Corporation (PBGC) recipient, then Form 8885 must be completed before using the worksheet. In addition, Worksheet 6-A in IRS Publication 535 must be used if the taxpayer had more than one source of income subject to self-employment tax, paid for qualified long-term care insurance, or is filing Form 2555 to claim the exclusion foreign earned income or housing costs. If the taxpayer has more than one health plan and each plan is established under a different business, then a separate Worksheet 6-A must be used to figure each plan's net earnings limit.

Line 30, Penalty on Early Withdrawal of Savings

Enter any penalty for early withdrawal of savings or certificates from Form 1099-INT or Form 1099-OID on line 30.

Lines 31a and 31b, Alimony Paid

Alimony (also called spousal support, separate maintenance or maintenance and support) is deductible for the spouse who makes the payment on line 31 and taxable income of the spouse who receives the payment reported on line 11 (see page 1-17). Enter the amount of alimony paid on line 31a and the recipient's SSN on line 31b. For a discussion of the requirements for alimony, see Tab 13 and MTG ¶771-¶778.

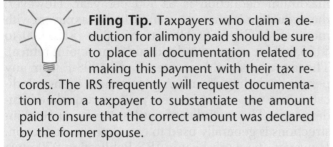

Filing Tip. Taxpayers who claim a deduction for alimony paid should be sure to place all documentation related to making this payment with their tax records. The IRS frequently will request documentation from a taxpayer to substantiate the amount paid to insure that the correct amount was declared by the former spouse.

Line 32, IRA Deduction

A taxpayer may claim a deduction for contributions to a traditional IRA (but not a Roth IRA). For 2013, the maximum contribution that can be made to an IRA is limited to the lesser of $5,500 ($6,500 for taxpayers who will be at least age 50 by the end of the year) or the taxpayer's taxable compensation for the year. If the taxpayer has more than one IRA, the limit applies to the total contributions made to all of his or her IRAs for the year.

Compensation for this purpose includes wages, salaries, tips, professional fees, bonuses, or other compensation reported in box 1 of Form W-2 (including scholarships and fellowships, but reduced by income received from a nonqualified deferred compensation plan or 457 plan as shown in box 11 of Form W-2, box 12 of Form W-2 with Code Z, or box 15b of Form 1099-MISC). It also includes net earnings from self employment (reduced by contributions made to retirement plans and the deduction for one-half of self-employment taxes reported on line 29), as well as any alimony or separate maintenance payments reported on line 11 (see page 1-17). Members of the U.S. Armed Forces may elect to include combat pay (normally excluded from gross income and reported in box 12 of Form W-2, Code Q) as part of their compensation for purposes of determining their maximum IRA contributions.

In the case of married taxpayers filing a joint return, each spouse may have a separate IRA. For 2013, the maximum contribution limit for the spouse with the least amount of compensation is the lesser of $5,500 (or $6,500 if age 50 or older) or the total compensation of both spouses. For this purpose, total compensation is reduced by:

- the IRA deduction for the year of the spouse with the greater compensation;

- any nondeductible contributions made for the year on behalf of the spouse with the greater compensation; and
- any contributions to a Roth IRA on behalf of the spouse with the greater compensation.

Example. Kris is 25 years old and is a full-time student with no taxable income. During 2013, she marries Chad who is 30 years old and has taxable income of $35,000. If the couple files a joint return for the tax year, they may both contribute $5,500 to a traditional IRA. This is because Kris can add Chad's compensation to her own (reduced by the amount of his IRA contribution) to figure her maximum contribution to a traditional IRA. In this case, her contribution limit is $5,500 because it is less than her compensation ($30,000).

Deduction Limit. A taxpayer's deduction for contributions to a traditional IRA may be reduced or eliminated if the taxpayer (or his or her spouse) is covered by an employer-provided retirement plan such as a 401(k) plan, depending on the taxpayer's filing status and modified AGI as shown in the table below. The worksheet in the 1040 instructions is generally used to calculate the amount of the deduction. However, if the taxpayer receives Social Security benefits, then use the worksheets in Appendix B of IRS Publication 590 to calculate the deduction.

2013 Phaseout- Ranges for IRA Deduction	
Filing Status	**Modified AGI**
Single or head of household	$59,000 to $69,000
Married filing jointly (taxpayer covered by employer plan)	$95,000 to $115,000
Married filing jointly (taxpayer not covered by employer plan but spouse is)	$178,000 to $188,000
Married filing separately*	Less than $10,000

* If the taxpayer did not live with his or her spouse at any time during the year, their filing status is considered single for this purpose. Under such circumstances, the taxpayer should enter "D" next to the dotted line next to line 32 or you may receive a math error notice from the IRS.

Caution. An individual only has to be eligible to participate in an employer-provided retirement plan for the limitation on deducting IRA contributions to apply. It does not matter if the individual actually does participate in the plan. For purposes of a defined contribution plan (for example, 401(k)), if any amount is contributed or allocated to the account by the taxpayer or the employer, then the taxpayer is considered covered by the plan. The taxpayer's employer should inform the taxpayer if he or she is eligible to participate in an employer-provided plan by checking box 13 of the individual's Form W-2. However, if box 13 is checked and the taxpayer believes that he or she is not covered, he or she should check with his or her employer and obtain a revised Form W-2 if needed.

Nondeductible Contributions. Although a taxpayer's deduction for contributions to a traditional IRA may be reduced or eliminated, contributions can still be made up to the maximum limit. Nondeductible contributions to a traditional IRA must be reported on Form 8606. A taxpayer has until the due date for filing his or her tax return (not including extensions) to make a contribution to an IRA for the year (April 15, 2014). Thus, the taxpayer does not have to designate a contribution to a traditional IRA as nondeductible until he or she files a return. See MTG ¶2153D.

Caution. Contributions to either a traditional or Roth IRA in excess of the maximum limit (whether deductible or nondeductible) are subject to a six-percent excise tax reported on line 58 (see page 1-37). To avoid the tax, the taxpayer may withdraw any excess contribution by the due date of the return (including extensions) for the year contributions are made. Any income earned on the excess contributions, however, must also be withdrawn and reported as 'Other Income' on line 21.

Caution. Taxpayers who are age 70½ or older at the end of the tax year may not deduct contributions to traditional IRAs or treat them as nondeductible contributions.

Line 33, Student Loan Interest Deduction

Individuals are allowed to deduct interest paid during the tax year on any qualified student loan. The maximum deduction is $2,500 per year. However, the deduction is phased out in 2013 for taxpayers with modified (AGI) of $60,000 to $75,000 ($125,000 to $155,000 for married individuals filing a joint return). The taxpayer should receive a Form 1098-E from any person (including a bank or government agency) indicating the amount of interest paid on a qualified student loan. The worksheet found in the Form 1040 instructions is generally used to calculate the deduction. However, the worksheet in IRS Publication 970 must be used if the taxpayer excludes income using Form 2555, 2555-EZ, or 4563, or from sources within Puerto Rico. See MTG ¶1082.

The deduction can only be claimed if the taxpayer is legally obligated to pay the interest on a qualified student loan. The interest must also be actually paid by the taxpayer or by someone else on the taxpayer's behalf. The deduction, however, cannot be claimed if someone else claims the taxpayer as a dependent in the tax year or if the interest can be deducted elsewhere (for example, as home mortgage interest). Married taxpayers must file a joint return in order to claim the deduction.

Example. Josh received a Form 1098-E from his bank indicating that he paid $1,100 of interest on his qualified student loan in 2013. Only he is legally obligated to make the payments on the loan. If Josh's parents claim him as a dependent on their 2013 return, then neither Josh nor his parents may deduct the student loan interest Josh paid in 2013. However, if Josh's parents do not claim him as a dependent on their return, then Josh may deduct the interest on his return.

Example. Darla obtained a qualified student loan to attend college. After Darla's graduation from college, she worked as an intern for a nonprofit organization. As part of the internship program, the nonprofit organization made an interest payment on behalf of Darla. This payment was reported in box 1 of her Form W-2. Assuming all other qualifications are met, Darla can deduct this payment of her student loan interest on her return.

Qualified Student Loan. A qualified student loan is a loan for qualified higher education expenses including tuition, fees, room and board, and related expenses such as books and supplies. The expenses must be for a degree, certificate, or similar program at a college, university, or vocational school eligible to participate in federal student aid programs. The student must be the taxpayer, the taxpayer's spouse, any person who was the taxpayer's dependent at the time the loan was taken out, or any person who could have been claimed as a dependent at the time the loan was taken out except that the person filed a joint return and had gross income of at least $3,900 for the year, or if taxpayer is married filing a joint return and either spouse could be claimed as a dependent on someone else's return. The student must carry at least half the normal full-time workload for the degree or certificate he or she is pursuing.

Line 34, Tuition and Fees Deduction

 Caution. Absent further legislation, the deduction for qualified tuition and fees is not available for tax years beginning after December 31, 2013.

A deduction may be claimed for qualified tuition expenses paid during the year for the taxpayer, the taxpayer's spouse, or the taxpayer's dependent for whom an exemption is claimed. The maximum deduction is $4,000 for taxpayers with an adjusted gross income (AGI) at or below $65,000 ($130,000 for joint filers). The maximum deduction is $2,000 for taxpayers whose AGI exceeds $65,000 but less than or equal to $80,000 ($130,000 and $160,000, respectively, for joint filers). Taxpayers whose AGI exceeded these limits, married taxpayers filing separately, nonresident aliens, and taxpayers who can be claimed as a dependent on another person's return are not allowed to claim the deduction. Form 8917 is used to calculate the deduction.

Qualified tuition expenses are amounts paid during the year for tuition and fees required for the student's enrollment at a college, university, or vocational school for an academic period beginning in the year and the first three months of the following year. They do not include expenses for room and board, insurance, medical expenses (including student health fees), transportation or other similar personal expenses. Qualified expenses also do not include books, supplies, equipment, or expenses for courses involving sports, games or hobbies, unless such courses are part of the student's degree program. The taxpayer should have received a Form 1098-T from the school indicating the amount of qualified expenses paid.

Qualified education expenses *can not* be deducted on line 34 to the extent:

- the expenses were deducted elsewhere, for example as a business expense;
- the American Opportunity (modified Hope) or lifetime learning Credit was claimed for the same student for the year (see Tab 13);
- the expenses were used to figure the tax-free portion of a distribution from a Coverdell ESA or qualified tuition program (529 plan);
- the expenses were paid with tax-free educational assistance such as scholarships and fellowships that were not included on line 7, employer-provided or other nontaxable education assistance (for example, Pell grants or veterans' education assistance), or other tax-free payments such as gifts or inheritance; or
- the expenses were paid with tax-free interest on U.S. savings bonds.

Line 35, Domestic Production Activities Deduction

Individuals engaged in a trade or business may deduct nine percent of the lesser their adjusted gross income (determined without regard to the deduction) or qualified production activities income (QPAI). However, the deduction may not exceed 50 percent of the W-2 wages paid by the taxpayer attributable to domestic production gross receipts.

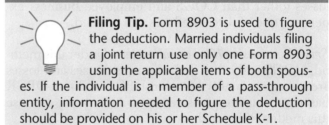 **Filing Tip.** Form 8903 is used to figure the deduction. Married individuals filing a joint return use only one Form 8903 using the applicable items of both spouses. If the individual is a member of a pass-through entity, information needed to figure the deduction should be provided on his or her Schedule K-1.

Qualified Activities. A taxpayer's QPAI is his or her domestic production gross receipts (DPGR), less the cost of goods sold allocable to DPGR and other expenses, losses or deductions allocable to DPGR. Generally, an individual's gross receipts derived from the following activities are DPGR:

- construction of real property performed by the taxpayer in the United States in a construction trade or business;
- engineering or architectural services performed by the taxpayer in the United States in a engineering or architectural services trade or business for the construction of real property in the United States; and
- any lease, rental, license, sale, exchange or other disposition of:
  - tangible personal property, computer software, and sound recordings that the taxpayer manufactured, produced, grew, or extracted in whole or in significant part in the United States;

- qualified film produced by the taxpayer; or
- electricity, natural gas, or potable water the taxpayer produced in the United States.

Activities from which the gross receipts will **not** be DPGR include:

- the sale of food and beverages at a retail establishment;
- property leased, rented or licensed between certain persons treated as a single employer;
- the lease, rental, license, sale, exchange or other disposition of land; and
- the transmission or distribution of electricity, natural gas, or potable water.

Allocation methods. To compute the deduction, a taxpayer must allocate all of its gross receipts between DPGR and non-DPGR. Any reasonable method may be used so long as it accurately identifies which gross receipts are DPGR. However, if less than five percent of the taxpayer's gross receipts are DPGR, all of the gross receipt may be treated as either DPGR or non-DPGR.

The taxpayer must use the same method to allocate cost of goods sold (COGS) to DPGR as used to allocate gross receipts, unless another method is more accurate. To allocate other deductions, expenses or losses (other than COGS and employee business expenses), one of three methods can be used.

Small business simplified overall method. Under this method, COGS and other deductions, expenses and losses are allocated ratably between DPGR and non-DPGR based on relative gross receipts. A taxpayer can use this method if he or she:

- has average annual gross receipts of $5 million or less;
- is engaged in a farming trade or business and is not required to use the accrual-method of accounting; or
- has average annual gross receipts of $10 million or less and is eligible to use the cash method of accounting.

Simplified deduction method. Under this method, trade or business deductions, expenses and losses (other than COGS and employee business expenses) are allocated ratably between DPGR and non-DPGR based on relative gross receipts. A taxpayer can use this method if total trade or business assets is $10 million or less at the end of the tax year or average annual gross receipts are $100 million or less.

Section 861 method. Under this method, trade or business expenses and losses (other than COGS and employee business expenses) are allocated using the tracing rules under Code Sec. 861.

Lines 36, 37, and 38, Adjusted Gross Income Calculations

Include in the sum on line 36 any of the following write-in adjustments on the dotted line next to line 36 by writing in the amount and identity of the deduction.

- Expenses related to income from rental of personal property reported on line 21 and engaged in for profit (identify as "PPR");
- Jury duty pay surrendered to an employer in exchange for regular compensation (identify as "Jury Pay");
- Deductible contributions to Archer MSAs as determined on Form 8853 (identify as "MSA");
- Repayment of supplemental unemployment benefits under the Trade Act of 1974 (identify as "Sub-Pay TRA");
- Contributions to certain pension plans under IRC §§403(b) or 501(c)(18)(D) (identify as "403(b)" and "501(c)(18)(D)," respectively);
- Attorney fees and court costs paid for prosecuting unlawful discrimination claims, but only to extent of gross income from such actions (identify as "UDC");
- Attorney fees and courts costs paid in connection with an IRS whistleblower award that substantially contributed to detection of tax law violations, but only to the extent of the amount of the award included in gross income (identify as "WBF");
- Reforestation amortization and expenses (see Tab 8 for more information) (identify as "RFST"); and
- Foreign housing deduction for qualified self-employed taxpayers as calculated on Form 2555 (identify as "Form 2555").

See MTG ¶1005 for a comprehensive list of above-the-line deductions.

Adjusted Gross Income. Lines 37 and 38 are the taxpayer's AGI. This is the primary value used in tax calculations, including calculation of the alternative minimum tax.

Tax and Credits, Lines 38-55

After AGI is determined, additional deductions may be taken to determine the taxpayer's taxable income. From this amount the taxpayer's tentative tax liability is calculated before any tax credits are subtracted dollar for dollar to determine the taxpayer's actual tax liability.

Lines 39 and 40, Itemized or Standard Deductions

Generally, taxpayers will lower their federal income tax liability by taking the larger of their itemized deductions on Schedule A (see Tab 2) or a standard deduction listed in the table below. Additions to the standard deduction are allowed if the taxpayer (or spouse if filing a joint return) is age 65 or older, or is totally or partially blind on the last day of the year. Check the appropriate box(es) on line 39a and enter the total number checked. If the taxpayer (or spouse if filing jointly) may be claimed as a dependent on someone else's return, the basic standard deduction amount will be limited and the worksheet in the 1040 instructions must be used to compute the amount to enter on line 40.

2013 Standard Deductions		
Filing Status	Standard Deduction	Age 65 or Older or Blind (Each)
Single	$6,100	$1,500
MFJ or QW/SS	$12,200	$1,200
MFS	$6,100	$1,200
HOH	$8,950	$1,500

Filing Tip. If the taxpayer is married filing a separate return and his or her spouse itemizes deductions for the year, then the taxpayer's standard deduction amount is zero (-0-), even if the taxpayer was age 65 or older or blind. The individual should itemize deductions under such circumstances. In either case, the box on line 39b must be checked.

Filing Tip. The standard deduction amount for a taxpayer who is a dual-status alien (both nonresident and resident alien during portions of the year) will also be zero (-0-), even if the taxpayer was age 65 or older or blind. Under such circumstance, the box on line 39b must be checked and "Dual-Status Return" should be written across the top of the taxpayer's return. However, a nonresident alien married to a U.S. citizen or resident alien at the end of the year may elect to be treated as a resident alien (see page 1-3).

Line 42, Calculation of Exemptions

In 2013, a taxpayer may claim a deduction of up to $3,900 for each exemption claimed in line 6d (see page 1-8). The dependency exemption amount is denied to claimants who fail to provide the dependent's correct taxpayer identification number on the return claiming the dependency exemption. Beginning in 2013, the personal and dependent exemption amounts are subject to phase out. The phase-out threshold amount is $300,000 for filing status of joint of surviving spouse, $275,000 for head of household filers, $250,000 for

unmarried and single filers; and $150,000 if using the married filing separately status. The exemption amount is reduced by two percent for every $2,500 of part thereof that the taxpayers AGI exceeds the threshold amount for their filing status. See MTG ¶133 for more information.

Line 43, Taxable Income

Subtract line 42 from line 41 to determine the taxpayer's taxable income. If line 42 is more than line 41, enter zero (-0-).

Line 44, Tax Rates

A taxpayer's tentative tax liability is reported on line 44. Generally, if taxable income (line 43) is less than $100,000, then the tax table reproduced in Tab 17 is used to determine the taxpayer's tentative liability. If taxable income is $100,000 or more, then the tax rate schedule reproduced in Tab 17 is used. Certain taxpayers, however, are required to calculate their tentative tax liability using alternative methods.

- Form 8615 must generally be used for certain children who had more than $2,000 of investment income (unless neither of the child's parents was alive at the end of 2013 or the child files a joint return for the year). See Tab 13.
- Schedule D Worksheet must be used if the taxpayer is required to file Schedule D and has gains that are subject to the 28 percent capital gains rate or any unrecaptured section 1250 gain. See Tab 4.
- Qualified Dividends and Capital Gain Tax Worksheet, in the 1040 instructions, must be used if the taxpayer does not have to use the Schedule D Worksheet, but reports qualified dividends on line 9b or capital gains on line 13. The Worksheet must also be used if the taxpayer is filing Schedule D and has net-long term capital gains or losses, or long-term capital loss carryovers. See Tab 4.
- Schedule J may be used by taxpayers who had income from farming or fishing. See Tab 3 and MTG ¶767.
- Foreign Earned Income Tax Worksheet in the 1040 instructions must be used by taxpayers who claimed the foreign earned income exclusion, housing exclusion, or housing deduction on Form 2555.

Include in the total on line 44 (checking the appropriate box) any of the following:

- tax from Form 8814, relating to a parent's election to report a child's investment income (see Tab 13);
- tax from Form 4972, relating to the tax on lump-sum distributions (see page 1-20);
- tax due to making a Code Sec. 962 election (the election made by a domestic shareholder of a controlled foreign corporation to be taxed at corporate rates); and
- recapture of an education credit if the credit was claimed in an earlier year and a refund or tax-free

educational assistance was received in 2013 for that year (enter the amount and write "ECR" in the space next to line 44). See Form 8863 for more information.

Line 45, Alternative Minimum Tax

All taxpayers subject to the regular federal income tax are also subject to the alternative minimum tax (AMT). Alternative minimum taxable income (AMTI) is calculated according to a different system than that for income subject to the regular tax. See Tab 10 for more information, as well as a worksheet to be used to determine whether the taxpayer must complete Form 6251 to calculate his or her AMT liability.

Line 46, Calculation of Tax Liability

Add line 44, regular income tax, and 45, alternative minimum tax, to determine the taxpayer's total tax liability.

Line 47, Foreign Tax Credit

Taxpayers who paid or accrued foreign income taxes on foreign-source income subject to U.S. tax may choose to claim a credit for such taxes or to include them as an itemized deductions on Schedule A. Form 1116 is generally used to calculate the credit. See Tab 10 for more information.

Line 48, Child and Dependent Care Credit

Taxpayers who paid someone to care for their child under age 13 or other qualifying dependent so they (or spouse, if filing a joint return) could work or look for work may claim a credit for such expenses. Form 2441 is used to calculate the credit. See Tab 10 for more information.

> **Caution.** A taxpayer cannot receive a double benefit by claiming a credit on dependent care benefits that are excluded from income on line 7 of Form 1040. Thus, a taxpayer must calculate the exclusion in Part III of Form 2441 first. Then the credit may be calculated in Part II of Form 2441 on any child and dependent care expenses not excluded from income.

Line 49, Education Credits

Two education credits are available to a taxpayer who incurred qualifying education expenses during the year for himself or herself, his or her spouse, or dependent to enroll in or attend an eligible education institution. The credits are the American Opportunity Tax Credit (a modified Hope Scholarship Credit) and the Lifetime Learning Credit. A taxpayer may only claim one of the credits for each student for the year. Form 8863 is used to calculate the credits. Forty percent of the American Opportunity (modified Hope) Credit is refundable and reported on line 66 (see page 1-41). See Tab 10 for more information.

Line 50, Retirement Savings Credit

Certain low- and middle-income taxpayers may be able to claim a nonrefundable credit for contributions made to a retirement plan. Form 8880 is used to calculate the credit. See Tab 10 for more information.

Line 51, Child Tax Credit

Taxpayers who have one or more qualifying child (see page 1-8) under the age of 17 may be entitled to a credit of $1,000 per child, subject to a phaseout limitation. A taxpayer should have checked the box in column 4 of line 6c for each dependent for whom the child tax credit is claimed. Generally, the credit is nonrefundable. However, a taxpayer may qualify for an additional child tax credit which may be refundable on line 65 (see page 1-40). See Tab 10 for more information.

Line 52, Residential Energy Credits

A taxpayer is allowed a nonbusiness energy property credit for the cost of qualified energy efficiency improvements and expenses for residential energy property relating to their principal residence. A taxpayer may claim a nonrefundable residential energy efficient property credit for amounts spent for qualified solar electric property, qualified solar water heating property, or qualified fuel cell property. Form 5695 is used to calculate the credits to be reported on line 52. See Tab 10 for more information.

Line 53, Other Tax Credits

A taxpayer reports the following various credits on line 53 by checking the appropriate box(es) and completing the form(s) indicated. If the taxpayer checks box c, then enter the form number in the space provided. See Tab 10 for more information about these credits.

- **Form 8396**, *Mortgage Interest Credit.* The credit can only be claimed if the taxpayer was issued a Mortgage Credit Certificate (MCC) by a state or local government.
- **Form 3800**, *General Business Credit.* The credit consists of a number of credits that usually only apply to individuals who are partners, S corporation shareholders, or self-employed, or have rental property. If the taxpayer claims only one business credit, Form 3800 need not be filed unless the taxpayer has one or more of the business credits to claim in a single year or a carryback or carryforward from previous years.
- **Schedule R, Form 1040**, *Credit for the Elderly or the Disabled.* Write "Sch R" in space next to box c.
- **Form 8936**, *Qualified Plug-in Electric Drive Motor Vehicle Credit.* The qualified plug-in electric drive motor vehicle credit is available for qualified vehicles placed in service during the year.

- **Form 8910**, *Alternative Motor Vehicle Credit.* The alternative motor vehicle credit can be claimed if the taxpayer placed an alternative motor vehicle in service during the year. See also Form 8911, *Alternative Fuel Vehicle Refueling Property Credit.*
- **Others.** Form 8801, *Credit for Prior Year Minimum Tax—Individuals, Estates, and Trusts;* Form 8912, *Credit for Clean Renewable Energy and Gulf Tax Credit Bonds.*

Lines 54 and 55, Total Credits

Lines 47 through 53 are added together to determine the taxpayer's total amount of tax credits claimed on line 54. This total is then subtracted from the taxpayer's tentative tax liability (line 46) and the result is entered on line 55. However, if the total amount of tax credits claimed on line 54 is more than the taxpayer's tentative liability, then enter zero (-0-) on line 55.

Other Taxes, Lines 56-61

Line 56, Self-Employment Tax

Self-employed taxpayers who have more than $400 of net earnings must pay a self-employment tax. The tax is computed on Schedule SE. See Tab 3 for more information. A taxpayer may claim a deduction from gross income for part of the self-employment tax paid on line 27 (see page 1-30).

Line 57, Unreported Social Security and Medicare Tax

A taxpayer must figure and report his or her share of uncollected Social Security and Medicare taxes due on tip income or wages received during the year. Check the appropriate box and enter the total amount of taxes from Form 4137 and Form 8919 for this purpose.

Form 4137 is used if the taxpayer received cash or charge tips of $20 or more in any month and did not report the full amount to their employer. The taxpayer must also pay uncollected Social Security and Medicare taxes on allocated tips shown on his or her Form W-2(s) and that are included on line 7.

Form 8919 is used if the taxpayer was an employee but was incorrectly treated as an independent contractor by his or her employer resulting in no Social Security or Medicare taxes being withheld from compensation received from the employer.

 Caution. If the taxpayer did not report tips to his or her employer as required, then he or she may be charged a penalty equal to 50 percent of the taxes calculated on Form 4137. To avoid the penalty, attach a statement to the return explaining why the taxpayer had reasonable cause for not reporting the tips to their employer. See IRS Publication 531.

Line 58, Additional Tax on IRAs and Other Qualified Retirement Plans, Etc.

Report on line 58 any additional taxes on qualified retirement plans (including IRAs), HSAs, Archer MSAs, Coverdell ESAs, and qualified tuition plans (529 plans) as calculated on Form 5329. In the case of a joint return, a separate Form 5329 must be completed for each spouse. The additional taxes include:

- the 10-percent additional tax on early distributions from a qualified retirement plan or IRA (including an early distribution from a Roth IRA that is not a qualifying distribution);
- the six-percent additional tax on excess contributions to a traditional IRA, Roth IRA, HSA, Archer MSA, or Coverdell ESA; and
- the 10-percent additional tax on distributions from a Coverdell ESA or qualified tuition plan (529 plan) which are not used for qualified education expenses.

If the taxpayer is only subject to the 10-percent additional tax on early distributions (code 1 in box 7 of Form 1099-R), then Form 5329 does not need to be filed. Instead, on line 58 enter 10 percent of the taxable amount of the distribution (as reported on line 15b, 16b or Form 4972) and enter "No" to the left of line 58. However, if code 1 is incorrectly shown in box 7 of Form 1099-R or an exception to the early distribution penalty applies (code 2 in box 7 of Form 1099-R), then Form 5329 must be filed (see Tab 9).

Lines 59a and 59b, Additional Taxes

Report on line 59a or 59b any household employment taxes from Schedule H repayment or any recapture of the first-time homebuyer credit. Check the appropriate box.

Household Employment Taxes. If the taxpayer pays cash wages of $1,800 or more in 2013 to any one household employee, then Social Security and Medicare (FICA) taxes must be paid. Similarly, if the taxpayer pays cash wages of $1,000 or more in any one calendar quarter in 2013 to all household employees, then federal unemployment taxes (FUTA) must be paid. Schedule H is used to calculate the taxes and the amount reported on line 59. However, Schedule

H does not have to be used and no amount is required to be reported on line 59 if the taxpayer chooses to pay the taxes for household employees with business or farm employment taxes on Form 941, Form 943, or Form 944.

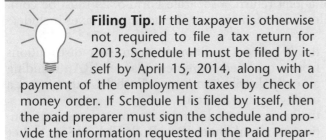

Planning Tip. A taxpayer is not required to withhold federal *income* taxes from wages paid to a household employee unless the employee requests the taxpayer to do so (using Form W-4) and the taxpayer agrees. If the withholding tables show no income tax should be withheld, then a notice (Copy B of Form W-2) should be given to the employee about the earned income credit (EIC).

Filing Tip. If the taxpayer is otherwise not required to file a tax return for 2013, Schedule H must be filed by itself by April 15, 2014, along with a payment of the employment taxes by check or money order. If Schedule H is filed by itself, then the paid preparer must sign the schedule and provide the information requested in the Paid Preparer's Use Only section.

Wages paid to certain household employees will not be subject to employment taxes. This includes wages paid to the taxpayer's spouse, the taxpayer's child who is under the age of 21, or the taxpayer's parent. However, FICA taxes must be paid if the parent is caring for the taxpayer's minor child who has a physical or mental condition and the taxpayer is divorced, a widow(er), or living with a spouse who is physically or mentally disabled. FICA taxes also do not have to paid for any employee under the age of 18 at any time during the year, unless providing household services is his or her principal occupation.

For these purposes, a household employee is any person hired by the taxpayer to do household work in and around his or her home. Examples include housekeepers, nannies, health aides, maids, yard workers, and similar domestic workers. However, the taxpayer must be able to control what work the individual does and how he or she does it in order to be considered an employee. For example, workers from an agency or a self-employed individual who can control how his or her work is done are not considered household employees.

A separate Form W-2 must be filed with the Social Security Administration (SSA) for each household employee the taxpayer paid wages of $1,800 or more subject to FICA or wages from which federal income

tax is withheld. A copy must also be given to the employee. If the taxpayer files one or more Form W-2, then Form W-3 must also be filed with the SSA. The taxpayer must obtain an employment identification number (EIN) to file Form W-2 or Schedule H. The taxpayer must also have verified that the employee can legally work in the United States by completing with the employee Form I-9 obtained from the U.S. Citizenship and Immigration Services.

First-Time Homebuyer Credit. A taxpayer who claimed the first-time homebuyer credit for a purchase of a home in 2008 must repay the credit ratably over a 15-year period beginning in 2010. If the taxpayer purchased the home in 2009 or 2010 (or before July 1, 2011, for purchases by eligible military, foreign service, or intelligence community personnel), and disposed of the home or stopped using it as a personal residence within 36 months of purchase, the taxpayer will have to repay the credit. The repayment or recapture of the credit in either situation is calculated on Form 5405. See Tab 10 for more information on the first-time homebuyer credit.

Line 60, Other Taxes.

This line is used to report other taxes not reported elsewhere on the return. The 1040 instructions list the taxes that should be listed here, along with the relevant form or publication, In the event that more room is required, attach a statement to the Form 1040 listing the amount of the tax and the relevant code. The total of all additional taxes should be entered on line 60.

Additional Medicare Tax. Beginning in 2013, individual taxpayers with wages and self-employment income in excess of specific thresholds determined by filing status will pay an additional 0.9-percent Medicare tax on the excess amount over the threshold. The threshold amounts are: for joint filiers, $250,000; for single, head-of-household, and surviving spouse filers, $200,000; and for those filing married but separate, $125,000. Taxpayers with income in excess of the threshold amount will complete Form 8959, check box a, enter the amount on line 60, and attach the form to their Form 1040. IRC §3101. See MTG ¶2648.

Net Investment Income Tax. Beginning in 2013, individual taxpayers with net investment income (NII) will pay an additional 3.8-percent tax on the lesser of the excess of their modified adjusted gross income over a threshold amount determined by filing status or the total of their net investment income for the year. The threshold amounts are: for joint filers, $250,000; for single, head-of-household, and surviving spouse filers, $200,000; and for married separate filers, $125,000. Net investment income is the sum of interest, dividends, annuities, royalties, rents other than that derived in the ordinary course of a trade or buisness, gross income derived from a trade or business that is a passive activity or trading in financial instruments or commodities, the net gain from disposition of property other than property held in a trade or business, less the allowable deduction properly allocable to such income or net gain. Modified adjusted gross income is adjusted gross income increased by the excess of the amount of excluded foreign earned income over the amount of deductions or exclusions taken into account with respect to the foreign earned income. Taxpayers will use Form 8960 to determine the amount of net investment income tax, check box b, enter the amount on line 60, and attach the form to their Form 1040. IRC §1411. See MTG ¶129.

- **Other Taxes.** In addition to the addition Medicare tax and the net investment income tax, other taxes that should be included by checking box c are:
- Additional tax on distributions from
  - health savings accounts, "HSA" (Form 8889)
  - Archer medical savings accounts, "MSA" (Form 8853)
  - Medicare Advantage MSAs, "Med MSA" (Form 8853)
  - nonqualified deferred compensation plans, "NQDC" (Form W-2, box 12, Code Z or Form 1099-MISC, box 15b)

- Additional tax for failure to maintain HDHP for a HSA, "HDHP" (Form 8889, Part III)
- Recapture of federal mortgage subsidy, "FMSR" (Form 8828)
- Recapture of COBRA premium assistance if modified AGI is more than $125,000 ($250,000 if married filing jointly), "COBRA"
- Section 72(m)(5) excess benefits tax, "72(m)(5)"
- Uncollected Social Security and Medicare tax on tips or group-term life insurance, "UT" (Form W-2, box 12, codes A and B or M and N)
- Golden parachute payments, "EPP" (Form W-2, box 12, code K or Form 1099-MISC, box 13)
- Tax on accumulation distribution of trusts, "ADT" (Form 4970)
- Interest on tax due on installment income from the sale of certain residential lots and timeshares "453(l)(3)"
- Interest on deferred tax on gain from certain installment sales over $150,000, "453A(c)"
- Lookback interest under Code Sec. 167(g) or 460(b), "From Form 8697" or "From Form 8866"
- Additional tax on recapture of charitable contribution deduction relating to fractional interest in tangible personal property, "FITPP"
- Excise tax on insider stock compensation from an expatriated corporation, "ISC"
- Additional tax on compensation received from a nonqualified deferred compensation plan described in IRC §457A, "457A"
- Any negative amount on Form 8885, line 5, because of advance payments of the health coverage tax credit, "HCTC"

- Recapture of the following credits
  - investment credit, "ICR" (Form 4255)
  - low-income housing credit, "LIHCR" (Form 8611)
  - qualified electric vehicle credit, "QEVCR" (Form 8834)
  - Indian employment credit, "IECR" (Form 8845)
  - new markets credit, "NMCR" (Form 8874)
  - credit for employer-provided child care facilities, "ECCFR" (Form 8882)
  - alternative motor vehicle credit, "AMVCR" (Form 8910)
  - alternative motor vehicle refueling property credit, "APRCR" (Form 8911)
  - qualified plug-in electric drive motor vehicle credit, "8936" (Form 8936)

 Caution. Eligible employees who have lost their jobs may qualify for a 65-percent subsidy for COBRA continuation premiums for up to nine months. Generally, the premium subsidy is not included in gross income. However, the subsidy must be recaptured as an addition to tax on line 60 and identified as "COBRA" when the individual's modified AGI exceeds $125,000 ($250,000 for joint returns). If the individual's modified AGI exceeds $145,000 ($290,000 for joint returns), then the full amount of the subsidy is recaptured. See MTG ¶896B for more information.

Line 61, Total Tax

A taxpayer computes his or her total tax liability by adding lines 56 through 60 together and entering the result on line 61.

Payments, Lines 62-72

Line 62, Federal Income Tax Withheld

Report on line 62 the sum of the federal income tax withheld shown in:

- box 2 of Forms W-2 and W-2G;
- box 4 of most types of Form 1099 (1099-DIV, 1099-G, 1099-R, etc.); and
- box 6 of Form SSA-1099.

If the taxpayer is married filing a separate return, enter only the tax withheld from his or her own income. Do not include any amount withheld from the income of the taxpayer's spouse unless the couple lives in a community property state. In such cases, each spouse can claim half of the total income tax withheld from their combined wages since each can report half of the wages.

Line 63, Estimated Tax Payments

Enter on line 63, estimated federal income tax payments made using Form 1040-ES and any overpayment from the taxpayer's 2012 return that was applied to his or her 2013 estimated tax. Also include any estimated taxes credited to the taxpayer from an estate or trust (box 13 of Schedule K-1 of Form 1041).

 Planning Tip. If any estimated taxes are credited to the taxpayer from an estate or trust, then they must be reported on Schedule E (see Tab 5). However, the taxes do not need to be included on line 37 of Schedule E. Instead, enter "ES payment claimed" and the amount next to line 37.

Married Filing Separate Returns. Joint estimated payments made by married taxpayers who are filing separate returns or who are divorced may be divided between the spouses in any way they agree. If the spouses cannot agree, then the couple must divide the joint payments in proportion to each spouse's individual tax as shown on their separate 2013 returns.

Example. Richard and Paula filed a joint return for 2012 that showed a $3,000 overpayment, which they applied to their 2013 estimated tax. The couple, however, are filing separate returns for 2013. Richard's tax liability for 2013 is $4,000 and Paula's tax liability for 2013 is $1,000. If the couple does not agree on how to divide the $3,000 overpayment made in 2012, then Richard's share will be $2,400 (80 percent of $3,000) and Paula's share will be $600 (20 percent of $3,000).

If the taxpayer claims a joint estimated payment on a separate return, then the other spouse's Social Security number (SSN) must be reported in the space provided on page 1 of the return. However, if a divorced taxpayer has remarried during the year, enter the present spouse's SSN on page 1 of his or her separate return. Enter the former spouse's SSN, followed by "DIV" to the left of line 63.

If a married couple paid separate estimated tax payments for 2013 but are filing a joint return, then the separate amounts may be added together on the return. However, if a married couple made separate estimated tax payments for 2013 and file separate returns for 2013, then each spouse may only claim credit for the estimated payments he or she made.

Example. Carla and Nick filed a joint return for 2012 that showed a $1,100 overpayment that they applied to their 2013 estimated tax. The couple, however, are filing separate returns for 2013. Carla's W-2 shows $1,000 withheld for 2013 and she has a tax liability of $2,700. Nick's W-2 shows $300 withheld for 2013 but he has no tax liability. Carla can enter $2,100 on line 62, claiming $1,000 for the amount withheld from her wages and the entire $1,100 of the 2012 overpayment since Nick has no tax liability for 2013. Carla, however, cannot claim the $300 withheld from Nick's wages even though she would have a tax liability of $600 remaining. Instead, Nick must claim the $300 on his separate return.

Name Change. If a taxpayer's name changed, and estimated payments were made using the former name, attach a statement to the return explaining all the payments made by the taxpayer (and spouse, if applicable), and the names and SSNs under which they were made.

Line 64, Earned Income Credit

A refundable credit is available to certain low-income individuals who have earned income. See Tab 10 for more information including the tables to determine the amount of credit that may be claimed on line 64a.

Members of the U.S. armed forces may elect to treat nontaxable combat pay as earned income for purposes of the credit. A taxpayer's nontaxable combat pay should be shown in box 12 of Form W-2, Code Q. The amount of pay that the taxpayer elects to be included as earned income is reported on line 64b. In the case of a joint return where both spouses receive nontaxable combat pay, both spouses may make the election and the total is reported on line 64b.

Filing Tip. Since electing to include nontaxable combat pay could potentially decrease the amount of earned income credit, the credit amount should be calculated both with and without the nontaxable combat pay included.

Line 65, Additional Child Tax Credit

Taxpayers who have at least one qualifying child for the child tax credit on line 51 (see page 1-36) may also qualify for the additional child tax credit. The additional child tax credit may give the taxpayer a refund even if no tax is owed. If the taxpayer claimed the child tax credit, or was not entitled to take the child tax credit only because no tax was owed, use Schedule 8812 to determine the amount of the additional child tax credit. See Tab 10 and MTG ¶1305 for more information.

Line 66, American Opportunity Credit

A taxpayer may be entitled to a refund of 40 percent of the American Opportunity (modified Hope) Credit claimed for 2013. Form 8863 is used to compute the credit including the refundable portion which is reported on line 66. See Tab 10 for more information.

Line 68, Payments Made With Extension Request

If the taxpayer filed Form 4868 to get an automatic extension to file his or her 2013 return, enter on line 68 any amount paid with the forms or by electronic funds withdrawal or credit card. If an amount was paid by credit card, the convenience fee is not included.

Line 69, Excess Social Security and Tier I RRTA Tax Withheld

If the taxpayer had more than one employer during 2013 and total wages of more than $113,700, too much Social Security or tier I Railroad Retirement taxes may have been withheld. For 2013, no more than $7,049.40 should have been withheld. Any excess may be claimed as a credit on line 69. Withheld Social Security and tier I RRTA taxes are reported in box 4 and box 14 of Form W-2, respectively. For taxpayers filing a joint return, each spouse must figure the excess separately. A taxpayer cannot add Social Security or tier I RRTA tax withheld from his or her spouse's income to the amount withheld from his or her own income.

 Caution. If any one employer withheld too much Social Security or tier I RRTA taxes, then the taxpayer cannot claim the credit. Instead, the employer should adjust the amount withheld. If the employer does not, the taxpayer must file a claim for refund using Form 843. If the taxpayer has any excess tier II RRTA taxes, Form 843 must also be used. For 2013, the maximum amount of tier II RRTA taxes that should have been withheld and reported in box 14 of Form W-2 is $3,709.20.

Lines 70 and 71, Other Payments

On lines 70 and 71, a taxpayer reports various other credits against his or her tax liability. On line 70, the taxpayer reports credit for federal tax paid on certain fuel as determined on Form 4136. On line 71, the taxpayer must check the appropriate box(es) and enter the amount from the following forms to receive credit for the payment of the following taxes:

- Form 2439, *Notice to Shareholders of Undistributed Long-Term Capital Gains* (box 2).
- Form 8801, *Credit for Prior Year Minimum Tax* (line 29) (see Tab 10).
- Form 8885, *Health Coverage Tax Credit* (line 5).

Line 72, Total Payments

Add lines 62, 63, 64a, and 65 through 71. This is the amount of 2013 federal income tax prepaid by the taxpayer, including refundable credits.

Refund or Amount Due, Lines 73-77

Line 73, Overpayment

If line 72 is more than line 61, then the taxpayer is entitled to a refund. However, if the overpayment is less than $1, the IRS will send a refund only on written request.

 Planning Tip. If the amount of overpayment is large, the taxpayer may want to file a new Form W-4 or recalculate the estimated tax amounts that will be paid with Form 1040-ES. See Tab 11 for more details.

Refund Offsets. All or part of a taxpayer's overpayment may be used to pay past-due debts including federal tax, state income tax, child or spousal support, or federal nontax debts such as student loans and unemployment benefits received by fraud. If offsets are made, the taxpayer will receive a notice showing the amount of the offset and the agency receiving it.

A spouse who files a joint return may file an injured spouse claim using Form 8379 to obtain a refund of his or her part of the overpayment if an offset is made to pay the other spouse's debts. If the form is attached to the taxpayer's return, then write "Injured Spouse" on page 1 of the return. Form 8379 may also be filed by itself. In such cases, it must show the Social Security numbers of both spouses in the same order as they appear on the taxpayer's return. Injured spouse relief is different from an innocent spouse relief request made on Form 8857.

Line 74, Amount of Refund

On line 74a, enter the portion of any overpayment that the taxpayer would like refunded (if any). The taxpayer may also have the overpayment applied to his or her 2014 estimated taxes (see page 1-43).

Direct Deposit. Normally, the IRS will issue a paper check to the taxpayer for any refund. However, a taxpayer may have the entire refund directly deposited into an account maintained in his or her name at a U.S. financial institution (such as a mutual fund, brokerage firm, or credit union). A taxpayer can choose to have a refund directly deposited into a checking or savings account, brokerage account, any type of IRA (except a SIMPLE IRA), health savings account (HSA), Archer MSA, or Coverdell ESA.

 Caution. Generally, a taxpayer cannot directly deposit a refund into someone else's account (even the account of the preparer for any fees preparing the return). The only exception is in the case of a joint return where the taxpayers can designate deposits to a joint account or to an account of only one spouse. In such cases, married taxpayers appoint their spouse as an agent to receive a refund of taxes.

 Caution. A taxpayer should check with his or her financial institution to make sure a direct deposit will be accepted. For example, some financial institutions will not allow a joint refund to be deposited into an individual account. If the direct deposit is rejected by the financial institution, the IRS will issue a paper check instead.

Split Refund. A taxpayer may choose to have a refund directly deposited in up to three different accounts in his or her name. To deposit the refund in a single account, include the routing and account number on line 74b and 74d, respectively (leaving any unused boxes blank). If the deposit is to an IRA, HSA, MSA, Coverdell, or brokerage account, the taxpayer must confirm with his or her financial institution as to whether the "Checking" or "Savings" box should be checked on line 74c.

 Caution. The taxpayer should also verify the correct routing and account numbers with his or her financial institution. The IRS is not responsible for a lost refund if incorrect account information is provided with the return.

If a taxpayer chooses to have a refund directly deposited into more than one account, then check the box at the end of line 74a and complete Form 8888. On the form, the taxpayer should indicate the amount of the refund allocated to each account, as well as the routing number, account type, and account number of each account. If the total amount allocated on Form 8888 does not equal the amount the taxpayer wants refunded as indicated on line 74a, then no di-

rect deposit will occur and the IRS will send a paper check to the taxpayer. Also, if the taxpayer's refund is adjusted (such as math error or refund offset), this will be reflected in the last account listed.

 Caution. A taxpayer cannot have a refund deposited into more than one account if he or she has filed for an injured spouse allocation using Form 8379.

Deposits in IRAs. For a refund to be deposited in an IRA, the account must be established before the request for the direct deposit is made. The deposit will count towards the taxpayer's annual deductible limit for contributions to his or her traditional IRAs. Thus, the taxpayer must notify the trustee of the account of the year to which the deposit applies. The taxpayer must also verify that the direct deposit is actually made to the IRA by the due date or his or her return, without regard to extensions.

 Example. Leon Rice files his 2013 individual return on April 9, 2014, indicating a $5,500 overpayment. Leon files Form 8888 with his return, indicating that he would like $5,000 of the overpayment directly deposited in his traditional IRA and the remaining $500 directly deposited into his savings account. Leon directs the trustee of his IRA that the deposit is a contribution to his IRA for the 2013 tax year.

The IRS deposits Leon's refund into his IRA and savings account on April 20, 2014. Since the deposit is made after the due date for Leon to file his return, the deposit cannot be considered a contribution to his IRA for 2013, but instead is a contribution for 2014. If Leon claimed the $5,000 deposit into his traditional IRA as a deductible contribution made in 2013, then he must file an amended 2013 return to reduce his IRA deduction and any retirement savings credit he claimed.

Planning Tip. To ensure that a deposit of a refund into an IRA may be claimed as deductible contribution on the taxpayer's return in the same year the return is filed, a taxpayer should be sure to file his or her return as soon as possible. Normally, taxpayers who file their returns electronically and opt for direct deposit can receive their refund in two weeks or less. However, the closer to the filing deadline a taxpayer waits to submit his or her return to the IRS, the longer it may take to deposit a refund into an IRA.

Line 75, Applied to 2014 Estimated Tax

Instead of having an overpayment of taxes refunded, a taxpayer may request that part or all of the overpayment be applied to the taxpayer's 2014 estimated tax by entering the appropriate amount on line 75. A married taxpayer may request that any overpayment be applied to a spouse's 2014 estimated tax instead of his or her own by attaching a statement to that effect and including the other spouse's Social Security number in the attachment.

 Caution. The election to apply part or all of any overpayment to 2014 estimated tax cannot be changed later.

Line 76, Amount Owed

If the amount of a taxpayer's total tax (line 61) is more than the total payments (line 72), then the taxpayer owes taxes and the amount is reported on line 76. Include any estimated tax penalty from line 77 in the amount reported on line 76.

Payment Methods. If the amount of taxes owed is less than $1, the taxpayer does not have to pay. However, if the taxpayer must pay taxes, they must be paid in full by April 15, 2014, to avoid interest and penalties. Payments may be made by check, money order, credit card, or electronic fund transfer through the Electronic Federal Tax Payment System (EFTPS) or Electronic Funds Withdrawal (EFW).

Make checks or money orders payable for the full amount due to the "United States Treasury." Include the taxpayer's name, address, daytime phone, Social Security number (SSN) and write "2013 Form 1040" on the front of the check or money order. If filing a joint return, enter the SSN shown first on the return. Enter the full amount tax owed from line 76 as $XXX.XX. Do not use dashes or lines. Form 1040-V is an optional payment voucher that may also be used which allows the IRS to process the payment more accurately.

Credit Card Payments. A taxpayer can pay any tax liability by American Express, Discover, MasterCard, or Visa. To pay by credit card, call or visit the website of one of the following service providers: Link2Gov Corporation (888-PAY-1040 or www.PAY1040.com); Official Payments Corporation (800-UPAY-TAX or www.officialpayments.com); or RBS WorldPay, Inc (1-888-9-PAY-TAX or www.payUSAtax.com). A convenience fee will be charged by the service provider based on the amount of tax being paid.

Unable to Pay. If a taxpayer cannot pay the full amount of tax shown on line 76 by April 15, 2014, then there are two options. First, the taxpayer may ask to make monthly installment payments by applying online or filing Form 9465. Generally, the IRS will respond to an installment payment request within 30 days. Even if the IRS agrees to let the taxpayer make installment payments, interest and penalties will still accrue on any tax not paid by April 15, 2014.

If paying the amount shown on line 76 would cause an undue hardship, then a taxpayer's second option is to ask for an extension of time to pay the tax by filing Form 1127 by April 15, 2014. An extension will not be granted for more than six months and interest will be charged on tax not paid by April 15, 2014. If the taxpayer does not pay the tax before the extension runs out, then penalties will be imposed on the amount of tax owed.

Line 77, Estimated Tax Penalty

The IRS will assess a penalty against the taxpayer if he or she failed to pay enough tax during the tax year either through withholding of by making estimated tax payments. The penalty will apply if *either* of the following applies:

- Line 76 is at least $1,000 and more than 10 percent of the tax shown on the return.
- The taxpayer did not pay enough estimated tax by any of the due dates even if the taxpayer is due a refund.

 Planning Tip. Form 2210 (Form 2210-F for farmers and fisherman) is used by a taxpayer to determine if he or she owes a penalty for underpayment of taxes and to figure the amount of the penalty. Since the penalty is complicated, line 77 may be left blank and the IRS will compute any penalty amount required to be paid.

Safe Harbor. No penalty will be owed for 2013 if the taxpayer's 2012 tax return was for 12 full months, any estimated tax payments were made on time, and *either* of the following applies:

- the taxpayer had no tax liability for 2012 and was a U.S. citizen or resident for all of 2012; or
- the total tax withheld on lines 62 and 69 on the taxpayer's 2013 return is at least as much as the tax liability shown on the 2012 return, or is at least 110 percent of the tax liability shown on the 2012 return if the 2012 AGI was over $150,000 (over $75,000 if married filing separately) and the taxpayer is not a farmer or fisherman.

See Tab 11 and MTG ¶2682 for more information.

Third-Party Designee

A taxpayer may designate any person to discuss his or her 2013 tax return with the IRS by checking "Yes" in the "Third Party Designee" section. Also, enter the designee's name, phone number, and any five digits the designee chooses as his or her personal identification number. However, if the taxpayer wants to allow the paid preparer who signed the return to discuss it with the IRS, enter only "Preparer" in the space for the designee's name.

By checking the "Yes" box, the taxpayer (and spouse, if filing a joint return) is authorizing the following:

- the IRS may call the designee to answer any questions that may arise during the processing of the taxpayer's return;
- the designee may provide any information that is missing on the return to the IRS;
- the designee may request information about the processing of the return or the status of the refund or payment;
- the IRS may send copies of notices or transcripts related to the return, upon request; and
- the designee may respond to certain IRS notices about math errors, offsets, and return preparation.

The designee is not authorized to receive any refund check or to represent the taxpayer before the IRS. In addition, the authorization is only good for one year after the due date of the return without extension (April 15, 2014, for most taxpayers). The authorization may be revoked at any time by sending a written statement signed by both the taxpayer and the third-party designee to the IRS. See IRS Publication 947.

Signature Requirements

All returns must be signed and dated by the taxpayer. The taxpayer must also enter his or her occupation. A daytime telephone number may be provided to help speed the processing of the return.

If a joint return is filed, then both spouses must generally sign and date the return, even if only one spouse had income. In addition, both spouses must enter their respective occupations. However, a domestic spouse may sign a joint return on behalf of the spouse serving in the U.S. Armed Forces oversees if the other spouse is:

- in a combat zone or qualified hazardous duty area;
- missing in a combat zone (domestic spouse can sign return for up to two years after end of combat zone activities);
- incapacitated; or
- died during the tax year, so long as the surviving spouse did not remarry before the end of the year.

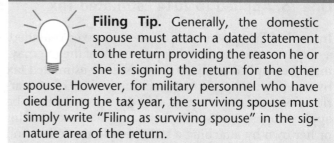

Filing Tip. Generally, the domestic spouse must attach a dated statement to the return providing the reason he or she is signing the return for the other spouse. However, for military personnel who have died during the tax year, the surviving spouse must simply write "Filing as surviving spouse" in the signature area of the return.

Form 2848. An agent may be appointed to sign the return on the taxpayer's behalf if the taxpayer is unable to sign because of a disease or injury, the taxpayer is absent from the United States for at least 60 days before the due date of the return, or the taxpayer has given the authority to have an agent sign on his or her behalf by the IRS. A return signed by an agent must have a power of attorney on Form 2848 attached to the return and it must state that the agent is granted authority to sign the return. There are several exceptions to this requirement.

Child. If the taxpayer is a child and cannot sign the return, either parent may sign the child's name and add "By (parent's signature), parent for minor child."

Deceased Taxpayer. If the taxpayer is deceased, then the return must be signed by the taxpayer's personal representative (executor or administrator). If it is a joint return, the surviving spouse must also sign. If no personal representative has been appointed, the surviving spouse should sign the return and write in the signature area "Filing as surviving spouse." If there is no personal representative or surviving spouse, the person in charge of the decedent's property must file and sign the return as "personal representative."

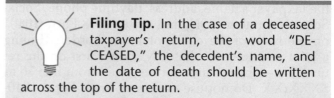

Filing Tip. In the case of a deceased taxpayer's return, the word "DECEASED," the decedent's name, and the date of death should be written across the top of the return.

Paid Preparers. An individual who prepares the return for a taxpayer(s) for a fee must also sign the return and provide his or her preparer tax identification number (PTIN). If the return is signed by a representative for the taxpayer, then a power of attorney (Form 2848) must also be attached to the return. See Tab 12 for more information on the PTIN requirements of paid preparers.

Electronic Returns. A taxpayer may sign an electronically filed income tax return by directly entering onto the return a self-selected personal identification number (PIN). If filing a joint return, both spouses must enter a self-selected PIN. A taxpayer establishes a five-digit PIN by verifying his or her identity and AGI from their originally filed federal income tax return from the prior year.

Alternatively, the practitioner may enter the taxpayer's PIN on the return or the electronic return originator (ERO) may select the taxpayer's PIN to be entered on the return. In either case, the taxpayer authorizes the practitioner or ERO to enter the PIN by completing the appropriate sections of Form 8879. The form does not have to be filed with the IRS, but must be retained by the practitioner or ERO for up to three years.

 Filing Tip. Form 8453 is used to send certain required paper forms or supporting documentation with an electronically filed return, including Form 2848. Form 8453 and supporting documents must be transmitted to the IRS within three business days after the taxpayer's electronically filed return has been accepted.

If the taxpayer signs the return using an electronic signature method, then the preparer must also sign the return with his or her preparer tax identification number (PTIN). The PTIN may be manually inputted or automatically entered by software. The PTIN must be entered in the e-file return.

 Caution. Tax preparation software may automatically enter the preparer's identifying information onto a return. However, some software may enter the preparer's business entity name and not the practitioner's name for the "name" area of the return. Sole proprietors often change this to their individual names.

Filing Details

For most individuals, Form 1040 must be filed for the 2013 tax year by April 15, 2014. For fiscal-year filers, the return must be filed on or before the 15th day of the fourth full month following the close of the tax year. Individuals are entitled to an automatic *six-month* extension of time to file their income tax return (October 15, 2014, for the 2013 tax year). The extension can be obtained by filing Form 4868 on or before the due date of the tax return. No reason must be given for the need for the extension, but a good-faith estimate of the tax liability must be provided.

 Caution. The automatic extension of time to file does not extend the amount of time to pay the tax. Thus, interest is charged from the original due date. Penalties may also apply.

Outside of the Country. U.S. citizens and residents outside the country will have an additional two months to file their return and pay taxes. For tax year 2013, this means the return is not due until June 16, 2014. To qualify, the individual must be living outside the United States and Puerto Rico, and his or her main place of business or post of duty is outside the United States and Puerto Rico on the due date of the return. Individuals in military service on duty outside the United States also qualify for this extension. If a joint return is filed, only one spouse has to qualify. If married taxpayers file separate returns, the extension only applies to the spouse who qualifies.

 Caution. No form is required for a taxpayer "outside of the country" to obtain the automatic two-month extension to file or pay taxes for the tax year. Instead, the taxpayer must attach a statement to his or her return showing that he or she meets the requirements for the extension. If any tax remains unpaid, interest is charged from the original due date of the return.

A taxpayer who is "out of the country" is generally given only an additional four-month extension (for a total of six months) if he or she files Form 4868 (October 15, 2014, for the 2013 tax year). However, the individual may get an extension of time beyond the normal six-month period if he or she expects to qualify for the foreign earned income or foreign housing exclusion and file Form 2555 by meeting either the bona fide resident or physical presence test after the due date for his or her return. In these circumstance, the taxpayer who is "out of the country" may request for additional time by filing Form 2350.

 Caution. If false or misleading information is provided on Form 2350, then any extension of time granted by the IRS is voided and the taxpayer will be responsible for late-filing penalties.

Serving in Combat Zone. The deadline for filing a tax return, paying any tax owed, and filing a claim for refund is automatically extended for taxpayers serving in a combat zone. This applies to members of the U.S. Armed Forces, as well as merchant marines serving aboard vessels under the operational control of the Department of Defense, Red Cross personnel, accredited correspondents, and civilians under the direction of the Armed Forces in support of the Armed Forces.

If a member of the Armed Forces is serving in a designated combat zone or is deployed in a contingency operation, or is hospitalized outside the United States due to injury received while serving in a combat zone or in a contingency operation, the due date of the member's return is postponed for the period of the combat service or hospitalization plus 180 days. The deadline will also be extended by the number of days the taxpayer had left to take action with the IRS before entering the combat zone. No interest or penalties will be assessed during this period. The extension is also available to the spouse of such service members wishing to file a joint return. See MTG ¶895 for a listing of combat zones.

Where to File Form 1040

In the following charts are the mailing addresses for filing individual income tax returns, either self-prepared or prepared by a tax professional. Per the IRS, if an addressed envelope came with the return, please use it. If you do not have one, or if you moved during the year, mail the return to the Internal Revenue Service Center for the state of residence. No street address is required. See MTG ¶5.

Where Taxpayers and Tax Professionals File Form 1040 for 2013

State of Taxpayer's Residence	Form 1040 (Filed by Taxpayer) No Payment Enclosed	Form 1040 (Filed by Taxpayer) Payment Enclosed
Alabama, Georgia, Kentucky, Missouri, New Jersey, North Carolina, South Carolina, Tennessee, Virgina	Department of the Treasury Internal Revenue Service Kansas City, MO 64999-0002	Internal Revenue Service P.O. Box 931000 Louisville, KY 40293-1000
Florida, Louisiana, Mississippi, Texas	Department of the Treasury Internal Revenue Service Austin, TX 73301-0002	Internal Revenue Service P.O. Box 1214 Charlotte, NC 28201-1214
Alaska, Arizona, California, Colorado, Hawaii, Idaho, Nevada, New Mexico, Oregon, Utah, Washington, Wyoming	Department of the Treasury Internal Revenue Service Fresno, CA 93888-0002	Internal Revenue Service P.O. Box 7704 San Francisco, CA 94120-7704
Arkansas, Illinois, Indiana, Iowa, Kansas, Michigan, Minnesota, Montana, Nebraska, North Dakota, Ohio, Oklahoma, South Dakota, Wisconsin	Department of the Treasury Internal Revenue Service Fresno, CA 93888-0002	Internal Revenue Service P.O. Box 802501 Cincinnati, OH 45280-2501
Connecticut, Delaware, District of Columbia, Maine, Maryland, Massachusetts, New Hampshire, New York, Pennsylvania, Rhode Island, Vermont, West Virginia	Department of the Treasury Internal Revenue Service Kansas City, MO 64999-0002	Internal Revenue Service P.O. Box 37008 Hartford, CT 06176-0008
A foreign country, U.S. possession or territory[1], or use and APO or FPO address, or file Form 2555, 2555-EZ, or 4563, or are a dual-status alien.	Department of the Treasury Internal Revenue Service Austin, TX 73301-0215 USA	Internal Revenue Service P.O. Box 1303 Charlotte, NC 28201-1303 USA

1 If you live in American Samoa, Puerto Rico, Guam, the U.S. Virgin Islands, or the Northern Mariana Islands, see Pub. 570.

Where Taxpayers and Tax Professionals File Form 4868 for 2013

State of Taxpayer's Residence	Form 4868 No Payment Enclosed	Form 4868 Payment Enclosed
Alabama, Georgia, Kentucky, Missouri, New Jersey, North Carolina, South Carolina, Tennessee, Virginia	Department of the Treasury Internal Revenue Service Kansas City, MO 64999-0045	Internal Revenue Service P.O. Box 931300 Louisville, KY 40293-1300
Florida, Louisiana, Mississippi, Texas	Department of the Treasury Internal Revenue Service Austin, TX 73301-0045	Internal Revenue Service P.O. Box 1302 Charlotte, NC 28201-1302
Connecticut, Delaware, District of Columbia, Maine, Maryland, Massachusetts, New Hampshire, New York, Pennsylvania, Rhode Island, Vermont, West Virginia	Department of the Treasury Internal Revenue Service Kansas City, MO 64999-0045	Internal Revenue Service P.O. Box 37009 Hartford, CT 06176-0009
Alaska, Arizona, California, Colorado, Hawaii, Idaho, Nevada, New Mexico, Oregon, Utah, Washington, Wyoming	Department of the Treasury Internal Revenue Service Fresno, CA 93888-0045	Internal Revenue Service P.O. Box 7122 San Francisco, CA 94120-7122
Arkansas, Illinois, Indiana, Iowa, Kansas, Michigan, Minnesota, Montana, Nebraska, North Dakota, Ohio, Oklahoma, South Dakota, Wisconsin	Department of the Treasury Internal Revenue Service Fresno, CA 93888-0002	Internal Revenue Service P.O. Box 802503 Cincinnati, OH 45280-2503
A foreign country, American Samoa1, or Puerto Rico or is excluding income under Code Sec. 933, use an APO or FPO address, or file Form 2555, 2555-EZ, or 4563, or are a dual-status alien, or are a nonpermanent resident of Guam1 or the U.S. Virgin Islands[2]	Department of the Treasury Internal Revenue Service Austin, TX 73301-0215 USA	Internal Revenue Service P.O. Box 1302 Charlotte, NC 28201-1302 USA
All Form 1040-SS, Form 1040-PR, Form 1040-NR and Form 1040-NR_EZ filers	Department of the Treasury Internal Revenue Service Austin, TX 73301-0215	Internal Revenue Service P.O. Box 1303 Charlotte, NC 28201-1303 USA

1 Permanent residents of Guam should use: Department of Revenue and Taxation, Government of Guam, P.O. Box 23607, GMF, GU 96921.
2 Permanent residents of U.S. Virgin Islands should use: V.I. Bureau of Internal Revenue, 9601 Estate Thomas, Charlotte Amalie, St. Thomas, VI 00802.

Before you begin: ✓ If you are the beneficiary of a deceased employee or former employee who died before August 21, 1996, include any death benefit exclusion that you are entitled to (up to $5,000) in the amount entered on line 2 below.

More than one pension or annuity. If you had more than one partially taxable pension or annuity, figure the taxable part of each separately. Enter the total of the taxable parts on Form 1040, line 16b. Enter the total pension or annuity payments received in 2013 on Form 1040, line 16a.

1. Enter the total pension or annuity payments from Form 1099-R, box 1. Also, enter this amount on Form 1040, line 16a . . . . 1.

2. Enter your cost in the plan at the annuity starting date . . . . 2.
   Note. If you completed this worksheet last year, skip line 3 and enter the amount from line 4 of last year's worksheet on line 4 below (even if the amount of your pension or annuity has changed). Otherwise, go to line 3.

3. Enter the appropriate number from Table 1 below. But if your annuity starting date was after 1997 and the payments are for your life and that of your beneficiary, enter the appropriate number from Table 2 below . . . . 3.

4. Divide line 2 by the number on line 3 . . . . 4.

5. Multiply line 4 by the number of months for which this year's payments were made. If your annuity starting date was before 1987, skip lines 6 and 7 and enter this amount on line 8. Otherwise, go to line 6 . . . . 5.

6. Enter the amount, if any, recovered tax free in years after 1986. If you completed this worksheet last year, enter the amount from line 10 of last year's worksheet . . . . . 6.

7. Subtract line 6 from line 2 . . . . 7.

8. Enter the smaller of line 5 or line 7 . . . . 8.

9. **Taxable amount.** Subtract line 8 from line 1. Enter the result, but not less than zero. Also, enter this amount on Form 1040, line 16b. If your Form 1099-R shows a larger amount, use the amount on this line instead of the amount from Form 1099-R. If you are a retired public safety officer, see *Insurance Premiums for Retired Public Safety Officers* before entering an amount on line 16b . . . . 9.

10. Was your annuity starting date before 1987?

    ☐ Yes. (STOP) Leave line 10 blank.

    ☐ No. Add lines 6 and 8. This is the amount you have recovered tax free through 2013. You will need this number when you fill out this worksheet next year . . . . 10.

Table 1 for Line 3 Above

IF the age at annuity starting date was . . .	AND your annuity starting date was—	
	before November 19, 1996, enter on line 3 . . .	after November 18, 1996, enter on line 3 . . .
55 or under	300	360
56–60	260	310
61–65	240	260
66–70	170	210
71 or older	120	160

Table 2 for Line 3 Above

IF the combined ages at annuity starting date were . . .	THEN enter on line 3 . . .
110 or under	410
111–120	360
121–130	310
131–140	260
141 or older	210

Social Security Benefits Worksheet—Lines 20a and 20b

Before you begin:	✓ Complete Form 1040, lines 21 and 23 through 32, if they apply to you.	
	✓ Figure any write-in adjustments to be entered on the dotted line next to line 36 (see the instructions for line 36).	
	✓ If you are married filing separately and you lived apart from your spouse for all of 2013, enter "D" to the right of the word "benefits" on line 20a. If you do not, you may get a math error notice from the IRS.	
	✓ Be sure you have read the **Exception** in the line 20a and 20b instructions to see if you can use this worksheet instead of a publication to find out if any of your benefits are taxable.	

1. Enter the total amount from **box 5 of all** your **Forms SSA-1099** and **Forms RRB-1099.** Also, enter this amount on Form 1040, line 20a . . . . **1.** _____

2. Enter one-half of line 1 . . . . **2.** _____

3. Combine the amounts from Form 1040, lines 7, 8a, 9a, 10 through 14, 15b, 16b, 17 through 19, and 21 . . . . **3.** _____

4. Enter the amount, if any, from Form 1040, line 8b . . . . **4.** _____

5. Combine lines 2, 3, and 4 . . . . **5.** _____

6. Enter the total of the amounts from Form 1040, lines 23 through 32, plus any write-in adjustments you entered on the dotted line next to line 36 . . . . **6.** _____

7. Is the amount on line 6 less than the amount on line 5?

   ☐ **No.** (STOP) None of your social security benefits are taxable. Enter -0- on Form 1040, line 20b.

   ☐ **Yes.** Subtract line 6 from line 5 . . . . **7.** _____

8. If you are:
   - Married filing jointly, enter $32,000
   - Single, head of household, qualifying widow(er), or married filing separately and you **lived apart** from your spouse for all of 2013, enter $25,000
   - Married filing separately and you lived with your spouse at any time in 2013, skip lines 8 through 15; multiply line 7 by 85% (.85) and enter the result on line 16. Then go to line 17

   . . . . **8.** _____

9. Is the amount on line 8 less than the amount on line 7?

   ☐ **No.** (STOP) None of your social security benefits are taxable. Enter -0- on Form 1040, line 20b. If you are married filing separately and you **lived apart** from your spouse for all of 2013, be sure you entered "D" to the right of the word "benefits" on line 20a.

   ☐ **Yes.** Subtract line 8 from line 7 . . . . **9.** _____

10. Enter: $12,000 if married filing jointly; $9,000 if single, head of household, qualifying widow(er), or married filing separately and you **lived apart** from your spouse for all of 2013 . . . . **10.** _____

11. Subtract line 10 from line 9. If zero or less, enter -0- . . . . **11.** _____

12. Enter the **smaller** of line 9 or line 10 . . . . **12.** _____

13. Enter one-half of line 12 . . . . **13.** _____

14. Enter the **smaller** of line 2 or line 13 . . . . **14.** _____

15. Multiply line 11 by 85% (.85). If line 11 is zero, enter -0- . . . . **15.** _____

16. Add lines 14 and 15 . . . . **16.** _____

17. Multiply line 1 by 85% (.85) . . . . **17.** _____

18. **Taxable social security benefits.** Enter the **smaller** of line 16 or line 17. Also enter this amount on Form 1040, line 20b . . . . **18.** _____

(TIP) *If any of your benefits are taxable for 2013 **and** they include a lump-sum benefit payment that was for an earlier year, you may be able to reduce the taxable amount. See Pub. 915 for details.*

DRAFT AS OF September 16, 2013

What's New in 2013

State and Local Sales Tax Deduction. The election to deduct state and local sales taxes in lieu of state and local income taxes has been reinstated for 2013.

Limitation on Itemized Deductions. For 2013, the amount of itemized deductions must be reduced if adjusted gross income is above $300,000 for MFJ/QW; $275,000 for HOH; $250,000 for single; or $150,000 for MFS.

Medical and Dental Expenses. For 2013, taxpayers can only deduct medical expenses that exceed 10% of adjusted gross income (7.5% for taxpayers age 65 or older).

Ponzi-Type Investment Schemes. There is a new section C on Form 4684 for individuals claiming a Rev. Proc. 2009-20 safe harbor theft loss deduction due to a Ponzi-type investment scheme.

Relevant IRS Publications

- ☐ IRS Publication 463, *Travel, Entertainment, Gift, and Car Expenses*
- ☐ IRS Publication 502, *Medical and Dental Expenses Including the Health Coverage Tax Credit*
- ☐ IRS Publication 514, *Foreign Tax Credit for Individuals*
- ☐ IRS Publication 523, *Selling Your Home*
- ☐ IRS Publication 526, *Charitable Contributions*
- ☐ IRS Publication 529, *Miscellaneous Deductions*
- ☐ IRS Publication 547, *Casualties, Disasters, and Thefts (Business and Nonbusiness)*
- ☐ IRS Publication 550, *Investment Income and Expenses*
- ☐ IRS Publication 561, *Determining the Value of Donated Property*
- ☐ IRS Publication 936, *Home Mortgage Interest Deduction*

Section at a Glance

Tax Preparer's Checklist

The following items are required:
- ☐ Records of medical expenses
- ☐ State tax returns
- ☐ Receipts showing state and local sales tax paid, if electing the state and local sales tax deduction
- ☐ Statement of mortgage interest and points (Form 1098)
- ☐ Required records for charitable contributions
- ☐ Detailed gambling logs
- ☐ Records of property tax payments
- ☐ Spouse's Schedule A if filing status is MFS

Itemized Deductions—2013 Schedule A

Category	Other Forms Needed	Limits and Reductions	High-Income Phaseout
Medical and dental expenses	None	Reduced by 10% of AGI (7.5% for 65 and over)	The high-income phaseout rules apply for 2013
Taxes paid	None	No reduction or floor	The high-income phaseout rules apply for 2013
Interest paid	Form 4952 (investment interest)	Investment interest limited to net investment income with carryover	The high-income phaseout rules apply for 2013
Gifts to charity	Form 8283 (noncash gifts greater than $500)	Maximum of 50%, 30%, or 20% of AGI, depending on receiver of gift	The high-income phaseout rules apply for 2013
Casualty and theft losses	Form 4684	Reduced by $100 per occurrence, then reduced by 10% of AGI	The high-income phaseout rules apply for 2013
Job expenses and most other misc. deductions	Form 2106 (certain job expenses)	Reduced by 2% of AGI	The high-income phaseout rules apply for 2013
Other misc. deductions	None	No reduction or floor	The high-income phaseout rules apply for 2013

Schedule A: Itemized Deductions

Schedule A should be used when a taxpayer's total itemized deductions are greater than the standard deduction for the applicable filing status. If a married taxpayer files separately and his or her spouse itemizes deductions, no standard deduction is allowed and Schedule A should be used to deduct any allowable deductions. The standard deduction for 2013 is $6,100 for single filers and married filing separately, $12,200 for married filing jointly and qualifying widow(er) filers, and $8,950 for head of household filers. Additional deductions for individuals who are over the age of 65 or blind are also available to those who take the standard deduction. See Tab 1.

National Guard and Reserve. Currently, National Guard and Reserve members have an above-the-line deduction for their nonreimbursable expenses for transportation, meals, and lodging when they had to travel away from home (and stay overnight) to attend meetings or drills. The expenses are tabulated on Form 2106 or 2106-EZ and reported on Form 1040. Schedule A is no longer used to claim these deductions. See Tab 1 and MTG ¶941E for details.

Medical and Dental Expenses, Lines 1-4

Line 1, Medical and Dental Expenses

Whose Medical Expenses Are Deductible? The taxpayer may deduct his or her own medical expenses and those of the taxpayer's spouse, and dependents. For the purpose of medical deductions on Schedule A, an individual the tax- payer could have claimed as a dependent except for the fact that they had gross income above the threshold or that they filed a joint return with their spouses can be considered dependents.

A child of divorced parents is treated as the dependent of both parents, regardless of which parent claims the child as a dependent.

See MTG ¶1015.

> **Example.** John Griffin contributes $9,000 per year toward his brother Joe's support, and he pays Joe's dental bills of $400. Since Joe has gross income of $7,000, John may not claim Joe as a dependent. However, John contributed more than half of Joe's support ($9,400 out of $16,400, assuming Joe spends all of his income on his own support and receives no other support), so he can deduct the $400 as a medical expense on Schedule A.

> **Example.** Sylvia Khalid furnished over half the support of her daughter Angela in 2013. Angela was married in October 2013 and filed a 2013 return jointly with her husband, who is required to file a return. Therefore, Sylvia cannot claim a dependent exemption for Angela. However, she can claim all medical expenses that she paid for Angela during the year on line 1 of Schedule A because all other dependency tests were met.

What Qualifies as a Deductible Medical Expense?
As a general rule, deductible medical expenses are the costs of diagnosis, cure, mitigation, treatment, or prevention of disease, and the costs for treatments affecting any part or function of the body. The following are some of the rules that apply to deductible medical expenses, including dental expenses:

- They must be primarily for the purpose of alleviating or preventing a physical or mental defect or illness.
- In many cases, the necessity of care or medicines must be determined by a licensed practitioner.
- They exclude expenses that are merely beneficial to general health, such as vitamins or a vacation.
- They can include the premiums paid for insurance that covers the expenses of medical care, and amounts paid for transportation to obtain medical care.
- They can also include medical expenses paid for qualified long-term care services and limited amounts paid for a qualified long-term care insurance contract.
- They include all physician-prescribed drugs and therapies for the purpose of treating medical conditions.

The IRS has clarified that, for purposes of the medical-expense deduction:

1. the deduction is not limited to amounts paid for the least expensive form of medical care applicable; and
2. a physician's recommendation, while often important to determine whether certain expenses are for medical or personal reasons, is unnecessary when the expenditures are for items wholly medical in nature and that serve no other function.

> **Gray Area.** Expenses for prescription drugs brought in or shipped from another country may not be deductible unless prescribed by a physician for a medical condition and the drugs are imported from a FDA approved country. Offlabel and alternative-source prescriptions are not treated differently for tax purposes provided they are FDA-approved drugs.

The following table provides an alphabetical list of the medical and dental expenses listed in IRS Publication 502, *Medical and Dental Expenses*, along with their treatment as specified by Code Sec. 213. MTG ¶59 and ¶1016 also list medical expenses.

Deductibility of Medical and Dental Expenses on 2013 Schedule A

Expense	Deductible (Subject to 10% AGI floor (7.5% for individuals age 65 or over))
Abortion	Costs of legal abortion deductible
Acupuncture costs	Deductible
Alcoholism treatment	Inpatient costs deductible, including meals and lodging; travel costs to AA meetings deductible
Ambulance costs	Deductible
Artificial limb costs	Deductible
Artificial teeth costs	Deductible
Babysitting, child care, and nursing services for a normal, healthy baby	Not deductible; such services for a sick child may be deductible
Bandages	Deductible
Breast reconstruction surgery	Deductible following a mastectomy
Birth control pills	Deductible
Braille books and magazines	Cost of such editions over and above the cost of regular publications of the same material deductible
Capital expenses	Deductible if reasonable and mainly for medical purposes; see discussion on page 2-6
Car	Modifications to accommodate disability, and medical transportation deductible; see discussion on page 2-5
Chiropractor fees	Deductible
Christian Science practitioner fees	Deductible
Contact lenses	Costs for contact lenses for which there is a medical reason deductible, i.e., for vision correction but not for solely cosmetic purposes
Controlled substances	No deduction for substances taken in violation of federal law, e.g., marijuana, even in states where its medical use is legal, qualify for deduction
Cosmetic surgery	All costs of cosmetic surgery to correct the effects of an accident or disease deductible; routine, elective cosmetic surgery is not deductible
Crutches	Costs of buying or renting are deductible [need not be prescribed (Rev. Rul. 2003-58)]
Dancing lessons	Not deductible, even if prescribed, if only for the improvement of general health, but deductible if prescribed as part of physical therapy to treat specific condition
Dental treatment	Nearly all expenses deductible except teeth whitening
Diagnostic devices	Deductible, including self-monitoring devices
Diaper service	Not deductible, unless needed for the effects of a disease
Disabled dependent care expenses	Can be deducted as a medical expense or can be applied to a credit for dependent care but cannot be used for both
Drug addiction treatment	Inpatient costs deductible, including meals and lodging
Drugs	Prescribed drugs and insulin deductible, but not over-the-counter or those for improvement of general health
Electrolysis or hair removal	Not deductible
Eye exams	Deductible if needed for medical reasons
Eyeglasses	Deductible if needed for medical reasons
Eye surgery	Deductible if used to treat defective vision, including corrective laser surgery
Fertility enhancement	All costs deductible, including those associated with in vitro fertilization or reversal of prior sterilization procedures; however, a fertile male taxpayer was denied a deduction for in vitro fertilization expenses paid with respect to an unrelated female gestational carrier because the taxpayer had no medical condition preventing him from procreating naturally and because the medical expenses did not affect the structure or function of the taxpayer's own body (*W. Magdalin*, CA-1)

Deductibility of Medical and Dental Expenses on 2013 Schedule A (Continued)

Expense	Deductible (Subject to 10% AGI floor (7.5% for individuals age 65 or over))
Founder's fee (advance payments to a retirement home)	Amount allocable to medical care deductible
Funeral expenses	Not deductible on a living person's return, but may be deductible on a decedent's return (see Tab 14)
Future medical care	Not deductible, but see exception under *Qualified Long-Term Care Services*, page 2-7
Guide dog or other, similar animal	All costs for purchase and care deductible
Hair transplant	Not deductible, except to correct effects of disease or accident
Health club dues	Not deductible, unless related to a specific medical condition
Health institute	Deductible only if prescribed by a physician; physician must also provide a statement of support
Health maintenance organization (HMO) fees	Deductible as insurance premiums
Health savings accounts (HSAs) contributions	Contributions not deductible as itemized medical expense (deductible directly on Form 1040)
Hearing aids	All costs, including batteries, deductible
Home care	See *Nursing Services*, page 2-7
Home improvements	See *Capital Expenses*, page 2-6
Household help	Not generally deductible, although there may be exceptions; see *Qualified Long-Term Care Services*, page 2-7 or *Nursing Services*, page 2-7
Illegal operations and treatments	Not deductible
Hospital services	Deductible, including meals and lodging
Insurance premiums	Generally deductible; see discussion on page 2-6
Laboratory fees	Deductible
Lead-based paint removal	Deductible only if necessary to keep such paint away from a child who has been diagnosed with lead poisoning; may be treated as capital expense (page 2-6) if covered, e.g., with wallboard or paneling, rather than removed
Learning disability	Costs of tutoring a child with a physician-diagnosed learning disability deductible
Legal fees	Deductible only if necessary to authorize treatment of mental illness; other legal fees not generally deductible
Lifetime care advance payments	Amount allocable to medical care deductible
Lodging	Lodging outside a hospital deductible up to $50 per night per person if the trip is made to enable treatment by a physician; if the person being treated needs to be accompanied, e.g., child accompanied by a parent, up to a total of $100 per night
Long-term care	See discussion on page 2-7
Maternity clothes	Not deductible
Meals and lodging	See discussion on page 2-5
Medical conferences	Costs of travel and admission to medical conferences concerning chronic condition of taxpayer, spouse, or dependent deductible; meals and lodging connected with the conference not deductible
Medical information plan	Deductible
Medical savings accounts (MSAs)	Contributions not deductible, nor are expenses paid with tax-free distributions
Medicines	Prescribed medicines deductible
Mentally retarded, special home for	Deductible, if recommended by a psychiatrist
Nonprescription drugs and medicines	Only insulin is deductible; other nonprescription drugs are not deductible, even if recommended by a physician
Nursing home	All costs deductible if the primary purpose of admission is medical; otherwise, only the medical costs are deductible
Nursing services	See discussion on page 2-7
Nutritional supplements	Deductible only if recommended by a medical practitioner for a condition diagnosed by a physician; not deductible if taken only to enhance general health

Deductibility of Medical and Dental Expenses on 2013 Schedule A (Continued)

Expense	Deductible (Subject to 10% AGI floor (7.5% for individuals age 65 or over))
Organ donors	All expenses deductible for taxpayer who is a donor or potential donor, or for patient who pays donor's expenses, including transportation
Osteopath	Deductible
Oxygen and related equipment	Deductible
Personal use items	Disposable personal use items, such as toothbrushes, not generally deductible
Physical therapy	All costs of physical therapy received as medical treatment are deductible
Prostheses	Deductible
Psychiatric care	Deductible, including costs of support of a mentally ill dependent in a special medical facility
Psychoanalysis	Deductible, unless part of training to be a psychoanalyst
Special education	Costs of tutoring a child with a physician-diagnosed learning disability are deductible; costs associated with sending such a child to a special school (meals, lodging, tuition) are also deductible [doctor's recommendation may not be necessary (*Lawrence F. Fay*, Dec. 37,721)]
Sterilization	Deductible
Stop-smoking programs	Fees for programs are deductible, but nonprescription drugs to aid smokers in quitting are not deductible
Surgery	Costs for all but unnecessary cosmetic surgery are deductible
Swimming lessons	Not deductible, even if prescribed, if only for the improvement of general health [may be deductible for therapeutic reasons (*R. Emanuel*, T.C. Summary Opinion, 2002-127)]
Teeth whitening	Not deductible, even if done by a dentist
Telephone	Special equipment for hearing-impaired is deductible
Television	Cost of equipment to display audio for hearing-impaired individual is deductible; if a specially equipped set is purchased, the deductible portion is the excess over the cost for a similar television without the special equipment
Transplants	All expenses deductible for taxpayer who is a donor or potential donor, or for patient who pays donor's expenses, including transportation
Transportation	Deductible if for essential medical care; see discussion below
Trips	Deductible if for essential medical care; see discussion below
Vasectomy	Deductible (reversal also deductible)
Veterinary fees	Not deductible, except for the care of guide dogs and other animals trained to help people with disabilities
Weight-loss program	Deductible if used to treat a physician-diagnosed disease; cost of special dietary food in such programs is generally not deductible without supporting statement from a physician
Wheelchair	Deductible, if used for a medical condition and not just for transportation
Wig	Deductible if hair loss is the result of disease
X-rays	Deductible

Medical Transportation and Trips.  Transportation expenses are deductible for trips that are primarily for and essential to medical care. The following expenses are included:

- Bus, taxi, train, plane, or ambulance service.
- Travel of parent who must go with a child needing medical care.
- Travel of a nurse or other person who can give injections, medications, or other treatments required by a patient who is traveling to get medical care and is unable to travel alone.

- Regular visits to see a mentally ill dependent, if these visits are recommended as a part of treatment.
- Travel expenses to a medical conference concerning a chronic condition of taxpayer, spouse, or dependent.

For this purpose, the standard mileage rate is 24¢ per mile for medical transportation expenses paid or incurred after January 1, 2013.

Meals and Lodging. Costs of meals and lodging at a hospital or similar institution are deductible if a principal reason for being there is to receive medical care. Lodging other than at a hospital may be deductible if all of the following apply:

- The lodging is primarily for and essential to the seeking of medical care.
- The medical care is provided by a doctor in a licensed hospital or in a medical care facility related to, or the equivalent of, a licensed hospital.
- The lodging is not lavish or extravagant under the circumstances.
- There is no significant element of personal pleasure, recreation, or vacation in the travel away from home.

The deductible amount for lodging cannot be more than $50 each night for each person.

The taxpayer can include lodging for a person traveling with the person receiving medical care. For example, a parent traveling with a sick child can deduct a total of $100 per night for lodging. Meals that are not part of inpatient care are not deductible.

Capital Expenses for Medical Care.

Costs for special equipment installed in a home, or for improvements to a home, are deductible if their main purpose is medical care for the taxpayer, spouse, or a dependent. Expenses incurred for personal reasons, such as for architectural or aesthetic purposes, are not deductible. Also, costs for permanent improvements must be reduced by any resulting increase in property value. The cost of operating and maintaining medical related improvements may also be deductible.

Example. Willie Smith has heart problems, and the Smiths' doctor recommends that they install an elevator in their home so that Willie does not have to climb stairs. In addition, the Smiths have some landscaping done to improve the grade from the driveway to the front door. The elevator costs $10,000 to construct, and the grading costs $1,000. An appraisal shows that the elevator increases the value of their home by $5,000 but the grading has no effect. The medical expense calculation for this scenario is as follows:

Total cost of the improvements	$11,000
Value of home with improvements	150,000
Value of home before the improvements	145,000
Increase in value of home	5,000
Medical expense (cost of improvements less increase in value)	6,000

Expenses to improve a home to accommodate individuals with disabilities usually do not increase the value of the home and thus are fully deductible.

These improvements include the following;

- Constructing entrance or exit ramps.
- Widening doorways at entrances or exits.
- Widening or otherwise modifying hallways and interior doorways.
- Installing railings, support bars, or other modifications in bathrooms.
- Lowering or modifying kitchen cabinets and equipment.
- Moving or modifying electrical outlets and fixtures.
- Installing porch lifts and other forms of lifts (elevators generally do add value to the house).
- Modifying fire alarms, smoke detectors, and other warning systems.
- Modifying stairways.
- Adding handrails or grab bars anywhere.
- Modifying hardware on doors.
- Modifying areas in front of entrance and exit doorways.
- Grading the ground to provide access to the residence.

Medical Insurance Premiums. Medical expenses include insurance premiums paid for policies that cover medical care. Policies may provide payment for any of the following;

- Hospitalization, surgical fees, X-rays, etc.
- Prescription drugs.
- Replacement of lost or damaged contact lenses.
- Membership in an association that gives cooperative, or "free-choice," medical service.
- Group hospitalization and clinical care.
- Qualified long-term care insurance contracts subject to additional limitations (see *Qualified Long-Term Care Insurance Contracts*, page 2-7).

If the policy provides payments that are not medically related, the premiums for the medical care part of the policy can be included if the charge for the medical part is reasonable. The cost of the medical part must be separately stated in the insurance contract or provided in a separate statement. For example, the premium for an automobile insurance policy that lumps all medical and nonmedical costs together is not deductible as a medical expense.

Caution. If advance payments of the health coverage tax credit were made on the taxpayer's behalf by an insurance company, these payments are not included in medical expense deductions.

The following premiums can be included as medical expenses;

- Medicare Part B,
- Medicare A tax (if taxpayer was not previously covered and then enrolled voluntarily), and
- Medicare Part D.

The following premiums are not medical expenses:

- Employer-sponsored health insurance plan (pretax plan) payments (unless included on the taxpayer's W-2 in box 1).
- Contributions made by a taxpayer's employer to provide coverage for qualified long-term care services under a flexible spending or similar arrangement.
- Health reimbursement arrangement (HRA) funded solely by an employer.
- Life insurance policies.
- Policies providing payment for loss of earnings.
- Policies for loss of life, limb, sight, etc.
- Policies that pay the taxpayer a guaranteed amount each week for a stated number of weeks if the taxpayer is hospitalized for sickness or injury.
- Car insurance premiums for a policy that provides medical insurance coverage for all persons injured in or by the taxpayer's car, unless the premium for the taxpayer, the taxpayer's spouse, and the taxpayer's dependents is stated separately from the premium for medical care for others.

 Planning Tip. The fees paid to a dependent's educational institution generally include a fee for insurance and medical care. The applicable portion is deductible as a medical expense.

Unused Sick Leave Used to Pay Premiums. If the taxpayer elects to use unused sick leave pay to pay for the cost of continuing participation in a health plan, this cost can be included as a medical expense, but it would also count as income. If this participation is required by the employer, however, it cannot be included as a medical expense, but the pay will not count as income.

Prepaid Insurance Premiums. Premiums paid before age 65 for medical insurance for medical care after the taxpayer reaches age 65 are medical care expenses in the year paid if both of the following are true:

- The premiums are payable in equal yearly or more frequent installments, and
- The premiums are payable for at least 10 years, or until the taxpayer reaches age 65 (but not for less than five years).

Qualified Long-Term Care Insurance Contracts. A qualified long-term care insurance contract is an insurance contract that provides coverage only for qualified long-term care services. The contract must:

1. Be guaranteed renewable;
2. Not provide for a cash surrender value;
3. Provide that refunds, other than refunds on the death of the insured or complete surrender or cancellation of the contract, be used only to reduce future premiums or increase future benefits; and
4. Generally not pay or reimburse expenses incurred for services or items that would be reimbursed under Medicare, unless Medicare is a secondary payor, and not pay per diem or other periodic payments without regard to expenses.

See MTG ¶1019.

Limit on Long-Term Care Premiums the Taxpayer May Deduct in 2013	
Age at End of 2013	**Maximum Deduction**
40 or under	$ 360
41-50	680
51-60	1,360
61-70	3,640
71 or older	4,550

Qualified Long-Term Care Services. Qualified long-term care services are necessary diagnostic, preventive, therapeutic, curing, treating, mitigating, or rehabilitative services, and maintenance and personal care services (defined below) that are required by a *chronically ill individual* and are provided according to a plan of care prescribed by a *licensed health care practitioner*. For these services, all unreimbursed expenses are deductible on Schedule A, as are insurance premiums up to the limits in the above table.

According to IRS Publication 502, an individual is defined as *chronically ill* if, within the previous 12 months, a licensed health care practitioner has certified that the individual meets either of the following descriptions:

- For at least 90 days, he or she is unable to perform at least two activities of daily living without substantial assistance from another individual, due to a loss of functional capacity. Activities of daily living are eating, toileting, transferring, bathing, dressing, and continence.
- He or she requires substantial supervision to be protected from threats to health and safety due to severe cognitive impairment.

Maintenance or personal care services consist of care that has as its primary purpose the providing of a chronically ill individual with needed assistance for his or her disabilities, including protection from threats to health and safety due to severe cognitive impairment.

Nursing Services. Nursing services provided in the home or in another facility are deductible. These services need not be performed by a nurse as long as they are services generally performed by a nurse—such as giving medicine or changing bandages—or if they are services connected with a disability, such as bathing a patient. Also includible as a medical expense are any payments of Social Security tax, FUTA, Medicare tax, and state employment taxes for nursing services.

If an attendant also provides household services such as cleaning or cooking, the wages and taxes paid for time spent on these tasks are not deductible, and the percentage of time spent on these tasks will have to be calculated.

Reimbursements as a Subtraction from Medical Expenses. Medical expenses can be deducted only if there was no insurance or other reimbursement payment made during the tax year. This includes payments from Medicare, but it does not include amounts received for loss of earnings or damages for injuries. If a policy overpays for certain expenses, the overpayment must be counted against other services that are not reimbursed.

Health Reimbursement Arrangement (HRA). A health reimbursement arrangement is an employer-funded plan that reimburses employees for medical care expenses and allows unused amounts to be carried forward. An HRA is funded solely by the employer, and the reimbursements for medical expenses, up to a maximum dollar amount for a coverage period, are not included in income and should not be included in deductions.

> **Example.** Betty Wiggins has insurance policies that cover her hospital and doctors' bills but not her nursing bills. After an operation that disables her for a while, she receives payment of $6,500 for her hospital and doctors' bills, which is $150 more than their charges. She requires home nursing services after the operation, which is not covered by her insurance. For these, she pays $800 to a nursing agency, which includes $100 for cleaning services. She can claim a deduction of $550: $800 minus the $100 nonqualified nursing services minus the $150 insurance payment.

Other Reimbursements That Do Not Reduce Medical Expenses. Generally, medical expenses are not reduced by payments received for the following:

- Permanent loss or loss of use of a member or function of the body (loss of limb, sight, hearing, etc.).
- Disfigurement to the extent the payment is based on the nature of the injury without regard to the amount of time lost from work.
- Loss of earnings.

However, the taxpayer must reduce medical expenses by any part of these payments that is designated for medical costs.

Insurance Reimbursements More than Medical Expenses. If an insurance reimbursement is greater than the total medical expenses, the excess may or may not be taxable, depending on who paid for the policy. If the policy was paid for by the taxpayer, the excess is tax-free and need not be reported. If, however, the taxpayer's employer paid for the policy, the excess is taxable and is reported on line 21 of Form 1040. If both the taxpayer and the employer paid for the policy (the usual arrangement), the excess is proportionately taxable.

Insurance Reimbursements in a Different Taxable Year. Often medical expenses are paid in one year but not reimbursed until the next. In this case, the expenses are deductible in the year paid. The reimbursement, when it comes, is treated as "other income" and reported on line 21 of Form 1040. If no deduction was taken for the expense, the reimbursement is tax-free.

Decedent Considerations. Medical expenses paid before death by the decedent are included in figuring any deduction for medical and dental expenses on the decedent's final income tax return. This includes expenses for the decedent's spouse and dependents. The survivor or personal representative of a decedent can choose to treat certain medical expenses paid by the decedent's estate as paid by the decedent at the time the medical services were provided. The expenses must be paid within the one-year period beginning with the day after the date of death.

The survivor or personal representative making this choice must attach a statement to the decedent's Form 1040, or the decedent's amended return, Form 1040X, saying that the expenses have not been and will not be claimed on the estate tax return. See MTG ¶1018.

What if the decedent's return had been filed and the medical expenses were not included? Form 1040X can be filed for the year or years the expenses are treated as paid, unless the period for filing an amended return for that year has passed. Generally, an amended return must be filed within three years of the date the original return was filed, or within two years from the time the tax was paid, whichever date is later.

> **Caution.** Qualified medical expenses paid before death by the decedent are not deductible if paid with a tax-free distribution from any HSA or Archer MSA.

Example. Willis Ferguson died on June 1, 2013. He had incurred $8,000 in medical expenses: $5,000 in 2012 and $3,000 in 2013. He had filed his 2012 return on April 15, 2013, and did not claim the $5,000 in medical expenses. His executor paid the entire $8,000 in August 2013. The executor can then file an amended return for 2012, claiming the $5,000 as a deduction in order to get a refund from the increase in deductions. The remaining $3,000 may be deducted on Willis's final return.

What if the taxpayer paid medical expenses of a deceased spouse or dependent? If the taxpayer paid medical expenses for the taxpayer's deceased spouse or dependent, the expenses should be treated as medical expenses on Form 1040 in the year paid, whether they are paid before or after the decedent's death.

Lines 2-4, Calculation

The amount of the allowed deduction on line 4 will be the amount of line 1 that exceeds 10% (7.5% if the taxpayer or his or her spouse is age 65 or older) of line 2, which is the taxpayer's adjusted gross income (AGI). (See Tab 1 for a discussion of AGI.)

Note that, for AMT purposes (see Tab 10), medical expenses are deductible only to the extent that they exceed 10% of AGI.

Partly because of the 10% floor (7.5% floor if age 65 or older), it may be beneficial for married couples who have medical expenses to file separately.

 Planning Tip. If a married client is filing separately and is using Schedule A, it's a good idea to ask for the spouse's Schedule A to ensure that both are itemizing, as required.

Taxes Paid, Lines 5-9

Taxes not directly connected with a business or with property held for production of income are generally deducted on lines 5-9 of Schedule A. See MTG ¶1021.

Nondeductible Taxes

The following taxes are not deductible;

- Federal income and excise taxes.
- Social Security, Medicare, federal unemployment (FUTA), and railroad retirement (RRTA) taxes.
- Customs duties.

 Caution. Filing separate returns can have many other adverse tax consequences. When making the decision whether clients should file separate returns, take all parts of the return into consideration. In the example below, Mrs. Miranda cannot elect to use the standard deduction and this may result in an increase in overall tax liability. See Tab 1 for considerations regarding married filing separately filing status.

Example. Leoni Wheeler is 55, her AGI is $50,000 and her deductible medical expenses are $15,000 (all of which she paid in 2013). The allowed deduction would be calculated as follows:

Line	Amount
1	$15,000
2	$50,000
3	$5,000
4	$10,000

Amount of medical expenses not deductible due to 10%-of-AGI reduction:

$50,000 × 10% = $5,000

Deductible amount:

$15,000 – $5,000 = $10,000

Example. Jorge Miranda, age 65, paid $1,100 for his own medical expenses, $800 for his wife Esperanza's medical expenses, and $1,450 for his dependent mother's medical expenses in 2013. Jorge's 2013 AGI is $22,000, and his wife's AGI is $23,000. If he and his wife file jointly, they cannot deduct any of the expenses [$3,350 of medical expenses – $3,375 (7.5% of $45,000 AGI) is less than zero].

If they file separate returns, however, their total medical deductions will be $900. While Esperanza cannot deduct her medical expenses [$800 of medical expenses - $2,300 (10% of $23,000 AGI) is less than zero], Jorge's deduction is $900 [$2,550 of medical expenses -$1,650 (7.5% of $22,000 AGI) = $900].

If the couple had records substantiating payment of Esperanza's medical expenses solely from Jorge's funds, the deduction could be as much as $1,700. Careful and detailed records are required.

- Federal estate and gift taxes.
- Gasoline tax.
- Car inspection fees.
- Assessments for sidewalks or other improvements to the taxpayer's property.
- Taxes paid for others.
- License fees (marriage, driver's, dog, etc.).

Who Can Deduct Taxes?

Taxes are deductible only by the person who owes and pays them. Thus, taxes paid on a child's property are not deductible by the parent, because they are not the parent's obligation, or by the child, because the child did not pay them, unless the parent paid on the child's behalf (the child treats the amount as a gift).

If, as part of a rental arrangement, a tenant pays taxes for his or her landlord on a business property, the tenant may be able to deduct the taxes, not as a tax expense but as additional rent, provided that the rent is deductible.

When Are Taxes Deducted?

Cash-basis taxpayers deduct taxes on the return for the year the taxes are paid. Accrual-basis taxpayers deduct taxes on the return for the year the taxes are accrued. Amended returns must be filed to deduct taxes in the correct year if they were not claimed on the original return.

Line 5, State and Local Income Taxes or General Sales Taxes

The taxpayer can elect to deduct *either* state and local general sales taxes *or* state and local income taxes, but not both. State and local income taxes include the following:

1. Amounts withheld from the taxpayer's salary (Form W-2) or other earnings (Form 1099) in 2013.
2. Taxes paid in 2013 for a prior year, not including penalties or interest.
3. State and local estimated tax payments made during 2013, including any part of a prior year's refund that the taxpayer chooses to have credited to the current year's state or local income taxes.
4. Mandatory contributions made to the Alaska, New Jersey, or Pennsylvania unemployment fund; California, New Jersey, or New York Nonoccupational Disability Benefit Fund; Rhode Island Temporary Disability Benefit Fund; or Washington State Supplemental Workmen's Compensation Fund.

 Planning Tip. The taxpayer can often make adjustments in paying the fourth-quarter estimated taxes to maximize deductions in one year and minimize them in another. Estimating whether itemizing deductions for 2013 will be advantageous in December allows planning for maximum benefit.

If a state tax refund was received in 2013 and a state tax deduction was claimed in 2012, the refund amount does not reduce the Schedule A tax deduction. Instead, the refund is included in gross income on Form 1040, line 10. If a standard deduction was claimed in 2012, the refund is *not* taxable.

 Caution. Some practitioners use the actual state income tax due rather than the total state tax withheld for Schedule A, thereby avoiding making the refund taxable in the subsequent year. Although doing so can be more favorable to the taxpayer, it could lead to a document matching inquiry by the IRS.

Line 6, Real Estate Taxes

State, local or foreign taxes based on the assessed value of nonbusiness real estate owned by a taxpayer (or spouse if married filing jointly) are deductible on line 6. Also, the assessment must be made uniformly on property throughout the community, and the proceeds must be used for general community or governmental purposes. The following amounts are not included:

- Itemized charges for services to specific property or persons. For example, a $20 monthly charge per house for trash collection, a $5 charge for every 1,000 gallons of water consumed, or a flat charge for mowing a lawn that had grown higher than permitted under a local ordinance.
- Charges for improvements that increase the value of the taxpayer's property. For example, an assessment to build a new sidewalk. The cost of a property improvement is added to the basis of the property. However, a charge is deductible if the funds are used only to maintain an existing public facility in service. For example, a charge to repair an existing sidewalk, and any interest included in that charge, if it meets the general requirements for deductible taxes.
- Amounts for refunds and rebates of current-tax-year real estate taxes.

If mortgage payments include real estate taxes, only the amount the mortgage company actually paid to the taxing authority during the tax year may be deducted.

Caution. States or municipalities may impose regular, uniform, or specific-purpose "benefit" taxes. Both intent of the tax and uniformity of application must be scrutinized to determine deductibility.

Real Estate Taxes Paid at Settlement or Closing. If real estate is sold, the deduction for real estate taxes is apportioned according to the number of days during the tax year that the buyer and seller each owned the home. For federal income tax purposes, the seller is treated as paying the property taxes up to, but not including, the date of sale. The buyer's tax-paying portion begins on the date of sale. The seller's and buyer's share of these taxes are each fully deductible, if each itemizes deductions. See MTG ¶¶1032-1038.

 Planning Tip. Examine real estate closing documents carefully to ensure that proration between buyer and seller is properly calculated based on the local real property tax year.

For federal income tax purposes, the buyer and the seller each are considered to have paid their own share of the taxes, even if one or the other paid the entire amount. If the buyer pays delinquent back taxes that have been imposed on the seller, the buyer may not deduct these payments, but they should be added to the basis of the property.

Example. Mr. and Mrs. Larsen bought their home on September 1, 2013. The property tax year in their area is the calendar year. The tax for the year was $1,000 and was due and paid by the seller on August 15. The deduction calculation for the Larsens would be as follows:

Total real estate taxes	$1,000
Number of days in the home (from September 1 to December 31)	122
Portion of the year (days in the home divided by days in the year: 122/365)	0.334
Total deduction	$ 334

Construction Period Taxes. Taxes (and interest) on real property paid during the construction period generally must be capitalized. However, homeowners are permitted to deduct real property taxes and qualified mortgage interest paid during the construction of a personal residence (Temporary Reg. §1.163-10T(p)(5)(i)). See MTG ¶991 and ¶993.

Line 7, Personal Property Taxes

To be deductible, personal property taxes must be based on value alone and be charged on a yearly basis.

 Example. Taxpayers in Larimer County, Colorado, pay a vehicle registration tax that includes an ownership tax based on the vehicle's value and a license fee based on the weight of the vehicle. If Jason paid a fee of $225 when registering his new $10,000 car, the deductible amount would be the portion attributable to the value of the car, $178.50 ($10,000 × 0.85 × 0.021). The $46.50 he paid based on the weight of the vehicle is not deductible.

Line 8, Other Taxes

Any other deductible taxes not listed on line 5, 6, or 7 should be listed on line 8 by type and amount. Taxes paid to a foreign country or U.S. possession are included on this line.

 Planning Tip. The taxpayer may want to take a credit for the foreign tax instead of a deduction. See the discussion of Form 1040, line 47 in Tab 1.

If the foreign tax credit is taken for any eligible foreign taxes, the taxpayer generally may not take any part of the year's foreign taxes as a deduction. However, even if the foreign tax credit is claimed, a deduction may be taken if:

- Foreign taxes are not allowed as a credit because of boycott provisions.
- Taxes are paid to certain foreign countries for which a credit has been denied (see IRS Publication 514).
- Taxes are paid on dividends that are not creditable because the taxpayer does not meet the stock holding period requirement, generally more than 15 days during a 30-day period, as described in IRS Publication 514.
- Certain taxes are paid or accrued to a foreign country in connection with the purchase or sale of oil or gas extracted in that country, as described in IRS Publication 514.

Planning Tip. Although a taxpayer claiming the credit for foreign taxes on an accrual basis will ordinarily use the average exchange rate for the relevant tax year, the taxpayer may elect to use the exchange rate on the date the taxes were paid, rather than an annual average.

See IRS Publication 514 and Tab 10 for details.

Line 9, Add Lines 5 through 8

The total of deductible taxes is entered on line 9.

Example. Leon Jones has had $1,220 in state income taxes withheld from his income in 2013, and he paid an additional $250 with his state tax return. He bought a new residence on May 15, 2013, and sold his previous residence (in the same state) on June 12, 2013. The annual real estate taxes on his first residence were $1,725 and on his second residence, $2,150. In addition, his new municipality levies an annual garbage collection charge of $250 with its property tax bill. In his new city of residence, he has also paid a vehicle registration tax, based entirely on book value, of $19. The calculation of his real estate tax is shown below. His total tax deductions would amount to $3,609.49 ($1,470 in state income taxes + $2,120.49 in real estate taxes + $19 in personal property taxes).

Days in first residence (January 1–June 11)	162
Tax deductible for first residence (162/365 × $1,725)	$765.62
Days in second residence (May 15–December 31)	231
Tax deductible for second residence (231/365 × $2,150)	$1,360.68
Total real estate tax (garbage collection fee not includible)	$2,126.30

Interest Paid, Lines 10-15

What Can Be Deducted on Schedule A?

Whether interest is deductible depends on the type and purpose of the debt on which the interest is paid.

- *Personal interest,* which is interest paid on nonbusiness car loans, credit cards, and the like, is not deductible.
- *Student loan interest,* is generally considered personal interest, but may be deductible from gross income on Form 1040 (see Tab 1).
- *Business interest* is interest incurred on debts that are used in a trade and business; it is deductible on Schedule C or F (see Tab 3), or, if the business involves rentals or other passive activities, on Schedule E or Form 4835 (see Tab 5).
- *Investment interest* is interest paid on money borrowed to buy or carry property that generates income such as interest, dividends, annuities, and royalties. In-

vestment interest is figured on Form 4952 and is generally reportable on Schedule A; it is deductible up to the amount of net investment income (see discussion on page 2-18).
- *Mortgage interest* is deductible on Schedule A, if the mortgage is on a qualified residence. In fact, outstanding personal loans can be converted into loans with deductible interest, for regular tax purposes only, if they are consolidated into qualified home equity loans or lines of credit.

Treatment of Tax Penalties and Tax Refunds

Interest paid due to tax underpayments, no matter what the jurisdiction, is nondeductible personal interest. Interest on tax refunds is counted as investment income to be netted against investment expenses.

Interest paid on another's debt is not deductible. Thus, mortgage payments made by a former spouse not legally liable for the debt will probably be treated as taxable alimony, and the interest will not be deductible by either party (*Linda J. Baxter*, TC Memo 1999-190). See Tab 13.

See IRS Publication 550, *Investment Income and Expenses,* and IRS Publication 936, *Home Mortgage Interest Deduction,* for more information.

Line 10, Home Mortgage Interest and Points Reported on Form 1098

Mortgage interest and points reported on Form 1098, *Mortgage Interest Statement,* are entered on line 10. If this form shows a refund of overpaid interest, the deduction is not reduced, but the overpayment is reported on Form 1040, line 21.

Home mortgage interest is any interest the taxpayer pays on a loan secured by his or her main home or second home. The loan may be a mortgage to buy the home, a second mortgage, a home equity line of credit, or a home equity loan. Home mortgage interest can be deducted only if all four of the following conditions are met:

- The taxpayer files Form 1040 and itemizes deductions on Schedule A.
- The taxpayer is legally liable for the loan.
- Both the taxpayer and the lender intend that the loan will be repaid and there must be a true debtor-creditor relationship between the taxpayer and the lender.
- The mortgage must be a *secured debt* on a *qualified* home. To be qualified, the home must be the taxpayer's main or second home, and it must be a structure, mobile or not, that has sleeping, cooking, and toilet facilities. A debt is not secured by the taxpayer's home if it is a security interest that attaches to the property without the taxpayer's consent, e.g., a mechanic's lien or judgment lien.

There are three types of qualified debt:

- home acquisition debt,
- home equity debt, and
- grandfathered debt.

Home Acquisition Debt. Home acquisition debt is a mortgage taken out after October 13, 1987, to buy, build, or substantially improve a qualified main or second home and secured by that home. If the mortgage is more than the cost of the home plus the cost of any substantial improvements, only the debt that equals the cost of the home plus improvements qualifies as home acquisition debt. The additional debt may qualify as *home equity debt.*

- *Home acquisition debt limit*–A taxpayer's home acquisition debt on a main home and second home cannot be more than $1 million ($500,000 for married filing separately). This limit is reduced, but not below zero, by the amount of *grandfathered debt.* Debt over this limit may qualify as *home equity debt.*
- *Refinanced home acquisition debt*–Any secured debt the taxpayer uses to refinance home acquisition debt is

Where to Deduct Interest on 2013 Return

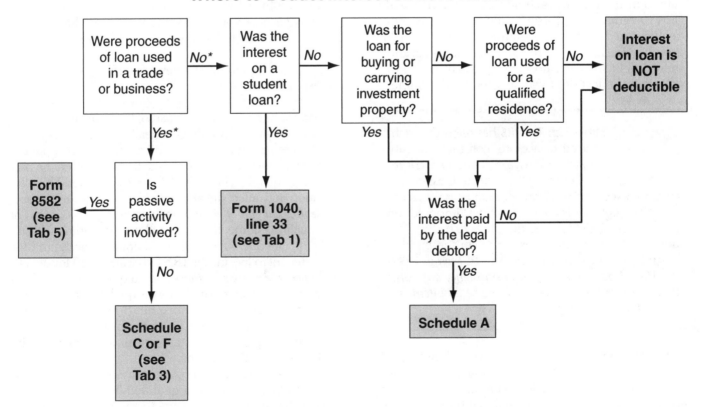

* If proceeds were used for both business and personal use, the interest must be allocated; see Reg. §1.163-8T and IRS Publication 535.

treated as home acquisition debt up to the balance of the old mortgage principal just before the refinancing. Any additional debt is not home acquisition debt, but may qualify as *home equity debt*. The IRS has confirmed that qualified home mortgage interest, which is deductible for AMT purposes, includes interest paid on a repeatedly refinanced home mortgage to the extent the mortgage indebtedness is not increased (Rev. Rul. 2005-11).

Home Equity Debt. If the taxpayer took out a loan for reasons other than to buy, build, or substantially improve the main or second home, it may qualify as home equity debt. In addition, debt the taxpayer incurred to buy, build, or substantially improve the home, to the extent that it is more than the home acquisition debt limit, may qualify as home equity debt. Home equity debt is a mortgage the taxpayer took out after October 13, 1987, that is secured by a qualified home but does not qualify as home acquisition debt.

- *Home equity debt limit*–The limit on the amount of debt that can be treated as home equity debt is the lesser of $100,000 ($50,000 if married filing separately) or the total of each home's fair market value (FMV) reduced, but not below zero, by its home acquisition debt and grandfathered debt. The FMV and the outstanding home acquisition and grandfathered debt for each home are determined on the date that the last debt was secured by the home.

> **Filing Tip.** The IRS has ruled that debt incurred to acquire, construct, or substantially improve a home can constitute home equity indebtedness to the extent it exceeds $1 million, although it is subject to the $100,000 and FMV limitations imposed on home equity indebtedness (Rev. Rul. 2010-25). This position, however, is inconsistent with the position taken by the Tax Court in *P.S. Pau, TC Memo. 1997-43. The IRS acknowledged the inconsistency but stated that it believes that its position is the better interpretation of IRC §163(h)(3).*

Grandfathered Debt. If the taxpayer took out a qualified mortgage before October 14, 1987, or refinanced a qualified mortgage, it will qualify as grandfathered debt if it was secured by the qualified home on October 13, 1987, and at all times after that date. All of the interest paid on grandfathered debt is fully deductible home mortgage interest, but the amount of grandfathered debt reduces the limits for home acquisition debt and home equity debt.

- *Refinanced grandfathered debt*–If grandfathered debt was refinanced after October 13, 1987, for an amount that was not more than the mortgage principal left on the debt, then it is still grandfathered debt. To the extent the new debt is more than the mortgage principal, it is treated as home acquisition or home equity debt, and the mortgage is a mixed-use mortgage. Grandfathered debt that was refinanced after October 13, 1987, is treated as grandfathered debt only for the term left on the debt that was refinanced. Then it has to be treated as home acquisition debt or home equity debt, depending on how the proceeds are used. There is an exception for balloon notes; see IRS Publication 936.
- *Line-of-credit mortgage*–If the taxpayer had a line-of-credit mortgage on October 13, 1987, and borrowed additional amounts against it after that date, the additional amounts are either home acquisition debt or home equity debt depending on how the proceeds were used. The balance on the mortgage before the taxpayer borrowed the additional amounts is grandfathered debt.

Home Considerations. An individual may consider interest on loans secured by two homes as deductible home mortgage interest:

- *Main home*–This is the home where the taxpayer ordinarily lives (only one at a time).
- *Second home*–A second home is a home that the taxpayer chooses to treat as a second home.

The following circumstances may affect mortgage interest deductibility:

- *Office in the home*–Only the part of the home used for residential living is considered a qualified home. Taxpayers who use part of it as a home office must divide both the cost and fair market value of the home between the part that is a qualified home and the part that is not. This allocation may affect the amount of home acquisition debt.
- *Renting out part of home*–If the taxpayer rents out part of a qualified home, the entire value of the home will still be qualified as long as there is not a separate unit for the tenant to live in. See IRS Publication 936 for details.
- *Home under construction*–The taxpayer can treat a home under construction as a qualified home for a period of up to 24 months, but only if it becomes a qualified home when it is ready for occupancy. The 24-month period can start any time on or after the day construction begins.
- *Home destroyed*–The taxpayer may be able to continue treating a home as a qualified home even after it is destroyed in a fire, storm, tornado, earthquake, or other casualty. See IRS Publication 936 for details.
- *Tenant-stockholders in a cooperative project*–Tenant-stockholders in an apartment house can deduct their portion of interest payments on the indebtedness of the cooperative. In addition, they can also deduct their share of the real estate taxes on the building.

The following considerations apply to second homes:

- *Second home not rented out at any time during the year*– The taxpayer can treat it as a qualified home, even if the home is not used during the year.
- *Second home rented out part of the year*–The taxpayer must use this home more than 14 days or more than 10% of the number of days during the year that the home is rented at a fair rental, whichever is greater. If this condition is not met, the unit is considered rental property rather than a second home.
- *More than one second home*–If the taxpayer has more than two homes, only one can be treated as the qualified second home during any year.
- *Time-sharing arrangements*–A time-shared home can be treated as a qualified home if it meets the requirements for a second home that is rented out.

 Filing Tip. A second home is any "structure" deemed by the taxpayer to be a second home. An RV, time share, or condominium may qualify, but the chosen second home must qualify as a residence under the local ordinance.

Example. Heather Brooks owns and occupies an apartment in a cooperative project. Her yearly carrying charges total $1,700: $1,000 for her share of the interest on the building's mortgage and $700 for her share of the real estate taxes. The $1,000 would be deductible on line 10 of Schedule A, and the $700 would be deductible on line 6 of Schedule A.

Limits on Home Mortgage Interest Deduction. Limits apply to the home mortgage interest expense deduction if the taxpayer has a home mortgage that does not fit into any of the previously discussed categories (see flowchart on page 2-16). The home mortgage interest deduction is limited to the interest on the part of the home mortgage debt that is not more than the qualified loan limit. This is the part of the taxpayer's home mortgage debt that is grandfathered debt or that is not more than the limits for home acquisition debt and home equity debt.

Whether all of the home mortgage interest is deductible depends on the date the taxpayer took out the mortgage, the amount of the mortgage, and the taxpayer's use of its proceeds. If all of the taxpayer's mortgages fit into one or more of the three categories already discussed at all times during the year, the taxpayer can deduct all of the interest on those mortgages.

The dollar limits for the home acquisition debt and the home equity debt categories apply to the combined mortgages on the taxpayer's main home and second home.

 Caution. Home equity interest deductions are subject to the alternative minimum tax.

Line 11, Home Mortgage Interest Not Reported on Form 1098

Deductible mortgage interest for which there is no Form 1098 is reported on line 11. If the home was purchased from the interest recipient, the recipient's name, identifying number, and address go on the dotted lines next to line 11. If the recipient is an individual, the identifying number is his or her Social Security number (SSN); otherwise, it is the employer identification number.

 Filing Tip. There is a $50 penalty for failure to show the required recipient information. If someone (other than the taxpayer's spouse, if filing jointly) was liable for, and paid interest on, the mortgage, and that person received the Form 1098, the payor's statement must be attached to the return showing the name and address of that person and the notation "See attached" added to the right of line 11.

Line 12, Points Not Reported on Form 1098

"Points" are certain charges paid, or treated as paid, by a homebuyer to obtain a mortgage for the purchase, construction, or substantial improvement of a main or second home. Points are deductible in the year paid, if the following conditions are met:

1. The amount is clearly shown on the settlement statement, e.g., the HUD-1 Settlement Statement, as points charged for the mortgage. The points may be shown as paid from either the buyer's funds or the seller's.
2. Amounts are a percentage of the stated principal loan amount.
3. Paying points is an established business practice in the area where the loan was made, and the points conform to the amounts generally charged in that area.
4. The loan is used to buy, build, or make substantial improvements to the taxpayer's main home, and it is secured by that home.
5. The amounts are paid directly by the homebuyer or by the seller for the homebuyer's mortgage.

Example. William and Jennifer Qian bought a home in 2004. Its current FMV is $125,000, and the balance on the mortgage on July 1, 2013, is $105,000. In order to consolidate some personal debts, they look into taking out a home equity loan. The best deal they find is from BBB Bank, which offers a loan of 120% of the FMV over the outstanding mortgage debt. (There are no other liens attached to the property.)

Currently, the Qians have $105,000 in home acquisition debt. Their loan from BBB is 120% × $125,000 − $105,000 = $45,000. Because their home acquisition debt is $105,000, their home equity debt is limited to $20,000, which is the amount by which their home's FMV exceeds the home acquisition debt. The interest they pay on their new home mortgage loan will have to be allocated between the qualified home equity part ($20,000), which will be fully deductible on Schedule A, and the rest ($25,000), which will be considered as personal interest and will not be deductible.

Is Home Mortgage Interest Fully Deductible on Schedule A?

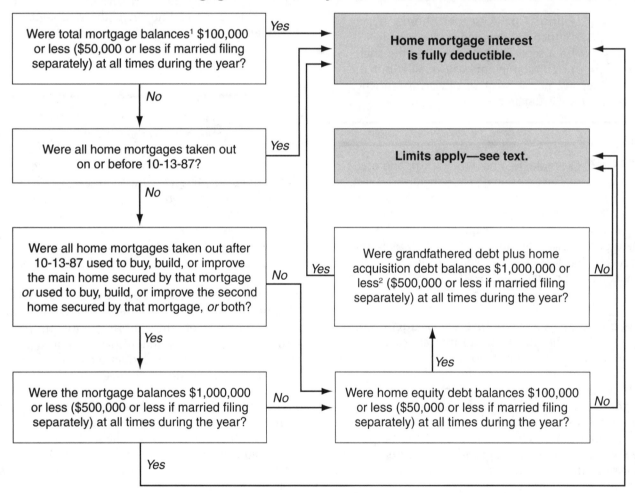

[1] Balances of ALL mortgages secured by main home and second home
[2] Amounts over the $1,000,000 limit ($500,000 if married filing separately) qualify as home equity debt if they are not more than the total home equity debt limit—see text

Planning Tip. Even if all five tests above are met, the taxpayer still has the option to deduct the points over the loan's lifetime. This option should be used in years in which points are paid but deductions are otherwise insufficient to itemize.

Points may also be called loan origination fees, maximum loan charges, loan discount, or discount points. Points paid to obtain a loan for the purchase of a principal residence are generally reported on Form 1098. A borrower is treated as having paid any points that a seller pays for the borrower's mortgage.

 Caution. All points paid on loans secured by the taxpayer's second home must be deducted only over the life of the loan.

Not Considered Points. Amounts charged by the lender for specific services connected to a loan are not considered interest, including;

- appraisal fees,
- notary fees,
- preparation fees for the mortgage note or deed of trust,
- mortgage insurance premiums, and
- VA funding fees, unless paid directly by the buyer.

These fees cannot be deducted as points either in the year paid or over the life of the mortgage.

 Gray Area. Points paid to refinance a mortgage are not fully deductible in the year paid unless they are paid in connection with the purchase or improvement of a home; they are deductible over the term of the loan. One appeals court, however, allowed a current deduction for points paid on a long-term mortgage refinancing a short-term balloon mortgage used to acquire the property because the refinancing was an integral part of the process of financing the purchase. *J.R. Huntsman*, 90-2 USTC ¶50,340, 905 F2d 1182 (8th Cir. 1990). A taxpayer or return preparer taking this position, outside the jurisdiction of the Eight Circuit Court of Appeals, may want to disclose this position in order to avoid the accuracy-related penalty if challenged by the IRS.

Points Paid by the Seller. The term points also includes loan placement fees that the seller pays to the lender to arrange financing for the buyer.

- *Treatment by seller*–The seller cannot deduct these fees as interest, but can use them as a selling expense to reduce the gain realized (see Tab 4).
- *Treatment by buyer*–The buyer reduces the basis of the home by the amount of the points paid by the seller and treats them as if he or she had paid them.

Qualified Mortgage Insurance Premiums

Certain qualified mortgage insurance premiums incurred before January 1, 2014, are deductible as qualified mortgage interest. However, the amount of the premium treated as interest is reduced by 10% for every $1,000 a taxpayer's AGI exceeds $100,000 ($500 and $50,000, respectively, for married filing separately).

Prepaid mortgage insurance premiums allocable to periods after the payment year are capitalized and treated as paid in the allocable periods. Prepaid premiums must be allocated ratably over the shorter of the stated term of the mortgage or 84 months, beginning with the month in which the insurance was obtained. If the mortgage is satisfied before the end of its term, no deduction is allowed for any premium allocable to periods after the mortgage is satisfied (see MTG ¶1055).

Line 14, Investment Interest

If the taxpayer borrows money to buy property held for investment purposes, the interest on that loan is investment interest. The taxpayer's deduction for investment interest is limited to the amount of net investment income. The taxpayer cannot deduct interest incurred to produce tax-exempt income (see MTG ¶1094 and ¶970).

Investment interest is deductible in the year paid for cash-basis taxpayers and in the year accrued for accrual-basis taxpayers. Interest paid in advance beyond year's end must be apportioned over the tax years to which the payment relates (see MTG ¶1055 and ¶1056).

Allocation of Interest Expense. If the same loan is used for business or personal purposes in addition to investment purposes, the debt must be allocated among those purposes. Regardless of what kind of property is used to secure the debt, only the portion of the interest attributable to the investment purpose is deductible on line 14 of Schedule A.

Limit on Deduction. The deduction for investment interest expense cannot exceed net investment income. The amount that cannot be deducted may be carried forward to the next tax year. The interest carried over is treated as investment interest paid or accrued in that next year. The taxpayer can carry over disallowed investment interest to the next tax year even if it is more

Example. The Qians paid a total of $12,000 of debt on their original home mortgage and their consolidation loan in 2013, and they use the table below, which is based on Table 1 from IRS Publication 936, to figure the amount of interest that is deductible, $8,640. Because the consolidation loan was entirely for personal reasons, none of the $3,360 nonallowable mortgage interest is deductible anywhere. In addition, the Qians paid $800 of points on the consolidation loan, but they cannot claim that amount as a deduction because it was not paid to purchase or improve their home. The total average balance of both mortgages on their home is $284,700. The Qians also paid $13,900 in investment interest in 2013. On their Schedule A, the Qians enter the $8,640 in mortgage interest on line 10 and the $13,900 in investment interest on line 14. The total of these amounts, $22,540, is entered on line 15.

Part I	Qualified Loan Limit		
1.	Enter the average balance of all your grandfathered debt. See line 1 instructions	1.	--------------
2.	Enter the average balance of all your home acquisition debt. See line 2 instructions	2.	105,000
3.	Enter $1,000,000 ($500,000 if married filing separately)	3.	1,000,000
4.	Enter the **larger** of the amount on line 1 or the amount on line 3	4.	1,000,000
5.	Add the amounts on lines 1 and 2. Enter the total here	5.	105,000
6.	Enter the **smaller** of the amount on line 4 or the amount on line 5	6.	105,000
7.	Enter $100,000 ($50,000 if married filing separately). See the line 7 instructions for a limit that may apply	7.	100,000
8.	Add the amounts on lines 6 and 7. Enter the total. This is your qualified loan limit	8.	205,000
Part II	**Deductible Home Mortgage Interest**		
9.	Enter the total of the average balances of all mortgages on all qualified homes. See line 9 instructions	9.	284,700
	• If line 8 is less than line 9, go on to line 10. • If line 8 is equal to or more than line 9, stop here. All of your interest on all the mortgages included on line 9 is deductible as home mortgage interest on Schedule A (Form 1040).		12,000
10.	Enter the total amount of interest that you paid. See line 10 instructions	10.	
11.	Divide the amount on line 8 by the amount on line 9. Enter the result as a decimal amount (rounded to three places)	11.	× .720
12.	Multiply the amount on line 10 by the decimal amount on line 11. Enter the result. This is your **deductible home mortgage interest.** Enter this amount on Schedule A (Form 1040)	12.	8,640
13.	Subtract the amount on line 12 from the amount on line 10. Enter the result. This is **not** home mortgage interest. See line 13 instructions	13.	3,360

than the taxpayer's taxable income in the year the interest was paid or accrued.

Form 4952, *Investment Interest Expense Deduction.* The investment interest expense deduction is figured on Form 4952, which is attached to Schedule A, and reported on line 14.

Definitions

- *Investment property*–Qualified investment property is property that produces interest, dividends, annuities, or royalties not derived in the ordinary course of a trade or business, but not an interest in a passive activity. Investment property also includes any interest in a trade or business activity in which the taxpayer did not materially participate, other than a passive activity.

- *Net investment income*–This is determined by subtracting investment expenses, other than interest expense, from all investment income.
- *Investment income*–This generally includes gross income derived from property held for investment. It does not include qualified dividends or net capital gain unless an election is made to include them–in which case capital gains and dividend rates do not apply.
- *Investment expenses*–Included in investment expenses are all income-producing expenses, other than interest expense, related to investment property after the 2%-of-AGI reduction is applied (see discussion of miscellaneous itemized deductions on page 2-27).

Line 15, Total Interest Deduction

The sum of lines 10 through 14 is reported on line 15. This is the total amount of deductible interest.

Gifts to Charity, Lines 16-19

Deductible Contributions

Generally, taxpayers can deduct contributions of money or property made to a qualified organization. A gift or contribution may also be deductible if given "for the use of" a qualified organization if held in a legally enforceable trust for the qualified organization or in a similar legal arrangement. The contributions must be made to a qualified organization and not set aside for use by a specific person. The fair market value of property given to a qualified organization is the amount of the deduction.

Qualified Organizations. Contributions can qualify for a charitable deduction only if made to one of the following:

- A corporation, trust, community chest, fund, or foundation that is organized and operated exclusively for a charitable, religious, educational, scientific, or literary purpose or for the prevention of cruelty to children or animals (up to a limit of 50% of AGI).
- The United States, a state, a territory, a city, or a political subdivision of any of these, if the contribution is made for a public purpose (up to a limit of 50% of AGI).
- Certain veterans' organizations or auxiliaries (up to a limit of 30% of AGI).
- Certain nonprofit cemetery companies (up to a limit of 30% of AGI).
- A domestic fraternity operating under the lodge system if the contribution is used solely for public purposes (up to a limit of 30% of AGI).

See MTG ¶1059 and ¶1061 for further details.

In addition, any qualifying organization must meet these requirements:

- No part of the net earnings may be used for the benefit of a private shareholder or individual.
- No substantial part of the activities of the organization may consist of carrying on lobbying activities or otherwise attempting to influence legislation.

Caution. A qualified charitable entity cannot act as a conduit to an individual regardless of the desires of the giver or the worthiness of the recipient. The IRS may disallow contributions it deems directed to an individual even if the gift was made through an organization.

Organizations should make their charitable status known when soliciting funds. IRS Publication 78, located online at www.irs.gov in a searchable format, has information on whether an organization is a qualified charity. If an organization is not on the IRS list, an inquiry may be sent to the Commissioner of Internal Revenue, Washington, DC 20224, Attention T:R:EO. The following organizations are usually qualified charities:

- Churches, temples, synagogues, mosques, and other religious organizations;
- Public recreation and park funds;
- Red Cross, Goodwill, Salvation Army, United Way, Boy/Girl Scouts, Boys/Girls Clubs of America, and other well-known charitable organizations; and
- Established veterans' groups such as the American Legion, the VFW, and Disabled American Veterans, although many newer veterans' groups' qualification should be checked in Publication 78.

Caution. The IRS lists charities that have recently had their tax-exempt status revoked. This list is published on a monthly basis in the Internal Revenue Bulletin. When an organization has had its exempt status revoked, contributions by individuals unaware of the revocation will still be deductible (1) until the date an announcement is published or (2) until the termination date stated in the announcement.

See IRS Publication 526, *Charitable Contributions*, and IRS Publication 561, *Determining the Value of Donated Property*, for more information.

Nondeductible Contributions

Contributions to the following are *not* deductible:

- Civic leagues (although membership dues to some civic organizations may be deductible as a business expense on Schedule C),
- Social clubs, and
- Any international or foreign organization (although gifts to certain Canadian, Israeli and Mexican charities may be deductible).

Caution. Contributions to an individual—no matter how needy that individual may be—are never deductible. This rule applies even to donations to qualified organizations if the gift is designated for the benefit of a specific individual.

Tuition for a Religious School. Tuition is *not* deductible on Schedule A. The IRS considers that all tuition payments go solely to the value of education. In the only significant challenge to this stance, a taxpayer tried to deduct 55% of his children's tuition to a religious school because that amount was for religious studies. However, the IRS prevailed in circuit court (M. *Sklar*, 2002-1 USTC ¶50,210, 279 F.3d 697 (9th Cir. 2002)).

Contributions made directly to a religious school aside from tuition, such as at a fundraiser, are deductible.

Services Rendered. The value of services rendered to any organization is not deductible, but unreimbursed expenses related to those services are deductible:

- Cost of uniforms required to be worn by Red Cross workers.
- Transportation expenses incurred (the standard automobile charitable mileage rate is a statutory 14 cents per mile).
- Expenses, i.e., travel, meals, lodging, etc., incurred while attending a qualified organization's convention as a delegate or officer of the organization. However, no expenses are deductible for attending in an unofficial capacity.

Contributions from Which the Donor Benefits. A taxpayer who receives a benefit as a result of making a contribution to a qualified organization can deduct only the amount of the contribution that exceeds the value of the benefit received. If the taxpayer pays more than fair market value to a qualified organization for merchandise, goods, or services, the amount paid over the value of the item can be deducted. For the excess amount to qualify, the taxpayer must pay it with the intent to make a charitable contribution.

> **Example.** John and Mary Kinsey pay $100 for two tickets to a dinner at their church. The church provides all contributors with a good-faith statement that says the FMV of the two dinners is $40. The Kinseys may take a $60 deduction on their joint return or, if filing separately, whoever paid for the tickets may take the deduction.

Token Items. If the value received in return for a contribution is a small item, such as a calendar or a mug, the benefit can be ignored in calculating the deduction. Benefits received in connection with a payment to a charity are considered to be insubstantial if the payment occurs in the context of a fund raising campaign in which the charity informs the donor of the amount of the contribution that is deductible, and, for 2013, either: (1) the fair market value of the benefits received does not exceed the lesser of 2% of the payment or $102; or (2) the payment is at least $51, the only items provided bear the charity's name or logo, and the cost of these items is within the $10.20 limit for "low-cost articles."

> **Gray Area.** Raffle tickets, a common fundraiser, benefit donors even if they do not win. Thus, amounts paid for chances to participate in raffles do not qualify as charitable contributions. Although in theory the amount by which the price of a raffle ticket exceeds the value of the chance to win the prize may be deductible if the taxpayer establishes the value of the chance of winning the prize, the taxpayer's unsubstantiated opinion of the chances of winning is not sufficient to satisfy the burden of proof.

Privilege to Purchase Athletic Tickets. 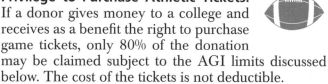 If a donor gives money to a college and receives as a benefit the right to purchase game tickets, only 80% of the donation may be claimed subject to the AGI limits discussed below. The cost of the tickets is not deductible.

Limits on Charitable Deductions

The amount of deductible charitable contributions is limited to 50% of AGI, and may be limited to 30% or 20% of AGI, depending on the type of property donated and the type of organization receiving it.

50% Limit. The deduction for charitable contributions cannot be more than 50% of AGI for the year.

> **Filing Tip.** An "exception" occurs for certain awards that are excludable from income (and therefore not deducted on Schedule A). Awards for scientific, artistic, literary, or civic achievement transferred unused to a government unit or tax-exempt charitable organization are nontaxable. See MTG ¶785.

For organizations listed as 50% limit organizations, total contributions up to 50% of AGI are permissible, except that a 30% limit applies to gifts of capital gain property for which the deduction is figured by using fair market value without reduction for appreciation. Examples of 50% limit organizations are churches and religious organizations, hospitals, medical research organizations, educational organizations (including public or private schools), and organizations that receive a substantial amount of public support, such as libraries, museums, and symphony orchestras. Also qualifying as 50% limit organizations are private foundations that distribute all contributions during the tax year in which they were received or within a 2.5-month period after the end of the year, and private foundations such as the United Way that pool contributions and allow contributors to name charities, as long as their income is distributed within 2.5 months of the end of the year.

30% Limit. A 30%-of-AGI limit applies to gifts to all qualified organizations other than 50% limit organizations. This includes gifts to veterans' organizations, fraternal societies, nonprofit cemeteries, and certain private nonoperating foundations.

20% Limit. A 20%-of-AGI limit applies to gifts to 30%-of-AGI organizations of capital gain property for which the deduction is figured by using fair market value without reduction for appreciation.

Figuring the Deduction When Limits Apply. If contributions are subject to more than one of the limits to a percentage of AGI, they can be deducted in the following order:

1. Contributions subject only to the 50% limit, up to 50% of the taxpayer AGI,
2. Contributions subject to the 30% limit, up to the lesser of (a) 30% of AGI, or (b) 50% of AGI minus contributions to 50% limit organizations, including contributions of capital gain property subject to the special 30% limit,
3. Contributions of capital gain property subject to the special 30% limit, up to the lesser of (a) 30% of AGI, or (b) 50% of AGI minus other contributions to 50% limit organizations, and
4. Contributions subject to the 20% limit.

Amounts of qualified contributions not allowable in 2013 may be carried over; see discussion on page 2-23.

> **Example.** Nancy Holdrege has AGI of $10,000. During 2013, she donates $700 to her church, $800 to her alma mater, both 50% organizations, and $3,300 to the Holdrege Family Foundation, a "private," 30% organization. Her deduction is calculated as follows: First, the $1,500 total contribution to 50% organizations is figured ($700 + $800). Since it is below the 50%-of-AGI maximum ($5,000), she can also deduct the 30% maximum of $3,000 for her contribution to the family's foundation, for a total of $4,500. The unused portion of the latter contribution can be carried over.

Contributions of Property

If the taxpayer contributes property to a qualified organization, the taxpayer's charitable contribution amount for deduction purposes is generally the fair market value of the property at the time of the contribution. However, if the property has increased in value, the taxpayer may have to make some adjustments to the deductible amount. See MTG ¶1058

> **Caution.** Charitable deductions for donated vehicles that have a value in excess of $500 are limited. Written acknowledgment by the donee is also required. Form 1098-C, *Contributions of Motor Vehicles, Boat, and Airplanes*, may be used for this purpose. The donor is required to attach the written acknowledgment to his or her return. In general, the deduction cannot be more than the price the organization receives when it sells the vehicle. If the organization does not sell the vehicle, it must provide certification of its intended use. See MTG ¶1070A.

In general, two questions have to be answered about gifts of property: What is the amount of the contribution based on–cost or value? What is the percentage limitation on the gift?

Capital Gain Property. Gifts of capital gain property held long-term are deductible at their FMV on the date of donation. Examples include personal property, stocks and other capital assets held long-term, and a portion of a business-use property that would generate long-term gains if sold. In a sense, the appreciation is not taxed, but it is taken into account when figuring the amount of contribution. If given to a 50% limit organization, these gifts cannot exceed 30% of AGI (20% if given to a 30% limit organization).

If stock is donated to a private foundation, no more than 10% of the outstanding stock may be given.

Election for Raising Limit. Instead of applying the 30% or 20% limit, a 50% limit may be used if the amount of contribution is reduced by *all* of the appreciation. If this election is made, all gifts–including carryovers–must be reduced by appreciation. The election is made with an attachment to Form 1040 simply stating that the election is being made. This election is not usually advisable unless there is minimal appreciation on all property donated.

Ordinary Income Property. If property would not generate long-term capital gain if sold, it is treated as ordinary income property. It is deductible at cost, and it is limited to 50% or 30% of AGI depending on the organization receiving it. Examples include capital assets held short term, inventory, taxpayer-produced creative works, and business-use property that would generate ordinary income if sold.

Tangible Personal Property. The deductible amount depends on how the recipient uses the donation. For the FMV to be deductible, the organization must use the gift for its exempt purpose. Otherwise, the deduction is limited to the original cost to the taxpayer. If the FMV is used, the 30% or 20% limit of AGI is used; otherwise, the 50% limit of AGI may be used.

> **Example.** George Reeder gives an old book to his church. He paid $100 for the book years ago, but it has appreciated in value to $5,000. The church sells it at a rummage sale. George can deduct only the $100 cost, up to the 50%-of-AGI limit. If, however, he had donated it to a library, he could have taken a $5,000 deduction, subject to the 30%-of-AGI limit.

Line 16, Gifts by Cash or Check

Cash contributions include any amounts paid by cash, check, credit card, or payroll deduction. They also include out-of-pocket expenses incurred while donating services.

Contributions of Less than $250. Substantiation requirements include:

• a canceled check or a legible and readable account statement,
• a receipt, a letter or other written communication from the organization showing its name, date of the contribution, and amount of the contribution. or
• other reliable (i.e., made near the time of contribution and regularly kept) written records with the relevant information just described.

Donors may not deduct monetary contributions unless they can produce a bank record or a receipt, letter or other written communication from the charitable organization.

Contributions of $250 or More. A deduction for a contribution of $250 or more in any one day must have an acknowledgment from the qualified organization or certain payroll deduction records.

The acknowledgment must be written, and it must be received by the earlier of the date the return is filed for the year of the contribution or the due date, including extensions, for filing the return.

For payroll deductions, a pay stub, Form W-2, or other document is required, accompanied by a pledge card or other document from the organization stating that the organization does not provide goods or services in return for any contribution made to it by payroll deduction.

Unreimbursed Expenses. For unreimbursed out-of-pocket expenses related to services performed for a charitable organization, the taxpayer must have adequate records to prove the amount of the expenses. The organization also has to provide, by the due date of the return, a written acknowledgment of those services.

Line 17, Other than by Cash or Check

For noncash contributions, e.g., tangible property, the taxpayer must have records that show all the following:

• The name of the charitable organization,
• The date and location of the charitable contribution,
• A reasonably detailed description of the property,
• FMV of the property and the appraisal method, and
• Any required reductions to the FMV (see "Contributions of Property" discussion on page 2-21).

Gifts of Partial Interest. In general, deductions cannot be claimed for property in which the giver retains an interest. There are, however, several exceptions, including:

• *Charitable remainder trusts.* The donor may deduct the present value of the remainder interest in a trust in which an income interest is retained for life or a term of not more than 20 years. It can be set up as a charitable remainder annuity trust or a charitable remainder unitrust and must meet strict requirements; see IRC §664(d) and Tab 14.
• *Pooled income funds.* The donor may deduct the present value of the remainder interest in a pooled income fund in which an income interest is retained for life.
• *Charitable interest in a personal residence or farm.* The donor may deduct the present value of the remainder interest in a home or farm in which the right to use the property is retained for life.

If less than the taxpayer's entire interest in the property is donated, there are additional requirements for record keeping: the amount claimed as a deduction for the tax year as a result of the contribution, the amount claimed as a deduction in any earlier years, the name of any person in possession of the property other than the organization to which it was contributed, and the name and address of each organization to which it was contributed.

Clothing and Household Items. Any donations of clothing and household items that are made to a charitable organization are not deductible unless the donated items are in "good" or better condition. This means that the IRS may deny a deduction for any item that has minimal monetary value. It also means that a donor of such items should be prepared to prove both the condition and the value of the donated items. There is one exception to this rule: if a single donated item is not in at least good condition, but it is worth more than $500, it is deductible, so long as a qualified appraisal is obtained at the time of the donation.

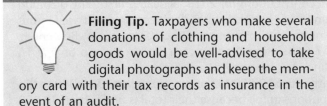

Filing Tip. Taxpayers who make several donations of clothing and household goods would be well-advised to take digital photographs and keep the memory card with their tax records as insurance in the event of an audit.

For purposes of this provision, "household items" include furniture, furnishing, electronics, appliances, linens, and other similar items. The term does not include food, paintings, antiques, other objects of art, jewelry, gems, or collections.

Contributions of Less than $250. Although all of the general recordkeeping requirements apply, it is not necessary to have a receipt if getting one would be difficult, such as at a drop-off site for donations or for a church-plate offering. Otherwise, a receipt showing the same things as the requirements for larger donations is needed.

Contributions of $250 to $500. For contributions of $250 and above, the taxpayer must get and keep an acknowledgment from the qualified organization showing the name and address of the organization, the date and location of the contribution, and a description of the property for each separate contribution of $250 or more. In addition, the acknowledgment must state whether the taxpayer received any goods or services in return for the donation.

Contributions of $501 to $5,000. In addition to the records necessary for the previous category, record-keeping requirements include the following:

- How the taxpayer originally obtained the property,
- The approximate date the property was obtained or completed,
- The cost or other basis, and any adjustments to the basis, of any property held less than 12 months, and
- The cost or other basis, and any adjustments to the basis, of property held 12 months or more, except publicly traded securities.

If the last requirement cannot be met, a statement of explanation must be attached to the return.

Caution. If the total deduction for non-cash contributions is over $500, Form 8283 must be attached.

Contributions of More than $5,000. To calculate whether the deduction is over $5,000, combine the claimed deductions for all similar items donated to any charitable organization during the year. All the requirements for lesser donations apply, and the taxpayer must obtain a qualified written appraisal of the donated property from a qualified appraiser (except for publicly traded stock; nonpublicly traded stock needs an appraisal only if over $10,000).

Filing Tip. The taxpayer must know when an appraisal is required and have the proper documentation. If there is no proof of cost or FMV, the value should be documented in some other way, such as with photographs. See IRS Publication 561, *Determining the Value of Donated Property*.

Line 18, Carryover from Prior Year
Contributions that cannot be deducted in the current year because they exceed the limitation on itemized deductions based on AGI (see Total Itemized Deductions, Line 29-30, below) can be carried forward for up to five years. Contributions for the current year are always deducted before the contributions that are carried over. If there are carryovers from two or more prior years, the earliest year's must be used first.

Contributions carried over are subject to the same percentage limits in the year to which they are carried. For example, contributions subject to the 20% limit in the year in which they are made are 20% limit contributions in the year to which they are carried. See MTG ¶ 1060.

Line 19, Calculation
Add lines 16 through 18. This is the total deductible gifts to charity. The total on line 19 should reflect any applicable 50%, 30%, or 20% AGI limitation.

Casualty and Theft Losses, Line 20

Casualties
A casualty loss results from the damage, destruction, or loss of property from a sudden, unexpected, or unusual event.

Deductible Losses. Examples of sudden, unusual events are automobile collisions, fires, floods, storms, shipwrecks, explosions, and hurricanes.

See IRS Publication 547, *Casualties, Disasters, and Thefts*, and MTG ¶ 1124 for more information.

Loss on Deposits. Loss on deposits occurs when a bank, credit union, or other financial institution becomes insolvent or bankrupt. If this happens, the taxpayer can choose whether to treat the loss as a casualty loss, an or-

> **Example.** Ben Halpern has an AGI of $50,000 in 2013. During 2013, he contributes $18,000 cash and $2,000 of artwork to his synagogue, a 50%-of-AGI limit organization, and $10,000 cash to a 30% limit organization. He has no other charitable contributions during the year and no carryover from prior year. He may deduct a total of $25,000 of his $30,000 of contributions for 2013, allocated first to his $20,000 contribution to the 50% limit organization and then to $5,000 of the 30% limit contribution. He fills out Form 8283, *Noncash Charitable Contributions*, for his $2,000 noncash contribution. On his Schedule A, Ben enters $23,000 on line 16 (gifts by cash or check), $2,000 on line 17 (gifts other than by cash or check), zero on line 18 (carryover from prior year), and $25,000 on line 19 (total of lines 16, 17, and 18).
>
> For 2014, Ben projects an AGI of $60,000. He plans to contribute $10,000 to the synagogue and $16,000 to the 30% limit organization. He will be able to deduct both contributions in full because their total is under the $30,000 (50% of $60,000) limit. Of his $5,000 carry over from 2013, he will be able to deduct only $2,000 (i.e., $18,000 – $16,000) because of the 30% limit carryover (30% of $60,000 is $18,000). Any remaining amount will be carried over to 2015 as a 30% limit contributions.

dinary loss, or a nonbusiness bad debt. It should be noted that an ordinary loss deduction is limited to $20,000 ($10,000 for married filing separately), is subject to the floor on miscellaneous itemized deductions, and it cannot be claimed if any part of the deposit is federally insured. See MTG ¶ 1128 for more information.

 Gray Area. Although usually limited to physical damage, casualty damages have been extended by courts to include permanent loss of FMV to a home (*Finkbohner v. United States*, 86-1 USTC ¶9393, 788 F.2d 723 (11th Cir. 1986)). This is a difficult case to prove, but even if it is not proven, there may be no penalty for claiming it (*Gerald Chamales v. Commissioner*, T.C. Memo 2000-33 (Feb. 3, 2000)).

Nondeductible Losses. Damage due to progressive deterioration is not a casualty loss because such damage is not sudden or unusual. For example, the weakening of a building brought on by ordinary wind or weather conditions is not a casualty loss, nor is damage from moths or termites. Deductions for losses from "sudden" infestations of termites and beetles have, however, occasionally been upheld in court (*Rosenberg v. Commissioner*, 52-2 USTC ¶9357, 198 F.2d 46 (8th Cir. 1952) (termites); *Black v. Commissioner*, Dec. 34,665(M), 36 T.C.M. 1347 (1977) (beetles)).

Similarly, drought losses are sometimes deductible and sometimes not. It is generally deductible if the drought is not of long duration (i.e., it meets the "suddenness" condition) and it involves reduction to FMV from damage to permanent landscaping features such as trees or shrubs or the building itself (*Winters v. U.S.*, D.C. Okla. 58-1 USTC ¶9205 (1958); *Stevens*, Dec. 41,343(M), T.C. Memo 1984-365).

The taxpayer's culpability in the incident is sometimes a factor. Losses resulting from a filer's drunk driving are not deductible, nor are those from a filer's deliberately setting a fire.

Theft

Theft losses are deductible if the property's taking is classified as a theft under state law. For example, if a contractor disappears after taking a down payment for a repair he never performs, the victim is allowed a deduction.

The following are not allowable theft losses:

- The loss of another's property in the filer's care, even if the filer had to pay the owner for the loss. The owner may deduct the loss, if the filer does not pay him or her for the loss.
- Anything confiscated by a foreign government. Such losses will qualify as business or investment losses if the property is used for business or investment, but not as theft losses of personal property.
- Anything legally confiscated by another. In some states, spouses who take personal property when permanently leaving a shared home are not committing a crime.

Mislaid or Lost Property. The mere disappearance of money or property is not a theft. However, an accidental loss or disappearance of property can qualify as a casualty if it results from an identifiable event, such as dropping a diamond ring down the drain.

Ponzi Schemes. Qualified investors who sustained losses from certain fraudulent investment arrangements known as Ponzi schemes may claim a theft loss. The loss is deductible as a loss on a transaction entered into for profit; therefore, deductibility is not limited to losses that exceed $100 and 10% of the investor's AGI (see page 2-26). Further, the loss is not subject to the 2%-of-AGI limit for miscellaneous itemized deductions (see page 2-32).

Guidance to assist victims of Ponzi-type investment schemes has been provided by the IRS. Although the guidance makes no mention of the Bernard Madoff scandal by name, Rev. Rul. 2009-9 clarifies the favorable tax treatment to which investors in that and similar schemes are entitled. Rev. Proc. 2009-20 provides optional safe harbor treatment that allows investors to deduct up to 95% of qualified losses from a fraudulent investment scheme, calculated by detailed definitions and formulas, if certain requirements are met. The procedure, which also provides guidance for investors choosing not to use the safe harbor, applies to investment fraud losses discovered in tax years after 2007.

A taxpayer making the safe harbor election must mark "Revenue Procedure 2009-20" at the top of Form 4684, *Casualties and Thefts,* for the tax year of the investor in which the indictment, information, or complaint is filed against the lead figure or the lead figure dies. The taxpayer must also complete section C of Form 4684. See MTG ¶1125 for further details.

When to Report

Casualty and theft losses are usually deductible only in the year they occur. This is true even if the property is not replaced or repaired until the following year. However, if a theft loss is discovered later than the year in which it occurs, the year of discovery is the year in which it is deductible. See MTG ¶1104.

If the extent of loss cannot be ascertained before the tax return's due date, Form 4868 can be filed for an automatic six-month extension of time to file.

Insurance and Other Reimbursement

The loss deduction must be reduced by the amount of reimbursement received. If the taxpayer expects with reasonable certainty to receive insurance or other compensation payments after the due date of the return, the loss must be reduced by the estimated amount of insurance or other compensation payment. If the amount ultimately received is less than the expected amount, the difference is deductible as a casualty loss in the following year.

 Caution. If property is covered by an insurance policy, the loss cannot be deducted unless an insurance claim has been made. For example, if a driver does not want to report an accident to his or her insurance company in order to keep rates low, the loss cannot be deducted on line 20.

If the reimbursement is greater than the loss, the taxpayer may defer recognition of the gain under the in-voluntary conversion rules by making an election and purchasing qualifying replacement property within the replacement period. See MTG ¶1124.

 Caution. If a loss is claimed in one year and an unexpected insurance or other recovery is received in the following year, the recovery will have to be reported as income in the year it is received. The return for the loss year cannot be amended, even if the tax year of the return is still open for amendment.

Records to Keep

To claim a deduction on line 20, the claimant must have records to show the following:

Casualty Loss Proof

- Type of casualty (car accident, fire, storm, etc.) and when it occurred.
- That the loss was a direct result of the casualty.
- That the taxpayer was the owner of the property, or if the taxpayer leased the property from someone else, that the taxpayer was contractually liable to the owner for the damage.
- Whether a claim for reimbursement exists for which there is a reasonable expectation of recovery.

Theft Loss Proof

- When it was discovered that the property was missing.
- That the property was stolen.
- That the taxpayer was the owner of the property.
- Whether a claim for reimbursement exists for which there is a reasonable expectation of recovery.

 Planning Tip. The costs of creating and keeping these records are reportable on line 23 of Schedule A.

Figuring the Loss

The following steps are required to figure the amount of the loss:

1. Determine the adjusted basis in the property before the casualty or theft (see Tab 4 for a discussion of adjusted basis).
2. Determine the decrease in FMV of the property as a result of the casualty or theft (for personal losses and nontotal business losses).
3. Take the smaller of 1 and 2.
4. Subtract any insurance or other reimbursement received or that the taxpayer is eligible to receive.

5. Determine whether the loss is a personal or business loss and apply the appropriate reduction ($100 per incident followed by 10% of AGI for personal losses).

> **Example.** Gale and Harry Adams' main residence has an adjusted basis of $112,000. They had a kitchen fire in 20132 that reduced their home's value from $188,000 before the fire to $175,000 immediately thereafter. They collected $10,000 from their insurance company and expect no more insurance payments. Their AGI for the year was $47,500.
>
> 1. The adjusted basis is $112,000.
> 2. The decrease in value is $188,000 – $175,000 = $13,000.
> 3. $13,000 is the smaller value.
> 4. $13,000 – $10,000 insurance = $3,000.
> 5. The loss is clearly a personal loss, so it has a $100 floor and is reduced by 10% of AGI (discussed below). The deduction is thus $3,000 – $100 – (0.10 × $47,500 = $4,750) < 0. Thus, they cannot claim a casualty loss deduction.

Personal Casualty Losses. Personal casualty losses are deductible only to the extent that the loss exceeds 10% of AGI; also, each separate casualty must be reduced by $100. If the taxpayer sustains more than one loss as the result of one casualty, or when the events of the casualty are closely related in origin, the resulting losses are subject to only one $100 reduction.

> **Example.** Jo Manning's vacation home sustained wind damage of $1,800 and flood damage of $1,200 from a single storm. Her AGI for 2013 was $28,000, and she had no insurance on the home. She reduces her $3,000 loss by only $100 because the damage was caused by closely related events, so Jo can deduct $100 ($3,000 - $100 = $2,900 – (0.10 × $28,000) $2,800) = $100).

For purposes of applying the limitations, a husband and wife with married filing jointly filing status are treated as one individual: only one $100 floor applies to each casualty. Couples with married filing separately filing status must apply all limitations separately. The $100 floor also applies to all individuals involved in a casualty loss, even if they are victims of the same event.

> **Filing Tip.** When reporting losses with multiple parts, the incident is the numbering sequence for electronic filing purposes, not the number of items related to the incident.

Business Casualty Loss. If business or income-producing property, such as rental property is stolen or completely destroyed, the decrease in FMV is not considered. The loss is figured as follows:

$$\text{Adjusted Basis} - \text{Salvage Value} - \text{Insurance Received or Expected}$$

It is advantageous to claim a business loss if possible, because there is no $100 floor and the 10%-of-AGI limit does not apply. Business casualty losses are netted against Section 1231 gain and reported above the line (see Tab 4).

If property is held for both business and personal use, the $100 floor and the 10%-of-AGI limit apply proportionally to the personal-use loss.

> **Example.** Roland and Rebecca Provenzano own a car used 50% in Mr. Provenzano's business and 50% for personal use. It sustains $1,000 damage in a collision in early 2013. The adjusted basis of the auto is $2,000, and the Provenzanos collected $900 from the insurance company, for a net loss of $100. The $50 business loss is deductible, but the personal loss of $50 is reduced by the $100 floor and, therefore, is not deductible. Nothing is reported on line 20 of Schedule A, although the Provenzanos will fill out and file Form 4684 to deduct their business loss.

Form 4684, Casualties and Thefts. Parts A and/or C of Form 4684 must be completed and the form must be attached to the return if any casualty or theft loss is claimed on line 20 of Schedule A.

Federally Declared Disaster Areas

For property in a federally declared disaster area (previously referred to as a presidentially declared disaster area), a special rule permits quick tax relief. Disaster losses during the current tax year can be deducted on the tax return filed for the previous year. The taxpayer may choose in which of the two years to take the deduction.

If the previous year is elected for taking the casualty loss, the deadline for filing the amended return is the due date, without extensions, for filing the return for the year in which the loss was incurred. For a calendar-year taxpayer who lives in an area that is declared a disaster area in 2013, the deadline for filing an amended 2012 return is April 15, 2014.

Other advantages for taxpayers with involuntary conversions in federal disaster zones are available (see Tab 4).

 Caution. The taxpayer's AGI for the year of the return elected will determine the 10% reduction amount.

If such disasters occur during tax-filing season, the IRS may postpone deadlines for up to 120 days.

 Planning Tip. Taxpayers claiming the disaster loss on the previous year's return should put the disaster designation in red ink at the top of the amended return so that the IRS can expedite the refund.

Job Expenses and Most Other Miscellaneous Deductions, Lines 21-27

Miscellaneous Deduction Facts

Employee business expenses typically represent the largest part of miscellaneous deductions subject to the 2%-of-AGI floor.

Line 21, Unreimbursed Employee Expenses

The taxpayer can deduct only unreimbursed employee expenses that meet three criteria:

1. They are paid or incurred during the tax year.
2. They are for carrying on the taxpayer's trade or business of being an employee.
3. They are ordinary and necessary:
   (a) An expense is ordinary if it is common and accepted in the taxpayer's trade or business.
   (b) An expense is necessary if it is appropriate and helpful to the taxpayer's trade or business.

 Caution. Many employee claims for business expense deductions have been denied because the employees could not prove that the employers *expected* them to make the expenditures. Taxpayers should request written authorization from the employer at the time the expense is incurred.

See IRS Publication 463, *Travel, Entertainment, Gift, and Car Expenses*, for more information.

Form 2106. Form 2106 (see Tab 6) must be completed and attached if either of the following applies:

- Travel, transportation, meal, or entertainment expenses are claimed.
- The employer has reimbursed any of the job expenses reportable on line 21.

If Form 2106 need not be attached, the expenses should be listed directly on the dotted lines by line 21; a separate page can be attached if there are too many to fit.

Work-Related Education. Education expenses are deductible, even if the education may lead to a degree, if the education meets at least one of two tests:

- It maintains or improves skills required in the taxpayer's present work.
- It is required by the taxpayer's employer or the law in order for the taxpayer to keep his or her salary, status, or job, and the requirement serves a business purpose of the taxpayer's employer.

If the education meets either of these tests, expenses for tuition, books, supplies, laboratory fees, and similar items, and even certain transportation costs, are deductible.

Nondeductible Job-Related Education. The taxpayer cannot deduct expenses for education, even if one or both of the preceding tests are met, if either of the following is true:

- The education is needed to meet the *minimum educational requirements* to qualify the employee in his or her trade or business.
- The education will lead to qualifying the taxpayer for a new trade or business. If the education qualifies the taxpayer for a new trade or business, expenses are not deductible even if there is no intention to enter that trade or business.

The "new trade or business" disqualification does not apply if the new duties involve the same general type of work.

Examples. A teacher who is required by his or her district to take summer school courses can deduct the course expenses. A teacher who takes courses to become qualified in an additional subject area or grade level has deductible expenses.

A teacher who takes courses to obtain a basic teaching certificate does not have qualified education expenses.

A computer technician who takes computer programming courses probably cannot deduct expenses, unless it could be shown that the programming was connected to his or her present position.

A dentist's expenses in studying to become an orthodontist have been ruled as deductible (Rev. Rul. 74-78).

A lawyer who takes a course to become qualified in another state has deductible educational expenses, but an accountant taking a CPA prep course does not (Rev. Rul. 69-292).

Planning Tip. The cost of educational travel may be a deductible business expense if it is linked to the trade or business of the traveler (e.g., a professor of Russian history traveling to do research in Russia).

Employee Home Expenses

- The cost of household employees such as maids or babysitters is not deductible on Schedule A (it may qualify for the dependent care credit; see Tab 10).
- The cost of long-distance phone calls made for business usually is deductible, as is the cost of business-related features such as call forwarding.

Planning Tip. Basic telephone service is always considered a personal expense. A cell phone used for business will be deductible only to the extent long distance and specific overage charges are attributable to the business if no other personal phone line is maintained by the taxpayer.

> ⚠️ **Caution.** In general, expenses of seeking a job outside one's current trade or business are not deductible.

Example. George works day shift as a typesetter. His computer is shared with a night-shift worker, but his employer wants him to occasionally put in overtime. However, the employer has no extra computer for George to work on, so George buys one to meet the employer's needs. William also works as a typesetter, but for a company that provides him with a computer and access to the building 24 hours per day. The employer permits William to work at home in the evenings to care for his children, but does not require him to. George may deduct depreciation on his computer, but William may not, because his computer is not being used for the employer's convenience.

- The cost of installing a second phone exclusively for business is deductible.
- Depreciation on a computer, a cell phone or any other IRC §179 property that is required by an employer is deductible. In this case Form 4562, Part V, must also be submitted, and the straight-line method over the ADS recovery period must be used. This deduction is available even if the device is used less than 50% of the time for business. If it is used more than 50% for business or is part of a home office, the accelerated depreciation deduction may be claimed. See Tab 7.
- Expenses for keeping an office at home for the employer's convenience are deductible.

Job Search Expenses. Certain expenses of looking for a new job in the taxpayer's present occupation are deductible, even if the search is not successful. The taxpayer has to be currently employed or recently unemployed. The following are deductible:

- Employment agency fees.
- Resume expenses—amounts spent for typing, printing, and mailing copies of a resume to prospective employers.
- Advertising expenses.
- Career counseling costs.
- 50% of meal and entertainment expenses.
- Travel and transportation expenses directly related to employment search. The amount of time spent on personal activity compared with the amount of time spent in looking for work is important in determining whether a trip is primarily personal or is primarily to look for a new job. Even if the travel expenses to and from an area are not deductible, the expenses of looking for a new job while in the area are deductible.

Employee Education Expenses

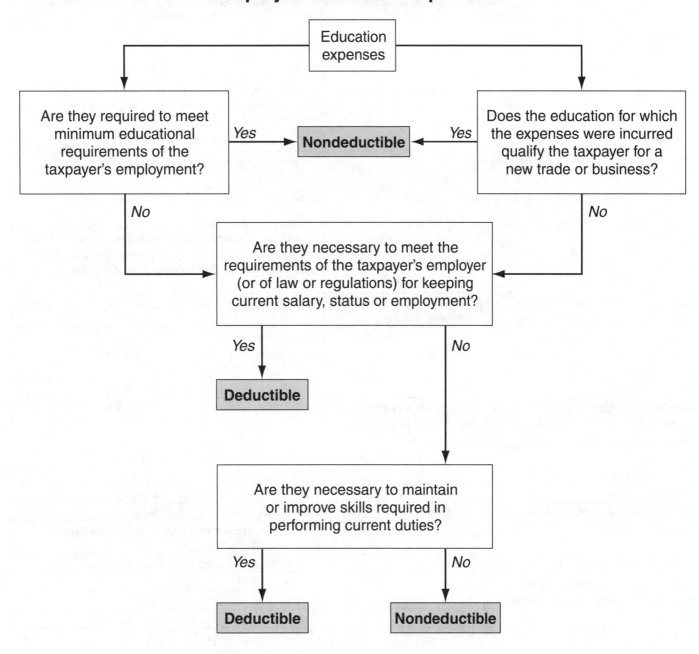

Miscellaneous Expenses 2013

Expense	Is It Deductible?
Annuities, unrecovered cost of, on decedent's final return	Fully deductible
Appraisal fees (charitable contributions and casualty losses)	Deductible, subject to 2%-of-AGI floor
Business bad debt	Deductible, subject to 2%-of-AGI floor
Cell phone	Depreciation is deductible, subject to 2% floor if cell phone is required by employer (line 21), or if used to produce other income (line 23)
Club dues	Not deductible with certain exceptions
Collecting interest or dividends, fees for	Deductible, subject to 2%-of-AGI floor
Commuting expenses, to regular place of employment	Not deductible
Commuting expenses, to temporary place of employment	Deductible subject to 2%-of-AGI floor (with Form 2106)
Computer	Depreciation is deductible, subject to 2%-of-AGI floor if computer is required by employer (line 21), or if used to produce other income (line 23)
Convenience fee charged by the card processor for paying income tax, including estimated tax payments, by credit or debit card	Deductible, subject to 2%-of-AGI floor
Credit card fees to pay taxes	Not deductible
Damages paid to former employer for breach of employment contract	Deductible, subject to 2%-of-AGI floor
Dividend reinvestment plans, service charges for	Deductible, subject to 2%-of-AGI floor
Employee business expenses: travel, 50% of meals and entertainment, professional books and journals, home office deductions, supplies, depreciation on property used for business	Deductible, subject to 2%-of-AGI floor
Estate taxes	Not deductible, generally (see Tab 14)
Funeral expenses	Not deductible
Gambling losses	Deductible, up to amount of winnings
Handicapped job-related expenses	Fully deductible
Hobby expenses	Deductible, subject to 2%-of-AGI floor and up to amount of hobby income
Homeowners' associations assessments	Not deductible except as business expense
House repairs or improvements (personal residence)	Not deductible
Investments, expenses (e.g., office help) for maintaining	Deductible, subject to 2%-of-AGI floor
IRA investments, loss on	Deductible, subject to 2%-of-AGI floor
Job-hunting expenses	Deductible, subject to 2%-of-AGI floor
Job-related education expenses	Deductible, subject to 2%-of-AGI floor
Legal fees: divorce, representation before IRS and courts, estate planning not related to tax matters, representation in lawsuits, except to protect business reputation	Not deductible
Legal fees: for collecting or producing taxable income, keeping a job, obtaining tax advice, filing business-related voluntary bankruptcy	Deductible, subject to 2%-of-AGI floor
Licenses (marriage, drivers, dog, etc.)	Not deductible
Life insurance	Not deductible
Loss on deposits	Deductible, subject to 2%-of-AGI floor
Malpractice insurance premiums	Deductible, subject to 2%-of-AGI floor
Medical exams, if required by employer	Deductible, subject to 2%-of-AGI floor
Miscellaneous investment expenses	Deductible, subject to 2%-of-AGI floor

Miscellaneous Expenses 2013 (Continued)

Expense	Is It Deductible?
Parking tickets and other fines for illegal acts, even if incurred for business purposes	Not deductible
Passport expense, if job-related	Deductible, subject to 2%-of-AGI floor
Pass-through entities, indirect miscellaneous deductions	Deductible, subject to 2%-of-AGI floor
Personal living expenses	Not deductible
Personal residence, loss on sale of	Not deductible
Political contributions	Not deductible
Professional dues	Deductible, subject to 2%-of-AGI floor
Repayment of income	Deductible, netted against reportable income, subject to 2%-of-AGI floor if under $3,000, or fully deductible over $3,000 (see page 2-32)
Research expenses (college professor)	Deductible, subject to 2%-of-AGI floor
Safe deposit box fees	Deductible, subject to 2%-of-AGI floor
Safe in home, installation costs	Deductible, subject to 2%-of-AGI floor
Sales tax, unless added to cost of business expenses	Not deductible (see page 2–10)
Tax preparation and other personal tax assistance	Deductible, subject to 2%-of-AGI floor
Teacher's classroom expenses	Deductible, subject to 2%-of-AGI floor
Telephone expenses of first line to personal residence	Not deductible, even if used for business
Tools, disposable within one year	Deductible, subject to 2%-of-AGI floor
Tools, useful life more than one year	Depreciation deductible, subject to 2%-of-AGI floor
Trust administration fees	Deductible, subject to 2%-of-AGI floor
Undeveloped land management, expenses	Deductible, subject to 2%-of-AGI floor
Union dues	Deductible, subject to 2%-of-AGI floor
Work clothes and uniforms, if not suitable for wear outside work	Deductible, subject to 2%-of-AGI floor

Work Clothes and Uniforms

- Wearing work clothes or uniforms must be a condition of employment to be deductible.
- The clothes must not be suitable for everyday wear.
- The cost of protective clothing, such as safety shoes or boots, safety glasses, hard hats, and work gloves, is deductible.

 Examples. Deductions are allowed for the cost of uniforms worn by delivery workers, firefighters, health care workers, law enforcement officers, letter carriers, professional athletes, and transportation workers (air, rail, bus, etc.). Musicians and entertainers can deduct the cost of theatrical clothing and accessories that are not suitable for everyday wear. However, according to the IRS, work clothing consisting of white cap, white shirt or jacket, white bib overalls, and standard work shoes, which a painter might be required by his union to wear on the job, is not distinctive in character or in the nature of a uniform.

Commuting

- Not deductible for travel between the home and the regular workplace.
- Deductible if traveling to a temporary workplace outside the metropolitan area that contains both the taxpayer's home and the permanent workplace. Work locations are considered temporary if the work is expected to last less than one year.
- Deductible if the taxpayer works at two places in a day, whether or not for the same employer; the expenses of getting from one workplace to the other are generally deductible.

Caution. A taxpayer who reports to a central dispatching location and then goes to a worksite is considered to be commuting. This travel is not deductible.

Line 22, Tax Preparation Fees

These fees are usually deductible in the year paid. Thus, fees paid in 2014 for preparing the taxpayer's 2013 return may be deducted. These fees can include the cost of tax preparation software programs and tax publications, legal and accounting fees, and any fee paid for electronic filing. Expenses for preparing Schedules C, E, and F should be deducted on the respective schedules; all other expenses are deducted on line 22.

Line 23, Other Expenses

The three basic categories for "other expenses" listed by the IRS in Publication 529 are expenses incurred:

- To produce or collect taxable income.
- To manage, conserve, or maintain property held for producing such income.
- To determine, contest, pay, or claim a refund of any tax.

Items listed as deductible subject to the 2% floor in the table beginning on page 2-30 are listed on line 23 if they are not employee related.

Return of Income. A taxpayer may sometimes have to return income that he or she was not entitled to, e.g., Social Security payments or unemployment compensation. If the mistake is found in the same year and the taxpayer repays it in the same year, the amount repaid is simply not entered on any form.

Under Code Sec. 1341, if the money is repaid in a later year, and it is $3,000 or less, the taxpayer should deduct the repayment amount on line 23. There is no way to recover the tax benefit if the taxpayer does not itemize deductions.

If the amount repaid in a later year is greater than $3,000, and the taxpayer can establish a claim of right (i.e., he or she appeared to have a right to the money), the taxpayer has a choice: claim the money on line 28 (no 2%-of-AGI floor) or claim a tax credit for the difference caused by the added income in the previous year's taxes.

> **Example.** Roger Hahn was mistakenly awarded $3,500 of unemployment compensation in 2012. This added $750 to his and his wife's joint tax total for 2012. He repaid all the money in 2013. They first figure their tax using the $3,500 as a deduction, but they do not have enough other deductions to make itemizing advantageous over taking the standard deduction. Therefore, they will take a tax credit for $750, the amount that they overpaid in 2012.

Code Sec. 1341 does not apply to:

- Deductions for bad debts.
- Deductions for sales to customers, such as returns

and allowances.
- Deductions for legal expenses of contesting the repayment.

Hobby Loss. Losses from hobbies that produce income are deducted here, but only to the extent that income was reported above the line. Making the distinction between a hobby and a business (where all expenses are deductible on different forms) can be a difficult call. See Tabs 3 and 16 for information on factors that go into determining whether an activity is a business or a hobby.

Lines 24-27, Calculation

> **Example.** John and Mary Wysocki have an AGI of $47,500 for 2013. Mary was required to use a cell phone and a laptop computer in her work, and she can claim $135 of depreciation on them for the year. In addition, they had an uninsured casualty loss of $8,000 on their personal residence, which required a $200 appraisal to calculate. John, a high school teacher, paid $240 in union dues and $975 in education expenses, including travel, for a course that he was required to take by his district. He had $125 in additional travel and meal expenses for attending required seminars. Also, 2014 is the first year that they have paid for tax preparation assistance.
>
> They can claim a $3,150 casualty loss on line 20, calculated as $8,000 − $100 − (0.10 × $47,500 = $4,750). They will also submit a Form 4684. They can claim a deduction of $1,475 on line 21 (they will also submit Forms 4562 and 2106) and a deduction of $200 on line 23. They get no deduction on line 22 because they did not pay any fees in 2013. Since 2% of their income is $950 (line 26), they enter $725 on line 27.

Other Miscellaneous Deductions, Line 28

Deductions Not Subject to the 2% Limit

- Amortizable premium on taxable bonds (usually claimed as an offset to investment income, but can be deducted here instead if an election to do so was made after 1998).
- Casualty and theft losses on income-producing property (note that this deduction is not subject to the $100 and 10% of AGI personal casualty floor).
- Gambling losses up to the amount of gambling winnings.
- Impairment-related work expenses of persons with disabilities.
- Repayments of more than $3,000 under a claim of right.
- Unrecovered investment in an annuity.

Gambling Losses. No gambling losses may be deducted unless gambling winnings are reported above the line. Gambling winnings must be reported as income even if no Form W-2G is issued.

 Caution. Even though gambling winnings may be offset on a Federal income tax return, this treatment is often not available on state income tax returns. The result could be a Federal refund and a sizable state tax liability.

Form W-2G must be issued by the payor when there is:

- $600 or more of winnings and the payout is 30 times or more greater than the stake.
- $1,200 or more in winnings from bingo or slot machines.
- $1,500 net winnings from keno.
- Any other net winnings over $5,000.

Gambling winnings and losses include lotteries, raffles, bets on athletic contests, bingo, bets on horse or dog racing, and all casino wagering, among other activities. Office pools and similar personal wagering activities are not included.

The taxpayer should keep an adequate log of winnings and losses. The log should include the date, location, amount, type of gambling, and results. Since winnings must be reported in full, not netted against losses, as income, winnings and losses should be kept separate on the log.

The IRS suggests the following notations in the diary for the following gambling activities:

- **Keno:** Copies of the keno tickets purchased that were validated by the gambling establishment, copies of casino credit records, and copies of casino check-cashing records.
- **Slot machines:** A record of the machine number and all winnings by date and time the machine was played.
- **Table games** (twenty-one, blackjack, craps, poker, baccarat, roulette, wheel of fortune, etc.): The number of the table; casino credit card data indicating whether the credit was issued in the pit or at the cashier's cage.
- **Bingo:** A record of the number of games played, cost of tickets purchased, and amounts collected on winning tickets, plus receipts from the casino, parlor, etc.
- **Racing (horse, harness, dog, etc.):** A record of the races, amounts of wagers, amounts collected on

winning tickets and amounts lost on losing tickets, plus unredeemed tickets and payment records from the racetrack.

- **Lotteries:** A record of ticket purchases, dates, winnings and losses, plus unredeemed tickets, payment slips, and winnings statements.

  Planning Tip. Getting information on losses and winnings is a vital part of the initial interview of new clients, and a vital part of planning for subsequent years.

 Filing Tip. Travel, meal, and entertainment expenses are not deductible for a nonprofessional gambler.

 Caution. For a joint gambling lottery venture, all participants should sign up in advance with allocations preset. Doing so after the fact can be a real problem.

Impairment-Related Work Expenses. A work expense that results from a physical or mental disability that limits the taxpayer's employment or substantially limits one or more of the taxpayer's major life activities—such as performing manual tasks, walking, speaking, breathing, learning, or working—is fully deductible on line 28. The definition of work expense for this deduction is the same as for other employee-related expenses: "ordinary" and "necessary."

Unrecovered Investment in Annuity. A retiree who contributed to the cost of an annuity can exclude from income a part of each payment received as a tax-free return of the retiree's investment. If the retiree dies before the entire investment is recovered tax-free, any unrecovered investment can be deducted on the retiree's final income tax return.

Filing Tip. Statutory employees (e.g., certain insurance agents and outside salespersons) can claim their business expenses on Schedule C and, therefore, are not subject to the 2% floor. See Tab 3 for more details on whether the client qualifies.

Filing Tip. If an expense is an annual payment, double up by paying on January 1 and December 31 one year and not at all the next, then repeat. This may get the deduction over the applicable limitation for itemizing.

Total Itemized Deductions, Lines 29-30

For 2013, higher-income individuals whose adjusted gross income (AGI) exceeds a threshold amount ($300,000 for married filing jointly or qualifying widow(er), $275,000 for head of household, $250,000 for single, and $150,000 for married filing separately)) must reduce the total amount of certain itemized deductions by the lesser of 3% of the amount of AGI above the threshold or 80 percent of the allowable itemized deductions reduced by the deductions for medical expenses, investment interest, casualty and theft losses and wagering losses. See MTG ¶1014.

Line 30 directs the taxpayer to check a box if the taxpayer elects to itemize deductions even though they are less than the taxpayer's standard deduction. This might be the case if, for example, the taxpayer would pay less total tax because the excess of the taxpayer's state standard deduction over the taxpayer's state itemized deductions is greater than the excess of the Federal itemized deductions over the Federal standard deduction.

Schedule B: Interest and Ordinary Dividends

Part I: Interest, Lines 1-4

Part I must be filled out if:

a. taxable interest income is greater than $1,500;
b. the exclusion of interest from series EE bonds issued after 1989 is being used;
c. any interest is being received as a nominee;
d. any interest was received from a seller-financed mortgage on a property the buyer used as a home;
e. a Form 1099-INT was received for interest on a bond bought between interest payment dates, for interest on frozen deposits, or for U.S. savings bond interest reported before 2003;
f. the taxpayer had any foreign account;
g. the taxpayer elects to reduce interest from bonds acquired after 1987 by any amortizable bond premium; or
h. there is a discrepancy between OID reported by the taxpayer and that shown on Form(s) 1099-OID.

See IRS Publication 550, *Investment Income and Expenses*, for detailed information.

Nominee Interest

A taxpayer may receive a Form 1099 as a nominee, meaning that the taxpayer does not own the proceeds. The following procedure must be used for reporting nominee interest:

- Report the interest amount as usual on line 1 of Schedule B.
- Under the last amount listed on line 1, total up all the amounts entered.
- On the line under this subtotal, write "Nominee Distribution" and enter the total interest received as a nominee.
- Subtract the nominee interest and enter the result on line 2.
- Issue a 1099-INT to the actual owner of the interest (unless the owner is the taxpayer's spouse).
- File a 1099-INT and Form 1096, *Annual Summary and Transmittal of U.S. Information Returns*, with the IRS.

An example illustrating the reporting of nominee interest appears below.

 Planning Tip. If your client is assigning someone as a nominee, he or she should do so in writing, which should lessen the chance of confusion in coming years.

Original Issue Discount (OID)
If a bond is issued for less than its stated redemption value, the difference is called OID. This is simply a form of interest. The bond issuer reports a portion of OID each year to the bondholder on Form 1099-OID.

- **Debt instruments issued after 1954 and before May 28, 1969 (before July 2, 1982, if a government instrument)**—OID is not reported until the year the obligation is sold, exchanged, or redeemed. If a gain results and the instrument is a capital asset, the gain equal to the OID is ordinary interest income and the rest is capital gain. If there is a loss on the sale, the entire loss is a capital loss and no reporting of OID is required. If a bond is purchased in the secondary market, the interest shown on the Form 1099-OID is not accurate unless the bond was purchased at exactly its original price, and the total OID has to be adjusted. Rules for adjusting the OID depend on when the debt instrument was issued and what kind it is.
- **Debt instruments issued after May 27, 1969 (after July 1, 1982, if a government instrument), and before 1985, i**f held as capital assets, include any discount on these debt instruments in gross income each year that the taxpayer owns the instruments. The taxpayer's basis in the instrument is increased by the amount of OID included in gross income.

- **Debt instruments issued after 1984**–Report the total OID that applies each year regardless of whether the taxpayer holds the debt instrument as a capital asset. The taxpayer's basis in the instrument is increased by the amount of OID included in gross income.

Details for calculating OID where necessary can be found in IRS Publication 1212, *Guide to Original Issue Discount (OID) Instruments*.

The OID reporting rules do not apply to the following debt instruments:

- Tax-exempt obligations (but must be accrued for increasing holder's basis to determine gain/loss if sold before maturity),
- U.S. savings bonds,
- Short-term debt instruments (less than one year to maturity),
- Obligations issued by an individual before March 2, 1984, or
- Most loans between individuals.

Stripped Bonds and Coupons. A *stripped bond* is a bond from which all of the interest coupons have been detached. *Stripped coupons* are the detached interest coupons. Without special rules, a bondholder could sell a stripped bond for less than he paid for the bond with the coupons and recognize a capital loss. Current law, however, prevents this scenario by mandating that the bondholder allocate the sale price between the bond without the coupons and the coupons. The bond and the coupons are then treated as having been issued with OID. The allocation must be based on the FMV of the bond and the coupons on the date that either the bond or a coupon is sold separately. In addition, the bondholder must report any accrued interest at the time of the bond's sale, and the bond's basis is adjusted accordingly. See MTG ¶1952.

Figuring the OID. A full discussion of the OID rules is contained in IRC §§1271–1288. The rules provide a formula for allocating the OID attributable to a bond, or other debt instrument, over the expected term of the bond. The objective of this formula is to amortize OID in a manner approximating the way in which interest would accrue on a bond that was issued for its face amount and paid a market interest rate.

The formula for allocating OID to particular tax periods is contained in IRC §1272(a)(3) and explained in the many pages of regulations under that section. The statutory formula provides a method for spreading the total OID attributable to a bond over the bond's term.

Line 1, List Name of Payer

Form 1099-INT. Interest income is generally reported on Form 1099-INT or Form 1099-OID, or a similar statement, by banks, savings and loans, and other payors of interest. This form, which shows the interest received during the year, should be kept for the taxpayer's records, but does not have to be attached to the tax return.

 Planning Tip. The name of the company or institution that issued the Form 1099 should always be used. Otherwise, the IRS's computer matching program will show unreported income.

Note that electronic filing enhances IRS access to matching 1099 information, leading to much faster CP-2000 follow-up letters.

Seller-Financed Mortgage. If the taxpayer has financed the sale of his or her personal residence during 2013, all interest paid by the buyer must be listed on line 1, along with the buyer's name, address, and Social Security number. In order to avoid a penalty, the seller also must provide his or her name, address and Social Security number to the buyer.

This information should precede all other entries on line 1.

Bank Accounts and Certificates of Deposit. Interest is usually taxable in the year it is earned. Thus, interest earned on a passbook savings account on December 31, 2013, is taxable in 2013, even though the interest was not credited in the passbook until 2014.

Interest on CDs is taxable in the year earned if the taxpayer has the right to use the income. Some short-term CDs do not give the depositor the right to use the interest until after the maturity date.

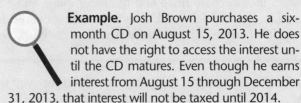 **Example.** Josh Brown purchases a six-month CD on August 15, 2013. He does not have the right to access the interest until the CD matures. Even though he earns interest from August 15 through December 31, 2013, that interest will not be taxed until 2014.

 Filing Tip. Amounts received from money market funds are taxable as dividends, *not* as interest income. Report them on line 5 of Schedule B.

REMICs and CMOs. Holders of REMICs (real estate mortgage investment conduits) or CMOs (collateralized mortgage obligations) have special reporting rules. Holders of these instruments should not count on written information on amounts to include on their returns until March 17, 2014, and then should follow instructions accompanying the written information.

Refunds on Adjustable-Rate Mortgages. If a taxpayer with an adjustable-rate mortgage on his or her principal residence receives a refund as a result of recalculation of the interest rate, the refund is considered interest income in the year paid.

 Caution. Failure to report interest income in the year received can result in backup withholding on future interest and dividends. The backup withholding rate for 2013 is 28%.

U.S. Treasury Bills, Notes, and Bonds
Treasury bills, notes, and bonds are direct debt obligations of the U.S. government, and interest on these is subject to federal income tax. However, interest income from Treasury bills, notes, and bonds is exempt from all state and local income taxes.

U.S. savings bonds currently outstanding include the following:

- Series HH bonds–The U.S. Treasury stopped issuing Series HH bonds after August 31, 2004. Outstanding bonds will continue to earn interest until maturity. These bonds were issued at face value. Interest is paid twice a year by direct deposit to a holder's bank account. A cash-method taxpayer must report interest on these bonds as income in the year received. Series HH bonds were first offered in 1980 and mature in 20 years.
- Series E and EE bonds–Interest on these bonds is payable when the bond is redeemed. The difference between the purchase price and the redemption value is taxable interest. Series EE bonds were first offered in July 1980 and have a maturity period of 30 years. Se-

ries E bonds are no longer issued. The bond's increase in value each year represents interest but for cash-basis taxpayers is not reportable until maturity unless the bond is cashed before that year. No further interest will be paid after maturity. Taxpayers may elect to report the income each year instead of reporting the entire amount at maturity. The election to report annually may be made in the year the bond is purchased or in any year thereafter. If the election is made in a later year, the entire amount of accrued interest must be reported in that year. Also, once the election is made, it applies to all bonds currently owned or acquired in the future, unless the IRS permits the taxpayer to change back to the lump-sum reporting method.

 Filing Tip. The election to report savings bond income annually is generally attractive to low-income elderly taxpayers and children not subject to the "Kiddie tax" because the small yearly interest may escape taxation altogether.

Series I bonds–Series I bonds were first offered in 1998. These are inflation-indexed bonds issued at their face amount with a maturity period of 30 years. The face value plus all accrued interest is payable at maturity.

Treasury Inflation-Indexed Debt Securities (TIPs). This relatively new type of Treasury obligation gives investors current interest and adjusts for inflation as well. If there is no significant purchase discount (less than $25 for a 10-year bond), these securities produce income each year, usually twice a year, that will be regarded as regular interest. Any adjustment based on inflation is then taken into account under the rules for OID (Reg. §1.1275-7). If the discount is greater than the *de minimis* amount, all income will be considered OID.

 Example. Pragnya Chakravarti received the interest payments shown on the following Schedule B. She also received nominee interest of $400.

1	List name of payer. If any interest is from a seller-financed mortgage and the buyer used the property as a personal residence, see instructions on back and list this interest first. Also, show that buyer's social security number and address ▶		Amount
	State Bank 1		400
	State Bank 2		1,500
	U.S. Government		730
	Local Bank A		950
	Subtotal		3,580
	Nominee Distribution	1	400
2	Add the amounts on line 1	2	3,180

Filing Tip. TIP bonds can produce significant income, and should usually be purchased for IRAs or other retirement plans in which the income tax can be deferred.

Changing the method of reporting is done by filing Form 3115, *Application for Change in Accounting Method,* with the tax return for the year of change, noting at the top that it is "Filed under Rev. Proc. 2008-52" and listing all bonds to which the change applies. Note that accrual-basis taxpayers cannot change the way they account for this bond income, because they automatically report income when it accrues.

 Planning Tip. For children who may be subject to the "kiddie tax," the use of series EE or I savings bonds is a way to defer interest income.

State or Local Government Obligations

Interest received on an obligation issued by a state or local government is generally not taxable for federal tax purposes. The issuer of tax-exempt state or local bond interest is required to furnish to the buyer Form 1099-INT, or a substitute statement, reporting the aggregate amount of tax-exempt interest. If the taxpayer invested in the obligation through a trust, fund, or other organization, that organization should issue this information.

Interest on state and local government bonds is taxable if the bonds are "private activity" bonds, unless a specific exemption is included in the IRC. The following state and local government bonds are nontaxable:

- Bonds for exempt facilities, such as airports and other commuting facilities, water-furnishing facilities, sewage facilities, residential rental projects, local furnishing of energy resources, and qualified hazardous-waste disposal facilities;
- Mortgage revenue bonds;
- Qualified small-issue bonds (less than $10 million and available for manufacturing facilities);
- Student loan bonds;
- Qualified development bonds; and
- Qualified 501(c)(3) bonds.

 Caution. Interest on "private activity" bonds issued after August 7, 1986, is a preference item that may be subject to AMT.

Interest on a bond used to finance government operations generally is not taxable if the bond is issued by a state, the District of Columbia, a U.S. possession, or any of their political subdivisions. Political subdivisions include:

- Port authorities;
- Toll road commissions;
- Utility services authorities;
- Community redevelopment agencies; and
- Qualified volunteer fire departments (for certain obligations issued after 1980).

Nongovernment Bonds

Interest on all nongovernment types of bonds is taxable.

Selling a Bond. If a bond is sold during 2013, part of its sale price is attributable to interest accrued up to the date of sale. The seller must report the interest accrued up to that time, and the buyer subtracts the accrued interest to that point from the full interest amount listed on Schedule B. The buyer's basis in the bond is also reduced by the amount of interest accrued up to the point of sale.

Below-Market Loans and Imputed Interest

Interest on below-market loans is considered interest income, and an additional amount of interest may be added to taxable interest income. A below-market loan is one on which interest is charged at a rate lower than market value or the applicable federal rate (AFR), sometimes at no interest whatsoever. If such loans were allowed without tax consequences, it could result in an untaxed shift of income from the lender to the borrower. It could also result in the recharacterization of income from interest income to capital gain income, which may be more favorably taxed. Under current law, however, the lender is treated as having:

1. made a loan to the borrower at the statutory rate, and
2. made a payment to the borrower.

This payment is treated as a gift, dividend, contribution to capital, compensation, or other payment, depending on the type of transaction. The size of the deemed payment depends on the imputed interest, which is based on how much the government has to spend to borrow money in a given month.

K-1 filers must be careful in handling loans. In the absence of documents showing intent or agreed process, the IRS can reclassify the "loan" as wages and assess accordingly or impute interest and then assess tax, penalty, and interest for underreporting.

Exceptions. If the loan is considered a "gift loan," there is no imputed interest if the amount of the loan is not over $10,000. Nor is there any imputed interest if a gift loan up to $100,000 is made to a child to help pay for a principal residence, if the child's investment income does not exceed $1,000. If the child's investment income is greater than $1,000, the imputed interest cannot be greater than the child's total investment income.

 Example. Jonas Livemore loaned his daughter $50,000 interest-free to help her purchase her home. If her investment income is $750 in 2013, Jonas has no tax liability on the imputed interest. If her investment income is $1,500, Jonas's imputed interest will be no more than $1,500.

The IRS publishes AFR tables every month for short-, mid-, and long-term loans. In the case of demand loans that were outstanding for all of 2013 with the principal balance constant, the IRS interest rate is 0.22% (Table 6, Rev. Rul. 2013-15).

Demand Loans versus Term Loans. A demand loan is any loan that is payable in full on demand of the lender, including those with indefinite maturity dates. Term loans are any other loans.

 Filing Tip. The $10,000 "gift loan" limit is unrelated to the $14,000 annual nontaxable-gift limit for 2013 (see Tab 14). However, the $10,000 limit does apply to all outstanding loans from the lender to a single borrower, including those charging interest.

Line 3, Excludable Interest on Series EE and I U.S. Savings Bonds Issued after 1989

Interest on series EE or I U.S. savings bonds issued after 1989 and cashed in 2013 may be excludable from income if used to pay qualified higher education costs. The following tests have to be met:

- The bondholder cashed qualified U.S. savings bonds in 2013 that were issued after 1989.
- The bondholder paid qualified higher education expenses in 2013 for self, spouse, or dependents, or to a qualified state tuition program or education IRA.
- The bondholder's filing status is any status except married filing separately, and the bondholder's modified AGI is less than $89,700 if single or head of household filing status, or $142,050 if married filing jointly or qualified widow(er) status. The exclusion begins to phase out for modified AGI over $74,700 for single and HOH, and $112,050 for MFJ and QW. "Modified" in this case means without regard to the foreign income exclusion and income

from U.S. possessions. The exclusion is not available to married taxpayers filing separate returns.
- The bondholder was at least 24 years old when the bonds were purchased.

The excludable portion of interest on Series EE or I U.S. savings bonds is computed on Form 8815.

Caution. The amount of higher education costs taken into account for figuring the exclusion of interest on college savings bonds has to be reduced by the expenses taken into account in figuring the American Opportunity credit (the modified Hope credit), the lifetime learning credit, or distributions from either a qualified tuition program (IRC 529) or a Coverdell education savings account (Coverdell ESA) (IRC 530) or both (see Tab 10).

Phaseout. The phaseout is calculated by multiplying a fraction by the amount of interest on Series EE bonds bought after 1989 and used for qualified education purposes, then subtracting the result from the amount otherwise excludable. The numerator of the fraction is the excess of modified AGI over the phaseout trigger, and the denominator is $15,000 for single or HOH and $30,000 for MFJ or QW.

Line 4, Subtract Line 3 from Line 2

If this amount is over $1,500, then Part III must be completed. The result entered on line 4 is also entered on line 8a of Form 1040.

Part II: Ordinary Dividends, Lines 5-6

See IRS Publication 550, Investment Income and Expenses, for detailed information.

Ordinary Dividends. Ordinary (taxable) dividends are the most common type of distribution from a corporation. They are paid out of the earnings and profits of a corporation and are ordinary income. This means that they are not capital gains. Any dividend received on common or preferred stock is an ordinary dividend unless the paying corporation tells the taxpayer otherwise. Ordinary dividends will be shown in box 1a on Form 1099-DIV.

Qualified Dividends. Qualified dividends are dividends received from a domestic or qualified foreign corporation that are taxed at the long-term capital gains rate. To qualify for the lower rates, investors are required to hold the stock from which the dividend is paid for more than 60 days in the 121-day period beginning 60 days before the ex-dividend date. They will be shown in box 1b Form on 1099-DIV.

Caution. Even though qualified dividends are taxable at the long-term capital gain rate, they may not be used to offset capital losses.

Filing Tip. The holding period for eligibility of dividends for capital gain treatment is more than 60 days; be sure the client knows how to count the holding period, i.e., don't count the day of acquisition. Also, the holding period is reduced if holdings are offset by a corresponding short position.

Nonqualified Dividends. Not all dividends are qualified for the capital gain rates. Common stock must be owned for at least 61 days during the 121-day period beginning 60 days before the ex-dividend date (see Tab 4). (Some preferred stock has a longer holding period; see IRS Publication 550.) Dividends paid by a foreign corporation qualify only if its stock trades on a U.S. exchange. The following are also not qualified dividends, even if shown as such in box 1b on Form 1099-DIV:

- Dividends from money market funds (for balanced funds, the portion allocated to stock holdings does qualify),
- Dividends from benevolent life insurance associations, credit unions, certain trusts, and tax-exempt farmers' cooperatives,
- Dividends paid on deposits in mutual savings banks, cooperative banks, domestic building savings and loan associations, and similar savings institutions,
- Dividends paid on employer securities held in retirement plans,
- Dividends received from REITs if certain requirements are met,
- Dividends generated by regulated investment companies, and
- Payments to the extent to which a taxpayer is under a payment obligation, as in a covered call.

Distributions from Savings Accounts. Distributions from savings accounts are not considered dividends. They should be reported as interest income and reported in Part I, if Part I has to be filled out.

"Dividends" on Insurance Policies. So-called dividends paid by insurance companies to holders of annuity, endowment, or unmatured life insurance policies are not true dividends. Since they serve simply to reduce the cost of the policy, they are not reportable as income, whether they are applied toward payment of the premiums or received in cash.

If total dividends *do* exceed the premiums paid, however, the excess is taxable as interest, not dividends. All dividends received after the policy has matured are also taxable as interest.

Dividends in Additional Stock. A corporation may issue dividends in the form of additional stock in the company rather than in cash. These dividends are tax free unless they raise the recipient's proportion of ownership in the company. If an option is offered to take either cash or stock, however, the dividends are taxable.

A dividend in the form of a right to acquire stock (*stock rights*) is taxed in much the same way as a stock dividend. It is not taxable unless there is a cash option, or percentage-of-ownership increase, or the distribution can be converted to preferred stock.

Liquidating Dividends. These dividends are paid when a corporation dissolves and disposes of all its assets. They are a return of the investor's capital and are not taxable unless they exceed the investment, in which case they are taxable as a capital gain on Form 1040. Upon complete liquidation, if total distributions are less than the investment, the difference may be treated as a capital loss on Form 8949, *Sales and other Dispositions of Capital Assets,* of Schedule D.

Mutual Fund Dividends. Distributions from a mutual fund could be one of three kinds: ordinary dividends, nontaxable return of capital distributions, and capital gain distributions. A mutual fund will notify its stockholders within 60 days of the close of its tax year what portion of the dividends distributed should be reported as long-term capital gains. It will also report what portion of the undistributed capital gains should be reported as long-term capital gains.

Ordinary dividends are reported as dividend income. Capital gains are reported as long-term capital gain (see Tab 4).

If the mutual fund has paid a tax on an undistributed capital gain, shareholders are entitled to a credit or refund of the tax, since it is deemed to have been paid by them. In such a case, the company should send Form 2439, *Notice to Shareholder of Undistributed Long-Term Capital Gains,* to indicate the tax paid.

Planning Tip. If dividends are not distributed to the investor, be sure to add the undistributed dividends to the basis of the fund shares.

Foreign Tax Paid. If a mutual fund invests overseas, it may be able to allocate foreign tax to its shareholders, as reported in box 6 of Form 1099-DIV. An investor who receives a foreign tax allocation has a choice: claim the foreign tax as an itemized deduction, or claim a foreign tax credit. The itemized deduction provides a small benefit, none at all for some taxpayers, but is easy to take. The tax credit usually provides a larger benefit; see Tab 10 for calculation of the foreign tax credit.

Filing Tip. Calculation of a foreign tax credit of over $300 ($600 for married filing jointly) requires knowledge of the names of countries the mutual fund was investing in. Such information is not usually available on the Form 1099-DIV but should be available in the fund's annual report.

Part III: Foreign Accounts and Trusts, Lines 7–8

Since the IRS is concerned about abusive tax shelters in other countries, it wants to know about every taxpayer's foreign investments. Because tax shelters tend to be used primarily by people with significant investment income, the IRS puts this mini-information return at the bottom of Schedule B.

Caution. Clients with foreign accounts and trusts merit close detail checking, since the IRS has placed these accounts near the top of its audit priorities.

Line 7, Signature Authority over Foreign Account

A taxpayer with signature authority or a financial interest in a foreign account may be required to file Form 8938, Statement of Specified Foreign Financial Assets, with his or her income tax return. Failure to file Form 8938 may result in penalties and an automatic extension of the statute of limitations.

Line 7a asks taxpayers, "At any time during 2013, did you have a financial interest in or signature authority over a financial account (such as a bank account, securities account, or brokerage account) located in a foreign country?...If 'Yes,' are you required to file FinCEN Form 114, Report of Foreign Bank and Financial Accounts (FBAR), formerly TD F 90.22-1, to report that financial interest or signature authority?"

Filing Tip. After July 1, 2013, all FBAR reports must be filed through the BSA E-Filing system on or before June 30th to avoid late-filing penalties. Additional information can be found at www.fincen.gov. Practitioners should register for e-filing privileges well before the filing date.

A taxpayer must check the "Yes" box on line 7a if either of the following applies:

1. The taxpayer owns more than 50% of the stock in any corporation that owns one or more foreign bank accounts.
2. At any time during the year the taxpayer had an interest in or signature or other authority over a financial account in a foreign country, i.e., a bank account, securities account, or other financial account. This does not apply to foreign securities held in a U.S. securities account.

A taxpayer with a foreign account has to check "Yes" here, unless one of the IRS's exceptions applies:

- The combined value of all accounts was $10,000 or less during the entire year.
- The accounts were with a U.S. military banking facility operated by a U.S. financial institution.
- The taxpayer was an officer or employee of a commercial bank supervised by the Comptroller of the Currency, the Board of Governors of the Federal Reserve System, or the Federal Deposit Insurance Corporation; the account was in an employer's name; and the taxpayer did not have a personal financial interest in the account.
- The taxpayer was an officer or employee of a domestic corporation with securities listed on national securities exchanges or with assets of more than $1 million and 500 or more shareholders of record; the account was in the employer's name; the taxpayer did not have a personal financial interest in the account; *and* the corporation's chief financial officer has given the taxpayer written notice that the corporation has filed a current report that includes the account.

The FBAR contains information needed to determine who is considered to have an interest in or signature authority over a financial account in a foreign country.

Caution. Anyone who checked the "Yes" box to Question 2 on line 7a must e-file an FBAR by June 30th of the year following the calendar year being reported. Do *not* attach it to Form 1040. Willful violations of the FBAR filing requirement may be subject to civil and criminal penalties.

Line 8, Foreign Trusts

Line 8 asks taxpayers, "During 2013, did you receive a distribution from, or were you the grantor of, or transferor to, a foreign trust? If 'Yes,' you may have to file Form 3520."

A taxpayer who received a distribution, including a loan, from a foreign trust must provide additional information, on either Form 3520, *Annual Return to Report Transactions with Foreign Trusts and Receipt of Certain Foreign Gifts,* or Form 926, *Return of a U.S. Transferor of Property to a Foreign Corporation.*

 Filing Tip. Do not attach Form 3520 to Form 1040. Instead file it at the address shown in the instructions.

 Caution. Anyone required to file an FBAR who fails to do so may have to pay a penalty of up to $10,000 (more in certain cases). If a taxpayer meets any of the requirements listed for checking "Yes" on line 7a, review the FBAR carefully.

Taxpayers who checked the "Yes" box on line 7a must also enter the name of the foreign country or countries in the space provided on 7b. A separate statement may be attached if more space is required.

SCHEDULE B
(Form 1040A or 1040)

Department of the Treasury
Internal Revenue Service (99)

Interest and Ordinary Dividends

▶ Attach to Form 1040A or 1040.
▶ Information about Schedule B (Form 1040A or 1040) and its instructions is at *www.irs.gov/scheduleb*.

OMB No. 1545-0074

2013

Attachment
Sequence No. **08**

Name(s) shown on return

Your social security number

Part I

Interest

(See instructions on back and the instructions for Form 1040A, or Form 1040, line 8a.)

Note. If you received a Form 1099-INT, Form 1099-OID, or substitute statement from a brokerage firm, list the firm's name as the payer and enter the total interest shown on that form.

		Amount
1	List name of payer. If any interest is from a seller-financed mortgage and the buyer used the property as a personal residence, see instructions on back and list this interest first. Also, show that buyer's social security number and address ▶	
		1
2	Add the amounts on line 1	**2**
3	Excludable interest on series EE and I U.S. savings bonds issued after 1989. Attach Form 8815	**3**
4	Subtract line 3 from line 2. Enter the result here and on Form 1040A, or Form 1040, line 8a . . . . ▶	**4**

Note. If line 4 is over $1,500, you must complete Part III.

Part II

Ordinary Dividends

(See instructions on back and the instructions for Form 1040A, or Form 1040, line 9a.)

Note. If you received a Form 1099-DIV or substitute statement from a brokerage firm, list the firm's name as the payer and enter the ordinary dividends shown on that form.

		Amount
5	List name of payer ▶	
		5
6	Add the amounts on line 5. Enter the total here and on Form 1040A, or Form 1040, line 9a . . . . ▶	**6**

Note. If line 6 is over $1,500, you must complete Part III.

Part III
Foreign Accounts and Trusts

(See instructions on back.)

You must complete this part if you **(a)** had over $1,500 of taxable interest or ordinary dividends; **(b)** had a foreign account; or **(c)** received a distribution from, or were a grantor of, or a transferor to, a foreign trust.

		Yes	No
7a	At any time during 2013, did you have a financial interest in or signature authority over a financial account (such as a bank account, securities account, or brokerage account) located in a foreign country? See instructions		
	If "Yes," are you required to file FinCEN Form 114, Report of Foreign Bank and Financial Accounts (FBAR), formerly TD F 90-22.1, to report that financial interest or signature authority? See FinCEN Form 114 and its instructions for filing requirements and exceptions to those requirements		
b	If you are required to file FinCEN Form 114, enter the name of the foreign country where the financial account is located ▶		
8	During 2013, did you receive a distribution from, or were you the grantor of, or transferor to, a foreign trust? If "Yes," you may have to file Form 3520. See instructions on back		

For Paperwork Reduction Act Notice, see your tax return instructions.   Cat. No. 17146N   **Schedule B (Form 1040A or 1040) 2013**

What's New in 2013

IRS Forms. At the time of publication, many 2013 IRS forms were not available. Visit CCHGroup.com/TaxUpdates for updates regarding IRS form information.

Section 179 Limit. The maximum Section 179 deduction for 2013 is $500,000. The investment threshold for reducing the deduction is $2 million.

Vehicle Expense Deduction Changes. The per mile standard mileage rate for 2013 is 56.5 cents per for business miles and 24 cents for medical and moving miles. The bonus depreciation cap remains at $8,000, which results in a maximum first year depreciation of $11,160 for autos and $11,360 for trucks and vans.

Simplified Home Office Deduction. Beginning in 2013, a simplified method is available for claiming a home office deduction. The maximum deduction is $1,500, based on multiplying a maximum of 300 square feet of the home used for business by $5.

Social Security Tax Wage Base Increased. The Social Security tax wage base for 2013 is increased to $113,700.

Social Security Self-Employment Tax Rate Increased. **The** Social Security portion of the self-employment tax returns to 12.4 percent for 2013. An additional 0.9 percent Medicare tax is imposed on self-employment income in excess of $200,000 ($250,000 for joint return, $125,000 for married filing separately).

Relevant IRS Publications

☐ IRS Publication 15, *Circular E, Employer's Tax Guide*

☐ IRS Publication 51, *Circular A, Agricultural Employer's Tax Guide*

☐ IRS Publication 225, *Farmer's Tax Guide*

☐ IRS Publication 334, *Tax Guide for Small Business*

☐ IRS Publication 535, *Business Expenses*

☐ IRS Publication 583, *Starting a Business and Keeping Records*

Section at a Glance

Tax Preparer's Checklist

☐ Existing businesses should have a taxpayer identification number; submit Form SS-4 if they do not.

☐ New businesses should obtain EINs as an identity protection issue for the business owners even if they do not have employees or retirement plans that would otherwise require them.

☐ Have copies of filed payroll documents to crosscheck: Forms 940, 941, W-3, SUI, and other state and local tax filings.

☐ Have copies or a record of state and local filing documents such as sales taxes.

☐ Request 1099-MISC and 1098 documents received and look for 1099-MISC filings.

☐ Keep and collect business mileage records.

☐ Keep records of ending inventory, if applicable.

Key 2013 Figures Relating to Self-Employment Income	
Net earnings threshold for filing Schedule SE	$ 400 ($433 x 92.35%)*
Income subject to Social Security or 4.2% railroad retirement tier 1 tax	$113,700
Self-employment tax rate	15.3%
Social Security portion	12.4%
Medicare portion	2.9%
Form 1040, line 27, deduction for one-half of self-employment tax paid	50% OASDI + 50% HI

*Church employee net income threshold is $100 ($108.28 x 92.35%).

Other 2013 Schedules and Forms that May Have to Be Filed with or because of Schedule C, C-EZ, or F

Schedule SE	To pay self-employment tax on income from any trade or business
Form 1065	In Lieu of a Schedule C if a business is a partnership
Form 4562	To claim depreciation and amortization deductions, to make an election under Section 179 to expense the cost of certain tangible property, and to provide information on the business and/or investment use of cars and other listed property (see Tab 7)
Form 4684	To report a casualty or theft gain or loss involving property used in trade or business or income-producing property (see Tab 2)
Form 4797	To report sales, exchanges and involuntary conversions (not from a casualty or theft) of trade or business property and to document recapture of Code Sec. 179 deductions (see Tab 4)
Form 8300	To report the receipt of more than $10,000 cash in one or more related transactions
Form 8824	To report like-kind exchanges (see Tab 4)
Form 8829	To claim expenses for business use of taxpayer's home
Form 8903	To take a deduction for income from domestic production activities
Employment Returns	Form 941, *Employer's Quarterly Federal Tax Return* Form 940, *Employer's Annual Federal Unemployment (FUTA) Tax Return* Form 943, *Employer's Annual Federal Tax Return for Agricultural Employees* Form 944, *Employer's Annual Federal Tax Return* Form W-2, *Wage and Tax Statement* Form W-3, *Transmittal of Wage and Tax Statements*
Information Returns	Form 1099-MISC, *Miscellaneous Income* Form 1096, *Annual Summary and Transmittal of U.S. Information Returns*

When to File Schedule C, Schedule C-EZ, Schedule F, and Schedule SE

Schedule C, *Profit and or Loss from Business* (Sole Proprietorship), Schedule C-EZ, *Net Profit from Business* (Sole Proprietorship), and Schedule F, *Profit or Loss from Farming*, are filed with Form 1040, *U.S. Individual Income Tax Return*, to report the income and expenses generated by an individual's participation as a sole proprietor in an active trade or business, along with pertinent information about the business. Income from separate businesses, even though owned by the same individual, must be reported on separate copies of Schedule C. Combining businesses on one Schedule C could lead to a tax penalty (IRC §6662 and Rev. Rul. 81-90).

An individual with a net self-employment income of $400 or more must file an income tax return and use Schedule SE to report that income, even if filing would not otherwise be required.

Business Owned Jointly by Spouses

Spouses who jointly own and operate an unincorporated business and share in the profits and losses are considered to be operating a partnership, even if no formal partnership agreement exists. A Form 1065,

U.S. Return of Partnership Income, should be filed in such situations, with the profit/loss and other items flowing through on Form 1065 Schedule K-1, *Partner's Share of Income, Credits, Deductions, etc.*

A qualified joint venture where the only members are a husband and wife filing a joint return can elect *not* to be treated as a partnership for federal tax purposes. Each spouse would take into account his or her income, gain, loss and other items as a sole proprietor and report their share of income on a separate Form 1040, *Schedule C*. A qualified joint venture is a joint venture involving the conduct of a trade or business if:

- the only members of the joint venture are the husband and wife;
- both spouses materially participate in the trade or business; and
- both spouses elect to have the qualified joint venture provision apply.

 Filing Tip. For 2013, as in 2012, qualified joint ventures reporting rental real estate income not subject to self-employment tax must report that income on Schedule E instead of Schedule C (unless the taxpayers provide substantial services).

If the material participation requirement is not satisfied, a married couple living in community property states can elect *not* to be treated as a partnership for federal tax purposes if their business is a qualified entity. To be a qualified entity:

- the business must be 100% owned by the couple as community property under the laws of a state, a foreign country, or a possession of the United States;
- no person, other than one or both spouses, may have an ownership interest in the property for federal tax purposes; and
- the business must not be treated as a corporation (Rev. Proc. 2002-69).

When one Schedule C is filed for a jointly owned business under these rules, self-employment income must be allocated on two Schedules SE.

 Filing Tip. Community property states are Arizona, California, Idaho, Louisiana, Nevada, New Mexico, Texas, Washington, and Wisconsin.

Shared and Allocated Expenses

If an individual operates a business in the same profession in which he or she is employed by someone else, records of expenses must be carefully allocated. Specific identification of expenses allocable to each activity is preferred, in order to properly file Schedule C (or C-EZ) and Form 2106, *Employee Business Expenses.* If specific identification is not possible, such expenses may be allocated on the basis of the relative gross income from each activity.

Sole Member of a Limited Liability Company (LLC)

The owner of a single-member domestic limited liability company (LLC) must file a Schedule C, C-EZ, or F, unless an election has been made to treat the LLC as a corporation. Form 8832, *Entity Classification Election,* is used to make that election. If the election has been made, the business income and expenses are reported on Form 1120, *U.S. Corporation Income Tax Return,* or Form 1120-S, *U.S. Income Tax Return for an S Corporation,* as appropriate.

 Caution. States handle LLCs in different ways. Some require a separate return for a single member LLC and charge annual fees.

Statutory Employees

The Form W-2, *Wage and Tax Statement,* of a statutory employee will have a checkmark in box 13. Wages and expenses of a statutory employee are reported on Schedule C or C-EZ.

Congress has declared certain employees to be statutory employees. Their position of being able to deduct expenses on Schedule C obviously gives them an advantage over other employees, who must itemize their deductions, subject to certain limitations, on Schedule A (see Tab 2).

Employers must withhold Social Security and Medicare taxes on the income of statutory employees and must give them a Form W-2 that reports this income and shows the payroll taxes that were withheld. Statutory employees must pay estimated income taxes on their net income since their employers are not required to withhold income taxes from their pay.

The following employees are considered statutory employees:

- Full-time traveling or local salespersons who solicit orders from wholesalers, retailers, contractors or operators of hotels, restaurants, or other similar establishments on behalf of a principal, if the goods sold are merchandise for resale or supplies for use in the customer's business;
- Drivers who distribute beverages other than milk, or who distribute meat, vegetable, fruit, or bakery products, or who pick up and deliver laundry or dry cleaning as an agent for the business or on commission;
- Full-time life insurance sales agents whose principal business is selling life insurance or annuity contracts primarily for one life insurance company; and
- Home workers performing work on material or goods furnished by the employer and to the employer's specifications.
- For more information see MTG ¶941B.

When to File Schedule C-EZ?

Schedule C-EZ is a simpler, less detailed version of Schedule C. Schedule C-EZ may be used in place of Schedule C on a 2013 return, provided that all of the following are true:

- The business had expenses of no more than $5,000.
- The business uses the cash method of accounting.
- The business did not have an inventory at any time during the year.
- The business did not have a net loss for the year.
- The taxpayer had only one business as either a sole proprietor or statutory employee during the year.

- The business had no employees during the year.
- The business is not required to file Form 4562, *Depreciation and Amortization (Including Information on Listed Property)*.
- The taxpayer does not deduct expenses for the business use of his or her home.
- There are no prior years' unallowed passive activity losses from this business.

When to File Schedule C?

Taxpayers who do not qualify to file Schedule C-EZ should file Schedule C to report income from a non-farm business.

When to File Schedule F?

Schedule F is used to report income generated and the related expense from the active conduct of a business involved in producing agricultural or horticultural commodities. Items to be reported include the following:

- Sales of livestock and other items bought for resale.
- Sales of livestock, produce, grains and so on that the taxpayer raised or produced.
- Distributions from cooperatives related to the farm business (from Form 1099-PATR).
- Government farm program payments, including commodity credit loans and certificates, disaster assistance, crop insurance proceeds and other income replacement insurance; also payments for damages to standing crops or crop replacement payments by responsible parties.
- Payments for custom hire or machine work (machine operator furnishes equipment).
- Federal and state fuel tax refunds and credits.

Gains from the sale of livestock held for draft, breeding, sport or dairy are reported on Form 4797, *Sales of Business Property*, as are the sales of farmland and depreciable farm equipment.

Rental of farmland and facilities that is based on a share of crops or livestock produced by a tenant is normally reported on Form 4835, *Farm Rental Income and Expenses*, and is not subject to SE tax, providing the owner does not materially participate in the operation or management of the farm.

Cash rent that represents a flat charge for the use of farmland and is not based on production is reported on Schedule E, *Supplemental Income and Loss*, and is not subject to SE tax.

Rental of farm equipment, soil testing, computer consulting, and other "farm-related" activities that are conducted as a separate trade or business are normally Schedule C activities.

Income from the rental of personal property, if not conducted for profit, is reported on Form 1040, line 21. Related expense is reported on Schedule A of Form 1040.

When to File Schedule SE

Schedule SE, *Self-Employment Tax*, is used to report net earning of $400 or more from self-employment. An individual is self-employed if they are in business for themselves or are a farmer. Receipt of Form 1099-MISC, *Miscellaneous Income*, does not necessarily mean that a Schedule SE must be filed. Often the sender of the 1099-MISC has mischaracterized the nature of the payment.

An individual is self-employed if:

- The taxpayer carried on a trade or business as a sole proprietor or an independent contractor;
- The taxpayer is a member of a partnership that carries on a trade or business; or
- The taxpayer is otherwise in business for themselves.

A trade or business is generally an activity carried on for a livelihood or in good faith to make a profit. The facts and circumstances of each case determine whether or not an activity is a trade or business. The regularity of activities and transactions and the production of income are important elements. A taxpayer does not need to actually make a profit to be in a trade or business as long as the taxpayer has a profit motive. However, the taxpayer does need to make ongoing efforts to further the interests of their business.

A taxpayer does not have to carry on regular full-time business activities to be self-employed. Having a part-time business in addition to a regular job or business may also be self-employment.

A taxpayer is a sole proprietor if they own an unincorporated business by themselves, in most cases. If the taxpayer is the sole member of a domestic limited liability company (LLC), they are a sole proprietor unless they elect to treat the LLC as a corporation. For more information see IRS Form 8832.

If the taxpayer is a member of a partnership that carries on a trade or business, the partnership should report the taxpayer's earnings subject to self-employment tax in box 14, of Form 1065, Schedule K-1 (using code A) or in box 9 of Form 1065-B, Schedule K-1 (using code J1), *Partner's Share of Income (Loss) From an Electing Large Partnership*. If the taxpayer is a general partner, the taxpayer may need to reduce these unreported earnings by the amounts the taxpayer has claimed as Code Sec. 179 deductions, unreimbursed partnership expenses, or depletion on oil and gas properties. If the amount reported is subject to the loss limitation rules (see Tab 5), the taxpayer should only include the deductible amount when figuring their total earnings subject to self-employment tax.

People such as doctors, dentists, veterinarians, lawyers, accountants, contractors, subcontractors, public stenographers, or auctioneers who are in an independent trade, business, or profession in which they offer services to the general public are generally independent contractors. However, whether these people are independent contractors or employees depends on the facts in each case. The general rule is that an individual is an independent contractor if the service recipient has the right to control or direct only the result of the work and not how it will be done. The earnings of a person who is working as an independent contractor are subject to self-employment tax.

A taxpayer is not an independent contractor if they perform services that can be controlled by an employer (i.e., what will be done and how it will be done). This applies even if the taxpayer is given freedom of action. What matters is that the employer has the legal right to control the details of how the services are performed. For more information regarding independent contractors, see IRS Publication 15-A, *Employer's Supplemental Tax Guide.*

Net earnings from self-employment consist of:

- Gross income derived from any trade or business, less allowable deductions attributable to the trade or business; and
- The taxpayer's distributive share of ordinary income or loss of a partnership engaged in a trade or business.

The term "trade or business" does not include services performed as an employee other than services relating to certain: (1) newspaper or magazine sales, (2) sharing of crops, (3) foreign organizations and (4) sharing of fishing catches.

Schedule SE must also be filed if an individual had church employee income of $108.28 or more. Self-employment tax must also be paid on certain partnership income and guaranteed payments. See IRS Publication 334, *Tax Guide for Small Business (For Individuals Who Use Schedule C or Schedule C-EZ)* and MTG ¶2670 for more information.

Rents from real estate and personal property leased with the real estate, and the attributable deductions are excluded from net earnings from self-employment unless received by the individual in his course of business as a real estate dealer. Termination payments received by former insurance salespeople are excluded under certain circumstances. For more information see MTG ¶2670.

There is also a Farm Optional Method for calculating net earnings from self-employment. See page 3-32.

The following are not subject to self-employment tax:

- Income from a hobby.
- Income received by a minister, member of the clergy, or member of a religious organization provided they have obtained an exemption.
- Wages earned as an employee.
- Retirement pay.
- Wages earned by a railroad employee.
- A distributive share of income or loss from a trade or business allocated to a limited partner.
- A distributive share of S corporation income or loss allocated to a shareholder and included on Schedule K-1.
- Periodic retirement payments.
- Some fishing crew members.
- State and local government employees.
- Public officials.
- Corporate employees.
- Nonprofessional fiduciaries such as an administrator or an executor of an estate.
- Indian fishing rights.
- Nonresident aliens, unless they are subject to an international agreement or are residents of a U.S. possession.
- US citizens or resident aliens residing abroad who are subject to the Social Security laws of the foreign country under a totalization agreement.

Chart of Business Entity Comparisons

Entity	Sole Proprietorship	General Partnership	Limited Partnership	C Corporation	S Corporation	Limited Liability Company
Tax Form	Form 1040–Schedule C, C-EZ, or F	Form 1065	Form 1065	Form 1120	Form 1120S	Forms 1065/1040 (Schedule C)/1120 or 1120S (election)
Taxation	Direct to proprietor	Flow-through	Flow-through	Direct to corporation	Flow-through	Various, based on election
Ownership	One owner	Unlimited number of general partners	Unlimited—must have one general partner	Unlimited number of stockholders	Up to 100 stockholders	Single-member or unlimited number of members

Chart of Business Entity Comparisons (Continued)

Entity	Sole Proprietorship	General Partnership	Limited Partnership	C Corporation	S Corporation	Limited Liability Company
Liability	Unlimited personal liability	Unlimited liability for general partners	Unlimited liability for general partners—limited to investment for limited partners	Shareholders have no personal liability for corporate obligations	Shareholders have no personal liability for corporate obligations	Members generally have no personal liability for business obligations
Management	Owner has complete control	Partners normally have equal voice unless otherwise agreed to	General partners manage business—possible restrictions from limited partners in agreement	Board of directors overall—officers day to day are responsible to board	Board of directors overall—officers day to day are responsible to board	Operating agreement with designated manager(s)
Legal Requirements	Easy to set up, easy to liquidate; minimal legal requirements	Few legal requirements; should have partnership agreement (not required in all states)	Distinction between general partners and limited partners	Must have board of directors, officers, and annual meetings—articles of incorporation and by-laws	Must have board of directors, officers, and annual meetings—articles of incorporation and by-laws	Organizational documentation—normally articles of organization; also operating agreement

Recordkeeping and Substantiation Requirements

A separate bank account should be kept for each business, in addition to a personal account for family living.

 Planning Tip. Although it is not required by law, an audit normally goes more smoothly if business and personal accounts are kept separate.

There is no requirement that business books be double-entry. A double-entry system, however, will make reconciliation of ending asset and liability balances easier.

No matter how the records are kept (13-column analysis pads, the traditional handwritten general ledger with supporting journals, basic computer spreadsheets, or sophisticated computer accounting programs), it is imperative that the supporting documentation be kept in an organized manner. In addition to the checkbook, canceled checks, deposit slips, and bank statements, the records that need to be maintained include sales slips, invoices, receipts, delivery receipts, inventory records, cost calculations and financial statements.

Canceled Checks. It is now rare that a bank returns the original canceled check to the customer. Copies of the cleared checks are normally included with the bank statement, along with a listing of the cleared checks by

number. The taxpayer should request that a copy of the check backs, in addition to the fronts, be included. Some banks are making the electronic images, front and back, available to the account holder online. Since a canceled check alone may not be sufficient documentation, the taxpayer should match the canceled check copies to the invoices and not the check number on the invoice.

To the extent possible, all disbursements should be made by check, rather than cash. Personal expenses should never be paid from the business account.

Accounting Methods

The taxpayer's accounting method is a set of rules as to when and how income and expenses are reported. Generally the same accounting method used for keeping the business's records must be used for completing Schedule C. The accounting method used in the year for which the first income tax return that includes the Schedule C for the business is filed is the accounting method the business is required to use in subsequent years. From then on, most changes in accounting method will require IRS approval. Kinds of accounting methods include the following:

- Cash method—used by most sole proprietors with no inventory. Items are included in income as they are actually or constructively received. Property or services received (i.e., bartering) must be valued and included in income at fair market value. Expenses are deducted in the tax year in which they are actually paid. There are some restrictions on advance payments that may not be deducted until applicable and some items (such as depreciable equipment) that must be capitalized.

- Accrual method–income is reported in the year earned (not necessarily received), and expenses are deducted in the year incurred.
- Special methods for certain items of income and expense.
- Combination method using elements of two or more of the above. It is quite common for taxpayers who must maintain an inventory in order to properly reflect income and expense to use the cash method for other expenses. The bottom line is that the method of accounting selected must be used consistently and must clearly show the income and expenses of the business.

Business and Personal Items

A taxpayer may account for business and personal items using different accounting methods. For example, a Schedule C business may be on the accrual method, while the taxpayer reports his or her personal items on a cash basis.

 Planning Tip. The timing of both receipt of income and payment of expenses can shift profits/losses to a more desirable year for a cash-basis taxpayer. It can also greatly influence other deductions or related expenditures, including Section 179 and bonus depreciation or retirement plan funding.

Determining how the client reports income can be simplified: cash if the client works from his or her checkbook balance, or accrual if the client reports/posts income and expenses by transactions/sales.

Two or More Businesses

If a taxpayer has two or more separate and distinct businesses, with separate books and records, he or she may use a different accounting method for each. The accounting method used must clearly reflect the income of each business. If the books are kept together and allocated at the end of the year in order to file the return, the books are not separate and distinct.

How Long Must Records Be Kept?

The statute of limitations for a tax return and supporting documentation is three years. The time frame increases to six years if gross income is understated by more than 25%. There is no limit if fraud is involved or false or fraudulent information is entered on the tax return. The statute of limitations does not begin to run until the return is filed, so if a return has not been filed, the statute remains open.

Some other events or items extend the statute of limitations:

- Net operating loss (NOL) or capital loss carryback extends the limitations period for the year in which the loss arose.
- Support and documentation of items that affect future returns extend the time as well. The support for depreciable assets must be kept for the statutory period after the last return on which depreciation for the asset is claimed. If like-kind exchanges are involved, the documentation for an asset originally purchased many years ago may need to be retained through subsequent trades.

Special Documentation for Some Business Deductions

Meals, entertainment, travel and gifts are subject to some special documentation requirements. Such expenditures must be ordinary and necessary expenses of carrying on the business to be deductible.

For *entertainment and meal expenses*, the following information should be maintained:

- Date and location.
- Business purpose or business benefit.
- Nature of business discussion or activity.
- If entertainment was directly before or after business discussion, keep the names of individuals who participated, as well as the date, place and nature of the business discussion.
- Record the professions/occupations/business relationship to the taxpayer of individuals present. Documentation must also show that the taxpayer or an employee participated if the entertainment was a business meal.

For *travel expenses*:

- Dates of departure and return and days spent for business versus personal days.
- Cost by category of expense, i.e., travel, lodging, meals and incidental expenses.
- Destination or travel area.
- Business purpose or business benefit of trip.
- See Tab 8 for additional rules.

For *gifts*:

- Date of gift.
- Description and cost of gift.
- Business purpose or business benefit of gift.
- Business relationship of taxpayer to recipient.

Schedule C Line-by-Line Instructions

General Business Information

Name of Proprietor and SSN

Be sure to include the name and Social Security number of the proprietor.

Lines A and B, Principal Business or Profession and Code

Enter on line A the activity that provided the principal source of income to be reported on line 1. The six-digit Principal Business or Professional Activity Codes are based on the North American Industry Classification System (NAICS) and are reproduced beginning on page 3-18 for convenience. Enter the code for the business on line B.

Lines C, D, and E, Business Name, EIN, and Address

If a business name is used, it goes on line C. If there is no separate business name or "doing business as"-type designation ("/dba"), line C is left blank.

The employer ID number (EIN) is entered on line D. A single-member disregarded LLC must enter the EIN of the LLC on this line. A person who has appointed an agent under IRC §3504 to pay or report employment taxes must put the EIN of the agent who files the employment tax returns. A person who leases employees must enter the EIN of the entity that provides the leased employees. If there is no EIN for the business and none is required, leave the line blank. Do not enter the taxpayer's Social Security number again.

There are several ways to apply for an EIN:

- Apply online at the IRS Web site: Go to www.irs. gov/Businesses and click on "Employer ID Numbers" under "Businesses Topics."
- Apply via fax: Complete Form SS-4 online, print it, and fax it to the taxpayer's state fax number.
- Apply via telephone at 800-829-4933. Have the completed SS-4 form in front of you ready to read the information to the IRS representative. The person making the call must be authorized to sign the form or be an authorized designee. The representative may or may not request that the signed Form SS-4 be mailed or faxed. International applicants must call (267) 941-1099 (Not a toll-free number).
- Apply by mail. The processing time frame for an EIN application received by mail is four weeks. Ensure that the Form SS-4 contains all of the required information. A copy of Form SS-4 with signature authorization should be maintained in a practitioner's records.

- Only one EIN per day can be assigned to a responsible party.

On line E, enter the address of the business, including suite or room number, as well as city, state, and zip.

Line F, Accounting Method

On line F, check Cash, Accrual, or Other. The mechanics of various accounting methods are discussed on pages 3-6 and 3-7. Of primary concern to the IRS is that the method used clearly reflects income. Unless the taxpayer meets the requirements as a qualifying taxpayer or a qualifying small business, the accrual method must be used for sales and purchases of inventory items. Exceptions apply to taxpayers with average annual gross receipts of $1 million or less and to service-type businesses with average annual gross receipts of $10 million or less.

It is possible to change accounting methods. Some changes require IRS approval. To change accounting methods, file Form 3115, *Application for Change in Accounting Method.* If a change is made, there may be adjustments to items of income and expense in order to prevent duplication or omission of any items. The adjustment is made under Code Sec. 481(a).

Line G, Material Participation

In general, material participation includes any work done in connection with an activity by an individual who owned an interest in the activity at the time the work was done. Marking this box "No" identifies the business as a passive activity. If the business is classified as a passive activity, allowable losses may be limited. See Tab 5 for information on passive activity losses and Form 8582, *Passive Activity Loss Limitations,* used to calculate the allowable loss.

According to the instructions for Schedule C, for purposes of the passive activity rules, the taxpayer materially participated in the operation of the trade or business activity during the year if he or she met any of the following seven tests:

1. The taxpayer participated in the activity for more than 500 hours during the tax year.
2. The taxpayer's participation in the activity for the tax year was substantially all of the total individual participation (including individuals who did not own any interest in the activity) for the tax year.
3. The taxpayer participated in the activity for more than 100 hours during the tax year, and participated at least as much as any other person for the tax year.
4. The activity is a significant participation activity for the tax year and the taxpayer participated in

all significant participation activities for more than 500 hours during the year. An activity is a "significant participation activity" if it involves the conduct of a trade or business, the taxpayer participated in the activity for more than 100 hours during the tax year, and the taxpayer did not materially participate under any of the material participation tests other than this one.

5. The taxpayer materially participated in the activity for any five (they do not need to be consecutive) of the 10 tax years prior to the tax year in question.

6. The activity is a personal service activity in which the taxpayer materially participated for any three prior tax years (need not be consecutive). A personal service activity is an activity that involves performing personal services in the fields of health, law, engineering, architecture, accounting, actuarial science, performing arts, consulting or any other trade or business in which capital is not a material income-producing factor.

7. Based on all the facts and circumstances, the taxpayer participated in the activity on a regular, continuous, and substantial basis during the tax year. For management activities to constitute participation under the facts and circumstances test: 1) there can be no individual other than the taxpayer who receives compensation (which is earned income) for management services; and 2) no other individual can put in more hours than the taxpayer in performing management services.

A taxpayer will not be treated as significantly participating in an activity if the taxpayer participated in the activity for 100 hours or less during any tax year.

Working interest in oil or gas property. There is an exception for a working interest in oil or gas property. The box should be checked "Yes" whether the working interest is owned directly or indirectly through an entity that does not limit liability. No matter the level of participation, the activity of owning a working interest is not a passive activity.

Investors. Work done as an investor in an activity is not treated as participation unless the individual was directly involved in the day-to-day management or operations of the activity. Work done as an investor includes:

- studying and reviewing financial statements or reports on the operation of the activity;
- preparing or compiling summaries or analyses of the finances or operations of the activity for the individual's own use; and
- monitoring the finances or operations in a nonmanagerial capacity.

Line H, New Business

If 2013 is the first year for the business for this taxpayer, check the box on line H. If a Schedule C or C-EZ was filed for the same business in 2012, leave the box blank.

Lines I and J, 1099s

On Line I, if you made any payment in 2013 that would require you to file any Forms 1099, check the "Yes" box. Otherwise, check "No." On Line J, indicate by checking the appropriate box if you filed all required Forms 1099 in 2013.

 Planning Tip. If a taxpayer operates multiple businesses, he or she may choose to include tax items from related businesses on the same Schedule C or to report tax items from each business on separate Schedule Cs. When a taxpayer's records cannot be separated by individual business, shared expenses are generally allocated on a pro rata basis by revenue.

Part I: Income

What Constitutes Business Income?

The term "trade or business" is used over and over again in the Internal Revenue Code. In most instances, there is no explanation or definition of the term. The explanations that do exist are not consistent across the Code.

Most tax professionals look at trade or business income as income that is generated by regular and continuous activity, not performed as an employee, and that is done with a profit motive. Trade or business activity may be engaged in on a full or part time basis. Many individuals have one or more Schedule C or F businesses in addition to full-time employment. Normally, investment activity is not considered trade or business activity.

Line 1, Gross Receipts or Sales

The term "gross receipts" includes all amounts received for the sale of goods or services (produced or purchased) in the normal course of business. Whether or not accounts receivable are a factor depends on the accounting method used for the business.

Income reported on Form 1099-MISC is normally reported as a part of gross receipts. All Forms 1099-MISC with entries in box 7 (nonemployee compensation) should be totaled and verified to ensure that they are included in gross receipts. If the total of the forms is more than income reported, attach an explanation and reconciliation of the totals. If a 1099-MISC is incorrect or was issued in error, the issuer should be contacted and a request for a correction made.

Bartering is a perfectly legal activity, but both parties must report their respective income for tax purposes. Include in gross receipts the fair market value (FMV) of property or services received in a bartering transaction. In order to avoid problems, both parties should agree to the FMV of items or services in advance of the actual trade.

Form 1099-B, *Proceeds from Broker and Barter Exchange Transactions*, or Form 1099-MISC, *Miscellaneous Income*, should be filed in bartering situations.

An individual may be a statutory employee, with income reported on a W-2, but reportable by him or her on a Schedule C or C-EZ. (See discussion on page 3-3.) Line 13 of Form W-2 contains a box that should be checked, if the individual is a statutory employee. The income and related expenses are reported on Schedule C or C-EZ and the "Statutory Employee" box is checked on Line 1 of Part I.

Social Security and Medicare tax is withheld and matched by the employer, so no self-employment tax is due on such earnings.

Filing Tip. If an individual has both income from self-employment and statutory employee income, he or she must file two Schedule Cs. The activities may not be combined on one Schedule C, and Schedule C-EZ is not allowed.

Filing Tip. Payments received in 2013 through merchant cards and third party networks are not reported separately from other gross receipts on Schedule C.

Line 2, Returns and Allowances

Report on line 2 returns, sales discounts, allowances, rebates and other items that reduce sales.

Line 3, Calculation

Subtract line 2 from line 1 and enter the result on line 3.

Line 4, Cost of Goods Sold

Line 4 is carried from line 42, Part III.

Line 5, Gross Profit

Subtract line 4 from line 3 and enter the result on line 5. This is the gross profit for the business.

Line 6, Other Income

Report as "Other income" income related to the trade or business, but not generated as a direct result of the principal trade or business activity. "Other income" items include the following:

- Federal fuel tax credit claimed on 2012 Form 1040
- State gasoline or fuel tax refunds received in 2013
- Finance reserve income
- Bad debts recovered
- Patronage dividends reported on Form 1099-PATR related to prior business purchases or business transactions with a cooperative sale of scrap or by-products
- Discount earned on timely sales tax filing
- Interest generated by accounts receivable finance charges
- Recapture of excess depreciation when business use of listed property falls below 50% before the end of the asset's recovery period (The recapture amount is calculated on Form 4797, Part III. See Tab 4.)
- *Note:* Not all receipts of money or property are included in income.

Sales tax is generally not reported as income. The tax is collected on sales and remitted to a state or local government authority. The amount is a flow-through. Most states require that the business owner remit to the state any excess sales tax collected. Some states do allow a discount for timely filing and remittance of sales tax. This discount should be reported on line 6, Other Income. Some states require that sales tax collected be reported as income, and the amount paid to the state is deducted.

The following items are **not income** and should not be reported as such:

- *Loans.* Money borrowed for operations or capital items, whether on a line of credit or a traditional note, is not income.
- *Asset appreciation.* Unrealized appreciation is not income until the asset is disposed of. At that point the disposition is reported on Form 4797, not Schedule C. See Tab 4.
- *Leasehold improvements.* Improvements paid for by a tenant on business or investment property may increase the value of the property, but are not considered income at that time. There is an exception if the facts and circumstances show that the improvements were actually a barter for rent payments.
- *Construction allowances.* Often a landlord will provide a tenant with a "construction allowance." The allowance is excluded from income provided both these conditions are met:
  - The arrangement is under a short-term lease (15 years or less) of retail space.
  - The allowance is to be used for constructing or improving nonresidential real property for use in the business at that retail space.
- *Like-kind exchange.* When business property is traded for like-kind replacement property (such as a business vehicle for a business vehicle), a gain is not taxable and a loss is not deductible. Form 8824, *Like-Kind Exchanges (and Section 1043 Conflict-of-Interest Sales)*, does

need to be included as part of the tax return for the year of trade. (See the discussion in Tabs 4 and 8.)

- *Consignments.* The title to merchandise consigned to someone else remains with the consignor until property is sold by the consignee. The property is considered inventory for the consignor until that time. Likewise, merchandise received on consignment is not a part of the consignee's inventory. The profit or commission is income to the consignee when the property is sold or payment received (subject to accounting method).

 Caution. Gross receipts (reported sales or revenues) should equal other reported receipts that the entity submits to any other third party: sales tax, workers' compensation payments and payments from the U.S. Department of Commerce, for example. Exceptions or deviations may be explained to the IRS in attached documentation.

Part II: Expenses

What Constitutes a Deductible Business Expense?

Ordinary and Necessary Business Expense. "Ordinary" and "necessary" have specific meanings with regard to business expenses.

- An **ordinary** expense is one that is common and accepted in that particular business or activity.
- A **necessary** expense is one that is helpful and appropriate for the trade or business. The expense does not have to be indispensable to be considered necessary.

Start-up Costs. The maximum amount of start-up expenses that may be deducted is $5,000, reduced by the amount by which start-up expenditures exceed $50,000. A taxpayer is deemed to have made an election to deduct and amortize start-up expenses for the taxable year in which the active trade or business to which the expenditures relate begins. A taxpayer may choose to forego the deemed election by clearly electing to capitalize its start-up expenditures on a timely filed federal income tax return, including extensions, for the taxable year in which the active trade or business to which the expenditures relate begins.

Expenses Paid after Business Is Closed and Ceases to Generate Revenue. For a cash-basis taxpayer, expenses incurred in prior years, but paid in the current year, are considered deductible. The taxpayer may continue to file a Schedule C in order to claim these expenses.

Line 8, Advertising

Expenditures for advertising costs are deducted on line 8 and must be reasonably related to the products and services offered by the business.

Lobbying. Note that advertising to influence legislation, contributions to candidates or office holders, and other such expenditures are not deductible for federal income tax.

Line 9, Car and Truck Expenses

Expenses related to the use of a car or truck may be deducted on Schedule C using one of two methods:

- *Standard mileage method.* The standard mileage method allows a taxpayer to deduct 56.5 cents per mile for business miles on up to four vehicles for 2013. This mileage amount covers all costs of owning and operating the vehicle except for interest on a vehicle loan, property taxes for the business percentage of the vehicle, parking, and tolls.
- *Actual cost method.* The actual cost method multiplies the percentage of business use by the actual cost of owning and operating the vehicle—depreciation, fuel, oil, repairs, insurance, license, maintenance and so on. Depreciation is reported on line 13 of schedule C, along with other business depreciation. If the vehicle is rented or leased, that expense goes on line 20a.

Information relative to the vehicle is reported in Part V of Form 4562, *Depreciation and Amortization (Including Information on Listed Property)*, providing that form is required for the return. If Form 4562 is not required for the return, complete the information in Part IV of Schedule C, *Information on Your Vehicle.*

This written information includes the date the vehicle was placed in service, the number of business, commuting, and other miles driven during the year, and questions regarding personal use and supporting evidence as to the business miles claimed.

Line 10, Commissions and Fees

Enter commissions and fees paid by the taxpayer on line 10.

Line 11, Contract Labor

On line 11, deduct the cost of services provided or labor performed by any individual who is not an employee. Contract labor normally does not include parts or materials.

A Form 1099-MISC must be filed if $600 or more is paid to one individual during 2013. A copy of Form 1099-MISC must be provided to the worker by January 31, 2014 (February 18, 2014, if reporting payments for boxes 8 or 14), and submitted to the IRS, along with a Form 1096 transmittal, by February 28, 2014 (March 31, 2014, if filed electronically).

Filing Tip. Be sure to report 1099-MISC income revenues as a separate line entry so that it may be identified easily.

1099-MISC nonemployee payouts should be segregated by activity, reported to the recipient, and shown as either a cost of goods (where appropriate) or as a business expense.

Form 1099-MISC is not required and should not be issued for any of the following:

- Payments to corporations.
- Payments for products, supplies, materials, or inputs.
- Payments to individuals for nonbusiness services, such as a plumber doing work on one's personal residence.
- Payments to employees.

 Caution. Because 1099-MISC nonreporting of compensation over $600 can result in a serious nonfiling penalty, obtain provider identification numbers. Use Form W-9 to obtain required SSNs as nonemployee workers are hired.

Line 12, Depletion

A depletion deduction is taken to offset the decrease in value of a taxpayer's economic interest in certain natural properties. These include mineral property, oil, gas, or geothermal wells and standing timber.

The depletion of standing timber is claimed on Form T (Timber), *Forest Activities Schedules*.

Line 13, Depreciation and Section 179 Expense Deduction

Depreciation and Section 179 expense deductions are taken on line 13 and detailed on Form 4562. Form 4562 must be completed and attached to the 2013 return only if one of the following are claimed:

- A Section 179 expense deduction.
- Depreciation on property placed in service during 2013.
- Depreciation on any vehicle or other listed property for 2013, regardless of when the property was placed in service.
- A deduction for any vehicled reported on a form other than Form 1040, Schedule C or Schedule C-EZ.
- Amortization of costs that begins in 2013.
- Depreciation on a corporate income tax return other than Form 1120S.

Depreciation spreads the recovery of the cost of property with an identifiable useful life over a period of years. Depreciation is not taken on inventory, stock in trade, land, or personal assets. See Tab 7.

 Planning Tip. Optional reporting of depreciation or election to expense of newly acquired assets should usually be a profit-based decision; discourage clients from making such depreciation decisions *only* on the basis of current tax consequences.

The maximum Section 179 deduction for 2013 is $500,000. The investment threshold for reducing the deduction is $2 million. For 2013, qualified real property is included as Section 179 property, but only $250,000 of the maximum $500,000 deduction can be for such property.

Temporary Bonus Depreciation. The first-year limit on depreciation for passenger automobiles is increased by $8,000 if bonus depreciation is claimed for a qualifying vehicle for a maximum first-year depreciation of 11,160 ($11,360 for vans or trucks).

Line 14, Employee Benefit Programs Other Than Pension and Profit-Sharing Plans

Contributions to employee benefit programs (other than pension and profit-sharing plans) are taken on line 14. These include accident and health plans, medical insurance, medical reimbursement plans, group term-life insurance, and dependent care assistance for employees.

Do not claim such expenses for the sole proprietor. In recent years, a popular move has been to hire the sole proprietor's spouse and provide family plan health insurance coverage to him or her as an employee benefit under a cafeteria plan. For the deduction to be allowable, the following conditions must be met:

- The spouse must be a true employee and must provide services as an employee to the business.
- The spouse must meet participation rules under an established medical reimbursement plan.
- The insurance coverage must be issued in the employee-spouse's name, not in the name of the employer-spouse.
- The employee-spouse may not be a joint owner, co-owner, or partner in the business.

Line 15, Insurance

Premiums paid for business insurance are reported on line 15. Insurance policies that qualify include the following:

- Casualty insurance—fire, theft, flood, and so on
- Credit insurance
- Business interruption insurance
- Overhead insurance
- Liability insurance

- Malpractice insurance
- Employee bonding
- Merchandise and inventory insurance
- Workers' compensation insurance

The following types of insurance policies do *not* qualify:

- Amounts credited to a reserve for self-insurance
- Premiums for a policy that pays for lost earnings due to the sickness or disability of the business owner
- Debt-driven life insurance on the business owner
- Health insurance for the business owner
- Long-term-care insurance for the business owner

 Filing Tip. Employing the taxpayer's spouse and providing health insurance benefits may increase deductions.

Line 16, Interest

Mortgage interest on business real property is deducted on line 16a. Generally, report on line 16a interest for which a bank or financial institution issued a Form 1098 to the taxpayer. The portion of home mortgage interest that applies to the business use of the taxpayer's personal residence is taken on Form 8829, *Expenses for Business Use of Your Home.* The personal portion of the home mortgage interest goes on Schedule A, *Itemized Deductions.*

Other business interest is reported on line 16b. This includes the interest on business operating loans, lines of credit, and the business-use portion of vehicle loans.

Generally, borrowing for business expenses is deductible and can be documented by using the tracing rules. Under the tracing rules, the use of the loan proceeds determines the nature of the interest and where and if it is deductible. IRS Publication 535, *Business Expenses,* gives details on tracing interest costs.

Interest charged on income tax owed is not deductible. It makes no difference that the tax problem that generated the interest charges was related to Schedule C.

Line 17, Legal and Professional Services

The cost of accounting and tax preparation related to Schedule C, Schedule E, *Supplemental Income and Loss,* and Schedule F, *Profit or Loss From Farming,* are properly deductible on each schedule. Ideally, the professional will provide information as to the portion of the fees allocable to each schedule. If not, allocation on the basis of income (including nonbusiness income) may be used. The personal portion of the tax preparation fee is reported on Schedule A.

Legal fees incurred in the normal operation of the business are deducted on the appropriate business schedule. Legal fees to acquire business assets must be added to the basis of depreciated assets over the life of the assets.

Line 18, Office Expenses

Office expenses, telephone, maintenance, office supplies, small tools, paper products, and so on are taken on line 18. This does not include business use of the home, which is reported on Form 8829 and flows to line 30 on Schedule C.

Line 19, Pension and Profit-Sharing Plans

Contributions made to pension, profit-sharing, and other retirement plans for the benefit of employees are claimed on line 19. Note that, even though a part of the same plan or program, contributions made for the benefit of the sole proprietor are claimed on the first page of Form 1040 as an adjustment to gross income.

Line 20, Rent or Lease

Line 20a is used for the rental of vehicles, machinery, and equipment.

 Caution. Rent-to-own contracts and purchase contracts are sometimes disguised as lease or rental arrangements. It is often necessary to look beneath the name of the contract or arrangement to its substance. If at the end of the lease or rental period, the asset belongs to the lessor for a small payment or no payment at all, the taxpayer has purchased the property. It is appropriately treated as acquired property and set up for depreciation. It may be necessary to add an inclusion amount to income. See Tab 8 for tables of inclusion amounts.

Line 20b is for amounts paid to rent or lease other property—office space, a retail shop, an entire building—used in the Schedule C business.

Line 21, Repairs and Maintenance

The cost of repairs and maintenance—ordinary upkeep, rather than improving or extending the life of the property involved—is a current deduction on line 21. Repairs related to an office in the home go on Form 8829 and ultimately on line 30 of Schedule C.

Line 22, Supplies

The cost of supplies purchased during the year for use in the ordinary course of business is deductible on line 22. The taxpayer may have a small amount of incidental supplies on hand, with no inventories or records of use and still deduct the cost of supplies purchased during the year, provided that this treatment clearly reflects income.

Line 23, Taxes and Licenses

The following taxes and licenses are deductible on line 23:

- State and local sales taxes imposed on taxpayer as seller of goods
- Real estate tax and personal property tax on business assets
- Licenses and regulatory fees, if paid every year
- Matching Social Security taxes (employer's share)
- Matching unemployment taxes (employer's share)
- Federal highway use tax
- Contributions to state unemployment insurance fund or disability benefit fund, if considered taxes under state law

The following items are *not* deductible on line 23:

- Federal income tax
- Self-employment tax
- Estate or gift taxes
- Taxes on home or personal use property
- Sales tax on purchase of business assets (add to basis and depreciate)
- Sales tax collected by taxpayer and paid over to state and local government (although any amounts allowed to be retained must be reported as income on Line 6)
- Taxes assessed to pay for improvements–paving and so on (reported on Form 4562)
- Employees' share of Social Security and Medicare tax, as well as federal income tax withheld from employees' wages (reported as part of gross wages on line 26)
- Taxes and license fees unrelated to business

 Caution. Many taxpayers list net wages here and also incorrectly report Social Security taxes under taxes. Withholdings are often omitted. Taxpayers and practitioners must carefully review. Be sure to reconcile payroll tax returns to numbers shown on Schedule C.

Line 24, Travel, Meals, and Entertainment

Lodging and transportation costs for overnight travel on business are reported on line 24a. The cost of travel for the taxpayer's spouse, dependent, or any other individual is not an allowable deduction unless the travel is for a bona fide business purpose, the person is an employee of the taxpayer, and the travel cost would have been deductible if the individual had paid for it himself or herself.

Expenses for foreign travel are not deductible unless directly related to the taxpayer's trade or business.

On line 24b, enter the cost of business meals and entertainment. In lieu of actual cost, the taxpayer may use the standard meal allowance.

Planning Tip. Be aware that records documenting the time, place, and purposes of the business meal or meals while traveling must still be kept, even if standard allowances are used.

A per diem that includes both meals and incidental expenses (M&IE) may be used. There is also a per diem that includes lodging–but that allowance may not be used by self-employed individuals. Actual facility receipts must support the lodging deduction.

The per diem rates can be found in Tab 6. IRS Publication 463 shows how to calculate the standard meal allowance. In order to be deductible, the business meals must be directly related to or associated with the active conduct of the trade or business, not lavish or extravagant, and they must be incurred while either the owner or an employee is present.

The following items are deductible without regard to whether they are directly related to or associated with the active conduct of the business (IRC §274(e)):

- Food and drink furnished on the employer's business premises primarily for employees (e.g., costs of a holiday office party).
- Recreational or social activities, including facilities primarily for employees (e.g., a summer golf outing, a company health club or an annual picnic).
- Entertainment and meal expenses for an employee if the employee reports their value as taxable compensation (e.g., a company-provided vacation for the top salesperson).
- Entertainment and meal expenses at business meetings of employees, stockholders, and directors (e.g., refreshments at a directors' meeting).
- Costs of items made available to the general public (e.g., soft drinks at a grand opening, free ham to the first 50 customers).
- Costs of entertainment and meals sold to customers (e.g., costs of food sold at an event).
- Reimbursed expenses if the employer does not include the reimbursements as compensation.
- Expenses directly related to and necessary for attendance at a business meeting of any tax-exempt group, such as a chamber of commerce, real estate board, or board of trade.

- Expenses incurred for goods, services, and facilities provided to nonemployees.

Generally, only 50% of the cost of business meals and entertainment is deductible,

Exceptions to the 50% Limitation. There are a number of situations involving meal and entertainment expenses when the 50% disallowance rule does not apply.

Reimbursement of expenses. The limitation does not apply to the extent the expense is reimbursed under an accountable plan. Instead, the limitation is imposed on the party making the reimbursement.

Excludable fringe benefits. The 50% limitation does not apply to fringe benefits that can be excluded, such as:

- De minimis fringe benefits (e.g., holiday turkeys, hams, and fruitcakes) given to employees
- Subsidized employee cafeterias
- Meals provided on the employer's premises for the convenience of the employer (e.g., for restaurant employees)

Self-employed. Taxpayers who are self-employed are not subject to the 50% limit if all of the following apply:

- The expenses are incurred as an independent contractor.
- The taxpayer's customer or client reimburses him or her for meal and entertainment expenses incurred in connection with services performed.
- The taxpayer provides adequate records of the expenses to the customer or client.

Promotional Activities. The limitation does not apply if the taxpayer provides meals and entertainment as a means of advertising (i.e., promoting goodwill in the community).

Recreational expenses for employees. The limitation does not apply to expenses for recreational, social, or similar activities (including facilities for such activities) incurred primarily for the benefit of employees (other than highly compensated employees).

Sales of meals or entertainment. The limitation does not apply if the taxpayer actually sells the meals or entertainment to the general public.

Charitable sporting events. The costs of tickets to a sporting event are generally not subject to the reduction rule if the event is for charity.

Department of Transportation workers. For workers subject to the Department of Transportation hours of service limitations, the deduction for 2013 is 80% of the total meal cost. This includes air transportation workers subject to Federal Aviation Administration regulations, as well as truck drivers, railroad workers, and others.

Line 25, Utilities

Direct utility costs for the business are deducted on line 25. Utilities costs for the business portion of the taxpayer's personal residence are reported on Form 8829.

If the taxpayer's home phone is used for business, the base rate of the first phone line into the residence is not deductible. The cost of a second line into the home is deductible to the extent of business use, including the base charges.

Line 26, Wages

Report on line 26 the gross wages paid to employees, reduced by employment credits and wages deducted under the calculation of the cost of goods sold. This is the net of the reportable wages, plus the employee's share of Social Security and Medicare withheld, the federal income tax withheld, and the state income tax withheld.

Reconcile the amount on line 26 to the Forms W-2 and W-3 filed for the business. For a cash-basis taxpayer, the gross wages are deductible when the net wages are paid to the employee. The employer's match for Social Security and Medicare is deductible when the government deposit is made.

 Filing Tip. Match reported wages—Forms 941 and W-2—with taxpayer's summarized wages. Do not include non–W-2 compensation with W-2 wages.

Line 27, Other Expenses

Deductible expenses not elsewhere identified on Schedule C are listed in Part V, with the total carried forward to line 27. This includes such items as bad debts, bank service charges, dues and subscriptions, trash removal, and others. It also includes the amortization of start-up costs.

Charitable contributions are not normally deductible on Schedule C; rather, they are claimed by the taxpayer on Schedule A. There are possible exceptions, however, that convert an otherwise charitable contribution to a business expense. A common situation is a contribution to a charity for which in return the business is listed or featured in a program brochure or advertised or promoted in some other way.

Lines 28 and 29, Calculations

Total expenses before including business use of home, the sum of lines 8 through 27a, are reported on line 28. This amount is then subtracted from line 7 to determine tentative profit or loss, which is reported on line 29.

Line 30, Expenses for Business Use of Home

Attach Form 8829 unless using the simplified method. Simplified method filers enter the square footage of the home and the part of the home used for business. The Simplified Method Worksheet is used to figure the amount to enter on line 30.

In order to qualify for the deduction, the taxpayer must meet two tests.

The business part of the home must be used in all of the following ways:

- *Exclusively.* A room or portion of a room in the home must be used only for the trade or business. It should be separately identifiable, but does not have to have a permanent partition.
- *Regularly.* The space must be used consistently and regularly for the business. Occasional or incidental use is not regular use.
- *For the trade or business.* If the space is used for a profit-seeking activity that is not a trade or business, the deduction is not allowable.

The business part of the home must be one of the following:

- The principal place of business. The space must be used exclusively and regularly for administrative or management activities of the trade or business and there must be no other fixed location where substantial administrative or management activities of the trade or business are conducted.
- A place used to meet or deal with patients, clients, or customers in the normal course of the trade or business.
- A separate structure, not attached to the home, and used for the trade or business.

 Planning Tip. Maintaining a guest book for all business visitors in which clients or customers sign in and out will support the deduction.

The business percentage of the home is calculated on Form 8829. The area of the home used for business is divided by the total area. The resulting percentage is the percentage applied to indirect expenses.

Expenses that can be included in calculating the business cost of the home include casualty losses, mortgage interest, real estate taxes, insurance, repairs and maintenance, utilities, and other operating expenses, including a security system.

Form 8829 has two columns so that expenses can be listed as direct or indirect in each category. Direct expenses

are those that benefit only the business portion of the home. Examples would be painting only the business area or putting in special security for that room only.

Indirect expenses are those that involve both the business and personal portions of the home. The full amount is entered in column b, with the business percentage from line 7 then applied to that amount.

Day care. A part of the home used for day care may be deducted, along with an appropriate percentage for day care expenses, even if the area is not used exclusively for business. The percentage calculation for day care takes into consideration the hours that day care is provided, rather than the square footage.

Line 31, Net Profit or (Loss)

Net profit or loss is entered on Form 1040, line 12 (or Form 1040NR, line 13), to become a part of the AGI calculation. The profit or loss is also entered on Schedule SE in order to calculate self-employment tax. If there is a loss, it is entered on line 32 of Schedule C.

Hobby Loss. The gain or loss generated by the business is effectively netted against other income on the first page of Form 1040. However, IRC §183 says that a loss that is generated by an activity not engaged in for profit may not be deducted against other income. A safe harbor provides that the IRS will not question the profit motive if a business generates a profit in three out of five consecutive years ending with the current tax year. The safe harbor is two out of seven consecutive years for horse breeding, showing and training.

 Planning Tip. What a lot of people think is the sole test is just a safe harbor; clients may therefore be overly timid about declaring hobby losses.

Failing to meet the safe harbor provision does not mean an automatic disallowance—only that the IRS may look into the situation and could disallow the loss. The IRS applies a facts and circumstances test to make a determination. Although the following list is not exhaustive, taken as a whole it does help gauge the existence of a profit motive:

1. Does the time and effort put into the activity indicate an intention to make a profit?
2. Does the taxpayer depend upon income from the activity?
3. If there are losses, are they due to circumstances beyond the taxpayer's control or did they occur in the start-up phase of the business?
4. Has the taxpayer changed methods of operation to improve profitability?

5. Does the taxpayer or his/her advisors have the knowledge needed to carry on the activity as a successful business?
6. Has the taxpayer made a profit in similar activities in the past?
7. Does the activity make a profit in some years?
8. Can the taxpayer expect to make a profit in the future from the appreciation of assets used in the activity? (IRS Fact Sheet, FS-2008-23).

 Planning Tip. Any client claiming consistent losses on a business should have, at the very least, a business plan that he or she can show to the IRS if necessary.

Line 32, Is Investment at Risk?

If the business generates a loss and all investments are at risk, check box 32a. If some of the investment is not at risk, check box 32b. If box 32a is checked, the loss is entered on both Form 1040, line 12 (or Form 1040NR, line 13) and on Scheduled SE, line 2. If box 32b is checked, Form 6198, *At-Risk Limitations*, must be attached.

Some possible non-at-risk items are the following:

- Nonrecourse loans used in the business, to acquire the business or to finance aspects of the business, but not secured by the taxpayer's own property (but there is an exception for some nonrecourse financing borrowed in connection with holding real property).
- The existence of a stop-loss agreement, guarantee, or other arrangement (other than insurance) that protects cash, property, or borrowed amounts used in the business.
- Amounts borrowed for business use from an individual who has an interest in the business, other than as a creditor.

Any loss that is disallowed under the at-risk rules on the 2013 return will be available to use as a deduction in the business for 2014. See Tab 5 for a discussion of the at-risk rules.

Part III: Cost of Goods Sold

If the production, purchase, or sale of merchandise is an income-producing factor for the business, inventories must be taken into account at the beginning and end of the tax year.

A taxpayer whose average annual gross receipts for the three previous years are $1 million or less, and whose business is not a tax shelter, may account for inventories in the same manner as materials and supplies that are not incidental. If the taxpayer has been in existence for less than three years, average annual gross receipts are determined by the number of years that the taxpayer has been in existence. So may a qualifying small business taxpayer whose average annual gross receipts for the three prior tax years are more than a $1 million but not more than $10 million, whose business is not a tax shelter, and whose principal business activity in not an ineligible activity per Rev. Proc. 2002-28.

Line 33, Inventory Method

The inventories may be valued at cost, the lower of cost or market, or any other method approved by the IRS. Indicate the method(s) used to value inventory.

 Caution. Note that taxpayers using the cash method of accounting are required to use cost.

Line 34, Changes in Inventory Method

An explanation must be attached if there was a change in determining quantities, costs, or valuations between the opening and closing inventory.

Line 35, Inventory at Beginning of Year

Enter the inventory at the beginning of the year and attach an explanation if the 2013 opening inventory differs from the 2012 closing inventory.

Line 36, Purchases Less Cost of Items Withdrawn for Personal Use

Enter the amount paid for purchasing items of inventory, less the cost of items used personally by the taxpayer.

 Filing Tip. Some inventory items, such as cosmetics, readily lend themselves to personal use by the taxpayer or as gifts. Take special note if this might be the case and verify inventory records.

Line 37, Cost of Labor

Be certain that amounts entered as labor here are not duplicated on line 26, Wages. Do not include any amount paid to the sole proprietor. If $600 or more was paid to one noncorporate entity, the 1099-MISC must be attached to the return.

Line 38, Materials and Supplies

Enter on line 38 the cost of materials and supplies used to produce or support inventory items.

Line 39, Other Costs

Enter other costs attributable directly to inventory or to the cost of goods sold on line 39. Warehousing costs or fees are included here.

Line 40, Calculation

The sum of lines 35 through 39 (costs related to inventory) is reported on line 40.

Line 41, Inventory at End of Year

The value of the inventory at year's end, preferably the result of a physical inventory, should be entered on line 41.

 Caution. Make sure you know whether the client is giving you retail or wholesale inventory numbers. Discourage anything but cost basis.

Table of Common Activity Codes

These codes for the Principal Business or Professional Activity classify sole proprietorships by the type of activity they are engaged in to facilitate the administration of the Internal Revenue Code. These six-digit codes are based on the North American Industry Classification System (NAICS).

Note. The following table is taken from the 2012 Instructions for Schedule C. The NAICS codes have been updated for 2013, but the IRS has not yet released the 2013 Schedule C or its instructions, which will contain the updated, categorized version of this table. The 2012 six-digit codes are available for download as a spreadsheet, without categorization, from the Census Bureau website at www.census.gov cgi-bin/sssd/naics/naicsrch?chart=2013.

Select the category that best describes your primary business activity (for example, Real Estate). Then select the activity that best identifies the principal source of your sales or receipts (for example, 531210, the code for offices of real estate agents and brokers) and **enter the six-digit code assigned to the activity on line B of Schedule C or C-EZ.**

Note. If your principal source of income is from farming activities, you should file **Schedule F**, *Profit or Loss From Farming*.

Accommodation, Food Services, & Drinking Places

Accommodation

721310 Rooming & boarding houses
721210 RV (recreational vehicle) parks & recreational camps
721100 Travel accommodation (including hotels, motels, & bed & breakfast inns)

Food Services and Drinking Places

722514 Cafeterias & buffets
722410 Drinking places (alcoholic beverages)
722110 Full-Service restaurants
722210 Limited-service eating places
722210 Snack and non-alcoholic beverage bars
722300 Special food services (including food service contractors & caterers)

Administrative & Support and Waste Management & Remediation Services

Administrative & Support Services

561430 Business service centers (including private mail centers & copy shops)

561740 Carpet & upholstery cleaning services
561440 Collection agencies
561450 Credit bureaus
561410 Document preparation services
561300 Employment services
561710 Exterminating & pest control services
561210 Facilities support (management) services
561600 Investigation & security services
561720 Janitorial services
561730 Landscaping services
561110 Office administrative services
561420 Telephone call centers (including telephone answering services & telemarketing bureaus)
561500 Travel arrangement & reservation services
561490 Other business support services (including repossession services, court reporting, & stenotype services)
561790 Other services to buildings & dwellings

561900 Other support services (including packaging & labeling services, & convention & trade show organizers)

Waste Management & Remediation Services

562000 Waste management & remediation services

Agriculture, Forestry, Hunting, & Fishing

112900 Animal production (including breeding of cats and dogs)
114110 Fishing
113000 Forestry & logging (including forest nurseries & timber tracts)
114210 Hunting & trapping

Support Activities for Agriculture & Forestry

115210 Support activities for animal production (including farriers)
115110 Support activities for crop production (including cotton ginning, soil preparation, planting, & cultivating)

115310 Support activities for forestry

Arts, Entertainment, & Recreation Amusement, Gambling, & Recreation Industries

713100 Amusement parks & arcades
713200 Gambling industries
713900 Other amusement & recreation services (including golf courses, skiing facilities, marinas, fitness centers, bowling centers, skating rinks, miniature golf courses)

Museums, Historical Sites, & Similar Institutions

712100 Museums, historical sites, & similar institutions

Performing Arts, Spectator Sports, & Related Industries

711410 Agents & managers for artists, athletes, entertainers, & other public figures
711510 Independent artists, writers, & performers
711100 Performing arts companies

711300 Promoters of performing arts, sports, & similar events

711210 Spectator sports (including professional sports clubs & racetrack operations)

Construction of Buildings

236200 Nonresidential building construction

236100 Residential building construction

Heavy and Civil Engineering Construction

237310 Highway, street, & bridge construction

237210 Land subdivision

237100 Utility system construction

237990 Other heavy & civil engineering construction

Specialty Trade Contractors

238310 Drywall & insulation contractors

238210 Electrical contractors

238350 Finish carpentry contractors

238330 Flooring contractors

238130 Framing carpentry contractors

238150 Glass & glazing contractors

238140 Masonry contractors

238320 Painting & wall covering contractors

238220 Plumbing, heating & air-conditioning contractors

238110 Poured concrete foundation & structure contractors

238160 Roofing contractors

238170 Siding contractors

238910 Site preparation contractors

238120 Structural steel & precast concrete construction contractors

238340 Tile & terrazzo contractors

238290 Other building equipment contractors

238390 Other building finishing contractors

238190 Other foundation, structure, & building exterior contractors

238990 All other specialty trade contractors

Educational Services

611000 Educational services (including schools, colleges, & universities)

Finance & Insurance

Credit Intermediation & Related Activities

522100 Depository credit intermediation (including commercial banking, savings institutions, & credit unions)

522200 Nondepository credit intermediation (including sales financing & consumer lending)

522300 Activities related to credit intermediation (including loan brokers)

Insurance Agents, Brokers, & Related Activities

524210 Insurance agencies & brokerages

524290 Other insurance related activities

Securities, Commodity Contracts, & Other Financial Investments & Related Activities

523140 Commodity contracts brokers

523130 Commodity contracts dealers

523110 Investment bankers & securities dealers

523210 Securities & commodity exchanges

523120 Securities brokers

523900 Other financial investment activities (including investment advice)

Health Care & Social Assistance

Ambulatory Health Care Services

621610 Home health care services

621510 Medical & diagnostic laboratories

621310 Offices of chiropractors

621210 Offices of dentists

621330 Offices of mental health practitioners (except physicians)

621320 Offices of optometrists

621340 Offices of physical, occupational & speech therapists, & audiologists

621111 Offices of physicians (except mental health specialists)

621112 Offices of physicians, mental health specialists

621391 Offices of podiatrists

621399 Offices of all other miscellaneous health practitioners

621400 Outpatient care centers

621900 Other ambulatory health care services (including ambulance services, blood, & organ banks)

Hospitals

622000 Hospitals

Nursing & Residential Care Facilities

623000 Nursing & residential care facilities

Social Assistance

624410 Child day care services

624200 Community food & housing, & emergency & other relief services

624100 Individual & family services

624310 Vocational rehabilitation services

Information

511000 Publishing industries (except Internet)

Broadcasting (except Internet) & Telecommunications

515000 Broadcasting (except Internet)

517000 Telecommunications

Internet Publishing & Broadcasting

516110 Internet publishing & broadcasting

Data Processing Services

518210 Data processing, hosting, & related services

519100 Other information services (including news syndicates & libraries, Internet publishing & broadcasting)

Motion Picture & Sound Recording

512100 Motion picture & video industries (except video rental)

512200 Sound recording industries

Manufacturing

315000 Apparel mfg.

312000 Beverage & tobacco product mfg.

334000 Computer & electronic product mfg.

335000 Electrical equipment, appliance, & component mfg.

332000 Fabricated metal product mfg.

337000 Furniture & related product mfg.

333000 Machinery mfg.

339110 Medical equipment & supplies mfg.

322000 Paper mfg.

324100 Petroleum & coal products mfg.

326000 Plastics & rubber products mfg.

331000 Primary metal mfg.

323100 Printing & related support activities

313000 Textile mills

314000 Textile product mills

336000 Transportation equipment mfg.

321000 Wood product mfg.

339900 Other miscellaneous mfg.

Chemical Manufacturing

325100 Basic chemical mfg.

325500 Paint, coating, & adhesive mfg.

325300 Pesticide, fertilizer, & other agricultural chemical mfg.
325410 Pharmaceutical & medicine mfg.
325200 Resin, synthetic rubber, & artificial & synthetic fibers & filaments mfg.
325600 Soap, cleaning compound, & toilet preparation mfg.
325900 Other chemical product & preparation mfg.

Food Manufacturing

311110 Animal food mfg.
311800 Bakeries, tortilla, & dry pasta mfg.
311500 Dairy product mfg.
311400 Fruit & vegetable preserving & speciality food mfg.
311200 Grain & oilseed milling
311610 Animal slaughtering & processing
311710 Seafood product preparation & packaging
311300 Sugar & confectionery product mfg.
311900 Other food mfg. (including coffee, tea, flavorings, & seasonings)

Leather & Allied Product Manufacturing

316210 Footwear mfg. (including leather, rubber, & plastics)
316110 Leather & hide tanning & finishing
316990 Other leather & allied product mfg.

Nonmetallic Mineral Product Manufacturing

327300 Cement & concrete product mfg.
327100 Clay product & refractory mfg.
327210 Glass & glass product mfg.
327400 Lime & gypsum product mfg.
327900 Other nonmetallic mineral product mfg.

Mining

212110 Coal mining
212200 Metal ore mining
212300 Nonmetallic mineral mining & quarrying
211110 Oil & gas extraction
213110 Support activities for mining

Other Services

Personal & Laundry Services

812111 Barber shops
812112 Beauty salons
812220 Cemeteries & crematories
812310 Coin-operated laundries & drycleaners
812320 Drycleaning & laundry services (except coin-operated) (including laundry & drycleaning dropoff & pickup sites)
812210 Funeral homes & funeral services
812330 Linen & uniform supply
812113 Nail salons
812930 Parking lots & garages
812910 Pet care (except veterinary) services
812920 Photofinishing
812190 Other personal care services (including diet & weight reducing centers)
812990 All other personal services

Repair & Maintenance

811120 Automotive body, paint, interior, & glass repair
811110 Automotive mechanical & electrical repair & maintenance
811190 Other automotive repair & maintenance (including oil change & lubrication shops & car washes)
811310 Commercial & industrial machinery & equipment (except automotive & electronic) repair & maintenance

811210 Electronic & precision equipment repair & maintenance
811430 Footwear & leather goods repair
811410 Home & garden equipment & appliance repair & maintenance
811420 Reupholstery & furniture repair
811490 Other personal & household goods repair & maintenance

Professional, Scientific, & Technical Services

541100 Legal services
541211 Offices of certified public accountants
541214 Payroll services
541213 Tax preparation services
541219 Other accounting services

Architectural, Engineering, & Related Services

541310 Architectural services
541350 Building inspection services
541340 Drafting services
541330 Engineering services
541360 Geophysical surveying & mapping services
541320 Landscape architecture services
541370 Surveying & mapping (except geophysical) services
541380 Testing laboratories

Computer Systems Design & Related Services

541510 Computer systems design & related services

Specialized Design Services

541400 Specialized design services (including interior, industrial, graphic, & fashion design)

Other Professional, Scientific, & Technical Services

541800 Advertising & related services
541600 Management, scientific, & technical consulting services
541910 Market research & public opinion polling

541920 Photographic services
541700 Scientific research & development services
541930 Translation & interpretation services
541940 Veterinary services
541990 All other professional, scientific, & technical services

Real Estate & Rental & Leasing

Real Estate

531100 Lessors of real estate (including miniwarehouses & self-storage units)
531210 Offices of real estate agents & brokers
531320 Offices of real estate appraisers
531310 Real estate property managers
531390 Other activities related to real estate

Rental & Leasing Services

532100 Automotive equipment rental & leasing
532400 Commercial & industrial machinery & equipment rental & leasing
532210 Consumer electronics & appliances rental
532220 Formal wear & costume rental
532310 General rental centers
532230 Video tape & disc rental
532290 Other consumer goods rental

Religious, Grantmaking, Civic, Professional, & Similar Organizations

813000 Religious, grantmaking, civic, professional, & similar organizations

Retail Trade

Building Material & Garden Equipment & Supplies Dealers

444130 Hardware stores
444110 Home centers

444200	Lawn & garden equipment & supplies stores
444120	Paint & wallpaper stores
444190	Other building materials dealers

Clothing & Accessories Stores

448130	Children's & infants' clothing stores
448150	Clothing accessories stores
448140	Family clothing stores
448310	Jewelry stores
448320	Luggage & leather goods stores
448110	Men's clothing stores
448210	Shoe stores
448120	Women's clothing stores
448190	Other clothing stores

Electronic & Appliance Stores

| 443142 | Electronics stores (including audio, video, computer, & camera stores) |
| 443141 | Household appliance stores |

Food & Beverage Stores

445310	Beer, wine, & liquor stores
445220	Fish & seafood markets
445230	Fruit & vegetable markets
445100	Grocery stores (including supermarkets & convenience stores without gas)
445210	Meat markets
445290	Other specialty food stores

Furniture & Home Furnishing Stores

| 442110 | Furniture stores |
| 442200 | Home furnishings stores |

Gasoline Stations

| 447100 | Gasoline stations (including convenience stores with gas) |

General Merchandise Stores

| 452000 | General merchandise stores |

Health & Personal Care Stores

446120	Cosmetics, beauty supplies, & perfume stores
446130	Optical goods stores
446110	Pharmacies & drug stores
446190	Other health & personal care stores

Motor Vehicle & Parts Dealers

441300	Automotive parts, accessories, & tire stores
441222	Boat dealers
441228	Motorcycle, ATV, & all other motor vehicle dealers
441110	New car dealers
441210	Recreational vehicle dealers (including motor home & travel trailer dealers)
441120	Used car dealers

Sporting Goods, Hobby, Book, & Music Stores

451211	Book stores
451120	Hobby, toy, & game stores
451140	Musical instrument & supplies stores
451212	News dealers & newsstands
451130	Sewing, needlework, & piece goods stores
451110	Sporting goods stores

Miscellaneous Store Retailers

453920	Art dealers
453110	Florists
453220	Gift, novelty, & souvenir stores
453930	Manufactured (mobile) home dealers
453210	Office supplies & stationery stores
453910	Pet & pet supplies stores
453310	Used merchandise stores

| 453990 | All other miscellaneous store retailers (including tobacco, candle, & trophy shops) |

Nonstore Retailers

454112	Electronic auctions
454111	Electronic shopping
454310	Fuel dealers (including heating oil & liquified petroleum)
454113	Mail-order houses
454210	Vending machine operators
454390	Other direct selling establishments (including door-to-door retailing, frozen food plan providers, party plan merchandisers, & coffee-break service providers)

Transportation & Warehousing

481000	Air transportation
485510	Charter bus industry
484110	General freight trucking, local
484120	General freight trucking, long distance
485210	Interurban & rural bus transportation
486000	Pipeline transportation
482110	Rail transportation
487000	Scenic & sightseeing transportation
485410	School & employee bus transportation
484200	Specialized freight trucking (including household moving vans)
485300	Taxi & limousine service
485110	Urban transit systems
483000	Water transportation
485990	Other transit & ground passenger transportation
488000	Support activities for transportation (including motor vehicle towing)

Couriers & Messengers

| 492000 | Couriers & messengers |

Warehousing & Storage Facilities

| 493100 | Warehousing & storage (except leases of miniwarehouses & self-storage units) |

Utilities

| 221000 | Utilities |

Wholesale Trade

Merchant Wholesalers, Durable Goods

423200	Furniture & home furnishing
423700	Hardware, & plumbing & heating equipment & supplies
423600	Household appliances & electrical & electronic goods
423940	Jewelry, watch, precious stone, & precious metals
423300	Lumber & other construction materials
423800	Machinery, equipment, & supplies
423500	Metal & mineral (except petroleum)
423100	Motor vehicle & motor vehicle parts & supplies
423400	Professional & commercial equipment & supplies
423930	Recyclable materials
423910	Sporting & recreational goods & supplies
423920	Toy & hobby goods & supplies
423990	Other miscellaneous durable goods

Merchant Wholesalers, Nondurable Goods

424300	Apparel, piece goods, & notions
424800	Beer, wine, & distilled alcoholic beverage
424920	Books, periodicals, & newspapers
424600	Chemical & allied products
424210	Drugs & druggists' sundries
424500	Farm product raw materials
424910	Farm supplies

424930 Flower, nursery stock, & florists' supplies	424100 Paper & paper products	424990 Other miscellaneous nondurable goods	425120 Wholesale trade agents & brokers
424400 Grocery & related products	424700 Petroleum & petroleum products	**Wholesale Electronic Markets and Agents & Brokers**	999999 Unclassified establishments (unable to classify)
424950 Paint, varnish, & supplies	424940 Tobacco & tobacco products	425110 Business to business electronic markets	

Schedule F
Line-by-Line Instructions

Schedule F is filed to report income and related expenses from the sale of livestock and other items bought for resale; the sale of livestock, produce, and other items raised; distributions from cooperatives; government farm program payments; and other income generated by the active conduct of production agriculture.

Schedule F may also be used to report the farm income for a trust or partnership.

Gray Area. When is a farmer not a farmer? A farmer is one who is engaged primarily in the business of farming. A taxpayer was not considered a farmer, due to his wife's separate income, because less than two-thirds of the aggregate gross income on the couple's joint return was from farming. Where only one spouse has substantial nonfarm income, the two-thirds farm income rule can be avoided by filing separate returns.

Farming and Self-Employment Tax

The net profit (earnings) on Schedule F is subject to self-employment (SE) tax. Farmers who have a loss can use the "farm optional method SE tax." This method allows individuals to continue paying SE tax for their Social Security coverage when their net profit for the year is small or they have a loss.

To qualify to use the "farm optional method SE tax" for 2013, gross income from farming must be $6,960 or less, or net farm profits must be less than $5,024. The amount that may be considered net earnings from farm self-employment income, and be taxed for SE purposes, is the smaller of $4,640 and two-thirds of gross farm income (not less than zero). Net earnings from self-employment of $4,640 is equivalent to net non-farm income of $5,024 (before the Code Sec.

1402(a)(12) deduction for one-half the sum of the self-employment OASDI and Medicare tax rates).

Farm Income Averaging

Farm income averaging was designed to allow farmers to "average" their income from a high-income year back over the last three years. Schedule J of Form 1040 is used to calculate 2013 tax by averaging, over the base years (the three previous years), all or part of a taxpayer's income from the trade or business of farming.

Farm income averaging may be used by an individual engaged in a farming business, a partner in a farm partnership, or a shareholder in an S corporation that is engaged in farming. Corporations, partnerships, S corporations, estates, and trusts cannot use farm income averaging.

Farm income, gains, losses, and deductions reported on the following forms are generally eligible for averaging:

- Form 1040, line 7–to the extent of wages and other compensation received as a shareholder in an S corporation engaged in a farming business
- Schedule D
- Schedule E, Part II
- Schedule F
- Form 4797
- Form 4835

Note two recent developments:

- Negative income in a base year now counts as negative income, rather than just zero.
- In calculating AMT, the regular tax before income averaging is compared to the tentative minimum tax.

Information About Farm Business

Name of Proprietor and SSN

The name of the proprietor goes on the first line of Schedule F, followed by the Social Security number at the end of that line (see line D). When Schedule F is used as a part of a Form 1041, 1065, or 1065B, use Employer ID Number, rather than a Social Security number.

Lines A and B, Principal Product and Code

Enter the principal crop or activity for 2013 on line A. On line B, enter one of the 14 principal agricultural codes. Select the code from the table below that best describes the largest source of income from Part IV of Schedule F.

Agricultural Principal Product Codes	
Agricultural, Forestry, Hunting & Fishing Agricultural	
112900	Animal production (including breeding of dogs and cats)
114110	Fishing
113000	Forestry and logging (including forest nurseries and timber tracts)
114210	Hunting and trapping
112300	Poultry and egg production
112400	Sheep and goat farming
112510	Animal aquaculture
112900	Other animal production
Support Activities for Agriculture & Forestry Agricultural	
115210	Support activities for animal production (including farriers)
115110	Support activities for crop production (including cotton ginning, soil preparation, planting and cultivating)
115310	Support activities for forestry

Line C, Accounting Method

Schedule F gives the taxpayer a choice of cash or accrual basis.

With the cash method, income is reported in the year it is actually or constructively received. Expenses are reported in the year they are paid, unless the expenditure creates an asset that has a useful life beyond the current year. In that case, the items may be only partially deductible in the current year. One example is the purchase of a tractor. It must be set up for depreciation. Another example is payment for liability insurance that includes the current year and the following two years. Only the portion applying to the current year is deductible on that year's return. A cash-basis taxpayer marks the "Cash" box and completes Parts I and II of Schedule F.

Caution. Is that farm implement a depreciable asset or a leased piece of equipment? Read the contract and also follow the payment and trade-in documentation.

Under the accrual method of accounting, income is reported in the year earned, while expenses are deducted in the year incurred. Accrual-basis taxpayers are on a cash basis for deducting business expenses owed to a related cash-basis taxpayer. A taxpayer who keeps an inventory must generally use an accrual method of accounting to determine gross income. There is an exception for farmers who average annual gross receipts of $1 million or less.

Under the accrual method of accounting, expenses are generally deducted or capitalized when the *all-events* test has been met and economic performance has occurred. The all-events test is met when all events have occurred that fix the fact of liability and the liability can be determined with reasonable accuracy.

An accrual basis farmer marks the "Accrual" box and completes Parts II and III and then Part I, line 9, of Schedule F.

Line D, EIN

Enter an employer identification number only if the business has a qualified retirement plan or is required to file an employment, excise, estate, trust, partnership, or alcohol, tobacco, and firearms tax return. If you do not have an EIN, leave Line D blank.

Line E, Material Participation

See the discussion of material participation under Schedule C, page 3-8.

Lines F and G, 1099s

On Line F, if you made any payment in 2013 that would require you to file any Forms 1099, check the "Yes" box. Otherwise, check "No." On Line G, indicate by checking the appropriate box if you filed all required Forms 1099 in 2013.

Part I: Farm Income—Cash Method

For items 1 through 8 of this section, include both cash actually or constructively received and the FMV of goods or other property received for these items. When an amount is credited to the taxpayer's account, or is set aside for his or her benefit, it is considered constructively received.

There is an exception for farm production flexibility contract payments received under the Federal Agriculture Improvement and Reform Act of 1996. They must be reported as income only in the year of actual receipt.

Do not include sales of livestock held for draft, breeding, sport, or dairy purposes on Schedule F. The sale or disposition of these animals is reported on Form 4797.

There is a special provision for livestock sold due to drought, flood, or other weather-related conditions. A Schedule F filer may elect to report the income from the sale in the year after the sale if all of these conditions are met:

- The taxpayer's main business is farming.
- Schedule F is filed on a cash basis.
- The excess animals would not have been sold under the taxpayer's normal business practices, but were instead sold solely because of the weather-related condition.
- The weather-related condition caused the area to be designated as eligible for federal assistance.

Lines 1a, 1b and 1c, Sales of Livestock and Other Resale Items

Enter on line 1a specified sales of livestock and other resale items (see instructions). Enter on line 1b the cost or other basis of livestock or other items reported on line 1a. Substract line 1b from line 1a and enter on line 1c.

Line 2, Sales of Livestock, Product, Grains and Other Products You Raised

Enter on line 2 the sales of livestock, produce, grains and other products that were raised.

Lines 3a and 3b, Cooperative Distributions [Form(s) 1099-PATR, *Taxable Distributions Received From Cooperatives*]

Patronage dividends reported by cooperatives are reported to the taxpayer on a Form 1099-PATR.

 Filing Tip. Cooperative distributions are often made in a combination of cash (check) and stock in the co-op. Both must be reported. Taxpayers often forget to report the stock portion, since it was quite likely not recorded in the record book.

Two spaces are provided on line 3 for patronage refunds (dividends). The entire amount reported to the taxpayer (received by the taxpayer) is reported on line 3a, the taxable portion is reported on line 3b. Only the amount that was generated by farming activity or purchases is reported on line 3b. Income generated from buying personal or family items or personal assets is included on line 3a, but not on line 3b.

Lines 4a and 4b, Agricultural Program Payments

Government farm program payments are reported to recipients on Form 1099-G, *Certain Government Payments,* or CCC-1099-G. The payments reported may be from price support payments, market gain on CCC loans, diversion payments, cost-share payments, conservation reserve payments, payments in the form of materials or services, and other farm program payments.

There are two spaces on line 4. Line 4a is for reporting the total amount received and line 4b is for reporting the taxable amount.

Example. Marvin Phillips elected to report CCC loan proceeds as income in 2012, the year he received it. There is no gain from redemption of the commodity in 2013 because the CCC loan proceeds have previously been reported as income. Marvin is treated as having repurchased the commodity for the amount of the loan repayment. The transaction is thus shown on line 4a.

If Marvin had not reported the CCC loan proceeds under the election in 2012, then he would have to report the market gain on line 4b.

Lines 5a, 5b, and 5c, Commodity Credit Corporation (CCC) Loans

Schedule F has three spaces for reporting CCC loans. Line 5a is for CCC loans taken out in 2013 which the taxpayer is electing to report as income. CCC loans forfeited are reported in full on line 5b, whether or not an election was made and the original loan was reported as income. The taxable amount of the loans forfeited is reported on line 5c; if the taxpayer did not elect to report the loan proceeds as income when the loan was taken out, then the loan is reported as income here.

Farming losses of a taxpayer other than a C corporation are limited if the taxpayer receives an applicable subsidy during the year. Any loss disallowed under this rule is carried forward as a deduction attributable to farming businesses in the next tax year.

Normally, there will not be an entry on line 5c if the loan proceeds were reported as income under the election. However, even if the election was made, if the amount forfeited is different from the basis in the commodity, there may be an entry on line 5c.

Lines 6a, 6b, 6c, and 6d, Crop Insurance Proceeds and Certain Disaster Payments

There are four spaces for reporting crop insurance proceeds. The total of all crop insurance payments (and certain disaster payments) received during 2013, even if they are to be included on the 2014 return, is entered on line 6a. The taxable amount is reported on 6b, but not including the amount that is intended to be included in income in 2014. Line 6c is checked to make an election to defer until 2014.

 Caution. Dating of contracts, CCC loans, and leases must be tied to actual service times and not as shell dates for contingency arrangements for income recognition or placed in service scheduling.

Line 6b may be "0" if, on line 6c, the taxpayer elects to defer insurance proceeds received in the current year to the following year.

Line 6d is for reporting the amount deferred from the prior year and is fully taxable.

Note that the Form 1099 received from the insurance company may well show more than the total of the checks received. This may happen because many companies net the amount of the insurance claim against the deferred premium. When crop insurance proceeds are reported, check to reconcile the amount received with the Form 1099. The remittance advice received with the check should detail the deduction for the premium. Enter the full 1099 amount as above and show the amount deducted as an expense on line 20 of Part II as crop insurance premiums.

Line 7, Custom Hire (Machine Work) Income

On this line, the taxpayer should report payments received from custom hire (machine work).

Line 8, Other Income

Enter other income including federal and state gasoline or the fuel tax credit or refund (see instructions).

 Caution. The use of working capital loans for payment of personal, non-business debt can change the nature of the loan from business to personal.

Line 9, Gross Income

Cash-method taxpayers add lines 1c, 2, 3b, 4b, 5a, 5c, 6b, 6d, 7 and 8. Accrual taxpayers enter the amount from Part III, line 50 (see instructions). This is the gross income from the farm business.

Part II: Farm Expenses—Cash and Accrual Method

Do not deduct the following in this section: personal or living expenses (such as taxes, insurance or home repairs costs) that do not produce income, expenses of raising anything that was used by the taxpayer or his or her family, the value of animals raised that died, inventory losses or personal losses. If the taxpayer was repaid for any part of an expense the taxpayer must subtract the amount that was repaid from the deduction.

 Filing Tip. Segregate recordkeeping for personal and farming activities to avoid subsequent confusion of source and use.

Line 10, Car and Truck Expenses
See Tab 8 for a full discussion of autos and listed property.

Taxpayers may use the standard mileage rate of 56.5 cents for business miles (24 cents for medical or moving miles; 14 cents for charitable miles) for vehicles operated in 2013 or track actual operating expenses.

The standard mileage rate covers depreciation, fuel, oil, repairs, insurance, license, tires, and so on. Only tolls, parking, and the appropriate part of interest and personal property taxes paid are additional expenses. costs include all costs.

Actual costs include all costs. A log of business use must be kept in order to determine the appropriate allocation between business and personal use.

There is a special rule (Temporary Reg. §1.274-6T(b)) under which a farmer may consider a pickup truck that is used the majority of each day for farm business as a business vehicle.

Line 11, Chemicals

The cost of chemicals is shown on line 11. Report the total amount paid on line 11. Report any reimbursements from a landlord on line 8, Part I.

Line 12, Conservation Expenses

Deductible soil and water conservation expenses include the cost of leveling, grading and terracing; contour furrowing; the construction, control and protection of diversion channels, drainage ditches, earthen dams, watercourses, outlets and ponds; the eradication of brush; and the planting of windbreaks. All these are expenses paid to prevent erosion of land used for farming. In order to be deductible, they must be consistent with a conservation plan approved by the Natural Resources Conservation Service of the U.S. Department of Agriculture.

The deduction may not exceed 25% of gross income from farming in each year (excluding gains from selling assets, such as machinery or land). Any amount that cannot be taken in the current year is carried forward and deducted in a later year.

Endangered species recovery expenditures. Endangered species recovery expenditures qualify for the deduction allowed by Code Sec. 175 for soil and water conservation expenditures and land erosion prevention expenditures. The credit is available for endangered species recovery expenditures paid or incurred after December 31, 2008.

Line 13, Custom Hire (Machine Work)

On line 13, enter the amount paid to a nonemployee to do a custom job for the taxpayer or to bring in his equipment and operate it. This includes both the cost of the machinery or implement and the cost of the operator.

 Caution. A taxpayer should not report the amount paid for rental or lease of equipment that he or she operates himself or herself on line 13. That is machine rental to be reported on line 24a.

Line 14, Depreciation and Section 179 Expense Deduction

See Tab 7 for a complete discussion of depreciation.

 Planning Tip. Land-clearing costs, costs of draining or filling wetlands, costs involved in preparing the land for center pivot irrigation systems, and other related costs are added to the basis of the land.

The expanded Section 179 expensing election has worked very well for farmers in helping to even out the ups and downs of farming.

Unicap refers to uniform capitalization rules under IRC §263A for both farmers and other businesses. There are some special unicap rules for farmers. For more discussion see MTG ¶999.

For individuals with a farming business, the unicap rules apply only for plants that have a preproductive period of more than two years. They also do not ap-

ply to the cost of replanting plants bearing a crop for human consumption that are damaged or lost due to freezing, disease, drought, pests or casualty.

For unicap, a farming business is defined as a trade or business involving the cultivation of land or the raising or harvesting of any agricultural or horticultural commodity.

 Caution. Section 263A costs for raising an animal need specialized attention.

The preproductive period for plants begins when the plant is first acquired or the seed is first planted and ends when a marketable crop is produced.

The rules for depreciating farm property may be found in IRS Publication 225, *Farmer's Tax Guide.*

Line 15, Employee Benefit Programs Other Than Pension and Profit-Sharing Plans

Here report accident and health insurance, group-term life insurance and other employee benefits not reportable elsewhere. Pension and profit-sharing plans are reported on line 23.

Do not include any contribution made on behalf of the sole proprietor or self-employed individual.

Line 16, Feed Purchased

Report the cost of feed purchased during the current year.

Prepaid feed (as well as fertilizer, lime, chemicals and other crop and livestock input items) to be used in the following year may be deducted. There are some rules that must be followed:

- This must be an actual purchase, not a deposit. Indicators of a deposit, rather than a payment, are the following:
  - The absence of specific quantity terms.
  - The right to a refund of any unapplied payment credit at the end of the contract.
  - The seller's treatment of the payment as a deposit.
  - The right to substitute other goods or products for those specified in the contract.
- The product must be delivered to the business, or if it remains with the vendor, it should be separately accounted for by the vendor. There is an exception here for feed that does allow for some substitute ingredients to vary the particular feed to the livestock's current diet requirements: neither this, nor a price adjustment to reflect market value at the date of delivery is, by itself, proof of a deposit when dealing with prepaid feed.

- There must be a business purpose for the prepayment. (Saving taxes is not a business purpose.) The purpose could be concern about a possible supply shortage or a concern about a price increase. It may even be some other preferential treatment. But there should be a business benefit for the purchase.
- The purchase should not materially distort income.

For a cash-basis business, the deduction for prepaid farm supplies, feed, seed, etc. in the year they are paid for 2013 is generally limited to 50% of the other deductible farm expenses for 2013 (that is, all Schedule F deductions except prepaid farm supplies). Any excess is deducted in the year of use. The 50% limit does not apply if:

- The prepaid farm supplies expense is more than 50% of other deductible farm expenses because of a change in business operations caused by unusual circumstances.
- The total prepaid farm supplies expense for the preceding three years is less than 50% of the total other deductible farm expenses for those three years.

Farm Property Recovery Periods

Assets	Recovery Period in Years	
	GDS	ADS
Agricultural structures (single purpose)	10	15
Automobiles	5	5
Calculators and copiers	5	6
Cattle (dairy or breeding)	5	7
Communication equipment[1]	7	10
Computer and peripheral equipment	5	5
Drainage facilities	15	20
Farm buildings[2]	20	25
Farm machinery and equipment	7	10
Fences (agricultural)	7	10
Goats and sheep (breeding)	5	5
Grain bin	7	10
Hogs (breeding)	3	3
Horses (age when placed in service)		
Breeding and working (12 years or less)	7	10
Breeding and working (more than 12 years)	3	10
Racing horses (more than 2 years)	3	12
Horticultural structures (single purpose)	10	15
Logging machinery and equipment[3]	5	6
Nonresidential real property[4]	39	40
Office furniture, fixtures, and equipment (not calculators, copiers, or typewriters)	7	10
Paved lots	15	20
Residential rental property	27.5	40
Tractor units (over-the-road)	3	4
Trees or vines bearing fruit or nuts	10	20
Truck (heavy duty, unloaded weight 13,000 lbs. or more)	5	6
Truck (actual weight less than 13,000 lbs)	5	5
Water wells	15	20

[1] Not including communication equipment listed in other classes.
[2] Not including single purpose agricultural or horticultural structures.
[3] Used by logging and sawmill operators for cutting of timber.
[4] For property placed in service after May 12, 1993; for property placed in service before May 13, 1993, the recovery period is 31.5 years.

These exceptions apply only to farm-related taxpayers. A farm-related taxpayer is one who either makes his or her main home on a farm or has farming as his or her principal business. Any individual will qualify if a family member meets either qualification.

Line 17, Fertilizers and Lime

Enter on this line the cost of fertilizer and lime applied or purchased during the current year.

Line 18, Freight and Trucking

On line 18 enter the amount paid for freight and trucking. Do not include the cost of transportation incurred in purchasing livestock held for resale–those costs should be added to the cost of the livestock and taken as a deduction when the animal is sold. Similarly, additional freight costs incurred in getting a depreciable farm asset to the farm should not be taken as freight and trucking, but rather added to the basis of the machinery or equipment and taken along with and in the same manner as the depreciation of the item.

Line 19, Gasoline, Fuel, and Oil

The cost of gasoline, fuel, and oil is entered here.

 Filing Tip. Be certain that documentation exists for any personal use of these items. This is something the IRS will question on audit. Separate tanks for farm and personal fuels can banish this problem. Another solution is to routinely buy personal fuel in town and keep the receipts.

Line 20, Insurance (Other Than Health)

Take farm liability insurance here–and be sure to separate out the portion that applies to the home if it is covered under the same policy. Also report crop insurance costs–and be sure to check whether the crop insurance premium was deducted from the benefits check. If that is the case, it may not appear in the taxpayer's records. Note that amounts credited to a reserve for self-insurance or premiums paid for a policy that pays for any lost earnings due to sickness or disability are not deductible.

Line 21, Interest

Two lines are provided for interest. Mortgage interest is reported on 21a. This is interest paid to a financial institution and for which the taxpayer received a Form 1098, *Mortgage Interest Statement.* Be sure to separate out the home mortgage portion if both farm and home are part of the mortgage. Interest for which no Form 1098 was received and other farm interest–on operation loans, equipment acquisitions and so on–is reported on 21b.

Line 22, Labor Hired (Less Employment Credits)

The gross amount of labor hired is reported on line 22. The employer matching portion for Social Security and Medicare is reported with taxes on line 29. Cross-check the amounts with Form 943, *Employer's Annual Federal Tax Return for Agricultural Employees,* and all W-2s issued, and also with other records.

If payments for work performed are paid to a spouse or children, they should be paid as wages, not as contract labor. They should be reported with a W-2, not a 1099-MISC. If the payments are reported with the 1099-MISC, the recipient will have to pay self-employment tax. This is especially significant for children under 18, since children under age 18 may work for a parent in a sole proprietorship and not be subject to Social Security or Medicare withholding or payment.

It is possible to pay "wages in commodities." This means that the employee receives his or her pay as a certain quantity of commodities: 5,000 bushels of soybeans, and so on. When using wages in commodities, it is important that the employee have "dominion and control" over the commodities. He or she should make decisions as to where, when, and for what price the commodities are sold. The employee is also generally responsible for the cost of storage and trucking.

Line 23, Pension and Profit-Sharing Plans

Report on line 23 the amount of contributions to employee pension, profit-sharing, or annuity plans. The sole proprietor's contribution for himself or herself is not reported here, but rather is taken as an above-the-line adjustment on Form 1040.

Some of these plans require reporting on a Form 5500, *Annual Return/Report of Employee Benefit Plan,* or a Form 5500-EZ, *Annual Return of One Participant (Owners and Their Spouses) Retirement Plan.*

Line 24, Rent or Lease

The rental or lease of vehicles, machinery and equipment is reported on line 24a. Be sure to check that items listed as being rented or leased are documented by an instrument that bears out the nature of the arrangement. Often a document that says "Lease" at the top is in reality a sale.

If the item is truly a purchase, rather than a lease, it should be set up for depreciation over the appropriate life.

Line 24b is for "Other" rentals. This is normally where cash rent for land and pasture is recorded.

Line 25, Repairs and Maintenance

The cost of repairs of farm assets and maintenance is reported here.

Filing Tip. This is an area that the IRS likes to look at on audit. The reason is that they often find large amounts in this account that should actually have been depreciated over a period of time. Repairs and small fixes to the home sometimes end up in this account. Be sure they are taken out.

Line 26, Seeds and Plants Purchased

Purchases of seeds and plants are reported on line 26.

Line 27, Storage and Warehousing

Storage and warehousing of commodities are reported on line 27.

Line 28, Supplies Purchased

Line 28 is for general farm supplies and may be anything from soap to ledger paper to a longer telephone cord. Often this is referred to as "supplies and small tools," and hammers, pliers, and so on are included as well.

Line 29, Taxes

Report on line 29 real estate taxes, personal property tax, and other assessments on farm business assets. Be sure to eliminate real estate taxes on the home and anything else that is personal or family property rather than a part of the farm business.

Report also the employer portion of Social Security and Medicare taxes, as well as federal unemployment tax and federal highway use tax.

Caution. Personal taxes cannot be taken here. Do not deduct federal income tax, estate and gift taxes, taxes assessed for improvements, such as for sewers, paving, and so on not related to the farm.

Line 30, Utilities

Deduct the business portion of payments for electricity, water, telephone, and gas. It is a great help if the taxpayer can have the farm and home electricity (and possibly gas) billed separately and recorded on separate meters.

Telephone. The base cost of having the first telephone line in a residence is not deductible. The cost of a second line, provided it is used entirely for farm business, is fully deductible.

Line 31, Veterinary, Breeding, and Medicine

The cost of veterinary service, medicine, breeding, and so on is taken on line 31.

Line 32, Other Expenses

Farm expenses and costs that do not fit anywhere else on Schedule F are taken on lines 34a through 34f and should be separately itemized to the extent possible. These items include, but are not limited to, the following:

- Amortization
- At-risk deduction disallowed from prior year
- Bad debts
- Business use of home (use the worksheet in IRS Publication 587 to calculate the deduction–do not use Form 8829)
- Legal and professional fees
- Travel, meals, and entertainment–noting that meals and entertainment costs must usually be reduced by 50%
- Preproductive period expenses

Line 33, Total Expenses

The sum of lines 10 through 32f is the total expenses for the farm business and is entered on line 33. If lien 32f is negative, see the instructions.

Line 34, Net Farm Profit or (Loss)

Subtract line 33 from line 9, and enter the result on line 34. If there is a profit, stop her and see the instructions for where to report it. If there is a loss, complete lines 35 and 36.

Line 35, Appplicable Subsidy Received

Check either Yes or No, depending on whether an applicable subsidy was received for 2013.

Schedule F loss limitation. The amount of net farm losses that can be claimed for any tax year in which a taxpayer, other than a C corporation, has received "applicable subsidies" to the "excess farm loss." This loss limitation is available for tax years beginning after December 31, 2009.

Line 36, At-Risk Investment

If Schedule F shows a loss and the taxpayer was not at risk for the activity, Form 6198 must be completed. If all of the amounts are at risk in this business, check box 36a. If you checked the "Yes" box on line E, enter the loss on line 34 and on Form 1040, line 18. If you checked "No" on line E, it may be necessary to complete Form 8582 to figure the allowable loss to enter on line 34. If some investment is not at risk, check box 36b. Check the box that describes your investment in this activity and see the instructions for where to report your loss.

Part III: Farm Income—Accrual Method

Taxpayers using the accrual method of accounting report income when it is earned, not when it is received. The taxpayer must include animals and crops in inventory if the accrual method is used.

Line 37, Sales of Livestock, Produce, Grains, and Other Products

Enter on line 37 specified sales of livestock, produce, grains and other products (see instructions).

Lines 38a and 38b, Cooperative Distributions

Enter the cooperative distributions (Form(s) 1099-PATR) on line 38a. Enter the taxable amount on line 38b.

Lines 39a and 39b, Agricultural Program Payments

Enter the agricultural program paymes on line 39a. Enter the taxable amount on line 39b.

Lines 40a through 40c, Commodity Credit Corporation (CCC) Loans

Enter the commodity credit corporation loans on line 40a. Enter commodity credit corporation loans forfeited on line 40b. Enter the taxable amount on line 40c.

Line 41, Crop Insurance Proceeds

Report crop insurance proceeds received during 2013 for 2012 and those receivable at the end of 2013 for 2013.

Line 42, Custom Hire Income

Report custom hire income (machine work) received during 2013, less that on receivables from prior years and that earned in 2013.

Line 43, Other Income

Report other income (see instructions).

Line 44, Calculation

The sum of lines 37 through 43 (37, 38b, 39b, 40a, 40c, 41, 42 and 43) is entered on line 44.

Line 45, Inventory of Livestock, Produce, Grains, and Other Products at Beginning of the Year

The amount on line 45 should match the final inventory on the taxpayer's 2011 return. If it does not, attach a statement explaining the discrepancy.

Line 46, Cost of Livestock, Produce, Grains, and Other Products Purchased during the Year

Enter the cost of livestock, produce, grains, and other products purchased during the year on line 46. Include those for which a liability has been incurred, but has not yet been paid.

Line 47

Add lines 45 and 46.

Line 48, Inventory of Livestock, Produce, Grains, and Other Products at End of Year

A physical inventory should be taken if possible. Enter the total inventory of livestock, produce, grains, and other products at year's end.

There are four common methods for valuing farm inventory:

- Cost
- Lower of cost or market price
- Farm-price method
- Unit-livestock method

In the farm-price method, each item is valued at its market price less the direct cost of disposition. Market price is the current price at the nearest market and cost includes commissions, freight, and other costs of disposition. In the unit-livestock method, the livestock are grouped according to type and age and a standard unit price is applied to each animal in a group.

Line 49, Calculation

The cost of livestock, produce, grains, and other products sold is calculated by subtracting line 48 from line 47. The result is entered on line 49. Exception: If the taxpayer uses the unit-livestock-price method or the farm-price method of valuing inventory and the amount on line 48 is larger than the amount on line 47, subtract line 47 from line 48 and enter the result on line 49.

Line 50, Gross Income

Subtract line 49 from line 44 and enter the result on line 50 and on Part I, line 9, unless the exception just mentioned at Line 49 above applies. In that case, add lines 44 and 49 and enter the result on line 50 and on Part I, line 9.

Schedule SE Line-by-Line Instructions

Schedule SE comprises two sections. For each taxpayer required to file the schedule, either Section A (Short Schedule SE) or Section B (Long Schedule SE) must be completed. Individuals generally may report self-employment income from multiple businesses on a single form. Joint filers must report their self-employment income separately, though they may use the same form if one must use the long form and the other may use the short form. The Schedule includes a flow chart to determine which form to use.

Schedule SE Short Form

Line 1a

Enter the net farm profit or loss from Schedule F, line 34 and Schedule K-1, box 14, code A.

Line 1b

If you received Social Security retirement or disability benefits, enter the amount of Conservation Reserve Program payments included on Schedule F, line 4b, or listed on Schedule K-1 (Form 1065), box 20, code Z.

Line 2

Enter net profit or loss from Schedule C line 31, Schedule C-EZ line 3, Schedule K-1 (Form 1065) box 14, code A (other than farming), and Schedule K-1 (Form 1065-B) box 9, code J1. Ministers need to include on this line the rental value of a home or allowance for a home, including utilities, furnished to them as well as the value of meals and lodging provided to them, their spouse and their dependents. Retired ministers should not include their retirement benefits or the value of a housing allowance that has been provided to them during retirement.

Line 3, Calculation

Add lines 1a, 1b, and 2.

Line 4, Calculation

Multiply line 3 by 92.35%. If the amount is less than $400, self-employment tax is not owed.

If the total amount from Line 4 (Short Schedule SE) of all of the individual's Schedules SE exceeds a threshold amount, the individual might be subject to a 0.9% Additional Medicare Tax. See the "Caution" on page 3-32 for more information.

Line 5, Self-employment Tax

If line 4 is $113,700 or less, multiply line 4 by 15.3%. Enter this result here and on Form 1040, line 56.

If line 4 is more than $113,700, multiply line 4 by 2.9%. Then add $14,098.80 to the result. Enter the total here and on Form 1040, line 56, or Form 1040NR, line 54.

Line 6, Deduction for one-half of self-employment

Multiply line 5 by 50% (.50). Enter the result here and on Form 1040, line 27, or Form 1040NR, line 27.

Schedule SE Long Form

Part I: Self-Employment Tax

If the individual's only income subject to self-employment tax is church employee income, skip lines 1-4b. Enter zero on line 4c and go to line 5a. Income from services performed as a minister or member of a religious order is not church employee income.

Box A

If the individual is a minister, member of a religious order or Christian Science practitioner and filed Form 4361, *Application for Exemption From Self-Employment for Use by Ministers, Members of Religious Orders and Christian Science Practitioners*, but had $400 or more of other net earnings from self-employment, check the box.

Line 1a

Enter the net farm profit or loss from Schedule F, line 34 and Schedule K-1 (Form 1065), box 14, code A. Skip this line if the farm optional method is used.

Line 1b

If you received Social Security retirement or disability benefits, enter the amount of Conservation Reserve Program payments included on Schedule F, line 4b, or listed on Schedule K-1 (Form 1065), box 20, code Z.

Line 2

Enter net profit or loss from Schedule C, line 31, Schedule C-EZ, line 3, Schedule K-1 (Form 1065), box 14, code A (other than farming), and Schedule K-1 (Form 1065-B), box 9, code J1. Ministers need to include on this line the rental value of a home or allowance for a home, including utilities, furnished to them as well as the value of meals and lodging provided to them, their spouse and their dependents. Retired ministers should not include their retirement benefits or the value of a housing allowance that has been provided to them during retirement.

Skip this line if the individual uses the nonfarm optional method (see instructions).

Line 3, Calculation

Add lines 1a, 1b, and 2.

Line 4a, Calculation

If line 3 is more than zero, multiply line 3 by 92.35%. Otherwise enter the amount from line 3. If line 4a is less than $400 due to Conservation Reserve Program payments on line 1b, see the instructions.

Line 4b

If the individual elected one or both of the optional methods, enter the totals from line 15 and 17 here.

Line 4c, Calculation

Add lines 4a and 4b. If the amount is less than $400, no self-employment tax is owed. The exception to this is if an individual also had church employee income. If so, enter zero on this line and continue.

Line 5a

Enter church employee income. Church employee income is wages received as an employee (other than a minister or a member of a religious order) of a church or qualified church-controlled organization that has a certificate in effect electing an exemption from employer Social Security and Medicare taxes.

Line 5b, Calculation

Multiply line 5a by 92.35%. If the amount is less than $100, enter zero.

Line 6, Net Earnings from Self-Employment

Add lines 4c and 5b.

If the total amount from Line 6 (Long Schedule SE) of all of the individual's Schedules SE exceeds a threshold amount, the individual might be subject to a 0.9% Additional Medicare Tax. See the "Caution" on this page for more information.

Line 7

The maximum amount of combined wages subject to Social Security tax or the 6.2% portion of the 7.65% railroad retirement (tier 1) tax for 2013 ($113,700 is already entered on the form).

Line 8a

Enter the total of boxes 3 and 7 on Form W-2 (Social Security wages and tips) and railroad retirement (tier 1) compensation. If $113,700 or more, skip line 8b through 10 and go to line 11.

Line 8b

Enter unreported tips subject to Social Security tax (from Form 4137, line 10).

Line 8c

Enter wages subject to Social Security tax (from Form 8919, Line 10).

Line 8d, Calculation

Add line 8a, 8b, and 8c.

Line 9, Calculation

Subtract line 8d from line 7. If zero or less, enter zero here and on line 10 and go to line 11.

Line 10, Calculation

Multiply the smaller of line 6 or line 9 by 12.4%.

Line 11, Calculation

Multiply line 6 by 2.9%.

Line 12, Self-employment Tax

Add lines 10 and 11. Enter here and on Form 1040, line 56 or Form 1040NR, line 54.

Line 13, Deduction for one-half self-employment tax

Multiply line 12 by 50% (.50). Enter the result here and on Form 1040, line 27, or 1040NR, line 27.

 Caution. Starting in 2013, a 0.9% Additional Medicare Tax may apply if the total amount from Line 4 (Short Schedule SE) or Line 6 (Long Schedule SE) of all of the taxpayer's Schedules SE exceeds a threshold amount (based on filing status)—

- $250,000 for married filing jointly;
- $125,000 for married filing separately; or
- $200,000 for Single, Head of Household, or Qualifying Widow(er) filers.

If the taxpayer has both wages and self-employment income, the threshold amount for applying the Additional Medicare Tax on the self-employment income is reduced (not below zero) by the amount of wages subject to the tax. Use Form 8959, *Additional Medicare Tax*, to calculate this tax.

Part II: Optional Methods to Figure Net Earnings

Farm Optional Method

This method can only be used if (a) the individual's gross farm income was not more than $6,960 or (b) the net farm profits were less than $5,024.

Line 14

The maximum income for the optional methods is $4,640.

Line 15

Enter the smaller of two-thirds of gross farm income (cannot be less than zero) or $4,640. Include this amount on line 4b.

Nonfarm Optional Method

This method can be used only if the individual's net farm profits were less than $5,024 and less than 72.189% of the individual's gross nonfarm income and the individual had net earnings from self-employment of at least $400 in 2 of the prior 3 years. This method can be used no more than 5 times.

Line 16, Calculation

Subtract line 15 from line 14.

Line 17

Enter the smaller of two-thirds of gross nonfarm income (not less than zero) or the amount on line 16. Also include this amount on line 4b.

KEY FACTS: Home Office Deduction

Expenses that qualify for the home office deduction (to the extent of the area reserved for the business relative to the total size of the home) include:

- Operating expenses
- Depreciation
- Mortgage interest
- Real estate taxes
- Rent (with the exception of rent paid by the employer for the area in question)
- Casualty and theft losses
- Utilities charges
- Cleaning and other services
- Homeowner's insurance
- Security system costs
- Repair costs (labor and supplies)

To qualify for the deduction, the area must meet the following conditions:

- The area is used *regularly* and *exclusively* for *trade or business purposes* as opposed to other profit-making activity.
  - **Exception:** The home is used as a day care facility for children, adults 65 or over, or individuals who are mentally or physically incapacitated.
  - **Exception:** The area is used for inventory or storage of produce (must be regular but not exclusive).
- The area is used for the *convenience of the employer.*
- The area represents the *primary place of business, or* the area is the *place of contact* with clients or customers in the normal course of the trade or business, *or* the area is a *separate structure* used in connection with the trade or business.

Direct vs. Indirect Expenses

Direct expenses are those that affect only the part of the home used for the trade or business, such as the cost of painting or furnishing an office. Direct costs are deductible in full. **Indirect** expenses involve the costs of maintaining the entire home of which the office is a part. Only the business use percentage of an indirect expense is deductible.

Formulas

$$\text{Business use \%} = \frac{\text{Area used for business}}{\text{Total area of home}}$$

$$\text{Day care deduction} = \text{Total costs to maintain the home}$$

$$\frac{\text{Area available and used regularly for day care each day}}{\text{Total area of home}}$$

$$\frac{\text{Total hours used for day care per year}}{\text{Total hours in year (8,760)}}$$

KEY FACTS: Hobby vs. Business

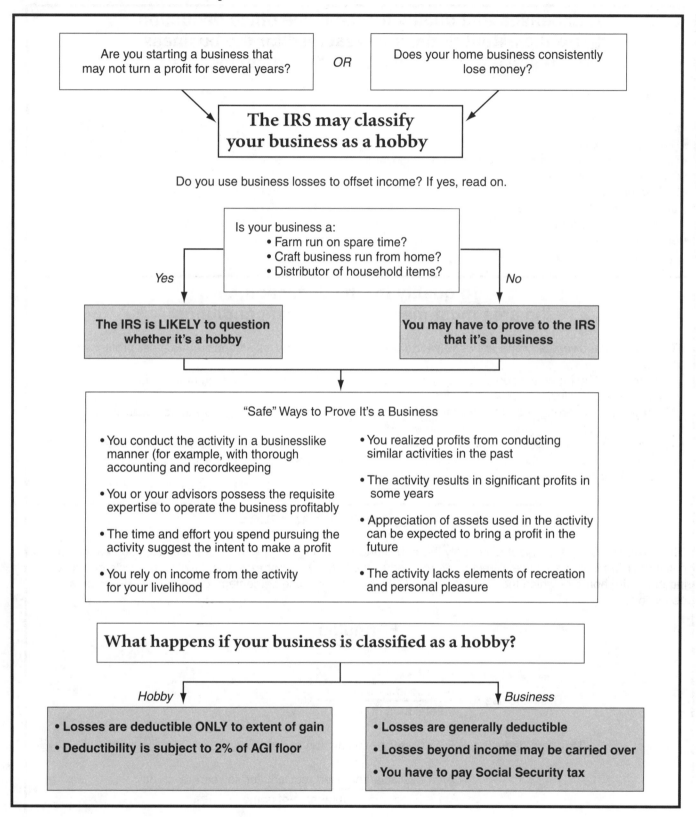

Are you starting a business that may not turn a profit for several years?

OR

Does your home business consistently lose money?

The IRS may classify your business as a hobby

Do you use business losses to offset income? If yes, read on.

Is your business a:
- Farm run on spare time?
- Craft business run from home?
- Distributor of household items?

Yes

The IRS is LIKELY to question whether it's a hobby

No

You may have to prove to the IRS that it's a business

"Safe" Ways to Prove It's a Business

- You conduct the activity in a businesslike manner (for example, with thorough accounting and recordkeeping

- You or your advisors possess the requisite expertise to operate the business profitably

- The time and effort you spend pursuing the activity suggest the intent to make a profit

- You rely on income from the activity for your livelihood

- You realized profits from conducting similar activities in the past

- The activity results in significant profits in some years

- Appreciation of assets used in the activity can be expected to bring a profit in the future

- The activity lacks elements of recreation and personal pleasure

What happens if your business is classified as a hobby?

Hobby

- **Losses are deductible ONLY to extent of gain**
- **Deductibility is subject to 2% of AGI floor**

Business

- **Losses are generally deductible**
- **Losses beyond income may be carried over**
- **You have to pay Social Security tax**

What's New in 2013

Capital Gains Rates for 2013. For sale or exchanges of capital assets in 2013, the capital gains rate for individuals is 20% if the individual is in the 39.6% income tax bracket, 15% if in the 25%, 28%, 33%, or 35% income tax bracket, and 0% if in the 10% or 15% income tax bracket. The capital gains rate is 25% for unrecaptured IRC §1250 gain, and 28% for collectibles and gain from the sale of qualified small business stock not excluded from income.

Form 8949. A taxpayer should enter on Form 8949 all sales and exchanges of capital assets during 2013 (including stocks, bonds, other securities), if those sales or exchanges are not reported on another form. Generally, all sales or exchanges of capital assets should be included even if the taxpayer did not receive a Form 1099-B or 1099-S. However, a taxpayer has the option for the 2013 tax year to report transactions on Form 8949 or Schedule D of Form 1040 if the taxpayer's basis is reported to the IRS on Form 1099-B and no basis adjustment is made.

Basis on Form 1099-B. If a taxpayer sold a covered security in 2013, his or her broker should send him a Form 1099-B (or similar statement) that shows the taxpayer's basis in the security. This will help complete Form 8949. Generally, a covered security is a security acquired after 2010, with certain exceptions.

Net Investment Income. Beginning in 2013, a 3.8% tax will be imposed on the lesser of an individual's net investment income or modified AGI in excess of certain threshold amounts. Net investment income includes any interest, dividends, annuities, royalties and rents, and other income attributable to an activity in which the taxpayer is a passive participant. The tax is calculated on Form 8960.

Relevant IRS Publications

- ☐ IRS Publication 523, *Selling Your Home*
- ☐ IRS Publication 530, *Tax Information for Homeowners*
- ☐ IRS Publication 537, *Installment Sales*
- ☐ IRS Publication 544, *Sales and Other Dispositions of Assets*
- ☐ IRS Publication 547, *Casualties, Disasters, and Thefts*
- ☐ IRS Publication 550, *Investment Income and Expenses (Including Capital Gains and Losses)*
- ☐ IRS Publication 551, *Basis of Assets*
- ☐ IRS Publication 946, *How to Depreciate Property*

Section at a Glance

General Summary of Basis Rules by Type of Acquisition

Type of Acquisition	Basis for Gain or Loss

Accounts receivable
   Accrual-basis taxpayer
   Cash-basis taxpayer
	
	Face value
	Zero

Bequest
   General rule:
   Property acquired from decedent's estate
   Property acquired in lieu of specific bequest
   If election is made for individuals dying in 2010:
   Property acquired from decedent's estate
   Property acquired in lieu of specific bequest
	
	Fair market value on date of death or alternate valuation date
	Value assigned in settlement
	
	Fair market value or decedent's adjusted basis on date of death
	Value assigned in settlement

Cash purchase	Cost
Community property survivor	See "Bequest" above, and Tab 14
Gift property	Donor's basis plus gift tax paid on appreciated property, **but** basis for loss is *limited* to the lesser of the donor's basis or fair market value at time of gift
Inherited property	See "Bequest" above, and Tab 14
Inventory goods	Last inventory value
Joint tenancy between spouses	Survivor's cost basis in one-half of property increased by one-half fair market value at date of death or on alternative valuation date (full estate tax value for property purchased by decedent before 1977)
Joint tenancy in general After death of one tenant after 1953	 Fair market value on date of death or alternative valuation date of portion included in estate
Life estate	Zero, if disposed of after October 9, 1969

Livestock
   Inventoried
   Purchased
   Raised by accrual-basis farmers
   Raised by cash-basis farmers
	
	Last inventory value
	Cost
	Cost of raising
	Zero, if costs expensed

Mortgage assumed (or property taken subject to mortgage)	Full price, including mortgage
Nontaxable exchange	Basis of property given up plus any recognized gain less any boot received
Marital property settlements	Transferor's basis

Repossessed property after installment sale
   Personal property
   Real property reacquired to satisfy purchaser's indebtedness secured by property
	
	Fair market value
	Adjusted basis of indebtedness plus gain resulting from reacquisition and reacquisition costs

Stock
   Acquired in wash sale
   Nontaxable stock dividend
   Received for services
	
	Cost of acquired stock plus loss not recognized
	Basis allocated among new total shares of stock on date declared
	Amount reported in income plus cash paid

Stock rights
   Taxable
   Nontaxable
	
	Fair market value when issued
	Allocable share of basis of stock, unless right's value is less than 15% of stock value, in which case basis is zero

Sale or Exchange of Property

Computing Gain or Loss

A taxpayer generally realizes gain or loss when property is sold, exchanged, or otherwise disposed. The amount of gain or loss depends on the taxpayer's adjusted basis in the property at the time of disposition. Gain is the excess of the amount realized by the taxpayer from the sale or exchange over his or her adjusted basis in the property. Loss is the excess of the taxpayer's adjusted basis in the property over the amount realized from the sale or exchange.

Basis

The basis for computing gain or loss from the sale or exchange of property is determined by reference to the cost of acquiring the property (referred to as the cost basis) (IRC §1012). The taxpayer's cost includes the sum of any cash paid, the face amount of any liability incurred or assumed, and the fair market value of other property transferred. Cost basis also includes costs incurred in acquiring or financing property, such as attorneys' or appraisal fees, sales and excise taxes, freight charges, and installation and testing costs.

A taxpayer who receives multiple properties in a single transaction or receives improved real estate is required to allocate the total cost among the properties based on their relative fair market values. Similarly, a taxpayer who sells or exchanges only a partial interest in property is required to allocate the basis between the interest sold and the interest retained.

The basis of real property includes settlement fees and closing costs including:

- abstract fees;
- charges for installing utility services;
- legal fees (including title search and preparation of the sales contract and deed);
- recording fees;
- survey costs;
- transfer taxes;
- owner's title insurance fees;
- amounts owed by the seller but paid by the buyer, such as back taxes or interest, recording or mortgage fees, charges for improvements or repairs, and sales commissions.

Settlement costs do not include amounts placed in escrow for future payments of items such as insurance and taxes. In addition, certain other settlement fees and closing costs cannot be included in the cost basis of property including casualty insurance premiums, rent and utility charges for occupancy before closing, and charges connected with getting a mortgage such as points mortgage insurance premiums, credit report costs, and loan assumption fees. See the table on page 4-30 for more information on the settlement costs for the sale of a personal residence.

Property Acquired by Gift. The basis of property acquired by gift is generally the donor's adjusted basis in the property at the time of the transfer (referred to as a carryover basis). If the property had an inherent loss at the time of the gift, however, the donee's basis for purposes of computing a loss is the property's fair market value at the time of the gift, rather than the donor's adjusted basis (IRC §1015). In either event, the basis is increased for certain gift taxes paid on the gift. See MTG ¶1630.

Property Inherited. The basis of property acquired from a decedent is generally its fair market value on the decedent's date of death (or on the alternative valuation date) (IRC §1014). This may result in either a stepped-up or stepped-down basis depending on whether the property has an inherent gain or loss. See MTG ¶1633. Special rules apply to prevent a taxpayer from receiving a stepped-up basis in appreciated property by transferring such property to an individual facing imminent death. See MTG ¶1639. Special rules also apply to determine the basis of property held in a joint tenancy (with a right of survivorship) or a tenancy by the entirety. See MTG ¶1634. Property acquired from a decedent that is subject to multiple interests has a single uniform basis for all income tax purposes and for all interest holders.

 Planning Tip. In the case of a decedent who died in 2010, the estate could have elected not to have the federal estate tax apply in which case modified carryover basis rules will apply to the property acquired from the decedent. See Tab 14 for more information.

Tax-Free Exchanges. The basis of property received in a tax-free exchange, such as a like-kind exchange, is generally the taxpayer's adjusted basis in the property given up (referred to as a substituted basis). The basis is increased by any gain recognized by the taxpayer in the exchange and decreased by the value of any boot received. See page 4-22 for more information. The basis of property that is converted from a nonbusiness use to a business use is the lesser of the adjusted basis of the property or its fair market value at the time of the conversion.

Additions to Basis of Property

In computing gain or loss on the sale or exchange of property, the cost or other basis of the property must be adjusted for certain expenditures, receipts, losses, or other items properly chargeable to capital account. This includes any improvements and additions to property having a useful life of more than one year. For example, the cost of an addition or new roof on a home, installation of central air conditioning, or rewiring of a home are added to the basis of the home. Additions to basis may also include taxes, interest, and carrying charges if elected by the taxpayer under IRC §266. See MTG ¶1611 and ¶1614.

Allowable depreciation, amortization, and depletion, whether or not claimed by the taxpayer, reduces the basis of property. Other returns of capital also decrease a taxpayer's basis in property, including various tax credits, deductions, and exclusions claimed in determining the taxpayer's taxable income. An assessment for improvements or other items that increase the value of property are added to the basis and not deducted as a tax. Such improvements may include streets, sidewalks, water mains, sewers, and public parking facilities. The amount of an assessment may be a depreciable asset. See MTG ¶1617.

Amount Realized

The gain or loss realized by a taxpayer on the sale or other disposition of property is the difference between the amount realized from the sale or disposition and the amount of the taxpayer's adjusted basis in the property. The amount realized is the amount of money received, plus the fair market value of other property received, including any third-party obligations. It also includes the amount of liabilities from which the taxpayer is relieved as a result of the sale or disposition. This includes all liabilities paid, assumed, or taken subject to by the purchaser, regardless of whether the liability is related to the property or whether it is recourse or nonrecourse. Discharge of recourse liabilities can also give rise to cancellation of indebtedness income. See Tab 1.

If a debt instrument is issued to the taxpayer in exchange for property, then the amount realized includes the value of the debt instrument and the sale or disposition is subject to the installment sale rules (see page 4-24). Any other consideration received by the seller must be taken into account in the year of sale or other disposition. If the installment method is not used or is not available, the amount of the purchaser's obligation that is included in the amount realized is determined by reference to the seller's method of accounting.

The amount realized is increased by property taxes that are the seller's obligation but which the buyer actually pays. On the other hand, the amount realized is reduced by property taxes that are the purchaser's obligation but which the seller pays. The amount realized is also generally reduced for expenses incurred by the seller in connection with the sale or other disposition. If more than one item of property is sold or otherwise disposed of, the amount realized must be allocated among the various properties, based on their relative fair market values.

Examples of Increases and Decreases to Basis

Increases to Basis	Decreases to Basis

o Capital improvements:
    Putting an addition on home
    Replacing an entire roof
    Paving driveway
    Installing central air conditioning
    Rewiring home
o Assessments for local improvements:
    Water connections
    Sidewalks
    Roads
o Casualty losses:
    Restoring damaged property
o Legal fees:
    Cost of defending and perfecting a title
o Zoning costs
	o Exclusion from income of subsidies for energy conservation measures
	o Casualty or theft loss deductions and insurance reimbursements
	o Vehicle credits
	o IRC §179 deduction
	o Deduction for clean-fuel vehicles and clean-fuel vehicle refueling property
	o Depreciation
	o Nontaxable corporate distributions

Capital and Noncapital Assets

The treatment of gain or loss from the sale or exchange of property is determined by the character of the property. Generally, gain or loss on the sale or exchange of property is recognized as ordinary income or deductible as an ordinary loss in determining adjusted gross income (AGI). A taxpayer includes the gain or deducts the loss for the tax year in which the gain or loss is realized.

Gain from the sale of a capital asset may be taxed at a lower rate than ordinary income. To be eligible for the lower capital gain rates, the taxpayer must hold the capital asset for more than 12 months (long-term capital gain). Gain from the sale of a capital asset held for 12 months or less (short-term capital gains) are taxed as ordinary income. In general, a taxpayer's holding period for a capital asset begins when the property is acquired and ends when it is sold (see page 4-7). Losses from the sale of a capital may be used to offset capital gains.

 Planning Tip. For sale or exchanges of capital assets in 2013, the capital gains rate for individuals is 20% if the taxpayer is in the 39.6% income tax bracket, 15% if in the 25%, 28%, 33%, or 35% income tax bracket, and 0% if in the 10% or 15% income tax bracket. The capital gains rate is 25% for unrecaptured IRC §1250 gain, and 28% for collectibles and gain from the sale of qualified small business stock not excluded from income.

 Caution. Capital gains from the sale of property that a taxpayer does not use in an active business are subject to a 3.8% net investment income (NII) tax beginning in 2013 to the extent the gains are not otherwise offset by capital losses (see page 4-37). The NII tax is in addition to the individual's tax liability on capital gains.

Capital assets consist of any property owned for personal purposes or for the purpose of generating income. A taxpayer's home, for example, is a capital asset, as is virtually everything in it. Stocks and bonds and all other investment instruments are also capital assets, as are collectibles. Property not considered a capital asset (i.e., a noncapital asset) includes property listed in IRC §1221, and is generally property that is used in a trade or business, including:

- stock in trade or other property held as inventory in a trade or business;
- property held primarily for sale to customers in the ordinary course of the taxpayer's trade or business;
- notes or accounts receivable acquired in the ordinary course of trade or business for services rendered or from the sale of stock in trade or property held for sale in the ordinary course of business;
- depreciable property used in a trade or business, even if fully depreciated;
- real property used in taxpayer's trade or business;
- copyrights, literary, musical, or artistic compositions, letters or memorandum, or similar property created by personal efforts of the taxpayer;
- U.S. government publications (including the Congressional Record) held by a taxpayer who received

it (or by another taxpayer in whose hands the publication would have a basis determined in whole or in part by reference to the taxpayer's basis) other than by purchase at the price at which the publication is offered to the public;
- certain commodities derivative financial instruments held by a dealer;
- hedging transactions entered into during the normal course of a trade or business; and
- supplies of a type regularly used or consumed by the taxpayer in the ordinary course of business.

 Planning Tip. A taxpayer can elect to treat a musical composition or a copyright in musical works as a capital asset if: (1) the taxpayer's personal effects created the property, or (2) the taxpayer acquired the property under circumstances (for example, by gift) entitling him or her to the basis of the person who created the work or for whom it was produced. The election is made on Form 8949 by treating the sale or exchange of the property as the sale or exchange of a capital asset. The election must be made on or before the date, including extensions, of the income tax return for the tax year of the sale or exchange. The election is revocable with consent of the IRS. Alternatively, the taxpayer may, within six months of filing the timely filed return, file an amended return treating the sale or exchange as the sale or exchange of property that is not a capital asset.

Reporting Gains and Losses

A taxpayer generally must complete and attach Schedule D to Form 1040 to report overall sales, exchanges, and other dispositions of capital assets. Before completing Schedule D, however, a taxpayer must complete the following forms.

Form 8949, *Sales and Other Dispositions of Capital Assets*, is used to report:

- the sale or exchange of capital assets *not* reported on another form or schedule (see page 4-6);
- gains from involuntary conversions (other than from casualty or theft) of capital assets *not* held for business or profit; and
- nonbusiness bad debts (see Tab 1 for exceptions).

 Filing Tip. Form 8949 must be completed before lines 1, 2, 3, 8, 9, or 10 of Schedule D of Form 1040. The combined totals from all Forms 8949 completed are reported on Schedule D.

Form 4797, *Sales of Business Property (Also Involuntary Conversions and Recapture Amounts under Sections 179 and 280F(b)(2))*, is used to report:

- gain or loss from the sale or exchange of: (1) property used in a trade or business; (2) depreciable and amortizable property; (3) oil, gas, geothermal, or other mineral properties; and (4) IRC §126 property acquired, improved, or modified as a result of the receipt of certain agricultural cost-sharing program payments for conservation purposes;
- dispositions of noncapital assets (other than inventory or property held primarily for sale to customers in the taxpayer's trade or business);
- dispositions of capital assets not reported on Schedule D;
- involuntary conversions (from other than casualty or theft) of property used in a trade or business and capital assets held in connection with a trade or business or a transaction entered into for profit;
- gain or loss allocated to partners and S corporation shareholders from dispositions of IRC §179 property by partnerships and S corporations; and
- the computation of recapture of deductions claimed in a prior year for IRC §179 property or listed property under IRC §280F(b)(2) because the business use of the property decreased to 50% or less.

 Caution. Traders in securities or commodities, including day traders must report gains or losses on Form 8949 and Schedule D unless they elect to use the mark-to-market method of accounting (see page 4–35). If that election is made, the transactions must be reported on Form 4797.

Form 2439, *Notice to Shareholder of Undistributed Long-Term Capital Gains*, is sent by regulated investment companies and real estate investment trusts to inform shareholders of their portion of undistributed capital gains and tax paid. See MTG ¶2305.

Form 4684, *Casualties and Thefts*, is used to report gains or losses from casualties and thefts. Gains may be deferred if insurance proceeds are used to purchase replacement property. See Tab 2.

Form 6252, *Installment Sale Income*, is used to report casual sales of real or personal property (other than inventory) if payments will be received in a tax year after the year of sale. See page 4-24 and MTG ¶1801 for more information on installment sales.

Form 8824, *Like-Kind Exchanges*, is used to report exchanges of qualifying business or investment property (not personal property) for property of a like-kind/

like-class. See page 4-21 and MTG ¶1721 for more information on like-kind exchanges.

Form 6781, *Gains and Losses from IRC §1256 Contracts and Straddles*, is used to report gains and losses on any regulated futures contract, foreign currency contract, nonequity option, dealer equity option, or dealer securities futures contract (IRC §1256 contracts or section 1256 contracts). Use Part II of Form 6781 to figure gains and losses on straddles before entering these amounts on Form 8949 and Schedule D.

Nondeductible Losses

Losses from transactions between related parties are nondeductible. See MTG ¶1717. Do *not* deduct a loss from the direct or indirect sale or exchange of property between any of the following:

- members of a family, including the individual's brothers and sisters (by whole or half blood), spouse, ancestors, and lineal descendents, including adopted children;
- a corporation and an individual owning more than 50% of the corporation's stock (unless the loss is from a distribution after the corporation has undergone complete liquidation);
- a grantor and a fiduciary of a trust;
- a fiduciary of one trust and fiduciary of another trust if both trusts were created by the same grantor;
- a fiduciary and a beneficiary of the same trust;
- a fiduciary of a trust and a beneficiary of another trust created by the same grantor;
- an executor of an estate and a beneficiary of that estate, unless the sale or exchange was to satisfy a bequest of money; and
- an individual and a tax-exempt organization controlled by the individual or the individual's family.

 Filing Tip. A sale or exchange of property between related parties that results in a nondeductible loss should be reported on Form 8949, but with the code "L" entered in column (f) and the amount of the loss reported as a positive number in column (g).

Form 8949

Sales and Other Dispositions of Capital Assets

Taxpayers should enter on Form 8949 all sales and exchanges of capital assets (including stocks, bonds, other securities), if those sales or exchanges are not reported on Form 4684, 4797, 6252, 6781, or 8824. All sales or exchanges of capital assets should be included even if the taxpayer did not receive a Form 1099-B, *Proceeds from Broker and Barter Exchange Transactions*, or 1099-S, *Proceeds from Real Estate Transactions*. Short-term capital gains are reported on line 1, and long-term capital gains are reported on line 3. Details of each transaction should generally be reported on separate lines. A taxpayer may use as many Forms 8949 as necessary.

 Filing Tip. A taxpayer has the option to report short term and long term transactions directly on Schedule D of Form 1040 rather than Form 8949 if the taxpayer receives a Form 1099-B for the transactions on which basis was reported to the IRS and the taxpayer has no adjustments to the basis. Alternatively, the taxpayer may include these transactions on Form 8949 by reporting short term transactions on line 1 (check box A) and long term transactions on line 3 (check box D).

Instead of reporting each transaction on a separate line, capital-gain and -loss transactions may be reported on an attachment to Form 8949. The attachment must contain the same information as required on Form 8949 and must use a similar format. As many attached statements may be used as are required. Combined totals from all attached statements should be entered on a copy of Form 8949 with the appropriate box checked.

 Filing Tip. If reporting transactions on a separate attachment, enter the name of the broker followed by the words "see attached statement" in column (a). Leave columns (b) and (c) blank, and enter "M" in column (f). If other codes also apply, enter all of them in column (f). If the taxpayer has statements from more than one broker, report the totals from each broker on a separate row. Do not enter "Available upon request" and summary totals in lieu of reporting the details of each transaction.

A separate Form 8949 must be used for each of the following situations. Box A, B, or C (short-term) or D, E, or F (long-term) should be checked, as appropriate. Only one box should be checked on each copy. If more than one situation applies, separate copies of Part I (short-term) or Part II (long-term) should be used.

Box A or D. Report separately short-term and long-term transactions for which the taxpayer received a Form 1099-B or 1099-S (or substitute) that shows cost or other basis in box 3, and check box A or box D. However, if the statement shows basis, but indicates that it was not reported to the IRS, then check box B or E.

Box B or E. Report short-term and long-term transactions for which the taxpayer received a Form 1099-B or 1099-S (or substitute) that does not show cost or other basis in box 3, and check box B or box E.

Box C or F. Report separately short-term and long-term transactions for which the taxpayer did not receive a Form 1099-B or 1099-S (or substitute), and check box C or box F.

 Filing Tip. Be sure to reconcile all Form 1099-Bs to insure that all transactions have been reported. Combining information on single lines of Form 8949 will lead to IRS follow up and added attention. Transaction-by-transaction listings allow the IRS to match all reported Form 1099-Bs and avoids the problem of future inquiries regarding net information.

Charitable Gift Annuities. Beneficiaries of charitable gift annuities should report the amount showing in box 3 of Form 1099-R, *Distributions From Pensions, Annuities, Retirement or Profit-Sharing Plans, IRAs, Insurance Contracts, etc.*, on line 3 of a Form 8949, Part II that has box F checked at the top. Enter "Form 1099-R" in column (a), the box 3 amount in column (d), and complete column (h).

E-filing. Taxpayers who e-file their returns may include sales and exchanges of capital assets in the electronic short- or long-term capital-gain (or loss) records, as appropriate. If the taxpayer chooses not report each transaction separately on the electronic return, then Form(s) 8949 must be included as a PDF file with the taxpayer's return or attach Form(s) 8949 (or a statement with the same information) to Form 8453, *U.S. Individual Income Tax Transmittal for an IRS e-file Return*, and mail the forms to the IRS.

Short-Term versus Long-Term Capital Gains

The holding period for the property determines whether capital gains are short or long term and whether they are reported on line 1 or line 3 of Form 8949. If the holding period is one year or less, the gain is short-term. If the holding period is more than one year, the gain is long term.

Begin counting the holding period on the day after the taxpayer acquired the property and include the day on which it was disposed. If the taxpayer disposed of property acquired by inheritance, the disposition is reported as a long-term gain or loss, regardless of the holding period for the property.

 Caution. Nonbusiness bad debts are reported as short-term capital losses. Worthless securities are treated as though they were capital assets sold on the last day of the tax year.

 Example. On March 15, 2013, Vasily Cherokov sold shares of stock A for $700 gain and shares of stock B for $400 gain. He had purchased the shares of stock A on March 15, 2012, and the shares of stock B on February 1, 2012. His gain on stock A is short-term gain because he held the stock one day less than one year, but his gain on the stock B shares is long-term gain because he held the stock at least one day more than one year after purchase.

Line 1(a) or 3(a), Description of Property

Enter a brief description of the property sold or exchange in column (a). For example, for a block of stock indicate the number of shares and the company name. Stock ticker symbols or abbreviations may be used to describe the property as long as they are based on the descriptions of the property on Form 1099-B or 1099-S.

Filing Tip. If the taxpayer inherited the property from someone who died in 2010 and the executor of the decedent's estate made the election to file Form 8939, also enter " INH-2010" in column (a). See Tab 14 for more information.

Line 1(b) or 3(b), Date Acquired

Enter the date the property was acquired in column (b). Use the trade date for stocks and bonds traded on an exchange or over-the-counter market. For stock or other property sold short, enter the date the stock or property was delivered to the broker or lender to close the short sale. The date acquired for an asset held on January 1, 2001, for which the taxpayer made an election to recognize any gain in a deemed sale is the date of the deemed sale and reacquisition.

For the sale of a block of stocks that were acquired over a period of time, "VARIOUS" may be entered

for the date of acquisition, but the short- and long-term gain for each acquisition must still be reported in the appropriate part of Form 8949.

 Filing Tip. If the taxpayer sells or otherwise disposes of property inherited, then generally: (1) report the sale or disposition as a long-term capital gain or loss, regardless of the decedent's or the taxpayer's holding period; and (2) enter "INHERITED" instead of the date acquired in column 3(b). If the property sold or disposed by the taxpayer was inherited from someone who died in 2010 and the decedent's executor filed Form 8939, then see IRS Publication 4895 to see whether the gain or loss is reported on line 1 or line 3.

Short Sales. A *short sale* is a sale of stock in which the seller borrows the stock that is delivered to the buyer. At a later date, the seller "closes" the short sale by covering the loan either with stock purchased for that purpose or with stock the seller held at the time of the short sale but did not wish to transfer at the earlier date. An investor who enters into a short sale realizes profits when the price of the stock declines.

The taxable event in a short sale is the closing of the transaction. Any gain or loss realized upon closing a short sale is treated as a capital gain or loss, provided that the stock used to close the short sale is a capital asset in the investor's hands. See MTG ¶1944 for more details.

Line 1(c) or 3(c), Date Sold

Enter the date the asset was sold in column (c). Use the trade date for stocks and bonds traded on an exchange or over-the-counter market. For stock or other property sold short, enter the date the taxpayer sold the stock or property borrowed to open the short-sale transaction.

In real estate sales, a sale occurs when the deed passes or when possession, and the burdens and benefits of ownership, are transferred to the buyer, whichever occurs first. The same rules apply to an executory contract, such as one involving a purchase option. The transaction is usually not considered to be closed until unconditional liability of the buyer for the purchase price is created by acquisition of title and right of possession. See MTG ¶1742.

Line 1(d) or 3(d), Sales Price

Brokers and barter exchanges use Form 1099-B to report proceeds from transactions to the taxpayer and the IRS. Form 1099-S is used to report the sale or exchange of real estate. Brokers are also allowed to issue substitute statements listing information that is identical to what appears on Form 1099-B.

Enter in column (d) either the gross sales price or the net sales price from the sale shown on Form 1099-B, 1099-S, or other statement received. If the proceeds received are more than shown on the Forms or other statement, then report the correct amount in column (d). If the taxpayer does not receive a Form 1099-B, 1099-S, or other statement, report the net proceeds from the transaction in column (d).

If the taxpayer sold stocks or bonds and received a Form 1099-B from his or her broker that shows the gross sales price, enter that amount. But if Form 1099-B (or substitute statement) indicates that gross proceeds minus commissions and option premiums were reported to the IRS, enter that net amount in column (d). If the net amount is entered in column (d), do not include the commissions and option premiums from the sale in the basis reported in column (e).

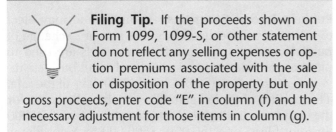

Filing Tip. If the proceeds shown on Form 1099, 1099-S, or other statement do not reflect any selling expenses or option premiums associated with the sale or disposition of the property but only gross proceeds, enter code "E" in column (f) and the necessary adjustment for those items in column (g).

Line 1(e) or 3(e), Cost or Other Basis

The cost or other basis of property is the cost to purchase the property, plus purchase commissions and improvements, minus depreciation, amortization, and depletion. If the taxpayer inherited the property, received it as a gift, or received it in a tax-free exchange, involuntary conversion, or wash sale of stock, he or she may not be able to use the actual cost as the basis. If the actual cost is not used, attach an explanation of the basis used. See page 4-3.

Increase the cost or other basis by any expense of sale, such as broker's fees, commissions, state and local transfer taxes, and option premiums, before making an entry in column (e), unless the net sales price was reported in column (d).

Stock. The basis of stocks or bonds of a taxpayer generally is the purchase price plus the costs of purchase, such as commissions and recording or transfer fees. If the taxpayer acquired stock or bonds other than by purchase, his or her basis is usually determined by fair market value or the previous owner's adjusted basis. If the taxpayer sold stock, adjust the basis by subtracting all nontaxable distributions received before the sale, while adjusting the basis for stock splits, if any. See page 4-36 for more information on the basis of stock.

If the taxpayer can adequately identify the shares of stock or bonds sold, his or her basis is the cost or other basis of the particular shares of stock or bonds. Adequate identification occurs if the taxpayer can show that certificates representing shares of stock from a lot that the taxpayer bought on a certain date or for a certain price were delivered to the taxpayer's broker or other agent. If the taxpayer sells stock directly rather than through a broker, adequate identification is made if the taxpayer maintains a written record of the particular stock that he or she intended to sell.

If the taxpayer buys and sells securities at various times in varying quantities during the tax year and cannot adequately identify the shares sold, the basis of the securities sold is the basis of the securities acquired first (first-in, first-out). Except for certain mutual fund shares, the taxpayer cannot use the average price per share to figure gain or loss on the sale of the shares.

Mutual Funds. The basis of shares in a mutual fund (or other regulated investment company) or a real estate investment trust (REIT) is generally figured in the same way as the basis of other stock and usually includes any commissions or load charges paid for the purchase. The taxpayer, however, can elect to use the average basis of mutual fund shares if he or she acquired the identical shares at various times and prices, or acquired the shares after December 31, 2010, in connection with a dividend reinvestment plan, and left them on deposit in an account. Shares are identical if they have the same Committee on Uniform Security Identification Procedure (CUSIP) number or other security identifier number permitted by the IRS.

The average basis is the total adjusted basis of all shares of identical security in an account regardless of how long held, and divided by the total number of shares in the account. For this purpose, shares of stock in a dividend reinvestment plan are not identical to shares of stock with the same CUSIP number that are not in a dividend reinvestment plan. The average basis method applies on an account by account basis.

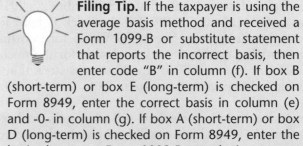

Filing Tip. If the taxpayer is using the average basis method and received a Form 1099-B or substitute statement that reports the incorrect basis, then enter code "B" in column (f). If box B (short-term) or box E (long-term) is checked on Form 8949, enter the correct basis in column (e) and -0- in column (g). If box A (short-term) or box D (long-term) is checked on Form 8949, enter the basis shown on Form 1099-B or substitute statement in column (e) even though incorrect, and make the appropriate adjustment in column (g).

Once the taxpayer elects to use an average basis, it must be used for all accounts in the same fund and the same method must continue to be used. However, the cost basis (or a different method of figuring the average basis) may be used for shares in other funds, even those within the same family of funds.

Filing Tip. A taxpayer elects the average basis method for covered securities by notifying the custodian or agent for the taxpayer's account in writing. The election must identify each account with the custodian or agent, including accounts the taxpayer later establishes with the custodian or agent. A taxpayer is allowed to change from the average basis method to another method prospectively at any time.

Line 1(f) or 3(f), Code

Enter the appropriate code to explain any adjustment to gain or loss in column (g). If more than one code applies, enter all the codes that apply in alphabetical order but do not separate by a space or comma (for example, "BOQ").

Line 1(g) or 3(g), Adjustments to Gain or Loss

Any adjustments to gain or loss required because of a code entered in column (f) should be entered in column (g). Negative amounts should be entered in parentheses. If more than one code is entered in column (f), the net adjustment should be entered in column (g). Use the worksheet in the Instructions to Form 8949 to figure the adjustment needed to be reported in column (g).

Qualified Small Business Stock. An individual can exclude from income 50% of the gain realized on the sale or exchange of qualified small business stock held for more than five years. The exclusion is 60% if the qualified stock is issued by a corporation in an empowerment zone. The exclusion is increased to 75% for qualified stock acquired after February 17, 2009, and before September 28, 2010, and to 100% for qualified stock acquired after September 27, 2010, and before January 1, 2014, if the stock is held for more than five years. See MTG ¶1905 for information on what qualified stock is eligible for the exclusion. Gain from qualified small business stock that is not excluded is taxed at a rate of 28%.

An individual may elect to roll over gain realized on the sale of qualified small business stock held for at least 6 months if used to purchase other qualified small business stock within 60 days of the sale. See MTG ¶1907 for more information.

Filing Tip. The election to exclude gain from the sale of qualified small business stock, or to roll over such gain, is made by reporting the sale or exchange on Form 8949. The taxpayer reports the sale or exchange as if he or she were not taking the exclusion or rolling over gain. Enter the amount excluded or rolled over as a negative number (in parentheses) in column (g), and entering code "Q" for the exclusion and code "R" for the rollover in column (f). If the transaction is reported as an installment sale on Form 6252, figure the exclusion amount for the year by multiplying the total amount of the exclusion by a fraction. The numerator is the amount of eligible gain to be recognized for the tax year and the denominator is the total amount of eligible gain.

Publicly Traded Securities. An individual may elect to roll over gain realized from the sale or exchange of publicly traded securities if the proceeds are used to purchase an interest in a specialized small business investment company (SSBIC) within 60 days of the sale. The amount of capital gain that may be rolled over for the tax year is limited to the lesser of $25,000 ($50,000 for joint filers) or $250,000 ($500,000 for joint filers), reduced by the gain excluded in prior tax years. In the case of joint return, the amount of gain excluded is allocated equally between the spouses for purposes of applying the limits in later tax years.

Filing Tip. The election to roll over gain from the sale of publicly traded securities is made by reporting the sale or exchange on Form 8949 as if the taxpayer were not rolling over the gain. Enter the amount rolled over as a negative number (in parentheses) in column (g), and entering code "R" in column (f).

Line 1(h) or 3(h), Gain or Loss

Figure gain or loss on each row in column (h) by subtracting the cost or other basis in column (e) from the proceeds (sales price) in column (d), and then taking into account any adjustments in column (g). Enter negative amounts in parentheses.

Line 2 or 4, Totals

Total the amounts in columns (d), (e), (g), and (h) for short-term or long-term capital gains and losses.

Schedule D

Capital Gains and Losses

Schedule D of Form 1040 is used to:

- figure the overall gain or loss from the sale or exchange of capital assets reported on Form 8949;
- report gain from installment sales (Form 6252), from IRC §1231 property (Part I of Form 4797), and undistributed long-term capital gains from regulated investment companies and real estate investment trusts (Form 2439);
- report gain or loss from casualties or thefts (Form 4684), like-kind exchanges (Form 8824), and IRC §1256 contracts and straddles (Form 6781);
- report a gain or loss from a partnership, S corporation, estate or trust (Schedule K-1s);
- report capital gain distributions not reported directly on Form 1040, line 13 (or effectively connected capital gain distributions not reported directly on Form 1040NR, line14), and
- report a capital loss carryover from 2012 to 2013.

 Filing Tip. A taxpayer has the option to report short term and long term transactions directly on Schedule D of Form 1040 rather than Form 8949 if the taxpayer receives a Form 1099-B for the transactions on which basis was reported to the IRS and the taxpayer has no adjustments to the basis. Alternatively, the taxpayer may include these transactions on Form 8949 by reporting short term transactions on line 1 (check box A) and long term transactions on line 3 (check box D).

 Filing Tip. Form 8949 must be completed before lines 1, 2, 3, 8, 9, or 10 of Schedule D of Form 1040. The combined totals from all Forms 8949 completed are reported on Schedule D.

Short-Term Capital Gains and Losses, Lines 1-7

Figure the taxpayer's short-term gain or loss in lines 1-3 from all Forms 8949 with Box A, B, or C checked in Part I, respectively. Gain or loss is calculated by subtracting the cost or basis in column (e) from the sales price in column (d), and then taking into account any adjustments in column (g). The gain or loss is entered in column (h). Losses should be entered in parentheses.

Enter on line 4 short-term gains from Form 6252, as well as gains or losses from Forms 4684, 8824, and 6781. Enter on line 5, the amount of net short-term capital gains or losses from Schedule K-1, Forms 1041, 1065, and 1120S. Instructions are included with Schedule K-1. See Tab 5 for a discussion of Schedule K-1.

Capital Loss Carryover. Individuals may carry over a net capital loss to future tax years until the loss is used. The carryover is figured on the Capital Loss Carryover Worksheet in the Schedule D instructions, reproduced on page 4-40. The allowable capital loss deduction is the lesser of:

- $3,000 ($1,500 if married filing separately); or
- the total net loss as shown on line 16 of Schedule D.

A capital loss that is carried over to a later tax year retains its original character as either long term or short term in the year to which it is carried. Thus, a short-term capital loss carried over from a preious tax year is reported on line 6 of Schedule D.

The amount of capital loss to be carried over to the next tax year is equal to the excess of the total net loss over the lesser of:

- the allowable capital loss deduction for the current tax year reported on line 16, or
- the taxpayer's taxable income for the current tax year increased by the allowable capital loss deduction, plus the personal exemption deductions.

If the deductions are more than the gross income for the tax year, use the negative taxable income in computing this item.

The result is that a short-term capital loss carryover first offsets short-term gain in the carryover year. If a net short-term capital loss remains, this loss then offsets net long-term capital gain, and then up to $3,000 of ordinary income. A long-term capital loss carryover first reduces long-term capital gain in the carryover year, then net short-term capital gain, and finally up to $3,000 of ordinary income.

 Filing Tip. When calculating the amount of a capital loss carryover to the next tax year, the allowable capital loss deduction for the current year must be taken into account regardless of whether claimed in, or filed a return for, the current tax year.

Net Short-Term Gain or Loss. The taxpayer combines column (h) of lines 1 through 6 and enter the total on line 7 for his or her net short-term capital gain or loss.

Example. Joel and Susan Cramer filed a joint return with an AGI of $30,000 and deductions of $11,000 in 2013. Their Schedule D shows a net short-term capital loss of $1,000 and a net long-term capital loss of $5,000. The $1,000 net short-term loss will be used to offset $1,000 of ordinary income; then the $2,000 of the net long-term capital loss will be used to offset $2,000 of ordinary income. The remaining $3,000 of the net long-term capital loss will be carried over to 2014.

Long-Term Capital Gains and Losses, Lines 8-15

Figure the taxpayer's long-term gain or loss in lines 8-10 from all Forms 8949 with Box D, E, or F checked in Part II, respectively. Gain or loss is calculated by subtracting the cost or basis in column (e) from the sales price in column (d), and then taking into account any adjustments in column (g). The gain or loss is entered in column (h). Losses should be entered in parentheses.

Enter on line 11, gain from the sale or exchange of property used in a trade or business, as well as from involuntary conversion (other than from casualty or thefts) from Part I of Form 4797. Also include long-term gains from Form 6252 and Form 2439, as well as long-term gains or losses from Forms 4684, 8824, and 6781. Enter on line 12, the amount of net long-term gain or loss from Schedule K-1, Forms 1041, 1065, and 1120S. Instructions are included with Schedule K-1. See Tab 5 for a discussion of Schedule K-1.

Distributions paid by a mutual fund (or other regulated investment company) or real estate investment trust from its net realized long-term capital gains are recorded on line 13. They are reported on Form 1099-DIV in box 2a. Distributions of net short-term capital gains are not treated as capital gains but are included on Form 1099-DIV as ordinary dividends and reported on Schedule B.

Capital gains received as a nominee are reported on line 13 of Schedule D but in only the amount that belongs to the taxpayer. A statement must be attached showing the full amount received and the amount received as a nominee. See Tab 2 for filing requirements by a nominee.

Capital Loss Carryover. As noted for short-term capital gains, individuals may carry over a net capital loss to future tax years until the loss is used. When a loss is carried over, it remains long or short term. The carryover is figured on the Capital Loss Carryover Worksheet in the Schedule D instructions and reproduced on page 4-40. The allowable capital loss deduction is the lesser of:

- $3,000 ($1,500 if married filing separately); or
- the total net loss as shown on line 16 of Schedule D.

A capital loss that is carried over to a later tax year retains its original character as either long term or short term in the year to which it is carried. Thus, if it is a long-term capital loss, it is reported on line 14 of Schedule D. A long-term capital loss carried over to the next year will reduce that year's long-term capital gain prior to reducing that year's short-term gains.

Joint or Separate Returns. If the taxpayer and his or her spouse filed separate returns in previous tax years and are now filing a joint return for 2013, then combine the couple's separate capital loss carryovers for the 2013 return. However, if the spouses filed jointly in previous tax years and are now filing separate returns for 2013, any capital loss carryover from a joint return must allocated to each spouse on the basis of their respective net capital loss from the preceding year.

Example. Jon and Margery filed joint returns from 2009 to 2012, but they chose married filing separately in 2013. Their 2012 return has a long-term capital loss of $6,000: $5,000 for Jon's investment activities and $1,000 for Margery's. The couple cannot split the $6,000 carryover equally; Margery can use only $1,000 of the total carryover in 2013, and Jon, assuming he can use the maximum $1,500 to offset gain or income, will carry over $3,500 of loss to 2014.

Net Long-Term Gain or Loss. The taxpayer combines column (h) of lines 8 through 14 and enters the total on line 15 for his or her long-term capital gain or loss.

Lines 16 and 17

Combine line 7, net short-term capital gain/loss, and line 15, net long-term capital gain/loss, and enter the result on line 16. Answer whether both lines 15 and 16 are gains and mark line 17 accordingly.

Line 18, Amount of 28% Rate Gain

A 28% tax rate applies for:

- capital gains realized from the sale or qualified small business stock under IRC §1202 to the extent not excluded from gross income; and
- collectibles held for more than one year, but only to the extent such gain is taken into account in computing gross income and any loss is taken into account in computing taxable income.

The 28% Rate Gain Worksheet in the Schedule D instructions (reproduced at page 4-40) is used to calculate the net amount of gain subject to the 28% rate by netting the gain reported against short-term capital losses from line 7 of Schedule D. If the result is positive, the amount is entered on line 18.

 Caution. The 28% rate applies to gains from qualified small business stock and collectibles regardless of the capital gains rate for gain from the sales and exchange of other capital assets.

Collectibles. A *collectibles gain or loss* is a long-term gain or loss from the sale or exchange of a collectible that is a capital asset. A collectible includes works of art, rugs, antiques, metals (i.e., gold, silver, and platinum bullion), gems, stamps, coins, alcoholic beverages, and certain other tangible property.

 Caution. Note that, although certain gold, silver, and platinum coins and bullion are not classified as collectibles for IRA investment purposes, these items are considered collectibles for purposes of the 28% capital gains rate.

Filing Tip. The sale or other disposition of collectibles is reported on Form 8949 the same as any other sale or exchange of a capital asset. When reporting the sale of a collectible, however, enter code "C" in column (f) and -0- in column (g) of Form 8949.

Gains (but not losses) from any sale of a partnership, S corporation, or trust that is attributable to unrealized appreciation of collectibles will also be taxed at 28%. The exclusion may be partially recaptured on the 28% Rate Gain Worksheet.

Qualified Small Business Stock. Gain from the sale of qualified small business stock that is not excluded from income is not eligible for the regular long-term capital gains rate that applies to assets held for more than 12 months. Instead, such gain is taxed at a maximum rate of 28%. See page 4-10 for more information on the exclusion of gain from the sale of qualified small business stock. For further details on what stock is eligible for the exclusion, see MTG ¶1905.

 Filing Tip. The election to exclude gain from the sale of qualified small business stock is made by reporting the sale or exchange on Form 8949. The taxpayer reports the sale or exchange as if he or she were not taking the exclusion, but with code "Q" entered in column (f) and the amount of the exclusion as a negative number (in parentheses) in column (g). If the transaction is reported as an installment sale on Form 6252, figure the exclusion amount for the year by multiplying the total amount of the exclusion by a fraction, the numerator of which is the amount of eligible gain to be recognized for the tax year and the denominator of which is the total amount of eligible gain.

Line 19, Unrecaptured IRC §1250 Gain

The Unrecaptured Section 1250 Gain Worksheet (reproduced on page 4-41) must be completed if *any* of the following conditions applied:

- the taxpayer sold or otherwise disposed of IRC §1250 property (generally, real property that the client depreciated) held more than one year (reported on Form 4797, Parts I and III);
- the taxpayer received installment payments for IRC §1250 property held more than one year for which taxpayer reported gain on the installment method on Form 6252;
- the taxpayer received Schedule K-1 from an estate or trust, partnership, or S corporation that shows "unrecaptured IRC §1250 gain";
- the taxpayer received Form 1099-DIV or Form 2439 from a mutual fund (or other regulated investment compnay) or real estate investment trust that reports "unrecaptured IRC §1250 gain"; or
- the taxpayer reported long-term capital gain from the sale or exchange of an interest in a partnership that owned IRC §1250 property.

As with the 28% Rate Gain Worksheet, the Unrecaptured IRC §1250 Gain Worksheet nets these unrecaptured gains against long-term and short-term capital gains from lines 15 and 7. If the result is positive, the amount has to be entered on line 19. See page 4-19 and MTG ¶1786 for more information.

Form 4797

Sale of Business Property

Form 4797 is used to report the following:

- gain or loss for partners and S corporation shareholders from the disposition of certain IRC §179 property by a partnership or S corporation;

- the computation of recapture amounts for IRC §179 property or listed property under IRC §280F(b)(2) because the business use of the property decreased to 50% or less;
- the sale or exchange of property used in a trade or business; depreciable an amortizable property; oil, gas, geothermal, or other mineral properties; and IRC §126 property acquired, improved, or modified as a of the receipt of certain agricultural cost-sharing program payments for conservation purposes;
- the involuntary conversion (from other than casualty or theft) of property used in a trade or business and capital assets held in connection with a trade or business or a transaction entered into for profit;
- the disposition of noncapital assets (other than inventory or property held primarily for sale to customers in the ordinary course of a trade or business); and
- the disposition of capital assets not reported on Form 8949 and Schedule D.

Form 4797 is divided into four main parts. The table on page 4-16 sets forth where to begin reporting most transactions. The taxpayer enters gross proceeds from all sales or exchanges that were reported on Form 1099-B or Form 1099-S or substitute statement on line 1 that are included on line 2, line 10, or line 20, of the various Parts, whichever is applicable.

Part I—IRC §1231 Transactions

Part I is used to determine gains or losses from the sales or exchanges of IRC §1231 property (see IRC §1231 property, following) that are not required to be reported in Part III.

Line 2(a), Description of Transaction

IRC §1231 property includes the following:

- property used in a trade or business, subject to depreciation and held more than one year;
- real property used in a trade or business and held for more than one year (but excluding property includible in inventory or held primarily for sale to customers);
- trade or business property (defined in the previous two items) held for more than one year and involuntarily converted;
- capital assets held for more than one year;
- an unharvested crop on land used in the trade or business and held for more than one year;
- livestock (except poultry and other birds) held for draft, breeding, dairy, or sporting purposes; and
- timber, domestic iron ore, or coal under certain conditions.

See MTG ¶1747–¶1751 for details and explanations.

As with capital assets, to qualify as IRC §1231 property, business property must be held for one day longer than a full calendar year. The holding period for IRC §1231 property begins the day after purchase and ends on the day of disposition.

IRC §1231 transactions do not include sales or exchanges of inventory or property held primarily for sale to customers; copyrights; literary, musical, or artistic compositions; letters or memoranda; or similar property. Also not included are U.S. government publications, including the Congressional Record, received from the government other than by purchase at the normal sales price or from someone who had received it in a similar way.

Involuntary Conversions. Also entered in Part I of Form 4797 are involuntary conversions of property or capital assets held more than one year in connection with a trade or business or a transaction entered into for profit. The conversion may result from partial or destruction of the property, theft or seizure, or requisition or condemnation (whether threatened or carried out).

If any recognized losses were from involuntary conversions from fire, storm, shipwreck, or other casualty or from theft, and the losses exceed the recognized gains from the conversions, any gains or losses should not be included in figuring IRC §1231 losses.

Line 2(b), Date Acquired

Note that the actual date acquired should be listed in column 2(b), even though the following day is used to determine length of holding period.

Filing Tip. If the taxpayer sells or otherwise disposes of IRC §1231 property inherited, then generally enter "INHERITED" instead of the date acquired in column (b). However, if the IRC §1231 property was inherited from someone who died in 2010 and the decedent's executor filed Form 8939, then see IRS Publication 4895.

Line 2(c), Date Sold

The date of sale is entered column 2(c).

Line 2(d), Sales Price

Enter in column 2(d) the gross sales price. See also the discussion of Form 8949, line 1(d) on page 4-8.

Line 2(e), Depreciation Allowed or Allowable since Acquisition

If depreciable or amortizable property was disposed of at a gain, all or part of the gain (even if otherwise nontaxable) may have to be recaptured and treated as ordinary income.

Caution. The allowable depreciation will be subtracted from the unadjusted basis to determine gain or loss, even if the depreciation has never been taken.

Line 2(f), Cost or Other Basis

The cost or other basis is the cost of the property plus purchase commissions, improvements, and sale expenses. An explanation of any basis used that is not the cost has to be attached. This may be necessary if the property was inherited, received as a gift, or received in a tax-free exchange, involuntary conversion, or wash sale of stock. For more information, see the discussion of basis beginning on page 4-3.

Line 2(g), Gain or (Loss)

To calculate the taxpayer's gain or loss for the entire year, subtract column (f) from the sum of columns (d) and (e). Enter total in column (g).

Line 3, Gain, If Any, from Form 4684, Line 39

Form 4684, *Casualties and Thefts*, is used to report gains and losses from casualties and thefts. See discussion in Tab 2.

Line 4, Section 1231 Gain from Installment Sales

See the discussion of installment sales beginning on page 4-24.

Line 5, Section 1231 Gain from Like-Kind Exchanges from Form 8824

See discussion of like-kind exchanges on page 4-21.

Line 6, Gain from Line 32 from Other than Casualty or Theft

Line 6 represents the total long-term gain reported in Part III, other than from casualty or theft.

Line 7, Net Gain/Loss

Combine on line 7 the amounts on lines 1 through 6. If the taxpayer is a partner in a partnership or shareholder in an S corporation, include the gain or loss from the Schedule K-1s in line 7 per the K-1 instructions.

If after totaling everything, line 7 is zero or a loss, it is carried to Part II (line 11), where it is netted against short-term gain/loss. If line 7 is a gain and there are no prior year IRC §1231 losses reported on line 8, then enter the gain as a long-term capital gain on Schedule D of the taxpayer's return.

Line 8, Nonrecaptured Net Section 1231 Losses from Prior Years

IRC §1231 gain on line 7 is treated as ordinary income to the extent of nonrecaptured IRC §1231 losses, which are simply net IRC §1231 losses sustained during the *five preceding tax years* that have not yet been applied against any net IRC §1231 gain.

Example. Raphael had net IRC §1231 losses of $4,000 and $5,000 in 2008 and 2010, respectively, and net IRC §1231 gains of $3,000 in 2012. After filing his 2012 return, he has $6,000 of unrecaptured loss ($9,000 – $3,000). In 2013, he had a net IRC §1231 gain of $2,000 which is entered on line 7, and the nonrecaptured net IRC §1231 loss of $6,000 is entered on line 8. The entire $2,000 net IRC §1231 gain on line 7 is treated as ordinary income and is entered on line 12 of Form 4797. For recordkeeping purposes, $1,000 was recaptured from 2008 and $1,000 from 2010. Thus, the $4,000 loss from 2008 is entirely recaptured ($3,000 in 2012 and $1,000 in 2013), and $4,000 of IRC §1231 losses from 2010 are left to be recaptured ($5,000 minus the $1,000 recaptured in 2013) in 2014.

Line 9, Net Gain (or Loss)

Subtract line 8 from line 7. If the result is zero or less, enter -0-. Whenever this line is greater than zero, all net IRC §1231 losses from prior years have been recaptured. Enter the gain as a long-term capital gain on Schedule D of the taxpayer's return.

Part II—Ordinary Gains and Losses

If a transaction is not reportable on Part I or III of Form 4797, and the property is not a capital asset, then gain or loss is reported in Part II as ordinary income, and then reported on line 14 of Form 1040.

Line 10, Ordinary Gains and Losses Not Included in Parts I and III

Report other ordinary gains and losses, including gains and losses from property held one year or less on line 10.

Securities or Commodities Held by a Trader Who Made a Mark-to-Market Election. Report on line 10 all gains and losses from sales and dispositions of securities or commodities held in connection with a trading business, including gains and losses from marking to market securities and commodities held at the end of the tax year. Attach a statement that shows the details of each transaction, using the same format as

Where To Make First Entry for Certain Items Reported on This Form

	(a) Type of property	(b) Held 1 year or less	(c) Held more than 1 year
1	Depreciable trade or business property		
a	Sold or exchanged at a gain	Part II	Part III (1245, 1250)
b	Sold or exchanged at a loss	Part II	Part I
2	Depreciable residential rental property:		
a	Sold or exchanged at a gain	Part II	Part III (1250)
b	Sold or exchanged at a loss	Part II	Part I
3	Farmland held less than 10 years upon which soil, water, or land clearing expenses were deducted:		
a	Sold at a gain	Part II	Part III (1252)
b	Sold at a loss	Part II	Part I
4	All other farmland	Part II	Part I
5	Disposition of cost-sharing payment property described in section 126	Part II	Part III (1255)
6	Cattle and horses used in a trade or business for draft, breeding, dairy, or sporting purposes:	**Held less than 24 months**	**Held 24 months or more**
a	Sold at a gain	Part II	Part III (1245)
b	Sold at a loss	Part II	Part I
c	Raised cattle and horses sold at a gain	Part II	Part I
7	Livestock other than cattle and horses used in a trade or business for draft, breeding, dairy, or sporting purposes:	**Held less than 12 months**	**Held 12 months or more**
a	Sold at a gain	Part II	Part III (1245)
b	Sold at a loss	Part II	Part I
c	Raised livestock sold at a gain	Part II	Part I

line 10 (that is, columns (a) through (g)). Separately show and identify securities or commodities held and marked to market at the end of the year. On line 10, enter *"Trader–see attached"* in column (a) and the totals from the statement in columns (d), (f), and (g).

Small Business Investment Company Stock. Report on line 10 ordinary losses from the sale or exchange (including worthlessness) of stock in a small business investment company operating under the Small Business Investment Act of 1958 (IRC §1242). Also attach a statement that includes the name and address of the small business investment company and, if applicable, the reason the stock is worthless and the approximate date it became worthless. See MTG ¶1913 for more information.

IRC §1244 (Small Business) Stock. Individuals report losses, up to $50,000 ($100,000 for joint filers) from the sale or exchange (including worthlessness) of IRC §1244 (small business) stock as ordinary losses on line 10. See MTG ¶1911 for more information. To qualify as IRC §1244 stock:

- the corporation's equity cannot exceed $1 million at the time of stock issuance;

- the stock must have been acquired directly by the taxpayer at original issue for money or property other than stock or securities; and
- in the five years preceding the loss, the corporation must have derived over half of its gross receipts from business operations (not simply from investments).

Special rules may limit the amount of IRC §1244 ordinary loss if:

- IRC §1244 stock was received in exchange for property with a basis in excess of its fair market value; or
- the holder's stock basis increased because of contributions to capital or otherwise.

 Filing Tip. If an ordinary loss from the sale, exchange, or worthlessness of IRC §1244 stock is more than the maximum amount that can be treated as an ordinary loss, then report the loss on both Form 4797 and Form 8949. On Form 8949, however, enter the loss claimed on Form 4797 in column (g) as a positive number, and Code "S" in column (f). A computation of the loss must be attached to Form 4797.

Filing Tip. It is advisable to include a statement with the return on which the taxpayer is claiming a loss (including worthlessness) on the sale or exchange of stock in a small business investment company. The statement should include the name and address of the company. If declaring the stock worthless, an explanation of why the stock is worthless along with the approximate date it became worthless.

Lines 11-17, Net Gain (or Loss) from All Transactions

Line 11 has the net capital loss from Part I, and line 12 is the gain or unrecaptured IRC §1231 losses from Part I. See the discussion of Part III below regarding gain reported on line 13. Lines 14-16 are for *ordinary gain or loss* from casualty and theft, installment sales, and like-kind exchanges.

Line 18a, Subtraction of Casualty/Theft Losses

Enter on line 18a the smaller of the loss on Form 4797, line 11, or the loss on Form 4684, line 35, column (b) (ii). To figure which loss is smaller, treat both losses as positive numbers. If the casualty loss is from income-producing property, the loss will be reported on line 28 of Schedule A and will not be subject to the 2% adjusted-gross-income (AGI) floor. If the loss was sustained as an employee, the loss is reported on line 23 of Schedule A but is subject to the 2% AGI floor. Be sure to identify the amount as from "Form 4797, line 18a." The taxpayer must redetermine the gain or loss, including any gain reported on line 3 of Form 4797, to account for the loss taken on line 18a. The results will be reported as ordinary income or loss on line 14 of Form 1040.

Caution. If deductions are not itemized in 2013, these losses will not be recovered.

Part III—Depreciation Recapture and Other Gains

Part III of Form 4797 is used to determine the recapture of depreciation and certain other items that must be reported as ordinary income upon the disposition of property held for one year or less.

Line 19, Description of Property

List separately each piece of IRC §1245, §1250, §1252, §1254, and §1255 property sold or disposed during the tax year, including dispositions of property for which

the IRC §179 expense deduction was separately reported on Schedule K-1 by a partnership or S corporation. If there are more than four properties to report, use additional Forms 4797.

Filing Tip. Do not combine properties; each property must have its own line.

Line 20, Gross Sales Price

The gross sales price includes money, the fair market value of other property received, and any existing mortgage or other debt the buyer assumes. For casualty or theft gains, include insurance or other reimbursement received or expected for each item. As with all casualty reporting, insurance coverage must be considered in expected payments even if no claim has been submitted or will be submitted.

Enter the amount realized for the sale, exchange, or involuntary conversion of IRC §126 property acquired, improved, or modified as a result of the receipt of certain agricultural cost-sharing program payments for conservation purposes (and subject to recapture under IRC §1255). If the property is disposed of in any other way, enter the fair market value.

Line 21, Cost or Other Basis Plus Expense of Sale

Any increase in the cost or other basis of the property from expenditures with respect to the property must be reduced by the amount of any enhanced oil recovery credit or disabled access credit claimed with respect to such property. No adjustment is made, however, to the cost or other basis for any of the items taken into account on line 22.

Line 22, Depreciation (or Depletion) Allowed or Allowable

Depreciation allowed must be reported on line 22 even if it was not taken by the taxpayer.

Planning Tip. Taxpayers who have failed to claim depreciation or claimed an impermissible amount can correct this error even in the year of disposition by filing Form 3115, *Application for Change of Accounting Method*, and requesting an automatic change. Details can be found in the form instructions and Rev. Proc. 2011-14, 2011-4 IRB 330.

To determine the correct amount to enter on line 22, first add any amounts from the following list of items:

- deductions allowed or allowable for depreciation (including any special bonus depreciation allowance), amortization, depletion, or preproduction expenses;
- the IRC §179 expense deduction;
- the commercial revitalization deduction for buildings placed in service before 2010;
- the downward basis adjustment under IRC §50(c) to investment credit property;
- the deduction for qualified clean-fuel vehicle property or refueling property;
- deductions under IRC §1253(2) or (3) for franchises, trademarks, and trade names generally acquired on or before August 10, 1993, as well as deductions for the removal of architectural barriers to the handicapped and elderly under IRC §190, and for qualified tertiary injectant expenses under IRC §193;
- the basis reduction for the qualified plug-in electric or qualified electric vehicle credit;
- the basis reduction for the employer-provided childcare facility credit;
- the deduction for qualified energy-efficient commercial building property;
- the basis reduction for the alternative motor vehicle credit; and
- the basis reduction for the alternative fuel vehicle refueling property credit.

From this total, subtract any amounts from the following list of items:

- any investment credit property recapture amount, if the basis of the property was reduced in the tax year the property was placed in service;
- any recapture of deductions for IRC §179 property or listed property under IRC §280F(b)(2) included in gross income in a prior tax year because the business use of the property decreased to 50% or less;
- any qualified clean-fuel vehicle property or refueling property deduction required to be recaptured;
- any basis increase for for qualified plug-in electric or qualified electric vehicle credit recapture;
- any basis increase for recapture of the employer-provided childcare facility credit;
- any basis increase for recapture of the alternative motor vehicle credit;
- any basis increase for recapture of the alternative fuel vehicle refueling property credit; and
- any qualified disaster expense recapture under IRC §198A.

To insure the correct amounts are recaptured as depreciation allowed or allowable, IRS Publication 544, *Sales and Other Dispositions of Assets*, should be reviewed.

A taxpayer may be a partner or an S corporation shareholder, and the partnership or S corporation may have given him or her a Schedule K-1 that separately reports information on the sale, exchange, or other disposition of property for which the IRC §179 expense deduction was claimed. This information will be separately reported on line 20 of Schedule K-1 (Form 1065) or on line 17 of Schedule K-1 (Form 1120S).

If this is the case, the taxpayer should complete the worksheet in the instructions to Form 4797.

 Filing Tip. It is possible that this calculation will turn a gain into a loss. If it does, that loss will be reported in Part I, not Part III.

Lines 23 and 24, Adjusted Basis and Total Gain

On line 23, calculate the adjusted basis of the property by subtracting the depreciation (or depletion) allowable on line 22 from the cost of other basis of the property on line 21. In the case of IRC §126 property acquired, improved, or modified as a result of the receipt of certain agricultural cost-sharing program payments for conservation purposes (and subject to recapture under IRC §1255), enter the adjusted basis of the property when sold or otherwise disposed. Enter on line 24, the gain from the sale or disposition of the property by subtracting the adjusted basis on line 23, from the gross sales price on line 20.

Lines 25a and 25b, Section 1245 Property Depreciation

Enter the amount of depreciation allowed or allowable with respect to IRC §1245 property on line 25a. IRC §1245 property is property that is depreciable or amortizable and is one of the following:

- personal property;
- elevators and escalators placed in service before 1987;
- real property (other than property described under tangible real property below) subject to amortization or deductions under IRC §169, §179, §179A, §179B, §179C, §179D, §179E, §185 (repealed), §188 (repealed), §190, §193, or §194;
- tangible real property (except buildings and their structural components) if used in any of the following ways:
  (a) as an integral part of manufacturing, production, or extraction or of furnishing transportation, communications, or certain public utility services,
  (b) as a research facility in these activities, and
  (c) for the bulk storage of fungible commodities (including commodities in a liquid or gaseous state) used in these activities;
- a single-purpose agricultural or horticultural structure, as defined in IRC §168(i)(13);
- a storage facility (not including a building or its structural components) used in connection with the distribution of petroleum or any primary petroleum product; and

- any railroad grading or tunnel bore, as defined in IRC §168(e)(4).

See IRC §1245(b) for exceptions and limits involving the following:

- gifts;
- transfers at death;
- certain tax-free transactions;
- certain like-kind exchanges, involuntary conversions, etc;
- property distributed by a partnership to a partner;
- transfers to tax-exempt organizations where the property will be used in an unrelated business; and
- timber property.

For example, if a taxpayer transfers IRC §1245 property to another by gift and the recipient later sells the property for a gain, the recipient must take into account any depreciation deducted by the donor in computing IRC §1245 income.

A special rule must be applied when disposing of IRC §197 intangibles (IRC §1245(b)(8)).

Example. Joanna Chung purchased IRC §1245 property for $10,000. She takes depreciation deductions of $2,000 before giving the property to her son, Bruce. The adjusted basis to the son is $8,000, the same as the mother's. Bruce later takes an additional $1,000 of depreciation, reducing his basis to $7,000. In 2013, he sells the property for $10,500, realizing a recognized gain of $3,500.

Lines 26a-g, IRC §1250 Property

IRC §1250 property is depreciable real property (other than IRC §1245 property). IRC §1250 recapture applies if the taxpayer used an accelerated depreciation method, claimed bonus depreciation, or claimed the commercial revitalization deduction. IRC §1250 recapture does not apply to dispositions of the following property placed in service after 1986 (or after July 31, 1986, if elected):

- 27.5-year (or 40-year, if elected) residential rental property (except for 27.5-year qualified New York Liberty Zone property acquired after September 10, 2001); and
- 22-, 31.5-, or 39-year (or 40-year, if elected) nonresidential real property (except for 39-year qualified New York Liberty Zone property acquired after September 10, 2001, and property for which the taxpayer elected to claim a commercial revitalization deduction).

Real property depreciable under ACRS (pre-1987 rules) is subject to recapture under IRC §1245, except for the following, which are treated as IRC §1250 property:

- 15-, 18-, or 19-year real property and low-income housing that is residential rental property;
- 15-, 18-, or 19-year real property and low-income housing that is used mostly outside the United States;
- 15-, 18-, or 19-year real property and low-income housing for which a straight-line election was made; and
- low-income rental housing described in IRC §1250(a)(1)(B).

See IRC §1250(d) for exceptions and limits involving the following:

- gifts;
- transfers at death;
- certain tax-free transactions;
- certain like-kind exchanges, involuntary conversions, etc;
- property distributed by a partnership to a partner;
- disposition of qualified low-income housing;
- transfers of property to tax-exempt organizations if the property will be used in an unrelated business; and
- dispositions of property as a result of foreclosure proceedings.

Additional Depreciation after 1975. For line 26a, *additional depreciation* is the excess of actual depreciation (including any special depreciation allowance or commercial revitalization deduction) over depreciation figured using the straight-line method. For this purpose, the basis for investment credit property under IRC §50(c)(1) (or the corresponding provision of prior law) should not be reduced to figure straight-line depreciation. Also, if a commercial revitalization deduction was claimed, figure straight-line depreciation using the property's applicable recovery period under IRC §168.

Applicable Percentage. The percentage entered on line 26b will be 100%, except for low-income housing described in IRC §1250(a)(1)(B), where the applicable percentage can be found.

Additional Depreciation after 1969 and before 1976. If straight-line depreciation is more than the actual depreciation for the period after 1975, line 26d is reduced by the excess, but not below zero.

Line 27, IRC §1252 Property

The taxpayer may have ordinary income on the disposition of certain farmland held more than a year but less than 10 years. Line 27 may be skipped if such farmland was disposed of 10 years or more after acquisition.

Enter 100% of line 27a on line 27b except as follows:

- 80% if the farmland was disposed of within the sixth year after it was acquired;
- 60% if disposed of within the seventh year;
- 40% if disposed of within the eighth year; or
- 20% if disposed of within the ninth year.

Partners enter applicable amounts in accordance with instructions from the partnership.

Line 28, Section 1254 Property

If the taxpayer had a gain on the disposition of oil, gas, or geothermal property placed in service before 1987, all or part of the gain is treated as ordinary income. Include on line 22 of Form 4797 any depletion allowed (or allowable) in determining the adjusted basis of the property.

If the taxpayer had a gain on the disposition of oil, gas, geothermal, or other mineral properties (IRC §1254 property) placed in service after 1986, he or she must recapture all expenses that were deducted as intangible drilling costs, depletion, mine exploration costs, and development costs.

If the property was placed in service before 1987, enter on line 28a the total expenses after 1975 that were deducted by the taxpayer or any previous owner as intangible drilling and development costs under IRC §263(c) (except previously expensed mining costs that were included in income upon reaching the producing state) and would have been reflected in the adjusted basis of the property if they had not been deducted.

If the property was placed in service after 1986, enter on line 28a the total expenses that were deducted under IRC §§263, 616, or 617 by the taxpayer or any other person, and that would have been included in the basis of the property if there had been no deduction, plus the deduction under IRC §611 that reduced the adjusted basis of the property.

Lines 29a and 29b, Section 1255 Property

Gain realized on the disposition of IRC §126 property with respect to which certain agricultural cost-sharing program payments for conservation purposes were excluded from income must be included in ordinary income to the extent of an applicable percentage of the aggregate payments that were excluded. Enter 100% of the payments on line 29a if the property is disposed of less than 10 years after receipt of payments excluded from income. Enter 100% minus 10% of the amount for each year, or part of a year, that the property was held over 10 years after receipt of the excluded payments; enter zero if 20 years or more.

If any part of the gain shown on line 24 is treated as ordinary income under IRC §§1231 through 1254 (for example, IRC §1252), enter the smaller of line 24 reduced by the part of the gain treated as ordinary income under the other provision, or line 29a.

Lines 30-32, Total Gains for All Properties

The recapture amounts are totaled on line 31 and subtracted from total gains on the transactions listed on line 24. The amount is then added to long-term capital gains in Part I.

Part IV— Recapture Amounts Under IRC § 179 and §280F(b)(2)

If the taxpayer took an IRC §179 expense deduction for property placed in service after 1986 (other than listed property defined by IRC §280F(d)(4)), and the business use of the property decreased to 50% or less in 2013, complete column (a) of lines 33 through 35 to figure the recapture amount.

Filing Tip. IRC §179 expense deduction recapture rules also apply to any qualified Gulf Opportunity Zone (GO Zone) property on which the 50% bonus depreciation was claimed and which has ceased to be qualified GO Zone property (IRC §1400N(d)(5)). See MTG ¶1208 and ¶1237.

If the taxpayer has listed property placed in service in a prior year and the business use decreased to 50% or less in 2013, figure the amount to be recaptured under IRC §280F(b)(2). Complete column (b), lines 33 through 35. See IRS Publication 463, *Travel, Entertainment, Gift, and Car Expenses*, for more details on recapture of excess depreciation.

Filing Tip. If the client has more than one property subject to the recapture rules, figure the recapture amounts separately for each property. Show these calculations on a separate statement and attach it to the tax return.

Line 33, IRC §179 Expense

In column (a), enter the IRC §179 expense deduction claimed when the property was placed in service. In column (b), enter the depreciation allowable on the property in prior tax years (plus any IRC §179 expense deduction claimed when the property was placed in service).

Line 34, Recomputed Depreciation

In column (a), enter the depreciation that would have been allowable on the IRC §179 property from the year the property was placed in service through (and including) the current year. See Tab 7, MTG ¶1208, and IRS Publication 946, *How to Depreciate Property*.

In column (b), enter the depreciation that would have been allowable if the property had not been used more than 50% in a qualified business. Figure the depreciation from the year it was placed in service up to (but not including) the current year.

Line 35, Recapture Amount

Subtract line 34 from line 33 and enter the recapture amount as "other income" on the same form or schedule on which the taxpayer took the deduction (Schedule C (Form 1040), for example).

 Caution. If the taxpayer has filed either Schedule C or F and the property was used in both the taxpayer's trade or business and for the production of income, the portion of the recapture amount attributable to the trade or business is subject to self-employment tax. The recapture amount on Line 35 needs to be properly allocated to the appropriate schedule. In addition, the taxpayer will need to remember to increase the basis of the property by the recapture amount.

Other Sales or Exchanges

Like-Kind Exchanges—Form 8824

For personal property, it makes no tax difference whether the property changed hands by a sale or an exchange. When business property changes hands, it may make a great deal of difference in the taxes paid.

If a taxpayer sells business or investment property, both gain and loss are recognized. If a taxpayer exchanges business or investment property for other business or investment property of a "like kind" or "like class," the gain or loss that is realized on the exchange is not recognized.

Nonrecognition of gain or loss does not apply to stock in trade or other property held primarily for sale to customers such as inventories. Thus, if an automobile dealer exchanges one of his or her cars held for sale to a customer for another automobile, the full amount of gain or loss realized will be recognized by the dealer for tax purposes. The same is true if a *dealer* in real estate exchanges one real estate property (if held for sale to customers) for another piece of real estate. If it were not for this restriction, storekeepers, dealers, and other sellers of merchandise could simply trade or barter their goods, instead of selling them outright, in order to avoid paying taxes on their profits.

 Planning Tip. The nonrecognition of gain on a like-kind transaction is a double-edged sword. On the one hand, it defers the immediate recognition of the taxpayer's gain. On the other hand, it reduces the taxpayer's basis and increases the taxpayer's gain in the event of a future taxable disposition.

The only way to tell whether nonrecognition in a given situation is desirable is to project the taxpayer's future income and tax picture. If it appears that nonrecognition would do more harm than good, it may be possible to sidestep the nonrecognition provisions by arranging the transaction in the form of a sale rather than as an exchange.

What Constitutes a Like-Kind Exchange?

The determination of whether property is of like kind is made by reference to the nature and character of the property, and not the property's grade or quality. For example, an exchange of real property for real property, or the exchange of specific class of personal property for other personal property in the same class are exchanges of like property. One kind or class of property, however, may not be exchanged for property of a different kind or class. Generally, this means that real property can be exchanged only for other real property, personal property can be exchanged only for other personal property.

The exchange of an apartment house for a factory building, or of improved land for an unimproved piece of land, would qualify because both are real property used in trade, business, or investment. Personal property is considered like-kind if they fall within the same general MACRS asset class. These asset classes relate to common types of property that are used in most businesses. For other personal property taxpayers should refer to the North American Industry Classification System (NAICS). Property with in the same NAICS product class are treated as like-kind. For additional information regarding the exchange of like-kind or like-class property, see IRS Publication 544, *Sales and Other Dispositions of Assets*.

For example, the exchange of a business car for a sports utility vehicle (SUV) is a like-kind exchange because both items are of the same MACRS general asset class. Similarly, the exchange of a pick-up truck for a panel truck is a like-kind exchange because they are both included in the same MACRS general asset class.

Real property located outside the United States cannot be treated as like-kind property unless it is the replacement of condemned real property located in the United States. Personal property used predominantly in the United States can be exchanged *only* for other like-kind property in a similar location. For example, a computer used within the United States exchanged for a computer used in Canada does not qualify for like-kind treatment.

Deferred Exchanges

A deferred exchange occurs when the property received in a like-kind exchange is received after the transfer of the property given up. The transaction must be an exchange (property for property), rather than a transfer of property for money used to buy replacement property. For a deferred exchange to qualify as like-kind, certain timing requirements must be met for identification and receipt of replacement property.

The taxpayer must generally identify the property to be received in the like-kind exchange within 45 days after the original property transfer. If more than one property is transferred as part of the transaction and they are transferred on different dates, the identification and exchange period begin on the date of the earliest transfer. Identification for this purpose means delivering to the other party involved in the exchange a written description of the replacement property. Up to three properties may generally be identified.

The taxpayer must receive the replacement property by the earlier of: (1) 180 days after the transfer of property given up in the exchange, or (2) the due date or his or her return, including extensions, for the tax year in which the transfer of the property given up occurs. The taxpayer must receive substantially the same property identified earlier.

 Caution. There are no extensions available for the 45- and 180-day identification and closing requirements for like-kind exchanges. The IRS strictly enforces the like-kind requirements.

Trade or Exchange Involving Both Property and Money

The nonrecognition of gain or loss on the exchange of certain property applies *solely* for like-kind property. If nonqualifying property (commonly referred as to boot) is part of the exchange, then the taxpayer recognizes gain from the transaction to the extent of the boot's fair market value. In addition, no loss from the exchange may be recognized to any extent if boot is received.

Boot may consist of cash, relief from debt, property that is not like-kind property being exchanged, or property excluded from like-kind treatment. Boot is often given to equalize the value of the like-kind properties being exchanged

If each party to a like-kind exchange assumes a liability of the other party, then the consideration given by one party (i.e., the liability assumed from the other party) is offset against the consideration received by that party and vice versa for purposes of determining the amount of boot received. In other words, the liabilities assumed by the parties are netted for purposes of determining the amount of boot received.

Example. A butcher exchanges a refrigerator with a basis of $600 for $150 in cash plus a meat-cutting machine with an fair market value of $700. He realizes a gain of $250 on the transaction ($850 amount realized, less the basis of property traded in ($600)). Since the refrigerator and the meat-cutting machine are items of the same class and both are held for productive use in the taxpayer's trade or business, the exchange of the property is tax free. However, because the butcher also received cash, he must recognize gain to the extent of the money received ($150).

If a taxpayer receives both like-kind property and property that is not like kind in an exchange, the fair market value of the non-like-kind property is treated as cash. This means that a gain, if any, is recognized only to the extent of the fair market value of the other property received.

Example. An investor exchanges farm property having a basis of $35,000 for a vacant building lot worth $36,000, an automobile worth $2,000, and a diamond ring worth $500. The amount realized is $38,500, thus realizing a gain of $3,500. The farm and the lot are like-kind property, but the automobile and ring are not like-kind property. Thus, the taxpayer will recognize gain of $2,500, the sum of the fair market value of the automobile and ring.

A loss is never recognized on the exchange of like-kind property held for productive use in a trade or business, even though other property or money is received or paid in addition to the exchange.

> **Example.** A farmer exchanges a combine with a basis of $15,000 for a tractor worth $10,000, a parcel of land worth $2,000, and $1,000 cash. The amount realized is $13,000, and the realized loss is, therefore, $2,000, no part of which is recognized.

A taxpayer who transfers property in a deferred like-kind exchange may recognize gain if he or she actually or constructively receives money or other property (boot) before he or she actually receives like-kind replacement property. In these circumstance, the transaction is treated as a sale and not a like-kind exchange even though the like-kind replacement property may later be received.

There are four safe harbors, the use of any one of which can avoid a determination that the party who has relinquished property is in actual or constructive receipt of money or other property before the actual receipt of the like-kind replacement property. A party may use more than one of the four, but the conditions of each must be separately satisfied. See MTG ¶ 1722. The safe harbors involve security or guarantee arrangements, qualified escrow accounts and qualified trusts, use of qualified intermediaries, and interest and growth factors.

For example, if a qualified intermediary is involved, the determination of whether that party is in actual or constructive receipt of money or other property before the actual receipt of like-kind replacement property is made as if the qualified intermediary is not the agent of that party. A qualified intermediary may be a safe harbor, however, only if the agreement between the party to the exchange and the intermediary expressly limits that party's rights to receive, pledge, borrow, or otherwise obtain the benefits of money or other property held by the qualified intermediary.

Where the like-kind exchange involves related parties (spouse, siblings, descendants, ancestors, or controlled entities) and property is disposed of within two years of that exchange, gain on the original exchange is triggered. Exceptions apply to dispositions because of death or involuntary conversion.

Reporting Like-Kind Exchanges

Report the exchange of like-kind property, even though no gain or loss is recognized, on Form 8824, *Like-Kind Exchanges.* See the instructions for Form 8824 for how to report the details of the exchange. If the taxpayer has any recognized gain because boot is received, report the gain on Schedule D, Form 4797, or Form 6252, whichever applies. Recognized gain may have to be reported as ordinary income from depreciation recapture (see page 4-17).

Exchanges of Securities

Although corporate stocks (shares) are usually held for investment, an exchange of stock for stock is not a tax-free, like-kind exchange, unless the stock is exchanged for the same class of stock in the same corporation. This means that the exchange of stock in one corporation for stock in another corporation or the exchange of common stock for preferred stock in the same corporation, or of stocks for bonds or vice versa, is not a like-kind exchange. Any gain or loss is therefore fully recognized.

Exchanges of Insurance Policies

No gain or loss is recognized if a taxpayer exchanges a life insurance policy for another life insurance policy, an endowment, or an annuity contract. Nonrecognition applies even if there is an outstanding loan on the policy, as long as the new policy has similar loan provisions. The same rule applies when one annuity contract is exchanged for another annuity contract, so long as the insured (the annuitant) remains the same.

Where one endowment policy is exchanged for another endowment policy, no gain or loss is recognized if the beginning date under the new contract is no later than the beginning date under the old contract. Nonrecognition also applies to the exchange of an endowment policy for an annuity contract.

> **Caution.** The exchange of an annuity contract for a life insurance policy or an endowment policy does not fall under this tax-free exchange rule.

If the insurance company is financially troubled (in rehabilitation, insolvency, conservatorship, or other state proceeding), a policyholder can surrender the policy and make a tax-free reinvestment of the proceeds in a new policy if the transfer is completed within 60 days.

How Nonrecognition Affects Basis

The basis of the property that a taxpayer receives in a fully or partially tax-free exchange, such as a like-kind exchange, must be reduced by the amount of any gain that was realized but not recognized. The reason for this reduction makes economic sense in that the new property is merely a continuation or substitution of the old. In other words, for tax purposes, the exchange never took place (which is the theory for nonrecognition of gain or loss on a like-kind exchange).

Example. Joan Haslan had a nonrecognized gain of $1,400 on the exchange of her truck, which had a basis of $12,600, for another truck worth $14,000. The basis of the new truck would be $12,600 ($14,000 less the $1,400 nonrecognized gain). Thus, if she shortly thereafter sold the new truck for $14,000, she would have a recognized gain of $1,400.

Installment Sales—Form 6252

Generally, Form 6252, *Installment Sale Income*, is used to report gain from casual sales of real or personal property (other than inventory) if the taxpayer will receive any payments in a tax year after the year of sale. The form must be filed in the year of sale, and in every later year in which a payment is received. If the sale of the property results in a loss, the installment method of reporting cannot be used and the loss can be deducted only in the year of sale if the property was used in a trade or business or for investment purposes.

Caution. The installment method of reporting may allow a taxpayer to reduce his or her total tax on the sale of property by spreading the gain out over a number of years. Care must be taken, however, when structuring an installment sale agreement to insure a sufficient payment is received in the year of sale to satisfy any tax liability caused by depreciation recapture. If property is sold for which the taxpayer claimed depreciation, then the depreciation is recaptured as ordinary income in the year of sale, whether or not an installment payment is received.

Part I of Form 6252 should be completed for the year of sale only. Part II should be completed for the year of sale and for any year in which payment is received or certain debts must be treated as a payment on installation obligations. Part III should not be completed if final payment is received in the current tax year.

Electing Out of Installment Method

The installment method of reporting is mandatory unless the taxpayer elects not to report the sale on the installment method. To elect out, do not report the sale on Form 6252, but report the full amount of gain on a timely filed return, including extensions, on Form 4797, Form 8949, or Schedule D of Form 1040, whichever applies. If the original form was filed on time without the election being made, the election may be made on an amended return filed no later than six month after due date of the tax return, excluding extensions. Write "Filed pursuant to section 301.9100-2" at the top of the amended return.

Because this is an election, look at the sale agreement to see if the potential exists for a favorable allocation of the selling price.

Planning Tip. Other consideration that need to be taken into account when determining whether to use an installment sale are: dealing with elderly clients who may inadvertently leave the installment agreement in their estate; clients having capital losses that are being carried forward; and the potential of an increase in capital gains rates in the future when the balance of the installment sale agreement is paid.

Figuring Adjusted Basis for Installment Sales

Use the following worksheet to figure adjusted basis in the property for installment sale purposes. The worksheet also determines the gross profit percentage necessary to figure installment sale income (gain) for the current year.

Worksheet for Figuring Adjusted Basis and Gross Profit Percentage on Installment Sales	
1. Enter the selling price for the property.	
2. Enter adjusted basis for the property.	
3. Enter selling expenses.	
4. Enter any depreciation recapture.	
5. Add lines 2, 3, and 4. This is the **adjusted basis for installment sale purposes**.	
6. Subtract line 5 from line 1. If $0 or less, enter -0-. This is **gross profit**.	
If the amount entered on line 6 is $0, **Stop** here. The installment method cannot be used.	
7. Enter the contract price for the property.	
8. Divide line 6 by line 7. This is the **gross profit percentage**.	

Involuntary Conversions

An involuntary conversion occurs when property is destroyed, stolen, condemned, or disposed of under the threat of condemnation and the taxpayer receives other property or money in payment (e.g., insurance proceeds or a condemnation award). Gain from an involuntary conversion of property is usually recognized for tax purposes. However, there are two specific sets of circumstances under which gain from an involuntary conversion of property is not recognized.

First, when property is involuntarily converted into other property that is similar or related in service or use, no gain is currently recognized. The basis of the old property is simply transferred to the new property. This nonrecognition rule is mandatory.

Second, when property is involuntarily converted into money (e.g., insurance proceeds after fire destroys a building) or into unlike property, the owner may elect to postpone gain by buying replacement property within a certain period. To postpone reporting all the gain, the taxpayer must buy replacement property costing at least as much as the amount realized for the condemned property. If the cost of the replacement property is less than the amount realized, the taxpayer must report the gain up to the unspent part of the amount realized.

The length of time allowed to replace involuntarily converted property depends on the character of the property converted and the cause of the conversion.

- For real property converted by destruction or theft, or personal property (regardless of the cause of the conversion), the replacement period is two years after the close of the first tax year in which any part of the gain on the conversion is realized.
- For business or investment real property converted by condemnations and other seizures, the replacement period is three years after the close of the first tax year in which any part of the gain on the conversion is realized.
- For principal residences and their contents damaged by federally declared disasters, the replacement period is four years after the close of the first tax year in which any part of the gain on the conversion is realized.

 Planning Tip. Victims of the tornados and storms that struck Kansas in the spring of 2007 and parts of the Midwest struck by violent weather in the spring of 2008 (the Midwestern disaster area) were given an extended period of time to replace both businesses and personal residences destroyed in the hurricane. The replacement period for both individuals and businesses is five years, if the property was originally located with the disaster area and the replacement property is also substantially located within the disaster area.

Loss

Loss from an involuntary conversion is deductible only if the converted property is used in a business or for the production of income. However, casualty or theft losses on personal property may be deductible.

Principal Residence

When an individual's principal residence has been involuntarily converted, the individual may exclude any realized gain, up to the $250,000/$500,000 maximum (see page 4-26) as if the home had been sold. If the total realized gain is more than the maximum exclusion, the individual may defer recognizing the excess if replacement property is purchased.

The sale of land within a reasonable period of time following the destruction of a principal residence qualifies as part of the involuntary conversion of the residence (Rev. Rul. 96-32).

Livestock

The destruction of livestock by disease, or the sale or exchange of livestock because of disease, is also treated as an involuntary conversion. Sales or exchanges of livestock (except poultry) solely on account of drought, flood, or other weather-related conditions that exceed the number normally sold by the taxpayer may also be entitled to involuntary conversion treatment. If, because of soil or other environmental contamination, it is not feasible for a farmer to reinvest the proceeds from involuntarily converted livestock in property similar or related in service or use, the proceeds may be invested in other property, including real property, used for farming. The replacement property will then be treated as property similar or related in service or use to the converted livestock.

Planning Tip. The IRS has provided for automatic extensions of the four-year replacement period for livestock treated as involuntarily converted. For farmers and ranchers in designated severe drought areas, the replacement period is extended to the first tax year ending after the first drought-free year for the applicable region. The IRS has declared that the 12-month period ending on August 31, 2013, is not a drought-free year for the listed regions. The replacement period will be extended for any county listed in the applicable regions. A list of counties in affected states can be found in Notice 2013-62.

Reporting Requirements for Involuntary Conversions

The election to defer all or part of the gain realized in the involuntary conversion is made by excluding the gain from gross income on the tax return for the year in which it is realized.

- Form 4797 is used to report the gain or loss from an involuntary conversion (other than from casualty or theft) of business property, or capital assets used in a business or in connection with a transaction entered into for profit.
- Form 4684 is used to report involuntary conversions from casualties and thefts.
- Form 8949 is used to report gains from involuntary conversions (other than from casualty or theft) of capital assets not held for business or profit.

Required Statement. The taxpayer is required to attach a statement to the tax return for the year in which gain is realized (e.g., the year in which insurance proceeds are received). The statement should include such information as the date and details of the involuntary conversion and the insurance or other reimbursement received. If replacement property is acquired before the tax return is filed, the statement must include information concerning a description of the replacement property, the date of acquisition, and the cost of the replacement property. If replacement is to be made after the year in which the gain is realized, the statement should also state that the taxpayer intends to replace the property within the required replacement period.

Sale of Principal Residence

A taxpayer may exclude from gross income a limited amount of gain realized on the sale or exchange of his or her principal residence. Generally, the home one lives in most of the time is one's principal residence; it can be a house, houseboat, mobile home, cooperative apartment, or condominium.

In order to exclude gain on the sale of a home, a taxpayer generally must have owned and used the property as his or her principal residence for at least two years during the five-year period ending on the date of sale.

The maximum gain that can be excluded is $250,000 for individuals and $500,000 for married couples filing jointly. Surviving spouses may claim the $500,000 exclusion on the sale of the main home provided that the sale occurs within two years of the date of deceased spouse's death. See the discussion on page 4-27.

The exclusion may be claimed only once every two years. A taxpayer who has owned and lived in the property for less than two years, however, can still claim an exclusion if he or she sold or exchanged the home because of changes in employment, health, or unforeseen circumstances. The maximum amount that can be excluded will, however, be reduced. See the discussion on page 4-28.

Planning Tip. Even though the rules for exclusion of gain on the sale of a principal residence mean that the majority of taxpayers will feel they do not need to keep detailed records on improvements to their homes and other additions to basis, all homeowners should be encouraged to keep such records. This is especially true in areas experiencing rapid appreciation in housing prices or when plans call for a long-term occupancy. Also, the exclusion could be modified or eliminated in the future and the current exclusion amounts are not inflation adjusted, leading to devaluation over time.

Ownership and Use Tests

To claim the exclusion of gain from the sale of a principal residence, then during the five-year period ending on the date of sale the seller must have:

- owned the home for at least two years or five years if the home was acquired in a like-kind exchange (the ownership test); and
- lived in the home as a main home for at least two years (the use test).

The required two years of ownership and use during the five-year period ending on the date of sale do not have to be continuous, nor do they both have to occur at the same time. A taxpayer meets the tests if he or she owned and lived in the property as his or her main home for either 24 full months or 730 days (365 × 2) during the five-year period ending on the date of sale.

In establishing the use of the property as a principal residence, occupancy of the residence by the taxpayer is required. The use of multiple residences over the five year period may allow more than one residence to qualify for the exclusion. Short temporary absences such as for vacation or other seasonal absence, even if accompanied with the rental of the residence, are also counted as periods of use.

Gray Area. A taxpayer with more than one home should have records that support the treatment of one home as his or her main residence for any given period of time. It may be advantageous for planning purposes to select the home that will be sold first as the main home. A main home is not necessarily the location where one spends the most time, but if the taxpayer spent the most time at another location, then proof of principal residency must be available supporting the exclusion.

Married Taxpayers. If a husband and wife file a joint return for the year of the sale or exchange of their principal residence, then the exclusion applies if either spouse meets the ownership and use requirements with respect to the property. However, to qualify for the $500,000 exclusion amount, both spouses must meet the use requirement. In addition, while the taxpayers must be married at the time of the sale to qualify for the exclusion, they are not required to have been married during the two years in which they satisfy the use requirement.

Widowed Taxpayer. A surviving spouse can exclude up to $500,000 in gain if the marital principal residence is sold within two years after the death of the spouse. A widow or widower's period of ownership and use of a residence includes the period during which the taxpayer's deceased spouse owned and used the residence as a principal residence. See page 4-26 for more information.

> **Example.** Jorge owned and lived in a house as his principal residence since 1997. Jorge and Miranda were married on May 1, 2012, and used Jorge's house as their principal residence. Jorge died on August 15, 2013, and Miranda inherited the residence. She sold the house for a $200,000 gain on December 1, 2013. Even though Miranda owned and used the house for less than two years, she is considered to have satisfied the ownership and use requirements because her period of ownership and use includes the time period that Jorge owned and used the property prior to his death.

Transfers Incident to Divorce. If a residence is transferred following a divorce, the time during which the taxpayer's spouse or former spouse owned the residence is added to the taxpayer's period of ownership. Also, a taxpayer who owns a residence is deemed to use it as a principal residence while the taxpayer's spouse or former spouse is given separate use of the residence under the terms of a divorce or separation decree. Thus, if the former spouse maintains an ownership interest and the other spouse is allowed to use the residence as a principal residence under a decree of divorce and separation for a number of years, each spouse will be allowed to exclude the gain from the sale of the former marital principal residence.

> **Example.** Jack and Laetitia divorced in 2008. Under terms of the divorce agreement, their house and adjacent property were divided equally between them, each retaining 50% ownership. Laetitia was allowed the full use of the house. They sold the house in 2013 at a gain of $90,000. Since Jack is deemed to use the home as his principal residence under the divorce agreement, both he and Laetitia are allowed to exclude their respective shares of the gain.

Unmarried Joint Owners. Taxpayers who jointly own a principal residence, but are not married, may each exclude up to $250,000 of gain attributable to their respective interests in the property so long as they meet the ownership and use test separately.

Military, Foreign Service, Intelligence Community, and Peace Corps Personnel. A special exception to the two-out-of-five-year rule exists for certain members of the military, foreign service, intelligence community and Peace Corps. A qualified taxpayer in one of these groups may elect to suspend the five-year test period by up to 10 years.

To qualify, the taxpayer or the taxpayer's spouse must be serving on qualified official extended duty. The term extended duty refers to any active duty lasting for a period in excess of 90 days or for an indefinite period, at a location which is at least 50 miles from the residence or requiring residence in Government quarters. The election to extend the five-year test period is made by the taxpayer in the year of the sale by not including the gain in gross income.

> **Planning Tip.** A member of the Peace Corps that may take advantage of the 10-year suspension period includes an individual who is serving outside the United States as an employee of the Peace Corps on qualified official extended duty or as an enrolled volunteer leader.

Trusts and Single-Owner Entities. If a residence is owned by a grantor trust, a taxpayer will be treated as owning the residence for the period that the taxpayer is treated as the owner of the trust or the portion of the trust that includes the residence. The sale or exchange of the residence by the trust will be treated as if the residence were sold or exchanged by the taxpayer.

Similarly, if a residence is owned by an eligible single-owner entity that is disregarded for federal tax purposes as an entity separate from its owner, the taxpayer-owner is treated as owning the residence for purposes of the two-year ownership requirement. The sale or exchange of the residence by the single-owner entity is treated as if the residence were sold or exchanged by the taxpayer

Limitation on Amount of Exclusion

As noted, the maximum gain that can be excluded from the sale of a principal residence is $250,000 for individuals and $500,000 for married couples filing jointly. The maximum $500,000 exclusion applies if:

- either spouse satisfies the ownership test with respect to the property;
- both spouses satisfy the use test with respect to the property; and
- neither spouse is ineligible for the benefits by reason of the one sale or exchange every two-years limitation.

If a married couple filing a joint return does not qualify for the $500,000 maximum exclusion, the amount of gain eligible for the exclusion is the sum of the amounts that each spouse would be entitled to claim if such spouses had not been married including a partial exclusion of gain

A surviving spouse may be eligible to exclude a maximum of $500,000 of gain. The increased inclusion amount applies to a sale or exchange by an unmarried individual whose spouse is deceased on the date of the sale and:

- the sale occurs no later than two years after the date of death of the spouse;
- immediately before the date of death, either spouse met the two-out-of-five year ownership requirement, both spouses met the two-out-of-five year use requirement; and
- neither spouse was ineligible to claim the exclusion because of another sale or exchange within the prior two years that qualified for the exclusion.

 Caution. The $500,000 maximum exclusion for surviving spouses only applies to an unmarried taxpayer whose spouse is deceased on the date of sale of the principal residence. Thus, if the taxpayer remarries and sells the home within two years after the date of death of the first spouse, the taxpayer would not be entitled to the $500,000 maximum exclusion for surviving spouses. It is also unlikely that the taxpayer who remarries would qualify for the $500,000 maximum exclusion amount for joint return filers because the new spouse would not have met the two-out-of-five year use requirement.

Nonqualified Use. The exclusion does not apply to any gain realized from the sale or exchange of a principal residence that is allocable to periods of nonqualified use or attributable to depreciation. A period of nonqualified use is any period during which the property is not used as the principal residence of the taxpayer, the taxpayer's spouse, or the taxpayer's former spouse, i.e., used as a vacation home, rental unit. There are certain exceptions to this rule. See MTG ¶1705.

 Caution. The rule for nonqualified use period prevents the exclusion from applying to gain accumulated while a home was being used as a vacation home before being used as a primary residence.

Reduced Exclusion Rules

An individual who fails to meet the ownership and use test if the sale is caused by an unforeseen event may be entitled to a reduced exclusion. The reduced exclusion is computed by multiplying the maximum allowable exclusion ($250,000, or $500,000 if filing jointly) by a fraction. The numerator of the fraction is the shortest of:

- the period of time that the individual owned the property as a principal residence during the five-year period ending on the date of sale or exchange;
- the period of time that the individual used the property as a principal residence during the five-year period ending on the date of sale; or
- the period between the date of the most recent prior sale to which the exclusion applied and the date of the current sale or exchange.

The numerator may be expressed in days or months. The denominator of the fraction is either 730 days or 24 months (depending on the measure of time used in the numerator).

Example. Romeo is an unmarried taxpayer who owned and used a house for 385 days before he moved out of the house in December 2011 because he was unable to care for himself after sustaining injuries in an auto accident. He sold the house in January 2013. Romeo had not excluded gain from the sale of a residence within the previous two years. He may exclude up to $131,849 of any gain that he realizes from the sale ($250,000 × 385/730 = $131,849). Even though he owned the house for more than 385 days, he must use the smaller of the days of use or the days of ownership.

The following events are "safe harbors" for entitlement to the use of the reduced exclusion. Other unforeseen events may also qualify.

- involuntary conversion;
- natural or man-made disaster, acts of war or terrorism, etc;
- death of a member of the household;
- change of employment;
- change in income that leaves the owner unable to meet household expenses;
- divorce or legal separation; or
- multiple births from same pregnancy.

 Example. James and Amy buy a house near an airport with considerable jet traffic. After one year, they come to the conclusion that they can no longer live with the noise of the airplanes, so they sell their house. They are not eligible for even a partial exclusion on the gain from the sale. The airplane noise could not be considered an unforeseen circumstance since it existed at the time they purchased the home.

Business Use of Home

If only a part of the property sold was used as a principal residence, the amount of gain realized must be allocated between the residential portion and any non-residential portion that is separate from the dwelling unit. Thus, if the property was used partially for residential purposes and partially for business purposes, and the portion used for business purposes was separate from the dwelling unit, only the part of the gain allocable to the residential portion may be excluded. If both the residential and non-residential portions of the property are within the same dwelling unit, allocation of gain is not required, but the exclusion nevertheless will not apply to gain to the extent of any depreciation adjustments that may have been made for periods after May 6, 1997.

 Caution. Post–May 6, 1997, depreciation is treated as an unrecaptured IRC §1250 gain, regardless of where the business portion of the home is located. Depreciation taken before that date can, however, be excluded if all other tests are met.

Although the taxpayer may take deductions of various kinds on such a business use of the home (see Tab 3 for deducting expenses on a home office), the exclusion on the sale of a residence will *not* apply to the business portion of the home, unless the office is within the same dwelling unit.

In most cases, the apportionment is made according to respective square footage occupied by each business and the home. Other methods of apportionment may, however, be used if they give a more realistic indicator of the relative worth of each space and have been used in computing depreciation or other expenses. See MTG ¶1707.

If business use of the home ceases for two years prior to the sale, the entire property can be considered a residence eligible for the exclusion, because the two-year use test is met for the whole dwelling. However, any depreciation that has been claimed on a business use must be used to reduce basis of the entire residence, thus increasing gain.

Reporting the Sale of a Residence

The reporting rules presented in the following list apply to gain from the sale of a principal residence.

- Gain on Personal Use–If the taxpayer has gain from the sale of a principal residence, the entire gain attributable to the personal-use portion of the residence should be reported on Form 8949. If all or a portion can be excluded, enter "H" in column (f) and enter the amount of the exclusion as a negative number in column (g).
- Loss on Personal Use–If the taxpayer has a loss from the sale of a principal residence for which a Form 1099-S is received, the sale must be reported on Form 8949, even though the loss may not be deducted. Because the loss is nondeductible, enter "L" in column (f) and enter the amount of the loss as a positive number in column (g).
- Gain on Business Use–If part of the home was used in a business or to produce rental income, the sale of the business or rental portion is reported on lines 20–24 of Form 4797 based on the business-use portion only. If there has been post-May 6, 1997, depreciation allowed, is reported on line 26.
- Form 6252–If the home was sold using the installment sale method, the part of the gain that cannot be excluded is reported on Form 6252. Enter the exclusion on line 15 of Form 6252.

Filing Tip. The sale of a principal residence must be reported with the taxpayer's tax return if: (1) the taxpayer has a gain but cannot exclude all of it; or (2) the taxpayer received Form 1099-S, *Proceeds from Real Estate Transaction*, from the sale or exchange.

Basis of the Residence

The cost or other basis of a principal residence for purposes of determining any gain or loss from its sale is the cost to purchase or build the home. What constitutes a part of the cost or basis of real estate depends on the law of the particular state in which the property is located. If the taxpayer acquired the home by gift or inheritance, however, the taxpayer's basis is either the fair market value of the property when it was acquired or the adjusted basis of the previous owner.

Expenditures to increase the value of a residence are generally added to basis. These includes additions or improvements that have a useful life of more than one year, special assessments, and amounts spent by the taxpayer after a casualty to restore the damaged property. Also, many settlement costs are treated as additions to basis. The following table is an example of settlement costs related to a personal residence.

Settlement Cost Table—Sale of Personal Residence		
Cost	Impact on Seller	Impact on Buyer
Attorneys' fees–finding property	Reduce amount realized	Increase basis
Attorneys' fees–obtaining mortgage	Reduce amount realized	No impact
Commissions	Reduce amount realized	Increase basis
Expenses owed by seller and paid by buyer	Adjust deductions on Schedule A	Increase basis
Points (loan origination)	Reduce amount realized	Deductible on Schedule A (even if paid by seller)
Loan processing fee	Reduce amount realized	No impact
Miscellaneous expenses concerning title or deed	Reduce amount realized	Increase basis
Miscellaneous closing costs	Reduce amount realized	No impact
Real estate taxes (see Tab 2)	Deductible on Schedule A	Deductible on Schedule A
Title policy fees or insurance	Reduce amount realized	Increase basis

Items that must be subtracted from the basis of a residence include:

- discharge of qualified principal debt that was excluded from income;

- some or all cancellation of debt income due to bankruptcy or insolvency;
- depreciation allowed or allowable on the portion of the home used for business;
- casualty deductions and insurance payments received (or expect to receive) for casualty losses;
- residential energy credits claimed between 1978 and 1985;
- credits claimed under either or both the nonbusiness energy and residential energy credits for energy property placed into service after 2005 (but not for 2008 for nonbusines energy property); and
- District of Columbia first-time homebuyer credit (but not the national first-time homebuyer credit under IRC §36).

Foreclosures

If a borrower does not make payments owed on a loan secured by property, the lender may foreclose on the loan and/or repossess the property. The foreclosure and/or repossession is treated as a sale or exchange from which the borrower may realize gain or loss, even if the property is voluntarily returned to the lender. The borrower may also realize ordinary income from cancellation of debt if the loan balance is more than the fair market value of the property.

 Filing Tip. For an overview on the treatment of an individual's tax issues related to foreclosure or cancellation of debt, review IRS Publication 4681, *Canceled Debts, Foreclosures, Repossessions, and Abandonments (for Individuals).*

Buyer's (Borrower's) Gain or Loss

Figure and report gain or loss from a foreclosure or repossession in the same way as gain or loss from a sale or exchange. The gain or loss is the difference between borrower's adjusted basis in the transferred property and the amount realized. Use the worksheet on page 4-31 to figure gain or loss from a foreclosure or repossession.

If the borrower is not personally liable for repaying the debt (nonrecourse debt) secured by the transferred property, the amount realized includes the full amount of the debt canceled by the transfer. The full amount of canceled debt is included even if the fair market value of the property is less than the canceled debt amount.

Table 1-1. **Worksheet for Foreclosures and Repossessions**

Keep for Your Records

Part 1. Complete Part 1 only if you were personally liable for the debt (even if none of the debt was canceled). Otherwise, go to Part 2.

1. Enter the amount of outstanding debt immediately before the transfer of property reduced by any amount for which you remain personally liable immediately after the transfer of property . . . . _____
2. Enter the fair market value of the transferred property . . . . _____
3. **Ordinary income from the cancellation of debt upon foreclosure or repossession.** Subtract line 2 from line 1. If less than zero, enter zero. Next, go to Part 2 . . . . _____

Part 2. Gain or loss from foreclosure or repossession.

4. Enter the **smaller** of line 1 or line 2. If you did not complete Part 1 (because you were not personally liable for the debt), enter the amount of outstanding debt immediately before the transfer of property . . . . _____
5. Enter any proceeds you received from the foreclosure sale . . . . _____
6. Add line 4 and line 5 . . . . _____
7. Enter the adjusted basis of the transferred property . . . . _____
8. **Gain or loss from foreclosure or repossession.** Subtract line 7 from line 6 _____

* The income may not be taxable. See chapter 1 for more details.

Example. Chet bought a new car for personal use for $15,000. He paid $2,000 down and borrowed the remaining $13,000 from the dealer's credit company. Chet is not personally liable for the loan (nonrecourse), but he pledged the new car as security. The credit company repossessed the car because he stopped making loan payments. The balance due after taking into account the payments Chet made was $10,000. The fair market value of the car when repossessed was $9,000. The amount Chet realized on the repossession is $10,000 (the amount of debt canceled by the repossession), even though the car's fair market value is only $9,000.

If the borrower is personally liable for the debt (recourse debt), the amount realized on the foreclosure or repossession does not include the canceled debt that is income from cancellation of debt. However, if the fair market value of the transferred property is less than the canceled debt, the amount realized includes the canceled debt up to the fair market value of the property. The taxpayer is treated as receiving ordinary income from the canceled debt for the part of the debt that is more than the fair market value.

Seller's (Lender's) Gain or Loss

If the seller financed a buyer's purchase of property and later acquires an interest in it through foreclosure and/or repossession, the seller may have a gain or loss on the acquisition. For more information, see "Repossession" in IRS Publication 537, *Installment Sales*.

Forms 1099-A and 1099-C

A lender who acquires an interest in a borrower's property in a foreclosure or repossession should send a Form 1099-A showing the information needed to figure gain or loss. However, if the lender also cancels part of the debt, they must also file Form 1099-C. The lender may include the information about the foreclosure or repossession on that form instead of on Form 1099-A. The lender must file Form 1099-C and send a copy to the borrower if the amount of debt canceled is $600 or more and the lender is a financial institution, credit union, federal government agency, or any organization that has a significant trade or business of lending money.

Filing Tip. Be sure to account for all 1099's that your clients receive, even if they have completed a bankruptcy proceeding. This is accomplished by filing a Form 982, *Reduction of Tax Attributes Due to Discharge of Indebtedness (and Section 1082 Basis Adjustment)*.

Transfers of Property to Spouses

Generally, no gain or loss is recognized by an individual on the transfer of property to (or in trust for the benefit of) (1) the individuals spouse, or (2) the individual's former spouse, but only if the transfer is incident to divorce. This rule applies even if the transfer was in exchange for cash, the release of marital rights, the assumption of liabilities, or other consideration. The individual's basis for the transferred property is carried over to his or her spouse or former spouse. In the case of a transfer to a former spouse, the transfer must occur within one year after the date the marriage ends, or is related to the ending of the marriage. See Tab 13.

The nonrecognition of gain on the transfer of property to a spouse or former spouse does not apply if the taxpayer's spouse or former spouse is a nonresident alien. In addition, if the property is transferred in trust for the benefit of the spouse or former spouse, gain will be recognized by the taxpayer to the extent of the sum of any liabilities assumed by the spouse (plus liabilities to which the property is subject), exceeds the total adjusted basis of the property. Gain will also be recognized on certain stock redemptions under a divorce or settlement agreement.

Securities Transactions

Wash Sales

Under the wash sale rules, a taxpayer who realizes a loss from the sale or other disposition of stock or securities may not claim a deduction for the loss unless the loss is incurred in the ordinary course of the taxpayer's business as a securities dealer. A wash sale occurs when a taxpayer sells or trades stock or securities at a loss, and within 30 days before or after the sale (the 61-day period) the taxpayer:

- buys substantially identical stock or securities;
- acquires substantially identical stock or securities in a fully taxable trade;
- acquired a contract or option to buy substantially identical stock or securities; or
- acquires substantially identical stock or securities for his or her traditional or Roth IRA.

If stock is sold and a spouse or closely held corporation buys substantially identical stock under the same conditions, the seller again has a wash sale.

 Caution. Watch for notes on Forms 1009-B or 1099-DIV from mutual funds; reinvestment of dividends can trigger wash sale treatment.

If a loss is disallowed because of the wash sale rules, the disallowed loss will be added to the cost of the new stock or securities. The result is the basis in the new stock or securities. This adjustment postpones the loss deduction until the disposition of the new stock or securities.

 Filing Tip. A wash sale transaction is reported on Form 8949 with code "W" entered in column (f) and the amount of the nondeductible loss entered in column (g) as a positive number.

The holding period for the new stock or securities begins on the same day as the holding period of the stock or securities sold, not the date of purchase of the new stock. When a loss is disallowed on the sale of stock due to the wash sale rules, the holding period for the newly acquired stock includes the holding period of the stock that was sold

Example. Dolores buys 100 shares of ABC stock for $1,000. She sells these shares for $750 on May 19, 2013, and buys 100 shares of the same stock for $800 on June 13, 2013. Because Dolores bought substantially identical stock within a 61 day period of selling her first lot of ABC stock, the loss of $250 on the sale cannot be deducted. However, she adds the disallowed loss of $250 to the cost of the new stock, $800, to obtain a basis of $1,050 in the new stock.

Example. Rory, an employee of Corporation Z, has an incentive pay plan. Under this plan, Rory was given 10 shares of the corporation's stock as a bonus in 2011. He included the fair market value of the stock ($600) in his gross income for the year as additional pay. Those shares are sold on April 8, 2013, for $500. He gets another 10-share bonus award on April 30, 2013, at which time the stock has bounced back to $60 per share. He must again include the $600 in his gross income for 2013, but he cannot deduct his loss on the April 8 sale because the new stock was acquired within the 61-day or his selling his original shares. His basis in the new stock is $700.

Options, Puts, and Calls

An option is a right to buy or sell property at a stipulated price on or before a specified date. Gain or loss from the sale or exchange of an option is considered gain or loss from the sale of the underlying property rather than the option itself. IRC §1234.

If the underlying property would have been a capital asset in the hands of the taxpayer, then any gain or loss on the sale or exchange of the option is treated as a capital gain or loss. The length of time the taxpayer held the option determines whether the capital gain or loss is short term or long term

If the underlying property of an option is IRC §1231 property used in a taxpayer's trade or business, then any gain or loss from the sale or exchange of the option may be IRC §1231 gain or loss (see page 4-14). If the underlying property of an option is neither a capital asset nor IRC §1231 property, then any gain or loss realized on the sale or exchange of the option is ordinary income or loss.

If the holder of an option incurs a loss on failure to exercise the option, then the option is deemed to have been sold or exchanged on the date that it expired and the holder's loss is considered a loss from the sale or exchange of the underlying property. Any gain realized by the holder of the option from the failure to exercise the option is considered ordinary income or loss. Similarly, any gain or loss realized by the grantor of the option as the result of a closing transaction, like repurchasing the option from the holder, is considered ordinary income or loss if the underlying property is stock, securities, commodities, or commodity futures.

If an option is exercised, the option price is added to the grantor's amount realized for purposes of determining his or her gain or loss on the sale or exchange of the underlying property. The holder of the option also increases his or her basis in the property acquired through the option by the amount of the option price.

Filing Tip. Gain or loss from the closing or expiration of an option that is a capital asset, but not a IRC §1256 contract, is reported on Form 8949. If the option was purchased by the taxpayer, enter the expiration date in column (c) and enter "EXPIRED" in column (d). If the option was granted to the taxpayer, enter the expiration date in column (b) and enter "EXPIRED" in column (e). Gain or loss on IRC §1256 contracts are reported on Form 6781. IRC §1256 contracts include regulated futures contracts, foreign currency contracts, nonequity options, and dealer equity options.

Planning Tip. Extensive capital loss carryforwards should be considered in a taxpayer's investment strategy. Gain on options is essentially tax free if loss carryforwards are available.

Puts and Calls

Option contracts can be either put or call options. Puts and calls are issued by writers (grantors) to holders for cash premiums. They are ended by exercise, closing transaction, or lapse.

A put option is a contract that entitles the the holder to sell a specified amount of property to the the writer for a fixed price within a specified period of time. In other words, the holder purchases the right to sell his or her property to someone else under the terms of the contract. In contrast, a call option is a contract that entitles the holder to purchase a specified amount of property (frequently but not exclusively stock, securities, or commodities) from the writer at a fixed price within a specified period of time.

The cost of purchasing a put or call option is a nondeductible capital expense. If the taxpayer is a holder of a put or call option and sells it before exercising the option, the difference between the cost of the put or call, and the amount received for the option is either a long-term or short-term capital gain or loss, depending on how long it was held. If the option expires, its cost is either long-term or short-term capital loss, depending on the taxpayer's holding period, which ends on the expiration date.

If the holder exercises a call option, its cost is added to the basis of the security purchased. If the holder exercises a put option, the amount realized on the sale of the underlying security is reduced by the cost of the put when computing gain or loss. That gain or loss is long term or short term depending on the taxpayer's holding period for the underlying security.

Example—Expiration. Ten call options were issued to Ronnie on April 8, 2013, for $4,000 from Scott. These equity options expired in December 2013 without being exercised. Ronnie recognizes a short-term capital loss of $4,000. Scott recognizes a short-term capital gain of $4,000.

Example—Closing Transaction. Assume the same facts as in the previous example, except that on May 10, 2013, the options were sold for $6,000 to a third party. Ronnie, the original buyer of the options, recognizes a short-term capital gain of $2,000. If Scott had bought them back, he would recognize a short-term capital loss of $2,000.

Filing Tip. If a call option sold by the taxpayer is exercised by the purchaser and any option premium received is not reflected in the sales price on Form 1099-B, then report it on Form 8949. Enter code "E" in column (f) and the premium amount as a positive number in column (g).

Employee Stock Options

Corporations may grant their employees the option to purchase stock in the corporation. If a taxpayer receives a stock option to buy or sell stock (or other property) as compensation for services, the taxpayer may have income when the option is granted, when the taxpayer exercises the option to buy or sell the stock or other property, or when the taxpayer sells or disposes of the option or the property acquired through exercise of the option. The timing, type, and amount of income inclusion depend on whether the taxpayer receives a statutory stock option or nonstatutory stock option.

Statutory or Qualified Stock Options

There are two kinds of statutory stock options: incentive stock options (ISOs) and options granted under employee stock purchase plans (ESPPs). In either case, no gain or loss is generally realized by an employee when a statutory option is granted or exercised. Instead, the taxpayer will have capital gain or loss when he or she sells or otherwise disposes of the stock acquired through the exercise of the stock option.

Caution. Although there may be no immediate regular tax consequences upon the exercise of an incentive stock option (ISO), there are significant alternative minimum tax (AMT) consequences. The exercise of an ISO is considered a tax preference item under the AMT rules. As a result, the taxpayer's alternative minimum taxable income (AMTI) is increased by the difference between the option price and the fair market value of the date of exercise. Unaware taxpayers will find they owe a larger than expected tax liability because of the increase in tax generated by the "phantom" income.

In addition, the basis of the ISO stock must be tracked for the purpose of calculating gain or loss upon sale or exchange for both the regular tax and for the AMT. Thus, stock acquired through the exercise of an ISO carries a dual basis. See Tab 10 for more information on the AMT.

The gain or loss from the sale of stock acquired in a statutory stock option is the difference between the amount paid by the taxpayer for the stock (the option price) and the amount received when it is sold. The gain or loss treated as capital gain or loss and reported on Form 8949 for the year of the sale. The taxpayer, however, may have ordinary income for the year of the sale if certain holding period requirements are not met or if the option was granted at a discount through an ESPP. If the gain is ordinary income, it is reported as wages on Form 1040, line 7, for the year of the sale.

Planning Tip. A taxpayer that exercises an ISO during 2013 should receive Form 3921, *Exercise of an Incentive Stock Option Under Section 422(b)*, or similar statement from the corporation for each transfer. The corporation must send or provide the form by January 31, 2014. The taxpayer should keep this information for his or her records.

Holding Period Requirement. A taxpayer may treat gains or losses from the sale of stock acquired through a statutory stock option as capital gains or losses so long he or she does not sell the stock until the end of the later of the 1-year period after the stock was transferred or the 2-year period after the option was granted. If these holding period requirements are not satisfied, the sale is considered a "disqualifying disposition," the gain at exercise will be taxed as ordinary income, and any subsequent appreciation is taxed as capital gains.

Option Granted at Discount. For stock acquired through an ESPP, if the option price was less than 100% of the fair market value (but not less than 85%) when the option was granted, then any gain or loss is treated as ordinary income or loss if the stock is sold or otherwise disposed after meeting the holding period requirements or the taxpayer dies while still owning the shares.

The taxpayer must include in income as compensation, the lesser of:

- the excess of the fair market value of the share at the time the option was granted over the option price, or
- the excess of the fair market value of the share at the time of the disposition or death over the amount paid for the share under the option.

For this purpose, if the option price was not fixed or determinable at the time the option was granted, the option price is figured as if the option had been exercised at the time it was granted. Any excess gain is capital gain. If the taxpayer has a loss from the sale, it is a capital loss, and the taxpayer does not have any ordinary income.

Nonstatutory Stock Options

A nonstatutory stock option is one that does not meet the requirements of a statutory option. A taxpayer realizes income when a nonstatutory option is granted or exercised depending on when the option has "readily ascertainable fair market value."

The fair market value of an option can be readily determined if it is actively traded on an established market. The fair market value of an option that is not traded on an established market can be readily determined only if all of the following conditions are met:

- the option must be transferable;
- the option must be exercisable immediately and in full when it is granted;
- there can be no condition or restriction on the option or the property that would have a significant effect on its fair market value.

Grant of Option. A nonqualified stock option is taxed when it is granted if the option has a readily ascertainable fair market value at that time. The option is treated like other restricted property received as compensation. The taxpayer has ordinary income equal to fair market value of the option on the grant date or when substantially vested, less any amount paid for the option. If the nonstatutory option does not have a readily ascertainable fair market value at the time granted, then it is subject to the restricted property rules when it is exercised or transferred. See MTG ¶713.

Exercise or Transfer of Options. If a taxpayer exercises a nonstatutory stock option that had a readily determinable value at the time the option was granted, no amount is required to be included. If a taxpayer exercises a nonstatutory stock option that did not have a readily determinable value at the time the option was granted, the restricted property rules apply to the property received. The taxpayer has ordinary income equal to fair market value of the option on the grant date or when substantially vested, less any amount paid for the option.

If the taxpayer transfers a nonstatutory stock option without a readily determinable value in an arm's-length transaction to an unrelated person, he or she must include in income the money or other property received, as if the option was exercised.

If the taxpayer transfers a nonstatutory stock option without a readily determinable value in a non-arm's-length transaction (for example, a gift), the option is not treated as exercised or closed at that time. The taxpayer must include in income, as compensation, any money or property received.

When the transferee exercises the option, the taxpayer must also include in income, as compensation, the excess of the fair market value of the stock acquired by the transferee over the sum of the exercise price paid and any amount the taxpayer included in income at the time he or she transferred the option. At the time of the exercise, the transferee recognizes no income and has a basis in the stock acquired equal to the fair market value of the stock. Any transfer of this kind of option to a related person is treated as a non-arm's-length transaction.

Sale of Stock. Stock acquired through the exercise of a nonstatutory stock option is treated as any other investment property. Any gain or loss recognized is treated as capital gain or loss and reported on Form 8949. The taxpayer's basis in the stock is the fair market value of the option on which he or she paid taxes, plus the amount paid for the stock. The taxpayer's holding period of the stock begins the day after the option was exercised.

Dealers, Investors, and Traders

In order to determine whether a taxpayer's gains or losses are ordinary or capital in nature, it must be determined whether the taxpayer entered into the transaction as dealer, investor, or trader.

Dealers in Securities

Capital gain and loss treatment does *not* apply to securities owned by a dealer, except for securities that are held primarily for personal investment. Securities that are held by a dealer for investment purposes must be clearly identified in the dealer's records before the close of the day on which they were acquired and must *never* be held primarily for sale to the dealer's customers. A dealer regularly purchases securities from, and sells securities to, customers in the ordinary course of a trade or business. Because dealers are in the business of buying and selling, their gains and losses are classified as ordinary gain or loss.

Dealers in securities must use the mark-to-market method of accounting for gains and losses on securities. Under the mark-to-market rules, any security that is inventory must be included in inventory at its fair market value. A securities dealer may use the fair market value as reported in the dealer's financial statements for this purpose.

Any security that is not classified as inventory in the dealer's hand and this is held at the close of the tax year is treated as if it were sold at its fair market value on the last business day of the year. The dealer must recognize any gain or loss that results from the deemed sale. Any gain or loss recognized is taken into account when calculating the dealer's gain or loss when the security is actually sold or exchanged.

Dealers must follow mark-to-market rules, and investors and traders may elect to use the rules. Investors and traders make an mark-to-market election by attaching a statement to an original and timely (not including an extension) filed tax return for the tax year directly preceding the election. If an election is made, the gains and losses are treated as ordinary income and are deemed to be sold on the last business day of the year at fair market value.

Traders in Securities

A securities trader (including a "day trader") is a trader in securities, that is in the business of buying and selling securities for his or her own account. To be engaged in business as a trader in securities, all of the following conditions must be met:

- the taxpayer must seek to profit from daily market movements in the prices of securities and not from dividends, interest, or capital appreciation;
- the taxpayer's activity must be substantial; and
- the taxpayer must carry on the activity with continuity and regularity.

The following facts and circumstances should be considered in determining if the taxpayer's activity is a securities trading business:

- typical holding periods for securities bought and sold;
- frequency and dollar amount of trades during the year;
- the extent to which the activity is pursued to produce income for a livelihood; and
- the amount of time devoted to the activity.

Because the securities that traders buy and sell are not held primarily for sale to customers, the gains and losses are generally treated as capital in nature and are reported on Form 8949. Traders may make a mark-to-market election that allows them to treat gains and losses as ordinary. Traders claim their business expenses on Schedule C, *Profit or Loss From Business*, because they are in the business of trading. For the rules concerning the commissions paid by traders when buying and selling securities, see MTG ¶ 1983.

Investors

An investor is a taxpayer whose activities are limited to occasional transactions for his or her own account. The level of activity is less than that associated with a trade or business. Gains and losses of an investor are subject to the capital gain and loss rules.

Basis of Stock

Part of the process of figuring gain or loss on stock sales is determining the stock basis–a value that starts out as the original cost of the stocks (what the buyer paid for them, plus any commissions), then gets adjusted up or down as the shares pay dividends, split, or rare subject to certain other events. Here are the basic steps for determining the basis of stock.

- Gather all the brokerage statements from the time the stocks were purchased until the time they were sold.
- Figure out how much was paid for the shares, including any purchase costs such as commissions. (The result is known as the *starting basis*.)
- If the company issued dividends in the form of shares of stock, or a return on capital, reduce the starting basis by those amounts. If the stock split, divide the basis accordingly. The result is an adjusted basis for computing the capital gain or loss.
- Figure out the net proceeds from selling the shares– the money received for the shares, minus any commission paid.
- Subtract the stock basis from the net proceeds to determine the capital gain or loss.

Adjustments to Stock Basis

If the stock has been held for a while, it may have gone through several stock splits, issued dividends, perhaps distributed a return of capital, or maybe a subsidiary has been spun off in a corporate reorganization. If any of these events has occurred while the client owned and held the stock, he or she must make adjustments to the starting basis in those shares.

- *Stock splits:* These make the basis per share less than it was, at the same time increasing the number of shares owned. For example, if Bette paid $80 per share for Hot Item stock and the company subsequently split 2 for 1 on two occasions, her basis per share is now $20 ($80 × 1/2 × 1/2).
- *Stock dividends:* The shares (not cash payments) earned as dividends reduce the basis in the stock; it is only dividends in the form of stocks that adjust the basis. For example, Willie owns 100 shares of High Echelon stock that he bought for $20 per share, total cost $2,000. High Echelon issues a dividend in the form of stock, and Willie gets 10 more shares as his "dividend." So Willie now has 110 shares of stock, but he still only paid $2,000. His basis per share now is $2,000 divided by 110, or $18.18 per share, so his basis per share actually went down. Even though those extra 10 shares were "free," Willie must allocate his original basis to cover those "free" shares as well.
- *Return of capital:* A return-of-capital distribution reduces basis dollar for dollar.
- *Spin-offs:* If a large company spins off a subsidiary to form a new company, with its own stock, the company will send out an announcement telling how to allocate the basis.
- *Modified Carry Over Basis:* For individuals dying after December 31, 2009, and before January 1,

2011, the executor of the individual's estate may elect to apply special carry over basis rules under IRC §1022. If the election is made, the basis will generally be equal to the lesser of the decedent's fair market value or the decedent's adjusted basis in the property on the date of death. However, estates may increase by $1.3 million the basis of certain property for nonspousal property and an additional increase of $3 million for spousal property. See IRC §1022.

Making Adjustments

If no records exist, it is still possible to calculate basis. One possible method is to check your local public library for a copy of CCH's *Capital Changes Reporter*, which tracks these corporate transactions. There are also websites available that can be used to track a specific companies stock history. Using the data, you are able to make the necessary adjustments to the basis of the stock.

Net Investment Income Tax

Application to Individuals

Beginning in 2013, an individual will be subject to a net investment income (NII) tax of 3.8% under IRC §1411 on the lesser of his or her:

- net investment income for the year; or
- modified AGI in excess of:
  - $250,000 if married filing jointly or surviving spouse,
  - $200,000 if single or head or household, or
  - $125,000 if married filing separately.

 Planning Tip. If the taxpayer has a short tax year (less than 12 months), the threshold amount is not prorated for the year. For example, if an unmarried individual dies on June 1, the threshold amount is $200,000 for the decedent's short tax year that began on January 1 and ended on June 1. However, if an individual has a short tax year as a result of a change in his or her accounting period, the threshold amount will be prorated.

The NII tax only applies if modified AGI exceeds the specified threshold amount and there is net investment income. Modified AGI means the individual's AGI for the tax year without regard to the exclusion of foreign earned income or foreign housing costs calculated on Form 2555 (if any).

 Caution. The NII tax is in addition to a taxpayer's regular income tax liability. The tax is not required to be withheld from any payment of income made to the taxpayer. As a result, a taxpayer may need to adjust any income tax withholding or estimated tax payments to account for the tax to avoid any penalties for underpayment of tax.

Example. Jim and Pam are married and file a joint return for 2013. They have combined wages of $230,000, and $15,000 of net investment income from capital gains and dividends. The couple's modified AGI is $245,000. Because this is less than the $250,000 threshold for married individuals filing jointly, Jim and Pam are not subject to the 3.8% net investment income tax for 2013.

Example. Dwight and Angela are married and file a joint return for 2013. They have combined wages of $230,000. They also received $90,000 from a passive partnership interest, which is considered net investment income. The couple's modified AGI is $320,000. Because their modified AGI exceeds the $250,000 threshold for married individuals filing jointly, Dwight and Angela are subject to the 3.8% NII tax. The tax is based on the lesser of their modified AGI exceeding the threshold ($70,000), or their net investment income ($90,000). Thus, Dwight and Angela owe a net investment income tax of $2,660 ($70,000 × 3.8%) for 2013.

The NII tax does not apply to nonresident aliens. In the event a nonresident alien is married to a U.S. citizen or resident alien, the spouses are treated as married filing separately for purposes of the NII tax and the U.S. citizen or resident alien spouse applies the $125,000 threshold.

If the couple is planning to make an election to treat the nonresident alien spouse as a resident alien for purposes of filing a joint return, special rules apply a similar election for NII tax purposes. The effect is that the spouses will include their combined income in the NII tax calculation and apply the $250,000 threshold for joint returns.

Net Investment Income

Investment income subject to the NII tax includes:

- gross income from interest, dividends, annuities, royalties and rents unless such income is derived in the ordinary course of an active trade or business;
- other gross income from any passive trade or business, or a trade or business trading in financial investments or commodities; and
- net gain included in computing taxable income that is attributable to the disposition of property other than property held in an active trade or business.

With regard to a trade or business, the NII tax applies if the trade or business is a passive activity with respect to the taxpayer (see Tab 5) or involves trading in financial instruments and commodities. However, the fact that the NII tax applies to income from one trade or business of the taxpayer does not mean that it automatically applies to other trades or businesses of the taxpayer whether conducted as a sole proprietor, partnership, or S corporation.

Example. Ian owns 50% of a partnership that conducts two separate activities: heavy equipment leasing and the manufacturing of widgets. He does not satisfy any of the standards for material participation with respect to the heavy equipment leasing business, but actively participates in the widget manufacturing business. Ian would be subject to the NII tax on his share of rental income attributable to the equipment leasing business, but he would not be subject to the NII tax on his share of income from the widget manufacturing.

Gross Income from Interest, Dividends, Etc.

In determining whether gross income from interest, dividends, annuities, royalties, rents, substitute interest payments, and substitute dividend payments is derived in a trade or business, the following rules apply.

- If the taxpayer owns or engages in a trade or business directly (or indirectly through a disregarded entity), the determination of whether such income is derived in a trade or business is made at the individual level.
- If the taxpayer owns an interest in a trade or business through a partnership or S corporation, the determination of whether such income is derived from a trade or business that is a passive activity is made at the owner level.
- If the taxpayer owns an interest in a trade or business through partnership or S corporation, the de-

termination of whether such income is derived from a trade or business of a trader trading in financial instruments or commodities is made at the entity level. If the entity is involved in the business, the income retains its character when passing through to the taxpayer.

Net Gain from the Disposition of Property

Investment income subject to the NII tax includes any net gain attributable to the disposition of property, other than property held in an active trade or business. This includes capital gains from the sale of property that the taxpayer did not use in an active business to the extent the gains are not otherwise offset by capital losses. Examples include gains from the sale of stock, bonds, mutual funds, and real estate investments.

It also includes gains from the sale of interests in a partnership or S corporation to the extent the taxpayer was a passive owner. This is the amount of the net gain or loss that would be taken into account by the individual if all property of the partnership or S corporation were sold at fair market value immediately before the disposition of his or her interest. However, only net gain or loss attributable to property held by the entity that is not property attributable to an active trade or business is taken into account.

Sale of Personal Residence. Because the NII tax applies to net gains from the disposition of property, it may apply to gain from the sale of the taxpayer's principal residence. However, the taxpayer is still allowed to exclude up to $250,000 of the gain ($500,000 if married filing jointly) from income before application of the tax. See the discussion of page 4-26. In addition, any remaining gain must exceed the applicable modified AGI thresholds before the NII tax applies.

Example. Cliff and Claire are married filing jointly in 2013. During the year, they sell their principal residence and realize a gain of $600,000. They are eligible, however, to exclude $500,000 of the gain. The remaining $100,000 is the couple's only net investment income for the year. If their modified AGI, including the net investment income, is only $240,000, then they are not subject to the NII tax because it is less than the $250,000 threshold for married individuals filing jointly. If their modified AGI, including the net investment income, is $300,000, then they owe a net investment income tax of $1,900 ($50,000 × 3.8%).

Deductions

The taxpayer is allowed to reduce his or her investment income or gain by any deductible expenses which are allocable to the income or gain. Examples include investment interest expenses, investment advisory and brokerage fees, expenses related to rental and royalty income, and state and local income taxes properly allocable to the investment income or gain.

 Planning Tip. Any deductions that are subject to the 2% floor on miscellaneous itemized deductions or the overall limit on itemized deductions are allowed in determining net investment income but only after application of the limitations. The amounts that may be deducted in determining net investment income after the application of the limits are then determined by formulas provided in Prop. Reg. §1.1411-4(f).

The deductions may not exceed the taxpayer's investment income or gain for purposes of the NII tax; thus, net investment income may not be less than zero and any excess deduction may not carried over to another tax year in calculating the NII tax. A net operating loss (NOL) deduction otherwise allowed to the taxpayer for regular income tax purposes is not used in determining net investment income.

 Caution. Under proposed regulations, a taxpayer may use losses deductible under IRC §165 in calculating the NII tax only in determining net gain attributable to the disposition of property. A net loss from the sale of property cannot be used to offset the other categories of investment income (interest, dividends, etc. and other gross income from any passive trade or business).

Exclusions from Net Investment Income

Net investment income does not include wages, alimony, unemployment compensation, tax-exempt interest, Social Security benefits, or veterans' benefits. It includes any income, gain, or loss that is attributable to an investment of working capital that is treated as not derived in the ordinary course of a trade or business. Thus, it does not include operating income from a business, including self-employment income, unless the taxpayer is a passive participant in that business.

Net investment income also does not include any income the taxpayer receives from the sale of an interest in a partnership or S corporation, to the extent the gain would be from an active trade or business. In addition, it does not include any distribution from an employer-provided qualified retirement plan, such as a 401(k), 403(b), or 457 plan, or distributions from a traditional or Roth IRA.

Reporting NII Tax—Form 8960

Form 8960, *Net Investment Income Tax*, is used by taxpayers to calculate the NII tax. It is divided into three parts: Part I – Investment Income; Part II – Investment Expenses Allocable to Investment Income and Modifications; and Part III – Tax Computation. The tax calculated on the form is reported on line 60 of Form 1040.

 Caution. At the time of publication, only a draft version of Form 8960 was available and draft Instructions to Form 8960 had yet to be released. For the latest information on Form 8960 and its instructions, visit CCHGroup.com/TaxUpdates.

Caution: At the time of publication, the final 2013 IRS worksheets were not available; the 2012 worksheets are displayed for demonstration purposes. Visit CCHGroup.com/TaxUpdates for the latest developments.

Capital Loss Carryover Worksheet—Lines 6 and 14

Use this worksheet to figure your capital loss carryovers from 2011 to 2012 if your 2011 Schedule D, line 21, is a loss and **(a)** that loss is a smaller loss than the loss on your 2011 Schedule D, line 16, **or (b)** the amount on your 2011 Form 1040, line 41 (or your 2011 Form 1040NR, line 39, if applicable) is less than zero. Otherwise, you do not have any carryovers.

If you and your spouse once filed a joint return and are filing separate returns for 2012, any capital loss carryover from the joint return can be deducted only on the return of the spouse who actually had the loss.

1. Enter the amount from your 2011 Form 1040, line 41, or your 2011 Form 1040NR, line 39. If a loss, enclose the amount in parentheses . . . .   **1.** _____

2. Enter the loss from your 2011 Schedule D, line 21, as a positive amount . . . .   **2.** _____

3. Combine lines 1 and 2. If zero or less, enter -0- . . . .   **3.** _____

4. Enter the **smaller** of line 2 or line 3 . . . .   **4.** _____

   If line 7 of your 2011 Schedule D is a loss, go to line 5; otherwise, enter -0- on line 5 and go to line 9.

5. Enter the loss from your 2011 Schedule D, line 7, as a positive amount . . . .   **5.** _____

6. Enter any gain from your 2011 Schedule D, line 15. If a loss, enter -0- . . . .   **6.** _____

7. Add lines 4 and 6 . . . .   **7.** _____

8. **Short-term capital loss carryover for 2012.** Subtract line 7 from line 5. If zero or less, enter -0-. If more than zero, also enter this amount on Schedule D, line 6 . . . .   **8.** _____

   If line 15 of your 2011 Schedule D is a loss, go to line 9; otherwise, skip lines 9 through 13.

9. Enter the loss from your 2011 Schedule D, line 15, as a positive amount . . . .   **9.** _____

10. Enter any gain from your 2011 Schedule D, line 7. If a loss, enter -0- . . . .   **10.** _____

11. Subtract line 5 from line 4. If zero or less, enter -0- . . . .   **11.** _____

12. Add lines 10 and 11 . . . .   **12.** _____

13. **Long-term capital loss carryover for 2012.** Subtract line 12 from line 9. If zero or less, enter -0-. If more than zero, also enter this amount on Schedule D, line 14 . . . .   **13.** _____

28% Rate Gain Worksheet—Line 18

1. Enter the total of all collectibles gain or (loss) from items you reported on Form 8949, Part II . . . .   **1.** _____

2. Enter as a positive number the amount of any section 1202 exclusion you reported in column (g) of Form 8949, Part II, with code "Q" in column (f), for which you excluded 50% of the gain, plus $^2/3$ of any section 1202 exclusion you reported in column (g) of Form 8949, Part II, with code "Q" in column (f), for which you excluded 60% of the gain . . . .   **2.** _____

3. Enter the total of all collectibles gain or (loss) from Form 4684, line 4 (but only if Form 4684, line 15, is more than zero); Form 6252; Form 6781, Part II; and Form 8824 . . . .   **3.** _____

4. Enter the total of any collectibles gain reported to you on:
   - Form 1099-DIV, box 2d;
   - Form 2439, box 1d; and
   - Schedule K-1 from a partnership, S corporation, estate, or trust. } . . . .   **4.** _____

5. Enter your long-term capital loss carryovers from Schedule D, line 14, and Schedule K-1 (Form 1041), box 11, code C . . . .   **5.** (_____)

6. If Schedule D, line 7, is a (loss), enter that (loss) here. Otherwise, enter -0- . . . .   **6.** (_____)

7. Combine lines 1 through 6. If zero or less, enter -0-. If more than zero, also enter this amount on Schedule D, line 18 . . . .   **7.** _____

Caution: At the time of publication, the final 2013 IRS worksheets were not available; the 2012 worksheets are displayed for demonstration purposes. Visit CCHGroup.com/TaxUpdates for the latest developments.

Unrecaptured Section 1250 Gain Worksheet—Line 19

Sample Worksheet

If you are not reporting a gain on Form 4797, line 7, skip lines 1 through 9 and go to line 10.

1. If you have a section 1250 property in Part III of Form 4797 for which you made an entry in Part I of Form 4797 (but not on Form 6252), enter the **smaller** of line 22 or line 24 of Form 4797 for that property. If you did not have any such property, go to line 4. If you had more than one such property, see instructions . . . . **1.** _____

2. Enter the amount from Form 4797, line 26g, for the property for which you made an entry on line 1 . . . . **2.** _____

3. Subtract line 2 from line 1 . . . . **3.** _____

4. Enter the total unrecaptured section 1250 gain included on line 26 or line 37 of Form(s) 6252 from installment sales of trade or business property held more than 1 year (see instructions) . . . . **4.** _____

5. Enter the total of any amounts reported to you on a Schedule K-1 from a partnership or an S corporation as "unrecaptured section 1250 gain" . . . . **5.** _____

6. Add lines 3 through 5 . . . . **6.** _____

7. Enter the **smaller** of line 6 or the gain from Form 4797, line 7 . . . . **7.** _____

8. Enter the amount, if any, from Form 4797, line 8 . . . . **8.** _____

9. Subtract line 8 from line 7. If zero or less, enter -0- . . . . **9.** _____

10. Enter the amount of any gain from the sale or exchange of an interest in a partnership attributable to unrecaptured section 1250 gain (see instructions) . . . . **10.** _____

11. Enter the total of any amounts reported to you as "unrecaptured section 1250 gain" on a Schedule K-1, Form 1099-DIV, or Form 2439 from an estate, trust, real estate investment trust, or mutual fund (or other regulated investment company) or in connection with a Form 1099-R . . . . **11.** _____

12. Enter the total of any unrecaptured section 1250 gain from sales (including installment sales) or other dispositions of section 1250 property held more than 1 year for which you did not make an entry in Part I of Form 4797 for the year of sale (see instructions) . . . . **12.** _____

13. Add lines 9 through 12 . . . . **13.** _____

14. If you had any section 1202 gain or collectibles gain or (loss), enter the total of lines 1 through 4 of the **28% Rate Gain Worksheet**. Otherwise, enter -0- . . . . **14.** _____

15. Enter the (loss), if any, from Schedule D, line 7. If Schedule D, line 7, is zero or a gain, enter -0- . . . . **15.** (_____)

16. Enter your long-term capital loss carryovers from Schedule D, line 14, and Schedule K-1 (Form 1041), box 11, code C* . . . . **16.** (_____)

17. Combine lines 14 through 16. If the result is a (loss), enter it as a positive amount. If the result is zero or a gain, enter -0- . . . . **17.** _____

18. **Unrecaptured section 1250 gain.** Subtract line 17 from line 13. If zero or less, enter -0-. If more than zero, enter the result here and on Schedule D, line 19 . . . . **18.** _____

*If you are filing Form 2555 or 2555-EZ (relating to foreign earned income), see the footnote in the Foreign Earned Income Tax Worksheet in the Form 1040 instructions before completing this line.

Form 8960

Department of the Treasury
Internal Revenue Service (99)

Net Investment Income Tax—
Individuals, Estates, and Trusts

☒ **Attach to Form 1040 or Form 1041.**
☒ **Information about Form 8960 and its separate instructions is at www.irs.gov/form8960.**

OMB No. XXXX-XXXX

2013

Attachment
Sequence No. **72**

Name(s) shown on Form 1040 or Form 1041

Your social security number or EIN

Part I	**Investment Income**		
	☐ Section 6013(g) election (see instructions)		
	☐ Regulations section 1.1411-10(g) election (see instructions)		
1	Taxable interest (Form 1040, line 8a; or Form 1041, line 1)	**1**	
2	Ordinary dividends (Form 1040, line 9a; or Form 1041, line 2a)	**2**	
3	Annuities from nonqualified plans (see instructions)	**3**	
4a	Rental real estate, royalties, partnerships, S corporations, trusts, etc. (Form 1040, line 17; or Form 1041, line 5) · · · · · **4a**		
b	Adjustment for net income or loss derived in the ordinary course of a non-section 1411 trade or business (see instructions) · · · **4b**		
c	Combine lines 4a and 4b	**4c**	
5a	Net gain or loss from disposition of property from Form 1040, combine lines 13 and 14; or from Form 1041, combine lines 4 and 7 **5a**		
b	Net gain or loss from disposition of property that is not subject to net investment income tax (see instructions) · · · · · **5b**		
c	Adjustment from disposition of partnership interest or S corporation stock (see instructions) · · · · · · · **5c**		
d	Combine lines 5a through 5c	**5d**	
6	Changes to investment income for certain CFCs and PFICs (see instructions) · · · ·	**6**	
7	Other modifications to investment income (see instructions) · · · · · · ·	**7**	
8	Total investment income. Combine lines 1, 2, 3, 4c, 5d, 6, and 7 · · · · · ·	**8**	
Part II	**Investment Expenses Allocable to Investment Income and Modifications**		
9a	Investment interest expenses (see instructions) · · · · · **9a**		
b	State income tax (see instructions) · · · · · · · **9b**		
c	Miscellaneous investment expenses (see instructions) · · · · **9c**		
d	Add lines 9a, 9b, and 9c · · · · · · · · · · · ·	**9d**	
10	Additional modifications (see instructions) · · · · · · · · ·	**10**	
11	Total deductions and modifications. Add lines 9d and 10 · · · · · ·	**11**	
Part III	**Tax Computation**		
12	Net investment income. Subtract Part II, line 11 from Part I, line 8. Individuals complete lines 13–17. Estates and trusts complete lines 18a–21. If zero or less, enter -0- · · · · · ·	**12**	
	Individuals:		
13	Modified adjusted gross income (see instructions) · · · · **13**		
14	Threshold based on filing status (see instructions) · · · · **14**		
15	Subtract line 14 from line 13. If zero or less, enter -0- · · · · **15**		
16	Enter the smaller of line 12 or line 15 · · · · · · · · · ·	**16**	
17	Net investment income tax for individuals. Multiply line 16 by 3.8% (.038). Enter here and on Form 1040, line 60 · · · · · · · · · · ·	**17**	
	Estates and Trusts:		
18a	Net investment income (line 12 above) · · · · · · · **18a**		
b	Deductions for distributions of net investment income and deductions under section 642(c) (see instructions) · · · · **18b**		
c	Undistributed net investment income. Subtract line 18b from 18a (see instructions) · · · · · · · · · · · **18c**		
19a	Adjusted gross income (see instructions) · · · · **19a**		
b	Highest tax bracket for estates and trusts for the year (see instructions) · · · · · · · · · · · **19b**		
c	Subtract line 19b from line 19a. If zero or less, enter -0- · · · **19c**		
20	Enter the smaller of line 18c or line 19c · · · · · · · · ·	**20**	
21	Net investment income tax for estates and trusts. Multiply line 20 by 3.8% (.038). Enter here and on Form 1041, Schedule G, line 4 · · · · · · · · · · · ·	**21**	

For Paperwork Reduction Act Notice, see your tax return instructions.

Cat. No. 59474M

Form **8960** (2013)

What's New in 2013

Standard Mileage Rates. The standard mileage rate for miles driven in connection with rental activities is 56.5 cents per mile.

Net investment Income Tax. Beginning in 2013, individuals, estates, and trusts may be subject to the net investment income tax (NIIT). NIIT is a 3.8% tax on the lesser of net investment income or the excess of modified adjusted gross in-come (MAGI) over the threshold amount. Net investment income may include rental and royalty income, income from partnerships, S corporations and trusts, and income from other passive activities reported on your Schedule E. Use Form 8960, *Net Investment Income Tax*, to figure this tax.

Relevant IRS Publications

- ☐ IRS Publication 527, *Residential Rental Property*
- ☐ IRS Publication 535, *Business Expenses*
- ☐ IRS Publication 544, *Sales and Other Dispositions of Assets*
- ☐ IRS Publication 550, *Investment Income and Expenses (Including Capital Gains and Losses)*
- ☐ IRS Publication 555, *Community Property*
- ☐ IRS Publication 925, *Passive Activity and At-Risk Rules*

Section at a Glance

Tax Preparer's Checklist

- ☐ Assemble all Forms 1099-MISC and 1098 payee documents and inquire whenever other evidence indicates that a document may be missing.
- ☐ Identify business versus investment activity sources.
- ☐ Assemble Schedule K-1 documents.

Supplemental Forms That May Be Required with Schedule E	
Form	**When Required**
Form 6198, *At-Risk Limitations*	The taxpayer reports a loss from a trade or business activity or from an activity engaged in for the production of income when some amounts invested in the activity are not at risk.
Form 8082, *Notice of Inconsistent Treatment or Administrative Adjustment Request (AAR)*	The taxpayer has received apparently incorrect partnership, S corporation, estate, or trust information.
Form 8582, *Passive Activity Loss Limitations*	The taxpayer reports a loss from activities in which the taxpayer did not materially participate.
Form 8886, *Reportable Transaction Disclosure Statement*	The taxpayer's federal income tax liability is affected by participation in any transaction that falls into one or more of the reportable categories (see page 5–6).
Form 8960, *Net Investment Income Tax–Individuals, Estates, and Trusts*	The taxpayer has certain income from rental and other passive activities, and has modified adjusted gross income in excess of certain threshold amounts (see Tab 4).

At-Risk Rules

Deductions or losses from any activity are limited to the investor's amount at risk. Any losses in excess of that amount are suspended until there is an increase in the amount at risk. The suspension is another form of carryforward. The suspended losses cannot be carried back. See MTG ¶2045 for further information.

 Caution. The at-risk rules cover any trade or business or investment activity other than certain real estate activities or equipment leasing activities. They are not limited to investments that produce portfolio income or loss or to those that produce passive income or loss.

Amount at Risk Defined

The amount at risk includes money contributed to the activity, debts for which the taxpayer is personally liable, and certain qualified nonrecourse financing. If the taxpayer has no personal liability but has pledged property that is not used in the activity as security for repayment of the debt, the amount at risk is the fair market value of the pledged property, less any superior liens. If the taxpayer pledges property that is used in the activity, the amount at risk does not include the value of the pledged property. A related rule provides that any loan from a co-venturer in the activity usually does not increase the borrower's amount at risk, even if the borrower is personally obligated to repay the loan.

Example. Susan acquires stock in SHV Corporation, an S corporation. She invests $10,000 of her own money and borrows $90,000 from SHV to purchase a total of $100,000 worth of stock. Her basis is $100,000 but her amount at risk is only $10,000 because the loan is from a co-venturer.

A taxpayer's amount at risk is increased for additional contributions of cash or property. It is also increased by the individual's share of any income that the venture produces.

In addition, a taxpayer can increase his or her amount at risk by changing a loan from nonrecourse to recourse. This refinancing would not affect the taxpayer's adjusted basis in his or her partnership interest, and it is unlikely that it would affect the basis of a shareholder in his or her S corporation stock or debt.

Finally, a rule that is a complete departure from the basis rules increases a taxpayer's amount at risk for any gain recognized on the disposition of the taxpayer's interest in the activity.

Passive Activity Loss (PAL) Rules

According to IRC §469, expenses related to passive activities can be deducted only to the extent of passive activity income. Suspended losses and credits (not available because of limitations) can be carried forward to offset passive income from future years. Suspended losses from a passive activity are allowed in full once the taxpayer disposes of his or her interest in the activity in a fully taxable transaction.

Example. Susan Johnson incurred a $30,000 passive loss and reported no passive income in the previous tax year. Therefore, the loss was not deductible in that year. Assume Susan reports $25,000 of passive income for the current tax year. Of the suspended loss, $25,000 will be allowed in the current year.

Passive Activity Defined

A passive activity is one that involves the conduct of a trade or business in which the taxpayer does not materially participate. In addition, a rental activity (whether or not the taxpayer materially participates) is generally considered a passive activity. However, the self-rental rule treats rental income from an item of property as nonpassive income if the property is rented for use in a trade or business in which the taxpayer materially participates. Special rules apply to real estate rentals. See MTG ¶2062 for more details.

Example. John Smith is a self-employed real estate appraiser. In the current tax year his appraisal business sustained a loss of $6,000. He had interest income of $10,000 and a $5,000 loss from an equipment rental business in which he did not materially participate. The loss from his appraisal business is allowable in full in the current tax year. However, the $5,000 loss from his rental activity is a passive loss and cannot offset John's interest income. John must report $4,000 of income for the current year, and carry the $5,000 passive loss forward.

Example. During the previous year, Ken invested $125,000 cash in KPB Partnership and received a 25% partnership interest, using $25,000 of his own funds plus $100,000 loaned to him by one of the other partners. In the current year, the partnership used cash plus $500,000 borrowed from First One Bank to purchase an office building for $1,000,000. The debt on the building was secured by a mortgage and was payable over 20 years with an interest rate of 6 percent. None of the partners were personally liable on the debt. Also during the current year, the partnership suffered a loss of $700,000.

Worksheet: Amount at Risk

1.	Amount at risk at beginning of year, or at acquisition date if acquired during year **1.**	$ 25,000
2.	Additions to amount at risk (CAUTION: Make sure that any debt amount at risk has been restored to the extent of prior reductions.) **2.**	125,000
a.	Add all taxable items **2a.**	0
b.	Add all tax-exempt income **2b.**	0
c.	Add any nonrecourse financing that has been reduced by cash payment or by refinancing with recourse debt **2c.**	0
d.	Add any gain from the sale of part or all of an interest in the activity **2d.**	0
3.	Subtotal (1 + 2 + 2a + 2b + 2c + 2d) **3.**	150,000
4.	Reductions of amount at risk **4.**	0
a.	Nondeductible expenses, not capitalized **4a.**	0
b.	Subtotal (3 - 4 - 4a) **4b.**	150,000
c.	Deductible expenses and losses **4c.**	175,000
d.	Amounts carried forward from last year **4d.**	0
e.	Subtotal (4b - 4c - 4d) (CAUTION: Do not reduce amount at risk below zero. Carry forward any excess expense to next year.) **4e.**	0
f.	Refinancing of amount at risk by nonrecourse debt **4f.**	0
5.	Ending amount at risk (4e - 4f) **5.**	0
6.	Amount carried forward to next year. **6.**	25,000

Ken's at-risk amount includes his $25,000 cash contribution plus his 25% of the partnership's $500,000 qualified nonrecourse debt. It does not include the $100,000 amount borrowed from the other partner. Since the building loan was borrowed from an unrelated commercial lender and not the seller, the loan is considered qualified nonrecourse financing. Ken's share of the partnership's loss is $175,000. However, his deduction is limited to his $150,000 at-risk amount and the remaining $25,000 is carried over until his at-risk basis is increased.

Nonpassive Activity Defined

A trade or business activity in which the taxpayer materially participates is a nonpassive activity.

In addition, a working interest in any oil or gas property that the taxpayer holds directly or as a general partner is considered nonpassive.

Example. Attorney Sam Jones owns and operates K&B Corporation, a law firm for which Sam works full-time. Sam and his wife lease a building that they own jointly to K&B Corporation. The corporation was the sole tenant. The rents received in the current tax year totaled $24,000. The amount received would not be considered passive income since Sam materially participates in the business of the corporation.

Material Participation

If a taxpayer materially participates in the operations of an activity on a regular, continuous and substantial basis, the income is not considered passive and losses generated are currently deductible against other forms of income. Treasury Regulations Sec. 1.469-5T outlines objective standards that look to the actual number of hours spent in the activity. An individual who meets the requirements of any one of seven tests is deemed to materially participate in an activity:

1. The individual participates for more than 500 hours during the tax year.
2. The individual's participation in the tax year constitutes substantially all of the participation in the activity.
3. The individual participates for more than 100 hours and no other individual spends more time on the activity.
4. Total participation in all significant participation activities exceeds 500 hours. A significant participation

activity is defined as one in which the taxpayer participates for more than 100 hours.

5. The individual materially participated in the activity for any five of the past ten tax years that immediately precede the current tax year.
6. The individual materially participated in a personal service activity for any three tax years (need not be consecutive) prior to the current year.
7. The individual satisfies a fact and circumstances test that requires the individual to show participation on a regular, continuous, and substantial basis for more than 100 hours during the year.

Example. Phil Smart is a teacher who earns extra income by contracting with some of his neighbors to plow private roads and driveways. He maintains and drives the truck. Assume that in the current tax year there is little snow and he only operates the truck for 10 hours. He is considered a material participant in the snow plowing business under the second test listed above.

Special Rules for Real Estate Rentals

$25,000 Limit. Rental operations are generally classified as passive. If a taxpayer who owns an interest in a rental real estate property does not satisfy the material participation standards described above but does actively participate in the management of that property, the activity will still be classified as passive. In this case, however, the taxpayer will be allowed a deduction for up to $25,000 in losses from the activity, in excess of income from other real estate activities. This relief is provided to individuals and certain estates, but not to trusts or corporations.

"Active" Participation. The difference between active participation and material participation is that the active participation test can be satisfied without regular, continuous and substantial involvement in operations, as long as the taxpayer participates in making management decisions or arranging for others to provide tenant services (such as repairs) in a significant and bona fide manner. The approvals of tenants, terms, major repairs, and capital expenditures are all evidence of active participation.

To qualify as actively participating, the taxpayer must also have at least a 10% ownership in the rental activity.

Example. Sidney owns and rents out an apartment that he formerly used as his primary residence. He hires a rental agent and uses a contractor to handle routine repairs. Sidney is likely to meet the active participation test.

AGI Phaseout. The $25,000 allowance starts being phased out when a taxpayer's adjusted gross income reaches $100,000. Once the adjusted gross income exceeds that amount, the allowance is reduced by 50% of the excess. Once adjusted gross income reaches $150,000, losses from rental real estate with active participation are treated in the same manner as other losses from passive activities. For this measurement, adjusted gross income is computed before any contribution to an IRA is deducted, before any Social Security benefits are included, and before any net passive loss is allowed. See MTG ¶2062 and ¶2063 for further information.

Example. Lisa Miller reports income of $10,000 from a passive activity on her current year tax return. She also reports a $47,000 loss from an apartment building that she owns and actively manages. She will use $10,000 of the loss from the rental property to offset income from the other passive activity. Of the remaining $37,000 loss, $25,000 may be claimed as a current year deduction and $12,000 will be carried forward.

Rental Activities as Nonpassive

Persons engaged in active real estate trades or businesses are allowed to treat real estate rental activities as non-rental trades or businesses. Thus, a qualifying owner can treat these activities as nonpassive if he or she meets the requirement of a material participation test.

A real estate professional is someone who performs more than half of the personal services he or she performs in all trades or businesses during the tax year in real property trades or businesses in which he or she materially participated. He or she must also spend more than 750 hours during the year in real estate business activities, which include management, operation, development, redevelopment, construction, conversion, rental, leasing and brokering.

Even if the taxpayer meets the real estate professional standard, he or she must still meet one of the material participation tests for the particular activity in question.

Example. John retired from the medical profession in 2011. Since then, he has acquired several properties that he has renovated and rented. He spent a total of 500 hours overseeing and working on renovations during 2012. During 2013, John bought several more properties and spent a total of 1,400 hours on renovations. John rented out all the properties purchased and renovated in 2012; however, he had vacant units in the properties purchased in 2013. In that year, John sustained a loss of $15,000 due to the vacant units. John did not qualify as a real estate professional in 2012, but in 2013 he meets the requirements as a real estate professional; therefore, he can deduct the $15,000 loss.

Where to Report Passive Activity Losses

Not all passive activity losses are reported on Schedule E. Some other forms on which these losses may be reported are Schedule C for PALs related to a business, Schedule D for capital gains and losses, Schedule F for PALs related to farming, Form 4797 for sales of business property, and Form 6252 for installment sales. See IRS Publication 925, *Passive Activity and At-Risk Rules* for more information.

Form 8886—Reportable Transaction Disclosure Statement

There are always creative new ways to avoid taxes. The financial press has been full of stories about abusive tax shelters, which have gone far beyond the legitimate structuring of businesses and investment matters. Promoters, which have included major accounting and law firms, have been penalized severely. Some have even gone out of business. Part of the government's response has been to require specific reporting by persons who promote such transactions and by persons who have invested in these ventures. The transaction categories that require this special reporting are:

1. "Listed" transactions, specifically designated by the IRS in published documents (Notice 2009-59 and subsequent modifications thereto) and any transactions "substantially similar" to those listed.
2. "Confidential transactions" for which the investor has signed an agreement with the advisors, agreeing to a limit of disclosure of the tax treatment of the transaction. In addition, the taxpayer must have paid the advisor a fee of at least $50,000, except in the case of corporations, in which case the fee must be at least $250,000.
3. "Transactions with contractual protection" for which the promoter has guaranteed a refund of the fee if the IRS disallows the anticipated tax treatment.

Gray Area. Multiple rental unit activity may require proper licensing (as a realtor or property manager). An investor must be able to substantiate tax treatment of rental income. Records should include how the property is managed, by whom, and time spent.

Taxpayers with rental losses, or losses incurred in a trade or business, must be careful to review the various participation rules. The definition of a real estate professional is not precise. At least one person who was a partial owner in several closely held businesses has found that merely inspecting and managing company-owned real estate does not constitute being a real estate professional. Thus the taxpayer was unable to deduct losses on certain real estate activities, even though he had met the material participation test, since the real estate rents were *per se* passive.

4. "Loss transactions" that result in a loss of at least $2 million in one year or $4 million in multiple years to an individual (except for foreign currency transactions that result in a loss of at least $50,000 in a single year). Different limits apply to other types of taxpayers.
5. "Transactions of interest," which are those identified by the IRS in published guidance. In Notice 2009-55, the IRS has provided a list of transactions identified as transactions of interest. For updates, see the IRS web page at www.irs.gov/businesses/corporations and click on "Abusive Tax Shelters and Transactions."

Under proposed regulations, "Patented transactions" would be a sixth category of reportable transactions. "Patented transactions" are transactions for which a taxpayer pays a fee to a patent holder or the patent holder's agent for the legal right to use a tax planning method that the taxpayer knows or has reason to know is the subject of a patent. Patented transactions also include transactions for which a taxpayer is the patent holder (or the patent holder's agent) and therefore has the right to payment for another person's use of a tax planning method that is the subject of a patent.

The taxpayer who participates in a reportable transaction must file Form 8886 and disclose the category, the person(s) to whom the taxpayer paid a fee for tax advice, and the nature and projected amount of tax benefits. Form 8886 does not feed directly into any other schedule. The losses and credits claimed from these ventures are reported on the usual schedules. Accordingly, if any of these transactions relate to rental or royalty activities, or are conducted through partnerships or S corporations, the losses would be reported on Schedule E.

Planning Tip. Having a taxpayer describe in writing the results they anticipated from particular financial or investment activities will greatly aid the preparer in addressing those unique tax issues. The preparer will also be able to incorporate the source of the intent and show during filer review whether the tax benefits were a principal factor in the transaction.

Schedule E: Supplemental Income and Loss

Part I: Income or Loss from Rental Real Estate or Royalties

Line A

Taxpayers should check "Yes" if they made any payments that would require them to file any form in series 1099. Otherwise they should check "No."

Filing Tip. Taxpayers are most likely to have to file Form 1099-Misc. See MTG ¶2565 for more information about the Form 1099 series.

Line B

If the taxpayer made payments in 2013 that require him to file Forms 1099, and the required forms were or will be filed, then the "Yes" box should be checked. Otherwise, the "No" box should be checked. If the taxpayer was not required to file any form in the 1099 series, neither box should be checked.

Line 1a, Physical Address of Property

For rental real estate property only, show the street address, city or town, state, and ZIP code. If the property is located in a foreign country, enter the city, province or state, country, and postal code. If there are more than three properties that produced rental income or royalties, additional schedules may be used to identify those properties. However, the total of all properties is only entered on one form.

Line 1b, Type of Property

For the type of property, enter one of the codes listed under Type of Property in Part I of the form.

Self-rental. Enter code type 7 for self-rental if you rent property to a trade or business in which you materially participated. See Rental of Property to a Nonpassive Activity in Pub. 925 for details about the tax treatment of income from this type of rental property.

Other. Enter code type 8 if the property is not one of the other types listed on the form. Attach a statement to your return describing the property.

Line 2, Personal Use vs. Fair Rental; Qualified Joint Ventures

On this line, the taxpayer must give the information necessary to determine whether or not the income and expense from the real property are subject to the vacation home rules, which limit most of the deductions so that they cannot exceed the gross rental income from the property. In other words, any net income is reportable, but a net loss under the vacation home rules does not even enter into the calculations on Form 8582.

For each property, taxpayers should enter the number of days in the year that the property was rented for fair market value in the left-hand column. They should enter the number of days the property was used for personal purposes in the middle column.

If the taxpayer uses the home for more than 14 days, it may pass the test only if the taxpayer's use is fewer than 10% of the days for which it is rented to others at a fair market rate.
If it passes the non-personal-use test, it is treated as a rental activity and all deductions in connection with the rental property are allowed, subject to the at-risk and passive activity loss restrictions, discussed below.

If the owner's use exceeds the greater of 14 days or 10% of the days the property was rented, the expenses may offset the gross income from the property. However, allowable deductions cannot exceed gross income from the property. The statute prescribes that the gross income shall be offset in the following order:

1. Interest, taxes, and casualty losses that are deductible without regard to the vacation home limits. Advertising, rental commissions, and such other expenses that can be associated only with rental income. If these expenses create a net loss, the loss may be deductible, subject to the passive activity loss limits.
2. Repairs and maintenance, utilities, and insurance, but only to the extent of the income remaining after the first category of expenses has been subtracted.

3. Depreciation, but only to the extent of the income remaining after the first two categories of expenses have been subtracted.

If the taxpayer cannot get beyond step 1, there is possible additional relief. If the interest is on a second (but not a third) home, the taxpayer may claim a deduction for the interest that is left over from Schedule E as an itemized deduction on Schedule A. Real property taxes are also deductible on Schedule A, without limit as to the number of properties.

 Gray Area. When the personal usage of a rental unit exceeds the greater of either 14 days or 10 percent of the rental days, according to the IRS, expenses attributable to the use of the rental unit are limited so that the total deductions may not exceed the gross rental income and only a percentage of expenses equalling the total days rented divided by the total days used is deductible. However, the Tax Court and the Ninth and Tenth Circuit Courts of Appeals, have rejected this formula and stated that mortgage interest and real estate taxes are not subject to the same percentage limitations as are other expenses because they are assessed on an annual basis without regard to the number of days that the property is used. The formula employed by the courts computes the percentage limitation for interest and taxes by dividing the total days rented by the total days in the year. Generally, the courts' formula allows higher expense deductions.

Qualified Joint Ventures. Married taxpayers who jointly own rental real estate and file joint tax returns may be able to elect to have their rental real estate properties held in a qualified joint venture. The primary advantage to holding the property in a qualified joint venture rather than a partnership is that income from a qualified joint venture may be entered directly on the taxpayers' Form 1040, with no requirement to file a separate Form 1065 for the jointly owned business. In order to be eligible to make the qualified joint venture election, the husband and wife must both materially participate (see MTG ¶2059) in the business and must be the business's only members.

 Filing Tip. When a husband and wife jointly own property, but the level of activity does not meet the material participation standard, the activity is not considered a trade or business, and they may not choose to be taxed as a qualified joint venture.

The qualified joint venture election is made by checking the "QJV" box in the right-hand column of line 2. If the election is made, each spouse files a separate Schedule E, entering their respective shares of applicable income, deduction or loss. The election may not be revoked without the permission of the IRS. However, the election remains valid only as long as the qualified-joint-venture requirements are met. Thus, if the couple files their tax returns separately or divorces, the qualified joint venture election terminates. A new election will be necessary for any subsequent tax years the taxpayers wish to treat their real estate business as a qualified joint venture.

 Planning Tip. Electing qualified joint venture status does not affect the application of the passive activity loss rules (see page 5-2) or self-employment tax provisions (see Tab 3). Rental real estate income is typically not included in self-employment income. However, losses from real estate activities typically are subject to the passive activity loss limitation rules.

Line 3, Rents Received

Report rental income from real estate (including personal property leased with real estate) on line 3. Use a separate column (A, B, or C) for each rental property. Include income received for renting a room or other space. If services or property, instead of money, are received as rent, report the fair market value of what was received as rental income.

If significant services were provided to the renter, such as maid service, report the rental activity on Schedule C or C-EZ, not on Schedule E. Significant services do not include the furnishing of heat and light, cleaning of public areas, trash collection, or similar services.

Real Estate Dealers. Real estate dealers include only the rent received from real estate (including personal property leased with this real estate) that was held for the primary purpose of renting to produce income. Do not use Schedule E to report income and expenses from rentals of real estate that was held for sale to customers in the ordinary course of your business as a real estate dealer. Instead use Schedule C or C-EZ for those rentals.

Rental Income From Farm Production or Crop Shares. Report farm rental in-come and expenses on Form 4835 if you are an individual, you received rental income based on crops or livestock produced by the tenant, and you did not materially participate in the management or operation of the farm.

Cash Method. Most individual taxpayers use the cash method of accounting. By this method, only amounts actually received during the reporting year are shown as income. Thus, if a tenant is late and makes a December payment in the following January, the income is not reported by the landlord until the tax year in which it is actually received. However, if a tenant pays early, the landlord must report that in the year received.

> **Example.** Ms. Jones owns a duplex and rents both halves in 2013. One tenant does not pay the December rent until January 5, 2014. The other tenant pays her January rent on December 17, 2013. Ms. Jones reports only the amounts she received in 2013 on line 3 of Schedule E.

Payments are usually in cash, although some lessors receive payment in the form of other property or services. The fair market value of noncash payments is reportable as income. One item that is usually not included as rental income is any improvement made by the lessee. The landlord takes no cost basis in this item and is unable to claim any deduction or depreciation related to the cost.

Security Deposits. A landlord who receives a security deposit that may be returned to the tenant at the end of the rental period usually must report the deposit as income when received and as a deduction when it is returned. However, if the landlord receives a deposit, segregates it in the accounting records, and actually pays the tenant interest on the deposit when all or a part of it is refunded, the landlord need not report the deposit as income until it is determined that all or a part of the deposit will not be returned. Any other deposit, for which no return is anticipated, must be reported in the year received, even if it is to cover more than one year of the lease term.

When to Use Schedule C. If a landlord provides significant services (such as maid services) to the renter, the rental activity should be reported on Schedule C or C-EZ (see Tab 3), rather than on Schedule E. For this purpose, significant services do not include the furnishing of heat or light, cleaning of public areas, trash collection, or other services typically provided by landlords to their tenants in the course of a lease.

Real estate dealers should only include rents from properties held primarily as rental properties. Rents from properties held primarily for sale in the ordinary course of the real estate dealer's business should be reported on Schedule C or C-EZ. Self-employed writers, artists, and inventors should report royalty income and expenses on Schedule C rather than Schedule E.

Line 4, Royalties Received

Royalty income from oil, gas, mineral, copyright, or patent properties is reported on line 4. However, if a payment for patent rights is termed a royalty, but is actually consideration for a sale of the patent rights, the seller may be able to claim capital gain treatment. Enter the gross amount of royalty income on line 4 even if state or local taxes were withheld from oil or gas payments received. Include taxes withheld by the producer on line 16. If you received $10 or more in royal-ties during 2013, the payer should send a Form 1099-MISC or similar statement by January 31, 2014, showing the amount you received.

Royalties received in the ordinary course of the business of being an author, composer, or other creator of intellectual property are reported as self-employment income on Schedule C or C-EZ.

Amounts received as royalties for the transfer of a patent or amounts received on the disposal of coal and iron ore may be treated as the sale of a capital asset. For details, see Pub. 544.

Line 5, Advertising

A cash-method taxpayer deducts advertising expenses when they are actually paid and not when they are billed by the agency or media outlet. These could be newspaper, radio, magazine, or other media promotions. They could also include fees paid to an advertising agency or fees paid to a property manager that are designated as advertising expense.

Line 6, Auto and Travel

Automobile expenses are deductible to the extent that the taxpayer uses his or her personal automobile for travel related to the rental activity. If the rental property is located away from the taxpayer's home, the taxpayer must be careful to separate business from rental purposes for a trip. This is an especially hot issue when there is a vacation home and the taxpayer deducts travel to that home. See Tab 3 and Tab 8.

> **Example.** Mr. Gray lives in Indiana and owns a condominium in Florida. After severe storms and tornadoes, he drove to Florida to inspect the damage and make arrangements for repairs to the condominium. If the majority of the days on this trip were devoted to the business matters of the condominium, he may deduct the expenses.

If the standard mileage rate is used, multiply the number of miles driven in connection with the rental activities by 56.5 cents per mile. Include this amount, along with parking fees and tolls, on line 6. Rental or lease payments, depreciation, or actual auto expenses cannot be deducted if the standard mileage rate is used.

If actual auto expenses are deducted, include on line 6 the rental activity portion of the cost of gasoline, oil, repairs, insurance, tires, license plates, etc. Also, Part V of Form 4562 and Form 4562 must be attached to the tax return. Auto rental or lease payments are shown on line 19 and depreciation is shown on line 18.

Documentation of automobile expense for any type of deduction is often challenged by the IRS. A mileage log, which has been filled out contemporaneously, may be essential to preserving this deduction.

Line 7, Cleaning and Maintenance

Cleaning and maintenance expenses are deductible in the year paid. These can sometimes be subject to challenge. The taxpayer is advised to keep careful records to distinguish maintenance from improvements to the property.

Line 8, Commissions

Commissions may be paid to real estate agents, owners' groups, or other property managers, based on the amounts of rent collected. If the agent is entitled to collect a portion of a tenant's rent, then the income is received and the commission is paid when the agent receives the rental income from the tenant.

Line 9, Insurance

Most property owners carry hazard insurance on property. The insurance premiums are deductible when paid. If they are paid by the lender out of an escrow account, the taxpayer claims the deduction in the year in which the lender pays the amount out of escrow. If a premium covers more than one year on a policy, the taxpayer should prorate it among the years covered. As a practical matter, the IRS approves the deduction of a one-year premium in the year paid.

 Example. In February, a taxpayer pays a one-year premium for hazard insurance. Assuming that the taxpayer follows the practice consistently, he or she may deduct the cost in the current year.

In addition to hazard insurance, a property owner may also carry personal liability insurance, private mortgage insurance, business interruption insurance and other specialty policies. These are generally deductible under the same rules as hazard insurance. However, credit life insurance, which will pay off the mortgage in the event of the insured's death or disability, is not deductible.

Line 10, Legal and Other Professional Fees

Legal expenses paid in the ordinary course of operating the rental property, such as those incurred for dealing with tenants, vendors, contractors, neighbors or other periodic concerns, are deductible when paid. Legal expenses paid in the ordinary course of operating the rental property, such as those incurred for dealing with tenants, vendors, contractors, neighbors or other periodic concerns are deductible when paid. Fees paid in connection with rental property must be segregated from fees incurred in connection with other business matters or those related to person or family matters. Legal fees paid in connection with the purchase of a property must be added to the cost of the property. Legal fees connected with the sale of the property are treated as reductions of the sale price and are reflected in determining the gain or loss on the sale or other disposition of the property.

Legal fees paid or incurred to defend or protect title to property, to recover property, or to develop or improve property cannot be deducted. Instead, these fees must be capitalized and added to the property's basis, Legal, accounting, and other professional fees related to tax preparation or tax advice are also deductible. If these fees are commingled with the owner's other tax and legal fees, there should be some sustainable method of segregating the portion of the fees attributable to the rental property.

Planning Tip. Tax preparation and other professional fees may have alternative minimum tax consequences when posted on Schedule A. Allocation of these expenses to income schedules (Schedules C, E, and F) can minimize AMT impact.

Line 11, Management Fees

Management fees have no special rules that are not applicable to deductions generally. If a property manager charges periodic fees for monitoring or supervision of the property, or for conducting business with tenants, these are deductible when paid. Amounts paid to family members may qualify, as long as the recipient reports it in his or her taxable income. Self-charged time, or the value of the owner's personal services, is not deductible under management fees or any other category of expenses.

Line 12, Mortgage Interest Paid to Banks, etc.

To determine the interest expense allocable to rental activities, records must be kept to show how the proceeds of each debt were used. Mortgage interest paid to banks and commercial lenders is deductible when paid. Prepaid interest is deductible in the year in which it is properly allocable, rather than the year in which it was paid. Points paid at time of loan origination are not immediately deductible and must be amortized over the term of the loan. If the mortgage is refinanced, the points paid at that time must be amortized over the life of the new loan. Any amortization remaining from prior financing should be deducted.

The lender should send Form 1098 to the borrower if the borrower paid $600 or more in mortgage interest during the year. If the amount on Form 1098 does not agree with the borrower's records, the borrower should prepare a note explaining the difference and attach it to his or her tax return. Mortgage interest paid to private lenders or when Form 1098 is not issued in the taxpayer's name should be reported on line 13.

Line 13, Other Interest

Interest paid to private lenders and other interest paid in connection with the rental activity is reported on line 13. Examples include interest paid on loans to improve, repair, or furnish the property, to replace appliances, and other expenditures. This line should also include interest paid to the seller of the property, and any other source of credit that is not required to file Form 1098.

Line 14, Repairs

This line shows the amount paid for repairs to the property, furnishings, or appliances. A taxpayer should be careful to distinguish repairs from improvements. Any expenditure that improves a property's income potential beyond what it was when the taxpayer acquired it is suspect as a repair deduction. However, repairs that merely restore the property to its normal operating condition are completely deductible. These can result from tenant damage, storms, vandalism, or any other occurrence. If the expenditure in question is an improvement, the taxpayer may be able to recover its cost gradually by claiming depreciation deductions. See line 18 for further discussion.

 Gray Area. Work done to prevent damage and protect an investment may qualify as repair expense rather than capital investment if the work prolongs the life of the property in its normal operating condition.

Line 15, Supplies

Supplies for cleaning, maintenance, tenant comfort, and other needs may be deducted when they are purchased. On occasion, the IRS may challenge the immediate deductibility of a large purchase of items in bulk quantities that may last more than one year. This is another area where the taxpayer needs to distinguish

routine supplies, such as furnace filters, from capital improvements, such as a new furnace. The former would be deductible when purchased, whereas the latter would need to be capitalized and depreciated according to its MACRS recovery period (see Tab 7).

Line 16, Taxes

Taxes assessed on the property by a local government, county, school district, or other taxing authority are deductible when paid. If paid by the lender from an escrow account, the taxes are deductible when the lender pays the tax. The primary trouble spots for this deduction are assessments for improvement of the property, which are not deductible. They must be added to the cost of the land. On occasion, a taxpayer attempts to deduct a portion of state or local income tax, to the extent it is attributable to net rental income. Personal income taxes are deductible only on Schedule A.

Sales taxes paid on supplies or services are deductible as part of those expenditures. Sales taxes paid on appliances, furnishings, or other long-lived assets must be added to the property's cost and recovered either through depreciation deductions or upon selling the property.

Line 17, Utilities

Utilities paid by the landlord for tenant use are deductible when the rental agreement provides that the landlord will pay the utilities. Any utility charges imposed on the landlord during a period of vacancy would also be deductible. The cost of ordinary and necessary telephone calls related to rental activities or royalty income can be deducted. However, the base rate (including taxes and other charges) for local telephone service for the first telephone line into your residence is a personal expense and is not deductible.

Line 18, Depreciation Expense or Depletion

Depreciation expense is computed for property used in the trade or business of renting. There is some depreciation on royalty-producing property, although it is not as common as depletion. Depletion is allowed only for oil, gas, or mineral royalty property. As similar as the terms depreciation and depletion may sound, they are really quite different.

Depreciation on real estate rental property is often divided into two major components: building and land. The building component is depreciated using the real property depreciation allowance rules. These generally allow deductions over 27.5 years, using the straight-line method for any residential property placed in service after 1986. Nonresidential property, which includes short term lodging facilities such as hotels and motels, is subject to a longer depreciation period. For most buildings placed in service after May 12, 1993, this period is 39 years. There are different rules for properties placed in service before these dates.

Personal property used in connection with the rental property may be depreciated over much shorter MACRS lives. Thus, it is wise to segregate the cost of furnishings, appliances and mechanical equipment from the cost of the building itself.

There is no depreciation deduction for the cost of the land. The only tax benefit resulting from land cost is its effect on gain or loss from the property's sale.

A taxpayer with depletable oil, gas, timber, or mineral interests should consult IRS Publication 535 for the rules governing these computations. They can become quite complicated, and they may vary by the nature of the property, the involvement of the royalty interest holder, and other conditions.

Line 19, Other Expenses

Enter on line 19 any ordinary and necessary expenses not listed on lines 5 through 18. Part or all of the cost of modifying existing commercial buildings to make them energy efficient may be deductible. Other expenses not listed above may be deductible if they are ordinary and necessary to the conduct of the rental activity. These might include the following:

- Wages and salaries paid in connection with the rental real estate activity.
- Some prizes or other incentives given to tenants, although there are strict substantiation requirements for anything construed as entertainment.
- The cost of an event such as a holiday picnic (may be subject to the 50% disallowance for meals and entertainment).

Line 20, Add Lines 5 Through 19

On this line, the taxpayer sums the expenses reported above. Note that this is computed before depreciation expense.

Line 21, Income (Loss) Calculation

Fill out line 21 using only the current year's income and deduction items. If the result on line 21 is positive income for any property, no more work may be necessary. If the result on line 21 shows a loss, the rental or royalty activity may be subject to the at-risk rules. The at-risk limitation should be calculated on Form

6198, and the allowable amount of the loss(es) should be entered on line 21. If the at-risk limitation reduces the amount of losses included in line 21, "Form 6198" should be entered to the left of line 21.

Filing Tip. Be sure to check prior years' Forms 6198 and 8582 for any previous losses, so that hidden deductions are not lost.

In general, the income and loss items from line 21 should also be posted to Form 8582 and its worksheets to determine the amount to report on line 22. However, if there are no properties for which losses are reported in the current year and no properties where there have been disallowed losses, the taxpayer may not need to fill out Form 8582.

If any rental or royalty activity shows a loss, the taxpayer must check the at-risk limitations. If a loss is limited by this rule, the loss on line 21 should be the amount from Form 6198, line 21.

Line 22, Deductible Rental Real Estate Loss

Caution. Losses from royalty interests should not be reported on line 22. Royalty losses should be reported on line 21 and line 25.

This line includes a net loss that has run through Form 8582 and is deductible on Schedule E for the current year. Up to $25,000 of passive activity loss may be deducted as a result of the taxpayer's passive activity income or according to the active participation rule. This line is also the proper place for deducting losses for taxpayers qualifying for "real estate professional" status, which allows the taxpayer to treat rental operations as a trade or business, rather than *per se* passive activities.

Line 22 should also include any prior-year loss that was disallowed under the passive activity loss rules, if the activity is completely disposed of in the current year. Also, report disallowed passive activity losses from prior years when there is passive income in the current year that can offset those losses.

Gray Area. According to the instructions to Form 6198, prior-year losses that were not deductible due to at-risk limitations should be reported on the appropriate form or schedule of the taxpayer's current year tax return. In most cases, prior-year disallowed losses from rental real estate activities will be reported on line 3c of Form 8582. However, they may be reported elsewhere on Form 8582 for some activities, and if the taxpayer is not required to file Form 8582 for the current tax year, generally these losses are entered directly on line 22 of Schedule E with an explanation on the dotted line next to line 22. The IRS recommends "PYA" (prior-year amount) for disallowed losses entered in Part II of Schedule E, so this is the recommended notation on line 22.

Lines 24, 25, and 26, Income and Loss Calculations

These totals involve self-evident calculations. If the taxpayer has no income or losses reportable in Part II, III, IV, or line 40, the amount from line 26 goes to Form 1040, line 17. If the taxpayer has income or deductions from partnerships, S corporations, trusts, estates, or residual interests in real estate mortgage investment conduits (REMICs; see page 5-15), the total from line 26 becomes part of the amount entered on Schedule E, line 41.

Part II: Income or Loss from Partnerships and S Corporations

Partnerships

Each partnership must provide Form 1065, Schedule K-1 to every partner. Most K-1s report income or loss that should be entered on Schedule E. However, there are other forms on which a taxpayer may need to report income or loss from his or her interest in a partnership. Schedule K-1 has fairly detailed instructions on where to report the amount from each line item. For example, if a partnership realizes interest income, it must report it as such to the partners on Schedule K-1 and this interest if reported on the partner's Form 1040, line 8a or Schedule B, not on the partner's Schedule E.

Filing Tip. Processing of Schedule K-1 (Form 1065) may delay preparation of the individual's Form 1040. If a partnership has not provided Schedule K-1, the individual should contact the person responsible. Individuals may estimate the information, file Form 1040, and file a later amended return if information on the K-1 is different from the estimate. Filing an extension until all information is received is the other option.

Not all income or loss may progress directly from Schedule K-1 to Schedule E. For example, any net rental income from a partnership, or net trade or business income from a partnership in which the taxpayer does not materially participate, must be routed through Form 8582 in order to compute the allowable losses from passive activities owned by the taxpayer.

Example. A taxpayer has net ordinary income of $15,000 from ABC Partnership. He also has $14,000 of ordinary losses from XYZ Partnership. Both of these items need to be entered on Schedule E. However, if the taxpayer does not materially participate in these activities or if they are rental activities, he must also report them on Form 8582.

A Schedule K-1 may show ordinary income or ordinary loss. If there is a loss, the taxpayer must ensure that the loss does not exceed his or her basis in the partnership interest. If the loss exceeds basis, the partner may deduct only the portion of the loss that does not exceed basis. Next, the partner must make sure that the loss does not exceed his or her amount at risk in the partnership. Only the portion that does not exceed the amount at risk moves to the next step, which is the passive activity loss limit, and only if the partner does not materially participate in the partnership's trade or business or if the loss is incurred in connection with a rental activity. Only the portion of the loss that is allocable from Form 8582 and its worksheets actually flows to Schedule E.

It is always a good idea to check prior years' tax returns for any losses or deductions that might have been disallowed due to one of these provisions. If the partner has acquired basis, increased his or her amount at risk, or currently meets one of the passive activity loss allowance criteria, he or she may be able to claim a deduction on the current year's return for prior year items.

A partnership must also report the partner's share of self-employment income. This amount is not always identical to the ordinary income shown in box 1 of Schedule K-1. Enter the amount from box 14 (with code A) of Schedule K-1 of Form 1065 or from box 9 (with code J1) of Schedule K-1 of Form 1065-B on Schedule SE after reducing this amount by any allowable expenses. These expenses may also qualify as an adjustment to self-employment income flowing from Schedule K-1. The self-employment income amount goes directly to Schedule SE and does not enter into any other calculations, including those on Form 8582.

In general, income from a partnership is not community income, but is the separate income of the partner. See IRS Publication 555. However, if the partnership is community property, the income or loss from the partnership is community income.

A U.S. citizen who is a member of a foreign partnership may be required to file Form 8865 to provide information similar to Form 1065, which U.S. partnerships must file. There are several categories of filers of this form. The level of required information varies with the level of ownership in the foreign partnership.

A partner may bear certain expenses outside of the partnership on its behalf, such as for the use of a personal automobile, or interest paid on loans to acquire the investment in the partnership. The partner should report these on line 28 of Schedule E with an appropriate explanation. Line 28 should also include any loss or deduction that had been disallowed in any prior year due to basis, at-risk, or passive activity loss limits.

S Corporations

The rules for reporting income and other items from S corporations are almost identical to the partnership reporting rules, with the following important differences.

There is no self-employment income reportable from the S corporation, so there is no feed to Schedule SE. If the S corporation shareholder is also an employee and incurs employee business expenses related to the S corporation, these are treated in the same manner as any other employee expenses. If the S corporation reimburses the shareholder-employee, the reimbursements do not appear on the return. If not reimbursed, the shareholder-employee may claim a deduction for unreimbursed employee business expenses by completing Form 2106 and entering the appropriate items on Schedule A as miscellaneous itemized deductions. This is quite different from the partner, who reports these items on Line 28 of Schedule E. However, if the shareholder borrows money to purchase stock in the S corporation, the interest paid on these loans is reported on Schedule E, in the same manner as a partner who has borrowed money to finance his or her interest in the partnership.

A final major difference between partnership income and S corporation income arises when there are distributions of accumulated earnings and profits from years before the corporation became an S corporation. These may be dividend income to the shareholder when received and should be reported on Form 1040, line 9a or 9b, or on Schedule B in the same manner as dividends from regular C corporations. They should not be duplicated on Schedule E. The S corporation should send Form 1099 to notify the shareholder of these distributions.

 Caution. Persons who are sole shareholders in S corporations have often made the mistake of trying to avoid social security taxes by taking little or no wages or salaries from the corporation, but by taking the profits out in the form of distributions. The IRS has had an active program of monitoring these corporations, and assessing FICA and FUTA taxes on the corporations. Often the penalties alone for failure to pay these taxes are more than the income that the shareholders have attempted to divert. Many of these assessments have been challenged in the courts, but to date the IRS has won every single case. Thus, every shareholder in an S corporation who performs services for the corporation, and withdraws money from the corporation should make sure to establish and maintain a reasonable level of compensation for the services he or she performs.

Losses from S corporations are subject to similar limitations as partnership losses. Therefore the shareholder should check prior years' tax returns for losses that may have been disallowed in an earlier year. If they are deductible in the current year they should be entered on line 28, Schedule E.

Line 27, Prior-Year Losses

On line 27, the "Yes" box should be checked if the taxpayer is reporting any prior year losses on the current return. These prior year losses must have been disallowed due to the at-risk, excess farm loss, or basis limitations, a prior year disallowed loss from a passive activity (if that loss was not reported on Form 8582), or unreimbursed partnership expenses. These items will not appear on Schedule K-1 or any other correspondence from a partnership or S corporation in the current year, so the taxpayer must be able to consult prior years' records to determine if it is necessary to check this box. The "No" box on line 27 should be checked if the taxpayer is not reporting such items, or if the taxpayer has prior years' losses but is unable to claim any of them in the current year.

Line 28, Income and Loss Details

Line 28 is divided into two sets of columns, passive and nonpassive. Nonpassive income or loss, as well as IRC §179 asset expensing, will be from partnerships and S corporations in which the taxpayer materially participates. However, even these entities might have some rental income that does not meet the active business exception. If that is the case, the income or loss might be divided between passive and nonpassive. This information should be readily available from the Schedule K-1 of the partnership or S corporation, possibly on attachments to the official form.

> **Example.** A taxpayer owns an interest in a limited liability company (LLC), which is treated as a partnership for federal income tax purposes. This year's Schedule K-1 shows that her share of the LLC's ordinary income from its business was $40,000 and her share of IRC §179 asset expensing was $15,000. The LLC also owned a rental property, which was separate from its business. The taxpayer was allocated $3,000 of net income from the rental activity this year. She will make three separate entries on line 28 for the LLC's activities reported on the K-1. These will include nonpassive income of $40,000, a nonpassive IRC §179 deduction of $15,000, and passive income of $3,000.

There may be two reasons why a prior year's disallowed nonpassive loss is reported in the current year. A taxpayer who lacked basis in his or her partnership interest or S corporation stock and debt in one or more prior years may have either invested additional amounts or reported income from the same entity in the current year. In either of these cases, some or all of the prior year's suspended loss may be deductible in the current year. If so, it is reported on line 28 with the notation PYA (for prior year amount).

> **Example.** A taxpayer owns stock in an S corporation. Last year the taxpayer's share of ordinary losses from the S corporation was $40,000, but his basis was only $25,000. His suspended loss from this corporation was $15,000. This year, he reports $60,000 of ordinary income from the S corporation. The taxpayer materially participated in the S corporation's business in both years. On line 28 this year he reports $60,000 of nonpassive income. On a separate line, with the notation "PYA," he should report a loss of $15,000.

A passive loss could have been disallowed in the prior year for lack of basis, lack of amount at risk, or from the passive activity loss (PAL) limits. The first two limits should not appear on the prior year's worksheet for Form 8582, but the PAL limit should come from that worksheet.

Lines 29-32, Calculations

Passive and nonpassive income from Schedule K-1 are totaled separately in columns (g) and (j) of line 29a, and the total of these is reported on line 30. Allowed passive loss is totaled on line 29b in column (f), and nonpassive losses from Schedule K-1 are totaled on line 29b in column (h). Totals of IRC §179 expense deductions in column (i) are also reported on line 29b. The total of the three sums on line 29b is reported on line 31, shown in parentheses to indicate it represents a loss.

Line 32 is the total partnership and S corporation income or loss, the result of combining lines 30 and 31. This amount is included in line 41.

Part III: Income or Loss from Estates and Trusts

Part III is quite similar to Part II. However, the information for this part is from the taxpayer's Schedule K-1 from estates and trusts. The flow-through amount from an estate or trust is calculated quite differently from partnership or S corporation amounts. The fiduciary bears the responsibility for those calculations. The taxpayer who receives income from these fiduciary entities will find that the estate and trust reporting requirements are almost identical to those for partnerships.

One principal difference is that a taxpayer will not normally report a loss from an estate or trust, unless the fiduciary entity is terminated in the reporting year. Another reporting difference is that there is no place for a IRC §179 asset expensing deduction, since this provision is prohibited for estates and trusts.

Trusts Not Reported on Schedule E. There are two types of trusts that do not require the taxpayer to report income or expenses on Schedule E. A grantor trust is one in which the taxpayer has sufficient control and the trust is disregarded entirely for tax purposes. A revocable living trust is a popular example of this type of trust. The taxpayer should report all items of income of the trust directly on his own return. Thus, the income from a grantor trust will be reported on Schedule E only if the income source is from a partnership, S corporation, another trust or estate, rental, or royalty activities.

The other type of trust not reporting to Schedule E is the electing small business trust (ESBT). An ESBT's sole purpose is to hold stock in one or more S corporations. This trust does not pass income or loss to its beneficiaries. Distributions from these trusts are not taxable to the beneficiary and are not reported on the individual beneficiary's tax return.

The taxation of trust activities can be quite complicated. A trust may pass through some of its income to a beneficiary on Schedule K-1 and may report that part of the income is from a grantor trust. This is reported directly by the beneficiary on the source schedule, such as Schedule B. Some trusts are actually split into three parts for one beneficiary, with some trust income reported on Schedule E, Part III, some reportable as grantor trust income, and some as distributions from an ESBT.

Line 33, Income and Loss Details

Line 33 serves the same purpose as line 28 does for income and deductions from partnerships and S corporations. Again, there is no column for IRC §179 expensing, since this deduction is not allowed for fiduciaries. The passive or nonpassive status of the income or loss is usually determined by the fiduciary's participation, rather than by the taxpayer's participation.

Lines 34a-37, Calculations

Line 35 is total income and line 36 is total loss from estates and trusts. The combination on line 37 is also included on line 41.

Form 8082

Form 8082 is filed by a taxpayer when he or she receives apparently incorrect partnership, S corporation, estate, or trust information, or does not receive a Schedule K-1. In this situation, the taxpayer will not be reporting the same amounts that are reported by the entity. He or she should use this form to explain the difference.

Form 3520 and Form 3520-A

These forms are filed by taxpayers who have certain dealings with foreign trusts, partnerships, or corporations. Preparation of these forms requires substantial knowledge of the tax and nontax laws of the affected jurisdiction.

Part IV: Income or Loss from Real Estate Mortgage Investment Conduits (REMICs)

Distributions from a REMIC are not reported on Schedule E. If the distribution does not exceed the taxpayer's basis in the REMIC, the holder reduces his or her basis in the REMIC investment. If a distribution from the REMIC exceeds the taxpayer's basis, the excess is reported as a gain from the sale of the interest in a REMIC. For the casual investor, this would be reported as a capital gain on Schedule D.

REMICs Defined

A REMIC is an entity formed for holding a pool of mortgages secured by real estate. For income tax purposes, its treatment is generally the same as that of a partnership, although it may be subject to certain taxes on its holdings.

REMIC income or loss is not passive activity income or loss. Therefore, it does not enter onto Form 8582, although some of it may be reported on Schedule E. The income from a "regular" interest is interest income. The taxpayer receives a Form 1099 from the REMIC and reports that amount on Form 1040, line 8a or Schedule B.

For the residual interest, the holder is treated like a partner in a partnership. Rather than sending a K-1 annually, the REMIC sends Form 1066, Schedule Q, each quarter. The holder's treatment of this income or loss is not passive activity income or loss, but has other complications.

If the taxpayer does not agree with the amounts reported by the REMIC, he or she should file Form 8082, discussed previously under Part III, to notify the IRS of the contrary position on the return. Note that this greatly increases the probability of examination, so Form 8082 should be filed with great care. However, it is probably better to file this form than to merely ignore the figures on Form 1066, Schedule Q, or to knowingly report erroneous items on a tax return.

Line 38, Income and Loss Details

Form 1066, Schedule Q, line 2c is the smallest amount reportable as taxable income or as alternative minimum taxable income (AMTI). This is really a black box calculation made by the REMIC. The holder reports this total for the year on Schedule E, line 38, column (c). The taxpayer must compare this total with his or her taxable income on line 43, Form 1040, as computed without this item. If this amount does not exceed the otherwise taxable income on line 43 of Form 1040, it does not enter into the income tax calculation, *per se*. However, the taxpayer must also compare this figure with the alternative minimum taxable income, calculated without regard to this amount, which is found on Form 6251, line 28. If line 28 exceeds column (c), no further action is necessary. However, if line 28 of Form 6251 is less than column (c), AMTI must be increased up to this amount.

Form 1066, Schedule Q lists the holder's share of net residual income on line 1b and the share of investment expenses on line 3b. These are entered on Schedule E, line 38, columns (d) and (e), respectively.

The individual holder must add these two together, even though it is intuitively illogical to include an item that is designated as an expense on Schedule Q as income on Schedule E. However, the amount on line 1b is net of the investment expenses, so the individual holder must gross it up for the amount of these expenses, and then report the expenses as a Schedule A itemized deduction, subject to the 2% adjusted gross income (AGI) limit.

Line 39, REMIC Total

Only columns (d) and (e) of line 38 are combined on line 39.

Part V: Summary

Line 40, Net Farm Rental Income or Loss

A taxpayer who receives rental income from farming may have up to three places to report his or her income.

A taxpayer who materially participates in the farming business and receives crop rents must report the income and deductions on Schedule F.

Cash rents that are not dependent upon production are reported on Schedule E, Part I, in the same manner as other real estate rental income.

Cash rents based on production, where the owner (or sublessor) does not materially participate, are reported on Form 4835 and then on Schedule E, line 40. This net income or loss from each identifiable farming activity must also be reported on Form 8582, unless the taxpayer is not required to submit this form. If this rental activity shows a loss for the year, it is subject to the cutback imposed by the passive activity loss rules before the amount allowable is transferred to line 40.

Line 41, Total Income or Loss

This line shows the total of all ordinary income or deductible loss from all of the activities reported on Schedule E. Although there are two additional lines on Schedule E, this is the final amount that flows to Form 1040. The taxpayer must enter this total on Form 1040, page 1, line 17.

Line 42, Reconciliation of Farming and Fishing Income

On line 42, the taxpayer shows the amount of gross income from farming and fishing. This amount is taken from Form 4835, line 7 and includes any gross income from farming and fishing reported to the taxpayer by partnerships, S corporations, estates, and trusts.

The major significance of this amount is its effect on estimated tax payments. To calculate estimated tax payments required, the amount from line 42 of Schedule E must be combined with gross income from Schedule F and with the gains from the sales of certain livestock on Form 4797. However, cash rents reported in Part I of Schedule E are not included in farming or fishing income. If less than two-thirds of the taxpayer's gross income from all sources is from farming and fishing, this figure has no other significance. However, if the gross income from farming and fishing is at least two-thirds of the taxpayer's gross income, there are special estimated tax rules.

If the taxpayer pays all tax due by January 15 of the following year, there is no penalty for failing to pay quarterly estimates. If the taxpayer misses this date, but files Form 1040 by March 1 of the succeeding year, and pays the tax due in full with the return, there is no penalty for failure to pay estimated tax.

If the taxpayer does not pay all tax due by January 15 and does not file and pay by March 1, the penalty period is from January 15 of the subsequent year to April 15, or three months. In addition, the required estimate is only two-thirds of the current tax, as opposed to 90% for most taxpayers. See Tabs 3 and 11 for more information about these special rules that apply to farmers and fishermen.

Example. Alistair Brown has $10,000 in tax liability for 2013, including all income tax, self-employment tax, and alternative minimum tax, after subtracting credits. His 2012 tax was higher than $10,000, so he does not qualify for an underpayment exception based on the prior year's tax. He files his return and pays his tax on April 15, 2014.

If he does not meet the farming gross income test, his estimated tax payments must be at least 90% of the tax due, or $9,000. The penalty dates for 2013 are April 15 for 25% of the $9,000, or $2,250; June 17 for $2,250; September 16 for $2,250; and January 15, 2014, for $2,250. If he does qualify for the farming exception his required estimated tax payment is only $6,667 and the penalty period for the entire amount runs from January 15 to April 17, 2014.

Line 43, Reconciliation for Real Estate Professionals

This line does not directly feed into any other schedule or form. It is the net income from real estate rental activities in which the taxpayer materially participated, if he or she is a real estate professional. The significance of this is that real estate rentals are treated as trades or businesses, rather than *per se* rental activities, if the taxpayer qualifies for this status.

Planning Tip. Electronic filing limits the number of Schedule Es to five forms. If more forms are required a paper return must be filed.

Comprehensive Example of Schedule E

Pam Stanley is a real estate dealer. In addition to $175,000 in real estate commissions reported on Form 1099, she has the following items for the current tax year:

Rental Duplexes. Pam spent 800 hours in the current year actively managing a number of rental duplexes. No other person participates in management of this activity. The current income is $14,000 and deductions are $18,000. In the previous tax year, $2,500 was disallowed due to at-risk limits. She invested an additional $10,000 in this activity in the current tax year. No passive activity loss deductions were suspended from a prior year.

Information on Pam's rental duplex activity comes from books, records and last year's Form 6198. Reporting is done on Schedule E, Part I. None of these items go to Form 8582, since she is a material participant, using the real estate professional rules.

Limited Real Estate Partnership. Pam has a limited real estate partnership interest, in which she does not participate. Her Schedule K-1 shows $3,000 rental loss and $2,000 interest income. $1,800 deductions were suspended from the prior year.

Information on Pam's limited real estate partnership comes from Form 1065, Schedule K-1, and last year's Form 8582. Interest income is not reported on Schedule E or Form 8582, but directly to Form 1040, Line 8a and Schedule B. Net rental loss from current year and prior year is reported on Form 8582, and any allowable amount will be reported on Schedule E, Part II.

Equipment Leasing Partnership. Pam holds a limited interest in an equipment leasing partnership. Her Schedule K-1 shows $4,000 net rental loss. There is a suspended passive activity loss of $6,000 from prior years.

Information on Pam's equipment leasing partnership comes from Form 1065, Schedule K-1 and last year's Form 8582. Net rental loss from current year and pri-

or year is reported on Form 8582, and any allowable amount will be reported on Schedule E, Part II.

Apartment Complex. Pam has a joint ownership in an apartment complex. She participated about 50 hours in the activity and others participated more. She had $2,500 net rental loss and $7,000 gain from the sale of her entire interest to an unrelated party. There is also a $1,500 suspended passive activity loss from the prior year.

Information from Pam's apartment complex activity comes from books, records, last year's Form 8582, and closing statement on sale. Gain from sale is reported on Form 8582, and then on Form 4797. Current and last year's loss are reported Form 8582, but only to offset gain. Net loss will be allowed in full on Schedule E, Part I, because the joint ownership arrangement does not constitute a partnership.

Pam needs to fill out the following schedules.

Schedule E Part I

Rental duplex, line 3	$ 14,000
Lines 5 through 20	18,000
Lines 21 and 22, including $2,500, noted on line 22 with notation "PYA." This does not feed into Form 8582, since she materially participates, and is a real estate professional.	(6,500)

Form 8582, Worksheets

There are no entries to worksheets 1 and 2, since Pam does not have any passive real estate rentals in which she actively participates. Moreover, her AGI is too high to claim any active participation loss. She has no commercial revitalization deduction expenses which would qualify for that special deduction. Worksheet 3 is where she will begin her inputs for this form.

Real Estate Partnership		Apartment	
Worksheet 3, column b	$ 3,000	Worksheet 3, column a	$7,000
Worksheet 3, column c	1,800	Worksheet 3, column b	2,500
Worksheet 3, column e	4,800	Worksheet 3, column c	1,500
		Worksheet 3, column d	3,000
Equipment Leasing Partnership		Totals for This Worksheet	
Worksheet 3, column b	$ 4,000	Column a	$7,000
Worksheet 3, column c	6,000	Column b	9,500
Worksheet 3, column e	10,000	Column c	9,300

These totals then go to the front page of Form 8582.

Line 3a	$ 7,000
Line 3b	(9,500)
Line 3c	(9,300)

Line 3d shows a loss of ($11,800.00). Since there are no entries on lines 1d or 2d, the same ($11,800.00) goes to line 4.

Line 15	$7,000
Line 16	7,000

Now she must return to the worksheets, and will use worksheet 5. This worksheet requires that she apportion the losses between all passive activities, and determine the disallowed portion. It is not an obvious transition from page 1. The loss in column a comes from the losses in column e of worksheet 3. The total of these losses is then prorated by percentage in column b. The total in column c is the total passive activity loss for the year from line 4 of page 1 ($11,800) less the sum of the special allowance for rental real estate activities with active participation from line 10 of page 1 ($0) and the special allowance for commercial revitalization deductions from rental real estate activities ($0).

Activity	Form or Schedule Where Reported	(a) Loss	(b) Ratio	(c) Unallowed Loss
Limited real estate partnership	E	$ 4,800	.3243	$ 3,827
Equipment leasing partnership	E	10,000	.6757	7,973
Total		14,800	1.00	11,800

For this year, Pam's final step in completing Form 8582 is to fill out worksheet 6, as follows:

Activity	Form or Schedule Where Reported	(a) Loss	(b) Unallowed Loss	(c) Allowed Loss
Limited real estate partnership	E	$ 4,800	$ 3,827	$ 973
Equipment leasing partnership	E	10,000	7,973	2,027
Total		14,800	11,800	3,000

Now Pam returns to Schedule E, where she needs to complete the following:

Part I, line 25		$ 10,500
Part I, line 26		(10,500)
Part II, line 27		Check no
Part II, line 28	a	(name of partnership)
	b	Enter p
		Check if foreign
	c	EIN
	d	Do not check
	e	973
	f	2,027
Part II, line 29	f	3,000
Part II, line 31		3,000
Part II, line 32		(3,000)
Part V, line 41		(13,500)
Schedule E, line 43		(10,500)

What's New in 2013

Business Mileage Rate. In 2013, the standard rate for business miles driven is 56.5 cents per mile for miles driven.

High-Low Rates. In 2013, for travel from January 1 through September 30, the per diem rates under the "high-low" substantiation method are $242 for "high-cost" localities and $163 for all other localities. For travel on and after October 1, the rates are $251 for "high-cost" localities and $170 for all other localities.

Tax Preparer's Checklist

The following items are required:

☐ Review employer pay stubs for deductions and reimbursements.

☐ Verify employer's policy for travel and entertainment reimbursements.

☐ Interview filer for ordinary and necessary work-related expenses.

☐ Compile mileage records, with vehicle type and odometer readings.

☐ Review meal and entertainment expense documentation.

Section at a Glance

Relevant IRS Publications

☐ IRS Publication 463, *Travel, Entertainment, Gift, and Car Expenses*

☐ IRS Publication 529, *Miscellaneous Deductions*

☐ IRS Publication 535, *Business Expenses*

2013 Federal Per Diem Rates for Some Common U.S. Destinations		Maximum Lodging		Meals and Incidental Rate		Max Per Diem Rate	
City		Before Oct. 1*	After Sept. 30	Before Oct. 1*	After Sept. 30	Before Oct. 1*	After Sept. 30
Atlanta, GA		$133	$133	56	56	$189	$189
Chicago, Ill.	Jan. 1 – Feb. 28	130	128	71	71	$201	$199
	Mar. 1 – Mar. 31	130	186	71	71	$201	$257
	Apr. 1 – June 30	171	186	71	71	$242	$257
	July 1 - Aug. 31	155	166	71	71	$226	$237
	Sept. 1 - Nov. 30	190	209	71	71	$261	$280
	Dec. 1 - Dec. 31	130	128	71	71	$201	$199
Houston, TX (L.B. Johnson Space Center)		109	118	71	71	$180	$189
Las Vegas, NV		99	92	71	71	$170	$163
Los Angeles, CA		125	133	71	71	$196	$204
Manhattan, NY	Jan. 1 – Feb. 28	204	191	71	71	$275	$262
	Mar. 1 – Mar. 31	204	267	71	71	$275	$338
	Apr. 1 – June 30	241	267	71	71	$312	$338
	July 1 - Aug. 31	216	229	71	71	$287	$300
	Sept. 1 - Dec. 31	295	303	71	71	$366	$374
Orlando, Fla	Jan. 1 - Apr. 30	111	123	56	56	$167	$179
	May 1 - May 31	111	101	56	56	$167	$157
	June 1 - Dec. 31	97	101	56	56	$153	$157

* Note that this may be used for all of 2013; see text. Complete per diem listings begin on page 6-18.

Employee Business Expenses

Substantiation and Reporting of Expenses

The treatment and reporting of an employee's business expenses differs depending on whether and how the expenses are reimbursed.

Most employees account for their expenses to their employers and then receive reimbursements. If the reimbursement arrangement constitutes an "accountable plan" as defined by the IRS, the reimbursement normally is equivalent to the expenses, and nothing appears on the employee's tax return. If the expenses are not reimbursed or the reimbursement is less than the expenses incurred, or the reimbursement arrangement does not qualify as an "accountable plan," the unreimbursed expenses are reported on Form 2106 and are treated as miscellaneous itemized deductions on Schedule A. (See page 6-13, "Accountable and Nonaccountable Plans".)

If the reimbursements received from the employer are reported in box 1 of Form W-2 as gross wages, a determination should be made as to whether this is the proper treatment. Normally, reimbursements for expenses that are properly accounted for should not be treated as wages. See MTG ¶942 and ¶952A.

Substantiation Requirements for 2013 Expenses

| Category of Expense | Details Required in Records | | | |
	Amount	Time	Place or Description	Business Purpose and Business Relationship
Travel	Cost of each separate expense for travel, lodging, and meals. Incidental expenses may be totaled in reasonable categories such as taxis, daily meals for traveler, etc.	Dates taxpayer left and returned for each trip and number of days spent on business.	Destination or area of taxpayer's travel (name of city, town, or other designation).	**Purpose:** Business purpose for the expense or the business benefit gained or expected to be gained. **Relationship:** N/A
Entertainment	Cost of each separate expense. Incidental expenses such as taxis, telephones, etc., may be totaled on a daily basis.	Date of entertainment. (Also see *Business Purpose.*)	Name and address or location of place of entertainment. Type of entertainment if not otherwise apparent. (Also see *Business Purpose.*)	**Purpose:** Business purpose for the expense or the business benefit gained or expected to be gained. For entertainment, the nature of the business discussion or activity. If the entertainment was directly before or after a business discussion: the date, place, nature, and duration of the business discussion, and the identities of the persons who took part in both the business discussion and the entertainment activity. **Relationship:** Occupations or other information (such as names, titles, or other designations) about the recipients that shows their business relationship to taxpayer. For entertainment, must also prove that taxpayer or taxpayer's employee was present if the entertainment was a business meal.
Gifts	Cost of the gift. (Deduction limited to $25 per recipient per year.)	Date of the gift.	Description of the gift.	(See Entertainment, above.)
Transportation	Cost of each separate expense. For car expenses: cost of the car and any improvements, date taxpayer started using it for business, mileage for each business use, and total miles for the year.	Date of the expense. For car expenses, the date of the use of the car.	Taxpayer's business destination.	**Purpose:** Business purpose for the expense. **Relationship:** N/A

Statutory Employees. An important rule applies to "statutory employees," such as outside salesmen (e.g., traveling salesmen), life insurance salesmen, certain agent or commission drivers and certain homeworkers. These taxpayers can report their unreimbursed deductible expenses on Schedule C. Thus a statutory employee avoids both having to itemize deductions and the 2% of AGI limitation imposed on miscellaneous itemized deductions. Employers normally check box 13 on Form W-2 to indicate that the taxpayer is a statutory employee. If the employee is a statutory employee and the employer has failed to check this box, the employee should contact the employer to obtain a corrected Form W-2 with box 13 checked. See Tab 3.

 Caution. Don't assume that the taxpayer is a "statutory employee" simply because he or she fits into a category mentioned above. Advise the employee to verify the classification with his or her employer.

Employee Business Expenses That Are Not Reimbursed

Unreimbursed employee expenses are treated as miscellaneous itemized deductions and are deductible to the extent that total miscellaneous itemized deductions exceed 2% of AGI. Miscellaneous itemized deductions that exceed 2% are generally added back to the income base in determining the alternative minimum tax. See Tab 2.

Employee Business Expenses Reimbursed under an Accountable Plan

Employee expenses reimbursed under an accountable plan are not deductible by the employee, but the reimbursement is excludable from gross income. In effect, the reimbursement and expense offset each other, and there is no effect on the taxpayer's return.

An expense is considered "reimbursed" and eligible for this treatment only if the employer has an accountable plan.

Documentation

Under the *Cohan* rule, a reasonable estimate of an expense is normally considered sufficient documentation. However, the *Cohan* rule does not apply to travel and entertainment expenses. A taxpayer cannot deduct expenses for travel (including meals, unless the standard meal allowance is used), entertainment, gifts, or use of a car or other listed property (such as a computer) unless the taxpayer maintains records to prove five elements of the expense:

- Time;
- Place;
- Business purpose;
- Business relationship (for entertainment and gifts); and
- Amount.

The taxpayer must also keep receipts for all lodging expenses regardless of the amount (unless per diem allowances for lodging, meals and incidental expenses are used under an accountable plan), and for any other expense of $75 or more. The IRS provides a table in Publication 463 (reproduced on page 6-2) explaining the documentation required.

Note that documentation is required to substantiate the time, place, and purpose of travel (but not actual amounts paid), even if a per diem rate is used. See MTG ¶953 and ¶954.

 Planning Tip. By itself, a receipt is insufficient to meet the substantiation standards. A diary or some other type of record should be used to document the five elements, particularly the business purpose and business relationship, which are never included on the receipt. Records should be prepared at or near the time of the expense in order to meet the contemporaneous recordkeeping requirement. Court decisions have allowed calendars and other types of substantiation. A pocket calendar, PDA, or any other recordkeeping mechanism should work.

Per Diems and Car Allowances

The taxpayer can use a per diem or car allowance to satisfy the adequate accounting requirements for employee business expense amounts only if all of the following conditions apply:

- The employer reasonably limits payments of the taxpayer's expenses to those that are ordinary and necessary in the conduct of the business.
- The allowance is similar in form to and not more than the federal rate.
- The taxpayer proves the time, place and business purposes of his or her employee expenses to the employer within a reasonable time.
- The taxpayer is not related to his or her employer.

The taxpayer is related to the employer if any of the following apply:

- The employer is the taxpayer's spouse, brother, sister, half-brother, half-sister, ancestor or lineal descendant.
- The employer is a corporation in which the taxpayer owns, directly or indirectly, more than 10% in value of the outstanding stock.

Who Must File 2013 Form 2106?

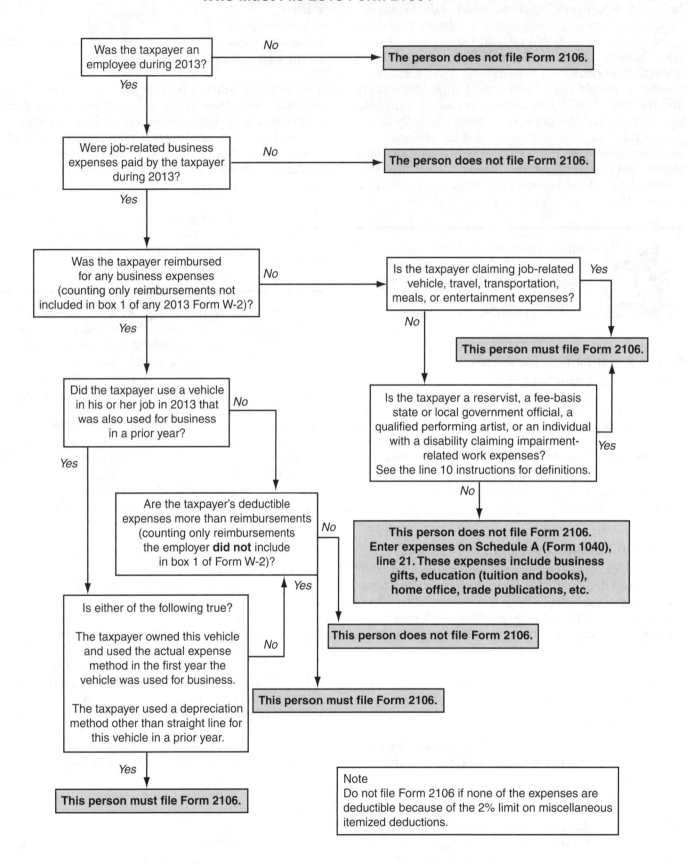

Was the taxpayer an employee during 2013? → *No* → **The person does not file Form 2106.**

Yes ↓

Were job-related business expenses paid by the taxpayer during 2013? → *No* → **The person does not file Form 2106.**

Yes ↓

Was the taxpayer reimbursed for any business expenses (counting only reimbursements not included in box 1 of any 2013 Form W-2)? → *No* → **Is the taxpayer claiming job-related vehicle, travel, transportation, meals, or entertainment expenses?** → *Yes* → **This person must file Form 2106.**

Yes ↓   (from "Is the taxpayer claiming..." *No* ↓)

Did the taxpayer use a vehicle in his or her job in 2013 that was also used for business in a prior year? → *No* ↓

Is the taxpayer a reservist, a fee-basis state or local government official, a qualified performing artist, or an individual with a disability claiming impairment-related work expenses? See the line 10 instructions for definitions. → *Yes* → **This person must file Form 2106.**

No ↓

This person does not file Form 2106. Enter expenses on Schedule A (Form 1040), line 21. These expenses include business gifts, education (tuition and books), home office, trade publications, etc.

Yes ↓ (from "Did the taxpayer use a vehicle...")

Are the taxpayer's deductible expenses more than reimbursements (counting only reimbursements the employer did not include in box 1 of Form W-2)? → *No* → **This person does not file Form 2106.**

Yes → **This person must file Form 2106.**

No →

Is either of the following true?

The taxpayer owned this vehicle and used the actual expense method in the first year the vehicle was used for business.

The taxpayer used a depreciation method other than straight line for this vehicle in a prior year.

→ *No* → (to "Are the taxpayer's deductible expenses...")

Yes ↓

This person must file Form 2106.

Note
Do not file Form 2106 if none of the expenses are deductible because of the 2% limit on miscellaneous itemized deductions.

- A grantor, fiduciary or beneficiary relationship exists between the taxpayer, a trust, and the employer.

Per Diems for Travel. For business travel within the continental United States (CONUS), the IRS provides taxpayers a choice of two per diem methods: high-low and regular federal per diem rate. Under the high-low method, expenses for travel to certain localities (see Tables 1 and 2, beginning at page 6-18) are deductible at a higher rate: $242 ($177 for lodging, $65 for meals and incidental expenses (M&IE)), effective through September 30, 2013; $251 ($186 for lodging, $65 for M&IE), effective October 1, 2013. Expenses for travel to localities that are within CONUS but not specifically listed in the per diem tables or within the boundary definition of a listed locality are deductible at a lower rate: $163 ($111 for lodging, $52 for M&IE), effective through September 30, 2013; $170 ($118 for lodging, $52 for M&IE), effective October 1, 2013.

The regular federal per diem rate method provides specific rates for many localities (see Tables 3 and 4, beginning at page 6-20). For localities that are within CONUS but not specifically listed in the per diem tables or within the boundary definition of a listed locality, a standard rate applies. Before October 1, 2013, the standard rate is $123 ($77 for lodging, $46 for M&IE); after September 30, 2013, the standard rate moves $129 ($83 for lodging, $46 for M&IE). See MTG ¶954 and ¶954A.

> **Planning Tip.** The IRS has *stopped* updating IRS Publication 1542, *Per Diem Rates*. Going forward, taxpayers should consult the U.S. General Services Administration (GSA) website (http://www.gsa.gov/portal/category/21287) for current per diem rates for locations within CONUS. For locations outside the continental U.S. (OCONUS), such as Alaska, Hawaii, Guam, etc., and for foreign locations, see the "Per Diem Rates" page of the U.S. Department of Defense Travel Management Office website (http://www.defensetravel.dod.mil/site/perdiem.cfm). Other per diem rate information, including substantiation methods and transition rules, can be found in IRS Publication 463, *Travel, Entertainment, Gift, and Car Expenses*.

To assist our customers, for fiscal years 2013 and 2014, CCH has compiled tables for localities treated as high cost localities under the high-low substantiation method (Tables 1 and 2, beginning at page 6-18), and for the regular maximum federal per diem rates published by GSA (Tables 3 and 4, beginning at page 6-20). These are similar to the tables published for previous years in IRS Publication 1542.

Use by Employees and the Self-Employed. Employees and self-employed individuals who are not reimbursed may compute their allowable deductions for *meals and incidental expenses* while away from home by using the applicable federal M&IE rate. The time, place, and business purpose of the travel must still be substantiated. However, for *lodging expenses,* they must apply the actual amount, not the per diem rate, and must substantiate with the required documentation. See MTG ¶954B.

Prorated M&IE Rate. The M&IE rate is for a full 24-hour day of travel (i.e., 12:01 a.m. to 12 midnight). If the travel is only for a partial day, compute the M&IE rate (or the M&IE portion of the high-low or regular federal per diem rates) by either (1) allowing 75% of the M&IE rate for each partial day during which the employee or self-employed individual is traveling away from home on business, or (2) prorating the M&IE rate by using any method that is consistently applied and in accordance with reasonable business practice. See MTG ¶954A.

Standard Mileage Rate. See "Section B: Standard Mileage Rate" on page 6-16 for details.

Do You Need Form 2106?

Taxpayers normally report employee business expenses on Form 2106, Employee Business Expenses. The preparer should consult the flowchart on page 6-4 (similar to that in the Instructions to Form 2106) for determining whether or not the form should be filed.

Form 2106 is divided into Part I and Part II:

- Part I (page 1) is used to report deductible employee business expenses and reimbursements related to those expenses.
- Part II (page 2) is used to report information that must be provided if deductions are claimed for employee vehicle expenses. Total vehicle expenses calculated here are entered on line 1 of Part I.

> **Filing Tip.** Form 2106-EZ, Unreimbursed Employee Business Expenses, is a one-page form which may be used if the taxpayer uses the standard mileage rate (if claiming vehicle expenses) and was not reimbursed for *any* expenses.

Part I: Employee Business Expenses and Reimbursements

Step 1: Enter Your Expenses

Unreimbursed employee business expenses are miscellaneous itemized deductions. This treatment is reflected in Part I of Form 2106. All expenses are reported in step 1 (lines 1-6). All reimbursements are reported in step 2 (line 7). The expenses identified in step 1 are reduced by any reimbursement reported in step 2, and the net amount appears in step 3 (line 8). The net effect is that neither the reimbursements nor the reimbursed expenses have any effect on the taxpayer's taxable income.

Part I includes two columns: column A, "Other Than Meals and Entertainment," and column B, "Meals and Entertainment." Column A requires information about all employee business expenses except those for meals and entertainment. Meals and entertainment are reported separately in column B, to accommodate the limitation imposed on their deduction. The deduction for unreimbursed meals and entertainment expenses is generally limited to 50% of their actual cost. Note that the 50% limitation is applied before the 2% of AGI floor for miscellaneous itemized deductions.

Line 1, Vehicle Expenses

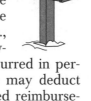 This information is carried over from line 22 or line 29. The costs of operating a vehicle in a trade or business are generally deductible (see Tab 8 for more information). Such expenses are computed in Part II and the total is entered here.

Rural Mail Carriers. Employees of the U.S. Postal Service (USPS) who collect and deliver the mail on rural routes are subject to a special rule. If the employee received qualified reimbursements (i.e., certain equipment maintenance allowance amounts) for vehicle expenses incurred in performing services for USPS, he or she may deduct actual expenses that exceed the qualified reimbursements. In such case, total vehicle expenses from line 29 of Part II are carried over to line 1, and the qualified reimbursement amount is entered on line 7.

If vehicle expenses are less than or equal to the qualified reimbursement amount, the rural mail carrier does not have to file Form 2106 unless he or she has deductible employee business expenses other than vehicle expenses. In such case, the qualified reimbursement amount is not entered on line 7.

> **Caution.** Rural mail carriers who receive qualified reimbursements cannot use the standard mileage rate.

Line 2, Parking Fees, Tolls, and Transportation

The costs of transportation incurred in a trade or business are deductible to the extent they are not the costs of commuting to and from work. Transportation expenses that do not involve overnight travel are reported on line 2. (Travel expenses that involve overnight stays are reported on line 3.) See MTG ¶945. Examples of expenses to report on line 2 include:

- Parking fees incurred while visiting customers or clients, but not those for parking at the taxpayer's regular place of business, which are considered nondeductible commuting costs.
- Tolls.
- Fares for transportation by train, bus, subway, taxi, or other form of paid conveyance.

Commuting. Costs of commuting between the taxpayer's home and his or her place of employment are nondeductible personal expenses, regardless of how far the taxpayer lives from work.

If the taxpayer carries tools, equipment, or similar items while commuting to and from work, a deduction may be allowed for additional expenses incurred (such as renting a trailer towed by the taxpayer's car to carry the equipment), notwithstanding the ban on deducting commuting expenses.

The IRS measures the taxpayer's "additional expenses" by applying the "same mode" test. Under this test, a deduction is allowed for the excess cost of commuting by one mode with the tools over the cost of commuting by the same mode without the tools. Thus, a carpenter who drives a truck would not be allowed a transportation deduction simply by loading it with tools, since carrying the tools created no additional expense. The fact that the carpenter might or would have used a less expensive mode of transportation were it not for the tools is immaterial.

Commuting from Home Office. If the taxpayer maintains an office in his or her home and qualifies for the home office deduction, the IRS permits a deduction specifically for the costs of transportation from the home to another work location in the same trade or business.

Commuting to a Temporary Work Location. If a taxpayer commutes to a temporary work location, the commuting expenses are deductible transportation costs if either of the following conditions is met:

- The taxpayer has no regular place of work, and the temporary work location is *outside* the metropolitan area where the taxpayer lives and normally works.
- The taxpayer has one or more regular work locations away from his or her residence and the temporary work location is *in the same trade or business*, regardless of the distance. If this condition applies, then the expenses of commuting between the taxpayer's residence and a temporary work location *within* the metropolitan area where the taxpayer lives and normally works are deductible.

A taxpayer's work location is *temporary* if he or she is realistically expected to be (and is in fact) employed at that location for one year or less.

> **Example.** Marguerite is a claims adjuster for an insurance company that has its office in downtown Dallas. Marguerite works about 20% of the time in her employer's office, and the remaining 80% is spent at various sites throughout the state. Marguerite may deduct the costs of commuting between her residence and the site of an insurance claim because the site is a temporary work location and Marguerite otherwise has a regular place of business (i.e., her employer's office).

> **Example.** Ed is an electrician. He works for EZS Inc. as an electrical contractor. Most of his assignments are located within about 25 miles of his employer's office. This year he spent most of his time installing electrical systems at two apartment complexes. Although Ed is assigned to temporary work locations, he is not allowed to deduct any of his commuting expenses because he does not otherwise have a regular place of business.

Union Members' Trips from a Union Hall. If a taxpayer obtains work assignments at a union hall and then proceeds to the assigned place of work, the costs of getting from the union hall to the place of work are nondeductible commuting expenses.

> **Caution.** Merely displaying advertising on an automobile does not convert use of the car from personal to business use. Similarly, the cost of using a taxpayer's car in a nonprofit car pool are not deductible. Any payments received from passengers are not included in income but are considered reimbursements of expenses.

Line 3, Travel Expenses

Deductible expenses for overnight travel include lodging, airline, car rental, and similar costs. *Do not* include meals and entertainment on line 3. See MTG ¶952.

Travel Away from Home. A deduction is permitted for travel expenses while "away from home" in the pursuit of a trade or business. The taxpayer is considered to be "away from home" if (1) the taxpayer's duties require him or her to be away from his or her "tax home" for substantially longer than an ordinary day's work, and (2) the taxpayer needs sufficient time to sleep or rest to meet the demands of work while away from home. The taxpayer does not need to be away from his or her tax home for a whole day or even from dusk to dawn, as long as the taxpayer is relieved from work duties long enough to get necessary sleep or rest. Taking naps in the car does not satisfy the rest requirement. See MTG ¶949.

The IRS and the Tax Court have defined the term *tax home* to mean the business location of the taxpayer or the general vicinity of the taxpayer's employment, regardless of the location of the taxpayer's personal residence. If the taxpayer has more than one regular place of business, his or her tax home is the main place of business.

> **Example.** Sasha is a traveling salesman living in St. Louis. His employer's office is also in St. Louis. The majority of his customers live in St. Louis. Sasha drove to Kansas City to call on several customers. He spent the night there and drove back home to St. Louis the next day. St. Louis is Sasha's tax home, the general vicinity of his employment. Sasha meets the away-from-home test since he was away overnight from his tax home, St. Louis. Thus Sasha may deduct his travel expenses to and from Kansas City as well his meals and lodging.

If the taxpayer has no principal place of business, his or her tax home is normally his or her residence. But if the taxpayer has no permanent place of residence, the taxpayer is considered an itinerant whose tax home is wherever his or her work is done.

Local Lodging Expenses. The IRS will allow deduction of lodging expenses *not* incurred while an employee is "traveling away from home" if (1) the lodging is temporary, and necessary for the employee to participate in or be available for the employer's bona fide business meeting or function; and (2) the expenses are or would otherwise be deductible by the employee as a business expense.

Business Straddling Weekend. A taxpayer may have away-from-home business that straddles a weekend. For example, the taxpayer may have to attend business meetings on Friday and Monday. If the taxpayer remains at the location for business reasons (i.e., to attend the Monday meeting), the weekend days (Saturday and Sunday) should be treated as business days, the travel expenses for which are deductible.

Weekend Travel Home. If a taxpayer is out of town on a temporary business assignment for an extended period of time, he or she may decide to fly home for a weekend. The costs of the weekend trip home (transportation, plus meals and lodging en route) are deductible up to the amount the traveler would have spent on meals and lodging at the out-of-town location. Note, however, that this rule applies only if the traveler checks out of the out-of-town hotel before leaving for the weekend trip home and then re-registers. If the traveler retains the hotel room, the cost of the hotel room is deductible, and the deduction for the trip home (e.g., the airfare) is limited to what the traveler would have spent on meals during the weekend at the out-of-town location. The costs of meals and lodging purchased while at home for the weekend are not deductible.

Temporary Assignments. Taxpayers may deduct travel expenses incurred away from the principal place of business if an assignment away from home is temporary and not indefinite. Assignments in a single location lasting more than one year are not temporary but are considered indefinite. If a taxpayer anticipates an assignment to last more than a year or it actually exceeds one year, none of the taxpayer's travel expenses is deductible. See MTG ¶951.

Combined Business and Personal Travel. If a taxpayer travels within the United States (including all 50 states and the District of Columbia) combining business and personal activities, the taxpayer may deduct *all* of the costs of travel to and from the destination if the trip is *primarily* for business. The costs of side trips for personal purposes are not deductible. If the travel is primarily for personal purposes, none of the travel costs is deductible even though some business is conducted. However, any expenses incurred while at the destination that are directly related to business may be deducted. Observe

that the taxpayer deducts either *all* of the *to-and-from* travel expenses or none of them—there is no allocation.

Travel Expenses for Another Individual. The taxpayer generally cannot deduct the travel expenses of a spouse, dependent, or other individual who accompanies the taxpayer on a business trip. However, a deduction is allowed for the travel expenses of someone who goes with the taxpayer if that person: (1) is the taxpayer's employee or a business associate (e.g., a current or prospective customer, client, supplier, agent, partner, or professional advisor); (2) has a bona fide business purpose for the travel; and (3) would otherwise be allowed to deduct the travel expenses. A bona fide business purpose exists if the taxpayer can prove a real business purpose for the individual's presence; incidental services are not enough to make the expenses deductible. See MTG ¶952.

> **Example.** David drives to Philadelphia on business and takes his wife, Linda, with him. Linda is not David's employee, but occasionally types notes and performs other similar services for David, and joins him for lunches and dinners. Linda's services do not establish that her presence on the trip is necessary to the conduct of David's business, so her expenses are not deductible. David pays $145 per day for a double occupancy room; a single occupancy room costs $128 per day. He can deduct the total cost of driving his car to and from Philadelphia, but only $128 per day for his hotel room. If he uses public transportation, David can deduct only his fare.

Saturday Night Stayovers. Although an employee's out-of-town business work concludes on Friday, he or she may be asked to extend the business trip to take advantage of a low-priced airfare requiring a "Saturday night stayover." The savings in airfare may outweigh the costs of the additional meals and lodging. Meals and lodging expenses for a Saturday night stayover are deductible to the same extent as they would be for "normal" business travel away from home.

Travel Outside the United States. Transportation expenses incurred for travel to and from a foreign destination and other travel expenses must be allocated between business and personal activities. However, the foreign travel will be considered "entirely for business" and travel expenses will be fully deductible without allocation, even if the taxpayer did not spend all of his or her time on business activities, if *at least one* of the following conditions is satisfied:

- *Travel outside the United States does not exceed one week* (seven consecutive days). In counting the days outside of the United States, the day of departure from the United States is excluded but the day of return to the United States is included.

- *More than 75% of the days on the trip were devoted to business.* In determining whether a day is business or personal, a day is treated as a business day if during any part of the day the taxpayer's presence is required at a particular place for a business purpose, even if the taxpayer spends more time during normal working hours engaged in nonbusiness activity than in business activity. Weekends, holidays, or other "standby" days that fall between the taxpayer's business days are also considered business days. However, such days are not business days if they fall at the end of the taxpayer's business activities and the taxpayer elects to stay merely for personal purposes. The day of departure and the day of return are both treated as business days.
- *A personal vacation was not a major consideration in making the trip.*
- *The taxpayer had no substantial control over arranging the business trip.* The taxpayer does not have "substantial control" over the trip if he or she is an employee who was reimbursed or paid a travel expense allowance, is not related to the employer, and is not a managing executive.

If none of those conditions is satisfied, the to-and-from travel expenses must be allocated. A deduction for the to-and-from travel expenses is not allowed if the trip is primarily personal. However, expenses that are directly related to the taxpayer's business upon arriving at the destination are deductible. See MTG ¶955.

> **Example.** Claudia is the chief financial officer of an international company located in Los Angeles. She called a meeting of the controllers of the European units, to be held in Madrid. Claudia leaves Los Angeles on Monday morning, and arrives in Madrid on Tuesday morning. On Tuesday afternoon, she takes a sightseeing tour of the city. On Wednesday, Claudia meets all day with the controllers. On Thursday, she leaves Madrid and arrives back in Los Angeles. Because Claudia was outside of the U.S. for less than a week, her trip is considered entirely for business. She may deduct all of her travel expenses subject to the normal rules for travel expenses.

Luxury Water Travel. Deductions for transportation by water are limited to twice the highest per diem amount allowable at the time of travel to federal employees while away from home but serving in the 48 contiguous states. See MTG ¶957.

Foreign Conventions. No deduction is allowed for travel expenses to attend a convention, seminar, or similar meeting outside of North America unless the taxpayer establishes *both* of the following:

- The meeting is directly related to the active conduct of his or her trade or business.
- It is as reasonable to hold the meeting outside North America as within North America.

North America includes the United States, its possessions, Canada, Mexico, jurisdictions that have entered into Compacts of Free Association with the U.S., and certain beneficiary countries (see IRS Publication 463 for a complete list). See MTG ¶960.

Cruise Ships. No deduction is allowed for the cost of attending a meeting conducted on a cruise ship unless all four of the following conditions are met:

- The ship is a vessel registered in the United States and sails *only* between ports in the United States or its possessions;
- The meeting is directly related to the taxpayer's business;
- The taxpayer signs and attaches to the return a statement regarding total days of the trip, total hours each day devoted to scheduled business activities, and a program of the activities; and
- The taxpayer attaches to the return a written statement signed by an officer of the organization or group sponsoring the meeting which includes a schedule of business activities of each day of the meeting, and the number of hours which the taxpayer attended the scheduled business activities.

For qualifying cruises, the maximum deduction is $2,000 per calendar year for each taxpayer.

> **Example.** Teresa traveled by cruise ship to Nassau for a business meeting in September 2013. The cruise took five days at a total cost of $5,000. Since the highest federal per diem rate allowed in September 2013 is $366, under the luxury water travel limitation, Teresa's deduction can be no more than ($366 × 2) × 5 = $3,660. However, because she did not attend a conference or similar meeting *on* the cruise ship, her trip is not subject to the $2,000 annual deduction limit for meetings held on cruise ships.

Line 4, Business Expenses Not Included on Lines 1 through 3

All deductible employee business expenses not listed on any other line of the form are entered on line 4. These include such expenses as business gifts, education (tuition and books), home office costs, trade publications, union dues, professional license fees, etc. Do not include the costs of meals and entertainment on line 4. See Tab 2 for details on other common employee business expenses.

Qualifying Education Expenses. An employee may deduct education expenses if the expenses satisfy *either* of the following conditions *and* are not considered personal or capital in nature, as discussed below:

- The education maintains or improves skills required of the taxpayer in his or her present work.
- The education meets express requirements imposed by either the individual's employer or applicable law, and the taxpayer must meet such requirements to retain his or her job, position, or rate of compensation.

Education expenses that meet either of these conditions are *not* deductible if they are considered personal or capital expenditures under either of the following two tests:

- The education is necessary to meet the minimum educational requirements of the taxpayer's trade or business.
- The education qualifies the taxpayer for a new trade or business.

Travel as a form of education. No deduction is allowed for travel alone, notwithstanding the fact that it may be educational. Deductions are allowed for travel only when the education activity otherwise qualifies and the travel expense is necessary to pursue such activity. For example, a deduction for travel expenses would be allowed where a professor of French literature travels to France to take courses that are offered only at the Sorbonne.

Types of deductible education expenses. Typical deductible education expenses are for continuing professional education programs, professional development courses, college courses related to the taxpayer's trade or business, vocational courses, or similar courses or seminars. Deductible expenses include costs of tuition, books, supplies, typing, transportation, and travel (including meals, lodging, and similar expenses).

Transportation expenses for going between the taxpayer's place of work and the educational location are deductible. If the taxpayer goes home before going to the educational location, however, the expense of going from home to the location is deductible, but only to the extent that it does not exceed the costs of going directly to the location from work.

According to IRS Publication 970, *Tax Benefits for Education,* if the taxpayer is regularly employed and goes directly from home to school on a temporary basis, the cost of round-trip transportation between home and school is deductible, regardless of the school's location, the distance traveled, or whether the taxpayer attends school on nonwork days. A taxpayer attends school on a "temporary basis" if his or her attendance is realistically expected to last–and does last–one year or less. If, at a later date, the taxpayer later reasonably expects attendance to last longer, attendance is temporary only up to that later date. Attendance is not temporary if facts and circumstances indicate otherwise.

 Caution. The Tax Court has both disallowed the deduction for transportation costs between home and school (*E.J. Zimmerman; D.M. Jouett*), and allowed the deduction to the extent of the excess of commuting costs between home and work (*G.F. Boerner; O. Gilliam*).

Line 5, Meal and Entertainment Expenses

Although meal and entertainment expenses may contain personal elements, such costs may be deducted if they are business related. Generally, expenses for meals are deductible if the taxpayer is traveling away from home on business and must stop for substantial sleep or rest to properly perform his or her duties, and the meals are not lavish or extravagant under the circumstances. See MTG ¶949 and ¶952.

Entertainment includes any activity generally considered to provide entertainment, amusement or recreation. Expenses for entertainment and "entertainment-related" meals (see "Entertainment-Related Business Meals" discussion on page 6-11) are deductible only if they:

- Represent an ordinary and necessary expense incurred in carrying on the taxpayer's trade or business; *and*
- Are *either* "directly related to" *or* "associated with" the taxpayer's business.

The taxpayer must meet strict substantiation requirements. For exceptions to the entertainment rules, see Tab 3 and MTG ¶915.

Directly Related Expenses. Expenses for entertainment and entertainment-related meals are considered *directly related* to the business if the taxpayer can show all of the following:

- More than a general expectation of deriving some income or other specific benefit (other than goodwill) existed as a result of making the expenditure; no resulting benefit must be shown, however.

- Business was actually discussed or engaged in during the entertainment or meal.
- The main purpose of the combined business and entertainment or meal was the active conduct of business.

"Associated With" Expenses. Expenses for entertainment and entertainment-related meals are considered *associated with* the taxpayer's business if the taxpayer can show that:

- He or she had a clear business purpose in making the expenditure, such as to obtain new business or to encourage the continuation of an existing business relationship; and
- The entertainment or meal occurs immediately before or after a substantial and bona fide business discussion.

In determining whether the expenses are "immediately before or after," it is sufficient if the entertainment or meal takes place on the same day as the business activity. In some cases, the entertainment or meal may take place on the day before or after the business activity.

Example. The Cadillac division of General Motors provides a golf clinic for its franchise owners on the day before a business meeting. The clinic is deductible under the "associated with" test.

Entertainment-Related Business Meals. Entertainment includes the cost of a meal the taxpayer *provides to a customer or client,* whether the meal is part of other entertainment or by itself. Like other entertainment expenses, entertainment-related meal expenses are deductible only if they satisfy the "directly related" or "associated with" test. In addition, the meal must not be lavish or extravagant under the circumstances, and the taxpayer or his or her employee normally must be present at the meal. For example, if the taxpayer merely reserves a table for dinner at a restaurant for a customer but does not attend the dinner, no deduction is allowed. See MTG ¶914.

The IRS allows the taxpayer a deduction for his or her own business meal except in abusive situations where it is apparent that substantial personal expenditures are being deducted. The taxpayer cannot claim the cost of his or her business meal both as an entertainment expense and a travel expense.

Entertainment Facilities. Costs related to the ownership, rental or use of any entertainment facility (e.g., yacht, skybox, hunting lodge) are not deductible. However, out-of-pocket expenses incurred while at the entertainment facility for such items as food or beverage are deductible, assuming they meet the "directly related" or "associated with" test. See MTG ¶913.

Club Dues. No deduction is allowed for the cost of membership in any club organized for business, pleasure, recreation, or any other social purpose. The rule applies not only to country clubs but to all types of clubs, including luncheon, social, athletic, airline, and hotel clubs. However, dues paid to civic organizations, such as the Kiwanis or Rotary Club, or to professional organizations, such as a bar association, are deductible as long as the organization's principal purpose is not entertainment. Any specific expense incurred at a club, such as a business meal, is deductible to the extent that it meets the other applicable requirements for business expenses. See MTG ¶913A.

Standard Meal Allowance. To calculate the amount of meal expenses, before reimbursement and application of the 50% limit, taxpayers may either use the actual cost of their meals or a "standard meal allowance" provided by the IRS. The standard meal allowance allows taxpayers to use a set amount for their daily meals and incidental expenses (M&IE) incurred in connection with business travel away from home. The amount differs by travel location. The standard meal allowance cannot be used if the taxpayer is related to his or her employer, unless the taxpayer receives an allowance from the employer *only* for M&IE. There are two methods for determining M&IE under the standard meal allowance: high-low and the regular federal per diem rate (see "Per Diems and Car Allowances" on page 6-3 for more details).

Meals & Incidentals Breakdown for 2013						
M&IE Rate	$46	$51	$56	$61	$66	$71
Breakfast	7	8	9	10	11	12
Lunch	11	12	13	15	16	18
Dinner	23	26	29	31	34	36
Incidentals	5	5	5	5	5	5

Notice 2013-65 announced that "Incidental expenses" will only include fees and tips to porters, baggage carriers, behllhops, hotel maids, stewards or stewardesses and others on ships, and hotel servants in foreign countries. No longer will incidental expenses include the costs of transportation between place of lodgings or business and places where meals are taken; and mailing costs associated with filing travel vouchers and paying employer-sponsored charge card billings.

A taxpayer has the option of deducting only incidental expenses if no meal expenses are incurred. The amount of this deduction is $5 a day for travel during 2013 and also $5 a day for travel during 2014. See MTG ¶954B.

Per diem rates change on October 1 of each year, but a taxpayer may elect to use the "before Sept. 30" rates for the entire year. See the "transition rule" for the high-low substantiation method on page 6-18, and for the standard federal per diem method on page 6-36.

Transportation industry workers. A special standard meal allowance applies to taxpayers whose work (1) directly involves moving people or goods by airplane, barge, bus, ship, train, or truck; and (2) regularly requires travel away from home which, during any single trip, usually involves travel to localities with differing federal M&IE rates. Before October 1, 2013, the special rate is $59 per day ($65 per day for travel outside the continental United States (OCONUS)); after September 30, 2013, the special rate remains at $59 per day ($65 per day for OCONUS travel).

Entertainment Expenses for Spouses. The taxpayer generally cannot deduct the cost of entertainment for his or her spouse or for the spouse of a customer. However, these costs are deductible if the taxpayer can show that he or she had a clear business purpose for providing the entertainment, rather than a personal or social purpose.

> **Example.** Kevin entertains a customer. The cost is an ordinary and necessary business expense and is allowed under the entertainment rules. The customer's spouse joins them because it is impractical to entertain the customer without the spouse. Kevin can deduct the cost of entertaining the customer's spouse. If Kevin's spouse joins the party because the customer's spouse is present, the cost of entertaining Kevin's spouse is also deductible.

50% Limitation. The amount that can be deducted for meals and entertainment is limited to 50% of the allowable expense. For employees whose entertainment expenses are *not reimbursed* or are reimbursed under a non-accountable plan, the 50% limitation is applied before the 2% of AGI floor for itemized deductions. See Tab 2.

Expenses subject to the 50% limitation include the costs of taxes, tips, and parking related to a meal or an entertainment activity. Costs of transportation to and from the activity are not subject to the limitation.

The 50% reduction is calculated on column B of line 9. Therefore, the full amount of qualifying meal and entertainment expenses should be entered on line 5.

> **Example.** Dale, an employee, pays $2,500 for entertaining clients, including meals. He was not reimbursed. The amount of the 50% limitation is calculated as follows:
>
> Total unreimbursed meals
> and entertainment expenses............$2,500
> Less: 50% reduction
> (50% × $2,500)............................(1,250)
> Amount reported on line 9
> (col. B) of Form 2106 1,250

Certain transportation workers are allowed to deduct more than 50% of the cost of their meals consumed while away from home. Individuals subject to Department of Transportation hours of service rules may deduct 80% of their meal expenses. The hours of service rules apply to such workers as airplane pilots, crew, dispatchers, mechanics, and control tower operators under Federal Aviation Administration regulations; interstate truck operators and bus drivers under Department of Transportation regulations; certain railroad employees such as engineers, conductors, train crews, dispatchers, and control operations personnel under Federal Railroad Administration regulations; and certain merchant mariners under Coast Guard regulations. The special rule exists because workers in these industries are frequently forced to eat meals away from home in circumstances where their choices are limited, prices are comparatively high, and the opportunity for lavish meals is remote.

For exceptions to the 50% limitation on meal and entertainment expenses, see Tab 3 and MTG ¶917.

Line 6, Total Expenses

In column A, the sum of lines 1 through 4 is entered on line 6. In column B, the amount from line 5 is entered on line 6.

Step 2: Enter Reimbursements Received from Your Employer for Expenses Listed in Step 1

Line 7, Employer Reimbursements

Note: If the taxpayer was not reimbursed for any expenses in step 1, skip line 7 and enter the amount from line 6 on line 8.

Enter reimbursements received from an employer that were not reported in box 1 of Form W-2. If the amounts were included in gross wages on the W-2, they are not reported here.

Include any reimbursements reported under code L in box 12 of Form W-2. The code L amounts are reimbursements made to the employee under an accountable plan arrangement. Reimbursements paid under an accountable plan are not reported as income.

Accountable and Nonaccountable Plans. The tax treatment of an employee's business expenses depends upon whether his or her employer's reimbursement or expense allowance arrangement is an accountable or nonaccountable plan. An arrangement is an *accountable plan* if it satisfies the following:

- The employee must properly substantiate the expenses to the employer;
- In the case of advances or allowances (i.e., per diems), the employee must return to the employer any amount in excess of substantiated expenses; and
- The expenses must have a business connection.

Amounts paid under an accountable plan are excluded from gross income, are not reported on the employee's Form W-2, and are exempt from employment taxes (i.e., Social Security and unemployment). If expenses equal reimbursements, the taxpayer does not need to complete Form 2106 and has no business expense deduction.

If the arrangement does not meet one or more of the accountable plan requirements, it is considered a *nonaccountable plan*, in which case the following treatment applies:

- Reimbursements and advances made to the employee must be reported in the employee's gross income, are included on Form W-2, and are subject to employment taxes.
- The employee taxpayer must complete Form 2106 or Form 2106-EZ and itemize deductions in order to deduct his or her business expenses. The taxpayer must substantiate the full amount of his or her expenses, including any that are treated as reimbursed under an accountable plan.
- The expense is treated as a miscellaneous itemized deduction subject to the 2% of AGI floor, and meals and entertainment expenses are subject to the 50% limitation.

 Planning Tip. Taxpayers should encourage their employers to establish accountable plans if such arrangements are not offered, or they could face greater tax burdens. If the employer's plan is not accountable or if there is no plan, all or part of the business expense deduction could be lost if the taxpayer cannot meet the 2% of AGI floor. See Tab 2.

The taxpayer is deemed to have properly substantiated an expense if either:

Reporting Reimbursements	
IF the type of reimbursement (or other expense allowance) arrangement is under	**THEN the employer reports on Form W-2**
An accountable plan with:	
Actual expense reimbursement: Adequate accounting made and excess returned	No amount.
Actual expense reimbursement: Adequate accounting and return of excess both required but excess not returned	The excess amount as wages in box 1.
Per diem or mileage allowance up to the federal rate: Adequate accounting made and excess returned	No amount.
Per diem or mileage allowance up to the federal rate: Adequate accounting and return of excess both required but excess not returned	The excess amount as wages in box 1. The amount up to the federal rate is reported only in box 12–it is not reported in box 1.
Per diem or mileage allowance exceeds the federal rate: Adequate accounting made up to the federal rate only and excess not returned	The excess amount as wages in box 1. The amount up to the federal rate is reported only in box 12–it is not reported in box 1.
A nonaccountable plan with:	
Either adequate accounting or return of excess, or both, not required by plan	The entire amount as wages in box 1.
No reimbursement plan	The entire amount as wages in box 1.

- The employer gave the taxpayer a fixed travel allowance, such as a per diem, that falls within the government guidelines, and the taxpayer reports the time, place, and business purpose of the expenditure. In this case, the employee need not return any allowance received that exceeded expenses.
- The employer reimburses vehicle expenses at the standard mileage rate, and the taxpayer substantiates the date of each trip, mileage, and business purpose of the vehicle use.

Step 3: Figure Expenses to Deduct on Schedule A (Form 1040)

Line 8, Subtract Line 7 from Line 6

If the result is zero or less, enter -0-. However, if line 7 is greater than line 6 in column A, report the excess as income on Form 1040, line 7.

Note: If both columns of line 8 are zero, do not deduct employee business expenses. Stop here and attach Form 2106 to the return.

In step 3, the taxpayer compares the total reimbursements to total expenses. If reimbursements exceed expenses, the taxpayer reports the excess as income on line 7 of Form 1040. If the expenses exceed the reimbursements, the taxpayer proceeds with the computation of the final deduction to be claimed on line 21 of Schedule A. The amount in column A representing all business expenses other than meals and entertainment is the amount of the deduction subject to the 2% of AGI limitation on miscellaneous itemized deductions that is applied on Schedule A. No other calculation is required. The amount in column B is the deduction for meals and entertainment before reduction for the 50% disallowance.

Line 9

In Column A, Enter the Amount from Line 8. This is the amount of the deduction for employee business expenses, other than meals and entertainment, that is subject to the 2% of AGI limitation on Schedule A.

In Column B, Multiply Line 8 by 50% (0.50). In line 9, column B, the 50% limitation on meals and entertainment expenses is computed. The 50% limitation applies only to the unreimbursed expenses, and is applied before the 2% of AGI limitation is applied on Schedule A.

The deductible percentage of the cost of meals consumed while away from home on business is increased to 80% for transportation workers subject to Department of Transportation hours-of-service rules.

For more details, see "50% Limitation" on page 6-12.

Line 10, Add the Amounts on Line 9 of Both Columns

Total employee business expenses are the combination of the meals and entertainment expenses (after taking into account the appropriate percentage limitation) on line 9, column B, and all other employee business expenses in line 9, column A. This total is entered on line 10, and is transferred to line 21 of Schedule A (Form 1040), where it is aggregated with all other miscellaneous itemized deductions. This aggregate amount is potentially deductible as an itemized deduction to the extent it exceeds 2% of AGI. See Tab 2.

Special Rules for Certain Occupations

Armed Forces Reservists. Members of an armed forces reserve component who travel *more than 100 miles away from home* in connection with the performance of services as reservists can include those line 10 expenses for travel over 100 miles from home as an above-the-line deduction on line 24 of Form 1040. The expenses are not miscellaneous itemized deductions subject to the 2% of AGI limitation. The above-the-line deduction is limited to the regular federal per diem rate (for lodging, meals, and incidental expenses; see page 6-5) and the standard mileage rate (for car expenses; see page 6-16) plus any parking fees, ferry fees, and tolls. Any excess over those amounts is treated as a miscellaneous itemized deduction. See MTG ¶941E.

Members of a reserve component include individuals in the Army, Navy, Marine Corps, Air Force, or Coast Guard Reserve; the Army National Guard; the Air National Guard; or the Reserve Corps of the Public Health Service.

Fee-Basis State or Local Government Officials. A fee-basis state or local government official is an official who is an employee of a state or political subdivision of a state and is compensated in whole or in part on a fee basis. These individuals are entitled to include their line 10 employee business expenses incurred in that job on line 24 of Form 1040. The expenses are not miscellaneous itemized deductions subject to the 2% of AGI limitation. See MTG ¶941D.

Qualified Performing Artists. Employee business expenses of qualified performing artists should be reported on line 10 and also in the total on line 24 of Form 1040. A qualified performing artist meets all of the following tests:

(1) Performs services in the performing arts for at least two employers during the tax year;
(2) Has earnings of at least $200 from each employer;
(3) Has total performing-arts business deductions that exceed 10% of gross income from such services; and
(4) Has AGI before business deductions of $16,000 or less.

If the individual is married, he or she must file a joint return, and tests (1), (2) and (3) must be determined separately for each spouse; test (4) is determined using the spouses' combined AGIs.

If the individual fails to meet these tests, any unreimbursed employee business expenses are considered miscellaneous itemized deductions. See MTG ¶941A.

Disabled Individuals. Handicapped individuals are entitled to deduct the ordinary and necessary business expenses incurred for attendant care services at their place of employment, or for other expenses in connection with the place of employment that are necessary for the individual to be able to work. Handicapped persons include individuals who have a physical or mental disability (including those who are blind or deaf) that limits employment, or a physical or mental impairment (including sight or hearing impairment) that substantially limits one or more major life activities. See MTG ¶1013.

If an employee is not reimbursed for these impairment-related work expenses, they are treated as itemized deductions but are not subject to the 2% of AGI limitation. The portion of the total employee business expenses from line 10 of Form 2106 that constitutes impairment-related work expenses is reported on line 28 of Schedule A (Form 1040), rather than line 21 of Schedule A.

Part II: Vehicle Expenses

Section A: General Information, Lines 11-21

An employee's vehicle expenses are reported in Part II of Form 2106. There are two methods for computing vehicle expenses: the actual expense method and the standard mileage rate. See Tab 8 for more details on vehicle expenses.

Part II has four sections:

- Section A requests general information about mileage driven, including business use, personal use, and commuting. Section A also asks whether evidence exists to support the deduction for vehicle expenses and whether it is written.
- Section B is used to compute the deduction using the standard mileage rate.
- Section C is used to compute the deduction using actual expenses.
- Section D is used to compute the amount of depreciation to be reported in Section C.

Only the sections necessary for the reporting method selected should be completed.

Line 11, Enter the Date the Vehicle Was Placed in Service
The date the vehicle was placed in service is generally the date the taxpayer first started using the vehicle for business. See Tab 8.

Line 12, Total Miles Driven in 2013
Record the total number of miles driven for each vehicle used during 2013 (both business and personal). If the taxpayer converted a vehicle during the year from personal to business use (or from business to personal use), record the total miles for only the months the taxpayer drove the vehicle for business.

Line 13, Business Miles
Record the total business miles driven during the year. Do not include commuting mileage, which is not considered business mileage. (See the discussion of line 15, below, for what constitutes "commuting.")

Line 14, Percent of Business Use

Determine the business use percentage by dividing line 13 business miles by line 12 total miles.

> **Caution.** If the taxpayer has converted the vehicle from personal use to business use during the tax year but does not have mileage records for the period before the change, an additional calculation may be required to determine the business use percentage for the depreciation deduction. See IRS Pub. 463.

Line 15, Average Daily Round-Trip Commuting Distance
Report the taxpayer's daily round-trip commuting distance. If the taxpayer commutes to more than one work location, the average daily commuting distance should be reported.

According to the IRS, commuting is travel between the taxpayer's home and a work location. However, travel in the following situations is not "commuting":

- The taxpayer has at least one regular work location away from home (e.g., an insurance agent has an office), and the travel is to a temporary work location in the same trade or business regardless of the distance (e.g., a client's location). A temporary work location is one where employment is expected to last one year or less.
- The travel is to a temporary work location outside the metropolitan area where the taxpayer lives and normally works.
- The taxpayer maintains a qualified home office that is the principal place of business (see Tab 3), and the travel is to another work location in the same

trade or business, regardless of whether that location is regular or temporary and regardless of distance.

Line 16, Commuting Miles

Report the total actual miles that the taxpayer used the vehicle for commuting during the year. If the actual commuting miles are unknown, multiply the average daily commuting miles by the number of days during the year that the vehicle was used for commuting. However, if the taxpayer converted the vehicle during the year from personal to business use (or vice versa), only the commuting miles for the period the vehicle was driven for business are reported.

Line 17, Other Miles

Add the business miles on line 13 and commuting miles on line 16, subtract this sum from the total miles on line 12, and enter the result on line 17.

Lines 18-21, Vehicle Business Expense Support

Due to the strict recordkeeping requirements of IRC §274(d), the IRS must ask the following questions concerning substantiation:

	Yes	No
Line 18: Was your vehicle available for personal use during off-duty hours?	❏	❏
Line 19: Do you (or your spouse) have another vehicle available for personal use?	❏	❏
Line 20: Do you have evidence to support your deduction?	❏	❏
Line 21: If "Yes," is the evidence written?	❏	❏

Section B: Standard Mileage Rate

Line 22, Multiply Line 13 by 56.5¢

A taxpayer may use the standard mileage rate for a vehicle that is either owned or leased by the taxpayer. The taxpayer may deduct an amount equal to the standard rate times the number of business miles driven during the year. The deduction is in lieu of all actual vehicle expenses allocable to business use (i.e., maintenance, repairs, depreciation, insurance, license fees, etc.). Parking fees, tolls, personal property taxes, and interest relating to the vehicle's purchase may be deducted separately. Interest on a vehicle loan is deductible only if the taxpayer is self-employed and used the vehicle in the business.

The rate is 56.5¢ a mile for all business miles driven from January 1, 2013, through December 31, 2013. This is an increase from the 55.5¢ rate in effect during 2012.

The new twelve-month rate for computing deductible medical or moving expenses increases to 24¢ for 2013. The rate for providing services for charitable organizations remains at 14¢ for 2013.

Taxpayers will always have the option of calculating the actual costs of using their vehicle rather than using the standard mileage rates.

2013 Mileage Rates	
Purpose	**Rates 1/1 through 12/31/13**
Business	56.5
Medical/Moving	24
Charitable	14

To use the standard mileage rate, the taxpayer generally must do so in the first year the vehicle is placed in service. The standard mileage rate may not be available for all vehicles. See Tab 8.

Section C: Actual Expenses, Lines 23-29

In lieu of using the standard mileage rate to determine the vehicle expense deduction, taxpayers may report actual expenses, which normally include the costs for gas, oil, tires, repairs, insurance, depreciation, etc. See MTG ¶946.

Business-related parking fees and tolls that were not incurred in overnight travel or commuting to and from work are listed separately on line 2 of Form 2106.

Business-related personal property taxes on motor vehicles may be deductible on Schedule A (Form 1040). See Tab 2.

An employee cannot deduct any interest paid on a car loan, even if the car is used 100% for business. A self-employed taxpayer may be able to deduct the business-use part of car loan interest, but that deduction would appear on Schedule C (Form 1040), not Form 2106. See Tab 3.

Actual expenses are reported on the following lines:

- *Line 23:* Gasoline, oil, repairs, vehicle insurance, etc.
- *Line 24a:* Vehicle rentals. Enter the cost of renting or leasing the vehicle if the taxpayer rented the vehicle.
- *Line 24b:* Inclusion amount. The rent deduction for certain leased vehicles might be reduced by an inclusion amount if the lease term is 30 days or more. To prevent taxpayers from avoiding the limitation on the depreciation deduction for luxury automobiles, a certain amount must be included in income as an offset to the lease expense deduction. To determine the inclusion amount, see IRS Publication 463 and MTG ¶1215. See Tab 8 for inclusion amount tables.
- *Line 24c:* Subtract line 24b from line 24a.
- *Line 25:* Value of employer-provided vehicle. If the employer provided the taxpayer with a vehicle for business use and included 100% of its annual lease val-

ue in box 1 of the taxpayer's W-2, enter that amount on line 25. If less than 100% was included in box 1, then skip line 25.

- *Line 26:* Add lines 23, 24c, and 25.
- *Line 27:* Multiply line 26 by the business use percentage on line 14.
- *Line 28:* Depreciation. Enter amount from line 38 below if applicable.
- *Line 29:* Add lines 27 and 28. Enter total here and on line 1.

 Filing Tip. If the taxpayer has the option of using either the standard mileage rate or the actual expenses method, he or she should calculate expenses both ways, and then fill in the form using the method that provides the larger vehicle expense amount.

Section D: Depreciation of Vehicles, Lines 30-38

Note: Use Section D only if the taxpayer owned the vehicle and is using actual expenses rather than the standard mileage rate to calculate the vehicle expense deduction.

Line 30, Enter the Cost or Other Basis

Enter the vehicle's actual cost (including sales tax) or other basis, unadjusted for prior years' depreciation. If the taxpayer converted the vehicle from personal to business use, the basis for depreciation is the smaller of the vehicle's adjusted basis or its fair market value on the conversion date. See Tab 8 for more details.

Line 31, Enter Section 179 Deduction and Special Depreciation Allowance

An employee using the actual expense method to compute vehicle expenses is entitled to claim a deduction for depreciation, subject to a variety of limitations. The depreciation deduction, including the Section 179 limited expensing amount, is computed on lines 32-38. Calculation of vehicle depreciation and the Section 179 expense are covered in detail in Tab 8.

Lines 32-38, Calculations

Line 32: Multiply line 30 by line 14 (the business use percentage) to determine the basis for depreciation,

then subtract the full amount of any Section 179 deduction and special allowance.

Line 33: Enter depreciation method and percentage. See Tab 8 for the applicable vehicle depreciation methods and percentages.

Line 34: Multiply line 32 by the depreciation percentage on line 33. If the taxpayer sold or exchanged a vehicle during the year, see IRS Publication 463 for special rules.

Line 35: Add lines 31 and 34.

Line 36: Enter applicable depreciation limit. See Tab 8 and MTG ¶1214 for depreciation limits.

Line 37: Multiply line 36 by the percentage on line 14.

Line 38: Enter the smaller of line 35 or line 37. If lines 36 and 37 were skipped, enter amount from line 35. Enter the line 38 amount on line 28.

 Planning Tip. The taxpayer should retain the following information for each vehicle for at least four years after it is removed from service:

- Vehicle's bill-of-sale from purchase, or lease contract;
- Receipts from all maintenance or repairs;
- Total mileage driven each year, broken down into personal, commuting, and business miles; and
- Dates of each use for business, with an explanation of the purpose of the expense.

The taxpayer should keep a daily log or diary to achieve adequate substantiation of vehicle expenses. Odometer readings should be entered for each trip, but multiple short trips may be combined (see below). The taxpayer should make entries when gasoline, oil, or any other purchase for the vehicle is made.

The taxpayer can use a single record to account for several uses of the vehicle that can be considered as part of a single use (for example, a round trip to make business deliveries, or uninterrupted business use). Minimal personal use, such as a lunch stop between business stops, is not considered an interruption of business use.

Table 1. Localities Eligible for $242 ($65 M&IE) Per Diem Amount Under the High-Low Substantiation Method (Effective October 1, 2012)[1,2]

Note: The standard ("low") rate of $163 ($111 for lodging and $52 for M&IE) applies to all locations within the continental United States (CONUS) not specifically listed below or encompassed by the boundary definition of a listed point.

State	Key City	County and/or Other Defined Location	Effective Date of $242 Rate
Arizona	Sedona	City limits of Sedona	3/1 – 4/30
California	Monterey	Monterey	All year
	Napa	Napa	10/1 – 11/30, 4/1 – 9/30
	San Diego	San Diego	All year
	San Francisco	San Francisco	All year
	Santa Barbara	Santa Barbara	All year
	Santa Monica	City limits of Santa Monica	All year
	Yosemite National Park	Mariposa	6/1 – 8/31
Colorado	Aspen	Pitkin	12/1 – 3/31, 6/1 – 8/31
	Denver/Aurora	Denver, Adams, Arapahoe, and Jefferson	All year
	Steamboat Springs	Routt	12/1 – 3/31
	Telluride	San Miguel	12/1 – 3/31
	Vail	Eagle	12/1 – 8/31
District of Columbia	Washington D.C. (also the cities of Alexandria, Falls Church, and Fairfax, and the counties of Arlington and Fairfax, in Virginia; and the counties of Montgomery and Prince George's in Maryland) (See also Maryland and Virginia)		All year
Florida	Fort Lauderdale	Broward	1/1 – 5/31
	Fort Walton Beach/De Funiak springs	Okaloosa and Walton	6/1 – 7/31
	Key West	Monroe	All year
	Miami	Miami-Dade	12/1 – 3/31
	Naples	Collier	1/1 – 4/30
Illinois	Chicago	Cook and Lake	10/1 – 11/30, 4/1 – 9/30
Louisiana	New Orleans	Orleans, St. Bernard, Jefferson and Plaquemine Parishes	10/1 – 6/30
Maine	Bar Harbor	Hancock	7/1 – 8/31
Maryland	Baltimore City	Baltimore City	10/1 – 11/30, 3/1 – 9/30
	Cambridge/St. Michaels	Dorchester and Talbot	6/1 – 8/31
	Ocean City	Worcester	6/1 – 8/31
	Washington, DC Metro Area	Montgomery and Prince George's	All year
Massachusetts	Boston/Cambridge	Suffolk, City of Cambridge	All year
	Falmouth	City limits of Falmouth	7/1 – 8/31
	Martha's Vineyard	Dukes	7/1 – 8/31
	Nantucket	Nantucket	6/1 – 9/30
New Hampshire	Conway	Carroll	7/1 – 8/31
New York	Floral Park/Garden City/Great Neck	Nassau	All year
	Glens Falls	Warren	7/1 – 8/31
	Lake Placid	Essex	7/1 – 8/31
	Manhattan (includes the boroughs of Manhattan, Brooklyn, the Bronx, Queens and Staten Island)	Bronx, Kings, New York, Queens, Richmond	All year
	Saratoga Springs/Schenectady	Saratoga and Schenectady	7/1 – 8/31
	Tarrytown/White Plains/New Rochelle	Westchester	All year
North Carolina	Kill Devil	Dare	6/1 – 8/31
Pennsylvania	Philadelphia	Philadelphia	All year
Rhode Island	Jamestown/Middletown/Newport	Newport	10/1 – 10/31, 5/1 – 9/30
Utah	Park City	Summit	1/1 – 3/31
Virginia	Washington, DC Metro Area	Cities of Alexandria, Fairfax, and Falls Church; counties of Arlington and Fairfax	All year
	Virginia Beach	City of Virginia Beach	6/1 – 8/31
Washington	Seattle	King	All year
Wyoming	Jackson/Pinedale	Teton and Sublette	7/1 – 8/31

[1] **Transition rule.** A payor who uses the high-low substantiation method in Table 1 for an employee during the first 9 months of calendar year 2013 must continue to use the high-low substantiation method for the remainder of calendar year 2013 for that employee. For travel on or after October 1, 2013, and before January 1, 2014, the payor may continue to use the rates and high-cost localities published in Table 1 or the updated rates and high-cost localities published in the revenue procedure or notice that supersedes Revenue Procedure 2011-47 and Notice 2012-63, as long as those rates and localities are used consistently during this period for all employees reimbursed under this method.

[2] Revenue Procedure 2011-47, in Internal Revenue Bulletin 2011-42, and Notice 2012-63, in Internal Revenue Bulletin 2012-42.

Table 2. Localities Eligible for $251 ($65 M&IE) Per Diem Amount Under the High-Low Substantiation Method (Effective October 1, 2013)[1,2]

Note: The standard ("low") rate of $170 ($118 for lodging and $52 for M&IE) applies to all locations within the continental United States (CONUS) not specifically listed below or encompassed by the boundary definition of a listed point.

State	Key City	County and/or Other Defined Location	Effective Date of $251 Rate
Arizona	Sedona	City limits of Sedona	3/1 – 4/30
California	Monterey	Monterey	7/1 - 8/31
	Napa	Napa	10/1 – 11/30, 4/1 – 9/30
	San Diego	San Diego	All year
	San Francisco	San Francisco	All year
	Santa Barbara	Santa Barbara	All year
	Santa Cruz	Santa Cruz	6/1 - 8/31
	Santa Monica	City limits of Santa Monica	All year
	Yosemite National Park	Mariposa	6/1 – 8/31
Colorado	Aspen	Pitkin	12/1 – 3/31, 6/1 – 8/31
	Denver/Aurora	Denver, Adams, Arapahoe, and Jefferson	All year
	Steamboat Springs	Routt	12/1 – 3/31
	Telluride	San Miguel	12/1 – 3/31, 6/1 – 9/30
	Vail	Eagle	12/1 – 8/31
District of Columbia	Washington D.C. (also the cities of Alexandria, Falls Church, and Fairfax, and the counties of Arlington and Fairfax, in Virginia; and the counties of Montgomery and Prince George's in Maryland) (See also Maryland and Virginia)		All year
Florida	Boca Raton/Delray Beach/Jupiter	Palm Beach/Hendry	1/1 - 4/30
	Fort Lauderdale	Broward	1/1 – 5/31
	Fort Walton Beach/De Funiak springs	Okaloosa and Walton	6/1 – 7/31
	Key West	Monroe	All year
	Miami	Miami-Dade	12/1 – 3/31
	Naples	Collier	1/1 – 4/30
Illinois	Chicago	Cook and Lake	10/1 – 11/30, 3/1 – 9/30
Louisiana	New Orleans	Orleans, St. Bernard, Jefferson and Plaquemine Parishes	10/1 – 6/30
Maine	Bar Harbor	Hancock	7/1 – 8/31
Maryland	Baltimore City	Baltimore City	10/1 – 11/30, 3/1 – 9/30
	Cambridge/St. Michaels	Dorchester and Talbot	6/1 – 8/31
	Ocean City	Worcester	6/1 – 8/31
	Washington, DC Metro Area	Montgomery and Prince George's	All year
Massachusetts	Boston/Cambridge	Suffolk, City of Cambridge	All year
	Falmouth	City limits of Falmouth	7/1 – 8/31
	Martha's Vineyard	Dukes	7/1 – 8/31
	Nantucket	Nantucket	6/1 – 9/30
New Hampshire	Conway	Carroll	7/1 – 8/31
New York	Floral Park/Garden City/Great Neck	Nassau	All year
	Glens Falls	Warren	7/1 – 8/31
	Lake Placid	Essex	7/1 – 8/31
	Manhattan (includes the boroughs of Manhattan, Brooklyn, the Bronx, Queens and Staten Island)	Bronx, Kings, New York, Queens, Richmond	All year
	Saratoga Springs/Schenectady	Saratoga and Schenectady	7/1 – 8/31
	Tarrytown/White Plains/New Rochelle	Westchester	All year
North Carolina	Kill Devil	Dare	6/1 – 8/31
Pennsylvania	Philadelphia	Philadelphia	All year
Rhode Island	Jamestown/Middletown/Newport	Newport	10/1 – 10/31, 5/1 – 9/30
South Carolina	Charleston	Charleston, Berkeley and Dorchester	3/1 - 5/31
Texas	Midland	Midland	All year
Utah	Park City	Summit	12/1 – 3/31
Virginia	Washington, DC Metro Area	Cities of Alexandria, Fairfax, and Falls Church; counties of Arlington and Fairfax	All year
	Virginia Beach	City of Virginia Beach	6/1 – 8/31
Washington	Seattle	King	All year
Wyoming	Jackson/Pinedale	Teton and Sublette	7/1 – 8/31

[1] **Transition rule.** A payor who uses the high-low substantiation method in Table 2 for an employee during the first 9 months of calendar year 2014 must continue to use the high-low substantiation method for the remainder of calendar year 2014 for that employee. For travel on or after October 1, 2014, and before January 1, 2015, the payor may continue to use the rates and high-cost localities published in Table 2 or the updated rates and high-cost localities published in the revenue procedure or notice that supersedes Revenue Procedure 2011-47 and Notice 2013-65, as long as those rates and localities are used consistently during this period for all employees reimbursed under this method.

[2] Revenue Procedure 2011-47, in Internal Revenue Bulletin 2011-42, and Notice 2013-65, in Internal Revenue Bulletin 2013–44.

Table 3: Maximum Federal Per Diem Rates (Effective for 10/1/2012 - 9/30/2013 and updated on 4/1/2013).

State	Primary Destination	County	Season Begin Date	Season End Date	Lodging Rate	M&IE Rate	
	Standard CONUS rate applies to all counties not specifically listed. Cities not listed may be located in a listed county.				$77	$46	$123
	NOTE: The locations listed to the right were updated as of Apr. 1, 2013 as a result of midyear reviews. Their previous rates expired on Mar. 31, 2013. No assumptions about previous rates being seasonal should be assumed. No other changes were made to rates in other locations.	Enid, OK (Garfield County) Midland, TX (Midland County)					
AL	Birmingham	Jefferson and Shelby			$ 86	$ 56	$ 142
AL	Gulf Shores	Baldwin	Oct. 1	May 31	$ 100	$ 51	$ 151
AL	Gulf Shores	Baldwin	June 1	July 31	$ 117	$ 51	$ 168
AL	Gulf Shores	Baldwin	Aug. 1	Sept. 30	$ 100	$ 51	$ 151
AL	Huntsville	Madison and Limestone			$ 87	$ 51	$ 138
AL	Mobile	Mobile			$ 94	$ 51	$ 145
AL	Montgomery / Prattville	Montgomery / Autauga			$ 80	$ 51	$ 131
AR	Hot Springs	Garland			$ 101	$ 46	$ 147
AR	Little Rock	Pulaski			$ 86	$ 61	$ 147
AZ	Grand Canyon / Flagstaff	Coconino / Yavapai less the city of Sedona	Oct. 1	Oct. 31	$ 97	$ 66	$ 163
AZ	Grand Canyon / Flagstaff	Coconino / Yavapai less the city of Sedona	Nov. 1	Feb. 28	$ 77	$ 66	$ 143
AZ	Grand Canyon / Flagstaff	Coconino / Yavapai less the city of Sedona	Mar. 1	Sept. 30	$ 97	$ 66	$ 163
AZ	Kayenta	Navajo	Oct. 1	Apr. 30	$ 79	$ 46	$ 125
AZ	Kayenta	Navajo	May 1	Sept. 30	$ 90	$ 46	$ 136
AZ	Phoenix / Scottsdale	Maricopa	Oct. 1	Dec. 31	$ 105	$ 71	$ 176
AZ	Phoenix / Scottsdale	Maricopa	Jan. 1	May 31	$ 128	$ 71	$ 199
AZ	Phoenix / Scottsdale	Maricopa	June 1	Aug. 31	$ 80	$ 71	$ 151
AZ	Phoenix / Scottsdale	Maricopa	Sept. 1	Sept. 30	$ 105	$ 71	$ 176
AZ	Sedona	City Limits of Sedona	Oct. 1	Feb. 28	$ 127	$ 66	$ 193
AZ	Sedona	City Limits of Sedona	Mar. 1	Apr. 30	$ 145	$ 66	$ 211
AZ	Sedona	City Limits of Sedona	May 1	Sept. 30	$ 127	$ 66	$ 193
AZ	Sierra Vista	Cochise			$ 83	$ 46	$ 129
AZ	Tucson	Pima	Oct. 1	Jan. 31	$ 90	$ 56	$ 146
AZ	Tucson	Pima	Feb. 1	May 31	$ 103	$ 56	$ 159
AZ	Tucson	Pima	June 1	Aug. 31	$ 77	$ 56	$ 133
AZ	Tucson	Pima	Sept. 1	Sept. 30	$ 90	$ 56	$ 146
AZ	Yuma	Yuma			$ 78	$ 46	$ 124
CA	Antioch / Brentwood / Concord	Contra Costa			$ 101	$ 66	$ 167
CA	Bakersfield / Ridgecrest	Kern County			$ 86	$ 51	$ 137
CA	Barstow / Ontario / Victorville	San Bernardino			$ 96	$ 56	$ 152
CA	Benicia / Dixon / Fairfield	Solano			$ 80	$ 56	$ 136
CA	Death Valley	Inyo			$ 91	$ 46	$ 137
CA	Eureka / Arcata / McKinleyville	Humboldt	Oct. 1	May 31	$ 83	$ 61	$ 144
CA	Eureka / Arcata / McKinleyville	Humboldt	June 1	Aug. 31	$ 96	$ 61	$ 157

Table 3: Maximum Federal Per Diem Rates (Effective for 10/1/2012 - 9/30/2013 and updated on 4/1/2013).

State	Primary Destination	County	Season Begin Date	Season End Date	Lodging Rate	M&IE Rate	
CA	Eureka / Arcata / McKinleyville	Humboldt	Sept. 1	Sept. 30	$ 83	$ 61	$ 144
CA	Fresno	Fresno			$ 86	$ 61	$ 147
CA	Los Angeles	Los Angeles, Orange, Ventura, and Edwards AFB, less the city of Santa Monica			$ 125	$ 71	$ 196
CA	Mammoth Lakes	Mono			$ 114	$ 61	$ 175
CA	Mill Valley / San Rafael / Novato	Marin			$ 113	$ 56	$ 169
CA	Modesto	Stanislaus			$ 81	$ 51	$ 132
CA	Monterey	Monterey	Oct. 1	June 30	$ 134	$ 71	$ 205
CA	Monterey	Monterey	July 1	Aug. 31	$ 149	$ 71	$ 220
CA	Monterey	Monterey	Sept. 1	Sept. 30	$ 134	$ 71	$ 205
CA	Napa	Napa	Oct. 1	Nov. 30	$ 147	$ 66	$ 213
CA	Napa	Napa	Dec. 1	Mar. 31	$ 117	$ 66	$ 183
CA	Napa	Napa	Apr. 1	Sept. 30	$ 147	$ 66	$ 213
CA	Oakhurst	Madera	Oct. 1	Apr. 30	$ 79	$ 56	$ 135
CA	Oakhurst	Madera	May 1	Aug. 31	$ 90	$ 56	$ 146
CA	Oakhurst	Madera	Sept. 1	Sept. 30	$ 79	$ 56	$ 135
CA	Oakland	Alameda			$ 99	$ 61	$ 160
CA	Palm Springs	Riverside	Oct. 1	Dec. 31	$ 99	$ 71	$ 170
CA	Palm Springs	Riverside	Jan. 1	May 31	$ 115	$ 71	$ 186
CA	Palm Springs	Riverside	June 1	Aug. 31	$ 82	$ 71	$ 153
CA	Palm Springs	Riverside	Sept. 1	Sept. 30	$ 99	$ 71	$ 170
CA	Point Arena / Gualala	Mendocino			$ 90	$ 66	$ 156
CA	Redding	Shasta			$ 87	$ 61	$ 148
CA	Sacramento	Sacramento			$ 99	$ 61	$ 160
CA	San Diego	San Diego			$ 133	$ 71	$ 204
CA	San Francisco	San Francisco	Oct. 1	Oct. 31	$ 184	$ 71	$ 255
CA	San Francisco	San Francisco	Nov. 1	Aug. 31	$ 155	$ 71	$ 226
CA	San Francisco	San Francisco	Sept. 1	Sept. 30	$ 184	$ 71	$ 255
CA	San Luis Obispo	San Luis Obispo	Oct. 1	June 30	$ 103	$ 66	$ 169
CA	San Luis Obispo	San Luis Obispo	July 1	Aug. 31	$ 121	$ 66	$ 187
CA	San Luis Obispo	San Luis Obispo	Sept. 1	Sept. 30	$ 103	$ 66	$ 169
CA	San Mateo / Foster City / Belmont	San Mateo			$ 111	$ 61	$ 172
CA	Santa Barbara	Santa Barbara	Oct. 1	June 30	$ 139	$ 66	$ 205
CA	Santa Barbara	Santa Barbara	July 1	Aug. 31	$ 180	$ 66	$ 246
CA	Santa Barbara	Santa Barbara	Sept. 1	Sept. 30	$ 139	$ 66	$ 205
CA	Santa Cruz	Santa Cruz	Oct. 1	May 31	$ 97	$ 66	$ 163
CA	Santa Cruz	Santa Cruz	June 1	Aug. 31	$ 131	$ 66	$ 197
CA	Santa Cruz	Santa Cruz	Sept. 1	Sept. 30	$ 97	$ 66	$ 163
CA	Santa Monica	City limits of Santa Monica			$ 169	$ 71	$ 240
CA	Santa Rosa	Sonoma			$ 110	$ 61	$ 171
CA	South Lake Tahoe	El Dorado			$ 118	$ 71	$ 189
CA	Stockton	San Joaquin			$ 83	$ 56	$ 139
CA	Sunnyvale / Palo Alto / San Jose	Santa Clara			$ 121	$ 56	$ 177
CA	Tahoe City	Placer			$ 82	$ 61	$ 143

Table 3: Maximum Federal Per Diem Rates (Effective for 10/1/2012 - 9/30/2013 and updated on 4/1/2013).

State	Primary Destination	County	Season Begin Date	Season End Date	Lodging Rate	M&IE Rate	
CA	Truckee	Nevada	Oct. 1	Nov. 30	$ 96	$ 71	$ 167
CA	Truckee	Nevada	Dec. 1	Feb. 28	$ 120	$ 71	$ 191
CA	Truckee	Nevada	Mar. 1	Sept. 30	$ 96	$ 71	$ 167
CA	Visalia / Lemoore	Tulare and Kings			$ 81	$ 61	$ 142
CA	West Sacramento / Davis	Yolo			$ 100	$ 51	$ 151
CA	Yosemite National Park	Mariposa	Oct. 1	May 31	$ 127	$ 71	$ 198
CA	Yosemite National Park	Mariposa	June 1	Aug. 31	$ 166	$ 71	$ 237
CA	Yosemite National Park	Mariposa	Sept. 1	Sept. 30	$ 127	$ 71	$ 198
CO	Aspen	Pitkin	Oct. 1	Nov. 30	$ 104	$ 71	$ 175
CO	Aspen	Pitkin	Dec. 1	Mar. 31	$ 207	$ 71	$ 278
CO	Aspen	Pitkin	Apr. 1	May 31	$ 111	$ 71	$ 182
CO	Aspen	Pitkin	June 1	Aug. 31	$ 150	$ 71	$ 221
CO	Aspen	Pitkin	Sept. 1	Sept. 30	$ 104	$ 71	$ 175
CO	Boulder / Broomfield	Boulder and Broomfield			$ 109	$ 61	$ 170
CO	Colorado Springs	El Paso			$ 83	$ 66	$ 149
CO	Cortez	Montezuma	Oct. 1	May 31	$ 90	$ 51	$ 141
CO	Cortez	Montezuma	June 1	Aug. 31	$ 112	$ 51	$ 163
CO	Cortez	Montezuma	Sept. 1	Sept. 30	$ 90	$ 51	$ 141
CO	Crested Butte / Gunnison	Gunnison	Oct. 1	May 31	$ 78	$ 51	$ 129
CO	Crested Butte / Gunnison	Gunnison	June 1	Aug. 31	$ 96	$ 51	$ 147
CO	Crested Butte / Gunnison	Gunnison	Sept. 1	Sept. 30	$ 78	$ 51	$ 129
CO	Denver / Aurora	Denver, Adams, Arapahoe, and Jefferson			$ 149	$ 66	$ 215
CO	Douglas County	Douglas			$ 99	$ 61	$ 160
CO	Durango	La Plata	Oct. 1	May 31	$ 95	$ 61	$ 156
CO	Durango	La Plata	June 1	Sept. 30	$ 133	$ 61	$ 194
CO	Fort Collins / Loveland	Larimer			$ 84	$ 56	$ 140
CO	Glenwood Springs / Grand Junction	Garfield / Mesa			$ 84	$ 51	$ 135
CO	Montrose	Montrose	Oct. 1	May 31	$ 80	$ 56	$ 136
CO	Montrose	Montrose	June 1	Sept. 30	$ 95	$ 56	$ 151
CO	Silverthorne / Breckenridge	Summit	Oct. 1	Nov. 30	$ 92	$ 56	$ 148
CO	Silverthorne / Breckenridge	Summit	Dec. 1	Mar. 31	$ 144	$ 56	$ 200
CO	Silverthorne / Breckenridge	Summit	Apr. 1	Sept. 30	$ 92	$ 56	$ 148
CO	Steamboat Springs	Routt	Oct. 1	Nov. 30	$ 99	$ 56	$ 155
CO	Steamboat Springs	Routt	Dec. 1	Mar. 31	$ 181	$ 56	$ 237
CO	Steamboat Springs	Routt	Apr. 1	Sept. 30	$ 99	$ 56	$ 155
CO	Telluride	San Miguel	Oct. 1	Nov. 30	$ 92	$ 71	$ 163
CO	Telluride	San Miguel	Dec. 1	Mar. 31	$ 160	$ 71	$ 231
CO	Telluride	San Miguel	Apr. 1	May 31	$ 90	$ 71	$ 161
CO	Telluride	San Miguel	June 1	Sept. 30	$ 126	$ 71	$ 197
CO	Vail	Eagle	Oct. 1	Nov. 30	$ 116	$ 71	$ 187
CO	Vail	Eagle	Dec. 1	Mar. 31	$ 296	$ 71	$ 367
CO	Vail	Eagle	Apr. 1	Aug. 31	$ 148	$ 71	$ 219
CO	Vail	Eagle	Sept. 1	Sept. 30	$ 116	$ 71	$ 187
CT	Bridgeport / Danbury	Fairfield			$ 113	$ 71	$ 184

Table 3: Maximum Federal Per Diem Rates (Effective for 10/1/2012 - 9/30/2013 and updated on 4/1/2013).

State	Primary Destination	County	Season Begin Date	Season End Date	Lodging Rate	M&IE Rate	
CT	Cromwell / Old Saybrook	Middlesex			$ 81	$ 61	$ 142
CT	Hartford	Hartford			$ 104	$ 56	$ 160
CT	Lakeville / Salisbury	Litchfield			$ 95	$ 66	$ 161
CT	New Haven	New Haven			$ 87	$ 61	$ 148
CT	New London / Groton	New London			$ 97	$ 61	$ 158
DC	District of Columbia	Washington DC (also the cities of Alexandria, Falls Church and Fairfax, and the counties of Arlington and Fairfax, in Virginia; and the counties of Montgomery and Prince George's in Maryland)	Oct. 1	Oct. 31	$ 226	$ 71	$ 297
DC	District of Columbia	Washington DC (also the cities of Alexandria, Falls Church and Fairfax, and the counties of Arlington and Fairfax, in Virginia; and the counties of Montgomery and Prince George's in Maryland)	Nov. 1	Feb. 28	$ 183	$ 71	$ 254
DC	District of Columbia	Washington DC (also the cities of Alexandria, Falls Church and Fairfax, and the counties of Arlington and Fairfax, in Virginia; and the counties of Montgomery and Prince George's in Maryland)	Mar. 1	June 30	$ 224	$ 71	$ 295
DC	District of Columbia	Washington DC (also the cities of Alexandria, Falls Church and Fairfax, and the counties of Arlington and Fairfax, in Virginia; and the counties of Montgomery and Prince George's in Maryland)	July 1	Aug. 31	$ 169	$ 71	$ 240
DC	District of Columbia	Washington DC (also the cities of Alexandria, Falls Church and Fairfax, and the counties of Arlington and Fairfax, in Virginia; and the counties of Montgomery and Prince George's in Maryland)	Sept. 1	Sept. 30	$ 226	$ 71	$ 297
DE	Dover	Kent	Oct. 1	Apr. 30	$ 77	$ 46	$ 123
DE	Dover	Kent	May 1	Sept. 30	$ 90	$ 46	$ 136
DE	Lewes	Sussex	Oct. 1	June 30	$ 83	$ 46	$ 129
DE	Lewes	Sussex	July 1	Aug. 31	$ 122	$ 46	$ 168
DE	Lewes	Sussex	Sept. 1	Sept. 30	$ 83	$ 46	$ 129
DE	Wilmington	New Castle			$ 114	$ 56	$ 170
FL	Altamonte Springs	Seminole	Oct. 1	Dec. 31	$ 77	$ 61	$ 138
FL	Altamonte Springs	Seminole	Jan. 1	Mar. 31	$ 82	$ 61	$ 143
FL	Altamonte Springs	Seminole	Apr. 1	Sept. 30	$ 77	$ 61	$ 138
FL	Boca Raton / Delray Beach / Jupiter	Palm Beach	Oct. 1	Dec. 31	$ 84	$ 71	$ 155
FL	Boca Raton / Delray Beach / Jupiter	Palm Beach	Jan. 1	Apr. 30	$ 118	$ 71	$ 189
FL	Boca Raton / Delray Beach / Jupiter	Palm Beach	May 1	Sept. 30	$ 84	$ 71	$ 155
FL	Bradenton	Manatee	Oct. 1	Dec. 31	$ 80	$ 56	$ 136
FL	Bradenton	Manatee	Jan. 1	Apr. 30	$ 97	$ 56	$ 153
FL	Bradenton	Manatee	May 1	Sept. 30	$ 80	$ 56	$ 136
FL	Cocoa Beach	Brevard			$ 99	$ 51	$ 150

Table 3: Maximum Federal Per Diem Rates (Effective for 10/1/2012 - 9/30/2013 and updated on 4/1/2013).

State	Primary Destination	County	Season Begin Date	Season End Date	Lodging Rate	M&IE Rate	
FL	Daytona Beach	Volusia	Oct. 1	Jan. 31	$ 82	$ 51	$ 133
FL	Daytona Beach	Volusia	Feb. 1	July 31	$ 101	$ 51	$ 152
FL	Daytona Beach	Volusia	Aug. 1	Sept. 30	$ 82	$ 51	$ 133
FL	Fort Lauderdale	Broward	Oct. 1	Dec. 31	$ 124	$ 71	$ 195
FL	Fort Lauderdale	Broward	Jan. 1	Mar. 31	$ 164	$ 71	$ 235
FL	Fort Lauderdale	Broward	Apr. 1	May 31	$ 137	$ 71	$ 208
FL	Fort Lauderdale	Broward	June 1	Sept. 30	$ 101	$ 71	$ 172
FL	Fort Myers	Lee	Oct. 1	Dec. 31	$ 85	$ 56	$ 141
FL	Fort Myers	Lee	Jan. 1	Apr. 30	$ 115	$ 56	$ 171
FL	Fort Myers	Lee	May 1	Sept. 30	$ 85	$ 56	$ 141
FL	Fort Walton Beach / De Funiak Springs	Okaloosa and Walton	Oct. 1	Oct. 31	$ 109	$ 51	$ 160
FL	Fort Walton Beach / De Funiak Springs	Okaloosa and Walton	Nov. 1	Feb. 28	$ 77	$ 51	$ 128
FL	Fort Walton Beach / De Funiak Springs	Okaloosa and Walton	Mar. 1	May 31	$ 121	$ 51	$ 172
FL	Fort Walton Beach / De Funiak Springs	Okaloosa and Walton	June 1	July 31	$ 154	$ 51	$ 205
FL	Fort Walton Beach / De Funiak Springs	Okaloosa and Walton	Aug. 1	Sept. 30	$ 109	$ 51	$ 160
FL	Gainesville	Alachua			$ 90	$ 51	$ 141
FL	Gulf Breeze	Santa Rosa	Oct. 1	Feb. 28	$ 97	$ 51	$ 148
FL	Gulf Breeze	Santa Rosa	Mar. 1	May 31	$ 117	$ 51	$ 168
FL	Gulf Breeze	Santa Rosa	June 1	Aug. 31	$ 128	$ 51	$ 179
FL	Gulf Breeze	Santa Rosa	Sept. 1	Sept. 30	$ 97	$ 51	$ 148
FL	Jacksonville / Jacksonville Beach / Mayport Naval Station	Duval / Nassau			$ 80	$ 51	$ 131
FL	Key West	Monroe	Oct. 1	Nov. 30	$ 150	$ 71	$ 221
FL	Key West	Monroe	Dec. 1	Jan. 31	$ 190	$ 71	$ 261
FL	Key West	Monroe	Feb. 1	Apr. 30	$ 221	$ 71	$ 292
FL	Key West	Monroe	May 1	Sept. 30	$ 150	$ 71	$ 221
FL	Kissimmee	Osceola	Oct. 1	Dec. 31	$ 77	$ 46	$ 123
FL	Kissimmee	Osceola	Jan. 1	May 31	$ 79	$ 46	$ 125
FL	Kissimmee	Osceola	June 1	Sept. 30	$ 77	$ 46	$ 123
FL	Lakeland	Polk			$ 82	$ 46	$ 128
FL	Miami	Miami-Dade	Oct. 1	Nov. 30	$ 105	$ 66	$ 171
FL	Miami	Miami-Dade	Dec. 1	Mar. 31	$ 152	$ 66	$ 218
FL	Miami	Miami-Dade	Apr. 1	May 31	$ 125	$ 66	$ 191
FL	Miami	Miami-Dade	June 1	Sept. 30	$ 105	$ 66	$ 171
FL	Naples	Collier	Oct. 1	Dec. 31	$ 109	$ 61	$ 170
FL	Naples	Collier	Jan. 1	Apr. 30	$ 156	$ 61	$ 217
FL	Naples	Collier	May 1	Sept. 30	$ 96	$ 61	$ 157
FL	Ocala	Marion			$ 79	$ 46	$ 125
FL	Orlando	Orange	Oct. 1	Dec. 31	$ 97	$ 56	$ 153
FL	Orlando	Orange	Jan. 1	May 31	$ 111	$ 56	$ 167
FL	Orlando	Orange	June 1	Sept. 30	$ 97	$ 56	$ 153
FL	Panama City	Bay	Oct. 1	Feb. 28	$ 79	$ 51	$ 130
FL	Panama City	Bay	Mar. 1	July 31	$ 103	$ 51	$ 154
FL	Panama City	Bay	Aug. 1	Sept. 30	$ 79	$ 51	$ 130

Table 3: Maximum Federal Per Diem Rates (Effective for 10/1/2012 - 9/30/2013 and updated on 4/1/2013).

State	Primary Destination	County	Season Begin Date	Season End Date	Lodging Rate	M&IE Rate	
FL	Pensacola	Escambia			$ 102	$ 46	$ 148
FL	Punta Gorda	Charlotte	Oct. 1	Jan. 31	$ 77	$ 51	$ 128
FL	Punta Gorda	Charlotte	Feb. 1	Apr. 30	$ 85	$ 51	$ 136
FL	Punta Gorda	Charlotte	May 1	Sept. 30	$ 77	$ 51	$ 128
FL	Sarasota	Sarasota	Oct. 1	Dec. 31	$ 87	$ 56	$ 143
FL	Sarasota	Sarasota	Jan. 1	Apr. 30	$ 112	$ 56	$ 168
FL	Sarasota	Sarasota	May 1	Sept. 30	$ 87	$ 56	$ 143
FL	Sebring	Highlands	Oct. 1	Dec. 31	$ 80	$ 46	$ 126
FL	Sebring	Highlands	Jan. 1	Mar. 31	$ 120	$ 46	$ 166
FL	Sebring	Highlands	Apr. 1	Sept. 30	$ 80	$ 46	$ 126
FL	St. Augustine	St. Johns			$ 95	$ 56	$ 151
FL	Stuart	Martin	Oct. 1	Dec. 31	$ 81	$ 51	$ 132
FL	Stuart	Martin	Jan. 1	Apr. 30	$ 100	$ 51	$ 151
FL	Stuart	Martin	May 1	Sept. 30	$ 81	$ 51	$ 132
FL	Tallahassee	Leon			$ 85	$ 46	$ 131
FL	Tampa / St. Petersburg	Pinellas and Hillsborough	Oct. 1	Dec. 31	$ 93	$ 51	$ 144
FL	Tampa / St. Petersburg	Pinellas and Hillsborough	Jan. 1	Apr. 30	$ 112	$ 51	$ 163
FL	Tampa / St. Petersburg	Pinellas and Hillsborough	May 1	Sept. 30	$ 93	$ 51	$ 144
FL	Vero Beach	Indian River	Oct. 1	Jan. 31	$ 99	$ 51	$ 150
FL	Vero Beach	Indian River	Feb. 1	Apr. 30	$ 132	$ 51	$ 183
FL	Vero Beach	Indian River	May 1	Sept. 30	$ 99	$ 51	$ 150
GA	Athens	Clarke			$ 91	$ 46	$ 137
GA	Atlanta	Fulton, Dekalb and Cobb			$ 133	$ 56	$ 189
GA	Augusta	Richmond			$ 83	$ 51	$ 134
GA	Columbus	Muscogee			$ 82	$ 46	$ 128
GA	Jekyll Island / Brunswick	Glynn	Oct. 1	Nov. 30	$ 112	$ 56	$ 168
GA	Jekyll Island / Brunswick	Glynn	Dec. 1	Mar. 31	$ 91	$ 56	$ 147
GA	Jekyll Island / Brunswick	Glynn	Apr. 1	Sept. 30	$ 112	$ 56	$ 168
GA	Savannah	Chatham			$ 95	$ 56	$ 151
IA	Cedar Rapids	Linn			$ 80	$ 51	$ 131
IA	Dallas County	Dallas			$ 98	$ 51	$ 149
IA	Des Moines	Polk			$ 84	$ 51	$ 135
ID	Bonner's Ferry / Sandpoint	Bonner / Boundary / Shoshone	Oct. 1	June 30	$ 78	$ 61	$ 139
ID	Bonner's Ferry / Sandpoint	Bonner / Boundary / Shoshone	July 1	Aug. 31	$ 100	$ 61	$ 161
ID	Bonner's Ferry / Sandpoint	Bonner / Boundary / Shoshone	Sept. 1	Sept. 30	$ 78	$ 61	$ 139
ID	Coeur d'Alene	Kootenai	Oct. 1	May 31	$ 81	$ 61	$ 142
ID	Coeur d'Alene	Kootenai	June 1	Aug. 31	$ 114	$ 61	$ 175
ID	Coeur d'Alene	Kootenai	Sept. 1	Sept. 30	$ 81	$ 61	$ 142
ID	Driggs / Idaho Falls	Bonneville / Fremont / Teton			$ 81	$ 46	$ 127
ID	Sun Valley / Ketchum	Blaine	Oct. 1	May 31	$ 84	$ 71	$ 155
ID	Sun Valley / Ketchum	Blaine	June 1	Aug. 31	$ 102	$ 71	$ 173
ID	Sun Valley / Ketchum	Blaine	Sept. 1	Sept. 30	$ 84	$ 71	$ 155
IL	Bolingbrook / Romeoville / Lemont	Will			$ 85	$ 51	$ 136
IL	Chicago	Cook and Lake	Oct. 1	Nov. 30	$ 190	$ 71	$ 261
IL	Chicago	Cook and Lake	Dec. 1	Mar. 31	$ 130	$ 71	$ 201

Table 3: Maximum Federal Per Diem Rates (Effective for 10/1/2012 - 9/30/2013 and updated on 4/1/2013).

State	Primary Destination	County	Season Begin Date	Season End Date	Lodging Rate	M&IE Rate	
IL	Chicago	Cook and Lake	Apr. 1	June 30	$ 171	$ 71	$ 242
IL	Chicago	Cook and Lake	July 1	Aug. 31	$ 155	$ 71	$ 226
IL	Chicago	Cook and Lake	Sept. 1	Sept. 30	$ 190	$ 71	$ 261
IL	O'Fallon / Fairview Heights / Collinsville	Bond, Calhoun, Clinton, Jersey, Macoupin, Madison, Monroe and St. Clair			$ 104	$ 56	$ 160
IL	Oak Brook Terrace	Dupage			$ 92	$ 61	$ 153
IL	Springfield	Sangamon			$ 81	$ 56	$ 137
IN	Bloomington	Monroe			$ 97	$ 56	$ 153
IN	Ft. Wayne	Allen			$ 84	$ 56	$ 140
IN	Hammond / Munster / Merrillville	Lake			$ 84	$ 46	$ 130
IN	Indianapolis / Carmel	Marion, Hamilton			$ 91	$ 61	$ 152
IN	Lafayette / West Lafayette	Tippecanoe			$ 82	$ 51	$ 133
IN	Michigan City	La Porte			$ 78	$ 56	$ 134
IN	South Bend	St. Joseph			$ 86	$ 56	$ 142
IN	Valparaiso / Burlington Beach	Porter			$ 78	$ 51	$ 129
KS	Kansas City / Overland Park	Wyandotte / Johnson / Leavenworth			$ 99	$ 61	$ 160
KS	Wichita	Sedgwick			$ 86	$ 56	$ 142
KY	Boone County	Boone			$ 87	$ 51	$ 138
KY	Kenton County	Kenton			$ 118	$ 56	$ 174
KY	Lexington	Fayette			$ 100	$ 61	$ 161
KY	Louisville	Jefferson	Oct. 1	Jan. 31	$ 97	$ 61	$ 158
KY	Louisville	Jefferson	Feb. 1	May 31	$ 109	$ 61	$ 170
KY	Louisville	Jefferson	June 1	Sept. 30	$ 97	$ 61	$ 158
LA	Alexandria / Leesville / Natchitoches	Allen / Jefferson Davis / Natchitoches / Rapides / Vernon Parishes			$ 80	$ 61	$ 141
LA	Baton Rouge	East Baton Rouge Parish			$ 93	$ 56	$ 149
LA	Covington / Slidell	St. Tammany Parish			$ 89	$ 56	$ 145
LA	Lafayette	Lafayette Consolidated Government			$ 85	$ 56	$ 141
LA	New Orleans	Orleans, St. Bernard, Jefferson and Plaquemine Parishes	Oct. 1	June 30	$ 135	$ 71	$ 206
LA	New Orleans	Orleans, St. Bernard, Jefferson and Plaquemine Parishes	July 1	Sept. 30	$ 101	$ 71	$ 172
MA	Andover	Essex			$ 87	$ 56	$ 143
MA	Boston / Cambridge	Suffolk, city of Cambridge	Oct. 1	Oct. 31	$ 221	$ 71	$ 292
MA	Boston / Cambridge	Suffolk, city of Cambridge	Nov. 1	Mar. 31	$ 158	$ 71	$ 229
MA	Boston / Cambridge	Suffolk, city of Cambridge	Apr. 1	June 30	$ 201	$ 71	$ 272
MA	Boston / Cambridge	Suffolk, city of Cambridge	July 1	Aug. 31	$ 183	$ 71	$ 254
MA	Boston / Cambridge	Suffolk, city of Cambridge	Sept. 1	Sept. 30	$ 221	$ 71	$ 292
MA	Burlington / Woburn	Middlesex less the city of Cambridge			$ 111	$ 71	$ 182
MA	Falmouth	City limits of Falmouth	Oct. 1	Apr. 30	$ 98	$ 51	$ 149
MA	Falmouth	City limits of Falmouth	May 1	June 30	$ 115	$ 51	$ 166
MA	Falmouth	City limits of Falmouth	July 1	Aug. 31	$ 167	$ 51	$ 218
MA	Falmouth	City limits of Falmouth	Sept. 1	Sept. 30	$ 98	$ 51	$ 149
MA	Hyannis	Barnstable less the city of Falmouth	Oct. 1	June 30	$ 87	$ 56	$ 143
MA	Hyannis	Barnstable less the city of Falmouth	July 1	Aug. 31	$ 128	$ 56	$ 184

Table 3: Maximum Federal Per Diem Rates (Effective for 10/1/2012 - 9/30/2013 and updated on 4/1/2013).

State	Primary Destination	County	Season Begin Date	Season End Date	Lodging Rate	M&IE Rate	
MA	Hyannis	Barnstable less the city of Falmouth	Sept. 1	Sept. 30	$ 87	$ 56	$ 143
MA	Martha's Vineyard	Dukes	Oct. 1	June 30	$ 111	$ 71	$ 182
MA	Martha's Vineyard	Dukes	July 1	Aug. 31	$ 207	$ 71	$ 278
MA	Martha's Vineyard	Dukes	Sept. 1	Sept. 30	$ 111	$ 71	$ 182
MA	Nantucket	Nantucket	Oct. 1	May 31	$ 133	$ 61	$ 194
MA	Nantucket	Nantucket	June 1	Sept. 30	$ 249	$ 61	$ 310
MA	Northampton	Hampshire			$ 94	$ 56	$ 150
MA	Pittsfield	Berkshire	Oct. 1	June 30	$ 111	$ 61	$ 172
MA	Pittsfield	Berkshire	July 1	Aug. 31	$ 135	$ 61	$ 196
MA	Pittsfield	Berkshire	Sept. 1	Sept. 30	$ 111	$ 61	$ 172
MA	Plymouth / Taunton / New Bedford	Plymouth / Bristol			$ 90	$ 56	$ 146
MA	Quincy	Norfolk			$ 115	$ 51	$ 166
MA	Springfield	Hampden			$ 94	$ 51	$ 145
MA	Worcester	Worcester			$ 93	$ 61	$ 154
MD	Aberdeen / Bel Air / Belcamp	Harford			$ 83	$ 56	$ 139
MD	Annapolis	Anne Arundel	Oct. 1	Oct. 31	$ 116	$ 61	$ 177
MD	Annapolis	Anne Arundel	Nov. 1	Apr. 30	$ 101	$ 61	$ 162
MD	Annapolis	Anne Arundel	May 1	Sept. 30	$ 116	$ 61	$ 177
MD	Baltimore City	Baltimore City	Oct. 1	Nov. 30	$ 145	$ 71	$ 216
MD	Baltimore City	Baltimore City	Dec. 1	Feb. 28	$ 121	$ 71	$ 192
MD	Baltimore City	Baltimore City	Mar. 1	Sept. 30	$ 145	$ 71	$ 216
MD	Baltimore County	Baltimore			$ 97	$ 61	$ 158
MD	Cambridge / St. Michaels	Dorchester and Talbot	Oct. 1	Oct. 31	$ 133	$ 61	$ 194
MD	Cambridge / St. Michaels	Dorchester and Talbot	Nov. 1	Mar. 31	$ 105	$ 61	$ 166
MD	Cambridge / St. Michaels	Dorchester and Talbot	Apr. 1	May 31	$ 120	$ 61	$ 181
MD	Cambridge / St. Michaels	Dorchester and Talbot	June 1	Aug. 31	$ 164	$ 61	$ 225
MD	Cambridge / St. Michaels	Dorchester and Talbot	Sept. 1	Sept. 30	$ 133	$ 61	$ 194
MD	Centreville	Queen Anne			$ 106	$ 51	$ 157
MD	Columbia	Howard			$ 105	$ 61	$ 166
MD	Frederick	Frederick			$ 95	$ 56	$ 151
MD	Hagerstown	Washington			$ 79	$ 56	$ 135
MD	La Plata / Indian Head / Waldorf	Charles			$ 83	$ 51	$ 134
MD	Lexington Park / Leonardtown / Lusby	St. Mary's and Calvert			$ 102	$ 61	$ 163
MD	Ocean City	Worcester	Oct. 1	Oct. 31	$ 105	$ 71	$ 176
MD	Ocean City	Worcester	Nov. 1	Mar. 31	$ 77	$ 71	$ 148
MD	Ocean City	Worcester	Apr. 1	May 31	$ 88	$ 71	$ 159
MD	Ocean City	Worcester	June 1	Aug. 31	$ 195	$ 71	$ 266
MD	Ocean City	Worcester	Sept. 1	Sept. 30	$ 105	$ 71	$ 176
ME	Bar Harbor	Hancock	Oct. 1	Oct. 31	$ 123	$ 61	$ 184
ME	Bar Harbor	Hancock	Nov. 1	June 30	$ 97	$ 61	$ 158
ME	Bar Harbor	Hancock	July 1	Aug. 31	$ 154	$ 61	$ 215
ME	Bar Harbor	Hancock	Sept. 1	Sept. 30	$ 123	$ 61	$ 184
ME	Kennebunk / Kittery / Sanford	York	Oct. 1	Oct. 31	$ 97	$ 56	$ 153
ME	Kennebunk / Kittery / Sanford	York	Nov. 1	Mar. 31	$ 77	$ 56	$ 133
ME	Kennebunk / Kittery / Sanford	York	Apr. 1	June 30	$ 89	$ 56	$ 145

Table 3: Maximum Federal Per Diem Rates (Effective for 10/1/2012 - 9/30/2013 and updated on 4/1/2013).

State	Primary Destination	County	Season Begin Date	Season End Date	Lodging Rate	M&IE Rate	
ME	Kennebunk / Kittery / Sanford	York	July 1	Aug. 31	$ 124	$ 56	$ 180
ME	Kennebunk / Kittery / Sanford	York	Sept. 1	Sept. 30	$ 97	$ 56	$ 153
ME	Portland	Cumberland / Sagadahoc	Oct. 1	June 30	$ 92	$ 56	$ 148
ME	Portland	Cumberland / Sagadahoc	July 1	Sept. 30	$ 117	$ 56	$ 173
ME	Rockport	Knox	Oct. 1	June 30	$ 81	$ 56	$ 137
ME	Rockport	Knox	July 1	Sept. 30	$ 105	$ 56	$ 161
MI	Ann Arbor	Washtenaw			$ 90	$ 56	$ 146
MI	Benton Harbor / St. Joseph / Stevensville	Berrien			$ 80	$ 51	$ 131
MI	Detroit	Wayne			$ 91	$ 56	$ 147
MI	East Lansing / Lansing	Ingham and Eaton			$ 81	$ 51	$ 132
MI	Grand Rapids	Kent			$ 82	$ 51	$ 133
MI	Holland	Ottawa			$ 82	$ 56	$ 138
MI	Kalamazoo / Battle Creek	Kalamazoo / Calhoun			$ 88	$ 51	$ 139
MI	Mackinac Island	Mackinac	Oct. 1	June 30	$ 77	$ 66	$ 143
MI	Mackinac Island	Mackinac	July 1	Aug. 31	$ 80	$ 66	$ 146
MI	Mackinac Island	Mackinac	Sept. 1	Sept. 30	$ 77	$ 66	$ 143
MI	Midland	Midland			$ 88	$ 46	$ 134
MI	Mount Pleasant	Isabella			$ 78	$ 51	$ 129
MI	Muskegon	Muskegon	Oct. 1	May 31	$ 77	$ 46	$ 123
MI	Muskegon	Muskegon	June 1	Aug. 31	$ 93	$ 46	$ 139
MI	Muskegon	Muskegon	Sept. 1	Sept. 30	$ 77	$ 46	$ 123
MI	Petoskey	Emmet	Oct. 1	June 30	$ 79	$ 51	$ 130
MI	Petoskey	Emmet	July 1	Aug. 31	$ 105	$ 51	$ 156
MI	Petoskey	Emmet	Sept. 1	Sept. 30	$ 79	$ 51	$ 130
MI	Pontiac / Auburn Hills	Oakland			$ 86	$ 56	$ 142
MI	South Haven	Van Buren	Oct. 1	May 31	$ 77	$ 56	$ 133
MI	South Haven	Van Buren	June 1	Aug. 31	$ 92	$ 56	$ 148
MI	South Haven	Van Buren	Sept. 1	Sept. 30	$ 77	$ 56	$ 133
MI	Traverse City and Leland	Grand Traverse and Leelanau	Oct. 1	June 30	$ 77	$ 51	$ 128
MI	Traverse City and Leland	Grand Traverse and Leelanau	July 1	Aug. 31	$ 120	$ 51	$ 171
MI	Traverse City and Leland	Grand Traverse and Leelanau	Sept. 1	Sept. 30	$ 77	$ 51	$ 128
MN	Duluth	St. Louis	Oct. 1	Oct. 31	$ 99	$ 56	$ 155
MN	Duluth	St. Louis	Nov. 1	May 31	$ 82	$ 56	$ 138
MN	Duluth	St. Louis	June 1	Sept. 30	$ 99	$ 56	$ 155
MN	Eagan / Burnsville / Mendota Heights	Dakota			$ 83	$ 56	$ 139
MN	Minneapolis / St. Paul	Hennepin and Ramsey			$ 121	$ 71	$ 192
MN	Rochester	Olmsted			$ 101	$ 51	$ 152
MO	Columbia	Boone			$ 80	$ 51	$ 131
MO	Jefferson City	Cole			$ 79	$ 51	$ 130
MO	Kansas City	Jackson, Clay, Cass, Platte			$ 99	$ 61	$ 160
MO	St. Louis	St. Louis, St. Louis City and St. Charles, Crawford, Franklin, Jefferson, Lincoln, Warren and Washington			$ 104	$ 66	$ 170
MO	St. Robert	Pulaski			$ 80	$ 46	$ 126
MS	Gulfport / Biloxi	Harrison			$ 82	$ 56	$ 138

Table 3: Maximum Federal Per Diem Rates (Effective for 10/1/2012 - 9/30/2013 and updated on 4/1/2013).

State	Primary Destination	County	Season Begin Date	Season End Date	Lodging Rate	M&IE Rate	
MS	Hattiesburg	Forrest and Lamar			$ 84	$ 51	$ 135
MS	Oxford	Lafayette			$ 96	$ 51	$ 147
MS	Picayune	Pearl River / Hancock			$ 82	$ 56	$ 138
MS	Southaven	Desoto			$ 87	$ 46	$ 133
MS	Starkville	Oktibbeha			$ 95	$ 46	$ 141
MT	Big Sky / West Yellowstone	Gallatin	Oct. 1	May 31	$ 82	$ 61	$ 143
MT	Big Sky / West Yellowstone	Gallatin	June 1	Aug. 31	$ 110	$ 61	$ 171
MT	Big Sky / West Yellowstone	Gallatin	Sept. 1	Sept. 30	$ 82	$ 61	$ 143
MT	Butte	Silver Bow			$ 89	$ 51	$ 140
MT	Helena	Lewis and Clark			$ 83	$ 56	$ 139
MT	Missoula / Polson / Kalispell	Missoula / Lake / Flathead	Oct. 1	June 30	$ 87	$ 51	$ 138
MT	Missoula / Polson / Kalispell	Missoula / Lake / Flathead	July 1	Aug. 31	$ 110	$ 51	$ 161
MT	Missoula / Polson / Kalispell	Missoula / Lake / Flathead	Sept. 1	Sept. 30	$ 87	$ 51	$ 138
MT	Sidney / Glendive	Richland / Dawson	Oct. 1	Mar. 31	$ 96	$ 56	$ 152
MT	Sidney / Glendive	Richland / Dawson	Apr. 1	May 31	$ 90	$ 56	$ 146
MT	Sidney / Glendive	Richland / Dawson	June 1	Sept. 30	$ 96	$ 56	$ 152
NC	Asheville	Buncombe	Oct. 1	Oct. 31	$ 95	$ 51	$ 146
NC	Asheville	Buncombe	Nov. 1	June 30	$ 86	$ 51	$ 137
NC	Asheville	Buncombe	July 1	Sept. 30	$ 95	$ 51	$ 146
NC	Atlantic Beach / Morehead City	Carteret	Oct. 1	May 31	$ 85	$ 56	$ 141
NC	Atlantic Beach / Morehead City	Carteret	June 1	Aug. 31	$ 116	$ 56	$ 172
NC	Atlantic Beach / Morehead City	Carteret	Sept. 1	Sept. 30	$ 85	$ 56	$ 141
NC	Chapel Hill	Orange			$ 83	$ 56	$ 139
NC	Charlotte	Mecklenburg			$ 97	$ 51	$ 148
NC	Durham	Durham			$ 91	$ 51	$ 142
NC	Fayetteville	Cumberland			$ 94	$ 51	$ 145
NC	Greensboro	Guilford			$ 86	$ 56	$ 142
NC	Greenville	Pitt			$ 79	$ 51	$ 130
NC	Kill Devil	Dare	Oct. 1	May 31	$ 89	$ 61	$ 150
NC	Kill Devil	Dare	June 1	Aug. 31	$ 144	$ 61	$ 205
NC	Kill Devil	Dare	Sept. 1	Sept. 30	$ 89	$ 61	$ 150
NC	New Bern / Havelock	Craven			$ 93	$ 46	$ 139
NC	Raleigh	Wake			$ 91	$ 66	$ 157
NC	Wilmington	New Hanover			$ 91	$ 56	$ 147
NC	Winston-Salem	Forsyth			$ 82	$ 56	$ 138
ND	Dickinson / Beulah	Stark / Mercer/ Billings	Oct. 1	Nov. 30	$ 104	$ 56	$ 160
ND	Dickinson / Beulah	Stark / Mercer/ Billings	Dec. 1	Mar. 31	$ 118	$ 56	$ 174
ND	Dickinson / Beulah	Stark / Mercer/ Billings	Apr. 1	Sept. 30	$ 104	$ 56	$ 160
ND	Minot	Ward	Oct. 1	Mar. 31	$ 112	$ 56	$ 168
ND	Minot	Ward	Apr. 1	June 30	$ 100	$ 56	$ 156
ND	Minot	Ward	July 1	Sept. 30	$ 112	$ 56	$ 168
ND	Williston	Williams/ Mountrail / McKenzie	Oct. 1	Mar. 31	$ 96	$ 56	$ 152
ND	Williston	Williams/ Mountrail / McKenzie	Apr. 1	May 31	$ 90	$ 56	$ 146
ND	Williston	Williams/ Mountrail / McKenzie	June 1	Sept. 30	$ 96	$ 56	$ 152
NE	Omaha	Douglas	Oct. 1	Mar. 31	$ 91	$ 61	$ 152

Table 3: Maximum Federal Per Diem Rates (Effective for 10/1/2012 - 9/30/2013 and updated on 4/1/2013).

State	Primary Destination	County	Season Begin Date	Season End Date	Lodging Rate	M&IE Rate	
NE	Omaha	Douglas	Apr. 1	June 30	$ 102	$ 61	$ 163
NE	Omaha	Douglas	July 1	Sept. 30	$ 91	$ 61	$ 152
NH	Concord	Merrimack	Oct. 1	May 31	$ 81	$ 51	$ 132
NH	Concord	Merrimack	June 1	Sept. 30	$ 89	$ 51	$ 140
NH	Conway	Caroll	Oct. 1	Feb. 28	$ 120	$ 61	$ 181
NH	Conway	Caroll	Mar. 1	June 30	$ 103	$ 61	$ 164
NH	Conway	Caroll	July 1	Aug. 31	$ 145	$ 61	$ 206
NH	Conway	Caroll	Sept. 1	Sept. 30	$ 120	$ 61	$ 181
NH	Durham	Strafford			$ 97	$ 46	$ 143
NH	Laconia	Belknap	Oct. 1	Oct. 31	$ 104	$ 51	$ 155
NH	Laconia	Belknap	Nov. 1	May 31	$ 86	$ 51	$ 137
NH	Laconia	Belknap	June 1	Sept. 30	$ 104	$ 51	$ 155
NH	Lebanon / Lincoln / West Lebanon	Grafton / Sullivan			$ 103	$ 56	$ 159
NH	Manchester	Hillsborough			$ 87	$ 56	$ 143
NH	Portsmouth	Rockingham	Oct. 1	June 30	$ 100	$ 61	$ 161
NH	Portsmouth	Rockingham	July 1	Sept. 30	$ 130	$ 61	$ 191
NJ	Atlantic City / Ocean City / Cape May	Atlantic and Cape May			$ 96	$ 66	$ 162
NJ	Belle Mead	Somerset			$ 119	$ 56	$ 175
NJ	Cherry Hill / Moorestown	Camden and Burlington			$ 90	$ 61	$ 151
NJ	Eatontown / Freehold	Monmouth			$ 108	$ 56	$ 164
NJ	Edison / Piscataway	Middlesex			$ 108	$ 51	$ 159
NJ	Flemington	Hunterdon			$ 107	$ 61	$ 168
NJ	Newark	Essex, Bergen, Hudson and Passaic			$ 120	$ 61	$ 181
NJ	Parsippany	Morris			$ 121	$ 56	$ 177
NJ	Princeton / Trenton	Mercer			$ 119	$ 61	$ 180
NJ	Springfield / Cranford / New Providence	Union			$ 95	$ 56	$ 151
NJ	Toms River	Ocean	Oct. 1	May 31	$ 77	$ 51	$ 128
NJ	Toms River	Ocean	June 1	Aug. 31	$ 105	$ 51	$ 156
NJ	Toms River	Ocean	Sept. 1	Sept. 30	$ 77	$ 51	$ 128
NM	Albuquerque	Bernalillo			$ 81	$ 56	$ 137
NM	Carlsbad	Eddy			$ 89	$ 51	$ 140
NM	Las Cruces	Dona Ana			$ 84	$ 56	$ 140
NM	Los Alamos	Los Alamos			$ 87	$ 51	$ 138
NM	Santa Fe	Santa Fe	Oct. 1	Oct. 31	$ 105	$ 71	$ 176
NM	Santa Fe	Santa Fe	Nov. 1	May 31	$ 83	$ 71	$ 154
NM	Santa Fe	Santa Fe	June 1	Sept. 30	$ 105	$ 71	$ 176
NM	Taos	Taos			$ 90	$ 66	$ 156
NV	Incline Village / Reno / Sparks	Washoe	Oct. 1	June 30	$ 94	$ 51	$ 145
NV	Incline Village / Reno / Sparks	Washoe	July 1	Aug. 31	$ 121	$ 51	$ 172
NV	Incline Village / Reno / Sparks	Washoe	Sept. 1	Sept. 30	$ 94	$ 51	$ 145
NV	Las Vegas	Clark			$ 99	$ 71	$ 170
NV	Stateline, Carson City	Douglas, Carson City			$ 91	$ 61	$ 152
NY	Albany	Albany			$ 104	$ 61	$ 165
NY	Binghamton / Owego	Broome and Tioga			$ 92	$ 46	$ 138

Table 3: Maximum Federal Per Diem Rates (Effective for 10/1/2012 - 9/30/2013 and updated on 4/1/2013).

State	Primary Destination	County	Season Begin Date	Season End Date	Lodging Rate	M&IE Rate	
NY	Buffalo	Erie			$ 100	$ 56	$ 156
NY	Floral Park / Garden City / Great Neck	Nassau			$ 142	$ 66	$ 208
NY	Glens Falls	Warren	Oct. 1	June 30	$ 94	$ 66	$ 160
NY	Glens Falls	Warren	July 1	Aug. 31	$ 138	$ 66	$ 204
NY	Glens Falls	Warren	Sept. 1	Sept. 30	$ 94	$ 66	$ 160
NY	Ithaca / Waterloo / Romulus	Tompkins and Seneca			$ 118	$ 46	$ 164
NY	Kingston	Ulster			$ 105	$ 66	$ 171
NY	Lake Placid	Essex	Oct. 1	Nov. 30	$ 108	$ 61	$ 169
NY	Lake Placid	Essex	Dec. 1	Feb. 28	$ 126	$ 61	$ 187
NY	Lake Placid	Essex	Mar. 1	June 30	$ 99	$ 61	$ 160
NY	Lake Placid	Essex	July 1	Aug. 31	$ 151	$ 61	$ 212
NY	Lake Placid	Essex	Sept. 1	Sept. 30	$ 108	$ 61	$ 169
NY	Manhattan (includes the boroughs of Manhattan, Brooklyn, the Bronx, Queens and Staten Island)	Bronx, Kings, New York, Queens, Richmond	Oct. 1	Dec. 31	$ 295	$ 71	$ 366
NY	Manhattan (includes the boroughs of Manhattan, Brooklyn, the Bronx, Queens and Staten Island)	Bronx, Kings, New York, Queens, Richmond	Jan. 1	Mar. 31	$ 204	$ 71	$ 275
NY	Manhattan (includes the boroughs of Manhattan, Brooklyn, the Bronx, Queens and Staten Island)	Bronx, Kings, New York, Queens, Richmond	Apr. 1	June 30	$ 241	$ 71	$ 312
NY	Manhattan (includes the boroughs of Manhattan, Brooklyn, the Bronx, Queens and Staten Island)	Bronx, Kings, New York, Queens, Richmond	July 1	Aug. 31	$ 216	$ 71	$ 287
NY	Manhattan (includes the boroughs of Manhattan, Brooklyn, the Bronx, Queens and Staten Island)	Bronx, Kings, New York, Queens, Richmond	Sept. 1	Sept. 30	$ 295	$ 71	$ 366
NY	Niagara Falls	Niagara	Oct. 1	May 31	$ 77	$ 51	$ 128
NY	Niagara Falls	Niagara	June 1	Aug. 31	$ 103	$ 51	$ 154
NY	Niagara Falls	Niagara	Sept. 1	Sept. 30	$ 77	$ 51	$ 128
NY	Nyack / Palisades	Rockland			$ 105	$ 61	$ 166
NY	Poughkeepsie	Dutchess			$ 99	$ 66	$ 165
NY	Riverhead / Ronkonkoma / Melville	Suffolk	Oct. 1	May 31	$ 112	$ 71	$ 183
NY	Riverhead / Ronkonkoma / Melville	Suffolk	June 1	Aug. 31	$ 127	$ 71	$ 198
NY	Riverhead / Ronkonkoma / Melville	Suffolk	Sept. 1	Sept. 30	$ 112	$ 71	$ 183
NY	Rochester	Monroe			$ 96	$ 51	$ 147
NY	Saratoga Springs / Schenectady	Saratoga and Schenectady	Oct. 1	June 30	$ 104	$ 56	$ 160
NY	Saratoga Springs / Schenectady	Saratoga and Schenectady	July 1	Aug. 31	$ 148	$ 56	$ 204
NY	Saratoga Springs / Schenectady	Saratoga and Schenectady	Sept. 1	Sept. 30	$ 104	$ 56	$ 160
NY	Syracuse / Oswego	Onondaga and Oswego			$ 94	$ 56	$ 150
NY	Tarrytown / White Plains / New Rochelle	Westchester			$ 136	$ 71	$ 207
NY	Troy	Rensselaer			$ 96	$ 51	$ 147
NY	Watertown	Jefferson			$ 99	$ 56	$ 155
NY	West Point	Orange			$ 108	$ 51	$ 159
OH	Akron	Summit			$ 87	$ 51	$ 138
OH	Canton	Stark			$ 89	$ 51	$ 140
OH	Cincinnati	Hamilton / Clermont			$ 118	$ 56	$ 174

Table 3: Maximum Federal Per Diem Rates (Effective for 10/1/2012 - 9/30/2013 and updated on 4/1/2013).

State	Primary Destination	County	Season Begin Date	Season End Date	Lodging Rate	M&IE Rate	
OH	Cleveland	Cuyahoga			$ 101	$ 56	$ 157
OH	Columbus	Franklin			$ 94	$ 56	$ 150
OH	Dayton / Fairborn	Greene, Darke and Montgomery			$ 82	$ 56	$ 138
OH	Hamilton	Butler and Warren			$ 92	$ 51	$ 143
OH	Medina / Wooster	Wayne and Medina			$ 86	$ 51	$ 137
OH	Mentor	Lake			$ 86	$ 46	$ 132
OH	Sandusky / Bellevue	Erie / Huron	Oct. 1	Jan. 31	$ 77	$ 46	$ 123
OH	Sandusky / Bellevue	Erie / Huron	Feb. 1	Aug. 31	$ 84	$ 46	$ 130
OH	Sandusky / Bellevue	Erie / Huron	Sept. 1	Sept. 30	$ 77	$ 46	$ 123
OH	Youngstown	Mahoning and Trumbull			$ 84	$ 51	$ 135
OK	Enid	Garfield	Oct. 1	Mar. 31	$ 77	$ 46	$ 123
OK	Enid	Garfield	Apr. 1	Sept. 30	$ 103	$ 56	$ 159
OK	Oklahoma City	Oklahoma			$ 81	$ 66	$ 147
OR	Ashland / Crater Lake	Jackson / Klamath			$ 82	$ 56	$ 138
OR	Beaverton	Washington			$ 93	$ 51	$ 144
OR	Bend	Deschutes	Oct. 1	June 30	$ 89	$ 61	$ 150
OR	Bend	Deschutes	July 1	Aug. 31	$ 114	$ 61	$ 175
OR	Bend	Deschutes	Sept. 1	Sept. 30	$ 89	$ 61	$ 150
OR	Clackamas	Clackamas			$ 88	$ 61	$ 149
OR	Eugene / Florence	Lane			$ 97	$ 51	$ 148
OR	Lincoln City	Lincoln	Oct. 1	June 30	$ 84	$ 56	$ 140
OR	Lincoln City	Lincoln	July 1	Aug. 31	$ 105	$ 56	$ 161
OR	Lincoln City	Lincoln	Sept. 1	Sept. 30	$ 84	$ 56	$ 140
OR	Portland	Multnomah			$ 113	$ 66	$ 179
OR	Seaside	Clatsop	Oct. 1	June 30	$ 96	$ 51	$ 147
OR	Seaside	Clatsop	July 1	Aug. 31	$ 131	$ 51	$ 182
OR	Seaside	Clatsop	Sept. 1	Sept. 30	$ 96	$ 51	$ 147
PA	Allentown / Easton / Bethlehem	Lehigh and Northampton			$ 83	$ 51	$ 134
PA	Bucks County	Bucks			$ 95	$ 71	$ 166
PA	Chester / Radnor / Essington	Delaware			$ 95	$ 51	$ 146
PA	Erie	Erie			$ 84	$ 46	$ 130
PA	Gettysburg	Adams	Oct. 1	Oct. 31	$ 98	$ 51	$ 149
PA	Gettysburg	Adams	Nov. 1	Mar. 31	$ 77	$ 51	$ 128
PA	Gettysburg	Adams	Apr. 1	Sept. 30	$ 98	$ 51	$ 149
PA	Harrisburg / Hershey	Dauphin	Oct. 1	May 31	$ 108	$ 51	$ 159
PA	Harrisburg / Hershey	Dauphin	June 1	Aug. 31	$ 134	$ 51	$ 185
PA	Harrisburg / Hershey	Dauphin	Sept. 1	Sept. 30	$ 108	$ 51	$ 159
PA	Lancaster	Lancaster			$ 95	$ 56	$ 151
PA	Malvern / Frazer / Berwyn	Chester			$ 118	$ 51	$ 169
PA	Mechanicsburg	Cumberland			$ 85	$ 56	$ 141
PA	Montgomery County	Montgomery			$ 116	$ 66	$ 182
PA	Philadelphia	Philadelphia	Oct. 1	Nov. 30	$ 143	$ 66	$ 209
PA	Philadelphia	Philadelphia	Dec. 1	Aug. 31	$ 137	$ 66	$ 203
PA	Philadelphia	Philadelphia	Sept. 1	Sept. 30	$ 143	$ 66	$ 209
PA	Pittsburgh	Allegheny			$ 119	$ 71	$ 190

Table 3: Maximum Federal Per Diem Rates (Effective for 10/1/2012 - 9/30/2013 and updated on 4/1/2013).

State	Primary Destination	County	Season Begin Date	Season End Date	Lodging Rate	M&IE Rate	
PA	Reading	Berks			$ 86	$ 56	$ 142
PA	Scranton	Lackawanna			$ 82	$ 56	$ 138
PA	State College	Centre			$ 88	$ 56	$ 144
RI	East Greenwich / Warwick / North Kingstown	Kent and Washington			$ 86	$ 56	$ 142
RI	Jamestown / Middletown / Newport	Newport	Oct. 1	Oct. 31	$ 149	$ 71	$ 220
RI	Jamestown / Middletown / Newport	Newport	Nov. 1	Apr. 30	$ 93	$ 71	$ 164
RI	Jamestown / Middletown / Newport	Newport	May 1	Sept. 30	$ 149	$ 71	$ 220
RI	Providence / Bristol	Providence / Bristol			$ 121	$ 71	$ 192
SC	Aiken	Aiken			$ 86	$ 46	$ 132
SC	Charleston	Charleston, Berkeley and Dorchester			$ 137	$ 56	$ 193
SC	Columbia	Richland / Lexington			$ 85	$ 51	$ 136
SC	Greenville	Greenville			$ 79	$ 56	$ 135
SC	Hilton Head	Beaufort	Oct. 1	Oct. 31	$ 105	$ 61	$ 166
SC	Hilton Head	Beaufort	Nov. 1	Mar. 31	$ 87	$ 61	$ 148
SC	Hilton Head	Beaufort	Apr. 1	Aug. 31	$ 123	$ 61	$ 184
SC	Hilton Head	Beaufort	Sept. 1	Sept. 30	$ 105	$ 61	$ 166
SC	Myrtle Beach	Horry	Oct. 1	Oct. 31	$ 84	$ 51	$ 135
SC	Myrtle Beach	Horry	Nov. 1	Mar. 31	$ 77	$ 51	$ 128
SC	Myrtle Beach	Horry	Apr. 1	May 31	$ 89	$ 51	$ 140
SC	Myrtle Beach	Horry	June 1	Aug. 31	$ 126	$ 51	$ 177
SC	Myrtle Beach	Horry	Sept. 1	Sept. 30	$ 84	$ 51	$ 135
SD	Hot Springs	Fall River and Custer	Oct. 1	May 31	$ 77	$ 46	$ 123
SD	Hot Springs	Fall River and Custer	June 1	Aug. 31	$ 110	$ 46	$ 156
SD	Hot Springs	Fall River and Custer	Sept. 1	Sept. 30	$ 77	$ 46	$ 123
SD	Rapid City	Pennington	Oct. 1	May 31	$ 77	$ 51	$ 128
SD	Rapid City	Pennington	June 1	Aug. 31	$ 126	$ 51	$ 177
SD	Rapid City	Pennington	Sept. 1	Sept. 30	$ 77	$ 51	$ 128
SD	Sturgis / Spearfish	Meade, Butte and Lawrence	Oct. 1	May 31	$ 77	$ 51	$ 128
SD	Sturgis / Spearfish	Meade, Butte and Lawrence	June 1	Aug. 31	$ 114	$ 51	$ 165
SD	Sturgis / Spearfish	Meade, Butte and Lawrence	Sept. 1	Sept. 30	$ 77	$ 51	$ 128
TN	Brentwood / Franklin	Williamson			$ 97	$ 56	$ 153
TN	Chattanooga	Hamilton			$ 94	$ 56	$ 150
TN	Knoxville	Knox			$ 86	$ 56	$ 142
TN	Memphis	Shelby			$ 93	$ 61	$ 154
TN	Nashville	Davidson			$ 107	$ 66	$ 173
TN	Oak Ridge	Anderson			$ 91	$ 46	$ 137
TX	Arlington / Fort Worth / Grapevine	Tarrant County and City of Grapevine			$ 139	$ 56	$ 195
TX	Austin	Travis			$ 108	$ 71	$ 179
TX	Beaumont	Jefferson			$ 79	$ 51	$ 130
TX	College Station	Brazos			$ 93	$ 56	$ 149
TX	Corpus Christi	Nueces			$ 88	$ 51	$ 139
TX	Dallas	Dallas County			$ 113	$ 71	$ 184
TX	El Paso	El Paso			$ 88	$ 51	$ 139
TX	Galveston	Galveston	Oct. 1	May 31	$ 82	$ 56	$ 138

Table 3: Maximum Federal Per Diem Rates (Effective for 10/1/2012 - 9/30/2013 and updated on 4/1/2013).

State	Primary Destination	County	Season Begin Date	Season End Date	Lodging Rate	M&IE Rate	
TX	Galveston	Galveston	June 1	July 31	$ 100	$ 56	$ 156
TX	Galveston	Galveston	Aug. 1	Sept. 30	$ 82	$ 56	$ 138
TX	Greenville	Hunt County			$ 86	$ 51	$ 137
TX	Houston (L.B. Johnson Space Center)	Montgomery, Fort Bend and Harris			$ 109	$ 71	$ 180
TX	Laredo	Webb			$ 82	$ 56	$ 138
TX	McAllen	Hidalgo			$ 84	$ 56	$ 140
TX	Midland	Midland	Oct. 1	Mar. 31	$ 95	$ 51	$ 146
TX	Midland	Midland	Apr. 1	Sept. 30	$ 161	$ 56	$ 217
TX	Plano	Collin			$ 99	$ 61	$ 160
TX	Round Rock	Williamson			$ 88	$ 51	$ 139
TX	San Antonio	Bexar			$ 106	$ 66	$ 172
TX	South Padre Island	Cameron	Oct. 1	May 31	$ 86	$ 56	$ 142
TX	South Padre Island	Cameron	June 1	July 31	$ 106	$ 56	$ 162
TX	South Padre Island	Cameron	Aug. 1	Sept. 30	$ 86	$ 56	$ 142
TX	Waco	McLennan			$ 82	$ 51	$ 133
UT	Moab	Grand	Oct. 1	Oct. 31	$ 104	$ 56	$ 160
UT	Moab	Grand	Nov. 1	Feb. 28	$ 77	$ 56	$ 133
UT	Moab	Grand	Mar. 1	Sept. 30	$ 104	$ 56	$ 160
UT	Park City	Summit	Oct. 1	Dec. 31	$ 94	$ 71	$ 165
UT	Park City	Summit	Jan. 1	Mar. 31	$ 163	$ 71	$ 234
UT	Park City	Summit	Apr. 1	Sept. 30	$ 94	$ 71	$ 165
UT	Provo	Utah			$ 81	$ 51	$ 132
UT	Salt Lake City	Salt Lake and Tooele			$ 96	$ 61	$ 157
VA	Abingdon	Washington			$ 88	$ 46	$ 134
VA	Blacksburg	Montgomery			$ 95	$ 46	$ 141
VA	Charlottesville	City of Charlottesville, Albemarle, Greene			$ 115	$ 56	$ 171
VA	Chesapeake / Suffolk	Cities of Chesapeake and Suffolk	Oct. 1	May 31	$ 77	$ 56	$ 133
VA	Chesapeake / Suffolk	Cities of Chesapeake and Suffolk	June 1	Aug. 31	$ 86	$ 56	$ 142
VA	Chesapeake / Suffolk	Cities of Chesapeake and Suffolk	Sept. 1	Sept. 30	$ 77	$ 56	$ 133
VA	Chesterfield / Henrico Counties	Chesterfield / Henrico			$ 83	$ 51	$ 134
VA	Fredericksburg	City of Fredericksburg / Spotsylvania / Stafford / Caroline			$ 88	$ 56	$ 144
VA	Loudoun County	Loudoun			$ 108	$ 61	$ 169
VA	Lynchburg	Campbell, Lynchburg City			$ 80	$ 51	$ 131
VA	Norfolk / Portsmouth	Cities of Norfolk and Portsmouth			$ 89	$ 61	$ 150
VA	Prince William County / Manassas	Prince William and City of Manassas			$ 88	$ 56	$ 144
VA	Richmond	City of Richmond			$ 112	$ 66	$ 178
VA	Roanoke	City limits of Roanoke			$ 96	$ 51	$ 147
VA	Virginia Beach	City of Virginia Beach	Oct. 1	May 31	$ 89	$ 56	$ 145
VA	Virginia Beach	City of Virginia Beach	June 1	Aug. 31	$ 151	$ 56	$ 207
VA	Virginia Beach	City of Virginia Beach	Sept. 1	Sept. 30	$ 89	$ 56	$ 145
VA	Wallops Island	Accomack	Oct. 1	June 30	$ 85	$ 56	$ 141
VA	Wallops Island	Accomack	July 1	Aug. 31	$ 127	$ 56	$ 183
VA	Wallops Island	Accomack	Sept. 1	Sept. 30	$ 85	$ 56	$ 141

Table 3: Maximum Federal Per Diem Rates (Effective for 10/1/2012 - 9/30/2013 and updated on 4/1/2013).

State	Primary Destination	County	Season Begin Date	Season End Date	Lodging Rate	M&IE Rate	
VA	Warrenton	Fauquier			$ 92	$ 46	$ 138
VA	Williamsburg / York	James City and York Counties, City of Williamsburg	Oct. 1	Oct. 31	$ 77	$ 51	$ 128
VA	Williamsburg / York	James City and York Counties, City of Williamsburg	Nov. 1	Aug. 31	$ 96	$ 51	$ 147
VA	Williamsburg / York	James City and York Counties, City of Williamsburg	Sept. 1	Sept. 30	$ 77	$ 51	$ 128
VT	Burlington / St. Albans	Chittenden and Franklin	Oct. 1	Oct. 31	$ 112	$ 66	$ 178
VT	Burlington / St. Albans	Chittenden and Franklin	Nov. 1	Apr. 30	$ 94	$ 66	$ 160
VT	Burlington / St. Albans	Chittenden and Franklin	May 1	Sept. 30	$ 112	$ 66	$ 178
VT	Manchester	Bennington			$ 86	$ 71	$ 157
VT	Middlebury	Addison			$ 117	$ 61	$ 178
VT	Montpelier	Washington			$ 101	$ 61	$ 162
VT	Stowe	Lamoille	Oct. 1	Mar. 31	$ 129	$ 71	$ 200
VT	Stowe	Lamoille	Apr. 1	May 31	$ 102	$ 71	$ 173
VT	Stowe	Lamoille	June 1	Sept. 30	$ 129	$ 71	$ 200
VT	White River Junction	Windsor	Oct. 1	Feb. 28	$ 101	$ 56	$ 157
VT	White River Junction	Windsor	Mar. 1	May 31	$ 89	$ 56	$ 145
VT	White River Junction	Windsor	June 1	Sept. 30	$ 101	$ 56	$ 157
WA	Anacortes / Coupeville / Oak Harbor	Skagit, Island, San Juan			$ 89	$ 61	$ 150
WA	Everett / Lynnwood	Snohomish			$ 96	$ 61	$ 157
WA	Ocean Shores	Grays Harbor	Oct. 1	June 30	$ 97	$ 51	$ 148
WA	Ocean Shores	Grays Harbor	July 1	Aug. 31	$ 117	$ 51	$ 168
WA	Ocean Shores	Grays Harbor	Sept. 1	Sept. 30	$ 97	$ 51	$ 148
WA	Olympia / Tumwater	Thurston			$ 88	$ 61	$ 149
WA	Pasco	Franklin			$ 93	$ 46	$ 139
WA	Port Angeles / Port Townsend	Clallam and Jefferson	Oct. 1	June 30	$ 93	$ 61	$ 154
WA	Port Angeles / Port Townsend	Clallam and Jefferson	July 1	Aug. 31	$ 123	$ 61	$ 184
WA	Port Angeles / Port Townsend	Clallam and Jefferson	Sept. 1	Sept. 30	$ 93	$ 61	$ 154
WA	Richland	Benton			$ 93	$ 46	$ 139
WA	Seattle	King			$ 137	$ 71	$ 208
WA	Spokane	Spokane			$ 87	$ 61	$ 148
WA	Tacoma	Pierce			$ 105	$ 61	$ 166
WA	Vancouver	Clark, Cowlitz and Skamania			$ 113	$ 56	$ 169
WI	Appleton	Outagamie			$ 82	$ 46	$ 128
WI	Brookfield / Racine	Waukesha / Racine			$ 88	$ 56	$ 144
WI	Lake Geneva	Walworth	Oct. 1	May 31	$ 91	$ 51	$ 142
WI	Lake Geneva	Walworth	June 1	Sept. 30	$ 118	$ 51	$ 169
WI	Madison	Dane			$ 89	$ 56	$ 145
WI	Milwaukee	Milwaukee			$ 97	$ 61	$ 158
WI	Sheboygan	Sheboygan			$ 79	$ 51	$ 130
WI	Sturgeon Bay	Door	Oct. 1	June 30	$ 77	$ 56	$ 133
WI	Sturgeon Bay	Door	July 1	Sept. 30	$ 83	$ 56	$ 139
WI	Wisconsin Dells	Columbia	Oct. 1	June 30	$ 77	$ 61	$ 138
WI	Wisconsin Dells	Columbia	July 1	Aug. 31	$ 90	$ 61	$ 151
WI	Wisconsin Dells	Columbia	Sept. 1	Sept. 30	$ 77	$ 61	$ 138

Table 3: Maximum Federal Per Diem Rates (Effective for 10/1/2012 - 9/30/2013 and updated on 4/1/2013).

State	Primary Destination	County	Season Begin Date	Season End Date	Lodging Rate	M&IE Rate	
WV	Charleston	Kanawha			$ 97	$ 51	$ 148
WV	Morgantown	Monongalia			$ 82	$ 46	$ 128
WV	Shepherdstown	Jefferson and Berkeley			$ 83	$ 51	$ 134
WV	Wheeling	Ohio			$ 94	$ 46	$ 140
WY	Cody	Park	Oct. 1	May 31	$ 91	$ 51	$ 142
WY	Cody	Park	June 1	Sept. 30	$ 120	$ 51	$ 171
WY	Evanston / Rock Springs	Sweetwater / Uinta			$ 79	$ 51	$ 130
WY	Gillette	Campbell	Oct. 1	May 31	$ 79	$ 51	$ 130
WY	Gillette	Campbell	June 1	Aug. 31	$ 88	$ 51	$ 139
WY	Gillette	Campbell	Sept. 1	Sept. 30	$ 79	$ 51	$ 130
WY	Jackson / Pinedale	Teton and Sublette	Oct. 1	June 30	$ 113	$ 56	$ 169
WY	Jackson / Pinedale	Teton and Sublette	July 1	Aug. 31	$ 163	$ 56	$ 219
WY	Jackson / Pinedale	Teton and Sublette	Sept. 1	Sept. 30	$ 113	$ 56	$ 169
WY	Sheridan	Sheridan	Oct. 1	May 31	$ 77	$ 56	$ 133
WY	Sheridan	Sheridan	June 1	Aug. 31	$ 88	$ 56	$ 144
WY	Sheridan	Sheridan	Sept. 1	Sept. 30	$ 77	$ 56	$ 133

NOTES:

Standard rate: The standard rate of $123 ($77 for lodging and $46 for M&IE) applies to all locations within the continental United States (CONUS) not specifically listed above or encompassed by the boundary definition of a listed point. However, the standard CONUS rate applies to all locations within CONUS, including those defined above, for certain relocation allowances. (See parts 302-2,302-4 and 302-5 of 41 CFR.)

Transition rule. In lieu of the updated GSA rates that will be effective October 1, 2013 (Table 4), taxpayers may continue to use the CONUS rates in effect for the first 9 months of 2013 (Table 3) for expenses of all CONUS travel away from home that are paid or incurred during calendar year 2013. A taxpayer must consistently use either these rates or the updated rates for the period of October 1, 2013, through December 31, 2013.

Per diem locality. Unless otherwise specified, the perdiem locality is defined as "all locations within, or entirely surrounded by, the corporate limits of the key city, including independent entities located within those boundaries."

Per diem localities with county defintions shall include "all locations within, or entirely surrounded by, the corporate limits of the key city as well as the boundaries of the listed counties, including independent entities within the boundaries of the key city and the listed counties (unless otherwise listed separately)."

When a military installation or Government-related facility (whether or not specifically named) is located partially within more than one city or county boundary, the aplicable per diem rate for the entire installation or facility is the higher of the two rates which apply to the cities and /or counties, even though part(s) of such activities may be located outside the defined per diem locality.

Recognizing that all locations are not incorporated cities, the term "city limits" has been used as a general phrase to denote the commonly recginzed local boundaries of the location cited.

[Sources: Revenue Procedure 2011-47, in Internal Revenue Bulletin 2011-42; U.S. General Services Administration, Domestic Per Diem Rates (available at http://www.gsa.gov)]

Table 4: Maximum Federal Per Diem Rates (Effective for 10/01/2013 - 9/30/2014)

State	Primary Destination	County	Season Begin Date	Season End Date	Lodging Rate	M&IE Rate	Total
	Standard CONUS rate applies to all counties not specifically listed. Cities not listed may be located in a listed county.				$83	$46	$129
AL	Birmingham	Jefferson and Shelby			$90	$56	$146
AL	Gulf Shores	Baldwin	Oct. 1	May 31	$104	$51	$155
AL	Gulf Shores	Baldwin	June 1	July 31	$133	$51	$184
AL	Gulf Shores	Baldwin	Aug. 1	Sept. 30	$104	$51	$155
AL	Huntsville	Madison and Limestone			$88	$51	$139
AL	Mobile	Mobile	Oct. 1	Dec. 31	$86	$51	$137
AL	Mobile	Mobile	Jan. 1	Feb. 28	$95	$51	$146
AL	Mobile	Mobile	Mar. 1	Sept. 30	$86	$51	$137
AR	Hot Springs	Garland			$99	$46	$145
AR	Little Rock	Pulaski			$87	$61	$148
AZ	Grand Canyon / Flagstaff	Coconino / Yavapai less the city of Sedona	Oct. 1	Oct. 31	$101	$66	$167
AZ	Grand Canyon / Flagstaff	Coconino / Yavapai less the city of Sedona	Nov. 1	Feb. 28	$83	$66	$149
AZ	Grand Canyon / Flagstaff	Coconino / Yavapai less the city of Sedona	Mar. 1	Sept. 30	$101	$66	$167
AZ	Phoenix / Scottsdale	Maricopa	Oct. 1	Dec. 31	$106	$71	$177
AZ	Phoenix / Scottsdale	Maricopa	Jan. 1	Apr. 30	$133	$71	$204
AZ	Phoenix / Scottsdale	Maricopa	May 1	Aug. 31	$88	$71	$159
AZ	Phoenix / Scottsdale	Maricopa	Sept. 1	Sept. 30	$106	$71	$177
AZ	Sedona	City Limits of Sedona	Oct. 1	Feb. 28	$123	$66	$189
AZ	Sedona	City Limits of Sedona	Mar. 1	Apr. 30	$147	$66	$213
AZ	Sedona	City Limits of Sedona	May 1	Sept. 30	$123	$66	$189
AZ	Tucson	Pima	Oct. 1	Jan. 31	$86	$56	$142
AZ	Tucson	Pima	Feb. 1	May 31	$99	$56	$155
AZ	Tucson	Pima	June 1	Aug. 31	$83	$56	$139
AZ	Tucson	Pima	Sept. 1	Sept. 30	$86	$56	$142
CA	Antioch / Brentwood / Concord	Contra Costa			$117	$66	$183
CA	Bakersfield / Ridgecrest	Kern County			$94	$51	$145
CA	Barstow / Ontario / Victorville	San Bernardino			$99	$56	$155
CA	Death Valley	Inyo			$94	$46	$140
CA	Eureka / Arcata / McKinleyville	Humboldt	Oct. 1	May 31	$87	$61	$148
CA	Eureka / Arcata / McKinleyville	Humboldt	June 1	Aug. 31	$102	$61	$163
CA	Eureka / Arcata / McKinleyville	Humboldt	Sept. 1	Sept. 30	$87	$61	$148
CA	Fresno	Fresno			$85	$61	$146
CA	Los Angeles	Los Angeles, Orange, Ventura, and Edwards AFB, less the city of Santa Monica			$133	$71	$204
CA	Mammoth Lakes	Mono			$129	$61	$190
CA	Mill Valley / San Rafael / Novato	Marin			$122	$56	$178
CA	Modesto	Stanislaus			$84	$51	$135
CA	Monterey	Monterey	Oct. 1	June 30	$123	$71	$194
CA	Monterey	Monterey	July 1	Aug. 31	$156	$71	$227
CA	Monterey	Monterey	Sept. 1	Sept. 30	$123	$71	$194

Table 4: Maximum Federal Per Diem Rates (Effective for 10/01/2013 - 9/30/2014)

State	Primary Destination	County	Season Begin Date	Season End Date	Lodging Rate	M&IE Rate	Total
CA	Napa	Napa	Oct. 1	Nov. 30	$163	$66	$229
CA	Napa	Napa	Dec. 1	Mar. 31	$127	$66	$193
CA	Napa	Napa	Apr. 1	Sept. 30	$163	$66	$229
CA	Oakhurst	Madera	Oct. 1	Apr. 30	$83	$56	$139
CA	Oakhurst	Madera	May 1	Sept. 30	$102	$56	$158
CA	Oakland	Alameda			$112	$61	$173
CA	Palm Springs	Riverside	Oct. 1	Dec. 31	$105	$71	$176
CA	Palm Springs	Riverside	Jan. 1	May 31	$125	$71	$196
CA	Palm Springs	Riverside	June 1	Aug. 31	$86	$71	$157
CA	Palm Springs	Riverside	Sept. 1	Sept. 30	$105	$71	$176
CA	Point Arena / Gualala	Mendocino			$93	$66	$159
CA	Redding	Shasta			$89	$61	$150
CA	Sacramento	Sacramento			$102	$61	$163
CA	San Diego	San Diego			$139	$71	$210
CA	San Francisco	San Francisco	Oct. 1	Oct. 31	$226	$71	$297
CA	San Francisco	San Francisco	Nov. 1	Dec. 31	$172	$71	$243
CA	San Francisco	San Francisco	Jan. 1	Aug. 31	$189	$71	$260
CA	San Francisco	San Francisco	Sept. 1	Sept. 30	$226	$71	$297
CA	San Luis Obispo	San Luis Obispo	Oct. 1	June 30	$105	$66	$171
CA	San Luis Obispo	San Luis Obispo	July 1	Aug. 31	$126	$66	$192
CA	San Luis Obispo	San Luis Obispo	Sept. 1	Sept. 30	$105	$66	$171
CA	San Mateo / Foster City / Belmont	San Mateo	Oct. 1	Oct. 31	$140	$61	$201
CA	San Mateo / Foster City / Belmont	San Mateo	Nov. 1	Jan. 31	$129	$61	$190
CA	San Mateo / Foster City / Belmont	San Mateo	Feb. 1	Sept. 30	$140	$61	$201
CA	Santa Barbara	Santa Barbara	Oct. 1	June 30	$148	$66	$214
CA	Santa Barbara	Santa Barbara	July 1	Aug. 31	$193	$66	$259
CA	Santa Barbara	Santa Barbara	Sept. 1	Sept. 30	$148	$66	$214
CA	Santa Cruz	Santa Cruz	Oct. 1	May 31	$122	$66	$188
CA	Santa Cruz	Santa Cruz	June 1	Aug. 31	$159	M&IE	$225
CA	Santa Cruz	Santa Cruz	Sept. 1	Sept. 30	$122	$66	$188
CA	Santa Monica	City limits of Santa Monica	Oct. 1	May 31	$183	$71	$254
CA	Santa Monica	City limits of Santa Monica	June 1	Aug. 31	$216	$71	$287
CA	Santa Monica	City limits of Santa Monica	Sept. 1	Sept. 30	$183	$71	$254
CA	Santa Rosa	Sonoma			$114	$61	$175
CA	South Lake Tahoe	El Dorado			$109	$71	$180
CA	Stockton	San Joaquin			$89	$56	$145
CA	Sunnyvale / Palo Alto / San Jose	Santa Clara			$144	$56	$200
CA	Tahoe City	Placer			$84	$61	$145
CA	Truckee	Nevada			$107	$71	$178
CA	Visalia / Lemoore	Tulare and Kings			$84	$61	$145
CA	West Sacramento / Davis	Yolo			$106	$51	$157
CA	Yosemite National Park	Mariposa	Oct. 1	May 31	$133	$71	$204
CA	Yosemite National Park	Mariposa	June 1	Aug. 31	$178	$71	$249
CA	Yosemite National Park	Mariposa	Sept. 1	Sept. 30	$133	$71	$204
CO	Aspen	Pitkin	Oct. 1	Nov. 30	$122	$71	$193

Table 4: Maximum Federal Per Diem Rates (Effective for 10/01/2013 - 9/30/2014)

State	Primary Destination	County	Season Begin Date	Season End Date	Lodging Rate	M&IE Rate	Total
CO	Aspen	Pitkin	Dec. 1	Mar. 31	$247	$71	$318
CO	Aspen	Pitkin	Apr. 1	May 31	$120	$71	$191
CO	Aspen	Pitkin	June 1	Aug. 31	$213	$71	$284
CO	Aspen	Pitkin	Sept. 1	Sept. 30	$122	$71	$193
CO	Boulder / Broomfield	Boulder and Broomfield			$111	$61	$172
CO	Colorado Springs	El Paso			$87	$66	$153
CO	Cortez	Montezuma	Oct. 1	May 31	$87	$51	$138
CO	Cortez	Montezuma	June 1	Sept. 30	$109	$51	$160
CO	Crested Butte / Gunnison	Gunnison	Oct. 1	May 31	$83	$51	$134
CO	Crested Butte / Gunnison	Gunnison	June 1	Aug. 31	$94	$51	$145
CO	Crested Butte / Gunnison	Gunnison	Sept. 1	Sept. 30	$83	$51	$134
CO	Denver / Aurora	Denver, Adams, Arapahoe, and Jefferson			$156	$66	$222
CO	Douglas County	Douglas			$104	$61	$165
CO	Durango	La Plata	Oct. 1	May 31	$97	$61	$158
CO	Durango	La Plata	June 1	Sept. 30	$138	$61	$199
CO	Fort Collins / Loveland	Larimer			$91	$56	$147
CO	Glenwood Springs / Grand Junction	Garfield / Mesa			$84	$51	$135
CO	Montrose	Montrose	Oct. 1	May 31	$83	$56	$139
CO	Montrose	Montrose	June 1	Sept. 30	$92	$56	$148
CO	Silverthorne / Breckenridge	Summit	Oct. 1	Nov. 30	$92	$56	$148
CO	Silverthorne / Breckenridge	Summit	Dec. 1	Mar. 31	$132	$56	$188
CO	Silverthorne / Breckenridge	Summit	Apr. 1	May 31	$86	$56	$142
CO	Silverthorne / Breckenridge	Summit	June 1	Sept. 30	$92	$56	$148
CO	Steamboat Springs	Routt	Oct. 1	Nov. 30	$99	$56	$155
CO	Steamboat Springs	Routt	Dec. 1	Mar. 31	$158	$56	$214
CO	Steamboat Springs	Routt	Apr. 1	Sept. 30	$99	$56	$155
CO	Telluride	San Miguel	Oct. 1	Nov. 30	$107	$71	$178
CO	Telluride	San Miguel	Dec. 1	Mar. 31	$222	$71	$293
CO	Telluride	San Miguel	Apr. 1	May 31	$129	$71	$200
CO	Telluride	San Miguel	June 1	Sept. 30	$221	$71	$292
CO	Vail	Eagle	Oct. 1	Nov. 30	$114	$71	$185
CO	Vail	Eagle	Dec. 1	Mar. 31	$297	$71	$368
CO	Vail	Eagle	Apr. 1	Aug. 31	$142	$71	$213
CO	Vail	Eagle	Sept. 1	Sept. 30	$114	$71	$185
CT	Bridgeport / Danbury	Fairfield			$121	$71	$192
CT	Cromwell / Old Saybrook	Middlesex			$92	$61	$153
CT	Hartford	Hartford			$112	$56	$168
CT	Lakeville / Salisbury	Litchfield			$100	$66	$166
CT	New Haven	New Haven			$92	$61	$153
CT	New London / Groton	New London			$97	$61	$158
DC	District of Columbia	Washington DC (also the cities of Alexandria, Falls Church and Fairfax, and the counties of Arlington and Fairfax, in Virginia; and the counties of Montgomery and Prince George's in Maryland)	Oct. 1	Oct. 31	$219	$71	$290

Table 4: Maximum Federal Per Diem Rates (Effective for 10/01/2013 - 9/30/2014)

State	Primary Destination	County	Season Begin Date	Season End Date	Lodging Rate	M&IE Rate	Total
DC	District of Columbia	Washington DC (also the cities of Alexandria, Falls Church and Fairfax, and the counties of Arlington and Fairfax, in Virginia; and the counties of Montgomery and Prince George's in Maryland)	Nov. 1	Feb. 28	$184	$71	$255
DC	District of Columbia	Washington DC (also the cities of Alexandria, Falls Church and Fairfax, and the counties of Arlington and Fairfax, in Virginia; and the counties of Montgomery and Prince George's in Maryland)	Mar. 1	June 30	$224	$71	$295
DC	District of Columbia	Washington DC (also the cities of Alexandria, Falls Church and Fairfax, and the counties of Arlington and Fairfax, in Virginia; and the counties of Montgomery and Prince George's in Maryland)	July 1	Aug. 31	$167	$71	$238
DC	District of Columbia	Washington DC (also the cities of Alexandria, Falls Church and Fairfax, and the counties of Arlington and Fairfax, in Virginia; and the counties of Montgomery and Prince George's in Maryland)	Sept. 1	Sept. 30	$219	$71	$290
DE	Dover	Kent	Oct. 1	Apr. 30	$83	$46	$129
DE	Dover	Kent	May 1	Sept. 30	$103	$46	$149
DE	Lewes	Sussex	Oct. 1	June 30	$88	$46	$134
DE	Lewes	Sussex	July 1	Aug. 31	$133	$46	$179
DE	Lewes	Sussex	Sept. 1	Sept. 30	$88	$46	$134
DE	Wilmington	New Castle			$115	$56	$171
FL	Boca Raton / Delray Beach / Jupiter	Palm Beach / Hendry	Oct. 1	Dec. 31	$93	$71	$164
FL	Boca Raton / Delray Beach / Jupiter	Palm Beach / Hendry	Jan. 1	Apr. 30	$142	$71	$213
FL	Boca Raton / Delray Beach / Jupiter	Palm Beach / Hendry	May 1	Sept. 30	$93	$71	$164
FL	Bradenton	Manatee	Oct. 1	Jan. 31	$83	$56	$139
FL	Bradenton	Manatee	Feb. 1	Apr. 30	$105	$56	$161
FL	Bradenton	Manatee	May 1	Sept. 30	$83	$56	$139
FL	Cocoa Beach	Brevard			$103	$51	$154
FL	Daytona Beach	Volusia	Oct. 1	Jan. 31	$83	$51	$134
FL	Daytona Beach	Volusia	Feb. 1	July 31	$97	$51	$148
FL	Daytona Beach	Volusia	Aug. 1	Sept. 30	$83	$51	$134
FL	Fort Lauderdale	Broward	Oct. 1	Dec. 31	$134	$71	$205
FL	Fort Lauderdale	Broward	Jan. 1	Mar. 31	$180	$71	$251
FL	Fort Lauderdale	Broward	Apr. 1	May 31	$147	$71	$218
FL	Fort Lauderdale	Broward	June 1	Sept. 30	$108	$71	$179
FL	Fort Myers	Lee	Oct. 1	Dec. 31	$88	$56	$144
FL	Fort Myers	Lee	Jan. 1	Apr. 30	$128	$56	$184
FL	Fort Myers	Lee	May 1	Sept. 30	$88	$56	$144
FL	Fort Walton Beach / De Funiak Springs	Okaloosa and Walton	Oct. 1	Oct. 31	$126	$51	$177
FL	Fort Walton Beach / De Funiak Springs	Okaloosa and Walton	Nov. 1	Feb. 28	$83	$51	$134

Table 4: Maximum Federal Per Diem Rates (Effective for 10/01/2013 - 9/30/2014)

State	Primary Destination	County	Season Begin Date	Season End Date	Lodging Rate	M&IE Rate	Total
FL	Fort Walton Beach / De Funiak Springs	Okaloosa and Walton	Mar. 1	May 31	$142	$51	$193
FL	Fort Walton Beach / De Funiak Springs	Okaloosa and Walton	June 1	July 31	$188	$51	$239
FL	Fort Walton Beach / De Funiak Springs	Okaloosa and Walton	Aug. 1	Sept. 30	$126	$51	$177
FL	Gainesville	Alachua			$91	$51	$142
FL	Gulf Breeze	Santa Rosa			$87	$51	$138
FL	Key West	Monroe	Oct. 1	Nov. 30	$167	$71	$238
FL	Key West	Monroe	Dec. 1	Jan. 31	$210	$71	$281
FL	Key West	Monroe	Feb. 1	Apr. 30	$246	$71	$317
FL	Key West	Monroe	May 1	Sept. 30	$167	$71	$238
FL	Miami	Miami-Dade	Oct. 1	Dec. 31	$140	$66	$206
FL	Miami	Miami-Dade	Jan. 1	Mar. 31	$187	$66	$253
FL	Miami	Miami-Dade	Apr. 1	May 31	$138	$66	$204
FL	Miami	Miami-Dade	June 1	Sept. 30	$109	$66	$175
FL	Naples	Collier	Oct. 1	Dec. 31	$121	$61	$182
FL	Naples	Collier	Jan. 1	Apr. 30	$186	$61	$247
FL	Naples	Collier	May 1	Sept. 30	$105	$61	$166
FL	Orlando	Orange	Oct. 1	Dec. 31	$101	$56	$157
FL	Orlando	Orange	Jan. 1	Apr. 30	$123	$56	$179
FL	Orlando	Orange	May 1	Sept. 30	$101	$56	$157
FL	Panama City	Bay	Oct. 1	Feb. 28	$83	$51	$134
FL	Panama City	Bay	Mar. 1	July 31	$113	$51	$164
FL	Panama City	Bay	Aug. 1	Sept. 30	$83	$51	$134
FL	Pensacola	Escambia			$102	$46	$148
FL	Punta Gorda	Charlotte	Oct. 1	Jan. 31	$83	$51	$134
FL	Punta Gorda	Charlotte	Feb. 1	Mar. 31	$100	$51	$151
FL	Punta Gorda	Charlotte	Apr. 1	Sept. 30	$83	$51	$134
FL	Sarasota	Sarasota	Oct. 1	Jan. 31	$94	$56	$150
FL	Sarasota	Sarasota	Feb. 1	Apr. 30	$128	$56	$184
FL	Sarasota	Sarasota	May 1	Sept. 30	$94	$56	$150
FL	Sebring	Highlands	Oct. 1	Dec. 31	$83	$46	$129
FL	Sebring	Highlands	Jan. 1	Mar. 31	$117	$46	$163
FL	Sebring	Highlands	Apr. 1	Sept. 30	$83	$46	$129
FL	St. Augustine	St. Johns			$102	$56	$158
FL	Stuart	Martin	Oct. 1	Dec. 31	$83	$51	$134
FL	Stuart	Martin	Jan. 1	Apr. 30	$96	$51	$147
FL	Stuart	Martin	May 1	Sept. 30	$83	$51	$134
FL	Tallahassee	Leon	Oct. 1	Dec. 31	$83	$46	$129
FL	Tallahassee	Leon	Jan. 1	Apr. 30	$94	$46	$140
FL	Tallahassee	Leon	May 1	Sept. 30	$83	$46	$129
FL	Tampa / St. Petersburg	Pinellas and Hillsborough	Oct. 1	Dec. 31	$99	$51	$150
FL	Tampa / St. Petersburg	Pinellas and Hillsborough	Jan. 1	Apr. 30	$116	$51	$167
FL	Tampa / St. Petersburg	Pinellas and Hillsborough	May 1	Sept. 30	$99	$51	$150
FL	Vero Beach	Indian River	Oct. 1	Jan. 31	$101	$51	$152

Table 4: Maximum Federal Per Diem Rates (Effective for 10/01/2013 - 9/30/2014)

State	Primary Destination	County	Season Begin Date	Season End Date	Lodging Rate	M&IE Rate	Total
FL	Vero Beach	Indian River	Feb. 1	Apr. 30	$139	$51	$190
FL	Vero Beach	Indian River	May 1	Sept. 30	$101	$51	$152
GA	Athens	Clarke			$90	$46	$136
GA	Atlanta	Fulton, Dekalb and Cobb			$133	$56	$189
GA	Augusta	Richmond			$91	$51	$142
GA	Jekyll Island / Brunswick	Glynn	Oct. 1	Nov. 30	$143	$56	$199
GA	Jekyll Island / Brunswick	Glynn	Dec. 1	Feb. 28	$110	$56	$166
GA	Jekyll Island / Brunswick	Glynn	Mar. 1	Sept. 30	$143	$56	$199
GA	Savannah	Chatham			$98	$56	$154
IA	Cedar Rapids	Linn			$86	$51	$137
IA	Dallas County	Dallas			$109	$51	$160
IA	Des Moines	Polk			$93	$51	$144
ID	Bonner's Ferry / Sandpoint	Bonner / Boundary / Shoshone	Oct. 1	June 30	$83	$61	$144
ID	Bonner's Ferry / Sandpoint	Bonner / Boundary / Shoshone	July 1	Aug. 31	$107	$61	$168
ID	Bonner's Ferry / Sandpoint	Bonner / Boundary / Shoshone	Sept. 1	Sept. 30	$83	$61	$144
ID	Coeur d'Alene	Kootenai	Oct. 1	May 31	$85	$61	$146
ID	Coeur d'Alene	Kootenai	June 1	Aug. 31	$126	$61	$187
ID	Coeur d'Alene	Kootenai	Sept. 1	Sept. 30	$85	$61	$146
ID	Driggs / Idaho Falls	Bonneville / Fremont / Teton			$84	$46	$130
ID	Sun Valley / Ketchum	Blaine	Oct. 1	June 30	$93	$71	$164
ID	Sun Valley / Ketchum	Blaine	July 1	Aug. 31	$116	$71	$187
ID	Sun Valley / Ketchum	Blaine	Sept. 1	Sept. 30	$93	$71	$164
IL	Bolingbrook / Romeoville / Lemont	Will			$88	$51	$139
IL	Chicago	Cook and Lake	Oct. 1	Nov. 30	$209	$71	$280
IL	Chicago	Cook and Lake	Dec. 1	Feb. 28	$128	$71	$199
IL	Chicago	Cook and Lake	Mar. 1	June 30	$186	$71	$257
IL	Chicago	Cook and Lake	July 1	Aug. 31	$166	$71	$237
IL	Chicago	Cook and Lake	Sept. 1	Sept. 30	$209	$71	$280
IL	Oak Brook Terrace	Dupage			$100	$61	$161
IL	O'Fallon / Fairview Heights / Collinsville	Bond, Calhoun, Clinton, Jersey, Macoupin, Madison, Monroe and St. Clair			$108	$56	$164
IL	Springfield	Sangamon			$85	$56	$141
IN	Bloomington	Monroe			$102	$56	$158
IN	Ft. Wayne	Allen			$87	$56	$143
IN	Hammond / Munster / Merrillville	Lake			$89	$46	$135
IN	Indianapolis / Carmel	Marion, Hamilton			$95	$61	$156
IN	Lafayette / West Lafayette	Tippecanoe			$86	$51	$137
IN	South Bend	St. Joseph			$88	$56	$144
KS	Kansas City / Overland Park	Wyandotte / Johnson / Leavenworth			$106	$61	$167
KS	Wichita	Sedgwick			$92	$56	$148
KY	Boone County	Boone			$88	$51	$139
KY	Kenton County	Kenton			$127	$56	$183
KY	Lexington	Fayette			$95	$61	$156
KY	Louisville	Jefferson	Oct. 1	Jan. 31	$100	$61	$161

Table 4: Maximum Federal Per Diem Rates (Effective for 10/01/2013 - 9/30/2014)

State	Primary Destination	County	Season Begin Date	Season End Date	Lodging Rate	M&IE Rate	Total
KY	Louisville	Jefferson	Feb. 1	May 31	$115	$61	$176
KY	Louisville	Jefferson	June 1	Sept. 30	$100	$61	$161
LA	Alexandria / Leesville / Natchitoches	Allen / Jefferson Davis / Natchitoches / Rapides / Vernon Parishes			$84	$61	$145
LA	Baton Rouge	East Baton Rouge Parish			$97	$56	$153
LA	Covington / Slidell	St. Tammany Parish			$91	$56	$147
LA	New Orleans	Orleans, St. Bernard, Jefferson and Plaquemine Parishes	Oct. 1	Dec. 31	$140	$71	$211
LA	New Orleans	Orleans, St. Bernard, Jefferson and Plaquemine Parishes	Jan. 1	June 30	$151	$71	$222
LA	New Orleans	Orleans, St. Bernard, Jefferson and Plaquemine Parishes	July 1	Sept. 30	$108	$71	$179
MA	Andover	Essex			$98	$56	$154
MA	Boston / Cambridge	Suffolk, city of Cambridge	Oct. 1	Oct. 31	$237	$71	$308
MA	Boston / Cambridge	Suffolk, city of Cambridge	Nov. 1	Mar. 31	$170	$71	$241
MA	Boston / Cambridge	Suffolk, city of Cambridge	Apr. 1	June 30	$229	$71	$300
MA	Boston / Cambridge	Suffolk, city of Cambridge	July 1	Aug. 31	$207	$71	$278
MA	Boston / Cambridge	Suffolk, city of Cambridge	Sept. 1	Sept. 30	$237	$71	$308
MA	Burlington / Woburn	Middlesex less the city of Cambridge			$124	$71	$195
MA	Falmouth	City limits of Falmouth	Oct. 1	Apr. 30	$103	$51	$154
MA	Falmouth	City limits of Falmouth	May 1	June 30	$122	$51	$173
MA	Falmouth	City limits of Falmouth	July 1	Aug. 31	$175	$51	$226
MA	Falmouth	City limits of Falmouth	Sept. 1	Sept. 30	$103	$51	$154
MA	Hyannis	Barnstable less the city of Falmouth	Oct. 1	June 30	$93	$56	$149
MA	Hyannis	Barnstable less the city of Falmouth	July 1	Aug. 31	$147	$56	$203
MA	Hyannis	Barnstable less the city of Falmouth	Sept. 1	Sept. 30	$93	$56	$149
MA	Martha's Vineyard	Dukes	Oct. 1	June 30	$128	$71	$199
MA	Martha's Vineyard	Dukes	July 1	Aug. 31	$264	$71	$335
MA	Martha's Vineyard	Dukes	Sept. 1	Sept. 30	$128	$71	$199
MA	Nantucket	Nantucket	Oct. 1	May 31	$138	$61	$199
MA	Nantucket	Nantucket	June 1	Sept. 30	$267	$61	$328
MA	Northampton	Hampshire			$102	$56	$158
MA	Pittsfield	Berkshire	Oct. 1	June 30	$110	$61	$171
MA	Pittsfield	Berkshire	July 1	Aug. 31	$134	$61	$195
MA	Pittsfield	Berkshire	Sept. 1	Sept. 30	$110	$61	$171
MA	Plymouth / Taunton / New Bedford	Plymouth / Bristol			$98	$56	$154
MA	Quincy	Norfolk			$129	$51	$180
MA	Springfield	Hampden			$102	$51	$153
MA	Worcester	Worcester			$102	$61	$163
MD	Aberdeen / Bel Air / Belcamp	Harford			$93	$56	$149
MD	Annapolis	Anne Arundel	Oct. 1	Oct. 31	$121	$61	$182
MD	Annapolis	Anne Arundel	Nov. 1	Apr. 30	$101	$61	$162
MD	Annapolis	Anne Arundel	May 1	Sept. 30	$121	$61	$182
MD	Baltimore City	Baltimore City	Oct. 1	Nov. 30	$147	$71	$218
MD	Baltimore City	Baltimore City	Dec. 1	Feb. 28	$119	$71	$190

Table 4: Maximum Federal Per Diem Rates (Effective for 10/01/2013 - 9/30/2014)

State	Primary Destination	County	Season Begin Date	Season End Date	Lodging Rate	M&IE Rate	Total
MD	Baltimore City	Baltimore City	Mar. 1	Sept. 30	$147	$71	$218
MD	Baltimore County	Baltimore			$98	$61	$159
MD	Cambridge / St. Michaels	Dorchester and Talbot	Oct. 1	Oct. 31	$134	$61	$195
MD	Cambridge / St. Michaels	Dorchester and Talbot	Nov. 1	Mar. 31	$114	$61	$175
MD	Cambridge / St. Michaels	Dorchester and Talbot	Apr. 1	May 31	$137	$61	$198
MD	Cambridge / St. Michaels	Dorchester and Talbot	June 1	Aug. 31	$170	$61	$231
MD	Cambridge / St. Michaels	Dorchester and Talbot	Sept. 1	Sept. 30	$134	$61	$195
MD	Centreville	Queen Anne			$115	$51	$166
MD	Columbia	Howard			$104	$61	$165
MD	Frederick	Frederick			$100	$56	$156
MD	Lexington Park / Leonardtown / Lusby	St. Mary's and Calvert			$98	$61	$159
MD	Ocean City	Worcester	Oct. 1	Oct. 31	$97	$71	$168
MD	Ocean City	Worcester	Nov. 1	Mar. 31	$83	$71	$154
MD	Ocean City	Worcester	Apr. 1	May 31	$87	$71	$158
MD	Ocean City	Worcester	June 1	Aug. 31	$189	$71	$260
MD	Ocean City	Worcester	Sept. 1	Sept. 30	$97	$71	$168
ME	Bar Harbor	Hancock	Oct. 1	Oct. 31	$119	$61	$180
ME	Bar Harbor	Hancock	Nov. 1	June 30	$95	$61	$156
ME	Bar Harbor	Hancock	July 1	Aug. 31	$155	$61	$216
ME	Bar Harbor	Hancock	Sept. 1	Sept. 30	$119	$61	$180
ME	Kennebunk / Kittery / Sanford	York	Oct. 1	June 30	$105	$56	$161
ME	Kennebunk / Kittery / Sanford	York	July 1	Aug. 31	$142	$56	$198
ME	Kennebunk / Kittery / Sanford	York	Sept. 1	Sept. 30	$105	$56	$161
ME	Portland	Cumberland / Sagadahoc	Oct. 1	June 30	$98	$56	$154
ME	Portland	Cumberland / Sagadahoc	July 1	Sept. 30	$128	$56	$184
ME	Rockport	Knox			$86	$56	$142
MI	Ann Arbor	Washtenaw			$99	$56	$155
MI	Benton Harbor / St. Joseph / Stevensville	Berrien			$91	$51	$142
MI	Detroit	Wayne			$100	$56	$156
MI	East Lansing / Lansing	Ingham and Eaton			$86	$51	$137
MI	Grand Rapids	Kent			$88	$51	$139
MI	Holland	Ottawa			$93	$56	$149
MI	Kalamazoo / Battle Creek	Kalamazoo / Calhoun			$89	$51	$140
MI	Mackinac Island	Mackinac	Oct. 1	June 30	$83	$66	$149
MI	Mackinac Island	Mackinac	July 1	Aug. 31	$94	$66	$160
MI	Mackinac Island	Mackinac	Sept. 1	Sept. 30	$83	$66	$149
MI	Midland	Midland			$94	$46	$140
MI	Muskegon	Muskegon	Oct. 1	May 31	$83	$46	$129
MI	Muskegon	Muskegon	June 1	Aug. 31	$102	$46	$148
MI	Muskegon	Muskegon	Sept. 1	Sept. 30	$83	$46	$129
MI	Petoskey	Emmet	Oct. 1	June 30	$83	$51	$134
MI	Petoskey	Emmet	July 1	Aug. 31	$112	$51	$163
MI	Petoskey	Emmet	Sept. 1	Sept. 30	$83	$51	$134

Table 4: Maximum Federal Per Diem Rates (Effective for 10/01/2013 - 9/30/2014)

State	Primary Destination	County	Season Begin Date	Season End Date	Lodging Rate	M&IE Rate	Total
MI	Pontiac / Auburn Hills	Oakland			$90	$56	$146
MI	South Haven	Van Buren	Oct. 1	May 31	$83	$56	$139
MI	South Haven	Van Buren	June 1	Aug. 31	$102	$56	$158
MI	South Haven	Van Buren	Sept. 1	Sept. 30	$83	$56	$139
MI	Traverse City and Leland	Grand Traverse and Leelanau	Oct. 1	June 30	$87	$51	$138
MI	Traverse City and Leland	Grand Traverse and Leelanau	July 1	Aug. 31	$150	$51	$201
MI	Traverse City and Leland	Grand Traverse and Leelanau	Sept. 1	Sept. 30	$87	$51	$138
MN	Duluth	St. Louis	Oct. 1	Oct. 31	$106	$56	$162
MN	Duluth	St. Louis	Nov. 1	May 31	$88	$56	$144
MN	Duluth	St. Louis	June 1	Sept. 30	$106	$56	$162
MN	Eagan / Burnsville / Mendota Heights	Dakota			$86	$56	$142
MN	Minneapolis / St. Paul	Hennepin and Ramsey			$133	$71	$204
MN	Rochester	Olmsted			$108	$51	$159
MO	Kansas City	Jackson, Clay, Cass, Platte			$106	$61	$167
MO	St. Louis	St. Louis, St. Louis City and St. Charles, Crawford, Franklin, Jefferson, Lincoln, Warren and Washington			$108	$66	$174
MS	Hattiesburg	Forrest and Lamar			$85	$51	$136
MS	Oxford	Lafayette			$102	$51	$153
MS	Southaven	Desoto			$92	$46	$138
MS	Starkville	Oktibbeha			$99	$46	$145
MT	Big Sky / West Yellowstone	Gallatin	Oct. 1	May 31	$83	$61	$144
MT	Big Sky / West Yellowstone	Gallatin	June 1	Sept. 30	$117	$61	$178
MT	Butte	Silver Bow			$88	$51	$139
MT	Glendive / Sidney	Dawson / Richland			$105	$56	$161
MT	Helena	Lewis and Clark			$88	$56	$144
MT	Missoula / Polson / Kalispell	Missoula / Lake / Flathead	Oct. 1	June 30	$89	$51	$140
MT	Missoula / Polson / Kalispell	Missoula / Lake / Flathead	July 1	Aug. 31	$114	$51	$165
MT	Missoula / Polson / Kalispell	Missoula / Lake / Flathead	Sept. 1	Sept. 30	$89	$51	$140
NC	Asheville	Buncombe			$97	$51	$148
NC	Atlantic Beach / Morehead City	Carteret	Oct. 1	May 31	$83	$56	$139
NC	Atlantic Beach / Morehead City	Carteret	June 1	Aug. 31	$105	$56	$161
NC	Atlantic Beach / Morehead City	Carteret	Sept. 1	Sept. 30	$83	$56	$139
NC	Chapel Hill	Orange			$92	$56	$148
NC	Charlotte	Mecklenburg			$110	$51	$161
NC	Durham	Durham			$89	$51	$140
NC	Fayetteville	Cumberland			$95	$51	$146
NC	Greensboro	Guilford			$90	$56	$146
NC	Kill Devil	Dare	Oct. 1	May 31	$95	$61	$156
NC	Kill Devil	Dare	June 1	Aug. 31	$155	$61	$216
NC	Kill Devil	Dare	Sept. 1	Sept. 30	$95	$61	$156
NC	New Bern / Havelock	Craven			$90	$46	$136
NC	Raleigh	Wake			$96	$66	$162
NC	Wilmington	New Hanover			$92	$56	$148
ND	Dickinson / Beulah	Stark, Mercer, Billings Counties			$120	$56	$176

Table 4: Maximum Federal Per Diem Rates (Effective for 10/01/2013 - 9/30/2014)

State	Primary Destination	County	Season Begin Date	Season End Date	Lodging Rate	M&IE Rate	Total
ND	Minot	Ward County			$125	$56	$181
ND	Williston	Williams, Mountrail, McKenzie			$105	$56	$161
NE	Omaha	Douglas			$100	$61	$161
NH	Concord	Merrimack			$88	$51	$139
NH	Conway	Caroll	Oct. 1	Feb. 28	$112	$61	$173
NH	Conway	Caroll	Mar. 1	June 30	$95	$61	$156
NH	Conway	Caroll	July 1	Aug. 31	$155	$61	$216
NH	Conway	Caroll	Sept. 1	Sept. 30	$112	$61	$173
NH	Durham	Strafford			$96	$46	$142
NH	Laconia	Belknap	Oct. 1	Oct. 31	$117	$51	$168
NH	Laconia	Belknap	Nov. 1	May 31	$96	$51	$147
NH	Laconia	Belknap	June 1	Sept. 30	$117	$51	$168
NH	Lebanon / Lincoln / West Lebanon	Grafton / Sullivan			$112	$56	$168
NH	Manchester	Hillsborough			$91	$56	$147
NH	Portsmouth	Rockingham	Oct. 1	June 30	$100	$61	$161
NH	Portsmouth	Rockingham	July 1	Sept. 30	$129	$61	$190
NJ	Atlantic City / Ocean City / Cape May	Atlantic and Cape May			$92	$66	$158
NJ	Belle Mead	Somerset			$133	$56	$189
NJ	Cherry Hill / Moorestown	Camden and Burlington			$96	$61	$157
NJ	Eatontown / Freehold	Monmouth			$104	$56	$160
NJ	Edison / Piscataway	Middlesex			$118	$51	$169
NJ	Flemington	Hunterdon			$110	$61	$171
NJ	Newark	Essex, Bergen, Hudson and Passaic			$132	$61	$193
NJ	Parsippany	Morris			$133	$56	$189
NJ	Princeton / Trenton	Mercer			$124	$61	$185
NJ	Springfield / Cranford / New Providence	Union			$110	$56	$166
NJ	Toms River	Ocean	Oct. 1	May 31	$83	$51	$134
NJ	Toms River	Ocean	June 1	Aug. 31	$100	$51	$151
NJ	Toms River	Ocean	Sept. 1	Sept. 30	$83	$51	$134
NM	Carlsbad	Eddy			$105	$51	$156
NM	Las Cruces	Dona Ana			$88	$56	$144
NM	Los Alamos	Los Alamos			$86	$51	$137
NM	Santa Fe	Santa Fe			$88	$71	$159
NM	Taos	Taos			$90	$66	$156
NV	Incline Village / Reno / Sparks	Washoe	Oct. 1	June 30	$93	$51	$144
NV	Incline Village / Reno / Sparks	Washoe	July 1	Aug. 31	$125	$51	$176
NV	Incline Village / Reno / Sparks	Washoe	Sept. 1	Sept. 30	$93	$51	$144
NV	Las Vegas	Clark			$92	$71	$163
NV	Stateline, Carson City	Douglas, Carson City			$88	$61	$149
NY	Albany	Albany			$111	$61	$172
NY	Binghamton / Owego	Broome and Tioga			$97	$46	$143
NY	Buffalo	Erie			$107	$56	$163
NY	Floral Park / Garden City / Great Neck	Nassau			$150	$66	$216

Table 4: Maximum Federal Per Diem Rates (Effective for 10/01/2013 - 9/30/2014)

State	Primary Destination	County	Season Begin Date	Season End Date	Lodging Rate	M&IE Rate	Total
NY	Glens Falls	Warren	Oct. 1	June 30	$99	$66	$165
NY	Glens Falls	Warren	July 1	Aug. 31	$154	$66	$220
NY	Glens Falls	Warren	Sept. 1	Sept. 30	$99	$66	$165
NY	Ithaca / Waterloo / Romulus	Tompkins and Seneca			$113	$46	$159
NY	Kingston	Ulster			$111	$66	$177
NY	Lake Placid	Essex	Oct. 1	Nov. 30	$113	$61	$174
NY	Lake Placid	Essex	Dec. 1	Feb. 28	$133	$61	$194
NY	Lake Placid	Essex	Mar. 1	June 30	$107	$61	$168
NY	Lake Placid	Essex	July 1	Aug. 31	$169	$61	$230
NY	Lake Placid	Essex	Sept. 1	Sept. 30	$113	$61	$174
NY	Manhattan (includes the boroughs of Manhattan, Brooklyn, the Bronx, Queens and Staten Island)	Bronx, Kings, New York, Queens, Richmond	Oct. 1	Dec. 31	$303	$71	$374
NY	Manhattan (includes the boroughs of Manhattan, Brooklyn, the Bronx, Queens and Staten Island)	Bronx, Kings, New York, Queens, Richmond	Jan. 1	Feb. 28	$191	$71	$262
NY	Manhattan (includes the boroughs of Manhattan, Brooklyn, the Bronx, Queens and Staten Island)	Bronx, Kings, New York, Queens, Richmond	Mar. 1	June 30	$267	$71	$338
NY	Manhattan (includes the boroughs of Manhattan, Brooklyn, the Bronx, Queens and Staten Island)	Bronx, Kings, New York, Queens, Richmond	July 1	Aug. 31	$229	$71	$300
NY	Manhattan (includes the boroughs of Manhattan, Brooklyn, the Bronx, Queens and Staten Island)	Bronx, Kings, New York, Queens, Richmond	Sept. 1	Sept. 30	$303	$71	$374
NY	Niagara Falls	Niagara	Oct. 1	May 31	$83	$51	$134
NY	Niagara Falls	Niagara	June 1	Sept. 30	$99	$51	$150
NY	Nyack / Palisades	Rockland			$112	$61	$173
NY	Poughkeepsie	Dutchess			$102	$66	$168
NY	Riverhead / Ronkonkoma / Melville	Suffolk			$119	$71	$190
NY	Rochester	Monroe			$101	$51	$152
NY	Saratoga Springs / Schenectady	Saratoga and Schenectady	Oct. 1	June 30	$114	$56	$170
NY	Saratoga Springs / Schenectady	Saratoga and Schenectady	July 1	Aug. 31	$164	$56	$220
NY	Saratoga Springs / Schenectady	Saratoga and Schenectady	Sept. 1	Sept. 30	$114	$56	$170
NY	Syracuse / Oswego	Onondaga and Oswego			$96	$56	$152
NY	Tarrytown / White Plains / New Rochelle	Westchester			$139	$71	$210
NY	Troy	Rensselaer			$100	$51	$151
NY	Watertown	Jefferson			$96	$56	$152
NY	West Point	Orange			$106	$51	$157
OH	Akron	Summit			$99	$51	$150
OH	Canton	Stark			$105	$51	$156
OH	Cincinnati	Hamilton / Clermont			$127	$56	$183
OH	Cleveland	Cuyahoga			$111	$56	$167
OH	Columbus	Franklin			$99	$56	$155
OH	Dayton / Fairborn	Greene, Darke and Montgomery			$87	$56	$143
OH	Hamilton	Butler and Warren			$92	$51	$143
OH	Medina / Wooster	Wayne and Medina			$93	$51	$144

Table 4: Maximum Federal Per Diem Rates (Effective for 10/01/2013 - 9/30/2014)

State	Primary Destination	County	Season Begin Date	Season End Date	Lodging Rate	M&IE Rate	Total
OH	Mentor	Lake			$87	$46	$133
OH	Sandusky / Bellevue	Erie / Huron			$90	$46	$136
OH	Youngstown	Mahoning and Trumbull			$92	$51	$143
OK	Enid	Garfield			$106	$56	$162
OK	Oklahoma City	Oklahoma			$87	$66	$153
OR	Beaverton	Washington			$106	$51	$157
OR	Bend	Deschutes	Oct. 1	June 30	$89	$61	$150
OR	Bend	Deschutes	July 1	Aug. 31	$107	$61	$168
OR	Bend	Deschutes	Sept. 1	Sept. 30	$89	$61	$150
OR	Clackamas	Clackamas			$90	$61	$151
OR	Eugene / Florence	Lane			$94	$51	$145
OR	Lincoln City	Lincoln	Oct. 1	June 30	$94	$56	$150
OR	Lincoln City	Lincoln	July 1	Aug. 31	$121	$56	$177
OR	Lincoln City	Lincoln	Sept. 1	Sept. 30	$94	$56	$150
OR	Portland	Multnomah			$126	$66	$192
OR	Seaside	Clatsop	Oct. 1	June 30	$96	$51	$147
OR	Seaside	Clatsop	July 1	Aug. 31	$138	$51	$189
OR	Seaside	Clatsop	Sept. 1	Sept. 30	$96	$51	$147
PA	Allentown / Easton / Bethlehem	Lehigh and Northampton			$87	$51	$138
PA	Bucks County	Bucks			$99	$71	$170
PA	Chester / Radnor / Essington	Delaware			$96	$51	$147
PA	Erie	Erie			$90	$46	$136
PA	Gettysburg	Adams	Oct. 1	Oct. 31	$96	$51	$147
PA	Gettysburg	Adams	Nov. 1	Mar. 31	$83	$51	$134
PA	Gettysburg	Adams	Apr. 1	Sept. 30	$96	$51	$147
PA	Harrisburg	Dauphin County excluding Hershey			$106	$51	$157
PA	Hershey	Hershey	Oct. 1	May 31	$103	$51	$154
PA	Hershey	Hershey	June 1	Aug. 31	$148	$51	$199
PA	Hershey	Hershey	Sept. 1	Sept. 30	$103	$51	$154
PA	Lancaster	Lancaster			$97	$56	$153
PA	Malvern / Frazer / Berwyn	Chester			$124	$51	$175
PA	Mechanicsburg	Cumberland			$88	$56	$144
PA	Montgomery County	Montgomery			$126	$66	$192
PA	Philadelphia	Philadelphia	Oct. 1	Nov. 30	$163	$66	$229
PA	Philadelphia	Philadelphia	Dec. 1	Aug. 31	$155	$66	$221
PA	Philadelphia	Philadelphia	Sept. 1	Sept. 30	$163	$66	$229
PA	Pittsburgh	Allegheny			$125	$71	$196
PA	Reading	Berks			$88	$56	$144
PA	Scranton	Lackawanna			$88	$56	$144
PA	State College	Centre			$89	$56	$145
RI	East Greenwich / Warwick / North Kingstown	Kent and Washington			$90	$56	$146
RI	Jamestown / Middletown / Newport	Newport	Oct. 1	Oct. 31	$158	$71	$229
RI	Jamestown / Middletown / Newport	Newport	Nov. 1	Apr. 30	$91	$71	$162
RI	Jamestown / Middletown / Newport	Newport	May 1	Sept. 30	$158	$71	$229

Table 4: Maximum Federal Per Diem Rates (Effective for 10/01/2013 - 9/30/2014)

State	Primary Destination	County	Season Begin Date	Season End Date	Lodging Rate	M&IE Rate	Total
RI	Providence / Bristol	Providence / Bristol			$130	$71	$201
SC	Aiken	Aiken			$89	$46	$135
SC	Charleston	Charleston, Berkeley and Dorchester	Oct. 1	Oct. 31	$150	$56	$206
SC	Charleston	Charleston, Berkeley and Dorchester	Nov. 1	Feb. 28	$133	$56	$189
SC	Charleston	Charleston, Berkeley and Dorchester	Mar. 1	May 31	$173	$56	$229
SC	Charleston	Charleston, Berkeley and Dorchester	June 1	Sept. 30	$150	$56	$206
SC	Columbia	Richland / Lexington			$89	$51	$140
SC	Hilton Head	Beaufort	Oct. 1	Oct. 31	$101	$61	$162
SC	Hilton Head	Beaufort	Nov. 1	Mar. 31	$86	$61	$147
SC	Hilton Head	Beaufort	Apr. 1	Aug. 31	$128	$61	$189
SC	Hilton Head	Beaufort	Sept. 1	Sept. 30	$101	$61	$162
SC	Myrtle Beach	Horry	Oct. 1	Oct. 31	$86	$51	$137
SC	Myrtle Beach	Horry	Nov. 1	Mar. 31	$83	$51	$134
SC	Myrtle Beach	Horry	Apr. 1	May 31	$102	$51	$153
SC	Myrtle Beach	Horry	June 1	Aug. 31	$140	$51	$191
SC	Myrtle Beach	Horry	Sept. 1	Sept. 30	$86	$51	$137
SD	Hot Springs	Fall River and Custer	Oct. 1	Oct. 31	$85	$46	$131
SD	Hot Springs	Fall River and Custer	Nov. 1	May 31	$83	$46	$129
SD	Hot Springs	Fall River and Custer	June 1	Aug. 31	$119	$46	$165
SD	Hot Springs	Fall River and Custer	Sept. 1	Sept. 30	$85	$46	$131
SD	Rapid City	Pennington	Oct. 1	May 31	$83	$51	$134
SD	Rapid City	Pennington	June 1	Aug. 31	$131	$51	$182
SD	Rapid City	Pennington	Sept. 1	Sept. 30	$83	$51	$134
SD	Sturgis / Spearfish	Meade, Butte and Lawrence	Oct. 1	May 31	$83	$51	$134
SD	Sturgis / Spearfish	Meade, Butte and Lawrence	June 1	Aug. 31	$108	$51	$159
SD	Sturgis / Spearfish	Meade, Butte and Lawrence	Sept. 1	Sept. 30	$83	$51	$134
TN	Brentwood / Franklin	Williamson			$102	$56	$158
TN	Chattanooga	Hamilton			$95	$56	$151
TN	Knoxville	Knox			$90	$56	$146
TN	Memphis	Shelby			$99	$61	$160
TN	Nashville	Davidson			$122	$66	$188
TN	Oak Ridge	Anderson			$88	$46	$134
TX	Arlington / Fort Worth / Grapevine	Tarrant County and City of Grapevine			$140	$56	$196
TX	Austin	Travis			$120	$71	$191
TX	Big Spring	Howard			$128	$46	$174
TX	College Station	Brazos			$97	$56	$153
TX	Corpus Christi	Nueces			$97	$51	$148
TX	Dallas	Dallas County	Oct. 1	Oct. 31	$123	$71	$194
TX	Dallas	Dallas County	Nov. 1	Dec. 31	$108	$71	$179
TX	Dallas	Dallas County	Jan. 1	Sept. 30	$123	$71	$194
TX	El Paso	El Paso			$90	$51	$141

Table 4: Maximum Federal Per Diem Rates (Effective for 10/01/2013 - 9/30/2014)

State	Primary Destination	County	Season Begin Date	Season End Date	Lodging Rate	M&IE Rate	Total
TX	Galveston	Galveston	Oct. 1	May 31	$91	$56	$147
TX	Galveston	Galveston	June 1	Aug. 31	$119	$56	$175
TX	Galveston	Galveston	Sept. 1	Sept. 30	$91	$56	$147
TX	Greenville	Hunt County			$86	$51	$137
TX	Houston (L.B. Johnson Space Center)	Montgomery, Fort Bend and Harris			$118	$71	$189
TX	Laredo	Webb			$96	$56	$152
TX	McAllen	Hidalgo			$86	$56	$142
TX	Midland	Midland			$164	$56	$220
TX	Pearsall	Frio, Medina, and La Salle			$151	$46	$197
TX	Plano	Collin			$104	$61	$165
TX	Round Rock	Williamson			$91	$51	$142
TX	San Antonio	Bexar			$110	$66	$176
TX	South Padre Island	Cameron	Oct. 1	May 31	$85	$56	$141
TX	South Padre Island	Cameron	June 1	July 31	$103	$56	$159
TX	South Padre Island	Cameron	Aug. 1	Sept. 30	$85	$56	$141
TX	Waco	McLennan			$87	$51	$138
UT	Moab	Grand	Oct. 1	Oct. 31	$128	$56	$184
UT	Moab	Grand	Nov. 1	Feb. 28	$114	$56	$170
UT	Moab	Grand	Mar. 1	Sept. 30	$128	$56	$184
UT	Park City	Summit	Oct. 1	Nov. 30	$99	$71	$170
UT	Park City	Summit	Dec. 1	Mar. 31	$211	$71	$282
UT	Park City	Summit	Apr. 1	Sept. 30	$99	$71	$170
UT	Provo	Utah			$85	$51	$136
UT	Salt Lake City	Salt Lake and Tooele	Oct. 1	Dec. 31	$103	$61	$164
UT	Salt Lake City	Salt Lake and Tooele	Jan. 1	Mar. 31	$115	$61	$176
UT	Salt Lake City	Salt Lake and Tooele	Apr. 1	Sept. 30	$103	$61	$164
VA	Abingdon	Washington			$95	$46	$141
VA	Blacksburg	Montgomery			$97	$46	$143
VA	Charlottesville	City of Charlottesville, Albemarle, Greene			$126	$56	$182
VA	Chesapeake / Suffolk	Cities of Chesapeake and Suffolk	Oct. 1	May 31	$83	$56	$139
VA	Chesapeake / Suffolk	Cities of Chesapeake and Suffolk	June 1	Aug. 31	$85	$56	$141
VA	Chesapeake / Suffolk	Cities of Chesapeake and Suffolk	Sept. 1	Sept. 30	$83	$56	$139
VA	Fredericksburg	City of Fredericksburg / Spotsylvania / Stafford / Caroline			$85	$56	$141
VA	Loudoun County	Loudoun			$105	$61	$166
VA	Lynchburg	Campbell, Lynchburg City			$85	$51	$136
VA	Norfolk / Portsmouth	Cities of Norfolk and Portsmouth			$89	$61	$150
VA	Prince William County / Manassas	Prince William and City of Manassas			$88	$56	$144
VA	Richmond	City of Richmond			$114	$66	$180
VA	Roanoke	City limits of Roanoke			$97	$51	$148
VA	Virginia Beach	City of Virginia Beach	Oct. 1	May 31	$94	$56	$150
VA	Virginia Beach	City of Virginia Beach	June 1	Aug. 31	$166	$56	$222
VA	Virginia Beach	City of Virginia Beach	Sept. 1	Sept. 30	$94	$56	$150
VA	Wallops Island	Accomack	Oct. 1	June 30	$88	$56	$144

Table 4: Maximum Federal Per Diem Rates (Effective for 10/01/2013 - 9/30/2014)

State	Primary Destination	County	Season Begin Date	Season End Date	Lodging Rate	M&IE Rate	Total
VA	Wallops Island	Accomack	July 1	Aug. 31	$133	$56	$189
VA	Wallops Island	Accomack	Sept. 1	Sept. 30	$88	$56	$144
VA	Warrenton	Fauquier			$111	$46	$157
VA	Williamsburg / York	James City and York Counties, City of Williamsburg	Oct. 1	Mar. 31	$83	$51	$134
VA	Williamsburg / York	James City and York Counties, City of Williamsburg	Apr. 1	Aug. 31	$93	$51	$144
VA	Williamsburg / York	James City and York Counties, City of Williamsburg	Sept. 1	Sept. 30	$83	$51	$134
VT	Burlington / St. Albans	Chittenden and Franklin	Oct. 1	Oct. 31	$124	$66	$190
VT	Burlington / St. Albans	Chittenden and Franklin	Nov. 1	Apr. 30	$102	$66	$168
VT	Burlington / St. Albans	Chittenden and Franklin	May 1	Sept. 30	$124	$66	$190
VT	Manchester	Bennington	Oct. 1	Oct. 31	$100	$71	$171
VT	Manchester	Bennington	Nov. 1	May 31	$86	$71	$157
VT	Manchester	Bennington	June 1	Sept. 30	$100	$71	$171
VT	Middlebury	Addison			$130	$61	$191
VT	Montpelier	Washington			$107	$61	$168
VT	Stowe	Lamoille	Oct. 1	Mar. 31	$129	$71	$200
VT	Stowe	Lamoille	Apr. 1	May 31	$102	$71	$173
VT	Stowe	Lamoille	June 1	Sept. 30	$129	$71	$200
VT	White River Junction	Windsor			$96	$56	$152
WA	Anacortes / Coupeville / Oak Harbor	Skagit, Island, San Juan			$91	$61	$152
WA	Everett / Lynnwood	Snohomish			$104	$61	$165
WA	Ocean Shores	Grays Harbor	Oct. 1	June 30	$83	$51	$134
WA	Ocean Shores	Grays Harbor	July 1	Aug. 31	$105	$51	$156
WA	Ocean Shores	Grays Harbor	Sept. 1	Sept. 30	$83	$51	$134
WA	Olympia / Tumwater	Thurston			$94	$61	$155
WA	Port Angeles / Port Townsend	Clallam and Jefferson	Oct. 1	June 30	$95	$61	$156
WA	Port Angeles / Port Townsend	Clallam and Jefferson	July 1	Aug. 31	$122	$61	$183
WA	Port Angeles / Port Townsend	Clallam and Jefferson	Sept. 1	Sept. 30	$95	$61	$156
WA	Richland / Pasco	Benton / Franklin			$90	$46	$136
WA	Seattle	King			$152	$71	$223
WA	Spokane	Spokane			$88	$61	$149
WA	Tacoma	Pierce			$106	$61	$167
WA	Vancouver	Clark, Cowlitz and Skamania			$126	$56	$182
WI	Appleton	Outagamie			$86	$46	$132
WI	Brookfield / Racine	Waukesha / Racine			$93	$56	$149
WI	Lake Geneva	Walworth	Oct. 1	May 31	$93	$51	$144
WI	Lake Geneva	Walworth	June 1	Sept. 30	$129	$51	$180
WI	Madison	Dane	Oct. 1	Oct. 31	$111	$56	$167
WI	Madison	Dane	Nov. 1	Aug. 31	$94	$56	$150
WI	Madison	Dane	Sept. 1	Sept. 30	$111	$56	$167
WI	Milwaukee	Milwaukee			$104	$61	$165
WI	Sheboygan	Sheboygan	Oct. 1	May 31	$83	$51	$134
WI	Sheboygan	Sheboygan	June 1	Aug. 31	$96	$51	$147
WI	Sheboygan	Sheboygan	Sept. 1	Sept. 30	$83	$51	$134

Table 4: Maximum Federal Per Diem Rates (Effective for 10/01/2013 - 9/30/2014)

State	Primary Destination	County	Season Begin Date	Season End Date	Lodging Rate	M&IE Rate	Total
WI	Sturgeon Bay	Door	Oct. 1	June 30	$83	$56	$139
WI	Sturgeon Bay	Door	July 1	Aug. 31	$87	$56	$143
WI	Sturgeon Bay	Door	Sept. 1	Sept. 30	$83	$56	$139
WI	Wisconsin Dells	Columbia	Oct. 1	May 31	$89	$61	$150
WI	Wisconsin Dells	Columbia	June 1	Aug. 31	$106	$61	$167
WI	Wisconsin Dells	Columbia	Sept. 1	Sept. 30	$89	$61	$150
WV	Charleston	Kanawha			$102	$51	$153
WV	Morgantown	Monongalia			$96	$46	$142
WV	Wheeling	Ohio			$106	$46	$152
WY	Cody	Park	Oct. 1	May 31	$93	$51	$144
WY	Cody	Park	June 1	Sept. 30	$132	$51	$183
WY	Evanston / Rock Springs	Sweetwater / Uinta			$89	$51	$140
WY	Gillette	Campbell	Oct. 1	May 31	$83	$51	$134
WY	Gillette	Campbell	June 1	Aug. 31	$88	$51	$139
WY	Gillette	Campbell	Sept. 1	Sept. 30	$83	$51	$134
WY	Jackson / Pinedale	Teton and Sublette	Oct. 1	June 30	$117	$56	$173
WY	Jackson / Pinedale	Teton and Sublette	July 1	Aug. 31	$180	$56	$236
WY	Jackson / Pinedale	Teton and Sublette	Sept. 1	Sept. 30	$117	$56	$173
WY	Sheridan	Sheridan	Oct. 1	May 31	$83	$56	$139
WY	Sheridan	Sheridan	June 1	Aug. 31	$88	$56	$144
WY	Sheridan	Sheridan	Sept. 1	Sept. 30	$83	$56	$139

NOTES:

Standard rate: The standard rate of $129 ($83 for lodging and $46 for M&IE) applies to all locations within the continental United States (CONUS) not specifically listed above or encompassed by the boundary definition of a listed point. However, the standard CONUS rate applies to all locations within CONUS, including those defined above, for certain relocation allowances. (See parts 302-2,302-4 and 302-5 of 41 CFR.)

Transition rule. In lieu of the updated GSA rates that will be effective October 1, 2014, taxpayers may continue to use the CONUS rates in effect for the first 9 months of 2014 (Table 4) for expenses of all CONUS travel away from home that are paid or incurred during calendar year 2014. A taxpayer must consistently use either these rates or the updated rates for the period of October 1, 2014, through December 31, 2014.

Per diem locality. Unless otherwise specified, the per diem locality is defined as "all locations within, or entirely surrounded by, the corporate limits of the key city, including independent entities located within those boundaries."

Per diem localities with county definitions shall include "all locations within, or entirely surrounded by, the corporate limits of the key city as well as the boundaries of the listed counties, including independent entities within the boundaries of the key city and the listed counties (unless otherwise listed separately)."

When a military installation or Government-related facility (whether or not specifically named) is located partially within more than one city or county boundary, the applicable per diem rate for the entire installation or facility is the higher of the two rates which apply to the cities and /or counties, even though part(s) of such activities may be located outside the defined per diem locality.

Recognizing that all locations are not incorporated cities, the term "city limits" has been used as a general phrase to denote the commonly recognized local boundaries of the location cited.

[Sources: Revenue Procedure 2011-47, in Internal Revenue Bulletin 2011-42; Notice 2013-65, in Internal Revenue Bulletin 2013–44; U.S. General Services Administration, Domestic Per Diem Rates (available at http://www.gsa.gov)]

Sample Weekly Traveling Expense and Entertainment Record

From: _____   To: _____   Name: _____

Expenses	SUN		MON		TUE		WED		THU		FRI		SAT		Total	
Travel Expenses:																
Airlines																
Excess baggage																
Bus – Train																
Cab and Limousine																
Tips																
Porter																
Meals and Lodging:																
Breakfast																
Lunch																
Dinner																
Hotel and Motel (Detail in Section B)																
Entertainment (Detail in Section C)																
Other Expenses:																
Postage																
Telephone, Internet Access																
Stationery, Printing																
Stenographer																
Sample Room																
Advertising																
Assistant(s), Model(s)																
Trade Shows																
Car Expenses: (List all car expenses – the division between business and personal expenses may be made at the end of the year.) (Detail mileage in Section A)																
Gas, oil, lube, wash																
Repairs, parts																
Tires, supplies																
Parking fees, tolls																
Other (identify)																
Total																

Note: Attach receipted bills for (1) ALL lodging and (2) any other expenses of $75.00 or more.

Section A – Car							
Mileage: End							
Start							
Total							
Business Mileage							

Section B – Lodging								
Hotel or Motel	Name:							
	City:							

Section C – Entertainment					
Date	Item	Place	Amount	Business Purpose	Business Relationship

WEEKLY REIMBURSEMENTS:

Travel and transportation expenses _____

Other reimbursements _____

TOTAL _____

Form **2106**	**Employee Business Expenses**	OMB No. 1545-0074

Form **2106**

Department of the Treasury
Internal Revenue Service (99)

Employee Business Expenses

▶ Attach to Form 1040 or Form 1040NR.

▶ **Information about Form 2106 and its separate instructions is available at** *www.irs.gov/form2106.*

OMB No. 1545-0074

2013

Attachment
Sequence No. **129**

Your name	Occupation in which you incurred expenses	Social security number

---

Part I **Employee Business Expenses and Reimbursements**

Step 1 Enter Your Expenses

		Column A Other Than Meals and Entertainment		Column B Meals and Entertainment	
1	Vehicle expense from line 22 or line 29. (Rural mail carriers: See instructions.)	**1**			
2	Parking fees, tolls, and transportation, including train, bus, etc., that **did not** involve overnight travel or commuting to and from work .	**2**			
3	Travel expense while away from home overnight, including lodging, airplane, car rental, etc. **Do not** include meals and entertainment .	**3**			
4	Business expenses not included on lines 1 through 3. **Do not** include meals and entertainment	**4**			
5	Meals and entertainment expenses (see instructions)	**5**			
6	**Total expenses.** In Column A, add lines 1 through 4 and enter the result. In Column B, enter the amount from line 5	**6**			

Note: *If you were not reimbursed for any expenses in Step 1, skip line 7 and enter the amount from line 6 on line 8.*

Step 2 Enter Reimbursements Received From Your Employer for Expenses Listed in Step 1

7	Enter reimbursements received from your employer that were **not** reported to you in box 1 of Form W-2. Include any reimbursements reported under code "L" in box 12 of your Form W-2 (see instructions).	**7**			

Step 3 Figure Expenses To Deduct on Schedule A (Form 1040 or Form 1040NR)

8	Subtract line 7 from line 6. If zero or less, enter -0-. However, if line 7 is greater than line 6 in Column A, report the excess as income on Form 1040, line 7 (or on Form 1040NR, line 8)	**8**			
	Note: *If **both columns** of line 8 are zero, you cannot deduct employee business expenses. Stop here and attach Form 2106 to your return.*				
9	In Column A, enter the amount from line 8. In Column B, multiply line 8 by 50% (.50). (Employees subject to Department of Transportation (DOT) hours of service limits: Multiply meal expenses incurred while away from home on business by 80% (.80) instead of 50%. For details, see instructions.)	**9**			
10	Add the amounts on line 9 of both columns and enter the total here. **Also, enter the total on Schedule A (Form 1040), line 21** (or on **Schedule A (Form 1040NR), line 7**). (Armed Forces reservists, qualified performing artists, fee-basis state or local government officials, and individuals with disabilities: See the instructions for special rules on where to enter the total.) . . . . . ▶	**10**			

For Paperwork Reduction Act Notice, see your tax return instructions.   Cat. No. 11700N   Form **2106** (2013)

Part II	Vehicle Expenses

Section A—General Information (You must complete this section if you are claiming vehicle expenses.)

			(a) Vehicle 1	**(b)** Vehicle 2
11	Enter the date the vehicle was placed in service	11	/ /	/ /
12	Total miles the vehicle was driven during 2013	12	miles	miles
13	Business miles included on line 12	13	miles	miles
14	Percent of business use. Divide line 13 by line 12	14	%	%
15	Average daily roundtrip commuting distance	15	miles	miles
16	Commuting miles included on line 12	16	miles	miles
17	Other miles. Add lines 13 and 16 and subtract the total from line 12 . .	17	miles	miles
18	Was your vehicle available for personal use during off-duty hours?		☐ Yes ☐ No
19	Do you (or your spouse) have another vehicle available for personal use?		☐ Yes ☐ No
20	Do you have evidence to support your deduction?		☐ Yes ☐ No
21	If "Yes," is the evidence written?		☐ Yes ☐ No

Section B—Standard Mileage Rate (See the instructions for Part II to find out whether to complete this section or Section C.)

22	Multiply line 13 by 56.5¢ (.565). Enter the result here and on line 1	22	

Section C—Actual Expenses

			(a) Vehicle 1		**(b)** Vehicle 2	
23	Gasoline, oil, repairs, vehicle insurance, etc.	23				
24a	Vehicle rentals	24a				
b	Inclusion amount (see instructions) .	24b				
c	Subtract line 24b from line 24a .	24c				
25	Value of employer-provided vehicle (applies only if 100% of annual lease value was included on Form W-2—see instructions)	25				
26	Add lines 23, 24c, and 25. . .	26				
27	Multiply line 26 by the percentage on line 14	27				
28	Depreciation (see instructions) .	28				
29	Add lines 27 and 28. Enter total here and on line 1	29				

Section D—Depreciation of Vehicles (Use this section only if you owned the vehicle and are completing Section C for the vehicle.)

			(a) Vehicle 1		**(b)** Vehicle 2	
30	Enter cost or other basis (see instructions)	30				
31	Enter section 179 deduction and special allowance (see instructions)	31				
32	Multiply line 30 by line 14 (see instructions if you claimed the section 179 deduction or special allowance).	32				
33	Enter depreciation method and percentage (see instructions) .	33				
34	Multiply line 32 by the percentage on line 33 (see instructions) . .	34				
35	Add lines 31 and 34	35				
36	Enter the applicable limit explained in the line 36 instructions . . .	36				
37	Multiply line 36 by the percentage on line 14	37				
38	Enter the **smaller** of line 35 or line 37. If you skipped lines 36 and 37, enter the amount from line 35. Also enter this amount on line 28 above	38				

Form **2106** (2013)

Form **2106-EZ**	**Unreimbursed Employee Business Expenses**	OMB No. 1545-0074
Department of the Treasury Internal Revenue Service (99)	▶ Attach to Form 1040 or Form 1040NR. ▶ Information about Form 2106 and its separate instructions is available at *www.irs.gov/form2106*.	20**13** Attachment Sequence No. **129A**

Your name	Occupation in which you incurred expenses	Social security number

You Can Use This Form Only if All of the Following Apply.

• You are an employee deducting ordinary and necessary expenses attributable to your job. An ordinary expense is one that is common and accepted in your field of trade, business, or profession. A necessary expense is one that is helpful and appropriate for your business. An expense does not have to be required to be considered necessary.

• You **do not** get reimbursed by your employer for any expenses (amounts your employer included in box 1 of your Form W-2 are not considered reimbursements for this purpose).

• If you are claiming vehicle expense, you are using the standard mileage rate for 2013.

Caution: *You can use the standard mileage rate for 2013* **only if: (a)** *you owned the vehicle and used the standard mileage rate for the first year you placed the vehicle in service,* **or (b)** *you leased the vehicle and used the standard mileage rate for the portion of the lease period after 1997.*

Part I — Figure Your Expenses

1	Complete Part II. Multiply line 8a by 56.5¢ (.565). Enter the result here	1	
2	Parking fees, tolls, and transportation, including train, bus, etc., that **did not** involve overnight travel or commuting to and from work	2	
3	Travel expense while away from home overnight, including lodging, airplane, car rental, etc. **Do not** include meals and entertainment	3	
4	Business expenses not included on lines 1 through 3. **Do not** include meals and entertainment	4	
5	Meals and entertainment expenses: $ _____ × 50% (.50). (Employees subject to Department of Transportation (DOT) hours of service limits: Multiply meal expenses incurred while away from home on business by 80% (.80) instead of 50%. For details, see instructions.)	5	
6	**Total expenses.** Add lines 1 through 5. Enter here and on **Schedule A (Form 1040), line 21** (or on **Schedule A (Form 1040NR), line 7**). (Armed Forces reservists, fee-basis state or local government officials, qualified performing artists, and individuals with disabilities: See the instructions for special rules on where to enter this amount.)	6	

Part II — Information on Your Vehicle. Complete this part **only** if you are claiming vehicle expense on line 1.

7 When did you place your vehicle in service for business use? (month, day, year) ▶ _____ / _____ / _____

8 Of the total number of miles you drove your vehicle during 2013, enter the number of miles you used your vehicle for:

a Business _____ b Commuting (see instructions) _____ c Other _____

9 Was your vehicle available for personal use during off-duty hours? . . . . ☐ Yes ☐ No

10 Do you (or your spouse) have another vehicle available for personal use? . . . . ☐ Yes ☐ No

11a Do you have evidence to support your deduction? . . . . ☐ Yes ☐ No

b If "Yes," is the evidence written? . . . . ☐ Yes ☐ No

For Paperwork Reduction Act Notice, see your tax return instructions.   Cat. No. 20604Q   Form **2106-EZ** (2013)

Record Retention Table

If you have expenses for . . .	THEN you must keep records that show details of the following elements . . .			
	Amount	Time	Place or Description	Business Purpose Business Relationship
Travel	Cost of each separate expense for travel, lodging, and meals. Incidental expenses may be totaled in reasonable categories such as taxis, fees and tips, etc.	Dates you left and returned for each trip and number of days spent on business.	Destination or area of your travel (name of city, town, or other designation).	Purpose: Business purpose for the expense or the business benefit gained or expected to be gained. Relationship: N/A
Entertainment	Cost of each separate expense. Incidental expenses such as taxis, telephones, etc., may be totaled on a daily basis.	Date of entertainment. (Also see Business Purpose.)	Name and address or location of place of entertainment. Type of entertainment if not otherwise apparent. (Also see Business Purpose.)	Purpose: Business purpose for the expense or the business benefit gained or expected to be gained. For entertainment, the nature of the business discussion or activity. If the entertainment was directly before or after a business discussion: the date, place, nature, and duration of the business discussion, and the identities of the persons who took part in both the business discussion and the entertainment activity. Relationship: Occupations or other information (such as names, titles, or other designations) about the recipients that shows their business relationship to you. For entertainment, you must also prove that you or your employee was present if the entertainment was a business meal.
Gifts	Cost of the gift.	Date of the gift.	Description of the gift.	
Transportation	Cost of each separate expense. For car expenses, the cost of the car and any improvements, the date you started using it for business, the mileage for each business use, and the total miles for the year.	Date of the expense. For car expenses, the date of the use of the car.	Your business destination.	Purpose: Business purpose for the expense. Relationship: N/A

NOTES

Form 4562: Depreciation

What's New in 2013

IRC §179 Limits. The maximum IRC §179 deduction is $500,000 in 2013. The threshold investment for a reduction in these limits is $2,000,000 in 2013.

Additional First Year Depreciation Allowance. The special 50% first-year additional deprecation allowance provided for qualified property has been extended to apply to property placed in service on or before December 31, 2013.

Special Expensing Provision for Films is Extended. The special deduction for film and television productions allowed under IRC §181 has been extended to apply to expenses incurred in film and television productions commencing on or before December 31, 2013.

Qualified Property. The 15-year recovery period for qualified leasehold improvement property, qualified restaurant property, and qualified retail improvement property is extended two additional years to apply to property placed in service before January 1, 2014.

Motorsports Entertainment Complexes. The seven-year recovery period for motorsports entertainment complexes is extended two years to apply to property placed in service on or before December 31, 2013.

Section at a Glance

Relevant IRS Publications

- ☐ IRS Publication 463, *Travel, Entertainment, Gift, and Car Expenses*
- ☐ IRS Publication 534, *Depreciating Property Placed in Service Before 1987*
- ☐ IRS Publication 535, *Business Expenses*
- ☐ IRS Publication 544, *Sales and Other Dispositions of Assets*
- ☐ IRS Publication 551, *Basis of Assets*
- ☐ IRS Publication 946, *How to Depreciate Property*

MACRS Property Classes

MACRS Class	Examples
3 years	Special manufacturing tools, race horses, tractors, and property with a class life of 4 years or less
5 years	Automobiles, trucks, computers and peripheral equipment (such as printers, external disk drives, and modems), typewriters, copiers, R&E equipment, and property with a class life of more than 4 years and less than 10 years
7 years	Office furniture, fixtures, office equipment, most machinery, street light assets, property with a class life of 10 years or more but less than 16 years, and property with no assigned class life
10 years	Single-purpose agricultural and horticultural structures, assets used in petroleum refining and manufacturing of tobacco and certain food products, and property with a class life of 16 years or more but less than 20 years
15 years	Land improvements (such as sidewalks, roads, irrigation systems, sewers, fences, and landscaping), service stations, billboards, telephone distribution plants, and property with a class life of 20 years or more but less than 25 years
20 years	Municipal sewers and property with a class life of 25 years or more, farm buildings
27.5 years	Residential rental real estate, including apartment buildings, duplexes, etc.
39 years	Nonresidential real estate, including office buildings, warehouses, and factories

Filing Requirements

Form 4562, Depreciation and Amortization, is required for reporting:

- depreciation for property placed in service during the tax year;
- any IRC §179 expense deduction, including any carryover from a previous year;
- depreciation on a vehicle or other listed property including bonus depreciation, regardless of when it was placed in service;
- a deduction for any vehicle reported on a form other than Schedule C or C-EZ of Form 1040; and
- amortization of costs beginning during 2013.

A separate Form 4562 should be filed for each business activity on the taxpayer's return. If the taxpayer is an employee deducting job-related vehicle expenses, use Form 2106, Employee Business Expenses (See Tab 6).

IRC §179 Deduction (Part I, Lines 1-13)

General Rule

The IRC §179 expense deduction is an election to deduct part or all of the cost of qualifying depreciable property (i.e., section 179 property) in the year that it is placed in service. All taxpayers other than estates and trusts are entitled to elect the IRC §179 expensing deduction. If a partnership or S corporation elects to use IRC §179, limitations on the deduction apply at both the entity and owner levels.

 Planning Tip. In determining whether to use the IRC §179 expense deduction in any particular year, it is important to coordinate the deduction with net profit planning, the future income potential, and subsequent liquidation of the asset. Generally, a taxpayer will make the IRC §179 election on Form 4562 filed with their original return for the tax year the section 179 property is placed in service. However, a taxpayer can also make an election on an amended return that is filed within the three-year limitation period for filing an amended return. For tax years 2003 through 2013, a taxpayer may also revoke a IRC §179 election on an amended return without consent of the IRS. See MTG ¶1208.

Line 1, Maximum Amount

Generally, the maximum deduction allowed for section 179 property placed in service in a tax year beginning in 2013 is $500,000, which should be entered on Line 1 of Form 4562.

 Caution. If any section 179 property placed in service during the tax year ceases to be used in a trade or business in a empowerment or renewal zone, then the increased IRC §179 deduction claimed for such property must be reported as "Other income" on Line 21 of Form 1040. Recapture is also required in any tax year during the recovery period that qualified section 179 disaster assistance property ceases to be qualified section 179 disaster assistance property.

Line 2, Total Cost of Section 179 Property

Line 2 of Form 4562 is used to enter the total cost of section 179 property placed in service during 2013. Include in this amount the cost of any *listed property* (described on page 7-13). In the case of a married individual, also include the cost of section 179 property placed in service by his or her spouse, even if filing separately.

Eligible property. Property generally qualifies as section 179 property eligible for expensing if it is:

- tangible personal property (i.e., section 1245 property);
- depreciable under the Modified Accelerated Cost Recovery System or MACRS (see below); and
- acquired by purchase from a nonrelated party and used primarily (i.e., greater than 50%) in the active conduct of a trade or business (as opposed to property held for the production of income).

Off-the-shelf computer software that is placed in service in a tax year beginning after 2002 and before 2014 may be considered section 179 property.

For tax years beginning in 2010 through 2013, a taxpayer can elect the section 179 deduction for up to $250,000 of any qualified real property that is depreciable and acquired by purchase for use in the active conduct of a trade or business. The amount of qualified real property expensed counts toward the overall $500,000 limitation. "Qualified real property" is:

- qualified leasehold improvement property, as described in IRC §168(e)(6);
- qualified restaurant property, as described in IRC §168(e)(7); and
- qualified retail improvement property, as described in IRC §168(e)(8) (IRC §179(f)(2)).

Section 179 property does not include portable air conditioners and heating units, nor property that is used:

- predominantly outside the United States;
- predominantly in connection with furnishing lodging;
- by a tax-exempt organization, unless it is used mainly in a taxable activity unrelated to its exempt function; or
- by a governmental unit, or a foreign person or entity.

For more information about qualifying and nonqualifying property, see MTG ¶ 1208.

Lines 3-4, Investment Limitation

The maximum allowable IRC §179 deduction for the tax year is reduced dollar for dollar for any section 179 property placed in service during the tax year that exceeds an investment threshold amount. For tax years beginning in 2013, the threshold amount is $2,000,000. The amount of any reduction due to the investment limitation is recorded on Line 4.

 Example. HMO Inc., a calendar-year taxpayer, purchases a piece of equipment to be used in its business. The cost of the machine is $2,010,000. Because this cost exceeds the investment threshold for 2013 by $10,000, HMO's dollar limitation for the section 179 property for 2013 must be reduced by $10,000 and HMO records $490,000 on Line 4, assuming it places no other section 179 property in service in 2013.

Line 5, Dollar Limitation for the Tax Year

On Line 5, record the taxpayer's dollar limitation for the tax year (i.e., the maximum annual limit from Line 1, reduced by the investment limitation from Line 4, but not below zero). If the amount is zero, then the taxpayer cannot elect to deduct the cost of any section 179 property during the tax year. However, any disallowed deduction may be carried over to the next tax year (Line 13).

The dollar amount recorded on Line 5 must be shared by spouses filing separately. The couple may choose to allocate the limitation in any manner they wish (e.g., 50% to each, or 60% to wife and 40% to husband). In addition, the dollar limit on Line 5 must be allocated by a partnership or S corporation to its partners or shareholders according to their respective holdings in the entity.

 Planning Tip. If a partnership or S corporation elects to use IRC §179, then the annual dollar and investment limits are applied separately at the entity level and at the partner or shareholder level. For example, assume that Mary and Linda form a calendar-year business partnership that purchases equipment for $650,000 in 2013. Assuming that the equipment is section 179 property, the partnership may deduct $500,000 of the cost. Mary and Linda may deduct $250,000 each. In addition, each may deduct an additional $250,000 (subject to the investment limitation) on any other section 179 property placed in service in 2013 individually or through another partnership.

Line 6, Description of Property, Cost and Elected Cost

Each item of section 179 property the taxpayer is electing to deduct the cost of during 2013 should be briefly described in Line 6. In column 6(a) provide the description of the property (e.g., type of equipment, office furniture).

Caution. Listed property should not be reported on Line 6. Instead it is included on Line 26. See page 7-13 for a discussion of listed property.

The total cost of section 179 property is reported in column 6(b). For this purpose, if the property was acquired in a like-kind exchange (e.g., a trade-in), only the excess of the cost of the property over the value of the property traded in is reported (i.e., the amount attributable to any boot given in the exchange). The portion of the new asset's basis attributable to the old asset cannot be expensed under IRC §179.

In column 6(c), the portion of the section 179 property's cost that the taxpayer elects to expense is reported. The taxpayer may allocate the IRC §179 allowance in any manner. Normally, the section 179 property that has the longest useful life and that would take the longest to depreciate is expensed. Note that any portion of the asset may be expensed. Any portion that is not expensed under IRC §179 may be depreciated in the normal manner.

Example. Tanya purchased five-year property for $255,000 and seven-year property for $445,000 during 2013. Both assets may be expensed subject to the limitations of IRC §179. The maximum amount that can be expensed for the 2013 tax year is $500,000. To maximize current tax savings from limited expensing and depreciation deductions, she should expense the full $445,000 of the seven-year property rather than the five-year property because the cost of the five-year property can then be recovered more quickly, resulting in higher depreciation. The remaining IRC §179 allowance of $55,000 should be used to expense the five-year property. In such case the total deduction for the five-year property in 2013 would be $175,000, computed as follows:

Original cost	$255,000
Expensed portion	− 55,000
Depreciable basis	200,000
Bonus depreciation	− 100,000
Remaining depreciable basis	100,000
Depreciation percentage	× 20.00%
Depreciation deduction	20,000
IRC §179 deduction	+ 55,000
Bonus depreciation	+100,000
Total deduction	$ 175,000

Taxpayers who are entitled to a share of a IRC §179 expense deduction from a partnership or an S corporation should write "from Schedule K-1 (Form 1065)" or "from Schedule K-1 (Form 1120S)" across columns (a) and (b).

Line 7, Listed Property

The amount of any IRC §179 deduction that may be claimed for "listed property" is limited. To determine the amount of the deduction for "listed property," including motor vehicles, see the discussion beginning on page 7-13.

Line 8, Total Elected Cost of Section 179 Property

The sum of the amounts in column 6(c) and the cost of any listed property (see below) recorded on Line 7 is the total IRC §179 election reported on Line 8.

Line 9, Tentative Deduction

If the Line 8 amount is less than the dollar limitation for the tax year on Line 5, then the Line 8 amount is the taxpayer's tentative deduction for 2013 and should be reported on Line 9. However, if the the Line 8 amount is more than the taxpayer's dollar limitation for the tax year, then report the Line 5 dollar limitation on Line 9.

Line 10, Carryover of Disallowed Prior-Year Deduction

If, in a prior year, the amount of the IRC §179 deduction was limited due to the taxable income limitation (see Line 11), the amount not used may be carried over to future years until there is sufficient taxable income to utilize it. The amount of carryover from the previous year to report on Line 10 is the amount from Line 13 of the taxpayer's 2012 Form 4562.

Line 11, Business Income Limitation

The IRC §179 deduction is limited to the aggregate taxable income derived from all of the taxpayer's trades or businesses during the year. Thus, the smaller of business income (but not less than zero) or Line 5 is entered on Line 11.

For this purpose, taxable income includes: section 1231 gains or losses (see Tab 4); interest from the working capital of a taxpayer's trade or business; and wages, salaries, tips, and other compensation earned as an employee. It is computed prior to consideration of the IRC §179 deduction, the deduction for self-employment tax, any net operating loss carryover, and any unreimbursed employee business expense. Married individuals filing a joint return combine their incomes for this purpose.

 Planning Tip. Any amount that cannot be deducted due to the taxable income limitation can be carried over indefinitely to following years to be used against future income. The maximum amount that can be expensed in subsequent years is not increased by the carryover amount, however. Rather than carry over the amount that could not be expensed because of the taxable income limitation, the taxpayer may want to consider reducing the election amount so that there is no carryover. This will allow an increased depreciation deduction in the current tax year.

Partnerships. In determining the taxable business income from a partnership or LLC, the taxpayer aggregates the partnership's items of income and expense from any trade or business that the partnership actively conducted. Items of tax-exempt income and the IRC §179 deduction are not taken into account in determining the partner's share of partnership income. Guaranteed payments from the partnership to the partner are generally treated as taxable business income to the partner only if such payments are for services or are otherwise treated as derived by the partner from the conduct of a trade or business.

S Corporations. In determining the taxable business income from an S corporation, the taxpayer aggregates the income and expense of the S corporation from any trade or business the corporation actively conducted. Items of tax-exempt income and the IRC §179 deduction are not considered in calculating the amount of taxable business income allocated to the shareholder by the S corporation. Wages received by a shareholder-employee of an S corporation are included in taxable business income.

 Caution. Amounts attributable to qualified real property (see above) that are disallowed under the business income limitation cannot be carried over to a tax year beginning after 2013. Such disallowed amounts are treated as if no IRC §179 election had been made with respect to them. Any disallowed amount attributable to qualified real property that would otherwise be carried over from 2010, 2011 or 2012 to 2014 is treated as if the property was placed in service on the first day of the taxpayer's last tax year beginning in 2013 (IRC §179(f)(4)).

Line 12, Total IRC §179 Expense Deduction

The sum of the current-year tentative deduction (Line 9) and carryover from prior years (Line 10) is entered on Line 12, if it does not exceed the amount on Line 11. Otherwise, the amount on Line 11 is also entered on Line 12 and the difference is reported on Line 13.

The reduction in the IRC §179 allowance for purchases exceeding $2,000,000 and the taxable income limitation apply to the taxpayer, and not to each separate business or activity. If the taxpayer has more than one business or activity, the allowable IRC §179 expense deduction may be allocated among them. To do so, the taxpayer should write "Summary" at the top of Part I of the separate Form 4562 filed for each business. The remainder of the form should not be completed. On Line 12 of the Form 4562 prepared for each separate business or activity, the amount allocated to the business or activity from the "Summary" should be reported. No other entry is required in Part I of the separate Form 4562.

Recapture. If section 179 property is no longer used more than 50% in a trade or business in a tax year during the property's recovery period, then the taxpayer may have to recapture all or part of the amount deducted under IRC §179 as ordinary income. The amount recaptured is equal to the excess of the amount deducted under IRC §179 over the amount of MACRS depreciation that would have been allowable on the property from the year it was placed in service, including the tax year of recapture. This calculation is made in Part IV of Form 4797. The taxpayer's basis in the property must also be increased by the recaptured amount.

In addition, the IRC §179 expense deduction will be treated as depreciation for recapture purposes. Thus, gain realized on the sale, exchange or other disposition of the property will be characterized as ordinary income to the extent of the IRC §179 deduction claimed, plus any depreciation claimed. If the property is disposed of through an installment sale, then the IRC §179 deduction is immediately recaptured as ordinary income to the extent gain is recognized on the disposition.

Line 13, Carryover of Disallowed Deduction to 2014

Any portion of the IRC §179 allowance that is disallowed due to the taxable income limitation is reported on Line 13 and may be carried over to the next year and deducted as if it were incurred in that year. There is no limit on the carryover period.

Special Depreciation Allowance and Other Depreciation (Part II, Lines 14-16)

Line 14, Special Depreciation Allowance

For certain qualified property, an additional special (bonus) depreciation allowance applies for the first year the property is placed in service. For 2013, taxpayers are allowed to claim bonus depreciation in the amount of 50% of the property's depreciable basis. In order to claim bonus depreciation on property, it must be one of the following: (1) property eligible for the modified accelerated cost recovery system (MACRS) with a depreciation period of 20 years or less; (2) water utility property; (3) computer software; or (4) qualified leasehold improvement property.

Caution. Taxpayers were allowed 100% bonus depreciation for property the original use of which began with the taxpayer after September 8, 2010, where the taxpayer acquired the property after September 8, 2010, and before January 1, 2012. However, the 100% bonus depreciation allowance has expired for property placed in service on or after January 1, 2012 (on or after January 1, 2013, for certain long production or noncommercial aircraft property).

Time Requirements. To qualify for 50% bonus depreciation, these three requirements must be met: (1) the original use of the property must begin with the taxpayer after December 31, 2007; (2) the taxpayer must acquire the property after December 31, 2007, and before January 1, 2014 (with no binding contract in place prior to January 1, 2008), or acquire the property pursuant to a written binding contract entered into after December 31, 2007, and before January 1, 2014; and (3) the property must be placed in service before January 1, 2014 (before January 1, 2015, for certain long production or noncommercial aircraft property).

> **Example.** A taxpayer enters into a written binding contract on September 1, 2010, for the purchase of a machine. The machine is acquired after September 8, 2010, and placed in service before January 1, 2012. The machine will qualify for special bonus depreciation at the 100% rate even though a binding contract was in effect prior to September 9, 2010, because the binding contract was entered into after December 31, 2007. If the machine had been placed in service in 2012, the 50% rate would apply.

Original Use Requirement. To qualify for the bonus depreciation allowance, the original use requirement must be met. This is the first use to which property is put. Costs incurred to recondition or rebuild property acquired or owned satisfy the original use requirement. However, the cost incurred to purchase reconditioned or rebuilt property does not. Under a safe harbor provision, property that contains used parts will not be treated as reconditioned or rebuilt property if the cost of the used parts is not more than 20% of the cost of the property.

Special Depreciation Allowed for Qualified Real Property. Qualified leasehold improvement property is eligible for the 50% additional first-year depreciation deduction. Qualified leasehold improvement property includes any improvement to an interior portion of a building that is nonresidential real property, as long as the improvement is made under or pursuant to a lease either by the lessee or sublessee or the lessor of that portion of the building. The improved portion must be occupied exclusively by the lessee or sublessee, and the improvement must be placed in service more than three years after the building was first placed in service. It does not include any improvement for which the expenditure is attributable to the enlargement of the building, any elevator or escalator, any structural component benefiting a common area, or the internal structural framework of the building (IRC §168(k)(3)).

Election Out of Bonus Depreciation. Bonus depreciation must be claimed unless the taxpayer elects out. Once made, such an election cannot be revoked without IRS consent. The election out must be for all property of the same class. Thus, if the taxpayer elects out of bonus depreciation for some 5-year property, the election must apply to all 5-year property. The manner of making the election is described in the instructions for Form 4562.

Line 15, Property Subject to Section 168(f)(1) Election

Depreciation for property the taxpayer elects to depreciate under the unit-of-production method or another method not based on a term of years is reported on Line 15. The election is made by reporting the taxpayer's depreciation for the property on Line 15 and attaching a statement to Form 4562 providing a description of the property and the depreciation method, as well as the taxpayer's adjusted basis in the property.

Line 16, Other Depreciation (Including ACRS)

If property may not be depreciated under the Modified Accelerated Cost Recovery System (MACRS) (see below), then total depreciation is reported on Line 16. This generally includes depreciation on the following types of property.

ACRS Property (pre-1987). Tangible personal property placed in service during 1981 through 1986 is normally depreciated using the Accelerated Cost Recovery System (ACRS). Certain antichurning rules exist to prevent taxpayers from taking advantage of MACRS for property owned or used prior to 1987. However, these rules do not apply to:

- residential rental property or nonresidential real property; and
- property for which in the tax year when it was placed in service, the deduction under ACRS was more than the deduction under MACRS using the half-year convention.

> **Planning Tip.** Improvements made after 1986 to property placed in service before 1987 must be depreciated using MACRS and not ACRS.

Personal property. Subject to the preceding exceptions, MACRS cannot be used for personal property (i.e., section 1245 property) if:

1. the taxpayer or someone related to the taxpayer owned or used the property in 1986;
2. the taxpayer acquired the property from a person who owned it in 1986 and the user of the property did not change as a result of the transaction;

3. the taxpayer leased the property to a person (or someone related to the person) who owned or used the property in 1986; or
4. the taxpayer acquired the property in a transaction in which the user of the property did not change, and the property was not MACRS property in the hands of the person from whom the taxpayer acquired it by virtue of restriction 2 or 3.

Real property. Subject to the exceptions to the antichurning rules, a taxpayer generally cannot use MACRS for real property (i.e., IRC §1250 property) if restrictions (1) and (3) applicable to personal property above apply. Also MACRS may not be used if the taxpayer acquired the real property in a like-kind exchange, involuntary conversion, or repossession of property that the taxpayer (or someone related to the taxpayer) owned in 1986. MACRS applies only to that part of the basis in the acquired real property that represents cash paid or unlike property given up. It does not apply to the carried-over part of the basis.

Property Placed in Service Before 1981. Property placed in service before 1981 generally is depreciated using a facts-and-circumstances method subject to certain limitations (e.g., property acquired from related persons).

Certain Nonrecognition Transactions. In the following nonrecognition transactions, the transferee of MACRS property steps into the transferor's shoes and must continue to depreciate the transferor's adjusted basis in the transferred property as if the transfer did not take place (IRC Section 168(i)(7)):

- a distribution in complete liquidation of a subsidiary;
- a transfer to a corporation controlled by the transferor;
- an exchange of property solely for corporate stock or securities in a reorganization;
- a contribution of property to a partnership in exchange for a partnership interest; and
- a partnership distribution of property to a partner.

Intangibles. Intangibles are normally depreciated using the straight-line method. However, the income forecast method (discussed below) can be elected for certain property. See also the discussion of Amortization beginning on page 7-16.

Motor Vehicles. If a taxpayer elects to depreciate the cost of a motor vehicle for which the standard mileage rate had been used in a previous tax year, then the straight-line method must be used over the vehicle's estimated remaining useful life.

Certain Sound Recordings, Motion Pictures and Videotapes. MACRS cannot be used to depreciate sound recordings, motion picture films and video tapes. For this purpose, sound recordings are discs, tapes, or other phonorecordings resulting from the fixation of a series of sounds. Depreciation for this type of property is computed using the straight-line method or the income forecast method. Taxpayers in the business of renting videos can depreciate only those videos bought for rental. If the video has a useful life of one year or less, the cost may be deducted as a business expense.

Income Forecast Method. A taxpayer may choose to use the income forecast method or straight-line method to depreciate certain intangible property including sound recordings, motion pictures, videotapes, copyrights, books, and patents. Under the income forecast method, each year's depreciation deduction is equal to the cost of the property, less its salvage value, multiplied by a fraction. The numerator of the fraction is the current year's net income from the property, and the denominator is the total income anticipated from the property through the end of the 10th tax year following the tax year the property is placed in service.

MACRS Depreciation (Part III, Lines 17-20)

General Information

A taxpayer who buys or acquires a capital asset, such as a building, a machine, or equipment, is generally not permitted to deduct the total cost of the item in the tax year of acquisition. Instead, the cost of such an item must be written off and deducted over a period of tax years that begins generally with the year of acquisition. This write-off is permitted by means of a depreciation deduction.

For this purpose, property is depreciable if:

- it is used in a trade or business or for the production of income;
- it has a useful life exceeding one year;
- if it is *tangible*, it is subject to wear and tear; and
- if it is *intangible*, it must generally be known to have a limited life that can be estimated with reasonable accuracy. See MTG ¶1201.

Trade or Business Requirement. No deduction is allowed for depreciation unless the property is used in a trade or business or other income-producing activity. In other words, no deduction is allowed for depreciation while property is being used for personal purposes.

If the taxpayer held property for personal use and subsequently converted it to business or income-producing use, the property can be depreciated. In such circumstances, the depreciable basis is the lesser of:

- the fair market value of the property on the date of the change in use; *or*
- the original cost increased by the cost of any permanent improvements or additions and other costs that must be added to basis, and decreased by any deductions the taxpayer claimed for casualty and theft losses and other items reducing the taxpayer's basis.

If an asset is used for *both* personal and business or income production purposes, the taxpayer is permitted to deduct depreciation on the portion of the asset used for business or production of income purposes. An allocation of the property's basis must be made to determine the portion of the asset that is subject to depreciation.

Wear and Tear Requirement. The deduction for depreciation is permitted only for property that wears out or becomes obsolete. Property, such as land, that does not wear out cannot be depreciated. The IRS takes the position that works of art cannot be amortized or depreciated since they normally are not subject to wear and tear.

Modified Accelerated Cost Recovery System (MACRS)

For most tangible property placed in service after 1986, taxpayers must compute depreciation using the Modified Accelerated Cost Recovery System (MACRS). See MTG ¶ 1238. MACRS is not used to depreciate *intangible* assets, such as patents or copyrights, which are amortized using a straight-line depreciation method (see discussion on page 7-16).

Under MACRS, there are two depreciation systems, the general depreciation system (GDS) and the alternative depreciation system (ADS). Under both systems, the cost of tangible depreciable property (not including salvage value) must be recovered using the applicable depreciation method, recovery period, and accounting convention. The GDS normally will be used unless the taxpayer is specifically required by the Code or elects to use the ADS to compute her depreciation under MACRS.

General Depreciation System. Under the GDS, each piece of property is assigned to a prescribed asset class based on its useful life. For each asset class, an applicable depreciation method, recovery period and accounting convention are provided. A table of asset classes and applicable recovery periods under the GDS is provided beginning at page 7-19.

 Caution. Classification is critical because the recovery periods, methods, and accounting conventions to be used in calculating depreciation can vary among the different classes of property. Carefully review the class descriptions and the characteristics of the specific property.

The depreciation method and accounting convention that may be used in computing depreciation depends on the asset class the property is assigned and the recovery period for that class. The recovery period for a particular class is the number or years over which the taxpayer's cost or basis in the property may be recovered. There are generally eight recovery periods under the GDS including 3, 5, 7, 10, 15, 20, 27.5 and 39 years.

 Caution. Nonresidential real property placed in service before May 13, 1993, is depreciated under MACRS over 31.5 years.

Depreciation Methods. MACRS provides three depreciation methods under the GDS. The cost of property with a 3-, 5-, 7- or 10-year recovery period must be recovered using the 200% declining-balance depreciation method. The cost of property with a 15 or 20-year recovery period must be recovered using the 150%-declining-balance depreciation method. The cost of property recovered over 27.5 or 39 years is recovered using the straight-line method.

Declining-balance methods. Under the declining-balance methods, an applicable depreciation rate is determined by dividing the specified declining-balance percentage (i.e., 200 or 150 percent) by the applicable recovery period. This rate will then apply for each tax year in which the declining-balance method is used and applied to the unrecovered basis of the property. For example, the 200% declining-balance method applied to property with a 5-year recovery period results in an applicable depreciation rate of 40% in each of the five years.

Straight-line method. Under the straight-line method, a new applicable depreciation rate is determined for each tax year in the applicable recovery period. For any tax year, the applicable depreciation rate is determined by dividing one by the length of the recovery period remaining as of the beginning of the tax year. The rate is applied to the unrecovered basis of the property.

For example, the straight-line method applied to property with a 5-year recovery period results in applicable depreciation rates of 20, 25, 33.33, 50, and 100%, computed for five full years. If, as of the beginning of any tax year, the remaining recovery period is less than one year, the applicable depreciation rate for that year is 100%.

Special Elections. In lieu of using the applicable 150% or 200% DB depreciation method, a taxpayer may irrevocably elect to use the straight-line method over the regular recovery period. A taxpayer may also elect to use the 150%-declining-balance depreciation method over the regular 3-, 5-, 7- or 10-year recovery periods for property otherwise depreciated using the 200% DB method. If made, either election will apply to all property in the particular MACRS class that is placed in service during the tax year. A separate election is required for each property class.

 Caution. If a taxpayer places personal property in service in a farming business during the tax year, then the 150%-declining-balance or straight-line depreciation methods must be used, unless the property must be depreciated under the ADS.

Accounting Conventions. Certain accounting conventions are used to determine the amount of depreciation in the year of acquisition and the year of disposition. Like the depreciation methods, what convention applies under the GDS is dependent on the applicable recovery period of the property.

Property with a 3-, 5-, 7-, 10-, 15- or 20-year recovery period must use the half-year convention (unless the mid-quarter convention applies). Property with 27.5 or 39 year recovery period must use a mid-month convention.

Half-Year Convention. Under the half-year convention, only one-half year of depreciation is allowed in the first tax year, regardless of when the asset is placed in service or sold during the year (i.e., ½ × the annual depreciation as normally computed). As a consequence, the recovery period is effectively extended one year so that the remaining one-half may be claimed. If the half-year convention applies, the depreciation tables automatically take this into account.

Mid-Month Convention. The mid-month convention is used for residential and nonresidential real property. Under the mid-month convention, one-half month of depreciation is allowed for the month the asset is

placed in service or sold, and a full month of depreciation is allowed for each additional month of the year that the asset is in service.

For example, if a calendar-year taxpayer places a building in service on March 4, the annual depreciation allowed is 9.5/12 (a half-month's depreciation for March and nine months' depreciation for April through December). The MACRS depreciation tables automatically take this into account.

Mid-Month (MM) Convention		
Month	Placed in Service	Disposed Of
1	0.9583	0.0417
2	0.8750	0.1250
3	0.7917	0.2083
4	0.7083	0.2917
5	0.6250	0.3750
6	0.5417	0.4583
7	0.4583	0.5417
8	0.3750	0.6250
9	0.2917	0.7083
10	0.2083	0.7917
11	0.1250	0.8750
12	0.0417	0.9583

Mid-Quarter Convention. The mid-quarter convention applies to tangible personal property only if more than 40% of the aggregate bases of all personal property placed in service during the tax year is placed in service during the last three months of the year. For this purpose, property placed in service and disposed of during the same tax year is not taken into account. Similarly, property that is not depreciated using MACRS is omitted.

Also not taken into account is any amount expensed under IRC §179 or property used for personal purposes. Unlike the section 179 deduction, bonus depreciation does not reduce the basis of property for purposes of applying the 40% test. If the 40% test is satisfied, the mid-quarter convention applies to *all* personal property placed in service during the year (regardless of the quarter in which it was actually placed in service).

The mid-quarter convention treats all personal property as being placed in service in the middle of the quarter of the taxable year in which it was actually placed in service. Therefore, one-half of a quarter's depreciation—one-eighth (½ × ¼) or 12.5% of the annual depreciation—is allowed for the quarter in which the asset is placed in service or sold. In addition, a full quarter's depreciation is allowed for each additional quarter that the asset is in service.

For example, if the mid-quarter convention applies, personal property placed in service on March 3 would be treated as having been placed in service in the middle of the first quarter, and the taxpayer would be able to claim 3½ quarters–3.5/4 or 87.5%–of the annual amount of depreciation.

Mid-Quarter (MQ) Convention		
Quarter	Placed in Service	Disposed Of
1	0.875	0.125
2	0.625	0.375
3	0.375	0.625
4	0.125	0.875

Alternative Depreciation System. Instead of depreciating property under the MACRS general depreciation system (GDS), a taxpayer may make an irrevocable election to use the alternative depreciation system (ADS) with respect to any classification of property for the tax year. The election will cover all property in the same property class placed in service in the tax year. However, for real property (i.e., nonresidential and residential rental property), the election may be made on a property-by-property basis.

Mandatory Use of ADS. The taxpayer must use ADS for depreciating the following property:

- "listed property" (see page 7-13) that is not used more than 50% for business purposes;
- tangible property used outside the United States during the tax year;
- property used by a tax-exempt entity;
- property financed by the issuance of tax-exempt bonds;
- property used predominantly in a farming business and placed in service during any tax year in which an election was made not to apply the uniform capitalization rules; and
- property imported into the United States for which an executive order of the president of the United States is in effect.

Planning Tip. ADS depreciation periods are generally longer than the regular depreciation periods. By electing ADS for a class of property, a taxpayer can defer depreciation deductions over a greater period of time.

Caution. If a taxpayer is required to use ADS to depreciate property, then bonus depreciation may not be claimed for the property.

ADS is similar to GDS in that the same accounting conventions must be followed. The major difference between GDS and ADS is that ADS has longer recovery periods for most assets and the straight-line depreciation method is required for all classes of property.

Line 17, MACRS Deductions for Assets Placed in Service before 2013

For assets placed in service in tax years beginning before 2013, the amount of depreciation that may be claimed in 2013 under MACRS is reported on Line 17. Note that the taxpayer should maintain separate records of depreciation for each tax year. However, only the total amount of depreciation for all such assets is entered on Line 17. The taxpayer does not have to separately state the amount of depreciation for each asset placed in service before 2013.

Line 18, Election to Group Assets

To simplify the computation of MACRS depreciation, a taxpayer may establish *general asset accounts* (GAAs) for groups of assets and then depreciate each account as a single item. Each GAA must include only assets that are placed in service in the same tax year and have the same asset class, depreciation method, recovery period and convention.

Assets without an asset class, but which have the rest of the preceding characteristics in common,

Comparison of MACRS GDS and ADS			
MACRS Property Class	MACRS GDS	ADS (Use ADS Life)	Accounting Convention
3-year, 5-year, 7-year, 10-year	200% DB 150% DB SL	SL	Half-year or mid-quarter
15-year, 20-year	150% DB SL	SL	Half-year or mid-quarter
Residential rental real estate	27.5 years SL	40 years SL	Mid-month
Nonresidential real estate	39 years SL	40 years SL	Mid-month

may be grouped in a single general asset account. In addition, the following rules apply in grouping property into GAAs:

- Property subject to the mid-quarter convention can be grouped only in a GAA with property placed in service in the same quarter.
- Property subject to the mid-month convention can be grouped only in a GAA with property placed in service in the same month.
- Passenger automobiles subject to the limits on passenger automobile depreciation must be grouped in a separate GAA (see Tab 8).
- A taxpayer cannot include property in a GAA if it is used for both personal and business purposes.
- Property that generates foreign-source income is subject to special rules.

Disposition of GAA Property. When a taxpayer disposes of property included in a GAA, the entire amount of the proceeds *realized* (i.e., the property is treated as having an adjusted basis of zero) is generally recognized as ordinary income. However, the unadjusted basis of the disposed property is left in the GAA to be fully recovered through depreciation in future years. A taxpayer who chooses to apply temporary GAA regulations to tax years beginning after 2011 may make an election to recognize gain or loss by reference to the adjusted basis of the disposed-of property (Temp. Reg. §1.168(i)-1T).

If all the assets, or the last asset, in a GAA are disposed of, then the taxpayer may treat the GAA as terminated. Under such circumstances, gain or loss for the GAA is the amount realized on the disposition over the adjusted basis of the GAA. A transfer of all of the assets in a GAA in a like-kind exchange or involuntary conversion, will be treated as a termination for this purpose. Alternatively, a taxpayer may continue to depreciate the adjusted basis of the GAA.

 Planning Tip. Work with clients to discuss acquisitions and liquidations as they occur, rather than well after the fact or after the year end. Some projects run beyond the filing-year deadline and involved parties may or may not be available to assist you in return preparation.

Line 19, Assets Placed in Service During the 2013 Tax Year Using the General Depreciation System (Section B)

For property placed in service in 2013, a taxpayer uses Line 19 of Form 4562 to depreciate assets under the MACRS general depreciation system (GDS).

The taxpayer must sort property into one of the nine classifications listed on Lines 19a-19i in column (a). A table of asset classes and applicable recovery periods under GDS is provided beginning at page 7-19 to help in this process.

Month and Year Placed in Service. In column (b), the month and year residential rental property and nonresidential real property was placed in service must be provided.

Basis for Depreciation. A taxpayer's adjusted basis in property placed in service during the tax year, is entered in column (c). If the asset is used for both business and personal purposes, only the portion of the basis attributable to business (or income-producing use) is depreciated.

Normally, a taxpayer's basis in property is the cost to purchase the asset. However, basis must be adjusted for several factors. For example, a taxpayer's basis in property must be reduced for any IRC §179 deduction claimed on the property on Line 12. In addition, basis must be reduced for any "additional special/bonus" depreciation claimed on the property on Line 14. Basis for depreciation purposes must also be reduced for: the deduction for removal of barriers to the disabled and elderly; disabled access credit; and the credit for employer-provided childcare facilities and services.

Recovery Period. The recovery period of the depreciable property must be entered in column (d). The recovery period generally follows the asset class of the property (e.g., 3-year property has a 3-year recovery period).

Convention. The accounting convention that must be used in computing depreciation is entered in column (e). If the half-year convention applies, then "HY" is entered. If the mid-month convention applies, then "MM" is entered. If the mid-quarter convention applies, then "MQ" is entered.

Method. The depreciation method that may be used in computing depreciation is entered in column (f). As noted before, the depreciation method used normally depends on the classification of the property. However, different options may be available for a particular class. If the taxpayer is using either the 200%- or 150%-declining-balance method, then enter "200 DB" or "150 DB" in the column. If the taxpayer is using the straight-line method, then enter "S/L" instead.

Depreciation Deduction. Computation of depreciation for each classification of property is made using the basis and the applicable statutory percentage provided in IRS tables. The tables incorporate the appropriate convention. The result is entered for each classification of property in column (g) of Line 19. Some of the most common used MACRS depreciation tables are reproduced beginning on page 7-29.

 Caution. Information needed to compute the depreciation deduction (basis, method, etc.) must be part of the permanent records even if it is not sent with the return. *The date placed in service is key to when a taxpayer may start taking the deduction.*

Line 20, Assets Placed in Service During 2013 Tax Year Using the Alternative Depreciation System (Section C)

A taxpayer uses Line 20 of Form 4562 to record depreciation on property placed in service in 2013 for which the Alternative Depreciation System (ADS) under MACRS is elected. Like the GDS, the taxpayer must sort property into the one of the classifications listed on Lines 20a-20c in column (a).

Example. On May 1, 2013, Daniel Muzrahi purchased a copier to be used solely for business for $10,000. He did not elect IRC §179 expensing and elected out of bonus depreciation. The copier was his only acquisition during the year. It had a class life of four years. Under MACRS, the recovery period is specified based on the classification of the property. Copiers are considered five-year property, so the recovery period is five years.

Daniel has several options regarding the depreciation method: 200% or 150% declining balance, MACRS straight line using a five-year life, or ADS straight line using a six-year life. The accounting convention prescribed for five-year property is the half-year convention.

Daniel elects to compute his depreciation using the 200% declining-balance method (switching to straight line where appropriate), a five-year recovery period, and the half-year convention. Depreciation would be computed as follows:

Year	Unadjusted Recovery Basis	Accelerated Annual Percentage	Depreciation
2013	$10,000	20.00%	$2,000
2014	10,000	32.00	3,200
2015	10,000	19.20	1,920
2016	10,000	11.52	1,152
2017	10,000	11.52	1,152
2018	10,000	5.76	576
		100.00%	$10,000

The depreciation for most property is based on the property's class life and is entered on Line 20a. A table of asset classes and applicable recovery periods under ADS is provided below to help in this process. Property that does not have a class life is entered as 12-year property on Line 20b. Nonresidential real property and residential rental property is entered as 40-year property on Line 20c.

The rest of Line 20 is completed similarly to Line 19 under the GDS. Column (b) is used to record the month and year nonresidential real property and residential rental property is placed in service. Column (c) is where basis is reported. The ADS recovery period is entered in column (d). Only straight-line depreciation is allowed to be used for ADS property.

The total ADS depreciation for each classification of property is entered on column (g) of Line 20. Computation of depreciation for each classification is made using the basis and the applicable statutory percentage provided in IRS tables. The tables are available in IRS Publication 946, How to Depreciate Property.

Depreciation Summary (Part IV, Lines 21-23)

The total amount of depreciation being claimed in 2013 is reported on Line 22. The total includes the sum of the amount of any:

- IRC §179 deduction (Line 12);
- bonus/additional depreciation (Line 14);
- depreciation under the unit-of-production method or another method not based on term of year (Line 15);
- depreciation not computed under MACRS (Line 16);
- depreciation under the MACRS general depreciation system (GDS) (Line 19(g));
- depreciation under the MACRS alternative depreciation system (ADS) (Line 20(g)); and
- depreciation on any listed property (Line 21).

A taxpayer that is a partnership or an S corporation, should not include any IRC §179 deduction in the total on Line 22. Instead, the deduction is passed through to each partner or shareholder (and reported on Schedule K-1) based on their respective interest in the entity. If any assets being depreciated in 2013 are subject to the uniform capitalization rules under IRC §263A, then the increase in basis from costs that the taxpayer must capitalize is entered on Line 23.

Recapture. If a taxpayer sells or otherwise disposes of property that was depreciated under MACRS, any gain on the sale may be recaptured as ordinary income up to the amount of the depreciation previously allowed. Generally, the gain treated as ordinary income is the *lesser* of: (1) the depreciation allowed or allowable on the property; or (2) the gain *realized* on the sale or disposition. Part III Form 4797 is used to figure this amount.

For this purpose, depreciation includes any additional special/bonus depreciation allowed, as well as any IRC §179 deduction claimed on the property. Gain on MACRS section 1250 property, such as residential rental property and nonresidential real property, is subject to recapture as ordinary income to the extent the depreciation claimed exceeds the amount of straight-line depreciation that is allowed. Since MACRS residential rental property and nonresidential real property is depreciated using the straight-line method, there is no depreciation recapture. However, if bonus depreciation is claimed on section 1250 property, it is treated as an accelerated deduction and is subject to recapture to the extent it exceeds the amount of straight-line depreciation that would be allowed on the bonus deduction. Where a section 179 deduction is claimed on section 1250 property, such as qualified real property discussed above, the entire section 179 is subject to recapture (to the extent of gain) as if the section 1250 property were section 1245 property.

 Caution. All depreciation recapture is reported as ordinary income in the year the personal property is sold, even if the gain from the sale is reported using the installment method over the term of the contract. It may be advisable to make sure that the installment sale agreement includes an initial payment large enough to pay for any tax owed on the recapture income.

Listed Property (Part V, Lines 24-41)

Depreciation and Other Information (Section A)

The amount of depreciation as well as the IRC §179 deduction that may be claimed for "listed property" is limited if such property is not used predominantly (more than 50%) for business. If the property is not used more than 50% for business in the year it is placed in service, then:

- expensing under IRC §179 is not allowed; and
- the MACRS general depreciation system (GDS) may not be used, but instead the property must be depreciated using the MACRS alternative depreciation system (ADS).

In certain cases, depreciation may be denied.

For this purpose, "listed property" includes:

- passenger automobiles weighing 6,000 pounds or less (see Tab 8 for a discussion of depreciation limits for passenger automobiles);

- any property used for transportation if the nature of the property lends itself to personal use (e.g., motorcycles, pick-up trucks, SUVs);
- any property used for entertainment or recreational purposes (e.g., photographic, phonographic, communication, and video recording equipment); and computers or peripheral equipment.

Exceptions. Listed property does not include property used for entertainment or recreational purposes if it is used exclusively in a taxpayer's trade or business or at the taxpayer's regular business establishment. Computers and peripheral equipment are not listed property if used exclusively at a regular business establishment and owned or leased by the person who operates the business establishment. For this purpose, a portion of the taxpayer's home can be treated as a regular business establishment only if it meets the requirements for the home office deduction.

Line 24, Evidence for Use

A taxpayer cannot take any depreciation or IRC §179 deduction unless the business/investment use of the listed property is substantiated with adequate records or with sufficient evidence to support the taxpayer's own statements. The following information should be included in the records:

- the amount of each separate expenditure, such as the cost of acquiring the item, maintenance and repair costs, capital improvement costs, lease payments, and any other expenses;
- the amount of each business and investment use (based on an appropriate measure, such as mileage for vehicles and time for other listed property), and the total use of the property for the tax year;
- the date of the expenditure or use; and
- the business or investment purpose of the expenditure.

The information above should be recorded on a timely basis. The IRS takes the position that the expense must be recorded when the taxpayer has full knowledge of the elements of an expenditure. An expense account statement made from an account book, diary, or similar record prepared or maintained at or near the time of the expenditure or use generally is considered a timely record if, in the regular course of business:

- the statement is given by an employee to the employer; or
- the statement is given by an independent contractor to the client or customer.

For example, a log maintained on a weekly basis, that accounts for use during the week, will be considered a record made at or near the time of use.

Line 25, Special Depreciation Allowance

If the taxpayer placed listed property in service in the tax year and it is used more than 50% in a *qualified business use* (see below), any bonus depreciation claimed on the property should be entered on Line 25. However, the amount of the deduction for passenger automobiles that may be claimed for the tax year is limited (see Tab 8). For a discussion of the special depreciation allowance, see page 7-5.

A 50% first-year special depreciation deduction can be claimed for most new cars acquired after December 31, 2007, and before January 1, 2014, (with no binding contract in place prior to January 1, 2008) and placed in service before January 1, 2014. The aggregate of the bonus depreciation, section 179, and regular first-year depreciation deductions that can be claimed on the 2013 return will be limited to the first-year cap of $11,160 for passenger autos that are rated at an unloaded gross vehicle weight of 6,000 pounds or less ($11,360 for trucks, vans, and SUVs). Trucks, vans, and SUVs are not subject to the caps if they have a gross weight in excess of 6,000 pounds.

Lines 26–29, Depreciation for Listed Property

A taxpayer uses Line 26 to compute depreciation for listed property used more than 50% in a qualified business use. Line 27 is used to computed depreciation for listed property used 50% or less in a qualified business use.

In determining whether the property is used more than 50% for business, only *qualified business use* is considered. Generally, *qualified business use* means any use in a trade or business of the taxpayer, rather than use in an investment or other activity conducted for the production of income. Qualified business use does not include:

- leasing listed property to a five-percent owner or related person;
- use of listed property as compensation for services performed by a five-percent owner or related person (unless the property in question is an airplane, in which case use will be qualified business use if at least 25% of the total use during the tax year is for a qualifying business use); or
- use of listed property as compensation for services performed by any person (who is not a five-percent owner or related person), unless an amount is included in that person's income for the use of the property and, if required, income tax is withheld on that amount.

Employee's Use of Own Listed Property. An employee's use of his or her own listed property in connection with employment is not considered business use unless it is for the *convenience of the employer* and is *required as a condition of employment*. Thus, a statement by the employer expressly requiring the employee to use the property

is insufficient for this purpose. Ordinarily, the property is considered required only if it enables the employee to properly perform the duties of his or her employment.

Computing Depreciation. The taxpayer must describe the type of listed property being depreciated in column (a) of Lines 26 and 27. Automobiles and other vehicles must be listed first, followed by any other listed property the taxpayer placed in service in the tax year.

The date on which depreciation begins is entered in column (b) of Lines 26 and 27. Depreciation begins when the asset is placed in service. This is not always the same as the time the asset is purchased. An asset is considered placed in service when it is in a state of readiness and availability for the assigned function of the activity.

In column (c) of Lines 26 and 27, the taxpayer enters the percentage of business/investment use (as opposed to personal use). For automobiles and other vehicles, this percentage is determined by dividing the number of miles driven during the tax year for trade or business purposes (or for the production of income) by the total number of miles driven for the tax year (see Tab 8). Commuting expenses are not included in business/investment use.

Basis for Depreciation. Column (d) of Lines 26 and 27 is used to record the taxpayer's basis (i.e., cost) of the listed property (unadjusted for prior years' depreciation). If the listed property was converted from personal use to business use, then the taxpayer's basis is the smaller of the property's adjusted basis or its fair market value on the date of conversion.

> **Filing Tip.** For an automobile or other vehicle, the basis of the property is reduced for any qualified electric vehicle credit or deduction for clean-fuel vehicles claimed in previous years.

If the asset is used for both business and personal purposes, only the portion of the basis attributable to business (or income-producing) use is depreciated. This amount is entered in column (e) of Lines 26 and Line 27. It is calculated by multiplying the taxpayer's cost or other basis in column (d) by the percentage of business/investment use in column (c). This amount should then be reduced by any IRC §179 deduction, as well as the credit for employer-provided childcare facilities or service, and the investment tax credit.

Depreciation Methods. In columns (f) and (g) of Lines 26 and 27, the taxpayer should enter the appropriate recovery period, depreciation method and accounting convention. For listed property used more than 50% in qualified business use (Line 26), these are determined under the same rules for nonlisted property under MACRS (see page 7-8). For listed property used 50% or less in a qualified business use (Line 27), the taxpayer must use recovery periods under the MACRS alternative depreciation system (ADS) and the straight-line depreciation method.

Using the recovery period, depreciation method and accounting convention, compute the depreciation deduction for each listed property in column (h) of Lines 26 and 27 using the IRS tables (see page 7-29). However, the amount of the deduction for passenger automobiles that may be claimed for the tax year is limited (see Tab 8). Add the amount in column (h) for Lines 25, 26, and 27 (subject to the limits for automobiles), and enter the total on Line 28 and on Line 21.

IRC §179 Deduction. A taxpayer may elect the IRC §179 expense deduction for "listed property" that meets the 50-percent qualified business test (see above). The amount expensed is reported in column (i) of Line 26. The total expensed amount is entered on Line 29 and on Line 7. "Listed property" that fails to meet the 50-percent qualified business use requirement (Line 27) does not qualify for the IRC §179 deduction.

Expensing Limit for SUVs. A taxpayer may not expense more than $25,000 of the cost of certain motor vehicles, including a sport utility vehicle (SUV), under IRC §179. This rule applies to any vehicle:

- primarily designed or used to carry passengers over public streets, roads, or highways;
- not subject to the depreciation limits on motor vehicles (e.g., gross vehicle weight exceeds 6,000 pounds) (see discussion under Tab 8); and
- that has a gross vehicle weight not exceeding 14,000 pounds.

A pick-up truck that weighs more than 6,000 pounds is not subject to the $25,000 limit unless it has a bed less than 6 feet long.

Recapture. If listed property is predominantly used (more than 50%) for business in the year in which it is placed in service but fails to be predominantly used for business in a later tax year, then the taxpayer will have to recapture depreciation deductions. The recaptured amount is equal to the excess of any MACRS deprecation allowable for tax years before business use fell to 50% or less, over the depreciation that would have been allowable in those years under the alternative depreciation system (ADS). Depreciation for this purpose includes any IRC §179 deduction claimed and any bonus depreciation.

Form 4797 is used to figure the recapture amount and it is reported as other income on the same form or schedule on which the taxpayer claimed the depreciation deduction (Schedule C or Form 2106).

Information on Use of Vehicles (Section B)

If a motor vehicle is identified as "listed property" on Lines 26 and 27, then the taxpayer may have to provide certain information on the vehicle on Lines 30 through 36, including (see Tab 8 for a definition of some of these terms):

Line 30: Total business/investment miles

Line 31: Total commuting miles

Line 32: Total other personal miles

Line 33: Total miles

Line 34: Available for personal use

Line 35: Used by greater than five-percent owner

Line 36: Availability of another vehicle for personal use.

This information only has to be provided for vehicles used by a sole proprietor, a partner, any "more than 5% owner," or a related person. However, a taxpayer will be not required to complete Lines 30 through 36 if they provide the vehicle for use by their employees who are *not* a "more than 5% owner" or a related person and answer **Yes** to all of the requirements of Section C below.

Questions for Employers Who Provide Vehicles for Use by Their Employees (Section C)

Employers who provide vehicles to their employees must meet substantiation requirements by maintaining a written policy statement that either:

- prohibits personal use of a vehicle *including* commuting; or
- prohibits personal use of a vehicle *except* for commuting.

For either written policy statement, there must be evidence that would enable the IRS to determine whether use of the vehicle meets these conditions. An employee does not need to keep separate records for vehicles satisfying these written policy statement rules.

Line 37, Written Policy Prohibiting Personal Use (Including Commuting)

A written policy statement that prohibits personal use (including commuting) must meet *all* of the following conditions:

- The employer owns or leases the vehicle and provides it to one or more employees for use in the employer's trade or business.
- When the vehicle is not used in the employer's trade or business, it is kept on the employer's business

premises, unless temporarily located elsewhere (e.g., for maintenance or because of a mechanical failure).

- No employee using the vehicle lives at the employer's business premises.
- No employee may use the vehicle for personal purposes, other than *de minimis* personal use (e.g., a stop for lunch between two business deliveries).
- Except for *de minimis* use, the employer reasonably believes that no employee uses the vehicle for any personal purpose.

Line 38, Written Policy Prohibiting Personal Use (Excluding Commuting)

A written policy statement that prohibits personal use (except for commuting) is *not* available if the commuting employee is an officer, director, or 1%-or-more owner. This policy must meet *all* of the following conditions:

- The employer owns or leases the vehicle and provides it to one or more employees for use in the employer's trade or business, and it is used in the employer's trade or business.
- For bona fide noncompensatory business reasons, the employer requires the employee to commute to and/or from work in the vehicle.
- The employer establishes a written policy under which the employee may not use the vehicle for personal purposes, other than commuting or de minimis personal use (e.g., a stop for a personal errand between a business delivery and the employee's home).
- Except for *de minimis* use, the employer reasonably believes that the employee does not use the vehicle for any personal purpose other than commuting.
- The value of commuting use is included in the employee's gross income.

Line 39, All Vehicle Use as Personal

If all use of vehicles by employees is treated as personal use (and is therefore included as taxable wages), check "Yes."

Line 40, More than Five Vehicles to Employees

An employer that provides more than five vehicles to its employees who are not 5% owners or related persons need not complete Section B for such vehicles. Instead, the employer must obtain the information from its employees and retain the information received.

Line 41, Qualified Automobile Demonstration

- If an automobile is a demonstrator, the value of the automobile is a nontaxable fringe benefit to the employee and all of the related costs are deductible by the employer. An automobile meets the requirements for qualified demonstration use if the employer maintains a written policy statement that: prohibits use of the vehicle by individuals other than full-time automobile salespersons;

- prohibits use for personal vacation trips;
- prohibits storage of personal possessions in the automobile; and
- limits the total mileage outside the salesperson's normal working hours.

Amortization (Part VI, Lines 42-44)

Amortization is the recovery of certain capital expenditures that are not ordinarily deductible, over a fixed period of time. Amortization is therefore similar to straight-line depreciation. A taxpayer may elect to amortize certain property, while other property *must be* amortized.

 Caution. The portion of the basis of property that is amortized, will not qualify for depreciation under MACRS or the IRC §179 deduction.

Line 42, Amortization of Costs for 2013 Tax Year

Line 42 is used to report the amortization of costs beginning during the tax year. Column (a) is used to provide a description of the costs. Columns (b), (c), and (e) are used to enter respectively, the date the amortization period begins, the total amount being amortized, and the amortization period or percentage (whichever applies). These are provided by various Code sections which permit the amortization of certain costs. The particular Code section must be entered in column (d).

The amortization deduction for 2013 is computed in column (f) in one of two ways:

- by dividing the total amortizable amount in column (c) by the number of months over which the costs are to be amortized in column (e) and multiplied by the number of the amortization months that occur in 2013; or
- by multiplying the total amortizable amount in column (c) by the amortizable percentage in column (e).

Section 197 Intangibles. One of the most common costs that are *required* to be amortized are section 197 intangibles. Such costs must be amortized over 15 years (180 months) starting with the month they were acquired or the month the trade or business activity engaged in begins, whichever is later. A longer amortization period may apply to section 197 intangibles leased to a tax-exempt organization, government, or foreign person.

A section 197 intangible includes:

- goodwill;
- going concern value;
- workforce in place;
- business books and records, operating systems, or any other information base;
- a patent, copyright, formula, process, design, pattern, know-how, format, or similar item;
- a customer-based intangible (e.g., composition of market or market share);
- a supplier-based intangible;
- any license, permit, or other right granted by a governmental unit;
- any covenant not to compete entered into in connection with the acquisition of a business; and
- any franchise (other than a sports franchise), trademark, or trade name.

Assets which are not section 197 intangibles and not eligible to be amortized include:

- any interest in a corporation, partnership, trust or estate;
- any interest in land;
- computer software; and
- any interest under an existing lease of tangible property, or a debt that was in existence when the interest was acquired.

 Caution. A section 197 intangible will be treated as depreciable property used in the taxpayer's trade or business. Thus, a taxpayer who sells or otherwise disposes of a section 197 intangible held for more than one year may have to recapture any gain as ordinary income. Generally, the gain treated as ordinary income is the *lesser* of the amortization allowed or allowable on the property, or the gain realized on the sale or disposition.

If the taxpayer sells more than one section 197 intangible during the tax year, recapture must be calculated as if all of the taxpayer's section 197 intangibles sold or disposed of were a single asset. Thus, any gain realized on the sale or other disposition of the intangibles is recaptured as ordinary income to the extent of amortization claimed on any of the intangibles. For this purpose, the gain is calculated in Part III of Form 4797.

Start-Up Costs. A taxpayer is deemed to elect to deduct up to $5,000 of start-up expenses paid or incurred in the 2013 tax year when she begins a trade or business. The deduction must be reduced on a dollar-by-dollar basis as the amount of expenses exceeds $50,000. The taxpayer is not required to attach a statement to his or her return or specifically identify the deducted amounts as start-up expenses. Rather, the taxpayer will be deemed to have made such an election. A taxpayer can forego the deemed election by clearly electing to capitalize start-up expenses on a timely filed federal income tax return for the tax year in which the business begins operations. The election either to deduct start-up expenses or to capitalize such amounts is irrevocable and applies to all start-up expenses. Start-up expenses that are not currently deductible must be amortized over a 180-month (15-year) period beginning with the month the taxpayer begins business operations.

Start-up expenses are expenses paid or incurred in connection with: (1) investigating the creation or acquisition of an active trade or business; (2) creating an active trade or business; or (3) any activity engaged in for profit or for the production of income before the day on which the active trade or business begins. In addition, start-up expenses are allowable as a deduction if they were paid or incurred in connection with an existing active business in the same field as that entered into by the taxpayer. Start-up expenses do not include deductible interest, taxes, or research and experimental expenses.

 Caution. The deduction and amortization of start-up expenses is allowed to the taxpayer who incurs the start-up expenditures and subsequently enters the business. In the case of a sole proprietor, this means the deduction is allowed for the business with respect to which the start-up costs were incurred. If the business is organized into a corporation or partnership, then only the corporation or partnership may elect to deduct and amortize the start-up expenses it incurs. However, an individual taxpayer may elect to deduct and amortize expenses incurred to investigate an interest in an existing partnership when the individual acquires the interest.

If the taxpayer does not subsequently enter the trade or business to which the start-up expenses relate, then the taxpayer may not deduct and amortize the expenses but instead may be able to deduct them as losses. Similarly, if the trade or business is disposed of completely by the taxpayer before the end of the amortization period, then any remaining start-up expenses which were deferred through amortization are deductible only to the extent they qualify as a loss from a business.

Planning Tip. In addition to the deduction for start-up expenses, a corporation or partnership may deduct $5,000 of any organizational expenses in the tax year the business begins. This deduction is subject to a $50,000 limitation similar to the limitations for start-up costs, and any remaining organizational expenses must be amortized over a 180-month period.

Other Amortizable Costs. Other costs which may be amortized include the following:

- Premiums paid on taxable bonds acquired after 1987 may be amortized over the life of the bond (IRC §171).
- Research and experimental expenditures may either be deducted as business expenses in the tax year incurred or amortized over a 60-month period or more (up to 120 months) (IRC §174).

 Planning Tip. Any deduction for research expenditures must be reduced by the amount of the research tax credit under IRC §41 for the same expenses. Capitalized research expenses must also be reduced by the amount of the research credit that exceeds the amount otherwise allowable as a deduction for such expenses. As an alternative to reducing the otherwise allowable deduction or capitalized amount, the taxpayer may elect to claim a reduced credit on Form 6765. A taxpayer will want to calculate which alternative will allow him to achieve the lowest tax liability. The research tax credit is available for qualifying expenses paid or incurred before January 1, 2014.

- The cost of acquiring a lease must be amortized over the term of the lease (IRC §178).
- Up to $10,000 of qualified reforestation costs may be deducted in the year incurred. Any remaining costs may be amortized over an 84-month period (IRC §194).
- Pollution control facilities may be amortized over a 60-month period (IRC §169).

Line 43, Amortization of Costs That Began In Prior Years

The amortization of costs that began before the tax year is reported on Line 43. However, if the taxpayer is not required to file Form 4562 for any other reason, then Form 4562 does not have to be filed merely to report these costs. Instead, the amortization of costs that began before the tax year are reported as "Other expenses" on Schedule C or F of Form 1040.

Line 44, Total Amortization Costs

The total amortization claimed for the tax year is reported on Line 44 (the sum of column (f) Lines 42 and 43). The total is reported as "Other expenses" on Schedule C or F of Form 1040.

Table B-1. Table of Class Lives and Recovery Periods

Asset class	Description of assets included	Recovery Periods (in years)		
		Class Life (in years)	GDS (MACRS)	ADS
	SPECIFIC DEPRECIABLE ASSETS USED IN ALL BUSINESS ACTIVITIES, EXCEPT AS NOTED:			
00.11	**Office Furniture, Fixtures, and Equipment:** Includes furniture and fixtures that are not a structural component of a building. Includes such assets as desks, files, safes, and communications equipment. Does not include communications equipment that is included in other classes.	10	7	10
00.12	**Information Systems:** Includes computers and their peripheral equipment used in administering normal business transactions and the maintenance of business records, their retrieval and analysis. Information systems are defined as: 1) Computers: A computer is a programmable electronically activated device capable of accepting information, applying prescribed processes to the information, and supplying the results of these processes with or without human intervention. It usually consists of a central processing unit containing extensive storage, logic, arithmetic, and control capabilities. Excluded from this category are adding machines, electronic desk calculators, etc., and other equipment described in class 00.13. 2) Peripheral equipment consists of the auxiliary machines which are designed to be placed under control of the central processing unit. Nonlimiting examples are: Card readers, card punches, magnetic tape feeds, high speed printers, optical character readers, tape cassettes, mass storage units, paper tape equipment, keypunches, data entry devices, teleprinters, terminals, tape drives, disc drives, disc files, disc packs, visual image projector tubes, card sorters, plotters, and collators. Peripheral equipment may be used on-line or off-line. Does not incude equipment that is an integral part of other capital equipment that is included in other classes of economic activity, i.e., computers used primarily for process or production control, switching, channeling, and automating distributive trades and services such as point of sale (POS) computer systems. Also, does not include equipment of a kind used primarily for amusement or entertainment of the user.	6	5	5
00.13	**Data Handling Equipment; except Computers:** Includes only typewriters, calculators, adding and accounting machines, copiers, and duplicating equipment.	6	5	6
00.21	**Airplanes (airframes and engines), except those used in commercial or contract carrying of passengers or freight, and all helicopters (airframes and engines)**	6	5	6
00.22	**Automobiles, Taxis**	3	5	5
00.23	**Buses**	9	5	9
00.241	**Light General Purpose Trucks:** Includes trucks for use over the road (actual weight less than 13,000 pounds)	4	5	5
00.242	**Heavy General Purpose Trucks:** Includes heavy general purpose trucks, concrete ready mix-trucks, and ore trucks, for use over the road (actual unloaded weight 13,000 pounds or more)	6	5	6
00.25	**Railroad Cars and Locomotives, except those owned by railroad transportation companies**	15	7	15
00.26	**Tractor Units for Use Over-The-Road**	4	3	4
00.27	**Trailers and Trailer-Mounted Containers**	6	5	6
00.28	**Vessels, Barges, Tugs, and Similar Water Transportation Equipment, except those used in marine construction**	18	10	18
00.3	**Land Improvements:** Includes improvements directly to or added to land, whether such improvements are section 1245 property or section 1250 property, provided such improvements are depreciable. Examples of such assets might include sidewalks, roads, canals, waterways, drainage facilities, sewers (not including municipal sewers in Class 51), wharves and docks, bridges, fences, landscaping shrubbery, or radio and television transmitting towers. Does not include land improvements that are explicitly included in any other class, and buildings and structural components as defined in section 1.48-1(e) of the regulations. Excludes public utility initial clearing and grading land improvements as specified in Rev. Rul. 72-403, 1972-2 C.B. 102.	20	15	20
00.4	**Industrial Steam and Electric Generation and/or Distribution Systems:** Includes assets, whether such assets are section 1245 property or 1250 property, providing such assets are depreciable, used in the production and/or distribution of electricity with rated total capacity in excess of 500 Kilowatts and/or assets used in the production and/or distribution of steam with rated total capacity in excess of 12,500 pounds per hour for use by the taxpayer in its industrial manufacturing process or plant activity and not ordinarily available for sale to others. Does not include buildings and structural components as defined in section 1.48-1(e) of the regulations. Assets used to generate and/or distribute electricity or steam of the type described above, but of lesser rated capacity, are not included, but are included in the appropriate manufacturing equipment classes elsewhere specified. Also includes electric generating and steam distribution assets, which may utilize steam produced by a waste reduction and resource recovery plant, used by the taxpayer in its industrial manufacturing process or plant activity. Steam and chemical recovery boiler systems used for the recovery and regeneration of chemicals used in manufacturing, with rated capacity in excess of that described above, with specifically related distribution and return systems are not included but are included in appropriate manufacturing equipment classes elsewhere specified. An example of an excluded steam and chemical recovery boiler system is that used in the pulp and paper manufacturing equipment classes elsewhere specified. An example of an excluded steam and chemical recovery boiler system is that used in the pulp and paper manufacturing industry.	22	15	22

Table B-2. **Table of Class Lives and Recovery Periods**

Asset class	Description of assets included	Recovery Periods (in years)		
		Class Life (in years)	GDS (MACRS)	ADS
	DEPRECIABLE ASSETS USED IN THE FOLLOWING ACTIVITIES:			
01.1	**Agriculture:** Includes machinery and equipment, grain bins, and fences but no other land improvements, that are used in the production of crops or plants, vines, and trees; livestock; the operation of farm dairies, nurseries, greenhouses, sod farms, mushroom cellars, cranberry bogs, apiaries, and fur farms; the performance of agriculture, animal husbandry, and horticultural services.	10	7	10
01.11	**Cotton Ginning Assets**	12	7	12
01.21	**Cattle, Breeding or Dairy**	7	5	7
01.221	**Any breeding or work horse that is 12 years old or less at the time it is placed in service****	10	7	10
01.222	**Any breeding or work horse that is more than 12 years old at the time it is placed in service****	10	3	10
01.223	**Any race horse that is more than 2 years old at the time it is placed in service****	*	3	12
01.224	**Any horse that is more than 12 years old at the time it is placed in service and that is neither a race horse nor a horse described in class 01.222****	*	3	12
01.225	**Any horse not described in classes 01.221, 01.222, 01.223, or 01.224**	*	7	12
01.23	**Hogs, Breeding**	3	3	3
01.24	**Sheep and Goats, Breeding**	5	5	5
01.3	**Farm buildings except structures included in Class 01.4**	25	20	25
01.4	**Single purpose agricultural or horticultural structures (within the meaning of section 168(i)(13) of the Code)**	15	10***	15
10.0	**Mining:** Includes assets used in the mining and quarrying of metallic and nonmetallic minerals (including sand, gravel, stone, and clay) and the milling, beneficiation and other primary preparation of such materials.	10	7	10
13.0	**Offshore Drilling:** Includes assets used in offshore drilling for oil and gas such as floating, self-propelled and other drilling vessels, barges, platforms, and drilling equipment and support vessels such as tenders, barges, towboats and crewboats. Excludes oil and gas production assets.	7.5	5	7.5
13.1	**Drilling of Oil and Gas Wells:** Includes assets used in the drilling of onshore oil and gas wells and the provision of geophysical and other exploration services; and the provision of such oil and gas field services as chemical treatment, plugging and abandoning of wells and cementing or perforating well casings. Does not include assets used in the performance of any of these activities and services by integrated petroleum and natural gas producers for their own account.	6	5	6
13.2	**Exploration for and Production of Petroleum and Natural Gas Deposits:** Includes assets used by petroleum and natural gas producers for drilling of wells and production of petroleum and natural gas, including gathering pipelines and related storage facilities. Also includes petroleum and natural gas offshore transportation facilities used by producers and others consisting of platforms (other than drilling platforms classified in Class 13.0), compression or pumping equipment, and gathering and transmission lines to the first onshore transshipment facility. The assets used in the first onshore transshipment facility are also included and consist of separation equipment (used for separation of natural gas, liquids, and in Class 49.23), and liquid holding or storage facilities (other than those classified in Class 49.25). Does not include support vessels.	14	7	14
13.3	**Petroleum Refining:** Includes assets used for the distillation, fractionation, and catalytic cracking of crude petroleum into gasoline and its other components.	16	10	16
15.0	**Construction:** Includes assets used in construction by general building, special trade, heavy and marine construction contractors, operative and investment builders, real estate subdividers and developers, and others except railroads.	6	5	6
20.1	**Manufacture of Grain and Grain Mill Products:** Includes assets used in the production of flours, cereals, livestock feeds, and other grain and grain mill products.	17	10	17
20.2	**Manufacture of Sugar and Sugar Products:** Includes assets used in the production of raw sugar, syrup, or finished sugar from sugar cane or sugar beets.	18	10	18
20.3	**Manufacture of Vegetable Oils and Vegetable Oil Products:** Includes assets used in the production of oil from vegetable materials and the manufacture of related vegetable oil products.	18	10	18
20.4	**Manufacture of Other Food and Kindred Products:** Includes assets used in the production of foods and beverages not included in classes 20.1, 20.2 and 20.3.	12	7	12
20.5	**Manufacture of Food and Beverages—Special Handling Devices:** Includes assets defined as specialized materials handling devices such as returnable pallets, palletized containers, and fish processing equipment including boxes, baskets, carts, and flaking trays used in activities as defined in classes 20.1, 20.2, 20.3 and 20.4. Does not include general purpose small tools such as wrenches and drills, both hand and power-driven, and other general purpose equipment such as conveyors, transfer equipment, and materials handling devices.	4	3	4

* Property described in asset classes 01.223, 01.224, and 01.225 are assigned recovery periods but have no class lives.
** A horse is more than 2 (or 12) years old after the day that is 24 (or 144) months after its actual birthdate.
*** 7 if property was placed in service before 1989.

Table B-2. **Table of Class Lives and Recovery Periods (Continued)**

Asset class	Description of assets included	Class Life (in years)	GDS (MACRS)	ADS
		Recovery Periods (in years)		
21.0	**Manufacture of Tobacco and Tobacco Products:** Includes assets used in the production of cigarettes, cigars, smoking and chewing tobacco, snuff, and other tobacco products.	15	7	15
22.1	**Manufacture of Knitted Goods:** Includes assets used in the production of knitted and netted fabrics and lace. Assets used in yarn preparation, bleaching, dyeing, printing, and other similar finishing processes, texturing, and packaging, are elsewhere classified.	7.5	5	7.5
22.2	**Manufacture of Yarn, Thread, and Woven Fabric:** Includes assets used in the production of spun yarns including the preparing, blending, spinning, and twisting of fibers into yarns and threads, the preparation of yarns such as twisting, warping, and winding, the production of covered elastic yarn and thread, cordage, woven fabric, tire fabric, braided fabric, twisted jute for packaging, mattresses, pads, sheets, and industrial belts, and the processing of textile mill waste to recover fibers, flocks, and shoddies. Assets used to manufacture carpets, man-made fibers, and nonwovens, and assets used in texturing, bleaching, dyeing, printing, and other similar finishing processes, are elsewhere classified.	11	7	11
22.3	**Manufacture of Carpets and Dyeing, Finishing, and Packaging of Textile Products and Manufacture of Medical and Dental Supplies:** Includes assets used in the production of carpets, rugs, mats, woven carpet backing, chenille, and other tufted products, and assets used in the joining together of backing with carpet yarn or fabric. Includes assets used in washing, scouring, bleaching, dyeing, printing, drying, and similar finishing processes applied to textile fabrics, yarns, threads, and other textile goods. Includes assets used in the production and packaging of textile products, other than apparel, by creasing, forming, trimming, cutting, and sewing, such as the preparation of carpet and fabric samples, or similar joining together processes (other than the production of scrim reinforced paper products and laminated paper products) such as the sewing and folding of hosiery and panty hose, and the creasing, folding, trimming, and cutting of fabrics to produce nonwoven products, such as disposable diapers and sanitary products. Also includes assets used in the production of medical and dental supplies other than drugs and medicines. Assets used in the manufacture of nonwoven carpet backing, and hard surface floor covering such as tile, rubber, and cork, are elsewhere classified.	9	5	9
22.4	**Manufacture of Textile Yarns:** Includes assets used in the processing of yarns to impart bulk and/or stretch properties to the yarn. The principal machines involved are falsetwist, draw, beam-to-beam, and stuffer box texturing equipment and related highspeed twisters and winders. Assets, as described above, which are used to further process man-made fibers are elsewhere classified when located in the same plant in an integrated operation with man-made fiber producing assets. Assets used to manufacture man-made fibers and assets used in bleaching, dyeing, printing, and other similar finishing processes, are elsewhere classified.	8	5	8
22.5	**Manufacture of Nonwoven Fabrics:** Includes assets used in the production of nonwoven fabrics, felt goods including felt hats, padding, batting, wadding, oakum, and fillings, from new materials and from textile mill waste. Nonwoven fabrics are defined as fabrics (other than reinforced and laminated composites consisting of nonwovens and other products) manufactured by bonding natural and/or synthetic fibers and/or filaments by means of induced mechanical interlocking, fluid entanglement, chemical adhesion, thermal or solvent reaction, or by combination thereof other than natural hydration bonding as occurs with natural cellulose fibers. Such means include resin bonding, web bonding, and melt bonding. Specifically includes assets used to make flocked and needle punched products other than carpets and rugs. Assets, as described above, which are used to manufacture nonwovens are elsewhere classified when located in the same plant in an integrated operation with man-made fiber producing assets. Assets used to manufacture man-made fibers and assets used in bleaching, dyeing, printing, and other similar finishing processes, are elsewhere classified.	10	7	10
23.0	**Manufacture of Apparel and Other Finished Products:** Includes assets used in the production of clothing and fabricated textile products by the cutting and sewing of woven fabrics, other textile products, and furs; but does not include assets used in the manufacture of apparel from rubber and leather.	9	5	9
24.1	**Cutting of Timber:** Includes logging machinery and equipment and roadbuilding equipment used by logging and sawmill operators and pulp manufacturers for their own account.	6	5	6
24.2	**Sawing of Dimensional Stock from Logs:** Includes machinery and equipment installed in permanent or well established sawmills.	10	7	10
24.3	**Sawing of Dimensional Stock from Logs:** Includes machinery and equipment in sawmills characterized by temporary foundations and a lack, or minimum amount, of lumberhandling, drying, and residue disposal equipment and facilities.	6	5	6
24.4	**Manufacture of Wood Products, and Furniture:** Includes assets used in the production of plywood, hardboard, flooring, veneers, furniture, and other wood products, including the treatment of poles and timber.	10	7	10
26.1	**Manufacture of Pulp and Paper:** Includes assets for pulp materials handling and storage, pulp mill processing, bleach processing, paper and paperboard manufacturing, and on-line finishing. Includes pollution control assets and all land improvements associated with the factory site or production process such as effluent ponds and canals, provided such improvements are depreciable but does not include buildings and structural components as defined in section 1.48-1(e)(1) of the regulations. Includes steam and chemical recovery boiler systems, with any rated capacity, used for the recovery and regeneration of chemicals used in manufacturing. Does not include assets used either in pulpwood logging, or in the manufacture of hardboard.	13	7	13

Asset class	Description of assets included	Recovery Periods (in years)		
		Class Life (in years)	GDS (MACRS)	ADS
26.2	**Manufacture of Converted Paper, Paperboard, and Pulp Products:** Includes assets used for modification, or remanufacture of paper and pulp into converted products, such as paper coated off the paper machine, paper bags, paper boxes, cartons and envelopes. Does not include assets used for manufacture of nonwovens that are elsewhere classified.	10	7	10
27.0	**Printing, Publishing, and Allied Industries:** Includes assets used in printing by one or more processes, such as letter-press, lithography, gravure, or screen; the performance of services for the printing trade, such as bookbinding, typesetting, engraving, photo-engraving, and electrotyping; and the publication of newspapers, books, and periodicals.	11	7	11
28.0	**Manufacture of Chemicals and Allied Products:** Includes assets used to manufacture basic organic and inorganic chemicals; chemical products to be used in further manufacture, such as synthetic fibers and plastics materials; and finished chemical products. Includes assets used to further process man-made fibers, to manufacture plastic film, and to manufacture nonwoven fabrics, when such assets are located in the same plant in an integrated operation with chemical products producing assets. Also includes assets used to manufacture photographic supplies, such as film, photographic paper, sensitized photographic paper, and developing chemicals. Includes all land improvements associated with plant site or production processes, such as effluent ponds and canals, provided such land improvements are depreciable but does not include buildings and structural components as defined in section 1.48-1(e) of the regulations. Does not include assets used in the manufacture of finished rubber and plastic products or in the production of natural gas products, butane, propane, and by-products of natural gas production plants.	9.5	5	9.5
30.1	**Manufacture of Rubber Products:** Includes assets used for the production of products from natural, synthetic, or reclaimed rubber, gutta percha, balata, or gutta siak, such as tires, tubes, rubber footwear, mechanical rubber goods, heels and soles, flooring, and rubber sundries; and in the recapping, retreading, and rebuilding of tires.	14	7	14
30.11	**Manufacture of Rubber Products—Special Tools and Devices:** Includes assets defined as special tools, such as jigs, dies, mandrels, molds, lasts, patterns, specialty containers, pallets, shells; and tire molds, and accessory parts such as rings and insert plates used in activities as defined in class 30.1. Does not include tire building drums and accessory parts and general purpose small tools such as wrenches and drills, both power and hand-driven, and other general purpose equipment such as conveyors and transfer equipment.	4	3	4
30.2	**Manufacture of Finished Plastic Products:** Includes assets used in the manufacture of plastics products and the molding of primary plastics for the trade. Does not include assets used in the manufacture of basic plastics materials nor the manufacture of phonograph records.	11	7	11
30.21	**Manufacture of Finished Plastic Products—Special Tools:** Includes assets defined as special tools, such as jigs, dies, fixtures, molds, patterns, gauges, and specialty transfer and shipping devices, used in activities as defined in class 30.2. Special tools are specifically designed for the production or processing of particular parts and have no significant utilitarian value and cannot be adapted to further or different use after changes or improvements are made in the model design of the particular part produced by the special tools. Does not include general purpose small tools such as wrenches and drills, both hand and power-driven, and other general purpose equipment such as conveyors, transfer equipment, and materials handling devices.	3.5	3	3.5
31.0	**Manufacture of Leather and Leather Products:** Includes assets used in the tanning, currying, and finishing of hides and skins; the processing of fur pelts; and the manufacture of finished leather products, such as footwear, belting, apparel, and luggage.	11	7	11
32.1	**Manufacture of Glass Products:** Includes assets used in the production of flat, blown, or pressed products of glass, such as float and window glass, glass containers, glassware and fiberglass. Does not include assets used in the manufacture of lenses.	14	7	14
32.11	**Manufacture of Glass Products—Special Tools:** Includes assets defined as special tools such as molds, patterns, pallets, and specialty transfer and shipping devices such as steel racks to transport automotive glass, used in activities as defined in class 32.1. Special tools are specifically designed for the production or processing of particular parts and have no significant utilitarian value and cannot be adapted to further or different use after changes or improvements are made in the model design of the particular part produced by the special tools. Does not include general purpose small tools such as wrenches and drills, both hand and power-driven, and other general purpose equipment such as conveyors, transfer equipment, and materials handling devices.	2.5	3	2.5
32.2	**Manufacture of Cement:** Includes assets used in the production of cement, but does not include assets used in the manufacture of concrete and concrete products nor in any mining or extraction process.	20	15	20
32.3	**Manufacture of Other Stone and Clay Products:** Includes assets used in the manufacture of products from materials in the form of clay and stone, such as brick, tile, and pipe; pottery and related products, such as vitreous-china, plumbing fixtures, earthenware and ceramic insulating materials; and also includes assets used in manufacture of concrete and concrete products. Does not include assets used in any mining or extraction processes.	15	7	15

Asset class	Description of assets included	Recovery Periods (in years)		
		Class Life (in years)	GDS (MACRS)	ADS
33.2	**Manufacture of Primary Nonferrous Metals:** Includes assets used in the smelting, refining, and electrolysis of nonferrous metals from ore, pig, or scrap, the rolling, drawing, and alloying of nonferrous metals; the manufacture of castings, forgings, and other basic products of nonferrous metals; and the manufacture of nails, spikes, structural shapes, tubing, wire, and cable.	14	7	14
33.21	**Manufacture of Primary Nonferrous Metals—Special Tools:** Includes assets defined as special tools such as dies, jigs, molds, patterns, fixtures, gauges, and drawings concerning such special tools used in the activities as defined in class 33.2, Manufacture of Primary Nonferrous Metals. Special tools are specifically designed for the production or processing of particular products or parts and have no significant utilitarian value and cannot be adapted to further or different use after changes or improvements are made in the model design of the particular part produced by the special tools. Does not include general purpose small tools such as wrenches and drills, both hand and power-driven, and other general purpose equipment such as conveyors, transfer equipment, and materials handling devices. Rolls, mandrels and refractories are not included in class 33.21 but are included in class 33.2.	6.5	5	6.5
33.3	**Manufacture of Foundry Products:** Includes assets used in the casting of iron and steel, including related operations such as molding and coremaking. Also includes assets used in the finishing of castings and patternmaking when performed at the foundry, all special tools and related land improvements.	14	7	14
33.4	**Manufacture of Primary Steel Mill Products:** Includes assets used in the smelting, reduction, and refining of iron and steel from ore, pig, or scrap; the rolling, drawing and alloying of steel; the manufacture of nails, spikes, structural shapes, tubing, wire, and cable. Includes assets used by steel service centers, ferrous metal forges, and assets used in coke production, regardless of ownership. Also includes related land improvements and all special tools used in the above activities.	15	7	15
34.0	**Manufacture of Fabricated Metal Products:** Includes assets used in the production of metal cans, tinware, fabricated structural metal products, metal stampings, and other ferrous and nonferrous metal and wire products not elsewhere classified. Does not include assets used to manufacture non-electric heating apparatus.	12	7	12
34.01	**Manufacture of Fabricated Metal Products—Special Tools:** Includes assets defined as special tools such as dies, jigs, molds, patterns, fixtures, gauges, and returnable containers and drawings concerning such special tools used in the activities as defined in class 34.0. Special tools are specifically designed for the production or processing of particular machine components, products, or parts, and have no significant utilitarian value and cannot be adapted to further or different use after changes or improvements are made in the model design of the particular part produced by the special tools. Does not include general small tools such as wrenches and drills, both hand and power-driven, and other general purpose equipment such as conveyors, transfer equipment, and materials handling devices.	3	3	3
35.0	**Manufacture of Electrical and Non-Electrical Machinery and Other Mechanical Products:** Includes assets used to manufacture or rebuild finished machinery and equipment and replacement parts thereof such as machine tools, general industrial and special industry machinery, electrical power generation, transmission, and distribution systems, space heating, cooling, and refrigeration systems, commercial and home appliances, farm and garden machinery, construction machinery, mining and oil field machinery, internal combustion engines (except those elsewhere classified), turbines (except those that power airborne vehicles), batteries, lamps and lighting fixtures, carbon and graphite products, and electromechanical and mechanical products including business machines, instruments, watches and clocks, vending and amusement machines, photographic equipment, medical and dental equipment and appliances, and ophthalmic goods. Includes assets used by manufacturers or rebuilders of such finished machinery and equipment in activities elsewhere classified such as the manufacture of castings, forgings, rubber and plastic products, electronic subassemblies or other manufacturing activities if the interim products are used by the same manufacturer primarily in the manufacture, assembly, or rebuilding of such finished machinery and equipment. Does not include assets used in mining, assets used in the manufacture of primary ferrous and nonferrous metals, assets included in class 00.11 through 00.4 and assets elsewhere classified.	10	7	10
36.0	**Manufacture of Electronic Components, Products, and Systems:** Includes assets used in the manufacture of electronic communication, computation, instrumentation and control system, including airborne applications; also includes assets used in the manufacture of electronic products such as frequency and amplitude modulated transmitters and receivers, electronic switching stations, television cameras, video recorders, record players and tape recorders, computers and computer peripheral machines, and electronic instruments, watches, and clocks; also includes assets used in the manufacture of components, provided their primary use is products and systems defined above such as electron tubes, capacitors, coils, resistors, printed circuit substrates, switches, harness cables, lasers, fiber optic devices, and magnetic media devices. Specifically excludes assets used to manufacture electronic products and components, photocopiers, typewriters, postage meters and other electromechanical and mechanical business machines and instruments that are elsewhere classified. Does not include semiconductor manufacturing equipment included in class 36.1.	6	5	6
36.1	**Any Semiconductor Manufacturing Equipment:** Includes equipment used in the manufacturing of semiconductors if the primary use of the semiconductors so produced is in products and systems of the type defined in class 36.0.	5	5	5

Asset class	Description of assets included	Recovery Periods (in years)		
		Class Life (in years)	GDS (MACRS)	ADS
37.11	**Manufacture of Motor Vehicles:** Includes assets used in the manufacture and assembly of finished automobiles, trucks, trailers, motor homes, and buses. Does not include assets used in mining, printing and publishing, production of primary metals, electricity, or steam, or the manufacture of glass, industrial chemicals, batteries, or rubber products, which are classified elsewhere. Includes assets used in manufacturing activities elsewhere classified other than those excluded above, where such activities are incidental to and an integral part of the manufacture and assembly of finished motor vehicles such as the manufacture of parts and subassemblies of fabricated metal products, electrical equipment, textiles, plastics, leather, and foundry and forging operations. Does not include any assets not classified in manufacturing activity classes, e.g., does not include any assets classified in asset guideline classes 00.11 through 00.4. Activities will be considered incidental to the manufacture and assembly of finished motor vehicles only if 75 percent or more of the value of the products produced under one roof are used for the manufacture and assembly of finished motor vehicles. Parts that are produced as a normal replacement stock complement in connection with the manufacture and assembly of finished motor vehicles are considered used for the manufacture assembly of finished motor vehicles. Does not include assets used in the manufacture of component parts if these assets are used by taxpayers not engaged in the assembly of finished motor vehicles.	12	7	12
37.12	**Manufacture of Motor Vehicles—Special Tools:** Includes assets defined as special tools, such as jigs, dies, fixtures, molds, patterns, gauges, and specialty transfer and shipping devices, owned by manufacturers of finished motor vehicles and used in qualified activities as defined in class 37.11. Special tools are specifically designed for the production or processing of particular motor vehicle components and have no significant utilitarian value, and cannot be adapted to further or different use, after changes or improvements are made in the model design of the particular part produced by the special tools. Does not include general purpose small tools such as wrenches and drills, both hand and powerdriven, and other general purpose equipment such as conveyors, transfer equipment, and materials handling devices.	3	3	3
37.2	**Manufacture of Aerospace Products:** Includes assets used in the manufacture and assembly of airborne vehicles and their component parts including hydraulic, pneumatic, electrical, and mechanical systems. Does not include assets used in the production of electronic airborne detection, guidance, control, radiation, computation, test, navigation, and communication equipment or the components thereof.	10	7	10
37.31	**Ship and Boat Building Machinery and Equipment:** Includes assets used in the manufacture and repair of ships, boats, caissons, marine drilling rigs, and special fabrications not included in asset classes 37.32 and 37.33. Specifically includes all manufacturing and repairing machinery and equipment, including machinery and equipment used in the operation of assets included in asset class 37.32. Excludes buildings and their structural components.	12	7	12
37.32	**Ship and Boat Building Dry Docks and Land Improvements:** Includes assets used in the manufacture and repair of ships, boats, caissons, marine drilling rigs, and special fabrications not included in asset classes 37.31 and 37.33. Specifically includes floating and fixed dry docks, ship basins, graving docks, shipways, piers, and all other land improvements such as water, sewer, and electric systems. Excludes buildings and their structural components.	16	10	16
37.33	**Ship and Boat Building—Special Tools:** Includes assets defined as special tools such as dies, jigs, molds, patterns, fixtures, gauges, and drawings concerning such special tools used in the activities defined in classes 37.31 and 37.32. Special tools are specifically designed for the production or processing of particular machine components, products, or parts, and have no significant utilitarian value and cannot be adapted to further or different use after changes or improvements are made in the model design of the particular part produced by the special tools. Does not include general purpose small tools such as wrenches and drills, both hand and power-driven, and other general purpose equipment such as conveyors, transfer equipment, and materials handling devices.	6.5	5	6.5
37.41	**Manufacture of Locomotives:** Includes assets used in building or rebuilding railroad locomotives (including mining and industrial locomotives). Does not include assets of railroad transportation companies or assets of companies which manufacture components of locomotives but do not manufacture finished locomotives.	11.5	7	11.5
37.42	**Manufacture of Railroad Cars:** Includes assets used in building or rebuilding railroad freight or passenger cars (including rail transit cars). Does not include assets of railroad transportation companies or assets of companies which manufacture components of railroad cars but do not manufacture finished railroad cars.	12	7	12
39.0	**Manufacture of Athletic, Jewelry, and Other Goods:** Includes assets used in the production of jewelry; musical instruments; toys and sporting goods; motion picture and television films and tapes; and pens, pencils, office and art supplies, brooms, brushes, caskets, etc. **Railroad Transportation:** Classes with the prefix 40 include the assets identified below that are used in the commercial and contract carrying of passengers and freight by rail. Assets of electrified railroads will be classified in a manner corresponding to that set forth below for railroads not independently operated as electric lines. Excludes the assets included in classes with the prefix beginning 00.1 and 00.2 above, and also excludes any non-depreciable assets included in Interstate Commerce Commission accounts enumerated for this class.	12	7	12

Table B-2. **Table of Class Lives and Recovery Periods (Continued)**

Asset class	Description of assets included	Class Life (in years)	GDS (MACRS)	ADS
		Recovery Periods (in years)		
40.1	**Railroad Machinery and Equipment:** Includes assets classified in the following Interstate Commerce Commission accounts: **Roadway accounts:** (16) Station and office buildings (freight handling machinery and equipment only) (25) TOFC/COFC terminals (freight handling machinery and equipment only) (26) Communication systems (27) Signals and interlockers (37) Roadway machines (44) Shop machinery **Equipment accounts:** (52) Locomotives (53) Freight train cars (54) Passenger train cars (57) Work equipment	14	7	14
40.2	**Railroad Structures and Similar Improvements:** Includes assets classified in the following Interstate Commerce Commission road accounts: (6) Bridges, trestles, and culverts (7) Elevated structures (13) Fences, snowsheds, and signs (16) Station and office buildings (stations and other operating structures only) (17) Roadway buildings (18) Water stations (19) Fuel stations (20) Shops and enginehouses (25) TOFC/COFC terminals (operating structures only) (31) Power transmission systems (35) Miscellaneous structures (39) Public improvements construction	30	20	30
40.3	**Railroad Wharves and Docks:** Includes assets classified in the following Interstate Commerce accounts: (23) Wharves and docks (24) Coal and ore wharves	20	15	20
40.4	**Railroad Track**	10	7	10
40.51	**Railroad Hydraulic Electric Generating Equipment**	50	20	50
40.52	**Railroad Nuclear Electric Generating Equipment**	20	15	20
40.53	**Railroad Steam Electric Generating Equipment**	28	20	28
40.54	**Railroad Steam, Compressed Air, and Other Power Plan Equipment**	28	20	28
41.0	**Motor Transport—Passengers:** Includes assets used in the urban and interurban commercial and contract carrying of passengers by road, except the transportation assets included in classes with the prefix 00.2.	8	5	8
42.0	**Motor Transport—Freight:** Includes assets used in the commercial and contract carrying of freight by road, except the transportation assets included in classes with the prefix 00.2.	8	5	8
44.0	**Water Transportation:** Includes assets used in the commercial and contract carrying of freight and passengers by water except the transportation assets included in classes with the prefix 00.2. Includes all related land improvements.	20	15	20
45.0	**Air Transport:** Includes assets (except helicopters) used in commercial and contract carrying of passengers and freight by air. For purposes of section 1.167(a)-11(d)(2)(iv)(a) of the regulations, expenditures for "repair, maintenance, rehabilitation, or improvement," shall consist of direct maintenance expenses (irrespective of airworthiness provisions or charges) as defined by Civil Aeronautics Board uniform accounts 5200, maintenance burden (exclusive of expenses pertaining to maintenance buildings and improvements) as defined by Civil Aeronautics Board accounts 5300, and expenditures which are not "excluded additions" as defined in section 1.167(a)-11(d)(2)(vi) of the regulations and which would be charged to property and equipment accounts in the Civil Aeronautics Board uniform system of accounts.	12	7	12
45.1	**Air Transport (restricted):** Includes each asset described in the description of class 45.0 which was held by the taxpayer on April 15, 1976, or is acquired by the taxpayer pursuant to a contract which was, on April 15, 1976, and at all times thereafter, binding on the taxpayer. This criterion of classification based on binding contract concept is to be applied in the same manner as under the general rules expressed in section 49(b)(1), (4), (5) and (8) of the Code (as in effect prior to its repeal by the Revenue Act of 1978, section 312(c)(1), (d), 1978-3 C.B. 1, 60).	6	5	6
46.0	**Pipeline Transportation:** Includes assets used in the private, commercial, and contract carrying of petroleum, gas and other products by means of pipes and conveyors. The trunk lines and related storage facilities of integrated petroleum and natural gas producers are included in this class. Excludes initial clearing and grading land improvements as specified in Rev. Rul. 72-403, 1972-2; C.B. 102, but includes all other related land improvements.	22	15	22

Asset class	Description of assets included	Class Life (in years)	GDS (MACRS)	ADS
			Recovery Periods (in years)	
48.11	**Telephone Communications:** Includes the assets classified below and that are used in the provision of commercial and contract telephonic services such as: **Telephone Central Office Buildings:** Includes assets intended to house central office equipment, as defined in Federal Communications Commission Part 31 Account No. 212 whether section 1245 or section 1250 property.	45	20	45
48.12	**Telephone Central Office Equipment:** Includes central office switching and related equipment as defined in Federal Communications Commission Part 31 Account No. 221. Does not include computer-based telephone central office switching equipment included in class 48.121. Does not include private branch exchange (PBX) equipment.	18	10	18
48.121	**Computer-based Telephone Central Office Switching Equipment:** Includes equipment whose functions are those of a computer or peripheral equipment (as defined in section 168(i)(2)(B) of the Code) used in its capacity as telephone central office equipment. Does not include private exchange (PBX) equipment.	9.5	5	9.5
48.13	**Telephone Station Equipment:** Includes such station apparatus and connections as teletypewriters, telephones, booths, private exchanges, and comparable equipment as defined in Federal Communications Commission Part 31 Account Nos. 231, 232, and 234.	10	7*	10*
48.14	**Telephone Distribution Plant:** Includes such assets as pole lines, cable, aerial wire, underground conduits, and comparable equipment, and related land improvements as defined in Federal Communications Commission Part 31 Account Nos. 241, 242.1, 242.2, 242.3, 242.4, 243, and 244.	24	15	24
48.2	**Radio and Television Broadcastings:** Includes assets used in radio and television broadcasting, except transmitting towers. **Telegraph, Ocean Cable, and Satellite Communications (TOCSC)** includes communications-related assets used to provide domestic and international radio-telegraph, wire-telegraph, ocean-cable, and satellite communications services; also includes related land improvements. If property described in Classes 48.31–48.45 is comparable to telephone distribution plant described in Class 48.14 and used for 2-way exchange of voice and data communication which is the equivalent of telephone communication, such property is assigned a class life of 24 years under this revenue procedure. Comparable equipment does not include cable television equipment used primarily for 1-way communication.	6	5	6
48.31	**TOCSC—Electric Power Generating and Distribution Systems:** Includes assets used in the provision of electric power by generation, modulation, rectification, channelization, control, and distribution. Does not include these assets when they are installed on customers premises.	19	10	19
48.32	**TOCSC—High Frequency Radio and Microwave Systems:** Includes assets such as transmitters and receivers, antenna supporting structures, antennas, transmission lines from equipment to antenna, transmitter cooling systems, and control and amplification equipment. Does not include cable and long-line systems.	13	7	13
48.33	**TOCSC—Cable and Long-line Systems:** Includes assets such as transmission lines, pole lines, ocean cables, buried cable and conduit, repeaters, repeater stations, and other related assets. Does not include high frequency radio or microwave systems.	26.5	20	26.5
48.34	**TOCSC—Central Office Control Equipment:** Includes assets for general control, switching, and monitoring of communications signals including electromechanical switching and channeling apparatus, multiplexing equipment patching and monitoring facilities, in-house cabling, teleprinter equipment, and associated site improvements.	16.5	10	16.5
48.35	**TOCSC—Computerized Switching, Channeling, and Associated Control Equipment:** Includes central office switching computers, interfacing computers, other associated specialized control equipment, and site improvements.	10.5	7	10.5
48.36	**TOCSC—Satellite Ground Segment Property:** Includes assets such as fixed earth station equipment, antennas, satellite communications equipment, and interface equipment used in satellite communications. Does not include general purpose equipment or equipment used in satellite space segment property.	10	7	10
48.37	**TOCSC—Satellite Space Segment Property:** Includes satellites and equipment used for telemetry, tracking, control, and monitoring when used in satellite communications.	8	5	8
48.38	**TOCSC—Equipment Installed on Customer's Premises:** Includes assets installed on customer's premises, such as computers, terminal equipment, power generation and distribution systems, private switching center, teleprinters, facsimile equipment and other associated and related equipment.	10	7	10
48.39	**TOCSC—Support and Service Equipment:** Includes assets used to support but not engage in communications. Includes store, warehouse and shop tools, and test and laboratory assets. **Cable Television (CATV):** Includes communications-related assets used to provide cable television community antenna television services. Does not include assets used to provide subscribers with two-way communications services.	13.5	7	13.5

* Property described in asset guideline class 48.13 which is qualified technological equipment as defined in section 168(i)(2) is assigned a 5-year recovery period.

Asset class	Description of assets included	Class Life (in years)	GDS (MACRS)	ADS
			Recovery Periods (in years)	
48.41	**CATV—Headend:** Includes assets such as towers, antennas, preamplifiers, converters, modulation equipment, and program non-duplication systems. Does not include headend buildings and program origination assets.	11	7	11
48.42	**CATV—Subscriber Connection and Distribution Systems:** Includes assets such as trunk and feeder cable, connecting hardware, amplifiers, power equipment, passive devices, directional taps, pedestals, pressure taps, drop cables, matching transformers, multiple set connector equipment, and convertors.	10	7	10
48.43	**CATV—Program Origination:** Includes assets such as cameras, film chains, video tape recorders, lighting, and remote location equipment excluding vehicles. Does not include buildings and their structural components.	9	5	9
48.44	**CATV—Service and Test:** Includes assets such as oscilloscopes, field strength meters, spectrum analyzers, and cable testing equipment, but does not include vehicles.	8.5	5	8.5
48.45	**CATV—Microwave Systems:** Inlcudes assets such as towers, antennas, transmitting and receiving equipment, and broad band microwave assets is used in the provision of cable television services. Does not include assets used in the provision of common carrier services.	9.5	5	9.5
49.11	**Electric, Gas, Water and Steam, Utility Services:** Includes assets used in the production, transmission and distribution of electricity, gas, steam, or water for sale including related land improvements. **Electric Utility Hydraulic Production Plant:** Includes assets used in the hydraulic power production of electricity for sale, including related land improvements, such as dams, flumes, canals, and waterways.	50	20	50
49.12	**Electric Utility Nuclear Production Plant:** Includes assets used in the nuclear power production and electricity for sale and related land improvements. Does not include nuclear fuel assemblies.	20	15	20
49.121	**Electric Utility Nuclear Fuel Assemblies:** Includes initial core and replacement core nuclear fuel assemblies (i.e., the composite of fabricated nuclear fuel and container) when used in a boiling water, pressurized water, or high temperature gas reactor used in the production of electricity. Does not include nuclear fuel assemblies used in breader reactors.	5	5	5
49.13	**Electric Utility Steam Production Plant:** Includes assets used in the steam power production of electricity for sale, combusion turbines operated in a combined cycle with a conventional steam unit and related land improvements. Also includes package boilers, electric generators and related assets such as electricity and steam distribution systems as used by a waste reduction and resource recovery plant if the steam or electricity is normally for sale to others.	28	20	28
49.14	**Electric Utility Transmission and Distribution Plant:** Includes assets used in the transmission and distribution of electricity for sale and related land improvements. Excludes initial clearing and grading land improvements as specified in Rev. Rul. 72-403, 1972-2 C.B. 102.	30	20	30
49.15	**Electric Utility Combustion Turbine Production Plant:** Includes assets used in the production of electricity for sale by the use of such prime movers as jet engines, combustion turbines, diesel engines, gasoline engines, and other internal combustion engines, their associated power turbines and/or generators, and related land improvements. Does not include combustion turbines operated in a combined cycle with a conventional steam unit.	20	15	20
49.21	**Gas Utility Distribution Facilities:** Includes gas water heaters and gas conversion equipment installed by utility on customers' premises on a rental basis.	35	20	35
49.221	**Gas Utility Manufactured Gas Production Plants:** Includes assets used in the manufacture of gas having chemical and/or physical properties which do not permit complete interchangeability with domestic natural gas. Does not include gas-producing systems and related systems used in waste reduction and resource recovery plants which are elsewhere classified.	30	20	30
49.222	**Gas Utility Substitute Natural Gas (SNG) Production Plant (naphtha or lighter hydrocarbon feedstocks):** Includes assets used in the catalytic conversion of feedstocks or naphtha or lighter hydrocarbons to a gaseous fuel which is completely interchangeable with domestic natural gas.	14	7	14
49.223	**Substitute Natural Gas—Coal Gasification:** Includes assets used in the manufacture and production of pipeline quality gas from coal using the basic Lurgi process with advanced methanation. Includes all process plant equipment and structures used in this coal gasification process and all utility assets such as cooling systems, water supply and treatment facilities, and assets used in the production and distribution of electricity and steam for use by the taxpayer in a gasification plant and attendant coal mining site processes but not for assets used in the production and distribution of electricity and steam for sale to others. Also includes all other related land improvements. Does not include assets used in the direct mining and treatment of coal prior to the gasification process itself.	18	10	18
49.23	**Natural Gas Production Plant**	14	7	14
49.24	**Gas Utility Trunk Pipelines and Related Storage Facilities:** Excluding initial clearing and grading land improvements as specified in Rev. Rul. 72-40.	22	15	22
49.25	**Liquefied Natural Gas Plant:** Includes assets used in the liquefaction, storage, and regasification of natural gas including loading and unloading connections, instrumentation equipment and controls, pumps, vaporizers and odorizers, tanks, and related land improvements. Also includes pipeline interconnections with gas transmission lines and distribution systems and marine terminal facilities.	22	15	22

Asset class	Description of assets included	Class Life (in years)	GDS (MACRS)	ADS
		Recovery Periods (in years)		
49.3	**Water Utilities:** Includes assets used in the gathering, treatment, and commercial distribution of water.	50	20***	50
49.4	**Central Steam Utility Production and Distribution:** Includes assets used in the production and distribution of steam for sale. Does not include assets used in waste reduction and resource recovery plants which are elsewhere classified.	28	20	28
49.5	**Waste Reduction and Resource Recovery Plants:** Includes assets used in the conversion of refuse or other solid waste or biomass to heat or to a solid, liquid, or gaseous fuel. Also includes all process plant equipment and structures at the site used to receive, handle, collect, and process refuse or other solid waste or biomass in a waterwall, combustion system, oil or gas pyrolysis system, or refuse derived fuel system to create hot water, gas, steam and electricity. Includes material recovery and support assets used in refuse or solid refuse or solid waste receiving, collecting, handling, sorting, shredding, classifying, and separation systems. Does not include any package boilers, or electric generators and related assets such as electricity, hot water, steam and manufactured gas production plants classified in classes 00.4, 49.13, 49.221, and 49.4. Does include, however, all other utilities such as water supply and treatment facilities, ash handling and other related land improvements of a waste reduction and resource recovery plant.	10	7	10
50.	**Municipal Wastewater Treatment Plant**	24	15	24
51.	**Municipal Sewer**	50	20***	50
57.0	**Distributive Trades and Services:** Includes assets used in wholesale and retail trade, and personal and professional services. Includes section 1245 assets used in marketing petroleum and petroleum products.	9	5	9*
57.1	**Distributive Trades and Services—Billboard, Service Station Buildings and Petroleum Marketing Land Improvements:** Includes section 1250 assets, including service station buildings and depreciable land improvements, whether section 1245 property or section 1250 property, used in the marketing of petroleum and petroleum products, but not including any of these facilities related to petroleum and natural gas trunk pipelines. Includes car wash buildings and related land improvements. Includes billboards, whether such assets are section 1245 property or section 1250 property. Excludes all other land improvements, buildings and structural components as defined in section 1.48-1(e) of the regulations. See *Gas station convenience stores* in chapter 3.	20	15	20
79.0	**Recreation:** Includes assets used in the provision of entertainment services on payment of a fee or admission charge, as in the operation of bowling alleys, billiard and pool establishments, theaters, concert halls, and miniature golf courses. Does not include amusement and theme parks and assets which consist primarily of specialized land improvements or structures, such as golf courses, sports stadia, race tracks, ski slopes, and buildings which house the assets used in entertainment services.	10	7	10
80.0	**Theme and Amusement Parks:** Includes assets used in the provision of rides, attractions, and amusements in activities defined as theme and amusement parks, and includes appurtenances associated with a ride, attraction, amusement or theme setting within the park such as ticket booths, facades, shop interiors, and props, special purpose structures, and buildings other than warehouses, administration buildings, hotels, and motels. Includes all land improvements for or in support of park activities (e.g., parking lots, sidewalks, waterways, bridges, fences, landscaping, etc.), and support functions (e.g., food and beverage retailing, souvenir vending and other nonlodging accommodations) if owned by the park and provided exclusively for the benefit of park patrons. Theme and amusement parks are defined as combinations of amusements, rides, and attractions which are permanently situated on park land and open to the public for the price of admission. This guideline class is a composite of all assets used in this industry except transportation equipment (general purpose trucks, cars, airplanes, etc., which are included in asset guideline classes with the prefix 00.2), assets used in the provision of administrative services (asset classes with the prefix 00.1) and warehouses, administration buildings, hotels and motels.	12.5	7	12.5
	Certain Property for Which Recovery Periods Assigned: A. Personal Property With No Class Life Section 1245 Real Property With No Class Life		7 7	12 40
	B. Qualified Technological Equipment, as defined in section 168(i)(2).	**	5	5
	C. Property Used in Connection with Research and Experimentation referred to in section 168(e)(3)(B).	**	5	class life if no class life—12
	D. Alternative Energy Property described in sections 48(1)(3)(viii) or (iv), or section 48(1)(4) of the Code.	**	5	class life if no class life—12
	E. Biomass property described in section 48(1)(15) and is a qualifying small production facility within the meaning of section 3(17)(c) of the Federal Power Act (16 U.S.C. 796(17)(C)), as in effect on September 1, 1986.	**	5	class life if no class life—12

* Any high technology medical equipment as defined in section 168(i)(2)(C) which is described in asset guideline class 57.0 is assigned a 5-year recovery period for the alternate MACRS method.

** The class life (if any) of property described in classes B, C, D, or E is determined by reference to the asset guideline classes. If an item of property described in paragraphs B, C, D, or E is not described in any asset guideline class, such item of property has no class life.

*** Use straight line over 25 years if placed in service after June 12, 1996, unless placed in service under a binding contract in effect before June 10, 1996, and at all times until placed in service.

3-, 5-, 7-, 10-, 15-, and 20-Year Property
Half-Year Convention

Year	Depreciation rate for recovery period					
	3-year	5-year	7-year	10-year	15-year	20-year
1	33.33%	20.00%	14.29%	10.00%	5.00%	3.750%
2	44.45	32.00	24.49	18.00	9.50	7.219
3	14.81	19.20	17.49	14.40	8.55	6.677
4	7.41	11.52	12.49	11.52	7.70	6.177
5		11.52	8.93	9.22	6.93	5.713
6		5.76	8.92	7.37	6.23	5.285
7			8.93	6.55	5.90	4.888
8			4.46	6.55	5.90	4.522
9				6.56	5.91	4.462
10				6.55	5.90	4.461
11				3.28	5.91	4.462
12					5.90	4.461
13					5.91	4.462
14					5.90	4.461
15					5.91	4.462
16					2.95	4.461
17						4.462
18						4.461
19						4.462
20						4.461
21						2.231

Residential Rental Property
Mid-Month Convention
Straight Line—27.5 Years

Year	Month property placed in service											
	1	2	3	4	5	6	7	8	9	10	11	12
1	3.485%	3.182%	2.879%	2.576%	2.273%	1.970%	1.667%	1.364%	1.061%	0.758%	0.455%	0.152%
2–9	3.636	3.636	3.636	3.636	3.636	3.636	3.636	3.636	3.636	3.636	3.636	3.636
10	3.637	3.637	3.637	3.637	3.637	3.637	3.636	3.636	3.636	3.636	3.636	3.636
11	3.636	3.636	3.636	3.636	3.636	3.636	3.637	3.637	3.637	3.637	3.637	3.637
12	3.637	3.637	3.637	3.637	3.637	3.637	3.636	3.636	3.636	3.636	3.636	3.636
13	3.636	3.636	3.636	3.636	3.636	3.636	3.637	3.637	3.637	3.637	3.637	3.637
14	3.637	3.637	3.637	3.637	3.637	3.637	3.636	3.636	3.636	3.636	3.636	3.636
15	3.636	3.636	3.636	3.636	3.636	3.636	3.637	3.637	3.637	3.637	3.637	3.637
16	3.637	3.637	3.637	3.637	3.637	3.637	3.636	3.636	3.636	3.636	3.636	3.636
17	3.636	3.636	3.636	3.636	3.636	3.636	3.637	3.637	3.637	3.637	3.637	3.637
18	3.637	3.637	3.637	3.637	3.637	3.637	3.636	3.636	3.636	3.636	3.636	3.636
19	3.636	3.636	3.636	3.636	3.636	3.636	3.637	3.637	3.637	3.637	3.637	3.637
20	3.637	3.637	3.637	3.637	3.637	3.637	3.636	3.636	3.636	3.636	3.636	3.636
21	3.636	3.636	3.636	3.636	3.636	3.636	3.637	3.637	3.637	3.637	3.637	3.637
22	3.637	3.637	3.637	3.637	3.637	3.637	3.636	3.636	3.636	3.636	3.636	3.636
23	3.636	3.636	3.636	3.636	3.636	3.636	3.637	3.637	3.637	3.637	3.637	3.637
24	3.637	3.637	3.637	3.637	3.637	3.637	3.636	3.636	3.636	3.636	3.636	3.636
25	3.636	3.636	3.636	3.636	3.636	3.636	3.637	3.637	3.637	3.637	3.637	3.637
26	3.637	3.637	3.637	3.637	3.637	3.637	3.636	3.636	3.636	3.636	3.636	3.636
27	3.636	3.636	3.636	3.636	3.636	3.636	3.637	3.637	3.637	3.637	3.637	3.637
28	1.97	2.273	2.576	2.879	3.182	3.485	3.636	3.636	3.636	3.636	3.636	3.636
29							0.152	0.455	0.758	1.061	1.364	1.667

Nonresidential Real Property
Mid-Month Convention
Straight Line—31.5 Years

Year	Month property placed in service											
	1	**2**	**3**	**4**	**5**	**6**	**7**	**8**	**9**	**10**	**11**	**12**
1	3.042%	2.778%	2.513%	2.249%	1.984%	1.720%	1.455%	1.190%	0.926%	0.661%	0.397%	0.132%
2–7	3.175	3.175	3.175	3.175	3.175	3.175	3.175	3.175	3.175	3.175	3.175	3.175
8	3.175	3.174	3.175	3.174	3.175	3.174	3.175	3.175	3.175	3.175	3.175	3.175
9	3.174	3.175	3.174	3.175	3.174	3.175	3.174	3.175	3.175	3.174	3.175	3.175
10	3.175	3.174	3.175	3.174	3.175	3.174	3.175	3.174	3.175	3.174	3.175	3.174
11	3.174	3.175	3.174	3.175	3.174	3.175	3.174	3.175	3.174	3.175	3.174	3.175
12	3.175	3.174	3.175	3.174	3.175	3.174	3.175	3.174	3.175	3.174	3.175	3.174
13	3.174	3.175	3.174	3.175	3.174	3.175	3.174	3.175	3.174	3.175	3.174	3.175
14	3.175	3.174	3.175	3.174	3.175	3.174	3.175	3.174	3.175	3.174	3.175	3.174
15	3.174	3.175	3.174	3.175	3.174	3.175	3.174	3.175	3.174	3.175	3.174	3.175
16	3.175	3.174	3.175	3.174	3.175	3.174	3.175	3.174	3.175	3.174	3.175	3.174
17	3.174	3.175	3.174	3.175	3.174	3.175	3.174	3.175	3.174	3.175	3.174	3.175
18	3.175	3.174	3.175	3.174	3.175	3.174	3.175	3.174	3.175	3.174	3.175	3.174
19	3.174	3.175	3.174	3.175	3.174	3.175	3.174	3.175	3.174	3.175	3.174	3.175
20	3.175	3.174	3.175	3.174	3.175	3.174	3.175	3.174	3.175	3.174	3.175	3.174
21	3.174	3.175	3.174	3.175	3.174	3.175	3.174	3.175	3.174	3.175	3.174	3.175
22	3.175	3.174	3.175	3.174	3.175	3.174	3.175	3.174	3.175	3.174	3.175	3.174
23	3.174	3.175	3.174	3.175	3.174	3.175	3.174	3.175	3.174	3.175	3.174	3.175
24	3.175	3.174	3.175	3.174	3.175	3.174	3.175	3.174	3.175	3.174	3.175	3.174
25	3.174	3.175	3.174	3.175	3.174	3.175	3.174	3.175	3.174	3.175	3.174	3.175
26	3.175	3.174	3.175	3.174	3.175	3.174	3.175	3.174	3.175	3.174	3.175	3.174
27	3.174	3.175	3.174	3.175	3.174	3.175	3.174	3.175	3.174	3.175	3.174	3.175
28	3.175	3.174	3.175	3.174	3.175	3.174	3.175	3.174	3.175	3.174	3.175	3.174
29	3.174	3.175	3.174	3.175	3.174	3.175	3.174	3.175	3.174	3.175	3.174	3.175
30	3.175	3.174	3.175	3.174	3.175	3.174	3.175	3.174	3.175	3.174	3.175	3.174
31	3.174	3.175	3.174	3.175	3.174	3.175	3.174	3.175	3.174	3.175	3.174	3.175
32	1.720	1.984	2.249	2.513	2.778	3.042	3.175	3.174	3.175	3.174	3.175	3.174
33							0.132	0.397	0.661	0.926	1.190	1.455

Nonresidential Real Property
Mid-Month Convention
Straight Line—39 Years

Year	Month property placed in service											
	1	**2**	**3**	**4**	**5**	**6**	**7**	**8**	**9**	**10**	**11**	**12**
1	2.461%	2.247%	2.033%	1.819%	1.605%	1.391%	1.177%	0.963%	0.749%	0.535%	0.321%	0.107%
2–39	2.564	2.564	2.564	2.564	2.564	2.564	2.564	2.564	2.564	2.564	2.564	2.564
40	0.107	0.321	0.535	0.749	0.963	1.177	1.391	1.605	1.819	2.033	2.247	2.461

150% Declining Balance Method
Half-Year Convention

Year	Recovery periods in years												
	2.5	3	3.5	4	5	6	6.5	7	7.5	8	8.5	9	9.5
1	30.0%	25.0%	21.43%	18.75%	15.00%	12.50%	11.54%	10.71%	10.00%	9.38%	8.82%	8.33%	7.89%
2	42.0	37.5	33.67	30.47	25.50	21.88	20.41	19.13	18.00	16.99	16.09	15.28	14.54
3	28.0	25.0	22.45	20.31	17.85	16.41	15.70	15.03	14.40	13.81	13.25	12.73	12.25
4		12.5	22.45	20.31	16.66	14.06	13.09	12.25	11.52	11.22	10.91	10.61	10.31
5				10.16	16.66	14.06	13.09	12.25	11.52	10.80	10.19	9.65	9.17
6					8.33	14.06	13.09	12.25	11.52	10.80	10.19	9.64	9.17
7						7.03	13.08	12.25	11.52	10.80	10.18	9.65	9.17
8							6.13	11.52	10.80	10.19	9.64	9.17
9								6.13	11.52	10.80	10.18	9.65	9.17
10										5.40	10.18	9.65	9.17
												4.82	9.16

(Continued)

Year	Recovery periods in years												
	10	10.5	11	11.5	12	12.5	13	13.5	14	15	16	16.5	17
1	7.50%	7.14%	6.82%	6.52%	6.25%	6.00%	5.77%	5.56%	5.36%	5.00%	4.69%	4.55%	4.41%
2	13.88	13.27	12.71	12.19	11.72	11.28	10.87	10.49	10.14	9.50	8.94	8.68	8.43
3	11.79	11.37	10.97	10.60	10.25	9.93	9.62	9.33	9.05	8.55	8.10	7.89	7.69
4	10.02	9.75	9.48	9.22	8.97	8.73	8.51	8.29	8.08	7.70	7.34	7.17	7.01
5	8.74	8.35	8.18	8.02	7.85	7.69	7.53	7.37	7.22	6.93	6.65	6.52	6.39
6	8.74	8.35	7.98	7.64	7.33	7.05	6.79	6.55	6.44	6.23	6.03	5.93	5.83
7	8.74	8.35	7.97	7.64	7.33	7.05	6.79	6.55	6.32	5.90	5.55	5.39	5.32
8	8.74	8.35	7.98	7.63	7.33	7.05	6.79	6.55	6.32	5.90	5.55	5.39	5.23
9	8.74	8.36	7.97	7.64	7.33	7.04	6.79	6.55	6.32	5.91	5.55	5.39	5.23
10	8.74	8.35	7.98	7.63	7.33	7.05	6.79	6.55	6.32	5.90	5.55	5.39	5.23
11	4.37	8.36	7.97	7.64	7.32	7.04	6.79	6.55	6.32	5.91	5.55	5.39	5.23
12			3.99	7.63	7.33	7.05	6.78	6.55	6.32	5.90	5.55	5.39	5.23
13					3.66	7.04	6.79	6.56	6.32	5.91	5.54	5.38	5.23
14							3.39	6.55	6.31	5.90	5.55	5.39	5.23
15									3.16	5.91	5.54	5.38	5.23
16										2.95	5.55	5.39	5.23
17											2.77	5.38	5.23
18													2.62

(Continued)

Year	Recovery periods in years												
	18	19	20	22	24	25	26.5	28	30	35	40	45	50
1	4.17%	3.95%	3.750%	3.409%	3.125%	3.000%	2.830%	2.679%	2.500%	2.143%	1.875%	1.667%	1.500%
2	7.99	7.58	7.219	6.586	6.055	5.820	5.500	5.214	4.875	4.194	3.680	3.278	2.955
3	7.32	6.98	6.677	6.137	5.676	5.471	5.189	4.934	4.631	4.014	3.542	3.169	2.866
4	6.71	6.43	6.177	5.718	5.322	5.143	4.895	4.670	4.400	3.842	3.409	3.063	2.780
5	6.15	5.93	5.713	5.328	4.989	4.834	4.618	4.420	4.180	3.677	3.281	2.961	2.697
6	5.64	5.46	5.285	4.965	4.677	4.544	4.357	4.183	3.971	3.520	3.158	2.862	2.616
7	5.17	5.03	4.888	4.627	4.385	4.271	4.110	3.959	3.772	3.369	3.040	2.767	2.538
8	4.94	4.69	4.522	4.311	4.111	4.015	3.877	3.747	3.584	3.225	2.926	2.674	2.461
9	4.94	4.69	4.462	4.063	3.854	3.774	3.658	3.546	3.404	3.086	2.816	2.585	2.388
10	4.94	4.69	4.461	4.063	3.729	3.584	3.451	3.356	3.234	2.954	2.710	2.499	2.316
11	4.94	4.69	4.462	4.063	3.729	3.583	3.383	3.205	3.072	2.828	2.609	2.416	2.246
12	4.95	4.69	4.461	4.063	3.729	3.584	3.383	3.205	2.994	2.706	2.511	2.335	2.179
13	4.94	4.69	4.462	4.064	3.730	3.583	3.383	3.205	2.994	2.590	2.417	2.257	2.114
14	4.95	4.69	4.461	4.063	3.729	3.584	3.383	3.205	2.994	2.571	2.326	2.182	2.050
15	4.94	4.69	4.462	4.064	3.730	3.583	3.383	3.205	2.994	2.571	2.253	2.110	1.989
16	4.95	4.69	4.461	4.063	3.729	3.584	3.383	3.205	2.994	2.571	2.253	2.039	1.929
17	4.94	4.69	4.462	4.064	3.730	3.583	3.383	3.205	2.994	2.571	2.253	2.005	1.871
18	4.95	4.70	4.461	4.063	3.729	3.584	3.383	3.205	2.994	2.571	2.253	2.005	1.815
19	2.47	4.69	4.462	4.064	3.730	3.583	3.383	3.205	2.994	2.571	2.253	2.005	1.806
20		2.35	4.461	4.063	3.729	3.584	3.384	3.205	2.993	2.571	2.253	2.005	1.806
21			2.231	4.064	3.730	3.583	3.383	3.205	2.994	2.571	2.253	2.005	1.806
22				4.063	3.729	3.584	3.384	3.205	2.993	2.571	2.253	2.005	1.806
23				2.032	3.730	3.583	3.383	3.205	2.994	2.571	2.253	2.005	1.806
24					3.729	3.584	3.384	3.205	2.993	2.571	2.253	2.004	1.806
25					1.865	3.583	3.383	3.205	2.994	2.571	2.253	2.005	1.806
26						1.792	3.384	3.205	2.993	2.571	2.253	2.004	1.806
27							3.383	3.205	2.994	2.571	2.253	2.005	1.806
28								3.205	2.993	2.572	2.253	2.004	1.806
29								1.602	2.994	2.571	2.253	2.005	1.806
30									2.993	2.572	2.253	2.004	1.806
31									1.497	2.571	2.253	2.005	1.806
32										2.572	2.253	2.004	1.806
33										2.571	2.252	2.005	1.806
34										2.572	2.253	2.004	1.806
35										2.571	2.252	2.005	1.806
36										1.286	2.253	2.004	1.806
37											2.252	2.005	1.806
38											2.253	2.004	1.806
39											2.252	2.005	1.806
40											2.253	2.004	1.806
41											1.126	2.005	1.806
42												2.004	1.805
43												2.005	1.806
44												2.004	1.805
45												2.005	1.806
46												1.002	1.805
47													1.806
48													1.805
49													1.806
50													1.805
51													0.903

Table A-8. **Straight Line Method**
Half-Year Convention

Year	Recovery periods in years												
	2.5	3	3.5	4	5	6	6.5	7	7.5	8	8.5	9	9.5
1	20.0%	16.67%	14.29%	12.5%	10.0%	8.33%	7.69%	7.14%	6.67%	6.25%	5.88%	5.56%	5.26%
2	40.0	33.33	28.57	25.0	20.0	16.67	15.39	14.29	13.33	12.50	11.77	11.11	10.53
3	40.0	33.33	28.57	25.0	20.0	16.67	15.38	14.29	13.33	12.50	11.76	11.11	10.53
4		16.67	28.57	25.0	20.0	16.67	15.39	14.28	13.33	12.50	11.77	11.11	10.53
5				12.5	20.0	16.66	15.38	14.29	13.34	12.50	11.76	11.11	10.52
6					10.0	16.67	15.39	14.28	13.33	12.50	11.77	11.11	10.53
7						8.33	15.38	14.29	13.34	12.50	11.76	11.11	10.52
8								7.14	13.33	12.50	11.77	11.11	10.53
9										6.25	11.76	11.11	10.52
10												5.56	10.53

Table A-8. *(Continued)*

Year	Recovery periods in years												
	10	10.5	11	11.5	12	12.5	13	13.5	14	15	16	16.5	17
1	5.0%	4.76%	4.55%	4.35%	4.17%	4.0%	3.85%	3.70%	3.57%	3.33%	3.13%	3.03%	2.94%
2	10.0	9.52	9.09	8.70	8.33	8.0	7.69	7.41	7.14	6.67	6.25	6.06	5.88
3	10.0	9.52	9.09	8.70	8.33	8.0	7.69	7.41	7.14	6.67	6.25	6.06	5.88
4	10.0	9.53	9.09	8.69	8.33	8.0	7.69	7.41	7.14	6.67	6.25	6.06	5.88
5	10.0	9.52	9.09	8.70	8.33	8.0	7.69	7.41	7.14	6.67	6.25	6.06	5.88
6	10.0	9.53	9.09	8.69	8.33	8.0	7.69	7.41	7.14	6.67	6.25	6.06	5.88
7	10.0	9.52	9.09	8.70	8.34	8.0	7.69	7.41	7.14	6.67	6.25	6.06	5.88
8	10.0	9.53	9.09	8.69	8.33	8.0	7.69	7.41	7.15	6.66	6.25	6.06	5.88
9	10.0	9.52	9.09	8.70	8.34	8.0	7.69	7.41	7.14	6.67	6.25	6.06	5.88
10	10.0	9.53	9.09	8.69	8.33	8.0	7.70	7.40	7.15	6.66	6.25	6.06	5.88
11	5.0	9.52	9.09	8.70	8.34	8.0	7.69	7.41	7.14	6.67	6.25	6.06	5.89
12			4.55	8.69	8.33	8.0	7.70	7.40	7.15	6.66	6.25	6.06	5.88
13					4.17	8.0	7.69	7.41	7.14	6.67	6.25	6.06	5.89
14							3.85	7.40	7.15	6.66	6.25	6.06	5.88
15									3.57	6.67	6.25	6.06	5.89
16										3.33	6.25	6.06	5.88
17											3.12	6.07	5.89
18													2.94

Table A-8. *(Continued)*

Year	\multicolumn{13}{c}{Recovery periods in years}

Year	18	19	20	22	24	25	26.5	28	30	35	40	45	50
1	2.78%	2.63%	2.5%	2.273%	2.083%	2.0%	1.887%	1.786%	1.667%	1.429%	1.25%	1.111%	1.0%
2	5.56	5.26	5.0	4.545	4.167	4.0	3.774	3.571	3.333	2.857	2.50	2.222	2.0
3	5.56	5.26	5.0	4.545	4.167	4.0	3.774	3.571	3.333	2.857	2.50	2.222	2.0
4	5.55	5.26	5.0	4.545	4.167	4.0	3.774	3.571	3.333	2.857	2.50	2.222	2.0
5	5.56	5.26	5.0	4.546	4.167	4.0	3.774	3.571	3.333	2.857	2.50	2.222	2.0
6	5.55	5.26	5.0	4.545	4.167	4.0	3.774	3.571	3.333	2.857	2.50	2.222	2.0
7	5.56	5.26	5.0	4.546	4.167	4.0	3.773	3.572	3.333	2.857	2.50	2.222	2.0
8	5.55	5.26	5.0	4.545	4.167	4.0	3.774	3.571	3.333	2.857	2.50	2.222	2.0
9	5.56	5.27	5.0	4.546	4.167	4.0	3.773	3.572	3.333	2.857	2.50	2.222	2.0
10	5.55	5.26	5.0	4.545	4.167	4.0	3.774	3.571	3.333	2.857	2.50	2.222	2.0
11	5.56	5.27	5.0	4.546	4.166	4.0	3.773	3.572	3.333	2.857	2.50	2.222	2.0
12	5.55	5.26	5.0	4.545	4.167	4.0	3.774	3.571	3.333	2.857	2.50	2.222	2.0
13	5.56	5.27	5.0	4.546	4.166	4.0	3.773	3.572	3.334	2.857	2.50	2.222	2.0
14	5.55	5.26	5.0	4.545	4.167	4.0	3.773	3.571	3.333	2.857	2.50	2.222	2.0
15	5.56	5.27	5.0	4.546	4.166	4.0	3.774	3.572	3.334	2.857	2.50	2.222	2.0
16	5.55	5.26	5.0	4.545	4.167	4.0	3.773	3.571	3.333	2.857	2.50	2.222	2.0
17	5.56	5.27	5.0	4.546	4.166	4.0	3.774	3.572	3.334	2.857	2.50	2.222	2.0
18	5.55	5.26	5.0	4.545	4.167	4.0	3.773	3.571	3.333	2.857	2.50	2.222	2.0
19	2.78	5.27	5.0	4.546	4.166	4.0	3.774	3.572	3.334	2.857	2.50	2.222	2.0
20		2.63	5.0	4.545	4.167	4.0	3.773	3.571	3.333	2.857	2.50	2.222	2.0
21			2.5	4.546	4.166	4.0	3.774	3.572	3.334	2.857	2.50	2.222	2.0
22				4.545	4.167	4.0	3.773	3.571	3.333	2.857	2.50	2.222	2.0
23				2.273	4.166	4.0	3.774	3.572	3.334	2.857	2.50	2.222	2.0
24					4.167	4.0	3.773	3.571	3.333	2.857	2.50	2.222	2.0
25					2.083	4.0	3.774	3.572	3.334	2.857	2.50	2.222	2.0
26						2.0	3.773	3.571	3.333	2.857	2.50	2.222	2.0
27							3.774	3.572	3.334	2.857	2.50	2.223	2.0
28								3.571	3.333	2.858	2.50	2.222	2.0
29								1.786	3.334	2.857	2.50	2.223	2.0
30									3.333	2.858	2.50	2.222	2.0
31									1.667	2.857	2.50	2.223	2.0
32										2.858	2.50	2.222	2.0
33										2.857	2.50	2.223	2.0
34										2.858	2.50	2.222	2.0
35										2.857	2.50	2.223	2.0
36										1.429	2.50	2.222	2.0
37											2.50	2.223	2.0
38											2.50	2.222	2.0
39											2.50	2.223	2.0
40											2.50	2.222	2.0
41											1.25	2.223	2.0
42												2.222	2.0
43												2.223	2.0
44												2.222	2.0
45												2.223	2.0
46												1.111	2.0
47–50													2.0
51													1.0

What's New in 2013

Standard Mileage Rates. For 2013 the standard mileage rate is 56.5¢ per mile for business, 14¢ per mile for charitable miles driven, 24¢ for medical and moving miles, and 23¢ for depreciation miles.

Depreciation Limitation for Cars and Trucks Increases. The limitation on first-year depreciation of a car purchased in 2013 is $3,160, while the limitation for trucks remains at $3,360.

Bonus Depreciation. In 2013, the bonus depreciation allowance for the first year depreciation limit remains at $11,160 for cars and $11,360 for trucks and vans.

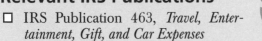
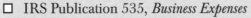

Relevant IRS Publications

- ☐ IRS Publication 463, *Travel, Entertainment, Gift, and Car Expenses*
- ☐ IRS Publication 535, *Business Expenses*
- ☐ IRS Publication 544, *Sales and Other Dispositions of Assets*
- ☐ IRS Publication 551, *Basis of Assets*
- ☐ IRS Publication 946, *How to Depreciate Property*
- ☐ Form 2106, *Employee Business Expenses*

Section at a Glance

Tax Preparer's Checklist

- ☐ The following items are required: Logs of usage for all vehicles, cell phones, computers, etc., used in a small enterprise or home office; copy of lease, if applicable
- ☐ Vehicle type, date placed in service, and odometer readings on January 1, 2013, and December 31, 2013, in addition to all actual business travel in logs
- ☐ All receipts for vehicle expenses if actual expense method is elected or required. Invoice or other evidence of purchase or acquisition amount for each item of property

Vehicle Depreciation Percentages and 2013 Depreciation Limits*

Year of Ownership	MACRS % Assuming Half-Year Convention** (More than 50% Business Use)	150% DB Optional Method (More than 50% Business Use)	Straight Line Optional Method or for 50% Business Use or Less	Total Depreciation Limitation Car	Total Depreciation Limitation Truck or Van
First year (bonus deprec.)	20.00%	15.00%	10.00%	11,160	11,360
First year (no bonus)	20.00%	15.00%	10.00%	3,160	3,360
Second year	32.00%	25.50%	20.00%	5,100	5,400
Third year	19.20%	17.85%	20.00%	3,050	3,250
Fourth year	11.52%	16.66%	20.00%	1,875	1,975
Fifth year	11.52%	16.66%	20.00%	1,875	1,975
Sixth year	5.76%	8.33%	10.00%	1,875	1,975
Seventh year and later	If vehicle is not fully depreciated after the sixth year, a maximum amount may be claimed based on business use percentage.			1,875	1,975

*Limits are for vehicles first placed in service in 2013.
**If using the mid-quarter convention, these amounts do not apply; see IRS Publication 463 for rates.

Business Vehicles

If a taxpayer purchases a vehicle for use in a business, or uses a personal vehicle for business purposes, all or a portion of the cost of owning and using that vehicle may be claimed as a business expense. Purchase cost and costs of having a vehicle overhauled or reconditioned are usually claimed through depreciation. Expenses and repairs related to business vehicles may also qualify to be deducted as a business expense.

Vehicle Recordkeeping

As for all deductions, substantiation requirements must be met when claiming vehicle expenses.

For every vehicle, records must indicate both general vehicle information and specific details of use:

- Vehicle make and model.
- Whether unloaded gross vehicle weight is more than or less than 6,000 pounds.
- Date of purchase and invoice, receipt, or other evidence of amount paid.
- Date vehicle was placed in service for business.
- Odometer readings on January 1 and December 31.
- All actual business travel, with mileage and date and purpose of trip (and which vehicle was used if more than one vehicle is in service).

If the vehicle was purchased or converted from solely personal use during the year, the odometer reading on the date placed in service may take the place of the January 1 reading.

Records must be kept at least as long as the statute of limitations on IRS examinations of returns runs or the item remains in use thereafter. Records of vehicle purchase and business use should be kept as long as the vehicle is owned, or at least three years after the last return is filed on which any deductions relating to that vehicle are taken, whichever is longer.

 Caution. Lines 20 and 21 of Part II of Form 2106 ask whether the taxpayer has evidence to support the deduction and whether that evidence is written. Lack of written records may lead to inability to take the deduction.

Choice of Deduction Method

Taxpayers can choose to deduct actual expenses, including depreciation, gas, registration fees, repairs, maintenance, and insurance. Or they can choose to use the standard mileage method. Either way, individuals can also deduct business-related tolls, parking fees, and personal property tax. Self-employed individuals can also deduct loan interest on business vehicles.

Business-Use Percentage

If a vehicle is used for both personal and business purposes, the costs related to the vehicle must be divided based on the mileage driven for each purpose.

 Example. Leo is the sole proprietor of a small business. He has only one vehicle, which he uses for both personal and business purposes. The odometer reading on January 1, 2013, was 31,522. The odometer reading on December 31, 2013, was 74,373. He keeps a log of each business trip, including miles driven, which indicates that he drove 18,130 miles on business during 2013. The business-use percentage for his vehicle is 18,130/(74,373 − 31,522) = 42.3%.

Some benefits are only available if a vehicle is used more than 50% for business. If business use varies from year to year, special rules may apply; see the discussion of depreciation recapture on page 8-8.

 Planning Tip. To maximize deductible business miles, to the extent that the taxpayer can plan out his or her day with multiple business trips, the first and last destinations should be closest to home. Also, taxpayers who use a vehicle for both business and personal use may consider the benefits of renting a vehicle for personal vacations, particularly if this prevents the business-use percentage from falling below 50%.

Caution. The IRS assumes that individuals require a vehicle for personal use, so 100% business use of a vehicle in a situation where there is no other vehicle available is closely scrutinized. Line 19 of Part II of Form 2106 asks the question, "Do you (or your spouse) have another vehicle available for personal use?" Answering "No" may be incompatible with claiming 100% business use of the vehicle.

Qualified Business Use

Qualified business use is any use in a trade or business. Records must indicate the business purpose of each trip. Note that use of a vehicle for investment activities (use for production of income) is not a qualified business use, but mileage for investment activities

When Are Local Transportation Expenses Deductible?

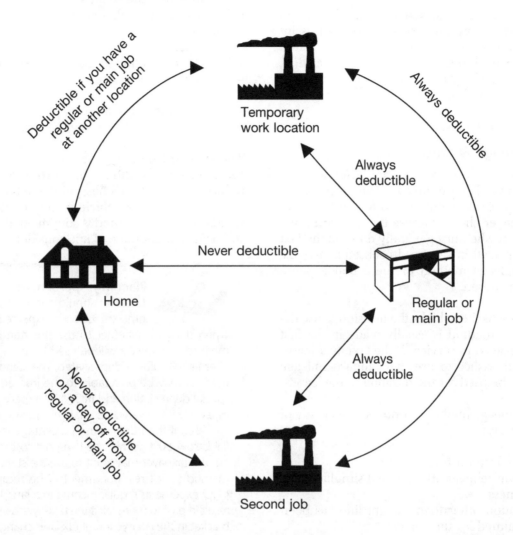

is combined with qualified business use in calculating the depreciation deduction.

Deductible Commuting

Transportation expenses for travel between jobs or to clients' locations are generally deductible. Travel between a regular job and a temporary jobsite, or between a regular job and a second job, is also deductible. Additionally, travel between a second job location and a temporary job or client's office is deductible. The general rule is that the travel must be for work, but not for the taxpayer's regular commute. The cost of traveling between the taxpayer's home and regular place of business is never deductible, even if the vehicle used displays advertising or if business telephone calls or business discussions are conducted while traveling.

Office in Home as Main Place of Work. If a taxpayer's main place of business is an office in the home, then the cost of traveling from there to clients' offices or other places of business is deductible. However, the cost of traveling to another main job location is not deductible.

See MTG ¶961 for further information.

Example. Donna has a regular place of business. The cost of traveling from her home to that business and back is not deductible. She is assigned to a different location for a week. The cost of traveling from her home to this temporary assignment is deductible.

Example. Frances does not have a regular place of business, nor does she have an office in her home. She leaves her home and visits several clients and then returns. The cost of traveling from her home to the first client and the cost of traveling from the last client back to her home is not deductible. The amount in between clients is deductible. If she had an office in her home, the entire trip would be deductible.

Mileage Deduction Methods

Either the standard mileage deduction may be taken or actual expenses may be used. Depreciation is included in the standard mileage method, so an election to use MACRS or another method of depreciation, or to claim any IRC §179 expense, requires that the actual expense method be used.

See MTG ¶947 for details.

Standard Mileage Method

The standard mileage method may be elected whether or not the taxpayer is reimbursed by an employer. It may be used for leased vehicles and for owned vehicles. If the taxpayer chooses to use the standard mileage method, he or she must generally do so in the first year the car is placed in service. In subsequent years, the standard mileage method or the actual expense method may be chosen.

If the taxpayer owns the vehicle, the decision to use the standard mileage method is usually made in the first year the car is placed in service. If the taxpayer leases the vehicle, and wishes to use the standard mileage method, it must be used for the duration of the lease.

The standard mileage method cannot be used if any of the following apply:

- The vehicle is used for hire.
- More than four vehicles are operated simultaneously in the business.
- Any depreciation other than straight line has been previously claimed for the vehicle.
- An IRC §179 deduction has been taken for the vehicle.
- Actual expenses on this vehicle have been claimed in a previous year and the vehicle is leased.
- The taxpayer is a rural mail carrier and received a qualified reimbursement.

 Caution. Using the standard mileage method in the first year precludes using any accelerated depreciation methods in subsequent years (including IRC §179 deductions). Taking accelerated depreciation deductions on a vehicle (including IRC §179) precludes using the standard mileage method in future years.

Expenses Included in the Standard Mileage Allowance. The standard business allowance in 2013 is 56.5 cents per mile. This allowance is intended to cover all costs of operating the vehicle, and includes the following expenses:

- Depreciation.
- Maintenance and repairs.
- Gasoline and gasoline taxes.
- Oil.
- Insurance.
- Vehicle registration fees and license fees that are not personal property taxes.

Actual payments for these expenses may not be deducted in addition to the standard rate.

The standard mileage rate covers depreciation at 23 cents per mile for 2013. This portion of the deduction reduces the taxpayer's basis in the vehicle, but not below zero. Once the vehicle is fully depreciated, if the standard mileage method is continued, the full rate may still be taken, but none of it is considered depreciation.

 Planning Tip. For maximum benefit, a taxpayer should consider the length of time vehicles are expected to be used when deciding whether to use the standard mileage method. If a vehicle will be used for many years, long after its full value is depreciated, the standard mileage method may be preferable to the immediate value of special depreciation and IRC §179 expense deduction, especially if the vehicle is relatively inexpensive.

Also, if the business-use percentage is expected to fall below 50% within the five-year cost-recovery period, the taxpayer may want to use the standard mileage method for all reimbursements. The recapture of IRC §179 expense as regular income in a later tax year may result in paying more tax if the taxpayer is in a higher tax bracket in the later year or if tax laws change.

Expenses Not Included in the Standard Mileage Allowance. Some expenses are not included in the standard rate. These include the following:

- Parking fees.
- Tolls.
- The personal property tax portion (if any) of license fees.
- Interest on auto loan.

These expenses may be deducted in addition to the standard mileage amount. Employees and statutory employees may not deduct interest on auto loans. They also may not include fees paid to park at their place of employment or tolls paid during their regular commute, as these are considered nondeductible commuting expenses. Other parking fees and tolls paid in the course of their work may be deductible job expenses.

Parking and tolls are deductible if paid in the course of business use. The portion of other expenses that is deductible is based on the percentage of use of the vehicle in business.

The personal property tax on the vehicle may be split on a pro rata basis. The business portion is deductible against self-employment income and the amount not related to business may be taken as an itemized deduction on Schedule A.

Actual Expense Method

The taxpayer must use the actual expense method if any accelerated depreciation (ACRS, MACRS, or any method other than straight line) or IRC §179 expense has been claimed on the vehicle, the vehicle is used for hire, more than four vehicles are operated simultaneously in the business, or actual expenses on this vehicle have been claimed in a previous year and the vehicle is leased (after 1997). Rural mail carriers who received a qualified reimbursement must also use the actual expense method.

If the taxpayer chooses to deduct actual expenses, this will include all costs of operating and maintaining the vehicle: gas, oil, maintenance, repairs, tires, licenses, registration, insurance, parking, tolls, garage fees, etc. Additionally, the taxpayer can take straight line or another form of depreciation on the vehicle. If the taxpayer uses the vehicle for both personal and business use, then the expenses must be either allocated between the two (as in the case of insurance) or traced directly to the type of use (as in the case of parking fees). Most expenses can be allocated on the basis of the number of miles driven for business and personal use.

Example. Oliver uses his car for both personal and business use. During the year he drove 12,000 personal miles and 18,000 business miles. He paid $800 for insurance for the year. The business portion of that insurance expense would be ($800 × 18/30) = $480. He also has several receipts for tolls paid. One was for $20 he paid while taking his family on vacation. Another is for $10 paid while making a sales call. The first one is a personal expense and not deductible. The $10 is deductible as a business expense.

Charitable Use of Automobile

If the taxpayer uses his or her car to drive to a qualified charity to perform volunteer work, a portion of the costs of the car's charitable use is deductible as a charitable expense. If the actual expense method is chosen, the costs must be directly related to the miles driven for a charitable purpose, such as gasoline. If the car is used exclusively for charitable purposes, maintenance and repairs on the car are deductible. If the car is used for both charitable and noncharitable purposes, no general maintenance or repairs can be deducted. Rather, only those costs directly attributable to the car's use for charitable purposes can be deducted.

If the taxpayer does not wish to track actual expenses, then a standard rate of 14 cents per mile may be used instead. Ad-

ditionally, any parking fees or tolls incurred while using the vehicle for a charitable purpose may be deducted. Records must be kept to substantiate any deductions.

If the charitable travel is combined with personal pleasure time, it is generally not deductible.

Example. Quentin travels to San Francisco on a weekend pleasure outing. While he is there he volunteers at a qualified soup kitchen for half a day. He did not schedule the charity work before traveling to San Francisco. His mileage is not deductible.

Example. Ruth travels to Chicago to work at a qualified charity all day. On the way home she stops and watches a movie she has been wanting to see. The travel is deductible, but the cost of the movie is not.

Employer-Provided Vehicle

If an employee drives a vehicle provided by an employer, that is a fringe benefit and the value of the benefit is usually taxable. The employee can deduct actual expenses paid for use of the vehicle, such as for gasoline, that are in excess of what is reimbursed. The standard mileage method may not be used.

Planning Tip. Employer-provided vehicles may present unique difficulties if no other vehicle is available. If strictly a business vehicle and no personal vehicle exists, include the personal use as income on the person's W-2. If strictly business and another personal vehicle exists, then keep it that way—avoid any commuting.

Depreciating and Expensing Vehicles

A vehicle is a capital asset and thus can be depreciated if used for business. An IRC §179 deduction is also available. There are restrictions on depreciation and IRC §179 deductions based on the value of the vehicle, the type of usage, the percentage of business use, and who owns the vehicle.

A car (referred to in the statute as a "passenger automobile") is defined as a four-wheeled vehicle with an *unloaded* gross vehicle weight of 6,000 pounds or less and which is made primarily for use on public roads. A truck or van is considered to be a car if it has a *loaded* gross vehicle weight of 6,000 pounds or less. Vehicles with a weight in excess of this amount are not considered to be cars, and are subject to higher depreciation caps (discussed below). Also not considered to be cars are ambulances and hearses.

Trucks and vans (including SUVs and minivans that are built on a truck chassis) weighing less than 6,000 pounds while loaded are subject to a separate set of depreciation caps, which are slightly higher than those for cars.

A truck or van that is a "qualified nonpersonal use vehicle" is not considered to be a car, and is not subject to the annual depreciation cap. A qualified nonpersonal use vehicle is a vehicle which has been specially modified in such a way that more than a small amount of personal use is unlikely. One example of such vehicles would be taxis, while another would be delivery vans with built-in shelves and no passenger seating.

A taxpayer may elect to expense, rather than depreciate, a portion of the cost of business property for the first year that the property is placed in service. Expensing under IRC §179 (discussed further below) is usually subject to a limitation of $500,000 (for 2013).

For purposes of the IRC §179 expensing limitations, heavy SUVs (i.e., weighing more than 6,000 pounds) are ordinarily limited to $25,000. Trucks and vans in excess of 6,000 pounds are included in the statutory definition of SUV (and thus subject to the $25,000 expensing limitation) unless the truck or van has (a) seating for more than nine people behind the driver, (b) a bed (cargo area) of six feet or more in interior length, or (c) no seating behind the driver and no part of the vehicle body extending more than 30 inches past the windshield (i.e., cargo vans).

 Caution. Simply placing advertising on a vehicle does not qualify it as a nonpersonal use vehicle, though it can result in advertising expenses qualified for deduction.

Limits

There are limits on depreciation as follows:

Purchased in 2013	Car	Truck or Van
General limit	$11,160	$11,360
If special depreciation allowance is not allowed or not taken	$3,160	$3,360
If the vehicle is used less than 100% for business, then the limit must be multiplied by the percentage of business use (for example, a vehicle with 60% business use that qualified and took the special depreciation allowance)	$6,696 (for 60% business use)	$6,816 (for 60% business use)

Limitations on depreciation for previous years are different. See MTG ¶1211 and ¶1214 for depreciation limitations and further information.

If the taxpayer's vehicle weighs over 6,000 pounds, it is not subject to the same depreciation limitations. However, such vehicles are still listed property, and if the business use is below 50% they are therefore not eligible for accelerated depreciation or for IRC §179 expensing.

Basis

Basis is the amount paid for the vehicle, which includes cash, loan money, and property (or services) traded in. The total of sticker price, taxes, title and document fees, and a dealer's transportation charge is the basis in the purchased vehicle. Generally, to calculate depreciation, the basis must be used. However, sometimes the taxpayer's adjusted basis is used. If the vehicle was converted from personal use to business use, the basis is the lesser of the adjusted basis and fair market value.

Unadjusted Basis. Unadjusted basis, or "basis for depreciation," is the basis including sales tax, destination charge, and dealer preparation fees plus the cost of any significant improvements made that extend the value or life expectancy of the car (e.g., new engine or overhaul), less IRC §179 deductions, diesel fuel tax credit, clean-fuel vehicle deduction, and qualified electric vehicle credit.

Generally, when a vehicle is traded in on a new vehicle, and both cars are 100% business use, the basis is the adjusted basis in the old car plus the price paid for the new car.

Example. Gary has a car with an adjusted basis of $1,000 that he trades in along with $14,000 for a new car. Both cars are used exclusively for business. No IRC §179 deduction was taken for the old car; all proper elections made. The new car has a basis of $15,000.

Example. Hannah purchased a car exclusively for business in 2011 for $20,000. For 2011 through 2013, she deducted $10,910 for depreciation. On February 1, 2014, she traded in the car, along with $10,000 cash, for another car to be used exclusively in business. Under the half-year convention, she took $1,152 in depreciation for 2014. Her adjusted basis in the old car is ($20,000 − $10,910 − $1,152) = $7,938. Her basis in the new car is ($7,938 + $10,000) = $17,938. Note that the taxpayer could depreciate the $7,938 using the old schedule and for the old remaining life, while the $10,000 starts out as new MACRS property. Alternatively, the taxpayer could elect out of that method and could depreciate the entire $17,938 as new property.

Vehicle Depreciation Percentages and 2013 Depreciation Limits*

Year of Ownership	MACRS % Assuming Half-Year Convention** (More than 50% Business Use)	150% DB Optional Method (More than 50% Business Use)	Straight Line Optional Method or for 50% Business Use or Less	Total Depreciation Limitation	
				Car	Truck or Van
First year (bonus depr.)	20.00%	15.00%	10.00%	$11,160	$11,360
First year (no bonus)	20.00%	15.00%	10.00%	3,160	3,360
Second year	32.00%	25.50%	20.00%	5,100	5,400
Third year	19.20%	17.85%	20.00%	3,050	3,250
Fourth year	11.52%	16.66%	20.00%	1,875	1,975
Fifth year	11.52%	16.66%	20.00%	1,875	1,975
Sixth year	5.76%	8.33%	10.00%	1,875	1,975
Seventh year and later	If vehicle is not fully depreciated after the sixth year, a maximum amount may be claimed based on business use percentage.			1,875	1,975

*Limits are for vehicles first placed in service in 2013.

**If using the mid-quarter convention, these amounts do not apply; see IRS Publication 463 for rates.

Example. Isaac purchased a car that he uses 60% for business in 2011 and 2012 for $20,000. He did not claim any IRC §179 expense. In 2011 and 2012 he took a total of $4,776 in depreciation deductions. On February 1, 2013, he traded that car in for another car, paying an additional $10,000 cash. Under MACRS, he took a half-year's depreciation deduction for 2013 of $1,152 (the lesser of ($20,000 × 19.20% (3rd year percentage) × 50% (for half-year convention) × 60% = $1,152) or ($2,950 (3rd year limit) × 60% = $1,770)). Actual depreciation taken for 2011, 2012, and 2013 was ($4,776 + $1,152) $5,928. Isaac's adjusted basis in the old car was ($20,000 − $5,928) $14,072, which is added to the amount paid for the new car for a preliminary basis of ($14,072 + $10,000) = $24,072. However, since the car was not 100% business use, he must calculate what the allowable depreciation on the old car would have been if it had been 100% business use:

2013	$20,000 × 19.20% x 50% (limit of $2,950)	$1,920
2012	$20,000 × 32% (limit of $4,900)	$4,900
2011	$20,000 × 20% (limit of $3,060)	$3,060
Total		$9,880

The excess of the allowable depreciation over actual depreciation taken is ($9,880 − $5,928) $3,952. The adjusted basis on his old car was $14,072, but his adjusted basis in the new vehicle is ($24,072 − $3,952) $20,120.

If the old car is not a 100% business-use vehicle, then an adjustment must be made to the basis of the trade-in vehicle. Add the adjusted basis of the old car to the amount paid for the new car then subtract the amount that would have been allowed as depreciation on the old car if it had been 100% business use to the extent that it exceeds the actual depreciation taken.

Date Placed in Service

A car is placed in service when it first becomes available to the taxpayer for use in his or her business or other income-producing activity. The date an order was placed is irrelevant. For a car that was personal use that is converted to business use, the date placed in service is the date of conversion (the earliest date used for business purposes).

IRC §179 Expensing

An IRC §179 deduction can only be claimed on a vehicle in the first year for which that vehicle was placed in service for business use (whether or not such use was made of it). The vehicle must be used for business more than 50% of the time. If the vehicle is used for personal use and then in a later year converted to business use, an IRC §179 deduction may not be taken for that vehicle.

Generally, up to $500,000 (for 2013) in IRC §179 deductions can be taken. However, there are limits on how much total IRC §179 and depreciation can be taken on individual vehicles:

- If the car was acquired in 2005 or 2006, the limit is $2,960.
- If the car was acquired in 2007, the limit is $3,060.
- If the car was acquired in 2008 or 2009, the limit is $2,960 (or $10,960 if special depreciation is taken).
- If the car was acquired in 2010 or 2011, the limit is $3,060 (or $11,060 if special depreciation is taken).
- If the car was acquired in 2012 and 2013, the limit is $3,160 (or $11,160 if special depreciation is taken).

The above limits are for passenger cars. Trucks and vans have somewhat higher limits. These limits are reduced ratably if the car is used less than 100% for business purposes.

See MTG ¶1208 and Tab 7 for more information about IRC §179 deductions.

The basis in the new car is limited to the cash paid for it plus the adjusted basis (not value) of the traded-in vehicle.

 Caution. An IRC §179 deduction can only be taken in the year the vehicle was purchased AND placed in service. A personal use vehicle placed in service in subsequent years does not qualify.

 Filing Tip. Employees elect to expense property under IRC §179 on Form 2106, Employee Business Expenses. Everyone else uses Form 4562, Depreciation and Amortization (Including Information on Listed Property).

Special Depreciation Allowance

For 2013, the taxpayer is allowed to claim first-year bonus depreciation equal to 50% of the adjusted basis of qualifying property eligible for depreciation using the modified accelerated cost recovery system (MACRS) with a depreciation period of 20 years or less. The first-year limit on depreciation for vehicles placed in service in 2013 ($3,160 for passenger vehicles and $3,360 for vans and trucks) is increased by $8,000, if bonus depreciation is claimed, for a total limit on vehicle depreciation of $11,160 for passenger vehicles and $11,360 for vans and trucks.

Only new vehicles qualify for bonus depreciation. Those who choose to claim this allowance must reduce the adjusted basis of the car by the amount of the allowance. The special depreciation allowance is calculated after the IRC §179 deduction, but before calculating the MACRS depreciation deduction. If the vehicle is not used more than 50 percent for business in a subsequent year, then the bonus depreciation taken must be recaptured.

Bonus depreciation must be claimed for both regular tax and alternative minimum tax liability, unless the taxpayer makes an election out. Once made, an election out cannot be revoked without IRS consent.

MACRS Calculation

Generally, cars are depreciated using the MACRS method. However, if the standard mileage method was used the first year the car was placed in service, MACRS cannot be used. Additionally, the car must be used more than 50% for business in each of the recovery years. If the business use is less than 50%, MACRS cannot be used. If the business use falls below 50% in subsequent years, the taxpayer must switch to straight-line depreciation (and may have to recapture excess depreciation). Once the taxpayer has calculated the IRC §179 deduction, if any, he or she may then determine the amount of the MACRS deduction.

 Filing Tip. If a car is placed in service and disposed of in the same year, no depreciation deduction may be taken on it.

Less than 50% Business Use. If the taxpayer's car is used less than 50% for business purposes, no IRC §179 deduction is allowed. Additionally, the straight-line method must be used. The other limits remain the same.

If the business percentage varies from year to year, just use the applicable rate in the calculations for the depreciation amount and for the limit.

Depreciation Recapture

If the taxpayer's car drops to below 50% business use in a year after MACRS or other accelerated depreciation has been taken, it must convert to straight line. Additionally, excess depreciation over straight line that has been taken in previous years must be recovered and added to income.

Example. Maureen buys a new car for 100% business use in 2013. She elects not to take an IRC §179 expensing deduction, and she elects out of special depreciation. Her basis in the car is $20,000. She elects to use the regular MACRS method. Her depreciation deductions are:

Year	Calculation	Amount of Depreciation	Limit	Depreciation Allowed	Basis after Depreciation
2013	$20,000 × 20%	$4,000	$3,160	$3,160	$16,840
2014	$20,000 × 32%	6,400	5,100	5,100	11,740
2015	$20,000 × 19.2%	3,840	3,050	3,050	8,690
2016	$20,000 × 11.52%	2,304	1,875	1,875	6,815
2017	$20,000 × 11.52%	2,304	1,875	1,875	4,940
2018	$20,000 × 5.76%	1,152	1,875	1,152	3,788
2019	$3,788 (unrecovered basis) × 100%	3,788	1,875	1,875	1,913
2020	$1,913 × 100%	1,913	1,875	1,875	38
2021	$38 × 100%	38	1,875	38	0

Example. The limitations on allowed deductions may make it advisable not to claim the IRC §179 expensing deduction. Lisa buys a new car for 100% business use in 2013. She elects not to expense any of its cost, and the car qualifies for the 50% first-year special depreciation allowance. Her basis in the car is $30,000. She elects to use the regular MACRS method. Her depreciation deductions are:

Year	Calculation	Amount of Depreciation	Limit	Depreciation Allowed	Basis after Depreciation
2013	Bonus depreciation	15,000			
	$15,000 × 20%	3,000	$11,160	$11,160	$18,840
2014	$15,000 × 32%	4,800	5,100	4,800	14,040
2015	$15,000 × 19.2%	2,880	3,050	2,880	11,160
2016	$15,000 × 11.52%	1,728	1,875	1,728	9,432
2017	$15,000 × 11.52%	1,728	1,875	1,728	7,704
2018	$15,000 × 5.76%	864	1,875	864	6,840
2019	$6,840 (unrecovered basis) × 100%	6,840	1,875	1,875	4,965
2020	$4,965 × 100%	4,965	1,875	1,875	3,090
2021	$3,090 × 100%	3,090	1,875	1,875	1,215
2022	$1,215 × 100%	1,215	1,875	1,215	0

Even though Lisa is eligible to claim an IRC §179 deduction in addition to the special depreciation allowance, her first-year depreciation deductions have already reached the limit and it would do her no good. *(This Example continues on page 8-10.)*

Assume the same facts, except that the car's initial basis was $12,000. Without the IRC §179 deduction, her depreciation deductions are as follows:

Year	Calculation	Amount of Depreciation	Limit	Depreciation Allowed	Basis after Depreciation
2013	Bonus depreciation	$6,000			
	$6,000 × 20%	1,200	$11,160	$7,200	$4,800
2014	$6,000 × 32%	1,920	5,100	1,920	2,880
2015	$6,000 × 19.2%	1,152	3,050	1,152	1,728
2016	$6,000 × 11.52%	691	1,875	691	1,037
2017	$6,000 × 11.52%	691	1,875	691	346
2018	$6,000 × 5.76%	346	1,875	346	0

Here are the calculations for the same situation, but with the IRC §179 deduction taken into account:

Year	Calculation	Amount of Depreciation	Limit	Depreciation Allowed	Basis after Depreciation
2013	IRC §179 Expensing	$9,900			
	Bonus depreciation	1,050			
	$1,050 × 20%	210	$11,160	$11,160	$840
2014	$1,050 × 32%	336	5,100	336	504
2015	$1,050 × 19.2%	202	3,050	202	302
2016	$1,050 × 11.52%	121	1,875	121	181
2017	$1,050 × 11.52%	121	1,875	121	60
2018	$1,050 × 5.76%	60	1,875	60	0

In this case, Lisa is able to recover her basis in the car much faster with the IRC §179 deduction than without. The amount of IRC §179 deduction taken was that amount which, when added to the allowable special and regular depreciation deductions, reached the cap amount.

Example. Mark buys a used car in 2013 for $20,000. Because he plans to use it only 40% for business purposes, he is not eligible for bonus depreciation or IRC §179 expensing, and must use straight-line depreciation. His depreciation deductions are as follows:

Year	Calculation	Amount of Depreciation	Limit*	Depreciation Allowed	Basis after Depreciation
2013	$20,000 × 10% × 40%	$ 800	$1,264	$ 800	$18,000
2014	$20,000 × 20% × 40%	1,600	2,040	1,600	14,000
2015	$20,000 × 20% × 40%	1,600	1,220	1,220	10,950
2016	$20,000 × 20% × 40%	1,600	750	750	9,075
2017	$20,000 × 20% × 40%	1,600	750	750	7,200
2018	$20,000 × 10% × 40%	800	750	750	5,325
2019	$5,325 (unrecovered basis) × 40%	2,130	750	750	3,450
2020	$3,450 × 40%	1,380	750	750	1,575
2021	$1,575 × 40%	630	750	630	0

*Limit is calculated by taking the statutory limit and multiplying by the percentage of business use.

Example. Kevin buys a used car for 80% business use in 2013. He elects not to take IRC §179 expensing, and a used vehicle is ineligible for bonus depreciation. His basis in the car is $20,000. He elects to use the regular MACRS method. His depreciation deductions are:

Year	Calculation	Amount of Depreciation	Limit*	Depreciation Allowed	Basis after Depreciation
2013	$20,000 × 20% × 80%	$3,200	$2,528	$2,528	$16,840
2014	$20,000 × 32% × 80%	5,120	4,080	4,080	11,740
2015	$20,000 × 19.2% × 80%	3,072	2,440	2,440	8,690
2016	$20,000 × 11.52% × 80%	1,843	1,500	1,500	6,815
2017	$20,000 × 11.52% × 80%	1,843	1,500	1,500	4,940
2018	$20,000 × 5.76% × 80%	922	1,500	922	3,788
2019	$3,788 (unrecovered basis) × 80%	3,030	1,500	1,500	1,913
2020	$1,913 × 80%	1,530	1,500	1,500	38
2021	$38 × 80%	30	1,500	30	0

*Limit is calculated by taking statutory limit and multiplying by the percentage of business use.

If business use varies from year to year, change the percentages and calculate the limits accordingly. Assume the same facts as in the previous example except that Kevin's business use changes from year to year. His depreciation deductions are:

Year	Percent Business Use	Calculation	Amount of Depreciation	Limit*	Depreciation Allowed	Basis After Depreciation
2013	80%	$20,000 × 20% × 80%	$3,200	$2,528	$2,528	$16,840
2014	60%	$20,000 × 32% × 60%	3,840	3,060	3,060	11,740
2015	70%	$20,000 × 19.2% × 70%	2,688	2,135	2,135	8,690
2016	80%	$20,000 × 11.52% × 80%	1,843	1,500	1,500	6,815
2016	60%	$20,000 × 11.52% × 60%	1,382	1,125	1,125	4,940
2018	70%	$20,000 × 5.76% × 70%	806	1,313	806	3,788
2019	80%	$3,788 (unrecovered basis) × 80%	3,030	1,500	1,500	1,913
2020	40%	$1,913 × 40%	765	750	750	38
2021	40%	$38 × 40%	15	750	15	0

*Limit is calculated by taking the statutory limit and multiplying by the percentage of business use.

Example. Joanne buys a used car for 100% business use in 2013. She does not elect to take IRC §179 expensing. Her basis in the car is $20,000. She is not eligible for bonus depreciation, and elects to use the regular MACRS method. She planned to use the car solely for business, but in the fourth year the business use dropped to 40%. First, she must calculate how much depreciation would have been allowed in the first three years using the straight-line method:

Year	Calculation*	Amount of Depreciation	Limit	Depreciation Allowed	Basis after Depreciation
2013	$20,000 × 10%	$2,000	$3,160	$2,000	$18,000
2014	$20,000 × 20%	4,000	5,100	4,000	14,000
2015	$20,000 × 20%	4,000	3,050	3,050	10,950

*Because her first three years were at 100%, no need exists regarding multiplying by business-use percentage here.

Her first three years looked like this before the business-use percentage dropped below 50%:

Year	Calculation	Amount of Depreciation	Limit	Depreciation Allowed	Basis after Depreciation
2013	$20,000 × 20%	$4,000	$3,160	$3,160	$16,840
2014	$20,000 × 32%	6,400	5,100	5,100	11,740
2015	$20,000 × 19.2%	3,840	3,050	3,050	8,690

She actually took ($3,160 + $5,100 + $3,050) = $11,310 depreciation. Under the straight-line method, she would only have been allowed ($2,000 + $4,000 + $3,050) = $9,050. Therefore she has to claim a recapture of ($11,310 – $9,050) = $2,260 on Form 4797. She adds the $2,260 basis back to her calculated basis to arrive at her new basis of ($2,260 + $8,690) = $10,950, which matches what her basis would have been if she'd used the straight-line method all along. For future years she continues with straight-line depreciation:

Year	Calculation	Amount of Depreciation	Limit	Depreciation Allowed	Basis after Depreciation
2016	$20,000 × 20% × 40%	$1,600	$750	$750	$9,075
2017	$20,000 × 20% × 40%	1,600	750	750	7,200
2018	$20,000 × 10% × 40%	800	750	750	5,325
2019	$5,325 (unrecovered basis) × 40%	2,130	750	750	3,450
2020	$3,450 × 40%	1,380	750	750	1,575
2021	$1,575 × 40%	630	750	630	0

*Limit is found by taking statutory limit and multiplying by business-use percentage.

The following example pertains to the trade-in of a business vehicle, which is discussed on page 8-13.

Example. Nina used the standard mileage method on her old car and is now trading it in along with an additional $15,000 cash payment on a new car. Her basis, before depreciation, in the old car was $12,000. Mileage and depreciation calculations are:

Year	Mileage	Rate	Depreciation
2013	11,200	0.23	$2,576
2012	10,600	0.23	2,438
2011	11,500	0.22	2,530
2010	10,750	0.23	2,473
2009	10,900	0.21	2,289
		Total	$12,306

Her new car's basis is $15,000 + ($12,000 – $12,306) = $14,694.

Disposition of Cars

Sale of Business Vehicle. The basis for computing gain or loss is generally the original cost reduced by the depreciation allowed. For vehicles that were used for both personal and business purposes, the gain or loss is computed by treating the vehicle as two separate pieces of property. The basis and selling price are allocated to two portions of the vehicle based on business-use percentage. Depreciation is allocated entirely to the business portion of the basis. The business-use percentage to be used in this calculation is determined for the entire life of the vehicle:

$$\text{Business use percentage} = \frac{\text{Sum of business miles driven in all years}}{\text{Total miles driven in all years}}$$

Trade-In of Business Vehicle. At the time of a trade in of one business vehicle for another, the basis of the old vehicle plus any amount paid for the new vehicle becomes the new vehicle's basis. The basis of the old vehicle must be reduced by any depreciation. If the standard mileage method was used, then a portion of that was for depreciation. The amount-per-mile considered allowed as depreciation is as follows:

Year	Amount
2012-2013	$0.23
2011	0.22
2010	0.23
2008-2009	0.21
2007	0.19
2005-2006	0.17

See MTG ¶947.

Charitable Donation of Vehicle. If the taxpayer donates his or her vehicle to charity, it is deductible at fair market value. One source of information for the fair market value of a vehicle is the Blue Book Value, available at dealers and online. However, the condition of the vehicle and mileage must be taken into consideration. In the case of a donated vehicle with a value of greater than $500, the contribution must be substantiated by a contemporaneous written acknowledgment containing the name and taxpayer identification number of the donor, the vehicle identification number, and certain certifications. The acknowledgment must be obtained within 30 days of the contribution or the disposition of the vehicle by donee organization, as applicable. If the vehicle is valued at between $250 and $500, the general rules for substantiation of a charitable contribution of property valued at $250 or more must be met. If the vehicle is resold, the deduction is limited to the amount realized by the charity on resale.

Alternative Motor Vehicles

The alternative motor vehicle credit may be applied to property placed in service after December 31, 2005.

See MTG ¶1345 for additional information.

The alternative motor vehicle credit is the sum of five credits:

- Qualified fuel cell motor vehicle credit – for a vehicle using a hydrogen-oxygen-based fuel cell.
- Advanced lean burn technology motor vehicle credit – for a vehicle with an internal combustion engine with direct injection, using more air than is necessary for complete fuel combustion.
- Qualified hybrid motor vehicle credit – for a vehicle using both internal combustion and a rechargeable energy storage system.
- Qualified alternative fuel motor vehicle credit – for a vehicle fueled by an alternative fuel, such as liquefied natural gas, hydrogen, methanol, or a mixture of one of these with petroleum-based fuel that meets certain requirements.
- Plug-in conversion credit – for a vehicle which is converted to a plug-in electric drive motor vehicle.

 Caution. Of these five component credits, only the qualified fuel cell motor vehicle credit is available to be claimed currently.

Although these component credits have their own unique characteristics, they share in common the requirements that (1) the vehicle's original use begins with the taxpayer claiming the credit, (2) the vehicle is acquired for use or lease by the taxpayer, and not for resale, (3) the vehicle is made by a "manufacturer" (as defined at 42 USC 7550(1)), and (4) the vehicle is used primarily in the United States.

If the vehicle is used in a trade or business, the taxpayer will claim the credit as part of, and as subject to the rules governing, the general business credit. Any unused part of the credit can therefore be carried back three years or forward 20 years (although it cannot be carried back to years before the credit first became available).

The credit may also be claimed by an individual as a personal credit, subject to various limitations. Specifically, the credit is reduced by the amount of certain other credits. If the personal portion of the credit cannot be used because of these limitations, it is lost, and may not be carried to other tax years. The nonrefundable personal use portion of the alternative motor vehicle credit can be used to offset both regular and minimum tax liability.

 Filing Tip. The claiming of the credit is at the election of the taxpayer. The credit is claimed by filing Form 8910, Alternative Motor Vehicle Credit, with one's tax return. This form includes separate sections for the "business/investment" and "personal use" parts of the vehicle.

Ordinarily, the credit is claimed by the buyer of the vehicle. However, if a qualified vehicle is sold (but not leased) to a tax-exempt entity, a governmental unit, or a foreign entity, the seller can claim the credit. To do so, the seller must give written notice to the buyer of the seller's intent to claim the credit, as well as the amount claimed.

The basis of a vehicle is reduced by the amount of alternative motor vehicle credit allowed. Also, the credit reduces the amount of any other deduction or credit applicable to the vehicle for the tax year.

 Planning Tip. A qualified vehicle must comply with safety and air emissions standards. This includes more stringent emissions standards applicable in some states. The taxpayer should verify that the vehicle complies with the specific standards applicable in his or her state.

If the vehicle no longer qualifies for the credit, the taxpayer must recapture part or all of the credit.

 Caution. In the case of the credit for a hybrid vehicle, the amount of the credit is limited based on sales of the vehicles. The credit amount will be phased out when a particular manufacturer has sold 60,000 vehicles. The full credit will be available for all certified hybrids sold during the calendar quarter in which 60,000 sales are reached. For the next two calendar quarters, the credit will be limited to 50 percent of the allowable credit. For the following two quarters, the credit will be limited to 25 percent. After that time, no credit will be allowed.

Listed Property

Listed property is subject to deduction limitations if used partly for business and partly for personal use. Listed property includes the following types of assets:

- Any passenger vehicle as defined under "Business Vehicles"
- Any other property used for transportation, such as a trailer
- Any property generally used for entertainment, recreation, or amusement, such as video cameras, photography equipment, etc.
- Computer equipment and peripherals (unless used exclusively for business at a permanent business establishment)

 Filing Tip. Cellular telephones and personal communications devices are no longer classified as listed property.

Although other listed property is not subject to the same dollar caps on depreciation as automobiles, all of the other requirements applicable to the automobiles also apply to these properties. Thus, the taxpayer must keep written documentation to support the deductions, and the 50% business-use tests apply. Thus if the taxpayer's initial use does not exceed 50% for business, he or she is limited to straight-line depreciation. If the initial use is greater than 50%, and then drops to that amount or less, the taxpayer may need to recapture prior deductions.

Business-use percentage is determined for listed property by hours of use.

See IRS Publication 946 and MTG ¶1211 for further information. See also Tab 7.

Lease or Buy Decision

Whether a client should buy or lease a vehicle may come up for discussion with the person who prepares their taxes. Following is a chart that briefly highlights the advantages both forms of acquisition pose. The answer, as always, depends on the client's preferences and awareness of the benefits of either mode.

Who Should Buy and Who Should Lease in 2013

Buying is likely to be more favorable if . . .	Leasing is likely to be more favorable if . . .
The vehicle is driven more than 15,000 miles per year	The vehicle is driven less than 15,000 miles per year
The vehicle is primarily for personal use Interest not deductible Depreciation deductible Standard mileage rate is available	The vehicle is primarily for business use Interest deductible Greatly simplified calculation If standard mileage rate used, it must be for life of lease
The vehicle is less valuable (or used)	The vehicle is more valuable
Making a large down payment is possible	Down payment can be avoided
The vehicle will be kept longer than 3-4 years	The vehicle will be traded in 2-4 years
Changes in lifestyle and vehicle requirements are likely and flexibility is needed	Flexibility in terms of contract not needed
Poor credit rating is an issue	Credit rating is excellent
Higher monthly payments are acceptable to build equity	Lower monthly payments are a priority (30-60% lower)

Negotiating the Lease Agreement

The following list highlights some key points affecting the cost involved in leasing a vehicle.

Checklist for Lease Agreement

Early return: Terms may be negotiable; determine any penalty fees before signing.

Insurance: Be sure to get additional coverage to take care of the immediate, driving-off-the-lot depreciation. Otherwise, should the vehicle be stolen or severely damaged in the first few months, the insurance payoff would not be enough to make up for the difference between the vehicle's value and what you owe.

Lease Rate: This "money factor" is used to calculate the interest portion of the monthly payment. Just like interest rates for purchase, these are negotiable.

Residual Value: The anticipated market value of the vehicle at the end of the lease should be clearly spelled out in the lease contract.

Warranty: Verify that the warranty for the vehicle encompasses the whole time of the lease.

Leased Vehicle Tables

Limitations on deductions for leased vehicles are similar to those for vehicles that are owned by the taxpayer.

Passenger cars with FMV greater than $19,000 that are leased in 2013 for a term of 30 days or more trigger an annual income inclusion amount. Similarly, trucks and vans with FMV greater than $19,000 that are leased for 2013 for a term of 30 days or more trigger an annual income inclusion amount.

The inclusion amount is determined by prorating the amount listed in the appropriate table for the number of days of the lease term that are included in the applicable year, prorated by the percentage of business and investment use for the year.

See IRS Publication 463 and MTG ¶1215 for further details.

Where to Report the Inclusion Amount

Self-employed taxpayers reduce their lease expense by the business-use portion of the lease inclusion amount and enter the result on line 20a of Schedule C.

Employees report the inclusion amount on lines 24a and 24b of Part II of Form 2106. See Tab 6 for instructions.

Inclusion Amounts for Passenger Automobiles (That Are Not Trucks or Vans) with a Lease Term Beginning in Calendar Year 2013

Fair Market Value		Tax Year During Lease[1]				
Over	Not Over	1st	2nd	3rd	4th	5th & later
$19,000	$19,500	2	4	6	7	8
19,500	20,000	2	5	6	9	9
20,000	20,500	2	5	8	9	11
20,500	21,000	3	6	8	10	12
21,000	21,500	3	6	10	11	13
21,500	22,000	3	7	10	13	14
22,000	23,000	4	8	11	14	16
23,000	24,000	4	9	14	16	18
24,000	25,000	5	10	15	18	21
25,000	26,000	5	12	16	21	23
26,000	27,000	6	12	19	23	25
27,000	28,000	6	14	20	25	28
28,000	29,000	7	15	22	27	30
29,000	30,000	7	16	24	29	33
30,000	31,000	8	17	26	31	35
31,000	32,000	8	19	27	33	38
32,000	33,000	9	20	29	35	40
33,000	34,000	10	21	31	37	43
34,000	35,000	10	22	33	39	45
35,000	36,000	11	23	35	41	48
36,000	37,000	11	25	36	43	50
37,000	38,000	12	26	38	45	53
38,000	39,000	12	27	40	47	55
39,000	40,000	13	28	42	49	58
40,000	41,000	13	29	44	52	59
41,000	42,000	14	30	45	54	63
42,000	43,000	14	32	47	56	64
43,000	44,000	15	33	48	59	67
44,000	45,000	15	34	51	60	69
45,000	46,000	16	35	52	63	72
46,000	47,000	17	36	54	65	74
47,000	48,000	17	38	55	67	77
48,000	49,000	18	39	57	69	79
49,000	50,000	18	40	59	71	82
50,000	51,000	19	41	61	73	84
51,000	52,000	19	42	63	75	87
52,000	53,000	20	43	65	77	89
53,000	54,000	20	45	66	79	92
54,000	55,000	21	46	68	81	94
55,000	56,000	21	47	70	84	96
56,000	57,000	22	48	72	85	99
57,000	58,000[2]	22	50	73	88	101

[1] For the last year of the lease, use the dollar amount for the preceding year.
[2] See IRS Revenue Procedure 2013-21, 2013-13 IRB 660 for inclusion amounts for vehicles with fair market value over $58,000.

Inclusion Amounts for Passenger Automobiles (That Are Not Trucks or Vans) with a Lease Term Beginning in Calendar Year 2012

Fair Market Value		Tax Year During Lease[1]				
Over	Not Over	1st	2nd	3rd	4th	5th & later
$18,500	$19,000	2	4	5	6	8
19,000	19,500	2	4	7	7	9
19,500	20,000	2	5	8	8	10
20,000	20,500	3	5	9	10	11
20,500	21,000	3	6	9	12	12
21,000	21,500	3	7	10	12	14
21,500	22,000	3	8	11	13	16
22,000	23,000	4	8	13	15	17
23,000	24,000	4	10	15	17	20
24,000	25,000	5	11	17	19	23
25,000	26,000	6	12	19	21	26
26,000	27,000	6	14	20	24	28
27,000	28,000	7	15	22	26	31
28,000	29,000	7	16	25	28	33
29,000	30,000	8	18	25	32	35
30,000	31,000	9	19	27	34	38
31,000	32,000	9	20	30	36	41
32,000	33,000	10	21	32	38	43
33,000	34,000	10	23	33	41	46
34,000	35,000	11	24	35	43	49
35,000	36,000	12	25	37	45	52
36,000	37,000	12	27	39	47	54
37,000	38,000	13	28	41	49	57
38,000	39,000	13	29	43	52	59
39,000	40,000	14	30	45	54	62
40,000	41,000	14	32	47	56	65
41,000	42,000	15	33	49	58	68
42,000	43,000	16	34	51	61	70
43,000	44,000	16	36	52	63	73
44,000	45,000	17	37	54	66	75
45,000	46,000	17	38	57	67	78
46,000	47,000	18	39	59	70	80
47,000	48,000	19	40	61	72	83
48,000	49,000	19	42	62	75	86
49,000	50,000	20	43	64	77	89
50,000	51,000	20	45	66	79	91
51,000	52,000	21	46	68	81	94
52,000	53,000	21	47	70	84	96
53,000	54,000	22	48	72	86	99
54,000	55,000	23	49	74	88	102
55,000	56,000	23	51	76	90	104
56,000	57,000	24	52	78	92	107
57,000	58,000	24	54	79	95	110
58,000	59,000[2]	25	55	81	97	113

[1] For the last year of the lease, use the dollar amount for the preceding year.
[2] See IRS Revenue Procedure 2012-23, 2012-14 IRB 712 for inclusion amounts for vehicles with fair market value over $59,000.

Inclusion Amounts for Passenger Automobiles (That Are Not Trucks or Vans) with a Lease Term Beginning in Calendar Year 2011

Fair Market Value		Tax Year during Lease[1]				
Over	Not Over	1st	2nd	3rd	4th	5th & later
$18,500	$19,000	3	8	11	13	16
19,000	19,500	4	9	13	15	18
19,500	20,000	4	10	15	17	20
20,000	20,500	5	11	16	19	23
20,500	21,000	5	12	18	21	25
21,000	21,500	6	13	19	24	26
21,500	22,000	6	14	21	26	29
22,000	23,000	7	16	23	29	32
23,000	24,000	8	18	27	32	37
24,000	25,000	9	20	30	36	42
25,000	26,000	10	23	33	40	46
26,000	27,000	11	25	36	44	51
27,000	28,000	12	27	40	48	55
28,000	29,000	13	29	43	52	60
29,000	30,000	14	31	47	55	65
30,000	31,000	15	34	49	60	69
31,000	32,000	16	36	53	63	73
32,000	33,000	17	38	56	68	77
33,000	34,000	18	40	60	71	82
34,000	35,000	19	42	63	75	87
35,000	36,000	20	45	66	79	91
36,000	37,000	21	47	69	83	96
37,000	38,000	22	49	73	87	100
38,000	39,000	23	51	76	91	105
39,000	40,000	24	53	80	94	110
40,000	41,000	25	56	82	99	114
41,000	42,000	26	58	86	102	119
42,000	43,000	27	60	89	107	123
43,000	44,000	28	62	93	110	128
44,000	45,000	29	64	96	114	133
45,000	46,000	30	67	98	119	137
46,000	47,000	31	69	102	122	141
47,000	48,000	32	71	105	127	145
48,000	49,000	33	73	109	130	150
49,000	50,000	34	76	111	134	155
50,000	51,000	35	78	115	138	159
51,000	52,000	36	80	118	142	164
52,000	53,000	37	82	122	146	168
53,000	54,000	38	84	125	150	173
54,000	55,000	39	87	128	153	178
55,000	56,000	40	89	131	158	182
56,000	57,000	41	91	135	161	187
57,000	58,000	42	93	138	166	191
58,000	59,000[2]	43	95	142	169	196

[1] For the last year of the lease, use the dollar amount for the preceding year.
[2] See IRS Revenue Procedure 2011-21, 2011-12 IRB 560 for inclusion amounts for vehicles with fair market value over $59,000.

Inclusion Amounts for Passenger Automobiles (That Are Not Trucks or Vans) with a Lease Term Beginning in Calendar Year 2010

Fair Market Value		Tax Year during Lease[1]				
Over	Not Over	1st	2nd	3rd	4th	5th & later
$ 16,700	$ 17,000	3	7	10	11	14
17,000	17,500	4	8	13	15	16
17,500	18,000	5	10	16	19	21
18,000	18,500	6	13	18	23	26
18,500	19,000	7	15	22	26	31
19,000	19,500	8	17	25	30	35
19,500	20,000	9	19	29	34	39
20,000	20,500	10	21	32	38	44
20,500	21,000	11	23	35	42	48
21,000	21,500	12	26	38	45	53
21,500	22,000	13	28	41	50	57
22,000	23,000	14	31	46	56	63
23,000	24,000	16	36	52	63	73
24,000	25,000	18	40	59	71	81
25,000	26,000	20	44	66	78	90
26,000	27,000	22	49	71	86	100
27,000	28,000	24	53	78	94	108
28,000	29,000	26	57	85	101	118
29,000	30,000	28	61	92	109	126
30,000	31,000	30	66	97	117	135
31,000	32,000	32	70	104	125	144
32,000	33,000	34	74	111	132	153
33,000	34,000	36	79	117	140	161
34,000	35,000	38	83	123	148	171
35,000	36,000	40	87	130	156	179
36,000	37,000	42	92	136	163	188
37,000	38,000	44	96	143	170	198
38,000	39,000	46	100	149	179	206
39,000	40,000	48	105	155	186	215
40,000	41,000	50	109	162	194	224
41,000	42,000	52	113	169	201	233
42,000	43,000	54	118	174	210	241
43,000	44,000	56	122	181	217	251
44,000	45,000	58	126	188	225	259
45,000	46,000	60	131	194	232	269
46,000	47,000	61	135	201	240	277
47,000	48,000	63	140	207	248	286
48,000	49,000	65	144	213	256	295
49,000	50,000	67	148	220	263	304
50,000	51,000	69	153	226	271	313
51,000	52,000	71	157	232	279	322
52,000	53,000	73	161	239	287	331
53,000	54,000	75	166	245	294	340
54,000	55,000[2]	77	170	252	302	348

[1] For the last year of the lease, use the dollar amount for the preceding year.
[2] See IRS Revenue Procedure 2010-18, 2010-9 IRB 427 for inclusion amounts for vehicles with fair market value over $55,000.

Inclusion Amounts for Passenger Automobiles (That Are Not Trucks or Vans) with a Lease Term Beginning in Calendar Year 2009

Fair Market Value		Tax Year during Lease[1]				
Over	Not Over	1st	2nd	3rd	4th	5th & later
$18,500	$19,000	9	19	28	34	38
19,000	19,500	10	21	32	38	43
19,500	20,000	11	24	36	42	48
20,000	20,500	12	27	39	46	54
20,500	21,000	13	29	43	51	58
21,000	21,500	15	31	47	55	64
21,500	22,000	16	34	50	60	68
22,000	23,000	17	38	56	66	76
23,000	24,000	20	42	64	75	86
24,000	25,000	22	47	71	84	96
25,000	26,000	24	52	78	93	107
26,000	27,000	26	58	85	101	117
27,000	28,000	29	62	93	110	127
28,000	29,000	31	67	100	119	138
29,000	30,000	33	72	108	128	147
30,000	31,000	35	77	115	137	157
31,000	32,000	38	82	122	146	167
32,000	33,000	40	87	129	155	178
33,000	34,000	42	92	137	163	188
34,000	35,000	44	97	144	172	199
35,000	36,000	47	102	151	181	208
36,000	37,000	49	107	159	189	219
37,000	38,000	51	112	166	199	228
38,000	39,000	53	117	173	208	239
39,000	40,000	56	122	180	216	250
40,000	41,000	58	127	188	225	259
41,000	42,000	60	132	195	234	269
42,000	43,000	62	137	203	242	280
43,000	44,000	65	141	210	252	290
44,000	45,000	67	146	218	260	300
45,000	46,000	69	151	225	269	311
46,000	47,000	71	157	232	278	320
47,000	48,000	74	161	240	286	331
48,000	49,000	76	166	247	296	340
49,000	50,000	78	171	255	304	351
50,000	51,000	80	176	262	313	361
51,000	52,000	83	181	269	322	371
52,000	53,000	85	186	276	331	381
53,000	54,000	87	191	284	339	392
54,000	55,000[2]	89	196	291	349	401

[1] For the last year of the lease, use the dollar amount for the preceding year.
[2] See IRS Publication 463 for inclusion amounts for vehicles with fair market value over $55,000.

Inclusion Amounts for Trucks and Vans with a Lease Term Beginning in Calendar Year 2013

Fair Market Value		Tax Year During Lease[1]				
Over	Not Over	1st	2nd	3rd	4th	5th & later
19,000	19,500	1	3	4	5	6
19,500	20,000	2	3	5	6	7
20,000	20,500	2	4	6	7	8
20,500	21,000	2	5	7	8	9
21,000	21,500	2	5	8	9	11
21,500	22,000	3	6	8	10	12
22,000	23,000	3	7	10	11	14
23,000	24,000	4	8	11	14	16
24,000	25,000	4	9	14	16	18
25,000	26,000	5	10	15	18	21
26,000	27,000	5	12	17	20	23
27,000	28,000	6	13	18	23	25
28,000	29,000	6	14	20	25	28
29,000	30,000	7	15	22	27	30
30,000	31,000	7	16	24	29	33
31,000	32,000	8	17	26	31	35
32,000	33,000	8	19	27	33	38
33,000	34,000	9	20	29	35	41
34,000	35,000	10	21	31	37	43
35,000	36,000	10	22	33	39	46
36,000	37,000	11	23	35	41	48
37,000	38,000	11	25	36	43	51
38,000	39,000	12	26	38	45	53
39,000	40,000	12	27	40	48	55
40,000	41,000	13	28	42	49	58
41,000	42,000	13	29	44	52	60
42,000	43,000	14	30	46	54	62
43,000	44,000	14	32	47	56	65
44,000	45,000	15	33	48	59	67
45,000	46,000	15	34	51	60	70
46,000	47,000	16	35	52	63	72
47,000	48,000	17	36	54	65	74
48,000	49,000	17	38	55	67	77
49,000	50,000	18	39	57	69	79
50,000	51,000	18	40	59	71	82
51,000	52,000	19	41	61	73	84
52,000	53,000	19	42	63	75	87
53,000	54,000	20	43	65	77	89
54,000	55,000	20	45	66	80	91
55,000	56,000[2]	21	46	68	81	94

[1] For the last year of the lease, use the dollar amount for the preceding year.
[2] See IRS Revenue Procedure 2013-21, 2013-13 IRB 660 for inclusion amounts for vehicles with fair market value over $56,000.

Inclusion Amounts for Trucks and Vans with a Lease Term Beginning in Calendar Year 2012

Fair Market Value		Tax Year During Lease[1]				
Over	Not Over	1st	2nd	3rd	4th	5th & later
19,000	19,500	1	4	5	6	7
19,500	20,000	2	4	6	7	9
20,000	20,500	2	5	7	8	10
20,500	21,000	2	5	8	10	11
21,000	21,500	3	6	9	10	13
21,500	22,000	3	6	10	12	14
22,000	23,000	3	8	11	14	15
23,000	24,000	4	9	13	16	18
24,000	25,000	4	10	15	19	21
25,000	26,000	5	11	17	21	24
26,000	27,000	6	12	19	23	26
27,000	28,000	6	14	21	25	29
28,000	29,000	7	15	23	27	32
29,000	30,000	7	17	24	30	34
30,000	31,000	8	18	26	32	37
31,000	32,000	9	19	28	34	40
32,000	33,000	9	20	31	36	42
33,000	34,000	10	21	33	39	44
34,000	35,000	10	23	34	41	48
35,000	36,000	11	24	36	44	50
36,000	37,000	12	25	38	46	53
37,000	38,000	12	27	40	48	55
38,000	39,000	13	28	42	50	58
39,000	40,000	13	29	44	53	60
40,000	41,000	14	31	45	55	63
41,000	42,000	14	32	48	57	66
42,000	43,000	15	33	50	59	69
43,000	44,000	16	34	52	61	72
44,000	45,000	16	36	53	64	74
45,000	46,000	17	37	55	66	77
46,000	47,000	17	38	58	68	79
47,000	48,000	18	40	59	70	82
48,000	49,000	19	41	61	73	84
49,000	50,000	19	42	63	75	87
50,000	51,000	20	43	65	78	89
51,000	52,000	20	45	66	80	93
52,000	53,000	21	46	68	83	95
53,000	54,000	21	48	70	84	98
54,000	55,000	22	49	72	87	100
55,000	56,000[2]	23	50	74	89	103

[1] For the last year of the lease, use the dollar amount for the preceding year.
[2] See IRS Revenue Procedure 2012-23, 2012-14 IRB 712 for inclusion amounts for vehicles with fair market value over $56,000.

Inclusion Amounts for Trucks and Vans with a Lease Term Beginning in Calendar Year 2011

Fair Market Value		Tax Year during Lease[1]				
Over	Not Over	1st	2nd	3rd	4th	5th & later
$19,000	$19,500	3	7	9	12	13
19,500	20,000	3	8	11	14	15
20,000	20,500	4	9	13	15	18
20,500	21,000	4	10	15	17	20
21,000	21,500	5	11	16	20	22
21,500	22,000	5	12	18	22	24
22,000	23,000	6	14	20	24	29
23,000	24,000	7	16	24	28	32
24,000	25,000	8	18	27	32	37
25,000	26,000	9	20	31	36	41
26,000	27,000	10	23	33	40	46
27,000	28,000	11	25	37	43	51
28,000	29,000	12	27	40	48	55
29,000	30,000	13	29	43	52	60
30,000	31,000	14	31	47	56	64
31,000	32,000	15	34	49	60	69
32,000	33,000	16	36	53	63	74
33,000	34,000	17	38	56	68	78
34,000	35,000	18	40	60	71	83
35,000	36,000	19	43	62	76	87
36,000	37,000	20	45	66	79	92
37,000	38,000	21	47	69	83	97
38,000	39,000	22	49	73	87	101
39,000	40,000	23	51	76	91	105
40,000	41,000	24	54	79	95	109
41,000	42,000	25	56	82	99	114
42,000	43,000	26	58	86	103	118
43,000	44,000	27	60	89	107	123
44,000	45,000	28	62	93	110	128
45,000	46,000	29	65	95	115	132
46,000	47,000	30	67	99	118	137
47,000	48,000	31	69	102	123	141
48,000	49,000	32	71	106	126	146
49,000	50,000	33	73	109	130	151
50,000	51,000	34	76	112	134	155
51,000	52,000	35	78	115	138	160
52,000	53,000	36	80	118	143	164
53,000	54,000	37	82	122	146	169
54,000	55,000	38	84	125	150	173
55,000	56,000	39	87	128	154	177
56,000	57,000	40	89	131	158	182
57,000	58,000	41	91	135	162	186
58,000	59,000	42	93	138	166	191
59,000	60,000	43	95	142	169	196
60,000	62,000	45	99	146	175	203
62,000	64,000	47	103	153	183	212
64,000	66,000[2]	49	107	160	191	221

[1] For the last year of the lease, use the dollar amount for the preceding year.
[2] See IRS Revenue Procedure 2011-21, 2011-12 IRB 560 for inclusion amounts for vehicles with fair market value over $66,000.

Inclusion Amounts for Trucks and Vans with a Lease Term Beginning in Calendar Year 2010

Fair Market Value		Tax Year during Lease[1]				
Over	Not Over	1st	2nd	3rd	4th	5th & later
$17,000	$17,500	3	6	9	10	11
17,500	18,000	4	8	12	14	16
18,000	18,500	5	10	15	18	21
18,500	19,000	6	12	19	22	24
19,000	19,500	7	15	21	26	29
19,500	20,000	8	17	25	29	34
20,000	20,500	9	19	28	33	38
20,500	21,000	10	21	31	37	43
21,000	21,500	11	23	35	41	47
21,500	22,000	12	25	38	45	51
22,000	23,000	13	29	42	51	58
23,000	24,000	15	33	49	58	67
24,000	25,000	17	37	56	66	76
25,000	26,000	19	42	62	73	85
26,000	27,000	21	46	68	82	93
27,000	28,000	23	50	75	89	103
28,000	29,000	25	55	81	97	111
29,000	30,000	27	59	88	104	121
30,000	31,000	29	63	94	113	129
31,000	32,000	31	68	100	120	138
32,000	33,000	33	72	107	127	148
33,000	34,000	35	76	114	135	156
34,000	35,000	37	81	119	143	165
35,000	36,000	39	85	126	151	174
36,000	37,000	41	89	133	158	183
37,000	38,000	43	94	139	166	191
38,000	39,000	45	98	145	174	201
39,000	40,000	47	102	152	182	209
40,000	41,000	49	106	159	189	218
41,000	42,000	51	111	164	198	227
42,000	43,000	53	115	171	205	236
43,000	44,000	55	119	178	213	245
44,000	45,000	57	124	184	220	254
45,000	46,000	59	128	190	228	263
46,000	47,000	60	133	197	235	272
47,000	48,000	62	137	203	244	280
48,000	49,000	64	142	209	251	290
49,000	50,000	66	146	216	259	298
50,000	51,000	68	150	223	266	308
51,000	52,000	70	154	229	275	316
52,000	53,000	72	159	235	282	325
53,000	54,000	74	163	242	290	334
54,000	55,000	76	167	249	297	343
55,000	56,000	78	172	254	305	352
56,000	57,000	80	176	261	313	361
57,000	58,000	82	180	268	320	370
58,000	59,000	84	185	274	328	378
59,000	60,000[2]	86	189	280	336	388

[1] For the last year of the lease, use the dollar amount for the preceding year.
[2] See IRS Publication 463 for inclusion amounts for vehicles with fair market value over $60,000.

Inclusion Amounts for Trucks and Vans with a Lease Term Beginning in Calendar Year 2009

Fair Market Value		Tax Year during Lease[1]				
Over	Not Over	1st	2nd	3rd	4th	5th & later
$18,500	$18,000	8	17	25	30	35
19,000	19,500	9	19	29	35	40
19,500	20,000	10	22	33	38	45
20,000	20,500	11	25	36	43	50
20,500	21,000	12	27	40	48	55
21,000	21,500	13	30	43	52	60
21,500	22,000	15	32	47	56	66
22,000	23,000	16	36	52	64	72
23,000	24,000	18	41	60	72	83
24,000	25,000	21	45	68	81	93
25,000	26,000	23	50	75	90	103
26,000	27,000	25	56	82	98	114
27,000	28,000	27	61	89	107	124
28,000	29,000	30	65	97	116	134
29,000	30,000	32	70	104	125	144
30,000	31,000	34	75	112	134	154
31,000	32,000	36	80	119	143	164
32,000	33,000	39	85	126	151	175
33,000	34,000	41	90	134	160	184
34,000	35,000	43	95	141	169	195
35,000	36,000	45	100	148	178	205
36,000	37,000	48	105	155	187	215
37,000	38,000	50	110	163	195	226
38,000	39,000	52	115	170	204	236
39,000	40,000	55	120	177	213	246
40,000	41,000	57	125	185	221	256
41,000	42,000	59	130	192	231	266
42,000	43,000	61	135	199	240	276
43,000	44,000	64	139	207	249	286
44,000	45,000	66	144	215	257	296
45,000	46,000	68	149	222	266	307
46,000	47,000	70	155	229	274	317
47,000	48,000	73	159	237	283	327
48,000	49,000	75	164	244	292	338
49,000	50,000	77	169	251	301	348
50,000	51,000	79	174	259	310	357
51,000	52,000	82	179	266	318	368
52,000	53,000	84	184	273	328	378
53,000	54,000	86	189	281	336	388
54,000	55,000	88	194	288	345	399
55,000	56,000	91	199	295	354	408
56,000	57,000	93	204	302	363	419
57,000	58,000	95	209	310	371	429
58,000	59,000	97	214	317	381	439
59,000	60,000[2]	100	219	324	389	450

[1] For the last year of the lease, use the dollar amount for the preceding year.
[2] See IRS Publication 463 for inclusion amounts for vehicles with fair market value over $60,000.

KEY FACTS: Automobiles and Taxes

Automobiles for Personal Use: Expenses are generally not deductible.
- Interest on a home equity loan may be deductible, even if the amount is used to purchase personal-use items such as an automobile.
- Use of personal vehicles to obtain medical treatment and to do volunteer work is deductible, either as the actual portion of automobile expenses related, or at the standard medical rate of 24¢ per mile or the charitable rate of 14¢ per mile.

Automobiles for Business Use: Business portion of expenses is generally deductible.

Documentation Required

Standard mileage method
- Total miles driven during year
- Business miles driven during year
- Date vehicle was placed in service
- Basis in vehicle

Actual expense method
All of the documentation required for standard mileage method, *plus* records of actual expenses paid during year

Choice of Method

Standard mileage method required if
- The vehicle is leased and the standard mileage method has previously been used for the same vehicle during the lease period
- Mileage records are available but actual expense records are not available

Actual expense method required if
- The vehicle is used for hire (such as a taxi)
- ACRS, MACRS, or any method other than straight-line depreciation has been claimed on the vehicle
- Section 179 expense has been claimed
- More than four vehicles are used in the business (before 2004, the rule was two or more)
- Actual expenses have been previously used

Standard Mileage Rate [The 2013 rates, per mile, are: 56.5¢ (business) 24¢ (medical/moving), and 14¢ (charitable)]

Includes: *(These expenses cannot be deducted in addition to the standard rate.)*
- Depreciation
- Maintenance and repairs
- Gasoline and gasoline taxes
- Oil
- Insurance
- Vehicle registration fees

Excludes: *(These expenses may be deducted in addition to the standard rate, if deductible.)*
- Parking fees
- Tolls
- Personal property taxes
- Interest on auto loan

Converting a Vehicle to or from Business Use:

To Business Use:
- If records are available for the entire year, business use percentage for the first year is calculated using mileage for the entire year.
- If records are not available for the portion of the year before the vehicle was placed in service, business use percentage must be annualized based on the portion of the year that the vehicle was used for business.

To Less Than 50% Business Use or Personal Use:
- Earlier MACRS deductions must be recaptured if the recovery period is not complete.
- When the vehicle is sold, a taxable gain over depreciated basis may be realized.

What's New in 2013

IRA Contributions. The maximum contribution amount to a traditional or Roth IRA is $5,500. The maximum catch-up contribution amount is $1,000.

IRA Deductions. The deduction phaseout range for contributions to a traditional IRA by an active participant in an employer-provided plan is $59,000-$69,000 if single or a head of household, and $95,000-$115,000 if married filing jointly. The contribution phaseout range for contributions to a Roth IRA is $112,000-$127,000 if single or a head of household, and $178,000-$188,000 if married filing jointly. The phaseout range for IRAs and Roth IRAs remains $0-$10,000 if married filing separately.

Elective Deferrals. The maximum elective deferral that an employee can make to all 401(k) plans, 403(b) tax-sheltered annuities, or SARSEP IRAs is $17,500. The maximum catch-up contribution is $5,500.

IRA Distributions. Before 2014, an individual age 70½ or older can distribute up to $100,000 of an IRA balance to a charitable organization without recognizing income.

Hurricane Sandy. 401(k)s and similar plans were able to make loans and hardship distributions to employee-victims of Hurricane Sandy by February 1, 2013.

Social Security Tax. The employee tax rate for Social Security is increased to 6.2%, the same as for employers. The rate for self-employed individuals is increased to 12.4%.

Medicare Tax. An additional 0.9 percent Medicare tax is imposed on wages and self-employment income over $200,000 ($250,000 if married filing jointly, $125,000 if married filing seperately).

Relevant IRS Publications

- ☐ IRS Pub. 517, *Social Security and Other Information for Members of the Clergy and Religious Workers*
- ☐ IRS Pub. 554, *Tax Guide for Seniors*
- ☐ IRS Pub. 560, *Retirement Plans for Small Business (SEP, SIMPLE, and Qualified Plans)*
- ☐ IRS Pub. 571, *Tax-Sheltered Annuity Plans (403(b) Plans)*
- ☐ IRS Pub. 575, *Pension and Annuity Income*
- ☐ IRS Pub. 590, *Individual Retirement Arrangements (IRAs)*
- ☐ IRS Notice 703, *Read This to See if Your Social Security Benefits May Be Taxable*
- ☐ IRS Pub. 721, *Tax Guide to U.S. Civil Service Retirement Benefits*
- ☐ IRS Pub. 915, *Social Security and Equivalent Railroad Retirement Benefits*
- ☐ IRS Pub. 939, *General Rule for Pensions and Annuities*

Section at a Glance

Tax Preparer's Checklist

- ☐ The following items may be required:
- ☐ Forms RRB-1099 and SSA-1099
- ☐ Forms 1099-R, *Distributions from Pensions, Annuities, Retirement or Profit-Sharing Plans, IRAs, Insurance Contracts, etc.*
- ☐ Forms 1099-INT, *Interest Income*
- ☐ Form 5329, *Additional Taxes on Qualified Plans (Including IRAs) and Other Tax-Favored Accounts*
- ☐ Form 5498, *IRA Contribution Information*
- ☐ Form 8606, *Nondeductible IRAs*
- ☐ Form 8959, *Additional Medicare Tax*
- ☐ Estimation tools
- ☐ Documents showing the accumulated deposits and year-end balances in investment accounts, IRAs and employer plans

Retirement Contribution Limits for 2013 and 2014

Limit	2013	2014
IRA contributions	$5,500	$5,500
Catch-up IRA contributions	1,000	1,000
Total standard and designated Roth deferrals to 401(k), 403(b), and 501(c)(18) plans, SARSEPs and SIMPLEs	17,500 (no more than 12,000 in a SIMPLE)	17,500 (no more than 12,000 in a SIMPLE)
Catch-up deferrals	5,500	5,500

Social Security Disability and SSI Key Figures for 2013 and 2014

Key Figure	2013	2014
Social Security disability thresholds for substantial gainful activity (SGA)		
Nonblind	$1,040/month	$1,070/month
Blind	$1,740/month	$1,800/month
Trial work period (TWP)	$750/month	$770/month
SSI federal payment standard		
Individual	$710/month	$721/month
Couple	$1,066/month	$1,082/month
SSI resources limits		
Individual	$2,000	$2,000
Couple	$3,000	$3,000
SSI student exclusion limits		
Monthly limit	$1,730	$1,750
Annual limit	$6,960	$7,060

Social Security

The Social Security system is a federal government program set up to provide retirement, survivor and disability benefits for workers and their families.

Basic Elements of the System

Individuals become eligible for Social Security benefits by accumulating credits. Credits are based on an individual's total wages and self-employment income during the year, no matter when the actual work is performed. The amount of earnings it takes to qualify for a credit changes each year. For 2013, one credit is given for each $1,160 of earnings, so that any individual who earns at least $4,640 during the year will get the maximum of four credits. For 2014, one credit will be given for each $1,200 of earnings, so any individual who earns at least $4,800 during the year will get the maximum of four credits.

Everyone born in 1929 or later needs 40 Social Security credits to be eligible for retirement benefits. Fewer credits are required for eligibility for survivor or disability benefits.

Average Monthly Social Security Benefits Payable in 2013

Recipient(s)	Amount
All retired workers	$1,261
Aged couple, both receiving benefits	2,048
Young widow or widower and two children	2,592
Aged widow(er) alone	1,214
Disabled worker (under retirement age), spouse, and one or more children	1,919
All disabled workers	1,132

Paying into the System

Workers and employers pay into the Social Security system. Self-employed individuals, employers, and employees are taxed on earned income up to the Social Security wage base ($113,700 for 2013 and $117,000 for 2014). For

Comparison of Social Security Key Figures for 2013 and 2014

Key Figure	2013	2014
Maximum earnings taxable		
Social Security	$113,700	$117,000
Medicare	No limit	No limit
Earnings required for one quarter of coverage	$1,160	$1,200
Maximum Social Security benefit		
Worker retiring at *full retirement age*	$2,533/month	$2,642/month
Retirement earnings test exempt amounts		
Under full retirement age[1]	$15,120/year ($1,260/month)	$15,480/year ($1,290/month)
Year individual reaches *full retirement age*[2]	$40,080/year ($3,340/month)	$41,400/year ($3,450/month)

[1] One dollar in benefits will be withheld for every $2 in earnings above the limit.
[2] Applies only to earnings for months prior to attaining full retirement age. One dollar in benefits will be withheld for every $3 in earnings above the limit. There is no limit on earnings beginning the month an individual attains full retirement age.

2013, the Social Security rate is 12.4%. The employee tax rate is increased to 6.2%, while the employer tax rate remains unchanged at 6.2%. The rate for self-employed individuals is increased to 12.4%. See MTG ¶2648 and ¶2664 for discussion of Social Security tax rates.

Similarly, workers and employers pay a Medicare tax to help fund Medicare benefits. There is no limit on wages subject to the Medicare tax. The general Medicare tax rate is 2.9 percent. Again, employers and employees split the rate, each contributing 1.45 percent; self-employed individuals pay the entire 2.9 percent. Beginning in 2013, employees and self-employed individuals are subject to an additional 0.9 percent Medicare tax on wages and self-employment income over a threshold amount. The threshold is $250,000 for married taxpayers filing a joint return, $125,000 for married taxpayers filing separate returns, and $200,000 for all other individuals. Employers are only required to withhold the additional tax on wages or income exceeding $200,000. Any over- or under-withheld amount is taken into account on the individual's Form 1040 by using Form 8959, *Additional Medicare Tax*.

Employees pay Social Security and Medicare taxes through payroll withholding. Self-employed individuals pay self-employment tax (Social Security and Medicare taxes) by completing Schedule SE. See Tab 3 for more information.

Types of Benefits

Social Security provides more than just retirement benefits. Payments are also made to family members of retirees or deceased workers, and to disabled workers. The supplemental security income (SSI) program provides additional benefits to dis-abled, blind or elderly individuals who have low income and resources.

Retirement. Retirement benefits are paid on a monthly basis. The full amount of benefits available to an individual are paid if he or she waits until reaching full retirement age to begin receiving benefits. Full retirement age varies depending on the individual's year of birth. If an individual's birthday is on January 1, their benefit is calculated as if their birthday was in the previous year. Individuals born after January 2, 1947, and before January 2, 1948, reached full retirement age in 2013. The amount of the full benefit is determined by a complex formula that takes into account the individual's earnings during the 35 years in which the individual had the highest earnings (indexed for inflation).

Age to Receive Full Social Security Benefits (as of 2013)	
Year of Birth	**Full Retirement Age**
1937 or earlier	65
1938	65 and 2 months
1939	65 and 4 months
1940	65 and 6 months
1941	65 and 8 months
1942	65 and 10 months
1943-1954	66
1955	66 and 2 months
1956	66 and 4 months
1957	66 and 6 months
1958	66 and 8 months
1959	66 and 10 months
1960 and later	67

Planning Tip. Consider the impact of beginning Social Security retirement benefits at different ages. Individuals can choose to begin receiving their Social Security retirement benefits as early as age 62. Receiving retirement benefits before reaching full retirement age has a benefit and a drawback. On the positive side, a person will receive payments. However, the monthly benefit paid is permanently lower if payments begin before the recipient has reached full retirement age. Individuals choosing to begin receiving retirement benefits at age 62 in 2014 will receive monthly benefits equal to about 70% of what they would have received if they had waited until full retirement age. By factoring in life expectancy and the time value of money, a person may compare these trade-offs.

For individuals who begin receiving benefits before they reach full retirement age, benefits are reduced further if their earned income exceeds an annual earned income limit. For 2014, the earned income limit is $1,290/month ($15,480/year). For every $2 above that limit that a person receives as wages, salary, or self-employment income, his or her Social Security benefit is reduced by $1. A special version of the limit applies in the year in which the person reaches full retirement age. This reduction of benefits stops once the recipient reaches full retirement age.

Individuals who delay the start of their Social Security benefits past full retirement age receive larger monthly payments. Individuals reaching full retirement age in 2014 will increase their monthly benefits by approximately 25% if they delay the start of benefits until they reach age 70. Each year of delayed retirement increases benefits by 8% annually until the individual reaches age 70, after which there is no additional increase from delaying Social Security benefits.

The Social Security Web site, at www.ssa.gov, is extremely helpful in planning for retirement. For a chart showing the effect of starting benefits at various ages, see: www.ssa.gov/OACT/ProgData/ar_drc.html.

Example. Assuming that any Social Security money received can earn an 8% investment rate of return and is subject to a 3% inflation rate, a person who retires at 65 will have to collect benefits for 12 years before being better off than someone who retires at 62. A person who retires at 67 will go over their breakeven point after 14 years.

An individual can choose to begin receiving Social Security benefits as early as age 62, instead of waiting until full retirement age. However, the monthly benefit received is permanently reduced if the individual chooses to begin receiving benefits before reaching full retirement age. This permanent reduction is intended to result, on average, in lifetime payments of the same total amount as full benefits beginning at full retirement age. The formula to determine the reduced benefits is complicated. An online calculator for computing benefits for specific combinations of retirement age and annual earnings can be found on the Social Security website at www.ssa.gov.

An additional temporary reduction may apply if an individual who chooses to begin receiving benefits early is still working. The temporary reduction ceases once the individual reaches full retirement age. For an individual who is working and receiving benefits in 2014 but has not reached full retirement age by the end of the year, benefits are reduced by $1 for every $2 the individual earns over $15,480 ($1,290 per month). For an individual who reaches full retirement age during 2014, benefits are reduced by $1 for every $3 the individual earns over $41,400 ($3,450 per month) until the month the individual reaches retirement age.

If an individual delays the start of payments beyond full retirement age, then his or her monthly retirement benefit will be increased. Delaying the start of payments beyond age 70, however, has no additional effect. Individuals should sign up for Medicare when they reach age 65, even if they do not plan to begin receiving Social Security retirement benefits then.

Benefit Increases for Delaying Retirement to Age 70 (as of 2013)	
Year of Birth	Yearly Rate of Increase
1930	4.5%
1931-1932	5.0
1933-1934	5.5
1935-1936	6.0
1937-1938	6.5
1939-1940	7.0
1941-1942	7.5
1943 or later	8.0

Survivor. Social Security pays survivor benefits to certain family members of a deceased worker. Eligible survivors receive a percentage of the deceased worker's benefit. A family will receive about 150 to 180 percent of the deceased worker's benefit. Survivor benefits may be available to the following individuals:

- a surviving spouse who is age 60 or older;
- a disabled surviving spouse who is age 50 or older;
- a surviving spouse of any age who is caring for the deceased worker's child, if that child is younger than age 16 or disabled and receiving Social Security benefits;
- an unmarried child of the deceased who is under age 18, who is age 18 or 19 and not out of high school, or who becomes disabled before age 22;
- parents of the deceased, age 62 or older, who were dependent on the deceased for at least half of their support;
- a former spouse who reaches full retirement age (age 60 for reduced benefits or age 50 if disabled), if the marriage lasted at least 10 years;
- a former spouse of any age who is caring for the deceased worker's child, if that child is eligible for benefits based on the deceased worker's record.

A former spouse can get these benefits only if she is not eligible for an equal or higher benefit based on her own work and she is not currently married (unless the remarriage occurred after age 60).

Disability and Supplemental Security Income. Social Security pays disability benefits to certain individuals who cannot work because they have a medical condition that is expected to last at least one year or result in death. The Social Security Administration (SSA) maintains an extensive list of conditions that qualify an individual for disability benefits. This list is provided in SSA Publication No. 64-039, entitled *Disability Evaluation under Social Security*, available online at www.ssa.gov/disability/professionals/bluebook.

A disabled adult qualifies for Social Security disability benefits if she satisfies two tests: a "duration of work" test to show that she worked long enough under Social Security; and a "recent work" test to show that she was working for significant portions of the period just prior to the time she became disabled. For example, an individual who becomes disabled at age 50 must have worked for at least seven years total and for five of the last 10 years. Certain blind workers only have to meet the "duration of work" test.

Disabled children can qualify for disability payments through the Supplemental Security Income (SSI) program. SSI is funded by general tax revenues and administered by the SSA. SSI benefits for children are payable to disabled children under age 18 who have limited income and resources, or who come from homes with limited income and resources.

A person who is disabled or blind may also receive SSI benefits if he or she has limited income and resources. The benefit available under this program is the same for all eligible individuals ($710 per month for 2013 and $721 per month for 2014). This amount may be supplemented in certain states. For more information, see SSA Publication No. 05-11053, *What You Need to Know When You Get Supplemental Security Income (SSI)* from www.ssa.gov/pubs/10153.html.

Social Security Statements

Workers can access their Social Security statements online at www.socialsecurity.gov/myaccount. In 2011, the SSA discontinued sending paper statements to workers, but in 2012, it resumed sending statements to workers age 60 or older if they are not already receiving Social Security benefits, and to workers in the year they reach age 25. Each statement contains a brief explanation of Social Security and Medicare, the individual's estimated benefits (including his or her earnings record), and the estimated amount Social Security and Medicaid taxes paid. The estimated benefits portion of the statement specifies the estimated amount of benefits the taxpayer is eligible to receive per month for retirement (including early retirement) or disability, and his or her survivor benefits. The earnings record included in the statement provides a chart of the taxpayer's Social Security earnings and Medicare earnings for every year the taxpayer has worked.

If the earnings statement or any other information on the taxpayer's personalized statement is incorrect, the SSA provides a toll-free number to call (800-772-1213) to correct the information.

Social Security Benefit Planning

Maximizing Social Security Benefits. Workers do not lose accumulated Social Security benefits. However, a worker who has not earned the minimum number of credits may not be entitled to Social Security benefits. In addition, maximum benefits may not be earned if an individual ceases working prior to reaching full retirement age. An individual should determine whether continuing to work will result in increased earnings that would boost his or her average salary for the most lucrative 35 years of his or her working life, as this is the basis used to determine the individual's Social Security benefit. Review of the individual's annual Social Security Statement may be useful in making these decisions.

Diminishing Benefit from Increased Earnings. Social Security taxes are not imposed on income above the taxable wage base ($113,700 for 2013 and $117,000 for 2014). Workers who have 35 years of earnings at or above the taxable wage base should consider these maximums when deciding whether to continue working beyond the earliest age in which they could begin receiving Social Security benefits.

Taxation of Benefits

Social Security benefits are nontaxable for most recipients. Taxpayers must calculate their modified adjusted gross income (MAGI) to determine if social security benefits are subject to tax. A portion of the Social Security benefits received are taxable to individuals whose MAGI exceeds certain thresholds.

Calculation of Taxable Portion of Social Security Benefits for 2013

Filing Status	MAGI		Amount Taxed
	Over	But Not Over	
Single, HOH, QW, or MFS (living apart from spouse for entire tax year)	$25,000	$34,000	*Step 1:* Lesser of (1) 50% of benefits or (2) 50% × (MAGI - $)
	$34,000	Unlimited	*Step 2:* Lesser of (1) Step 1 amount not to exceed $ + 85% × (MAGI - $) or (2) 85% of benefits
MFJ	$32,000	$44,000	*Step 1:* Lesser of (1) 50% of benefits or (2) 50% × (MAGI - $)
	$44,000	Unlimited	Step 2: Lesser of (1) Step 1 amount not to exceed $ + 85% × (MAGI - $) or (2) 85% of benefits
MFS (and lived with spouse for part of tax year)	Any		Lesser of (1) 85% MAGI or (2) 85% of benefits

MAGI is computed as follows:

Adjusted gross income
+ 1/2 of Social Security benefits
+ Tax-exempt income
+ Certain exclusions

Modified adjusted gross income

 Caution. Note that certain tax-exempt interest is reported to the IRS and the recipient. Review all Forms 1099-INT or substitute statements for tax-exempt interest to be included in the taxpayer's MAGI.

Depending on the taxpayer's MAGI and filing status, the percentage of Social Security benefits to be taxed can be up to 85 percent. For 2013 returns, taxpayers whose MAGI is less than the first threshold ($25,000 for unmarried taxpayers, $32,000 for joint filers) are not taxed on their Social Security benefits. If MAGI is between $25,000 and $34,000 for single filers, or $32,000 and $44,000 for joint filers, the amount of benefits taxed is the lesser of 50 percent of the Social Security benefits received or 50 percent of the excess of MAGI over the specified threshold. If the MAGI is higher than the second threshold ($34,000 for unmarried taxpayers, $44,000 for joint filers), up to 85 percent of the Social Security benefits could be taxable. The instructions to Forms 1040, 1040A, and 1040EZ include worksheets to be used to determine the amount of taxable Social Security benefits (see Tab 1). If any Social Security benefits are taxable, the taxpayer cannot use Form 1040EZ. See MTG ¶716 for discussion of the taxability of Social Security benefits.

Tax Planning Ideas

Managing the Retirement Portfolio. Taxpayers whose benefits are subject to tax may be able to reduce or avoid the tax by properly structuring their portfolios. Taxation of Social Security benefits is dependent on the taxpayer's MAGI. Taxation cannot be avoided merely by investing in securities that produce tax-exempt income, such as state and local bonds, since such income is included in the MAGI calculation. However, the unrealized appreciation of investments is not treated as income in calculating MAGI. Consequently, investment in growth stocks should be considered. Similarly, the growth element in series E or EE savings bonds is not included in income.

Managing Taxable Income. If Social Security benefits are included in gross income, the impact may be reduced or eliminated if the taxpayer is able to reduce

overall taxable income (including Social Security benefits). For example, if a taxpayer has itemized deductions that offset their income, then the amount of tax due can be reduced. The taxpayer may be able to manage deductions (e.g., charitable contributions) in such a way that the standard deduction is used in one year and in the alternate year the taxpayer itemizes deductions.

Managing Distributions from Other Retirement Plans. Careful consideration should also be given to the effects on MAGI when the taxpayer makes withdrawals from retirement plans. Such income is generally included in the MAGI calculation (Roth distributions are an exception). By reducing or eliminating such withdrawals, the amount of Social Security income that is taxed may be reduced. Alternatively, withdrawals prior to the receipt of Social Security benefits may help to minimize the impact such payments have on taxation.

Medicare

Medicare is a federal health insurance program, enacted by Congress in 1965, to benefit people 65 years of age and older and some disabled people under age 65. The program currently covers over 40 million people. An individual is eligible for Medicare if he or she worked for at least 10 years in Medicare-covered employment (or his or her spouse did so), is at least 65 years old, and is a citizen or permanent resident of the United States. Younger people may also qualify for coverage if they have a disability or end-stage renal disease. Medicare benefits include hospital insurance (Part A), medical insurance (Part B), Medicare Advantage plans (Part C), and prescription drug benefits (Part D).

The basic Medicare coverage is referred to as Part A compulsory hospitalization insurance. Financed through payroll taxes, it is provided free to anyone who qualifies for Medicare benefits. Individuals who do not qualify for free coverage can purchase Part A coverage. For 2013, the premium for seniors with at least 30 quarters of covered employment is $243 per month. The premium for seniors with fewer than 30 quarters of covered employment is $441 per month. Individuals should apply for Medicare benefits three months before their 65th birthday.

The deductible for hospitalization coverage under Part A is $1,184 per benefit period for 2013, and the required coinsurance for hospitalization is $296 a day for the 61st through 90th day of each benefit period, and $592 a day for each lifetime reserve day (the total of 60 lifetime reserve days is nonrenewable). All costs of hospitalization beyond 150 days are paid by the individual.

Part A also covers the full cost of the individual's first 20 days in a skilled nursing facility during a benefit period. For 2013, the individual pays $148 a day in coinsurance for days 21 through 100 in each benefit period. All costs of care in a skilled nursing facility beyond 100 days are paid by the individual.

A benefit period begins the day an individual goes to a hospital or skilled nursing facility. The benefit period ends when the individual has not received any hospital care or skilled care for 60 days in a row. If an individual goes into the hospital or a skilled nursing facility after one benefit period has ended, a new benefit period begins.

Medicare Part B, supplementary medical insurance, covers physician, outpatient and preventive services and is paid for by the insured individual via an enrollment program. For 2013, the standard monthly Part B premium is $104.90. For most individuals, this is a $5.50 increase over 2012. People who get Part B beginning January 1, 2013, or later, will pay the standard monthly premium rate. Individual beneficiaries with modified adjusted gross income (MAGI) two years ago (in 2011) over $85,000 (and married couples with MAGI in excess of $170,000) pay higher premiums that are based on the amount of their income. Part B premiums are deductible as medical expenses. See MTG ¶1019. The coverage has a $147 annual deductible and a 20 percent-per-service coinsurance in 2013.

Medicare Part C, Medicare Advantage, is a collection of private plans, including HMOs and PPOs, that provide Part A, Part B and Part D benefits to enrollees. The costs for individuals electing to join a Medicare Advantage plan vary based on the terms of the plan.

Medicare Part D is a prescription drug benefit. Medicare recipients can join a prescription drug plan (and get other Medicare benefits from the traditional program) or join a Medicare Advantage plan, which will cover all Medicare benefits. Prescription drug plans are offered by private insurers and subsidized by Medicare. Each plan must offer at least the Medicare standard minimum level of coverage.

Planning Tip. In choosing a Medicare drug plan, enrollees should keep in mind their current prescriptions, their location, and their preferred pharmacy. The Medicare website (www.medicare.gov) provides useful tools for comparing plans. Nevertheless, enrollees should double check with the plans they are considering to confirm that the information on the web is still correct. In particular, plans have great flexibility to change the list of drugs that they cover. An enrollee may change drug plans on a yearly basis.

The SSA determines entitlement to Medicare, and Medicare benefits are administered by the Centers for Medicare & Medicaid Services (CMS). For more information regarding Medicare benefits, call 800-MEDICARE or log on to www.cms.gov or www.medicare.gov.

Planning Tip. The Medicare portion or premium subsidy amount is reduced for certain beneficiaries of the Voluntary Prescription Drug Benefit Program under Medicare Part D, namely, for beneficiaries whose modified adjusted gross income (as defined by the Social Security Act) exceeds the thresholds used under Part B.

Medigap Insurance

The private insurance industry has created special policies designed to supplement Medicare coverage, known as Medigap policies. There are 10 standard Medigap policies designated by the letters A, B, C, D, F, G, K, L, M, and N. Medigap policies are standardized in a different way in Massachusetts, Minnesota and Wisconsin.

Medicare SELECT versions of the Medigap policies are available in some states. A Medicare SELECT policy pays full benefits only for care provided at specific hospitals and, in some cases, by specific doctors. Some basic benefits are included in Medigap plans while other benefits vary.

For more information regarding Medigap plans, log on to www.medicare.gov/Publications/Pubs/pdf/02110. pdf and see Choosing a Medigap Policy: A Guide to Health Insurance for People with Medicare.

Pensions and Retirement Plans

Individual Retirement Accounts (IRAs)

An IRA is a trust created or organized in the United States for the exclusive benefit of an individual or his or her beneficiaries. See MTG ¶2152 and following paragraphs for discussions of IRAs. IRAs must meet the following requirements to receive tax-favored status:

- Annual contributions to the trust in 2013 must not exceed the lesser of $5,500 (plus allowable catch-up contributions for individual's 50 years or older of $1,000) or the individual's compensation.
- The trustee must be a bank or other entity/person that demonstrates that the manner in which the trust is administered will be consistent with the statutory requirements, if such entity/person is approved by the IRS.
- The trust's investment funds cannot be invested in life insurance contracts.
- The account holder's interest in the trust must be nonforfeitable.
- The assets of the trust must be maintained separately from other funds.

Medigap Plans in 2013										
Medigap Benefits	A	B	C	D	F*	G	K	L	M	N
Medicare Part A Coinsurance and Hospital costs up to an additional 365 days after Medicare benefits are used up	✓	✓	✓	✓	✓	✓	✓	✓	✓	✓
Medicare Part B Coinsurance or Copayment	✓	✓	✓	✓	✓	✓	50%	75%	✓	✓***
Blood (First 3 Pints)	✓	✓	✓	✓	✓	✓	50%	75%	✓	✓
Part A Hospice Care Coinsurance or Copayment	✓	✓	✓	✓	✓	✓	50%	75%	✓	✓
Skilled Nursing Facility Care Coinsurance			✓	✓	✓	✓	50%	75%	✓	✓
Medicare Part A Deductible		✓	✓	✓	✓	✓	50%	75%	50%	✓
Medicare Part B Deductible			✓		✓					
Medicare Part B Excess Charges					✓	✓				
Foreign Travel Emergency (Up to Plan Limits)**			✓	✓	✓	✓			✓	✓
Out-of-Pocket Limit**							$4,800	$2,400		

* Plan F also offers a high-deductible plan. If you choose this option, this means you must pay for Medicare-covered costs up to the deductible amount of $2,110 in 2013 before your Medigap plan pays anything.

** After you meet your out-of-pocket yearly limit and your yearly Part B deductible ($147 in 2013), the Medigap plan pays 100% of covered services for the rest of the calendar year.

***Plan N pays 100% of the Part B coinsurance, except for a copayment of up to $20 for some office visits and up to a $50 copayment for emergency room visits that don't result in an inpatient admission.

- The trust must impose the minimum distribution rules required by the Code and regulations.

IRA Contributions. Contributions to a traditional IRA may be fully or partially deductible, depending on whether the individual is covered by an employer's plan and on the individual's gross income for the year. The maximum deduction may not exceed the *smaller* of the compensation includible in the taxpayer's gross income or the applicable statutory limit. If a married couple files jointly, the lower-paid spouse can take the higher paid spouse's compensation into account when calculating the compensation limit. See MTG ¶2153A and following paragraphs for discussions of IRA deduction and contribution limits. Contributions to a Roth IRA are not deductible.

Example. Irina who has no compensation, files a joint return with Oscar, who earns $42,000 (taxable compensation) in 2013 and plans to contribute the maximum $5,500 to his traditional IRA (Irina and Oscar are both under 50). Irina can contribute an additional $5,500 to her own IRA because this amount is smaller than Oscar's compensation ($42,000) plus her own ($0), minus Oscar's $5,500 contribution ($42,000 – $5,500 = $36,500).

IRA contributions for a tax year can be made until the due date (without extension) of the return for that year. For 2013, contributions must be made by April 15, 2014.

If total contributions to the IRA are less than the maximum allowed by law, the taxpayer *cannot* make up the difference after the due date of the return. If contributions exceed the legal limit, the excess portion may be withdrawn or applied to a later year in which total contributions would otherwise fall below the limit. However, if the excess contribution is not withdrawn before the date the return is due, a six percent tax applies.

Contributions may be made for any year before the taxpayer turns 70½ in which either the taxpayer or his or her spouse has compensation (i.e., wages, salary, commissions, self-employment income, etc.). A spouse's compensation can be taken into account only if the couple files a joint return.

Planning Tip. A nonrefundable tax credit is available to assist low- and middle-income taxpayers in saving for retirement. The credit is in addition to the usual tax advantages of making contributions to a qualified retirement plan or an IRA. See Tab 10 for more information on the retirement savings contributions credit.

Withdrawals. IRA assets can be withdrawn at any time, though penalties are imposed to discourage early withdrawals. Distributions from a traditional IRA are generally taxable as ordinary income in the year received unless they are rolled over to another retirement arrangement. An additional 10 percent tax generally applies to any withdrawals made before the owner reaches the age of 59½. Before 2014, an individual age 70½ or older can distribute up to $100,000 of their IRA balance to a charitable organization without recognizing income on the distribution. In addition, an individual can elect to exclude from income an IRA distribution that is directly rolled over into his or her health savings account (HSA) in a trustee-to-trustee transfer. Generally, an individual is allowed to exclude only one such transfer during his or her lifetime. The dollar amount excluded from income cannot exceed the annual limit on the individual's HSA contribution for the year. If the individual ceases to be eligible to make HSA contributions within the 12 months following the HSA funding distribution, the exclusion is lost and an additional 10 percent tax also applies. The amount transferred is not deductible as an HSA contribution. See Tab 1 for more information.

 Planning Tip. Basis in traditional IRAs is the total of all nondeductible contributions and nontaxable amounts included in rollovers made to traditional IRAs minus the total of all nontaxable distributions.

Distributions from IRAs to which only deductible contributions were made are fully taxable, but distributions from IRAs that include some nondeductible contributions are only partly taxable. The portion of the distribution representing nondeductible contributions (the cost basis) is tax free and is calculated on Form 8606, *Nondeductible IRAs.*

Distributions representing income earned in a traditional IRA are taxed. Losses from an IRA investment can be recognized only if all the IRA assets have been distributed and their total is less than the unrecovered basis. The loss can be claimed as an itemized deduction on Schedule A, subject to the two-percent of adjusted gross income limit. See MTG ¶2153G for discussion of the taxation of IRA distributions.

Exceptions to the tax on early distributions. The 10 percent additional tax on distributions made before the owner reaches age 59½ does not apply to any withdrawal of contributions that occurs before the original due date of the return for the year in which the contributions were made. The additional tax also does not apply to early distributions if:

- the distributions are not more than the amount of the taxpayer's deductible medical expenses (even if the taxpayer does not itemize deductions);
- the distributions are not more than the cost of medical insurance (in certain unemployment situations);
- the taxpayer is disabled;
- the taxpayer is the beneficiary of a deceased IRA owner;

- the taxpayer is receiving distributions in the form of an annuity;
- the distributions are not more than certain higher education expenses for the taxpayer or the taxpayer's spouse, child or grandchild;
- the distributions (not exceeding $10,000 during the individual's lifetime) are used to buy, build, or rebuild a first home;
- the distribution is due to an IRS levy on the IRA; or
- the distribution was taken by an individual called on active duty.

See MTG ¶2153H, ¶2153I and ¶2124C for discussion of the tax on early distributions from IRAs.

Required minimum distributions. IRA owners who are generally required to take minimum distributions from their accounts beginning April 1 of the calendar year following the year he or she turns 70½ and every year thereafter. The required minimum distribution (RMD) for a given year is determined by dividing the account balance as of the end of the preceding year by the applicable distribution period or life expectancy generally determined in tables in IRS Publication 590, *Individual Retirement Arrangements (IRAs).* See MTG ¶2124B and ¶2153F for more information.

A 50 percent excise tax is assessed on amounts not distributed as required. Any distributions exceeding the RMD for a given year may not be credited against the minimum for a later year. RMDs also cannot be rolled over into another qualified plan or IRA. When an individual who is receiving RMDs passes away, the entire RMD for the year of death must still be made.

Rollovers and Trustee-to-Trustee Transfers. IRA assets are held by a trustee, usually a bank or mutual fund company. The account owner can choose to move IRA assets from one trustee to another. If the transfer of assets is accomplished by a trustee-to-trustee transfer (without a distribution to the account owner), there is no distribution, and no taxable event. If the account owner actually receives a distribution, it will be subject to tax, and possibly to the additional tax on early distributions, unless it is rolled over to another IRA or eligible plan within 60 days. Required distributions cannot be rolled over. Rollover contributions to an IRA or other plan cannot be deducted but must be reported on the return for the tax year in which they occur. See MTG ¶2125 and following for discussion of rollovers.

IRA-to-IRA rollovers may be made from or moved into a particular IRA only once per year. The time period begins on the date a distribution is received by the account owner. Trustee-to-trustee transfers are not subject to this limitation.

IRA Facts for 2013

Attribute	Traditional IRA	Roth IRA
Age limit on contributions	Taxpayer must not have reached age $70^1/_2$ by the end of the year.	Any age.
Limit on contributions (if the taxpayer earned more than the dollar limit)	For 2013, a taxpayer can contribute $5,500 ($6,500 if 50 or older by the end of 2013) to his or her traditional and Roth IRAs.	For 2013, a taxpayer may be able to contribute $5,500 ($6,500 if 50 or older by the end of 2013) to a Roth IRA but the amount may be less than that depending on income, filing status, and whether contributions are made to a traditional IRA.
Contributions deductible?	Yes. Contributions to a traditional IRA are deductible, depending on income, filing status, and whether the taxpayer (or his or her spouse) is covered by a retirement plan at work.	No. Contributions to a Roth IRA are never deductible.
Form to file when contributions are made	None, unless nondeductible contributions are made to a traditional IRA. In that case, Form 8606, *Nondeductible IRAs*, must be filed.	None. Although no form must be filed when the taxpayer contributes to a Roth IRA, records of the amount and date of contributions must be kept.
Required distributions	The taxpayer must begin receiving required minimum distributions by April 1 of the year following the year he or she reaches age $70^1/_2$.	The owner of a Roth IRA is not required to take any distributions regardless of age, though required minimum distributions must be made from an inherited non-spousal Roth IRA.
Tax treatment of distributions	Distributions from a traditional IRA are taxed as ordinary income, but if nondeductible contributions were made, not all of the distribution is taxable.	Distributions from a Roth IRA are not taxed as long as certain criteria are met.
Form to file when distributions are received	None, unless nondeductible contributions have been made. In that case file Form 8606.	File Form 8606 when distributions are received from a Roth IRA (other than a rollover, recharacterization, certain qualified distributions, or a return of certain contributions).

Distributions from any of the following types of arrangements may be rolled over into a traditional or Roth IRA:

- a traditional IRA;
- an employer-provided qualified retirement plan;
- a Section 457 plan (discussed later); or
- a tax-sheltered annuity (Section 403) plan (discussed later).

Distributions from a traditional IRA may be rolled over to any of those types of plans, if the plan allows it. Distributions from a traditional IRA or employer plan may also be contributed to a new or existing Roth IRA account, or all or a portion of a traditional IRA may be converted to a Roth IRA.

 Planning Tip. A taxpayer can rollover distributions from an eligible retirement plan to a Roth IRA without regard to the taxpayer's income and without regard to whether the taxpayer is a married individual filing a separate return.

It may also be possible to make a non-Roth rollover within the same plan. A 401(k), 403(b), or governmental 457(b) plan that includes a qualified Roth contribution program may permit a qualified rollover contribution from a participant's non-Roth account to the participant's designated Roth account within the same plan (Code Sec. 402A(c)(4)(B)).

Penalties and Additional Taxes. Penalties or additional taxes may be imposed if IRA funds are used for prohibited transactions or if one of the following occurs:

- investment in collectibles;
- excess contributions;
- early withdrawals;
- failure to take required minimum distributions.

Additional taxes on these events are reported on Form 5329.

Prohibited transactions involving a traditional IRA include the following:

- borrowing money from the account;
- selling property to the account;
- receiving unreasonable compensation for managing the account;
- using it as security for a loan; or
- buying property for personal use with IRA funds.

If the account owner or a beneficiary engages in a prohibited transaction with an IRA, the account ceases to be an IRA, and it is treated as if its assets were distributed to the holder of the account.

Types of IRAs (Employee Funded)

Traditional. A traditional IRA is any IRA that is not a Roth IRA or a SIMPLE IRA. See MTG ¶2153 for discussion of traditional IRAs.

Eligibility to Make Contributions–An individual who has compensation (or whose spouse has compensation, if filing a joint return), and has not reached age 70½ by the end of the year is eligible to make contributions to a traditional IRA.

Contribution Limits–For 2013, an eligible individual may contribute the *lesser* of $5,500 ($6,500 if the individual was born before January 1, 1964) *or* an amount equal to the individual's compensation for the tax year to their traditional and/or Roth IRAs. A married couple filing jointly can make IRA contributions on behalf of both spouses, even if one has no compensation for the year. For the lower compensated spouse, the limit is the *smaller* of the dollar limit *or* the total compensation of both spouses, reduced by the traditional and Roth IRA contributions made on behalf of the higher paid spouse.

Phaseout Ranges for Deductible Contributions–Contributions to traditional IRAs are generally deductible. However, the deduction is reduced or eliminated completely for high-income individuals who are covered by an employer's retirement plan or who file jointly with a spouse who is covered by such a plan. The deduction is phased out over a range of modified adjusted gross incomes (MAGI), with different ranges depending on the individual's filing status. For individuals who are not covered by an employer plan, but file jointly with a spouse who is covered, the phaseout range is from MAGI of $178,000 to $188,000 for 2013 and $181,000 to $191,000 for 2014.

Distributions–Distributions from a traditional IRA are taxable as ordinary income, except for the return of nondeductible contributions. Minimum distributions are required once the account owner has died or reached age 70½.

Pre-Retirement Liquidity–The account owner may withdraw amounts from a traditional IRA, but a 10 percent additional tax may be imposed (in addition to the regular income tax). The additional tax is not imposed after age 59½ or if another exception applies.

Roth. A Roth IRA is an IRA that the owner has designated to be a Roth IRA. See MTG ¶2154 and following paragraphs for discussions of Roth IRAs.

Eligibility to Make Contributions–An individual who has compensation (or whose spouse has compensation, if filing a joint return) is eligible to make contributions to a Roth IRA. Contributions can be made after age 70½. Eligibility to make Roth IRA contributions is eliminated by a phaseout based on the taxpayer's modified adjusted gross income (MAGI).

Roth IRA Contribution Phaseout Ranges		
Filing Status	**2013 MAGI**	**2014 MAGI**
MFJ or QW	$178,000-$188,000	$181,000-$191,000
Single, HOH	112,000-127,000	114,000-129,000
MFS	0-10,000	0-10,000

Contribution Limits–For 2013, an eligible individual may contribute the lesser of $5,500 ($6,500 if the individual is 50 or older by the end of 2013) *or* an amount equal to the individual's compensation for the tax year to their traditional and/or Roth IRAs. As with traditional IRAs, joint filers can "share" their compensation.

Traditional IRA Deduction Phaseout Ranges		
Filing Status	**2013 MAGI**	**2014 MAGI**
MFJ or QW	$95,000-$115,000	$96,000-$116,000
Single, HOH	59,000-69,000	60,000-70,000
MFS	0-10,000	0-10,000

Annual Retirement Contribution Limits for Individuals		
	2013	**2014**
IRA contributions	$5,500	$5,500
Catch-up IRA contributions	1,000	1,000
Total standard deferrals to 401(k), 403(b), 501(c)(18) plans, and SARSEPs	17,500	17,500
Standard deferrals to SIMPLEs	12,000	12,000
Catch-up deferrals to SIMPLE accounts	2,500	2,500
Catch-up deferrals to 401(k), 403(b) and 457 plans	5,500	5,500

Planning Tip. When a member of the military is killed in action or during training, his survivor may receive a military death gratuity or payment under the Servicemembers' Group Life Insurance Program. The survivor can make a Roth IRA contribution up to the amount of such payments received without regard to the annual limit on contributions or the income-based phaseout of that limit. The contribution must be made within one year of the survivor's receipt of the underlying payment.

Deductibility—Contributions to Roth IRAs are not deductible.

Distributions—Qualified distributions are not taxable. A distribution is qualified if it is made after the five year period beginning with the first tax year for which a contribution was made to a Roth IRA by or on behalf of the taxpayer, and is made:

- on or after the taxpayer attains age 59½;
- because the taxpayer is disabled;
- to the estate or beneficiary of the account owner after his or her death; or
- a qualified first-time home purchase.

The minimum distribution requirements do not apply to Roth IRAs while the account owner is alive. Minimum distribution requirements do apply after the account owner's death.

Pre-Retirement Liquidity—Amounts may be withdrawn from a Roth IRA at any time. Qualified distributions are completely excluded from income. Withdrawals that are not qualified are tax free up to the amount of the regular after-tax contributions to the account. Nonqualified withdrawals of earnings may be taxable, and may be subject to the additional 10 percent tax on early withdrawals, which is computed and reported on Form 5329.

Qualified Defined Contribution Plans

General Principles. Qualified defined contribution plans are employer sponsored retirement plans that provide benefits based on participants' individual account balances. See MTG ¶2105 for discussion of defined contribution plans. The accounts are increased by contributions made by the employer and/or employee. The account balance will also fluctuate depending on investment earnings and fees assessed to the account. If investments perform poorly, the participant's account decreases, and the reverse is true if investments perform well. Therefore, investment risk is borne by the employee.

For 2013, the maximum annual addition to a participant's account is the lesser of $51,000 or 100% of the participant's compensation. For 2014, the maximum annual addition to a participant's account is the lesser of $52,000 or 100% of the participant's compensation. Annual additions include employer and employee contributions and any forfeitures. Employer contributions and an employee's elective deferrals to a defined contribution plan (such as a 401(k) plan) are generally excluded from the employee's income. For 2013 and 2014, the maximum elective deferral that an employee can make is $17,500 ($23,000 for individuals age 50 or older). The employer's contributions are deductible. However, the employer's deduction is limited to 25 percent of the compensation paid or accrued during the tax year to plan participants.

Penalty for Excess Contributions. Excess contributions to a defined contribution plan may be taxed and penalized. An employer that contributes more to a plan than it can deduct may be permitted to carry over the excess contribution to the next year. However, depending on the circumstances, an excise penalty may also apply.

Excess elective deferrals are not excluded from the employee's income, and are subject to tax again upon distribution. Excess deferrals by an employee should generally be returned to the employee by April 15 of the tax year immediately following the year in which the deferral is made.

If excess deferrals are not properly returned to participants, the plan's tax-favored status may be jeopardized. Excess contributions on behalf of highly compensated employees will subject the employer to a 10 percent excise tax.

Setup and Administration. A defined contribution plan is generally sponsored by an employer. The employer must comply with the Employee Retirement Income Security Act of 1974 (ERISA) and the Internal Revenue Code in order to maintain a retirement plan. Plan design requirements are very complicated (e.g., eligibility requirements, employer contributions, vesting requirements, funding obligations). See MTG ¶2114 and following paragraphs. The employer must ensure the plan is administered in a manner consistent with regulations issued by the Internal Revenue Service and the Department of Labor.

A tax credit may be available for certain start-up costs associated with creation of a new plan. The small employer pension start-up cost credit is an amount equal to 50 percent of the qualified start-up costs paid or incurred by the taxpayer during the taxable year. The credit may not exceed $500 for the first credit year and each of the two tax years immediately following the first credit year, and is not available for any other tax year. A small employer is defined as one that had no more than 100 employees who received at least

$5,000 of compensation from the employer for the preceding year. A qualified start-up cost is an ordinary and necessary expense of an employer that is paid or incurred in connection with the establishment or administration of an employer plan or the retirement-related education of employees with respect to such a plan. See MTG ¶1365U for discussion of the credit.

Types of Defined Contribution Plans

SEP IRA. A simplified employee pension (SEP) plan allows a small employer to contribute to employees' IRAs without setting up a profit-sharing or other type of qualified plan. Contributions must be made on behalf of every eligible employee. This includes any individual who is 21 years old, has been employed by the employer during at least three of the last five years, and receives at least $550 in compensation from the employer during 2013 ($550 in 2014). For 2013, employers are permitted to contribute to the SEP the lesser of 25 percent of an employee's compensation or $51,000 ($52,000 for 2014). See MTG ¶2156 for a discussion of SEPs.

Pre-Retirement Liquidity. Withdrawals are permitted prior to retirement to the extent allowed under the IRA rules. In addition, the 10 percent additional tax is imposed on certain early withdrawals.

 Caution. Since contribution limits apply to all retirement plan contributions, employers should require employees to certify that they will disclose their participation in any other qualified retirement plans.

SIMPLE IRA. A savings incentive match plan for employees (SIMPLE) IRA may be sponsored by an employer that employs fewer than 100 employees (regardless of their eligibility to participate in the plan) who received $5,000 or more in compensation for the preceding plan year, and that does not sponsor any other qualified plans (except for collective bargaining plans) from the start-up year of the SIMPLE plan. Any employee who received at least $5,000 in compensation during any two earlier years and is reasonably expected to receive $5,000 in the current calendar year is eligible to participate. An employer sponsoring a SIMPLE IRA plan can choose to impose less restrictive eligibility requirements. See MTG ¶2155 and following paragraphs for discussions of SIMPLEs.

Contribution Limits. Under a SIMPLE IRA plan, employees are allowed to make elective deferrals, and the employer must make either matching contributions on behalf of employees who make deferrals or nonelective contributions on behalf of all employees. Elective deferrals under a SIMPLE IRA are limited to $12,000 for 2013 and 2014 ($14,500 for employees age 50 or older). Employers generally must make either matching contributions of up to three percent of an employee's compensation, or fixed nonelective contributions equal to two percent of each eligible employee's compensation.

Pre-Retirement Liquidity. Withdrawals are permitted prior to retirement to the extent allowed under the IRA rules. However, the 10 percent additional tax is imposed on certain early withdrawals and the 10 percent rate is increased to 25 percent for withdrawals made within the first two years of plan participation.

401(k) Plan. Employers, including self-employed individuals, can set up 401(k) plans. Employees will be permitted to participate in the plan according to the plan's written document. The plan will also be required to provide for protection of plan assets (e.g., via a trust document, annuity, etc.). A 401(k) plan allows eligible employees to make elective deferrals of salary. The amounts deferred are excluded from the employees' incomes. A 401(k) plan may also allow participants to treat all or a portion of their contributions as designated Roth contributions. Designated Roth contributions are included in the employee's current income, but qualified distributions of such contributions and the income on them are excluded from income. See MTG ¶2106 and following paragraphs for discussions of 401(k) plans.

Contribution Limits. For 2013 and 2014, participants are limited to contributing $17,500 ($23,000 for employees age 50 or older) to their 401(k) accounts. Contributions in excess of the annual limit are included in the employee's income, but may generally be withdrawn before April 15 of the year following the year they were included as income. A 10-percent additional tax is imposed on the employer for excess contributions, unless the excess is recharacterized or distributed within two months following the applicable plan year. In addition, the employer is free to make matching contributions that are not subject to the annual limit on elective deferrals. Matching contributions and elective deferrals are subject to special discrimination tests.

Pre-Retirement Liquidity. In-service withdrawals are permitted, but are included in gross income and subject to the additional 10 percent tax if the withdrawal occurs prior to the participant's reaching age 59½. The 10-percent additional tax does not apply if the participant has separated from service after reaching age 55. Loans may also be permitted, depending on provisions of the plan document.

Section 457 Plan. An employer that is a state or local government or nongovernmental tax-exempt entity may sponsor a Section 457 plan under which participants may defer part of their compensation. See MTG ¶2161 for discussion of Section 457 plans.

Contribution Limits. For 2013 and 2014, participants are allowed to contribute the lesser of 100 percent of includible compensation or $17,500 ($23,000 for participants age 50 or older). Additional catch-up contributions calculated under a special formula are permitted for each of the last three years ending before the participant reaches normal retirement age under the plan.

Distributions. Amounts deferred under a Section 457 plan must not be distributed before the calendar year in which the participant turns 70½, is severed from employment, or is faced with an unforeseen emergency. Distributions before age 59½ are normally subject to the same 10-percent additional tax as early distributions from 401(k) plans. However, the exclusion for distributions after severance from employment after age 55 is expanded to cover distributions from governmental plans to former public safety officers (police officers, firefighters, and emergency medical services technicians) who separate from service after attaining age 50. Also, a retired public safety officer may elect to have up to $3,000 deducted from distributions from a government plan and paid directly to an insurance company or self-insured plan for health insurance without such amounts excluded from income.

403(b) Plan. Certain nonprofit entities (e.g., public schools, colleges, universities, churches, public hospitals, or Section 501(c)(3) entities) are permitted to sponsor 403(b) tax-sheltered annuity plans. See MTG ¶2160 for discussion of Section 403(b) plans.

Contribution Limits. The annual additions that may be made to an employee's 403(b) account are limited. Annual additions include elective contributions by the employee, nonelective contributions by the employer, and after-tax contributions by the employee. For 2013, the annual addition cannot exceed the lesser of $51,000 ($52,000 for 2014) or 100 percent of the employee's compensation.

For 2013 and 2014, an employee's elective deferrals are limited to $17,500 ($23,000 for employees age 50 or older). All of an individual's elective deferrals under any 401(k) plan, SIMPLE, SEP or 403(b) plan are combined and compared against this limit. See IRS Publication 571, *Tax-Sheltered Annuity Plans (403(b) Plans)*.

Pre-Retirement Liquidity. Generally, distributions are not permitted until the employee attains age 59½, severs from employment, dies or becomes disabled. Elective deferral amounts may be distributable upon financial hardship.

Money Purchase Plans. Money purchase plans involve mandatory employer contributions that are set by the plan document. Employers, including self-employed individuals, can set up a money purchase plan. Employees will be permitted to participate in the plan according to the plan's written document. The plan will also be required to provide protection of plan assets (e.g., through a trust document, annuity, etc.). See MTG ¶2107 for discussion of money purchase plans.

Contribution Limits. For 2013, employer contributions to a money purchase plan are limited to the lesser of $51,000 ($52,000 for 2014) or 100 percent of a participant's compensation.

Pre-Retirement Liquidity. In-service withdrawals are permitted, but are included in gross income and subject to the 10-percent additional tax if the withdrawal occurs prior to the participant's reaching age 59½. The 10-percent additional tax does not apply if the participant has separated from service after reaching age 55. Loans may also be permitted, depending on the plan document.

 Caution. Due to the mandatory nature of the employer contributions, certain funding requirements must be satisfied for money purchase plans.

Profit-Sharing Plans. Profit-sharing plans are defined contribution plans funded by discretionary employer contributions. Employees will be permitted to participate in the plan according to the plan's written document. The plan will also be required to provide protection of plan assets (e.g., by means of a trust document, annuity, etc.). See MTG ¶2108 for discussion of profit-sharing plans.

Contribution Limits. For 2013, the maximum annual additions to a profit sharing plan on account of a particular employee are limited to the lesser of $51,000 or 100 percent of the participant's compensation. For 2014, the maximum annual addition amount is the lesser of $52,000 or 100 percent of the participant's compensation. Annual additions include both employer and employee contributions and any forfeitures. Employer contributions must be allocated to employees according to a specific written formula. The employer's contributions are deductible. However, the deduction is limited to 25 percent of the compensation paid or accrued during the tax year to plan participants.

Pre-Retirement Liquidity. In-service withdrawals are permitted, but are included in gross income and subject to the 10-percent additional tax if the withdrawal occurs prior to the participant's reaching age 59½. The 10-percent additional tax does not apply if the participant has separated from service after reaching age 55. Loans may also be permitted, depending on the plan document.

KEY FACTS: Retirement Plans Side by Side

Comparison of Features	SEP IRA	SIMPLE IRA	Profit-Sharing Plan	401(k) (pre-tax and Roth)	Defined Benefit Plan
Eligibility	Anyone with SE income, or employee 21 or over with income >$550 for 2013 ($550 for 2014)	Employer must have <100 employees and no other retirement programs; must be offered to all employees who earn >$5,000	Plan can restrict participation to employees at least 21 with one year of service	Plan can restrict participation to employees at least 21 with one year of service	Plan can restrict participation to employees at least 21 with one year of service
Maximum employee contribution (for 2013 and 2014)	N/A; note that SEP IRAs do not count against individual IRA limits	Lesser of $12,000 for 2013 ($12,000 for 2014) or earned income; catch-up (over 50), $2,500 for 2013 ($2,500 for 2014)	N/A	$17,500 for 2013 ($17,500 for 2014); catch-up (over 50), $5,500 for 2013 ($5,500 for 2014)	N/A
Maximum employer contribution (for 2013 and 2014)	25% of wages up to $51,000 for 2013 ($52,000 for 2014) or 20% of SE net income	(a) 2% of compensation (for all employees) or (b) matching contribution up to 3% for employees making a deferral contribution	Lesser of $51,000 for 2013 ($52,000 for 2014) or 100% of compensation; deduction limit, 25% of total compensation of participants	Employer/employee total: Lesser of 25% of compensation or $51,000 for 2013 ($52,000 for 2014)	Actuarially determined (annual benefit promised cannot exceed $205,000 for 2013 ($210,000 for 2014)
Penalties for early withdrawal	10%	10% (25% if in first 2 years of program)	10%	10%	10%
Penalties for excess contributions	6% SE and employees; 10% employers	10%	10%	10% if not distributed within 2.5 months after end of year	10%
When withdrawals must begin	70½ (but contributions can still be made if there is earned income)	70½ (but contributions can still be made if there is earned income)	70½ or year of retirement, whichever is later	70½ or year of retirement, whichever is later	70½ or year of retirement, whichever is later

Qualified distributions from each of these plans generally can be rolled over into IRAs or qualified employer plans. In addition, a 401(k) can be rolled into another employer's 401(k).

KEY FACTS: Principal Characteristics of IRAs and 401(k)s

Characteristic	Traditional IRA	Roth IRA	401(k) Traditional	401(k) Roth
Age Limitations on Contributions or Participation	No contributions allowed if participant will be 70½ by year-end	No age requirement for ending contributions	Plan may impose minimum age and service requirements (up to age 21 and 1 year of service) for participation. Contributions may continue as long as participant is employed.	
Due Date of Contributions	April 15th of following year	April 15th of following year	Employer must deposit deferred amounts as soon as is reasonably possible, and not later than the 15th day of the following month.	
Deductibility of Contributions	Full deduction available in current year unless individual participates in employer-sponsored retirement plan If participating in employer plan, deduction for 2013 contributions phases out for modified AGI: S, HOH $59,000-69,000 FJ, QW $95,000-115,000 MFS $0-10,000	Contributions are not deductible	Elective deferrals are excluded from income	Designated Roth contributions are included in income
Taxability of Distributions	Distributions taxable	Qualified distributions nontaxable	Distributions taxable Qualified distributions nontaxable	
Contribution Limits for 2013	Lesser of taxable compensation and $5,500 for those under age 50 or $6,500 for those age 50 or over	Contribution limits same as for traditional IRA **AGI phaseouts for contributions** S, HOH $112,000-127,000 MFJ, QW $178,000-188,000 MFS $0-10,000	Total elective contributions capped at $17,500, or $23,000 for those age 50 or over. Employer deduction cannot exceed 25% of all compensation. Total contributions cannot exceed 100% of wages up to $51,000.	
Distributions Permitted	Distributions permitted without penalty: • After participant turns 59½ • At death or disability • For qualified college costs • For qualified medical costs exceeding 10% of AGI • For qualified first-time home buyers • Distributions in the form of an annuity	Return of basis always tax free. Distributions made after five years of participation are qualified (tax-free) if made: • After participant turns 59½ • At death or disability • For qualified first-time home buyers	Distributions permitted without penalty: • After participant turns 59½ • At death or disability • After severance from employment after age 55 Hardship distributions from a traditional 401(k) are subject to income tax and the penalty for early withdrawals unless an exception applies. Hardship distributions from a designated Roth account are qualified (and excluded from income) if made after five years of participation and after participant turns 59½ or becomes disabled.	
Distributions Required	Distributions must begin by April 1 following the year participant turns 70½	Distributions required only at death of participant	Withdrawals required to begin at later of age 70½ or retirement	
Penalty for Early Withdrawal	10% penalty on nonqualified distributions	10% penalty for withdrawal before age 59½	10% penalty for withdrawal before age 59½ or for failure to distribute excess within 2½ months after close of plan year	
Rollovers	Rollover into another IRA or an employer plan permitted. Rollover into Roth IRA requires income recognition	Rollover to another Roth IRA permitted	Rollover to IRA or another employer plan permitted. Rollover into Roth IRA requires income recognition	Rollover to a Roth IRA or other employer Roth 401(k) permitted in some circumstances

What Retirement Plan Rollovers Are Allowed in 2013

ROLL FROM: \ ROLL TO:	Traditional IRA	SEP-IRA	SIMPLE IRA	Roth IRA	457(b)	403(b)	Qualified plan	Designated Roth Account (Roth 401(k), 403(b), or 457(b))
IRA	Yes	Yes	No	Yes, but must be included in income.	Yes, if destination 457(b) has separate accounts.	Yes	Yes	No
SEP-IRA	Yes	Yes	No	Yes, but must be included in income.	Yes, if destination 457(b) has separate accounts.	Yes	Yes	No
SIMPLE IRA	Yes, after two years of participation.	Yes, after two years of participation.	Yes	Yes, after two years of participation. Must be included in income.	Yes, after two years of participation. Destination 457(b) must have separate accounts.	Yes, after two years of participation.	Yes, after two years of participation.	No
Roth IRA	No	No	No	Yes	No	No	No	No
457(b)	Yes	Yes	No	Yes. Must be included in income.	Yes	Yes	Yes	Yes, if an in-plan rollover. Must be included in income.
403(b)	Yes	Yes	No	Yes. Must be included in income.	Yes, if destination 457(b) has separate accounts.	Yes	Yes	Yes, if an in-plan rollover. Must be included in income.
Qualified plan	Yes	Yes	No	Yes. Must be included in income.	Yes, if destination 457(b) has separate accounts.	Yes	Yes	Yes, if an in-plan rollover. Must be included in income.
Designated Roth Account (Roth 401(k), 403(b), or 457(b))	No	No	No	Yes	No	No	No	Yes, via direct trustee-to-trustee transfer only.

Qualified Defined Benefit Plans

Defined benefit plans are retirement plans that do not maintain individual accounts for each participant. Instead, benefits are calculated based on the plan's formula, and usually take the form of a monthly pension based on the employee's wages and years of service. Employers are required to contribute to the plan based on actuarial calculations of the amount necessary to fund the promised benefits. If investment returns are poor, the employer must contribute an increased amount to the trust to maintain the proper level of funding. However, if market returns are better than expected, the employer reaps the reward and may contribute less to maintain the proper level of funding. Therefore, unlike the defined contribution plans, the employer bears the investment risk associated with defined benefit plans. See MTG ¶2135 and following paragraphs for discussions of defined benefit plans.

Defined benefit plans vary in plan design. Participants should carefully review the plan's summary description and ask for clarification by the plan administrator where needed.

Social Security and Railroad Retirement. See discussion above and IRS Publication 915, *Social Security and Equivalent Railroad Retirement Benefits*, for information regarding taxation of these benefits.

Civil Service. See IRS Publication 721, *Tax Guide to U.S. Civil Service Retirement Benefits*, for information regarding taxation of these benefits.

412(i) Plans. Defined benefit plans that are fully insured and funded are Section 412(i) plans. These plans must be fully guaranteed by insurance products and are eligible for greater tax deductions than other defined benefit plans.

 Caution. How retirement plans interact when you are participating in more than one plan must be examined. Be aware of overall contribution limits.

 Planning Tip. Retirement planning for one's spouse as a Schedule C employee may be advantageous.

Pension and Retirement Plan Income

Taxable Distributions

Distributions received from traditional IRAs, qualified retirement plans, or nonqualified plans (including annuities) are taxable to the extent they have not been previously taxed. For example, if nondeductible contributions have been made to an IRA, the taxpayer will need to calculate the taxable portion of distributions from the account. The taxpayer will be responsible for paying taxes only on the amount of the distribution that has not been previously taxed. Specifically, the taxable portion of the distribution will include any before-tax contributions and earnings on before- or after-tax contributions.

Taxation of Annuity Benefits. If the taxpayer has no basis in a periodic distribution from a retirement plan (an annuity), the entire amount of each payment is taxable. If the taxpayer has a basis in a periodic distribution, a portion of that basis is recovered in each payment, determined under either the "simplified method" or the "general rule." The appropriate method is set at the time payments begin and cannot be changed.

The simplified method must be used if the payments are from a qualified plan or tax-sheltered annuity if the annuity starting date is after November 18, 1996, and on that date the recipient was under age 75 or was entitled to less than five years of guaranteed payments. Under this method, the nontaxable portion of a distribution is calculated by dividing the cost by the expected number of payments. The expectation is based on either the lifetime of the recipient (in which case life expectancy tables are used) or the set number of payments for the annuity. The instructions to Form 1040 include a worksheet for using the simplified method. The worksheet is reproduced at page 9-42.

Individuals with annuity starting dates before November 19, 1996, but after July 1, 1986, had the option to choose either the simplified method or the general rule if they met the requirements for the simplified method described above and the annuity was payable for life (or for the lives of the annuitant and one survivor). The taxable portion of other types of distributions, most notably distributions from nonqualified plans, is determined under the general rule.

The general rule calculates the nontaxable portion of each payment by dividing the cost by the total expected return, and multiplying that by the amount of each payment. Examples of this calculation are provided in IRS Publication 939, *General Rule for Pensions and Annuities*.

Taxation of Nonperiodic Payments. A nonperiodic distribution (any distribution other than an annuity payment) must be taxed when distributed unless some portion of the distribution has already been taxed. A nonperiodic distribution received after annuity payments have started will be treated as fully taxable unless it results in a reduction of the annuity payments received. A nonperiodic distribution received before annuity payments have begun is treated as a pro rata return of capital.

Generally, taxable lump-sum distributions are treated as ordinary income and taxed at ordinary income tax rates. However, certain older taxpayers may be eligible to tax a portion of their distributions at capital gains tax rates and may employ a 10-year tax option on the portion of the distribution not taxed at capital gains rates. This optional method is available only to taxpayers born before January 2, 1936. See MTG ¶2124A for discussion of the 10-year tax option. In addition, certain distributions will not qualify for the optional method treatment, regardless of the taxpayer's date of birth. For a list of such distributions, see IRS Publication 575, *Pension and Annuity Income*. If the optional method is elected, the taxpayer must use Form 4972, *Tax on Lump-Sum Distributions*, to report the distributions. Form 4972 should be completed and attached to the taxpayer's Form 1040 or 1040A.

If a taxpayer's entire cost is not recovered before his or her benefit is fully distributed, the taxpayer may claim the loss on his or her tax return. However, the loss may be recouped only if the taxpayer itemizes deductions. The loss should be reported on the taxpayer's Schedule A as a miscellaneous deduction.

Required Minimum Distributions. Taxpayers must generally begin receiving minimum distributions from traditional IRAs and other retirement plans by April 1 of the year that follows the later of year of the taxpayer's retirement from the employer maintaining the plan or the year the taxpayer reaches age 70½. Required minimum distributions (RMDs) are subject to the general rules for taxation of distributions.

Divorce Issues and QDROs. Qualified domestic relations orders (QDROs) are court orders instructing a retirement plan to assign a plan participant's retirement benefits to an alternate payee. Generally, ERISA preempts state law interference with qualified retirement plans; however, if a court order qualifies as a QDRO, the plan must comply with the order. ERISA and the Internal Revenue Code have specific requirements regarding the qualifications for a QDRO. The specificity is intended to ensure that the plan has clear directions regarding whom to pay benefits to and how much of the participant's benefit should be directed to that alternate payee. Distributions to a spouse or former spouse under a QDRO are taxable to the alternate payee who receives them, and not to the employee. A distribution to a child or other dependent under a QDRO is taxable to the employee. For further discussion of QDROs, see Tab 13 and MTG ¶2124D.

Financial Planning

The Financial Planning Process

Careful financial planning allows people to anticipate opportunities, prepare for contingencies, and navigate competently through the life stages of education, employment, marriage and divorce, home ownership, parenting, eldercare, retirement, and ultimately death. Wherever a person is in life, the financial planning process includes several basic steps:

- taking an inventory of current assets, income, expenditures, debt, and existing planning documents;
- identifing and quantify goals;
- determining a path that will meet these goals;

- implementing the plan; and
- reviewing and revising the plan as necessary and as circumstances change.

A simple financial planning system will take anyone through these basic steps.

Starting Point

Financial planning primarily focuses on the future, but knowledge of one's financial past and the present circumstances it has produced is critical for effective planning.

Inventory of Assets and Liabilities. The first step in determining a financial planning starting point is to create an organized list of current assets and liabilities. The list of assets need not be the type of detailed, whole-house inventory that might be done in connection with a homeowner's or renter's insurance policy (though it is a good idea to have that as well). It is simply a list of all major assets, indicating the date acquired, purchase price, current value, and what income (if any) they generate. The emphasis of this list is on investments, that is, assets that are held with a view to their likely appreciation in value (such as real estate or collectible coins or stamps) and/or generation of income (such as stocks or bonds). Married couples should also note whether each asset is owned by one spouse or jointly.

Similarly, the list of liabilities should include a brief description of each liability, including to whom the debt is owed, when it was incurred, the interest rate, the amount of the unpaid balance, the amount of each payment and the frequency of payments (such as monthly), the date when the debt is expected to be completely repaid, and, if the debt is secured, the security or collateral (such as a house or car).

Net worth is the sum of assets less the sum of liabilities. If liabilities are more than assets, net worth is negative. Individuals may use the personal financial statement on page 9-38 to account for their current financial situation.

Assemble Current Documents

Existing legal documents and arrangements will have an effect on future financial plans. Documents such as wills, trusts, business contracts, and alimony agreements are an important part of the snapshot of any current financial situation. Some of these arrangements may be readily changeable, such as wills, trusts, and powers of attorney. Others, such as contracts and marriage dissolution agreements, may be difficult or impossible to amend. Still others can be changed for a fee, such as variable annuities, or mortgages that can be refinanced.

Existing legal arrangements have an impact on the current cash flow situation and also affect the types of choices available. The following are some of the legal documents that must be taken into consideration wherever they would be relevant to life planning, investments, and estate planning:

- marriage dissolution agreements, including alimony, property settlements, prenuptial agreements, and child support agreements;
- business organization documents and materials for the self-employed;
- business transfer/continuation agreements and plans, including insurance policies;
- contracts;
- wills and trusts;
- property tax records, including information about jointly owned property;
- evidence of gifts of money or property worth more than $10,000 to individuals or charitable organizations;
- insurance policies;
- living wills;
- powers of attorney; and
- tax returns.

Setting Goals

To create a workable personal financial plan and follow through long enough to reap the benefits, it is important to identify personal financial goals. Goal setting is important because it identifies the correct financial direction and provides a way to measure progress. Goals must meet certain criteria to be useful for financial planning:

- list several goals and clearly prioritize them;
- have some goals that are short term and some that are long term;
- goals must be realistic; if they are too easy to achieve, little benefit is gained; if they are so difficult that they are practically impossible to reach, sticking with the plan will be difficult;
- concrete images motivate people emotionally; envisioning a goal is important for creating the drive to make financial sacrifices;
- goals must be measurable; in order to make progress measurable, reduce the goal to a monetary amount and set a deadline to reach the goal.

Build a Budget

A personal budget is a tool to help individuals reach their personal financial goals. It is intended to be an organized way to compare income and expenditures over a relatively short time frame (often one month or one year), and to forecast income and expenses, monitor progress, and make changes as needed to achieve stated goals.

A personal budget provides a detailed picture of how money comes in and how it is spent. Be sure to include income fluctuations, especially if any income is from self-employment.

Keeping track of all expenditures–no matter how small–is the key to effective budgeting. The best way to do this is to track payments shown in checkbooks and on credit card statements for the last six months or so, to determine how much is spent each month in various categories of expenses. To account for out-of-pocket cash expenses, it may make sense to record actual expenses for a week or more and compare these amounts to cash withdrawals. The following general categories should be considered:

- **Housing.** For most people, housing expenses are the major drain on their finances. This category includes all housing-related expenses: rent, mortgage payments, utilities (gas, water, electricity), telephone, garbage disposal, property taxes, home maintenance and repairs, and furnishings.
- **Taxes.** This includes federal, state, and local taxes on income and property, including employment taxes.
- **Food.** This includes grocery purchases, beverage purchases (alcoholic and nonalcoholic), and restaurant costs.
- **Clothing.** Annualize costs.
- **Support of children and other relatives.** These expenses can be included in other categories, if paid in conjunction with those personal expenses.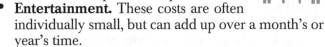
- **Entertainment.** These costs are often individually small, but can add up over a month's or year's time.
- **Transportation.** Given the increasing cost of gas, these expenses are a big chunk of most people's budget. 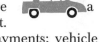 Other costs to factor in are car payments; vehicle modifications due to physical handicap; car repairs; licenses, registration, and fees; tolls; parking; and public transportation.
- **Personal care.** This category includes the costs of personal grooming items, cosmetics, haircuts, manicures, facials, pedicures, mud baths, and body wraps.
- **Health care.** These costs cover everything from routine medical and dental check-ups, glasses, and prescription and nonprescription medicines to major surgery.
- **Insurance.** Include the various forms of personal insurance. Usually, this includes health, auto, home, life, and disability insurance.
- **Debt.** Payment toward credit cards and other debt not included in other categories must be included in the overall budget.

- **Gifts.** Charitable donations and gifts to family members should be included in budget planning.
- **Retirement savings.** Include individual accounts and amounts withheld by an employer.
- **Savings (other than for retirement).** This category should not be considered "leftover;" pay yourself first.
- **Miscellaneous.** The specific categories probably cover most major expenses. However, there may be other expenses to consider.

A personal budget can be used to match income with expenses to clearly show what needs cutting back, or where increases must be made. An interactive electronic budget is easier to use and provides more useful information than a budget done on paper. It is also easier to update and saves time.

Fundamentals of Financial Planning

Time Value of Money

The time value of money is the foundation of all financial planning. A dollar received today is worth more than a dollar to be received at some point in the future, because today's dollar can earn interest starting now (and inflation has not eroded the value of today's dollar). A variety of financial calculators are available that help with the understanding and use of this important concept.

Compounding Interest. The two most common methods of calculating interest are the simple interest and compound interest formulas. Simple interest is based on the amount borrowed (the principal), the interest rate, and the amount of time for which the principal is borrowed. The formula used to find simple interest is

$$\text{Interest} = \text{Principal} \times \frac{\text{Rate of}}{\text{Interest}} \times \frac{\text{Amount of time}}{\text{the loan}}_{\text{is outstanding}}$$

or $I = P \times R \times t$. The future repayment amount is the principal plus interest, so $F = P \times (1 + Rt)$.

Unlike simple interest, compound interest calculates interest not only on the principal, but also on all interest already accrued. The formula for calculating compound interest is

$$\frac{\text{Future Repayment}}{\text{value}} = \text{Principal} \times \left(1 + \frac{\text{Rate of}}{\text{interest}}\right)^{\text{amount of time}}$$

or

$$F = P \times (1 + R)^t$$

Most consumer loans use monthly or even daily compounding. The interest rate used in the calculation must be the rate for the period of compounding, and the time must be in the same units.

> **Example.** Adam borrows $1,000 at 10 percent simple annual interest and repays it in one lump sum at the end of three years. He will pay interest of $1,000 $\times$ 0.10 $\times$ 3 = $300 in addition to the principal, for a total payment due of $1,300.
>
> Suppose instead Adam borrows $1,000 at 10% interest, compounded monthly, and repays it in one lump sum at the end of three years. To find the amount that must be repaid, he first converts the 10 percent annual interest rate into a monthly interest rate: 0.10/12 = 0.00833
>
> Plugging this number into the formula yields
> $F = \$1,000 \times (1 + .00833)^{36}$
> $\quad = \$1,000 \times (1.00833)^{36}$
> $\quad = \$1,000 \times (1.34802)$
> $\quad = \$1,348.02$
>
> The monthly compounding added $48.02 to the cost of the loan.

Discounting. The time value of money is a two-way street. Discounting is based on the premise that a future dollar is worth less in today's terms. Discounting is a way of expressing the loss of interest income and/or erosion by inflation that occurs before money is received at some future time. Discount rates can be determined by using a financial calculator or from standard tables.

The following table gives the present value of $1 at various interest rates if it is to be received after a given number of years.

Net Present Value of a Dollar				
Number of Years	9.0%	9.5%	10.0%	10.5%
1	$0.917431	$0.913242	$0.909091	$0.904977
2	0.841680	0.834011	0.826446	0.818984
3	0.772183	0.761654	0.751315	0.741162
4	0.708425	0.695574	0.683013	0.670735
5	0.649931	0.635228	0.620921	0.607000
6	0.596267	0.580117	0.564474	0.549321
7	0.547034	0.529787	0.513158	0.497123
8	0.501866	0.483824	0.466507	0.449885
9	0.460428	0.441848	0.424098	0.407136
10	0.422411	0.403514	0.385543	0.368449
11	0.387533	0.368506	0.350494	0.333438
12	0.355535	0.336535	0.318631	0.301754

Example. Erica is designing a building for a big client who wants her to agree to wait for payment of her fees until the building is built and rented out. The client needs five years for this. If Erica expects to earn 10 percent interest on her money, she would use the 10 percent column of the Present Value table and find the value of $1 in the 5-year row. Since the payment in five years is worth only 62 cents, she chooses to charge a higher fee for this delayed-payment scenario.

Opportunity Costs. Opportunity cost is the cost of choosing one use of money over another. Spending money on a party rather than investing it in a CD yielding four percent has an opportunity cost of four percent. There are also other, less obvious and more difficult-to-calculate opportunity costs.

Other opportunity costs include failure to use available sources of money, such as life insurance cash value and low-interest loans. However, opportunity cost is not the only factor to consider in saving money. The security of the investment and the risk of unguaranteed returns are also relevant considerations.

Example. Alice has decided that she will need to replace her current automobile in about two years. Moreover, anticipated changes in her lifestyle are going to dictate the need for a roomier vehicle capable of carrying more people and their things. Alice has chosen a vehicle that will probably cost $25,000 two years from now. Alice wants to pay for her new auto outright, instead of over time through a loan.

Alice has $60,000 in a secure low-interest savings account paying 3.5 percent annually, but feels uncomfortable liquidating any more than one-third of her account for the new vehicle. So she decides to move some money into a higher-interest investment to make up the shortfall in savings. She puts $20,000 into a mutual fund that ends up yielding 11.5 percent each of those two years, yielding a final value of $24,864.50. Had she left her $20,000 car purchase allowance in the savings account, she would have only $21,424.50 to spend on her new vehicle. If Alice had left the money where it was, her opportunity cost in terms of the annual interest rate would have been eight percent (11.5 – 3.5). In terms of dollars, her opportunity cost for doing nothing would have been $3,440.

Inflation

It is easy to overlook inflation when planning one's financial future. An inflation rate of four percent might not seem like much, but its effect on the purchasing power of money over the long term is substantial. Over 20 years, four percent inflation annually would drive the value of a dollar down to $0.44.

Factors for inflation rate calculations are provided in the table below. Multiply the amount of money at issue by an inflation factor from the table corresponding to the expected inflation rate and the number of years. For example, to have the same buying power as $1,000 today, $1,280 will be needed five years from now, assuming a five percent inflation rate ($1,000 × 1.28).

Inflation Factors for Selected Annual Inflation Rates over a Number of Years

Years	3% Inflation Rate	4% Inflation Rate	5% Inflation Rate
5	1.16	1.22	1.28
10	1.34	1.48	1.63
15	1.56	1.80	2.08
20	1.81	2.19	2.65
25	2.09	2.67	3.39
30	2.43	3.24	4.32
35	2.81	3.95	5.52
40	3.26	4.80	7.04

Procrastination Is Expensive

Compounding of interest makes early action the key to sound financial planning. Consider two 30-year-old individuals with different attitudes toward saving for retirement. One begins to save $100 per month, earning eight percent interest, compounded monthly. The other postpones saving until age 40. Even if the early saver stops contributing to his retirement nest egg after 10 years, he will have one and one-half times as much at age 65 as the procrastinator. It is never too early to start saving, and the bigger the goal, the more time is likely needed to achieve it.

Monthly Savings to Accumulate $100,000

Number of Years of Savings	Monthly Savings Required to Accumulate $100,000 (8% interest)
10	$550
20	170
30	70
40	30

Risk Tolerance

In implementing an investment plan, the first factor to consider is the risk level. Generally speaking, the riskier an investment is, the higher its expected return will have to be in order to entice investors. Factors affecting risk tolerance include the individual's family situation, age, business or employment situation, debt and liquidity, insurance, and emotional factors. Changes in any of these areas should be considered whenever the plan is updated.

Investments

Investing always involves forecasting the future. It is never possible to guarantee that predicted events will occur or that unexpected setbacks will not, but with more information, risk can be evaluated and kept within limits.

Requirements

Certain basic financial needs should be met before other investment strategies can be implemented:

- stable income (from employment, self-employment, or other sources);
- an emergency savings fund sufficient to cover three to six months of living expenses;
- a budget and financial plan; and
- adequate insurance coverage.

Diversification

A general rule is that a diversified group of investment holdings is the best protection against investment disaster. A diversified investment portfolio is another way of managing risk—having several kinds of investments, such as stocks, bonds (government and corporate), real estate, and precious metals greatly reduces the chance that a particular economic or legal change will devastate one's entire investment fund.

A diversified portfolio requires knowledge of the various investment vehicles. The different types of investments available include bank accounts, stocks, bonds, mutual funds, investments for education, real estate, and insurance. It is important to understand the basics about the types of investments available and to carefully investigate the options to achieve the best result.

Dollar-Cost Averaging. Dollar-cost averaging, that is, investing a specific amount of money in a specific mutual fund or stock on a regular schedule (usually monthly), is a method of diversifying by time. A good example of dollar-cost averaging is contributing to a 401(k) retirement plan through salary withholding.

The benefits are twofold. First, an investor using dollar-cost averaging buys more shares of his selected investment when its price is low, and fewer when the price is high. Second, a dollar-cost averaging program provides a schedule of regular investing, which provides necessary discipline for many investors. The disadvantage of dollar-cost averaging is that it eliminates the opportunity for the investor to take advantage of situations where the investor has determined that a particular security is underpriced at a particular time. Given the difficulty of making such determinations consistently, perhaps this is not a disadvantage for most investors.

Types of Investments

The general rule is that the safer the investment (the less likely the investor is to lose the principal invested), the lower the return. Investments offering greater potential returns will generally have a greater risk of loss.

Savings and Checking Accounts. An interest-bearing savings or checking account at a local bank or credit union is an investment. Bank accounts are a simple and important part of successful financial planning. Traditional savings accounts earn compound interest at a low rate. The federal government, through the Federal Deposit Insurance Corporation (FDIC), guarantees bank and credit union accounts for amounts up to $250,000 per depositor per insured bank. Most of these types of accounts allow withdrawals and deposits of funds without penalty.

A vital part of anyone's financial planning is an emergency savings fund, and a traditional savings account is the perfect place for it. A great way to have an emergency fund earn interest is to find a bank or credit union that offers checking accounts that earn interest. Usually a higher minimum balance is required for interest-bearing checking. Interest earned on savings and checking accounts is considered income for tax purposes.

	Comparison of Early and Late Start—Savings of $100 per Month (8% Interest)			
	Saves $100 per Month Starting at Age 30		Saves $100 per Month Starts Saving at Age 40	
Age	Contributions	Balance	Contributions	Balance
31	$ 1,200	$ 1,253	$ 0	$ 0
35	4,800	7,397	0	0
40	6,000	18,417	0	0
41	0	19,946	1,200	1,253
45	0	27,438	4,800	7,397
50	0	40,879	6,000	18,417
55	0	60,904	6,000	34,835
60	0	90,737	6,000	59,295
65	0	135,184	6,000	95,737
Total invested	$12,000		$24,000	

Certificates of Deposit. Certificates of deposit (CDs) are accounts that require an investment of money for a specific time period. CDs from insured banks are also insured by the FDIC. CDs usually have terms that range from three months to four years, but they can be shorter or longer. Some CDs are set up to automatically roll over, or reinvest the principal and interest in a new CD of the same term at the current interest rate. If this is the case, investors must keep track of the end-of-term dates if they want to withdraw funds to use or to invest elsewhere.

The disadvantage of CDs is their early withdrawal penalty, which can be substantial. CDs also tend to have a low interest rate. It is best to lock in the rate at a time when interest rates are relatively high. CD rates are generally higher than rates for saving accounts. Interest earned on CDs is considered income for tax purposes.

Money Market Accounts. Money market accounts are bank accounts that invest in vehicles such as government securities. There are two sources of money market accounts: mutual funds and savings institutions. This discussion concerns money markets through institutions such as banks and credit unions.

Money market accounts are very similar to traditional savings accounts offered by financial institutions. They may be guaranteed by the federal government up to $250,000 per account, and there is no penalty for early withdrawals. Like CDs, money market accounts typically earn higher interest than traditional savings accounts.

Money market accounts require a minimum deposit. The minimum starting deposit and minimum balance is typically $500, and often $1,000. Many financial institutions offer interest rates based on the amount in the money market account, so that a money market account with a $100,000 balance will earn a higher interest rate than a money market account with a $5,000 balance.

Some money market accounts function as checking accounts as well. Some financial institutions charge a maintenance fee for their money market accounts. Money market accounts are a safe, stable investment and a good alternative to traditional savings accounts for sizable deposit amounts. Money market accounts are not subject to the restrictions that come with investing in a CD, but their interest rates are comparable and usually higher than those of traditional savings accounts. Interest earned on money market accounts is considered income for tax purposes.

Stocks and Equities. A company's stock represents a piece, or a share, of that company. The stockholders of a company are its owners. This is the reason stocks are considered equity investments. Most individual investors buy and sell securities through brokerage firms that are registered with the NASD. Registered stock-

brokers buy and sell stocks through traders on the appropriate stock exchange. There are basic two types of stock: common stock and preferred stock.

Common stock is categorized by its expected rate of growth and income. For example, common stock can be in the low-income category, but be characterized as aggressive growth. Conversely, high-income stock can be in the low-growth category.

Preferred stock is so labeled because it has priority over common stock. If dividends are paid or the company is liquidated, owners of preferred stock are paid before owners of common stock. Preferred stock in a company usually carries a higher price tag than common stock in the same company.

Stock options are the right to purchase or sell a specific amount of shares in a company for a specific price and for a defined time period. The price is generally the stock's market price at the time the option is granted. Stock options fall in an investment vehicle category known as derivatives. For most investors, unless their mutual funds participate in stock options, involvement with stock options is limited to employee benefit plans.

Derivatives include options contracts or futures contracts that enable or obligate the holder to buy or sell stock at a certain price. Options and futures contracts are called derivatives because the price is derived from the value and characteristics of some underlying asset.

The two primary stock investment goals are income and growth. Although growth and income may coexist in a particular stock investment, most stocks have one primary strength.

Growth stock is stock in a company that does not pay cash dividends, but instead reinvests its profits into the company in hopes of "growing" the value of the business and the stock price. Income stock is stock in well-established companies that do not need to reinvest their profits internally and therefore use them to pay dividends to stockholders. Income stock is often more expensive than most growth stock because the income stream and security of the investment is greater.

Stock investing is sometimes seen as a get-rich-quick scheme. However, the only strategy that has proven successful for investing in stocks is to pick wisely, and then hold on for the long term. Bull markets (when the stock market is on an upswing) and bear markets (when stock prices are going down) are part of the inevitable cycle that is the stock market. No one—not even the experts—can reliably predict which way the market is headed until it is too late to turn a quick profit.

Bonds. Bonds are a way to invest by loaning money to an entity such as a corporation or the government, whether federal, state, or local. Bonds usually pay interest at a fixed rate for a fixed period of time, from a few months to over 20 years. When the bond matures, the borrower pays the face amount of the bond to the holder.

In general, when interest rates go up, bonds decrease in value. Conversely, when interest rates go down, bonds are more valuable because their interest rate is higher than the interest rate available from other investments. Investing in bonds carries varying degrees of risk depending on the type of bond.

Municipal bonds are bonds that are issued by state and local governments. The interest earned on municipal bonds is not subject to federal income tax. In addition, residents of the state or locality that issues the bonds generally do not have to pay state and local income tax. Because of this attractive tax feature, municipal bonds typically pay interest at rates lower than other types of bonds. However, for those in higher tax brackets, the tax savings may offset the lower interest rate.

Zero coupon bonds are bonds that are sold at a discount, and when they mature, the owner receives the full face value of the bond. Zero coupon bonds do not make periodic interest payments. However, the interest is taxed as it is earned. Investing in zero coupon bonds has the primary advantage of locking in a good interest rate. But the locking-in feature of zero coupon bonds can also be its downfall if interest rates are rising.

Treasury bonds are sold by the U.S. government at auction and have a set interest rate for 30 years. The minimum amount they are issued for is $100. Interest is paid every six months.

Treasury notes are sold by the U.S. government at auction and have a set interest rate for a specific term that ranges from two to 10 years. The minimum amount they are issued for is $100. Interest is paid every six months.

Treasury bills (T-bills) are sold by the U.S. government at auction and do not have a set interest rate. Investors purchase these bills for less than face value, and when the term is over, the investor receives the full face value of the T-bill. T-bills are available in $100 increments, with a minimum purchase amount of $100. Treasury bills are issued with terms of four, 13 and 26 weeks. Cash management bills may be issued for shorter or irregular terms.

Treasury inflation-protected securities (TIPS) are sold by the U.S. government at auction, with terms of five, 10, or 20 years, and with the interest rate determined at the auction. TIPS are sold in $100 increments. Interest is paid every six months. The interest rate is fixed, but the principal amount is adjusted for inflation (and deflation) throughout the term of the note, so that the amount of interest fluctuates as well. The principal paid at maturity is the greater of the adjusted principal or the original principal.

Collectively, Treasury bonds, bills, TIPS, and notes are referred to as "Treasuries" and are considered one of the lowest-risk investments because they are backed by the U.S. government. Treasuries can be purchased directly from the federal government or through a bank or brokerage. Treasuries can be held until they mature or be sold on the secondary market.

The interest on Treasuries is not taxed at the state or local level. This may help to offset the major disadvantage of Treasuries, namely that the interest rates that they pay are on the lower end of the scale. However, a low interest rate is to be expected with such a low-risk security.

U.S. savings bonds are also issued by the federal government. Series EE and series I U.S. savings bonds are currently available for purchase directly from the U.S. Treasury online. Online purchases can be made in any amount from $25 up to the maximums. Some employers offer payroll programs where deductions are made to purchase savings bonds.

Series EE savings bonds are sold as electronic bonds. Interest on the bonds is not actually paid until the bonds are cashed in. Federal income tax is not due until the bonds are cashed in. See Tab 2 for reporting of savings bond interest. In addition, the interest earned is exempt from state and local taxes. The electronic bonds are purchased through www.treasurydirect.gov and are sold at face value. The buyer can choose any dollar amount between $25 and $5,000. Buyers can purchase up to $5,000 in electronic bonds each year. Series EE savings bonds earn interest for 30 years. They can be redeemed at any time after one year has passed for the purchase price and any accrued interest, except that if they are redeemed before five years have passed, the last three months of interest is forfeited.

Series EE savings bonds issued after April 1997 and before May 2005 earn interest based on 90 percent of the average yields on five-year Treasury securities for the preceding six months. These bonds increase in value every month and interest is compounded semiannually. Their interest rate is adjusted every six months, on May 1 and November 1. Series EE bonds issued after April 2005 earn a fixed rate of interest. This rate has ranged from .2 to 3.7 percent.

Series I bonds are designed to protect the bondholder against inflation. Electronic I bonds can be purchased at face value in any amount from $25 to $5,000, up to a maximum of $5,000 per calendar year. Upon redemption the holder of an I bond receives the face value of the bond plus accrued interest. Similar to Series EE bonds, Series I bonds can be redeemed at any time after one year has passed for the purchase price and any accrued interest, except that if they are redeemed before five years have passed, the last three months of interest is forfeited.

Planning Tip. Paper bonds are no longer sold at financial institutions. The SmartExchange program allows Treasury Direct account owners to convert their Series E, EE, and I paper savings bonds to electronic securities. For more information, see *Electronic EE Bonds* at http://www.treasurydirect.gov/indiv/research/indepth/ebonds/res_e_bonds.htm.

Caution. Series HH savings bonds are no longer available to the public. Series HH savings bonds issued through August 2004 will continue to earn interest until they reach maturity 20 years after issue.

Corporate bonds are issued by a company at a specific interest rate for a specific period of time. Corporate bonds have maturity dates ranging anywhere from 10 to 30 years. The interest rate on corporate bonds depends on several factors, including the length of the maturity. Generally, longer-term bonds pay higher interest rates as an incentive for investors to lock in their funds for such a long period of time.

The interest rate on corporate bonds depends even more heavily on the strength of a corporation's finances. The stronger a corporation's credit record is, the lower the interest rate on bonds it issues. The safest bonds, those issued by financially strong corporations, will attract investors for the safety of their investment. Credit ratings issued by firms such as Standard & Poor's and Moody's Investors Service, which assign letter grades to the credit history of corporations, range from a high of AAA all the way down to C.

In general, corporate bonds pay higher interest rates than Treasuries that mature in the same time period. As safe an investment as the best-rated corporate bond may be, a comparable Treasury will be safer still with the U.S. government as its backer. Therefore, investors have to sacrifice a higher interest rate for less risk if they choose Treasuries over corporate bonds.

Junk bonds are simply corporate bonds that are considered to be particularly high risk. This means that bond-rating services such as Standard & Poor's and Moody's Investors Service have assigned them a low rating in terms of the company's ability to meet its obligations. To offset the risk involved, these bonds offer higher interest rates than other corporate bonds.

Mutual Funds. Most people invest in securities through mutual funds, which pool investors' money to invest in stocks, bonds, and other assets. Many people are introduced to mutual fund investing by the opportunity to choose investments for their account under an employer's 401(k) plan. The most important advantages of investing in mutual funds are diversification, simplicity, and professional management. Index mutual funds are often excellent choices because they generally have lower administrative costs than actively managed funds.

The choice of a particular fund should be based on several factors, including:

- performance, measured by annual average return over an appropriate period;
- performance record of individuals managing the fund;
- investment objective (growth vs. income);
- risk tolerance;
- reliability and customer service of fund family
- fees.

Load fees are actually a sales charge paid to the financial advisor or broker who sells Class A shares in a mutual fund. There are no-load funds, in which shares are purchased directly from the mutual fund company. Even though no-load funds are free of sales charges, they still have costs. No-load funds are generally Class B or Class C shares, which may have back-end load fees or redemption charges if shares are sold within a specific time period, usually four to six years.

Management fees are fees that mutual fund investors pay for management services (for example, salaries and expenses). Management fees range from less than 0.5 to three percent of the value of an investor's fund. Generally, they are automatically deducted annually.

Many funds charge an annual marketing fee (also known as a 12b-1 fee) of generally 0.25 to one percent of assets managed. No-load funds are particularly likely to charge a marketing fee (although it must be below a certain percentage in order for the fund to be labeled no-load) to make up for not charging load fees.

The length of time a manager has been with a fund and whether there is high turnover in a fund's management are also important factors. If a fund's management changes, the methodology it uses to achieve its objective can change, and it may not be as successful or as good a fit for a particular investor.

Mutual funds can be categorized by their general investment strategies. Some mutual funds invest in companies of a particular size, as measured by the companies' total market values, or market capitalization. Other funds are categorized by the weight their investment strategy places on seeking growth or income. The two goals are not mutually exclusive, but many actively managed funds focus heavily on one or the other.

 Planning Tip. Fees and expenses are one of the factors that impact investment returns and the amount of retirement income. For more information, see *A Look At 401(k) Plan Fees* at http://www.dol.gov/ebsa/publications/401k_employee.html.

Growth funds have the primary objective of a high return on investment in the form of appreciation. This type of fund is generally not aimed at obtaining an income stream, such as dividends.

Growth and income funds or equity return funds are a more conservative version of a basic growth fund, usually investing in companies that consistently pay dividends and are also expected to grow.

Income funds have the primary objective of a high return on investment in the form of dividends and interest, rather than capital appreciation.

Funds are also categorized by other dimensions of their strategies.

Index funds are mutual funds that invest in all the stocks in a particular stock index. For example, a mutual fund that uses the Standard & Poor's 500 stock index would buy stock in all the companies that make up the index. Investment management fees for index funds are much lower than for actively managed funds. An index fund will generally not beat the market, but it will usually outperform most of the actively managed funds owning a similar mix of securities.

Balanced funds are mutual funds that invest in both stocks and bonds. In order to be considered a balanced fund, federal securities law requires that a fund have at least 25 percent of its holdings in bonds and 25 percent of its holdings in stocks. The remaining holdings can vary but are usually based on how the stock market is doing at that particular time. Balanced funds are more stable than growth funds and produce higher returns than bond funds.

Foreign equity funds or international equity funds invest in stocks of companies outside the United States. Funds that invest in the stock of companies in one country outside the United States are known as single-country or country funds.

Global equity funds invest in the stock of both domestic and international companies.

Sector funds invest in one particular industry or sector of the economy. Examples of these sectors include technology, financial services, and precious metals. The greatest risk inherent in sector funds is lack of diversification. A sector fund may invest in several different companies, but all the companies will be in the same line of business. The performance of the fund tends to go up and down based on how the industry is doing as a whole.

Socially responsible funds or conscious funds are mutual funds that are defined more by what they do not invest in than by what they do invest in. Socially responsible funds choose not to invest in companies that engage in activities that go against a particular social cause, political ideology, or value system. Examples of the types of companies that these funds may not buy stock in are drug companies that conduct tests on animals, tobacco companies, and gun manufacturers.

Option funds invest in stock options as opposed to actually purchasing stocks. A variation on basic option funds are funds that actually purchase stocks and then issue options on the stocks they purchased. This type of option fund can produce dividends for investors because of the options being sold, but does not rate highly in terms of growth, because the options are exercised if the price of the stock purchased goes up.

Money market funds invest in items such as certificates of deposit and Treasuries. The most common type of money market fund invests in various items, including Treasuries, certificates of deposit, and commercial paper. Some money market funds invest in securities guaranteed by the federal government. Money market funds are one of the safest types (and can be the safest depending on what items make up the fund) of mutual fund. Also, money market funds usually have conveniences attached, such as the ability to write checks on the account. They provide little opportunity for growth of the investor's capital.

Investment Real Estate

For most people, the single largest investment they have is their home. Investing in other real estate also has its advantages.

Fixer-uppers. Buying houses, condominiums, or other buildings that need some work at a bargain price and fixing them up is a common method of investing in real estate. Different tax rules apply to the purchase and sale of a home if it is not used as the owner's principal residence.

Rental Property. Rental real estate can produce income. In addition, if the property appreciates in value, the investor may be able to sell it at a profit. Some investors hire a property manager or management company to manage their investment real estate.

 Planning Tip. A popular method of investing in real estate for many investors is to not sell their present home when they buy a new one, but rent it out instead. This is especially common for those who move from a condominium or starter home to a bigger home in the same general area. If the proceeds from the sale of the present home are not needed to purchase a new home, this may be an investment alternative. However, keeping the home as a rental for more than three years will eliminate the opportunity to exclude any gain realized on the sale of the property under Code Sec. 121. (See Tab 4.)

Seller financing, or holding a mortgage for a new homeowner and receiving an income stream from his or her mortgage payments, is another alternative for those who own a home outright with no mortgage liens.

Second Homes. Second homes or vacation homes should be purchased primarily for vacation purposes, not investment purposes. Most people end up with a loss on their vacation home properties because the costs of owning the home often exceed the rental income it produces, and resale values in resort areas may be more vulnerable to the effects of a general economic downturn.

Timeshares. Timeshares are best defined as the purchase of a set period of time (usually one or two weeks) during a certain time of the year at a certain location (for example, a condominium in Florida or a villa in France). This provides a fixed vacation cost each year, and often weeks and locations can be traded with other timeshare owners in the same company. Approach such "investments" as vacation rentals, not as investments. It may be telling that in bankruptcy cases, timeshares are often assigned zero value as an asset.

Real Estate Investment Trusts (REITs). These trusts invest in real estate through actual property or mortgage portfolios. Pooling investor funds for REITs also allows investors to invest in larger-scale properties such as hotels and office buildings, which would be financially impossible for most of us to do on our own dime. Another important selling point for using a REIT to invest in real estate is liquidity. It is much easier to sell or transfer a share of a REIT than to sell or transfer actual real estate. Like real estate, REITs may provide an income stream from rents and offer a very good possibility of long-term appreciation if the real estate market goes up.

Investments for Education

Investments for education, including Coverdell education savings accounts (CESAs), state-sponsored educational investment accounts and prepaid tuition plans, and education savings bonds, college certificates of deposit, and financial aid are covered in Tab 13 and IRS Publication 970, *Tax Benefits for Higher Education.*

Planning for Retirement

Most people have done little or no planning for retirement, even though many may spend as much as a third of their lives in retirement.

Most individuals who consider themselves financially successful rely on the "three-legged stool" of personal savings and holdings, company retirement benefits, and Social Security to fund retirement. It is important to actually estimate what retirement income and expenses will be rather than to simply take a comfortable retirement on faith.

Being Late Is Never Better. People often start planning for retirement later in life. Although it is never too late to begin retirement planning, the number of options available decreases with time.

Company Retirement Benefits Alone Are Not Always Enough. People commonly misunderstand how company retirement benefits work and what they offer.

Social Security Is Not a Safety Net. The Social Security system has never been and never will be a safety net for those who retire with no assets or income. At most, it provides a cushion to soften the blow when employees retire.

 Planning Tip. Social Security benefits will not be decreased by the amount of employer-provided pensions an individual receives if Social Security taxes were paid on the earnings from that employer. On the other hand, pensions based on work that is not covered by Social Security (such as the federal civil service and some state, local, or foreign government systems) will probably reduce the amount of Social Security benefits.

Medicare Is Not Enough to Cover Health Care Costs. For most older individuals, Medicare will be the main source of health insurance coverage. Unfortunately, Medicare costs increase regularly, and any shortfall in coverage will have to come from individual retirees.

It Does Not Cost Less to Live During Retirement. In addition to increased health care costs, leisure and entertainment costs tend to increase sharply after retirement. Families who started having children late in life may find their resources strained under the burden of funding college tuition. Finally, inflation becomes a major factor.

Retirement Needs as a Percentage of Income

The simplest method for estimating future retirement needs is to use a percentage of current income. The general rule of thumb is that retirement expenses will be 60 to 80 percent of after-tax preretirement income.

Using a factor of 80 percent or more provides a more conservative approach to estimating potential retirement expenses. Conversely, the lower the percentage used in the calculations, the lower the safety cushion. Using any percentage below 60 percent would be likely to lead to a major shortfall in retirement funds.

Another method of figuring how much is needed for retirement involves the use of budget calculations, by comparing a current budget with a projected retirement budget. Although more time consuming and complicated, this method can provide a more realistic idea of what will be needed during retirement.

Pension Benefits. These benefits include income from employer-provided retirement plans, self-employed plans, and savings from the various forms of IRAs. Unlike Social Security benefits, an individual has some control over this potential source of income. The amount of control, however, is limited to participating (as opposed to not participating) in a plan, selecting investment options, and switching to employers that offer better retirement benefits.

Personal Savings. If either of the other legs in the model comes up short, it is personal savings that will have to support the three-legged stool.

401(k) Plans. A 401(k) plan is often an important retirement planning device for employees and participation is generally advantageous. As an initial benefit, contributions to a 401(k) are made on a pretax basis, so the employee sees an immediate tax savings. In addition, the money in a 401(k) will grow on a tax-deferred basis, making it even easier to save for retirement. Yet another benefit of most 401(k) plans is that the employer will match employee contributions or otherwise make additional contributions to the plan.

Meeting Your Savings Goal			
Your Age	Annual Savings Necessary to Reach $100,000 by Age 65 (8% Interest Rate)	Your Age	Annual Savings Necessary to Reach $100,000 by Age 65 (8% Interest Rate)
18	$ 204	37	$ 962
19	221	38	1,049
20	239	39	1,145
21	259	40	1,251
22	280	41	1,368
23	303	42	1,498
24	329	43	1,642
25	356	44	1,803
26	386	45	1,983
27	419	46	2,185
28	454	47	2,413
29	492	48	2,670
30	534	49	3,298
31	580	50	3,683
32	630	51	4,130
33	685	52	4,652
34	745	53	5,270
35	811	54	6,008
36	883		

Credit and Debt

Personal credit, if used wisely, has its advantages. Consumer credit falls into two broad categories: closed-end and open-end. Closed-end credit is used for a specific purpose, for a specific amount, and for a specific period of time. Payments are usually of equal amounts. Mortgage loans and automobile loans are common examples of closed-end credit. With open-end, or revolving credit, loans are made on a continuous basis, and the lender bills the borrower periodically to make at least partial payment. Credit cards issued by a store, bank cards such as VISA or MasterCard, and overdraft protection are examples of open-end credit.

Debit cards deduct payments directly from a bank account and are not considered credit cards because funds are not borrowed.

Cost of Credit

Credit costs money. Because a dollar invested today can earn interest over time, a dollar today is worth more than a dollar at some point in the future. Many people think that the cheapest loan is the one with the lowest interest rate and the lowest payments. However, the length of the loan and its fees are essential in figuring the loan's real cost.

The Consumer Credit Protection Act requires creditors to state the cost of borrowing in a common language so that the consumer understands exactly what the charges will be. With that information, consumers can compare costs and shop around for the best credit deal.

Annual Percentage Rate. The Annual Percentage Rate (APR) combines the fees with a year of interest charges to give the true annual interest rate. All lenders are required to disclose the effective annual percentage rate as well as the total finance charge in dollars. In this way, credit alternatives can be compared on equal terms.

The APR is the ratio of the total finance charge, not just the interest charge, to the average amount of credit in use during the life of the loan and is expressed as a percentage rate per year. The calculation of the APR depends on whether the loan is repaid in a single payment or in installments.

Debt and Income Tax Laws. The cost of credit is increased because individuals cannot generally deduct interest paid on auto, credit cards, education, and other consumer loans.

In addition, only a limited amount of qualified residence (mortgage) interest is deductible. Qualified residence interest is the interest paid or accrued on acquisition or home equity loans with respect to an individual's principal residence and one other residence, usually a "vacation home." The total amount of acquisition loans is limited to $1 million and the total amount of home equity loans is limited to $100,000. Interest on any debt over these limits is considered to be personal, consumer interest that is not deductible. See Tab 2 for details about the home mortgage interest deduction.

Tips to Lower Credit Card Costs

There are effective strategies for minimizing the cost of credit in any financial situation:

- pay off the entire amount within the grace period if at all possible;
- pay off card balances as quickly as possible; paying only the minimum payment required each month may prolong the debt for a decade or more;
- charge new purchases on lower-interest-rate cards;
- carry only one or two cards for emergencies (such as gas and telephone cards) and only a few selected store or bank cards, arranged in a way to remind you which cards offer the lowest rates;
- cancel any unneeded cards, especially those that charge annual fees;
- pay off high-interest, high-fee card balances first;
- avoid late-payment and overlimit penalties;
- use overnight delivery or on-line payments to save charges and fees if necessary. Because many credit card companies now assess hefty late payment fees

($15, $20, or more), consider whether you could avoid these fees by sending a payment by overnight delivery; and
- negotiate with creditors for better credit terms.

Credit Reports and Credit Bureaus

Every consumer should review his or her credit report periodically to ensure that no errors have slipped in, and also to uncover fraud or identity theft. Credit reports contain the name, address, Social Security number, birth date, information about past and current employers and incomes, home ownership information, and detailed credit information of an individual.

Creditors inform the credit bureaus of account numbers and the amount and type of credit and payments, the outstanding balance, the number and the amounts of payments past due, and the frequency of 30, 60, or 90-day lateness. Commonly, credit files indicate the largest amount of credit an individual has had and each inquiry and credit refusal. Any lawsuits, judgments, or tax liens may appear as well.

Creditors who deny credit to an applicant must send a written rejection notice within 30 days of the decision, stating the specific reasons for the rejection and providing the name and address of any credit bureau that issued a report. Consumers have the right to view their credit files.

 Caution. Small business owners often have more trouble than employees in obtaining personal credit. One of the reasons for this is that creditors may feel that the income stream from a small business is less secure than income received as an employee. Also, the creditors may worry about verifying the amount of income actually generated by the small business. Faced with these difficulties in obtaining credit, some small business owners may be tempted to "fudge" their income numbers, that is, inflate the amount received from their businesses. Such "creative accounting" is ill advised: not only can a loan be denied if untrue information is supplied, but the applicant can be criminally prosecuted.

At the center of the credit reporting system are three national credit bureaus: Equifax, Experian, and Trans-Union. The credit bureaus are private, for-profit businesses. Under federal law, consumers may obtain a free copy of their credit report from each of these companies once each year. The free reports are available through a single website sponsored by the credit bureaus, at www.annualcreditreport.com, by calling

1-877-322-8228, or by filling out and mailing in a request form (available at the website). Consumers may obtain additional credit reports from any of the credit bureaus by visiting their websites–www.equifax.com, www.transunion.com, and www.experian.com.

The credit bureaus simply collect and collate credit information and make it available to businesses that subscribe to their service. They do not deny credit; they merely report the information they have gathered.

Time Limits on Adverse Data. Most of the information in an individual's credit file may be reported for only seven years. Personal bankruptcy, however, may be reported for 10 years. After that time, the past information in a credit file cannot be disclosed by a credit-reporting agency except with regard to an application for credit of $150,000 or more, to purchase life insurance for $150,000 or more, or for employment at an annual salary of $75,000 or more. In those situations, the time limits on releasing the information in a credit file do not apply. Nor do those time limits apply if the creditor chooses to use prior adverse information to deny a credit application.

Incorrect Credit File Information. Credit bureaus are required to follow reasonable procedures to ensure that subscribing creditors report information accurately. However, mistakes do occur. When a consumer notifies a credit bureau that he or she disputes the accuracy of information, the credit bureau must investigate and modify or remove inaccurate data. If investigation does not resolve the dispute, a consumer may place a statement of 100 words or less in his or her file explaining why the record is inaccurate. The credit bureau must then include the statement about disputed data or a coded version of that statement with the credit report.

Mortgage Credit

Mortgage lenders traditionally use a 28/36 ratio test to figure out the mortgage an applicant qualifies for. That is, the sum of the monthly mortgage payment, homeowner's insurance, and property taxes should equal no more than 28 percent of household monthly gross income. The second part of the ratio is that monthly debts, including the mortgage payment, should equal no more than 36 percent of monthly income.

$$\text{Gross monthly income} \times 0.28 = \text{Maximum monthly mortgage payment}$$

$$\text{Gross monthly income} \times 0.36 = \text{Maximum total monthly debt}$$

For information on the tax advantages of owning a home, see Tab 2.

Managing Substantial Debt

Overwhelming debt has become a common problem in America. There are a number of solutions, with bankruptcy as a last resort.

Information Is Key. The book NCLC Guide to Surviving Debt, from the National Consumer Law Center, is available through most local libraries or from NCLC at (617) 542-8010.

Consumer credit counseling services (CCCSs) are not-for-profit organizations that provide debt counseling services for families and individuals with serious financial problems, for a modest fee. A credit counselor meets with debtors and analyzes their total financial situation. The counselor may develop a repayment plan and contact creditors to arrange new repayment terms. These services also offer education and help design a budget.

The IRS has been reviewing the not-for-profit status of many of these organizations and has revoked that status in many cases, on the grounds that the organization was operating for a profit rather than engaged in educational activities for the benefit of the public. Consumers are encouraged to check that the organization offers advice and counseling, rather than promises of easy escape from debt for a fee.

Loan Consolidation. Loan consolidation companies specialize in loaning people money to pay off all their other debts. The advantages include having to deal with only one creditor and one payment each month, the fact that loans are usually long term, and the monthly payments often being lower than before consolidation. However, the interest charged by loan consolidators may be very high, and there may be a fee for paying off the loan ahead of schedule. Another danger is that a consolidation loan does nothing to resolve the habits and tendencies that may have caused the credit problems in the first place.

Home Equity Loans. The most common loan consolidation technique is to roll as much debt as possible into a home equity loan, which may have tax advantages (see Tab 2).

Most credit counselors advocate the general rule that individuals should not convert unsecured debt to secured debt. Following this rule would mean not using home equity to collateralize credit card debt. Although this is certainly a logical and prudent rule, there are exceptions. For instance, a home equity loan may be appropriate if most or all of the following factors are true:

- you have been able to make only the minimum monthly payment required on your credit cards;
- your credit card debt carries very high interest rates compared with what you could obtain for a home equity loan;
- you meet the qualifications that would make interest paid on the home equity loan deductible on your federal income tax return;
- you will pay back the home equity loan on a relatively short payment schedule–preferably five years, but no more than 10 years;
- you have an adequate and dependable source of income available to repay the home equity loan; and
- you have made the adjustments to your lifestyle and personal finances necessary to ensure that you will not slide back into the credit card debt morass once (or worse, before) your existing credit balances are extinguished.

Bankruptcy: The Last Resort

The United States Constitution provides a method whereby individuals burdened by excessive debt can obtain a fresh financial start and pursue newly productive lives unimpaired by past financial problems. It is an important alternative for persons mired deep in financial difficulty.

The federal bankruptcy laws were enacted to provide debtors with a fresh start and to establish a ranking and equity among all the creditors who are clamoring for the debtor's limited resources. Bankruptcy helps people avoid the kind of permanent discouragement that can prevent them from ever reestablishing themselves as hard-working members of society. Also, creditors are ranked so that the debtor's nonexempt property can be fairly distributed according to established rules guaranteeing identical treatment to all creditors of the same rank.

This discussion is intended only as a brief overview of the types of bankruptcy filings and of what a bankruptcy filing can and cannot do. Anyone considering this course of action is encouraged to seek the advice and assistance of an attorney specializing in bankruptcy law.

Types of Bankruptcy. The Bankruptcy Code is divided into chapters. The chapters that usually apply to consumer debtors are Chapter 7, known as a liquidation, and Chapter 13, known as an adjustment of the debts of an individual with regular income.

An important feature applicable to all types of bankruptcy filings is the automatic stay. The automatic stay means that the mere request for bankruptcy protection automatically "stays," or forces an abrupt halt to, repossessions, foreclosures, evictions, garnishments, attachments, utility shut-offs, and debt collection harassment. Creditors cannot take any further action against the debtor or the property without permission from the bankruptcy court.

Chapter 7. In a Chapter 7, or liquidation, case, the bankruptcy court appoints a trustee to examine the debtor's assets and divide them into exempt and nonexempt property. Exempt property is limited to a certain amount of equity in the debtor's residence, motor vehicle, household goods, life insurance, health aids, specified future earnings such as Social Security benefits and alimony, and certain other personal property. The trustee may then sell the nonexempt property and distribute the proceeds among the unsecured creditors. Although a liquidation case can rarely help with secured debt (the secured creditor still has the right to repossess the collateral), the debtor will be discharged from the legal obligation to pay unsecured debts such as credit card debts, medical bills, and utility arrearages. Certain types of unsecured debt are allowed special treatment and cannot be discharged. These include some student loans, alimony, child support, criminal fines, and some taxes.

Chapter 13. In a Chapter 13 case, the debtor puts forward a plan, following the rules set forth in the bankruptcy laws, to repay all creditors over a period of time, usually from future income. A Chapter 13 case may be advantageous in that the debtor is allowed to get caught up on mortgages or car loans without the threat of foreclosure or repossession and is allowed to keep both exempt and nonexempt property. The debtor's plan is a simple document outlining to the bankruptcy court how the debtor proposes to pay current expenses while paying off all the old debt balances. The debtor's property is protected from seizure from creditors, including mortgage and other lien holders, as long as the proposed payments are made. The plan generally requires monthly payments to the bankruptcy trustee over a period of three to five years. Arrangements can be made to have these payments made automatically through payroll deductions.

For information about bankruptcy and taxes, see Tab 12.

Insurance

In most cases, risks that are large or unpredictable are best transferred to a reliable insurance carrier. Lines of insurance such as homeowner's or renter's, auto, life, disability, health, and business coverage protect individuals from varying degrees of risk depending on the likelihood of an adverse occurrence.

Health Insurance

Private health insurance costs have risen much more than inflation in recent years. Many employees receive insurance under group policies provided or subsidized by their employers; others must seek individual policies or do without. Medicare is a federal health insurance program for people 65 years of age and older and some disabled people under age 65. For discussion of Medicare costs and coverages, see the discussion earlier in this Tab.

 Planning Tip. Beginning in 2014, individuals may be subject to a penalty for failing to maintain minimum essential health care coverage. Generally, individuals not covered by an employer-sponsored policy or by a government-sponsored program such as Medicare, or for whom an employer-sponsored policy is unafforadable, may purchase coverage through a Health Benefit Exchange. Tax credits and subsidies are available to low-income individuals to help lower the costs of such coverage.

Disability Insurance

There are two types of disability insurance: short-term and long-term.

Short-term disability insurance is designed to provide income to employees who become disabled due to sickness or an accident, and are unable to work after an initial waiting period (generally, one to seven days). Short-term benefits are usually expressed in terms of the maximum number of weeks that the plan will pay (the industry standard is 26 weeks). These benefits typically replace 50 percent to 67 percent of an employee's income.

Long-term disability policies take up where short-term coverage leaves off for those who become disabled and unable to work for longer periods of time (generally six months or longer), and typically provide 50 percent to 60 percent of pay. In most plans, benefits are paid for the duration of the disability up to the age of 65.

Life Insurance and Annuities

Life insurance offers important benefits, including income replacement for survivors, forced savings, possible collateral, and a ready source of emergency cash.

Term versus Cash Value? Life insurance policies can be divided into two main categories, term insurance and cash-value insurance.

Term Insurance. Term insurance provides a death benefit only. If the insured dies within the specified term, the insurance company pays the benefit amount. Such a policy is pure protection only; it has no investment (cash value) component to it. Although it is called "term" insurance because the coverage runs for a specified term (such as a year), many modern term policies may be renewed at the option of the insured for as long as he or she is willing to pay the premiums. Term insurance is generally less expensive than cash-value insurance.

The simplest form of term insurance must be renewed annually. Many term policies are now written for much longer terms (five, 10, or 15 years). Although the cost of term insurance usually rises as the insured gets older, level-term policies are also available. These policies keep the premium at the same dollar amount throughout the term (although the premium would jump more sharply for the next term than would be the case for the year-to-year rise for an annual term policy).

Cash-Value Insurance. There sometimes appear to be a nearly unlimited number of types of cash-value (or whole-life) policies. Although they have important differences, they all boil down to this: They provide a death benefit (equivalent to term protection) and they also provide a savings feature in their cash value. Cash-value insurance is much more expensive than term (particularly at younger ages), but typically provides insurance throughout the insured's lifetime at a level premium. The extra expense of cash-value insurance (over term insurance) funds the cash value feature.

A policyholder normally can receive the benefit of the cash value during lifetime in one of two ways: (1) by taking a loan against them or (2) by cashing in the policy (the policy will no longer be in force, but the policyholder will receive the cash surrender value). If the cash value remains in the policy, it increases without any tax consequence to the policyholder. Thus, an individual who lacks the discipline to follow through on an independent investment plan may benefit from the "forced savings" under a cash-value insurance policy.

Annuities. An annuity is sometimes referred to as an "upside-down life insurance policy." With a life insurance policy, the insured's relatively small periodic payments (premiums) are invested to fund a large sum to be paid in the future. With an annuity the purchaser makes one or more payments to fund a series of periodic payments (starting immediately or at some point in the future) over an extended period of time. A life insurance policy primarily protects the insured's dependents against the economic harm of premature death. An annuity is meant to protect individuals (and their dependents) from the economic harm of outliving their life savings and other resources.

Annuities are available in various forms. A fixed annuity is one designed to assure the buyer of a lifetime (or other fixed period) of payments of a guaranteed set amount. The amount of these payments is based on the age of the annuitant (the person whose life the annuity is computed on) at the time the payments are to commence, the sex of the annuitant, and the rate of interest that the insurer assumes will be made from the purchase funds paid by the annuitant.

A variable annuity (also known as a "market value account") is one in which the insurer invests the premiums (less investment charges) in a portfolio of securities. The value of the annuity provided varies with the performance of the portfolio. A variable annuity is purchased with the hope that the performance of the underlying securities will outstrip the return that would have been obtained from a fixed annuity.

Both the amounts that build up within the annuity (during the accumulation phase) and the amounts that are received as annuity payments (during the distribution phase) can qualify for favorable federal income tax treatment. Thus, purchasing an annuity can become a tax-deferred method of saving for retirement.

Homeowner's Insurance

There are several different types of homeowner's policies in terms of the risks that are covered. The most common type of homeowner's policy in use today (known as "comprehensive coverage," or HO-3 in the insurance industry) covers a variety of risks. Here are some of the major kinds of risks that are covered by a comprehensive-coverage homeowner's policy:

- damage to home and personal property caused by fire, lightning, wind, or storm;
- medical payments for occupants for injuries caused by fire, lightning, wind, or storm;
- medical and legal liabilities to persons injured by accident while in the home;
- loss or theft of personal property, even if not in the home, with some restrictions on things like jewelry or laptop computers;
- liability to others for accidental damage to their property, even if not in the home;
- liability for unintentional personal injury to others caused by the homeowner or his or her family;
- liability for intentional personal injury to others caused by the homeowner's children who are below a specified age;
- liability to others hurt because of the homeowner's participation in a sporting event (for example, while playing golf, the homeowner accidentally strikes someone with a golf ball);

- liability for damage or injury caused by pets (but damage caused by exotic pets is not covered);
- damage caused by vandalism, riot, or civil unrest; and
- damage caused by falling objects (such as tree limbs).

What's Not Covered by a Homeowner's Policy? It is important to know the types of risks a homeowner's policy does not cover. The main risks that a comprehensive policy normally does not cover are the following:

- flood damage (including the water damage caused by a hurricane);
- damage caused by ground movement (such as earthquakes and soil erosion); and
- claims arising from a business use of the premises.

Claims arising from a business use of the premises are, by far, the most important exclusion for home business operators.

The phrase "normally does not cover" is used because some states require insurance companies to cover some of these risks (for example, California requires coverage of earthquakes) and because coverage can often be obtained by purchasing a policy rider, at an additional premium cost, or other specific insurance, such as through the National Flood Insurance Program.

 Caution. Home-based business owners should consult with their insurance advisors to be sure that their home and business needs are all covered.

Auto Insurance

Auto insurance has two main components: liability insurance and insurance for property damage. Liability insurance is the most important. It provides compensation to persons who would be able to sue for personal injuries, medical payments, loss of earnings, or damage to their property arising out of an auto accident.

Property damage insurance includes collision and comprehensive coverage, which compensates the policyholder for assorted damage to the car caused by collisions and such things as fire, theft, and vandalism.

Business Insurance

General liability insurance will protect you from payments required to be made for bodily injury or property damage to a third party, for medical expenses arising from the underlying incident, for the cost of defending lawsuits including investigations and settlements, and for any bonds or judgments required during an appeal procedure.

This type of coverage comes with exclusions and limitations. The exclusions typically include war and sometimes property of others entrusted to you (such as clothing if you own a dry-cleaning business). Liability for the property of others can be removed as an exclusion, usually for an additional premium or via separate coverage. Limitations will be akin to those on your personal auto policy–for example, $100,000 per person and $300,000 per accident. In addition to general liability coverage, depending on what kind of business you are in, you may need one or more of the other kinds of liability coverage.

Product liability insurance can cover products you may manufacture or sell or your services if you are, say, a mechanic or house painter. Under the name of malpractice insurance, this is the classification of coverage that will cover physicians, dentists, accountants, and lawyers. In today's world, a minimum of $1 million is the recommended coverage for businesses dealing with the general public. It is also a good idea to have the name of your business added to your supplier's insurance riders as an "additional named" insured. This adds another explicit layer of protection should a product liability suit arise, generally costs nothing, and has become common practice for companies in food retailing, wholesaling, marketing, and manufacturing.

Auto liability insurance for a business, just as for your personal vehicles, should be of the comprehensive type. This is especially important if you have employees who drive for your business.

Workers' compensation insurance is required by law in all states and protects an employer from liability for an accident involving an employee. This type of insurance will pay for medical expenses and lost wages for an injured employee and, in cases of death or disability, provide lump sums or annuities. Maintaining a safe working environment will go a long way toward controlling the cost of this type of coverage, but a careless or accident-prone employee can raise your insurance rates out of the realm of affordability very quickly. Proper selection and training must be practiced to minimize this risk. In some states this coverage is not required for family members who may be working in the business. Your agent will know if any exceptions apply to your situation.

Umbrella liability insurance is an all-inclusive option that can cover enormous liabilities exceeding the normal limits of your basic policy at a fairly low cost. This coverage is almost always worth considering since it provides a valuable safety net for you and your business.

Malpractice, errors and omissions (E&O), or professional liability coverage is needed if you provide advice or services to the public where significant liability could result if something went wrong. You may want to consider obtaining professional insurance for a couple of reasons. First, depending on your profession, you may be required to carry such insurance by law. Second, certain policies will provide you with low-cost legal representation in the event you are sued. Even if your work is flawless, a customer could still claim that you did something wrong. A good professional insurance policy would help you defray the costs of any lawsuit, regardless of whether the underlying claim has merit.

Planning Investments for Tax Advantages

Tax planning is a process of looking at various tax options in order to determine when, whether, and how to conduct business and personal transactions so that taxes are eliminated or reduced. There are countless tax planning strategies available, particularly for small-business owners. Regardless of how simple or how complex a tax strategy is, it will be based on structuring the transaction to accomplish one or more of these goals:

- reducing the amount of taxable income;
- reducing the tax rate;
- controlling the time when the tax must be paid;
- claiming any available tax credits; and
- controlling the effects of the alternative minimum tax.

Tax-Favored Investments

In addition to deductions and exclusions from income, certain items (generally, capital gains (other than gains on collectibles) and qualified dividends) are taxed at lower rates.

Tax Avoidance

Tax evasion is illegal. Tax avoidance is the legal planning of transactions to take full advantage of the tax laws. Frequently, what sets tax evasion apart from tax avoidance is the IRS's finding that there was some fraudulent intent on the part of the taxpayer. The following are four areas commonly identified by IRS examiners as pointing to possible fraud:

- a failure to report substantial amounts of income, such as a shareholder's failure to report dividends, or a store owner's skimming from the cash register without including it in the daily business receipts;
- a claim for fictitious or improper deductions on a return, such as a sales representative's substantial overstatement of travel expenses, or a taxpayer's claim of a large deduction for charitable contributions when no verification exists;
- accounting irregularities, such as a business's failure to keep adequate records, or a discrepancy between

amounts reported on a corporation's return and amounts reported on its financial statements; and

- improper allocation of income to a related taxpayer who is in a lower tax bracket, such as where a corporation makes distributions to the controlling shareholder's children.

In contrast, the following techniques may result in a lower tax bill without breaking the law:

- shifting income from a high-bracket taxpayer to a lower-bracket taxpayer (such as a child); one fairly simple way to do this is to shift investment assets to minor children; owners of small businesses can hire their children; another possibility is to make one or more children part owners of a small business, so that net profits of the business are shared among a larger group; the tax laws limit the usefulness of this strategy for shifting *unearned* income to children under age 18, but some tax saving opportunities still exist (see Tab 13);

- structuring an investment or transaction so that payments are classified as capital gains. Long-term capital gains earned by noncorporate taxpayers are subject to lower tax rates than other income; and

- choosing the optimal form of organization for a business (such as sole proprietorship, partnership, or corporation); if business income is under $75,000 and the business is not a personal-service business such as medicine, law, architecture, engineering, accounting, the arts, or consulting, incorporating may result in tax savings; otherwise, the sole proprietorship or pass-through entities (partnerships, LLCs, S corporations) usually offer more tax benefits; of course, nontax factors must be taken into account as well.

Timing of Income and Deductions

In broad terms, taxes can be minimized in the current year by postponing the receipt of income so that more of it will be taxed next year, and by accelerating deductions into the current year.

Postponing Income, Accelerating Deductions. If the current year's tax bracket is expected to be as high or higher than next year's, strategies for postponing taxable income until the next tax year will reduce current tax liability. Even if the tax bracket is expected to stay the same, because of the time value of money, it is often best to postpone tax liability. There are several methods to do this:

- **Delay collections**–Year-end billings can be delayed until late enough in the year that payments come in the following year.
- **Delay dividends**–Corporations may arrange for any dividends to be paid after the end of the year.
- **Delay capital gains**–Sell assets that have appreciated in value after the first of the year.
- **Accelerate payments**–Where possible, prepay deductible business expenses, including rent, interest, taxes, insurance, etc.
- **Accelerate large purchases**–Close the purchase of depreciable personal property or real estate within the current year.
- **Accelerate operating expenses**–Accelerate the purchase of equipment, supplies, or the making of repairs.
- **Accelerate depreciation**–Elect to expense the cost of new equipment if eligible to do so, rather than to depreciate the equipment.

A "How Much Life Insurance Do You Need?" Worksheet	
1. Estimated annual living expenses of survivors (spouse, children, etc.) Estimate 75% of current family living expenses	$_____ (1)
2. Less expected annual benefits	
A. Social Security benefits	$_____
B. Survivor's pension benefits	$_____
C. Survivor's earned income	$_____
D. Other income	$_____
Total expected annual benefits	$_____ (2)
3. Net living expense shortage (or surplus) (1) MINUS (2) =	$_____ (3)
4. Amount of capital required to cover living expense shortage: Inflation-adjusted rate of return (example: 8% interest less 3% inflation = 5%) $_____ (3) DIVIDED BY _____ % =	_____ % $_____ (4)
5. Plus other lump-sum expenses	
A. Final expenses/estate costs	$_____
B. Mortgage cancellation	$_____
C. Education fund or other	$_____
D. Emergency fund	$_____
Total lump-sum expenses	$_____ (5)
6. Total capital required (4) PLUS (5) =	$_____ (6)
7. Less present capital	
A. Income-producing assets	$_____
B. Present life insurance	$_____
Total present capital	$_____ (7)
8. Additional life insurance needed (6) MINUS (7) =	$_____

Many of these strategies are much easier to accomplish under the cash method of accounting. Although strategies aimed at changing the year in which income and deductions will be accounted for are usually more difficult to accomplish using the accrual method, this does not mean that they cannot be done.

To delay an accrual basis taxpayer's recognition of an item of income, make sure that all events fixing the liability for payment of that income are not met by year's end. For instance, when selling goods, delay shipment until next year.

To accelerate a deductible expense into the current year, make sure that all events fixing the liability and amount of payment as well as the economic performance have been completed by year's end. If purchasing goods, services, or the use of property, make sure that a valid contract covering all necessary terms is in effect and that the goods, services, or properties are delivered, performed, or used by year's end.

Accelerating Income, Postponing Deductions. If the current year's tax bracket is expected to be lower than next year's, maximize the amount of income that will be taxed in the present tax year. This can be accomplished by accelerating income and postponing expenses into the following year. In most cases, the opposite of the suggestions listed in the previous section apply. For example, instead of delaying billings, send out year-end bills early and try to collect payments before year's end.

FINANCIAL PLANNING CHECKUP STATEMENT

CONFIDENTIAL

Personal Financial Statement as of _____

Name(s): _____

_____

Home Address: _____

_____

Home Phone: _____

E-Mail–Home: _____

E-Mail–Office: _____

Social Security #: _____

Spouse's Social Security #: _____

Assets	Amount	Liabilities and Net Worth	Amount
Cash on hand and in banks	$	Notes payable	$
U.S. government securities		Notes payable–Relatives	
Listed securities		Notes payable–Other	
Unlisted securities		Accounts and bills due	
Other equity interests		Unpaid taxes	
Accounts and notes receivable		Real estate mortgages payable	
Real estate owned		Land contracts payable	
Mortgages and land contracts receivable		Life insurance loans	
Cash value life insurance		Other liabilities: Itemize	
Retirement accounts			
Other assets: Itemize			
TOTAL ASSETS	$	TOTAL LIABILITIES	$
		NET WORTH	$
		TOTAL LIABILITIES AND NET WORTH	$

Sources of Income	Amount	General Information	
Salary	$	Employer	
Bonus and Commissions		Position or Profession	No. Years
Dividends		Employer's Address	
Real Estate Income			
*Other Income: Itemize		Phone No.	
TOTAL INCOME	$	Partner, officer, or owner in any other venture? No ___ Yes ___ If so, explain:	
		Are any assets pledged? No ___ Yes ___ (Detail in Schedule A)	
		Income taxes settled through (Date)	

*Alimony, child support, or separate maintenance payments need not be disclosed unless relied
 upon as a basis for extension of credit. If disclosed, payments received under:
(circle) court order written agreement oral understanding.

Contingent Liabilities	Amount	General Information (Continued)
As endorser, comaker, or guarantor	$	Are you a defendant in any suits or legal action? No ___ Yes ___
On leases		If so, explain:
Legal claims		Have you ever filed for bankruptcy? No ___ Yes ___
Provision for federal income taxes		If so, explain:
Other special debt, e.g., recourse or repurchase liability		Do you have a will? No ___ Yes ___ With whom?
		Do you have a trust? No ___ Yes ___ With whom?
TOTAL	$	Number of dependents _____ Age(s) _____

Banks, Brokers, Savings & Loan Associations, Finance Companies, or Credit Unions

List the names of all the institutions at which you maintain a deposit account and/or where you have obtained loans.

Name of Institution	Name on Account	Balance on Deposit	High Credit	Amount Owing	Monthly Payment	Secured by What Assets
	TOTAL					

Stocks (Listed & Unlisted), Bonds (Gov't & Comm.), and Partnership Interests (General & Ltd.)

Number of Shares, Face Value (Bonds), or % of Ownership	Indicate: 1. Agency or name of company issuing security or name of partnership 2. Type of investment or equity classification 3. Number of shares, bonds or % of ownership held 4. Basis of valuation*	In Name Of	*Market Value	Pledged	
				Yes	No
		TOTAL			

*If unlisted security or partnership interest, provide current financial statements to support basis for valuation.

Real Estate Owned (and related debt, if applicable)

Description of Property or Address	Name on Title	Date Acquired	Cost Improvements	Present Mkt. Value	Mortgage or Land Contract Payable		
					Bal. Owing	Mo. Payt.	Holder
	TOTAL						

Real Estate: Mortgages & Land Contracts Receivable (and related debt, if applicable)

Description of Property or Address	Name on Title	Date Acquired	Balance Receivable	Monthly Payment	Mortgage or Land Contract Payable		
					Bal. Owing	Mo. Payt.	Holder
TOTAL							

Life Insurance Carried

Name of Company	Beneficiary	Cash Surrender Value	Loans	Face Amount
			TOTAL	

Retirement Accounts

Description of Account	Institution	Beneficiary	Balance	Nondeductible Contributions
			TOTAL	

Social Security Benefits Worksheet—Lines 20a and 20b

Before you begin:	✓ Complete Form 1040, lines 21 and 23 through 32, if they apply to you.	
	✓ Figure any write-in adjustments to be entered on the dotted line next to line 36 (see the instructions for line 36).	
	✓ If you are married filing separately and you lived apart from your spouse for all of 2013, enter "D" to the right of the word "benefits" on line 20a. If you do not, you may get a math error notice from the IRS.	
	✓ Be sure you have read the **Exception** in the line 20a and 20b instructions to see if you can use this worksheet instead of a publication to find out if any of your benefits are taxable.	

1. Enter the total amount from **box 5** of **all** your **Forms SSA-1099** and **Forms RRB-1099.** Also, enter this amount on Form 1040, line 20a . . . .   **1.** _____

2. Enter one-half of line 1 . . . .   **2.** _____

3. Combine the amounts from Form 1040, lines 7, 8a, 9a, 10 through 14, 15b, 16b, 17 through 19, and 21 . . . .   **3.** _____

4. Enter the amount, if any, from Form 1040, line 8b . . . .   **4.** _____

5. Combine lines 2, 3, and 4 . . . .   **5.** _____

6. Enter the total of the amounts from Form 1040, lines 23 through 32, plus any write-in adjustments you entered on the dotted line next to line 36 . . . .   **6.** _____

7. Is the amount on line 6 less than the amount on line 5?

    ☐ **No.** (STOP)   None of your social security benefits are taxable. Enter -0- on Form 1040, line 20b.

    ☐ **Yes.** Subtract line 6 from line 5 . . . .   **7.** _____

8. If you are:
    - Married filing jointly, enter $32,000
    - Single, head of household, qualifying widow(er), or married filing separately and you **lived apart** from your spouse for all of 2013, enter $25,000
    - Married filing separately and you lived with your spouse at any time in 2013, skip lines 8 through 15; multiply line 7 by 85% (.85) and enter the result on line 16. Then go to line 17

    . . . .   **8.** _____

9. Is the amount on line 8 less than the amount on line 7?

    ☐ **No.** (STOP)   None of your social security benefits are taxable. Enter -0- on Form 1040, line 20b. If you are married filing separately and you **lived apart** from your spouse for all of 2013, be sure you entered "D" to the right of the word "benefits" on line 20a.

    ☐ **Yes.** Subtract line 8 from line 7 . . . .   **9.** _____

10. Enter: $12,000 if married filing jointly; $9,000 if single, head of household, qualifying widow(er), or married filing separately and you **lived apart** from your spouse for all of 2013 . . . .   **10.** _____

11. Subtract line 10 from line 9. If zero or less, enter -0- . . . .   **11.** _____

12. Enter the **smaller** of line 9 or line 10 . . . .   **12.** _____

13. Enter one-half of line 12 . . . .   **13.** _____

14. Enter the **smaller** of line 2 or line 13 . . . .   **14.** _____

15. Multiply line 11 by 85% (.85). If line 11 is zero, enter -0- . . . .   **15.** _____

16. Add lines 14 and 15 . . . .   **16.** _____

17. Multiply line 1 by 85% (.85) . . . .   **17.** _____

18. **Taxable social security benefits.** Enter the **smaller** of line 16 or line 17. Also enter this amount on Form 1040, line 20b . . . .   **18.** _____

> (TIP) *If any of your benefits are taxable for 2013 **and** they include a lump-sum benefit payment that was for an earlier year, you may be able to reduce the taxable amount. See Pub. 915 for details.*

Before you begin: √   If you are the beneficiary of a deceased employee or former employee who died **before** August 21, 1996, include any death benefit exclusion that you are entitled to (up to $5,000) in the amount entered on line 2 below.

More than one pension or annuity. If you had more than one partially taxable pension or annuity, figure the taxable part of each separately. Enter the total of the taxable parts on Form 1040, line 16b. Enter the total pension or annuity payments received in 2013 on Form 1040, line 16a.

---

1. Enter the total pension or annuity payments from Form 1099-R, box 1. Also, enter this amount on Form 1040, line 16a . . . . **1.** _____

2. Enter your cost in the plan at the annuity starting date . . . . **2.** _____

   Note. If you completed this worksheet last year, skip line 3 and enter the amount from line 4 of last year's worksheet on line 4 below (even if the amount of your pension or annuity has changed). Otherwise, go to line 3.

3. Enter the appropriate number from **Table 1** below. **But** if your annuity starting date was **after** 1997 **and** the payments are for your life and that of your beneficiary, enter the appropriate number from **Table 2** below . . . . **3.** _____

4. Divide line 2 by the number on line 3 . . . . **4.** _____

5. Multiply line 4 by the number of months for which this year's payments were made. If your annuity starting date was **before** 1987, skip lines 6 and 7 and enter this amount on line 8. Otherwise, go to line 6 . . . . **5.** _____

6. Enter the amount, if any, recovered tax free in years after 1986. If you completed this worksheet last year, enter the amount from line 10 of last year's worksheet . . . . . **6.** _____

7. Subtract line 6 from line 2 . . . . **7.** _____

8. Enter the **smaller** of line 5 or line 7 . . . . **8.** _____

9. **Taxable amount.** Subtract line 8 from line 1. Enter the result, but not less than zero. Also, enter this amount on Form 1040, line 16b. If your Form 1099-R shows a larger amount, use the amount on this line instead of the amount from Form 1099-R. If you are a retired public safety officer, see *Insurance Premiums for Retired Public Safety Officers* before entering an amount on line 16b . . . . **9.** _____

10. Was your annuity starting date before 1987?

    ☐ **Yes.** (STOP) Leave line 10 blank.

    ☐ **No.**   Add lines 6 and 8. This is the **amount you have recovered tax free** through 2013. You will need this number when you fill out this worksheet next year . . . . **10.** _____

Table 1 for Line 3 Above

	AND your annuity starting date was—	
IF the age at annuity starting date was . . .	**before** November 19, 1996, enter on line 3 . . .	**after** November 18, 1996, enter on line 3 . . .
55 or under	300	360
56–60	260	310
61–65	240	260
66–70	170	210
71 or older	120	160

Table 2 for Line 3 Above

IF the combined ages at annuity starting date were . . .	**THEN enter on line 3 . . .**
110 or under	410
111–120	360
121–130	310
131–140	260
141 or older	210

What's New in 2013

Form 1040. At the time of publication, the IRS had not released a final version of 2013 Form 1040 or the instructions. Line references are based on the 2013 draft version of the form. For the latest information, visit CCHGroup.com/TaxUpdates.

Alternative Minimum Tax. For tax years beginning after 2012, for the first time, certain dollar amounts used in calculating the AMT of individuals will be adjusted for inflation, including the AMTI threshold for applying the 26- or 28-percent AMT rate, and the threshold for the phaseout of the AMT exemption amounts. For 2013, the AMTI threshold for applying the 26- or 28-percent AMT rate rises to $179,500, while the exemption phaseout threshold amount increases to $153,900 for joint filers and qualifying widow(er)s, $115,400 for singles or heads-of-household, and $76,950 for married filing separately.

Motor Vehicle Credits. Only one component credit of the alternative motor vehicle credit, the fuel cell motor vehicle credit, remains available for vehicles purchased in 2013. Also available for vehicles acquired during 2013 are: (1) the plug-in electric drive motor vehicle credit; and (2) the 2- or 3-wheeled plug-in electric vehicle credit.

Education Credits. The American Opportunity Tax Credit, which is a modified version of the Hope Scholarship tax credit, has been extended and is available on an annual basis to taxpayers who pay education-related expenses through 2017.

Adoption Credit. The maximum credit amount for parents who adopted a child in 2013 is $12,970 per child. The credit is phased out if the parent has a modified AGI of $194,580 or higher, and is completely disallowed for parents with an AGI at or above $234,580.

Tax Preparer's Checklist

- ☐ Interview client to see whether anything affecting the tax credits claimed last year has changed or created the potential for claiming additional tax credit.
- ☐ Review AGI phaseout limitation of credits.
- ☐ Review the alternative minimum tax rules and exemption amounts for potential AMT liability.
- ☐ Review prior year return for any long-term unused alternative minimum tax credit, part or all of which may be refundable.
- ☐ Review tax planning to maximize the use of tax credits and flexible spending arrangements.

Section at a Glance

Relevant IRS Publications

- ☐ IRS Publication 502, *Medical and Dental Expenses (Including the Coverage Tax Credit)*, and Form 8885, *Health Coverage Tax Credit*
- ☐ IRS Publication 503, *Child and Dependent Care Expenses*, and Form 2441, *Child and Dependent Care Expenses*
- ☐ IRS Publication 514, *Foreign Tax Credit for Individuals*, Publication 901, *U.S. Tax Treaties*, and Form 1116, *Foreign Tax Credit (Individual, Estate, or Trust)*
- ☐ IRS Publication 524, *Credit for the Elderly or the Disabled*, and Schedule R of Form 1040, *Credit for the Elderly or the Disabled*
- ☐ IRS Publication 530, *Tax Information for Homeowners*, Form 5405, *First-Time Homebuyer Credit and Repayment of the Credit*, and Form 8396, *Mortgage Interest Credit*
- ☐ IRS Publication 590, *Individual Retirement Arrangements (IRAs)*, and Form 8880, *Credit for Qualified Retirement Savings Contributions*
- ☐ IRS Publication 596, *Earned Income Credit*, and Schedule EIC of Form 1040, *Earned Income Credit Qualifying Child Information*
- ☐ IRS Publication 970, *Tax Benefits for Education*, and Form 8863, *Education Credits (American Opportunity and Lifetime Learning Credits)*
- ☐ IRS Publication 972, *Child Tax Credit*, and Schedule 8812 (Form 1040), *Child Tax Credit*

Tax Credits

Tax credits are subtracted directly from a taxpayer's tax liability and they reduce his or her tax, dollar for dollar, by the amount of the allowable credit. The advantage of a tax credit over a tax deduction is that the credit amount is subtracted from the tax liability rather than from taxable income. Thus, a tax credit results in a greater benefit than a tax deduction of the same dollar amount. Tax credits also allow all taxpayers who qualify to obtain a tax benefit, regardless of whether they itemize or take the standard deduction, since credits are available even to those who do not itemize on Schedule A of Form 1040.

A refundable credit will generate a refund in the amount that it exceeds the current year's tax liability. A nonrefundable credit that exceeds the tax liability of the current year will not generate a refund. However, some nonrefundable credits may be carried back or forward to offset income taxes in other years.

See MTG Chapter 13, Tax Credits.

Nonrefundable Credits

The order in which the nonrefundable credits are claimed, which is specified in the Internal Revenue Code, is important both because credit amounts are limited by the taxpayer's tax liability and because not *all* credits allow carryback or carryforward treatment. The nonrefundable credits are:

- the foreign tax credit,
- the child and dependent care credit,
- the elderly and disabled credit,
- the adoption credit,
- the educational credits,
- the retirement savings contributions credit,
- the child tax credit,
- the home mortgage interest credit,
- the first-time homebuyer in the District of Columbia credit,
- the residential energy credit,
- the electric vehicle credit,
- the general business credit,
- the alternative motor vehicle credit (personal use portion),
- the alternative fuel vehicle refueling property credit (residential installation),
- the credit for holders of tax credit bonds, and
- the prior year alternative minimum tax credit.

Child and Dependent Care Credit

A nonrefundable credit is allowed for a portion of qualifying child or dependent care expenses paid for the purpose of allowing the taxpayer to be gainfully employed (IRC §21). The credit is claimed by filing Form 2441, *Child and Dependent Care Expense,* and reporting the credit on Form 1040, line 48.

Eligibility. To be eligible for the child and dependent care credit, the taxpayer must maintain a household for him- or herself and one of the following individuals:

1. A dependent as defined in IRC §152(a)(1), i.e., a qualifying child, that has not yet attained the age of 13. See Tab 1 for the definition of a qualifying child.
2. A dependent who is physically or mentally incapable of caring for him- or herself and has the same principal place of abode as the taxpayer for more than one-half of the year.
3. The taxpayer's spouse who is physically or mentally incapable of caring for him- or herself and has the same principal place of abode of more than one-half of the year.

Taxpayers must provide each dependent's taxpayer identification number, usually a Social Security number, and the identifying number of the service provider (either a Social Security number or an employer identification number (EIN)) in order to claim the credit.

The maximum amount of qualifying expenses eligible for the child and dependent care credit is $3,000 for taxpayers with one qualifying individual, and $6,000 for taxpayers with two or more qualifying individuals. Eligible expenses are further limited to the smaller of the earned income of either the taxpayer or their spouse. Generally, if one spouse is not working, no credit is allowed. However, if the nonworking spouse is a full-time student at an educational institution for at least five months during the calendar year or is mentally or physically incapable of self-care, the law assumes for each month of disability or school attendance an earned income of $250 if there is one qualifying child or dependent and $500 if there are two or more qualifying children or dependents.

 Planning Tip. Depending on the tax bracket of the taxpayer, the number of dependents, and amount of qualifying expenses, comparing the use of the dependent care credit to an employer's dependent care benefit plan is in order to help the taxpayer maximize their tax benefits.

Expenses paid for child and dependent care may qualify for tax benefits under the following methods:

- Taxpayer claims a credit on Form 1040, line 48 and attaches Form 2441, *Child and Dependent Care Expenses.*
- Taxpayer's employer provides a dependent care benefit (DCB) plan that may be either;

- an employer paying incurred expenses for the care of a qualifying dependent directly to the taxpayer or his/her care provider;
- receiving the fair market value for use of an employer-provided daycare center; or
- pre-tax contributions made by the taxpayer to a daycare flexible spending arrangement (FSA).

The maximum amount that may be set aside under an employer's DCB plan to cover qualifying dependent care is $5,000 ($2,500 if the taxpayer's status is married filing separately).

 Caution. The credit may *not* be claimed for expenses that were paid with pre-tax employer-provided benefits or with funds from a pre-tax dependent care flexible spending account. Even though the taxpayer may be unable to use these expenses to claim a credit, the pre-tax benefits must be reconciled on Form 2441.

Example. Gina paid $8,000 in qualifying child care expenses for two children during the year. Her employer reimbursed her for $2,500 of those expenses. The $6,000 maximum is reduced by the $2,500 reimbursement, leaving $3,500 of expenses eligible for the credit.

Married Taxpayers Who File Separate Returns Are Generally Ineligible. Generally, a married taxpayer must file a joint return to claim the credit. However, a married person living apart from his or her spouse may be considered unmarried for this purpose, unless the spouse was a member of the household during the last six months of the tax year. The requirements for being considered unmarried for this purpose are the same as those for Head of Household filing status described in Tab 1.

Divorced Taxpayers. A divorced or legally separated taxpayer with custody of a child who is disabled or under the age of 13 is entitled to the credit even though the taxpayer has released the right to a dependency exemption for the child.

Amount of the Credit. The amount of the child and dependent care credit is from 20% to 35% of eligible expenses, depending on the taxpayer's AGI. To calculate the credit, multiply the amount of qualifying expenses by the percentage (%) for the appropriate AGI range. Qualifying expenses are limited to $3,000 for one qualifying individual or $6,000 for two or more qualifying individuals.

Child and Dependent Care Credit Rates

Adjusted Gross Income (AGI)	%	Adjusted Gross Income (AGI)	%
$ 0 - 15,000	0.35	$29,001 - 31,000	0.27
15,001 - 17,000	0.34	31,001 - 33,000	0.26
17,001 - 19,000	0.33	33,001 - 35,000	0.25
19,001 - 21,000	0.32	35,001 - 37,000	0.24
21,001 - 23,000	0.31	37,001 - 39,000	0.23
23,001 - 25,000	0.30	39,001 - 41,000	0.22
25,001 - 27,000	0.29	41,001 - 43,000	0.21
27,001 - 29,000	0.28	43,001 - No limit	0.20

 Caution. If an employee's W-2 form includes an amount for DCB, Part III of Form 2441 must be completed to report qualified expenses incurred, even if the child and dependent care credit is not claimed. DCBs may result in taxable income if not enough qualified expenses are paid for child or dependent care.

Example. Tony had $4,000 in pre-tax earnings withheld through a DCB plan. He was reimbursed for the entire $4,000, but incurred only $3,500 of qualified child care expenses for the year. Result: $500 of benefits must be included on line 7 of Form 1040 as taxable income.

See MTG ¶ 1301.

Credit for the Elderly or the Disabled

A 15% nonrefundable credit is available to low-income taxpayers who are age 65 or older, or permanently and totally disabled and retired (IRC §22). The credit is claimed by filing Schedule R, *Credit for the Elderly and Disabled.* The credit amount is reported on Form 1040, line 53 by checking box c and writing "Sch R" in space next to the box. The maximum amount of this credit is $1,125.

To qualify, the AGI must be equal to or less than;

- the cutoff for the taxpayer's filing status, or
- the total of nontaxable income from Social Security and other nontaxable pensions must be equal to or less than the cutoff for the taxpayer's filing status.

See the following chart for the cutoff amounts for each filing status.

AGI Limitations for the Elderly or the Disabled Credit

Filing Status	AGI Cutoff	Cutoff for Total of Non-taxable Social Security and Other Nontaxable Pensions
Single, Head of Household, or Qualifying Widow(er)	$17,500	$5,000
Married Filing Jointly **and** both spouses qualify	$25,000	$7,500
Married Filing Jointly **and** only one spouse qualifies	$20,000	$5,000
Married Filing Separately **and** spouses did not live together at any time during the year	$12,500	$3,750

Individuals are considered retired on disability if they have stopped working because of a permanent and total disability, even if they did not formally retire. A physi-

cian must complete a statement certifying that the permanent and total disability existed on the date of retirement and is expect to last at least 12 months or more. This statement should be retained with their income tax records. For more information, see IRS Publication 554, *Credit for the Elderly or the Disabled,* and MTG ¶1302.

Unless they lived apart at all times during the tax year, married taxpayers must file a joint tax return to claim the credit.

Amount of the Credit. For individuals age 65 or older, the initial amount of allowable credit varies with filing status (see the chart below). This initial amount is then reduced by amounts received as pension, annuity or disability benefits that are excludable from gross income and are payable under the Social Security Act (Title II), the Railroad Retirement Act of 1974, or a Veterans Administration program, or that are excludable under a non-Code provision. No reduction is made for pension, annuity or disability benefits for personal injuries or sickness resulting from active service in the armed forces of any country, the National Oceanic and Atmospheric Administration, the Public Health Service, or as a disability annuity payable under the provisions of §808 of the Foreign Service Act of 1980.

Amounts Required to Calculate the Credit for the Elderly or the Disabled

Filing Status	Age and Disability Status	Initial (Maximum) Amount	Reduced by One-Half of AGI Over
Single, Head of Household, or Qualifying Widow(er)	Age 65 or older or under age 65 and retired on permanent and total disability[1]	$5,000	$7,500
Married Filing Jointly	Both age 65 or older or one age 65 or older and the other retired on permanent and total disability or both retired on permanent and total disability[1]	$7,500	$10,000
Married Filing Jointly	Both under age 65 and one retired on permanent and total disability[1] or one 65 or older and the other under age 65 and not retired on permanent and total disability[1]	$5,000	$10,000
Married Filing Separately and spouses did not live together at any time during the year	Age 65 or older or under age 65 and retired on permanent and total disability[1]	$3,750	$5,000

[1] For permanently and totally disabled individuals under age 65, the applicable initial amount may not exceed the amount of taxable disability income.

Adoption Credit

Adoptive parents in 2013 may be able to take either a nonrefundable credit (IRC §23) or an adoption assistance income exclusion (IRC §137) for qualifying adoption expenses incurred in the legal adoption of a child under age 18 or an incapacitated or special needs person. Both a credit and an exclusion may be claimed for the same adoption; however, the same expenses cannot be used to claim both the credit and the exclusion. For 2013, there is a $12,970 per child maximum on qualifying expenses. The credit is phased out for modified AGI between $194,580 and $234,580. File Form 8839, *Qualified Adoption Expenses,*

to claim the credit or exclusion. For further information regarding the adoption credit, such as expense limitations and eligibility requirements, see MTG ¶1307.

Education Credits—American Opportunity (modified Hope Scholarship), and Lifetime Learning Credits

Two nonrefundable tax credits are available to persons who incur expenses for higher education (IRC §25A). Taxpayers claim an education credit on Form 8863, *Education Credits (American Opportunity and Life-*

time Learning Credits), and enter the amounts on Line 49 of Form 1040.

Requirements and Rules for Education Credits. The credits are available for qualified tuition and related expenses of the taxpayer, the taxpayer's spouse, or a dependent of the taxpayer claimed on the taxpayer's return. The credits are not available to married taxpayers filing separate returns, unless one of the taxpayers can qualify under the filing status rules as unmarried for filing purposes.

The American Opportunity Tax Credit (modified Hope Scholarship tax credit) phases out in 2013 for modified AGI between $80,000 and $90,000 if Single, Head of Household or Qualifying Widow(er), or between $160,000 and $180,000 if Married Filing Jointly. The lifetime learning credit phases out in 2013 for modified AGI between $53,000 and $63,000 if Single, Head of Household or Qualifying Widow(er), or between $107,000 and $127,000 if Married Filing Jointly. AGI must be increased by any exclusion or deduction for foreign earned income, foreign housing cost, income for residents of American Samoa and income from Puerto Rico.

A taxpayer may not claim both an American Opportunity and lifetime learning credits for the same student in the same year.

A taxpayer may claim either the tuition and fees deduction under IRC §222 or an educational credit, but not both, for the same student in the same year. See Tab 13 for information on the tuition and fees deduction.

Dependent Claimed on Another Person's Return. If a parent claims a child as a dependent, only that parent, or, in some cases, the other parent (see IRS Publication 970, *Tax Benefits for Education*), may claim the education credit for the child. If the parent does not claim an eligible child, who is a student, as a dependent, only the student can claim the education credit. Qualifying expenses paid by a student are considered to have been paid by the parent if the student is claimed as a dependent on the parent's tax return.

 Planning Tip. It may be advantageous for upper-income parents, whose adjusted gross income either partially or completely phases out the educational credit and most or all of the dependency exemption, to forego claiming the eligible child, who is a student, as a dependent. This would allow the child to claim the full amount of the education credit, assuming the child has a tax liability. This would result in a lower family tax liability than if the parents claimed the student as a dependent.

 Caution. If upper income parents forego claiming an eligible child who is a student as a dependent, to maximize the use of an education credit, this does not mean the child may claim the personal exemption for themselves.

Third-Party Tuition Payments. If a third party (such as a grandparent) makes a payment directly to an eligible educational institution for a student's qualified expenses, the student is treated as receiving the payment from a third party and, in turn, paying the qualified expenses. If the student is not claimed as a dependent on another person's return, the student claims the education credit (if otherwise eligible). If the student is claimed as a dependent on another person's return, the expenses treated as paid by the student are treated as paid by the person claiming the dependency deduction and that person claims the education credit.

Qualified Expenses. The taxpayer may include tuition and fees required for the enrollment or attendance of a student at an eligible educational institution. Fees are included only if the fees must be paid to the institution as a condition of enrollment or attendance. For the American Opportunity Tax Credit, qualifying expenses will also include course materials.

Expenses qualify in the tax year paid. Payments must be for an academic period (such as a quarter, semester, or trimester) that begins either in the same tax year or in the first three months of the following tax year. For institutions that use credit hours or clock hours and not academic periods, each payment period may be treated as an academic period.

An eligible educational institution is any accredited college, university, vocational school or other accredited post-secondary education institution.

See Tab 13 and MTG ¶1303.

Payment with Borrowed Funds. The American Opportunity and lifetime learning credits can be claimed for qualified tuition and related expenses paid with the proceeds of a loan. The expenses are used to figure the credit for the year in which the expenses are paid, not the year in which the loan is repaid.

Caution. The Hope Scholarship credit has been replaced by the American Opportunity Tax Credit (IRC §25A(i)) for 2009 through 2017. Absent further legislation, the Hope credit will return for 2018 and the American Opportunity Tax Credit will terminate.

Hope Scholarship Credit. The Hope Scholarship credit is a nonrefundable tax credit of 100% of the first $1,000 and 50% of the next $1,000 for each of the first two years of post-secondary tuition and fees. The amount of tuition and fees to be used each year in calculating the credit amount is adjusted for inflation.

The following restrictions apply to the Hope credit:

- Students must be enrolled in a program that leads to a degree, certificate, or other recognized educational credential.
- Student must take at least one-half of the normal full-time workload for the student's course of study for at least one academic period beginning during the year.
- The student must be free of any felony conviction for possessing or distributing a controlled substance.
- The first two years of post-secondary education may include two one-year certificate programs. A student who completes a one-year post-secondary certificate program and in a later year completes another one-year post-secondary certificate program may claim the Hope credit for both years if all other requirements are met.

Planning Tip. The Hope credit is claimed per student per year. A family may have more than one eligible student in a year.

American Opportunity Tax Credit. For 2009 through 2017, a modified version of the Hope Scholarship credit, called the American Opportunity Tax Credit, is available. The amount of the credit is 100 percent of the tuition and related expenses paid by the taxpayer during the tax year for education furnished to the eligible student during any academic period beginning in the tax year up to $2,000, and 25 percent of the next $2,000 of the same expenses, for a maximum credit of $2,500. Qualified expenses are the same as for purposes of the Hope Scholarship credit, except that they include course materials, whether or not they are required as a condition of enrollment. The American Opportunity Tax Credit is allowed for first four years of post-secondary education per student at an eligible educational institution (IRC §25A(i)).

Unlike the Hope credit, the American Opportunity Tax Credit is refundable up to 40 percent of the credit amount and is allowed against the alternative minimum tax (AMT). However, no portion of the credit is refundable for any taxpayer that is subject to the kiddie tax.

Lifetime Learning Credit. The lifetime learning credit is a nonrefundable tax credit of 20% of up to $10,000 of qualified tuition and fees paid during the tax year. The maximum credit allowed is $2,000. There is no limit on the number of years for which the credit can be claimed. The credit is per taxpayer and does not vary based on the number of students in a family. The credit is not workload-based; it is allowed for students taking one or more courses. Both degree and nondegree courses are counted. The credit is available for undergraduate, graduate, and professional degree students and for students acquiring or improving job skills.

Residential Energy Credits
Nonbusiness (Residential) Energy Property Credit

This credit is to assist taxpayers in defraying the expenses of either improving their principal residence's energy efficiency or replacing heating and cooling systems with more efficient units (IRC §25C). For property placed in service in 2013, the credit amount is equal to (a) 10 percent of the taxpayer's residential energy property expenditures, plus (b) the cost of qualified energy efficiency improvements for the tax year. The amount of credit a taxpayer may claim is limited to a maximum of $500 over the lifetime of the taxpayer, and separate annual limitations apply to different types of property. These are: $200 for exterior windows and skylights, reduced by the aggregate amount of previously allowed credits for windows and skylights; $50 for any advanced main air circulating fan; $150 for any qualified natural gas, propane, or oil furnace or hot water boiler; and $300 for any item of energy-efficient building property. The credit is to be treated as a nonrefundable personal credit allowing the credit to be claimed against both a taxpayer's regular and alternative minimum tax liabilities.

The taxpayer must be the original owner and place the property into use prior to January 1, 2014. Any increase in the basis of the residential property must be reduced by the credit amount claimed. The credit will be claimed on Form 5695, *Residential Energy Credits*.

Planning Tip. Typically, the amount paid with respect to any improvements to property that improved its energy efficiency will increase the taxpayer's basis in the property. The reduction for the credit would, presumably, partially or fully offset this increase.

Qualified energy efficiency improvements include the following building envelope components that are installed on or in the taxpayer's main home located in the United States:

- insulation material or system that is specifically and primarily designed to reduce the heat loss or gain of a home when installed in or on that home and that meet certain efficiency criteria;
- exterior windows and doors, including skylights and certain storm doors; and
- any metal roofs, but only if this roof has appropriate pigmented coatings or cooling granules that are specifically and primarily designed to reduce the heat gain of the home.

These components must be new, and they must be expected to remain in use for at least five years.

 Caution. The costs for onsite preparation, assembly or original installation of the qualified energy efficiency improvements *cannot* be included in the amounts used to determine the amount of credit.

Qualified residential energy property is any of the following:

- certain electric heat pump water heaters, electric heat pumps, central air conditioners, and natural gas, propane, oil water, or biomass fueled heaters;
- qualified natural gas, propane, or oil furnaces or hot water boilers; and
- certain advanced main air circulating fans used in natural gas, propane, or oil furnaces.

The costs of onsite preparation, assembly, or original installation of residential energy property (unlike such costs related to qualified energy efficiency improvements) are included in the amount of costs to be used for determining the credit amount.

 Planning Tip. Married taxpayers who maintain separate main residences but still file jointly can each claim the nonbusiness energy property credit. Each figures their credit amount on their own Form 5695, which is attached to Form 1040. The total amount is written in on line 52 with the phrase "more than one main home" written on the dotted line to the left of the box.

 Caution. Qualified nonbusiness energy property must meet certain energy performance and quality standards to be able to claim the credit. The manufacturer's written certification may be relied upon but should be retained with tax records.

For further information on the nonbusiness (residential) energy property credit, see MTG at ¶1341.

Residential Energy Efficient Property Credit

This energy credit allows taxpayers to claim a credit in an amount equal to 30 percent of the expenditures, including installation costs, for qualified solar water heating, solar electric equipment, including but not limited to photovoltaic equipment, fuel cell energy property, geothermal heat pump property, and small wind energy property (IRC §25D). The credit for fuel cell property, however, is $500 per half kilowatt of capacity. Any unused credit due to the tax liability limitation rules may be carried forward to succeeding tax years. The property must be installed and used in a home in the United States. The credit will also be claimed on Form 5695, *Residential Energy Credits*.

 Planning Tip. Qualified residential solar energy property installed and used in a home in the United States does *not* have to be on the taxpayer's principal or main home.

Qualified solar water heating property expenditures are for property used to heat water for use in a home, with at least one-half of the energy used being derived from the sun. The property must be certified by the nonprofit Solar Rating Certification Corporation or a comparable entity endorsed by the government of the state in which the property is installed.

 Caution. Costs allocated to solar water heating property of a swimming pool, hot tub, or any other energy storage medium which has a function other than storage do not qualify for purposes of claiming the residential energy efficient property credit.

Qualified solar electric property expenditures are for property that uses solar energy to generate electricity for use in a home and includes costs related to solar panels or other property installed as a roof or a portion of a roof.

Planning Tip. There is no lifetime maximum, as for the nonbusiness energy credit, for the residential energy efficient property credit. A taxpayer could install a solar heating system and a solar electrical system in the same year and potentially be eligible to claim the full amount of both credits.

Qualified fuel cell property expenditures are for an integrated system comprising a fuel cell stack assembly and associated balance of plant components that converts a fuel into electricity using electrochemical means. The fuel cell property must have a nameplate capacity of at least one-half kilowatt of electricity using an electrochemical process and an electricity-only generation efficiency of greater than 30 percent to qualify for the credit.

Caution. If installing qualified fuel cell property, the installation must be in a home located in the United States, which must be the taxpayer's principal residence. This is different from the rules for solar water heating or electrical generation property, which only requires installation in a home used by the taxpayer in the United States.

Qualifying small wind energy property expenditures are for property that uses a wind turbine to generate electricity for use in connection with the taxpayer's residence located in the United States. If the residence is occupied by two or more taxpayers, the total credit amount for the year *cannot* exceed the annual maximum limit.

Qualifying geothermal heat pump property expenditures are for property that uses ground water as a thermal energy source to heat a U.S. residential dwelling unit, or as a thermal heat energy sink to cool the unit that meets the Energy Star program requirements.

For further information on the residential energy efficient property credit, see MTG at ¶1342

Planning Tip. For 2013, the residential energy efficient property credit is allowed to the full extent of the taxpayer's regular tax liability, reduced by any foreign tax credit, and alternative minimum tax liability. If the amount of the residential energy efficient property credit exceeds this limit, the excess can be carried to the next tax year and added to the credit allowable during that year.

Foreign Tax Credit

A taxpayer may choose between claiming a foreign tax credit (IRC §27) or a tax deduction on Schedule A of Form 1040 for taxes paid to a foreign government or a U.S. possession on income that is also subject to U.S. federal income tax. A taxpayer cannot take both the credit and claim the deduction on the same foreign tax. However, the deduction on Schedule A is allowed for certain taxes that do not qualify for the foreign tax credit due to boycott provisions or limitations imposed by IRC §901(j)(2).

Election Not to File Form 1116, Foreign Tax Credit. Taxpayers are allowed to claim the foreign tax credit on line 47 of Form 1040 without regard to the foreign tax credit limitation and without filing Form 1116 if all of the following apply:

1. The foreign taxes paid or accrued during the year do not exceed $300 ($600 for joint filers).
2. All foreign income is "passive income" (such as dividends, interest, annuities, and rents and royalties not from an active trade or business).
3. All foreign income is reported on Form 1099-DIV, 1099-INT, or a similar statement.

No excess foreign taxes may be carried over to or from a tax year to which the election applies, but carryovers to and from other years are unaffected.

Form 1116, Foreign Tax Credit. A separate Form 1116 must be filed for each category of income listed above Part I of the form.

In *Part I, Taxable Income or Loss From Sources Outside the United States,* the taxpayer begins by entering the gross income from sources within the country named for the category of income designated on the form. This does not include any income that has been excluded on Form 2555, *Foreign Earned Income.*

Caution. The taxpayer must include income even if it is not taxable by the foreign country.

Deductions and losses definitely related to earning this income, plus a pro-rata share of other expenses and losses, are then subtracted from the gross income figure.

In *Part II, Foreign Taxes Paid or Accrued,* the taxpayer must enter the foreign tax paid in both the foreign currency denominations and converted to U.S. dollars. Foreign tax on passive income does not have to be entered in foreign currency amounts.

In *Part III, Figuring the Credit,* the foreign taxes paid, from Part II, are adjusted to arrive at total foreign taxes available for credit. Adjustments include carrybacks and carryovers of foreign taxes and taxes on income excluded on Form 2555. If only part of the taxpayer's income is excluded on Form 2555, pro-rate the adjustment for this item. Adjustments are also made for dividends and lump sum distributions. The maximum foreign tax credit is generally limited to the allocated amount of U.S. tax imposed on the foreign income or the actual foreign tax paid, whichever is less.

Part IV, Summary of Credits from Separate Parts III, is filled out if more than one Form 1116 is being filed. Combine the credits from each form and enter the total in Part IV.

Child Tax Credit

The child tax credit allows an individual to claim a credit for each qualifying child, as defined in IRC §152(c), who is under age 17 on the last day of the tax year (IRC §24). See Tab 1 for the definition of a qualifying child. The child tax credit amount is $1,000 per qualifying child.

 Caution. A child is a qualifying child of the taxpayer only if the taxpayer *can and does* claim an exemption for the child. The child must be younger than the taxpayer.

Part I of Schedule 8812 (Form 1040), *Child Tax Credit,* must be completed for each child who has an individual taxpayer identification number (ITIN) and for whom the taxpayer is claiming the credit. The taxpayer must indicate whether or not the child has met the "substantial presence" test.

Phaseout Based on Modified AGI. The child tax credit is phased out for individuals with modified AGI over $75,000 for single taxpayers, $110,000 for married individuals filing jointly, and $55,000 for married individuals filing separately. Specifically, the credit is reduced by $50 for each $1,000 (or fraction thereof) of modified AGI (MAGI) over the threshold. Therefore, a $1,000 credit will be completely phased out at $20,000 of income over the threshold, but because excess income must be increased to the next $1,000 rather than being rounded down, the full benefit actually is lost at $19,001 of income over the threshold amount. Thus, the actual phaseout range for a single individual with one qualifying child is between $75,000 and $94,001 of MAGI. The actual phaseout range for a single individual with two qualifying children is between $75,000 and $114,001. MAGI (modified adjusted gross income) is adjusted gross income determined without regard to the exclusion for foreign earned income, the exclusion for foreign housing costs, and exclusion of income from certain U.S. possessions and Puerto Rico.

Additional Child Tax Credit May Be Available. The additional child tax credit allows a portion of the child tax credit to be refundable for certain taxpayers who get less than the full amount of the child tax credit. For details, see *Additional Child Tax Credit* under Refundable Credits.

Tax Liability Limitation. In 2013, the nonrefundable portion of the child tax credit is allowed to the full extent of the taxpayer's regular tax liability, minus any applicable foreign tax credit, plus alternative minimum tax liability.

Retirement Savings Contributions Credit

This nonrefundable credit is targeted toward low- and middle-income taxpayers who make contributions to a retirement plan (IRC §25B). The credit amount is determined by multiplying the applicable percentage for the taxpayer's filing status and AGI (see the table below) by their contribution amount to a qualified retirement plan, except that the total amount of credit claimed cannot exceed $2,000. Taxpayers are allowed both a deduction for contributions to a qualified retirement plan and an exclusion for the retirement savings contributions credit (also referred to as the "saver's credit"). The total amount of the saver's credit claimed by a taxpayer is allowed to the full extent of the taxpayer's regular tax liability, reduced by any applicable foreign tax credit, and alternative minimum tax liability. Form 8880, *Credit for Qualified Retirement Savings Contributions,* is used to claim the credit.

Retirement Savings Credit Limitations

Adjusted Gross Income			% of AGI Allowed as Credit
MFJ	HOH	Single, MFS, QW	
$0 - $35,500	$0 - $26,625	$0 - $17,750	50%
$35,501 - $38,500	$26,626 - $28,875	$17,751 - $19,250	20%
$38,501 - $59,000	$28,876 - $44,250	$19,251 - $29,500	10%
$59,001 or more	$44,251 or more	$29,501 or more	0%

Mortgage Interest Credit

This nonrefundable credit is targeted toward low-income homeowners who obtain qualified mortgage credit certificates (MCCs) from state or local governments (IRC §25). The credit amount is equal to the percentage as listed on the MCC of the interest paid on the mortgage amount. Only the taxpayer's main home/principal residence is eligible. The credit rate is provided on the MCC and cannot be less than 10% or more than 50%. If the certificate credit rate is more than 20%, a $2,000 limit applies to the credit. Any unused credit amount due to the tax liability limitation rule imposed by IRC §26 may be carried forward for three years. Mortgage interest deducted on Schedule A, Form 1040 must be reduced by any credit allowed under this provision. Form 8396, *Mortgage Interest Credit,* is used to claim the credit.

See MTG ¶1306.

 Planning Tip. Taxpayers need to be aware that if the main home/principal residence upon which the mortgage interest certificate is issued is disposed of before the tenth year, a portion of the credit amount must be recaptured under the formula in IRC §143(m).

District of Columbia First-Time Homebuyer Credit

First-time homebuyers who purchased a principal residence in the District of Columbia before January 1, 2012, were eligible to claim a credit of up to $5,000 ($2,500 in the case of a married person filing separately) (IRC §1400C). The credit was phased out ratably between AGI of $70,000 and $90,000 ($110,000 to $130,000, for joint filers). Although the residence must have been purchased before 2012, any unused credit is carried forward indefinitely. The taxpayer's basis in the home must be reduced by the amount of credit claimed.

See MTG ¶1308.

Alternative Motor Vehicle Credit

To encourage taxpayers to use cars powered by alternative fuel sources, the alternative motor vehicle credit was enacted. The credit is actually the sum of five separate credits each based on the alternative propulsion system used to power the car (IRC §30B). The credit amounts are determined by the IRS using numerous factors including, but not limited to, the car's weight, the annual fuel consumption and the percentage increase in miles per gallon over the base year, 2002. The amount of the credit that may be claimed is further limited by the tax liability limitation under IRC §30B(g)(2). For individual taxpayers, the credit is allowed to the full extent of the taxpayer's regular income tax, reduced by the foreign tax credit, plus any alternative minimum tax liability. Although the credit for all the components of the alternative motor vehicle credit is claimed on Form 8910, *Alternative Motor Vehicle Credit,* for vehicles purchased in 2013, only one component credit, the fuel cell motor vehicle credit (discussed below), remains. One other component credit, the plug-in conversion credit, was available for conversions completed prior to January 1, 2012. The other three component credits, the hybrid motor vehicle credit, the alternative fuel motor vehicle credit, and the lean-burn technology credit, were available for vehicles purchased prior to January 1, 2011. See MTG ¶1345-¶1349.

Fuel Cell Motor Vehicle Credit

The qualified fuel cell motor vehicle credit is available for vehicles purchased before January 1, 2015. Fuel cell motor vehicles are vehicles propelled by power derived from one or more cells that convert chemical energy directly into electricity by combining oxygen with hydrogen fuel that is stored on board the vehicle and may or may not require reformation before use, and in the case of a passenger automobile or light truck, is certified to meet certain emission standards (IRC §30B(b)). The amount of the credit is based on the weight class of the vehicle. A complete list of qualifying vehicles and credit amounts can be found on the IRS website at http://www.irs.gov/Businesses/Corporations/Qualified-Fuel-Cell-Vehicles.

Alternative Fuel Vehicle Refueling Property Credit

The alternative fuel vehicle refueling credit is available to taxpayers who install in their residence the necessary equipment to refuel their alternative fuel motor vehicles (IRC §30C). The credit is available for property placed in service before January 1, 2014, except for property related to hydrogen, which is available for property placed in service prior to January 1, 2015. The credit amount is 30 percent of each property's cost, limited to a per-location total of $30,000 for property of a character subject to an allowance for depreciation and $1,000 for other property. This amount could be further reduced by the tax liability limitation, which limits the credit amount that may be claimed to the excess of the regular tax liability less the sum of all nonrefundable personal credits, the foreign tax credit, and the alternative motor vehicle credit over the alternative minimum tax (IRC §30C(d)(2)). The credit is claimed on Form 8911, *Alternative Fuel Vehicle Refueling Property Credit*.

Electric Drive Motor Vehicle Credits

New Qualified Plug-in Electric Drive Motor Vehicle Credit

The plug-in electric drive motor vehicle credit for 2013 is equal to $2,500 plus $417 for each kilowatt hour of battery capacity over five kilowatts up to $5,000. The maximum credit amount cannot exceed $7,500. A new qualified plug-in electric drive motor vehicle must meet requirements similar to those of the alternative motor vehicle credit. A vehicle meets the requirements of the credit if it:

- is first used by taxpayer,
- is acquired for use or lease and not resale,
- is made by a manufacturer,
- is used in the United States,
- is treated as a motor vehicle for purposes of title II of the Clean Air Act,
- has a gross vehicle weight rating (GVWR) of less than 14,000 lbs., and
- is propelled to a significant extent by an electric motor which draws electricity from a battery having a capacity of not less than four kilowatt hours and is rechargeable from an external source.

A vehicle used in a trade or business will be treated as a component of the general business credit. The personal use of such a vehicle will be treated as a nonrefundable personal credit. The credit begins to phase out after 200,000 vehicles have been sold for use in the United States. The phaseout period begins with the second calendar quarter following the calendar quarter in which the 200,000th unit is sold. Certain other requirements apply, including satisfying clean air standards. A list of qualifying vehicles can be found on the IRS website at http://www.irs.gov/Businesses/Qualified-Vehicles-Acquired-after-12-31-2009.

For further information, see MTG ¶1351.

2- and 3-Wheeled Plug-in Electric Vehicles

The plug-in electric drive motor vehicle credit has been extended to cover 2- and 3-wheeled plug-in electric vehicles acquired during 2012 or 2013 (IRC §30D(g)). The credit is equal to the applicable amount with respect to each new qualified 2- or 3-wheeled plug-in electric drive vehicle. The applicable amount is equal to the lesser of:

1. 10 percent of the cost of the qualified 2- or 3-wheeled plug-in electric drive vehicle; or
2. $2,500.

In order for a vehicle to qualify as a 2- or 3-wheeled plug-in electric drive vehicle, the vehicle must have 2 or 3 wheels, be made by a manufacturer, and be acquired for use or lease by the taxpayer and not resale. The original use of the vehicle must begin with the taxpayer.

For more information, see MTG ¶1351.

Credit for Prior Year Minimum Tax

This credit can be carried forward indefinitely and is for the amount of the AMT that was attributable to deferral items (timing preferences and adjustments). Any amount of the AMT generated by "exclusion items," including but not limited to state and local taxes, employee business and investment expenses, personal exemptions, and private activity bond interest does *not* generate a prior year minimum tax credit amount. Form 8801, *Credit for Prior Year Minimum Tax—Individuals, Estates, and Trusts,* is used to claim the credit.

General Business Credit

The general business credit is a limited nonrefundable credit against income tax that is claimed after all other nonrefundable credits. In Part I of Form 3800, *General Business Credit*, the taxpayer determines the current tax year credit for credits not allowed against the tentative minimum tax. In Part II, the taxpayer determines the allowable credit for the current tax year. Part III, which must be completed before filling out Parts I and II, lists the various credits that are being claimed. Form 3800 must be filed to claim any of the general business credits.

Generally, if the taxpayer cannot use part or all of the credit because of the tax liability limit, he or she may carry the unused credit back one tax year. To carry back an unused credit, file an amended Form 1040 for the prior tax year or apply for a tentative refund on Form 1045, *Application for Tentative Refund*.

If the taxpayer has unused credit after carrying it back, he or she may carry it forward to each of the 20 tax years after the year of the credit.

Filing Tip. Several of the general business credits are no longer subject to the general business credit limitation rule (IRC §38(c)(4)). The limitation on the amount of these credits is calculated separately and the tentative tax is to be treated as zero. This will allow for the maximum use of these credits against both the regular and the alternative minimum tax liabilities. These credits are:

- the alcohol used as fuels credit;
- the low income housing credit;
- the credit for portion of employer Social Security taxes paid with respect to employee cash tips;
- the railroad tax maintenance credit;
- the investment credit, to the extent attributable to the energy credit or to the rehabilitation credit;
- the work opportunity tax credit;
- the small employer health insurance credit; and
- the renewable electricity production credit to the extent it is attributable to electricity or refined coal produced at facilities originally placed into service after October 22, 2004, and during the four year period beginning on the date the facility was originally placed in service.

For further information, see MTG ¶1365–¶1365LL.

 Caution. The effective date language would indicate that any carryforwards of these credits from prior years would still be subject to the tax liability limitation rule of the general business credit in effect in the year the credit amount was generated.

 Planning Tip. Certain of the general business credits are allowed to be taken as a deduction in the year after the taxpayer ceases to exist or the 20-year carryforward period ends (IRC §196).

Tax Liability Limitation

Limitation on the Use of Nonrefundable Personal Credits

In 2013, all nonrefundable personal credits that may be claimed are allowed to the full extent of the regular tax liability for the tax year, reduced by any applicable foreign tax credit and alternative minimum tax liability (IRC §26(a)(1)). Certain specified nonrefundable credits are excluded from application of this rule and are subject to special limitations and claiming order. These specified credits are: the child tax credit, the adoption credit, the American Opportunity tax credit, the retirement savings contributions (saver's) credit, the residential energy efficient property credit, the alternative motor vehicle credit, and the new plug-in electric drive motor vehicle credit.

.

Refundable Credits

First-Time Homebuyer Credit.

The first-time homebuyer credit could be claimed on the purchase of a principal residence before May 1, 2010, but there were two exceptions. The first exception was for members of the military, foreign service, or intelligence community who were on extended active duty for at least 90 days between December 31, 2008, and May 1, 2010; they had until before May 1, 2011, to purchase a principal residence, or enter into a written binding contract which called for the purchase to be completed prior to July 1, 2011. The second exception was for taxpayers who entered into a written binding contract prior to May 1, 2010, and contracted to complete the purchase before July 1, 2010. Due to the financial sector's slow response time on issuing new mortgages, the closing date for contracts entered into prior to May 1, 2010, was extended until September 30, 2010. For all taxpayers, the credit may be recaptured in years after the purchase. The credit has not been available for purchases after 2011; any recapture of the credit is reported on Form 5405, *Repayment of the First-Time Homebuyer Credit.*

Recapture of First-Time Homebuyer Credit. Taxpayers who purchased and claimed the first-time homebuyer credit in 2008 will continue to recapture the credit amount claimed over a 15-year period that began in 2010. The recapture amount is equal to one-fifteenth (or six and-two-thirds percent) of the credit amount claimed. The recapture of the credit amount is accelerated if the home is disposed of or ceases to be the taxpayer's principal residence. Thus, in the year of the sale or cessation of use as the taxpayer's principal residence, the tax liability for the year is increased by the balance of the credit amount. A safe harbor for taxpayers is that the recapture amount cannot exceed the amount of gain from the sale of the home. For purposed of determining the amount of gain, which might limit the accelerated recapture amount, the taxpayer's basis in the home before the sale is reduced by the amount of unrecaptured credit amount.

There are three exceptions to the accelerated recapture of the first-time homebuyer credit:

- in the event of the death of the taxpayer;
- upon an involuntary or compulsory conversion of

the home, as long as a new principal residence is acquired within two years; and

- upon transfer of the property to a spouse or former spouse incident to a divorce.

 Caution. The modifications to the first-time homebuyer credit regarding recapture were not made retroactive. For purchases made between April 8, 2008, and December 31, 2008, the original recapture rules still apply.

 Filing Tip. Taxpayers who purchased and claimed the maximum first-time homebuyer credit in 2008 should have begun to recapture the credit amount on their 2010 income tax returns. The recapture amount at the maximum credit amount is $500 and is an addition to tax.

Earned Income Credit

A refundable credit is available to certain low-income individuals who have earned income, meet adjusted gross income thresholds, and do not have disqualifying income (IRC §32). The IRS has developed an online assistant, the Earned Income Tax Credit Assistant, to assist taxpayers, as well as professional tax preparers, in determining eligibility for the earned income credit. The online assistant is available at http://www.irs.gov/Individuals/Earned-Income-Tax-Credit-(EITC)-%E2%80%93--Use-the-EITC-Assistant-to-Find-Out-if-You-Should-Claim-it.

Qualifying Taxpayer

To qualify for the EIC, a taxpayer must meet the following requirements:

1. The taxpayer has earned income.
2. The taxpayer's investment income is not more than $3,300 in 2013.
3. The taxpayer's filing status is not married filing separately.
4. The taxpayer, his or her spouse (if married), and any qualifying children have Social Security numbers. Other identifying numbers, such as ITINs, do not qualify.
5. Neither the taxpayer nor his or her spouse (if married) is the qualifying child of another person.
6. The taxpayer did not exclude any 2013 income by filing Form 2555 or Form 2555-EZ.
7. The taxpayer was not a nonresident alien for any part of the year. (See IRS Publication 596, *Earned Income Credit (EIC)*, for exceptions to this rule.)

 Filing Tip. Special rules apply for military personnel stationed outside the U.S. See IRS Publication 596, *Earned Income Credit*, for more information.

Taxpayers without Qualifying Children

The following additional rules apply to taxpayers without qualifying children:

1. The taxpayer's earned income and AGI for 2013 must each be less than $14,340 ($19,680 for joint filers).
2. The taxpayer must be at least 25 years old but less than 65 years old at the end of the tax year. If married, either spouse can meet the age requirement.
3. The taxpayer (and spouse, if married) cannot qualify as a dependent on any other return.
4. The taxpayer cannot be a qualifying child for another person.
5. The taxpayer's main home must be in the U.S. for more than half the year.

Taxpayers with Qualifying Children

The following additional rules apply to taxpayers with qualifying children:

1. The taxpayer's earned income and AGI must each be less than $37,870 ($43,210 for joint filers) with one qualifying child, or $43,038 ($48,378 for joint filers) with two qualifying children or $46,227 ($51,567 for joint filers) with three or more qualifying children.
2. Schedule EIC must be completed and attached to the taxpayer's return to provide information about qualifying child(ren).

The qualifying child must meet the requirements under the uniform definition of a qualifying child, which are:

1. Relationship–The child must be the taxpayer's:
   - Son, daughter, adopted child, stepchild, or a descendant (for example, grandchild) of any of them, or eligible foster child; or
   - Brother, sister, stepbrother, stepsister, or a descendant (for example, niece or nephew) of any of them.
2. Age–The qualifying child must be:
   - Under age 19 at the end of 2013 or under 24 and a student or permanently and totally disabled at any time during the year, regardless of age.

 Example. Jack's son turned 19 on December 10. Unless he was disabled or a full-time student, he is not a qualifying child because, at the end of the year, he was not under age 19.

3. Residency–has the same principal place of abode with the taxpayer for more than one-half of the year.
4. Income–child has not provided more than one-half of his or her own support during the year.
5. Dependency–claimed by the taxpayer as a dependent on line 6c of Form 1040 or 1040A.

Foster/Adopted Child

A foster child is eligible only if the child is placed with the taxpayer by any authorized placement agency or by judgment or decree of a court of competent jurisdiction. An adopted child is eligible only if the child is either legally adopted by the taxpayer or placed by an authorized agency with the taxpayer for adoption.

Kidnapped Child

A kidnapped child is treated as having lived with the taxpayer for more than one-half of the year if the child resided with the taxpayer for more than one-half of the year prior to the date of the kidnapping. Additionally, authorities must determine that the child was not kidnapped by a person related to the child. A taxpayer may continue to claim a kidnapped child until the child either has been determined to be deceased or has reached his or her 18th birthday.

 Caution. The tie-breaker rules apply when two or more taxpayers can claim the same qualifying child.

Tie-Breaker Rules

Sometimes a child is a qualifying child of more than one person for purposes of the EIC. However, only one person can treat that child as a qualifying child in order to claim the earned income credit. If two or more persons have the same qualifying child, they must decide who will claim the credit using that qualifying child. But if they cannot agree and two or more persons wish to claim the credit using the same child, the tie-breaker rule applies. If the other person is a spouse and they file a joint return, this rule does not apply.

Under the tie-breaker rule, only the following taxpayers may treat the child as a qualifying child:

1. The parents, if they file a joint return.
2. The parent, if only one of the persons is the child's parent.
3. The parent with whom the child lived the longest during the tax year, if two of the persons are the child's parents and they do not file a joint return together.
4. The parent with the highest AGI if the child lived with each parent for the same amount of time during the tax year and they do not file a joint return together.

5. The person with the highest AGI, if none of the persons is the child's parent.
6. If the parents of an individual may claim the individual as a qualifying child but neither actually do so, the individual may be claimed as the qualifying child of another taxpayer if the adjusted gross income of the taxpayer is higher than the highest adjusted gross income of either parent.

 Caution. The IRS issued Notice 2006-86 clarifying the tie-breaker rules. It is important to note that if two taxpayers may claim a qualifying child only the taxpayer actually claiming the child may claim any of the tax benefits that adopted the uniform definition of a child. The only exception that will allow the tax benefits to be divided between two taxpayers is for the child's parents that meet the requirements under IRC §152(e):

- the child is in the custody of one or both parents for more than one-half of the year;
- the child receives over one-half of the child's support during the calendar year from the child's parents; and
- the parents are separated or divorced under a written decree or separation agreement, or have lived separate and apart at all times during the last six months of the calendar year.

Investment Income

Disqualified income, $3,300 for 2013, includes an individual's capital gain net income and net passive income in addition to interest, dividends, tax-exempt interest, and nonbusiness rents or royalties.

Earned Income Defined

This credit is based on earned income, which includes all wages, salaries, tips, and other employee compensation (including strike benefits), plus the amount of the taxpayer's net earnings from self-employment, determined with regard to the deduction for one-half of self-employment taxes. Earned income is determined without regard to community property laws.

 Caution. Remember the rental value of housing or the housing allowance for ministers that is provided as part of their compensation is excludable for income tax purposes, but is includible in net earnings for self-employment purposes. Thus, for earned income credit purposes, the rental value or housing allowance is includible in earned income.

Earned income does **not** include:

- Interest and dividends
- Welfare benefits (including AFDC payments)
- Veteran's benefits
- Pensions or annuities
- Alimony and child support
- Social Security and railroad retirement benefits
- Worker's compensation
- Unemployment compensation
- Taxable scholarships or fellowships that are not reported on Form W-2
- Income of nonresident alien individuals not connected with U.S. business
- Amounts received for services performed by prison inmates while in prison
- Salary deferrals, such as contributions to 401(k) plans
- Nontaxable military pay (including combat pay (but see exception following), the Basic Allowance for Housing (BAH), and the Basic Allowance for Subsistence (BAS))

Exception for Nontaxable Combat Pay

Members of the military are allowed to elect to include nontaxable combat pay in their earned income for purposes of the earned income tax credit. The purpose of this election is to increase the amounts of earned income tax credit available to families where the majority of their income is excludable combat pay.

 Filing Tip. To ensure that the maximum amount of the earned income tax credit for military taxpayers is claimed, the credit should be calculated twice: once electing to include nontaxable combat pay as earned income and once excluding nontaxable combat pay in earned income.

 Caution. The IRS will treat a claimed earned income credit as a mathematical error if the Federal Case Registry of Child Support Orders shows that the taxpayer is the noncustodial parent of a child claimed as a qualifying child for EIC or the qualifying child's social security number and last name fails to match the information on file with the Social Security Administration.

Additional Child Tax Credit

Though the child tax credit is generally nonrefundable, a portion of the credit is refundable regardless of the amount of the taxpayer's regular tax or alternative minimum tax liability (IRC §24(d)).

The child tax credit is refundable to the extent of 15 percent of the taxpayer's earned income in excess of $3,000 up to the per-child amount. The amount of the nonrefundable credit is reduced by the amount of the refundable credit.

For taxpayers with one or more qualifying children, the additional child tax credit is the smaller of:

1. The amount of the child tax credit remaining after reducing regular tax and AMT to zero, or
2. Fifteen percent of the taxpayer's earned income in excess of $3,000.

For taxpayers with three or more qualifying children, the additional child tax credit is the greater of:

1. The result of the above calculation for all taxpayers with one or more qualifying children, or
2. The taxpayer's employee share of FICA taxes (plus one-half SE tax liability, if any) in excess of the Earned Income Credit (EIC), limited to the amount of the child tax credit remaining after reducing regular tax and AMT to zero.

For purposes of the additional child tax credit, earned income is defined as it is for the EIC, but only to the extent included in taxable income.

Taxpayers who have more than $3,000 of earned income must complete Schedule 8812, *Child Tax Credit*, of Form 1040 to compute the refundable portion of the credit

Credit for Federal Tax Paid on Fuels

Use Form 4136, *Credit for Federal Tax Paid on Fuels*, to claim a credit for fuel used on a farm, for off-highway business use, and for other qualifying uses (IRC §34). No credit is allowed if the fuel or mixture is produced outside the United States for use outside the United States (IRC §6426(i) and 6427(e)(5)).

Health Coverage Tax Credit

A credit of up to 72.5% is available for months beginning after February 12, 2011, and before January 1, 2014, of health insurance premiums paid is available to members of the following groups:

- Eligible Trade Adjustment Assistance (TAA) recipients under Act Sec. 231 of the Trade Act of 1974
- Eligible alternative TAA recipients as defined under Act Sec. 246 of the Trade Act of 1974
- Eligible Pension Benefit Guaranty Corporation (PBGC) recipients (IRC §35).

Qualified individuals will claim the health coverage tax credit using Form 8885, *Health Coverage Tax Credit*.

See MTG ¶ 1332.

Alternative Minimum Tax (AMT)

Congress enacted the alternative minimum tax (AMT) in 1969 in an effort to ensure that wealthy taxpayers are unable to avoid significant federal tax liability through the use of tax shelters and other means. This was the response of Congress after learning that, in the 1966 tax year, 155 taxpayers with adjusted gross income of $200,000 or more paid no federal income tax at all.

An unintended result in more recent years has been that more and more middle-income taxpayers must complete Form 6251, *Alternative Minimum Tax–Individuals,* and pay AMT. Congress has repeatedly provided short-term relief to some taxpayers, extended the increased AMT exemption amounts and provided waivers that ensure that the AMT did not render personal tax credits useless. Despite these past modifications, many more taxpayers still found themselves paying AMT. Although Congress enacted many technical changes over past decades, the basic AMT rules have remained intact.

 Gray Area. The difficulty of projecting AMT tax liability in advance makes it challenging for taxpayers to compute it for the purpose of making required estimated tax payments; this can result in penalties. The "no estimate" safe harbor is the safest bet; see Tab 11.

Specific Provisions

The AMT is a separate system from the regular income tax, with its own rules governing taxable and nontaxable income and the timing of deductions and credits (IRC §55).

Complex Computation. For most taxpayers, the first step for determining whether they must complete Form 6251, *Alternative Minimum Tax–Individuals*, is to use the web-based "AMT Assistant" provided by the IRS, which is found at http://www.irs.gov/Businesses/Small-Businesses-&-Self-Employed/Alternative-Minimum-Tax-(AMT)-Assistant-for-Individuals. Then, taxpayers may have to complete Form 6251, a 60-line form, possibly to find out they owe little or no AMT. Other taxpayers, such as those claiming one or more of the general business credits, must complete Form 6251 even though they are not subject to the AMT, simply to substantiate their entitlement to the tax credits.

Taxpayers subject to the AMT must calculate their tax twice, once under the regular income tax rules and again under AMT rules. The mechanics and computation of AMT tax liability are so complex that many taxpayers may not even realize they are subject to the tax.

The determination of AMT liability involves the following steps:

1. Calculate the taxpayer's regular tax. The regular income tax rules provide preferred treatment for certain types of income and allow taxpayers to claim certain exemptions, deductions, exclusions, and credits.
2. Determine whether the taxpayer is subject to additional tax under the AMT system. The web-based "AMT Assistant" (at http://www.irs.gov/Businesses/ Small-Businesses-&-Self-Employed/Alternative-Minimum-Tax-(AMT)-Assistant-for-Individuals) may be used for this purpose.
3. Compute the alternative minimum taxable income (AMTI) on Form 6251, using the first 28 lines of the form. This computation generally requires taxpayers to give up the benefit of tax preference items to which they are entitled under the regular income tax system. These items commonly include dependency exemptions; the standard deduction; and itemized deductions for medical and dental expenses, state and local taxes, and miscellaneous deductions on line 27, Schedule A (Form 1040).
4. Determine the "exemption amount" to which the taxpayer is entitled based on filing status. The "exemption amount" replaces both the standard deduction and the personal exemption for purposes of computing the AMT.
5. Compute the "taxable excess" by subtracting the exemption amount from the AMTI.
6. Taxpayers with a positive "taxable excess" must compute the "tentative minimum tax." For 2013, a "taxable excess" of $179,500 ($89,750 for married filing separately) or less is taxed at a 26% rate and any additional "taxable excess" is taxed at a 28% rate. The total amount is the tentative minimum tax.
7. Compute the "alternative minimum tax." The AMT is equal to the excess of the taxpayer's tentative minimum tax, if any, over the regular tax liability (reduced by any tax from Form 4972, *Tax on Lump-Sum Distributions* and the foreign tax credit, if any) from Form 1040. If the net result is a negative number or zero, the taxpayer does not owe AMT.
8. If the taxpayer owes AMT, compute the final tax liability by adding the regular income tax and the AMT liability.

Who Must File Form 6251

Most taxpayers are exempt from AMT. Higher-income taxpayers and those who itemize deductions are the primary targets of this tax. Form 6251 is also used to figure the tax liability limit on any of the general business credits, the empowerment zone and renewal community employment credit, the qualified electric vehicle credit, the alternative motor vehicle credit, the alternative fuel vehicle refueling property credit, or the credit for prior-year minimum tax, which now includes the refundable AMT credit (see *Refundable AMT Credit* discussion following).

Form 6251 must be attached to any return if deductions taken are greater than AGI, or alternative minimum taxable income (AMTI) is above the exemption amount for the taxpayer's filing status, or if any general business credits, the empowerment zone and renewal community employment credit, the qualified electric vehicle credit, the alternative motor vehicle credit, the alternative fuel vehicle refueling property credit, or the credit for prior-year minimum tax is claimed.

AMT Exemption Amounts

Filing Status	2013
Single	$51,900
Head of Household	$51,900
Joint Return	$80,800
Qualifying Widow(er)	$80,800
Married Filing Separately	$40,400

 Caution. At one time, the exemption phaseout threshold amounts had never been adjusted for inflation. That is no longer true. For tax years beginning in 2013, the exemption phaseout threshold amounts are $153,900 for joint filers and qualifying widow(er)s, $115,400 for singles or heads-of-household, and $76,950 for married filing separately.

See the Example on page 10-19 for the different AMT results from different filing statuses.

Nonresident Aliens. If you are a nonresident alien and you disposed of U.S. real property interests at a gain, you must make a special computation. Fill in Form 6251 through line 30. If your net gain from the disposition of U.S. real property interests and the amount on line 28 are both greater than the tentative amount you figured for line 30, replace the amount on line 30 with the smaller of that net gain or the amount on line 28. Also, write "RPI" on the dotted line next to line 30. Otherwise, do not change line 30.

 Filing Tip. If you are filing Form 1040NR, treat any reference in these instructions or on Form 6251 to a line on Form 1040 as a reference to the corresponding line on Form 1040NR.

 Planning Tip. For effective tax planning, it is essential to identify clients who may be subject to the AMT. The AMT and Regular Income Tax Compared chart below shows the most common differences between the AMT and regular income tax bases. For a complete list of adjustments, see IRC §56 and §57.

AMT and Regular Income Tax Compared

AMT Computation		Regular Income Tax Computation	
Adjusted Gross Income		Adjusted Gross Income	
Plus	AMT adjustments and preferences	Less	Regular income tax personal and dependency exemptions
Less	AMT itemized deductions	Less	The greater of total itemized deductions or the standard deduction
Equals	AMT income	Equals	Taxable income
Less	AMT exemption	Times	Regular tax rate
Equals	AMT base	Equals	Regular income tax before credits
Times	AMT tax rate	Plus	Actual AMT
Equals	Tentative AMT liability	Less	Nonrefundable credits followed by refundable credits
Less	Regular income tax before credits	Plus	Other taxes
Equals	Actual AMT	Equals	Total tax

 Caution. The AMT basis in stock acquired through an incentive stock option is likely to differ from the regular tax basis. Therefore, adequate records are required for both the AMT and regular tax so that adjusted gain or loss can be determined.

Example. Jennifer, a single individual, has regular taxable income of $80,000 in 2013 and tax preference items (TPIs) totaling $150,000. Her regular tax on the regular taxable income using tax rate schedules is $15,929. To compute her AMT, she must first establish her AMTI by adding her TPIs to her regular taxable income ($230,000). Next, her tentative minimum tax must be computed by first subtracting her pro rata exemption amount, since her AMTI exceeds the phase out threshold for her filing status ($115,400), of $23,250 from AMTI of $230,000 to arrive at the amount of $206,750. Since $206,750 exceeds $179,500, add 26% of $179,500, or $46,670, to 28% of $27,250 ($206,750 minus $179,500) to arrive at a tentative minimum tax of $54,300. Assuming there is no alternative minimum tax foreign tax credit, the $38,371 excess of the $54,300 tentative minimum tax over the $15,929 regular tax is Jennifer's AMT and must be paid in addition to her regular tax.

A taxpayer who is subject to the AMT accrues AMT credits. However, these credits are generated only by timing items, not by exclusion items. Timing items are those accounted for in different tax years in the regular tax and AMT systems. For example, the AMT in some instances requires taxpayers to depreciate property over a longer period of time. Exclusion items are adjustments and tax preference items that result in the permanent disallowance of certain tax benefits such as the standard deduction, personal exemption, and certain itemized deductions. AMT credits can only be used when the regular tax liability, reduced by other nonrefundable credits, exceeds the tentative minimum tax for the year. (For tax years 2007 through 2012, unused long-term AMT credits were refundable.)

Planning Options

Schedule A itemized deductions continue to be a source of inconsistent treatment for middle-income taxpayers. Because the AMT does not treat itemized deductions uniformly, the type of Schedule A itemized deduction is a key factor in determining whether an AMT obligation is triggered. A married couple with three children living in a high-tax area or incurring high employee business expenses is more likely to owe AMT than a similar family that had other itemized deductions, such as mortgage interest or charitable contributions, which are not taken into account for AMT purposes.

Taxpayers who are subject to the AMT may consider accelerating income so that it is subject to the AMT rates, which are still lower than the regular tax rates.

Taxpayers who are not subject to the AMT may consider accelerating deductions, such as itemized deductions and state income tax payments, that would otherwise trigger the AMT. These taxpayers will still be able to enjoy the full benefit of these deductions.

Because certain expenses are treated as deferral items that give rise to a minimum tax credit, taxpayers who are subject to the AMT may wish to adopt a strategy of incurring expenses that are not deductible for AMT purposes. This can provide a benefit in future years. Examples of deferral items include depletion, certain depreciation, and the spread between the exercise and market value prices of incentive stock options.

Caution. Taxpayers with incentive stock options (ISOs) need to work carefully with tax professionals to time the exercise of their options, since the spread between the value of the option and the exercise price is an adjustment to income for AMT purposes and could trigger or increase AMT liability.

Example. In 2013, a married New York resident with three children earned $50,000, received $50,000 as a lump-sum settlement from a job-related discrimination lawsuit, and incurred legal fees of $26,400 for the settlement. He reports 100% of the settlement income and deducts the $24,400 legal fees ($26,400 minus $2,000 (2% of AGI)) as miscellaneous itemized deductions on Schedule A. (Assume for simplicity that he has no other itemized deductions.) If he is married and files a joint return (and his spouse has no income), he owes $4,992 AMT and his total tax is $12,515. If he is married and files a separate liability return (claiming his children as dependents), he and his wife would be required to file separate returns and would have an AMT of $6,065 and a total tax liability of $16,994. If the man is not married and has custody of his three children, he would file as HOH and be liable for $3,003 in AMT and a total tax liability of $12,506.

Example: AMT and Filing Status

Filing Status	MFJ	MFS	HOH
Adjusted Gross Income	$100,000	$100,000	$100,000
Schedule A Miscellaneous Deductions subject to 2%-of-AGI floor	$26,400	$26,400	$26,400
Tentative Minimum Tax	$12,515	$16,994	$12,506
Regular Tax (2013 tax rates)	$7,523	$10,929	$9,503
AMT	$4,992	$6,065	$3,003
Total Tax	$12,515	$16,994	$12,506

Earned Income Credit

Qualifying Child Information

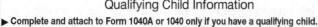
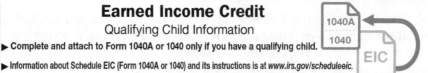

▶ Complete and attach to Form 1040A or 1040 only if you have a qualifying child.

▶ Information about Schedule EIC (Form 1040A or 1040) and its instructions is at *www.irs.gov/scheduleeic*.

OMB No. 1545-0074

20**13**

Attachment
Sequence No. **43**

Name(s) shown on return

Your social security number

Before you begin:

- See the instructions for Form 1040A, lines 38a and 38b, or Form 1040, lines 64a and 64b, to make sure that **(a)** you can take the EIC, and **(b)** you have a qualifying child.
- Be sure the child's name on line 1 and social security number (SSN) on line 2 agree with the child's social security card. Otherwise, at the time we process your return, we may reduce or disallow your EIC. If the name or SSN on the child's social security card is not correct, call the Social Security Administration at 1-800-772-1213.

> ⚠️ **CAUTION**
>
> - *If you take the EIC even though you are not eligible, you may not be allowed to take the credit for up to 10 years. See the instructions for details.*
> - *It will take us longer to process your return and issue your refund if you do not fill in all lines that apply for each qualifying child.*

Qualifying Child Information	Child 1		Child 2		Child 3	
1 Child's name If you have more than three qualifying children, you only have to list three to get the maximum credit.	First name	Last name	First name	Last name	First name	Last name
2 Child's SSN The child must have an SSN as defined in the instructions for Form 1040A, lines 38a and 38b, or Form 1040, lines 64a and 64b, unless the child was born and died in 2013. If your child was born and died in 2013 and did not have an SSN, enter "Died" on this line and attach a copy of the child's birth certificate, death certificate, or hospital medical records.						
3 Child's year of birth	Year ___ ___ ___ ___ *If born after 1994 **and** the child was younger than you (or your spouse, if filing jointly), skip lines 4a and 4b; go to line 5.*		Year ___ ___ ___ ___ *If born after 1994 **and** the child was younger than you (or your spouse, if filing jointly), skip lines 4a and 4b; go to line 5.*		Year ___ ___ ___ ___ *If born after 1994 **and** the child was younger than you (or your spouse, if filing jointly), skip lines 4a and 4b; go to line 5.*	
4 a Was the child under age 24 at the end of 2013, a student, and younger than you (or your spouse, if filing jointly)?	☐ **Yes.** *Go to line 5.*	☐ **No.** *Go to line 4b.*	☐ **Yes.** *Go to line 5.*	☐ **No.** *Go to line 4b.*	☐ **Yes.** *Go to line 5.*	☐ **No.** *Go to line 4b.*
b Was the child permanently and totally disabled during any part of 2013?	☐ **Yes.** *Go to line 5.*	☐ **No.** The child is not a qualifying child.	☐ **Yes.** *Go to line 5.*	☐ **No.** The child is not a qualifying child.	☐ **Yes.** *Go to line 5.*	☐ **No.** The child is not a qualifying child.
5 Child's relationship to you (for example, son, daughter, grandchild, niece, nephew, foster child, etc.)						
6 Number of months child lived with you in the United States during 2013 • If the child lived with you for more than half of 2013 but less than 7 months, enter "7." • If the child was born or died in 2013 and your home was the child's home for more than half the time he or she was alive during 2013, enter "12."	_____ months *Do not enter more than 12 months.*		_____ months *Do not enter more than 12 months.*		_____ months *Do not enter more than 12 months.*	

For Paperwork Reduction Act Notice, see your tax return instructions.

Cat. No. 13339M

Schedule EIC (Form 1040A or 1040) 2013

Purpose of Schedule

After you have figured your earned income credit (EIC), use Schedule EIC to give the IRS information about your qualifying child(ren).

To figure the amount of your credit or to have the IRS figure it for you, see the instructions for Form 1040A, lines 38a and 38b, or Form 1040, lines 64a and 64b.

Taking the EIC when not eligible. If you take the EIC even though you are not eligible and it is determined that your error is due to reckless or intentional disregard of the EIC rules, you will not be allowed to take the credit for 2 years even if you are otherwise eligible to do so. If you fraudulently take the EIC, you will not be allowed to take the credit for 10 years. You may also have to pay penalties.

Future developments. For the latest information about developments related to Schedule EIC (Form 1040A or 1040) and its instructions, such as legislation enacted after they were published, go to *www.irs.gov/scheduleeic.*

 You may also be able to take the additional child tax credit if your child was your dependent and under age 17 at the end of 2013. For more details, see the instructions for line 39 of Form 1040A or line 65 of Form 1040.

Qualifying Child

A qualifying child for the EIC is a child who is your . . .

Son, daughter, stepchild, foster child, brother, sister, stepbrother, stepsister, half brother, half sister, or a descendant of any of them (for example, your grandchild, niece, or nephew)

was . . .

Under age 19 at the end of 2013 and younger than you (or your spouse, if filing jointly)
or
Under age 24 at the end of 2013, a student, and younger than you (or your spouse, if filing jointly)
or
Any age and permanently and totally disabled

Who is not filing a joint return for 2013
or is filing a joint return for 2013 only to claim
a refund of withheld income tax or estimated tax paid

Who lived with you in the United States for more than half of 2013. If the child did not live with you for the required time, see *Exception to time lived with you* in the instructions for Form 1040A, lines 38a and 38b, or Form 1040, lines 64a and 64b.

 If the child was married or meets the conditions to be a qualifying child of another person (other than your spouse if filing a joint return), special rules apply. For details, see Married child *or* Qualifying child of more than one person *in the instructions for Form 1040A, lines 38a and 38b, or Form 1040, lines 64a and 64b.*

2013 Earned Income Credit (EIC) Table
Caution. This is **not** a tax table.

1. To find your credit, read down the "At least - But less than" columns and find the line that includes the amount you were told to look up from your EIC Worksheet.

2. Then, go to the column that includes your filing status and the number of qualifying children you have. Enter the credit from that column on your EIC Worksheet.

Example. If your filing status is single, you have one qualifying child, and the amount you are looking up from your EIC Worksheet is $2,455, you would enter $842.

If the amount you are looking up from the worksheet is—		And your filing status is—			
		Single, head of household, or qualifying widow(er) and the number of children you have is—			
At least	But less than	0	1	2	3
		Your credit is—			
2,400	2,450	186	825	970	1,091
2,450	2,500	189	842	990	1,114

If the amount you are looking up from the worksheet is—		Single, head of household, or qualifying widow(er) and the number of children you have is—				Married filing jointly and the number of children you have is—			
At least	But less than	0	1	2	3	0	1	2	3
		Your credit is—				Your credit is—			
$1	$50	$2	$9	$10	$11	$2	$9	$10	$11
50	100	6	26	30	34	6	26	30	34
100	150	10	43	50	56	10	43	50	56
150	200	13	60	70	79	13	60	70	79
200	250	17	77	90	101	17	77	90	101
250	300	21	94	110	124	21	94	110	124
300	350	25	111	130	146	25	111	130	146
350	400	29	128	150	169	29	128	150	169
400	450	33	145	170	191	33	145	170	191
450	500	36	162	190	214	36	162	190	214
500	550	40	179	210	236	40	179	210	236
550	600	44	196	230	259	44	196	230	259
600	650	48	213	250	281	48	213	250	281
650	700	52	230	270	304	52	230	270	304
700	750	55	247	290	326	55	247	290	326
750	800	59	264	310	349	59	264	310	349
800	850	63	281	330	371	63	281	330	371
850	900	67	298	350	394	67	298	350	394
900	950	71	315	370	416	71	315	370	416
950	1,000	75	332	390	439	75	332	390	439
1,000	1,050	78	349	410	461	78	349	410	461
1,050	1,100	82	366	430	484	82	366	430	484
1,100	1,150	86	383	450	506	86	383	450	506
1,150	1,200	90	400	470	529	90	400	470	529
1,200	1,250	94	417	490	551	94	417	490	551
1,250	1,300	98	434	510	574	98	434	510	574
1,300	1,350	101	451	530	596	101	451	530	596
1,350	1,400	105	468	550	619	105	468	550	619
1,400	1,450	109	485	570	641	109	485	570	641
1,450	1,500	113	502	590	664	113	502	590	664
1,500	1,550	117	519	610	686	117	519	610	686
1,550	1,600	120	536	630	709	120	536	630	709
1,600	1,650	124	553	650	731	124	553	650	731
1,650	1,700	128	570	670	754	128	570	670	754
1,700	1,750	132	587	690	776	132	587	690	776
1,750	1,800	136	604	710	799	136	604	710	799
1,800	1,850	140	621	730	821	140	621	730	821
1,850	1,900	143	638	750	844	143	638	750	844
1,900	1,950	147	655	770	866	147	655	770	866
1,950	2,000	151	672	790	889	151	672	790	889
2,000	2,050	155	689	810	911	155	689	810	911
2,050	2,100	159	706	830	934	159	706	830	934
2,100	2,150	163	723	850	956	163	723	850	956
2,150	2,200	166	740	870	979	166	740	870	979
2,200	2,250	170	757	890	1,001	170	757	890	1,001
2,250	2,300	174	774	910	1,024	174	774	910	1,024
2,300	2,350	178	791	930	1,046	178	791	930	1,046
2,350	2,400	182	808	950	1,069	182	808	950	1,069
2,400	2,450	186	825	970	1,091	186	825	970	1,091
2,450	2,500	189	842	990	1,114	189	842	990	1,114

If the amount you are looking up from the worksheet is—		Single, head of household, or qualifying widow(er) and the number of children you have is—				Married filing jointly and the number of children you have is—			
At least	But less than	0	1	2	3	0	1	2	3
		Your credit is—				Your credit is—			
2,500	2,550	193	859	1,010	1,136	193	859	1,010	1,136
2,550	2,600	197	876	1,030	1,159	197	876	1,030	1,159
2,600	2,650	201	893	1,050	1,181	201	893	1,050	1,181
2,650	2,700	205	910	1,070	1,204	205	910	1,070	1,204
2,700	2,750	208	927	1,090	1,226	208	927	1,090	1,226
2,750	2,800	212	944	1,110	1,249	212	944	1,110	1,249
2,800	2,850	216	961	1,130	1,271	216	961	1,130	1,271
2,850	2,900	220	978	1,150	1,294	220	978	1,150	1,294
2,900	2,950	224	995	1,170	1,316	224	995	1,170	1,316
2,950	3,000	228	1,012	1,190	1,339	228	1,012	1,190	1,339
3,000	3,050	231	1,029	1,210	1,361	231	1,029	1,210	1,361
3,050	3,100	235	1,046	1,230	1,384	235	1,046	1,230	1,384
3,100	3,150	239	1,063	1,250	1,406	239	1,063	1,250	1,406
3,150	3,200	243	1,080	1,270	1,429	243	1,080	1,270	1,429
3,200	3,250	247	1,097	1,290	1,451	247	1,097	1,290	1,451
3,250	3,300	251	1,114	1,310	1,474	251	1,114	1,310	1,474
3,300	3,350	254	1,131	1,330	1,496	254	1,131	1,330	1,496
3,350	3,400	258	1,148	1,350	1,519	258	1,148	1,350	1,519
3,400	3,450	262	1,165	1,370	1,541	262	1,165	1,370	1,541
3,450	3,500	266	1,182	1,390	1,564	266	1,182	1,390	1,564
3,500	3,550	270	1,199	1,410	1,586	270	1,199	1,410	1,586
3,550	3,600	273	1,216	1,430	1,609	273	1,216	1,430	1,609
3,600	3,650	277	1,233	1,450	1,631	277	1,233	1,450	1,631
3,650	3,700	281	1,250	1,470	1,654	281	1,250	1,470	1,654
3,700	3,750	285	1,267	1,490	1,676	285	1,267	1,490	1,676
3,750	3,800	289	1,284	1,510	1,699	289	1,284	1,510	1,699
3,800	3,850	293	1,301	1,530	1,721	293	1,301	1,530	1,721
3,850	3,900	296	1,318	1,550	1,744	296	1,318	1,550	1,744
3,900	3,950	300	1,335	1,570	1,766	300	1,335	1,570	1,766
3,950	4,000	304	1,352	1,590	1,789	304	1,352	1,590	1,789
4,000	4,050	308	1,369	1,610	1,811	308	1,369	1,610	1,811
4,050	4,100	312	1,386	1,630	1,834	312	1,386	1,630	1,834
4,100	4,150	316	1,403	1,650	1,856	316	1,403	1,650	1,856
4,150	4,200	319	1,420	1,670	1,879	319	1,420	1,670	1,879
4,200	4,250	323	1,437	1,690	1,901	323	1,437	1,690	1,901
4,250	4,300	327	1,454	1,710	1,924	327	1,454	1,710	1,924
4,300	4,350	331	1,471	1,730	1,946	331	1,471	1,730	1,946
4,350	4,400	335	1,488	1,750	1,969	335	1,488	1,750	1,969
4,400	4,450	339	1,505	1,770	1,991	339	1,505	1,770	1,991
4,450	4,500	342	1,522	1,790	2,014	342	1,522	1,790	2,014
4,500	4,550	346	1,539	1,810	2,036	346	1,539	1,810	2,036
4,550	4,600	350	1,556	1,830	2,059	350	1,556	1,830	2,059
4,600	4,650	354	1,573	1,850	2,081	354	1,573	1,850	2,081
4,650	4,700	358	1,590	1,870	2,104	358	1,590	1,870	2,104
4,700	4,750	361	1,607	1,890	2,126	361	1,607	1,890	2,126
4,750	4,800	365	1,624	1,910	2,149	365	1,624	1,910	2,149
4,800	4,850	369	1,641	1,930	2,171	369	1,641	1,930	2,171
4,850	4,900	373	1,658	1,950	2,194	373	1,658	1,950	2,194
4,900	4,950	377	1,675	1,970	2,216	377	1,675	1,970	2,216
4,950	5,000	381	1,692	1,990	2,239	381	1,692	1,990	2,239

(Continued)

If the amount you are looking up from the worksheet is–		Single, head of household, or qualifying widow(er) and the number of children you have is–				Married filing jointly and the number of children you have is–			
At least	But less than	0	1	2	3	0	1	2	3
		Your credit is–				Your credit is–			
5,000	5,050	384	1,709	2,010	2,261	384	1,709	2,010	2,261
5,050	5,100	388	1,726	2,030	2,284	388	1,726	2,030	2,284
5,100	5,150	392	1,743	2,050	2,306	392	1,743	2,050	2,306
5,150	5,200	396	1,760	2,070	2,329	396	1,760	2,070	2,329
5,200	5,250	400	1,777	2,090	2,351	400	1,777	2,090	2,351
5,250	5,300	404	1,794	2,110	2,374	404	1,794	2,110	2,374
5,300	5,350	407	1,811	2,130	2,396	407	1,811	2,130	2,396
5,350	5,400	411	1,828	2,150	2,419	411	1,828	2,150	2,419
5,400	5,450	415	1,845	2,170	2,441	415	1,845	2,170	2,441
5,450	5,500	419	1,862	2,190	2,464	419	1,862	2,190	2,464
5,500	5,550	423	1,879	2,210	2,486	423	1,879	2,210	2,486
5,550	5,600	426	1,896	2,230	2,509	426	1,896	2,230	2,509
5,600	5,650	430	1,913	2,250	2,531	430	1,913	2,250	2,531
5,650	5,700	434	1,930	2,270	2,554	434	1,930	2,270	2,554
5,700	5,750	438	1,947	2,290	2,576	438	1,947	2,290	2,576
5,750	5,800	442	1,964	2,310	2,599	442	1,964	2,310	2,599
5,800	5,850	446	1,981	2,330	2,621	446	1,981	2,330	2,621
5,850	5,900	449	1,998	2,350	2,644	449	1,998	2,350	2,644
5,900	5,950	453	2,015	2,370	2,666	453	2,015	2,370	2,666
5,950	6,000	457	2,032	2,390	2,689	457	2,032	2,390	2,689
6,000	6,050	461	2,049	2,410	2,711	461	2,049	2,410	2,711
6,050	6,100	465	2,066	2,430	2,734	465	2,066	2,430	2,734
6,100	6,150	469	2,083	2,450	2,756	469	2,083	2,450	2,756
6,150	6,200	472	2,100	2,470	2,779	472	2,100	2,470	2,779
6,200	6,250	476	2,117	2,490	2,801	476	2,117	2,490	2,801
6,250	6,300	480	2,134	2,510	2,824	480	2,134	2,510	2,824
6,300	6,350	484	2,151	2,530	2,846	484	2,151	2,530	2,846
6,350	6,400	487	2,168	2,550	2,869	487	2,168	2,550	2,869
6,400	6,450	487	2,185	2,570	2,891	487	2,185	2,570	2,891
6,450	6,500	487	2,202	2,590	2,914	487	2,202	2,590	2,914
6,500	6,550	487	2,219	2,610	2,936	487	2,219	2,610	2,936
6,550	6,600	487	2,236	2,630	2,959	487	2,236	2,630	2,959
6,600	6,650	487	2,253	2,650	2,981	487	2,253	2,650	2,981
6,650	6,700	487	2,270	2,670	3,004	487	2,270	2,670	3,004
6,700	6,750	487	2,287	2,690	3,026	487	2,287	2,690	3,026
6,750	6,800	487	2,304	2,710	3,049	487	2,304	2,710	3,049
6,800	6,850	487	2,321	2,730	3,071	487	2,321	2,730	3,071
6,850	6,900	487	2,338	2,750	3,094	487	2,338	2,750	3,094
6,900	6,950	487	2,355	2,770	3,116	487	2,355	2,770	3,116
6,950	7,000	487	2,372	2,790	3,139	487	2,372	2,790	3,139
7,000	7,050	487	2,389	2,810	3,161	487	2,389	2,810	3,161
7,050	7,100	487	2,406	2,830	3,184	487	2,406	2,830	3,184
7,100	7,150	487	2,423	2,850	3,206	487	2,423	2,850	3,206
7,150	7,200	487	2,440	2,870	3,229	487	2,440	2,870	3,229
7,200	7,250	487	2,457	2,890	3,251	487	2,457	2,890	3,251
7,250	7,300	487	2,474	2,910	3,274	487	2,474	2,910	3,274
7,300	7,350	487	2,491	2,930	3,296	487	2,491	2,930	3,296
7,350	7,400	487	2,508	2,950	3,319	487	2,508	2,950	3,319
7,400	7,450	487	2,525	2,970	3,341	487	2,525	2,970	3,341
7,450	7,500	487	2,542	2,990	3,364	487	2,542	2,990	3,364
7,500	7,550	487	2,559	3,010	3,386	487	2,559	3,010	3,386
7,550	7,600	487	2,576	3,030	3,409	487	2,576	3,030	3,409
7,600	7,650	487	2,593	3,050	3,431	487	2,593	3,050	3,431
7,650	7,700	487	2,610	3,070	3,454	487	2,610	3,070	3,454
7,700	7,750	487	2,627	3,090	3,476	487	2,627	3,090	3,476
7,750	7,800	487	2,644	3,110	3,499	487	2,644	3,110	3,499
7,800	7,850	487	2,661	3,130	3,521	487	2,661	3,130	3,521
7,850	7,900	487	2,678	3,150	3,544	487	2,678	3,150	3,544
7,900	7,950	487	2,695	3,170	3,566	487	2,695	3,170	3,566
7,950	8,000	487	2,712	3,190	3,589	487	2,712	3,190	3,589

If the amount you are looking up from the worksheet is–		Single, head of household, or qualifying widow(er) and the number of children you have is–				Married filing jointly and the number of children you have is–			
At least	But less than	0	1	2	3	0	1	2	3
		Your credit is–				Your credit is–			
8,000	8,050	483	2,729	3,210	3,611	487	2,729	3,210	3,611
8,050	8,100	479	2,746	3,230	3,634	487	2,746	3,230	3,634
8,100	8,150	475	2,763	3,250	3,656	487	2,763	3,250	3,656
8,150	8,200	472	2,780	3,270	3,679	487	2,780	3,270	3,679
8,200	8,250	468	2,797	3,290	3,701	487	2,797	3,290	3,701
8,250	8,300	464	2,814	3,310	3,724	487	2,814	3,310	3,724
8,300	8,350	460	2,831	3,330	3,746	487	2,831	3,330	3,746
8,350	8,400	456	2,848	3,350	3,769	487	2,848	3,350	3,769
8,400	8,450	452	2,865	3,370	3,791	487	2,865	3,370	3,791
8,450	8,500	449	2,882	3,390	3,814	487	2,882	3,390	3,814
8,500	8,550	445	2,899	3,410	3,836	487	2,899	3,410	3,836
8,550	8,600	441	2,916	3,430	3,859	487	2,916	3,430	3,859
8,600	8,650	437	2,933	3,450	3,881	487	2,933	3,450	3,881
8,650	8,700	433	2,950	3,470	3,904	487	2,950	3,470	3,904
8,700	8,750	430	2,967	3,490	3,926	487	2,967	3,490	3,926
8,750	8,800	426	2,984	3,510	3,949	487	2,984	3,510	3,949
8,800	8,850	422	3,001	3,530	3,971	487	3,001	3,530	3,971
8,850	8,900	418	3,018	3,550	3,994	487	3,018	3,550	3,994
8,900	8,950	414	3,035	3,570	4,016	487	3,035	3,570	4,016
8,950	9,000	410	3,052	3,590	4,039	487	3,052	3,590	4,039
9,000	9,050	407	3,069	3,610	4,061	487	3,069	3,610	4,061
9,050	9,100	403	3,086	3,630	4,084	487	3,086	3,630	4,084
9,100	9,150	399	3,103	3,650	4,106	487	3,103	3,650	4,106
9,150	9,200	395	3,120	3,670	4,129	487	3,120	3,670	4,129
9,200	9,250	391	3,137	3,690	4,151	487	3,137	3,690	4,151
9,250	9,300	387	3,154	3,710	4,174	487	3,154	3,710	4,174
9,300	9,350	384	3,171	3,730	4,196	487	3,171	3,730	4,196
9,350	9,400	380	3,188	3,750	4,219	487	3,188	3,750	4,219
9,400	9,450	376	3,205	3,770	4,241	487	3,205	3,770	4,241
9,450	9,500	372	3,222	3,790	4,264	487	3,222	3,790	4,264
9,500	9,550	368	3,239	3,810	4,286	487	3,239	3,810	4,286
9,550	9,600	365	3,250	3,830	4,309	487	3,250	3,830	4,309
9,600	9,650	361	3,250	3,850	4,331	487	3,250	3,850	4,331
9,650	9,700	357	3,250	3,870	4,354	487	3,250	3,870	4,354
9,700	9,750	353	3,250	3,890	4,376	487	3,250	3,890	4,376
9,750	9,800	349	3,250	3,910	4,399	487	3,250	3,910	4,399
9,800	9,850	345	3,250	3,930	4,421	487	3,250	3,930	4,421
9,850	9,900	342	3,250	3,950	4,444	487	3,250	3,950	4,444
9,900	9,950	338	3,250	3,970	4,466	487	3,250	3,970	4,466
9,950	10,000	334	3,250	3,990	4,489	487	3,250	3,990	4,489
10,000	10,050	330	3,250	4,010	4,511	487	3,250	4,010	4,511
10,050	10,100	326	3,250	4,030	4,534	487	3,250	4,030	4,534
10,100	10,150	322	3,250	4,050	4,556	487	3,250	4,050	4,556
10,150	10,200	319	3,250	4,070	4,579	487	3,250	4,070	4,579
10,200	10,250	315	3,250	4,090	4,601	487	3,250	4,090	4,601
10,250	10,300	311	3,250	4,110	4,624	487	3,250	4,110	4,624
10,300	10,350	307	3,250	4,130	4,646	487	3,250	4,130	4,646
10,350	10,400	303	3,250	4,150	4,669	487	3,250	4,150	4,669
10,400	10,450	299	3,250	4,170	4,691	487	3,250	4,170	4,691
10,450	10,500	296	3,250	4,190	4,714	487	3,250	4,190	4,714
10,500	10,550	292	3,250	4,210	4,736	487	3,250	4,210	4,736
10,550	10,600	288	3,250	4,230	4,759	487	3,250	4,230	4,759
10,600	10,650	284	3,250	4,250	4,781	487	3,250	4,250	4,781
10,650	10,700	280	3,250	4,270	4,804	487	3,250	4,270	4,804
10,700	10,750	277	3,250	4,290	4,826	487	3,250	4,290	4,826
10,750	10,800	273	3,250	4,310	4,849	487	3,250	4,310	4,849
10,800	10,850	269	3,250	4,330	4,871	487	3,250	4,330	4,871
10,850	10,900	265	3,250	4,350	4,894	487	3,250	4,350	4,894
10,900	10,950	261	3,250	4,370	4,916	487	3,250	4,370	4,916
10,950	11,000	257	3,250	4,390	4,939	487	3,250	4,390	4,939

(Continued)

Earned Income Credit (EIC) Table - Continued

(Caution. This is not a tax table.)

DRAFT AS OF September 16, 2013

If the amount you are looking up from the worksheet is— At least	But less than	Single, head of household, or qualifying widow(er) — 0	1	2	3	Married filing jointly — 0	1	2	3
11,000	11,050	254	3,250	4,410	4,961	487	3,250	4,410	4,961
11,050	11,100	250	3,250	4,430	4,984	487	3,250	4,430	4,984
11,100	11,150	246	3,250	4,450	5,006	487	3,250	4,450	5,006
11,150	11,200	242	3,250	4,470	5,029	487	3,250	4,470	5,029
11,200	11,250	238	3,250	4,490	5,051	487	3,250	4,490	5,051
11,250	11,300	234	3,250	4,510	5,074	487	3,250	4,510	5,074
11,300	11,350	231	3,250	4,530	5,096	487	3,250	4,530	5,096
11,350	11,400	227	3,250	4,550	5,119	487	3,250	4,550	5,119
11,400	11,450	223	3,250	4,570	5,141	487	3,250	4,570	5,141
11,450	11,500	219	3,250	4,590	5,164	487	3,250	4,590	5,164
11,500	11,550	215	3,250	4,610	5,186	487	3,250	4,610	5,186
11,550	11,600	212	3,250	4,630	5,209	487	3,250	4,630	5,209
11,600	11,650	208	3,250	4,650	5,231	487	3,250	4,650	5,231
11,650	11,700	204	3,250	4,670	5,254	487	3,250	4,670	5,254
11,700	11,750	200	3,250	4,690	5,276	487	3,250	4,690	5,276
11,750	11,800	196	3,250	4,710	5,299	487	3,250	4,710	5,299
11,800	11,850	192	3,250	4,730	5,321	487	3,250	4,730	5,321
11,850	11,900	189	3,250	4,750	5,344	487	3,250	4,750	5,344
11,900	11,950	185	3,250	4,770	5,366	487	3,250	4,770	5,366
11,950	12,000	181	3,250	4,790	5,389	487	3,250	4,790	5,389
12,000	12,050	177	3,250	4,810	5,411	487	3,250	4,810	5,411
12,050	12,100	173	3,250	4,830	5,434	487	3,250	4,830	5,434
12,100	12,150	169	3,250	4,850	5,456	487	3,250	4,850	5,456
12,150	12,200	166	3,250	4,870	5,479	487	3,250	4,870	5,479
12,200	12,250	162	3,250	4,890	5,501	487	3,250	4,890	5,501
12,250	12,300	158	3,250	4,910	5,524	487	3,250	4,910	5,524
12,300	12,350	154	3,250	4,930	5,546	487	3,250	4,930	5,546
12,350	12,400	150	3,250	4,950	5,569	487	3,250	4,950	5,569
12,400	12,450	146	3,250	4,970	5,591	487	3,250	4,970	5,591
12,450	12,500	143	3,250	4,990	5,614	487	3,250	4,990	5,614
12,500	12,550	139	3,250	5,010	5,636	487	3,250	5,010	5,636
12,550	12,600	135	3,250	5,030	5,659	487	3,250	5,030	5,659
12,600	12,650	131	3,250	5,050	5,681	487	3,250	5,050	5,681
12,650	12,700	127	3,250	5,070	5,704	487	3,250	5,070	5,704
12,700	12,750	124	3,250	5,090	5,726	487	3,250	5,090	5,726
12,750	12,800	120	3,250	5,110	5,749	487	3,250	5,110	5,749
12,800	12,850	116	3,250	5,130	5,771	487	3,250	5,130	5,771
12,850	12,900	112	3,250	5,150	5,794	487	3,250	5,150	5,794
12,900	12,950	108	3,250	5,170	5,816	487	3,250	5,170	5,816
12,950	13,000	104	3,250	5,190	5,839	487	3,250	5,190	5,839
13,000	13,050	101	3,250	5,210	5,861	487	3,250	5,210	5,861
13,050	13,100	97	3,250	5,230	5,884	487	3,250	5,230	5,884
13,100	13,150	93	3,250	5,250	5,906	487	3,250	5,250	5,906
13,150	13,200	89	3,250	5,270	5,929	487	3,250	5,270	5,929
13,200	13,250	85	3,250	5,290	5,951	487	3,250	5,290	5,951
13,250	13,300	81	3,250	5,310	5,974	487	3,250	5,310	5,974
13,300	13,350	78	3,250	5,330	5,996	487	3,250	5,330	5,996
13,350	13,400	74	3,250	5,350	6,019	482	3,250	5,350	6,019
13,400	13,450	70	3,250	5,372	6,044	479	3,250	5,372	6,044
13,450	13,500	66	3,250	5,372	6,044	475	3,250	5,372	6,044
13,500	13,550	62	3,250	5,372	6,044	471	3,250	5,372	6,044
13,550	13,600	59	3,250	5,372	6,044	467	3,250	5,372	6,044
13,600	13,650	55	3,250	5,372	6,044	463	3,250	5,372	6,044
13,650	13,700	51	3,250	5,372	6,044	459	3,250	5,372	6,044
13,700	13,750	47	3,250	5,372	6,044	456	3,250	5,372	6,044
13,750	13,800	43	3,250	5,372	6,044	452	3,250	5,372	6,044
13,800	13,850	39	3,250	5,372	6,044	448	3,250	5,372	6,044
13,850	13,900	36	3,250	5,372	6,044	444	3,250	5,372	6,044
13,900	13,950	32	3,250	5,372	6,044	440	3,250	5,372	6,044
13,950	14,000	28	3,250	5,372	6,044	436	3,250	5,372	6,044

If the amount you are looking up from the worksheet is— At least	But less than	Single, head of household, or qualifying widow(er) — 0	1	2	3	Married filing jointly — 0	1	2	3
14,000	14,050	24	3,250	5,372	6,044	433	3,250	5,372	6,044
14,050	14,100	20	3,250	5,372	6,044	429	3,250	5,372	6,044
14,100	14,150	16	3,250	5,372	6,044	425	3,250	5,372	6,044
14,150	14,200	13	3,250	5,372	6,044	421	3,250	5,372	6,044
14,200	14,250	9	3,250	5,372	6,044	417	3,250	5,372	6,044
14,250	14,300	5	3,250	5,372	6,044	413	3,250	5,372	6,044
14,300	14,350	*	3,250	5,372	6,044	410	3,250	5,372	6,044
14,350	14,400	0	3,250	5,372	6,044	406	3,250	5,372	6,044
14,400	14,450	0	3,250	5,372	6,044	402	3,250	5,372	6,044
14,450	14,500	0	3,250	5,372	6,044	398	3,250	5,372	6,044
14,500	14,550	0	3,250	5,372	6,044	394	3,250	5,372	6,044
14,550	14,600	0	3,250	5,372	6,044	391	3,250	5,372	6,044
14,600	14,650	0	3,250	5,372	6,044	387	3,250	5,372	6,044
14,650	14,700	0	3,250	5,372	6,044	383	3,250	5,372	6,044
14,700	14,750	0	3,250	5,372	6,044	379	3,250	5,372	6,044
14,750	14,800	0	3,250	5,372	6,044	375	3,250	5,372	6,044
14,800	14,850	0	3,250	5,372	6,044	371	3,250	5,372	6,044
14,850	14,900	0	3,250	5,372	6,044	368	3,250	5,372	6,044
14,900	14,950	0	3,250	5,372	6,044	364	3,250	5,372	6,044
14,950	15,000	0	3,250	5,372	6,044	360	3,250	5,372	6,044
15,000	15,050	0	3,250	5,372	6,044	356	3,250	5,372	6,044
15,050	15,100	0	3,250	5,372	6,044	352	3,250	5,372	6,044
15,100	15,150	0	3,250	5,372	6,044	348	3,250	5,372	6,044
15,150	15,200	0	3,250	5,372	6,044	345	3,250	5,372	6,044
15,200	15,250	0	3,250	5,372	6,044	341	3,250	5,372	6,044
15,250	15,300	0	3,250	5,372	6,044	337	3,250	5,372	6,044
15,300	15,350	0	3,250	5,372	6,044	333	3,250	5,372	6,044
15,350	15,400	0	3,250	5,372	6,044	329	3,250	5,372	6,044
15,400	15,450	0	3,250	5,372	6,044	326	3,250	5,372	6,044
15,450	15,500	0	3,250	5,372	6,044	322	3,250	5,372	6,044
15,500	15,550	0	3,250	5,372	6,044	318	3,250	5,372	6,044
15,550	15,600	0	3,250	5,372	6,044	314	3,250	5,372	6,044
15,600	15,650	0	3,250	5,372	6,044	310	3,250	5,372	6,044
15,650	15,700	0	3,250	5,372	6,044	306	3,250	5,372	6,044
15,700	15,750	0	3,250	5,372	6,044	303	3,250	5,372	6,044
15,750	15,800	0	3,250	5,372	6,044	299	3,250	5,372	6,044
15,800	15,850	0	3,250	5,372	6,044	295	3,250	5,372	6,044
15,850	15,900	0	3,250	5,372	6,044	291	3,250	5,372	6,044
15,900	15,950	0	3,250	5,372	6,044	287	3,250	5,372	6,044
15,950	16,000	0	3,250	5,372	6,044	283	3,250	5,372	6,044
16,000	16,050	0	3,250	5,372	6,044	280	3,250	5,372	6,044
16,050	16,100	0	3,250	5,372	6,044	276	3,250	5,372	6,044
16,100	16,150	0	3,250	5,372	6,044	272	3,250	5,372	6,044
16,150	16,200	0	3,250	5,372	6,044	268	3,250	5,372	6,044
16,200	16,250	0	3,250	5,372	6,044	264	3,250	5,372	6,044
16,250	16,300	0	3,250	5,372	6,044	260	3,250	5,372	6,044
16,300	16,350	0	3,250	5,372	6,044	257	3,250	5,372	6,044
16,350	16,400	0	3,250	5,372	6,044	253	3,250	5,372	6,044
16,400	16,450	0	3,250	5,372	6,044	249	3,250	5,372	6,044
16,450	16,500	0	3,250	5,372	6,044	245	3,250	5,372	6,044
16,500	16,550	0	3,250	5,372	6,044	241	3,250	5,372	6,044
16,550	16,600	0	3,250	5,372	6,044	238	3,250	5,372	6,044
16,600	16,650	0	3,250	5,372	6,044	234	3,250	5,372	6,044
16,650	16,700	0	3,250	5,372	6,044	230	3,250	5,372	6,044
16,700	16,750	0	3,250	5,372	6,044	226	3,250	5,372	6,044
16,750	16,800	0	3,250	5,372	6,044	222	3,250	5,372	6,044
16,800	16,850	0	3,250	5,372	6,044	218	3,250	5,372	6,044
16,850	16,900	0	3,250	5,372	6,044	215	3,250	5,372	6,044
16,900	16,950	0	3,250	5,372	6,044	211	3,250	5,372	6,044
16,950	17,000	0	3,250	5,372	6,044	207	3,250	5,372	6,044

(Continued)

* If the amount you are looking up from the worksheet is at least $14,300 but less than $14,340, and you have no qualifying children, your credit is $2.
If the amount you are looking up from the worksheet is $14,340 or more, and you have no qualifying children, you cannot take the credit.

Earned Income Credit (EIC) Table - *Continued*

(**Caution.** This is **not** a tax table.)

If the amount you are looking up from the worksheet is—		Single, head of household, or qualifying widow(er) and the number of children you have is—				Married filing jointly and the number of children you have is—			
At least	But less than	0	1	2	3	0	1	2	3
		Your credit is—				Your credit is—			
17,000	17,050	0	3,250	5,372	6,044	203	3,250	5,372	6,044
17,050	17,100	0	3,250	5,372	6,044	199	3,250	5,372	6,044
17,100	17,150	0	3,250	5,372	6,044	195	3,250	5,372	6,044
17,150	17,200	0	3,250	5,372	6,044	192	3,250	5,372	6,044
17,200	17,250	0	3,250	5,372	6,044	188	3,250	5,372	6,044
17,250	17,300	0	3,250	5,372	6,044	184	3,250	5,372	6,044
17,300	17,350	0	3,250	5,372	6,044	180	3,250	5,372	6,044
17,350	17,400	0	3,250	5,372	6,044	176	3,250	5,372	6,044
17,400	17,450	0	3,250	5,372	6,044	173	3,250	5,372	6,044
17,450	17,500	0	3,250	5,372	6,044	169	3,250	5,372	6,044
17,500	17,550	0	3,250	5,372	6,044	165	3,250	5,372	6,044
17,550	17,600	0	3,243	5,363	6,034	161	3,250	5,372	6,044
17,600	17,650	0	3,235	5,352	6,023	157	3,250	5,372	6,044
17,650	17,700	0	3,227	5,341	6,013	153	3,250	5,372	6,044
17,700	17,750	0	3,219	5,331	6,002	150	3,250	5,372	6,044
17,750	17,800	0	3,211	5,320	5,992	146	3,250	5,372	6,044
17,800	17,850	0	3,203	5,310	5,981	142	3,250	5,372	6,044
17,850	17,900	0	3,195	5,299	5,971	138	3,250	5,372	6,044
17,900	17,950	0	3,187	5,289	5,960	134	3,250	5,372	6,044
17,950	18,000	0	3,179	5,278	5,950	130	3,250	5,372	6,044
18,000	18,050	0	3,171	5,268	5,939	127	3,250	5,372	6,044
18,050	18,100	0	3,163	5,257	5,929	123	3,250	5,372	6,044
18,100	18,150	0	3,155	5,247	5,918	119	3,250	5,372	6,044
18,150	18,200	0	3,147	5,236	5,908	115	3,250	5,372	6,044
18,200	18,250	0	3,139	5,226	5,897	111	3,250	5,372	6,044
18,250	18,300	0	3,131	5,215	5,887	107	3,250	5,372	6,044
18,300	18,350	0	3,123	5,205	5,876	104	3,250	5,372	6,044
18,350	18,400	0	3,115	5,194	5,866	100	3,250	5,372	6,044
18,400	18,450	0	3,107	5,184	5,855	96	3,250	5,372	6,044
18,450	18,500	0	3,099	5,173	5,844	92	3,250	5,372	6,044
18,500	18,550	0	3,091	5,162	5,834	88	3,250	5,372	6,044
18,550	18,600	0	3,083	5,152	5,823	85	3,250	5,372	6,044
18,600	18,650	0	3,075	5,141	5,813	81	3,250	5,372	6,044
18,650	18,700	0	3,067	5,131	5,802	77	3,250	5,372	6,044
18,700	18,750	0	3,059	5,120	5,792	73	3,250	5,372	6,044
18,750	18,800	0	3,051	5,110	5,781	69	3,250	5,372	6,044
18,800	18,850	0	3,043	5,099	5,771	65	3,250	5,372	6,044
18,850	18,900	0	3,035	5,089	5,760	62	3,250	5,372	6,044
18,900	18,950	0	3,027	5,078	5,750	58	3,250	5,372	6,044
18,950	19,000	0	3,019	5,068	5,739	54	3,250	5,372	6,044
19,000	19,050	0	3,011	5,057	5,729	50	3,250	5,372	6,044
19,050	19,100	0	3,004	5,047	5,718	46	3,250	5,372	6,044
19,100	19,150	0	2,996	5,036	5,708	42	3,250	5,372	6,044
19,150	19,200	0	2,988	5,026	5,697	39	3,250	5,372	6,044
19,200	19,250	0	2,980	5,015	5,687	35	3,250	5,372	6,044
19,250	19,300	0	2,972	5,005	5,676	31	3,250	5,372	6,044
19,300	19,350	0	2,964	4,994	5,665	27	3,250	5,372	6,044
19,350	19,400	0	2,956	4,983	5,655	23	3,250	5,372	6,044
19,400	19,450	0	2,948	4,973	5,644	20	3,250	5,372	6,044
19,450	19,500	0	2,940	4,962	5,634	16	3,250	5,372	6,044
19,500	19,550	0	2,932	4,952	5,623	12	3,250	5,372	6,044
19,550	19,600	0	2,924	4,941	5,613	8	3,250	5,372	6,044
19,600	19,650	0	2,916	4,931	5,602	4	3,250	5,372	6,044
19,650	19,700	0	2,908	4,920	5,592	*	3,250	5,372	6,044
19,700	19,750	0	2,900	4,910	5,581	0	3,250	5,372	6,044
19,750	19,800	0	2,892	4,899	5,571	0	3,250	5,372	6,044
19,800	19,850	0	2,884	4,889	5,560	0	3,250	5,372	6,044
19,850	19,900	0	2,876	4,878	5,550	0	3,250	5,372	6,044
19,900	19,950	0	2,868	4,868	5,539	0	3,250	5,372	6,044
19,950	20,000	0	2,860	4,857	5,529	0	3,250	5,372	6,044
20,000	20,050	0	2,852	4,847	5,518	0	3,250	5,372	6,044
20,050	20,100	0	2,844	4,836	5,508	0	3,250	5,372	6,044
20,100	20,150	0	2,836	4,825	5,497	0	3,250	5,372	6,044
20,150	20,200	0	2,828	4,815	5,486	0	3,250	5,372	6,044
20,200	20,250	0	2,820	4,804	5,476	0	3,250	5,372	6,044
20,250	20,300	0	2,812	4,794	5,465	0	3,250	5,372	6,044
20,300	20,350	0	2,804	4,783	5,455	0	3,250	5,372	6,044
20,350	20,400	0	2,796	4,773	5,444	0	3,250	5,372	6,044
20,400	20,450	0	2,788	4,762	5,434	0	3,250	5,372	6,044
20,450	20,500	0	2,780	4,752	5,423	0	3,250	5,372	6,044
20,500	20,550	0	2,772	4,741	5,413	0	3,250	5,372	6,044
20,550	20,600	0	2,764	4,731	5,402	0	3,250	5,372	6,044
20,600	20,650	0	2,756	4,720	5,392	0	3,250	5,372	6,044
20,650	20,700	0	2,748	4,710	5,381	0	3,250	5,372	6,044
20,700	20,750	0	2,740	4,699	5,371	0	3,250	5,372	6,044
20,750	20,800	0	2,732	4,689	5,360	0	3,250	5,372	6,044
20,800	20,850	0	2,724	4,678	5,350	0	3,250	5,372	6,044
20,850	20,900	0	2,716	4,668	5,339	0	3,250	5,372	6,044
20,900	20,950	0	2,708	4,657	5,329	0	3,250	5,372	6,044
20,950	21,000	0	2,700	4,646	5,318	0	3,250	5,372	6,044
21,000	21,050	0	2,692	4,636	5,307	0	3,250	5,372	6,044
21,050	21,100	0	2,684	4,625	5,297	0	3,250	5,372	6,044
21,100	21,150	0	2,676	4,615	5,286	0	3,250	5,372	6,044
21,150	21,200	0	2,668	4,604	5,276	0	3,250	5,372	6,044
21,200	21,250	0	2,660	4,594	5,265	0	3,250	5,372	6,044
21,250	21,300	0	2,652	4,583	5,255	0	3,250	5,372	6,044
21,300	21,350	0	2,644	4,573	5,244	0	3,250	5,372	6,044
21,350	21,400	0	2,636	4,562	5,234	0	3,250	5,372	6,044
21,400	21,450	0	2,628	4,552	5,223	0	3,250	5,372	6,044
21,450	21,500	0	2,620	4,541	5,213	0	3,250	5,372	6,044
21,500	21,550	0	2,612	4,531	5,202	0	3,250	5,372	6,044
21,550	21,600	0	2,604	4,520	5,192	0	3,250	5,372	6,044
21,600	21,650	0	2,596	4,510	5,181	0	3,250	5,372	6,044
21,650	21,700	0	2,588	4,499	5,171	0	3,250	5,372	6,044
21,700	21,750	0	2,580	4,489	5,160	0	3,250	5,372	6,044
21,750	21,800	0	2,572	4,478	5,150	0	3,250	5,372	6,044
21,800	21,850	0	2,564	4,467	5,139	0	3,250	5,372	6,044
21,850	21,900	0	2,556	4,457	5,128	0	3,250	5,372	6,044
21,900	21,950	0	2,548	4,446	5,118	0	3,250	5,372	6,044
21,950	22,000	0	2,540	4,436	5,107	0	3,250	5,372	6,044
22,000	22,050	0	2,532	4,425	5,097	0	3,250	5,372	6,044
22,050	22,100	0	2,524	4,415	5,086	0	3,250	5,372	6,044
22,100	22,150	0	2,516	4,404	5,076	0	3,250	5,372	6,044
22,150	22,200	0	2,508	4,394	5,065	0	3,250	5,372	6,044
22,200	22,250	0	2,500	4,383	5,055	0	3,250	5,372	6,044
22,250	22,300	0	2,492	4,373	5,044	0	3,250	5,372	6,044
22,300	22,350	0	2,484	4,362	5,034	0	3,250	5,372	6,044
22,350	22,400	0	2,476	4,352	5,023	0	3,250	5,372	6,044
22,400	22,450	0	2,468	4,341	5,013	0	3,250	5,372	6,044
22,450	22,500	0	2,460	4,331	5,002	0	3,250	5,372	6,044
22,500	22,550	0	2,452	4,320	4,992	0	3,250	5,372	6,044
22,550	22,600	0	2,444	4,310	4,981	0	3,250	5,372	6,044
22,600	22,650	0	2,436	4,299	4,970	0	3,250	5,372	6,044
22,650	22,700	0	2,428	4,288	4,960	0	3,250	5,372	6,044
22,700	22,750	0	2,420	4,278	4,949	0	3,250	5,372	6,044
22,750	22,800	0	2,412	4,267	4,939	0	3,250	5,372	6,044
22,800	22,850	0	2,404	4,257	4,928	0	3,250	5,372	6,044
22,850	22,900	0	2,396	4,246	4,918	0	3,250	5,372	6,044
22,900	22,950	0	2,388	4,236	4,907	0	3,242	5,360	6,032
22,950	23,000	0	2,380	4,225	4,897	0	3,234	5,350	6,021

(Continued)

* If the amount you are looking up from the worksheet is at least $19,650 but less than $19,680, and you have no qualifying children, your credit is $1.
If the amount you are looking up from the worksheet is $19,680 or more, and you have no qualifying children, you cannot take the credit.

Earned Income Credit (EIC) Table - Continued

(**Caution.** This is **not** a tax table.)

If the amount you are looking up from the worksheet is— At least	But less than	Single, head of household, or qualifying widow(er) and the number of children you have is— 0	1	2	3	Married filing jointly and the number of children you have is— 0	1	2	3
23,000	23,050	0	2,372	4,215	4,886	0	3,226	5,339	6,011
23,050	23,100	0	2,364	4,204	4,876	0	3,218	5,329	6,000
23,100	23,150	0	2,356	4,194	4,865	0	3,210	5,318	5,990
23,150	23,200	0	2,348	4,183	4,855	0	3,202	5,308	5,979
23,200	23,250	0	2,340	4,173	4,844	0	3,194	5,297	5,969
23,250	23,300	0	2,332	4,162	4,834	0	3,186	5,287	5,958
23,300	23,350	0	2,324	4,152	4,823	0	3,178	5,276	5,948
23,350	23,400	0	2,316	4,141	4,813	0	3,170	5,266	5,937
23,400	23,450	0	2,308	4,131	4,802	0	3,162	5,255	5,927
23,450	23,500	0	2,300	4,120	4,791	0	3,154	5,245	5,916
23,500	23,550	0	2,292	4,109	4,781	0	3,146	5,234	5,906
23,550	23,600	0	2,284	4,099	4,770	0	3,138	5,224	5,895
23,600	23,650	0	2,276	4,088	4,760	0	3,130	5,213	5,884
23,650	23,700	0	2,268	4,078	4,749	0	3,122	5,202	5,874
23,700	23,750	0	2,260	4,067	4,739	0	3,114	5,192	5,863
23,750	23,800	0	2,252	4,057	4,728	0	3,106	5,181	5,853
23,800	23,850	0	2,244	4,046	4,718	0	3,098	5,171	5,842
23,850	23,900	0	2,236	4,036	4,707	0	3,090	5,160	5,832
23,900	23,950	0	2,228	4,025	4,697	0	3,082	5,150	5,821
23,950	24,000	0	2,220	4,015	4,686	0	3,074	5,139	5,811
24,000	24,050	0	2,212	4,004	4,676	0	3,066	5,129	5,800
24,050	24,100	0	2,205	3,994	4,665	0	3,058	5,118	5,790
24,100	24,150	0	2,197	3,983	4,655	0	3,050	5,108	5,779
24,150	24,200	0	2,189	3,973	4,644	0	3,042	5,097	5,769
24,200	24,250	0	2,181	3,962	4,634	0	3,034	5,087	5,758
24,250	24,300	0	2,173	3,952	4,623	0	3,026	5,076	5,748
24,300	24,350	0	2,165	3,941	4,612	0	3,018	5,066	5,737
24,350	24,400	0	2,157	3,930	4,602	0	3,010	5,055	5,727
24,400	24,450	0	2,149	3,920	4,591	0	3,002	5,045	5,716
24,450	24,500	0	2,141	3,909	4,581	0	2,994	5,034	5,705
24,500	24,550	0	2,133	3,899	4,570	0	2,986	5,023	5,695
24,550	24,600	0	2,125	3,888	4,560	0	2,978	5,013	5,684
24,600	24,650	0	2,117	3,878	4,549	0	2,970	5,002	5,674
24,650	24,700	0	2,109	3,867	4,539	0	2,962	4,992	5,663
24,700	24,750	0	2,101	3,857	4,528	0	2,954	4,981	5,653
24,750	24,800	0	2,093	3,846	4,518	0	2,946	4,971	5,642
24,800	24,850	0	2,085	3,836	4,507	0	2,938	4,960	5,632
24,850	24,900	0	2,077	3,825	4,497	0	2,930	4,950	5,621
24,900	24,950	0	2,069	3,815	4,486	0	2,922	4,939	5,611
24,950	25,000	0	2,061	3,804	4,476	0	2,914	4,929	5,600
25,000	25,050	0	2,053	3,794	4,465	0	2,906	4,918	5,590
25,050	25,100	0	2,045	3,783	4,455	0	2,898	4,908	5,579
25,100	25,150	0	2,037	3,772	4,444	0	2,890	4,897	5,569
25,150	25,200	0	2,029	3,762	4,433	0	2,882	4,887	5,558
25,200	25,250	0	2,021	3,751	4,423	0	2,874	4,876	5,548
25,250	25,300	0	2,013	3,741	4,412	0	2,866	4,866	5,537
25,300	25,350	0	2,005	3,730	4,402	0	2,858	4,855	5,526
25,350	25,400	0	1,997	3,720	4,391	0	2,850	4,844	5,516
25,400	25,450	0	1,989	3,709	4,381	0	2,842	4,834	5,505
25,450	25,500	0	1,981	3,699	4,370	0	2,834	4,823	5,495
25,500	25,550	0	1,973	3,688	4,360	0	2,826	4,813	5,484
25,550	25,600	0	1,965	3,678	4,349	0	2,818	4,802	5,474
25,600	25,650	0	1,957	3,667	4,339	0	2,810	4,792	5,463
25,650	25,700	0	1,949	3,657	4,328	0	2,802	4,781	5,453
25,700	25,750	0	1,941	3,646	4,318	0	2,794	4,771	5,442
25,750	25,800	0	1,933	3,636	4,307	0	2,786	4,760	5,432
25,800	25,850	0	1,925	3,625	4,297	0	2,778	4,750	5,421
25,850	25,900	0	1,917	3,615	4,286	0	2,770	4,739	5,411
25,900	25,950	0	1,909	3,604	4,276	0	2,762	4,729	5,400
25,950	26,000	0	1,901	3,593	4,265	0	2,754	4,718	5,390
26,000	26,050	0	1,893	3,583	4,254	0	2,746	4,708	5,379
26,050	26,100	0	1,885	3,572	4,244	0	2,738	4,697	5,369
26,100	26,150	0	1,877	3,562	4,233	0	2,730	4,686	5,358
26,150	26,200	0	1,869	3,551	4,223	0	2,722	4,676	5,347
26,200	26,250	0	1,861	3,541	4,212	0	2,714	4,665	5,337
26,250	26,300	0	1,853	3,530	4,202	0	2,706	4,655	5,326
26,300	26,350	0	1,845	3,520	4,191	0	2,698	4,644	5,316
26,350	26,400	0	1,837	3,509	4,181	0	2,690	4,634	5,305
26,400	26,450	0	1,829	3,499	4,170	0	2,682	4,623	5,295
26,450	26,500	0	1,821	3,488	4,160	0	2,674	4,613	5,284
26,500	26,550	0	1,813	3,478	4,149	0	2,666	4,602	5,274
26,550	26,600	0	1,805	3,467	4,139	0	2,658	4,592	5,263
26,600	26,650	0	1,797	3,457	4,128	0	2,650	4,581	5,253
26,650	26,700	0	1,789	3,446	4,118	0	2,642	4,571	5,242
26,700	26,750	0	1,781	3,436	4,107	0	2,634	4,560	5,232
26,750	26,800	0	1,773	3,425	4,097	0	2,626	4,550	5,221
26,800	26,850	0	1,765	3,414	4,086	0	2,618	4,539	5,211
26,850	26,900	0	1,757	3,404	4,075	0	2,610	4,529	5,200
26,900	26,950	0	1,749	3,393	4,065	0	2,602	4,518	5,190
26,950	27,000	0	1,741	3,383	4,054	0	2,594	4,507	5,179
27,000	27,050	0	1,733	3,372	4,044	0	2,586	4,497	5,168
27,050	27,100	0	1,725	3,362	4,033	0	2,578	4,486	5,158
27,100	27,150	0	1,717	3,351	4,023	0	2,570	4,476	5,147
27,150	27,200	0	1,709	3,341	4,012	0	2,562	4,465	5,137
27,200	27,250	0	1,701	3,330	4,002	0	2,554	4,455	5,126
27,250	27,300	0	1,693	3,320	3,991	0	2,546	4,444	5,116
27,300	27,350	0	1,685	3,309	3,981	0	2,538	4,434	5,105
27,350	27,400	0	1,677	3,299	3,970	0	2,531	4,423	5,095
27,400	27,450	0	1,669	3,288	3,960	0	2,523	4,413	5,084
27,450	27,500	0	1,661	3,278	3,949	0	2,515	4,402	5,074
27,500	27,550	0	1,653	3,267	3,939	0	2,507	4,392	5,063
27,550	27,600	0	1,645	3,257	3,928	0	2,499	4,381	5,053
27,600	27,650	0	1,637	3,246	3,917	0	2,491	4,371	5,042
27,650	27,700	0	1,629	3,235	3,907	0	2,483	4,360	5,032
27,700	27,750	0	1,621	3,225	3,896	0	2,475	4,350	5,021
27,750	27,800	0	1,613	3,214	3,886	0	2,467	4,339	5,011
27,800	27,850	0	1,605	3,204	3,875	0	2,459	4,328	5,000
27,850	27,900	0	1,597	3,193	3,865	0	2,451	4,318	4,989
27,900	27,950	0	1,589	3,183	3,854	0	2,443	4,307	4,979
27,950	28,000	0	1,581	3,172	3,844	0	2,435	4,297	4,968
28,000	28,050	0	1,573	3,162	3,833	0	2,427	4,286	4,958
28,050	28,100	0	1,565	3,151	3,823	0	2,419	4,276	4,947
28,100	28,150	0	1,557	3,141	3,812	0	2,411	4,265	4,937
28,150	28,200	0	1,549	3,130	3,802	0	2,403	4,255	4,926
28,200	28,250	0	1,541	3,120	3,791	0	2,395	4,244	4,916
28,250	28,300	0	1,533	3,109	3,781	0	2,387	4,234	4,905
28,300	28,350	0	1,525	3,099	3,770	0	2,379	4,223	4,895
28,350	28,400	0	1,517	3,088	3,760	0	2,371	4,213	4,884
28,400	28,450	0	1,509	3,078	3,749	0	2,363	4,202	4,874
28,450	28,500	0	1,501	3,067	3,738	0	2,355	4,192	4,863
28,500	28,550	0	1,493	3,056	3,728	0	2,347	4,181	4,853
28,550	28,600	0	1,485	3,046	3,717	0	2,339	4,171	4,842
28,600	28,650	0	1,477	3,035	3,707	0	2,331	4,160	4,831
28,650	28,700	0	1,469	3,025	3,696	0	2,323	4,149	4,821
28,700	28,750	0	1,461	3,014	3,686	0	2,315	4,139	4,810
28,750	28,800	0	1,453	3,004	3,675	0	2,307	4,128	4,800
28,800	28,850	0	1,445	2,993	3,665	0	2,299	4,118	4,789
28,850	28,900	0	1,437	2,983	3,654	0	2,291	4,107	4,779
28,900	28,950	0	1,429	2,972	3,644	0	2,283	4,097	4,768
28,950	29,000	0	1,421	2,962	3,633	0	2,275	4,086	4,758

(Continued)

Earned Income Credit (EIC) Table - *Continued*

(Caution. This is **not** a tax table.)

If the amount you are looking up from the worksheet is– At least	But less than	Single, head of household, or qualifying widow(er) and the number of children you have is– 0	1	2	3	Married filing jointly and the number of children you have is– 0	1	2	3
29,000	29,050	0	1,413	2,951	3,623	0	2,267	4,076	4,747
29,050	29,100	0	1,406	2,941	3,612	0	2,259	4,065	4,737
29,100	29,150	0	1,398	2,930	3,602	0	2,251	4,055	4,726
29,150	29,200	0	1,390	2,920	3,591	0	2,243	4,044	4,716
29,200	29,250	0	1,382	2,909	3,581	0	2,235	4,034	4,705
29,250	29,300	0	1,374	2,899	3,570	0	2,227	4,023	4,695
29,300	29,350	0	1,366	2,888	3,559	0	2,219	4,013	4,684
29,350	29,400	0	1,358	2,877	3,549	0	2,211	4,002	4,674
29,400	29,450	0	1,350	2,867	3,538	0	2,203	3,992	4,663
29,450	29,500	0	1,342	2,856	3,528	0	2,195	3,981	4,652
29,500	29,550	0	1,334	2,846	3,517	0	2,187	3,970	4,642
29,550	29,600	0	1,326	2,835	3,507	0	2,179	3,960	4,631
29,600	29,650	0	1,318	2,825	3,496	0	2,171	3,949	4,621
29,650	29,700	0	1,310	2,814	3,486	0	2,163	3,939	4,610
29,700	29,750	0	1,302	2,804	3,475	0	2,155	3,928	4,600
29,750	29,800	0	1,294	2,793	3,465	0	2,147	3,918	4,589
29,800	29,850	0	1,286	2,783	3,454	0	2,139	3,907	4,579
29,850	29,900	0	1,278	2,772	3,444	0	2,131	3,897	4,568
29,900	29,950	0	1,270	2,762	3,433	0	2,123	3,886	4,558
29,950	30,000	0	1,262	2,751	3,423	0	2,115	3,876	4,547
30,000	30,050	0	1,254	2,741	3,412	0	2,107	3,865	4,537
30,050	30,100	0	1,246	2,730	3,402	0	2,099	3,855	4,526
30,100	30,150	0	1,238	2,719	3,391	0	2,091	3,844	4,516
30,150	30,200	0	1,230	2,709	3,380	0	2,083	3,834	4,505
30,200	30,250	0	1,222	2,698	3,370	0	2,075	3,823	4,495
30,250	30,300	0	1,214	2,688	3,359	0	2,067	3,813	4,484
30,300	30,350	0	1,206	2,677	3,349	0	2,059	3,802	4,473
30,350	30,400	0	1,198	2,667	3,338	0	2,051	3,791	4,463
30,400	30,450	0	1,190	2,656	3,328	0	2,043	3,781	4,452
30,450	30,500	0	1,182	2,646	3,317	0	2,035	3,770	4,442
30,500	30,550	0	1,174	2,635	3,307	0	2,027	3,760	4,431
30,550	30,600	0	1,166	2,625	3,296	0	2,019	3,749	4,421
30,600	30,650	0	1,158	2,614	3,286	0	2,011	3,739	4,410
30,650	30,700	0	1,150	2,604	3,275	0	2,003	3,728	4,400
30,700	30,750	0	1,142	2,593	3,265	0	1,995	3,718	4,389
30,750	30,800	0	1,134	2,583	3,254	0	1,987	3,707	4,379
30,800	30,850	0	1,126	2,572	3,244	0	1,979	3,697	4,368
30,850	30,900	0	1,118	2,562	3,233	0	1,971	3,686	4,358
30,900	30,950	0	1,110	2,551	3,223	0	1,963	3,676	4,347
30,950	31,000	0	1,102	2,540	3,212	0	1,955	3,665	4,337
31,000	31,050	0	1,094	2,530	3,201	0	1,947	3,655	4,326
31,050	31,100	0	1,086	2,519	3,191	0	1,939	3,644	4,316
31,100	31,150	0	1,078	2,509	3,180	0	1,931	3,633	4,305
31,150	31,200	0	1,070	2,498	3,170	0	1,923	3,623	4,294
31,200	31,250	0	1,062	2,488	3,159	0	1,915	3,612	4,284
31,250	31,300	0	1,054	2,477	3,149	0	1,907	3,602	4,273
31,300	31,350	0	1,046	2,467	3,138	0	1,899	3,591	4,263
31,350	31,400	0	1,038	2,456	3,128	0	1,891	3,581	4,252
31,400	31,450	0	1,030	2,446	3,117	0	1,883	3,570	4,242
31,450	31,500	0	1,022	2,435	3,107	0	1,875	3,560	4,231
31,500	31,550	0	1,014	2,425	3,096	0	1,867	3,549	4,221
31,550	31,600	0	1,006	2,414	3,086	0	1,859	3,539	4,210
31,600	31,650	0	998	2,404	3,075	0	1,851	3,528	4,200
31,650	31,700	0	990	2,393	3,065	0	1,843	3,518	4,189
31,700	31,750	0	982	2,383	3,054	0	1,835	3,507	4,179
31,750	31,800	0	974	2,372	3,044	0	1,827	3,497	4,168
31,800	31,850	0	966	2,361	3,033	0	1,819	3,486	4,158
31,850	31,900	0	958	2,351	3,022	0	1,811	3,476	4,147
31,900	31,950	0	950	2,340	3,012	0	1,803	3,465	4,137
31,950	32,000	0	942	2,330	3,001	0	1,795	3,454	4,126

If the amount you are looking up from the worksheet is– At least	But less than	Single, head of household, or qualifying widow(er) and the number of children you have is– 0	1	2	3	Married filing jointly and the number of children you have is– 0	1	2	3
32,000	32,050	0	934	2,319	2,991	0	1,787	3,444	4,115
32,050	32,100	0	926	2,309	2,980	0	1,779	3,433	4,105
32,100	32,150	0	918	2,298	2,970	0	1,771	3,423	4,094
32,150	32,200	0	910	2,288	2,959	0	1,763	3,412	4,084
32,200	32,250	0	902	2,277	2,949	0	1,755	3,402	4,073
32,250	32,300	0	894	2,267	2,938	0	1,747	3,391	4,063
32,300	32,350	0	886	2,256	2,928	0	1,739	3,381	4,052
32,350	32,400	0	878	2,246	2,917	0	1,732	3,370	4,042
32,400	32,450	0	870	2,235	2,907	0	1,724	3,360	4,031
32,450	32,500	0	862	2,225	2,896	0	1,716	3,349	4,021
32,500	32,550	0	854	2,214	2,886	0	1,708	3,339	4,010
32,550	32,600	0	846	2,204	2,875	0	1,700	3,328	4,000
32,600	32,650	0	838	2,193	2,864	0	1,692	3,318	3,989
32,650	32,700	0	830	2,182	2,854	0	1,684	3,307	3,979
32,700	32,750	0	822	2,172	2,843	0	1,676	3,297	3,968
32,750	32,800	0	814	2,161	2,833	0	1,668	3,286	3,958
32,800	32,850	0	806	2,151	2,822	0	1,660	3,275	3,947
32,850	32,900	0	798	2,140	2,812	0	1,652	3,265	3,936
32,900	32,950	0	790	2,130	2,801	0	1,644	3,254	3,926
32,950	33,000	0	782	2,119	2,791	0	1,636	3,244	3,915
33,000	33,050	0	774	2,109	2,780	0	1,628	3,233	3,905
33,050	33,100	0	766	2,098	2,770	0	1,620	3,223	3,894
33,100	33,150	0	758	2,088	2,759	0	1,612	3,212	3,884
33,150	33,200	0	750	2,077	2,749	0	1,604	3,202	3,873
33,200	33,250	0	742	2,067	2,738	0	1,596	3,191	3,863
33,250	33,300	0	734	2,056	2,728	0	1,588	3,181	3,852
33,300	33,350	0	726	2,046	2,717	0	1,580	3,170	3,842
33,350	33,400	0	718	2,035	2,707	0	1,572	3,160	3,831
33,400	33,450	0	710	2,025	2,696	0	1,564	3,149	3,821
33,450	33,500	0	702	2,014	2,685	0	1,556	3,139	3,810
33,500	33,550	0	694	2,003	2,675	0	1,548	3,128	3,800
33,550	33,600	0	686	1,993	2,664	0	1,540	3,118	3,789
33,600	33,650	0	678	1,982	2,654	0	1,532	3,107	3,778
33,650	33,700	0	670	1,972	2,643	0	1,524	3,096	3,768
33,700	33,750	0	662	1,961	2,633	0	1,516	3,086	3,757
33,750	33,800	0	654	1,951	2,622	0	1,508	3,075	3,747
33,800	33,850	0	646	1,940	2,612	0	1,500	3,065	3,736
33,850	33,900	0	638	1,930	2,601	0	1,492	3,054	3,726
33,900	33,950	0	630	1,919	2,591	0	1,484	3,044	3,715
33,950	34,000	0	622	1,909	2,580	0	1,476	3,033	3,705
34,000	34,050	0	614	1,898	2,570	0	1,468	3,023	3,694
34,050	34,100	0	607	1,888	2,559	0	1,460	3,012	3,684
34,100	34,150	0	599	1,877	2,549	0	1,452	3,002	3,673
34,150	34,200	0	591	1,867	2,538	0	1,444	2,991	3,663
34,200	34,250	0	583	1,856	2,528	0	1,436	2,981	3,652
34,250	34,300	0	575	1,846	2,517	0	1,428	2,970	3,642
34,300	34,350	0	567	1,835	2,506	0	1,420	2,960	3,631
34,350	34,400	0	559	1,824	2,496	0	1,412	2,949	3,621
34,400	34,450	0	551	1,814	2,485	0	1,404	2,939	3,610
34,450	34,500	0	543	1,803	2,475	0	1,396	2,928	3,599
34,500	34,550	0	535	1,793	2,464	0	1,388	2,917	3,589
34,550	34,600	0	527	1,782	2,454	0	1,380	2,907	3,578
34,600	34,650	0	519	1,772	2,443	0	1,372	2,896	3,568
34,650	34,700	0	511	1,761	2,433	0	1,364	2,886	3,557
34,700	34,750	0	503	1,751	2,422	0	1,356	2,875	3,547
34,750	34,800	0	495	1,740	2,412	0	1,348	2,865	3,536
34,800	34,850	0	487	1,730	2,401	0	1,340	2,854	3,526
34,850	34,900	0	479	1,719	2,391	0	1,332	2,844	3,515
34,900	34,950	0	471	1,709	2,380	0	1,324	2,833	3,505
34,950	35,000	0	463	1,698	2,370	0	1,316	2,823	3,494

(Continued)

Earned Income Credit (EIC) Table - *Continued* (Caution. This is **not** a tax table.)

If the amount you are looking up from the worksheet is—		Single, head of household, or qualifying widow(er) and the number of children you have is—				Married filing jointly and the number of children you have is—			
At least	But less than	0	1	2	3	0	1	2	3
		Your credit is—				Your credit is—			
35,000	35,050	0	455	1,688	2,359	0	1,308	2,812	3,484
35,050	35,100	0	447	1,677	2,349	0	1,300	2,802	3,473
35,100	35,150	0	439	1,666	2,338	0	1,292	2,791	3,463
35,150	35,200	0	431	1,656	2,327	0	1,284	2,781	3,452
35,200	35,250	0	423	1,645	2,317	0	1,276	2,770	3,442
35,250	35,300	0	415	1,635	2,306	0	1,268	2,760	3,431
35,300	35,350	0	407	1,624	2,296	0	1,260	2,749	3,420
35,350	35,400	0	399	1,614	2,285	0	1,252	2,738	3,410
35,400	35,450	0	391	1,603	2,275	0	1,244	2,728	3,399
35,450	35,500	0	383	1,593	2,264	0	1,236	2,717	3,389
35,500	35,550	0	375	1,582	2,254	0	1,228	2,707	3,378
35,550	35,600	0	367	1,572	2,243	0	1,220	2,696	3,368
35,600	35,650	0	359	1,561	2,233	0	1,212	2,686	3,357
35,650	35,700	0	351	1,551	2,222	0	1,204	2,675	3,347
35,700	35,750	0	343	1,540	2,212	0	1,196	2,665	3,336
35,750	35,800	0	335	1,530	2,201	0	1,188	2,654	3,326
35,800	35,850	0	327	1,519	2,191	0	1,180	2,644	3,315
35,850	35,900	0	319	1,509	2,180	0	1,172	2,633	3,305
35,900	35,950	0	311	1,498	2,170	0	1,164	2,623	3,294
35,950	36,000	0	303	1,487	2,159	0	1,156	2,612	3,284
36,000	36,050	0	295	1,477	2,148	0	1,148	2,602	3,273
36,050	36,100	0	287	1,466	2,138	0	1,140	2,591	3,263
36,100	36,150	0	279	1,456	2,127	0	1,132	2,580	3,252
36,150	36,200	0	271	1,445	2,117	0	1,124	2,570	3,241
36,200	36,250	0	263	1,435	2,106	0	1,116	2,559	3,231
36,250	36,300	0	255	1,424	2,096	0	1,108	2,549	3,220
36,300	36,350	0	247	1,414	2,085	0	1,100	2,538	3,210
36,350	36,400	0	239	1,403	2,075	0	1,092	2,528	3,199
36,400	36,450	0	231	1,393	2,064	0	1,084	2,517	3,189
36,450	36,500	0	223	1,382	2,054	0	1,076	2,507	3,178
36,500	36,550	0	215	1,372	2,043	0	1,068	2,496	3,168
36,550	36,600	0	207	1,361	2,033	0	1,060	2,486	3,157
36,600	36,650	0	199	1,351	2,022	0	1,052	2,475	3,147
36,650	36,700	0	191	1,340	2,012	0	1,044	2,465	3,136
36,700	36,750	0	183	1,330	2,001	0	1,036	2,454	3,126
36,750	36,800	0	175	1,319	1,991	0	1,028	2,444	3,115
36,800	36,850	0	167	1,308	1,980	0	1,020	2,433	3,105
36,850	36,900	0	159	1,298	1,969	0	1,012	2,423	3,094
36,900	36,950	0	151	1,287	1,959	0	1,004	2,412	3,084
36,950	37,000	0	143	1,277	1,948	0	996	2,401	3,073
37,000	37,050	0	135	1,266	1,938	0	988	2,391	3,062
37,050	37,100	0	127	1,256	1,927	0	980	2,380	3,052
37,100	37,150	0	119	1,245	1,917	0	972	2,370	3,041
37,150	37,200	0	111	1,235	1,906	0	964	2,359	3,031
37,200	37,250	0	103	1,224	1,896	0	956	2,349	3,020
37,250	37,300	0	95	1,214	1,885	0	948	2,338	3,010
37,300	37,350	0	87	1,203	1,875	0	940	2,328	2,999
37,350	37,400	0	79	1,193	1,864	0	933	2,317	2,989
37,400	37,450	0	71	1,182	1,854	0	925	2,307	2,978
37,450	37,500	0	63	1,172	1,843	0	917	2,296	2,968
37,500	37,550	0	55	1,161	1,833	0	909	2,286	2,957
37,550	37,600	0	47	1,151	1,822	0	901	2,275	2,947
37,600	37,650	0	39	1,140	1,811	0	893	2,265	2,936
37,650	37,700	0	31	1,129	1,801	0	885	2,254	2,926
37,700	37,750	0	23	1,119	1,790	0	877	2,244	2,915
37,750	37,800	0	15	1,108	1,780	0	869	2,233	2,905
37,800	37,850	0	7	1,098	1,769	0	861	2,222	2,894
37,850	37,900	0	*	1,087	1,759	0	853	2,212	2,883
37,900	37,950	0	0	1,077	1,748	0	845	2,201	2,873
37,950	38,000	0	0	1,066	1,738	0	837	2,191	2,862
38,000	38,050	0	0	1,056	1,727	0	829	2,180	2,852
38,050	38,100	0	0	1,045	1,717	0	821	2,170	2,841
38,100	38,150	0	0	1,035	1,706	0	813	2,159	2,831
38,150	38,200	0	0	1,024	1,696	0	805	2,149	2,820
38,200	38,250	0	0	1,014	1,685	0	797	2,138	2,810
38,250	38,300	0	0	1,003	1,675	0	789	2,128	2,799
38,300	38,350	0	0	993	1,664	0	781	2,117	2,789
38,350	38,400	0	0	982	1,654	0	773	2,107	2,778
38,400	38,450	0	0	972	1,643	0	765	2,096	2,768
38,450	38,500	0	0	961	1,632	0	757	2,086	2,757
38,500	38,550	0	0	950	1,622	0	749	2,075	2,747
38,550	38,600	0	0	940	1,611	0	741	2,065	2,736
38,600	38,650	0	0	929	1,601	0	733	2,054	2,725
38,650	38,700	0	0	919	1,590	0	725	2,043	2,715
38,700	38,750	0	0	908	1,580	0	717	2,033	2,704
38,750	38,800	0	0	898	1,569	0	709	2,022	2,694
38,800	38,850	0	0	887	1,559	0	701	2,012	2,683
38,850	38,900	0	0	877	1,548	0	693	2,001	2,673
38,900	38,950	0	0	866	1,538	0	685	1,991	2,662
38,950	39,000	0	0	856	1,527	0	677	1,980	2,652
39,000	39,050	0	0	845	1,517	0	669	1,970	2,641
39,050	39,100	0	0	835	1,506	0	661	1,959	2,631
39,100	39,150	0	0	824	1,496	0	653	1,949	2,620
39,150	39,200	0	0	814	1,485	0	645	1,938	2,610
39,200	39,250	0	0	803	1,475	0	637	1,928	2,599
39,250	39,300	0	0	793	1,464	0	629	1,917	2,589
39,300	39,350	0	0	782	1,453	0	621	1,907	2,578
39,350	39,400	0	0	771	1,443	0	613	1,896	2,568
39,400	39,450	0	0	761	1,432	0	605	1,886	2,557
39,450	39,500	0	0	750	1,422	0	597	1,875	2,546
39,500	39,550	0	0	740	1,411	0	589	1,864	2,536
39,550	39,600	0	0	729	1,401	0	581	1,854	2,525
39,600	39,650	0	0	719	1,390	0	573	1,843	2,515
39,650	39,700	0	0	708	1,380	0	565	1,833	2,504
39,700	39,750	0	0	698	1,369	0	557	1,822	2,494
39,750	39,800	0	0	687	1,359	0	549	1,812	2,483
39,800	39,850	0	0	677	1,348	0	541	1,801	2,473
39,850	39,900	0	0	666	1,338	0	533	1,791	2,462
39,900	39,950	0	0	656	1,327	0	525	1,780	2,452
39,950	40,000	0	0	645	1,317	0	517	1,770	2,441
40,000	40,050	0	0	635	1,306	0	509	1,759	2,431
40,050	40,100	0	0	624	1,296	0	501	1,749	2,420
40,100	40,150	0	0	613	1,285	0	493	1,738	2,410
40,150	40,200	0	0	603	1,274	0	485	1,728	2,399
40,200	40,250	0	0	592	1,264	0	477	1,717	2,389
40,250	40,300	0	0	582	1,253	0	469	1,707	2,378
40,300	40,350	0	0	571	1,243	0	461	1,696	2,367
40,350	40,400	0	0	561	1,232	0	453	1,685	2,357
40,400	40,450	0	0	550	1,222	0	445	1,675	2,346
40,450	40,500	0	0	540	1,211	0	437	1,664	2,336
40,500	40,550	0	0	529	1,201	0	429	1,654	2,325
40,550	40,600	0	0	519	1,190	0	421	1,643	2,315
40,600	40,650	0	0	508	1,180	0	413	1,633	2,304
40,650	40,700	0	0	498	1,169	0	405	1,622	2,294
40,700	40,750	0	0	487	1,159	0	397	1,612	2,283
40,750	40,800	0	0	477	1,148	0	389	1,601	2,273
40,800	40,850	0	0	466	1,138	0	381	1,591	2,262
40,850	40,900	0	0	456	1,127	0	373	1,580	2,252
40,900	40,950	0	0	445	1,117	0	365	1,570	2,241
40,950	41,000	0	0	434	1,106	0	357	1,559	2,231

(Continued)

* If the amount you are looking up from the worksheet is at least $37,850 but less than $37,870, and you have one qualifying child, your credit is $2.
If the amount you are looking up from the worksheet is $37,870 or more, and you have one qualifying child, you cannot take the credit.

Earned Income Credit (EIC) Table - *Continued*

(Caution. This is **not** a tax table.)

If the amount you are looking up from the worksheet is–		Single, head of household, or qualifying widow(er) and the number of children you have is–				Married filing jointly and the number of children you have is–			
At least	But less than	0	1	2	3	0	1	2	3
		Your credit is–				Your credit is–			
41,000	41,050	0	0	424	1,095	0	349	1,549	2,220
41,050	41,100	0	0	413	1,085	0	341	1,538	2,210
41,100	41,150	0	0	403	1,074	0	333	1,527	2,199
41,150	41,200	0	0	392	1,064	0	325	1,517	2,188
41,200	41,250	0	0	382	1,053	0	317	1,506	2,178
41,250	41,300	0	0	371	1,043	0	309	1,496	2,167
41,300	41,350	0	0	361	1,032	0	301	1,485	2,157
41,350	41,400	0	0	350	1,022	0	293	1,475	2,146
41,400	41,450	0	0	340	1,011	0	285	1,464	2,136
41,450	41,500	0	0	329	1,001	0	277	1,454	2,125
41,500	41,550	0	0	319	990	0	269	1,443	2,115
41,550	41,600	0	0	308	980	0	261	1,433	2,104
41,600	41,650	0	0	298	969	0	253	1,422	2,094
41,650	41,700	0	0	287	959	0	245	1,412	2,083
41,700	41,750	0	0	277	948	0	237	1,401	2,073
41,750	41,800	0	0	266	938	0	229	1,391	2,062
41,800	41,850	0	0	255	927	0	221	1,380	2,052
41,850	41,900	0	0	245	916	0	213	1,370	2,041
41,900	41,950	0	0	234	906	0	205	1,359	2,031
41,950	42,000	0	0	224	895	0	197	1,348	2,020
42,000	42,050	0	0	213	885	0	189	1,338	2,009
42,050	42,100	0	0	203	874	0	181	1,327	1,999
42,100	42,150	0	0	192	864	0	173	1,317	1,988
42,150	42,200	0	0	182	853	0	165	1,306	1,978
42,200	42,250	0	0	171	843	0	157	1,296	1,967
42,250	42,300	0	0	161	832	0	149	1,285	1,957
42,300	42,350	0	0	150	822	0	141	1,275	1,946
42,350	42,400	0	0	140	811	0	134	1,264	1,936
42,400	42,450	0	0	129	801	0	126	1,254	1,925
42,450	42,500	0	0	119	790	0	118	1,243	1,915
42,500	42,550	0	0	108	780	0	110	1,233	1,904
42,550	42,600	0	0	98	769	0	102	1,222	1,894
42,600	42,650	0	0	87	758	0	94	1,212	1,883
42,650	42,700	0	0	76	748	0	86	1,201	1,873
42,700	42,750	0	0	66	737	0	78	1,191	1,862
42,750	42,800	0	0	55	727	0	70	1,180	1,852
42,800	42,850	0	0	45	716	0	62	1,169	1,841
42,850	42,900	0	0	34	706	0	54	1,159	1,830
42,900	42,950	0	0	24	695	0	46	1,148	1,820
42,950	43,000	0	0	13	685	0	38	1,138	1,809
43,000	43,050	0	0	*	674	0	30	1,127	1,799
43,050	43,100	0	0	0	664	0	22	1,117	1,788
43,100	43,150	0	0	0	653	0	14	1,106	1,778
43,150	43,200	0	0	0	643	0	6	1,096	1,767
43,200	43,250	0	0	0	632	0	**	1,085	1,757
43,250	43,300	0	0	0	622	0	0	1,075	1,746
43,300	43,350	0	0	0	611	0	0	1,064	1,736
43,350	43,400	0	0	0	601	0	0	1,054	1,725
43,400	43,450	0	0	0	590	0	0	1,043	1,715
43,450	43,500	0	0	0	579	0	0	1,033	1,704

If the amount you are looking up from the worksheet is–		Single, head of household, or qualifying widow(er) and the number of children you have is–				Married filing jointly and the number of children you have is–			
At least	But less than	0	1	2	3	0	1	2	3
		Your credit is–				Your credit is–			
43,500	43,550	0	0	0	569	0	0	1,022	1,694
43,550	43,600	0	0	0	558	0	0	1,012	1,683
43,600	43,650	0	0	0	548	0	0	1,001	1,672
43,650	43,700	0	0	0	537	0	0	990	1,662
43,700	43,750	0	0	0	527	0	0	980	1,651
43,750	43,800	0	0	0	516	0	0	969	1,641
43,800	43,850	0	0	0	506	0	0	959	1,630
43,850	43,900	0	0	0	495	0	0	948	1,620
43,900	43,950	0	0	0	485	0	0	938	1,609
43,950	44,000	0	0	0	474	0	0	927	1,599
44,000	44,050	0	0	0	464	0	0	917	1,588
44,050	44,100	0	0	0	453	0	0	906	1,578
44,100	44,150	0	0	0	443	0	0	896	1,567
44,150	44,200	0	0	0	432	0	0	885	1,557
44,200	44,250	0	0	0	422	0	0	875	1,546
44,250	44,300	0	0	0	411	0	0	864	1,536
44,300	44,350	0	0	0	400	0	0	854	1,525
44,350	44,400	0	0	0	390	0	0	843	1,515
44,400	44,450	0	0	0	379	0	0	833	1,504
44,450	44,500	0	0	0	369	0	0	822	1,493
44,500	44,550	0	0	0	358	0	0	811	1,483
44,550	44,600	0	0	0	348	0	0	801	1,472
44,600	44,650	0	0	0	337	0	0	790	1,462
44,650	44,700	0	0	0	327	0	0	780	1,451
44,700	44,750	0	0	0	316	0	0	769	1,441
44,750	44,800	0	0	0	306	0	0	759	1,430
44,800	44,850	0	0	0	295	0	0	748	1,420
44,850	44,900	0	0	0	285	0	0	738	1,409
44,900	44,950	0	0	0	274	0	0	727	1,399
44,950	45,000	0	0	0	264	0	0	717	1,388
45,000	45,050	0	0	0	253	0	0	706	1,378
45,050	45,100	0	0	0	243	0	0	696	1,367
45,100	45,150	0	0	0	232	0	0	685	1,357
45,150	45,200	0	0	0	221	0	0	675	1,346
45,200	45,250	0	0	0	211	0	0	664	1,336
45,250	45,300	0	0	0	200	0	0	654	1,325
45,300	45,350	0	0	0	190	0	0	643	1,314
45,350	45,400	0	0	0	179	0	0	632	1,304
45,400	45,450	0	0	0	169	0	0	622	1,293
45,450	45,500	0	0	0	158	0	0	611	1,283
45,500	45,550	0	0	0	148	0	0	601	1,272
45,550	45,600	0	0	0	137	0	0	590	1,262
45,600	45,650	0	0	0	127	0	0	580	1,251
45,650	45,700	0	0	0	116	0	0	569	1,241
45,700	45,750	0	0	0	106	0	0	559	1,230
45,750	45,800	0	0	0	95	0	0	548	1,220
45,800	45,850	0	0	0	85	0	0	538	1,209
45,850	45,900	0	0	0	74	0	0	527	1,199
45,900	45,950	0	0	0	64	0	0	517	1,188
45,950	46,000	0	0	0	53	0	0	506	1,178

(Continued)

* If the amount you are looking up from the worksheet is at least $43,000 but less than $43,038, and you have two qualifying children, your credit is $4.
If the amount you are looking up from the worksheet is $43,038 or more, and you have two qualifying children, you cannot take the credit.
** If the amount you are looking up from the worksheet is at least $43,200 but less than $43,210, and you have one qualifying child, your credit is $1.
If the amount you are looking up from the worksheet is $43,210 or more, and you have one qualifying child, you cannot take the credit.

Earned Income Credit (EIC) Table - *Continued*

(**Caution.** This is **not** a tax table.)

If the amount you are looking up from the worksheet is—		And your filing status is—							
		Single, head of household, or qualifying widow(er) and the number of children you have is—				Married filing jointly and the number of children you have is—			
At least	But less than	0	1	2	3	0	1	2	3
		Your credit is—				Your credit is—			
46,000	46,050	0	0	0	42	0	0	496	1,167
46,050	46,100	0	0	0	32	0	0	485	1,157
46,100	46,150	0	0	0	21	0	0	474	1,146
46,150	46,200	0	0	0	11	0	0	464	1,135
46,200	46,250	0	0	0	*	0	0	453	1,125
46,250	46,300	0	0	0	0	0	0	443	1,114
46,300	46,350	0	0	0	0	0	0	432	1,104
46,350	46,400	0	0	0	0	0	0	422	1,093
46,400	46,450	0	0	0	0	0	0	411	1,083
46,450	46,500	0	0	0	0	0	0	401	1,072
46,500	46,550	0	0	0	0	0	0	390	1,062
46,550	46,600	0	0	0	0	0	0	380	1,051
46,600	46,650	0	0	0	0	0	0	369	1,041
46,650	46,700	0	0	0	0	0	0	359	1,030
46,700	46,750	0	0	0	0	0	0	348	1,020
46,750	46,800	0	0	0	0	0	0	338	1,009
46,800	46,850	0	0	0	0	0	0	327	999
46,850	46,900	0	0	0	0	0	0	317	988
46,900	46,950	0	0	0	0	0	0	306	978
46,950	47,000	0	0	0	0	0	0	295	967
47,000	47,050	0	0	0	0	0	0	285	956
47,050	47,100	0	0	0	0	0	0	274	946
47,100	47,150	0	0	0	0	0	0	264	935
47,150	47,200	0	0	0	0	0	0	253	925
47,200	47,250	0	0	0	0	0	0	243	914
47,250	47,300	0	0	0	0	0	0	232	904
47,300	47,350	0	0	0	0	0	0	222	893
47,350	47,400	0	0	0	0	0	0	211	883
47,400	47,450	0	0	0	0	0	0	201	872
47,450	47,500	0	0	0	0	0	0	190	862
47,500	47,550	0	0	0	0	0	0	180	851
47,550	47,600	0	0	0	0	0	0	169	841
47,600	47,650	0	0	0	0	0	0	159	830
47,650	47,700	0	0	0	0	0	0	148	820
47,700	47,750	0	0	0	0	0	0	138	809
47,750	47,800	0	0	0	0	0	0	127	799
47,800	47,850	0	0	0	0	0	0	116	788
47,850	47,900	0	0	0	0	0	0	106	777
47,900	47,950	0	0	0	0	0	0	95	767
47,950	48,000	0	0	0	0	0	0	85	756
48,000	48,050	0	0	0	0	0	0	74	746
48,050	48,100	0	0	0	0	0	0	64	735
48,100	48,150	0	0	0	0	0	0	53	725
48,150	48,200	0	0	0	0	0	0	43	714
48,200	48,250	0	0	0	0	0	0	32	704
48,250	48,300	0	0	0	0	0	0	22	693
48,300	48,350	0	0	0	0	0	0	11	683
48,350	48,400	0	0	0	0	0	0	**	672
48,400	48,450	0	0	0	0	0	0	0	662
48,450	48,500	0	0	0	0	0	0	0	651

If the amount you are looking up from the worksheet is—		And your filing status is—							
		Single, head of household, or qualifying widow(er) and the number of children you have is—				Married filing jointly and the number of children you have is—			
At least	But less than	0	1	2	3	0	1	2	3
		Your credit is—				Your credit is—			
48,500	48,550	0	0	0	0	0	0	0	641
48,550	48,600	0	0	0	0	0	0	0	630
48,600	48,650	0	0	0	0	0	0	0	619
48,650	48,700	0	0	0	0	0	0	0	609
48,700	48,750	0	0	0	0	0	0	0	598
48,750	48,800	0	0	0	0	0	0	0	588
48,800	48,850	0	0	0	0	0	0	0	577
48,850	48,900	0	0	0	0	0	0	0	567
48,900	48,950	0	0	0	0	0	0	0	556
48,950	49,000	0	0	0	0	0	0	0	546
49,000	49,050	0	0	0	0	0	0	0	535
49,050	49,100	0	0	0	0	0	0	0	525
49,100	49,150	0	0	0	0	0	0	0	514
49,150	49,200	0	0	0	0	0	0	0	504
49,200	49,250	0	0	0	0	0	0	0	493
49,250	49,300	0	0	0	0	0	0	0	483
49,300	49,350	0	0	0	0	0	0	0	472
49,350	49,400	0	0	0	0	0	0	0	462
49,400	49,450	0	0	0	0	0	0	0	451
49,450	49,500	0	0	0	0	0	0	0	440
49,500	49,550	0	0	0	0	0	0	0	430
49,550	49,600	0	0	0	0	0	0	0	419
49,600	49,650	0	0	0	0	0	0	0	409
49,650	49,700	0	0	0	0	0	0	0	398
49,700	49,750	0	0	0	0	0	0	0	388
49,750	49,800	0	0	0	0	0	0	0	377
49,800	49,850	0	0	0	0	0	0	0	367
49,850	49,900	0	0	0	0	0	0	0	356
49,900	49,950	0	0	0	0	0	0	0	346
49,950	50,000	0	0	0	0	0	0	0	335
50,000	50,050	0	0	0	0	0	0	0	325
50,050	50,100	0	0	0	0	0	0	0	314
50,100	50,150	0	0	0	0	0	0	0	304
50,150	50,200	0	0	0	0	0	0	0	293
50,200	50,250	0	0	0	0	0	0	0	283
50,250	50,300	0	0	0	0	0	0	0	272
50,300	50,350	0	0	0	0	0	0	0	261
50,350	50,400	0	0	0	0	0	0	0	251
50,400	50,450	0	0	0	0	0	0	0	240
50,450	50,500	0	0	0	0	0	0	0	230
50,500	50,550	0	0	0	0	0	0	0	219
50,550	50,600	0	0	0	0	0	0	0	209
50,600	50,650	0	0	0	0	0	0	0	198
50,650	50,700	0	0	0	0	0	0	0	188
50,700	50,750	0	0	0	0	0	0	0	177
50,750	50,800	0	0	0	0	0	0	0	167
50,800	50,850	0	0	0	0	0	0	0	156
50,850	50,900	0	0	0	0	0	0	0	146
50,900	50,950	0	0	0	0	0	0	0	135
50,950	51,000	0	0	0	0	0	0	0	125

(Continued)

* If the amount you are looking up from the worksheet is at least $46,200 but less than $46,227, and you have three qualifying children, your credit is $3.
If the amount you are looking up from the worksheet is $46,227 or more, and you have three qualifying children, you cannot take the credit.
** If the amount you are looking up from the worksheet is at least $48,350 but less than $48,378, and you have two qualifying children, your credit is $3.
If the amount you are looking up from the worksheet is $48,378 or more, and you have two qualifying children, you cannot take the credit.

Earned Income Credit (EIC) Table - *Continued*

If the amount you are looking up from the worksheet is–		And your filing status is–							
		Single, head of household, or qualifying widow(er) and the number of children you have is–				Married filing jointly and the number of children you have is–			
		0	1	2	3	0	1	2	3
At least	But less than	Your credit is–				Your credit is–			
51,000	51,050	0	0	0	0	0	0	0	114
51,050	51,100	0	0	0	0	0	0	0	104
51,100	51,150	0	0	0	0	0	0	0	93
51,150	51,200	0	0	0	0	0	0	0	82
51,200	51,250	0	0	0	0	0	0	0	72
51,250	51,300	0	0	0	0	0	0	0	61
51,300	51,350	0	0	0	0	0	0	0	51
51,350	51,400	0	0	0	0	0	0	0	40
51,400	51,450	0	0	0	0	0	0	0	30
51,450	51,500	0	0	0	0	0	0	0	19
51,500	51,550	0	0	0	0	0	0	0	9
51,550	51,567	0	0	0	0	0	0	0	2

Form **8801**

Department of the Treasury
Internal Revenue Service (99)

**Credit for Prior Year Minimum Tax—
Individuals, Estates, and Trusts**

☒ Information about Form 8801 and its separate instructions is at *www.irs.gov/form8801*.
☒ **Attach to Form 1040, 1040NR, or 1041.**

OMB No. 1545-1073

2013

Attachment
Sequence No. **74**

Name(s) shown on return | Identifying number

Part I	Net Minimum Tax on Exclusion Items		
1	Combine lines 1 and 10 of your 2012 Form 6251. Estates and trusts, see instructions	**1**	
2	Enter adjustments and preferences treated as exclusion items (see instructions)	**2**	
3	Minimum tax credit net operating loss deduction (see instructions)	**3**	( )
4	Combine lines 1, 2, and 3. If zero or less, enter -0- here and on line 15 and go to Part II. If more than $232,500 and you were married filing separately for 2012, see instructions	**4**	
5	Enter: $78,750 if married filing jointly or qualifying widow(er) for 2012; $50,600 if single or head of household for 2012; or $39,375 if married filing separately for 2012. Estates and trusts, enter $22,500	**5**	
6	Enter: $150,000 if married filing jointly or qualifying widow(er) for 2012; $112,500 if single or head of household for 2012; or $75,000 if married filing separately for 2012. Estates and trusts, enter $75,000	**6**	
7	Subtract line 6 from line 4. If zero or less, enter -0- here and on line 8 and go to line 9 . . .	**7**	
8	Multiply line 7 by 25% (.25)	**8**	
9	Subtract line 8 from line 5. If zero or less, enter -0-. If under age 24 at the end of 2012, see instructions	**9**	
10	Subtract line 9 from line 4. If zero or less, enter -0- here and on line 15 and go to Part II. Form 1040NR filers, see instructions	**10**	
11	• If **for 2012** you filed Form 2555 or 2555-EZ, see instructions for the amount to enter. • If **for 2012** you reported capital gain distributions directly on Form 1040, line 13; you reported qualified dividends on Form 1040, line 9b (Form 1041, line 2b(2)); **or** you had a gain on both lines 15 and 16 of Schedule D (Form 1040) (lines 14a and 15, column (2), of Schedule D (Form 1041)), complete Part III of Form 8801 and enter the amount from line 45 here. Form 1040NR filers, see instructions. • **All others:** If line 10 is $175,000 or less ($87,500 or less if married filing separately for 2012), multiply line 10 by 26% (.26). Otherwise, multiply line 10 by 28% (.28) and subtract $3,500 ($1,750 if married filing separately for 2012) from the result. Form 1040NR filers, see instructions.	**11**	
12	Minimum tax foreign tax credit on exclusion items (see instructions)	**12**	
13	Tentative minimum tax on exclusion items. Subtract line 12 from line 11	**13**	
14	Enter the amount from your 2012 Form 6251, line 34, or 2012 Form 1041, Schedule I, line 55 . .	**14**	
15	**Net minimum tax on exclusion items.** Subtract line 14 from line 13. If zero or less, enter -0- . .	**15**	

For Paperwork Reduction Act Notice, see instructions.

Cat. No. 10002S

Form **8801** (2013)

Part II	Minimum Tax Credit and Carryforward to 2014

16	Enter the amount from your 2012 Form 6251, line 35, or 2012 Form 1041, Schedule I, line 56 . .	**16**		
17	Enter the amount from line 15	**17**		
18	Subtract line 17 from line 16. If less than zero, enter as a negative amount	**18**		
19	**2012 credit carryforward.** Enter the amount from your 2012 Form 8801, line 28	**19**		
20	Enter your 2012 unallowed qualified electric vehicle credit (see instructions)	**20**		
21	Combine lines 18 through 20. If zero or less, stop here and see the instructions	**21**		
22	Enter your 2013 regular income tax liability minus allowable credits (see instructions) . . .	**22**		
23	Enter the amount from your 2013 Form 6251, line 33, or 2013 Form 1041, Schedule I, line 54 . .	**23**		
24	Subtract line 23 from line 22. If zero or less, enter -0-	**24**		
25	**Minimum tax credit.** Enter the **smaller** of line 21 or line 24. Also enter this amount on your 2013 Form 1040, line 53 (check box **b**); Form 1040NR, line 50 (check box **b**); or Form 1041, Schedule G, line 2c	**25**		
26	**Credit carryforward to 2014.** Subtract line 25 from line 21. Keep a record of this amount because you may use it in future years	**26**		

Form **8801** (2013)

Part III	Tax Computation Using Maximum Capital Gains Rates

Caution. If you did not complete the 2012 Qualified Dividends and Capital Gain Tax Worksheet, the 2012 Schedule D Tax Worksheet, or Part V of the 2012 Schedule D (Form 1041), see the instructions before completing this part.

27　Enter the amount from Form 8801, line 10. If you filed Form 2555 or 2555-EZ for 2012, enter the amount from line 3 of the Foreign Earned Income Tax Worksheet in the instructions **27**

Caution. If **for 2012** you filed Form 1040NR, 1041, 2555, or 2555-EZ, see the instructions before completing lines 28, 29, and 30.

28　Enter the amount from line 6 of your 2012 Qualified Dividends and Capital Gain Tax Worksheet, the amount from line 13 of your 2012 Schedule D Tax Worksheet, or the amount from line 22 of the 2012 Schedule D (Form 1041), whichever applies* **28**

If you figured your 2012 tax using the 2012 **Qualified Dividends and Capital Gain Tax Worksheet**, skip line 29 and enter the amount from line 28 on line 30. Otherwise, go to line 29.

29　Enter the amount from line 19 of your 2012 Schedule D (Form 1040), or line 14b, column (2), of the 2012 Schedule D (Form 1041) **29**

30　Add lines 28 and 29, and enter the **smaller** of that result or the amount from line 10 of your 2012 Schedule D Tax Worksheet **30**

31　Enter the **smaller** of line 27 or line 30 . . . . **31**

32　Subtract line 31 from line 27 . . . . **32**

33　If line 32 is $175,000 or less ($87,500 or less if married filing separately for 2012), multiply line 32 by 26% (.26). Otherwise, multiply line 32 by 28% (.28) and subtract $3,500 ($1,750 if married filing separately for 2012) from the result. Form 1040NR filers, see instructions . . . . ▶ **33**

34　Enter:
　　• $70,700 if married filing jointly or qualifying widow(er) for 2012,
　　• $35,350 if single or married filing separately for 2012,
　　• $47,350 if head of household for 2012, or
　　• $2,400 for an estate or trust.
　　Form 1040NR filers, see instructions **34**

35　Enter the amount from line 7 of your 2012 Qualified Dividends and Capital Gain Tax Worksheet, the amount from line 14 of your 2012 Schedule D Tax Worksheet, or the amount from line 23 of the 2012 Schedule D (Form 1041), whichever applies. If you did not complete either worksheet or Part V of the 2012 Schedule D (Form 1041), enter -0-. Form 1040NR filers, see instructions **35**

36　Subtract line 35 from line 34. If zero or less, enter -0- **36**

37　Enter the **smaller** of line 27 or line 28 . . . . **37**

38　Enter the **smaller** of line 36 or line 37 . . . . **38**

39　Subtract line 38 from line 37 . . . . **39**

40　Multiply line 39 by 15% (.15) . . . . ▶ **40**

If line 29 is zero or blank, skip lines 41 and 42 and go to line 43. Otherwise, go to line 41.

41　Subtract line 37 from line 31 . . . . **41**

42　Multiply line 41 by 25% (.25) . . . . ▶ **42**

43　Add lines 33, 40, and 42 . . . . **43**

44　If line 27 is $175,000 or less ($87,500 or less if married filing separately for 2012), multiply line 27 by 26% (.26). Otherwise, multiply line 27 by 28% (.28) and subtract $3,500 ($1,750 if married filing separately for 2012) from the result. Form 1040NR filers, see instructions **44**

45　Enter the **smaller** of line 43 or line 44 here and on line 11. If you filed Form 2555 or 2555-EZ for 2012, do not enter this amount on line 11. Instead, enter it on line 4 of the Foreign Earned Income Tax Worksheet in the instructions **45**

* The 2012 Qualified Dividends and Capital Gain Tax Worksheet is in the 2012 Instructions for Form 1040. The 2012 Schedule D Tax Worksheet is in the 2012 Instructions for Schedule D (Form 1040) (or the 2012 Instructions for Schedule D (Form 1041)).

Form **8801** (2013)

Estimated Payments, Penalties, and Amended Returns

What's New in 2013

Itemized Deductions and Personal Exemptions Limited. Beginning in 2013, the phaseout of itemized deductions and personal and dependency exemptions for higher-income taxpayers has been reinstated. As a result, the amount of these otherwise allowable deductions and exemptions will be reduced or eliminated if adjusted gross income exceeds certain threshold amounts.

Last Estimated Tax Payment. An individual is not required to make the fourth and final installment payment of 2013 estimated tax if his or her return for 2013 is filed no later than January 31, 2014, and any balance of tax is paid at that time.

Relevant IRS Publications

☐ IRS Publication 505, *Tax Withholding and Estimated Tax*

☐ Instructions for Form 1040-ES, *Estimated Tax for Individuals*

☐ Instructions for Form 2210, *Underpayment of Estimated Tax by Individuals, Estates and Trusts*

Tax Preparer's Checklist

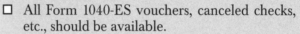

☐ Prior year's returns provide much of the information necessary for determining estimated tax requirements and safe harbor calculations.

☐ All Form 1040-ES vouchers, canceled checks, etc., should be available.

☐ Ensure that clients understand the civil and criminal penalties for tax code violations.

Rates for Individual (Noncorporate) Overpayments and Underpayments 2010-2013

Calendar Quarter	Interest Rate
1-1-10 to 3-31-10	4
4-1-10 to 6-30-10	4
7-1-10 to 9-30-10	4
10-1-10 to 12-31-10	4
1-1-11 to 3-31-11	3
4-1-11 to 6-30-11	4
7-1-11 to 9-30-11	4
10-1-11 to 12-31-11	3
1-1-12 to 3-31-12	3
4-1-12 to 6-30-12	3
7-1-12 to 9-30-12	3
10-1-12 to 12-31-12	3
1-1-13 to 3-31-13	3
4-1-13 to 6-30-13	3
7-1-13 to 9-30-13	3
10-1-13 to 12-31-13	3

Rates for Large Corporate Overpayments and Underpayments 2011-2013

Quarter	Overpayment Interest Rate	Underpayment Interest Rate
1-1-11 to 3-31-11	0.5	5
4-1-11 to 6-30-11	1.5	6
7-1-11 to 9-30-11	1.5	6
10-1-11 to 12-31-11	0.5	5
1-1-12 to 3-31-12	0.5	5
4-1-12 to 6-30-12	0.5	5
7-1-12 to 9-30-12	0.5	5
10-1-12 to 12-31-12	0.5	5
1-1-13 to 3-31-13	0.5	5
4-1-13 to 6-30-13	0.5	5
7-1-13 to 9-30-13	0.5	5
10-1-13 to 12-31-13	0.5	5

Estimated Payment Due Dates for 2013 and 2014

Installment	2013	2014	Fiscal - Year Filers
1	April 15, 2013	April 15, 2014	15th day of fourth month of fiscal year
2	June 17, 2013	June 16, 2014	15th day of sixth month of fiscal year
3	September 16, 2013	September 15, 2014	15th day of ninth month of fiscal year
4	January 15, 2014	January 15, 2015	15th day of the first month after fiscal year ends

Estimated Payments

Federal income tax is a pay-as-you-go tax. Unless the total tax shown on the taxpayer's return minus the amount paid through withholding will be less than $1,000, the taxpayer generally must make quarterly estimated tax payments. Taxpayers whose entire income is subject to withholding and who do not owe special taxes, such as household employment taxes, generally do not need to make separate estimated payments. IRS Publication 505, *Tax Withholding and Estimated Tax*, provides more information.

Who Must Make Estimated Payments

Taxpayers who have income that is not subject to withholding (earnings from self-employment, interest, dividends, rents, alimony, etc.) must determine whether they are required to make estimated payments. In addition, estimated tax payments may be required on unemployment compensation and the taxable portion of Social Security benefits if the taxpayer did not elect voluntary withholding.

Increased Withholding Preferable. There are advantages to increasing withholding rather than making estimated payments. The IRS assesses penalties for late payment, or underpayment, of estimated tax, even when the total amount paid for the year meets or exceeds the tax liability for that year. Withholding is credited ratably against each respective quarter's required estimated tax payment even if the tax was not withheld evenly throughout the year. Therefore, increased withholding later in the year may make up a shortfall that would otherwise result in an underpayment penalty for an earlier quarter. Taxpayers may elect to treat withheld taxes as paid on the date withheld. If they choose this option, they must file Form 2210.

Filing Tip. Taxpayers who have some income subject to withholding may choose to increase the amount of income tax withheld from wages in order to reduce the anticipated tax due with their tax return to below the amount at which quarterly payments are required (generally $1,000).

How to Increase Withholding. To increase the amount of tax withheld from wages, the taxpayer files Form W-4, *Employee's Withholding Allowance Certificate*, with his or her employer. Taxpayers may also choose to have tax withheld from pension or annuity payments (Form W-4P, *Withholding Certificate for Pension or Annuity Payments*), from sick pay that is received from a party other than the taxpayer's employer (Form W-4S, *Request for Federal Income Tax Withholding from Sick Pay*), and from certain government payments, including Social Security payments (Form W-4V, *Voluntary Withholding Request*). Most farm income is not subject to withholding, although voluntary withholding may be elected on certain government payments. IRS Publication 225, *Farmer's Tax Guide*, explains the tax treatment of commodity credit loans and crop disaster payments.

Gambling Winnings. Gambling winnings of more than $5,000 from sweepstakes, wagering pools, or lotteries are subject to income tax withholding at a flat rate. Poker tournament sponsors are required to report, but not withhold, winnings of more than $5,000. Any other wager is subject to withholding if the proceeds are at least 300 times the amount of the bet. Gambling winnings from bingo, keno, and slot machines are generally not subject to withholding. Taxpayers who receive gambling winnings not subject to withholding may need to pay estimated tax.

General Rule

At least 90% of an individual's final income tax is to be paid through either withholding or estimated tax payments. The estimated tax is the amount of income and self-employment tax (as well as other taxes reported on Form 1040–including household employment taxes computed on Form 1040, Schedule H) that an individual estimates will have to be paid for the tax year after subtracting any estimated credits against tax.

Planning Tip. Windfalls, unanticipated revenues, multiple W-2s from different employers, and a variable cash flow from self-employment all affect the estimated tax process in various ways. Practitioners must obtain current information from clients. Taxpayers should contact their tax preparers if their situation changes and estimates may need to be revised.

No underpayment penalty is assessed if the tax shown on the tax return for the year (or, if no return is filed, the tax due), reduced by income tax withheld from wages (including excess Social Security and railroad retirement tax withholding), is less than $1,000.

Also, an individual who was a U.S. citizen or resident alien for the entire previous tax year need not pay estimated tax if he or she had no tax liability for that tax year, provided it was a 12-month period.

Caution. Rules for individuals are different from rules for corporations, estates, trusts, and taxable income of tax-exempt organizations. Don't assume all taxpayers are treated the same! See MTG ¶241 for corporations, MTG ¶511 for estates and trusts, and MTG ¶658 for tax-exempt organizations.

Under circumstances of hardship or following an individual's retirement or disability, the penalty for underpayment of estimated tax may be waived. Form 2210, *Underpayment of Estimated Tax by Individuals, Estates, and Trusts,* must be filed when a waiver of the penalty is requested.

Safe Harbor Estimates

Individuals may avoid the penalty for failure to pay estimated tax by meeting one of the three "safe harbor" provisions:

1. Estimated payments and withholding are at least 90% of the tax shown on the current year's return.
2. Estimated payments and withholding are at least 100% of the tax shown on the prior year's return (the no-estimate safe harbor), provided the prior year's return covered a 12-month period. An individual with adjusted gross income in excess of $150,000 ($75,000 for a married individual filing separately) in 2013 can avoid the estimated tax penalty by paying 110% of the tax shown on the prior year's tax return, provided the prior year was a full year. No estimate of the current year's income is required if this option is available.
3. Estimated payments are made on a current basis under an annualized income installment method.

Married Couples

Married couples may make joint estimated tax payments, even if they are not living together and even if they file separate returns. Married couples cannot make joint estimated tax payments if any of the following three criteria applies:

1. They are legally separated under a decree of divorce or separate maintenance.
2. Either spouse is a nonresident alien (unless an election is made under Code Sec. 6013 to treat the spouse as a resident alien or the spouse becomes a resident alien during the tax year).
3. The spouses have different tax years.

Whether joint or separate estimated tax payments are made will not affect the choice of filing a joint tax return or separate returns. Form 2210 must be filed if 2013 tax is used to figure 2014 estimated payments and a joint return is filed for only one of the years.

2013 Separate Returns and 2014 Joint Return. Taxpayers who plan to file a joint return for 2014, but filed separate returns for 2013, must use the total of the tax shown on the separate 2013 returns in calculating 2013 tax for the no-estimate safe harbor. Returns filed as single, head of household, or married filing separately are considered separate returns.

2013 Joint Return and 2014 Separate Returns. If the taxpayer plans to file a separate return for 2014, but filed a joint return for 2013, the 2013 tax is his or her share of the tax on the joint return.

To figure each spouse's share of the tax on a joint return, first figure the tax both spouses would have paid had they filed separate returns for 2013 using the same filing status as they intend to use for 2014. Then multiply the tax on the joint return by the following fraction:

$$\frac{\text{The tax one spouse would have paid had separate returns been filed}}{\text{The total tax both spouses would have paid had separate returns been filed}}$$

Farmers and Fishermen

Farmers and fishermen may ignore the first three installment due dates and either: 1) pay all their estimated tax by January 15, 2014, and file their tax return by the regular due date; or 2) file their tax return by March 3, 2014, and pay all tax that is due. Estimated payments and withholding need only be two-thirds of the tax liability in 2013. The rule that 110% of the prior year's tax must be used for taxpayers with higher adjusted gross income for 2013 does not apply to farmers and fishermen.

An individual is a farmer or fisherman if at least two-thirds of their gross income for 2013 or 2014 is from farming or fishing. Installments may be based on 66 2/3 percent of the tax shown on the return (or the tax due if no return is filed) for the current tax year.

Gross Income from Farming. Income from cultivating the soil or raising agricultural commodities is considered income from farming. It includes the following amounts:

1. Income from operating a stock, dairy, poultry, bee, fruit, or truck farm.
2. Income from a plantation, ranch, nursery, range, orchard, or oyster bed.
3. Crop shares for the use of the taxpayer's land.
4. Gains from sales of draft, breeding, dairy, or sporting livestock.

These amounts may be shown on Schedule F of Form 1040, *Profit or Loss From Farming;* on Form 4835, *Farm Rental Income and Expenses;* as the taxpayer's share of a partnership's or S corporation's gross income from farming; or as the taxpayer's share of distributable net income from farming of an estate or trust. Gains from sales of draft, breeding, dairy, or sporting livestock are normally shown on Form 4797, *Sales of Business Property.*

Caution. Wages received as a farm employee and wages received from a farm corporation are not gross income from farming.

Gross Income from Fishing. Income from catching, taking, harvesting, cultivating, or farming any kind of fish, shellfish (for example, clams or mussels), crustaceans (for example, lobsters, crabs, or shrimp), sponges, seaweeds, or other aquatic forms of animal and vegetable life is considered income from fishing.

Gross income from fishing includes the following amounts:

1. Income for services as an officer or crew member of a vessel while the vessel is engaged in fishing.
2. The taxpayer's share of partnership, S corporation, estate or trust gross income from fishing.
3. Income for services normally performed in connection with fishing, such as shore service as an officer or crew member of a vessel engaged in fishing, and services that are necessary for the immediate preservation of the catch, such as cleaning, icing, and packing the catch.

See MTG ¶2691 for estimated tax information for farmers and fishermen.

Nonresident Aliens

Generally, a foreign person is subject to U.S. tax withholding on all U.S.-source income. Most types of U.S.-source income received by a foreign person are subject to U.S. tax of 30%. A reduced rate, including exemption, may apply if there is a tax treaty between the foreign person's country of residence and the United States. The tax is generally withheld (NRA withholding) from the payment made to the foreign person.

If too little tax is withheld, three estimated tax payments are required of most nonresident aliens: first installment, 50%, due June 15; second installment, 25%, due September 15; and third installment, 25%, due the following January 15. However, if any wages are subject to the same withholding rules that apply to U.S. citizens, the due dates for U.S. citizens apply. Nonresident aliens must make estimated payments or have withholding of at least (1) 90% of the tax to be shown on the current year's income tax return, or (2) 100% (110% if adjusted gross income for 2013 was more than $150,000, or $75,000 for married filing separately) of the tax shown on the prior year's income tax return, if that return covered 12 months and U.S. tax was owed.

Nonresident aliens use Form 1040-ES (NR) to figure and pay estimated tax, unless they expect to be a resident of Puerto Rico during the entire year, in which case they must use Form 1040-ES or Form 1040-ES (PR) (in Spanish).

Estimated Payment Calculation

Form 1040-ES includes worksheets to figure the amount to pay. A simplified worksheet is included on page 11-6. All taxable income, including the taxable portion of Social Security and railroad retirement benefits, must be included in gross income used to figure estimated payments. See Tab 9 for a table to figure the taxable portion of these benefits. Itemized deductions and adjustments to income may be taken into consideration when calculating estimated payments.

Taxpayers whose income varies during the year may choose to use the annualized income method to estimate tax (see next section).

Unexpected Income

If a taxpayer has unexpected income after March 31 or was not liable for estimated tax on March 31, but after that date his or her tax situation changes, the amount of tax must be recalculated and estimated taxes paid ratably over the remaining installment due dates.

 Caution. Tax rate schedules or tax tables, deductions, and credits for the year in which income is earned must be used to figure estimated payment amounts. Do not use rates or amounts from the prior year.

Annualized Income Method of Estimating Tax

The annualization method is suitable for taxpayers whose income is received or accrued more heavily in one part of the year.

 Gray Area. Annualization may or may not result in lower estimated tax payments. The option is always available, but its use should be weighed carefully.

Estimated tax penalties are computed from the quarter in which a shortfall in the required payment occurs. Normally, this means that the year's income tax is allocated equally across all four quarters. If a taxpayer uses the annualized income installment alterna-

When Unexpected Changes in Income During 2014 Affect Estimated Payments		
Estimated Tax Refigured	**Next Installment Due Date**	**Payment Amount on Due Date**
After March 31 but before June 1	June 16	50% of refigured amount minus prior payments
After May 31 but before September 1	September 15	75% of refigured amount minus prior payments
After August 31 but before December 31	January 15, 2015	100% of refigured amount minus prior payments

tive to calculate the amount of a quarterly installment, he or she can avoid the estimated tax penalty even if an installment of estimated tax is lower than the otherwise required installment. Under this alternative, any difference between an earlier installment paid and the amount required must be made up by increasing the next installment so that the applicable percentage of tax is paid as of that time.

If the annualized income installment method is used to figure estimated tax payments, Form 2210 *must be* filed with the taxpayer's return.

When Estimated Payments Are Due

Any underpayment of tax must be made up by a payment with the final return, and any overpayment is either refunded or credited against the estimated tax for the next year, whichever the taxpayer elects.

See MTG ¶2685 and table on page 11-1.

Installment	**Applicable Percentage**
1	22.5
2	45
3	67.5
4	90

Last Estimated Tax Payment. A taxpayer is not required to make the fourth installment payment if his or her return for the year is filed on or before January 31, 2014, and any balance of tax is paid at that time. Fiscal-year filers may file their returns and pay the tax due by the last day of the first month after the end of their fiscal year instead of paying the last installment. Farmers and fishermen need not make the January 15 payment if they file and pay the entire tax due by March 3, 2014.

See Tab 12 for information about collections, extensions of time to pay, and payment options for taxpayers unable to pay the full amount due.

Where to File Taxes for Form 1040-ES During 2014	
Taxpayer's State of Residence	**Send to: Internal Revenue Service**
Alabama, Georgia, Kentucky, Missouri, New Jersey, North Carolina, South Carolina, Tennessee, Virginia	P.O. Box 105225 Atlanta, GA 30348-5225
Florida, Louisiana, Mississippi, Texas	P.O. Box 1300 Charlotte, NC 28201-1300
Alaska, Arizona, California, Colorado, Hawaii, Idaho, Nevada, New Mexico, Oregon, Utah, Washington, Wyoming	P.O. Box 510000 San Francisco, CA 94151-5100
Arkansas, Illinois, Indiana, Iowa, Kansas, Michigan, Minnesota, Montana, Nebraska, North Dakota, Ohio, Oklahoma, South Dakota, Wisconsin	P.O. Box 802502 Cincinnati, OH 45280-2502
Connecticut, Delaware, District of Columbia, Maine, Maryland, Massachusetts, New Hampshire, New York, Pennsylvania, Rhode Island, Vermont, West Virginia	P.O. Box 37007 Hartford, CT 06176-0007
A foreign country, American Samoa, or Puerto Rico, or use an APO or FPO address, or file Form 2555, 2555-EZ, or 4563, or are a dual-status alien or non-permanent resident of Guam or the Virgin Islands	P. O. Box 1300 Charlotte, NC 28201-1300
Guam: Bona fide residents	Department of Revenue and Taxation Government of Guam P.O. Box 23607 GMF, GU 96921
Virgin Islands: Bona fide residents	V.I. Bureau of Internal Revenue 6115 Estate Smith Bay, Suite 225 St. Thomas, VI 00802

2014 Estimated Tax Worksheet

If filing a joint return, enter combined amounts.

1	Adjusted gross income expected in 2014. It may be easiest to estimate this by starting with 2013 AGI and adding and subtracting changes expected to take effect in 2014.	1
2	Estimated standard deduction for 2014 filing status ($6,200 for Single or MFS, $9,100 for HOH, or $12,400 for MFJ or QW) or total of estimated itemized deductions for 2014. Caution: If line 1 above is over: $305,050 if married filing jointly or qualifying widow(er); $279,650 if head of household; $254,200 if single; or $152,525 if married filing separately, the itemized deduction amount is reduced. See IRS Publication 505 for details and include the reduction in the amount entered.	2
3	Subtract line 2 from line 1.	3
4	Exemptions. Multiply $3,950 by the number of personal exemptions. Caution: If line 1 above is over: $305,050 if married filing jointly or qualifying widow(er); $279,650 if head of household; $254,200 if single; or $152,525 if married filing separately, the deduction for exemptions is reduced. See IRS Publication 505 for details and include the reduction in the amount entered.	4
5	Subtract line 4 from line 3.	5
6	Tax for the amount on line 5 from the 2014 Tax Rate Schedules. Also include tax on net capital gains.	6
7	Alternative minimum tax from Form 6251.	7
8	Add lines 6 and 7. Also include any tax from Forms 4972 and 8814 and any recapture of education credits.	8
9	Credits. Do not include any income tax withholding on this line. Do not include credits listed on line 13b below.	9
10	Subtract line 9 from line 8. If zero or less, enter -0-.	10
11	Self-employment tax. If estimate of 2014 net earnings (92.35% of total net profit) from self-employment is $117,000 or less, multiply the amount by 15.3%; if more than $117,000, multiply the amount by 2.9%, add $14,508 to the result, and enter the total. For a joint return, figure the self-employment tax separately for each spouse and add the amounts. Caution: If any wages are also subject to social security tax, the amount of self-employment tax may be reduced if the total income subject to social security tax is $117,000 or more.	11
12	Other taxes. Enter all other taxes expected to be owed in 2014, including additional taxes on IRA and qualified plan distributions and the additional Medicare and net investment income taxes (applicable to individuals whose income exceeds $200,000 ($250,000 for joint returns, $125,000 if married filing separately). Include household employment taxes owed in 2014 only if Federal income tax will be withheld on some income or estimated tax payments would be required, even if these taxes were not included. Do not include: • Tax on recapture of a Federal mortgage subsidy • Uncollected employee Social Security and Medicare tax or RRTA tax on tips or group-term life insurance	12
13a	Add lines 10 through 12.	13a
b	Earned income credit, additional child tax credit, refundable American opportunity credit, and credits from Form 4136, Form 2439, and Form 8885.	b
c	Total 2014 estimated tax. Subtract line 13b from line 13a. If zero or less, enter -0-.	c
14a	Multiply line 13c by 90% (66.67% for farmers and fishermen).	14a
b	Enter the tax shown on the taxpayer's 2013 return (110% of that amount if not a farmer or fisherman and the AGI shown on that return is more than $150,000 or, if married filing separately for 2014, more than $75,000).	b
c	Required annual payment to avoid a penalty. Enter the smaller of line 14a or 14b.	c
15	Income tax estimated to be withheld during 2014 (including income tax withholding on pensions, annuities, certain deferred income, etc.). If line 13c minus line 15 is less than $1,000, no estimated payments are required.	15
16	Subtract line 15 from line 14c. If the amount on line 16 is zero or less, no estimated payments are required.	16
17	If the first payment is due April 15, 2014, enter 25% of line 16 (minus any 2013 overpayment that was applied to this installment) here, and on the payment voucher(s).	17

> **Example.** Garrett, a single taxpayer who itemizes deductions, has adjusted gross income from January 1, 2014, to March 31, 2014, of $6,500 and applicable itemized deductions for the period of $1,000. His annualized income minus annualized deductions for the year is $22,000 [($6,500 – $1,000) × 12/3]. He is entitled to a $3,950 personal exemption; therefore, his taxable income is $18,050. The tax on $18,050 is projected to be $2,254 for a single taxpayer. The first annualized installment equals $507 ($2,254 × 22.5%). To compute the second installment, Garrett must use his adjusted gross income from January 1 through May 31, which is $17,000, and his itemized deductions for the same period, which total $5,700. The annualized amount is $27,120 ($11,300 × 12/5), and his annualized taxable income is $23,170. The tax on $23,170 is projected to be $3,022. His second annualized installment is $853 [($3,022 × 45%) – $507].

How to File Estimated Payments

There are five ways to pay estimated tax.

1. **Credit an overpayment** on the previous year's return to the current year's estimated tax. If the taxpayer asks that an overpayment be credited to his or her estimated tax for the next year, the payment is considered to have been made on the due date of the first estimated tax installment (April 15 for calendar-year taxpayers). The taxpayer cannot have any of that amount refunded to him or her, or use that overpayment in any other way, after that due date until the close of that tax year.
2. **Mail each payment** with a payment voucher from Form 1040-ES to the appropriate address shown in the table on page 11-5. Make checks payable to "United States Treasury."
3. **Pay electronically** using the Electronic Federal Tax Payment System (EFTPS). For EFTPS information, call 800-555-4477 or visit the website at https://www.eftps.gov/eftps/.
4. **Use electronic funds withdrawal** if Form 1040 or Form 1040A is filed electronically. Taxpayers may make up to four 2014 estimated tax payments when they electronically file their 2013 Form 1040 or Form 1040A by authorizing an electronic funds withdrawal from a checking or savings account. Whether or not a balance is due on the 2013 electronically filed tax return, the taxpayer may schedule estimated tax payments with an effective date of April 15, 2014, June 16, 2014, September 15, 2014, and January 15, 2015. *Do not* send in a Form 1040-ES payment voucher when an estimated tax payment by electronic funds withdrawal is scheduled.
5. **Pay by credit or debit card** using a pay-by-phone system or the Internet. American Express®, Discover®, MasterCard®, or Visa® credit cards may be used to make estimated tax payments. Call or access by Internet one of the service providers listed in Tab 1 and follow the instructions of the provider. Each provider will charge a convenience fee based on the amount of the payment.

> **Example.** When Kathleen filed her 2012 tax return, it showed that she had overpaid her taxes by $750. Kathleen knew that she would owe additional tax in 2013, so she credited $600 of the overpayment to her 2013 estimated tax and had the remaining $150 refunded to her. In September, she amended her 2012 return by filing Form 1040X, *Amended U.S. Individual Income Tax Return*. It turned out that she owed $250 more in tax than she had thought. This reduced her 2012 overpayment from $750 to $500. Because the $750 had already been applied to her 2013 estimated tax or refunded to her, the IRS billed her for the additional $250 she owed, plus penalties and interest. Kathleen could not use any of the $600 she had credited to her 2013 estimated tax to pay this bill.

Interest

The interest rate that taxpayers must pay for underpayment of taxes is equal to the federal short-term rate plus three percentage points (short-term rate plus five percentage points for large corporate underpayments). In case of overpayment of taxes, the amount of interest owed by the Treasury is also equal to the federal short-term rate plus three percentage points (short-term rate plus 0.5 percentage point for large corporate overpayments). These interest rates are adjusted quarterly, with the new rates becoming effective two months after the date of each adjustment.

Abatement of Interest

The IRS may abate interest if it is excessive, if it is assessed after the statute of limitations on collections expires, or if it is illegally or erroneously assessed. Interest may also be abated if collection of a small balance would not be cost-effective. In addition, unreasonable delays or errors caused by IRS personnel performing ministerial or managerial acts may be cause for abatement of interest.

Interest is not charged during the period of extension designated for presidentially declared disaster areas.

For erroneous refunds of $50,000 or less made due to IRS error, interest is abated until the date the IRS demands repayment.

A taxpayer may request an abatement of interest attributable to IRS delays by filing Form 843, *Claim for Refund and Request for Abatement* (see page 11-18).

If the IRS denies a request for abatement of interest, eligible taxpayers may bring action in Tax Court within 180 days after the date the IRS mails its final determination not to abate interest. Generally, individuals with net worth up to $2 million and businesses with net worth up to $7 million are eligible.

 Gray Area. As the instructions for the form state, there are several ways to calculate penalties on Form 2210. Annualized or other calculations may be applied if they conform to IRS regulations and their use can be supported. It is to the taxpayer's advantage to calculate the penalty using each allowable method to determine which results in the lowest penalty.

Taxpayer Penalties

Penalties may be imposed for improperly reporting information on tax returns, for failure to file a return, for failure to pay tax or to make timely estimated tax payments, and for other infractions. These penalties are in addition to interest charged on unpaid balances.

Calculation of Penalties

Taxpayers may calculate the late-filing and late-payment penalty owed on Form 2210, *Underpayment of Estimated Tax by Individuals, Estates, and Trusts*, or may let the IRS calculate the penalty and bill them. Interest is not charged if the taxpayer timely filed the return and paid any penalty by the due date on the bill.

Date Return Considered Filed and Tax Considered Paid

To calculate penalties and interest owed, the date returns are filed and tax payments are considered paid is determined according to the following rules:

- Returns and payments received by the IRS on or before the due date are considered filed and paid on the due date.
- Returns and payments postmarked on or before due date are considered paid on either the original or extended due date (whichever applies). This "mailbox rule" also applies to original returns claiming a refund postmarked before the three-year deadline. An amended return is considered filed on the postmark date.
- Returns and payments postmarked after the due date are considered filed or paid when received by the IRS.

For the purposes of the mailbox rule, a return or payment is "postmarked" on the date of a U.S. mail postmark, on the date of an official foreign country's postmark, on the date of the electronic postmark if the return is e-filed, or the date received by a private delivery service designated by the IRS. There are 12 designated private delivery services provided by three carriers:

Civil and Criminal Taxpayer Penalties Applicable in 2013		
Code Section	**Violation**	**Amount of Penalty**
6651(a)(1)	Failure to file return	• 5% for each month or fraction thereof that the return is late, up to a maximum of 25% of the tax owed, less any penalty for failure to pay tax for the same month • A minimum of $135 or the tax due, whichever is less, if the return is more than 60 days late
6651(a)(2), 6651(a)(3), 6651(d), and 6651(h)	Failure to pay tax	• 0.5% for each month or fraction thereof that there is an unpaid balance, up to a maximum of 25% of tax owed • 1% per month after notice and demand for immediate payment is given, or 10 days after the IRS issues a notice of intent to levy, whichever date is earlier • 0.25% per month if an installment agreement is in effect and the return was filed on time For amounts not shown on a return, the penalty begins 21 calendar days from the date the IRS demands payment (10 business days if amount is $100,000 or more)

Civil and Criminal Taxpayer Penalties Applicable in 2013 (Continued)

Code Section	Violation	Amount of Penalty
6651(f)	Fraudulent failure to file return	• 15% for each month or fraction thereof that the return is late, up to a maximum of 75% of the tax owed, less any penalty for failure to pay tax for the same month • A minimum of $135 or the tax due, whichever is less, if the return is more than 60 days late
6652(b)	Failure to report tips	50% of the employee's portion of the FICA tax or railroad retirement tax for the tip amount not reported
6654 and 6655	Underpayment of estimated tax	Interest at federal rate (see tables on page 11-1)
6662	Accuracy-related penalty, including negligence, substantial understatement (10% of tax required to be shown on return or $5,000, whichever is greater) of tax, substantial overstatement of pension liabilities, undisclosed foreign financial asset understatement	20% of the portion of the underpayment (40% for undisclosed foreign financial asset understatement)
6663	Fraud	75% of the portion of the underpayment attributable to fraud
6673	Frivolous or delaying Tax Court actions	Up to $25,000 for frivolous actions or for actions brought primarily for delay
6682	False information on Form W-4 (including claims of withholding allowances that reduce the amount of tax withheld)	$500 for each false statement (W-4)
6702	Filing a frivolous return, including alteration or deletion of "penalties of perjury" statement	$5,000 per return deemed to be frivolous
7201	Willful attempt to evade or defeat tax	Felony punishable by a fine of up to $100,000 ($500,000 for corporations), imprisonment up to five years, or both, and costs of prosecution
7203	Willful failure to pay tax or file a return	Misdemeanor punishable by a fine of up to $25,000 ($100,000 for corporations), imprisonment up to one year, or both, and costs of prosecution
7205	Fraudulent withholding exemption certificate or statement that backup withholding does not apply	Misdemeanor punishable by a fine of up to $1,000, imprisonment of up to one year, or both
7206	Fraud	Felony punishable by a fine up to $100,000 ($500,000 for corporations), up to three years in prison, or both

- DHL Express (DHL): DHL Same Day Service
- Federal Express (FedEx): FedEx Priority Overnight, FedEx Standard Overnight, FedEx 2Day, FedEx International Priority, and FedEx International First
- United Parcel Service (UPS): UPS Next Day Air, UPS Next Day Air Saver, UPS 2nd Day Air, UPS 2nd Day Air A.M., UPS Worldwide Express Plus, and UPS Worldwide Express

Reasonable Cause for Late Filing and Late Payments

The IRS will waive the penalties for late filing and late payment if the taxpayer can show that delay was due to reasonable cause and not willful neglect. Although there is no clear definition of reasonable cause that applies to all penalty provisions, there is a recognized list of circumstances that the IRS considers to be "administratively acceptable" as justification for abatement of a penalty. Reasonable cause for filing a late return includes death or illness of the taxpayer or a close relative, unavoidable absence of the taxpayer, and destruction of the taxpayer's residence, business, or records due to fire, hurricane, etc. Reasonable cause for late payment of tax may be related to unexpected financial circumstances, but the taxpayer must show that he or she exercised ordinary business care and prudence. Standards used by the IRS for determining "reasonable cause" are set out in Internal Revenue Manual §20.1.1.3.2 (11-25-2011).

What Is and What Is Not Reasonable Cause. Forgetfulness, reliance on another person to perform required acts, and ignorance of the law are generally not accepted as reasonable cause for delay absent special circumstances. However, reliance on the advice of a competent tax advisor or on written advice of the IRS generally constitutes reasonable cause. In evaluating reasonable cause, IRS agents evaluate each case on its own merits.

Taxpayers can request abatement of late-filing and late-payment penalties by filing Form 843, *Claim for Refund and Request for Abatement.* It should be mailed to the service center where the current year return would be filed.

Planning Tip. Whenever there is sufficient doubt as to a taxpayer's liability or circumstances regarding tax penalties, an authorized representative may file the claim for abatement for the taxpayer.

Abatement of Accuracy-Related and Fraud Penalties

Accuracy-related penalties and penalties for fraudulent failure to file a return and fraud may be abated if they were illegally or erroneously assessed [IRC §6404(a)] or if the taxpayer can prove that the penalty does not apply under the statute. IRS agents consider payment patterns, penalty history, and whether the taxpayer acted with ordinary business care and prudence when considering an abatement request. A repetition of a penalty situation could indicate lack of ordinary business care and prudence. The Internal Revenue Manual sets out the standards for determining "ordinary business care and prudence" under the circumstances in §20.1.1.3.2.2 (2-22-2008).

Appeals. Penalties can be appealed through a claim for refund if the penalty has been paid, or after assessment through the post-assessment penalty appeal program.

The taxpayer may appeal a denial of a request for abatement or nonassertion. This is done by filing a protest to the Office of Appeals in the standard manner of income tax protests. It is important to note that the time limit for filing such appeals will be specified in the IRS letter to the taxpayer.

The case is then submitted to an appeals officer, and a conference is held, following which Appeals will either sustain the penalty, reject it, or compromise. Another route to take to contest a penalty is by paying the penalty and filing a claim for refund. If denied, refund suit may be brought in a U.S. District Court or the U.S. Court of Federal Claims.

Tax Return Preparer Penalties

Signing Prepared Returns
If the client retains the right to make all final decisions on the return, the preparer may not have to sign the return. For example, a certified public accountant who was asked to review a client's income tax return and to furnish a recommendation affecting an entry on the return was not a tax return preparer required to sign the client's return. In this case the client's tax director had retained the right to make all final decisions on the return.

Final Review. A final comprehensive review will likely result in bestowing a reviewer with primary responsibility if it includes (1) evaluating the information provided by other preparers; (2) applying to this information the final reviewer's knowledge of the taxpayer's affairs, if any; (3) observing that the preparer-employer's policies and practices have been followed; and (4) making the final determinations with respect to the proper application of the tax laws to the taxpayer's tax liability.

The fact that a return preparer is the last person to look at the return does not mean that he or she is the preparer with primary responsibility for its accuracy.

If a taxpayer sends a person his or her books and records and the person sends back a composite statement of all the necessary information so that it is merely a mechanical process for the taxpayer to fill out the return, the individual is an income tax return preparer with a duty to sign the return.

When Preparers Sign. The preparer must sign the completed return before its presentation to the taxpayer for signature, thereby ensuring that the taxpayer has had an opportunity to review the final return before signing it.

Example. Andrey and Andrey, an accounting partnership, entered into an agreement with Mark Young Inc. to prepare income tax returns for its clients. Under the agreement, where the law was unclear, the partnership was to resolve questions of law in favor of Young's clients if a reasonable justification for that position existed. Although the partnership prepared the returns, the partners were not responsible for the overall substantive accuracy of the returns because, prior to completion, questionable entries on the returns were discussed with Young and, after completion, the returns were submitted to Young for final review. Therefore, the partners were not required to sign the returns.

Specific Penalties. A return preparer who willfully, recklessly, or intentionally understates a taxpayer's liability or understates a liability due to an unreasonable position on a return is subject to penalty.

The Fifth Amendment protection against self-incrimination may not be claimed by tax return preparers in actions where the penalties imposed against them are civil and not criminal in nature. See the table on page 11-12 for a list of current penalties.

Regarding penalties for failure to perform a required act or for negotiating a client's refund check, an income tax return preparer can appeal the imposition of these penalties only after payment. Form 6118, *Claim for Refund of Income Tax Return Preparer and Promoter Penalties*, may be used for this purpose.

See MTG ¶2518 and ¶2894 for further information.

Unreasonable Positions and Willful Understatement

If a tax return preparer is assessed a penalty based upon understatements due to unreasonable positions (Code Sec. 6694(a)) or to willful or reckless conduct (Code Sec. 6694(b)), the IRS generally will issue a 30-day letter notifying the preparer of the proposed penalty and giving the preparer an opportunity to pursue administrative remedies prior to the assessment of the penalty. If the penalty is assessed, the preparer must, within 30 days, either pay the assessment in full or pay at least 15% of the penalty and file a claim for refund of the amount paid. The IRS may counterclaim for the balance of the penalty. Form 6118 is also used for this purpose. If the IRS denies the claim for refund, or if six months have passed since the day the claim was filed and the IRS has not made a determination, the return preparer must file suit in U.S. District Court within 30 days after the date the claim was denied or the six-month period expired, whichever is sooner, if he or she wants to pursue the claim further.

If a final administrative or judicial action determines that there was no understatement of the liability for which the penalty was assessed, any penalty assessed against a preparer for the understatement will be abated or, if paid, refunded.

Fraud

In its hunt for return preparer fraud, the IRS is looking for (1) inflated or bogus personal or business expenses, (2) false deductions, (3) unallowable or fraudulent credits, and (4) excessive exemptions.

The agency's Criminal Investigation Division has a special program that focuses on enforcing compliance among return preparers. In FY 2012, the IRS initiated 443 investigations into preparer fraud: 276 cases were recommended to the Justice Department for prosecution, resulting in 202 indictments/informations. Sentences were handed down in 178 cases.

Assessment of Penalties-Limitations Periods

A penalty may be assessed against a return preparer at any time during a three-year period following the filing of the return. The three-year period begins to run on the statutory due date of the return, in the case of an early or timely filed return, and on the actual date the return was filed, for a late-filed return. Extensions of the three-year period may be arranged by agreement between the IRS and the return preparer. The IRS may assess return preparer penalties prior to the statutory due date of a return where the return has been filed before such date. Although premature assessments are not usually made, the power to make them is necessary to permit the processing of returns before the due date.

The filing of a second, correct return prior to the statutory due date of the first return will cure preparer deficiencies on the first return. A letter or a list filed by the return preparer may also be accepted by the IRS as curing an incorrect first return, although the IRS is not required to accept anything less than a complete return.

Advertising Restrictions

The IRS has issued rules regarding advertising and solicitation of employment in tax-related matters by attorneys, certified public accountants, and enrolled agents, allowing tax practitioners a freedom to advertise that is roughly equivalent to that currently enjoyed by lawyers and CPAs in general.

Permissible Advertising. Among the permissible forms of solicitation under these rules are the announcement of fixed fees for specific, routine tax services and the use of professional listings, telephone directory listings, and the print media, radio, and television. If fees are advertised, the practitioner has to state clearly that they apply only to matters of average complexity and that they may vary for more involved matters (if applicable). Radio and television commercials must be prerecorded, and the practitioner must maintain a recording of the advertisements. A preparer is not prohibited from indicating a past or present connection with the IRS.

Civil and Criminal Tax Return Preparer Penalties Applicable in 2013

Code Section	Violation	Applies to Employer (including Partnerships) and Self-Employed Preparer	Applies to Employee Preparer (including Partners)	Amount of Penalty
6694(a)	Understatement of taxpayer's liability due to unreasonable positions	Yes	Yes	Greater of $1,000 or 50% of the income derived (or to be derived) by the preparer with respect to the return
6694(b)	Willful attempt to understate liability or reckless or intentional disregard of rules or regulations	Yes	Yes	Greater of $5,000 or 50% of the income derived (or to be derived) by the preparer with respect to the return, reduced by penalty paid under Code Sec. 6694(a)
6695(a)	Failure to furnish copy of return to taxpayer	Yes	No	$50 per failure, up to $25,000 per preparer
6695(b)	Failure of preparer to sign return	Yes	Yes	$50 per failure, up to $25,000 per preparer
6695(c)	Failure to furnish identifying numbers	Yes	No	$50 per failure, up to $25,000 per preparer
6695(d)	Failure to retain copies of returns prepared or to maintain a listing	Yes	No	$50 per failure, up to $25,000 per preparer
6695(e)	Failure to (1) retain and make available a record of the preparers employed (or engaged) during a return period and (2) set forth an item, as required by Code Sec. 6060	Yes	No	$50 per failure, up to $25,000 per preparer
6695(f)	Endorsing or negotiating a tax refund check	Yes	Yes	$500 per check
6695(g)	Failure to be diligent in determining eligibility for the earned income tax credit	Yes	Yes	$500 per failure
6701	Aiding and abetting understatements	Yes	Yes	$1,000 per return ($10,000 per corporate return) per preparer
6713	Unauthorized disclosure or use of information	Yes	Yes	$250 per disclosure or use, up to $10,000 per year
7206	Fraud and false statements	Yes	Yes	Maximum $100,000 fine ($500,000 for corporations), or three years imprisonment, or both, and prosecution costs
7207	Willful delivery or disclosure of fraudulent documents or information to IRS	Yes	Yes	Maximum $10,000 fine ($50,000 for corporations), or one year imprisonment, or both
7216	Unauthorized disclosure of taxpayer information	Yes	Yes	Maximum $1,000 fine, or one year imprisonment, or both, and prosecution costs

The IRS supports individual electronic return originators' (EROs) advertising and promotional efforts by annually creating and distributing an IRS e-file Marketing Tool Kit. New EROs receive a kit when they are accepted into the IRS e-file program. The kit contains professionally developed material that EROs can customize for use in advertising campaigns and promotional efforts.

 Caution. Advertising language requires careful scrutiny. Testimonials are allowed, but promising more than can be delivered or exaggerating possible results is not.

False Advertising. An individual tax return preparer is prohibited from using any advertising containing a false, fraudulent, misleading, deceptive, unduly influencing, coercive, or unfair statement or claim. The use or disclosure in marketing or advertising of statistical compilations identifying dollar amounts of refunds, credits, or deductions associated with tax returns, or percentages relating thereto, is not authorized. A practitioner may, however, publish certain fee information, including fixed fees for specific routine services, hourly rates, a range of fees for particular services and fees charged for initial consultation. Fee information may be communicated in professional lists, telephone directories, the print media, mailings, electronic mail, facsimile, hand delivered flyers, radio, and television and any other method.

A tax return preparer who engages in false or deceptive advertising may be subject to censure, suspension or disbarment from practice before the IRS, as well as a monetary penalty.

Electronic Filers

Electronic filing must be done through the IRS or through an electronic filing participant. Upon acceptance into the electronic filing program, a participant is referred to as an authorized IRS e-file provider. There are six categories of electronic filers, and, depending on the functions performed, an electronic filer may fall into more than one category at a time.

1. Electronic return originators (EROs) originate the electronic submission of income tax returns.
2. Software developers develop software for the purposes of formatting the electronic portion of returns according to IRS e-file specifications and/or transmitting the electronic portion of returns directly to the IRS. The IRS requires that all software developers complete acceptance or assurance testing for each return type.
3. Transmitters transmit the electronic portion of a return directly to the IRS.
4. Intermediate service providers receive tax return information from EROs or from taxpayers who file electronically from home via an Internet site or commercial tax preparation software. The intermediate service provider processes the return and either forwards the information to a transmitter or sends the information back to the ERO or taxpayer.
5. Reporting agents are accounting services, banks, or other entities that comply with IRS procedures and are authorized to sign and electronically file Forms 940, 941, and 944 for a taxpayer.

6. Online providers allow taxpayers to self-prepare returns by entering return data directly on commercially available software, on downloadable software, or through an online Internet site.

Filing Tip. Free File, a free federal income tax preparation and electronic filing program, is administered by the IRS through a partnership with the Free File Alliance, a group of private sector tax software companies. This program generally provides individual taxpayers, with an adjusted gross income of less than a designated amount ($57,000 for 2012 returns), a free interview-based software option for online filing. An alternative Free File Fillable Forms option is open to virtually all individual taxpayers, regardless of income. This option offers "self-service" online versions of paper forms that can be e-filed for free. Information is available at www.irs.gov.

Electronic filing provides the following advantages to taxpayers: (1) electronic returns are filed simultaneously and are easier to process than paper returns; (2) the taxpayer receives confirmation from the IRS within one or two days that the return was accurately received; and (3) the time period for receipt of a refund is shortened to about 3 weeks, and can be even shorter with direct deposit. The IRS also finds electronic filing advantageous because electronic returns have a lower error rate, are easier to store and retrieve, and are processed at a lower cost compared with paper returns. More information is available for tax return preparers and e-filers in IRS Publication 1345, *Handbook for Authorized IRS e-file Providers of Individual Income Tax Returns.*

Amended Returns

Taxpayers should file an amended return if filing status, total income, deductions, or credits were reported incorrectly. Taxpayers may also want to file an amended return to take advantage of changes in the tax law that are retroactive. However, an amended return cannot be filed to make retroactive changes in accounting method or as a means of obtaining a notice of deficiency required to bring an action in Tax Court.

Also, taxpayers who suffered losses in a federally declared disaster area can claim disaster-related casualty losses on either their current year's tax return or the return for last year.

Taxpayers may use Form 1045, *Application for Tentative Refund,* instead of Form 1040X to apply for a refund based on the carryback of a net operating loss, an unused general business credit, or a net Section 1256 contracts loss, or on a claim of right adjustment under Section 1341(b)(1). Form 1045 must be filed within one year after the end of the year in which the loss, credit, or claim of right adjustment arose. For more details, see the instructions for Form 1045.

How to Fill Out Form 1040X

Check the box or enter the year of the return being amended at the top of Form 1040X. If amended returns are being submitted for more than one tax return, use a separate 1040X for each one and mail each in a separate envelope.

Form 1040X (see pages 11-16 and 11-17) has three columns. Column A is used to show original or adjusted figures from the original return. Column C is used to show the corrected figures. The difference between the figures in columns A and C is shown in column B. There is an area on page two of the form for explaining the specific changes being made on the return and the reason for each change. The reason for filing the amended return should be clearly stated. If the changes involve another schedule or form, attach it to the 1040X.

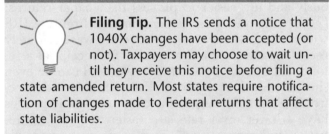 **Filing Tip.** The IRS sends a notice that 1040X changes have been accepted (or not). Taxpayers may choose to wait until they receive this notice before filing a state amended return. Most states require notification of changes made to Federal returns that affect state liabilities.

Filing Tip. When preparing amended returns, try to provide the person reviewing the return with all the documentation they might need to evaluate the taxpayer's claim and quickly make a decision to accept it. Failure to do so may result in delays, lack of acceptance, or, worse yet, the desire by the IRS to delve more completely into the taxpayer's return.

Deceased Taxpayer. If filing an amended return for a deceased taxpayer, enter "Deceased," the deceased taxpayer's name, and the date of death across the top of Form 1040X. A surviving spouse should enter "Filing as surviving spouse" in the signature area of the return. If someone else is the personal representative, he or she must also sign. If a refund is claimed by anyone other than a surviving spouse, Form 1310, *Statement of Person Claiming Refund Due a Deceased Taxpayer*, is required.

When to File an Amended Return

Taxpayers who wish to file a claim for an additional refund should wait until they have received the original refund before filing Form 1040X. If additional tax is owed, Form 1040X should be filed and the tax paid by the due date of the original return to avoid any penalty and interest.

Generally, to claim a refund, Form 1040X must be filed within three years from the date the original return was filed or within two years from the date the tax was paid, whichever is later. A Form 1040X based on a bad debt or worthless security generally must be filed within seven years after the due date of the return for the tax year in which the debt or security became worthless.

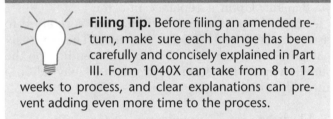 **Filing Tip.** Before filing an amended return, make sure each change has been carefully and concisely explained in Part III. Form 1040X can take from 8 to 12 weeks to process, and clear explanations can prevent adding even more time to the process.

Only the original return operates to start or extend the limitations period for assessment and collection. A second return is merely an amendment or supplement to a return already in the files and does not toll a limitation period that has begun to run.

The open-ended assessment period applicable to fraudulent returns cannot be cut off by the later filing of a nonfraudulent amended return.

Where to File Form 1040X During 2014

State of Taxpayer's Residence	Filing Address
Florida, Louisiana, Mississippi, Texas	Department of the Treasury Internal Revenue Service Center Austin, TX 73301
Alaska, Arizona, Arkansas, California, Colorado, Hawaii, Idaho, Illinois, Indiana, Iowa, Kansas, Michigan, Minnesota, Montana, Nebraska, Nevada, New Mexico, North Dakota, Ohio, Oklahoma, Oregon, South Dakota, Utah, Washington, Wisconsin, Wyoming	Department of the Treasury Internal Revenue Service Center Fresno, CA 93888-0422
Alabama, Connecticut, Delaware, District of Columbia, Georgia, Kentucky, Maine, Maryland, Massachusetts, Missouri, New Hampshire, New Jersey, New York, North Carolina, Pennsylvania, Rhode Island, South Carolina, Tennessee, Vermont, Virginia, West Virginia	Department of the Treasury Internal Revenue Service Center Kansas City, MO 64999
American Samoa, the Commonwealth of the Northern Mariana Islands, non-bona fide residents of Guam or the Virgin Islands, Puerto Rico, dual status taxpayers, non-resident aliens, U.S. citizens or tax residents in a foreign country, all APO or FPO addresses and anyone filing Form 2555, 2555-EZ, or 4563 (see IRS Publication 570, *Tax Guide for Individuals with Income from U.S. Possessions*, for additional information)	Department of the Treasury Internal Revenue Service Center Austin, TX 73301-0215
Guam: Bona fide residents	Department of Revenue and Taxation PO Box 23607 GMF, GU 96921
Virgin Islands: Bona fide residents	V.I. Bureau of Internal Revenue 6115 Estate Smith Bay Suite 225 St. Thomas, VI 00802

Form 1040X
(Rev. December 2013)

Department of the Treasury—Internal Revenue Service

Amended U.S. Individual Income Tax Return

☒ Information about Form 1040X and its separate instructions is at *www.irs.gov/form1040x.*

OMB No. 1545-0074

This return is for calendar year ☐ 2013 ☐ 2012 ☐ 2011 ☐ 2010

Other year. Enter one: calendar year ____ **or** fiscal year (month and year ended): ____

Your first name and initial	Last name	Your social security number
If a joint return, spouse's first name and initial	Last name	Spouse's social security number
Home address (number and street). If you have a P.O. box, see instructions.	Apt. no.	Your phone number
City, town or post office, state, and ZIP code. If you have a foreign address, also complete spaces below (see instructions).		
Foreign country name	Foreign province/state/county	Foreign postal code

DRAFT AS OF October 29, 2013 DO NOT FILE

Amended return filing status. You **must** check one box even if you are not changing your filing status.
Caution. In general, you cannot change your filing status from joint to separate returns after the due date.

☐ Single ☐ Married filing jointly ☐ Married filing separately
☐ Qualifying widow(er) ☐ Head of household (If the qualifying person is a child but not your dependent, see instructions.)

Use Part III on the back to explain any changes

			A. Original amount or as previously adjusted (see instructions)	**B. Net change—** amount of increase or (decrease)— explain in Part III	**C. Correct amount**
Income and Deductions					
1	Adjusted gross income. If net operating loss (NOL) carryback is included, check here . . . . ☒ ☐	**1**			
2	Itemized deductions or standard deduction	**2**			
3	Subtract line 2 from line 1	**3**			
4	Exemptions. **If changing, complete Part I on page 2 and enter the amount from line 28**	**4**			
5	Taxable income. Subtract line 4 from line 3	**5**			
Tax Liability					
6	Tax. Enter method used to figure tax (see instructions): _____	**6**			
7	Credits. If general business credit carryback is included, check here . . . . ☒ ☐	**7**			
8	Subtract line 7 from line 6. If the result is zero or less, enter -0- . . .	**8**			
9	Other taxes	**9**			
10	Total tax. Add lines 8 and 9	**10**			
Payments					
11	Federal income tax withheld and excess social security and tier 1 RRTA tax withheld (**if changing**, see instructions)	**11**			
12	Estimated tax payments, including amount applied from prior year's return	**12**			
13	Earned income credit (EIC)	**13**			
14	Refundable credits from Schedule(s) ☐ 8812 or ☐ M or Form(s) ☐ 2439 ☐ 4136 ☐ 5405 ☐ 8801 ☐ 8812 (2010 or 2011) ☐ 8839 ☐ 8863 ☐ 8885 or ☐ other (specify): _____	**14**			
15	Total amount paid with request for extension of time to file, tax paid with original return, and additional tax paid after return was filed	**15**			
16	Total payments. Add lines 11 through 15	**16**			
Refund or Amount You Owe *(Note. Allow 8–12 weeks to process Form 1040X.)*					
17	Overpayment, if any, as shown on original return or as previously adjusted by the IRS	**17**			
18	Subtract line 17 from line 16 (If less than zero, see instructions) . . .	**18**			
19	**Amount you owe.** If line 10, column C, is more than line 18, enter the difference	**19**			
20	If line 10, column C, is less than line 18, enter the difference. This is the amount **overpaid** on this return	**20**			
21	Amount of line 20 you want **refunded to you**	**21**			
22	Amount of line 20 you want **applied to your** (enter year): ____ estimated tax .	**22**			

Complete and sign this form on Page 2.

For Paperwork Reduction Act Notice, see instructions.   Cat. No. 11360L   Form **1040X** (Rev. 12-2013)

| **Part I** | **Exemptions** |

Complete this part **only** if you are increasing or decreasing the number of exemptions (personal and dependents) claimed on line 6d of the return you are amending.

See *Form 1040 or Form 1040A instructions and Form 1040X instructions.*

			A. Original number of exemptions or amount reported or as previously adjusted	**B. Net change**	**C. Correct number or amount**
23	Yourself and spouse. ***Caution.*** *If someone can claim you as a dependent, you cannot claim an exemption for yourself*	23			
24	Your dependent children who lived with you	24			
25	Your dependent children who did not live with you due to divorce or separation	25			
26	Other dependents	26			
27	Total number of exemptions. Add lines 23 through 26	27			
28	Multiply the number of exemptions claimed on line 27 by the exemption amount shown in the instructions for line 28 for the year you are amending. Enter the result here and on line 4 on page 1 of this form . .	28			

29 List **ALL** dependents (children and others) claimed on this amended return. If more than 4 dependents, see instructions.

(a) First name Last name	**(b)** Dependent's social security number	**(c)** Dependent's relationship to you	**(d)** Check box if qualifying child for child tax credit (see instructions)
			☐
			☐
			☐
			☐

| **Part II** | **Presidential Election Campaign Fund** |

Checking below will not increase your tax or reduce your refund.

☐ Check here if you did not previously want $3 to go to the fund, but now do.

☐ Check here if this is a joint return and your spouse did not previously want $3 to go to the fund, but now does.

| **Part III** | **Explanation of changes.** In the space provided below, tell us why you are filing Form 1040X. |

⊠ Attach any supporting documents and new or changed forms and schedules.

Sign Here

Remember to keep a copy of this form for your records.

Under penalties of perjury, I declare that I have filed an original return and that I have examined this amended return, including accompanying schedules and statements, and to the best of my knowledge and belief, this amended return is true, correct, and complete. Declaration of preparer (other than taxpayer) is based on all information about which the preparer has any knowledge.

⊠ _____   ⊠ _____

Your signature   Date   Spouse's signature. If a joint return, **both** must sign.   Date

Paid Preparer Use Only
⊠

Preparer's signature   Date   Firm's name (or yours if self-employed)

Print/type preparer's name   Firm's address and ZIP code

                    ☐ Check if self-employed

PTIN   Phone number   EIN

For forms and publications, visit IRS.gov.

Form **843**
(Rev. August 2011)
Department of the Treasury
Internal Revenue Service

Claim for Refund and Request for Abatement

☒ **See separate instructions.**

OMB No. 1545-0024

Use Form 843 if your claim or request involves:

(a) a refund of one of the taxes (other than income taxes or an employer's claim for FICA tax, RRTA tax, or income tax withholding) or a fee, shown on line 3,

(b) an abatement of FUTA tax or certain excise taxes, or

(c) a refund or abatement of interest, penalties, or additions to tax for one of the reasons shown on line 5a.

Do not use Form 843 if your claim or request involves:

(a) an overpayment of income taxes or an employer's claim for FICA tax, RRTA tax, or income tax withholding (use the appropriate amended tax return),

(b) a refund of excise taxes based on the nontaxable use or sale of fuels, or

(c) an overpayment of excise taxes reported on Form(s) 11-C, 720, 730, or 2290.

Name(s)	Your social security number
Address (number, street, and room or suite no.)	Spouse's social security number
City or town, state, and ZIP code	Employer identification number (EIN)
Name and address shown on return if different from above	Daytime telephone number

1 **Period.** Prepare a separate Form 843 for each tax period or fee year.

From _____ to _____

2 **Amount** to be refunded or abated:
$

3 **Type of tax or fee.** Indicate the type of tax or fee to be refunded or abated or to which the interest, penalty, or addition to tax is related.

☐ Employment ☐ Estate ☐ Gift ☐ Excise ☐ Income ☐ Fee

4 **Type of penalty.** If the claim or request involves a penalty, enter the Internal Revenue Code section on which the penalty is based (see instructions). IRC section:

5a **Interest, penalties, and additions to tax.** Check the box that indicates your reason for the request for refund or abatement. (If none apply, go to line 6.)

☐ Interest was assessed as a result of IRS errors or delays.

☐ A penalty or addition to tax was the result of erroneous written advice from the IRS.

☐ Reasonable cause or other reason allowed under the law (other than erroneous written advice) can be shown for not assessing a penalty or addition to tax.

b Date(s) of payment(s) ☒ _____

6 **Original return.** Indicate the type of fee or return, if any, filed to which the tax, interest, penalty, or addition to tax relates.

☐ 706 ☐ 709 ☐ 940 ☐ 941 ☐ 943 ☐ 945
☐ 990-PF ☐ 1040 ☐ 1120 ☐ 4720 ☐ Other (specify) ☒

7 **Explanation.** Explain why you believe this claim or request should be allowed and show the computation of the amount shown on line 2. If you need more space, attach additional sheets.

Signature. If you are filing Form 843 to request a refund or abatement relating to a joint return, both you and your spouse must sign the claim. Claims filed by corporations must be signed by a corporate officer authorized to sign, and the officer's title must be shown.

Under penalties of perjury, I declare that I have examined this claim, including accompanying schedules and statements, and, to the best of my knowledge and belief, it is true, correct, and complete. Declaration of preparer (other than taxpayer) is based on all information of which preparer has any knowledge.

Signature (Title, if applicable. Claims by corporations must be signed by an officer.)	Date
Signature (spouse, if joint return)	Date

Paid Preparer Use Only	Print/Type preparer's name	Preparer's signature	Date	Check ☐ if self-employed	PTIN
	Firm's name ☒			Firm's EIN ☒	
	Firm's address ☒			Phone no.	

For Privacy Act and Paperwork Reduction Act Notice, see separate instructions.

Cat. No. 10180R

Form **843** (Rev. 8-2011)

Tax Representation Issues and Filings

What's New in 2013

Return Preparers. The IRS has suspended its requirement that tax return preparers register to practice before the agency, including the requirement of continuing education.

Proposed Changes to Circular 230. Changes that have been proposed include elimination of the covered opinion rules, expansion of matters subject to expedited procedures, clarification of the prohibition against attorneys taking their fee from a taxpayer's refund, and a reasonableness standard to be applied to employee benefit attorneys.

Appeals Procedure. The IRS is developing new processes for its Appeals Office, including the Rapid Appeals Process.

Section at a Glance

Tax Preparer's Checklist

- ☐ The Internal Revenue Manual, Audit Technique Guides, and other instructions the IRS provides to examiners are freely available. In addition, the IRS website offers numerous calculators and other practice aids to help preparers.

- ☐ Authorization to file Form 2848, *Power of Attorney and Declaration of Representative*, and Form 8821, *Tax Information Authorization*, are available electronically to those who file five or more returns.

- ☐ The IRS offers "Free File," which allows taxpayers with adjusted gross income of less than a given amount to choose a preparer's website on which they can prepare their tax return.

- ☐ The IRS offers the Oral Disclosure Consent (ODC) and the Oral Tax Information Authorization (OTIA), which allow disclosure of tax information to a designee of the taxpayer.

Relevant IRS Publications

- ☐ Treasury Department Circular No. 230, *Regulations Governing Practice before the Internal Revenue Service*
- ☐ IRS Publication 1, *Your Rights as a Taxpayer*
- ☐ IRS Publication 5, *Your Appeal Rights and How to Prepare a Protest If You Don't Agree*
- ☐ IRS Publication 556, *Examination of Returns, Appeal Rights, and Claims for Refund*
- ☐ IRS Publication 594, *The IRS Collection Process*
- ☐ IRS Publication 947, *Practice Before the IRS and Power of Attorney*
- ☐ IRS Publication 3498, *The Examination Process*
- ☐ IRS Publication 4245, *Power of Attorney*
- ☐ Form 656-B, *Offer in Compromise Booklet*
- ☐ Instructions for Form 2848, *Power of Attorney and Declaration of Representative*
- ☐ Form 8821, *Tax Information Authorization*

Statute of Limitations Effective in 2013

Action	Period of Limitation
IRS examination of return and assessment of additional tax	Later of 3 years from due date of timely filed return or 3 years from receipt of late filed returns
Claim for credit or refund	Later of 3 years from date return filed or 2 years from date tax was paid, extended by any period during which the taxpayer was unable to manage his or her affairs due to terminal or prolonged illness that began during that time
Income not reported that is more than 25% of the gross income shown on return	6 years
Fraudulent return	Unlimited
Return not filed	Unlimited
Claim for a loss from worthless securities or a bad debt deduction	7 years
IRS collection action	10 years from assessment

Taxpayer Representation

Taxpayers have the right to representation during IRS examinations of tax returns and when dealing with other tax matters before the IRS. The taxpayer's representative may be an attorney, a certified public accountant, an enrolled agent, or any other person permitted to practice before the IRS who has written power of attorney to act on the taxpayer's behalf.

Practice Before the IRS

Matters relating to presentations to the IRS or any of its officers or employees relating to a taxpayer's rights, privileges, or liabilities under laws or regulations administered by the IRS are "practice before the IRS." Preparing and filing documents, corresponding and communicating with the IRS, and representing a taxpayer at conferences, hearings, and meetings are all considered practice before the IRS. "Practice before the IRS" also includes the rendering of written advice on any entity, transaction, plan, or arrangement that has a potential for tax avoidance or evasion. However, attorneys and CPAs are not required to file a power of attorney (Form 2848) in order to issue that advice.

Treasury Department Circular 230, *Regulations Governing Practice Before the Internal Revenue Service* (Title 31 CFR Subtitle A, Part 10, revised as of August 2011), provides regulations governing tax practice.

Caution. The IRS has suspended its requirement that tax return preparers register in order to practice before the IRS. Regulations that required the designation of registered tax return preparers and made them subject to Circular 230 were invalidated by a federal district court in March 2013, which granted a permanent injunction requiring the IRS to shut down its registered tax return preparer program. This court ruling does not affect the regulatory practice requirements for CPAs, attorneys, enrolled agents, enrolled retirement plan agents or enrolled actuaries. The IRS is currently appealing this decision but, in the meantime, it has refunded fees collected from preparers who had registered to practice before the IRS and were scheduled to take examinations that have now been cancelled. Return preparers may still obtain a Preparer Tax Identification Number (PTIN), however, and PTINs remain valid.

The IRS posts on its website final decisions regarding sanctions for violating Circular 230 imposed against tax practitioners who practiced before the IRS.

Social Media. The IRS provides free assistance to both taxpayers and practitioners using a variety of social media. The agency offers a smartphone app, IRS2Go, a YouTube channel containing instructional videos, Twitter for news for tax professionals, Tumblr, a Return Preparer Facebook page, and Podcasts, for which audio files and transcripts are available.

Who Can Practice Before the IRS. There are several categories of individuals who may practice before the IRS (see Circular 230 for details).

- **Attorneys** who are not currently under suspension or disbarment from practice before the IRS may file a written declaration stating that they are currently qualified as an attorney and authorized to represent the party or parties on whose behalf they act.
- **Certified Public Accountants** who are not currently under suspension or disbarment from practice before the IRS and who are qualified to practice public accountancy in any state may file a written declaration that they are currently qualified as a certified public accountant and are authorized to represent the party or parties on whose behalf they act.
- **Enrolled Agents** who are not currently under suspension or disbarment from practice before the IRS may file a written declaration stating that they are authorized to represent the party or parties on whose behalf they act.
- **Enrolled Actuaries** who are enrolled by the Joint Board for the Enrollment of Actuaries pursuant to 29 U.S.C. 1242 and are not currently under suspension or disbarment from practice before the IRS may practice before the IRS by filing a written declaration stating that they are currently qualified as an enrolled actuary and are authorized to represent the party or parties on whose behalf they act. Practice as an enrolled actuary is limited to representation with respect to issues involving certain specified statutory provisions requiring actuarial expertise, generally those relating to employee retirement plans.
- **Enrolled Retirement Plan Agents** are individuals who provide technical services to plan sponsors to maintain a plan's tax qualified status. Practice is limited to representation with respect to issues involving forms filed by plans and certain IRS employee plans programs, including the Determination Letter program, the Compliance Resolution System, and the Prototype and Volume Submitter program.
- **Others.** Anyone who satisfies the compliance and suitability checks provided in the regulations, or anyone not otherwise eligible to practice but who is authorized by the IRS to do so in a particular matter, may practice before the IRS.
- **Unenrolled Return Preparers and Individual Taxpayers** practicing in limited capacity. Those in this category may practice before the IRS in very limited situations. Individuals may appear on their

own behalf. In addition, unenrolled individuals may practice before the IRS with limited authority in the following circumstances:

- An individual may represent a member of his or her immediate family.
- An employer may be represented by a regular full-time employee.
- A partnership may be represented by a general partner or a regular full-time employee of the partnership.
- An association, corporation (including a parent, subsidiary, or affiliated corporation), or other organized group may be represented by an officer or full-time employee of the group.
- A trust, receivership, guardianship, or estate may be represented by a trustee, receiver, guardian, personal representative, administrator, executor, or regular full-time employee.
- An officer or a regular employee of a governmental unit, authority, or agency may, in the course of his or her official duties, represent that governmental unit.
- An individual may represent any individual or entity outside the United States when the representation takes place outside the United States.

The IRS's Office of Professional Responsibility (OPR) reviews applications from individuals and administers the rules for practice before the IRS as set forth in Treasury Department Circular 230.

The IRS Return Preparer Office administers PTIN applications, competency testing, and continuing education (although these last two functions are on hold due to the current injunction against enforcement of the testing and continuing education requirements for return preparers). Although the OPR will continue to enforce Circular 230 provisions related to practitioner conduct and discipline, the Return Preparer Office will manage other matters specifically pertinent to preparers of returns. Circular 230 now omits most references to the OPR, and the IRS can delegate necessary authorities to appropriate offices.

The IRS maintains a computerized system of records, called CAF, that contains information on authorized representatives of taxpayers. A CAF number is assigned to a tax practitioner when a Form 2848 or Form 8821 is filed.

Who Cannot Practice Before the IRS. Some individuals are not allowed to practice before the IRS.

- Any individual who has been disbarred from professional practice is prohibited from practicing before the IRS.
- An officer or employee of the executive, legislative, or judicial branch of the U.S. government; an officer or employee of the District of Columbia; a Member of Congress; or a Resident Commissioner may not practice before the IRS if such practice violates 18 U.S.C. 203 or 205.

- An officer or employee of any state, or subdivision of any state, whose duties require him or her to pass upon, investigate, or deal with tax matters for such state or subdivision, may not practice before the IRS, if such employment may disclose facts or information applicable to federal tax matters.

 Planning Tip. The IRS has proposed changes to Circular 230, which have yet to be implemented. One proposed change is to clarify that a practitioner must possess the necessary competence when engaged in practice before the IRS. Competent practice requires the knowledge, skill, thoroughness, and preparation necessary for the matter for which the practitioner is engaged. Other proposed changes include elimination of the current complex rules governing covered opinions, which would be replaced by a more streamlined procedure, expansion of the categories of violations subject to expedited proceedings, and clarification of the scope of responsibility of the Office of Professional Responsibility. Another proposed change would clarify the existing prohibition against practitioners taking their fee out of a portion of their clients' tax refunds. Finally, proposed "reasonableness" standards would apply to employee benefit attorneys, and would make clear that they may not rely on information from plan sponsors when providing written advice to clients. A higher standard of review would apply to practitioners who know, or have reason to know, that their tax advice will be used to recommend, market, or promote investment plans or other arrangements whose primary purpose is to avoid paying taxes.

Power of Attorney

Form 2848, *Power of Attorney and Declaration of Representative*, is used to confer necessary powers on the taxpayer's representative. A Form 2848 must be signed and dated by the taxpayer, and also signed by the representative. A non-IRS form containing the same information may be used in place of the Form 2848. Power of attorney allows the taxpayer's representative to act in all matters relating to IRS issues. If the appointed representative is not qualified to sign the form, however, the form will not be honored. The IRS no longer treats such invalid forms as authority for the person named to receive tax information.

Joint filers must complete and submit separate Forms 2848. The form offers checkboxes to identify specific acts that the representative may perform.

Third Party Designee

A taxpayer may designate another person to discuss his or her tax return with the IRS by checking the "Yes" box in the *Third Party Designee* area of the return. This checkbox authority may be used to allow an employee of the taxpayer's business, a return preparer, a friend, a family member, or another third party to discuss the tax return with the IRS. The taxpayer must enter the designee's name, phone number, and any five numbers as a personal identification number (PIN).

Preparer as Designee. To allow the paid preparer who signed the return to discuss it with the IRS, "*Preparer*" is entered in the space for the designee's name, and no other information is required.

Scope of Authorization. Designation of a third party authorizes the IRS to call the designee to answer any questions relating to the information reported on the tax return. It also authorizes the designee to:

- Exchange information concerning the return with the IRS,
- Call the IRS for information about the processing of the return or the status of any refund or payments,
- Request and receive written tax return information relating to the tax return, including copies of notices, correspondence, and account transcripts, and
- Respond to certain IRS notices about math errors, offsets, and return preparation.

A designee is not authorized to receive any refund check, bind the taxpayer to anything (including additional tax liability), or otherwise represent the taxpayer before the IRS. Power of attorney is required to expand the designee's authority.

Automatic Expiration. The designee authorization automatically expires on the due date for the next year's tax return (for the 2013 return, that would be April 15, 2014, for most people). The authorization may be revoked by the taxpayer (or the representative may withdraw) during this time by sending a written statement of revocation to the Internal Revenue Service Center at the address where the return was filed. The statement of revocation must indicate that the authority of the designee is revoked, list the tax return, and be signed and dated by the taxpayer or designee.

Disclosure of Returns

The IRS is generally prohibited from disclosing tax returns and tax return information in its files, but it may disclose tax returns to persons having a material interest under specified circumstances. The right to inspect an income tax return in the possession of the IRS is statutorily conferred on a limited number of persons, all of whom must have a material interest in the contents of that return.

Information subject to the disclosure rules is of two types: returns and return information. The former includes any tax or information return, declaration of estimated tax, or claim for refund, together with any amendments, supplements, supporting schedules, attachments, or lists that were part of such returns. "Return information" includes the taxpayer's identity and the nature, source, or amount of the taxpayer's income, payments, receipts, deductions, exemptions, credits, assets, liabilities, net worth, tax liability, tax withheld, deficiencies, overassessments, or tax payments.

The IRS may also disclose returns and return information to any person for purposes of tax administration, in connection with the processing, storage, transmission, or reproduction of returns. The regulation allowing this has been held to allow the IRS to contract out the processing of tax returns to third parties. Amendments to this regulation clarify the circumstances in which disclosure is allowed, and also set forth appropriate safeguards and notification requirements that must be met by those to whom the information is disclosed. Finally, these requirements apply regardless of the form of the contract under which the third party will process the returns.

Taxpayer. An individual taxpayer is entitled to inspect his or her own return. If a joint return was filed, either spouse may examine it. A spouse who files a joint return has waived the right to confidentiality of return information with respect to the other spouse.

A copy of a return and all attachments to a return may be obtained by submitting Form 4506, along with the $57 fee, to the IRS RAIVS Team address given in the instructions for Form 4506 for the state in which the taxpayer lived when the return was filed.

Form 4506-T may be used to request a transcript of information for a tax year. A return transcript includes most of the line items on the return as filed. An account transcript contains information on the financial status of the account. Transcripts of W-2s, 1099s and other information returns filed for a year are also available. There is no charge for a transcript.

An individual may file Form 8821, *Tax Information Authorization*, to allow another person (an appointee) to view his or her tax information. A Form 8821 appointee is not empowered to represent the taxpayer unless Form 2848 is also filed. Each individual or entity must sign and file a separate Form 8821.

Spouses and Children. A spouse who filed a joint return is entitled to examine the return, but spouses who file separate returns are not entitled to examine each other's returns. A separation agreement that requires a taxpayer to furnish his or her tax returns to the ex-spouse for the purpose of ensuring compliance with alimony and child support obligations would most likely not be sufficient to authorize disclosure. Regulations require that a taxpayer's authorization for disclosure be in the form of a separate written document pertaining solely to the authorized disclosure. The document must also, at the time it is signed, state the taxable years it covers.

If a deficiency with respect to a joint return is assessed, and the individuals filing the return are no longer married or sharing the same household, the IRS must disclose its collection activities, including whether the other party was contacted and how much of the debt has been paid, upon the written request of one of the individuals. The IRS may omit the current home address and business location of a former spouse.

A child or a child's legal representative is considered a person having a material interest in the disclosure of returns or return information and may examine the parents' returns. This rule is to facilitate the administration of the rules under which unearned income of certain minor children is subject to tax at a parent's tax rate.

Others Who May Examine Returns. Returns of partnerships, corporations, estates (including bankruptcy estates), and trusts may be examined by individuals who have a material interest in the returns.

- In the case of a partnership, one who was a partner during any part of the time covered by a partnership return is permitted to examine such return. However, a partner of a partnership, or a shareholder of an S corporation, is not entitled to the disclosure of information regarding tax deficiency challenges filed by other partners or shareholders since the disclosure of such information constitutes the disclosure of the individuals' and not the entity's confidential return information.

 Caution. Some practitioners routinely distribute copies of 1120/1120S/1065 returns to all shareholders or partners at the time of preparation. This is generally acceptable. However, it is important to be aware of other information related to partnerships and S corporations that may require permission for disclosure.

- In bankruptcy proceedings, the trustee of the bankruptcy estate of an individual may examine any returns of the debtor for the tax year in which the bankruptcy proceedings are commenced or for any prior years by making a written request. If the bankruptcy is involuntary, the court's permission is required for such examination. With regard to prior

years' returns, a finding by the IRS that the returns contain relevant information is required.
- Estate returns may be examined by the administrator, executor, or trustee of the estate. Estate returns may also be examined by any heir at law, next of kin, or beneficiary under the will of the decedent if the IRS determines that such person has a material interest that will be affected by the information contained in the return. This rule applies even if the decedent died intestate. However, the Tax Court has the power to issue a protective order preventing the IRS from giving information sought from a decedent's estate when such disclosure will contribute to harassment of the estate with spurious and protracted litigation and when the requestor can obtain such information through subsequent discovery proceedings in any civil action he may bring.
- Returns of a decedent may be examined by the same people who are entitled to examine his estate return.
- Trust returns may be inspected by the trustee or trustees, and by any individual who was a beneficiary of the trust during any part of the time covered by the return, if the IRS finds that the trust beneficiary has a material interest that will be affected by return information.
- A corporate return may be examined by (1) any person designated by action of its board of directors, (2) any officer or employee upon written request signed by any principal officer and attested to by the secretary or other officer, (3) the attorney in fact, (4) in the case of a dissolved corporation, any person who might have inspected at the date of dissolution, (5) the receiver or trustee in bankruptcy holding the property, or his attorney in fact, and (6) a bona fide shareholder of record owning 1 percent or more of the outstanding stock (the 1 percent requirement does not apply in the case of an S corporation). No power of attorney can be accepted, however, because the privilege to the shareholder is personal. The executor of an estate holding 2 percent of a corporation's outstanding stock is regarded as the shareholder and is entitled to inspect the corporate return.
- If an individual is legally incompetent, the committee, trustee, or guardian of the estate is entitled to inspect his or her return.

Privilege

Communications between a taxpayer and his or her federally authorized representative are protected by privilege similar to the privilege that exists between clients and attorneys. The representative may not be compelled to disclose the information in court unless the taxpayer waives the privilege. This confidentiality applies to all facts communicated by the taxpayer in the process of seeking tax advice from the representative, in an area within the scope of the representative's authority to practice before the IRS. Confidentiality does not apply to communications relating to the preparation of tax returns, general accounting services, or business advice, or to any information that can be obtained from other sources.

 Caution. Taxpayers have for some time been able to treat communications with federally authorized tax representatives as confidential and privileged (with some exceptions, in the case of criminal matters). The privilege, however, does not apply to any written communication regarding tax shelters. This exception to the privilege formerly applied only to communications regarding corporate tax shelters, but has now been expanded to include any tax shelter.

The Kovel Doctrine. Communications by a client with a nonattorney tax professional engaged by counsel to perform services to assist the attorney in rendering legal services (i.e., providing legal advice regarding tax matters) may be protected from disclosure by the attorney-client privilege. The landmark case in this area is *U.S. v. Kovel,* 62-1 USTC ¶9111, 296 F2d 918 (2nd Cir. 1961).

 Caution. The federally authorized tax representative privilege does not apply to communications between a taxpayer and a tax return preparer, since the advice the latter usually renders is intended to be reflected on a tax return and is not intended to be confidential or privileged.

Information Return Filing Requirements

Taxpayers engaged in a trade or business are required to file various information returns if they make or receive certain payments. It is important for taxpayers to be aware of information returns that may be filed by financial institutions, government agencies, and businesses with which they conduct transactions because the IRS compares information on these returns with individual tax returns.

Taxpayer Responsibilities

Recordkeeping. Taxpayers are required to keep adequate records relating to items reported on tax returns for at least the period covered by the statute of limitations for assessment of tax relating to the return, usually three years. Some records must be kept longer. The absence of adequate books and records may be treated as evidence of intent to engage in civil fraud or commit tax crimes. Records do not have to be kept in any specific form; any records that reflect income adequately and clearly on the basis of an annual accounting period are sufficient.

Example. A farmer sells depreciable farming equipment at auction for $75,000. He had not maintained any books or records as to the assets' original costs, useful lives, or dates of acquisition. Because he is unable to furnish any written proof that the farm equipment had a remaining basis at the time of the sale, he is subject to 100-percent recapture, and the auction proceeds are taxable as ordinary income.

After a sale or exchange, a lack of records can result in a zero basis and a large taxable gain.

Individual taxpayers who derive their incomes from the business of farming, or from salaries, wages, and similar compensation for personal services, need not maintain formal, permanent books, but they must maintain records sufficient to determine the correct amount of their taxable incomes and to prove any deductions or credits claimed on any return.

An approximation of business expenses based on credible evidence other than actual documentation was allowed in *Cohan* [39 F.2d 540 (2nd Cir. 1930)]. The Cohan rule may be applied in cases where records are incomplete or inadequate unless stricter substantiation requirements are specified by statute. Also, if a taxpayer has established that records have been lost due to circumstances beyond the taxpayer's control, such as destruction by fire or flood, then the taxpayer has the right to substantiate claimed deductions by a reasonable reconstruction of the financial information.

Information Return Filing Requirements as of 2013				
Form	Who Must File	Information Reportable	Where Filed	Due Date
W-2	Employer required to withhold	Employee names, wages, tips, other compensation, certain fringe benefits, advance earned income credit (EIC) payments, withheld income, Medicare, and FICA taxes	Social Security Administration (PA) Data Operations Center	February 28 (paper) March 31 (electronic) (to recipient January 31)

Information Return Filing Requirements as of 2013 (Continued)

Form	Who Must File	Information Reportable	Where Filed	Due Date
W-2G	Payers of gambling winnings from bingo, lotteries, horse racing, dog racing, jai alai, poker tournaments, etc.	Generally, payments of $600 or more if winnings are at least 300 times the amount of the wager; $1,200 or more in bingo or slot machine winnings; $1,500 or more in keno winnings; $5,000 or more in poker winnings	See General Instructions for Certain Information Returns	February 28 (paper) March 31 (electronic) (to recipient January 31)
W-3	Employer required to withhold	Total of amounts reported on wage and tax statements	Social Security Administration (PA) Data Operations Center	February 28 (paper) March 31 (electronic)
W-8	Noncitizens and nonresidents having gain not effectively connected with a U.S. trade or business, who meet certain residency requirements	Qualifications for exemption from withholding or notice of change in status	With payer of the qualifying income who is the withholding agent	Before a payment is made
W-9	Taxpayers desiring to avoid backup withholding on interest and dividends and other forms of nonwage income	Taxpayer Identification Number (TIN)	With payer, middleman, broker, or barter exchange	When TIN is requested
56	Fiduciary	Identification, authority, tax notices, revocation or termination of notice, and court or administrative proceedings	Service Center for principal's tax return	When a fiduciary relationship is first created or when it is terminated
90-22.1	U.S. person having authority over, or interest in, a foreign financial account valued at over $10,000	Name, institution, location, valuation of account	U.S. Treasury Dept., Detroit, MI, or hand carry to local IRS office	June 30 of the year following the calendar year reported
926	Transferor of property to foreign corporation	Foreign transferee information, indication if transfer was exempt from excise tax, and calculation of excise tax	Service Center for tax return	Due date of transferor's return
945	Persons who withhold tax from nonpayroll payments (employers)	Income tax withheld from nonpayroll payments, including pensions, annuities, IRAs, military retirement, gambling winnings, voluntary withholding on certain government payments, and backup withholding	See instructions for form	January 31 February 10 if timely deposits made in full payment of taxes
972	Shareholder evidencing consent to receive dividend (with corporation claiming deduction)	Amount of dividend, name and address of corporations, shares, class of stock	Office for income tax return as attachment to Form 973	Due date of corporation's return for year consent dividend claimed as deduction
973	Corporation claiming a deduction for consent dividends	Class of stock, amount of shares, amount of dividends distributed	Office for income tax return as an attachment to return	Due date of corporation's return
990	Organizations exempt under Code Sec. 501(c)	Income, expenses, balance sheet, contributions, substantial contributors, and other information	Service Center, Ogden, UT	Fifteenth day of fifth month after accounting period of organization ends
1040-C, 2063	Departing alien	Income (for certificate of compliance)	Local IRS office	Before alien leaves U.S.

Information Return Filing Requirements as of 2013 (Continued)

Form	Who Must File	Information Reportable	Where Filed	Due Date
1042-S	Withholding agent for nonresident aliens	Name and address of payee and agent, gross amount and nature of income paid, withholding, per-country analysis	Service Center, Ogden, UT	March 15
1065	Limited liability company	Income, shareholders, shares	See instructions for form	April 15
1065	Partnership	Income, partners, shares	See instructions for form	April 15
1065	Religious or apostolic association/corporation	Members, shares of main office	See instructions for form	April 15
1096	Payers, brokers, trustees of IRAs, mortgage interest recipients, barterers, creditors, persons reporting real estate transactions, and lenders who acquire an interest in secured property	Transmittals of Forms W-2G, 1097, 1098, 1099, 3921, 3922, 5498, 5498-ESA and 5498-SA	See instructions for form	February 28 (W-2G, 1097, 1098, 1099, 3921, 3922) June 2 (5498, 5498-ESA, 5498-SA)
1098	Mortgage lender	Mortgage interest payments of $600 or more received in course of trade or business, including certain points	See instructions for form	February 28 (paper) March 31 (electronic) (to payer/borrower January 31)
1098-C	Donees of contributed motor vehicles, boats, or airplanes valued at over $500	Information about a donated motor vehicle, boat, or airplane; gross proceeds over $500	See instructions for form	February 28 (paper) March 31 (electronic) To donor within 30 days of donation
1098-E	Payees of student loan payments	Qualified educational student loan interest payments of $600 or more during a covered period	See instructions for form	February 28 (paper) March 31 (electronic) (to payer/borrower January 31)
1098-T	Qualified educational institutions	Amount of qualified tuition and related expenses received on behalf of individual, amounts of refunds and reimbursements, and amounts of grants received by student that were processed through the institution	See instructions for form	February 28 (paper) March 31 (electronic) (to student January 31)
1099-A	Secured lender	Information about the acquisition or abandonment of property that is security for a debt	See instructions for form	February 28 (paper) March 31 (electronic) (to borrower January 31)
1099-B	Brokers and barter exchanges	Sales or redemptions of securities, futures transactions, commodities, and bartering exchange transactions	See instructions for form	February 28 (paper) March 31 (electronic) (to recipient February 18)
1099-C	Lender	Amount of canceled debt of $600 or more owed to a financial institution, credit union, RTC, FDIC, NCUA, or federal governmental agency	See instructions for form	February 28 (paper) March 31 (electronic) (to borrower January 31)

Information Return Filing Requirements as of 2013 (Continued)				
Form	Who Must File	Information Reportable	Where Filed	Due Date
1099-CAP	Domestic corporations after acquisition of control or substantial change in capital structure, unless exempt	Information about cash, stock, or other property from acquisition of control or change in capital structure of corporation	See instructions for form	February 28 (paper) March 31 (electronic) (to recipient January 31; if clearinghouse, January 5)
1099-DIV	Corporations (or associations taxable as such) or stockholders	Distributions, such as dividends (including ESOP dividends), capital gains or nontaxable distributions, that were paid on stock and that totaled $10 or more, distributions in liquidation of $600 or more, foreign tax paid on certain distributions and federal income tax withheld under the backup withholding rules	See instructions for form	February 28 (paper) March 31 (electronic) (to recipient January 31)
1099-G	Payer	Unemployment compensation and state and local income tax refunds aggregating $10 or more, or agricultural payments and taxable grants for $600 or more	See instructions for form	February 28 (paper) March 31 (electronic) (to recipient January 31)
1099-H	Qualified health insurance providers	Advance health insurance premiums received on behalf of certain individuals	See instructions for form	February 28 (paper) March 31 (electronic) (to recipient January 31)
1099-INT	Corporations, banks, and savings and loan institutions	Interest, not including interest on an IRA, generally aggregating $10 or more ($600 or more for certain interest paid in the course of a trade or business)	See instructions for form	February 28 (paper) March 31 (electronic) (to recipient January 31)
1099-INT	Real estate mortgage investment conduits, issuers of CDOs and broker-nominees holding interests in REMICs or CDOs	Interest, other than original issue discount, accrued to a REMIC regular interest holder	See instructions for form	February 28 (paper) March 31 (electronic) (to recipient January 31)
1099-K	Payment settlement entity; electronic payment facilitator	Annual and monthly gross amounts of payment card/third party network transactions; merchant category code; number of purchase transactions	See instructions for form	February 28 (paper) March 31 (electronic) (to recipient January 31)
1099-LTC	Payers	Payments from long-term care insurance plans or accelerated death benefits	See instructions for form	February 28 (paper) March 31 (electronic) (to insured and policyholder January 31)
1099-MISC	Payers	Attorney fees over $600	See instructions for form	February 28 (paper) March 31 (electronic) (to recipient January 31)
1099-MISC	Businesses, including nonprofit organizations	Amounts aggregating $600 or more such as rent, prizes, and awards, and $10 in royalty or broker payments	See instructions for form	February 28 (paper) March 31 (electronic) (to recipient January 31)

Information Return Filing Requirements as of 2013 (Continued)

Form	Who Must File	Information Reportable	Where Filed	Due Date
1099-MISC	Fishing boat owners and operators	Amounts paid to crew members as proceeds from sale of fish	See instructions for form	February 28 (paper) March 31 (electronic) (to recipient January 31)
1099-MISC	Persons in a trade or business	Payments aggregating $600 or more for services performed for a trade or business by people not treated as its employees, such as subcontractors or directors, including golden parachute payments	See instructions for form	February 28 (paper) March 31 (electronic) (to recipient January 31)
1099-MISC	Businesses making payments for services received	Payments aggregating $600 or more, with name, address, and identification number of service recipient	See instructions for form	February 28 (paper) March 31 (electronic) (to recipient January 31)
1099-MISC	Payers under health plan	Payments aggregating $600 or more to physicians, physicians' corporations, or others providing health and medical services	See instructions for form	February 28 (paper) March 31 (electronic) (to recipient January 31)
1099-MISC	Brokers	Substitute dividend and tax-exempt interest payments of $10 or more	See instructions for form	February 28 (paper) March 31 (electronic) (to recipient February 18)
1099-MISC	Direct sellers	Direct sales of $5,000 or more of consumer goods for resale	See instructions for form	February 28 (paper) March 31 (electronic) (to recipient January 31)
1099-MISC	Crop insurers	Crop insurance proceeds of $600 or more paid by an insurance company	See instructions for form	February 28 (paper) March 31 (electronic) (to recipient January 31)
1099-MISC	Attorneys	Gross proceeds of $600 or more paid to attorney	See instructions for form	February 28 (paper) March 31 (electronic) (to recipient February 18)
1099-OID	Bond, CD issuers, other institutions accepting deposits, brokers, nominees	Original issue discount aggregating $10 or more	See instructions for form	February 28 (paper) March 31 (electronic) (to recipient January 31)
1099-OID	REMICs and issuers of collateralized debt obligations	Accrued original issue discount of $10 or more	See instructions for form	February 28 (paper) March 31 (electronic) (to recipient January 31)
1099-PATR	Cooperatives	Patronage dividends aggregating $10 or more	See instructions for form	February 28 (paper) March 31 (electronic) (to recipient January 31)
1099-Q	Qualified tuition programs and account trustees	Distributions from qualified tuition programs or Coverdell education savings accounts	See instructions for form	February 28 (paper) March 31 (electronic) (to recipient January 31)

Information Return Filing Requirements as of 2013 (Continued)

Form	Who Must File	Information Reportable	Where Filed	Due Date
1099-R	Employers, plan administrators, and issuers of insurance or annuity contracts	All distributions aggregating more than $10 from retirement or profit-sharing plans, IRAs, SEPs, or insurance contracts	See instructions for form	February 28 (paper) March 31 (electronic) (to recipient January 31)
1099-S	Person responsible for closing certain real estate transactions	Gross proceeds from sale or exchange of certain real estate	See instructions for form	February 28 (paper) March 31 (electronic) (to transferor February 18)
1099-SA	Payers	Distributions, including earnings, from medical savings accounts	See instructions for form	February 28 (paper) March 31 (electronic) (to recipient January 31)
1120S	S corporation	Income, deductions, cost of goods sold, and each shareholder's pro rata share of each subchapter S item	See instructions for form	March 17 (15th day of third month after end of tax year)
2438	Regulated investment companies (RICs) and real estate investment trusts (REITs) for each mutual fund	Undistributed capital gains	Service Center, Covington, KY	30 days after close of the fund's tax year
3520	Grantor or fiduciary of foreign trusts	Preparer, name of trust or estate, country of creation, dates of creation and termination, foreign trustee, list of property transferred to trust, beneficiaries	Service Center, Ogden, UT	April 15
3520-A	Foreign trust with at least one U.S. owner	Preparer, name of trust, U.S. agent and foreign trustee, income and expenses, balance sheet, owner and beneficiary statement	Service Center, Ogden, UT	March 17 (file Form 3520-A, send copy of owner statement to grantor, send copy of beneficial statement to each beneficiary)
5227	Split-interest trusts treated the same as private foundations, e.g., pooled income funds, charitable remainder trusts, or charitable lead trusts	Income, deductions and capital gains or losses (for charitable remainder trusts), balance sheet, information on charitable activities and distribution	Service Center, Ogden, UT	April 15
5471	A U.S. citizen or resident who is an officer or director of a foreign corporation in which a U.S. person (citizen or resident or domestic partnership, corporation, estate or trust) initially acquires 10% or more stock ownership or subsequently acquires an additional 10% or more (by value or voting power) of the outstanding stock	Identifying information, Schedules G and O (Part I)	File with income tax return	March 17 for corporations; April 15 for individuals

Information Return Filing Requirements as of 2013 (Continued)

Form	Who Must File	Information Reportable	Where Filed	Due Date
5471	A U.S. person (a U.S. citizen, resident, partnership, corporation, estate, or trust) who, with respect to a foreign corporation; (1) acquires 10% ownership; (2) acquires additional stock that increases ownership to 10%; or (3) disposes of stock reducing ownership below 10%; also, a person who (1) is treated as a U.S shareholder under Code Sec. 953(c); or (2) becomes a U.S. person while meeting the 10% ownership requirement	Identifying information, Schedules A, B, C, E, F, G, and O (Pt II); statement on related person indebtedness and shareholder information	File with income tax return	March 17 for corporations; April 15 for individuals
5471	Controlling (50% or more) shareholders (a U.S. citizen, resident, partnership, corporation, estate, or trust) of a foreign corporation that exercised control for an uninterrupted period of at least 30 days during its annual accounting period	Identifying information, Schedules A, B, C, E, F, G, H, I, J, and M	File with income tax return	March 17 for corporations; April 15 for individuals
5471	A U.S. person (a U.S. citizen, resident, partnership, corporation, estate, or trust) who owns 10% of a controlled foreign corporation (CFC), or any stock of a CFC that is a captive insurance company, for 30 days during the CFC's tax year, as well as on the last day of that year.	Identifying information, Schedules G, H, I, and J	File with income tax return	March 17 for corporations; April 15 for individuals
5472	All foreign corporations engaged in a U.S. trade or business and all domestic corporations that are at least 25% foreign owned that engage in a reportable transaction	Sales and purchases of stock or other tangible property in trade, rents and royalties paid or received, consideration paid for specified services, commissions paid and received, amounts loaned or borrowed, interest, premiums for insurance and reinsurance	Same as corporation's income tax return	Same as corporation's income tax return
5498	Trustees or issuers of individual retirement arrangements (IRAs) or simplified employee pensions (SEPs)	Participant's name, address, SSN, amount of IRA or SEP contributions, cost of life insurance and value of IRA or SEP account	See instructions for form	June 2 (to participant January 31 for value of account and June 2 for contributions)
5498-ESA	Trustees or custodians of Coverdell ESAs	Participant's name, address, SSN, amount of Coverdell ESA contributions (including rollovers), and value of accounts	See instructions for form	June 2 (to beneficiary April 30)

Information Return Filing Requirements as of 2013 (Continued)

Form	Who Must File	Information Reportable	Where Filed	Due Date
5498-SA	Trustees or custodians of MSAs, HSAs, Medicare Advantage MSAs	Participant's name, address, SSN, amount of MSA or HSA contributions, year for which contribution is made, rollovers, fair market value of account	See instructions for form	June 2 (to participant June 2)
5500	Pension plan administrators and sponsors who maintain an employee benefit plan subject to ERISA	Specified information on the plan	See form instructions - Electronic filing only	The last day of the seventh month after the plan year ends
8027/ 8027-T	Existing large food or beverage establishments where tipping is customary and more than 10 persons are normally employed and new large food or beverage establishments where the average number of hours worked each business day by all employees during any two consecutive months exceeded 80 hours	Gross food and beverage sales receipts, total charge receipts, charged tips, number of tipped employees, wages paid and tips reported by each employee, allocation of employee tip income	Cincinnati Service Center - Electronic filing if more than 250 forms filed	February 28 (paper) March 31 (electronic) (allocable tips shown on W-2, furnished to recipients January 31)
8038	Issuers of certain tax-exempt private activity bonds	Date and type of issue, description of obligations including maturity date, total face amount of obligations and stated annual interest rate, description of financed property and its principal users unless a student, and approval of issue if industrial development bonds	Ogden Service Center	Fifteenth day of second month after the calendar quarter during which the bond was issued
8300	Persons engaged in a trade or business	Payment of over $10,000 in cash or foreign currency received in one transaction or two or more related transactions in the course of a trade or business; cash payments received with respect to the same transaction or a related transaction exceeding $10,000 in a 12-month period in the course of a trade or business	Detroit Computing Center or hand-carry to local office	Within 15 days after date of transaction (to payer January 31)
8300	Clerks of federal or state courts	Cash payment for bail of over $10,000 in aggregate for certain criminal offenses	Detroit Computing Center or hand-carry to local office	Within 15 days after date of transaction, or if multiple payments, 15 days after date of transaction that causes aggregate to exceed $10,000 (to payer January 31)

Information Return Filing Requirements as of 2013 (Continued)				
Form	**Who Must File**	**Information Reportable**	**Where Filed**	**Due Date**
8300	Casinos	Payment of over $10,000 in cash or foreign currency received in one transaction or two or more related transactions for nongaming activities (restaurants, shops, etc.)	Detroit Computing Center or hand-carry to local office	Within 15 days after date of transaction (to payer January 31)
8308	Partnership	Sale or exchange of partnership interest involving unrealized receivables or substantially appreciated inventory items	Service Center of main office	Attach and file by due date of Form 1065 (to transferor and transferee January 31)

Note: Form 8809 is used to request a 30-day extension of time to file Forms 1042-S, 1097, 1098, 1099, 3921, 3922, 5498 and 8027 with the IRS or Form W-2 or W-2G with the Social Security Administration. An extension of time to furnish required statements to recipients may be requested by sending a letter to the IRS Information Returns Branch in West Virginia.

Audits

Audits, also called examinations, are the main tool of the IRS for ensuring taxpayer compliance with tax laws.

The IRS reviews all returns it receives. Mathematical or clerical errors are corrected, and a notice of the correction is sent to the taxpayer along with a refund of any overpayment or a demand for payment of any additional tax resulting from the correction. A notice of correction does not give the taxpayer the right to appeal to the Tax Court.

Problems with returns that are treated as mathematical or clerical errors include:

- Failure to include a correct TIN for the taxpayer, spouse, or any dependent when claiming an exemption or when claiming the child care credit, child tax credit, any higher education credit, the earned income credit (EIC), etc.
- Failure to pay the proper amount of self-employment tax on returns on which the EIC is claimed on net earnings from self-employment.
- EIC claim by noncustodial parent.
- S corporation shareholder's return inconsistent with the corporation's return.
- In most cases, estate or trust beneficiary's return inconsistent with estate's or trust's return.

The IRS Restructuring and Reform Act of 1998 has driven many recent changes in the conduct of IRS audits, including a dramatic decline in individual and corporate audit rates. The Act provided that the IRS Mission Statement was to emphasize serving and educating the public and satisfying the needs of taxpayers rather than enforcement.

Selection of Returns for Audit

The IRS assigns an activity code that categorizes each return by the type of form used and by the level of the taxpayer's income, gross receipts, or assets (the "size" of the return). Under an annual examination plan, IRS employees select a predetermined percentage of the highest risk returns within each activity code.

The discriminant index function (sometimes called the discriminant inventory function) (DIF), the unreported income discriminant index function (UI DIF), and the National Research Program (NRP) are important features of the current return selection process.

DIF Score. The IRS determines which are the highest risk returns using the DIF, a complex, computer-based technique that evaluates multiple items on returns to determine the potential for changes, based on the IRS's past experience with similar returns. After all the relevant items on a return are scored, a total DIF score is calculated as a sum of the individual item scores. The higher the DIF score, the greater the audit potential for that return. The UI DIF uses similar methods to measure the potential for unreported income.

IRS Research Programs. The IRS uses data collected in the NRP to determine the DIF and UI DIF scores. The NRP employs annual individual studies using a multi-year rolling methodology. Audits under the NRP are similar to regular IRS examinations, and are less intrusive and time-consuming than those conducted under prior research programs.

Audit Techniques Guides. The IRS offers Audit Techniques Guides (ATGs) in order to train its examiners for a particular market segment. The ATGs include examination techniques, unique or common industry issues, business practices, terminology specific to particular industries, and other information that may assist examiners in performing examinations.

Planning Tip. No rules limit the information or documentation that can be attached to a return. If there is concern that a particular return item may increase audit potential, consider attaching a detailed explanation and some verification for that item. It may be possible to avoid an audit by taking advantage of the IRS's pre-audit screening process.

Examinations of Related or Associated Taxpayers. Sometimes the examining agent commences the audit with a substantial amount of information, documentary and sometimes testimonial, developed during the course of examining a third party's return.

A prime example would be the audit of a local check-cashing agency that routinely cashes the checks of its customers. While conducting a compliance audit of the check-cashing agency, the IRS would collect substantial information about the agency's customers, mindful that they may not have appropriately reported proceeds from the cashed checks as gross receipts. Similarly, audits of related taxpayers or the taxpayer's vendors or customers often lead to an audit of the taxpayer if the taxpayer has significant interactions with them.

Public Records and Government Agencies. Audits and examinations sometimes arise from a government agent's review of newspaper articles; local, state, or national publicity sources; or court records. There are also many information-sharing arrangements between the IRS and other federal agencies as well as various state agencies (including state taxing authorities).

Other Outside Sources. Many audits are prompted by information from people somehow connected to the taxpayer. Informants typically include disgruntled employees, ex-business partners, business competitors, ex-spouses, and others. The IRS may reward the informant with a percentage of the tax and penalty ultimately recovered and is precluded from disclosing the informant's identity.

Information Returns Processing (IRP). The IRS typically tries to match all information on a taxpayer's Form 1099, W-2, and Schedule K-1 with information in the taxpayer's return. If these do not match, and the taxpayer's response to an initial inquiry is insufficient, an audit may ensue.

Compliance Projects. Increased requirements for transaction and information reporting have provided the IRS with a great deal of information about currency-related transactions. The IRS performs compliance checks, or audits of businesses to determine whether information reporting requirements are being met. Audit potential is often determined during the compliance check. Currency and banking transaction information reports collected from all federal agencies are consolidated in the Currency and Banking Transaction Reporting System of the IRS. Many former IRS and Treasury forms are now used by (and renamed for) the Financial Crimes Enforcement Network (FinCEN). The Patriot Act and recent Treasury rules have greatly increased the amount of information that businesses must collect and maintain about their customers' financial lives; more businesses are required to report suspicious activities; and new rules step up information sharing between financial institutions and the government.

Financial Status Audits. Information not specifically related to an individual's tax return, such as a taxpayer's standard of living and credit reports, are considered by the IRS if it already has a reasonable indication that there is a likelihood of unreported income.

IRS Audit Priorities

Audit priorities of the IRS generally include key, high-risk areas of noncompliance, including offshore credit care users, high-risk, high-income taxpayers, abusive schemes and promoter investigations, high-income nonfilers, and filers with likely unreported income. In addition, each of the operating divisions within the IRS (Small Business/Self-Employed, Wage and Investment, Large Business and International, Tax Exempt and Government Entities, Criminal Investigation) has its own more specific audit priorities, which vary from year to year.

When the IRS Will Perform Examinations

The general statutory limitation on the IRS's power to assess additional taxes is three years from the due date of a timely filed return, or three years from the receipt of a return filed late.

A taxpayer will generally be notified that a return is going to be examined during the 26 months (27 months in the case of a corporation) after the date the return was due or filed. The statute of limitations begins running on the date the return was due if the return is filed on time or early, or on the date the return was received if the return was filed late.

If the IRS cannot complete an examination within the period of limitation, it may seek to extend the statute of limitations, subject to the consent of the taxpayer.

How Audits Are Conducted

Audits may take place through correspondence, at an IRS office, or at the taxpayer's home or place of business or the place of business of the taxpayer's representative (a field examination). The IRS is required to conduct its examination of taxpayers and their books and records in a reasonable fashion that does not unduly inconvenience the taxpayers.

Taxpayer Rights

During an IRS examination of a taxpayer's return, the taxpayer has specific rights.

- The IRS must provide a written statement detailing the taxpayer's rights and the IRS's obligations during the audit, appeals, refund, and collection process. The IRS must also explain the audit and collection process.
- A taxpayer is guaranteed the right to be represented by any individual currently permitted to practice before the IRS, unless the IRS notifies the taxpayer that the representative is responsible for unreasonable delay or hindrance. Further, unless it issues an administrative summons, the IRS cannot require the taxpayer to accompany the representative to the interview.
- If a taxpayer goes to an audit without a representative, any interview must be suspended when the taxpayer clearly requests the right to consult with a representative.
- The taxpayer has the right to make an audio recording of any in-person interview conducted by the IRS, upon 10 days' advance notice.
- The IRS is entitled to inspect the taxpayer's books only once, unless the taxpayer requests reexamination or the IRS provides written notification.
- The taxpayer has the right to claim additional deductions not claimed on the return during the audit if entitled to the deductions.
- The taxpayer may invoke his or her constitutional rights if questioned about possible criminal violations.
- After an audit, the taxpayer has the right to get a copy of the IRS's file. Case workpapers compiled by the examiner do not become a permanent part of the file, but may be obtained by the taxpayer after the examination is completed and before an appeal is filed. The taxpayer's right to his or her file is covered by the Freedom of Information Act, and the taxpayer may file a FOIA request with the responsible IRS official, as indicated in the regulation.

Taxpayer Representation During an Audit

During the course of an audit, the representative must remain aware of the many issues that might arise and any privileges that may apply. The representative must attempt to respond to each request for information in a timely manner. Effective representation requires adequate preparation, an understanding of the taxpayer's business, a fair presentation of the relevant facts and legal authorities, and a realistic evaluation of the relative hazards in the event of litigation.

Among a representative's key audit objectives should be to limit the scope of the agent's inquiry; maintain the appearance of reasonable cooperation; avoid presenting false or misleading information or statements; make certain no privileges are waived; and maintain a detailed schedule of all information and documents provided to the agent.

The IRS has the power to issue a summons to any person who has information that may be relevant to an IRS inquiry. This power may be invoked to require a person to produce books and records or to give testimony.

Unagreed Issues

If, as a result of an audit, adjustments are proposed with which the taxpayer does not agree, the taxpayer is given an opportunity to appeal the examiner's conclusions. If the examination takes place at an IRS office, the taxpayer may request a meeting with the examiner's supervisor. If that meeting fails to resolve the disagreement, or if the audit did not take place at an IRS office, the taxpayer may request an appeal. If the taxpayer requests such consideration, the case will be referred to the Appeals Office, which will afford the taxpayer the opportunity for a conference. The determination of tax liability by the Appeals Office is final insofar as the taxpayer's appeal rights within the IRS are concerned.

Fast-Track Mediation

If a taxpayer disagrees with the findings of an examination, or in certain other circumstances, it may be possible to resolve the issue with a mediator, outside of the federal court system. Most cases that are not docketed in any court qualify for fast-track mediation. IRS Publication 3605, *Fast Track Mediation*, describes the exceptions and procedure. In addition, the IRS offers specific fast-track mediation programs targeted toward business taxpayers. Small business/self-employed (SB/SE) fast-track mediation is an expedited process to resolve disputes within 40 days, compared to several months or longer for the regular appeals process. Large Business and International (LB&I) Division fast-track mediation aims to resolve issues within 120 days.

 Filing Tip. If fast-track mediation fails to resolve a dispute, the taxpayer retains the option of continuing with the traditional appeals process.

Collections

The IRS charges a late-payment penalty of 0.5% per month as well as interest at the federal rate on past-due tax payments. In addition, if a return is not filed by the due date, a late-filing penalty of 4.5% per month, up to 25% of the tax due, is charged. Extensions of time to file are obtained using Form 4868; see Tab 1. An extension of time to pay tax may be obtained using Form 1127, *Application for Extension of Time for Payment of Tax Due to Undue Hardship.* The taxpayer must show that timely payment would result in undue hardship.

Liens

A lien is a claim against property for the satisfaction of a debt. The IRS has an automatic lien on a taxpayer's property if the taxpayer owes tax that is not currently being disputed. The IRS may file a Notice of Federal Tax Lien to protect its right to the taxpayer's property if the tax is not paid.

The IRS must notify any person subject to a lien of the existence of the lien within five days of the lien being filed, with a notice given in person, left at the taxpayer's home or place of business, or sent by certified or registered mail to the person's last known address. The notice must explain (1) the amount of the unpaid tax, (2) the person's right to request a hearing during the 30-day period beginning on the fifth day after the lien is filed, (3) the available administrative appeals and their procedures, and (4) the procedures relating to the release of liens.

Any tax lien against an individual's property will be released within 30 days after the tax (along with applicable penalties and interest) is paid. In some circumstances, the IRS will release a tax lien while the tax is still owed. See IRS Publication 783, *Instructions on How to Apply for a Certificate of Discharge of Property from Federal Tax Lien*, and IRS Publication 1660, *Collection Appeal Rights*, for more information.

Levies

A levy is a seizure of property to satisfy a debt. The IRS must give 30 days' notice of its intent to seize a taxpayer's property. The IRS may generally levy any property the taxpayer owns at the time of the levy. Certain property is exempt from levy:

- Clothing and school books needed by the taxpayer and family members
- Furniture and personal effects in the taxpayer's household up to $8,790 in value (for 2013)
- Books and tools of the taxpayer's trade, business, or profession up to $4,400 in value (for 2013)
- Unemployment benefits, including any portion payable with respect to dependents
- Undelivered mail
- Annuity or pension payments under the Railroad Retirement Act; benefits under the Railroad Unemployment Insurance Act; special pension payments received by a person whose name has been entered on the Army, Navy, Air Force, and Coast Guard Medal of Honor roll; and annuities based on retired or retainer pay under chapter 73 of title 10 USC
- Worker's compensation, including any portion payable with respect to dependents
- Salary, wages, or other income necessary to comply with any child support judgment
- Wages or salary received by an individual for personal services, or income from other sources, up to the "exempt amount" stated in the statute. This amount consists of the sum of the individual's standard deduction and personal exemption for the tax year, divided by the number of payments during the year (for example, 52 in the case of weekly wage or salary payments).
- Certain amounts payable to an individual as a service-connected disability benefit
- Any amount payable to an individual as a recipient of public assistance under supplemental security income for the aged, blind, and disabled of the Social Security Act, or state or local government public assistance or public welfare programs for which eligibility is determined by a needs or income test
- Any amount payable to a participant under the Job Training Partnership Act (29 U.S.C. 1501 et seq.) from funds appropriated pursuant to that Act
- If the amount of the levy does not exceed $5,000, the residence of the taxpayer; or any real property of the taxpayer (other than that which is rented) used by any other individual as a residence

- The principal residence of the taxpayer (unless the levy is approved by a judge or magistrate of a federal district court), as well as tangible personal or real property (other than that which is rented) used in the trade or business of an individual taxpayer (unless the levy is approved by an appropriate IRS official, or it is determined that the collection of the tax is in jeopardy)

Personal property that is exempt from levy is not exempt from attachment by a federal tax lien.

Relief from Collection Activity

Delays of Collection Activities

If a taxpayer's income is below an amount based on the HHS poverty guidelines, the IRS may delay collection activities. Low-income taxpayers may file Form 433-A, *Collection Information Statement for Wage Earners and Self-Employed Individuals*, or Form 433-B, *Collection Information Statement for Businesses*, to prove that their income is insufficient to pay the tax owed and also meet basic living expenses, and that the taxpayer has no assets the IRS might levy to secure payment of the tax.

Taxpayer Advocate Service

Collection activity may be suspended if the taxpayer faces significant hardship. The Taxpayer Advocate Service assists taxpayers who have an issue that has not been resolved through normal channels. The taxpayer advocate independently represents taxpayer interests and concerns within the IRS. Taxpayer advocates are independent of other divisions of the IRS and report directly to the National Taxpayer Advocate. This service is provided for the following situations:

- The taxpayer is suffering, or is about to suffer, a significant hardship as a result of administration of the tax laws.
- The taxpayer is facing an immediate threat of adverse action.
- The taxpayer will incur significant costs in resolving the tax problem through normal channels (including fees for professional representation).
- The taxpayer will suffer irreparable injury or long-term adverse impact as a result of IRS action.
- There has been a delay of more than 30 days beyond normal processing times to resolve a tax account problem.
- A response has not been received by the date promised.

Situations are reviewed on a case-by-case basis. An issue is submitted for consideration by the Taxpayer Advocate Service in one of three ways:

- By phone at 877-777-4778 (for TTY/TDD, call 800-829-4059).

- By filing Form 911, *Request for Taxpayer Advocate Service Assistance (and Application for Taxpayer Assistance Order)*, with the Taxpayer Advocate Service.
- By telephone to, or in person at, the local Taxpayer Advocate office. See IRS Publication 1546, *Taxpayer Advocate Service is Here to Help*, for a list of local TAS offices with contact information.

Injured Spouse Claim

The IRS may offset overpayments of taxes for past-due federal debts, child support payments, and some other debts. If the debt is attributable to one spouse, and a joint return was filed, the other spouse may be entitled to receive a refund of his or her share of the overpayment by filing Form 8379, *Injured Spouse Allocation*.

Innocent Spouse Relief

If a joint return is filed, each spouse is responsible for the accuracy of the return and for the payment of the tax. Under certain circumstances, one spouse may claim relief by filing Form 8857, *Request for Innocent Spouse Relief*, no later than two years after the date on which the IRS first attempted to collect the tax. Married taxpayers who live in community property states may qualify for relief even if a joint return is not filed.

The following conditions must be met to qualify for innocent spouse relief:

1. The joint return had an understatement of tax due to erroneous items of the spouse or former spouse.
2. At the time the spouse requesting relief signed the joint return, he or she did not know or have reason to know that there was an understatement of tax.
3. Taking into account all the facts and circumstances, it would be unfair to hold the spouse requesting relief liable for the understatement of tax.

Relief by Separation of Liability. Under separation of liability, income, deductions, credits, and other items are allocated to each spouse in a method similar to that which would have been used if the spouses had filed separate returns, and each spouse is liable only for his or her portion of the tax. Only unpaid liabilities may be treated in this way. If the tax has been paid, relief by separation of liability is not available.

This type of relief applies only if the spouses are divorced or legally separated (or the other spouse has died), or if the spouses were not members of the same household at any time during the last 12 months. Also, the spouse applying for relief must not have had actual knowledge of the disputed items.

Equitable Relief. Spouses who do not qualify for innocent spouse relief or relief by separation of liability may qualify for equitable relief. The IRS automatically considers whether equitable relief is appropriate if an application for another form of relief is received and declined. This type of relief may apply to both understatement of tax and to underpayment of tax. An example would be where the taxpayer believes that his or her spouse paid the tax but the tax has in fact not been paid. The IRS has removed the former two-year limit to seek equitable relief.

See IRS Publication 971, *Innocent Spouse Relief*, for more details.

Appeals of Collections

There are various collection appeal procedures available to taxpayers who have received a bill or notice of deficiency from the IRS. The two main procedures are the Collection Due Process (CDP) hearing and the Collection Appeals Program (CAP).

 Caution. A practitioner who assists a taxpayer with a Collection Due Process claim when the taxpayer has not complied with payment and filing obligations may be subject to disciplinary proceedings. Because it is common knowledge that the IRS will reject a CDP claim due to taxpayer noncompliance, the IRS Office of Professional Responsibility scrutinizes such submissions. If the practitioner assists the taxpayer with knowledge that the claim will be rejected out of hand, the practitioner has violated the prohibition on attempting to delay tax administration proceedings.

Installment Agreements

Installment agreements are used when a taxpayer cannot fully and immediately pay the amount due. The IRS will generally grant an installment agreement in cases where the liability can be paid within three years and in "small dollar" cases, defined now as "streamlined agreements." A $105 fee is charged by the IRS for setting up an installment agreement ($52 for those with a direct debit agreement; $43 for those below a certain income level). If the tax is paid in full within 120 days, there are no fees. If a taxpayer has an installment agreement restructured or reinstated, the user fee is $45. An installment agreement reduces the late-payment penalty to 0.25% per month.

The IRS is authorized to enter into installment agreements with taxpayers that provide for partial payment of the tax liability (in contrast to prior law, which required an installment agreement to provide for payment in full of the tax liability). The IRS is required to review partial payment agreements every two years. If payment in full can be made within three years, however, and the taxpayer's liability is less than $10,000 (and if certain other conditions are met), the IRS can only accept an agreement providing for full payment, and the partial payment option is not available.

Offers in Compromise

Sometimes the IRS settles tax collection matters for less than the full amount of tax due. There are three potential grounds for an offer in compromise: doubt as to collectibility, doubt as to liability, and effective tax administration or special circumstances.

A taxpayer makes an offer using Form 656, *Offer in Compromise*, or, if the offer is based on doubt as to liability, Form 656-L *Offer in Compromise (Doubt as to Liability)*. A $150 application fee is required, but the fee may be waived for low-income taxpayers who file Form 656-A, *Income Certification for Offer in Compromise Application Fee*. If Form 656-L is filed, the fee may be waived. See Form 656-B, *Offer in Compromise Booklet*.

If an offer is accepted based on doubt as to collectibility, the IRS will determine the reasonable collection potential of a case (an amount less than the total debt owed), taking into account the taxpayer's basic living expenses. In addition, the agency may accept less than that amount if there are special circumstances. However, if a taxpayer's tax liability can be paid in full in a lump sum or through an installment agreement, the taxpayer will not be considered for an offer in compromise. The only exception is if the taxpayer can demonstrate special circumstances that would show the full payment of the liability would result in economic hardship or be detrimental to voluntary compliance.

In a case where the IRS accepts an offer based on the promotion of effective tax administration (that is, the IRS has decided that collecting the full amount owed would be possible, but would create economic hardship for the taxpayer or would be unfair or inequitable), the decision will be based on the taxpayer's individual circumstances. The structure of these agreements is based on the IRS's goal of collecting as much of the tax as possible in situations in which the taxpayer lacks the resources to meet the tax liability.

A taxpayer is required to make partial payments while an offer in compromise is being considered. If the offer is of a lump sum payment, then the taxpayer must make a nonrefundable downpayment of 20 percent of the amount of the offer. The relevant fee must also be submitted with the appropriate partial payment; that amount will be applied to the taxpayer's tax liability.

Bankruptcy and Taxes

A separate estate, for tax purposes, is created for an individual who files a petition under Chapter 7 or 11 of the Bankruptcy Code. A separate estate is not created under Chapter 12 or 13 of the Bankruptcy Code.

The individual taxpayer should continue to file the same federal income tax return, reporting all income received and deducting all allowable expenses. Debt canceled because of bankruptcy is not included in income, but may reduce certain losses and credits (to the extent that the taxpayer has them).

The estate is represented by a trustee appointed by the bankruptcy court to administer the estate and liquidate nonexempt assets. In Chapter 11, the debtor usually remains in control of the assets as a "debtor-in-possession."

A bankruptcy estate may produce its own income as well as incur its own expenses, and the trustee must file a tax return on Form 1041, *U.S. Income Tax Return for Estates and Trusts*, for the estate if its income is greater than the sum of the personal exemption amount and the basic standard deduction for a married individual filing separately. If a return is required, the trustee (or debtor-in-possession) completes the identification area at the top of the Form 1041 and lines 23-29 (the total tax amount on line 23 is taken from Form 1040), and signs and dates it. For bankruptcy estates, Form 1041 is used as a transmittal for Form 1040, *U.S. Individual Income Tax Return*. Complete Form 1040 and figure the tax using the tax rate schedule for a married person filing separately. In the top margin of Form 1040, write "Attachment to Form 1041. DO NOT DETACH." Attach Form 1040 to the Form 1041.

Advantages and Disadvantages of Tax Code and Bankruptcy Code Remedies as of 2013		
Remedy	Advantages	Disadvantages
Statute of Limitation on Collection	• Discharge of the tax liability without payment and release of underlying liens.	• Difficulty of withstanding 10 years of collection activity. • Heightened collection activity prior to the statute's expiration. • The IRS may renew the taxpayer's liability with a court proceeding.
Installment Agreement	• Creation of breathing space free from examination by the IRS. • Possibility of full payment. • Possibility of hardship status when payment is not possible. • Partial payment in satisfaction of liability may be accepted by IRS.	• Impossibly strict budget. • Likelihood that a notice of tax lien will be filed.
Offer in Compromise	• Discharge by the taxpayer of unsecured liabilities that are nondischargeable in bankruptcy. • Discharge of liabilities without payment in full. • Removal of the tax lien, which might otherwise remain attached to property after a Chapter 7 filing.	• Formulating an acceptable offer is incredibly difficult. • A taxpayer must find an outside source to fund/offer with cash equal to the proceeds that could be generated from a liquidation of the taxpayer's assets plus the net present value of a five-year installment agreement. • Taxpayer's tax refunds for all tax years up through and including the year in which the offer is accepted are taken by the IRS. • Filing of an offer stays the statute of limitation on collection, and the IRS receives an additional year (beyond the 10 it is already granted) to collect the tax if the offer is rejected, or if the offer is accepted and the taxpayer does not fulfill the obligation. • Interest continues to accrue. • Installment payments are required while offer is being considered by the IRS.
Chapter 7 Bankruptcy	• Discharge of unsecured income tax liabilities, regardless of size, for which the statute of limitation on assessment for the underlying tax year has run and the liability was neither assessed within the last 240 days nor the subject of an offer in compromise. • Payments above asset liquidation value are not required. • Bankruptcy Code exemptions are larger than the Tax Code exemptions used by the IRS for computing an offer. The taxpayer's tax refund may be protected.	• Provides no relief for relatively fresh tax liabilities. • It provides no relief for the Code Sec. 6672 responsible person penalty, regardless of assessment date. • It provides no relief from secured tax debt. • Relief against unsecured debt is limited in scope. • No relief if taxpayer did not file his or her tax returns for the tax years in question. Also, the returns must have been filed more than two years before the filing of the bankruptcy.

Advantages and Disadvantages of Tax Code and Bankruptcy Code Remedies as of 2013 (Continued)		
Remedy	**Advantages**	**Disadvantages**
Chapter 11 Bankruptcy	• Chapter 11 can be used when a taxpayer does not qualify for Chapter 13, cannot age Type 1 obligations into Type 3 obligations, and cannot pay priority taxes under terms and conditions available in an installment agreement.	• Chapter 11 is relatively uncommon for individuals. The Chapter 11 plan of reorganization is often more complicated, more expensive, and more time-consuming than Chapters 7 and 13. • All priority taxes must be paid.
Chapter 13 Bankruptcy	• Because of its $383,175 noncontingent, liquidated unsecured debt and $1,149,525 secured debt limitations, Chapter 13 works best to discharge moderate amounts of debt. Type 2 and Type 3 claims need only be paid out of disposable income for a three-year period. As compared with Chapter 7, this is an especially favorable treatment for the Type 2 claims. • Under current law old income tax liabilities (liabilities for tax periods over three years old) are dischargeable in Chapter 13 even if the taxpayer failed to file tax returns for one or more of the tax periods in question.	• Because a separate taxable entity is not created, the debtor retains tax attributes until the plan is completed and debt is discharged. Type 1 claims must be paid in full but without interest, at least during the life of the plan. Type 2 tax claims must be paid in full.
"Chapter 20" Bankruptcy	• "Chapter 20" is a Chapter 7 bankruptcy followed by a Chapter 13 (or vice versa); no Chapter 20 exists in the Bankruptcy Code. Chapter 20 works when the taxpayer has both large Type 3 claims that prevent the use of Chapter 13 and Type 1 claims that can be paid over the applicable three-year Chapter 13 period. The Type 3 claims are discharged in Chapter 7, the Type 2 claims are discharged in Chapter 13, and the Type 1 claims are paid in Chapter 13.	• In using Chapter 20, practitioners must be aware of case law increasing Bankruptcy Code time periods for determining priority and dischargeability by the time spent in the first bankruptcy. In addition, a court will scrutinize the second filing to ensure that the statutory good faith filing requirement is met. • There must be a minimum of four years between Chapter 7 and Chapter 13 filings. This will reduce the likelihood that a Chapter 20 will be of any use to a taxpayer.

Payment Options Comparison Chart					
	Total of All Liabilities	**Time Frame for Full Payment**	**Other Basic Requirements**	**Financial Information**	**Verification of Financial Information**
Guaranteed Installment Agreement (IA)*	Below $10,000	Within 36 months	Must stay current with all future taxes	Limited	No
Streamlined IA*	Below $25,000	Within 60 months	Must stay current with all future taxes	Limited	No
Full Pay IA < 60 months**	No limit	Up to 60 months	Leverage equity in assets Must stay current with all future taxes Conditional expenses may be allowed	Complete	Yes
Full Pay IA > 60 months**	No limit	61 months and up, prior to expiration of collection statute	Leverage equity in assets Must stay current with all future taxes Transition period for conditional expenses may be allowed for up to 12 months	Complete	Yes
Partial Pay IA	No limit	Payments made until collection statute expires	Leverage equity in assets Must stay current with all future taxes No conditional expenses allowed No transition period	Complete	Yes

Payment Options Comparison Chart (Continued)					
	Total of All Liabilities	Time Frame for Full Payment	Other Basic Requirements	Financial Information	Verification of Financial Information
Deferred Payment Offer in Compromise	No limit	Payments made until statute date or until accepted offer amount received	Net realizable equity must be accounted for in amount offered No conditional expenses allowed Must stay current with all future taxes	Complete	Yes

* 98 percent of all IA taxpayers fall into these first two categories
** Length of installment agreement determined by the financial analysis

Employer Identification Number. The trustee (or debt-or-in-possession) must obtain an employer identification number (EIN) for the bankruptcy estate if the estate must file any form, statement, or document with the IRS. The trustee uses this EIN on any tax return filed for the bankruptcy estate, including estimated tax returns. The trustee can obtain an EIN for a bankruptcy estate by filing Form SS-4, *Application for Employer Identification Number.*

Election to End Tax Year. Individuals who file a petition in bankruptcy court have the option of ending their tax year on the day before the bankruptcy petition is filed. This allows the tax due on that short-period return to be a claim against the bankruptcy estate. The election to end the tax year is made by filing Form 1040 for the short tax year on or before the fifteenth day of the fourth full month after the end of the short tax year. To avoid delays in processing the return, "Section 1398 Election" should be written at the top of the return. The taxpayer may also make the election by attaching a statement to an application for extension of time to file a tax return (Form 4868 or other) by the due date of the return for the short tax year ending on the day before the filing date of the bankruptcy. A debtor's spouse may also choose to elect the same short tax year, but only if the spouses file a joint return.

Tax Assessment During Bankruptcy

Generally, the automatic stay rules prevent a creditor (including the IRS) from taking actions to collect prepetition debts. However, the automatic stay does not apply to:

- An audit to determine tax liability.
- A demand for tax returns.
- The issuance of a notice of deficiency to the debtor.
- The making of an assessment for any tax and the sending of a notice and demand for payment of the tax assessed.

Under the Bankruptcy Abuse Prevention and Consumer Protection Act of 2005, postpetition actions are never barred by the automatic stay in a bankruptcy proceeding. The bankruptcy court may now determine not only postpetition tax liabilities, but also which taxable periods will be subject to the automatic stay.

In bankruptcy, debts are assigned priorities for payment. Most unsecured tax debts existing before the bankruptcy case was filed are classified as eighth-priority claims, including:

- Income taxes for tax years ending on or before the date of filing the bankruptcy petition, for which a return is due (including extensions) within three years of the filing date.
- Income taxes assessed within 240 days before the date of filing the petition. This 240-day period is increased by any time during which an offer in compromise that was made within 240 days after the assessment was pending, plus 30 days.
- Income taxes that were assessable but not assessed before the petition date, unless these taxes were still assessable solely because no return, a late return (within two years of the filing of the bankruptcy petition), or a fraudulent return was filed.
- Withholding taxes for which the debtor is liable in any capacity.
- Employer's share of employment taxes on wages, salaries, or commissions (including vacation, severance, and sick leave pay) paid as priority claims or for which a return is due within three years of the filing of the bankruptcy petition, including a return for which an extension of the filing date was obtained.
- Excise taxes on transactions occurring before the date of filing the bankruptcy petition, for which a return, if required, is due (including extensions) within three years of the filing of the bankruptcy petition. If a return is not required, these excise taxes include only those on transactions occurring during the three years immediately before the date of filing the petition.

Different rules apply to payment of eighth-priority prepetition taxes under Chapters 11, 12, and 13:

- Under Chapter 11, the debtor can pay these taxes over a period of six years from the date of assessment, including interest.

- Under Chapter 12, the debtor can pay such tax claims in deferred cash payments over time.
- Under Chapter 13, the debtor can pay such taxes over three years (or over five years with court approval).

Dismissal of Bankruptcy Case. If an individual's bankruptcy case began but was later dismissed by the bankruptcy court, the estate is not treated as a separate entity, and the taxpayer is treated as if the bankruptcy petition had never been filed in the first place. The taxpayer must file amended returns on Form 1040X to replace any returns previously filed. Include on any amended returns items of income, deductions, or credits that were or would have been reported by the bankruptcy estate on its returns. Administrative expenses the former estate could have claimed may be deductible. Also, the bankruptcy exclusion cannot be used to exclude debt that was canceled while the individual was under the bankruptcy court's protection. The other exclusions (such as insolvency) may apply.

Return Preparer Requirements

E-Filing Requirements

More and more preparers are choosing to, or are being required to, file the returns they prepare electronically. Preparers seeking to become authorized e-filers should review IRS Publication 3112, *IRS e-file Application and Participation*, and can file the e-file application electronically from the IRS website. Authorized e-filers can electronically transmit tax returns according to the procedures outlined in IRS Publication 1345, *Handbook for Authorized IRS e-File Providers of Individual Income Tax Returns.* (IRS Publication 1345A, *Filing Season Supplement for Authorized IRS e-file Providers*, has been deleted.)

Preparers of returns for 2013 are required to e-file if they prepare or file 11 or more returns.

Caution. The e-filing requirement applies to a preparer who either prepares or files more than the prescribed number of returns. Thus, if a preparer prepares more than 10 returns for 2013, all of those returns must be e-filed. Clients may independently choose to file on paper, but if so, the preparer should file Form 8948, Preparer Explanation for Not Filing Electronically.

Enrolled Agents

The Director, Office of Professional Responsibility, issues an enrollment card to each individual whose application for enrollment to practice before the Internal Revenue Service is approved. To maintain active enrollment to practice before the Internal Revenue Ser-

vice, each individual enrolled is required to renew his or her enrollment every three years.

Special Enrollment Examination. An individual may become an enrolled agent by getting a passing score on each part of the Special Enrollment Examination. The individual must then apply for enrollment and undergo a background check by the IRS. A computer-based version of the Special Enrollment Examination (SEE) is available. The examination is developed and administered by a nationwide private testing firm, Thomson Prometric. The examination comprises three parts, Individuals, Businesses, and Representation, Practice, and Procedures. Each part contains approximately 100 questions.

Renewal of Enrollment. Forms required for renewal may be obtained from the Director, Office of Professional Responsibility, Internal Revenue Service, 1111 Constitution Avenue NW, Washington, DC 20224. The three-year enrollment cycle applies to enrolled agents according to the last digit of his or her SSN or TIN:

- All enrolled individuals whose SSN or TIN ends with the number 0, 1, 2, or 3 must apply for renewal between November 1, 2015, and January 31, 2016. The renewal will be effective April 1, 2016.
- All enrolled individuals whose SSN or TIN ends with the number 4, 5, or 6 must apply for renewal between November 1, 2013, and January 31, 2014. The renewal will be effective April 1, 2014.
- All enrolled individuals whose SSN or TIN ends with the number 7, 8, or 9 must apply for renewal between November 1, 2014, and January 31, 2015. The renewal will be effective April 1, 2015.

Applications for renewal will be required between November 1 and January 31 of every subsequent third year according to the last number of the individual's SSN or TIN. Those individuals who receive initial enrollment after November 1 and before April 2 of the applicable renewal period will not be required to renew their enrollment before the first full renewal period following the receipt of their initial enrollment. The fee for renewal of enrollment is $30 (for actuaries, $250).

PTIN Program. Any individual who, for compensation, prepares or assists with the preparation of all, or substantially all, of a tax return or refund claim must have a preparer tax identification number (PTIN). The IRS has implemented a user fee for individuals who apply for a PTIN, as well as for those who renew their PTINs. The initial application fee is $64.25 and the renewal fee is $63. Attorneys, certified public accountants, enrolled agents and registered tax return preparers are eligible to apply for a PTIN. The PTIN user fee is separate from other fees, such as that required for enrollment. However, the IRS plans to coordinate all user fees.

An individual who is not an attorney, certified public accountant, enrolled agent, or registered tax return preparer may obtain a PTIN provided he or she is supervised by an attorney, certified public accountant, enrolled agent, enrolled retirement plan agent, or enrolled actuary who signs the tax return or refund claim when the individual prepares all, or substantially all, of the return or claim. These individuals are not required to pass the competency test or meet the continuing education requirements.

Registered Tax Return Preparers

The IRS implemented a program to register tax return preparers. The program classified return preparation as practice before the IRS and made return preparers subject to the requirements of Circular 230. Regulations required preparers of returns to register for a preparer tax identification number (PTIN), take required examinations to demonstrate competence in federal tax return preparation matters, and complete continuing education to maintain status as a registered tax return preparer. A federal district court held that preparation of returns does not constitute practice before the IRS and issued a permanent injunction invalidating the regulations allowing the IRS to regulate return preparers. PTINs remain valid, but the IRS has refunded fees collected for scheduled tax return preparer tests that have now been cancelled. The IRS is appealing this decision.

Computerized Return Preparation Services

A person who furnishes services consisting of typing, reproducing, or other mechanical assistance is not considered to be an income tax return preparer. However, persons or firms that furnish computerized tax return preparation services to tax practitioners are deemed to be return preparers, if the programs go beyond mere mechanical assistance.

> **Example.** A program that calculates the amount of applicable depreciation deductions goes beyond mechanical assistance, and the person or firm offering this service is a return preparer.

Continuing Education

To qualify for renewal of enrollment, an individual enrolled to practice before the IRS must certify on the application for renewal form that he or she has satisfied the continuing education (CE) requirements. For renewed enrollment, the following CE requirements must be met:

- A minimum of 72 hours of continuing education credit, including 6 hours of ethics or professional conduct, during each three-year renewal period (enrollment cycle).

- A minimum of 16 hours of continuing education credit, including 2 hours of ethics or professional conduct, in each year of an enrollment cycle.
- An individual who receives initial enrollment during an enrollment cycle must complete two (2) hours of qualifying continuing education credit for each month enrolled during the enrollment cycle. Enrollment for any part of a month is considered enrollment for the entire month.

Qualifying Programs. To qualify for CE credit, a course of learning must be a qualifying program designed to enhance professional knowledge in federal taxation or federal tax-related matters and be conducted by a continuing education provider.

Qualifying programs are formal, correspondence, or individual study programs that meet the criteria outlined in Circular 230. Generally, the programs must qualify in three areas:

- Registration or attendance must be required. CE providers must provide each attendee with a certificate of attendance. Other programs must provide a means of measuring completion by participants.
- CE programs must be conducted by a qualified instructor, discussion leader, or speaker.
- Programs must provide or require a written outline, textbook, or suitable electronic educational materials.
- Programs must satisfy the requirements established for qualified continuing education programs in Circular 230, sec. 10.9. Continuing education coursework is measured in contact hours. One contact hour is 50 minutes of continuous participation in a program. Credit is granted only for a full contact hour, i.e., 50 minutes or multiples thereof. For example, a program lasting more than 50 minutes but less than 100 minutes counts as one contact hour. No programs lasting less than 50 minutes earn CE credit. Individual segments at continuous conferences, conventions, etc., will be considered one total program.

For university or college courses, each semester hour credit equals 15 contact hours and a quarter-hour credit equals 10 contact hours.

CE Credit for Instructors. An instructor, discussion leader, or speaker will be awarded up to three hours of CE credit (up to two for subject preparation and one for the course itself) for every contact hour completed as an instructor, discussion leader, or speaker at qualifying programs. It is the responsibility of the individual claiming such credit to maintain records to verify preparation time. The maximum credit for instruction and preparation may not exceed six hours annually for enrolled agents and enrolled retirement plan agents. In addition, an instructor, discussion leader, or speaker who makes more than one presentation on the same subject matter during an enrollment cycle, will receive continuing education credit for only one such presentation for the enrollment cycle or registration year.

Recordkeeping Requirements. Each individual applying for renewal must retain records supporting qualifying CE credits for a period of three years following the date of renewal of enrollment.

CE Waivers. Waiver of the CE requirements for a given period may be granted for health reasons; for extended active military duty; for extended absence from the United States due to employment or other reasons, provided the individual does not practice before the IRS during such absence; and for other compelling reasons, considered on a case-by-case basis.

Individuals placed in inactive status and individuals ineligible to practice before the Internal Revenue Service may not state or imply that they are eligible to practice before the Internal Revenue Service, or use the term "enrolled agent," enrolled retirement plan agent, registered tax return preparer, the designation "E. A.," or other form of reference to eligibility to practice before the Internal Revenue Service. An individual placed in an inactive status may be reinstated to an active status by filing an application for renewal and providing evidence of the completion of all required continuing education hours for the enrollment cycle.

Contingent Fees

A contingent fee is any fee that is based, in whole or in part, on whether or not a position taken on a tax return or other filing avoids challenge by the IRS or is sustained either by the IRS or in litigation. A contingent fee includes any fee arrangement in which the practitioner will reimburse the client for all or a portion of the client's fee in the event that a position taken on a tax return or other filing is challenged by the IRS or is not sustained, whether pursuant to an indemnity agreement, a guarantee, rescission rights, or any other arrangement with a similar effect.

In general, a practitioner may not charge a contingent fee for services rendered in connection with any matter before the IRS. This prohibition encompasses the preparation or filing of an original return, or an amended return, as well as a claim for credit or refund. However, a practitioner is permitted to charge a contingent fee for services rendered in connection with any of the following:

- An IRS challenge to, or audit of, an original return;
- An IRS challenge to, or audit of, an amended return, or a claim for refund or credit, if the amended return or claim is filed within 120 days of the examination

notice (or if filed before the notice is given; written notice from the IRS is not a prerequisite to charging a contingent fee);

- A credit or refund claim filed solely to determine statutory interest or penalties assessed by the IRS;
- A whistleblower claim; or
- Any judicial proceeding arising under the Code.

 Caution. Practitioners who prepare tax returns to generate fees rather than informing the taxpayer that no return is required, such as by emphasizing the fact that a return may be filed even if not required, are subject to particular scrutiny.

Reasonable Belief Standard and Reliance on Information from Clients

A practitioner may not willfully, recklessly, or through gross incompetence sign or prepare a tax return or claim for refund containing a position, or advise a client to take a position on a return or refund claim, that (a) lacks a reasonable basis; (b) is an unreasonable position; or (c) is a willful attempt by the practitioner to understate the tax liability, or is a reckless or intentional disregard of rules or regulations. Also, a practitioner may not advise a client to take a position on a document, affidavit, or other paper submitted to the IRS that is frivolous, or designed to delay or impede the administration of tax law, or that contains information that shows an intentional disregard of a rule or regulation, unless the practitioner also advises the client to submit a document showing a good faith challenge to the rule or regulation.

A practitioner advising a client to take a position on a tax return, or preparing or signing a tax return as a preparer, must inform the client of the penalties reasonably likely to apply to the client with respect to the position advised, prepared, or reported. The practitioner must inform the client of any opportunity to avoid any such penalty by disclosure, if relevant, and of the requirements for adequate disclosure.

A practitioner generally may rely in good faith, without verification, on information furnished by the client. The practitioner may not, however, ignore the implications of information furnished to, or actually known by, the practitioner, and must make reasonable inquiries if the information appears to be incorrect, inconsistent with an important fact or another factual assumption, or incomplete.

Conflicts of Interest

A practitioner must be aware of possible conflicts of interest with respect to a particular taxpayer. A conflict exists if representation of one client of the practitioner's would be adverse to another client of the practitioner's. A conflict may exist if there is a significant risk that the representation of a client will be materially limited by the practitioner's responsibilities to another client, a former client, or a third party, or by a personal interest of the practitioner. However, the practitioner may represent a client despite a conflict if the practitioner believes he or she will be able to provide competent representation to each affected client, the representation is not otherwise prohibited, and each affected client gives informed, written consent. Examples of such situations include spouses on a joint return; former spouses, parent, and child on 1040s; trustee and beneficiaries on 1041s; limited and general partners on 1065s; and parent and child on gift tax returns.

Appeals Within the IRS

If a client disagrees with a proposed adjustment by an IRS tax examiner, a tax practitioner has several options. The most commonly used is to make a written appeal to the appropriate IRS Appeals Office. Alternatively, the taxpayer may skip over the IRS appeals process and proceed directly to Tax Court or, after payment in full of the deficiency, District or Claims Court. Similarly, if the IRS Appeals Office and the taxpayer cannot come to an agreement, the taxpayer may then proceed to court.

After an examination, if the return is accepted as filed, the taxpayer receives a "no change" letter. If the examiner proposes an adjustment, the taxpayer is informed by being sent a copy of the examination report, a transmittal letter (the "30-day letter"), information on appeal rights and procedures, and the appropriate waiver form for the taxpayer to sign if he or she agrees with the proposed adjustment. The most common form is Form 870, *Waiver of Restrictions on Assessment and Collection of Deficiency in Tax and Acceptance of Overassessment,* and its variations (870-E, 870-AD, etc.).

Written Request for Appeal and Protest. If the taxpayer disagrees with the examiner's findings, the taxpayer can respond with a request that the Appeals Office review the findings of the examiner. This requires a written request and a written protest, except in the cases of an office or correspondence examination, or a field examination where the amount of additional tax is $25,000 or less for a taxable period. The protest must contain:

- The name, address, and telephone number of the taxpayer;
- A statement that the taxpayer wants to appeal the conclusions of the IRS examiner to the Appeals Office;
- A copy of the letter showing the proposed changes and findings with which the taxpayer disagrees;
- The years or tax periods involved;
- A list of the changes with which the taxpayer disagrees, and the reasons for disagreement;

- The facts supporting the taxpayer's position on any issue with which the taxpayer disagrees;
- The law or authority on which the taxpayer intends to rely; and
- The taxpayer's signature, which must be under penalty of perjury.

The taxpayer must swear to the statement of facts under penalties of perjury. If the protest is prepared or filed by an attorney or agent, a substitute declaration may be used. The attorney or agent must state under penalty of perjury that he or she prepared the protest and knows of his or her own knowledge that the information contained in the protest is true.

Appeals Conference. The conference with the Appeals Office is held in an informal manner, by correspondence or telephone, or at a personal conference. The taxpayer is not required to have representation, but may choose to do so. He or she may be represented by an attorney, a CPA, an enrolled agent, or an enrolled actuary. The representative must be qualified to practice before the IRS. In general, the same confidentiality protection an individual has with an attorney is also applicable to communications between a taxpayer and a federally authorized practitioner.

 Planning Tip. A taxpayer can be represented by an attorney or agent at the Appeals conference. It may, in fact, be appropriate for the taxpayer not to attend with the representative, depending on the circumstances of the case and the temperment of the taxpayer. In some cases, the taxpayer's memory of relevant events will make his or her presence necessary. On the other hand, if the taxpayer is nervous, excessively timid or emotional, or too self-conscious, the attorney or agent might prefer to attend the conference alone. Similarly, a belligerent attitude on the part of the taxpayer might antagonize the IRS representative. This choice should be left to the judgment of the attorney or agent.

If the taxpayer is not going to attend the conference with the representative, the taxpayer must execute a power of attorney and provide it to the IRS before the representative can receive or inspect confidential information. The taxpayer may bring documents or witnesses supporting the taxpayer's position to the conference with the Appeals Office.

The IRS is developing new processes for its Appeals Office, including the Rapid Appeals Process (RAP). The new process allows both the IRS Examination personnel and the taxpayer to communicate with the Appeals Officer at the meeting, and is substantially faster than the existing process. Ideally, a case using the RAP process can be resolved in one or two meetings.

What's New in 2013

Adoption Credit. The adoption credit amount is $12,970 per eligible child and is nonrefundable for 2013. The per child amount also applies to adoption assistance programs.

American Opportunity (Modified Hope) Credit. The American Opportunity Tax Credit remains at a maximum of $2,500 per eligible student; qualifying expenses include text books and course materials; the credit is available for up to four years per eligible student; the income phaseout range for 2013 for nonmarried taxpayers is between $80,000 and $90,000 ($160,000 and $180,000 for joint filers); and up to 40 percent of the credit amount may be refundable.

Earned Income Tax Credit Amounts Increased. The maximum earned income tax credit amounts for 2013 are for taxpayers: with three or more children, $6,044; with two qualifying children, $5,372; with one qualifying child, $3,250; and with no children, $487.

Phaseout Thresholds for Earned Income Tax Credit Increased. The earned income tax credit phaseout threshold amount for single, head of household and surviving spouse filers begins at $17,530 for taxpayers with one or more children and $7,970 for taxpayers with no children. For those taxpayers, the phaseout is complete at $46,227 with three or more children, $43,038 with two children, $37,870 with one child and $14,340 with no children. For joint filers, the phaseout begins at $22,870 with one or more children and $13,310 with no children. For joint filers, the earned income credit completely phases out at $51,567 with three or more children, $48,378 with two children, $43,210 with only one qualifying child, and with no qualifying children at $19,680.

Section at a Glance

Relevant IRS Publications

- ☐ IRS Publication 501, *Exemptions, Standard Deduction, and Filing Information*
- ☐ IRS Publication 503, *Child and Dependent Care Expenses*
- ☐ IRS Publication 504, *Divorced or Separated Individuals*
- ☐ IRS Publication 929, *Tax Rules for Children and Dependents*
- ☐ IRS Publication 970, *Tax Benefits for Education*
- ☐ IRS Publication 972, *Child Tax Credit*

Tax Preparer's Checklist

- ☐ Date of birth, Social Security number, and accurate spelling of name as it appears in Social Security records of all dependents.
- ☐ All Forms W-2, 1098, and 1099 applicable to dependents.
- ☐ Form 1098-T, Tuition Statement, from school for students.
- ☐ Tuition, books, fees, and scholarship and fellowship documentation.
- ☐ Verify whether the dependent has already filed and, if so, whether they claimed a personal exemption.

Limits and Phaseout Ranges for Certain Education Tax Benefits			
Benefit	Student Loan Interest Deduction	American Opportunity (Modified Hope Credit)**	Lifetime Learning Credit
Limit	$2,500	$2,500 per student	$2,000 per family
Phaseout Range	$60,000-$75,000 ($125,000-$155,000 for MFJ)	$80,000-$90,000 ($160,000-$180,000 for MFJ)	$53,000-$63,000 ($107,000-$127,000 for MFJ)

** Available during tax years 2009 through 2017.

Children and Taxes

Taxpayers with children may enjoy tax advantages in many areas:

- **Filing status.** Taxpayers considered unmarried may be able to file as Head of Household if they have a qualifying child. See Tab 1.
- **Exemption for dependents.** If the child qualifies as a dependent, the taxpayer may be able to claim the dependency exemption. See Tab 1.
- **Other deductions.** Medical expenses, tuition and fee expenses, student loan interest, and child care expenses may all be deductible. See Tabs 1 and 2 for more information about deductions. Education deductions are discussed later in this Tab.
- **Credits.** The child tax credit and additional child tax credit, child and dependent care expense credit, earned income credit, adoption credit and educational credits may be available. These tax credits are discussed later in this Tab, and are also covered in Tab 10.
- **Exceptions to additional tax for IRA early distribution.** The 10% additional tax for early withdrawals from an individual retirement account (IRA) does not apply if the funds are used to pay the higher education expenses of the taxpayer, the taxpayer's spouse or the taxpayer's child and/or the health insurance premiums for an unemployed taxpayer or his or her spouse or dependents if the taxpayer has received unemployment compensation for at least 12 consecutive weeks under federal or state law.

 Caution. The exception to the early distribution tax only applies to IRAs, not to other types of qualified deferred plans or retirement accounts. Although the Tax Court sympathized with the taxpayer who received incorrect advice from the IRS, they noted that the law clearly states only withdrawals from IRAs may be exempted from the tax.

Who Qualifies as a Dependent?

A child is the taxpayer's dependent if he or she is either a qualifying child or a qualifying relative. The major difference is that a qualifying child must have a closer relationship to the taxpayer than a qualifying relative. See Tab 1.

 Planning Tip. Notice 2008-5 clarified the IRS position on claiming an unrelated child as a dependent when the same child is the qualifying child of another taxpayer. Essentially, the unrelated taxpayer may claim the dependent exemption for the child as a qualifying relative provided that the taxpayer for whom the child is a qualifying child is not required to file an income tax return or files only for the purpose of obtaining a refund.

A child born at any time during a tax year is considered a dependent for the entire tax year. If a child dies shortly after birth, the full exemption amount is taken; the exemption amount is not prorated. The question of what constitutes a child's being born alive depends on state or local law. To claim a dependency exemption for a child who was born and died during the same tax year, the taxpayer should have a birth certificate or other official documentation to show that the child was born alive. See Tab 1.

Individuals who are claimed as a dependent by another taxpayer may not also claim a personal exemption when filing their own tax return.

Taxpayers generally cannot claim an exemption for a dependent who files a joint return with a spouse, unless the joint return is filed merely as a claim for a refund and neither spouse would have had a tax liability if they were to file separately.

 Caution. Once an individual has been classified as a dependent, other tax consequences follow. Filing requirements differ, and some credits and deductions are not available to dependent individuals who file their own returns.

Each claimed dependent, including those born during the current tax year, must have a taxpayer identification number (TIN) or Social Security number. Resident and nonresident alien dependents who do not qualify for a Social Security number must have an individual taxpayer identification number (ITIN).

 Filing Tip. To obtain a Social Security number, file Form SS-5. For an ITIN, file Form W-7.

Filing Tip. Be sure to always enter the name on the return exactly as it appears on the Social Security card. A mismatch will prevent electronic filing and delay any refund.

Caution. Failure to provide the taxpayer identification number will be treated as a mathematical error. The IRS will recalculate the tax liability as if no exemption had been claimed, and may change the filing status or eliminate any deductions or credits related to the claimed exemption. This may reduce any refund amount or create a larger tax liability.

Adopted Children. An adopted child is always treated as the taxpayer's own child, even if the adoption is not final, provided the child has been placed for adoption with the taxpayer by a qualified adoption agency.

Filing Tip. To claim a child as a dependent during the adoption process before the Social Security number is issued, the taxpayer will need to obtain an adoption taxpayer identification number (ATIN) by filing Form W-7A.

Students. A dependency exemption is allowed for a taxpayer's child who is a full-time student under the age of 24, who does not file a joint return with his or her spouse and whose earned income does not exceed more than half of the child's own support. A full-time student is a student enrolled for at least the minimum number of hours or credits determined by the school to be considered in full-time attendance for some part of at least five months during the calendar year. The school must have:

- a regular teaching staff,
- an established curriculum, and
- a regularly enrolled body of students.

A school may be:

- an elementary school,
- a junior or senior high school,
- a college or university, or
- a technical, trade, or mechanical school.

On-the-job training courses, correspondence schools, online institutions and night schools do not qualify. However, individuals taking full-time on-farm training through an educational institution qualify as students.

Vocational high school students who work on jobs in private industry as part of their education are considered to be full-time students.

Planning Tip. Parents and college students should discuss in advance how to properly coordinate filing their income tax returns to avoid errors or confusion and minimize the family's total tax liability. College students often file their income tax returns before their parents and mistakenly believe they are entitled to claim a personal exemption, which entitles them to a large refund. When the parents, who are legally entitled to claim the child as a dependent, later file and claim the student as a dependent, they are denied the dependent exemption resulting in an unexpected increase in their tax liability.

Gray Area. Medical students, interns, and residents at hospitals are not considered students. However, an individual enrolled at a nursing school was considered to be a student even though part of the training included doing nursing work in a hospital.

Kidnapped Children. A kidnapped child under age 18 can be a qualifying child if the dependency tests and the qualifying child tests are met for the portion of the calendar year preceding the date of the kidnapping and the child is presumed by law enforcement officials to have been kidnapped by someone who is not a family member of the child or the taxpayer. The child is no longer considered a qualifying child in the calendar year after the year in which the child is determined to be deceased or would have turned 18, if earlier.

Children of Divorced or Separated Parents. Generally, as long as at least half of a child's support is provided by one or both parents, the parent who has custody of a child is entitled to the exemption. The exemption, however, may be relinquished by the custodial parent to the noncustodial parent. A child may be treated as the qualifying child of the noncustodial parent only if:

- the couple is divorced, legally separated, separated under a written separation agreement, or lived apart at all times during the last six months of the calendar year;
- one spouse (or both combined) provides more than half of the child's total support for the calendar year (determined without regard to any multiple support agreement);
- one spouse (or both combined) has custody of the child for more than half of the calendar year; and
- the custodial parent makes a written declaration that he or she will not claim the exemption and the non-

custodial parent attaches the declaration to his or her tax return for each year the exemption is claimed.

 Filing Tip. A custodial parent should sign Form 8332, *Release of Claim to Exemption for Child of Divorced or Separated Parents,* for the noncustodial parent to claim a dependent exemption for a child living with the other parent. A court order, divorce or separate maintenance agreement has no effect on allocating a dependency exemption.

Can a Child's Income Be Included on a Parent's Return?

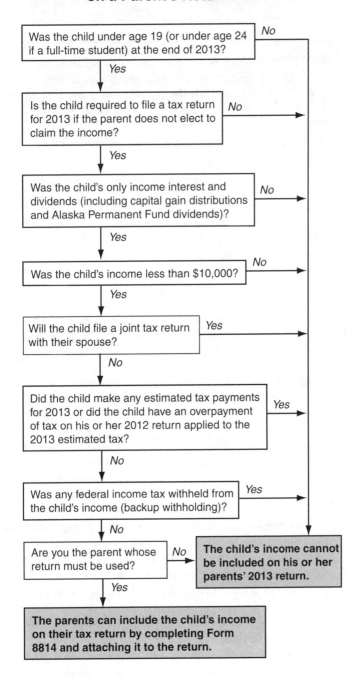

Was the child under age 19 (or under age 24 if a full-time student) at the end of 2013? — **No** →

↓ **Yes**

Is the child required to file a tax return for 2013 if the parent does not elect to claim the income? — **No** →

↓ **Yes**

Was the child's only income interest and dividends (including capital gain distributions and Alaska Permanent Fund dividends)? — **No** →

↓ **Yes**

Was the child's income less than $10,000? — **No** →

↓ **Yes**

Will the child file a joint tax return with their spouse? — **Yes** →

↓ **No**

Did the child make any estimated tax payments for 2013 or did the child have an overpayment of tax on his or her 2012 return applied to the 2013 estimated tax? — **Yes** →

↓ **No**

Was any federal income tax withheld from the child's income (backup withholding)? — **Yes** →

↓ **No**

Are you the parent whose return must be used? — **No** → **The child's income cannot be included on his or her parents' 2013 return.**

↓ **Yes**

The parents can include the child's income on their tax return by completing Form 8814 and attaching it to the return.

Taxation of a Child's Income

Most children are considered qualifying children for purposes of being claimed as dependents. See Tab 1 for filing requirements for dependents. If any federal income tax was withheld from a child's wages, the child should file a return to claim a refund of the withheld taxes even if he or she is not required to file a return.

If a child cannot sign his or her return, a parent or guardian can sign it in the space provided, followed by "By (signature), parent (or guardian) of minor child."

 Caution. A child with income who qualifies as a dependent cannot claim a personal exemption on his or her own tax return. The exemption can only be claimed by the parents, even if they choose not to claim it.

Special rules govern the taxation of income of children under age 19 or students under age 24 who have more than $1,900 in unearned income. See "Special Rules for Children Under 19 or Students Under 24" following.

Earned and Unearned Income. To determine whether a dependent must file a return, the amount of earned and unearned income must be known.

Earned income is money received as pay for work that was done, as well as certain scholarships, fellowships, and grants. It includes:

- Salaries and wages, including wages received as a household employee,
- Tips,
- Professional fees, and
- Taxable scholarships and fellowship grants (see "Education Tax Benefits," following).

For federal tax purposes, the income a child receives for his or her labor is considered his or her own, even if state law says it belongs to the parent. If a minor child does not pay tax on the income, the parent is liable.

Unearned income is income from investments, trusts and other payments that are not compensation for services. It includes:

- Interest,
- Dividends,
- Capital gains,
- Distributions from a trust, and
- Taxable Social Security payments.

Example. Robert and Ellen O'Connor maintain several investments for their eight-year-old son Joseph. Joseph did not have any earned income in 2013 but he did have taxable interest income of $2,000, tax-exempt interest of $35, and taxable dividend income of $2,500. Instead of filing a separate return for Joseph, Robert and Ellen, after determining the effect on their adjusted gross income dependent calculations, elect to report his income on their own joint return by attaching a completed Form 8814.

The first $1,000 of a child's unearned income is not taxable (this amount is equal to the standard deduction for dependents). The next $1,000 is taxed at the child's tax rate, and the amount greater than $2,000 is taxed at the parents' marginal tax rate. This is commonly known as the "kiddie tax." Kiddie tax is computed by adding the child's investment income to the income of the parents, so it is possible that the child's income will be taxed at a higher rate than the parents' income.

For purposes of imposing the kiddie tax on a child's unearned income of less than $10,000, the child must be:

- under the age of 18;
- under the age of 19 and whose earned income does not exceed one half of his or her own support; or
- under the age of 24, a full-time student, and whose earned income does not exceed one half of his or her own support.

See MTG ¶103 and ¶706.

Filing Tip. A child who is the beneficiary of a disability trust can treat the distributions as earned income. This income will not be subject to the kiddie tax rules.

Filing Tip. An account in a child's name and SSN, such as one set up under the Uniform Gifts to Minors Act, may be held by someone other than the child's parents, frequently a grandparent. Parents and tax return preparers must ensure that all Forms 1099-DIV are received and included when calculating the child's tax liability.

Special Rules for Children Under 19 or Full-Time Students Under 24. If a child is required to file a return, his or her parents may elect to report the child's income on their return if all of the following apply to their child:

1. The child is under age 19 at the end of 2013, or a full-time student under age 24.
2. The child has income only from interest and dividends (including Alaska Permanent Fund dividends and capital gain distributions).
3. The child's gross income is less than $10,000.
4. The child has no federal income tax withheld and did not make estimated tax payments for 2013.
5. The child does not file a joint tax return for the year.

Who Declares Income (Child or Parents)? Generally, a child under age 18, or a child under 19 or a full-time student under age 24 whose earned income does not exceed one half of his or her support must declare investment income of more than $2,000 by filing Form 8615, *Tax for Certain Children Who Have Unearned Income.*

Filing Tip. A minor child with unearned income of $10,000 or more will need to file his or her own return.

However, taxpayers may elect to include their child's unearned income on their own return if the child's income only comes from interest and dividends and is less than $10,000. These taxpayers will use Form 8814, *Parents' Election to Report Child's Interest and Dividends,* to determine the additional amount of tax to be added to the taxpayers' tax liability. If this election is made, then the child does not have to file a return or Form 8615. The amount on Form 8814 must be entered in the space provided on line 44 of Form 1040.

If a married couple decides to file separate returns and wishes to include the unearned income of a child, only the parent with the higher taxable income can make the election. Thus, the child's tax liability will be determined using the tax rate applicable to the parent with the higher taxable income.

Who Is a Qualifying Person for the Child and Dependent Care Credit?

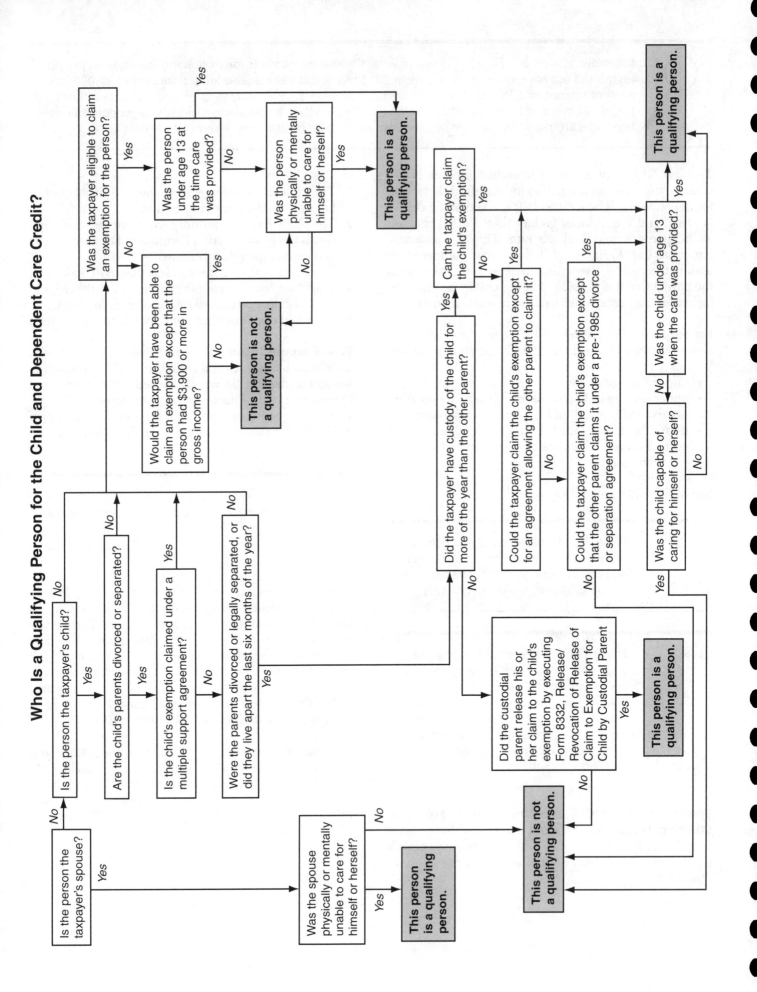

Can a Taxpayer Claim the Child and Dependent Care Credit?

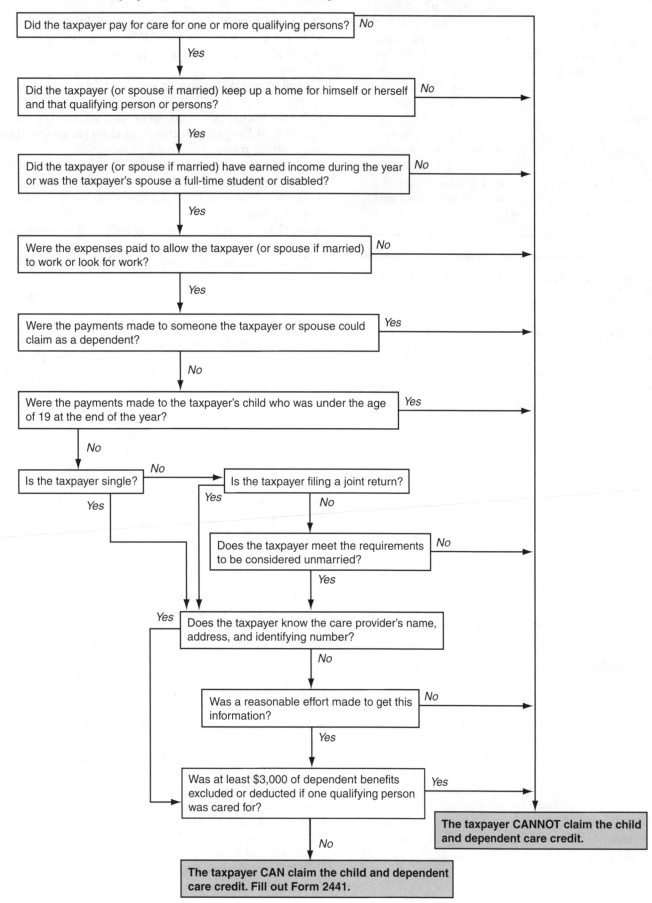

Did the taxpayer pay for care for one or more qualifying persons? — *No* →

↓ *Yes*

Did the taxpayer (or spouse if married) keep up a home for himself or herself and that qualifying person or persons? — *No* →

↓ *Yes*

Did the taxpayer (or spouse if married) have earned income during the year or was the taxpayer's spouse a full-time student or disabled? — *No* →

↓ *Yes*

Were the expenses paid to allow the taxpayer (or spouse if married) to work or look for work? — *No* →

↓ *Yes*

Were the payments made to someone the taxpayer or spouse could claim as a dependent? — *Yes* →

↓ *No*

Were the payments made to the taxpayer's child who was under the age of 19 at the end of the year? — *Yes* →

↓ *No*

Is the taxpayer single? — *No* → Is the taxpayer filing a joint return?

Yes (from "Is the taxpayer single?")

Is the taxpayer filing a joint return? — *Yes* → / ↓ *No*

Does the taxpayer meet the requirements to be considered unmarried? — *No* →

↓ *Yes*

Yes → Does the taxpayer know the care provider's name, address, and identifying number?

↓ *No*

Was a reasonable effort made to get this information? — *No* →

↓ *Yes*

Was at least $3,000 of dependent benefits excluded or deducted if one qualifying person was cared for? — *Yes* →

↓ *No*

The taxpayer CAN claim the child and dependent care credit. Fill out Form 2441.

The taxpayer CANNOT claim the child and dependent care credit.

Example. Aaron and Julia are married and will file separate tax returns. Their only child, Roxanne, is five years old. Roxanne received a Form 1099-INT showing $4,700 taxable interest income. Her parents decide to include that income on one of their returns so they will not have to file a return for Roxanne.

First, Aaron and Julia each figure their taxable income without regard to Roxanne's income. Aaron's taxable income is $141,200 and Julia's is $259,300. Because Julia's taxable income is greater, Roxanne's income is included on her return. She fills out Form 8814 and attaches it to her return.

Caution. Including the child's income on the parent's return affects AGI-sensitive calculations (e.g., the medical expense and miscellaneous itemized deductions), adjustments to gross income (e.g., the phaseout of the tuition and fees deduction), and credits (e.g., the phaseout of the education credits). The additional preparation time it takes to do the child's return is often rewarded with lower overall family tax liability.

These rules do *not* apply if either of the following is true:

- The child is *not* required to file a tax return.
- Neither of the child's parents were living at the end of the tax year.

For more information, see IRS Publication 17, *Your Federal Income Tax*, IRS Publication 929, *Tax Rules for Children and Dependents*, and MTG ¶103 and ¶706.

 Planning Tip. When investing for children, proper tax planning is essential to minimize the potential effects of the kiddie tax. Two possible investment strategies are:

Growth Investments. Invest in something that appreciates in value but does not pay dividends. The gain of investments of this nature is not realized until the asset is sold.

Savings Bonds. Put money in investments that accrue tax-deferred or tax-free interest. See Tab 4 and Tab 9 and MTG ¶730 for a discussion of the tax advantages of U.S. savings bonds.

Credits for Families with Children

Child Tax Credit. The maximum child tax credit is $1,000 for each qualifying child for whom the taxpayer claims a dependency exemption.

A qualifying child for purposes of the child tax credit must:

1. be the taxpayer's child, stepchild, adopted or foster child, sibling, stepbrother, stepsister, or descendant of any of them;
2. not have attained the age of 17 by the end of the calendar year;
3. share a home with the taxpayer for more than half of the year;
4. not have provided over one-half of their own support for the calendar year;
5. be claimed as a dependent on the taxpayer's 2013 return; and
6. not have filed a joint return with his or her spouse other than to claim a refund.

The $1,000 credit amount is reduced by $50 for each $1,000, or fraction thereof, by which the taxpayer's modified adjusted gross income exceeds a threshold amount of $75,000 ($55,000 if MFS, $110,000 if MFJ). The child tax credit may be used against both the regular and alternative minimum tax liability. The credit may not reduce the tax owed below zero; however, the additional child tax credit is refundable. See Tab 10 for a detailed discussion of the refundable additional child tax credit.

For more information, see details in IRS Publication 972, *Child Tax Credit,* Schedule 8812 (Form 1040), *Child Tax Credit* (per 2013 IRS draft form), *Schedule 8812 is to be attached to Form 1040 (if required), as indicated on Line 51 of Form 1040.* MTG ¶1305 and Tab 10.

Child and Dependent Care Credit. If a taxpayer resides in a household that includes a dependent child under the age of 13, or a dependent or spouse who is mentally or physically incapable of self-care, the taxpayer may claim this credit for expenses paid to provide care for the individual to enable the taxpayer to be employed or look for work. Generally:

- The credit ranges from 20% to 35% of qualifying expenses.
- Qualifying expenses must be paid to provide for the care and well-being of a dependent under the age of 13, or a dependent or spouse unable to care for themselves, to allow the taxpayer to work or look for work.
- The maximum 35% is available to taxpayers whose adjusted gross income (AGI) is less than $15,000. The credit is reduced by one percent for each $2,000 increase in AGI. Thus, taxpayers with AGI greater than $43,000 are limited to the minimum 20% credit for such expenses.

- The limit on the amount of eligible expenses is $3,000 for one qualifying individual and $6,000 for two or more qualifying individuals.

The amount on which the credit is computed is limited to the lower of eligible expenses, or, for married couples, the earned income of the lower-paid spouse. If the spouse is either a full-time student or not able to care for himself or herself, the amount of income he or she is treated as having earned is $250 a month if there is one qualifying person and $500 a month if there are two or more qualifying persons.

 Planning Tip. A dependent care flexible spending account (FSA) may offer significant tax savings. For two or more qualifying individuals, $5,000 could be withheld from a paycheck on a pre-tax basis. Should day-care expenses exceed $5,000, up to $1,000 of the excess could be used to claim the dependent care credit.

 Planning Tip. Beginning in 2013, health care reform legislation passed in March 2010 caps the amount that can be put into FSA(s) at $2,500 per employee.

Flow charts are provided on pages 13-6 and 13-7 to help determine whether an individual is a qualifying person for purposes of the dependent care credit and whether the taxpayer can claim the credit.

The child and dependent care credit is calculated on Form 2441, *Child and Dependent Care Expenses*, and reported on line 48 of Form 1040, *U.S. Individual Income Tax Return*. For more information, see Publication 503, *Child and Dependent Care Expenses*, MTG ¶ 1301 and Tab 10.

 Caution. Failure to reconcile dependent care benefits on page 2 of Form 2441 could result in the IRS recalculating the dependent care credit, adding the dependent care benefits back into income and sending a bill for tax due to the taxpayer.

Adoption Credit. The Patient Protection and Affordable Health Care Act increased the adoption credit amount and made it a refundable credit (IRC §23). The adoption credit amount that may be claimed on Form 8839, *Qualified Adoption Expenses*, is $12,970 for qualified adoption expenses for each eligible child. The credit is phased out ratably for taxpayers with modified gross incomes between $194,580 and $234,580. The credit amount is then reported on line 71 of Form 1040.

Taxpayers who adopt a child with special needs can claim an adoption credit of $12,970 regardless of actual expenses paid or incurred in the year the adoption becomes final. This increased amount was also extended to employer adoption assistance programs under IRC §137.

 Caution. The adoption credit is not refundable for 2013. The following expenses are *not* eligible for the adoption credit:
- Expenses incurred in connection with the adoption of a spouse's child.
- Costs associated with a surrogate parenting arrangement.

The adoption credit is coordinated with employer-provided adoption assistance programs. Expenses can only be used once either for claiming the exclusion under an assistance program or for claiming the credit.

 Planning Tip. For years after 2012, the adoption credit has been made permanent, with both the $10,000 dollar limitation and the income phase-out range adjusted for inflation. For 2013, the maximum adoption credit amount is $12,970 and is not refundable.

See MTG ¶ 1307.

Foster Care

Tax-Free Payments. Payments received from a state, political subdivision, or qualified foster care placement agency for providing foster care in the home are excluded from gross income as long as care is for:

- No more than five individuals over age 18; or
- In the case of any difficulty-of-care payments, no more than 10 individuals under age 19 and five individuals age 19 or older.

Taxable Payments. All foster care payments are taxable if the taxpayer:

- Maintains space in his or her home for emergency foster care;
- Provides care for more than five individuals age 19 or older; or
- In the case of difficulty-of-care payments, provides care for more than 10 qualified foster care individuals under the age of 19 and five individuals age 19 or over.

See MTG ¶ 883.

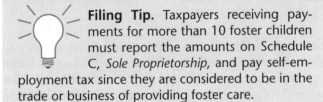
Foster Children as Dependents. A foster child may qualify as a dependent of the taxpayer if the dependency qualifications are met.

Family Income Tax Planning

Most families want to take steps to maximize their benefits—and minimize their tax liability—under the income tax laws. Careful planning and awareness of the requirements for specific tax credits and deductions will result in the most advantageous tax situation.

Shifting Income

Families can reduce their aggregate tax liability by shifting income from a higher-bracket family member to a lower-bracket family member, often from parents to children. There was a time when shifting income involved merely transferring assets from a family member in a higher tax bracket to a family member in a lower tax bracket. However, the kiddie tax limits this planning opportunity by taxing a child's net unearned income at the parents' marginal tax rate.

Employing Family Members. Taxpayers who operate their own business can shift income by employing other family members. A taxpayer who employs his or her child can deduct the wages paid as a business expense, and the child's earned income is not subject to the kiddie tax. In addition, if the taxpayer's business is a sole proprietorship or partnership, and the employed child is under age 18, the child's earned income is not subject to Social Security or Medicare taxes.

Wages paid to a parent employed by his or her child are not subject to federal unemployment tax (FUTA) (IRS Publication 15, Circular E).

Gifting Issues

A donor's gift of $14,000 or less to a single donee during the 2013 calendar year is not included in the total amount of the donor's taxable gifts during the year and, therefore, is not taxed and does not use up any of the donor's lifetime gift tax credit.

The annual exclusion is not applicable to gifts of future interests in property. Future interests include any interest, whether vested or contingent, that is not available for the donee's use, possession, or enjoyment until some future date or time.

Gifts to Minors

The annual exclusion is allowed for an outright gift to a minor whether made to the minor's legal guardian or to a custodian under a state statute such as the Uniform Gifts to Minors Act.

Uniform Gifts to Minors Act (UGMA) Accounts. The Uniform Gifts to Minors Act and Uniform Transfers to Minors Act allow taxpayers to set up custodial accounts for minors. Under state UGMA accounts, the custodian, often a parent, is responsible for managing the account, which is then transferred to the child when he or she is no longer a minor (age 18 or 21, depending on the state).

A transfer of property for the benefit of a minor pursuant to the Uniform Transfers to Minors Act, the Uniform Gifts to Minors Act, or the Model Gifts of Securities to Minors Act is considered to be a completed gift of the full fair market value of the property. No taxable gift occurs by reason of a subsequent resignation of the custodian or termination of the custodianship for federal gift tax purposes. Such a gift also qualifies for the annual gift tax exclusion ($14,000 in 2013).

Generation-Skipping Gifts

If a donor makes a generation-skipping transfer to a grandchild or lower generation, the transfer is a gift subject to the regular gift tax, and it may also be subject to the generation-skipping transfer tax. In computing the regular gift tax on such a transfer, the annual exclusion and gift-splitting provisions are available. Further, the regular gift tax is computed by using the unified tax rates based on cumulative gifts. If the generation-skipping transfer tax is applicable, it is payable as an additional tax in the year the transfer occurs. The annual exclusion and gift-splitting provisions are available in computing the amount subject to the generation-skipping transfer tax. For more information, see Tab 14.

Income-Producing Assets

Families can also shift income by giving income-producing property to a lower-bracket family member. When the donor retains no interest in the transferred property, the recipient generally is taxed on all the income generated by the property. In the case of minor children where the income discharges the parents' legal obligation of support, the income is taxed to the parents.

 Caution. Shifting assets to save income taxes could hurt college financial aid eligibility and could impact future support tests.

General Gifting Issues for Families

Gifts of property to members of a family, often motivated by a desire to spread the income and thereby reduce the tax on the donor and on the family as a whole, are not prohibited but may be carefully scrutinized by the IRS. The essential elements of a valid intra-family gift are:

1. A donor competent to make the gift.
2. A donee capable of receiving the gift.
3. A clear and unmistakable intention on the part of the donor to divest title, dominion, and control of the subject matter of the gift, immediately, absolutely, and irrevocably.
4. The irrevocable transfer of the present legal title and of the dominion and control of the entire gift to the donee, so the donor can exercise no further act of dominion or control over it.
5. Delivery by the donor to the donee of the property or of the means of controlling the property.
6. The donee's acceptance of the gift.

An assignment of income alone will be disregarded for tax purposes unless the taxpayer also assigns the income-producing property. For example, a taxpayer may not escape tax on wages by assigning part of a salary under a legally enforceable contract.

The gift itself results in no income to the recipient and is not deductible by the donor unless the gift qualifies as a deductible charitable contribution (MTG ¶1058), but it may result in liability of the donor for a gift tax (MTG ¶2903). Additionally, although the value of a gift is excluded from the recipient's income, any income from the gift, such as profit resulting from a sale of the gift, is taxable to the recipient (see MTG ¶849).

Family Loans

One effective means of shifting income from a high-bracket taxpayer to a low-bracket taxpayer is through use of an interest-free or below-market-interest loan. Upon receipt of the funds, the borrower can invest them in income-producing assets. Although the borrower must pay taxes on the income produced by the assets, the loan results in an overall lower tax liability within the family unit because the income is shifted away from the high-bracket taxpayer and taxed at lower rates.

Gift Loans

A below-market term loan is a gift loan because the foregone interest is in the nature of a gift; the excess of the amount loaned over the present value of all the payments is treated for gift tax purposes as being transferred to the borrower on the date the loan is made. In addition, the lender is considered to have received the foregone interest on the last day of the calendar year and must include the foregone interest in income.

See MTG ¶795 for the exceptions to gift loans.

Separation and Divorce

Divorce has many tax consequences. Issues of alimony, child support, and transfer of property all affect income tax. IRS Publication 504, *Divorced or Separated Individuals,* covers divorce-related tax issues in detail.

Filing Status

If the taxpayer is considered unmarried, his or her filing status is Single (or Head of Household if he or she qualifies according to the rules outlined in Tab 1). If the taxpayer is considered married, the status is either Married Filing Jointly or Married Filing Separately.

Situations in which taxpayers are considered unmarried:

- They have obtained a full decree of divorce, as determined by the law of their state of residence, by the last day of the tax year.
- They have obtained an annulment.

 Filing Tip. If a marriage has been annulled by a court, the marriage never legally existed. Any tax returns filed as married must be amended to reflect the taxpayers' single status if the tax year is still open under the statute of limitations (generally three years).

Situations in which taxpayers are considered married:

- They are separated but have not obtained a final divorce decree by the end of the tax year.

- Their common-law marriage is recognized by their state of residence.

There are exceptions to these general rules:

- If the husband and wife plan to remarry within one year, they may be considered married.
- In certain circumstances, if a couple lives apart they may be considered unmarried for tax purposes.

Alimony

Alimony is payment to or for a spouse or former spouse under a divorce or separation instrument. It is deductible by the payer and must be included in the recipient's income. Alimony payments made are deducted on line 31a of Form 1040, which must also include the former spouse's Social Security number. Alimony payments received are reported as income on line 11 of Form 1040.

Caution. If a taxpayer deducting alimony does not include the spouse's Social Security number, the deduction will be disallowed.

Only cash payments, including checks and money orders, qualify as alimony. The following do *not* qualify:

- Transfers of services or property (including a debt instrument of a third-party or an annuity contract)
- Execution of a debt instrument by the payor
- The use of property

Not all payments under a divorce or separation instrument are considered alimony. Alimony does *not* include the following:

- Child support.
- Noncash property settlements.
- Payments that are the spouse's or former spouse's part of community income.

- Payments to keep up the payer's property.
- Use of property.

See MTG ¶771.

Example. Under a written separation agreement, Donna lives rent-free in a home Josh owns. Josh must pay the mortgage, real estate taxes, insurance, repairs, and utilities for the home. Because Josh owns the home and the debts belong to him, these payments are not alimony. Neither is the value of Donna's use of the home. If the home were jointly owned, different rules would apply.

Underpayment of Support. If both child support and alimony are owed the payments apply first to child support and then to alimony.

Recapture of Alimony. In the event that alimony payments are reduced during the first three calendar years, the taxpayer may be subject to the alimony recapture rule. The rule is invoked if the alimony payments:

- decrease by more than $15,000 from the second to the third year; or
- decrease by more than $15,000 over the entire first three calendar years; or
- terminate.

Filing Tip. The recapture of alimony rule is not triggered by either the death of either spouse or the remarriage of the recipient spouse.

Taxpayers subject to this rule must include in income in the third year part of the alimony payments that were previously deducted. The spouse can deduct in the third year part of the alimony payments he or she previously included in income. See MTG ¶774 for further details.

Expenses for a Jointly-Owned Home in A Divorce: Who May Deduct on Form 1040?			
Ownership of Home	Expenses Considered Alimony if Paid by One Spouse for the Benefit of the Other	Expenses that Qualify as Itemized Deductions of Payor	Expenses That Qualify as Itemized Deductions of Other Spouse
Joint Tenancy	Half of the total mortgage payments (principal and interest) paid by spouse	Half of the interest as interest expense (if the home is a qualified home)	Half of the interest as interest expense (if the home is a qualified home)
Tenancy in Common	Half of the total real estate taxes and home insurance payments paid by spouse	Half of the real estate taxes	Half of the real estate taxes
Tenancy by the Entirety	None of the payments	All of the real estate taxes if required to pay by the divorce decree	Depends on the provisions of the divorce decree

The three-year period starts with the first calendar year during which the taxpayer makes a payment qualifying as alimony. No recapture is required if payments stop because of the death of either spouse or the remarriage of the payee, or if the amount of payments fluctuates because it is based on a fixed portion of a variable income.

Recapture of Alimony Worksheet

Note: Do not enter less than zero on any line.

1. Alimony paid in **2nd year**	1.
2. Alimony paid in **3rd year**	2.
3. Floor	3. $ 15,000
4. Add lines 2 and 3	4.
5. Subtract line 4 from line 1	5.
6. Alimony paid in **1st year**	6.
7. Subtract line 1 from line 5	7.
8. Alimony paid in **3rd year**	8.
9. Add lines 7 and 8	9.
10. Divide line 9 by 2	10.
11. Floor	11. $15,000
12. Add lines 10 and 11	12.
13. Subtract line 12 from line 6	13.
14. **Recaptured alimony.** Add lines 5 and 13	14. *

* If you deducted alimony paid, report this amount as income on line 11, Form 1040. If you reported alimony received, deduct this amount on line 31a on Form 1040.

Alimony recapture may be required if alimony payments are reduced or terminated because of a:Change in the divorce or separation instrument.

- Failure to make timely payments.
- Reduction in taxpayer's ability to provide support.
- Reduction in the spouse's support needs.

Child Support

Child support paid by the noncustodial parent is considered used for the child's support, even if it actually pays for other things. Child support is neither deductible by the payer nor taxable to the recipient. See MTG ¶776.

Individual Retirement Arrangements and Medical Savings Accounts

- **Spousal IRA:** If a couple is divorced by the end of the tax year, the taxpayer cannot deduct contributions to the former spouse's traditional individual retirement account (IRA). All taxable alimony received is treated as compensation for the contribution and deduction limits of traditional IRAs, so a former spouse who receives alimony can make and, if the general requirements are satisfied, deduct IRA contributions. See Tab 9.
- **Transfer of interest in an IRA to a spouse or former spouse:** The transfer of an interest in an IRA to a spouse or former spouse under a divorce or separation agreement is not considered a taxable transfer. Starting from the date of the transfer, the interest is treated as the former spouse's IRA.
- **Transfer of interest in an Archer medical savings account:** Similarly, the transfer of an interest in an Archer medical savings account (MSA) is not considered a taxable transfer. After the transfer, the interest is considered part of the spouse or former spouse's MSA.

Property Transferred Pursuant to Divorce—Where to Report on the Return

Nature of Property	Payor	Recipient	For More Information
Income-producing property (such as an interest in a business, rental property, stocks, or bonds)	Include on tax return any profit or loss, rental income or loss, dividends, or interest generated or derived from the property during the year until the property is transferred	Report any income or loss generated or derived after the property is transferred	Instructions for appropriate schedule (Schedule C, D, E, or F)
Interest in a passive activity with unused passive activity losses	Cannot deduct accumulated unused passive activity losses allocable to the transferred interest	Increase the adjusted basis of the transferred interest by the amount of the unused losses	IRS Publication 925, Passive Activity and At-Risk Rules
Investment credit property with recapture potential	Does not have to recapture any part of the credit	May have to recapture part of the credit if he or she disposes of the property or changes its use before the end of the recapture period	Form 4255, Recapture of Investment Credit
Nonstatutory stock options and nonqualified deferred compensation	Does not include any amount in gross income upon the transfer	Include an amount in gross income when the stock options are exercised or when the deferred compensation is paid or made available	IRS Publication 525, Taxable and Nontaxable Income, Rev. Rul. 2002-22, and Rev. Rul. 2004-60

Caution. Be sure to advise the client that any transfers from individual retirement accounts or medical savings accounts need to be a trustee-to-trustee transfer to avoid serious tax consequences. Monies withdrawn from such accounts to be directly paid to the other spouse will be taxed to the account holder with penalties and interest.

Property Settlements

There is no recognized gain or loss on the transfer of property between spouses or former spouses in the case of divorce. Retirement benefits held in a qualified plan are frequently a major asset of a divorcing couple. The plan will generally require a qualified domestic relations order (QDRO) to divide retirement benefits.

Qualified Domestic Relations Orders. A qualified domestic relations order (QDRO) is a judgment, decree, or court order under a domestic relations law that:

- allows someone other than the participant to receive benefits under a retirement plan, such as a tax-sheltered annuity, and most pension or profit-sharing plans;
- relates to payment of child support, alimony, or marital property rights to spouse, former spouse, child, or other dependent; and
- specifies the amount or portion of the participant's benefits to be transferred to the alternate payee.

Benefits paid to an alternate payee (spouse, ex-spouse, child or other dependent) are taxable to the payee, not to the participant. Benefits paid to a spouse or former spouse must be included in his or her income. A participant's contributions to the retirement plan are allocated to the distributions pro rata based on the present value of the benefits transferred to determine the taxable amount. See Tab 9.

See MTG ¶2124D for more information about QDROs.

Transfer of S Corporation Losses to Spouse or Incident to Divorce

Generally, suspended losses and deductions are disallowed and are not available to anyone once an S corporation shareholder transfers all of his or her shares to another person. However, if a shareholder's stock is transferred to his or her spouse, or to a former spouse incident to divorce, any suspended loss or deduction with respect to that stock will be treated as incurred by the S corporation in the succeeding tax year with respect to the transferee. Reg. §1.1366-2(a)(5)(ii) provides guidance on the handling of losses prior to and in the year of the transfer of stock incident to a divorce under IRC §1041(a).

Costs of Divorce

Taxpayers cannot deduct legal fees and court costs related to the divorce. However, taxpayers may be able to deduct legal fees paid for tax advice in connection with a divorce, and legal fees to get alimony. Deductions may also be taken for payments to appraisers, actuaries, and accountants for tax purposes or for help in obtaining alimony.

Planning Tip. Because some fees may be tax-deductible and others are not, based on the service for which the fee is paid, taxpayers should always request a breakdown of fees for each service performed by attorneys, accountants, and other professionals.

Education Tax Benefits

A variety of tax incentives are available for education expenses, including exclusion of scholarships, grants, and certain other income used for qualified education expenses from taxable income: two major above-the-line deductions (adjustments to gross income); and two major education tax credits.

For a summary of educational tax benefits, see the chart on page 13-18.

General Information

Qualified Education Expenses. For tax purposes, qualified education expenses generally include:

- Tuition and certain related expenses required to enroll in an eligible institution.
- Student activity fees and expenses for course-related books, supplies and equipment are included in qualified expenses only if the fees and expenses must be paid to the institution as a condition of enrollment.
- Expenses that do not qualify include room and board, travel, and clerical help.

Eligible Educational Institution. An eligible educational institution is one that maintains a regular facility and curriculum and normally has a regularly enrolled body of students.

Modified Adjusted Gross Income (MAGI). For most taxpayers, MAGI is adjusted gross income as figured on the federal income tax return (using Form 1040A, it is on line 21; on Form 1040, it is on line 37) modified by adding back certain deductions and exclusions, including:

- Foreign earned income exclusion.
- Foreign housing exclusion.

- Exclusion of income for residents of Guam, the Northern Mariana Islands, and American Samoa.
- Exclusion of income from Puerto Rico.

 Planning Tip. Students who have taxable income from any education benefits may need to make estimated tax payments if the payer does not withhold enough income tax. See Tab 11 for information about estimated tax.

No Double Benefits. When taking education-related deductions, taxpayers may not deduct the same expenses twice or claim both a credit and a deduction for the same expenses. The following double benefits are specifically disallowed:

- Claim of an American Opportunity (modified Hope) or lifetime learning credit and deduction of tuition and fees expenses for the same student in the same year.
- Claim of an American Opportunity (modified Hope) or lifetime learning credit based on the same expenses used to figure the tax-free portion of a distribution from a Coverdell education savings account (ESA) or a qualified tuition program (QTP).
- Claim of a credit based on qualified education expenses paid with a tax-free scholarship, grant, or employer-provided educational assistance.
- Claim of an exclusion of interest from U.S. savings bonds for qualified education expenses either used to claim another tax benefit or paid with a tax-free scholarship, grant, or employer-provided educational assistance.

Tax-Free Benefits

The taxability of various kinds of education assistance available while studying, teaching, or researching in the United States is covered in detail in IRS Publication 970, *Tax Benefits for Education.* Most scholarships, fellowships, need-based grants, and qualified tuition reductions are tax-free if they are used to pay qualified education expenses.

Scholarships and Fellowships. Generally, scholarships and fellowships received by a degree candidate and used for qualified education expenses are nontaxable. Taxpayers do not have to file a tax return if their only income is tax-free scholarships or fellowships. If all or part of the scholarships or fellowships is taxable, the taxpayer must file a return.

Other forms of educational assistance that may be tax-free include:

- Pell grants and other Title IV need-based education grants are treated like scholarships and are tax-free when used for qualified education express expenses.
- A Fulbright scholarship is generally treated as a scholarship or fellowship in figuring out how much of the grant is tax-free.
- Veterans' benefits received for education, training, or subsistence under any law administered by the Department of Veterans Affairs are tax-free.
- Payments to armed services academy cadets may be excluded if used for education expenses related to study at a U.S. military academy. Appointment to a U.S. military academy is now treated as a scholarship or fellowship. However, payments for services as a cadet or midshipman are taxable income.

Taxpayers may elect not to exclude scholarship or fellowship grants that can be used for room and board and other expenses. If these payments are reported as taxable income, they do not reduce the amount of qualifying expenses for the purpose of the American Opportunity (modified Hope) and lifetime learning credits.

Employer-Provided Assistance Excluded. Taxpayers who receive education assistance benefits from their employers under an education assistance program can exclude as much as $5,250 of those benefits each year. See MTG ¶871.

 Caution. The election to treat nontaxable scholarships as taxable does not extend to restricted scholarships, which must be used only for tuition and fees. Qualifying expenses must be reduced by the amount of these scholarships.

Education Tax Deductions

Unlike other tax benefits for education, the student loan interest deduction is an above-the-line (or adjustment to income) deduction. In addition, work-related education may be deductible as a business expense.

Student Loan Interest Deduction. This deduction is taken as a reduction in income on line 33 of Form 1040, so it can also be claimed even if taxpayers do not itemize. The maximum deduction is $2,500. The deduction is phased out for taxpayers with adjusted gross income between $60,000 and $75,000 ($125,000 and $155,000 for MFJ). See MTG ¶1082.

Work-Related Education Deduction. Some education expenses are deductible as employee business expenses. See Tab 6 and MTG ¶1082.

Planning Tip. *Tuition and Fees Deduction*–The deduction for qualified tuition and fees was extended for two years by the American Taxpayer Relief Act of 2012. It is available for qualified tuition and fees paid through December 31, 2013. The maximum deductible amount is $4,000 for taxpayers with AGI of $65,000 or less ($130,000 for joint filers) and $2,000 for taxpayers with AGI above $65,000 but less than or equal to $80,000 ($130,000 and $160,000, respectively, for joint filers). No deduction is available to taxpayers with AGI above $80,000 ($160,000 for joint filers). The deduction is claimed on Form 8917, which must submitted with Form 1040, and the deduction amount is entered on line 34 of Form 1040.

Tax-Free Transactions

Canceled Student Loans. Although the cancellation of a debt is usually treated as income to the debtor, certain cancellations of student loans are excluded from this rule. To qualify for tax-free treatment on a canceled loan, the loan must contain a provision that all or part will be forgiven if the taxpayer works for a certain period of time, in certain professions, and for any of a broad class of employers. Also, the loan generally must have been made by a government, a public corporation operating a hospital, or an educational institution. See MTG ¶885.

Student Loan Repayment Assistance. Student loan repayment assistance provided through the National Health Service Corps Loan Repayment Program or similar state programs is excluded from gross income. These programs provide subsidies to individuals providing primary health services in underserved areas. The IRS has expanded the exclusion to include recent law school graduates who accept loan repayment assistance from their law schools to enter public service, the non-profit sector, and underserved areas.

Qualified Tuition Programs (QTP) or 529 Plans. Qualified tuition programs, also known as 529 plans, are programs established by states or educational institutions that allow taxpayers to either prepay or contribute to an account for paying a student's qualified higher education expenses. Earnings in a qualified tuition program also accumulate tax-free. No tax is due on a distribution from a QTP unless the amount distributed is greater than the beneficiary's qualified higher education expenses. Excess distributions are included in the recipient's income and also are subject to an additional tax of 10%.

Contributions to a QTP cannot be more than the amount necessary to provide for the qualified education expenses of the beneficiary. See MTG ¶899.

Planning Tip. The change in the age for imposition of the "kiddie tax" makes the use of 529 plans more desirable for saving for a child's college education.

For ratings of various plans, see http://www.finaid.org/savings/.

Savings Bonds Used for Education. Taxpayers who cash series EE or I savings bonds issued after 1989 can exclude the interest from their income if they pay qualified education expenses for themselves, their spouse, or a dependent during the year. Qualified education expenses include college tuition and fees, contributions to a qualified tuition program, and contributions to a Coverdell education savings account. The exclusion phaseout begins for taxpayers with 2013 modified adjusted gross income in excess of $112,050 (if married filing jointly) or $74,700 (for other filers). The phaseout is complete at $142,050 for joint filers and $89,700 for other filers. Form 8815, *Exclusion of Interest from Series EE or I U.S. Savings Bonds Issued after 1989*, is used to calculate the exclusion. See MTG ¶730A.

To qualify for the exclusion, the bonds must be issued in the name of the taxpayer or the names of the taxpayer and the taxpayer's spouse, as co-owners, and the taxpayer must have been 24 or older when the bonds were issued. A bond purchased by a parent and issued in the name of his or her child under age 24 does *not* qualify for the exclusion by the parent or the child. See MTG ¶730A.

Coverdell Education Savings Accounts (ESAs). Taxpayers can contribute up to $2,000 to a Coverdell ESA created for a particular beneficiary. Contributions to the ESA are not deductible, but accumulations are tax-deferred until distributed. Beneficiaries must be under 18 or have special needs. Any individual, including the beneficiary, can contribute. The $2,000 amount is phased out for MAGI between $95,000 and $110,000 ($190,000 to $220,000 for joint filers).

The $2,000 annual limit also applies to all Coverdell ESAs set up for any one beneficiary. Contributions in excess of the $2,000 limit per contributor or per beneficiary are subject to a 6% excise tax if not withdrawn by June 1 of the following year.

Coverdell ESA distributions can be used to pay elementary and secondary education expenses, as well as higher education expenses.

If distributions exceed qualified education expenses, the excess is allocated to earnings and return of contributions. Earnings are taxable, but the amount attributable to the contributed basis in the account is not. IRS Publication 970 contains a worksheet to calculate the taxable amount of the distribution. Withdrawals in excess of qualified education expenses are also subject to a 10% penalty, which is calculated on Form 5329, *Additional Taxes on Qualified Plans (Including IRAs) and Other Tax Favored Accounts.*

Any balance remaining in a Coverdell ESA must be withdrawn within 30 days after the beneficiary's thirtieth birthday, unless the beneficiary has special needs that extend the length of time required for his or her education, or within 30 days after the beneficiary's death if he or she dies before reaching age 30. Rollovers to the following family members of the beneficiary (who are under age 30 at the time of the rollover) are allowed:

- Son, daughter, or descendant of son or daughter
- Stepson or stepdaughter
- Brother, sister, or son or daughter of a brother or sister
- Stepbrother or stepsister
- Father, mother, or ancestor of either
- Stepfather or stepmother
- Brother or sister of father or mother
- First cousin
- Son-in-law, daughter-in-law, brother-in-law, sister-in-law, mother-in-law, or father-in-law
- Spouse of original beneficiary or any relative listed except first cousin

Rollovers must be deposited within 60 days of withdrawal to avoid the 10% penalty. See MTG ¶898.

Education Tax Credits

American Opportunity (Modified Hope) Tax Credit and Lifetime Learning Credit. These two tax credits offset the cost of higher education by reducing the amount of income tax a student or his/her parents pays.

The American Opportunity (modified Hope) tax credit is available for the first four years of higher education, with a maximum credit amount of $2,500, includes the expenses of course materials as qualified expenses, and the phaseout begins at $80,000 for single filers ($160,000 for joint filers). For taxpayers with low or no tax liability, 40 percent of the credit amount may be claimed as a refundable credit. A student must be pursuing an undergraduate degree and must be enrolled at least half-time for an academic period beginning during the year to have his/her expenses qualify to be claim the American Opportunity (modified Hope) credit.

In contrast to the American Opportunity credit, the lifetime learning credit maximum of $2,000 is calculated per taxpayer and does not vary based on the number of eligible students in the taxpayer's family. A student is eligible for the lifetime learning credit if the student is enrolled in one or more courses at a qualified educational institution. The phaseout of the credits begins for at $107,000 for joint filers and $53,000 for other filers. The lifetime learning credit may not be claimed by married taxpayers who file separate returns (Code Sec. 25A(g)).

 Planning Tip. It may result in lower family tax liability if parents whose adjusted gross income results in the phaseout of the dependency exemption allow their student dependent to claim the education credit if the child has suficcient tax liability to offset the credit. However, this does not entitle the student dependent to claim a personal exemption on his or her tax return.

The credits are calculated on Form 8863, *Education Credits*, and reported on line 49 of Form 1040. Students may not claim both credits in the same year. Generally, the lifetime learning credit and the American Opportunity (modified Hope) credit are allowed for payments made in 2013 for an academic period beginning in 2013 or the first three months of 2014.

See Tab 10 and MTG ¶1303 for details.

Example. Charlie received a scholarship of $16,000 and has wages of $7,500 in 2013. He is not a dependent of any other taxpayer. His tuition, fees, and other expenses required for enrollment in his degree program totaled $13,500. He used the remaining $2,500 of his scholarship money toward his $5,000 expense for room and board (this use was allowed under the terms of the scholarship). He must include the $2,500 amount (and his wages) as taxable income on line 7 of Form 1040.

If he reports $10,000 taxable income, he may not claim any deduction or credit for education expenses because all qualifying expenses were paid with nontaxable income. After his $3,900 personal exemption and $6,100 standard deduction as a single filer, he has taxable income of $500 and pays $50 of tax.

Assume Charlie reports $12,000 taxable income on line 7 of Form 1040 (electing not to exclude an additional $2,000 of his scholarship, applying it to room and board rather than tuition). He then has $2,000 in qualifying education expenses for the the American Opportunity (modified Hope) tax credit, and can claim a $2,000 credit on line 49 of Form 1040. His tax on the taxable income of $2,500 is $250, but after he subtracts the American Opportunity credit, he owes no tax for 2013 (and can claim a full refund of any tax withheld from his wages by his employer).

Highlights of Tax Benefits for Education

	Scholarships, Fellowships, Grants, and Tuition Reductions	American Opportunity (Modified Hope Credit)**	Lifetime Learning Credit	Student Loan Interest Deduction	Coverdell Educational Savings Accounts (ESAs)*	Qualified Tuition Programs (QTPs)*	Education Savings Bond Program*	Employer-Provided Educational Assistance*	Educational Exception on Early IRA Distributions*
Benefit	Amounts received may not be taxable	Credit can reduce amount of tax owed	Credit can reduce amount of tax owed	Deduction can reduce taxable income	Earnings accumulate tax free	Earnings accumulate tax free	Interest not taxed	Employer benefits not taxed	No 10% penalty on early distribution
Annual Contribution Limit	None	$2,500 per student	$2,000 per family	Up to $2,500	Up to $2,000 per beneficiary	None	Amount of qualified education expenses	$5,250 exclusion	Amount of qualified education expenses
Adjusted Gross Income Phase Out Range	No phase out	Single — $80,000–$90,000; MFJ — $160,000–$180,000 (2009 through 2017)	Single — $53,000–$63,000; MFJ — $107,000–$127,000	Single — $60,000–$75,000; MFJ — $125,000–$155,000	Single — $95,000–$110,000; MFJ — $190,000–$220,000	No phase out	Single — $74,700–$89,700; MFJ — $112,050–$142,050	No phase out	No phase out
Qualifying Education	K – 12, undergraduate and graduate	1st 4 years of undergraduate (2009 through 2017)	Undergraduate and graduate courses to acquire or improve job skills	Undergraduate and graduate	K – 12, undergraduate and graduate	Undergraduate and graduate	Undergraduate and graduate	Undergraduate and graduate	Undergraduate and graduate
Qualifying Expenses (In addition to tuition and required enrollment fees)	Required books, supplies, and equipment	Course Materials (2009 through 2017)	None	Required books, supplies, & equipment; room & board, transportation, & other necessary expenses	Required books, supplies, & equipment; expenses for special needs services; payments to QTPs; Higher Education: Room and board, if at least a half-time student; K–12: Tutoring, room & board, uniforms, transportation, computer access, and supplementary expenses	Required books, supplies and equipment; room and board, if at least a half-time student, & expenses for special needs services	Payments to Coverdell ESAs and QTPs	Required books, supplies, and equipment	
Additional Requirements	• Must be a degree or vocational program • Payment of tuition and fees allowed under grant	• No felony drug conviction(s) • At least half-time in degree program	None	Must have been at least a half-time student in a degree program	Assets must be distributed at age 30 unless special needs beneficiary	None	Applies only to qualified series EE bonds issued after 1989 and series I bonds	None	None

*Any nontaxable distribution is limited to the amount that does not exceed qualified educational expenses.

**Available only during tax years 2009 through 2017.

What's New in 2013

Maximum Tax Rate. The maximum estate, gift, and generation-skipping transfer (GST) tax rate for 2013 is 40%. For gifts made in prior years, the 2013 tax rate must be used to compute both the gift tax on and the unified credit allowed for such gifts.

Applicable Exclusion Amount. The applicable exclusion amount for estate tax and gift tax, and the GST tax exemption amount, are all $5.25 million. The combined unified credit amount is $2,045,800.

Portability Election. Estates of decedents dying in 2013 can elect to allow the decedent's surviving spouse (or his or her estate) to use the unused portion of the predeceased spouse's unused exclusion amount. Portability is elected by filing a timely and complete Form 706. To opt out of portability, the predeceased spouse's estate must check a box on Form 706.

Same Sex Spouses. Legally married same-sex couples are treated as married for federal transfer tax purposes following the ruling in *E. Windsor*, SCt, 2013-2 USTC ¶60,667. The state of celebration controls for determining the legality of the marriage.

Due Dates of Required Forms

Form	Date
Form 1040, *U.S. Individual Income Tax Return*	Date the return would have been due if deceased taxpayer were still alive
Form 1041, *U.S. Income Tax Return for Estates and Trusts*	15th day of 4th month after close of the tax year
Form 706, *United States Estate (and Generation-Skipping Transfer) Tax Return*	9 months after date of death
Form 709, *United States Gift (and Generation-Skipping Transfer) Tax Return*	Earlier of Form 1040 due date or Form 706 due date

2013 Income Tax Rate Table for Trusts and Estates

Taxable Income Over	But Not Over	Pay +	% on Excess	Of the Amount Over—
$0–	$2,450	$0	15%	$0
2,450–	5,700	367.50	25	2,450
5,700–	8,750	1,180.00	28	5,700
8,750–	11,950	2,034.00	33	8,750
11,950–	......	3,090.00	39.6	11,950

Section at a Glance

Relevant IRS Publications

- ☐ IRS Publication 559, *Survivors, Executors, and Administrators*
- ☐ IRS Publication 950, *Introduction to Estate and Gift Taxes*

Tax Preparer's Checklist

Information Needed by Executor or Personal Representative

- ☐ Will
- ☐ Trust agreements
- ☐ Listing of assets and debts
- ☐ Decedent's checkbooks and bank statements for period including death
- ☐ Life insurance policies
- ☐ Recent credit card statements
- ☐ Titles to assets
- ☐ Inventory of safe deposit boxes
- ☐ Prior gift tax returns
- ☐ Death certificate
- ☐ Income tax returns for prior three years
- ☐ Buy-sell agreements (closely held corporations or partnerships)
- ☐ Prenuptial agreements and divorce decrees, if applicable
- ☐ For sole proprietorship:
  - • Balance sheet for valuation date and five preceding years
  - • Income statement for five preceding years
- ☐ Names, addresses, Social Security numbers, citizenship information, and dates of birth of heirs
- ☐ Basis of decedent in retirement accounts and annuities
- ☐ Amount of consideration provided by decedent for property owned jointly with individuals other than spouse
- ☐ Casualty insurance policies

What Tax Returns Must be Filed for a Deceased Taxpayer?

Form 1040, *U.S. Individual Income Tax Return*

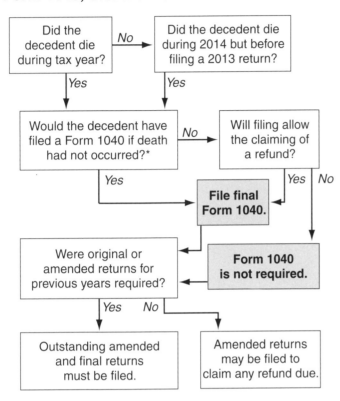

*If taxpayer was married and would have filed jointly with his or her spouse, see p.14–5.

Form 706, *United States Estate (and Generation-Skipping Transfer) Tax Return*

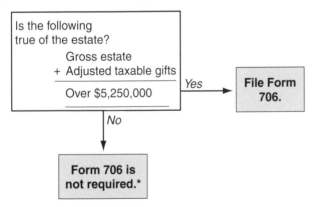

*Executors of estates that wish to elect portability must also file Form 706, regardless of the amount of the gross estate.

Form 1041, *U.S. Income Tax Return for Estates and Trusts*

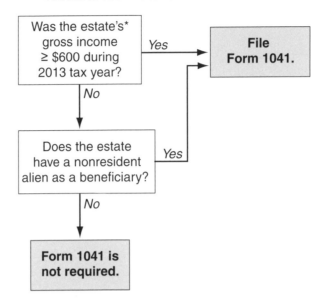

*Qualified revocable trusts may make an election to be treated as an estate; see Form 8855 and IRC §645.

Form 709, *United States Gift (and Generation-Skipping Transfer) Tax Return*

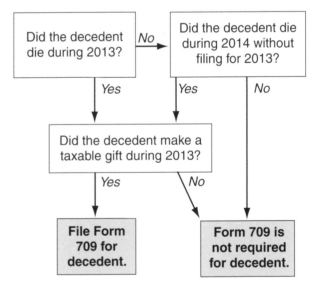

Death of a Taxpayer

This section discusses tax and other financial considerations concerning a taxpayer's death and related planning. One must understand what happens to a decedent's property at, and subsequent to, death.

Understanding Probate and Asset Administration

Person Responsible. Upon the death of an individual, a determination must be made as to who will be named the decedent's personal representative – the person responsible for handling the financial affairs of the decedent. The personal representative is charged with the following tasks:

- Accounting for all assets of the decedent, including collecting and valuing all assets.
- Collecting all income due during the period of administration.
- Paying all liabilities of the decedent.
- Paying expenses incurred during administration.
- Ensuring that the remaining assets of the decedent are transferred according to the decedent's will.
- Filing tax returns and paying taxes.
- Publishing notice of probate and acceptance of claims.
- Notifying creditors of death and providing information for making claims.
- Providing to the court and heirs an accounting of assets, income collected, and claims and expenses paid.

If the decedent had no will, the distribution of assets is governed by state law. The applicable law for real and tangible personal property is that of the state in which the property is located. The laws of the state of the decedent's residence at the time of death apply to all other property.

If the decedent had a will, the will specifies who is to be executor. If the decedent had no will, then local law provides rules as to who is to be the personal representative. (The terms "executor" and "personal representative" are used interchangeably throughout this chapter, unless otherwise indicated.) In either event, application is made to the court with jurisdiction to validate the will and/or appoint the personal representative. The court documents this by issuing *letters testamentary* or *letters of administration*.

The Probate Process. The formality of accounting for assets and liabilities of the decedent and the amount of court supervision depend on the total value of assets subject to probate. These may also depend on any anticipated controversy among heirs or creditors, or questions of title to assets.

Assets Subject to Probate. Assets subject to probate, generally, are any assets owned by the decedent at death to which title does not automatically pass to another person. Such assets must be reported to the probate court, which must authorize or approve the transfer or sale of such assets.

Examples of Probate Assets. Assets titled only in the name of the decedent, or as tenant-in-common with other persons:
- Checking account(s)
- Savings account(s)
- Brokerage account(s)
- Residence or other real estate
- Partnership interests
- Coin collection(s)
- Retirement accounts or other beneficiary accounts with no designated beneficiaries or for which the estate is named as beneficiary such as:
  - IRA(s)
  - Life insurance
  - Annuities

When Probate Is Required. Probate is generally required only when value of the total *probate* assets exceed a threshold dollar amount, depending on the state of jurisdiction (for example, $100,000). For probate estates under the threshold, a small estate affidavit or other similar procedure may be followed, obviating a formal probate procedure.

Examples of Non-Probate Assets. Assets with beneficiary designations (other than the estate) such as:
- Life insurance proceeds
- Retirement accounts [IRA, 401(k), 403(b), 457, SEP, SIMPLE]
- Annuities
- Annuities and other income interests that terminate on death
- Accounts that are "payable on death" (POD) or "transfer on death" (TOD)
- Beneficial interests in trusts created by others
- Land trusts
- Living trusts
- Social Security benefits
- Veterans Administration benefits
- Assets owned as joint tenants or as tenants-by-the-entirety

Filing Tip. Review decedent's prior income tax returns to ensure all sources of income have been identified and the related assets accounted for.

Caution. Once it is determined that the creation of an estate or trust is needed, obtain a tax identification number for the entity. This is required to open a separate checking account for the estate or trust. After establishing a separate checking account, deposit all income and proceeds from the liquidation of assets and pay all expenses from this account.

Caution. Depending on the terms of the will, it may be important to keep track of income separately from other receipts. Also, net income for probate purposes may not be the same as for income tax purposes.

Determining States Requiring Probate. The decedent's domicile within a state establishes jurisdiction. If the decedent owned real property or tangible personal property located in another state, an "ancillary" administration in that state may be required.

Caution. Depending on the property, an income tax return and/or an inheritance or estate tax return may also be required by the state.

Forms Required upon Death. The personal representative will need the following:

- Employer identification number (EIN) (Form SS-4)–Required for any income-producing assets of the decedent's estate. Apply for the EIN online, or by telephone (1-800-829-4933), fax, or mail. For more information, visit the IRS website, at http://www.irs.gov/Businesses/Small-Businesses-&-Self-Employed/How-to-Apply-for-an-EIN.

Filing Tip. Advise all payers of income as soon as you receive a tax identification number for the estate. This will reduce problems later when filing income tax returns.

- Notice of fiduciary relationship (Form 56)–File with the IRS Service Center where the person for whom you are acting is required to file tax returns. For the final 1040 and the 1041, note that more than one Form 56 may need to be filed. A separate Form 56 must be filed for each person for whom you are acting in a fiduciary capacity.

Income Tax Filing Requirements for Year of Death

The personal representative must file a final income tax return (Form 1040) for the year of death and any returns for prior years that have not been filed as of the date of death.

Example. Joe Black died July 15, 2013. He was married to Mabel at the time of his death. Joe received salary prior to death of $50,000. A payroll check for the month of his death and for unused sick and vacation pay was issued after his death for $15,237.75 ($16,500, less Social Security (6.2%) and Medicare (1.45%) taxes of $1,262.25). The check was made payable to Joe's estate. Mabel had wages of $55,000 for the year; $27,500 was earned prior to Joe's death. Joe and Mabel earned $1,200 on a joint savings account; $650 of this was earned prior to Joe's death. Joe owned stock on which he received $600 in dividends prior to death. A Form 1099 was received in Joe's name for $1,300, which included $700 of dividends paid to Joe's estate after death.

The first installment of property taxes on Joe and Mabel's residence, of $1,800, was paid prior to death. The residence was owned jointly. Mabel paid the second installment of $1,800 after Joe's death. In addition, Joe owned a vacation home in Florida. Mabel paid property taxes of $3,000 on this in November. Joe and Mabel can file a joint return for 2013. The joint return would include the following income:
- Joe's salary prior to death, $50,000
- Mabel's salary for the entire 12 months, $55,000
- Interest income on joint savings, $1,200
- Dividend income of $600 [$1,300 should be reported but then reduced by $700 as income not taxable in the final Form 1040 (reportable by Joe's estate)]

Income not includible in the final joint Form 1040:
- Final salary check of $15,237.75 (reportable in Joe's estate's Form 1041 as income in respect of a decedent (IRD))
- Dividend income of $700 (reportable in Joe's estate's Form 1041 as IRD)

The final joint return would include a deduction for property taxes of $3,600 but would not include the property taxes on the Florida property. The Florida property taxes would be deductible by Joe's estate on Form 1041 (and also on Form 706, if required).

IRS Publication 559, *Survivors, Executors, and Administrators*, provides further details.

 Example. John Smith, an unmarried taxpayer, died March 31, 2014, without having filed his 2013 income tax return. His personal representative must file a return for 2013 and a separate return for the period January 1, 2014, through John's date of death, March 31, 2014. The 2013 return is due April 15, 2014, and the 2014 return is due April 15, 2015.

If the decedent was married at the time of death and a joint return is to be filed, then the surviving spouse can sign the return as "Surviving Spouse." Note that the personal representative of the estate—*not* the surviving spouse—determines the filing status of the decedent's final return, unless the surviving spouse is also the personal representative. The return for the year of death will include income and deductions of the decedent up to the date of death, and the income and deductions of the surviving spouse for the entire year. See MTG ¶168, ¶178 and ¶182.

A widow or widower may qualify to use the lower Married Filing Jointly tax rates for the two years following the year of death if he or she:

- was entitled to file a joint return with the deceased spouse in the spouse's year of death;
- did not remarry before the end of the tax year;
- has a child, stepchild, adopted child, or foster child who qualifies as a dependent for the tax year; and
- provides more than half of the cost of maintaining the home, which is the principal residence of the child for the entire year except for temporary absences.

See MTG ¶175.

Planning Tip. A tax practitioner should consider working with an attorney when dealing with the financial affairs of a decedent, executor, or surviving spouse or other family members. State laws dictate requirements.

Decedent's Final Income Tax Return (Form 1040) Checklist

The purpose of this checklist is to ensure that all matters incident to death are considered in preparing the decedent's final income tax return.

1. Determine if a final tax return is required and the marital status at date of death. Check Form 1040 general instructions.

2. Separate all taxable income items actually or constructively received (per Treas. Reg. §1.451-2) to the date of death from items considered income in respect of decedent that are reportable on estate income tax return. See IRS Publication 559, Table B, Worksheet to Reconcile Amounts Reported in Name of Decedent on Information Returns.

3. If decedent had series E, EE, H, HH, or I savings bond interest, IRC §454(a) permits election of reporting all accrued interest on the final return.

4. Carryovers
   A. Capital loss—lost if not used on final return.
   B. Passive loss—additional passive losses may be allowed if suspended losses exceed the step-up in basis.
   C. Net operating loss—lost if not used on final return.
   D. Investment interest expense—lost if not used on final return.
   E. Charitable contribution—lost if not used on final return.

5. Complete preparation of return
   A. Input the same occupation as prior year in the "occupation" space of return.
   B. Enter date of death.
   C. Determine whether medical expenses of decedent paid by estate within one year after death will be deducted on Form 1040 or Form 706.
   D. Spouse can elect to treat deceased spouse's IRA as his or her own.
   E. Deduct any unamortized loan costs.
   F. Deduct any unrecovered basis in annuities.

6. Tax credit carryovers
   A. May deduct any unused "qualified business credits."
   B. Foreign tax credit carryovers may be used by decedent's estate or heirs.

7. If joint return is to be filed:

   A. Determine if payment of executor commissions to surviving spouse should be accelerated to the final joint return.

   B. Enter "Filing as surviving spouse" in the area where the surviving spouse will sign on behalf of the deceased taxpayer. Also write "Deceased" and the name and date of death above the "taxpayer's name" area.

   C. Determine the decedent's separate share of the joint tax liability (debt of decedent) as provided by Treas. Reg. §20.2053-6(f). The estate is liable for the decedent's allocable share of tax liability.

   D. Determine the surviving spouse's estimated tax obligation based on his or her separate share of income and expense items and estimated distributions from decedent's estate or trust.

   E. Consider the deduction for estate tax attributable to income in respect of a decedent.

8. If a refund is due, determine if Form 1310, Statement of Person Claiming Refund Due a Deceased Taxpayer (and corresponding state form) is necessary (see Form 1310 instructions).

9. Are Social Security numbers on Forms 1099 correct?

10. Are amounts on Forms 1099 correctly reported between individual and estate? If not, disclose in return amount per 1099 in return and then subtract amount not includible in return.

11. Are estimated tax vouchers for the succeeding year in the surviving spouse's name and Social Security number?

12. For taxation and reporting of income subsequent to death, see "Income Taxation after Death" on page 14-16.

Gift Tax Return Requirements for Year of Death

If the decedent made any reportable gifts in the year of death or any prior year, the personal representative is responsible for filing a gift tax return using Form 709, *United States Gift (and Generation-Skipping Transfer) Tax Return*. The personal representative can consent to "splitting" gifts with the decedent's spouse. See the discussion of gift tax beginning on page 14-14.

A gift tax return is generally due by April 15 in the year following the date of the gift. An exception exists where the gift and the decedent's death occur in the same year. In such cases, the gift tax return is due the earlier of the following two dates:

- April 15 of the year after the gift was made, or
- The due date of the estate tax return, Form 706

Example. Ben Newman makes a reportable gift on February 15, 2013. He dies March 1, 2013. The gift tax return is due December 1, 2013. Note that if Ben retained a power to amend or revoke the gift, the gifted property will be included in Ben's gross estate. See page 14-8 and MTG ¶2913.

Federal Estate and Gift Tax

The federal estate tax is a tax on the transfer of the decedent's property. It is in addition to and separate from the income tax. The federal gift tax is a tax on the transfer of property during one's lifetime. The gift tax is "integrated" with the estate tax; that is, transfers made by a person during life are included in the computation of that person's estate tax liability at death.

The applicable exclusion amount is the same for both gift and estate tax purposes, making the transfer tax system truly unified. Hence, the Internal Revenue Code (IRC) refers to a "unified credit." In 2013, both the estate tax applicable exclusion and the gift tax applicable exclusion are $5.25 million, making the unified credit equal to $2,045,800, (From 2004 through 2010, the gift and estate tax applicable exclusion amounts were "de-unified.") For 2013, any unified credit allocated to taxable gifts in prior periods must be redetermined using the current gift tax rate, not the rates in effect when the prior gifts were made.

The personal representative of the decedent is responsible for determining what transfers of assets are taxable at death and, depending on the value of total cumulative transfers, filing a federal estate tax return (Form 706) and paying any estate tax that may be due. In addition to the federal estate tax, it is necessary to determine whether the decedent will owe any state estate or inheritance tax requiring a separate tax return.

See IRS Publication 950, *Introduction to Estate and Gift Taxes*, for more information.

Federal Estate Tax

Estates of the following individuals are subject to federal estate tax:

- U.S. citizens, regardless of whether they are domiciled in the United States;
- Resident aliens; and
- Nonresident aliens, to the extent they own assets located in the United States.

Filing Requirements. Form 706 is required if the gross estate, plus adjusted taxable gifts and specific

Example. Margot Jones is the personal representative for John Smith, who died in 2013. To file Form 706 for John's estate, she calculates the estate tax as follows:

Gross estate	$6,500,000
Less: Allowable deductions	(60,000)
Taxable estate	6,440,000
Plus: Taxable gifts	100,000
Total	$6,540,000
Tentative tax on total	2,561,800
Less: Gift tax paid by decedent	0
Gross estate tax	2,561,800
Maximum unified credit	(2,045,800)
Total	$ 516,000
Net federal estate tax	$ 516,000

*State death tax deduction not taken into account. Example illustrates federal estate tax only.

exemptions, exceeds the applicable exclusion amount ($5,250,000 in 2013), even though there may be no tax liability. Estates of nonresident aliens must file Form 706-NA if the decedent's gross estate located in the United States exceeds $60,000 (after reduction for post-1976 taxable gifts and a special limited exemption).

Portability Election. Form 706 is required if the estate of a married decedent who died in 2013 wants to make an election allowing the decedent's surviving spouse (or the surviving spouse's estate) to use the deceased spousal unused exclusion (DSUE) amount. The predeceased spouse's estate must file Form 706 within the required filing period (including extensions), even if Form 706 is not otherwise required to be filed. See IRC §2010(c), Temp. Reg. §§20.2010-2T and 20.2010-3T, and Instructions to Form 706. See also MTG ¶2938.

Due Date. Form 706 is due nine months after the date of death. An automatic extension of six months is available by filing Form 4768.

Example. Hemberto Ruiz died in 2013. Prior to his death he had made $100,000 of taxable gifts. His gross estate is $5,200,000. His estate has deductions of $60,000. Form 706 must be filed, even though there is no federal estate tax liability, because his gross estate plus his amount of taxable gifts exceeds the $5.25 million applicable exclusion.

Tax Preparer's Checklist.
Assets includible in gross estate:

- ❖ Accrued interest
- ❖ Amounts due on sales contracts
- ❖ Annuities, IRAs, other retirement accounts
- ❖ Archer Medical Savings Accounts (MSA) or Health Savings Accounts (HSA)
- ❖ Autos, boats, etc.
- ❖ Bonds, certificates of deposit, savings accounts, etc.
- ❖ Cash
- ❖ Coin collections, other collectibles
- ❖ Dividends payable
- ❖ Gift tax paid on gifts within three years of death
- ❖ Includible portions of jointly owned property
- ❖ Jewelry, other significant personal property (review insurance policy)
- ❖ Life insurance on another
- ❖ Life insurance on decedent (need Form 712 from insurance company)
- ❖ Loans due decedent
- ❖ Partnership interests
- ❖ Property over which decedent had a general power of appointment
- ❖ Real estate
- ❖ Revocable transfers
- ❖ Section 529 gifts exceeding annual exclusion amounts
- ❖ Share of final income tax refund
- ❖ Stocks
- ❖ Transfers made for less than full and adequate consideration
- ❖ Transfers made within three years of death (see IRC §2035(a))
- ❖ Transfers taking effect after death (see IRC §2037)
- ❖ Unpaid salary
- ❖ Value of interest in qualified terminable interest property (QTIP) trust established upon prior death of spouse

Caution. Extending the time for filing does not extend the due date for payment of tax. See page 14–13 regarding provisions for extending the time for payment of tax.

Filing Tip. The IRS may grant a reasonable extension of time to make a regulatory or statutory election (e.g., IRC §2032A special use valuation election). See Treas. Reg. §301.9100-1.

Gross Estate

The gross estate includes all assets owned by the decedent, as well as certain legal rights or interests discussed in this section.

 Caution. The decedent's gross estate is not the same as the probate estate. It includes property, such as life insurance and retirement benefits, that is not part of probate.

 Filing Tip. Review the decedent's income tax returns for the last few years prior to death, to make sure all property and income sources have been identified and accounted for on the estate tax return. Also use these returns to identify all liabilities that may exist at the date of death.

Inventory the Contents of Safe Deposit Boxes. The IRS assumes the contents are owned by the decedent unless other ownership is established.

Property Owned Jointly with a Non-Spouse. The percentage of the cost of such property contributed by the decedent determines the amount includible in the decedent's estate.

Transfers During Life. Review any trusts created during the decedent's lifetime to determine if these are includible in the gross estate.

Powers of Appointment. Review trust agreements for any trusts in which the decedent had an interest. Determine if these are includible in the gross estate as the result of a general power of appointment.

Gifts Made Within Three Years of Death. The decedent's gross estate includes the amount of gift tax paid on any gift made within three years of death (IRC §2035(b)).

In addition, if the decedent transfers an interest in property (or relinquishes a power with respect to property) within three years of death, and the property would have been included in the decedent's gross estate under IRC §§2036-2038 and §2042 if the transferred property had been retained by the decedent, then the property is included in the gross estate. See IRC §2035(a). For example, if the decedent transfers a life insurance policy in which he has "incidents of ownership" within three years of death, the policy proceeds are includible in the decedent's gross estate. See IRC §2042. See the discussion at MTG ¶2914.

Valuation

When Valued. Generally, assets includible in the gross estate must be valued as of the date of death. An "alternate" valuation date election can be made to value property as of six months after the date of death (or for property disposed of prior to that date, the value at the date of disposition). This election should be considered if it results in reduced estate tax liability. The election is made by checking a box on Form 706. See MTG ¶1633 and ¶2922.

Valuation Guide	
Asset	**Comments**
Real estate	Attach copy of appraisal from qualified real estate appraiser to Form 706.
	• Be sure that the appraiser breaks out buildings and other land improvements from the land.
	• If an undivided or fractional interest is owned, consider whether a discount for lack of market-ability and/or cost to partition is appropriate. See, e.g., *E. Pillsbury Est.*, 64 TCM 284, CCH Dec. 48,378(M), TC Memo. 1992-425.
	• Consider whether the estate qualifies for special use valuation. See example on page 14–9. See Schedule A-1 and related instructions for Form 706.
	• Consider whether an exclusion for a qualified conservation easement applies. See Schedule U of Form 706.
Art, collectibles	Appraisals are needed for any item or collection of similar items valued in excess of $3,000 (e.g., jewelry, furs, silverware, paintings, etchings, engravings, antiques, books, statuary, vases, oriental rugs, coin or stamp collections). Review the insurance policy for any riders.
Closely held business	• Valuation needed of underlying business and assets, plus appraisal of decedent's ownership interest (i.e., stock or partnership interest). See Treas. Reg. §20.2031-2 when valuing stock and Reg. §20.2031-3 when valuing other business interests.
	• Determine if any buy-sell agreement exists. See *G. Blount Est.*, 87 TCM 1303, CCH Dec. 55,636(M), TC Memo. 2004-116, aff'd in part and rev'd and rem'd in part, CA-11, 2005-2 USTC ¶60,509 (factors for determining when price set in buy-sell agreement controls).

Valuation Guide (continued)

Asset	Comments
Stocks, bonds	Determine the mean between lowest and highest selling prices for publicly traded securities quoted on the valuation date.
Life insurance on another	Obtain Form 712 from insurance company for each policy.

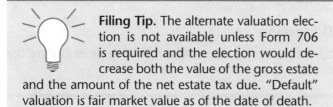

Filing Tip. The alternate valuation election is not available unless Form 706 is required and the election would decrease both the value of the gross estate and the amount of the net estate tax due. "Default" valuation is fair market value as of the date of death.

Valuation Rules. Fair market value is the standard used to value the decedent's property. See MTG ¶1633, ¶1695, ¶1697 and ¶2922.

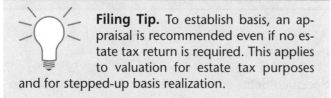

Filing Tip. To establish basis, an appraisal is recommended even if no estate tax return is required. This applies to valuation for estate tax purposes and for stepped-up basis realization.

The basis of real or personal property acquired from a decedent is generally "stepped up" to its fair market value on the decedent's date of death, or on the alternate valuation date or the special use valuation date. IRC §1014. Records indicating basis and appraisal value are important.

No step-up in basis is allowed for appreciated property acquired by the decedent through gift within one year of death if the property passes, directly or indirectly, from the donee-decedent to the original donor or the donor's spouse. See IRC §1014(e).

Special Use Valuation. An estate's personal representative may elect to value real property includible in a decedent's estate that is used for farming purposes or for closely held business use on the basis of the property's actual use, rather than on the traditional basis of "highest or best" use. The personal representative may make this election if the following conditions are met:

- The decedent must have been a resident or citizen of the United States.
- The property must pass to a qualified heir and a recapture agreement must be filed.
- The property must be devoted to a qualified use on the date of the decedent's death.
- The decedent or a member of the decedent's family must have owned the qualifying property and have ma-

terially participated in the operation of the farm or other business for a required period. See Reg. §20.2032A-3.
- The adjusted value of the real and personal property used in the farm or closely held business must comprise at least 50 percent of the adjusted value of the decedent's gross estate.
- At least 25 percent of the adjusted value of the gross estate must be qualified real property.

The amount by which the value of qualifying real property can be reduced under the special use valuation provisions is limited to $1,070,000 for 2013.

Example. Dick Brown, a widower, owns farmland worth $4,500,000, which he leases on a crop-share basis to a tenant. He has owned this land for 40 years. He is active in the management of the farm and shares crop expenses with the tenant. He reports the farm income as self-employment income. He has other assets of $2,000,000. His will provides that the farm land go to his two children equally. His son Darrell is interested in the farm and plans to take over the management of the farm upon his father's death. His other son, Dave, is not interested in farm management. A farm management fee will be paid to Darrell based on a percentage of farm income.

Upon Dick's death, his estate will be able to make an election to have the farm land valued pursuant to IRC §2032A. The property's value under the special use valuation provision is $3 million. The gross estate will be reduced by only $1,070,000. Although the difference in value is $1.5 million ($4.5 million less $3 million), IRC §2032A limits the reduction in the value of the land to $1,070,000 if Dick dies in 2013. Thus, Dick's taxable estate would be $5,430,000. The federal estate tax savings of electing §2032A will be $428,000.

*State death tax deduction not taken into account. Example illustrates federal estate tax only.

Note that the basis of the land to Dick's sons is its value as determined under the special-use valuation provision (i.e., the basis in the land would be $3 million).

To avoid losing this benefit, the farm must continue to be owned and managed by members of Dick's family for 10 years.

Planning Tip. A sole proprietor who operates an ongoing business and whose heirs may or may not be interested in continuing the business should discuss the handling of the business with legal counsel. Options available may include rolling the enterprise into the estate for disposition, or creating a new entity to enable business continuation.

Discounts. The valuation of a gross item may be subject to discounts. Discounts in value vary according to the type of property.

 Planning Tip. Family limited partnerships (FLPs) have been the subject of much attention and litigation between taxpayers and the IRS. The primary estate and gift tax benefit of an FLP is the ability to claim substantial discounts on the value of the partnership interest in some cases. FLPs, if properly set up and operated, are still an effective estate planning tool. See, *e.g., D. Kimbell, Sr., Exr.,* CA-5, 2004-1 USTC ¶60,486, 371 F3d 257, rev'g and rem'g DC Tex, 2003-1 USTC ¶60,455, 244 F Supp2d 700.

 Example. John Farmer transfers $2,000,000 of farmland to a family limited partnership. He then makes gifts of 10% interests in the partnership. Although the value of the farmland allocable to the 10% interests is $200,000, the value of a minority partnership interest is $120,000 if a 40% discount is applied.

For example, real estate may be discounted for the ownership of a fractional interest, market absorption, or potential environmental issues.

Stock, either publicly traded or closely held, may be subject to discounts for blockage, restricted securities, lack of marketability, minority interest, key-person, or built-in capital gains.

Deductions

Specified expenses are deductible in determining the taxable estate.

 Planning Tip. If expenses are of no benefit on Form 706 (e.g., not a taxable estate), consider claiming them as income tax deductions for the estate. See Treas. Reg. §1.642(g)-1 for the statement required to be attached to the income tax return.

Also deductible are any uncompensated casualty losses incurred by the estate.

Specified debts are deductible in determining the taxable estate.

Filing Tip. Some liabilities (e.g., property taxes, state income tax liability) are deductible on both Form 706 and for income tax purposes.

Liability Guide	
Liability	**Comments**
Mortgage and accrued interest expenses	Reference to the real property to which it relates on appropriate schedule.
Property taxes	Limited to the taxes accrued before death of decedent. See Treas. Reg. §20.2053-6(b).
State income taxes	Include for year of death and any prior year unpaid as of death. For Married Filing Jointly, determine decedent's share of joint liability. See Treas. Reg. §20.2053-6(f).
State intangible, personal property, other taxes	Determine if liability existed as of death.
Unpaid child support or alimony	Review divorce decree and property settlement.
Outstanding checks	If checks are in discharge of bona fide legal obligations or for charitable purposes and honored by the bank after death, then they reduce the bank balance. Gifts to noncharitable donees in the form of a check that are not paid until after the death of the decedent are includible in the gross estate. See, *e.g., J. Gagliardi Est.,* 89 TC 1207, CCH Dec. 44,393.

Filing Tip. Review amounts paid for at least six months after death to determine if the liability existed at the date of death. If it did not, then consider whether payment qualifies as an administrative expense.

State Death Taxes. For decedents dying after 2004, a deduction is available for state death taxes paid. This permanently replaces the credit for state death taxes that was phased out as a result of the Economic Growth and Tax Relief Reconciliation Act of 2001 (EGTRRA) (P.L. 107-16). The deduction is allowed for the amount of any estate, inheritance, legacy, or succession taxes paid to any state or the District of Columbia with respect to property included in the gross estate.

Marital Deduction. A married person's estate is allowed a deduction for property (both probate and non-probate) passing to the surviving spouse. Such amounts are reported on Schedule M of Form 706.

 Planning Tip. Legally married same-sex couples will be treated as surviving spouses for estate and gift tax marital deduction purposes (E. Windsor, SCt., 2013-2 USTC ¶60,667). The validity of the marriage is determined by the state of celebration, i.e. where the marriage took place, and not the couple's domicile (Rev. Rul. 2013-17).

Assets that pass tax-free to a spouse in this way include the following:

- Jointly owned property;
- Life insurance;
- Retirement benefits; and
- Bequests in the will or property passing in trust.

 Caution. If the surviving spouse is not a U.S. citizen, the marital deduction may be available only if the property passes through a qualified domestic trust (QDOT). See IRC §2056A.

If a surviving spouse is provided an income interest (only) in property, either outright or via a trust, then the personal representative needs to consider making a qualified terminable interest property (QTIP) election in order to qualify the interest for the marital deduction. See IRC §2056(b)(7).

 Example. Mark Thompson's will provides that all of his property, net of taxes and expenses, passes to a trust. His wife is entitled to all the income of the trust, to be paid quarterly. Upon her death, the trust terminates and passes to Mark's children by his first marriage. Mark dies in 2013. Mark's gross estate less expenses is $7,800,000. If the QTIP election is not made with Mark's estate tax return, his estate will owe federal tax of $1,020,000. By making the QTIP election as to one-third of the trust ($7,800,000 × 1/3 = $2,600,000), no estate taxes will be payable on Mark's death. One-third of the value of the trust at the time of his wife's death will be taxable in her estate. The estate taxes attributable to the inclusion of a portion of the trust in her estate are reimbursable out of the trust.

*State death tax deduction not taken into account. Example illustrates federal estate tax only.

Caution. The marital deduction is reduced to the extent it is chargeable for estate taxes or expenses.

Expense Guide

Expense	Comments
Funeral	Reduce by any amounts that were reimbursed, such as VA or Social Security death benefits.
Attorney, accountant	Can deduct reasonable amount that is not yet paid at time of filing, if amount is ascertainable with reasonable certainty and will be paid.
Executor commissions	If one is the sole beneficiary of the estate, it may be advantageous to claim these since the estate tax benefit will be more than the income tax cost. Generally, such fees are subject to income tax but not self-employment tax (if no business is being managed for the estate).
Maintaining or storing estate property	Deductible if it is not possible to immediately distribute property to beneficiaries. See Treas. Reg. §20.2053-3(d)(1). Also see *M. Millikin Est.*, 76 TCM 1076, CCH Dec. 53,009(M), TC Memo. 1998-456.
Selling expenses	Deductible if necessary to pay estate tax liabilities and expenses. Must not be for the benefit of beneficiaries. See Treas. Reg. §20.2053-3(d)(2) and *M. Millikin Est., above.*

Charitable Deductions. Amounts passing outright to qualified charitable organizations are fully deductible. If a partial interest is provided for (e.g., an income interest or a remainder interest to a charity), then specific requirements must be met to qualify for the estate tax charitable deduction.

The charitable deduction is reduced by any administrative expenses and death taxes allocable to the property being transferred to the charity. However, if the expenses are payable out of income generated during administration by assets allocable to a charitable trust, then the deduction is not reduced. See *O. Hubert Est.*, SCt, 97-1 USTC ¶60,261, 117 SCt 1124.

 Caution. Property passing to a charity by will cannot be deducted on the income tax return of the estate. Conversely, property transferred to a charity, but not pursuant to the will, does not qualify as an estate tax deduction but may be deductible for income tax purposes.

Be sure that charitable beneficiaries qualify for the deduction. Resources can be found at the "Exempt Organizations Select Check" page of the IRS website (http://www.irs.gov/Charities-&-Non-Profits/Exempt-Organizations-Select-Check). Donors can also confirm an organization's charitable status by calling the IRS at 1-877-829-5500 (toll-free).

Tax

The estate tax is based on the taxable estate. The taxable estate equals the gross estate less all allowable deductions and losses, plus any taxable gifts made after December 31, 1976. The resulting sum is the amount on which the tentative estate tax is calculated.

Credits against Tax

The following credits are available to reduce the estate tax:

- Applicable credit;
- Credit for gift taxes on pre-1977 gifts;
- Credit for foreign death taxes; and
- Credit for tax on prior transfers.

Applicable Credit. The applicable credit and exclusion are based on the year of death.

Applicable Credit and Exclusion 2003-2013

Year	Exclusion	Credit
2003	$1,000,000	$ 345,800
2004-2005	1,500,000	555,800
2006-2008	2,000,000	780,800
2009	3,500,000	1,455,800
2010-2011	5,000,000	1,730,800
2012	5,120,000	1,772,800
2013	5,250,000	2,045,800

Unified Transfer Tax Rate Schedule for Tax Years After 2012

Taxable Amount			
Over	Not Over	Tax	Rate of Tax on Excess over Lower Number of Taxable Amount Range (%)
$0	$10,000	$0	18
10,000	20,000	1,800	20
20,000	40,000	3,800	22
40,000	60,000	8,200	24
60,000	80,000	13,000	26
80,000	100,000	18,200	28
100,000	150,000	23,800	30
150,000	250,000	38,800	32
250,000	500,000	70,800	34
500,000	750,000	155,800	37
750,000	1,000,000	248,300	39
1,000,000		345,800	40

The applicable exclusion amount for a surviving spouse who dies in 2013 is the sum of the basic exclusion amount ($5.25 million), plus the aggregate deceased spousal unused exclusion amount. The DSUE amount is the lesser of (1) the surviving spouse's basic exclusion amount, or (2) the last deceased spouse's applicable exclusion amount minus the amount with respect to which the tentative tax is determined on the last deceased spouse's estate. In order for the surviving spouse's estate to use predeceased spouse's unused exclusion amount, each spouse must die after 2010, and the predeceased spouse's estate must have timely filed a complete Form 706 and not opted out of portability of the DSUE amount. See IRC §2010(c), Temp. Reg. §§20.2010-2T and 20.2010-3T, and Instructions to Form 706.

Credit for Taxes on Pre-1977 Gifts. A credit is allowed for gift taxes paid on pre-1977 gifts includible in the donor's gross estate under any one of the estate tax provisions that make prior gifts includible in the donor's estate. The credit is generally the same as the estate tax attributable to including the gift in the estate, but cannot be more than the gift tax paid.

Maximum Transfer Tax Rates 2003-2013	
2003	49%
2004	48%
2005	47%
2006	46%
2007-2009	45%
2010-2012	35%*
2013	40%

* For 2010 only: Estate may opt out of estate tax and apply modified carryover basis to property acquired from decedent; estate tax exclusion = $5 million; gift tax exclusion = $1 million

Credit for Foreign Death Taxes. A credit is available for foreign death taxes paid on property located in a foreign country but included in the gross estate of a U.S. citizen or resident. Because the United States has entered into estate tax conventions with many countries, determine whether a treaty applies. The estate must file Form 706-CE to claim the credit.

Credit for Tax on Prior Transfers. If the decedent owned property acquired from a person who died within 10 years before his or her death or 2 years after, then a credit, limited to the additional estate tax resulting from inclusion in the decedent's estate, is available for estate tax paid on the property in the transferor's estate.

State Estate Tax

Prior to 2002. Most states imposed an estate tax equal to the maximum credit allowed by the federal estate tax prior to the enactment of EGTRRA. Generally, a separate return was required by the state with payment at the same time as the federal tax.

Changes Enacted by EGTRRA. Starting in 2002, EGTRRA phased out the benefit of the state death tax credit. The credit was reduced by 25% for 2002, 50% for 2003, 75% for 2004, then fully phased out in 2005 and replaced with a deduction for state death taxes paid. The credit was permanently repealed by the American Taxpayer Relief Act of 2012 (P.L. 112-240) ("2012 Act").

As a result of the credit phaseout, many states have "de-coupled" from the federal tax law and reestablished the state estate tax as an amount equal to the federal credit before the phaseout. Specific state statutes should be examined.

Caution. As a result of states de-coupling from the federal estate tax, the marginal rate of the combined federal and state death tax has increased.

Planning Tip. Many states do not impose a gift tax. Thus, making gifts is an effective way to avoid state estate or inheritance tax. In some cases, "deathbed" gifts should be considered.

Pre-EGTRRA Exclusion Levels for De-coupled States		
Year	Exclusion	Credit
2002-2003	$700,000	$229,800
2004	$850,000	$287,300
2005	$950,000	$326,300
2006 and later	$1,000,000	$345,800

States that have de-coupled include the District of Columbia, Hawaii, Illinois (*re*-coupled estate tax to IRC only for estates of decedents dying in 2010), Massachusetts, Minnesota, New York, Rhode Island, and Vermont. Other states have adopted a alternative form of estate taxation, including Connecticut, Delaware, Iowa, Kentucky, Louisiana, Maine, Maryland, Nebraska, New Jersey, Ohio, Oregon, Pennsylvania, Tennessee and Washington. Arizona, Kansas, North Carolina, Ohio, and Oklahoma have repealed their state estate tax systems.

Caution. Executors and practitioners should consult the estate, inheritance, or death tax rules of the appropriate state.

Payment of Estate Tax

Generally, payment of the federal estate tax liability is due with the filing of the return, 9 months after the date of death. The IRS may extend the time for payment up to 12 months or, if reasonable cause exists, up to 10 years.

Election to Pay Estate Tax in Installments. If the value of a farm or other closely held business exceeds 35% of the "adjusted gross estate," then an election can be made to defer the tax attributable to such property. The tax subject to the election can be deferred up to 5 years (paying interest only) with installments payable after that up to 10 years. The adjusted gross estate for this purpose is:

> Gross estate
>   − Expenses, debts, and taxes
>   − Losses
> Adjusted gross estate

Conditions

- Must be an active business (i.e., must not consist of passive assets) except for persons holding real estate investments who have an active role in the property's management. See Rev. Rul. 2006-34.
- If an interest in a partnership or corporation, then such interest must represent 20% or more of the capital of a partnership or 20% or more of the value of the voting interests in the corporation.
- An aggregate disposition of 50% or more of the closely held business will result in an acceleration of the tax due.

Interest is payable on the unpaid tax as follows:

- 2% on the amount of estate tax if the taxable estate was $1,430,000 for decedents dying in 2013 plus the exemption equivalent amount ($5,250,000 for 2013) minus the applicable credit amount ($2,045,800 in 2013). The maximum amount eligible for the two-percent rate for 2013 is $572,000 (a $2,617,800 tentative tax on $6,680,000, less the applicable credit of $2,045,800). See IRC §6601(j).
- The interest rate on any tax deferred in excess of the above amount is 45% of the IRS rate being charged on underpayments, determined quarterly per IRC §6621. For fourth quarter 2013, the rate is 3%; therefore the §6166 rate is 1.35% (45% × 3%).

Caution. The interest expense is not deductible for income or estate tax purposes.

Example. Richard Freeman died June 30, 2013, owning 100% of the stock of Freeman, Inc., which is an active business. The value of the stock at his date of death is $5,000,000. Richard's other assets, net of expenses, total $1,500,000. Thus, his adjusted gross and taxable estate is $6,500,000. His federal estate tax is $500,000. The portion of this tax eligible for deferral under IRC §6166 is $384,615 ($500,000 × $5,000,000/$6,500,000). The balance of $115,385 is due March 30, 2014. The portion of the deferred tax eligible for the 2% interest rate is the entire amount of the deferral, $384,615, since this is less than the maximum amount eligible for the 2% rate, $572,500.
  * State death tax deduction not taken into account. Example illustrates federal estate tax only.

Redemption of Stock to Pay Estate Tax. If stock in a closely held corporation is 35% or more of the gross estate, then the corporation may redeem part or all of the stock to pay estate taxes and administrative expenses. A portion of the distribution in redemption qualifies for sale or exchange treatment (usually resulting in capital gain).

Federal Gift Tax

General Rule. The primary purpose of the gift tax is to prevent persons from avoiding the estate tax by gifting away their property during their lifetime. To that end, the gift tax is imposed using the same rate structure as the federal estate tax.

A gift given in the three years prior to a donor's death may be included in the donor's estate, if it was a gift of life insurance or of an interest in property over which the donor retained powers. See MTG ¶2914.

Valuation. Generally the same considerations apply to determining the amount of a gift as are used in determining one's gross estate (see pages 14-8 to 14-10), but there are no alternate valuation dates. The amount of a gift is the excess of the value of property transferred over any consideration received.

Exclusions and Deductions

Annual Exclusion. Each person is allowed an annual exclusion for 2013 of up to $14,000 per donee. The amount of the annual exclusion is subject to adjustment based on changes in the consumer price index. If a spouse consents to "splitting" a gift, then a person can give up to $28,000 per donee. A separate gift tax return must be filed for each spouse to effect the splitting.

Planning Tip. Legally married same-sex couples will be treated as surviving spouses for gift splitting purposes (E. Windsor, SCt., 2013-2 USTC ¶60,667). The validity of the marriage is determined by the state of celebration, i.e. where the marriage took place, and not the couple's domicile (Rev. Rul. 2013-17).

A person can pay another's educational or medical expenses and not have this count against the annual exclusion.

Caution. Educational or medical expenses of another person must be paid directly to the provider of services to be excludable from the annual tax-free gift limit.

To qualify for the annual exclusion, the gift must be of a present interest and not a future interest. For example, if one transfers property to a trust and keeps the income for 10 years and then provides that the property go to his son, the remainder interest passing to the son would not qualify as a present interest. An exception to this is a gift to a trust for the benefit of a minor if the minor will be entitled to the assets of the trust at age 21.

 Gray Area. The U.S. Court of Appeals for the 7th Circuit held in *A. Hackl*, CA-7, 2003-2 USTC ¶60,465, 335 F.3d 664, that gifts of membership interests in a limited liability company that owned tree farms did not qualify for the annual exclusion because they were gifts of future interests. In light of this case, consider giving donees of such interests a right to withdraw assets (*Crummey* power), or gift cash and then sell the interests to the donees.

Marital Gifts. A person can make unlimited gifts to his or her spouse, provided the spouse is a citizen. No return is required for gifts to a citizen spouse.

 Planning Tip. Legally married same-sex couples will be treated as surviving spouses for estate and gift tax marital deduction purposes (*E. Windsor*, SCt., 2013-2 USTC ¶60,667). The validity of the marriage is determined by the state of celebration, i.e. where the marriage took place, and not the couple's domicile (Rev. Rul. 2013-17).

Charitable Gifts. Outright transfers to qualifying organizations are not subject to gift tax or reporting requirements. However, if a return is required to report noncharitable gifts, then any gifts to charity must also be reported. See the discussion on pages 14-12 regarding charitable transfers for estate tax purposes.

Planning Tip. Charitable gifts of appreciated assets are deductible for income tax purposes at their fair market value. No tax is payable on the appreciation.

Gift Tax Exclusion. Each person has a lifetime exclusion from tax on taxable gifts up to $5.25 million for 2013 (as indexed for inflation).

Return Filing Requirements. An annual gift tax return is required for reporting any taxable gift and/or effecting gift splitting between spouses. Form 709 is due April 15 following the year of the gift. Any tax due is payable at that time also.

Basis to Recipients of Gifts. The donor's cost basis and holding period generally carry over to the recipient.

 Filing Tip. Be sure to notify, in writing, the persons to whom you made gifts, regarding your basis in the asset, its fair market value at the date of the gift, and the date you acquired the property.

Exception. If the fair market value of the property is less than the donor's basis at the date of gift, then upon a subsequent disposition of the property by the donee: (1) the basis, for purposes of determining loss, is the fair market value; and (2) for purposes of computing gain, the basis is equal to the donor's basis in the transferred property.

Federal Generation-Skipping Transfer Tax

The purpose of the generation-skipping transfer (GST) tax is to prevent families from avoiding estate tax in younger generations by skipping a generation and transferring property to the next generation. For example, suppose Jack Green dies with a $10,000,000 estate and leaves all his property in trust with income payable to his children, and upon their death the trust assets go to his grandchildren. Jack's estate will be subject to the estate tax. However, on the subsequent death of his children, none of the trust property will be taxable in the children's estate; the family would have "skipped" a generation of estate taxes. The GST tax is designed to minimize this result by imposing a tax comparable to the estate tax on the "skip."

Transfers Subject. There are three types of transfers subject to the GST tax:

- Direct skip (e.g., a transfer from grandparent to grandchild)
- Taxable distribution (e.g., in the above Jack Green example, if the trust makes a distribution of principal to the grandchildren)
- Taxable termination (e.g., in the above Jack Green example, a transfer upon the termination of the trust)

Exclusions. As is the case with the gift tax, an annual exclusion from the GST tax of $14,000 (for 2013) is generally available, as well as the exclusion for payment of medical and educational expenses. However, for gifts to trusts, the annual exclusion may not be available unless the trust provides the beneficiaries the right to withdraw an amount that does not exceed the gift tax annual exclusion amount.

Generation-Skipping Transfers: Filing the Return and Paying the Tax

Type of Transfer	Where Reported	When Due	Person Responsible
Direct skips at death	Form 706, Schedules R and R-1	With estate tax, generally nine months after death (IRC §6166 deferral may be available)	Executor or personal representative
Direct skips during life	Form 709	April 15 following year of transfer	Transferor
Taxable distributions	Form 706-GS(D)	April 15 following year of transfer	Transferee
Taxable terminations	Form 706-GS(T)	April 15 following year of transfer	Trustee

Exemption. Each individual has a lifetime exemption from the GST tax. The exemption is the same as the estate tax applicable exclusion amount ($5,250,000 in 2013).

Planning Tip. The GST tax exemption is not portable between spouses. Any unused portion of a decedent's available exemption is lost.

Rate of Tax. The GST tax rate is 40% for 2013.

Income Taxation After Death

Who Is Liable for Tax?

Income and expenses up to the date of death are reportable in the final Form 1040 of the decedent (and spouse, if filing jointly). (See pages 14-4 to 14-5 for discussion.) Income and expenses subsequent to death depend on the asset and the reason for the expense.

Probate Assets. Generally, probate assets do not pass directly to heirs but are subject to administration as part of the decedent's estate. Income on any assets that are subject to probate must be accounted for separately and reported on a fiduciary income tax return (Form 1041) for the estate. A separate estate checking account should be opened shortly after death by the personal representative, and all income and expenses should be paid out of that account. Also, all payers of income on probate assets should be notified as soon as possible of the change in ownership of the estate and provided with the estate's employer identification number (EIN). (See page 14-3 for probate asset examples, and page 14-4 for how to obtain an EIN.)

When probate assets are transferred to the heirs of the estate, the payers of income also should be notified of the transfer. Income and expenses related to such assets after transfer to the heir are reportable by the recipient.

Non-Probate Assets. The recipient of any assets passing outside of probate is responsible for reporting any income and related expenses subsequent to death.

Example. Jack Green owned 100 shares of XYZ company as a joint tenant with his son, Jim. Jack died on April 9, 2013. A dividend of $50 was paid to Jack and Jim on April 30, 2013. This dividend should be reported by Jim in his 2013 individual income tax return.

Basis of Assets Acquired from Decedent

The basis of assets acquired from a decedent, whether by probate or otherwise, is necessary in determining the following:

- Gain or loss on the subsequent disposition of the property.
- Depreciation on depreciable assets.

Current Law

In General. Under current law, the basis of assets acquired from a decedent is generally the fair market value at the date of death. If an estate tax return (Form 706) was filed and the alternate valuation election was made, then the basis is the value used for that purpose.

Example. Shirley makes a gift of XYZ stock on February 28, 2013, to her daughter. She originally purchased the stock on January 14, 2006, for $12,000. At the time of her gift, the value of the stock was $10,000. Her daughter sells the stock on March 15, 2013, for $9,000. Her daughter recognizes a long-term capital loss of $1,000. If she had sold it for $13,500, she would have recognized a long-term capital gain of $1,500. If she had sold it for $11,000, she would not have recognized a gain or a loss.

Filing Tip. Be sure to report to heirs the basis of assets distributed to or received by them.

 Caution. Although the adjustment of basis to fair market value at the date of death is referred to as "stepped-up basis," it can also result in a "step down" in basis if the fair market value is less than the decedent's basis.

 Example. Bob and Mary Carver owned, as joint tenants with the right of survivorship, a residential rental property that they had acquired for $150,000. They had allocated $15,000 to the cost of land and depreciated the balance of $135,000 using 27.5-year MACRS. Bob died on June 29, 2013. The property was appraised at $200,000, with $20,000 of that allocable to land. For the period before his death, Bob and Mary would be entitled to depreciation, using the mid-month convention, of $135,000/ 27.5 years × 5.5 months/12 months = $2,250. For the period after Bob's death, two calculations are necessary.

Calculation 1: Depreciation on Bob's interest would be based on one-half of the value at the date of his death (i.e., $90,000/27.5 years × 6.5 months/12 months, or $1,772.73).

Calculation 2: Depreciation on Mary's interest would be calculated using the MACRS depreciation formula used before Bob's death (i.e., $67,500/27.5 years × 6.5 months/12 months, or $1,329.55). Mary's interest in half of the property would continue to be reduced by one-half of the accumulated depreciation that had been claimed on the property prior to Bob's death.

Thus total depreciation to be claimed on the 2013 joint return would be $2,250.00 + $1,772.73 + $1,329.55 = $5,352.28.

 Planning Tip. As a matter of "deathbed" planning, consider selling "loss" assets prior to death.

Special Rules. The basis of property that is "income in respect of a decedent" (IRD) is not adjusted. See "Income and Deductions in Respect of a Decedent," following, for a discussion of IRD and how it is taxed.

One-half of the basis of property jointly owned with a spouse is adjusted to fair market value. The survivor's half is determined by reference to the basis prior to death.

 Caution. If the jointly owned property was acquired prior to 1977, then up to 100% of the property may be eligible for adjustment to fair market value at the date of death. See *T. Hahn,* 110 TC 140, CCH Dec. 52,606 (Acq.).

For property that was purchased and jointly owned with a nonspouse, the percentage of the cost of the property that the decedent contributed determines the amount includible in the decedent's estate. Basis is adjusted to this extent.

The surviving spouse's share of community property takes the same basis as the decedent's if at least one-half of the entire community interest is included in the gross estate. Thus, 100% of the basis is adjusted.

The basis of property subject to the special-use election is reduced by the amount of reduction in value. See the example on page 14-9.

Holding Period

Property acquired from a decedent is deemed to have been owned for more than one year, thus qualifying for more favorable long-term capital gain treatment.

 Example. John Smith owned 100 shares of XYZ company as a joint tenant with his son, Tom. John died on April 9, 2013. John had paid $2,000 for 100% of the stock. The value at the date of John's death was $5,000. Tom sells the stock on September 14, 2013, for $6,000. Tom has a long-term capital gain of $1,000.

Income and Deductions in Respect of a Decedent

Definition. Income in respect of a decedent (IRD) is any right to receive income as of the date of a decedent's death that would have been includible in the decedent's gross income had the decedent received it prior to death.

Examples of Income in Respect of Decedent

- Salary received after death
- Retirement income from IRAs (other than Roth), 401(k) plans, 403(b) plans, qualified profit sharing plans, etc.
- Interest income accrued but not paid as of death
- Dividends that are payable after death even though declared prior to death
- Increase in redemption value (interest) of U.S. savings bonds (series E, EE, H, HH, or I) if IRC §454(a) election to recognize income is not made
- Crops on hand held by landlord
- Installment obligations
- Life insurance commissions

Life insurance proceeds do not represent income in respect of a decedent and are not subject to income tax when received.

Deductions in respect of a decedent are obligations of the decedent that would have been deductible by the decedent had they been paid prior to death.

Examples of Deductions in Respect of a Decedent

- State income taxes due on final state income tax form
- Property taxes
- Business expenses

Income Taxation. Any IRD is taxable to the person who receives it. Thus, if the item is an asset subject to probate and is received by the estate, it is reportable by the estate. If it is received by a trust, then it is reportable by the trust. If received by an individual, then it is taxable to the individual when received.

The character of the income is the same as it would have been in the hands of the decedent (e.g., ordinary or capital gain).

For distributions from retirement plans, it is the actual distribution from the plan that is taxable, not the transfer of the interest in the plan.

Any item of IRD is taxable only to the extent it would have been taxable to the decedent (i.e., the decedent's basis in the item carries over).

Example. Jack Sage used the cash method of accounting. At the time of his death, he was entitled to receive $12,000 from clients for his services and he had accrued bond interest of $8,000, for a total income in respect of the decedent of $20,000. He also owed $5,000 for business expenses for which his estate is liable. The income and expenses are reported on Jack's estate tax return. The tax on Jack's estate is $11,250 after credits. The net value of the items included as income in respect of the decedent is $15,000 ($20,000 – $5,000). The estate tax determined without including the $15,000 in the taxable estate is $4,500, after credits. The estate tax that qualifies for the deduction is $6,750 ($11,250 – $4,500).

Recipient's deductible part. Wilma Krause is the recipient. Figure her part of the deductible estate tax by dividing the estate tax value of the items of income in respect of the decedent included in her income (the numerator) by the total value of all items included in the estate that represents income in respect of the decedent (the denominator). If the amount included in the recipient's income is less than the estate tax value of the item, use the lesser amount in the numerator.

As the beneficiary of Jack's estate, Wilma collects the $12,000 accounts receivable from his clients. She will include the $12,000 in her income in the tax year she receives it. If she itemizes her deductions in that tax year, she can claim an estate tax deduction of $4,050, figured as follows:

$$\frac{\text{Value included in income}}{\text{Total value of IRD}} \times \begin{array}{c}\text{The overall amount}\\\text{of estate tax that}\\\text{qualified for the}\\\text{deduction}\end{array} = \text{Deduction}$$

$$\frac{\$12{,}000}{\$20{,}000} \times \$6{,}750 = \$4{,}050$$

If the amount Wilma collects for the accounts receivable turns out to be more than $12,000, she would still claim $4,050 as an estate tax deduction because only the $12,000 actually reported on the estate tax return can be used in the above computation. However, if she collected less than the $12,000 reported on the estate tax return, she would use the smaller amount to figure the estate tax deduction.

Deductions in respect of a decedent are deductible when paid by the estate or the person who is liable for the obligation.

Deduction for Estate Tax Attributable to IRD. The person receiving and reporting an item of IRD is entitled to a deduction for the estate tax attributable to the income. See IRC §691(c). This is determined as follows:

1. Subtract all deductions in respect of a decedent from all items of income in respect of a decedent.
2. Determine estate tax on taxable estate excluding the net amount in step 1.
3. Subtract amount in step 2 from total estate tax.
4. Divide the amount of IRD being reported in the current return by the total IRD of the estate and multiply the result times the amount in step 3.

For individuals, the amount is deductible as an itemized deduction (not subject to the 2% limitation on miscellaneous itemized deductions). It is also deductible for alternative minimum tax purposes.

For estates, the amount is fully deductible.

Income Tax Considerations of an Estate

An estate is a separate taxable entity that must file a separate income tax return, Form 1041, if it has gross income of $600 or more. As discussed previously, income on any assets that are subject to probate must be accounted for separately and reported by the estate. The estate is generally entitled to the same deductions as an individual, with a few exceptions which are described in this section.

Administrative Expenses. Amounts paid in the administration of the estate are deductible for income tax purposes unless they have been claimed on Form 706 as deductions in arriving at the taxable estate.

The 2%-of-adjusted-gross-income floor on miscellaneous itemized deductions applies to administration expenses if they commonly or customarily would be incurred by a hypothetical individual holding the same property (*M.J. Knight, Trustee*, SCt, 2008-1 USTC ¶50,132; Proposed Reg. § 1.67-4). However, for tax years beginning before final regulations are published, estates are not required to determine the portion of a bundled fiduciary fee that is subject to the 2% floor, and may deduct 100% of the bundled fee (Notice 2011-37).

Exemption. An estate is entitled to an exemption of $600 even if the return is for a period of less than 12 months.

Investment Expenses. Investment expenses incurred by an estate are generally subject to the 2%-of-adjusted-gross-income floor. However, expenses that would not have been incurred if the property were not held by the estate are fully deductible.

Charitable Deductions. An estate is entitled to an unlimited charitable deduction for amounts that are paid or permanently set aside, pursuant to the will, out of gross income during the tax year. Amounts that are bequeathed per the will and are paid out of principal under state law are not deductible for income tax purposes.

Distributions to Beneficiaries. Income distributions made by an estate that are not payments of specific bequests are deductible by the estate and taxable to the beneficiaries. The amount of the income distributions deduction is limited to distributable net income as determined on Schedule B of Form 1041. The character of income to the beneficiaries is determined by reference to the character of the income to the estate.

Generally, capital gains are not includible in distributable net income and, therefore, are taxable to the estate. However, any capital gains in the year of termination are considered distributed to the beneficiaries and taxable to them. Details should be outlined in the governing document, and must be handled on a case-by-case basis based on a careful reading of the document.

Treatment of Payments after End of Tax Year. An estate can elect to treat distributions made up to 65 days after its tax year closes as made on the last day of that tax year.

 Planning Tip. Because the estate income tax brackets are very compressed (in 2013, the 39.6% bracket applies to taxable income over $11,950), the estate's taxable income should be determined (or at least estimated) before the 65-day period ends, and consideration given to making deductible distributions of income to the beneficiaries if they are expected to be in lower income tax brackets.
Be particularly alert if the estate has received any items of IRD, including withdrawals from qualified retirement plans.

Asset Distribution. An estate can distribute assets in lieu of cash to beneficiaries, in which case the distribution amount is the fair market value of the property at the time of distribution. No gain or loss is recognized on the distribution of property unless either of the following applies:

1. The distribution is in satisfaction of a specific bequest or designated amount.
2. The estate elects to recognize the gain or loss.

 Caution. Losses recognized on the distribution of property are not deductible because of the related-party rules of IRC §267(b).

If the estate has net capital losses or deductions in excess of income in its final year, they are passed on to the residuary beneficiaries in the year of termination.

Depreciation and Depletion. Depreciation and depletion of estate property is apportioned between the estate and its beneficiaries based on the income that is allocable to each. See IRC §167(h).

 Example. An estate has income on a rental property before depreciation of $50,000. Of this income, $20,000 is distributed to the beneficiaries of the estate. Depreciation for the year is $10,000. Depreciation of $4,000 is allocable to the beneficiaries (on Schedule K-1) ($10,000 × $20,000/$50,000); the balance of the depreciation, $6,000, is deductible by the estate.

Tax Year of an Estate. An estate's tax year starts with the date of the decedent's death. It can adopt any fiscal year end (not more than 12 months later).

 Example. Josh Burns dies February 21, 2013. The estate can adopt any month end as a fiscal year end up to January 31, 2014.

Distributions of income are deemed to be made on the last day of the tax year of the estate.

 Planning Tip. With the adoption of a fiscal year ending, January 31 in the above example, distributions of income made in 2013 would not be taxable to the beneficiaries until 2014.

Filing of Estate Income Tax Return and Payment of Tax. An estate income tax return is due the 15th day of the fourth month after the end of the tax year. Any estate income tax due is payable at such time. An estate is not required to pay estimated income tax for its first two tax years.

Caution. For the year of estate's termination, the final income tax return is due the 15th day of the fourth month after the month of termination.

Income Tax Considerations of Trusts

General Definition and Types of Trusts. A trust is a separate taxable entity for federal income tax purposes. A trust can be created pursuant to a trust agreement executed during one's lifetime or upon death pursuant to one's will (testamentary). The trustee takes title to the property in order to protect or conserve it for the beneficiaries pursuant to the directions of the grantor or decedent as expressed in the trust agreement or will.

Income Taxation. As a separate taxable entity, a trust reports all income received on assets owned by it and deducts all expenses paid by it that are otherwise deductible. It does so on Form 1041. However, if the grantor has sufficient control of trust income or principal as set forth in IRC §§671–679, the income is taxed directly to the grantor. A so-called "grantor trust" becomes a separate entity upon the grantor's death. See below for election to be treated as an estate.

Like an estate, a trust is entitled to a deduction for distributions made to its beneficiaries. Also like an estate, a trust must apportion depreciation between the trust and beneficiaries based on the income apportioned to each. However, if the trust agreement or applicable state law requires that the trust reserve from income an amount for depreciation, then depreciation, to that extent, is allocated to the trust.

A trust is entitled to an annual exemption of $300 if it is required under its terms to distribute all income currently (i.e., a simple trust); otherwise the exemption is $100.

> **Example.** A trust has income on a rental property, before depreciation, of $50,000. Of this income $20,000 is distributed to the beneficiaries of the trust. Depreciation for the year is $10,000. State law requires that the trustee reserve from income an amount for depreciation. Depreciation of $10,000 is so reserved. The $10,000 of depreciation is deductible only by the trust. The $20,000 distribution is fully taxable to the beneficiaries. The trust taxable income before exemption is $20,000 ($50,000 income less $10,000 depreciation and a deduction for distribution to beneficiaries of $20,000).

Calendar Year. Unlike an estate, a trust (other than certain charitable trusts) must be on a calendar-year basis.

Election to Be Treated as an Estate. A qualified revocable trust, upon the grantor's death, can elect along with the estate to be treated as part of the estate for income tax purposes. Making this election qualifies the trust for favorable tax treatment, including:

- The ability to report on a fiscal-year basis.
- No estimated income tax requirements for two tax years.
- Charitable deduction for amounts permanently set aside for charitable purposes.

- Deductibility of passive losses for first two tax years.
- Qualification for amortization of reforestation expenses.

The election is made by filing Form 8855 and, once made, cannot be revoked. A taxpayer identification number is necessary. This election allows the electing trust to be treated and taxed as part of its related estate during the election period. That period begins at the decedent's death and lasts for a minimum of two years. If an executor is appointed to the related estate after the election is made, the executor must agree to the election or it will terminate.

See Treas. Reg. §1.645-1 for more information.

Helping Clients Prepare Financially for Their Own Death

Whether or not an individual creates an estate plan can impact significantly what happens to the transfer of his or her property upon death, affecting:

- The probate process.
- The administration of one's financial affairs, including accounting for all assets, paying all claims, collecting income, and paying expenses during the period of administration.
- The application of income and transfer tax laws in the year of death and the subsequent period of administration.

It is prudent to plan for one's death. Failure to do so can have disastrous consequences, both financially and in terms of the survivors' well-being. This section discusses several key planning documents and considerations.

Will

The first and most important step in planning for death is to make a will. A will is a legal document that allows an individual to determine the administration and distribution of his or her estate. It also allows the individual to designate who will be responsible for his or her minor children.

Other Documents

Other documents to consider at the time of preparing or updating one's will are:

- **Living trust**–A living trust is a trust created to hold title to an individual's assets. The benefits include continuity of asset management if the individual becomes incapacitated and unable to take care of his or her financial affairs; avoidance of probate; privacy as to one's assets upon death; and possible reduced cost, time, and aggravation in settling one's estate.
- **Durable power of attorney**–This is a legal document in which an individual appoints a person to act as his or her agent as to certain personal and

financial matters in the event of specified events or at a specified time.

- **Living will**–A living will usually expresses an individual's desire not to receive extraordinary medical treatment and specifies the kind of medical care he or she would prefer under given circumstances.
- **Durable power of attorney for health care**–In this legal document, an individual designates someone to make health care decisions in the event he or she is unable to do so.

Ownership of Assets

Without careful preparation, an individual's assets at death may not go where he or she intended. Because of this, it is important to do a careful review of how one's assets are currently held. A will or living trust controls assets solely in an individual's name or in the trust's name as well as his or her portion of certain assets owned jointly with others. Assets in joint tenancy or tenancy by the entirety pass to the surviving joint owner under state law and not according to an individual's will. Assets owned as tenants in common are subject to an individual's will to the extent of his or her interest in the property.

A careful review should include beneficiary designations on the following:

- Life insurance.
- Group term life insurance.
- Annuities.
- IRAs and other retirement accounts.
- Deferred compensation contracts.

Individuals who are divorced should be especially alert to this. Although divorce generally terminates an ex-spouse's interest in probate assets, it does not terminate beneficiary designations.

It is important to consider providing for contingent or secondary beneficiaries, in case the primary beneficiary predeceases the individual or does not wish to take ownership of the asset.

Business Succession Planning

If an individual owns an interest in a closely held business, it is critically important to provide for disposition of the interest in the business and for an orderly transition after an individual's death. If the business is unincorporated, such as rental real estate or farming, the individual may consider transferring it to a family partnership or corporation. This might prevent the business assets from having to be divided up among the individual's heirs, and can facilitate management by those heirs that are active in the business.

Buy-Sell Agreement. A buy-sell agreement provides a set of rules for what is to happen to each owner's interest in the event of any of the following:

- Death.
- Disability.
- Termination of employment.
- An owner's desire to dispose of his or her interest during his or her lifetime.

This document should be reviewed at least once a year to make sure all parties agree with it and understand it.

The price set forth in the agreement may control the value to be reported in a deceased owner's estate.

 Caution. See *G. Blount Est.*, 87 TCM 1303, CCH Dec. 55,626(M), TC Memo 2004-116, aff'd in part and rev'd and rem'd in part, CA-11, 2005-2 USTC ¶60,509, for a discussion of factors that apply in determining whether a price in a buy-sell agreement is controlling for estate tax valuation purposes.

Estate Tax Planning

One of the purposes of estate tax planning is to ensure that an individual's assets are transferred to the persons or entities he or she chooses with the least federal and state estate tax cost. It is also important to consider the income tax consequences of the planned disposition of assets.

Inventory All Assets and Liabilities. The first step in estate tax planning is to prepare an inventory of all of the individual's assets and their approximate values. Note ownership (i.e., whether jointly owned and if so with whom). Also list all mortgages and other liabilities.

 Caution. Do not assume anything! Verify ownership and beneficiary designation by reference to written documents.

Who Is to Receive Income and/or Assets? Effective estate tax planning involves consideration of who is to receive interests in property and under what conditions, including transfers to:

- Spouse.
- Children.
- Other persons.
- Charitable causes.

Project Estate Tax. Based on the preceding information, project the potential estate and income taxes upon death. For a married couple, this needs to be done under two scenarios: the husband predeceasing the wife, and the wife predeceasing the husband.

Project Liquidity. Will there be enough cash to pay estate taxes and final expenses? Effective tax planning can reduce the need for cash, but even after planning, the availability of sufficient cash should be evaluated.

Checklist of Estate Planning Strategies under Current Law

Gifting

- Gifts up to the annual exclusion amount ($14,000 in 2013) completely avoid federal gift and estate tax (MTG ¶2905). Also, future appreciation on and income from the property gifted avoid estate tax.
- Gifts for education (tuition, books) and medical purposes paid directly to the institution can be made in addition to the annual exclusion amount. There is no limit on the amount of such gifts. See MTG ¶2907 for details.
- With a spouse's consent, one-half of gifts made by one spouse are deemed made by the other spouse. This increases the annual amount that can be given in 2013 with no transfer tax consequences from $14,000 to $28,000.
- Gifts to 529 plans, used to fund college education, avoid gift tax (MTG ¶899). Up to five times the annual exclusion amount (i.e., $70,000 for 2013) can be funded up front with no gift tax over a five-year period. If the donor lives five years, then the transfer is estate tax free also. Joining with a spouse can increase this limit to $140,000.
- Gifts in excess of the annual exclusion amounts should be considered. Although such gifts use some of the donor's lifetime exclusion ($5,250,000 in 2013), subsequent appreciation on such gifts avoids gift and estate taxes.

Example. Assume Jason Hamilton gifted $600,000 over and above his annual exclusion in 2000, using up $192,800 of his lifetime exemption (recalculated for 2013 rates). Assume the property appreciates to $1,000,000 by the time of his death in 2013. Also assume his remaining taxable estate is $6,000,000. His federal estate tax is $540,000. If he had not made the gift, his federal estate tax would have been $700,000—a savings of $160,000.

*State death tax deduction not taken into account. Example illustrates federal estate tax only.

- For a discussion of gifts in contemplation of death, see page 14-25.

Provide for and Optimize Marital Deduction

- The will or revocable trust can provide a formula for minimizing the amount of property passing to the surviving spouse while avoiding estate tax on the estate of the first spouse to die (i.e., maximizing the benefit of the decedent's applicable credit).
- Alternatively, a QTIP trust can be created by requiring, among other factors, that all income be payable at least annually to the surviving spouse (MTG ¶2926). Then, in connection with the filing of the estate tax return (Form 706) for the first spouse to die, a QTIP election can be made as to part or all of the trust property. This qualifies the property subject to the election for the marital deduction. On the death of the surviving spouse, the portion of the trust subject to the election is taxable to the surviving spouse's estate. (Provision should be made in the surviving spouse's will that taxes attributable to the QTIP are to be payable out of the QTIP trust.)
- Upon the death of the first spouse, a qualified disclaimer (MTG ¶2903) can be made as to property otherwise passing to the surviving spouse to keep it out of his or her taxable estate and to get full benefit of the decedent's applicable credit.
- *Portability election.* To eliminate the need for spouses to retitle property and create trusts solely to take full advantage of each spouse's basic exclusion amount, consider the portability election allowing the surviving spouses's estate to use the unused portion of the predeceased spouse's exclusion amount. See pages 14-7 and 14-12.

Sever and Avoid Joint Tenancy. Joint tenancy "preempts" any planning done through a will or living trust.

Charitable Planning. If a person has charitable interests, there are several planning considerations.

- Outright charitable bequests are fully deductible for estate tax and gift tax purposes.
- If a person wants to retain some amount of cash flow either for him- or herself or for an heir or heirs, a charitable trust may be appropriate (MTG ¶2932). For example, one could provide that, upon his death, his daughter would get an annuity equal to 5% of the amount going to a charitable trust. His estate would be entitled to a charitable deduction based on the value of the remainder interest going to the charity.
- By transferring a remainder interest in a residence or farm to a qualifying charity, one is entitled to an income tax charitable deduction and an estate tax charitable deduction.
- Consider naming a charity as beneficiary of qualified retirement plans. Upon death, qualified retirement plan assets are estate taxable as well as income taxable. By designating a charity as beneficiary of part or all of such assets, those assets go to the charity without any income or estate tax.

Life Insurance. If life insurance is a significant amount, then planning is obviously important.

- *Life insurance trust.* A life insurance trust is very effective in removing the death benefit from estate tax. An irrevocable trust is used that acquires ownership of the life insurance. Premiums are paid by the trust, usually from gifts received from the insured. Beneficiaries are usually given a right (*Crummey* power) to withdraw any gifts to the trust for a limited period of time in order to qualify the gifts as a present interest eligible for the annual exclusion amount ($14,000 in 2013). Upon the insured's death, the proceeds are paid to the trust. The trust can purchase nonliquid assets from the estate to provide cash to pay estate taxes. Such a trust usually provides for income to the surviving spouse as well as the ability to spend principal for education, medical expenses, or support and maintenance of the surviving spouse. Upon the surviving spouse's subsequent death, the trust may terminate and go to children and/or charity.

Example. Ted Blue has a taxable estate of $11,000,000, of which $4,000,000 is attributable to life insurance that Ted owns, with his wife designated as beneficiary. His will provides for the creation of a bypass trust to utilize his applicable exclusion amount, with the rest of his estate passing to his wife. Upon Ted's death in 2011, there is no estate tax payable because $5,000,000 will pass to the bypass trust (using Ted's applicable credit amount), and the remaining $6,000,000 (including the $4,000,000 in life insurance) will qualify for the marital deduction. Mrs. Blue dies in 2013, with a taxable estate of $6,000,000 (consisting of the $4,000,000 in life insurance and $2,000,000 in other property she received from Ted's estate). Mrs. Blue's estate will owe $300,000 in estate taxes.

If Ted had used a life insurance trust to acquire and hold the life insurance, and the proceeds were held in trust rather than paid outright to his wife, no estate taxes would have been payable at either Ted's death or his wife's death.

* State death tax deduction not taken into account. Example illustrates federal estate tax only, and assumes no portability election.

- *Second-to-die life insurance.* This insurance contract covers both spouses and does not pay a benefit until the second spouse dies. It is less expensive than normal life insurance. It provides funds to pay estate taxes when needed, which is usually on the second death.

Valuation. There are significant strategies to be considered that take advantage of either statutory reductions in value or valuation discounting principles.

- By qualifying for IRC §2032A, a significant discount (limited to $1,070,000 in 2013) can be achieved for qualifying farm land (MTG ¶2922).

- One should monitor the threshold requirement of 50% (i.e., qualifying farmland must meet or exceed 50% of the adjusted gross estate as defined). If one is close to this, then gifting of non-farm assets or purchasing additional farm land should be considered.
- Be sure to meet the material participation requirements either as to the owner or by providing for material participation by a "qualified heir."
- If properly structured and used, interests in family partnerships may be subject to significant discounts from the proportionate share of underlying assets.
- A properly structured buy-sell agreement can be effective to fix the value of a closely held business interest. See *H.A. True Jr., Est.*, 82 TCM 27, CCH Dec. 54 398(M), TC Memo. 2001-167, aff'd CA-10, 2004-2 USTC ¶60,495, 30 F3d 1210.

Payment of Taxes. Provisions exist that may assist the estate and heirs in financing the payment of estate taxes.

- Under IRC §6166, if a closely held business interest is more than 35% of the adjusted gross estate, then taxes allocable to such interest are eligible for up to a 14-year maximum payment period with a favorable interest rate. See page 14-13.
- IRC §303 provides that qualifying interests in closely held corporations may be redeemed by the corporation to provide cash to pay estate taxes and administrative expenses. Absent qualification under IRC §303, redemptions of stock may be treated as taxable dividend income to the estate.
- Consider acquiring life insurance if there will not be sufficient liquidity of an estate to pay taxes and expenses.

Loans. Loans to family members can effectively transfer wealth to heirs while reducing estate taxes.

- A person can loan up to $10,000 at no interest. If the loan recipient has less than $1,000 of investment income, up to $100,000 can be loaned interest free. See IRC §7872(c)(2) and (d), and Prop. Reg. §1.7872-8.
- Individuals can assist children and other heirs by loaning money (e.g., to purchase a house) at an interest rate based on the IRS adjusted federal rate (AFR), which is lower than the commercial rate that the child would otherwise borrow at. The AFR for short-term loans (three years or less) with monthly payments is published monthly.

Generation Skipping. If the children of an individual already have sizable estates, then passing part of the individual's estate to a generation-skipping trust will avoid additional estate tax on the children's death. Each individual has a generation-skipping transfer exemption ($5,250,000 in 2013). This is the maximum amount that can be transferred to the grandchildren without incurring generation-skipping transfer tax.

Example. George Street, a widower, has a $7,000,000 estate. His son Tom has an estate of $10,000,000. Tom has three children. If George dies in 2013 and leaves his estate to Tom, then Tom's estate is increased by $6,300,000 ($7,000,000 less $700,000 in federal estate taxes). Assuming a marginal estate tax bracket (federal) of 40%, this would result in $2,520,000 in additional taxes for Tom's estate. By providing that $5,250,000 of George's estate is to go to a generation-skipping trust, $2,100,000 of taxes could be avoided on Tom's death. The trust could provide for income to be payable to Tom or to Tom's children.

*State death tax deduction not taken into account. Example illustrates federal estate tax only.

Permanency of Transfer Taxes. Although the higher exclusion amount and portability, along with a higher maximum rate, were made permanent by the 2012 Act, uncertainty about the future of the federal transfer tax system remains.

Congress has considered repealing the estate tax, but so far has not done so. The status of the law leads to some uncertainty in estate planning and puts an emphasis on flexibility. Techniques that lend themselves to flexibility are:

- **Disclaimer**–By planning for the ability of survivors to disclaim part or all of their interest in the decedent's estate, one can take into account the estate and income tax law as of the time of death and use disclaimers to minimize estate tax.
- **QTIP interest**–The ability to vary the amount of property subject to the QTIP election provides the flexibility to take into account the estate and income tax law and financial factors at the time of death.

Deathbed Planning

The following strategies should be considered when a person is in failing health and/or does not expect to live much longer. If the person is not able to act because of incapacity, then an agent may be able to take action if he or she has authority under a power of attorney or as trustee of the individual's living trust.

Accelerate Distributions from Annuities and Retirement Plans. Generally, the amount in an annuity or retirement plan will be subject to income tax when received by the individual or by his or her heirs after the individual's death. Although the amount of the retirement account is taxable in one's estate, the income tax on the income (IRD) that is later payable by the heirs is not deductible for estate tax purposes. However, if the individual incurs the income tax liability prior to death, this reduces his or her taxable estate.

Charitable Gifts. Bequests provided for in one's will to a qualified charity will result in a deduction for estate tax purposes but not for income tax purposes. By making such gifts prior to death, the individual gets an income tax deduction (subject to the limitations based on adjusted gross income) and removes the gift from his or her estate.

Annual Exclusion Gifts. If the individual makes gifts that do not exceed the annual exclusion per donee ($14,000 in 2013), the amount gifted is not includible in his or her estate.

> ⚠️ **Caution.** Checks written as gifts prior to death must be cashed by the donees prior to death to be effective.

Additional Gifts. With the "de-coupling" of state estate taxes from the federal tax system, and given that most states do not impose a gift tax, additional gifts shortly prior to death can result in significant savings in estate taxes.

Recognize Losses. If the individual has unrealized losses, consider selling the assets with the losses prior to death. Upon death, the loss evaporates, with the adjustment of the basis to the (lower) fair market value at death. Taking the loss prior to death may offset other income in the individual's income tax return. Capital losses (e.g., on the sale of securities) are available only to offset capital gains and up to $3,000 of ordinary income. Potential ordinary (or IRC §1231) losses, such as on rental real estate used in a trade or business, are not limited. Also consider that the disposition of property with suspended passive losses prior to death will trigger full deductibility of the suspended loss (MTG ¶2076). Otherwise, the suspended loss is deductible in the year of death only to the extent it exceeds any increase in basis as a result of death.

> 🔍 **Example.** Ted Flynn dies in 2013. At the time of his death, he owns a rental property (passive activity) with a basis of $26,000 and suspended passive activity losses of $40,000. The property is appraised at $60,000 as of the date of Ted's death. Of the suspended loss, only $6,000 [$40,000 – increase in basis of $34,000 ($60,000 – $26,000)] is deductible on Ted's final individual income tax return.

Post-Mortem Tax Planning

Planning prior to death can be very effective. However, estate planning is often not done, or the plan created is not kept current with changes in one's financial situation and the tax laws. Nevertheless, there are still many opportunities to minimize taxes after death.

Preparing the Final Form 1040

The decedent's final tax return is discussed on pages 14-4 to 14-6. Post-mortem information must be included on the decedent's final Form 1040:

- Medical expenses incurred prior to death but paid within 12 months after death can be claimed on the final Form 1040.
- The election to report accrued series E and EE savings bond interest annually, rather than when received, may be made. In the year the election is made, previously unreported E and EE bond interest is recognized. This can be beneficial if the marginal income tax bracket of the decedent in his or her final return is lower than that of the estate or the ultimate beneficiaries.

Preparing the Estate Tax Return

The estate tax return, Form 706, is discussed on page 14-6.

- The election for alternate valuation can be made on a timely filed return, including extensions.
- An estate containing qualified farm or closely held business property passing to a qualified heir may use special valuation methods that value the property at its present use rather than its highest and best use (MTG ¶2922). The total reduction in value is limited to $1,070,000 for individuals dying in 2013.
- Personal representative's commissions, attorney's and accountant's fees, appraisal fees, court expenses, and other administrative costs can be claimed on either Form 706 or Form 1041.
- Consider maximizing executor fees if the marginal estate tax bracket is greater than the anticipated income tax bracket of the executor and the executor is the sole residuary beneficiary.
- The personal representative may elect to include in the marital deduction the value of qualified terminable interest property (QTIP), that is, property passing to the spouse, who is entitled to all the income from the property for life.
- Portability: For estates of married individuals who die in 2013, the deceased spouse's estate must timely file a complete Form 706 to allow the deceased spouse's unused exclusion amount to be used by the surviving spouse or his or her estate.
- A qualified disclaimer can be made, thus keeping the disclaimed property out of the estate of the person disclaiming and resulting in a tax-free transfer to those succeeding to the disclaimer's interest or in a charitable deduction to the estate. The disclaimer must be made within nine months of death.
- An extension of time to pay the estate tax due may be elected in the following circumstances:
  - For reasonable cause (extension up to 10 years, with interest at the statutory rate) (see IRC §6161).

- When a closely held business is a significant part of the estate (extension up to 14 years, with interest on part of the tax at 2% and on the remainder at 45% of the federal underpayment rate) (MTG ¶2939).
- When a remainder or reversionary interest is included in the estate (extension up to six months after the precedent interest terminates, with interest at the statutory rate) (see IRC §6163).
- Consider redeeming stock in a closely held corporation to provide funds to pay estate taxes and administrative expenses.

Preparing the Fiduciary Income Tax Return

A fiduciary (trustee or executor) files Form 1041 if required (see flowchart on page 14-2).

- Proper selection of a fiscal year may avoid bunching income into one tax year and allow deferral of income to the beneficiaries.
- All or part of the administration expenses may be deducted on Form 1041 as an income tax deduction rather than on Form 706 as an estate tax deduction (MTG ¶529).
- The partnership basis-adjustment election may be made in a timely filed partnership return. This results in an adjustment to fair market value to the extent of the deceased partner's interest in partnership assets (MTG ¶456).
- A distribution during administration, even a distribution of principal, is treated as a distribution of income (which is taxable to the beneficiaries in the tax year in which the estate's tax year ends) to the extent of the estate's distributable net income. This does not apply to a payment of a specific bequest of money that is distributed in not more than three installments (MTG ¶564).
- Consider distributions to spread income among the estate and beneficiaries.
- Consider an election to treat a revocable trust as part of an estate (MTG ¶516; see page 14-21).

Retirement Plan Accounts

IRAs require special attention at death. See Tab 9.

- Determine who the beneficiaries are, and advise them of minimum distribution requirements; see Treas. Reg. §§1.401(a)(9)-1 to -5 and 1.408-8.
- Advise beneficiaries of any basis in the accounts, and any related deduction for estate tax attributable to income in respect of a decedent (IRD).
- Consider a spousal rollover or the election to have a decedent's account treated as that of the spouse.
- Consider dividing IRA accounts so that each account has one beneficiary.

Caution. Information is current as of September 2013.

ALABAMA

Tax Agency Website: http://revenue.alabama.gov/index.cfm

2013 Individual Tax Rate Schedule

Single, Head of Family, Married Filing Separately:

$	0 –	500	× 2.000 %	minus	$	0
	501 –	3,000	× 4.000 %	minus		10
	3,001	and over	× 5.000 %	minus		40

Married Filing Jointly:

$	0 –	1,000	× 2.000 %	minus	$	0
	1,001 –	6,000	× 4.000 %	minus		20
	6,001	and over	× 5.000 %	minus		80

 http://www.revenue.alabama.gov/incometax/efilemain.htm

Mandated for tax preparers that filed 11 or more resident or part-year resident returns using tax preparation software. Not allowed for nonresidents. 2D barcode returns do not count as e-filed returns.

Taxpayer opt-out on Form EOO, *Taxpayer E-file Opt Out Election Form.* Attach Form EOO to tax return with 2D barcode printed on return. Reasonable cause is exception to mandate. No penalty for failure to e-file.

Filing Requirements

Form(s) to File: Form 40; Form 40NR

Due Date (General): April 15

Filing Status Options: Allowable state filing statuses include:

- Single
- Married Filing Jointly
- Married Filing Separately
- Head of Family

Alabama does not recognize same-sex marriages, civil unions, or domestic partnerships for filing status purposes.

Filing Thresholds: Residents must file if gross income exceeds threshold for applicable filing status (see below). Nonresidents must file if gross income from state sources exceeds allowable prorated personal exemption. Part-year residents must file if they meet the filing thresholds during the time they are residents. Dependents who are full-year or part-year residents must file if gross income meets the threshold amount.

Single: $4,000
Head of Family: $7,700
Married Filing Jointly (living with spouse): $10,500
Married Filing Separately (living with spouse): $5,250
Married (not living with spouse): $4,000

Where to Send Returns

Form 40, No Payment:

Alabama Department of Revenue
P.O. Box 154
Montgomery, AL 36135-0001

Form 40, Payment:

Alabama Department of Revenue
P.O. Box 2401
Montgomery, AL 36140-0001

Form 40NR:

Alabama Department of Revenue
P.O. Box 327469
Montgomery, AL 36132-7469

Alternative Minimum Tax?

No

IRC Conformity

IRC incorporated by reference as currently amended to extent of provisions directly referenced by state code.

Starting Point for Calculation of Taxable Income

Alabama gross income.

Credit for Taxes Paid to Another State Allowed?

Residents and Part-Year Residents: Yes

Nonresidents: No

Federal Return Attachment Required?

Complete copy of federal return must be attached to nonresident return if federal tax deduction is claimed; for resident and part-year resident returns, page 2 of federal return must be attached. Taxpayers must use and attach the appropriate federal form/schedule when making Alabama modifications. The state does not provide the following forms and schedules:

- Schedules C (business income) and F (farm income);
- Form 2106 (unreimbursed employee business expenses);
- Form 3903 (moving expenses);
- Form 4684 (casualty or theft losses);
- Form 4797 (other gains/losses);
- Form 6252 (installment sale income); and
- Form 8283 (noncash charitable contributions of $500 or more).

Deadline for Reporting Federal Changes

No deadline specified.

Estimated Tax Payments

Required if tax liability is at least $500.

ALASKA

Tax Agency Website: http://www.revenue.state.ak.us

Alaska does not collect personal income tax.

ARIZONA

Tax Agency Website: http://www.azdor.gov/

2013 Individual Tax Rate Schedule

Single, Married Filing Separately:

$	0	–	10,000	×	2.59 %	minus	$	0
	10,001	–	25,000	×	2.88 %	minus		29
	25,001	–	50,000	×	3.36 %	minus		149
	50,001	–	150,000	×	4.24 %	minus		589
	150,001		and over	×	4.54 %	minus		1,039

Married Filing Jointly, Head of Household:

$	0	–	20,000	×	2.59 %	minus	$	0
	20,001	–	50,000	×	2.88 %	minus		58
	50,001	–	100,000	×	3.36 %	minus		298
	100,001	–	300,000	×	4.24 %	minus		1,178
	300,001		and over	×	4.54 %	minus		2,078

Arizona is a community property state in which, generally, one-half of the community income is taxable to each spouse.

   http://www.azdor.gov/EServices. aspx

Allowed for resident, nonresident, and part-year resident returns.

Filing Requirements

Form(s) to File: Form 140; Form 140PY; Form 140NR

Due Date (General): April 15

Filing Status Options: Allowable state filing statuses include:

- Single
- Married Filing Jointly
- Married Filing Separately
- Unmarried Head of Household, including Surviving Spouse

Filing Thresholds: Residents, nonresidents, and part-year residents must file if income exceeds filing threshold for applicable filing status (see below).

> Single, Head of Household, Married Filing Separately: $5,500 (AGI) or $15,000 (gross income)
> Married Filing Jointly: $11,000 (AGI) or $15,000 (gross income)

Where to Send Returns
No Payment:

> Arizona Department of Revenue
> P.O. Box 52138
> Phoenix, AZ 85072-2138

Payment:

> Arizona Department of Revenue
> P.O. Box 52016
> Phoenix, AZ 85072-2016

Alternative Minimum Tax?
No

IRC Conformity
IRC incorporated by reference as of January 3, 2013, for tax years beginning after 2012.

Starting Point for Calculation of Taxable Income
Federal adjusted gross income.

Credit for Taxes Paid to Another State Allowed?
Yes. For nonresidents, credit allowed for taxes paid to state or country of residence if state or country of residence either exempts Arizona residents from tax on income derived from that state or country or allows Arizona residents a credit against taxes imposed by that state or country for taxes paid to Arizona. Other limitations apply.

Federal Return Attachment Required?
Copy of federal return not required. Taxpayers who itemize must attach copy of federal Schedule A.

Deadline for Reporting Federal Changes
File within 90 days after final determination of federal adjustment.

Estimated Tax Payments
Required if expected gross income exceeds $75,000 in current or preceding year ($150,000 if married filing jointly).

ARKANSAS

Tax Agency Website: http://www.state.ar.us/dfa/your_taxes.html

2012 Individual Tax Rate Schedule

$	0	–	4,099	× 1.000 %	minus	$	0
	4,100	–	8,199	× 2.500 %	minus		61.49
	8,200	–	12,199	× 3.500 %	minus		143.48
	12,200	–	20,399	× 4.500 %	minus		265.47
	20,400	–	33,999	× 6.000 %	minus		571.45
	34,000	and over		× 7.000 %	minus		911.44

Brackets indexed for inflation annually. Rates shown are 2012.

 http://www.dfa.arkansas.gov/offices/incomeTax/eFile/Pages/default.aspx

Allowed for resident, nonresident, and part-year resident returns.

Filing Requirements

Form(s) to File: Form AR1000F; Form AR1000NR

Due Date (General): April 15

Filing Status Options: Allowable state filing statuses include:

- Single
- Married Filing Jointly
- Married Filing Separately on Same Return
- Married Filing Separately on Different Returns
- Qualifying Widow or Widower with Dependent Child
- Head of Household

Filing Thresholds: Residents must file if gross income exceeds filing threshold for applicable filing status (see below). Nonresidents that received income from state sources must file regardless of income level. Part-year residents that received taxable income while a resident must file regardless of income level or source of income. If husband and wife live together and have aggregate gross income of at least $15,500, each must file a return unless income of each is included in single joint return.

> Single: $11,222
> Head of Household:
>> One or fewer dependents: $15,953
>> Two or more dependents: $19,017
> Married Filing Jointly:
>> One or fewer dependents: $18,923
>> Two or more dependents: $22,774
> Married Filing Separately: $3,999
> Surviving Spouse (with dependent child):
>> One or fewer dependents: $15,953
>> Two or more dependents: $19,017

Where to Send Returns

Tax Due:

> Arkansas State Income Tax
> P.O. Box 2144
> Little Rock, AR 72203-2144

Refund:

> Arkansas State Income Tax
> P.O. Box 1000
> Little Rock, AR 72203-1000

No Tax Due:

> Arkansas State Income Tax
> P.O. Box 8026
> Little Rock, AR 72203-8026

Alternative Minimum Tax?
No

IRC Conformity
Only certain IRC provisions are incorporated as amended through specified dates.

Starting Point for Calculation of Taxable Income
Arkansas gross income.

Credit for Taxes Paid to Another State Allowed?
Yes. For part-year residents and nonresidents, credit may not exceed what tax would be on the outside income, if added to the Arkansas income, and calculated at Arkansas income tax rates. Credit is limited to total income tax owed to other states on income reported as taxable income to both Arkansas and the other states, reported as income from all sources, and included as Arkansas income.

Federal Return Attachment Required?
Copy of federal return required for part-year residents and nonresidents. For residents, taxpayers must attach the following federal schedules and forms, if applicable:

- Schedule listing disaster loss;
- Schedule C (business income);
- Schedule D (capital gains/losses);
- Schedule E (rents, royalties, etc.);
- Schedule F (farm income);
- Form 2106 (unreimbursed employee business expenses);
- Form 2441 or 1040A, Schedule 2 (child care credit);
- Form 4684 (casualty or theft losses);
- Form 4797 (other gains/losses);
- Form 4952 (investment interest deduction);
- Form 5329 (IRA withdrawal);
- Form 8283 (noncash charitable contributions of $500 or more); and
- Form 8606 (nondeductible contributions to IRA).

Deadline for Reporting Federal Changes
File within 90 days from the receipt of the notice and demand for payment from the IRS.

Estimated Tax Payments

Required if expected liability is over $1,000.

CALIFORNIA

Tax Agency Website: http://www.ftb.ca.gov

2013 Individual Tax Rate Schedule

Single, Married Filing Separately, Registered Domestic Partner Filing Separately:

$	0 –	7,582	× 1.000 %	minus	$	0
	7,583 –	17,976	× 2.000 %	minus		75.82
	17,977 –	28,371	× 4.000 %	minus		435.34
	28,372 –	39,384	× 6.000 %	minus		1,002.76
	39,385 –	49,774	× 8.000 %	minus		1,790.44
	49,775 –	254,250	× 9.300 %	minus		2,437.50
	254,251 –	305,100	× 10.30 %	minus		4,980.00
	305,101 –	508,500	× 11.30 %	minus		8,031.00
	508,501	and over	× 12.30 %	minus		13,116.00

Married Filing Jointly, Registered Domestic Partner Filing Jointly, Qualifying Widow(er):

$	0 –	15,164	× 1.000 %	minus	$	0
	15,165 –	35,952	× 2.000 %	minus		151.64
	35,953 –	56,742	× 4.000 %	minus		870.68
	56,743 –	78,768	× 6.000 %	minus		2,005.52
	78,769 –	99,548	× 8.000 %	minus		3,580.88
	99,549 –	508,500	× 9.300 %	minus		4,875.00
	508,501 –	610,200	× 10.30 %	minus		9,960.00
	610,201 –	1,017,000	× 11.30 %	minus		16,062.00
	1,017,001	and over	× 12.30 %	minus		26,232.00

Head of Household:

$	0 –	15,174	× 1.000 %	minus	$	0
	15,175 –	35,952	× 2.000 %	minus		151.74
	35,953 –	46,346	× 4.000 %	minus		870.78
	46,347 –	57,359	× 6.000 %	minus		1,797.70
	57,360 –	67,751	× 8.000 %	minus		2,944.88
	67,752 –	345,780	× 9.300 %	minus		3,825.64
	345,781 –	414,936	× 10.30 %	minus		7,283.44
	414,937 –	691,560	× 11.30 %	minus		11,432.80
	691,561	and over	× 12.30 %	minus		18,348.40

An additional 1% tax is imposed on taxable income in excess of $1 million. Brackets are indexed for inflation annually.

http://www.ftb.ca.gov/
professionals/efile/index.shtml

Mandated for tax preparers that filed more than 100 resident, nonresident, and part-year resident returns and that file one or more returns for the current taxable year using tax preparation software.

Taxpayers can opt-out using Form FTB 8454. Form is retained. No exceptions or waivers to mandate. Penalty for failure to e-file of $50 per return, if due to willful neglect and not reasonable cause.

Filing Requirements

Form(s) to File: Form 540; Form 540NR

Due Date (General): April 15

Filing Status Options: Same as federal, except:

- married filing jointly or married filing separately must be used by same-sex married individuals/registered domestic partners;
- married filing separately may be used if one spouse was an active member of the military during taxable year; and
- married filing separately may be used if one spouse was a full-year nonresident and had no income from state sources during the taxable year.

Same-sex married individuals or RDPs may file as head of household only if considered to be unmarried or considered not in a domestic partnership.

Filing Thresholds: Residents, nonresidents, and part-year residents must file if their adjusted gross income (AGI) or their gross income exceeds certain filing thresholds (see below). The filing thresholds are adjusted on an annual basis.

No Dependents (Gross Income)
Single or Head of Household: $15,702
Single or Head of Household (65 years of age or older): $21,002
Married Filing Jointly or Separately: $31,406
Married Filing Jointly or Separately (one 65 years of age or older): $36,706
Married Filing Jointly or Separately (both 65 years of age or older): $42,006

1 Dependent (Gross Income)
Single or Head of Household: $26,569
Single or Head of Household (65 years of age or older): $29,152
Married Filing Jointly or Separately: $42,273
Married Filing Jointly or Separately (one 65 years of age or older): $44,856
Married Filing Jointly or Separately (both 65 years of age or older): $50,156
Surviving Spouse: $26,569
Surviving Spouse (65 years of age or older): $29,152

2 Dependents or More (Gross Income)
 Single or Head of Household: $34,719
 Single or Head of Household (65 years of age or older): $35,672
 Married Filing Jointly or Separately: $50,423
 Married Filing Jointly or Separately (one 65 years of age or older): $51,376
 Married Filing Jointly or Separately (both 65 years of age or older): $56,676
 Surviving Spouse: $34,719
 Surviving Spouse (65 years of age or older): $35,672

No Dependents (AGI)
 Single or Head of Household: $12,562
 Single or Head of Household (65 years of age or older): $17,862
 Married Filing Jointly or Separately: $25,125
 Married Filing Jointly or Separately (one 65 years of age or older): $30,425
 Married Filing Jointly or Separately (both 65 years of age or older): $35,725

1 Dependent (AGI)
 Single or Head of Household: $23,429
 Single or Head of Household (65 years of age or older): $26,012
 Married Filing Jointly or Separately: $35,992
 Married Filing Jointly or Separately (one 65 years of age or older): $38,575
 Married Filing Jointly or Separately (both 65 years of age or older): $43,875
 Surviving Spouse: $23,429
 Surviving Spouse (65 years of age or older): $26,012

2 Dependents or More (AGI)
 Single or Head of Household: $31,579
 Single or Head of Household (65 years of age or older): $32,532
 Married Filing Jointly or Separately: $44,142
 Married Filing Jointly or Separately (one 65 years of age or older): $45,095
 Married Filing Jointly or Separately (both 65 years of age or older): $50,395
 Surviving Spouse: $31,579
 Surviving Spouse (65 years of age or older): $32,532

Where to Send Returns
Payment:

 Franchise Tax Board
 P.O. Box 942867
 Sacramento, CA 94267-0001

No Payment:

 Franchise Tax Board
 P.O. Box 942840
 Sacramento, CA 94240-0001

Alternative Minimum Tax?
Yes

IRC Conformity
IRC incorporated as of January 1, 2009, with modifications for tax years beginning after 2009.

Starting Point for Calculation of Taxable Income
Federal adjusted gross income.

Credit for Taxes Paid to Another State Allowed?
Yes. For nonresidents, credit allowed only if state of residence either does not tax California residents on income from sources within its borders or allows California residents credit for California taxes imposed on income derived from the state. State of residence may not permit its residents a credit for the taxed income also taxed by California.

Federal Return Attachment Required?
Copy of federal return required for part-year residents and nonresidents. Resident taxpayers who attach federal forms or schedules other than Schedule A or B to federal Form 1040 must attach federal Form 1040 and all supporting schedules and forms. Taxpayers who itemize for state purposes, but not for federal purposes, must attach a pro forma copy of federal Schedule A to their state return.

If applicable, also attach federal Form 8886 (Reportable Transaction Disclosure Statement). If first time reportable transaction disclosure on return, send a duplicate copy of federal Form 8886 to the Franchise Tax Board (FTB). The FTB may impose penalties if the taxpayer fails to file federal Form 8886, Form 8918 (Material Advisor Disclosure Statement), or any other required information.

Deadline for Reporting Federal Changes
File within six months after final determination of federal adjustment or as otherwise required by the Franchise Tax Board.

Estimated Tax Payments
Required if expected liability is over $500 ($250 for married/registered domestic partner (RDP) filing separately).

Estimated payments are not required if taxpayer is a nonresident or new resident of California in the current tax year and did not have a California tax liability in previous tax year.

COLORADO

Tax Agency Website: http://www.colorado.gov/revenue

2013 Individual Tax Rate Schedule
Tax rate is 4.63% of federal taxable income, regardless of filing status. Individual taxpayers are subject to an alternative minimum tax equal to the amount by which 3.47% of

their Colorado alternative minimum taxable income exceeds their Colorado normal tax.

  http://www.colorado.gov/
cs/Satellite/Revenue-Main/
XRM/1213953995041

Allowed for resident, nonresident, and part-year resident returns.

Filing Requirements
Form(s) to File: Form 104; Form 104PN

Due Date (General): April 15

Filing Status Options: Allowable state filing statuses include:

- Single
- Married Filing Jointly
- Married Filing Separately
- Head of Household
- Qualifying Widow(er) with Dependent Child

Filing Thresholds: Residents must file if required to file federal return or have Colorado income tax liability. Nonresidents must file if required to file federal return and they received income from state sources. Filing required by part-year residents with taxable income during that part of the year they were residents.

Where to Send Returns
Colorado Department of Revenue
Denver, CO 80261-0005

Alternative Minimum Tax?
Yes

IRC Conformity
IRC incorporated by reference as currently amended.

Starting Point for Calculation of Taxable Income
Federal taxable income.

Credit for Taxes Paid to Another State Allowed?
Residents and Part-Year Residents: Yes

Nonresidents: No

Federal Return Attachment Required?
Copy of federal return not required.

Deadline for Reporting Federal Changes
File within 30 days after final determination of federal adjustment.

Estimated Tax Payments
Required if expected liability is over $1000.

CONNECTICUT

Tax Agency Website: http://www.ct.gov/drs

2013 Individual Tax Rate Schedule
Single, Married Filing Separately:

$	0	–	10,000	×	3.000 %	minus	$	0
	10,001	–	50,000	×	5.000 %	minus		200
	50,001	–	100,000	×	5.500 %	minus		450
	100,001	–	200,000	×	6.000 %	minus		950
	200,001	–	250,000	×	6.500 %	minus		1,950
	250,001	and over		×	6.700 %	minus		2,450

Filing Jointly, Qualifying Widow(er):

$	0	–	20,000	×	3.000 %	minus	$	0
	20,001	–	100,000	×	5.000 %	minus		400
	100,001	–	200,000	×	5.500 %	minus		900
	200,001	–	400,000	×	6.000 %	minus		1,900
	400,001	–	500,000	×	6.500 %	minus		3,900
	500,001	and over		×	6.700 %	minus		4,900

Head of Household:

$	0	–	16,000	×	3.000 %	minus	$	0
	16,001	–	80,000	×	5.000 %	minus		320
	80,001	–	160,000	×	5.500 %	minus		720
	160,001	–	320,000	×	6.000 %	minus		1,520
	320,001	–	400,000	×	6.500 %	minus		3,120
	400,001	and over		×	6.700 %	minus		3,920

Filing jointly includes:

- filing jointly for federal and state purposes; and
- filing jointly for state purposes only.

Filing separately includes:

- filing separately for federal and state purposes; and
- filing separately for state purposes only.

Resident estates and trusts are subject to 6.7% rate on all income.

  http://www.ct.gov/drs/
taxonomy/drs_taxonomy.
asp?DLN=40822&drsNav=|40822|

Mandated for tax preparers that filed 50 or more resident, nonresident, and part-year resident income tax returns during previous tax year.

Taxpayers can opt out by attaching a letter to the face of the return indicating that he/she has chosen not to e-file. Waivers are available for undue hardship. No penalties for failure to e-file.

Filing Requirements
Form(s) to File: Form CT-1040; Form CT-1040NR/PY

Due Date (General): April 15

Filing Status Options: Allowable state filing statuses include:

- Single
- Filing Jointly for Federal and State
- Filing Jointly for State Only
- Filing Separately for Federal and State
- Filing Separately for State Only
- Head of Household
- Qualifying Widow(er) with Dependent Child

Same-sex married couples must file using Filing Jointly for State Only or Filing Separately for State Only.

Filing Thresholds: Residents, nonresidents, and part-year residents must file if income exceeds filing threshold for applicable filing status (see below).

> Single: $14,000
> Head of Household: $19,000
> Married Filing Jointly: $24,000
> Married Filing Separately: $12,000

Where to Send Returns

Form CT-1040, Payment:

> Department of Revenue Services
> P.O. Box 2977
> Hartford, CT 06104-2977

Form CT-1040, No Payment:

> Department of Revenue Services
> P.O. Box 2976
> Hartford, CT 06104-2976

Form CT-1040NR/PY, Payment:

> Department of Revenue Services
> P.O. Box 2969
> Hartford, CT 06104-2969

Form CT-1040NR/PY, No Payment:

> Department of Revenue Services
> P.O. Box 2968
> Hartford, CT 06104-2968

Alternative Minimum Tax?
AMT imposed in addition to regular tax on:

- resident or part-year resident individuals, trusts, and estates that have federal AMT liability; and
- nonresident individuals, trusts, and estates with federal AMT liability and state source income.

AMT computed at rate equal to lesser of:

- 19% of adjusted federal tentative minimum tax; or
- 5.5% of adjusted federal AMT.

IRC Conformity
IRC incorporated by reference as currently amended.

Starting Point for Calculation of Taxable Income
Federal adjusted gross income.

Credit for Taxes Paid to Another State Allowed?
Residents and Part-Year Residents: Yes

Nonresidents: No

A domiciliary of another jurisdiction who is present in Connecticut more than 183 days of a tax year and has a permanent abode in Connecticut may claim a credit for certain taxes paid to the state of domicile.

Federal Return Attachment Required?
Copy of federal return not required. Attach, if applicable, federal Form 1310 (claiming refund due a deceased taxpayer).

Deadline for Reporting Federal Changes
File within 90 days after final determination of federal adjustment.

Estimated Tax Payments
Required if expected liability is $1,000 or more.

DELAWARE

Tax Agency Website: http://www.revenue.delaware.gov

2013 Individual Tax Rate Schedule

$			×		minus	$	
	0	–	2,000	× 0.000 %	minus	$	0
	2,001	–	5,000	× 2.200 %	minus		44.00
	5,001	–	10,000	× 3.900 %	minus		129.00
	10,001	–	20,000	× 4.800 %	minus		219.00
	20,001	–	25,000	× 5.200 %	minus		299.00
	25,001	–	60,000	× 5.550 %	minus		386.50
	60,001	and over		× 6.750 %	minus		1,106.50

   http://www.revenue.delaware.gov/services/online_svcs.shtml

Allowed for resident, nonresident, and part-year resident returns, except returns reporting a lump sum distribution; and returns on which the number of state exemptions claimed does not match the number of federal exemptions, excluding additional exemptions for taxpayers 60 years of age or older.

Filing Requirements
Form(s) to File: Form 200-01; Form 200-02

Due Date (General): April 30

Filing Status Options: Allowable state filing statuses include:

- Single, Divorced, Widow(er)
- Married Filing Jointly
- Married Filing Separately
- Married Filing Combined Separate Return
- Head of Household

Same-sex marriage is recognized effective July 1, 2013. No guidance had been issued at the time of publication regarding changes to filing status for married same-sex couples.

Civil union partners may file Joint, Separate, or Combined Separate returns effective for tax years after 2011.

Filing Thresholds: Residents must file if AGI for age and filing status exceeds filing threshold for applicable filing status (see below). Nonresidents must file if they had gross income from states sources. Part-year residents may choose to file as a resident or nonresident, whichever is more advantageous.

> Single, Head of Household, Surviving Spouse, Married Filing Separate or Combined Separate
> Under 60 years of age: $9,400
> 60 to 64 years of age: $12,200
> 65 years of age or older, or blind: $14,700
> 65 years of age or older, and blind: $17,200

> Married Filing Jointly
> Under 60 years of age: $15,450
> 60 to 64 years of age: $17,950
> 65 years of age or older, or blind: $20,450
> 65 years of age or older, and blind: $22,950

> Dependents:
> Under 60 years of age: $5,250
> 60 to 64 years of age: $5,250
> 65 years of age or older, or blind: $7,750
> 65 years of age or older, and blind: $10,250

Where to Send Returns

Form 200-01, Payment:

> Delaware Division of Revenue
> P.O. Box 508
> Wilmington, DE 19899-0508

Form 200-01, Refund:

> Delaware Division of Revenue
> P.O. Box 8765
> Wilmington, DE 19899-8765

Form 200-01, No Payment:

> Delaware Division of Revenue
> P.O. Box 8711
> Wilmington, DE 19899-8711

Form 200-02, Payment:

> Delaware Division of Revenue
> P.O. Box 8752
> Wilmington, DE 19899-8752

Form 200-02, Refund:

> Delaware Division of Revenue
> P.O. Box 8772
> Wilmington, DE 19899-8772

Form 200-02, No Payment:

> Delaware Division of Revenue
> P.O. Box 8711
> Wilmington, DE 19899-8711

Alternative Minimum Tax?
No

IRC Conformity
IRC incorporated by reference as currently amended.

Starting Point for Calculation of Taxable Income
Federal adjusted gross income.

Credit for Taxes Paid to Another State Allowed?
Residents and Part-Year Residents: Yes

Nonresidents: No

Federal Return Attachment Required?
Copy of pages 1 and 2 of federal return, plus all schedules required to be filed with federal return must be attached and, if applicable:

- Form 2106 or 2106EZ (unreimbursed employee expense credit);
- Form 2441 or 1040A Schedule 2 (child and dependent care expense credit);
- Schedule A;
- 1100S Schedule A-1 (credit for taxes paid by S corporations);
- Form 5884 (work opportunity credit); and
- Schedule EIC.

Effective for tax years after 2011, civil union individuals must include a pro forma federal return completed "as if" the filing status elected by the taxpayers for the Delaware return is married/civil union filing a joint, separate, or combined separate return.

Deadline for Reporting Federal Changes
File within 90 days after final determination of federal adjustment.

Estimated Tax Payments
Required if expected liability is over $400.

DISTRICT OF COLUMBIA

Tax Agency Website: http://otr.cfo.dc.gov/

2013 Individual Tax Rate Schedule

$					$	
0	–	10,000	× 4.000 %	minus	$	0
10,001	–	40,000	× 6.000 %	minus		200.00
40,001	–	350,000	× 8.500 %	minus		1,200.00
350,001	and over		× 8.950 %	minus		1,380.00

 e~file

http://otr.cfo.dc.gov/page/individual-income-tax-online-filing

Allowed for resident and nonresident returns. Not allowed for part-year resident returns.

Filing Requirements

Form(s) to File: Form D-40

Due Date (General): April 15

Filing Status Options: Allowable state filing statuses include:

- Single
- Married Filing Jointly
- Married Filing Separately
- Dependent Claimed by Someone Else
- Married Filing Separately on Same Return
- Head of Household
- Registered Domestic Partners Filing Jointly
- Registered Domestic Partners Filing Separately on Same Form

Filing Thresholds: Residents and part-year residents must file if required to file a federal return. Nonresidents are not subject to tax on net personal income.

In addition, a return must be filed if (1) the taxpayer's permanent residence was in the District of Columbia for part of or full taxable year; (2) the taxpayer lived in the District for 183 days or more during taxable year, even though permanent residence was outside the District; (3) the taxpayer was a member of the armed forces and his/her home of record was the District for either part of or the full taxable year; or (4) the taxpayer is a spouse of an exempt military person or of any other exempt person such as a nonresident presidential appointee or an elected official.

Where to Send Returns
Payment:

> Office of Tax and Revenue
> P.O. Box 7182
> Washington, DC 20044-7182

No Payment:

> Office of Tax and Revenue
> P.O. Box 209
> Washington, DC 20044-0209

Alternative Minimum Tax?
No

IRC Conformity
IRC incorporated by reference as currently amended.

Starting Point for Calculation of Taxable Income
Federal gross income.

Credit for Taxes Paid to Another State Allowed?
Residents: Yes. However, no credit is allowed for tax paid to another jurisdiction on income from intangible property, such as dividends or interest, the source of which is within the District of Columbia. A credit is permitted to (1) District domiciliaries required to pay tax to another jurisdiction on income from intangible property derived from sources within that jurisdiction, and (2) nondomiciliary statutory residents of the District required to pay tax on income from intangible property from sources other than the District to his or her state of domicile.

Part-Year Residents: Yes

Nonresidents: No. However, a credit is permitted to (1) District of Columbia domiciliaries required to pay tax to another jurisdiction on income from intangible property, such as dividends or interest, derived from sources within that jurisdiction, and (2) nondomiciliary statutory residents of the District required to pay tax on income from intangible property from sources other than the District to the state of his or her domicile.

Federal Return Attachment Required?
Copy of federal return not required.

Deadline for Reporting Federal Changes
File within 90 days after final determination of federal adjustment.

Estimated Tax Payments
Required if expected liability is over $100.

FLORIDA

Tax Agency Website: http://dor.myflorida.com/dor

Florida does not collect personal income tax.

GEORGIA

Tax Agency Website: http://www.etax.dor.ga.gov

2013 Individual Tax Rate Schedule
Single:

$	0	–	750	×	1.000 %	minus	$	0
	751	–	2,250	×	2.000 %	minus		7.50
	2,251	–	3,750	×	3.000 %	minus		30.00
	3,751	–	5,250	×	4.000 %	minus		67.50
	5,251	–	7,000	×	5.000 %	minus		120.00
	7,001	and over		×	6.000 %	minus		190.00

Married Filing Jointly, Head of Household:

$	0	–	1,000	×	1.000 %	minus	$	0
	1,001	–	3,000	×	2.000 %	minus		10.00
	3,001	–	5,000	×	3.000 %	minus		40.00
	5,001	–	7,000	×	4.000 %	minus		90.00
	7,001	–	10,000	×	5.000 %	minus		160.00
	10,001	and over		×	6.000 %	minus		260.00

Married Filing Separately:

$	0	–	500	×	1.000 %	minus	$	0
	501	–	1,500	×	2.000 %	minus		5.00
	1,501	–	2,500	×	3.000 %	minus		20.00
	2,501	–	3,500	×	4.000 %	minus		45.00
	3,501	–	5,000	×	5.000 %	minus		80.00

5,001	and over	×	6.000 %	minus	130.00

 https://etax.dor.ga.gov/

Mandated for resident, nonresident, and part-year residents that:

- are required to pay electronically;
- voluntarily pay electronically.

Mandated for any return preparer required to e-file federal return.

Filing Requirements
Form(s) to File: Form 500

Due Date (General): April 15

Filing Status Options: Allowable state filing statuses include:

- Single
- Married Filing Jointly
- Married Filing Separately
- Head of Household
- Qualifying Widow(er) with Dependent Child

Georgia does not recognize same-sex marriages, civil unions, or domestic partnerships for filing status purposes.

Filing Thresholds: Residents must file if required to file a federal return, income is subject to state income tax but not subject to federal income tax, or income exceeds standard deduction and personal exemptions (see below). Nonresidents must file if required to file a federal return and income was received from state sources, unless the only state activity consisted of employment services and wages do not exceed the lesser of 5% of income received in all places during taxable year or $5,000. Part-year residents must file if they are a legal state resident for part of the year and if required to file a federal return.

Single, Head of Household, Surviving Spouse
    Under 65 years of age: $5,000
    Under 65 years of age and blind: $6,300
    65 years of age or older: $6,300
    65 years of age or older and blind: $7,600

Married Filing Jointly
    Under 65 years of age: $8,400
    65 years of age or older (one): $9,700
    65 years of age or older (both): $11,000

Married Filing Jointly (one blind)
    Under 65 years of age: $9,700
    65 years of age or older (one): $11,000

Married Filing Jointly (both blind)
    Under 65 years of age (one): $11,000
    65 years of age or older (one): $12,300
    65 years of age or older (both): $13,600

Married Filing Separately
    Under 65 years of age: $4,200
    Under 65 years of age and blind: $5,500
    65 years of age or older: $5,500
    65 years of age or older and blind: $6,800

Where to Send Returns
Payment:

Georgia Department of Revenue
Processing Center
P.O. 740399
Atlanta, GA 30374-0399

Refunds:

Georgia Department of Revenue
Processing Center
P.O. 740380
Atlanta, GA 30374-0380

Alternative Minimum Tax?
No

IRC Conformity
IRC incorporated by reference as of January 3, 2013, with modifications, for taxable years beginning on or after January 1, 2012.

Starting Point for Calculation of Taxable Income
Federal adjusted gross income.

Credit for Taxes Paid to Another State Allowed?
Residents: Yes. Credit allowed if resident engages in employment, has an established business, or has investment property with taxable situs in another state that levies a tax upon net income.

Part-Year Residents: Yes

Nonresidents: No

Federal Return Attachment Required?
Copy of federal return not required. Taxpayers must attach the following federal schedules and forms, if applicable:

- Pages 1 and 2 of federal Form 1040, if federal adjusted gross income is $40,000 or more, or less than the total income on W-2(s);
- Form 2441 or 1040A Schedule 2 (child and dependent care expense credit);
- Schedule A (itemized deductions); and
- Copy of federal return when claiming combat zone pay exclusion.

Deadline for Reporting Federal Changes

File within 180 days after final determination of federal adjustment.

Estimated Tax Payments

Required if expected gross income exceeds personal exemption, plus credit for dependents, plus estimated deductions, plus $1,000 income not subject to withholding.

HAWAII

Tax Agency Website: http://www.state.hi.us/tax

2013 Individual Tax Rate Schedule

Single and Married Filing Separately:

$	0 –	2,400	×	1.400 %	minus	$	0
	2,401 –	4,800	×	3.200 %	minus		43.20
	4,801 –	9,600	×	5.500 %	minus		153.60
	9,601 –	14,400	×	6.400 %	minus		240.00
	14,401 –	19,200	×	6.800 %	minus		297.60
	19,201 –	24,000	×	7.200 %	minus		374.40
	24,001 –	36,000	×	7.600 %	minus		470.40
	36,001 –	48,000	×	7.900 %	minus		578.40
	48,001 –	150,000	×	8.250 %	minus		746.40
	150,001 –	175,000	×	9.000 %	minus		1,871.40
	175,001 –	200,000	×	10.000 %	minus		3,621.40
	200,001	and over	×	11.000 %	minus		5,621.40

Married Filing Jointly, Surviving Spouse:

$	0 –	4,800	×	1.400 %	minus	$	0
	4,801 –	9,600	×	3.200 %	minus		86.40
	9,601 –	19,200	×	5.500 %	minus		307.20
	19,201 –	28,800	×	6.400 %	minus		480.00
	28,801 –	38,400	×	6.800 %	minus		595.20
	38,401 –	48,000	×	7.200 %	minus		748.80
	48,001 –	72,000	×	7.600 %	minus		940.80
	72,001 –	96,000	×	7.900 %	minus		1,156.80
	96,001 –	300,000	×	8.250 %	minus		1,492.80
	300,001 –	350,000	×	9.000 %	minus		3,742.80
	350,001 –	400,000	×	10.000 %	minus		7,242.80
	400,001	and over	×	11.000 %	minus		11,242.80

Head of Household:

$	0 –	3,600	×	1.400 %	minus	$	0
	3,601 –	7,200	×	3.200 %	minus		64.80
	7,201 –	14,400	×	5.500 %	minus		230.40
	14,401 –	21,600	×	6.400 %	minus		360.00
	21,601 –	28,800	×	6.800 %	minus		446.40
	28,801 –	36,000	×	7.200 %	minus		561.60
	36,001 –	54,000	×	7.600 %	minus		705.60
	54,001 –	72,000	×	7.900 %	minus		867.60
	72,001 –	225,000	×	8.250 %	minus		1,119.60
	225,001 –	262,500	×	9.000 %	minus		2,807.10
	262,501 –	300,000	×	10.000 %	minus		5,432.10
	300,001	and over	×	11.000 %	minus		8,432.10

 e-file   http://www6.hawaii.gov/tax/b3_elf.htm

Allowed for resident, nonresident, and part-year resident returns.

Filing Requirements

Form(s) to File: Form N-11; Form N-15

Due Date (General): April 20

Filing Status Options: Same as federal, except for civil union partners. For taxable years beginning after 2011, civil union partners have the same Hawaii income tax filing status options as married couples.

Filing Thresholds: Residents, nonresidents, and part-year residents must file if income exceeds filing threshold for applicable filing status.

    Single, Legally Separated
        Under 65 years of age: $3,344
        65 years of age or older: $4,488

    Single, Head of Household
        Under 65 years of age: $4,356
        65 years of age or older: $5,500

    Married Filing Jointly
        Under 65 years of age: $6,688
        65 years of age or older (one): $7,832
        65 years of age or older (both): $8,976

    Married Filing Separately
        Under 65 years of age: $3,344
        65 years of age or older: $4,488

    Surviving Spouse (with dependent child)
        Under 65 years of age: $5,544
        65 years of age or older: $6,688

Where to Send Returns

Payment:

    Hawaii Department of Taxation
    Attn: Payment Section
    P.O. Box 1530
    Honolulu, HI 96806-1530

No Payment:

    Hawaii Department of Taxation
    P.O. Box 3559
    Honolulu, HI 96811-3559

Alternative Minimum Tax?

No

IRC Conformity

IRC incorporated by reference as amended through December 31, 2011, for tax years after 2011. Various IRC provisions inoperative.

Starting Point for Calculation of Taxable Income
Federal adjusted gross income.

Credit for Taxes Paid to Another State Allowed?
Residents: Yes. However, no credit is allowed to individuals who took up residence in Hawaii after age 65 and prior to July 1, 1976, who are treated as nonresidents for purposes of computing income.

Part-Year Residents: Yes

Nonresidents: No

Federal Return Attachment Required?
Copy of federal return required for part-year residents and nonresidents. Attach, if applicable:

- Form 1116 (foreign tax credit);
- Form 1128 (application to adopt, change, or retain tax year);
- Form 2106 or Form 2106-EZ (unreimbursed employee expense deduction);
- Form 2120 (multiple support declaration);
- Form 4562 (depreciation deduction);
- Form 4684 (casualty or theft losses);
- Form 4835 (farm rental income and expenses);
- Form 5213 (hobby losses);
- Form 6198 (at risk limitations);
- Form 6252 (installment sale income);
- Form 6781 (gains and losses);
- Form 8283 (charitable contributions over $500);
- Form 8332 (noncustodial parent dependent deduction);
- Form 8582 (passive activity loss limitations);
- Form 8814 (parent's election to report child's interest and dividends);
- Form 8824 (like-kind exchanges); and
- Form 8829 (business use of home expenses).

Copies of all federal forms used as substitutes for state forms also must be attached.

Deadline for Reporting Federal Changes
File within 90 days after final determination of federal adjustment.

Estimated Tax Payments
Required if expected tax liability is at least $500.

IDAHO

Tax Agency Website: http://www.tax.idaho.gov

2013 Individual Tax Rate Schedule
Single, Married Filing Separately:

$	0	–	1,408	×	1.600 %	minus	$	0
	1,409	–	2,817	×	3.600 %	minus		28.16
	2,818	–	4,226	×	4.100 %	minus		42.25
	4,227	–	5,635	×	5.100 %	minus		84.51
	5,636	–	7,044	×	6.100 %	minus		140.86
	7,045	–	10,567	×	7.100 %	minus		211.30
	10,568	and over		×	7.400 %	minus		243.00

Married Filing Jointly, Head of Household, Surviving Spouse:

$	0	–	2,817	×	1.600 %	minus	$	0
	2,818	–	5,635	×	3.600 %	minus		56.34
	5,636	–	8,453	×	4.100 %	minus		84.51
	8,454	–	11,271	×	5.100 %	minus		169.04
	11,272	–	14,089	×	6.100 %	minus		281.75
	14,090	–	21,135	×	7.100 %	minus		422.64
	21,136	and over		×	7.400 %	minus		486.04

Brackets indexed for inflation annually.

  http://www.tax.idaho.gov/i-1020.cfm

Allowed for resident, nonresident, and part-year resident returns.

Filing Requirements
Form(s) to File: Form 40; Form 43

Due Date (General): April 15

Filing Status Options: Allowable state filing statuses include:

- Single
- Married Filing Jointly
- Married Filing Separately
- Head of Household
- Qualifying Widow(er) with Dependent Child

Filing Thresholds: Filing required by residents, if required to file federal return. Filing required by nonresidents if income from state sources exceeds $2,500. Filing required by part-year residents if income from state sources while a nonresident and/or income from any source while a resident exceeds $2,500.

Where to Send Returns

Form 40:

> Idaho State Tax Commission
> P.O. Box 56
> Boise, ID 83756-0056

Form 43:

> Idaho State Tax Commission
> P.O. Box 56
> Boise, ID 83756-0056

Alternative Minimum Tax?
No

IRC Conformity
IRC incorporated by reference as of January 1, 2013, effective retroactively to January 1, 2013. IRC provisions added, amended, or deleted prior to conformity provision update, are applicable on effective date of federal changes, including retroactive provisions.

Starting Point for Calculation of Taxable Income
Federal adjusted gross income.

Credit for Taxes Paid to Another State Allowed?
Residents: Yes (must be domiciled in Idaho to qualify).

Part-Year Residents: Yes

Nonresidents: No

Federal Return Attachment Required?
Complete copy of the federal return must be attached.

Deadline for Reporting Federal Changes
File within 60 days after final determination of federal adjustment.

Estimated Tax Payments
Voluntary.

ILLINOIS

Tax Agency Website: http://www.revenue.state.il.us

2013 Individual Tax Rate Schedule
Tax rate is 5% of federal AGI with modifications, regardless of filing status.

   http://www.revenue.state.il.us/
ElectronicServices/index.htm

Mandated for tax preparers that filed 11 or more income tax returns during the previous tax year and who are required to e-file federal return. Taxpayers opt-out on Form IL-8948, Electronic Filing Opt-Out Declaration.

Filing Requirements
Form(s) to File: Form IL-1040

Due Date (General): April 15

Filing Status Options: Same as federal, except married filing separately may be used by an injured spouse or by a spouse who is a nonresident or part-year resident.

Civil union partners must file using Married Filing Jointly or Married Filing Separately for tax years after 2010. Beginning with the 2012 tax year, civil union partners must also complete and attach Schedule CU to the state return.

Filing Thresholds: Residents must file if required to file federal return or if base income for state tax purposes exceeds standard allowance of $2,050 for each exemption claimed on federal return. Additional exemptions: $1,000 for each individual 65 or over; $1,000 for each individual legally blind. Nonresidents must file if they earned enough taxable income from state sources to have tax liability. Part-year residents must file if they have earned income from any source while a resident or earned income from state sources while not a resident. Dependents must file if base income exceeds $2,050. For tax years 2013 and beyond, the standard exemption will be $2,050 plus a cost-of-living adjustment.

Where to Send Returns
Payment:

> Illinois Department of Revenue
> Springfield, IL 62726-0001

No Payment:

> Illinois Department of Revenue
> P.O. Box 1040
> Galesburg, IL 61402-1040

Alternative Minimum Tax?
No

IRC Conformity
IRC incorporated by reference as currently amended.

Starting Point for Calculation of Taxable Income
Federal adjusted gross income.

Credit for Taxes Paid to Another State Allowed?
Residents and Part-Year Residents: Yes

Nonresidents: No

Federal Return Attachment Required?
Copy of federal return not required. Taxpayers must attach the following federal schedules and forms, if applicable:

- Page 1 of Form 1040 or 1040A to support subtraction for Social Security, disability, and retirement income;
- Form 1099-R or Form SSA-1099, if Form 1040, page 1, does not clearly identify reported retirement income and Social Security benefits;
- Schedule D (capital gains and losses) for gain on sale or exchange of employer securities;

- Schedule B or Schedule 1, for interest and dividend income from U.S. retirement bonds; or
- Form 8886 (Reportable Transaction Disclosure Statement).

Deadline for Reporting Federal Changes
File within 120 days the federal adjustment is made or agreed to or the federal change is assessed or paid.

Estimated Tax Payments
Required if expected liability is over $500 after subtracting Illinois withholding, pass-through entity payments, credits and subtractions from Schedule 1299-C, credits for income tax paid to other states, property taxes paid on an Illinois residence, education expenses, and the earned income credit.

INDIANA

Tax Agency Website: http://www.in.gov/dor

2013 Individual Tax Rate Schedule
Tax rate is 3.4% of AGI, regardless of filing status. Counties may impose an adjusted gross income tax on residents or on nonresidents, or a county option income tax.

    http://www.in.gov/dor/index.htm

Mandated for tax preparers who filed 10 resident/nonresident returns in a calendar year after 2012.

Nonresidents and part-year residents may file online or through MeF. Taxpayers opt-out on Form IN-OPT, which should be retained by preparer for five years. No waivers/exceptions to mandate. Penalty of $50 per return if fail to e-file, up to $25,000 per year.

Filing Requirements
Form(s) to File: Form IT-40; Form IT-40PNR

Due Date (General): April 15

Filing Status Options: Allowable state filing statuses include:

- Single
- Married Filing Jointly
- Married Filing Separately

If joint return is filed by surviving spouse, surviving spouse should sign name and write "Filing as Surviving Spouse."

Filing Thresholds: Residents must file if taxable income exceeds standard allowance of $1,000 for each exemption claimed on federal return. Additional exemptions: $1,500 for certain dependent children; $1,000 for each individual 65 years of age or older; $1,000 for each individual legally blind; and $500 for each individual 65 years of age or older and federal AGI of less than $40,000. Nonresidents with income from state sources, except certain interest, dividends, or retirement income, must file. Part-year residents who had income while they were residents must file.

Where to Send Returns
Payment:

> Indiana Department of Revenue
> P.O. Box 7224
> Indianapolis, IN 46207-7224

No Payment:

> Indiana Department of Revenue
> P.O. Box 40
> Indianapolis, IN 46206-0040

Alternative Minimum Tax?
No

IRC Conformity
IRC incorporated by reference as of January 1, 2013, for taxable years beginning after 2012.

Starting Point for Calculation of Taxable Income
Federal adjusted gross income.

Credit for Taxes Paid to Another State Allowed?
Yes. For nonresidents, credit allowed only if other state grants substantially similar credit to Indiana residents subject to other state's income tax or imposes an income tax on its residents derived from sources in Indiana and exempts from taxation the income of Indiana residents.

Federal Return Attachment Required?
Copy of federal return not required. Taxpayers must attach federal Form 4972, Form 4868, Schedule A from federal Form 1045; and federal Schedule R, if applicable.

Deadline for Reporting Federal Changes
File within 180 days after the federal modification is made.

Estimated Tax Payments
Required if expected liability is $1,000 or more.

IOWA

Tax Agency Website: http://www.iowa.gov/tax

2013 Individual Tax Rate Schedule

$	0 – 1,494	×	0.360 %	minus	$	0
	1,495 – 2,988	×	0.720 %	minus		5.37
	2,989 – 5,976	×	2.430 %	minus		56.47
	5,977 – 13,446	×	4.500 %	minus		180.17
	13,447 – 22,410	×	6.120 %	minus		397.99
	22,411 – 29,880	×	6.480 %	minus		478.66
	29,881 – 44,820	×	6.800 %	minus		574.28
	44,821 – 67,230	×	7.920 %	minus		1,076.27
	67,231 and over	×	8.980 %	minus		1,788.90

An alternative minimum tax of 6.7% of alternative minimum income is imposed if the minimum tax exceeds the taxpayer's regular income tax liability. The minimum tax is 75% of the maximum regular tax rate.

Brackets indexed for inflation annually.

 http://www.iowa.gov/tax/elf/eservice.html

Allowed for resident, nonresident, and part-year resident returns.

Filing Requirements

Form(s) to File: Form IA 1040

Due Date (General): April 30

Filing Status Options: Allowable state filing statuses include:

- Single
- Married Filing Jointly
- Married Filing Separately
- Married and Filing Separately on Same Form
- Head of Household
- Qualifying Widow(er) with Dependent Child

Same sex married couples may file jointly, married filing separately on a combined return, or married filing separately.

Filing Thresholds: Residents must file a return if net income exceeds certain filing thresholds (see below). A return must be filed regardless of whether income exceeds the filing thresholds if the taxpayer is subject to either lump-sum or alternative minimum tax, or if the taxpayer wishes to receive a refund of tax already paid through estimates or withholding. Nonresidents and part-year residents must file a return if net income from Iowa sources was $1,000 or more, unless below the filing thresholds.

> Single
> Under 65 years of age: $9,001
> 65 years of age or older: $24,001

> Other Resident Taxpayers
> Under 65 years of age: $13,501
> 65 years of age or older: $32,001

Nonresidents
$1,000 attributable to state sources

Dependents
$5,000 or more

Where to Send Returns
Payment:

Iowa Income Tax - Document Processing
P.O. Box 9187
Des Moines, IA 50306-9187

No Payment:

Iowa Income Tax - Refund Processing
Hoover State Office Bldg
Des Moines, IA 50319-0120

Alternative Minimum Tax?
Yes

IRC Conformity
IRC incorporated by reference as of January 1, 2013, effective retroactively for tax years after 2012.

Starting Point for Calculation of Taxable Income
Federal adjusted gross income.

Credit for Taxes Paid to Another State Allowed?
Residents and Part-Year Residents: Yes

Nonresidents: No

Federal Return Attachment Required?
Copy of federal return not required, unless:

- nonresident or part-year resident credit is claimed; or
- Illinois resident is requesting refund for Iowa income tax withheld in error.

Attach, if applicable:

- Schedules C or C-EZ (net business income or loss), D (capital gains), E (rental, pass activity, and royalty losses), and F (farming income or losses);
- Form 3903 (moving expenses);
- Form 4797 (sales of business property);
- Form 1116 (foreign tax credit); and
- Form 2441 (child care expense credit).

Deadline for Reporting Federal Changes
Late payment penalty may be waived if taxpayer provides written notification of federal audit while it is in progress and voluntarily files an amended return within 60 days of final disposition of federal audit.

Estimated Tax Payments
Required if expected liability is $200 or more.

KANSAS

Tax Agency Website: http://www.ksrevenue.org

2013 Individual Tax Rate Schedule

Single, Head of Household, Married Filing Separately:

$	0 – 15,000	× 3.000 %	minus	$	0
	15,001 and over	× 4.900 %	minus		285.00

Married Filing Jointly:

$	0 – 30,000	× 3.000 %	minus	$	0
	30,001 and over	× 4.900 %	minus		570.00

 http://www.ksrevenue.org/eservices.htm

Mandated for paid tax preparer that prepares 50 or more resident, nonresident, and part-year resident income tax returns during any calendar year, in which case 90% of returns must be electronically filed. No taxpayer opt-out. Tax practitioner may request hardship waiver in writing. No penalty for failure to e-file.

Filing Requirements

Form(s) to File: Form K-40

Due Date (General): April 15

Filing Status Options: Allowable state filing statuses include:

- Single
- Married Filing Jointly
- Married Filing Separately
- Head of Household
- Qualifying Widow(er) with Dependent Child

If federal filing status is qualifying widow(er) with dependent child, check "Head of Household" box.

Filing Thresholds: Residents must file if required to file a federal return or adjusted gross income for state tax purposes is more than standard deduction and exemption allowance combined (see below). Dependants must file if base earned income exceeds $3,000 or if unearned income exceeds $500. Nonresidents must file if income is attributable to state sources. Part-year residents may file a return either as a resident or as a nonresident.

> Single, Married Filing Separately
> Under 65 years of age: $5,250
> 65 years of age or older, or blind: $6,100
> 65 years of age or older, and blind: $6,950

> Head of Household
> Under 65 years of age: $9,000
> 65 years of age or older, or blind: $9,850
> 65 years of age or older, and blind: $10,700

> Married Filing Jointly
> Under 65 years of age: $10,500
> 65 years of age or older (one): $11,200
> 65 years of age or older (both): $11,900

> Married Filing Jointly (one blind)
> Under 65 years of age: $11,200
> Under 65 years of age (one): $11,900
> 65 years of age or older (both): $12,600

> Married Filing Jointly (both blind)
> Under 65 years of age: $11,900
> 65 years of age or older: $13,300

Where to Send Returns

Kansas Income Tax
Kansas Department of Revenue
915 SW Harrison St.
Topeka, KS 66699-1000

Alternative Minimum Tax?

No

IRC Conformity

IRC incorporated by reference as currently amended.

Starting Point for Calculation of Taxable Income

Federal adjusted gross income.

Credit for Taxes Paid to Another State Allowed?

Residents and Part-Year Residents: Yes

Nonresidents: No

Federal Return Attachment Required?

Copy of federal return not required, unless taxpayer is a nonresident.

Attach, if applicable:

- Schedules A-F; and
- Form 1116 (foreign tax credit).

Deadline for Reporting Federal Changes

File within 180 days after the federal adjustment is paid, agreed to, or becomes final, whichever is earlier.

Estimated Tax Payments

Required if expected liability is over $500.

KENTUCKY

Tax Agency Website: http://www.revenue.ky.gov

2013 Individual Tax Rate Schedule

$	0 – 3,000	× 2.000 %	minus	$	0
	3,001 – 4,000	× 3.000 %	minus		30.00
	4,001 – 5,000	× 4.000 %	minus		70.00
	5,001 – 8,000	× 5.000 %	minus		120.00
	8,001 – 75,000	× 5.800 %	minus		184.00
	75,001 and over	× 6.000 %	minus		334.00

http://www.revenue.ky.gov/tax-pro/elf.htm

Mandated for tax preparers who submitted 11 or more resident, nonresident, and part-year resident returns for the previous tax year. Taxpayer may opt-out on Form 8948-K. Attach form to paper return. Waiver for tax preparer available if undue hardship. Penalty of $10 per return if fail to e-file.

Filing Requirements
Form(s) to File: Form 740; Form 740-NP

Due Date (General): April 15

Filing Status Options: Allowable state filing statuses include:

- Single
- Married Filing Jointly
- Married Filing Separately
- Married Filing Separately on Combined Return

Kentucky does not recognize same-sex marriages, civil unions, or domestic partnerships for filing status purposes.

Filing Thresholds: Residents, including dependents claimed on another taxpayer's return, must file if modified gross income exceeds the threshold for their family size and state adjusted gross income exceeds the threshold for age and filing status (see below). Nonresidents and part-year residents must file if gross income from state sources and gross income from all sources exceeds modified gross income for their family size, or if gross receipts from self-employment attributable to state sources exceeds modified gross income for their family size. The filing thresholds are adjusted on an annual basis.

    Modified gross income and family size threshold:
        Family size of 1: $ 11,170
        Family size of 2: $ 15,130
        Family size of 3: $ 19,090
        Family size of 4 or more: $ 23,050

    Adjusted gross income threshold (thresholds apply only if MGI exceeds family size amounts):
        Single, Under 65 years of age: $ 3,330
        Single, 65 years of age or older or blind: $ 5,330
        Single, 65 years of age or older and blind: $ 6,600
        Married, Under 65 years of age: $ 4,330
        Married, 65 years of age or older (one): $ 6,000
        Married 65 years of age or older (both): $ 7,100

Caution: The 2012 filing thresholds are shown above. At the time of publication, the 2013 filing thresholds were not available.

Where to Send Returns
Payment:

    Kentucky Department of Revenue
    Frankfort, KY 40619-0008

Refund:

    Kentucky Department of Revenue
    Frankfort, KY 40618-0006

Alternative Minimum Tax?
No

IRC Conformity
IRC incorporated by reference as amended on December 31, 2006. IRC §168 and §179 depreciation and expense deductions for property placed in service after September 10, 2001, have not been adopted.

Starting Point for Calculation of Taxable Income
Federal adjusted gross income.

Credit for Taxes Paid to Another State Allowed?
Residents and Part-Year Residents: Yes

Nonresidents: No

Federal Return Attachment Required?
Copy of federal return and all supporting schedules required for nonresidents and part-year residents. Not required for residents, unless farm, business, or rental income or loss is received.

Attach, if applicable:

- Schedules C (business income and losses), D (capital gains and losses), E (rent, royalty, partnership income), and F (farm income or losses);
- Form 2106 or Form 2106-EZ (employee business expenses);
- Form 2120 (multiple support declaration);
- Form 2441 (child and dependent care expenses);
- Form 4562 (depreciation and amortization);
- Form 4684 (casualties or thefts);
- Form 4797 (sales of business property);
- Form 4952 (investment interest expense deduction);
- Form 8283 (noncash charitable contributions);
- Form 8332 (custodial parent dependent exemption release); and
- Form 8889 (health savings account deduction).

Deadline for Reporting Federal Changes
Revenue Cabinet must be notified within 30 days of initiation of federal audit. Copy of final determination must be submitted within 30 days after conclusion of audit.

Estimated Tax Payments
Required if expected liability is over $500.

LOUISIANA

Tax Agency Website: http://www.rev.state.la.us

2013 Individual Tax Rate Schedule

Single, Head of household, Married Filing Separately:

$	0 –	12,500	× 2.000 %	minus	$	0
	12,501 –	50,000	× 4.000 %	minus		250.00
	50,001	and over	× 6.000 %	minus		1,250.00

Married Filing Jointly, Qualifying Widow(er):

$	0 –	25,000	× 2.000 %	minus	$	0
	25,001 –	100,000	× 4.000 %	minus		500.00
	100,001	and over	× 6.000 %	minus		2,500.00

Community property state in which, generally, one-half of the community income is taxable to each spouse.

 http://www.revenue.louisiana.gov/ sections/eservices/default.aspx

Mandated for tax preparers that prepare more than 100 resident, nonresident, and part-year resident returns in any calendar year as follows:

- 90% of the returns for returns due on or after January 1, 2012.

Taxpayer opt-out not available. Waiver available for undue hardship. Mandate authorized if taxpayer is required to file substantially same return for federal tax purposes.

Mandated for all returns filed by professional athletic teams or athletes. Penalty for failing to e-file athletic returns is $1000 per failure.

Filing Requirements

Form(s) to File: Form IT-540; Form IT-540B

Due Date (General): May 15

Filing Status Options: Allowable state filing statuses include:

- Single
- Married Filing Jointly
- Married Filing Separately
- Head of Household
- Qualifying Widow(er) with Dependent Child

Louisiana does not recognize same-sex marriages, civil unions, or domestic partnerships for filing status purposes. Same-sex married couples must file as Single or Head-of-Household, and recompute their federal income tax as if they were Single or Head-of-Household for federal purposes.

Filing Thresholds: Residents must file if required to file a federal return or had state income withheld. Nonresidents and part-year residents are required to file a federal return must file a Louisiana return if they received income from state sources.

Where to Send Returns

Payment:

Louisiana Department of Revenue
P.O. Box 3550
Baton Rouge, LA 70821-3550

No Payment:

Louisiana Department of Revenue
P.O. Box 3440
Baton Rouge, LA 70821-3440

Alternative Minimum Tax?

No

IRC Conformity

IRC incorporated by reference as currently amended.

Starting Point for Calculation of Taxable Income

Federal adjusted gross income.

Credit for Taxes Paid to Another State Allowed?

Residents: Yes

Part-Year Residents: A part-year resident has the option of filing either as a resident reporting all income earned regardless of the source, or a nonresident. To receive credit for taxes paid to another state, the part-year resident must file a resident form.

Nonresidents: No

Federal Return Attachment Required?

Copy of federal return not required. Taxpayers must attach federal return if Louisiana income tax withheld exceeds 10% of federal adjusted gross income or if claiming deduction for capital gain from sale of state business. Taxpayers must attach copies of federal return, federal Form 3800, and appropriate IRS forms substantiating credit amount if claimed federal disaster relief credits and/or IRC §280C expense adjustment on federal return as a result of Hurricane Katrina or Hurricane Rita.

Deadline for Reporting Federal Changes

File within 60 days of the taxpayer's receipt of the federal adjustments.

Estimated Tax Payments

Required if expected liability is over $1,000 ($2,000 if joint) after credits and taxes withheld.

MAINE

Tax Agency Website: http://www.maine.gov/revenue

2013 Individual Tax Rate Schedule

Single and Married Filing Separately:

$	0 – 5,199	× 0.000 %	minus	$	0
	5,200 – 20,899	× 6.500 %	minus		337.94
	20,900 and over	× 7.950 %	minus		640.97

Married Filing Jointly, Surviving Spouse:

$	0 – 10,449	× 0.000 %	minus	$	0
	10,450 – 41,849	× 6.500 %	minus		679.19
	41,850 and over	× 7.950 %	minus		1,286.00

Head of Household:

$	0 – 7,849	× 0.000 %	minus	$	0
	7,850 – 31,349	× 6.500 %	minus		510.19
	31,350 and over	× 7.950 %	minus		964.75

Brackets indexed for inflation annually.

 http://www.maine.gov/revenue/netfile/gateway2.htm

Mandated for tax preparers who submitted more than 10 resident, nonresident, and/or part-year resident returns for previous tax year. Taxpayer opt-out available. Written request required; tax preparer must note refusal in taxpayer's records. Waiver available for undue hardship (determined on case-by-case basis). Penalty of $50 per return for failure to e-file in absence of reasonable cause.

Filing Requirements

Form(s) to File: Form 1040ME

Due Date (General): April 15

Filing Status Options: Allowable state filing statuses include:

- Single
- Married Filing Jointly
- Married Filing Separately
- Head of Household
- Qualifying Widow(er) with Dependent Child

Same-sex married couples must file using Married Filing Jointly or Married Filing Separately.

Filing Thresholds: Residents must file if required to file a federal return or have income subject to state income tax, except residents with taxable income of $2,000 or less who claim a state exemption for themselves. Residents who do not have a state income tax liability and who file a federal income tax return for the sole purpose of claiming the federal earned income credit are not required to file a state income tax return. For tax years beginning after 2012, a resident whose federal AGI is less than a "threshold amount," and who is not subject to addition modifications, is not required to file a state income tax return. Nonresidents must file if they had income from state sources resulting in state income tax liability, unless (1) the number of days worked in the state performing is 12 or less during the tax year and $3,000 or less is earned during the year in the state from all sources or (2) the number of days present in the state on business is 12 or less during the tax year and $3,000 or less is earned during the year in the state from contractual or sales-related activities.

Where to Send Returns

Payment:

> Maine Revenue Services
> P.O. Box 1067
> Augusta, ME 04332-1067

Refund:

> Maine Revenue Services
> P.O. Box 1066
> Augusta, ME 04332-1066

Alternative Minimum Tax?

Yes, for tax years prior to 2012.

IRC Conformity

IRC incorporated by reference as amended on January 2, 2013, for taxable years beginning after 2012.

Starting Point for Calculation of Taxable Income

Federal adjusted gross income.

Credit for Taxes Paid to Another State Allowed?

Residents: Yes. Credit allowed only against regular income tax, not minimum tax.

Part-Year Residents: Yes.

Nonresidents: No. Separate nonresident credit is allowed to offset tax attributable to income not subject to Maine taxation.

Federal Return Attachment Required?

Copy of federal return not required, unless nonresident credit is claimed. Attach, if applicable:

- Form 4562 (depreciation and amortization); and
- Schedule K-1 (beneficiary's share of income, deductions, credits, etc.).

Deadline for Reporting Federal Changes

Effective July 1, 2011, file within 180 days after final determination of the federal change or correction or the filing of the federal amended return. Prior to July 1, 2011, file within 90 days after final determination of the federal change or correction or the filing of the federal amended return.

Estimated Tax Payments

Required if expected liability is $1,000 or more after withholding and allowable credits, and if prior year liability also exceeded $1,000.

MARYLAND

Tax Agency Website: http://taxes.marylandtaxes.com/

2013 Individual Tax Rate Schedule

Single, and Married Filing Separately:

$	0 –	1,000	×	2.000 %	minus	$ 0
	1,001 –	2,000	×	3.000 %	minus	10
	2,001 –	3,000	×	4.000 %	minus	30
	3,001 –	100,000	×	4.750 %	minus	52.50
	100,001 –	125,000	×	5.000 %	minus	302.50
	125,001 –	150,000	×	5.250 %	minus	615.00
	150,001 –	250,000	×	5.500 %	minus	990.00
	250,001	and over	×	5.750 %	minus	1,615.00

Married Filing Jointly, Head of Household, and Qualifying Widow/Widower:

$	0 –	1,000	×	2.000 %	minus	$ 0
	1,001 –	2,000	×	3.000 %	minus	10
	2,001 –	3,000	×	4.000 %	minus	30
	3,001 –	150,000	×	4.750 %	minus	52.50
	150,001 –	175,000	×	5.000 %	minus	427.50
	175,001 –	225,000	×	5.250 %	minus	865.00
	225,001 –	300,000	×	5.500 %	minus	1,427.50
	300,001	and over	×	5.750 %	minus	2,177.50

 http://taxes.marylandtaxes.com/ Resource_Library/Online_Services/ default.shtml

Mandated for tax preparer who prepares more than 100 personal income tax returns in prior tax year. Taxpayer opt-out by checking box on Form 502/505. Waiver available for undue hardship or reasonable cause. Penalty of $50 per return for failure to e-file, up to $500, unless failure is due to reasonable cause and not willful neglect.

Filing Requirements

Form(s) to File: Form 502; Form 505

Due Date (General): April 15

Filing Status Options: Allowable state filing statuses include:

- Single
- Married Filing Jointly
- Married Filing Separately
- Head of Household
- Qualifying Widow(er)
- Dependent Taxpayer

Same-sex married couples must file (with few exceptions) using Married Filing Jointly or Married Filing Separately.

Filing Thresholds: Residents must file if they are required to file a federal return or have sufficient federal gross income to be required to file a federal return. Nonresidents must file if required to file a federal return and if income was received from state sources.

Where to Send Returns

Comptroller of Maryland
Revenue Administration Division
110 Carroll Street
Annapolis, MD 21411-0001

Alternative Minimum Tax?

Yes

IRC Conformity

IRC incorporated by reference as currently amended, unless the Comptroller determines that impact of federal amendment on state income tax revenue for the fiscal year that begins during the calendar year in which amendment is enacted will be $5 million or more.

Starting Point for Calculation of Taxable Income

Federal adjusted gross income.

Credit for Taxes Paid to Another State Allowed?

Residents and Part-Year Residents: Yes. A taxpayer who has income subject to tax in both Maryland and another state may be eligible for the credit. The credit is not allowed for tax on income that is paid to another state during residency in that state (a subtraction from income is allowed for income received during period of non-residence).

Nonresidents: No

Federal Return Attachment Required?

Copy of federal return not required.

Deadline for Reporting Federal Changes

File within 90 days after final determination of federal adjustment.

Estimated Tax Payments

Required if expected liability is over $500.

MASSACHUSETTS

Tax Agency Website: http://www.mass.gov/dor/

2013 Individual Tax Rate Schedule

Part A income represents either interest and dividends or short-term capital gains. Part B income represents wages, salaries, tips, pensions, state bank interest, partnership income, business income, rents, alimony, winnings and certain other items of income. Part C income represents gains from the sale of capital assets held for more than one year.

- Part A income (short-term capital gains): 12.00%
- Part A income (interest and dividends): 5.25%
- Part B income: 5.25%
- Part C income: 5.25%

Mandated for all tax preparers unless preparers reasonably expect to file 10 or fewer resident, nonresident, and part-year resident returns during the previous calendar year. Taxpayer opt-out on Form EFO, which must be retained by tax practitioner. No exceptions/waivers to mandate. Penalty of $100 per return for failure to e-file.

Filing Requirements
Form(s) to File: Form 1; Form 1-NR/PY

Due Date (General): April 15

Filing Status Options: Allowable state filing statuses include:

- Single
- Married Filing Jointly
- Married Filing Separately
- Head of Household

Same sex couples should choose Married Filing Jointly and combine figures from separate federal returns.

Filing Thresholds: Residents, nonresidents, and part-year residents must file if income exceeds the filing threshold for the applicable filing status (see below). The filing thresholds are adjusted on an annual basis.

   Residents: more than $8,000
   Nonresidents: Single, Married Filing Separately $4,400
   Nonresidents: Head of Household $6,800
   Nonresidents: Married Filing Jointly $8,800

Caution: The 2012 filing thresholds are shown above. At the time of publication, the 2013 filing thresholds were not available.

Where to Send Returns
Payment:

   Massachusetts Department of Revenue
   P.O. Box 7003
   Boston, MA 02204-7003

No Payment:

   Massachusetts Department of Revenue
   P.O. Box 7000
   Boston, MA 02204-7000

Payment 2D-Barcode:

   Massachusetts Department of Revenue
   P.O. Box 7002
   Boston, MA 02204-7002

No Payment 2D-Barcode:

   Massachusetts Department of Revenue
   P.O. Box 7001
   Boston, MA 02204-7001

Alternative Minimum Tax?
No

IRC Conformity
IRC incorporated as amended on January 1, 2005, with exceptions.

Starting Point for Calculation of Taxable Income
Federal gross income.

Credit for Taxes Paid to Another State Allowed?
Residents and Part-Year Residents: Yes

Nonresidents: No

Federal Return Attachment Required?
Copy of federal return not required. Taxpayers may attach federal Schedule C-EZ (business/profession income or loss) in place of Massachusetts Schedule C, and must attach federal Schedule F (farm income or loss), if applicable.

Deadline for Reporting Federal Changes
One year.

Estimated Tax Payments
Required if expected liability is $400 or more.

MICHIGAN

Tax Agency Website: http://www.michigan.gov/taxes

2013 Individual Tax Rate Schedule
Tax rate is 4.25%.

http://www.michigan.gov/taxes/0,4676,7-238-43689-118045--,00.html

Mandated for tax preparers that file 11 or more resident, nonresident, and part-year resident returns. No taxpayer opt-out available. No exceptions or waivers to mandate. No penalty for failure to e-file.

Filing Requirements
Form(s) to File: Form MI-1040

Due Date (General): April 15

Filing Status Options: Allowable state filing statuses include:

- Single
- Married Filing Jointly
- Married Filing Separately

File as single if federal return was filed as head of household or qualifying widow(er).

Filing Thresholds: Residents must file if required to file a federal return or AGI exceeds exemption allowance for each exemption claimed on federal return. Nonresidents that received income from state sources must file regardless of income level. Dependents must file if AGI exceeds $1,500 and filing status is single or married filing separately, or $3,000 and filing status is married filing jointly.

Where to Send Returns
Payment:

Michigan Department of Treasury
Lansing, MI 48929

No Payment:

Michigan Department of Treasury
Lansing, MI 48956

Alternative Minimum Tax?
No

IRC Conformity
IRC incorporated as amended on January 1, 1996, or, at the option of the taxpayer, IRC in effect for current taxable year.

Starting Point for Calculation of Taxable Income
Federal adjusted gross income.

Credit for Taxes Paid to Another State Allowed?
Residents and Part-Year Residents: Yes

Nonresidents: No. If nonresident's state of residence exempts a Michigan resident from taxation on income earned for personal services performed in that state, a reciprocal agreement may provide a similar tax exemption for that state's residents on income earned for personal services performed in Michigan.

Federal Return Attachment Required?
Copy of federal return not required. Taxpayers must attach the following schedules and forms, if applicable:

- Schedule B or 1040A Schedule 1 (interest and dividend income if over $5,000);
- Schedule C or C-EZ (business income and losses);
- Schedule D (gains and losses);
- Schedule E (rent, royalty, partnership income);
- Schedule F (farm income or losses);
- Schedule R or 1040A Schedule 3 (credit for elderly or disabled);
- Form 1040NR (Nonresident Alien Income Tax Return);
- Form 2555 (foreign earned income);
- Form 3903 or 3903-F (moving expenses);
- Form 4797 (gains and losses);
- Form 6198 (deductible loss from activity);
- Form 8829 (expenses for business use of home); and
- Form 8839 (adoption expenses).

Taxpayers claiming credit for repayment of amounts previously reported as income must attach pages 1 and 2 of federal Form 1040 and Schedule A, if applicable.

Deadline for Reporting Federal Changes
File within 120 days after final determination of federal adjustment.

Estimated Tax Payments
Required if expected liability is over $500.

MINNESOTA

Tax Agency Website: http://www.revenue.state.mn.us/Pages/default.aspx

2013 Individual Tax Rate Schedule
Single:

$	0 –	24,270	× 5.350 %	minus	$	0
	24,271 –	79,730	× 7.050 %	minus		412.59
	79,731 –	150,000	× 7.850 %	minus		1,050.42
	150,001	and over	× 9.850 %	minus		4,050.42

Married Filing Jointly:

$	0 –	35,480	× 5.350 %	minus	$	0
	35,481 –	140,960	× 7.050 %	minus		603.16
	140,961 –	250,000	× 7.850 %	minus		1,730.84
	250,001	and over	× 9.850 %	minus		6,730.84

Married Filing Separately:

$	0 –	17,740	× 5.350 %	minus	$	0
	17,741 –	70,480	× 7.050 %	minus		301.58
	70,481 –	125,000	× 7.850 %	minus		865.42
	125,001	and over	× 9.850 %	minus		3,365.42

Head of Household:

$	0 –	29,880	× 5.350 %	minus	$	0
	29,881 –	120,070	× 7.050 %	minus		507.96
	120,071 –	200,000	× 7.850 %	minus		1,468.51
	200,001	and over	× 9.850 %	minus		5,468.51

A 6.75% alternative minimum tax is imposed. Brackets indexed for inflation annually.

  http://www.revenue.state.mn.us/individuals/individ_income/Pages/eServices.aspx

Mandated for tax preparers that reasonably expect to file more than 10 returns, including resident, nonresident, and part-year resident returns, for current year. Taxpayer opt-out available by checking box on return. Waiver available in rare circumstances. Penalty of $5 per return for each Form M1 return that is not filed electronically, including taxpayer opt-out returns.

Filing Requirements
Form(s) to File: Form M1

Due Date (General): April 15

Filing Status Options: Allowable state filing statuses include:

- Single
- Married Filing Jointly
- Married Filing Separately

- Head of Household
- Qualifying Widow(er) with Dependent Child

Filing Thresholds: Residents must file if required to file a federal return. Part-year residents and nonresidents must file if Minnesota gross income is $9,750 or more. The non-resident filing threshold is adjusted on an annual basis.

Caution: The 2012 filing thresholds are shown above. At the time of publication, the 2013 filing thresholds were not available.

Where to Send Returns
Minnesota Individual Income Tax
St. Paul, MN 55145-0010

Alternative Minimum Tax?
Yes

IRC Conformity
IRC adopted as amended through January 3, 2013, for 2012 tax year. IRC adopted as amended through April 14, 2011, for tax years beginning before 2012 and after 2012.

Starting Point for Calculation of Taxable Income
Federal taxable income.

Credit for Taxes Paid to Another State Allowed?
Yes. For nonresidents, the credit is allowed if the taxpayer is required to file a Minnesota return as a Minnesota resident and paid income tax to Minnesota and his or her state of residence. A credit is allowed for income taxes paid to a nonresident's domicile state if: (1) tax is from gain realized on the sale of a partnership interest assignable to Minnesota, and (2) the nonresident's state does not allow a credit for Minnesota taxes paid.

Federal Return Attachment Required?
Complete copy of federal return and schedules must be attached. Attach, if applicable:

- Form 6251 (alternative minimum tax return); and
- Form 8886 (reportable transaction disclosure statement).

A copy of federal Form 8886 also must be mailed to the Minnesota Department of Revenue when the taxpayer first discloses reportable transaction. Penalties apply for non-compliance.

Deadline for Reporting Federal Changes
File within 180 days after final determination of federal adjustment.

Estimated Tax Payments
Required if expected liability is $500 or more.

MISSISSIPPI

Tax Agency Website: http://www.dor.ms.gov/

2013 Individual Tax Rate Schedule

$	0	–	5,000	×	3.000 %	minus	$	0
	5,001	–	10,000	×	4.000 %	minus		50.00
	10,001	and over		×	5.000 %	minus		150.00

 http://www.dor.ms.gov/e-services.html

Allowed for resident, nonresident, and part-year resident returns. Mandate authorized, but not yet implemented.

Filing Requirements
Form(s) to File: Form 80-105; Form 80-205

Due Date (General): April 15

Filing Status Options: Allowable state filing statuses include:

- Single
- Married Filing Joint or Combined Return
- Married Spouse Died
- Married Filing Separate Returns
- Head of Family Individual

Filing Thresholds: Residents must file if income exceeds thresholds for applicable filing status (see below). Nonresidents and part-year residents with income taxed by Mississippi, other than gambling income, must file.

Single: $8,300, plus $1,500 per dependent
Head of Household: $12,900, plus $1,500 per dependent
Married Filing Jointly: $16,600, plus $1,500 per dependent
Married Filing Separately: $8,300, plus $1,500 per dependent

Where to Send Returns
Payment/No Tax Due:

Department of Revenue
P.O. Box 23050
Jackson, MS 39225-3050

Refund:

Department of Revenue
P.O. Box 23058
Jackson, MS 39225-3058

Alternative Minimum Tax?
No

IRC Conformity
IRC not incorporated.

Starting Point for Calculation of Taxable Income
Mississippi gross income.

Credit for Taxes Paid to Another State Allowed?
Residents: Yes

Nonresidents and Part-Year Residents: No

Federal Return Attachment Required?
Copy of federal return not required. Taxpayers must attach the following federal schedules and forms, if applicable:

- Schedule C or C-EZ (business income and losses);
- Schedule D (gains and losses);
- Schedule E (rent, royalty, partnership income);
- Schedule F (farm income or losses);
- Form 2106 (unreimbursed employee expense deduction);
- Form 3903 or 3903-F (moving expenses); and
- Form 4684 (casualty and theft losses).

If amount of state taxable income entered on Form 80-105 differs from amount of federal taxable income entered on a federal return, separate reconciling schedules must be attached.

Deadline for Reporting Federal Changes File within 30 days after agreeing to the federal change.

Estimated Tax Payments
Required if expected liability is over $200.

MISSOURI

Tax Agency Website: http://dor.mo.gov/

2013 Individual Tax Rate Schedule

$		0	–	1,000	×	1.500 %	minus	$	0
	1,001	–	2,000	×	2.000 %	minus		5.00
	2,001	–	3,000	×	2.500 %	minus		15.00
	3,001	–	4,000	×	3.000 %	minus		30.00
	4,001	–	5,000	×	3.500 %	minus		50.00
	5,001	–	6,000	×	4.000 %	minus		75.00
	6,001	–	7,000	×	4.500 %	minus		105.00
	7,001	–	8,000	×	5.000 %	minus		140.00
	8,001	–	9,000	×	5.500 %	minus		180.00
	9,001	and over	×	6.000 %	minus		225.00

  http://dor.mo.gov/electronic/

Allowed for resident, nonresident, and part-year resident returns.

Filing Requirements
Form(s) to File: Form MO-1040

Due Date (General): April 15

Filing Status Options: Allowable state filing statuses include:

- Single
- Dependent on Another Person's Federal Tax Return
- Married Filing Jointly
- Married Filing Separately
- Married Filing Separately (Spouse Not Filing)
- Head of Household
- Qualifying Widow(er) with Dependent Child

Filing Thresholds: Filing required if taxpayer is required to file a federal return, except:

- residents with less than $1,200 of state AGI;
- nonresidents with less than $600 of state income; or
- taxpayers with state AGI less than amount of standard deduction plus exemption amount for applicable filing status.

Where to Send Returns
Payment:

> Department of Revenue
> P.O. Box 329
> Jefferson City, MO 65107-0329

Refund:

> Department of Revenue
> P.O. Box 500
> Jefferson City, MO 65106-0500

Alternative Minimum Tax?
No

IRC Conformity
IRC incorporated by reference as currently amended.

Starting Point for Calculation of Taxable Income
Federal adjusted gross income.

Credit for Taxes Paid to Another State Allowed?
Residents and Part-Year Residents: Yes

Nonresidents: No

Federal Return Attachment Required?
Copy of federal return must be attached.

Attach, if applicable:

- Schedule A (itemized deductions);
- Form 1045 (net operating loss);
- Form 1099-R, Form W-2P, and/or Form SSA-1099 (pension, social security, and/or social security disability exemption);
- Form 4255 (recapture taxes);
- Form 4797 (capital gain exclusion on sale of low income housing);
- Form 4972 (lump sum distribution);
- Form 8611 (recapture taxes);
- Form 8826 (disabled access credit);
- Form 8828 (recapture taxes); and
- Schedule K-1.

Attachment of Form 8886 (reportable transaction disclosure statement), if applicable, is also recommended by Department of Revenue.

Deadline for Reporting Federal Changes
File within 90 days after final determination of federal adjustment.

Estimated Tax Payments
Required if expected liability is at least $100.

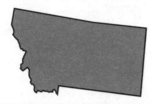

MONTANA

Tax Agency Website: http://revenue.mt.gov/default.mcpx

2013 Individual Tax Rate Schedule

$					$	
0	–	2,800	× 1.000 %	minus	$	0
2,801	–	4,900	× 2.000 %	minus		28.00
4,901	–	7,400	× 3.000 %	minus		77.00
7,401	–	10,100	× 4.000 %	minus		151.00
10,101	–	13,000	× 5.000 %	minus		252.00
13,001	–	16,700	× 6.000 %	minus		382.00
16,701	and over		× 6.900 %	minus		532.00

Minimum tax, $1. Brackets are indexed for inflation annually.

 http://revenue.mt.gov/forprofessionals/tax_preparers_practitioners/default.mcpx

Allowed for resident, nonresident, and part-year resident returns.

Filing Requirements
Form(s) to File: Form 2

Due Date (General): April 15

Filing Status Options: Allowable state filing statuses include:

- Single
- Married Filing Jointly
- Married Filing Separately on Same Form
- Married Filing Separately on Separate Forms
- Married Filing Separately and Spouse Not Filing
- Head of Household

Filing Thresholds: Residents, part-year residents, and non-residents must file if state-source income and federal gross income, excluding unemployment compensation, exceeds threshold for applicable filing status (see below). If taxpayer or spouse is blind, threshold amount is increased by $2,240. The filing thresholds are adjusted on an annual basis.

> Single, Married Filing Separately
> Under 65 years of age: $4,100
> 65 years of age or older: $6,340
> Head of Household
> Under 65 years of age: $5,960
> 65 years of age or older: $8,200

> Married Filing Jointly
> Under 65 years of age: $8,200
> 65 years of age or older (one): $10,440
> 65 years of age or older (both): $12,680

Caution: The 2012 filing thresholds are shown above. At the time of publication, the 2013 filing thresholds were not available.

Where to Send Returns
Payment:

> Montana Department of Revenue
> P.O. Box 6308
> Helena, MT 59604-6308

No Payment:

> Montana Department of Revenue
> P.O. Box 6577
> Helena, MT 59604-6577

Alternative Minimum Tax?
No

IRC Conformity
IRC incorporated by reference as currently amended.

Starting Point for Calculation of Taxable Income
Federal adjusted gross income.

Credit for Taxes Paid to Another State Allowed?
Residents and Part-Year Residents: Yes

Nonresidents: No

Federal Return Attachment Required?
Copy of federal return must be attached by nonresident and part-year resident taxpayers.

Pages 1 and 2 of federal return must be attached if head-of-household filing status is used. Attach, if applicable:

- Schedule B (interest and dividend income);
- Schedule C or C-EZ (business income and losses);
- Schedule D (gains and losses);
- Schedule E (rent, royalty, partnership income);
- Schedule F (farm income or losses);
- Schedule SE (self-employment tax);
- Form 1310 (statement of person claiming refund of deceased taxpayer);
- Form 2106 or 2106-EZ (unreimbursed employee business expenses);
- Form 3468 (historic property preservation credit);
- Form 3903 or 3903-F (moving expenses);
- Form 4797 (gains and losses);
- Form 4972 (lump sum distribution);
- Form 8839 (adoption expenses);
- Form 8889 (health savings account deduction); and
- Form 8903 (domestic production activities).

Deadline for Reporting Federal Changes

File within 90 days after receiving official notice of the federal change or correction.

Estimated Tax Payments

Required if expected liability is $500 or more after subtracting credits and withholding.

NEBRASKA

Tax Agency Website: http://www.revenue.ne.gov/

2013 Individual Tax Rate Schedule

Single:

$	0	–	2,400	× 2.460 %	minus	$ 0
	2,401	–	17,500	× 3.510 %	minus	25.20
	17,501	–	27,000	× 5.010 %	minus	287.70
	27,001	and over		× 6.840 %	minus	781.80

Married Filing Jointly, Surviving Spouse:

$	0	–	4,800	× 2.460 %	minus	$ 0
	4,801	–	35,000	× 3.510 %	minus	50.40
	35,001	–	54,000	× 5.010 %	minus	575.40
	54,001	and over		× 6.840 %	minus	1,563.60

Married Filing Separately:

$	0	–	2,400	× 2.460 %	minus	$ 0
	2,401	–	17,500	× 3.510 %	minus	25.20
	17,501	–	27,000	× 5.010 %	minus	287.70
	27,001	and over		× 6.840 %	minus	781.80

Head of Household:

$	0	–	4,500	× 2.460 %	minus	$ 0
	4,501	–	28,000	× 3.510 %	minus	47.25
	28,001	–	40,000	× 5.010 %	minus	467.25
	40,001	and over		× 6.840 %	minus	1,199.25

  http://www.revenue.ne.gov/electron/e-file.html

Mandated for tax preparers that file 25 or more resident, nonresident, and part-year resident returns in prior calendar year. Taxpayer opt-out available. Waiver for preparer if undue hardship. Preparer penalty for failing to comply is $100 per return.

Filing Requirements

Form(s) to File: Form 1040N

Due Date (General): April 15

Filing Status Options: Allowable state filing statuses include:

- Single
- Married Filing Jointly
- Married Filing Separately
- Head of Household
- Qualifying Widow(er) with Dependent Child

Filing Thresholds: Residents, nonresidents, and part-year residents must file if required to file federal return and report federal liability, or if taxpayer has $5,000 or more of state adjustments to federal AGI, including non-Nebraska state and local bond interest income exempt from federal tax.

Where to Send Returns

Payment:

Nebraska Department of Revenue
P.O. Box 98934
Lincoln, NE 68509-8934

No Payment:

Nebraska Department of Revenue
P.O. Box 98912
Lincoln, NE 68509-8912

Alternative Minimum Tax?

Yes. No, for tax years after 2013.

IRC Conformity

IRC incorporated by reference as currently amended.

Starting Point for Calculation of Taxable Income

Federal adjusted gross income.

Credit for Taxes Paid to Another State Allowed?

Residents: Yes

Nonresidents and Part-Year Residents: No

Federal Return Attachment Required?

Copy of federal return not required. Copy of pages 1 and 2 of federal return must be attached if claiming earned income credit. Taxpayers must attach the following federal schedules and forms, if applicable:

- Schedule D (special capital gain deduction);
- Schedule R or 1040A Schedule 3 (credit for elderly or disabled);
- Form 2441 or 1040A Schedule 2 (child/dependent care credit);
- Form 4972 (lump sum distributions);
- Form 5329 or copy of federal return if Form 5329 not required (early retirement plan distributions); and
- Form 6251 (alternative minimum tax recalculated under Revenue Ruling 22-03-1).

Deadline for Reporting Federal Changes

File within 60 days after a correction or change to the federal return.

Estimated Tax Payments

Required if expected liability is $500 or more.

NEVADA

Tax Agency Website: http://tax.state.nv.us/

Nevada does not collect personal income tax.

NEW HAMPSHIRE

Tax Agency Website: http://www.nh.gov/revenue

2013 Individual Tax Rate Schedule
Tax rate is 5% on interest and dividends only, regardless of filing status.

 https://www.efilenh.govconnect.com/web/introduction.asp

Allowed for residents and part-year resident returns. Non-residents are not subject to the interest and dividends tax.

Filing Requirements
Form(s) to File: Form DP-10

Due Date (General): April 15

Filing Status Options: Allowable state filing statuses include:

- Individual
- Joint

Same-sex married individuals may file jointly.

Filing Thresholds: Tax is imposed only on the income from interest and dividends. Filing is required for residents and part-year residents if interest and dividend taxable interest exceeds the threshold for the applicable filing status (see below).

Single: $2,400
Married Filing Jointly: $4,800

Where to Send Returns
NH Dept. of Revenue Administration
P.O. Box 2072
Concord, NH 03302-2072

Alternative Minimum Tax?
No

IRC Conformity
IRC incorporated.

Starting Point for Calculation of Taxable Income
New Hampshire gross income (tax on interest and dividends only).

Credit for Taxes Paid to Another State Allowed?
No

Federal Return Attachment Required?
Copy of federal return not required.

Deadline for Reporting Federal Changes
File within six months after final determination of federal adjustment.

Estimated Tax Payments
Required if expected liability is $500 or more.

NEW JERSEY

Tax Agency Website: http://www.state.nj.us/treasury/taxation

2013 Individual Tax Rate Schedule
Single, Married/Civil Union Partner Filing Separately:

$	0	–	20,000	×	1.400 %	minus	$	0
	20,001	–	35,000	×	1.750 %	minus		70.00
	35,001	–	40,000	×	3.500 %	minus		682.50
	40,001	–	75,000	×	5.525 %	minus		1,492.50
	75,001	–	500,000	×	6.370 %	minus		2,126.25
	500,001	and over		×	8.970 %	minus		15,126.25

Married/Civil Union Couple Filing Jointly, Head of Household, Qualifying Widow(er)/Surviving Civil Union Partner:

$	0	–	20,000	×	1.400 %	minus	$	0
	20,001	–	50,000	×	1.750 %	minus		70.00
	50,001	–	70,000	×	2.450 %	minus		420.00
	70,001	–	80,000	×	3.500 %	minus		1,154.50
	80,001	–	150,000	×	5.525 %	minus		2,775.00
	150,001	–	500,000	×	6.370 %	minus		4,042.50
	500,001	and over		×	8.970 %	minus		17,042.50

 http://www.state.nj.us/treasury/taxation/online.shtml

Mandated for tax preparers that reasonably expect to prepare 11 or more resident returns, including those prepared for trusts and estates, during the taxable year. Resident, nonresident, and part-year resident returns can be e-filed. Taxpayer opt-out available on Form NJ-1040-O. Tax preparer must maintain completed and signed form in file. No waivers or exceptions to mandate. Penalty of $50 per return if fail to e-file. Penalty may be abated if failure to e-file is due to reasonable cause.

Filing Requirements

Form(s) to File: Form NJ-1040; Form NJ-1040NR

Due Date (General): April 15

Filing Status Options: Allowable state filing statuses include:

- Single
- Married/Civil Union Filing Jointly
- Married/Civil Union Partner Filing Separately
- Head of Household
- Qualifying Widow(er)/Surviving Civil Union Partner

Filing Thresholds: Residents, nonresidents, and part-year residents must file if income exceeds filing thresholds (see below).

Single: $10,000
Head of Household: $20,000
Married Filing Jointly: $20,000
Married Filing Separately: $10,000
Surviving Spouse: $20,000

Where to Send Returns

Form NJ-1040, Payment:

NJ Division of Taxation
Revenue Processing Center
P.O. Box 111
Trenton, NJ 08645-0111

Form NJ-1040, Refund:

NJ Division of Taxation
Revenue Processing Center
P.O. Box 555
Trenton, NJ 08647-0555

Form NJ-1040NR:

State of New Jersey – TGI
Division of Taxation
Revenue Processing Center
P.O. Box 244
Trenton, NJ 08646-0244

Alternative Minimum Tax?

No

IRC Conformity

IRC not incorporated. Some income categories are treated in a manner similar to their treatment for federal income tax purposes.

Starting Point for Calculation of Taxable Income

New Jersey gross income.

Credit for Taxes Paid to Another State Allowed?

Residents and Part-Year Residents: Yes

Nonresidents: No

Federal Return Attachment Required?

Copy of federal return not required. Part-year residents with income below annual filing threshold ($10,000 single

or married filing separately, $20,000 married filing jointly) must attach copy of federal return. Taxpayers must attach the following federal schedules and forms, if applicable:

- Schedule B (interest and dividend income);
- Schedule C or C-EZ (business income and losses);
- Schedule F (farm income or losses);
- Form 2106 or 2106-EZ (unreimbursed employee business expenses);
- Form 3903 or 3903-F (moving expenses);
- Form 8283 (qualified conservation contributions);
- Form 8853 (Archer MSA contributions); and
- Schedule K-1.

Deadline for Reporting Federal Changes

Must report within 90 days and must either concede the accuracy of the determination or state the grounds upon which the taxpayer contends the determination is erroneous.

Estimated Tax Payments

Required if expected liability is more than $400 after withholding and credits.

NEW MEXICO

Tax Agency Website: http://www.tax.newmexico.gov/Pages/TRD-Homepage.aspx

2013 Individual Tax Rate Schedule

Single:

$	0 –	5,500	× 1.700 %	minus	$	0
	5,501 –	11,000	× 3.200 %	minus		82.50
	11,001 –	16,000	× 4.700 %	minus		247.50
	16,001	and over	× 4.900 %	minus		279.50

Married Filing Jointly, Qualifying Widow(er):

$	0 –	8,000	× 1.700 %	minus	$	0
	8,001 –	16,000	× 3.200 %	minus		120.00
	16,001 –	24,000	× 4.700 %	minus		360.00
	24,001	and over	× 4.900 %	minus		408.00

Married Filing Separately:

$	0 –	4,000	× 1.700 %	minus	$	0
	4,001 –	8,000	× 3.200 %	minus		60.00
	8,001 –	12,000	× 4.700 %	minus		180.00
	12,001	and over	× 4.900 %	minus		204.00

Head of Household:

$	0 –	8,000	× 1.700 %	minus	$	0
	8,001 –	16,000	× 3.200 %	minus		120.00
	16,001 –	24,000	× 4.700 %	minus		360.00
	24,001	and over	× 4.900 %	minus		408.00

Qualified nonresident taxpayers may pay alternative tax of 0.75% of gross receipts from sales in New Mexico.

http://www.tax.newmexico. gov/Tax-Professionals/Pages/ Electronic-Filing-Information.aspx

Mandated for tax preparers filing more than 25 resident, nonresident, and part-year resident returns per year. Taxpayer opt-out on Form RPD-41338, and checkbox in paid preparer's signature box on return must be marked. Tax preparer keeps copy of Form RPD-41338 for three years. No waivers or exceptions to mandate. Penalty of $5 per return if fail to e-file.

Filing Requirements

Form(s) to File: Form PIT-1

Due Date (General): April 15

Filing Status Options: Allowable state filing statuses include:

- Single
- Married Filing Jointly
- Married Filing Separately
- Head of Household
- Qualifying Widow(er) with Dependent Child

New Mexico does not recognize same-sex marriages, civil unions, or domestic partnerships for filing status purposes.

Filing Thresholds: Residents must file if required to file federal return. Nonresidents must file if required to file federal return and if income is received from any business transaction, property, or employment within the state.

Where to Send Returns

Payment:

> Taxation and Revenue Department
> P.O. Box 8390
> Santa Fe, NM 87504-8390

No Payment:

> Taxation and Revenue Department
> P.O. Box 25122
> Santa Fe, NM 87504-5122

Alternative Minimum Tax?
No

IRC Conformity
IRC incorporated by reference as currently amended.

Starting Point for Calculation of Taxable Income
Federal adjusted gross income.

Credit for Taxes Paid to Another State Allowed?
Residents: Yes. Credit limited to amount of taxpayer's New Mexico income tax liability on portion of income allocated or apportioned to New Mexico on which tax payable to other state is determined.

Part-Year Residents: Yes

Nonresidents: No

Federal Return Attachment Required?
Copy of federal return not required. However, state may request copy of federal return and attachments.

Deadline for Reporting Federal Changes
File within 180 days after final determination of federal adjustment (90 days prior to July 1, 2013).

Estimated Tax Payments
Required if expected liability is $1,000 or more.

NEW YORK

Tax Agency Website: http://www.tax.ny.gov/
2013 Individual Tax Rate Schedule

Single, Married Filing Separately:

$	0	–	8,200	× 4.000 %	minus	$	0
	8,201	–	11,300	× 4.500 %	minus		41.00
	11,301	–	13,350	× 5.250 %	minus		125.75
	13,351	–	20,550	× 5.900 %	minus		212.52
	20,551	–	77,150	× 6.450 %	minus		325.55
	77,151	–	205,850	× 6.650 %	minus		479.85
	205,851	–	1,029,250	× 6.850 %	minus		891.55
	1,029,251		and over	× 8.820 %	minus		21,167.77

Married Filing Jointly, Qualifying Widow(er):

$	0	–	16,450	× 4.000 %	minus	$	0
	16,451	–	22,600	× 4.500 %	minus		82.25
	22,601	–	26,750	× 5.250 %	minus		251.75
	26,751	–	41,150	× 5.900 %	minus		425.62
	41,151	–	154,350	× 6.450 %	minus		651.95
	154,351	–	308,750	× 6.650 %	minus		960.65
	308,751	–	2,058,550	× 6.850 %	minus		1,578.15
	2,058,551		and over	× 8.820 %	minus		42,131.58

Head of Household:

$	0	–	12,350	× 4.000 %	minus	$	0
	12,351	–	16,950	× 4.500 %	minus		61.75
	16,951	–	20,050	× 5.250 %	minus		188.88
	20,051	–	30,850	× 5.900 %	minus		319.20
	30,851	–	102,900	× 6.450 %	minus		488.87
	102,901	–	257,300	× 6.650 %	minus		694.67
	257,301	–	1,543,900	× 6.850 %	minus		1,209.27
	1,543,901		and over	× 8.820 %	minus		31,624.10

A supplemental tax is imposed to recapture the tax table benefit. Brackets indexed for inflation annually.

 http://www.tax.ny.gov/tp/

Mandated for tax preparers that prepared authorized tax documents for more than ten different taxpayers during any calendar year beginning after 2011, and that prepare one or more authorized tax documents using tax software in the subsequent calendar year.

Mandated for taxpayers preparing their own returns or other tax documents using tax software, applicable to documents filed during 2012 through 2016.

No taxpayer opt-out. No exception to mandate. Preparer penalty of $50 per return or extension if fail to e-file, unless there is reasonable cause. Penalty of $500 if charge separate e-file fee; $1,000 for later occurrences.

Preparers filing returns on or after December 31, 2009, are required to register electronically with New York Department of Taxation and Finance and pay an annual fee of $100.

Filing Requirements

Form(s) to File: Form IT-201; Form IT-203

Due Date (General): April 15

Filing Status Options: Same as federal, except married taxpayers filing jointly if:

- one spouse is state resident but other is nonresident or part-year resident;
- taxpayer is unable to file jointly for state purposes because address or whereabouts of one spouse is unknown; or
- one spouse refuses to sign joint state return.

Same sex married couples must file using a married filing status and recompute their federal income tax as if they were married for federal purposes.

Filing Thresholds: Residents must file if:

- required to file federal return;
- federal AGI plus state addition modifications is more than $4,000 or state standard deduction; or
- minimum tax is applicable.

Nonresidents and part-year residents must file if income from state sources and state AGI is more than standard deduction. Dependents must file if single and if federal AGI plus state addition modifications is more than $3,000.

Where to Send Returns

Payment:

State Processing Center
P.O. Box 15555
Albany, NY 12212-5555

No Payment:

State Processing Center
P.O. Box 61000
Albany, NY 12261-0001

Alternative Minimum Tax?

Yes

IRC Conformity

IRC not incorporated.

Starting Point for Calculation of Taxable Income

Federal adjusted gross income.

Credit for Taxes Paid to Another State Allowed?

Residents: Yes. Credit limited to items of income sourced to those other qualifying locations.

Part-Year Residents: Yes

Nonresidents: No

Federal Return Attachment Required?

Copy of federal return not required. Taxpayers must attach the following federal schedules and forms, if applicable:

- Schedule C or C-EZ (business income and losses);
- Schedule D (gains and losses);
- Schedule E (rent, royalty, partnership income);
- Schedule F (farm income or losses); and
- Form 4797 (gains and losses).

Copy of federal Form 8886 (Reportable Transaction Disclosure Statement) and any related information submitted to IRS must be attached, if applicable.

Deadline for Reporting Federal Changes

File within 90 days after final determination of federal adjustment.

Estimated Tax Payments

Required if expected liability is $300 or more after withholding and credits.

NORTH CAROLINA

Tax Agency Website: http://www.dor.state.nc.us

2013 Individual Tax Rate Schedule

Single:

$	0 – 12,750	× 6.000 %	minus	$	0
	12,751 – 60,000	× 7.000 %	minus		127.50
	60,001 and over	× 7.750 %	minus		577.50

Married Filing Jointly, Qualifying Widow(er):

$	0 – 21,250	× 6.000 %	minus	$	0
	21,251 – 100,000	× 7.000 %	minus		212.50
	100,001 and over	× 7.750 %	minus		962.50

Married Filing Separately:

$	0 – 10,625	× 6.000 %	minus	$	0
	10,626 – 50,000	× 7.000 %	minus		106.25
	50,001 and over	× 7.750 %	minus		481.25

Head of Household:

$	0 – 17,000	× 6.000 %	minus	$	0
	17,001 – 80,000	× 7.000 %	minus		170.00
	80,001 and over	× 7.750 %	minus		770.00

  http://www.dor.state.nc.us/electronic/index.html

Allowed for resident, nonresident, and part-year resident returns.

Filing Requirements

Form(s) to File: Form D-400

Due Date (General): April 15

Filing Status Options: Allowable state filing statuses include:

- Single
- Married Filing Jointly
- Married Filing Separately
- Head of Household
- Qualifying Widow(er) with Dependent Child

Filing Thresholds: Residents must file if income for taxable year equals or exceeds threshold for applicable filing status (see below). Nonresidents must file if income attributable to state sources equals or exceeds threshold for applicable filing status. Part-year residents must file if income received while a resident and/or income received from state sources while a nonresident equals or exceeds threshold for applicable filing status.

> Single
> Under 65 years of age: $5,500
> 65 years of age or older: $6,250
>
> Head of Household
> Under 65 years of age: $6,900
> 65 years of age or older: $7,650
>
> Married Filing Jointly
> Under 65 years of age: $11,000
> 65 years of age or older (one): $11,600
> 65 years of age or older (both): $12,200
>
> Married Filing Separately
> Any age: $2,500
>
> Surviving Spouse with dependent child
> Under 65 years of age: $8,500
> 65 years of age or older: $9,100

Where to Send Returns

No Refund:

> N.C. Department of Revenue
> P.O. Box 25000
> Raleigh, N.C. 27640-0640

Refund:

> N.C. Department of Revenue
> P.O. Box R
> Raleigh, NC 27634-0001

Alternative Minimum Tax?
No

IRC Conformity
IRC incorporated by reference as of January 2, 2013, for 2012 taxable year, except any federal amendments enacted after January 1, 2012, that increase state taxable income for the taxable year become effective beginning with the 2013 tax year.

Starting Point for Calculation of Taxable Income
For tax years after 2011, federal adjusted gross income.

Credit for Taxes Paid to Another State Allowed?
Residents and Part-Year Residents: Yes

Nonresidents: No

Federal Return Attachment Required?
Copy of federal return not required. Copy of federal return must be attached if federal return bears out-of-state address and taxpayer did not file electronically. Taxpayers with gross income meeting filing t hreshold who were not required to file federal return must complete and attach federal return. Taxpayers filing separate state return who filed joint federal return must complete and attach federal return as married filing separately or schedule showing computation of separate federal taxable income and include copy of joint federal return if that return bears out-of-state address.

Deadline for Reporting Federal Changes
File within six months of notification of correction or federal determination.

Estimated Tax Payments
Required if expected liability is $1,000 or more after subtracting credits and withholding.

NORTH DAKOTA

Tax Agency Website: http://www.nd.gov/tax

2013 Individual Tax Rate Schedule

Single:

$	0	–	36,250	× 1.220 %	minus	$	0
	36,251	–	87,850	× 2.270 %	minus		380.63
	87,851	–	183,250	× 2.520 %	minus		600.25
	183,251	–	398,350	× 2.930 %	minus		1,351.58
	398,351	and over		× 3.220 %	minus		2,506.79

Married Filing Jointly, Qualifying Widow(er):

$	0	–	60,650	× 1.220 %	minus	$	0
	60,651	–	146,400	× 2.270 %	minus		636.82
	146,401	–	223,050	× 2.520 %	minus		1,002.82
	223,051	–	398,350	× 2.930 %	minus		1,917.33
	398,351	and over		× 3.220 %	minus		3,072.54

Married Filing Separately:

$	0	–	30,325	× 1.220 %	minus	$	0
	30,326	–	73,200	× 2.270 %	minus		318.41
	73,201	–	111,525	× 2.520 %	minus		501.41
	111,526	–	199,175	× 2.930 %	minus		958.66
	199,176	and over		× 3.220 %	minus		1,536.27

Head of Household:

$	0 – 48,600	×	1.220 %	minus	$	0
	48,601 – 125,450	×	2.270 %	minus		510.30
	125,451 – 203,150	×	2.520 %	minus		823.92
	203,151 – 398,350	×	2.930 %	minus		1,656.84
	398,351 and over	×	3.220 %	minus		2,812.05

Brackets are indexed for inflation annually.

 http://www.nd.gov/tax/

Allowed for resident, nonresident, and part-year resident returns.

Filing Requirements

Form(s) to File: Form ND-1

Due Date (General): April 15

Filing Status Options: Allowable state filing statuses include:

- Single
- Married Filing Jointly
- Married Filing Separately
- Head of Household
- Qualifying Widow(er) with Dependent Child

Filing Thresholds: Residents must file if required to file federal return. Nonresidents must file if required to file federal return and income is received from state sources. Part-year residents must file if required to file a federal return and income is received from any source while a resident or income is received from states sources while a nonresident.

Where to Send Returns

State Tax Commissioner
P.O. Box 5621
Bismarck, ND 58506-5621

Alternative Minimum Tax?

No

IRC Conformity

IRC incorporated by reference as currently amended.

Starting Point for Calculation of Taxable Income

Federal taxable income.

Credit for Taxes Paid to Another State Allowed?

Residents and Part-Year Residents: Yes

Nonresidents: No

Federal Return Attachment Required?

Complete copy of federal return, including supplemental forms and schedules, must be attached.

Deadline for Reporting Federal Changes

File within 90 days after final determination of federal adjustment.

Estimated Tax Payments

Required if expected liability is $1,000 or more after withholding and credits.

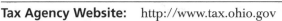

OHIO

Tax Agency Website: http://www.tax.ohio.gov

2013 Individual Tax Rate Schedule

$	0 – 5,200	×	0.537 %	minus	$	0
	5,201 – 10,400	×	1.074 %	minus		27.93
	10,401 – 15,650	×	2.148 %	minus		139.62
	15,651 – 20,900	×	2.686 %	minus		223.81
	20,901 – 41,700	×	3.222 %	minus		335.83
	41,701 – 83,350	×	3.760 %	minus		560.18
	83,351 – 104,250	×	4.296 %	minus		1,006.94
	104,251 – 208,500	×	4.988 %	minus		1,728.35
	208,501 and over	×	5.421 %	minus		2,631.16

 http://www.tax.ohio.gov/File.aspx

Mandated for tax preparers who prepare more than 11 original (resident, nonresident, part-year resident) individual tax returns during any calendar year that begins after 2012. Taxpayer opt-out available. Waivers determined on case-by-case. Penalty of $50 per return if fail to e-file.

Filing Requirements

Form(s) to File: Form IT-1040

Due Date (General): April 15

Filing Status Options: Allowable state filing statuses include:

- Single
- Married Filing Jointly
- Married Filing Separately
- Head of Household
- Qualifying Widow(er) with Dependent Child

Ohio does not recognize same-sex marriages, civil unions, or domestic partnerships for filing status purposes.

Filing Thresholds: Residents not required to file if no state income tax withheld and if:

- single and 65 years of age or older, federal AGI is $11,700 or less, and no state adjustments (Schedule A);
- married filing jointly and 65 years of age or older, federal AGI of $13,400 or less, and no state adjustments (Schedule A);
- only source of income is retirement income that is eligible for the retirement income credit, which is same or larger than tax liability before credits; or
- exemption amount is same or more than state AGI.

Nonresidents must file if they received income from state sources, unless they live in border states and their only income from state sources is from wages.

Caution: The 2012 filing thresholds are shown above. At the time of publication, the 2013 filing thresholds were not available.

Where to Send Returns
Payment:

> Ohio Department of Taxation
> P.O. Box 2057
> Columbus, OH 43218-2057

No Payment:

> Ohio Department of Taxation
> P.O. Box 2679
> Columbus, OH 43218-2679

Alternative Minimum Tax?
No

IRC Conformity
IRC incorporated by reference as amended on March 22, 2013.

Starting Point for Calculation of Taxable Income
Federal adjusted gross income.

Credit for Taxes Paid to Another State Allowed?
Yes. For nonresidents and part-year residents, the credit is allowed against tax due for that portion of Ohio adjusted gross income that is not allocable to Ohio.

Federal Return Attachment Required?
Copy of federal return not required. Taxpayers with zero or negative federal adjusted gross income must attach copy of page 1 of federal return to state return. Investors in pass-through entities claiming credit for tax paid on Ohio Form IT-4708 or IT-1140 must attach federal Form K-1s that reflect amount of Ohio tax paid.

Deadline for Reporting Federal Changes
File within 60 days after the federal adjustment has been agreed to or finally determined.

Estimated Tax Payments
Required if expected liability is over $500 after withholding.

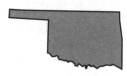

OKLAHOMA

Tax Agency Website: http://www.oktax.state.ok.us

2013 Individual Tax Rate Schedule
Single, Married Filing Separately:

$	0 –	1,000	× 0.500 %	minus	$	0
	1,001 –	2,500	× 1.000 %	minus		5.00
	2,501 –	3,750	× 2.000 %	minus		30.00
	3,751 –	4,900	× 3.000 %	minus		67.50
	4,901 –	7,200	× 4.000 %	minus		116.50
	7,201 –	8,700	× 5.000 %	minus		188.50
	8,701	and over	× 5.250 %	minus		210.25

Married Filing Jointly, Qualifying Widow(er), Head of Household:

$	0 –	2,000	× 0.500 %	minus	$	0
	2,001 –	5,000	× 1.000 %	minus		10.00
	5,001 –	7,500	× 2.000 %	minus		60.00
	7,501 –	9,800	× 3.000 %	minus		135.00
	9,801 –	12,200	× 4.000 %	minus		233.00
	12,201 –	15,000	× 5.000 %	minus		355.00
	15,001	and over	× 5.250 %	minus		392.50

 http://www.tax.ok.gov/online.html

Mandated for tax preparers that filed more than 10 resident returns for prior tax year. Nonresident and part-year resident returns allowed only through MeF. No taxpayer opt out. No exceptions to mandate. No penalties for failure to e-file.

Filing Requirements
Form(s) to File: Form 511; Form 511NR *Due Date (General):* April 15; April 20 for electronic filers.

Filing Status Options: Allowable state filing statuses include:

- Single
- Married Filing Jointly
- Married Filing Separately
- Head of Household
- Qualifying Widow(er) with Dependent Child

If federal filing status is married filing jointly and one taxpayer is a resident and the other is a nonresident (nonmilitary) state filing status must be:

- married filing separately; or
- married filing jointly as if both taxpayers were residents.

Oklahoma does not recognize same-sex marriages, civil unions, or domestic partnerships for filing status purposes.

Filing Thresholds: Residents must file if required to file federal return. Nonresidents and part-year residents must file if income from state sources is $1,000 or more.

Where to Send Returns
> Oklahoma Tax Commission
> Income Tax
> P.O. Box 26800
> Oklahoma City, OK 73126-0800

Alternative Minimum Tax?
No

IRC Conformity
IRC incorporated by reference as currently amended.

Starting Point for Calculation of Taxable Income
Federal adjusted gross income.

Credit for Taxes Paid to Another State Allowed?
Residents and Part-Year Residents: Yes. Credit only on taxes paid in another state for wages and compensation for personal services, including retirement income and gambling proceeds.

Nonresidents: No

Federal Return Attachment Required?

Copy of federal return must be attached if:

- State AGI differs from federal;
- Claiming earned income credit;
- Claiming child care credit;
- Medical or health savings account deduction;
- Police Corps Program deduction;
- Social security benefits subtracted;
- Lump sum distributions added;
- Out-of-state income; or
- Claiming exception to estimated payment requirements due to at least 66-2/3% of gross income this year or last year from farming.

Nonresidents and part-year residents must attach copy of federal return. Taxpayers must attach the following federal schedules and forms, if applicable:

- Schedule A (itemized deductions);
- Schedule D (gains from exempt federal obligations, capital gains);
- Schedule E (rent, royalty, partnership income);
- Schedule F (farm income);
- Form 2441 or 1040A Schedule 2 (child care expense credit);
- Form 4562 (depreciation);
- Form 8606 (nondeductible IRAs);
- Form 8885 and Form 3800 (Indian Employment Credit); and
- Copy of federal NOL computation.

Deadline for Reporting Federal Changes

File within one year after final determination of the federal adjustment.

Estimated Tax Payments

Required if expected liability is $500 or more after withholding.

OREGON

Tax Agency Website: http://www.oregon.gov/DOR

2013 Individual Tax Rate Schedule

Single, Married Filing Separately:

$						$	
0	–	3,250	× 5.000 %	minus	$	0
3,251	–	8,150	× 7.000 %	minus		65.00
8,151	–	125,000	× 9.000 %	minus		228.00
125,001	and over		× 9.900 %	minus		1,353.00

Married Filing Jointly, Qualifying Widow(er), Head of Household:

$						$	
0	–	6,500	× 5.000 %	minus	$	0
6,501	–	16,300	× 7.000 %	minus		130.00
16,301	–	250,000	× 9.000 %	minus		456.00
250,001	and over		× 9.900 %	minus		2,706.00

Brackets indexed for inflation annually, except for $125,000 or over brackets.

 http://www.oregon.gov/dor/ ESERV/Pages/elect-filing.aspx

Mandated for tax preparers who expect to file 11 or more returns. Taxpayer opt-out available on federal Form 8948. Tax preparer must must check box 1 and write his or her Oregon license number at the top of the form. Waiver for undue hardship.

Filing Requirements

Form(s) to File: Form 40; Form 40P; Form 40N

Due Date (General): April 15

Filing Status Options: Allowable state filing statuses include:

- Single
- Married Filing Jointly
- Registered Domestic Partners Filing Jointly
- Married Filing Separately
- Registered Domestic Partner Filing Separately
- Head of Household
- Qualifying Widow(er) with Dependent Child

Filing Thresholds: Residents must file if required to file federal return, gross income exceeds filing thresholds (see below), or $1 or more of state income tax was withheld from wages. Nonresidents and part-year residents must file if gross income exceeds filing thresholds. Dependents must file if gross income exceeds $950 or earned income plus $300, up to standard deduction amount for filing status. The filing thresholds are adjusted on an annual basis.

Single
    Under 65 years of age: $5,540
    65 years of age or older: $6,740

Head of Household
    Under 65 years of age: $6,925
    65 years of age or older: $8,125

Married Filing Jointly
    Under 65 years of age: $11,085
    65 years of age or older (one): $12,085
    65 years of age or older (both): $13,085

Married Filing Separately
    Under 65 years of age: $5,540
    65 years of age or older: $6,540

Surviving Spouse
    Under 65 years of age: $7,715
    65 years of age or older: $8,715

Caution: The 2012 filing thresholds are shown above. At the time of publication, the 2013 filing thresholds were not available.

Where to Send Returns
Payment:

> Oregon Department of Revenue
> P.O. Box 14555
> Salem, OR 97309-0940

Refund:

> Refund
> P.O. Box 14700
> Salem, OR 97309-0930

Alternative Minimum Tax?
No

IRC Conformity
IRC incorporated by reference as of January 3, 2013, for tax years after 2012, or if related to definition of taxable income, as applicable to tax year of taxpayer.

Starting Point for Calculation of Taxable Income
Federal adjusted gross income.

Credit for Taxes Paid to Another State Allowed?
Yes. For nonresidents, the credit is allowed only if the taxpayer's state of residence either (1) does not tax income of Oregon residents derived from sources within that state, or (2) allows Oregon residents a credit against that state's income tax for taxes paid or payable to Oregon.

Federal Return Attachment Required?
Copy of federal return must be attached. Federal schedules should not be attached, unless requested. Form 8886 checkbox must be marked on returns by taxpayers who are required to file federal disclosure form for listed or reportable transactions.

Deadline for Reporting Federal Changes
Must report within 90 days and must either concede the accuracy of the determination or state the grounds upon which the taxpayer contends the determination is erroneous.

Estimated Tax Payments
Required if expected liability is $1,000 or more after withholding.

PENNSYLVANIA

Tax Agency Website: http://www.revenue.state.pa.us

2013 Individual Tax Rate Schedule
Tax rate is 3.07% of taxable compensation, net profits, net gains from the sale of property, rent, royalties, patents or copyrights, income from estates or trusts, dividends, interest, and winnings.

 e~file   http://www.doreservices.state. pa.us/

Mandated for tax preparers who filed 50 or more resident, nonresident, and part-year resident returns (original or amended) for previous tax year. Threshold reduced to 10 or more returns, effective Jan. 1, 2014. Penalty for failure to e-file of 1% of tax due, up to $500, but not less than $10. Taxpayer opt-out by checking box on return. Waiver for undue hardship available.

Filing Requirements
Form(s) to File: Form PA-40

Due Date (General): April 15

Filing Status Options: Allowable state filing statuses include:

- Single
- Married Filing Jointly
- Married Filing Separately
- Final Return
- Deceased

Filing Thresholds: Residents, nonresidents, and part-year residents must file If total gross taxable income received is more than $33, even if no tax is due, or if there was a loss from any transaction as an individual, sole proprietor, partner in a partnership, S corporation shareholder, or association member.

Where to Send Returns
Form PA-40, Payment:

> PA Dept. of Revenue
> Payment Enclosed
> 1 Revenue Place
> Harrisburg, PA 17129-0001

Form PA-40, Refund:

> PA Dept. of Revenue
> Refund or Credit Requested
> 3 Revenue Place
> Harrisburg, PA 17129-0003

Form PA-40, No Payment:

> PA Dept. of Revenue
> No Payment or No Refund
> 2 Revenue Place
> Harrisburg, PA 17129-0002

Alternative Minimum Tax?
No

IRC Conformity
IRC incorporated by reference as amended to January 1, 1997. However, if a reference to the IRC of 1986 contains the phrase "as amended" and refers to no other date, the reference is to the IRC as it exists at the time the law is being applied.

Starting Point for Calculation of Taxable Income
Pennsylvania gross income.

Credit for Taxes Paid to Another State Allowed?
Residents: Yes

Nonresidents and Part-Year Residents: No

Federal Return Attachment Required?
Copy of federal return not required. Taxpayer must attach all applicable federal schedules, where allowed, if state schedules are not used. Federal Schedule K-1 must be attached if taxpayer did not receive the corresponding PA K-1, if applicable. Page 1 of federal Form 1040 must be attached if claiming deduction for medical savings account or health savings account contributions. Nonresident and part-year resident taxpayers who file paper copies of the PA-40 must also include a copy of page one of federal return.

Deadline for Reporting Federal Changes
File within 30 days after receipt of federal final change or correction.

Estimated Tax Payments
Required if current year withholding is less than the smaller of 90% (farmers, 66 2/3%) of expected current year tax liability (after employer incentive payments credit, job creation tax credit, research and development credit, special tax forgiveness credit, and credit for income tax paid to other states), or 100% of preceding year taxable income.

RHODE ISLAND

Tax Agency Website: http://www.tax.state.ri.us

2013 Individual Tax Rate Schedule
Single, Married Filing Jointly, Surviving Spouse, Married Filing Separately, Head of Household:

$	0 – 58,600	× 3.750 %	minus	$	0
	58,601 – 133,250	× 4.750 %	minus		586.00
	133,251 and over	× 5.990 %	minus		2,238.30

Brackets are indexed for inflation annually.

       http://www.tax.state.ri.us/

Mandated for tax preparers who prepare more than 100 resident, nonresident, and part-year resident returns in previous year. Taxpayer opt-out available by writing letter; attach letter to paper return. Waiver available for undue hardship. Preparers that fail to comply with mandate may, after a hearing to show cause, be precluded from preparing and filing state tax returns.

Filing Requirements
Form(s) to File: Form RI-1040; Form RI-1040NR

Due Date (General): April 15

Filing Status Options: Allowable state filing statuses include:

- Single
- Married Filing Jointly
- Married Filing Separately
- Head of Household
- Qualifying Widow(er) with Dependent Child

Filing Thresholds: Residents must file if required to file federal return or if state income exceeds sum of federal personal exemptions. Nonresidents must file if required to file federal return and if income is derived from or connected with state sources. Part-year residents must file if required to file federal return. Nonresidents and part-year residents who are not required to file federal returns may be required to file if they have state modifications increasing their federal AGI.

Where to Send Returns
Payments:

> The RI Division of Taxation
> One Capitol Hill
> Providence, RI 02908-5806

Refunds:

> The RI Division of Taxation
> One Capitol Hill
> Providence, RI 02908-5806

Alternative Minimum Tax?
Yes, applicable through 2010.

IRC Conformity
IRC incorporated by reference as currently amended.

Starting Point for Calculation of Taxable Income
Federal adjusted gross income.

Credit for Taxes Paid to Another State Allowed?
Residents: Yes. Other state's tax must be imposed regardless of taxpayer's residence or domicile.

Part-Year Residents: Yes

Nonresidents: No

Federal Return Attachment Required?
Copy of federal return not required.

Deadline for Reporting Federal Changes
File within 90 days after receipt of federal final determination of change.

Estimated Tax Payments
Required if expected liability is $250 or more.

SOUTH CAROLINA

Tax Agency Website: http://www.sctax.org

2013 Individual Tax Rate Schedule

$			×				$	
0	–	2,850	×	0.000 %	minus	$	0
2,851	–	5,700	×	3.000 %	minus		85
5,701	–	8,550	×	4.000 %	minus		142
8,551	–	11,400	×	5.000 %	minus		228
11,401	–	14,250	×	6.000 %	minus		342
14,251	and over		×	7.000 %	minus		485

Brackets indexed for inflation annually.

  http://www.sctax.org/
Electronic+Services/default.htm

Mandated for tax preparers that filed 100 or more resident, nonresident, and part-year resident returns for a tax period for same tax year. Taxpayer opt-out with form letter. Exception to mandate if financial hardship. Penalty of $50 per return if fail to e-file.

Filing Requirements
Form(s) to File: Form SC1040

Due Date (General): April 15

Filing Status Options: Allowable state filing statuses include:

- Single
- Married Filing Jointly
- Married Filing Separately
- Head of Household
- Qualifying Widow(er) with Dependent Child

South Carolina does not recognize same-sex marriages, civil unions, or domestic partnerships for filing status purposes. Same-sex married couples must file as Single or Head-of-Household.

Filing Thresholds: Residents must file if:

- required to file a federal income tax return;
- state income tax was withheld from wages;
- taxpayer is 65 years of age or older, and gross income is greater than federal gross income filing requirement amount plus $15,000; or
- married filing jointly, both age 65 years of age or older, and gross income is greater than federal gross income filing requirement amount plus $30,000.

Nonresidents must file if state income tax was withheld or income was taxed by the state. Part-year residents may choose to file as a resident or nonresident, whichever is more advantageous.

Where to Send Returns
Payment:

> Taxable Processing Center
> P.O. Box 101105
> Columbia, SC 29211-0105

No Payment:

> SC1040 Processing Center
> P.O. Box 101100
> Columbia, SC 29211-0100

Alternative Minimum Tax?
No

IRC Conformity
IRC incorporated by reference through January 2, 2013.

Starting Point for Calculation of Taxable Income
Federal taxable income.

Credit for Taxes Paid to Another State Allowed?
Residents: Yes.

Part-Year Residents: A part-year resident has the option of filing either as a full-year resident or a nonresident. If taxpayer elects to file as a full-year resident, all income is reported as though the taxpayer was a resident for the entire year and credit is allowed for taxes paid on income taxed by South Carolina and another state.

Nonresidents: No. However, the Department of Revenue may allow the credit where a taxpayer is considered a resident of South Carolina and a resident of another state.

Federal Return Attachment Required?
Complete copy of federal return and schedules must be attached if taxpayer has income or loss on federal Schedules C, D, E, or F or if filing Schedule NR (part-year resident/nonresident), Form SC1040TC (non-refundable credits), Form I-319 (tuition tax credit), or Form I-335 (active trade or business income). Taxpayers must attach federal Form 8332 (release of claim to exemption), if applicable.

Deadline for Reporting Federal Changes
File within 180 days after final determination of federal adjustment.

Estimated Tax Payments
Required if expected liability is $100 or more.

SOUTH DAKOTA

Tax Agency Website: http://dor.sd.gov/

South Dakota does not collect personal income tax.

TENNESSEE

Tax Agency Website: http://www.tn.gov/revenue/index.shtml

2013 Individual Tax Rate Schedule

Tax rate is 6% upon interest and dividend income of individuals.

 http://www.tn.gov/topics/Online+Services/Taxes

Allowed for resident, nonresident, and part-year resident returns. Electronic filing of returns available only through state's website at https://apps.tn.gov/etax.

Filing Requirements
Form(s) to File: Form INC-250

Due Date (General): April 15

Filing Status Options: Allowable state filing statuses include:

- Single
- Married Filing Jointly
- Married Filing Separately

Tennessee does not recognize same-sex marriages, civil unions, or domestic partnerships for filing status purposes.

Filing Thresholds: Residents, nonresidents, and part-year residents must file if income from interest and dividends exceeds filing thresholds for applicable filing status (see below).

    Single: $1,250
    Married Filing Jointly: $2,500

Where to Send Returns
    Tennessee Department of Revenue
    Andrew Jackson State Office Building
    500 Deaderick Street
    Nashville, TN 37242

Alternative Minimum Tax?
No

IRC Conformity
IRC not incorporated.

Starting Point for Calculation of Taxable Income
Certain dividends and interest income.

Credit for Taxes Paid to Another State Allowed?
Residents: Yes

Nonresidents and Part-Year Residents: No

Credit allowed to resident shareholder of S corporation incorporated and doing business in another state for tax paid to other state on income, distributions or dividends, if tax credit reciprocity agreement between Tennessee and other state.

Federal Return Attachment Required?
Copy of federal return not required.

Deadline for Reporting Federal Changes
No deadline specified.

Estimated Tax Payments
Voluntary.

TEXAS

Tax Agency Website: http://www.cpa.state.tx.us/taxes

Texas does not collect personal income tax.

UTAH

Tax Agency Website: http://www.tax.utah.gov

2013 Individual Tax Rate Schedule
Tax rate is 5%.

 http://taxexpress.utah.gov/

Mandated for tax preparers that filed 101 or more resident, nonresident, and part-year resident returns. Taxpayer opt-out on Form TC-831. Tax preparer retains form. Exception to mandate if undue hardship. No penalties for failure to e-file.

Filing Requirements
Form(s) to File: Form TC-40

Due Date (General): April 15

Filing Status Options: Allowable state filing statuses include:

- Single
- Married Filing Jointly
- Married Filing Separately
- Head of Household
- Qualifying Widow(er) with Dependent Child

Filing Thresholds: Residents, nonresidents, and part-year residents that have federal gross income derived from Utah sources must file if required to file a federal return.

Where to Send Returns
Payment:

Utah State Tax Commission
210 North 1950 West
Salt Lake City, UT 84134-0266

Refund:

Utah State Tax Commission
210 North 1950 West
Salt Lake City, UT 84134-0260

Alternative Minimum Tax?
No

IRC Conformity
IRC incorporated by reference as currently amended.

Starting Point for Calculation of Taxable Income
Federal adjusted gross income.

Credit for Taxes Paid to Another State Allowed?
Residents and Part-Year Residents: Yes

Nonresidents: No

Federal Return Attachment Required?
Copy of federal return not required. Attach, if applicable
Form 8379 (injured spouse allocation).

Deadline for Reporting Federal Changes
File within 90 days after final determination of federal adjustment.

Estimated Tax Payments
Voluntary.

VERMONT

Tax Agency Website: http://www.state.vt.us/tax/index.shtml

2013 Individual Tax Rate Schedule
Single:

$	0	–	36,250	×	3.550 %	minus	$	0
	36,251	–	87,850	×	6.800 %	minus		1,178.12
	87,851	–	183,250	×	7.800 %	minus		2,056.62
	183,251	–	398,350	×	8.800 %	minus		3,889.12
	398,351	and over		×	8.950 %	minus		4,486.65

Married Filing Jointly, Qualifying Widow(er), Civil Union Filing Jointly:

$	0	–	60,550	×	3.550 %	minus	$	0
	60,551	–	146,400	×	6.800 %	minus		1,967.87
	146,401	–	223,050	×	7.800 %	minus		3,431.87
	223,051	–	398,350	×	8.800 %	minus		5,662.37
	398,351	and over		×	8.950 %	minus		6,259.90

Married Filing Separately, Civil Union Filing Separately:

$	0	–	30,275	×	3.550 %	minus	$	0
	30,276	–	73,200	×	6.800 %	minus		983.94
	73,201	–	111,525	×	7.800 %	minus		1,715.94
	111,526	–	199,175	×	8.800 %	minus		2,831.19
	199,176	and over		×	8.950 %	minus		3,129.95

Head of Household:

$	0	–	48,600	×	3.550 %	minus	$	0
	48,601	–	125,450	×	6.800 %	minus		1,579.50
	125,451	–	203,150	×	7.800 %	minus		2,834.00
	203,151	–	398,350	×	8.800 %	minus		4,865.50
	398,351	and over		×	8.950 %	minus		5,463.03

The tax amount in the schedules is increased by 24% for: early withdrawals from qualified retirement plans, individual retirement accounts, and medical savings accounts; recapture of the federal investment tax credit; or tax on qualified lump-sum distributions of pension income not included in federal taxable income.

Brackets are indexed for inflation annually.

 http://www.state.vt.us/tax/practitionereservices.shtml

Allowed for resident, nonresident, and part-year resident returns.

Filing Requirements
Form(s) to File: Form IN-111

Due Date (General): April 15

Filing Status Options: Allowable state filing statuses include:

- Single
- Head of Household
- Married Filing Jointly
- Civil Union Partner Filing Jointly
- Married Filing Separately
- Civil Union Filing Separately
- Qualifying Widow(er) with Dependent Children

Filing Thresholds: Residents, nonresidents, and part-year residents required to file federal income tax return must file if:

- income earned or received in the state is $100 or more; or
- gross income from state sources is $1,000 or more.

Where to Send Returns
Payment:

VT Department of Taxes
P.O. Box 1779
Montpelier, VT 05601-1779

No Payment:

VT Department of Taxes
P.O. Box 1881
Montpelier, VT 05601-1881

Alternative Minimum Tax?
No

IRC Conformity
IRC incorporated by reference as in effect for 2012 taxable year, for tax years beginning after 2011. Federal amendments made subsequent to IRC conformity date impacting tax year at issue administratively recognized by Department of Taxes.

Starting Point for Calculation of Taxable Income
Federal taxable income.

Credit for Taxes Paid to Another State Allowed?
Residents and Part-Year Residents: Yes

Nonresidents: No

If taxpayer domiciled in other jurisdiction is deemed a resident of Vermont, income from intangibles not employed in a business, trade, or profession is considered derived from sources within jurisdiction of domicile and credit may be claimed if jurisdiction of domicile provides for a similar credit.

Federal Return Attachment Required?
Copy of pages 1 and 2 of federal Form 1040 and federal schedules reporting state income or loss must be attached, if applicable. Civil union partners filing jointly must complete federal Form 1040 on married filing jointly basis (partners filing separately complete federal return on married filing separately basis) and attach recomputed return along with copy of federal return actually filed. If married filing separately and one spouse is nonresident and has no state income, federal return must be completed on married filing separately basis and attached along with copy of federal return as actually filed. If taxpayer sold real estate in state and tax was withheld, taxpayer must attach copy of pages 1 and 2 of federal return and any federal schedule documenting income or loss from sale. Taxpayers must attach the following federal schedules and forms, if applicable:

- Schedule SE (self-employment);
- Form 1116 (foreign tax credit);
- Form 1310 (person claiming refund due a deceased taxpayer);
- Form 2210 (underpayment of estimated tax);
- Form 2441 (child and dependent care expenses); or
- Form 6252 (gain from installment sale of real estate).

Deadline for Reporting Federal Changes
File within 60 days after notice of federal change or filing federal amended return.

Estimated Tax Payments
Required if expected liability is $500 or more.

VIRGINIA

Tax Agency Website: http://www.tax.virginia.gov

2013 Individual Tax Rate Schedule

$							$	
0	–	3,000	×	2.000 %	minus	$	0
3,001	–	5,000	×	3.000 %	minus		30.00
5,001	–	17,000	×	5.000 %	minus		130.00
17,001	and over		×	5.750 %	minus		257.50

 http://www.tax.virginia.gov/site.cfm?alias=OnlineServicesCategory

Mandated for tax preparers that filed 50 or more resident, nonresident, and part-year resident returns during a previous tax year. Taxpayers opt out by providing code in election field on return. Request exception to mandate on Form VA-8454P, Paid Tax Preparer Hardship Waiver Request, and mail form in. No penalty for failure to e-file.

Filing Requirements
Form(s) to File: Form 760; Form 760PY; Form 763

Due Date (General): May 1

Filing Status Options: Allowable state filing statuses include:

- Single
- Married Filing Jointly
- Married Filing Separately

Filing Thresholds: Residents, part-year residents, and dependents must file if state AGI exceeds filing threshold for applicable filing status (see below). Nonresidents must file if income from state sources exceeds filing threshold for applicable filing status.

Single: $11,950
Married Filing Jointly: $23,900
Married Filing Separately: $11,950

Where to Send Returns
Payment:

Virginia Department of Taxation
P.O. Box 760
Richmond, VA 23218-0760

Refund:

Virginia Department of Taxation
P.O. Box 1498
Richmond, VA 23218-1498

Alternative Minimum Tax?
No

IRC Conformity
IRC incorporated by reference as of January 2, 2013, for taxable years beginning after 2011.

Starting Point for Calculation of Taxable Income
Federal adjusted gross income.

Credit for Taxes Paid to Another State Allowed?
Yes. For nonresidents, the taxpayer's state of residence must (1) allow a similar credit to Virginia residents, and (2) impose tax on income of its residents derived from Virginia sources and exempt income of Virginia residents.

Federal Return Attachment Required?
Copy of federal return not required. Nonresident and part-year resident taxpayers must attach complete copy of federal return. Taxpayers must attach federal Schedules C, C-EZ, E and F, and Form 1310 (person claiming refund due a deceased taxpayer), if applicable.

Deadline for Reporting Federal Changes
File within one year after final determination of a change or correction by the IRS or another state.

Estimated Tax Payments
Required if expected liability is over $150 and expected Virginia AGI is $11,650 or more, if single or married filing separately ($23,300 or more if married filing jointly).

WASHINGTON

Tax Agency Website: http://www.dor.wa.gov/Content/Home/Default.aspx

Washington does not collect personal income tax.

WEST VIRGINIA

Tax Agency Website: http://www.wva.state.wv.us/wvtax/default.aspx

2013 Individual Tax Rate Schedule
Single, Head of Household, Married Filing Jointly, Widow(er) with Dependent Child:

$	0 – 10,000	×	3.000 %	minus	$	0
	10,001 – 25,000	×	4.000 %	minus		100.00
	25,001 – 40,000	×	4.500 %	minus		225.00
	40,001 – 60,000	×	6.000 %	minus		825.00
	60,001 and over	×	6.500 %	minus		1,125.00

Married Filing Separately:

$	0 – 5,000	×	3.000 %	minus	$	0
	5,001 – 12,500	×	4.000 %	minus		50.00
	12,501 – 20,000	×	4.500 %	minus		112.50
	20,001 – 30,000	×	6.000 %	minus		412.50
	30,001 and over	×	6.500 %	minus		562.50

 http://www.wva.state.wv.us/wvtax/electronicServices.aspx

Mandated if preparer uses software to prepare more than 25 resident, nonresident, and part-year resident tax returns. Mandated for self filers who had total annual liability of $50,000 or more during prior tax year. Statutory and regulatory authority lower threshold to $25,000 for tax years after 2013, and $10,000 for tax years after 2014. However, department publication retains $100,000 threshold for tax years after 2012. Taxpayers opt-out on Opt Out Form, which is retained by preparer. Preparers may request waiver on Form HW-1, Income Tax Preparer Hardship Waiver Request. Penalty of $25 per return for failure to e-file.

Filing Requirements
Form(s) to File: Form WV/IT-140; Form WV/IT-140 NR/PY

Due Date (General): April 15

Filing Status Options: Allowable state filing statuses include:

- Single
- Married Filing Jointly
- Married Filing Separately
- Head of Household
- Qualifying Widow(er) with Dependent Child

West Virginia does not recognize same-sex marriages, civil unions, or domestic partnerships for filing status purposes.

Filing Thresholds: Residents, nonresidents, and part-year residents must file if required to file federal return or if state AGI is greater than personal exemption allowance of $2,000 per exemption or $500 (zero exemptions). Not required if taxpayer and/or spouse are 65 years of age or older.

Where to Send Returns
Payment:

West Virginia State Tax Department
P.O. Box 3694
Charleston, WV 25336-3694

Refund:

West Virginia State Tax Department
P.O. Box 1071
Charleston, WV 25324-1071

Alternative Minimum Tax?
No (expired for tax years beginning on or after January 1, 2010)

IRC Conformity
IRC and federal laws relating to determination of federal taxable income in effect after January 1, 2012 and prior to January 3, 2013, adopted for purposes of computing taxable income.

Starting Point for Calculation of Taxable Income
Federal adjusted gross income.

Credit for Taxes Paid to Another State Allowed?

Yes. For nonresidents, the credit is allowed only if there is reciprocity between West Virginia and the nonresident's state of residence.

Federal Return Attachment Required?

Copy of federal return not required. Copy of federal Schedule R (Part II) may be substituted for WV Schedule H (disabled taxpayer). If applicable, attach federal Form 8886 (Reportable Transaction Disclosure Statement).

Deadline for Reporting Federal Changes

File within 90 days after the final determination of the federal adjustment.

Estimated Tax Payments

Required if estimated tax liability is at least $600, unless that liability is less than 10% of the estimated tax.

WISCONSIN

Tax Agency Website: http://www.dor.state.wi.us

2013 Individual Tax Rate Schedule

Single, Head of Household:

$	0	–	10,750	×	4.400 %	minus	$	0
	10,751	–	21,490	×	5.840 %	minus		154.80
	21,491	–	236,600	×	6.270 %	minus		247.20
	236,601		and over	×	7.650 %	minus		3,512.28

Married Filing Jointly:

$	0	–	14,330	×	4.400 %	minus	$	0
	14,331	–	28,650	×	5.840 %	minus		206.35
	28,651	–	315,460	×	6.270 %	minus		329.54
	315,461		and over	×	7.650 %	minus		4,682.89

Married Filing Separately:

$	0	–	7,160	×	4.400 %	minus	$	0
	7,161	–	14,330	×	5.840 %	minus		103.10
	14,331	–	157,730	×	6.270 %	minus		164.72
	157,731		and over	×	7.650 %	minus		2,341.40

Brackets indexed for inflation annually.

 http://www.dor.state.wi.us/eserv/index.html

Mandated for tax preparers that filed 50 or more resident, nonresident, and part-year resident returns for prior tax year. Taxpayers may opt out by writing "no e-file" before signature on return. Exception to mandate for undue hardship; preparers submit written request. No penalty for failure to e-file.

Filing Requirements

Form(s) to File: Form 1; Form 1NPR

Due Date (General): April 15

Filing Status Options: Allowable state filing statuses include:

- Single
- Married Filing Jointly
- Married Filing Separately
- Head of Household

Filing Thresholds: Residents must file if gross income exceeds filing threshold for applicable filing status (see below). Part-year residents and nonresidents must file if gross income is $2,000 or more or, if married, combined gross income is $2,000 or more. Dependents must file if gross income is more than $950, including at least $301 of unearned income. The filing thresholds are adjusted on an annual basis.

Single
  Under 65 years of age: $10,460
  65 years of age or older: $10,710
  Dependent, any age: $9,760
Head of Household
  Under 65 years of age: $13,310
  65 years of age or older: $13,560
  Dependent, any age: $12,610

Married Filing Jointly
  Under 65 years of age: $18,980
  65 years of age or older (one): $19,230
  65 years of age or older (two): $19,480
  Dependent, any age: $17,580

Married Filing Separately
  Under 65 years of age: $9,050
  65 years of age or older: $9,300
  Dependent, any age: $8,350

Caution: The 2012 filing thresholds are shown above. At the time of publication, the 2013 filing thresholds were not available.

Where to Send Returns

Form 1, Payment:

Wisconsin Department of Revenue
P.O. 268
Madison, WI 53790-0001

Form 1, No Payment:

Wisconsin Department of Revenue
P.O. 59
Madison, WI 53785-0001

Form 1, Payment/No Payment (Homestead Credit claimed):

Wisconsin Department of Revenue
P.O. 34
Madison, WI 53786-0001

Form 1NPR, Payment:

Wisconsin Department of Revenue
P.O. 268
Madison, WI 53790-0001

Form 1NPR, No Payment:

> Wisconsin Department of Revenue
> P.O. 59
> Madison, WI 53785-0001

Alternative Minimum Tax?
Yes

IRC Conformity
IRC incorporated as amended to December 31, 2010, with exclusions.

Starting Point for Calculation of Taxable Income
Federal adjusted gross income.

Credit for Taxes Paid to Another State Allowed?
Residents and Part-Year Residents. Yes. However, the credit is not allowed for income tax paid to Illinois, Indiana, Kentucky, or Michigan on personal service income earned in those states included under a reciprocity agreement (reciprocity agreement with Minnesota terminated effective for tax years beginning after December 31, 2009).

Nonresidents: No

Federal Return Attachment Required?
Complete copy of federal return with supporting schedules and forms must be attached. Taxpayers itemizing deductions on federal, but not state, return are not required to attach federal Schedule A.

Deadline for Reporting Federal Changes
File within 90 days after the final determination of the federal adjustment.

Estimated Tax Payments
Required if expected liability is $200 or more after withholding and credits.

WYOMING

Tax Agency Website: http://revenue.wyo.gov/

Wyoming does not collect personal income tax.

SALES AND USE TAX TABLE OF RATES

State tax rates generally applicable to the retail sale of tangible personal property are listed below. Special rates may apply to specific categories of tangible personal property, and are not noted in this chart. Most states also authorize local jurisdictions to adopt sales and use taxes in addition to the state tax set forth below.

The following states do not impose a general sales and use tax: Alaska, Delaware, Montana, New Hampshire, and Oregon. Delaware imposes a merchants' and manufacturers' license tax and a use tax on leases.

	Sales	Use		Sales	Use
Alabama	4%	4%	Nebraska	5.5%	5.5%
Arizona	5.6%[2]	5.6%[2]	Nevada	6.85%[9]	6.85%[9]
Arkansas	6.5%[3]	6.5%[3]	New Jersey	7%	7%
California	7.5%[4]	7.5%[4]	New Mexico	5.125%	5.125%
Colorado	2.9%	2.9%	New York	4%	4%
Connecticut[1]	6.35%	6.35%	North Carolina	4.75%	4.75%
District of Columbia[1]	5.75%[5]	5.75%[5]	North Dakota	5%	5%
Florida	6%	6%	Ohio	5.75%[10]	5.75%[10]
Georgia	4%	4%	Oklahoma	4.5%	4.5%
Hawaii	4%	4%	Pennsylvania	6%	6%
Idaho	6%	6%	Rhode Island[1]	7%	7%
Illinois	6.25%	6.25%	South Carolina	6%	6%
Indiana[1]	7%	7%	South Dakota	4%	4%
Iowa	6%	6%	Tennessee	7%[11]	7%[11]
Kansas	6.15%[6]	6.15%[6]	Texas	6.25%	6.25%
Kentucky	6%	6%	Utah	4.7%	4.7%
Louisiana	4%	4%	Vermont	6%	6%
Maine[1]	5.5%[7]	5.5%[7]	Virginia	4.3%[12]	4.3%[12]
Maryland[1]	6%	6%	Washington	6.5%	6.5%
Massachusetts[1]	6.25%	6.25%	West Virginia[1]	6%	6%
Michigan[1]	6%	6%	Wisconsin	5%	5%
Minnesota	6.875%	6.875%	Wyoming	4%	4%
Mississippi[1]	7%	7%			
Missouri	4.225%[8]	4.225%[8]			

[1] Local general sales/use taxes not authorized or imposed. (Local governments may be authorized, however, to levy miscellaneous local taxes on specific types of transactions.)

[2] Arizona: 6.6% between June 1, 2010 and May 31, 2013.

[3] Arkansas: 6% prior to July 1, 2013.

[4] California: 7.25% prior to January 1, 2013.

[5] District of Columbia: 6% prior to October 1, 2013.

[6] Kansas: 6.3% prior to July 1, 2013.

[7] Maine: 5% prior to October 1, 2013 and after June 30, 2015.

[8] Missouri: Total rate of 4.225% consists of general sales/use tax of 4%, additional sales tax of 0.10% for soil/water conservation and state parks, and additional sales tax of 0.125% for wildlife conservation.

[9] Nevada: 6.5% before July 1, 2009 and after June 30, 2015. Tax rate consists of a 2% state rate under the general Sales and Use Tax Act, a 2.6% state rate under the Local School Support Tax Law (temporarily increased from 2.25% from July 1, 2009 through June 30, 2015), and a 2.25% state-mandated local rate under the City-County Relief Tax Law.

[10] Ohio: 5.5% prior to September 1, 2013.

[11] Tennessee: Additional tax of 2.75% imposed on any single item sold in excess of $1,600 but not more than $3,200.

[12] Virginia: 4% prior to July 1, 2013. Additional 1% local rate in all localities.

NOTES

NOTES

NOTES

NOTES

NOTES

NOTES

What's New in 2013

New Tax Laws. Most of the changes effective in 2013 are extensions of, or permanent changes to, tax laws already in effect for 2012. The American Taxpayer Relief Act of 2012 addressed numerous credits, deductions, amounts, and other items that are typically adjusted periodically or renewed for one or two years. In many cases, the adjustments are permanent, while in others the changes are extensions through 2013.

Benefits extended, amended, removed, reinstated or made permanent include a number of credits (adoption, child and dependent care, child tax, employer's differential wage payments, earned income, education, Indian employment, new markets, renewable electricity production, research, residential energy property, work opportunity), deductions (bonus depreciation, food inventory, educator expense, mortgage insurance, tuition), exclusions (qualified small business stock, scholarships, fringe benefits), and amounts (AMT exemption, capital gains tax rates, Coverdell ESA contribution limits, levy exemption, payroll tax).

Also modified are the use of nonrefundable credits against the AMT, benefits from empowerment zones, a number of elements of estate and gift tax, excise tax-es, phaseout of personal and dependency exemptions and of itemized deductions, depreciation of Indian reservation property, and income tax rates.

Actions taken by Congress or the IRS after publication that affect the 2013 tax year are discussed on the website at CCHGroup.com/TaxUpdates.

Tax Preparer's Checklist

☐ Use the Taxpayer Interview Form on page 16–11 to gather current tax information in one place.

Key Tax Law Changes for Individual Tax Returns		
Area	**Effective Date**	**Provisions of New Law**
Adoption credit	2013	The adoption credit and income exclusion for employer-provided adoption assistance have been made permanent by the American Taxpayer Relief Act of 2012. The inflation-adjusted credit and exclusion dollar limitation in 2013 is $12,970 and the credit is not refundable.
Alternative minimum tax - exemption amounts	2013	For tax years beginning in 2013, the alternative minimum tax (AMT) exemption amounts for individuals, estates and trusts have been increased to: • $51,900 for unmarried individuals, • $80,800 for married taxpayers filing jointly and surviving spouses, • $40,400 for married taxpayers filing separately and • $23,100 for estates and trusts. The $40,000 exemption amount for corporations remains unchanged.
Alternative minimum tax - nonrefundable credits	Tax years after 2011	The use of nonrefundable personal tax credits against an individual's regular tax and alternative minimum tax (AMT) liability has been made permanent. For this purpose, the regular tax liability is first reduced by the amount of any applicable foreign tax credit. The nonrefundable personal tax credits include: the dependent care credit, the credit for the elderly and disabled, the adoption credit, the child tax credit, the credit for interest on certain home mortgages, the Hope Scholarship and Lifetime Learning credits (including the American Opportunity tax credit), the retirement savings contributions credit, the credit for certain nonbusiness energy property, the credit for residential energy efficient property, and the plug-in electric drive motor vehicle credit.

Area	Effective Date	Provisions of New Law
Bonus depreciation	Property placed in service after December 31, 2012	The 50-percent additional depreciation allowance (bonus depreciation) applies to qualifying property acquired after December 31, 2007, and placed in service before January 1, 2014 (or before January 1, 2015, in the case of property with a longer production period and certain noncommercial aircraft).
Capital gains	Tax years ending after 2012	• The reduced maximum capital gains rate of 15 percent on adjusted net capital gain of noncorporate taxpayers (for regular tax and AMT purposes), and the zero percent capital gains rate on adjusted net capital gain of noncorporate taxpayers in the 10-percent or 15-percent income tax bracket, have been made permanent. The capital gains rate, however, is increased to 20 percent beginning in 2013 for adjusted net capital gains of individuals, estates, and trusts in the top income tax bracket.
		• Gains from the disposition of certain property held by individuals, estates, and trusts for more than five years will continue to be taxed in a manner similar to other long-term capital gains for tax years beginning after December 31, 2012, without special treatment. The maximum rate applicable to long-term capital gain from sales of such property will be either 20, 15, or 0 percent depending on the taxpayer's income tax bracket for the year. The special capital gain tax rates available specifically for "qualified five-year gain" have been permanently stricken.
Capital gains	Stock acquired after September 27, 2010	The 100-percent exclusion allowed for gain on the sale or exchange of qualified small business stock held for more than five years by noncorporate taxpayers has been extended for two years, and applies to stock acquired after September 27, 2010, and before January 1, 2014. Additionally, the alternative minimum tax preference treatment of seven percent of the amount of excluded gain on the sale or exchange of such stock has been made permanent for tax years beginning after December 31, 2012. The amount treated as a tax preference item will not increase to 42 percent of the excluded gain, or to 28 percent for stock with a holding period that began after December 31, 2000.
Charitable contributions	Contributions made after 2011	The enhanced deduction for charitable contributions of food inventory from any trade or business of a corporate or noncorporate taxpayer has been extended for two years, through December 31, 2013.
Charitable contributions	Tax years after 2011	• The exclusion from gross income of qualified charitable distributions from IRAs for individuals aged 70½ or older is extended two years to apply to distributions made in 2012 and 2013. Special relief is available for distributions for the 2012 calendar year as a result of the extension occurring after the end of the year.
		• The enhanced deduction for charitable contributions of real property for conservation purposes has been extended for two years, through December 31, 2013.
Child and dependent care credit	Tax years after 2012	The increased credit percentages and higher income limits for the child and dependent care expense credit have been made permanent for tax years beginning after December 31, 2012. The amount of the credit allowed is 35 percent of qualifying child or dependent care expenses. The maximum amount of qualifying expenses to which the credit may be applied is $3,000 for individuals with one qualifying child or dependent (for a maximum credit of $1,050), or $6,000 for individuals with two or more qualifying children or dependents (for a maximum credit of $2,100). For taxpayers with adjusted gross income (AGI) between $15,000 and $43,000, the 35-percent credit rate is reduced by one percentage point for each $2,000 of AGI until the credit percentage is 20 percent for taxpayers with AGI of $43,000.

Key Tax Law Changes for Individual Tax Returns (Continued)

Area	Effective Date	Provisions of New Law
Child care expenses	Tax years beginning after 2012	The income tax credit for qualified expenses incurred by an employer in providing child care for employees has been made permanent for tax years beginning after December 31, 2012. Qualified child care expenditures are any amounts paid or incurred: • to acquire, construct, rehabilitate or expand property that is to be used as a qualified child care facility of the taxpayer; • for the operating costs of a qualified child care facility, including the costs related to the training of employees, scholarship programs, and providing increased compensation for employees with high levels of child care training; or • under a contract with a qualified child care facility to provide child care services to the taxpayer's employees.
Child tax credit	Tax years after 2012	Temporary changes to the child tax credit have been made permanent for tax years beginning after December 31, 2012. This includes the increase in the credit amount to $1,000 per qualifying child, the refundable component of the credit available to all taxpayers, the repeal of the AMT offset applicable to the additional child credit for families with three or more children, and the repeal of the supplemental child credit under the earned income credit rules. Additionally, the reduced earned income threshold amount for purposes of the refundable component of the credit is extended for five years, through December 31, 2017.
Credit for employer's differential wage payments	Tax years after 2011	Small businesses with fewer than 50 employees can claim a credit equal to 20 percent of qualified differential wages paid to qualified workers called up for active military duty through 2013.
Deductions	Tax years after 2011	The election to claim an itemized deduction for state and local general sales taxes in lieu of state and local income taxes is extended two years and may be claimed for tax years beginning in 2012 and 2013.
Earned income credit	Tax years after 2012	The following changes to the earned income credit (EIC) have been made permanent for tax years beginning after December 31, 2012, as a result of the repeal of the EGTRRA sunset provision: (1) determining the EIC phaseout by multiplying the phaseout percentage by a taxpayer's AGI rather than modified AGI; (2) the increase in the phaseout amount for joint filers; (3) the requirement that wages, salaries, tips, and other employee compensation are treated as earned income only if included in gross income; (4) the rule allowing the EIC to be claimed against AMT liability; and (5) the authority to deny the EIC based on custody information obtained from the Department of Health and Human Services' child support database. In addition, the temporary increase in the credit percentage for taxpayers with three or more qualifying children from 40 percent to 45 percent has been extended through 2017. A temporary $5,000 increase in a joint filer's phaseout amount is also extended through 2017.
Education credits	2012	The American Opportunity (modified Hope Scholarship) credit is extended to apply to tax years beginning before 2018, including the $2,500 maximum credit per eligible student, the higher income phaseout ranges of $80,000 to $90,000 for single filers ($160,000 to $180,000 for joint filers), the eligibility extension to the first four years of post-secondary education, the inclusion of text books and course materials as eligible expenses, and the 40-percent refundable credit component.
Education savings accounts	Tax years after 2012	The increased annual contribution limits for Coverdell education savings accounts and certain corresponding rules and provisions regarding such accounts have been made permanent for tax years beginning after December 31, 2012.

Key Tax Law Changes for Individual Tax Returns (Continued)

Area	Effective Date	Provisions of New Law
Educator expense deduction	Tax years after 2011	The above-the-line deduction for eligible educator expenses for up to $250 in qualified expenses is extended two years and may be claimed for tax years beginning in 2012 and 2013.
Empowerment zones	After 2011	The tax benefits available to certain businesses and employers operating in financially distressed empowerment zones have been extended for two years, through December 31, 2013.
Estate and gift taxes	Estates of decedents dying after 2012	Changes made to the law governing federal estate, gift, and generation-skipping transfer (GST) taxes made by EGTRRA and the 2010 Tax Relief Act that were set to expire with respect to the estates of decedents dying and gifts and GSTs made after December 31, 2012, by operation of the sunset provision of EGTRRA, have been made permanent for estates of decedents dying, gifts made, or generation skipping transfers after December 31, 2012. However, the maximum transfer tax rate is 40 percent, rather than 35 percent as it had been under the 2010 Tax Relief Act.
Estate and gift taxes	Estates of decedents dying after 2012	Generally favorable changes to transfer tax rates that were to expire for the estates of decedents dying, gifts made, and GSTs after December 31, 2012, by operation of the sunset provision of EGTRRA, have been made permanent. However, the maximum tax rate imposed under the federal estate and gift taxes is now 40 percent with respect to the estates of decedents dying and gifts made in 2013 and later years, rather than 35 percent. The GST tax rate, which is tied to the maximum estate tax rate, also is 40 percent. In addition, the five-percent surtax, formerly imposed on estates and gifts in excess of $10 million and up to $17,184,000, is not imposed on the estates of decedents dying or gifts made in 2013 or later.
Estate and gift taxes	Estates of decedents dying after 2012	The increases in the estate tax and gift tax applicable exclusion amount and the GST tax exemption amount that were to expire for the estates of decedents dying, gifts made, and GSTs occurring after December 31, 2012, by operation of the sunset provision of EGTRRA, have been made permanent. Thus, the estate tax applicable exclusion amount for decedents dying in 2013 and later remains $5 million (adjusted for inflation to $5,250,000 in 2013). In addition, the gift tax applicable exclusion amount remains $5 million (adjusted for inflation to $5,250,000 in 2013) for gifts made in 2013 and later. Finally, the GST tax exemption amount is $5 million (adjusted for inflation to $5,250,000 in 2013). In conjunction with these extensions, the portability of a deceased spouse's unused exclusion amount is still available for the estates of decedents dying in 2013 and later.
Estate and gift taxes	Estates of decedents dying after 2012	The qualified family-owned business interest (QFOBI) deduction for estate tax purposes has been permanently repealed.
Estate and gift taxes	Estates of decedents dying after 2012	The state death tax credit allowed for estate, inheritance, legacy, or succession taxes paid to any state or the District of Columbia has been permanently repealed for the estates of decedents dying after December 31, 2012. Correspondingly, the state death tax deduction has been made permanent and is available for the estates of decedents dying after December 31, 2012.
Estate and gift taxes	Estates of decedents dying after 2012	The repeal of the distance requirements and clarification of the date used for determining the estate tax exclusion of a qualified conservation easement has been made permanent for the estates of decedents dying after December 31, 2012, as a result of the elimination of the EGTRRA sunset provision. Accordingly, the exclusion for a qualified conservation easement is available to any otherwise qualifying real property without regard to the distance requirement. The date to be used for determining the values to calculate the exclusion continues to be the date of contribution.

Area	Effective Date	Provisions of New Law
Estate and gift taxes	Estates of decedents dying after 2012	The stepped-up basis at death rules continue to generally apply to the property acquired from the estates of decedents dying after 2012. Under the stepped-up basis rules, the income tax basis of property acquired from a decedent at death generally is stepped-up (or stepped down) to equal its value as of the date of the decedent's death (or on the date six months after the date of death, if alternate valuation is elected on the decedent's estate tax return).
Estate and gift taxes	Estates of decedents dying, gifts made, or GSTs after December 31, 2012	The GST deemed allocation and retroactive allocation provisions have been made permanent as a result of the elimination of the EGTRRA sunset provision.
Exclusion of education expenses	Tax years after 2012	The exclusion from gross income and from wages of up to $5,250 annually of employer-provided educational assistance has been made permanent for tax years beginning after December 31, 2012. In addition, the application of the exclusion to payments for graduate level courses has also been made permanent for tax years beginning after December 31, 2012.
Exclusion of scholarships	Tax years after 2012	The exclusion from gross income for scholarships with obligatory service requirements received by degree candidates at qualified educational organizations from the National Health Service Corps Scholarship Program or the F. Edward Hebert Armed Forces Health Professions Scholarship and Financial Assistance Program has been made permanent for tax years beginning after December 31, 2012.
Exemptions	Tax years after 2012	The phaseout of personal and dependency exemptions for higher income individuals is reinstated for tax years beginning after December 31, 2012. As a result, the amount of otherwise allowable personal and dependency exemptions of a taxpayer for 2013 is reduced or eliminated if his or her adjusted gross income exceeds a threshold amount for the year based on filing status.
Fringe benefit exclusion	2013	For tax years beginning in 2013, the inflation-adjusted monthly exclusion amount for transit passes, van pool benefits, and qualified parking is increased to $245.
Health insurance	February 2011	Eligible individuals may claim a 72.5-percent refundable health coverage tax credit (HCTC) for the cost of qualified health insurance for themselves and qualified family members paid during each eligible coverage month beginning after February 12, 2011, and ending before January 1, 2014. The HCTC is available only to individuals receiving trade adjustment assistance (TAA) or TAA-alternative payments, and to retirees age 55 or older receiving Pension Benefit Guaranty Corporation benefits. Absent further congressional action, the HCTC is scheduled to terminate for coverage months beginning after December 31, 2013 (but it has been extended several times in the past).
Indian employment tax credit	2012-2013	The Indian employment tax credit is extended through December 31, 2013.
Information reporting	2012-2013	The IRS is permanently authorized to disclose to officers, employees and contractors of the Federal Bureau of Prisons and of State agencies that administer prisons any inmate return information if the inmate may have filed, or facilitated the filing of, a false return.

Key Tax Law Changes for Individual Tax Returns (Continued)

Area	Effective Date	Provisions of New Law
Investment income	2013	The net investment income tax (NIIT) applies at a rate of 3.8 percent to certain net investment income. The tax applies to individuals, estates, and trusts with income above certain statutory threshold amounts. The NIIT does not apply to nonresident aliens. This tax is subject to estimated tax rules, and is calculated on Form 8960. The tax amount is reported on Form 1040 for individuals and Form 1041 for estates and trusts. It is not required to be withheld from wages. Individuals will be subject to the NIIT if their modified adjusted gross income is over certain thresholds, which are not adjusted for inflation: • Married filing jointly, $250,000 • Married filing separately, $125,000 • Single, $200,000 • Head of household (with qualifying person), $200,000 • Qualifying widow(er) with dependent child, $250,000
IRS levies	2013	Levy exemption amounts have been adjusted for inflation. The exemption includes books and tools of the taxpayer's trade, business, or profession not exceeding $4,400 for 2013. Exempt household items include fuel, provisions, furniture, and other personal effects in the taxpayer's household, as well as arms for personal use, livestock, and poultry of the taxpayer, not exceeding $8,790 in value for 2013.
Itemized deductions	Tax years after 2012	The phaseout of itemized deductions for higher income individuals is reinstated for tax years beginning after December 31, 2012. As a result, the amount of otherwise allowable itemized deductions of a taxpayer for 2013 will be reduced or eliminated if his or her adjusted gross income exceeds a threshold amount for the tax year.
Medicare tax (0.9%)	2013	For tax years beginning after 2012, the employee's portion of the Medicare component of FICA taxes is increased by an additional 0.9 percent (to 2.35 percent) for wages in excess of $200,000 ($250,000 in the case of a joint return, $125,000 in the case of a married taxpayer filing separately). For a joint return, the additional tax is imposed on the couple's combined wages. Although the employer is generally required to withhold the employee's portion from the employee's wages, the employer is not obligated to withhold the additional Medicare tax unless (and until) the employee receives wages from the employer in excess of $200,000. The employee calculates the tax on Form 8959, which must be attached to Form 1040.
Mortgage insurance deduction	2012-2013	The treatment of qualified mortgage insurance premiums as deductible qualified residence interest has been extended two years for amounts paid or accrued in 2012 and 2013, so long as the premiums are not properly allocable to a period after 2013.
New markets tax credit	2012-2013	The new markets tax credit is extended for two years, through December 31, 2013. The carryover period for unused new markets tax credits is also extended for two years, through December 31, 2018.
Payroll tax	2013	For 2013, the rate of the old age, survivors, and disability insurance (OASDI) tax on self-employment income is reinstated at the former rate of 12.4 percent. The rate of the employee's OASDI portion of the payroll tax is also increased to its former level of 6.2 percent. The employer's share of OASDI remains at 6.2 percent.

Key Tax Law Changes for Individual Tax Returns (Continued)		
Area	**Effective Date**	**Provisions of New Law**
Qualified dividends	Tax years beginning after 2012	• The treatment of qualified dividend income passed through a regulated investment company, real estate investment trust, or other pass-through entity as qualified dividend income in the hands of the recipient has been made permanent and will continue to apply in tax years beginning after December 31, 2012.
		• The taxation of qualified dividends of noncorporate taxpayers at capital gains rates has been made permanent and will continue to apply in tax years beginning after December 31, 2012. Thus, qualified dividends will be subject to tax at a 0-, 15-, or 20-percent rate of tax beginning in 2013 depending on the taxpayers ordinary income tax rate for the year.
Qualified Indian reservation property	Property placed in service on or before December 31, 2013	The incentives pertaining to depreciation of qualified Indian reservation property are extended for two years to apply to property placed in service on or before December 31, 2013.
Qualified leasehold improvement property	Property placed in service before 2014	The 15-year recovery period for qualified leasehold improvement property, qualified restaurant property and qualified retail improvement property is extended two additional years to apply to property placed in service before January 1, 2014.
Qualified small business stock exclusion	Stock acquired after September 27, 2010, and before January 1, 2014	The 100-percent exclusion allowed for gain on the sale or exchange of qualified small business stock held for more than five years by noncorporate taxpayers has been extended for two years, and applies to stock acquired after September 27, 2010, and before January 1, 2014. Additionally, the alternative minimum tax (AMT) preference treatment of seven percent of the amount of excluded gain on the sale or exchange of such stock has been made permanent for tax years beginning after December 31, 2012. The amount treated as a tax preference item will not increase to 42 percent of the excluded gain, or to 28 percent for stock with a holding period that began after December 31, 2000.
Regulated investment companies	2012 and 2013	The provision that allows a regulated investment company (RIC) to report dividends paid to nonresident aliens or foreign corporations as interest-related dividends or short-term capital gain dividends is extended for two years. Dividends that are so reported are generally exempt from the 30-percent tax collected through withholding.
Renewable energy production credit	Facilities for which production begins before January 1, 2014	The credit for electricity produced from renewable resources for facilities that produce energy from wind has been extended through 2013. The credit for Indian coal facilities has also been extended for an additional year through 2013. Other energy-producing renewable resource facilities will qualify for the production tax credit if construction has begun on the facility before January 1, 2014, rather than the facility being required to be placed in service by that date. Recycled paper has been excluded from the definition of municipal solid waste for purposes of the credit.
Research credit	Amounts paid or incurred after 2011	The research credit is extended for two years, through December 31, 2013. Qualified research expenses that are paid or incurred by a taxpayer that disposes of a business or business unit in a tax year that includes or ends with a change in ownership are treated as current-year qualified research expenses of the disposing taxpayer. Such expenses are not treated as current-year qualified expenses of the acquiring taxpayer. The credit allowed to each member of a controlled group of corporations or a controlled group of businesses under common control must be determined on a proportionate basis to its share of the aggregate of qualified research expenses giving rise to the credit.

Key Tax Law Changes for Individual Tax Returns (Continued)

Area	Effective Date	Provisions of New Law
Residential energy property credit	Years prior to 2014	The nonbusiness energy property credit has been extended for two years through December 31, 2013. The lifetime credit limit remains at $500, and no more than $200 of the credit amount can be attributed to exterior windows and skylights.
Same-sex couples	2013	Same-sex marriages that are valid in the state where they were performed will be recognized for all federal tax purposes, even if the couple is domiciled in a state that does not recognize their marriage. These rules apply to income taxes, estate and gift taxes and payroll taxes related to employee benefits. As a result, legally married same-sex couples can no longer claim "unmarried" status on their federal tax returns, but instead must file joint or separate returns as married taxpayers. In general, federal tax provisions that have applied to a "husband and wife" now apply to members of a same-sex marriage.
Student loan interest deduction	Tax years after 2012	The increase in the modified adjusted gross income (AGI) phaseout ranges for eligibility for the student loan interest deduction has been made permanent for tax years beginning after December 31, 2012. In addition, the 60-month limitation on the deduction for student loan interest and the restriction that makes voluntary payments of interest nondeductible will not be reinstated beginning in 2013.
Tax rates	Tax years after 2012	The lower income tax rates imposed on individuals, estates, and trusts under EGTRRA have generally been made permanent for tax years beginning after December 31, 2012, as a result of the elimination of the EGTRRA sunset provision. Individuals, however, are subject to a top tax rate of 39.6 percent beginning in 2013, if their taxable income exceeds the applicable threshold amount of $450,000 for married individuals filing joint returns and surviving spouses, $425,000 for heads of households, $400,000 for single individuals, and $225,000 for married individuals filing separate returns. Estates and trusts are subject to a top tax rate of 39.6 percent on all taxable income in excess of the 33-percent tax bracket.
Tax rates	Tax years after 2012	Marriage penalty relief which increased the standard deduction amount for joint filers and surviving spouses to twice the inflation-adjusted amount of the standard deduction applicable to single taxpayers and married taxpayers filing separately has been made permanent for tax years beginning after December 31, 2012, as a result of the elimination of the EGTRRA sunset provision.
Tax refunds	Years after 2012	The treatment disregarding federal tax refunds and advance payments of refundable credits as income, or as resources for a 12-month period after receipt, in determining an individual's eligibility for federal assistance or federally financed State assistance, has been made permanent.
Tuition deduction	2012 and 2013	The above-the-line deduction for qualified tuition and related expenses is extended for two years through December 31, 2013.
Vaccines	2013	Seasonal vaccines that include four strains of virus have been added to the list of taxable influenza vaccines subject to the excise tax imposed under the Vaccine Injury Compensation Program (VICP). Under prior law, only vaccines that provide protection from three strains of virus were covered under the VICP, which operates like a no-fault alternative to tort law to resolve vaccine injury claims. The program requires that patients fund the VICP through a 75-cents-per-dose excise tax. The change is designed to encourage manufacturers to bring new vaccines to market.
Work opportunity credit	2012 and 2013	The work opportunity credit is extended through December 31, 2013.

Key Tax Figures 2010-2014

Year	2014	2013	2012	2011	2010
Income Threshold for Requirement to File Form 1040					
Single, under age 65	10,150	10,000	9,750	9,500	9,350
Single, age 65 or over	11,700	11,500	11,200	10,950	10,750
HOH, under age 65	13,050	12,850	12,500	12,200	12,050
HOH, age 65 or over	14,600	14,350	13,950	13,650	13,450
MFJ, under age 65, (both spouses)	20,300	20,000	19,500	19,000	18,700
MFJ, age 65 or over (one spouse)	21,500	21,200	20,650	20,150	19,800
MFJ, age 65 or over (both spouses)	22,700	22,400	21,800	21,300	20,900
MFS, any age	3,950	3,900	3,800	3,700	3,650
QW, under age 65	16,350	16,100	15,700	15,300	15,050
QW, age 65 or over	17,550	17,300	16,850	16,450	16,150
Standard Deduction					
MFJ or QW	12,400	12,200	11,900	11,600	11,400
Single	6,200	6,100	5,950	5,800	5,700
HOH	9,100	8,950	8,700	8,500	8,400
MFS	6,200	6,100	5,950	5,800	5,700
Additional for age 65 or over, or blind each (MFJ, QW, MFS)	1,200	1,200	1,150	1,150	1,100
Additional for age 65 or over, or blind each (Single, HOH)	1,550	1,500	1,450	1,450	1,400
Personal and Dependent Exemption					
Amount of deduction	3,950	3,900	3,800	3,700	3,650
Phaseout begins, MFJ or QW	305,050	300,000	No Phaseout	No Phaseout	No Phaseout
Phaseout begins, Single	254,200	250,000	No Phaseout	No Phaseout	No Phaseout
Phaseout begins, HOH	279,650	275,000	No Phaseout	No Phaseout	No Phaseout
Phaseout begins, MFS	152,525	150,000	No Phaseout	No Phaseout	No Phaseout
Maximum Earnings Subject To					
Social Security tax	117,000	113,700	110,100	106,800	106,800
Medicare tax	No Limit	No Limit	No Limit	No Limit	No Limit
Maximum Tax Paid For					
Employee Social Security	7,254	7,049.40	4,624.20	4,485.60	6,621.60
Employee Medicare	No Limit	No Limit	No Limit	No Limit	No Limit
SE Social Security	14,508	14,098.80	13,652.40	13,243.20	13,243.20
SE Medicare	No Limit	No Limit	No Limit	No Limit	No Limit
Maximum Earnings Allowed Without Reduction of Social Security Benefits					
Under full retirement age, benefits reduced by $1 for each $2 earned over:	15,480	15,120	14,640	14,160	14,160
Full retirement age and over	No Limit	No Limit	No Limit	No Limit	No Limit
Maximum Deductible 401(k) Contribution					
Under age 50	17,500	17,500	17,000	16,500	16,500
Age 50 or older	23,000	23,000	22,500	22,000	22,000
Auto Standard Mileage Allowances (cents per mile)					
Business	N/A	56.5	55.5	51/55.5[1]	50

Key Tax Figures 2010-2014 (Continued)

Year	2014	2013	2012	2011	2010
Medical/moving	N/A	24	23	19	16.5
Charity work	14	14	14	14	14

¹ Before 7-1-11: business rate is 51¢ per mile. After 6-30-11: business rate is 55.5¢ per mile.

Itemized Deduction Phaseout Begins

	2014	2013	2012	2011	2010
MFJ or QW	305,050	300,000	No Phaseout	No Phaseout	No Phaseout
Single	254,200	250,000	No Phaseout	No Phaseout	No Phaseout
HOH	279,650	275,000	No Phaseout	No Phaseout	No Phaseout
MFS	152,525	150,000	No Phaseout	No Phaseout	No Phaseout

Earned Income Credit

One qualifying child

	2014	2013	2012	2011	2010
Earned income amount	9,720	9,560	9,320	9,100	8,970
Maximum credit	3,305	3,250	3,169	3,094	3,050
Threshold phaseout	17,830	17,530	17,090	16,690	16,450
Complete phaseout	38,511	37,870	36,920	36,052	35,535
Threshold (MFJ)	23,260	22,870	22,300	21,770	21,460
Complete (MFJ)	43,941	43,210	42,130	41,132	40,545

Two qualifying children

	2014	2013	2012	2011	2010
Earned income amount	13,650	13,430	13,090	12,780	12,590
Maximum credit	5,460	5,372	5,236	5,112	5,036
Threshold phaseout	17,830	17,530	17,090	16,690	16,450
Complete phaseout	43,756	43,038	41,952	40,964	40,363
Threshold (MFJ)	23,260	22,870	22,300	21,770	21,460
Complete (MFJ)	49,186	48,378	47,162	46,044	45,373

Three or more qualifying children

	2014	2013	2012	2011	2010
Earned income amount	13,650	13,430	13,090	12,780	12,590
Maximum credit	6,143	6,044	5,891	5,751	5,666
Threshold phaseout	17,830	17,530	17,090	16,690	16,450
Complete phaseout	46,997	46,227	45,060	43,998	43,352
Threshold (MFJ)	23,260	22,870	22,300	21,770	21,460
Complete (MFJ)	52,427	51,567	50,270	49,078	48,362

No qualifying children

	2014	2013	2012	2011	2010
Earned income amount	6,480	6,370	6,210	6,070	5,980
Maximum credit	496	487	475	464	457
Threshold phaseout	8,110	7,970	7,770	7,590	7,480
Complete phaseout	14,590	14,340	13,980	13,660	13,460
Threshold (MFJ)	13,540	13,310	12,980	12,670	12,490
Complete (MFJ)	20,020	19,680	19,190	18,740	18,470

Kiddie Tax

	2014	2013	2012	2011	2010
Unearned income thresholds	1,000/2,000	1,000/2,000	950/1,900	950/1,900	950/1,900

Child Tax Credit Refund Threshold

	2014	2013	2012	2011	2010
Amount per child	3,000	3,000	3,000	3,000	3,000

Taxpayer Interview

Personal

Name: _____	Occupation: _____	SSN: _____	
Single	Married, living w/spouse	Separated	Divorced
Spouse: _____	Occupation: _____	SSN: _____	
Blind/disabled	Spouse blind/disabled		

Children: Name	Birthdate	SSN	Gross Income	Months in Home	% Support from Child

Filing status in 2012:	Single	MFJ	MFS	HOH	QW
List dependent children who filed an income tax return in 2012: _____					
List dependent children who have unearned income > $1,000 in 2013: _____					
Changes in exemptions from 2012: _____					
Educational expenses: _____		Documentation? _____			

Income

[Self] How many Forms W-2? _____	Have them all? _____
[Spouse] How many Forms W-2? _____	Have them all? _____
[Both] How many Forms 1099? _____	Have them all? _____
Income from mutual funds? _____	Complete records? _____
Income from sales of stock? _____	Basis information available? _____
Income from municipal bonds? _____	Amount from "private activity" bonds: _____
Income from sales of personal assets? _____	Basis information available? _____
Forgiveness of debt? _____	Loans with interest below AFR? _____ Gifts? _____
Rental Income–How many properties?_____	Income/expense records available? _____
Retirement–How many Forms 1099-R? ____	Forms SSA-1099 or RRB-1099? _____
Other Income: Forms 1099-G: _____	Gambling: _____ Alimony: _____
Tax refunds: _____	Tips: _____ Other not on W-2: _____

Business Income, Deductions, and Credits

Business activity: _____	Name: _____	Product: _____ Gain or loss: _____
Records clear and complete? _____		Multiple businesses' records kept separately? _____
Business jointly owned with spouse? _____		Is spouse an employee? _____
Gross income from sales: _____		Other income: _____
Income from sales of assets? _____	Basis information: _____	Recapture applicable? ____
Insurance expenses: _____		
Casualty/theft losses? _____	Insurance proceeds paid: ____	Insurance proceeds expected? _____

Bad debts written off in 2013? _____		
Office in home (% of home)? _____		Mortgage/rent on buildings: _____
Depreciable equipment? ____	Auto(s)/other vehicle(s)? _____	Records of use? _____
Records of taxes paid: _____	Records of purchases: _____	Records of improvements since purchase?
Records of travel/lodging expenses? _____		_____
Other expenses: _____		
Was any of the income related to farming? ___		Specific farming activities: _____
Credits. Rehabilitation: _____	Energy: _____	Employment: _____ Research: _____
Disabled access: _____		Other: _____

Personal Deductions

IRA contributions made? _____	Can they be made now? _____	HSA/MSA? ____
Student loan interest paid? ____	Tuition/fees paid? _____	
Alimony paid? _____		
Itemized deductions in past? ____	Big change in medical expenses/living quarters in 2013? ____	
Medical. Whose medical expenses did you pay? _____	Special-needs dependents? ____	
Medical expenses (less insurance): Major work: _____ Glasses: ____ Dental _____ Routine medical: _____ Prescription drugs: _____ Insurance premiums (list all) _____ Medical transportation: _____ Other: _____		
Taxes. State income taxes paid in 2013: _____ Local taxes: _____ Property taxes _____ Records of sales taxes paid? _____ Real property taxes on home: _____ Other real property taxes: _____ Personal property taxes: _____		
Casualty Losses. Was property used in a business (% used)? _____	Insurance proceeds paid: _____	Insurance proceeds expected _____
Charitable Contributions. Money directly donated: _____ To whom? _____ _____		Records? _____
Incidental expenses while donating services? _____	Goods donated: _____	Records? _____
Other. Employee expenses–Did you incur expenses for the convenience of your employer? ___	Auto: _____ Travel/lodging: _____ Auto expenses: _____ Telephone: _____ Supplies/tools: _____ Equipment: _____ Uniforms: _____	
Job-seeking expenses: _____	Investment expenses: _____	Records? _____
Gambling losses: _____		
Other: _____		

Payments and Credits

Estimated federal 2013 tax payments: Q1_____ Q2 _____ Q3 _____ Q4 _____	
Estimated state 2013 tax payments: Q1_____ Q2 _____ Q3 _____ Q4 _____	
Amount applied to estimated payments from 2012 return: _____	
Contributions to retirement funds:	
Child care expenses: _____	Any provided tax-free by employer? _____
Advance child credit payments received? _____	Adoption in 2013? _____
Taxes paid to foreign government? _____	
Family members in first 4 years of higher education? _____ Any family members in higher education? _____	
Certificate for mortgage interest credit? _____	
Paid AMT in prior 5 years? _____	

Miscellaneous

Tax returns and records available how far back?	Worker employed in home?

Requirements at a Glance:
Filing Returns for Recently Deceased Taxpayers

2013 Forms That May Be Required When Filing for Recently Deceased Taxpayers

Form	Form Title	Required If...	Date Due	Special Requirements
1040	*U.S. Individual Income Tax Return*	If decedent dies after end of calendar year but before due date of tax return (usually after January 1 and before April 15), and would normally have filed for the previous year, that return would have to be filed. A return may be filed to claim a refund or a refundable credit even if the return isn't required. A return must be filed if either of the following is true: • Decedent's income from beginning of tax year through date of death was large enough to require filing of Form 1040. • Decedent was required to file for some other reason (such as SE income); see Tab 1 for details. • Decedent did not have to file, but had tax withheld.	Same date that the decedent's return would have been due if still alive. Final return for a decedent who was a calendar year taxpayer is generally due on April 15 following the year of death.	Write the words "Deceased," the decedent's name, and the date of death across the top margin of the tax return. If refund is requested, and not filing MFJ, attach Form 1310, *Statement of Person Claiming Refund Due a Deceased Taxpayer,* to the return. If filing MFJ, enter "filing as surviving spouse" in the area where you sign the return.
1041	*U.S. Income Tax Return for Estates and Trusts*	File if either of the following is true: • The estate had more than $600 of income in the tax year. • Any beneficiary of the estate is a nonresident alien.	For fiscal-year filers, 15th day of fourth month following the end of the estate's tax year (beginning on the date of death). For calendar-year filers of 2013 returns, April 15, 2014.	Note that the gross income of an estate consists of all items of income received, i.e., dividends, interest, rents, royalties, gain from the sale of property (including personal residence if paid to the probate estate), and income from business, partnerships, trusts, and any other sources earned and received after the date of death.
706	*Estate Tax Return*	Gross estate over $5,250,000 for those dying in 2013.	Generally, due nine months after decedent's date of death.	Automatic six-month extension available by filing Form 4768.
709	*U.S. Gift (and Generation-Skipping Transfer) Tax Return*	The decedent made a taxable gift in either the year of death, or in the year preceding death without yet filing a return. Also, returns required for preceding years must be filed if decedent had not filed them.	Due date for IRC §6018 information return for "large transfers" at death (April 15, 2014)	Extension to file decedent's federal income tax return (Form 4868 or 2350) automatically extends time to file gift tax return. Otherwise, use Form 8892 to request automatic six-month filing extension.

KEY FACTS: Comparing Tax Benefits of Education Options

Tax Benefits for K-12

Tuition is NEVER deductible, except when required for special-needs children. Coverdell ESAs (Formerly education IRAs) can be used for tuition along with all other qualified expenses.

Coverdell ESA:

- Trust established to cover qualified education expenses of beneficiary
- Limited to contributions of $2,000 per child under 18 (exception: special-needs child)
- Elementary, secondary, postsecondary, and graduate education
- Tuition, books, supplies, equipment, registration fees, room and board (for attendance at least half-time), and qualified tuition program payments, as long as distribution is not used for expenses for which credit is claimed
- Hope or lifetime learning credit can be claimed in the same year as a Coverdell ESA distribution is excluded from income
- Contributions not deductible
- Earnings tax deferred
- Distributions tax-free
- 6% excise tax on excess contributions (including earnings) not withdrawn by June of the next year
- Phaseouts: MFJ, $190,000–220,000; others, $95,000–110,000

Tax Credits for Higher Education

Attribute	American Opportunity Tax Credit (modified Hope)	Lifetime Learning Credit
Benefit	Covers 100% of the first $2,000 and 25% of the second $2,000 of qualified expenses	Credit equals 20% of the first $10,000 of qualified education expenses for all eligible students
Limit	Limited to $2,500 per student	Limited to $2,000 per taxpayer
Education covered	Available through completion of first four post-secondary years	Available through all post-secondary years, and for job improvement or skill attainment coursework
Years covered	Limited to four years of education	Unlimited number of years education
Qualifying expenses	Tuition; related expenses (e.g., student-activity fees, course-related books, supplies, and equipment) only if they must be paid to the institution as a condition of enrollment or attendance. Hope Credit also covers "course materials" (e.g., books, supplies and equipment needed for a course of study whether or not they are purchased from the institution as a condition of enrollment or attendance).	
Qualifying education	Must be used in pursuit of undergraduate degree or other recognized credential; student must be enrolled at least half-time for academic period beginning in tax year	Cannot claim both Hope and Lifetime Learning credit for the same student in the same year.
Other requirements	No felony drug conviction on student's record	
Type of credit	Up to 40% refundable; 0% refundable if taxpayer claiming the credit is a child subject to the "kiddie tax"	Nonrefundable tax credit
Phaseout	MFJ: $160,000–$180,000; Others: $80,000–$90,000; MFS: $0	MFJ: $107,000–$127,000; Others: $53,000–$63,000; MFS: $0

Other Education Benefits

Qualified Tuition Program (Shop Around!!)

- No AGI limitations
- Distributions not exceeding costs of higher education excluded from income
- Can be used in conjunction with Coverdell ESA
- States and even private universities may offer programs; shopping around advisable

Scholarships and Fellowships

- Generally excluded from income unless payments for services are included
- No AGI limits

Series EE and I Savings Bonds

- All or part of interest excluded from income if used to cover college tuition or fees
- EE bond must have been issued since 12/31/89

NOTES

NOTES

NOTES

NOTES

_____

_____

_____

_____

_____

_____

_____

_____

_____

_____

_____

_____

_____

_____

_____

_____

_____

_____

_____

_____

_____

_____

_____

Comments or suggestions for CCH Express Answers?

If you have any questions or comments about Express Answers publications, please visit the
CCH Customer Support site at support.cch.com (first-time visitors will need to register).
You can also chat with us online at support.cch.com/chat/booksupport/ or email us at
CCHCustomerService@wolterskluwer.com.

What's New in 2013

Tax Rates. The lower income tax rates imposed on individuals, estates, and trusts under EGTRRA have generally been made permanent for tax years beginning after December 31, 2012, as a result of the elimination of the EGTRRA sunset provision. Individuals, however, are subject to a top tax rate of 39.6 percent beginning in 2013, if their taxable income exceeds the applicable threshold amount of $450,000 for married individuals filing joint returns and surviving spouses, $425,000 for heads of households, $400,000 for single individuals, and $225,000 for married individuals filing separate returns. Estates and trusts are subject to a top tax rate of 39.6 percent on all taxable income in excess of the 33-percent tax bracket.

Marriage Penalty Relief. For married taxpayers filing joint returns and for surviving spouses, the increase in the size of the 15-percent tax bracket to twice the size of the corresponding rate bracket for single filers, and the increase in the standard deduction to twice the inflation-adjusted amount of the deduction amount for single taxpayers and married taxpayers filing separately, have been made permanent for tax years beginning after December 31, 2012.

Capital Gains. The reduced maximum capital gains rate of 15 percent on adjusted net capital gain of noncorporate taxpayers (for regular tax and AMT purposes), and the zero-percent capital gains rate on adjusted net capital gain of noncorporate taxpayers in the 10-percent or 15-percent income tax bracket, have been made permanent. The capital gains rate, however, is increased to 20 percent beginning in 2013 for adjusted net capital gains of individuals, estates, and trusts in the top tax bracket.

Alternative Minimum Tax (AMT) Exemption Amount Increased. The AMT exemption amounts have increased for the 2013 tax year to $51,900 for unmarried individuals, $80,800 for married filing jointly or a qualifying widow(er), $40,400 for married filing separately, and $23,100 for estate or trusts.

Bonus Depreciation. The additional depreciation allowance (bonus depreciation) applies to qualifying property acquired after December 31, 2007, and placed in service before January 1, 2014 (or before January 1, 2015, in the case of property with a longer production period and certain noncommercial aircraft). The bonus depreciation allowance rate is 50 percent for qualified property.

Credits Made Permanent or Extended. Many credits, previously extended from year to year, have now been made permanent, including credits for adoption, child and dependent care, child care expenses, and child tax, as well as changes to the earned income credit. Other credits have been extended to 2013 or later, including credits for employer's differential wage payments, American Opportunity, Indian employment, new markets, renewable electricity production, research, residential energy property, and work opportunity.

Itemized Deduction Phaseout. The phaseout of itemized deductions for higher income individuals is reinstated for tax years beginning after December 31, 2012. As a result, the amount of otherwise allowable itemized deductions of a taxpayer for 2013 will be reduced or eliminated if his or her adjusted gross income exceeds a threshold amount for the tax year.

Sales Tax Deduction. The election to claim an itemized deduction for state and local general sales taxes in lieu of state and local income taxes is extended two years and may be claimed for tax years beginning in 2012 and 2013.

The table presented here is a draft version of the 2013 Tax Table. At the time of publication, the IRS had not released the final 2013 Tax Table. The 2013 Tax Computation Worksheet is also a draft version. For the latest information, see CCHGroup.com/TaxUpdates.

2013 Tax Table

CAUTION See the instructions for line 44 to see if you must use the Tax Table below to figure your tax.

Example. Mr. and Mrs. Brown are filing a joint return. Their taxable income on Form 1040, line 43, is $25,300. First, they find the $25,300-25,350 taxable income line. Next, they find the column for married filing jointly and read down the column. The amount shown where the taxable income line and filing status column meet is $2,906. This is the tax amount they should enter on Form 1040, line 44.

Sample Table

At Least	But Less Than	Single	Married filing jointly *	Married filing sepa-rately	Head of a house-hold
		Your tax is—			
25,200	**25,250**	3,338	2,891	3,338	3,146
25,250	**25,300**	3,345	2,899	3,345	3,154
25,300	**25,350**	3,353	(2,906)	3,353	3,161
25,350	**25,400**	3,360	2,914	3,360	3,169

If line 43 (taxable income) is—		And you are—			
At least	But less than	Single	Married filing jointly *	Married filing sepa-rately	Head of a house-hold
		Your tax is—			
0	5	0	0	0	0
5	15	1	1	1	1
15	25	2	2	2	2
25	50	4	4	4	4
50	75	6	6	6	6
75	100	9	9	9	9
100	125	11	11	11	11
125	150	14	14	14	14
150	175	16	16	16	16
175	200	19	19	19	19
200	225	21	21	21	21
225	250	24	24	24	24
250	275	26	26	26	26
275	300	29	29	29	29
300	325	31	31	31	31
325	350	34	34	34	34
350	375	36	36	36	36
375	400	39	39	39	39
400	425	41	41	41	41
425	450	44	44	44	44
450	475	46	46	46	46
475	500	49	49	49	49
500	525	51	51	51	51
525	550	54	54	54	54
550	575	56	56	56	56
575	600	59	59	59	59
600	625	61	61	61	61
625	650	64	64	64	64
650	675	66	66	66	66
675	700	69	69	69	69
700	725	71	71	71	71
725	750	74	74	74	74
750	775	76	76	76	76
775	800	79	79	79	79
800	825	81	81	81	81
825	850	84	84	84	84
850	875	86	86	86	86
875	900	89	89	89	89
900	925	91	91	91	91
925	950	94	94	94	94
950	975	96	96	96	96
975	1,000	99	99	99	99
1,000					
1,000	1,025	101	101	101	101
1,025	1,050	104	104	104	104
1,050	1,075	106	106	106	106
1,075	1,100	109	109	109	109
1,100	1,125	111	111	111	111
1,125	1,150	114	114	114	114
1,150	1,175	116	116	116	116
1,175	1,200	119	119	119	119
1,200	1,225	121	121	121	121
1,225	1,250	124	124	124	124
1,250	1,275	126	126	126	126
1,275	1,300	129	129	129	129
1,300	1,325	131	131	131	131
1,325	1,350	134	134	134	134
1,350	1,375	136	136	136	136
1,375	1,400	139	139	139	139
1,400	1,425	141	141	141	141
1,425	1,450	144	144	144	144
1,450	1,475	146	146	146	146
1,475	1,500	149	149	149	149
1,500	1,525	151	151	151	151
1,525	1,550	154	154	154	154
1,550	1,575	156	156	156	156
1,575	1,600	159	159	159	159
1,600	1,625	161	161	161	161
1,625	1,650	164	164	164	164
1,650	1,675	166	166	166	166
1,675	1,700	169	169	169	169
1,700	1,725	171	171	171	171
1,725	1,750	174	174	174	174
1,750	1,775	176	176	176	176
1,775	1,800	179	179	179	179
1,800	1,825	181	181	181	181
1,825	1,850	184	184	184	184
1,850	1,875	186	186	186	186
1,875	1,900	189	189	189	189
1,900	1,925	191	191	191	191
1,925	1,950	194	194	194	194
1,950	1,975	196	196	196	196
1,975	2,000	199	199	199	199
2,000					
2,000	2,025	201	201	201	201
2,025	2,050	204	204	204	204
2,050	2,075	206	206	206	206
2,075	2,100	209	209	209	209
2,100	2,125	211	211	211	211
2,125	2,150	214	214	214	214
2,150	2,175	216	216	216	216
2,175	2,200	219	219	219	219
2,200	2,225	221	221	221	221
2,225	2,250	224	224	224	224
2,250	2,275	226	226	226	226
2,275	2,300	229	229	229	229
2,300	2,325	231	231	231	231
2,325	2,350	234	234	234	234
2,350	2,375	236	236	236	236
2,375	2,400	239	239	239	239
2,400	2,425	241	241	241	241
2,425	2,450	244	244	244	244
2,450	2,475	246	246	246	246
2,475	2,500	249	249	249	249
2,500	2,525	251	251	251	251
2,525	2,550	254	254	254	254
2,550	2,575	256	256	256	256
2,575	2,600	259	259	259	259
2,600	2,625	261	261	261	261
2,625	2,650	264	264	264	264
2,650	2,675	266	266	266	266
2,675	2,700	269	269	269	269
2,700	2,725	271	271	271	271
2,725	2,750	274	274	274	274
2,750	2,775	276	276	276	276
2,775	2,800	279	279	279	279
2,800	2,825	281	281	281	281
2,825	2,850	284	284	284	284
2,850	2,875	286	286	286	286
2,875	2,900	289	289	289	289
2,900	2,925	291	291	291	291
2,925	2,950	294	294	294	294
2,950	2,975	296	296	296	296
2,975	3,000	299	299	299	299

* This column must also be used by a qualifying widow(er).

(Continued)

If line 43 (taxable income) is—		And you are—			
At least	But less than	Single	Married filing jointly *	Married filing sepa-rately	Head of a house-hold
		Your tax is—			
3,000					
3,000	3,050	303	303	303	303
3,050	3,100	308	308	308	308
3,100	3,150	313	313	313	313
3,150	3,200	318	318	318	318
3,200	3,250	323	323	323	323
3,250	3,300	328	328	328	328
3,300	3,350	333	333	333	333
3,350	3,400	338	338	338	338
3,400	3,450	343	343	343	343
3,450	3,500	348	348	348	348
3,500	3,550	353	353	353	353
3,550	3,600	358	358	358	358
3,600	3,650	363	363	363	363
3,650	3,700	368	368	368	368
3,700	3,750	373	373	373	373
3,750	3,800	378	378	378	378
3,800	3,850	383	383	383	383
3,850	3,900	388	388	388	388
3,900	3,950	393	393	393	393
3,950	4,000	398	398	398	398
4,000					
4,000	4,050	403	403	403	403
4,050	4,100	408	408	408	408
4,100	4,150	413	413	413	413
4,150	4,200	418	418	418	418
4,200	4,250	423	423	423	423
4,250	4,300	428	428	428	428
4,300	4,350	433	433	433	433
4,350	4,400	438	438	438	438
4,400	4,450	443	443	443	443
4,450	4,500	448	448	448	448
4,500	4,550	453	453	453	453
4,550	4,600	458	458	458	458
4,600	4,650	463	463	463	463
4,650	4,700	468	468	468	468
4,700	4,750	473	473	473	473
4,750	4,800	478	478	478	478
4,800	4,850	483	483	483	483
4,850	4,900	488	488	488	488
4,900	4,950	493	493	493	493
4,950	5,000	498	498	498	498
5,000					
5,000	5,050	503	503	503	503
5,050	5,100	508	508	508	508
5,100	5,150	513	513	513	513
5,150	5,200	518	518	518	518
5,200	5,250	523	523	523	523
5,250	5,300	528	528	528	528
5,300	5,350	533	533	533	533
5,350	5,400	538	538	538	538
5,400	5,450	543	543	543	543
5,450	5,500	548	548	548	548
5,500	5,550	553	553	553	553
5,550	5,600	558	558	558	558
5,600	5,650	563	563	563	563
5,650	5,700	568	568	568	568
5,700	5,750	573	573	573	573
5,750	5,800	578	578	578	578
5,800	5,850	583	583	583	583
5,850	5,900	588	588	588	588
5,900	5,950	593	593	593	593
5,950	6,000	598	598	598	598
6,000					
6,000	6,050	603	603	603	603
6,050	6,100	608	608	608	608
6,100	6,150	613	613	613	613
6,150	6,200	618	618	618	618
6,200	6,250	623	623	623	623
6,250	6,300	628	628	628	628
6,300	6,350	633	633	633	633
6,350	6,400	638	638	638	638
6,400	6,450	643	643	643	643
6,450	6,500	648	648	648	648
6,500	6,550	653	653	653	653
6,550	6,600	658	658	658	658
6,600	6,650	663	663	663	663
6,650	6,700	668	668	668	668
6,700	6,750	673	673	673	673
6,750	6,800	678	678	678	678
6,800	6,850	683	683	683	683
6,850	6,900	688	688	688	688
6,900	6,950	693	693	693	693
6,950	7,000	698	698	698	698
7,000					
7,000	7,050	703	703	703	703
7,050	7,100	708	708	708	708
7,100	7,150	713	713	713	713
7,150	7,200	718	718	718	718
7,200	7,250	723	723	723	723
7,250	7,300	728	728	728	728
7,300	7,350	733	733	733	733
7,350	7,400	738	738	738	738
7,400	7,450	743	743	743	743
7,450	7,500	748	748	748	748
7,500	7,550	753	753	753	753
7,550	7,600	758	758	758	758
7,600	7,650	763	763	763	763
7,650	7,700	768	768	768	768
7,700	7,750	773	773	773	773
7,750	7,800	778	778	778	778
7,800	7,850	783	783	783	783
7,850	7,900	788	788	788	788
7,900	7,950	793	793	793	793
7,950	8,000	798	798	798	798
8,000					
8,000	8,050	803	803	803	803
8,050	8,100	808	808	808	808
8,100	8,150	813	813	813	813
8,150	8,200	818	818	818	818
8,200	8,250	823	823	823	823
8,250	8,300	828	828	828	828
8,300	8,350	833	833	833	833
8,350	8,400	838	838	838	838
8,400	8,450	843	843	843	843
8,450	8,500	848	848	848	848
8,500	8,550	853	853	853	853
8,550	8,600	858	858	858	858
8,600	8,650	863	863	863	863
8,650	8,700	868	868	868	868
8,700	8,750	873	873	873	873
8,750	8,800	878	878	878	878
8,800	8,850	883	883	883	883
8,850	8,900	888	888	888	888
8,900	8,950	893	893	893	893
8,950	9,000	900	898	900	898
9,000					
9,000	9,050	908	903	908	903
9,050	9,100	915	908	915	908
9,100	9,150	923	913	923	913
9,150	9,200	930	918	930	918
9,200	9,250	938	923	938	923
9,250	9,300	945	928	945	928
9,300	9,350	953	933	953	933
9,350	9,400	960	938	960	938
9,400	9,450	968	943	968	943
9,450	9,500	975	948	975	948
9,500	9,550	983	953	983	953
9,550	9,600	990	958	990	958
9,600	9,650	998	963	998	963
9,650	9,700	1,005	968	1,005	968
9,700	9,750	1,013	973	1,013	973
9,750	9,800	1,020	978	1,020	978
9,800	9,850	1,028	983	1,028	983
9,850	9,900	1,035	988	1,035	988
9,900	9,950	1,043	993	1,043	993
9,950	10,000	1,050	998	1,050	998
10,000					
10,000	10,050	1,058	1,003	1,058	1,003
10,050	10,100	1,065	1,008	1,065	1,008
10,100	10,150	1,073	1,013	1,073	1,013
10,150	10,200	1,080	1,018	1,080	1,018
10,200	10,250	1,088	1,023	1,088	1,023
10,250	10,300	1,095	1,028	1,095	1,028
10,300	10,350	1,103	1,033	1,103	1,033
10,350	10,400	1,110	1,038	1,110	1,038
10,400	10,450	1,118	1,043	1,118	1,043
10,450	10,500	1,125	1,048	1,125	1,048
10,500	10,550	1,133	1,053	1,133	1,053
10,550	10,600	1,140	1,058	1,140	1,058
10,600	10,650	1,148	1,063	1,148	1,063
10,650	10,700	1,155	1,068	1,155	1,068
10,700	10,750	1,163	1,073	1,163	1,073
10,750	10,800	1,170	1,078	1,170	1,078
10,800	10,850	1,178	1,083	1,178	1,083
10,850	10,900	1,185	1,088	1,185	1,088
10,900	10,950	1,193	1,093	1,193	1,093
10,950	11,000	1,200	1,098	1,200	1,098
11,000					
11,000	11,050	1,208	1,103	1,208	1,103
11,050	11,100	1,215	1,108	1,215	1,108
11,100	11,150	1,223	1,113	1,223	1,113
11,150	11,200	1,230	1,118	1,230	1,118
11,200	11,250	1,238	1,123	1,238	1,123
11,250	11,300	1,245	1,128	1,245	1,128
11,300	11,350	1,253	1,133	1,253	1,133
11,350	11,400	1,260	1,138	1,260	1,138
11,400	11,450	1,268	1,143	1,268	1,143
11,450	11,500	1,275	1,148	1,275	1,148
11,500	11,550	1,283	1,153	1,283	1,153
11,550	11,600	1,290	1,158	1,290	1,158
11,600	11,650	1,298	1,163	1,298	1,163
11,650	11,700	1,305	1,168	1,305	1,168
11,700	11,750	1,313	1,173	1,313	1,173
11,750	11,800	1,320	1,178	1,320	1,178
11,800	11,850	1,328	1,183	1,328	1,183
11,850	11,900	1,335	1,188	1,335	1,188
11,900	11,950	1,343	1,193	1,343	1,193
11,950	12,000	1,350	1,198	1,350	1,198

* This column must also be used by a qualifying widow(er).

(Continued)

2013 Tax Table —Continued

If line 43 (taxable income) is—		And you are—			
At least	But less than	Single	Married filing jointly *	Married filing separately	Head of a household
		Your tax is—			
12,000					
12,000	12,050	1,358	1,203	1,358	1,203
12,050	12,100	1,365	1,208	1,365	1,208
12,100	12,150	1,373	1,213	1,373	1,213
12,150	12,200	1,380	1,218	1,380	1,218
12,200	12,250	1,388	1,223	1,388	1,223
12,250	12,300	1,395	1,228	1,395	1,228
12,300	12,350	1,403	1,233	1,403	1,233
12,350	12,400	1,410	1,238	1,410	1,238
12,400	12,450	1,418	1,243	1,418	1,243
12,450	12,500	1,425	1,248	1,425	1,248
12,500	12,550	1,433	1,253	1,433	1,253
12,550	12,600	1,440	1,258	1,440	1,258
12,600	12,650	1,448	1,263	1,448	1,263
12,650	12,700	1,455	1,268	1,455	1,268
12,700	12,750	1,463	1,273	1,463	1,273
12,750	12,800	1,470	1,278	1,470	1,279
12,800	12,850	1,478	1,283	1,478	1,286
12,850	12,900	1,485	1,288	1,485	1,294
12,900	12,950	1,493	1,293	1,493	1,301
12,950	13,000	1,500	1,298	1,500	1,309
13,000					
13,000	13,050	1,508	1,303	1,508	1,316
13,050	13,100	1,515	1,308	1,515	1,324
13,100	13,150	1,523	1,313	1,523	1,331
13,150	13,200	1,530	1,318	1,530	1,339
13,200	13,250	1,538	1,323	1,538	1,346
13,250	13,300	1,545	1,328	1,545	1,354
13,300	13,350	1,553	1,333	1,553	1,361
13,350	13,400	1,560	1,338	1,560	1,369
13,400	13,450	1,568	1,343	1,568	1,376
13,450	13,500	1,575	1,348	1,575	1,384
13,500	13,550	1,583	1,353	1,583	1,391
13,550	13,600	1,590	1,358	1,590	1,399
13,600	13,650	1,598	1,363	1,598	1,406
13,650	13,700	1,605	1,368	1,605	1,414
13,700	13,750	1,613	1,373	1,613	1,421
13,750	13,800	1,620	1,378	1,620	1,429
13,800	13,850	1,628	1,383	1,628	1,436
13,850	13,900	1,635	1,388	1,635	1,444
13,900	13,950	1,643	1,393	1,643	1,451
13,950	14,000	1,650	1,398	1,650	1,459
14,000					
14,000	14,050	1,658	1,403	1,658	1,466
14,050	14,100	1,665	1,408	1,665	1,474
14,100	14,150	1,673	1,413	1,673	1,481
14,150	14,200	1,680	1,418	1,680	1,489
14,200	14,250	1,688	1,423	1,688	1,496
14,250	14,300	1,695	1,428	1,695	1,504
14,300	14,350	1,703	1,433	1,703	1,511
14,350	14,400	1,710	1,438	1,710	1,519
14,400	14,450	1,718	1,443	1,718	1,526
14,450	14,500	1,725	1,448	1,725	1,534
14,500	14,550	1,733	1,453	1,733	1,541
14,550	14,600	1,740	1,458	1,740	1,549
14,600	14,650	1,748	1,463	1,748	1,556
14,650	14,700	1,755	1,468	1,755	1,564
14,700	14,750	1,763	1,473	1,763	1,571
14,750	14,800	1,770	1,478	1,770	1,579
14,800	14,850	1,778	1,483	1,778	1,586
14,850	14,900	1,785	1,488	1,785	1,594
14,900	14,950	1,793	1,493	1,793	1,601
14,950	15,000	1,800	1,498	1,800	1,609
15,000					
15,000	15,050	1,808	1,503	1,808	1,616
15,050	15,100	1,815	1,508	1,815	1,624
15,100	15,150	1,823	1,513	1,823	1,631
15,150	15,200	1,830	1,518	1,830	1,639
15,200	15,250	1,838	1,523	1,838	1,646
15,250	15,300	1,845	1,528	1,845	1,654
15,300	15,350	1,853	1,533	1,853	1,661
15,350	15,400	1,860	1,538	1,860	1,669
15,400	15,450	1,868	1,543	1,868	1,676
15,450	15,500	1,875	1,548	1,875	1,684
15,500	15,550	1,883	1,553	1,883	1,691
15,550	15,600	1,890	1,558	1,890	1,699
15,600	15,650	1,898	1,563	1,898	1,706
15,650	15,700	1,905	1,568	1,905	1,714
15,700	15,750	1,913	1,573	1,913	1,721
15,750	15,800	1,920	1,578	1,920	1,729
15,800	15,850	1,928	1,583	1,928	1,736
15,850	15,900	1,935	1,588	1,935	1,744
15,900	15,950	1,943	1,593	1,943	1,751
15,950	16,000	1,950	1,598	1,950	1,759
16,000					
16,000	16,050	1,958	1,603	1,958	1,766
16,050	16,100	1,965	1,608	1,965	1,774
16,100	16,150	1,973	1,613	1,973	1,781
16,150	16,200	1,980	1,618	1,980	1,789
16,200	16,250	1,988	1,623	1,988	1,796
16,250	16,300	1,995	1,628	1,995	1,804
16,300	16,350	2,003	1,633	2,003	1,811
16,350	16,400	2,010	1,638	2,010	1,819
16,400	16,450	2,018	1,643	2,018	1,826
16,450	16,500	2,025	1,648	2,025	1,834
16,500	16,550	2,033	1,653	2,033	1,841
16,550	16,600	2,040	1,658	2,040	1,849
16,600	16,650	2,048	1,663	2,048	1,856
16,650	16,700	2,055	1,668	2,055	1,864
16,700	16,750	2,063	1,673	2,063	1,871
16,750	16,800	2,070	1,678	2,070	1,879
16,800	16,850	2,078	1,683	2,078	1,886
16,850	16,900	2,085	1,688	2,085	1,894
16,900	16,950	2,093	1,693	2,093	1,901
16,950	17,000	2,100	1,698	2,100	1,909
17,000					
17,000	17,050	2,108	1,703	2,108	1,916
17,050	17,100	2,115	1,708	2,115	1,924
17,100	17,150	2,123	1,713	2,123	1,931
17,150	17,200	2,130	1,718	2,130	1,939
17,200	17,250	2,138	1,723	2,138	1,946
17,250	17,300	2,145	1,728	2,145	1,954
17,300	17,350	2,153	1,733	2,153	1,961
17,350	17,400	2,160	1,738	2,160	1,969
17,400	17,450	2,168	1,743	2,168	1,976
17,450	17,500	2,175	1,748	2,175	1,984
17,500	17,550	2,183	1,753	2,183	1,991
17,550	17,600	2,190	1,758	2,190	1,999
17,600	17,650	2,198	1,763	2,198	2,006
17,650	17,700	2,205	1,768	2,205	2,014
17,700	17,750	2,213	1,773	2,213	2,021
17,750	17,800	2,220	1,778	2,220	2,029
17,800	17,850	2,228	1,783	2,228	2,036
17,850	17,900	2,235	1,789	2,235	2,044
17,900	17,950	2,243	1,796	2,243	2,051
17,950	18,000	2,250	1,804	2,250	2,059
18,000					
18,000	18,050	2,258	1,811	2,258	2,066
18,050	18,100	2,265	1,819	2,265	2,074
18,100	18,150	2,273	1,826	2,273	2,081
18,150	18,200	2,280	1,834	2,280	2,089
18,200	18,250	2,288	1,841	2,288	2,096
18,250	18,300	2,295	1,849	2,295	2,104
18,300	18,350	2,303	1,856	2,303	2,111
18,350	18,400	2,310	1,864	2,310	2,119
18,400	18,450	2,318	1,871	2,318	2,126
18,450	18,500	2,325	1,879	2,325	2,134
18,500	18,550	2,333	1,886	2,333	2,141
18,550	18,600	2,340	1,894	2,340	2,149
18,600	18,650	2,348	1,901	2,348	2,156
18,650	18,700	2,355	1,909	2,355	2,164
18,700	18,750	2,363	1,916	2,363	2,171
18,750	18,800	2,370	1,924	2,370	2,179
18,800	18,850	2,378	1,931	2,378	2,186
18,850	18,900	2,385	1,939	2,385	2,194
18,900	18,950	2,393	1,946	2,393	2,201
18,950	19,000	2,400	1,954	2,400	2,209
19,000					
19,000	19,050	2,408	1,961	2,408	2,216
19,050	19,100	2,415	1,969	2,415	2,224
19,100	19,150	2,423	1,976	2,423	2,231
19,150	19,200	2,430	1,984	2,430	2,239
19,200	19,250	2,438	1,991	2,438	2,246
19,250	19,300	2,445	1,999	2,445	2,254
19,300	19,350	2,453	2,006	2,453	2,261
19,350	19,400	2,460	2,014	2,460	2,269
19,400	19,450	2,468	2,021	2,468	2,276
19,450	19,500	2,475	2,029	2,475	2,284
19,500	19,550	2,483	2,036	2,483	2,291
19,550	19,600	2,490	2,044	2,490	2,299
19,600	19,650	2,498	2,051	2,498	2,306
19,650	19,700	2,505	2,059	2,505	2,314
19,700	19,750	2,513	2,066	2,513	2,321
19,750	19,800	2,520	2,074	2,520	2,329
19,800	19,850	2,528	2,081	2,528	2,336
19,850	19,900	2,535	2,089	2,535	2,344
19,900	19,950	2,543	2,096	2,543	2,351
19,950	20,000	2,550	2,104	2,550	2,359
20,000					
20,000	20,050	2,558	2,111	2,558	2,366
20,050	20,100	2,565	2,119	2,565	2,374
20,100	20,150	2,573	2,126	2,573	2,381
20,150	20,200	2,580	2,134	2,580	2,389
20,200	20,250	2,588	2,141	2,588	2,396
20,250	20,300	2,595	2,149	2,595	2,404
20,300	20,350	2,603	2,156	2,603	2,411
20,350	20,400	2,610	2,164	2,610	2,419
20,400	20,450	2,618	2,171	2,618	2,426
20,450	20,500	2,625	2,179	2,625	2,434
20,500	20,550	2,633	2,186	2,633	2,441
20,550	20,600	2,640	2,194	2,640	2,449
20,600	20,650	2,648	2,201	2,648	2,456
20,650	20,700	2,655	2,209	2,655	2,464
20,700	20,750	2,663	2,216	2,663	2,471
20,750	20,800	2,670	2,224	2,670	2,479
20,800	20,850	2,678	2,231	2,678	2,486
20,850	20,900	2,685	2,239	2,685	2,494
20,900	20,950	2,693	2,246	2,693	2,501
20,950	21,000	2,700	2,254	2,700	2,509
21,000					
21,000	21,050	2,708	2,261	2,708	2,516
21,050	21,100	2,715	2,269	2,715	2,524
21,100	21,150	2,723	2,276	2,723	2,531
21,150	21,200	2,730	2,284	2,730	2,539
21,200	21,250	2,738	2,291	2,738	2,546
21,250	21,300	2,745	2,299	2,745	2,554
21,300	21,350	2,753	2,306	2,753	2,561
21,350	21,400	2,760	2,314	2,760	2,569
21,400	21,450	2,768	2,321	2,768	2,576
21,450	21,500	2,775	2,329	2,775	2,584
21,500	21,550	2,783	2,336	2,783	2,591
21,550	21,600	2,790	2,344	2,790	2,599
21,600	21,650	2,798	2,351	2,798	2,606
21,650	21,700	2,805	2,359	2,805	2,614
21,700	21,750	2,813	2,366	2,813	2,621
21,750	21,800	2,820	2,374	2,820	2,629
21,800	21,850	2,828	2,381	2,828	2,636
21,850	21,900	2,835	2,389	2,835	2,644
21,900	21,950	2,843	2,396	2,843	2,651
21,950	22,000	2,850	2,404	2,850	2,659
22,000					
22,000	22,050	2,858	2,411	2,858	2,666
22,050	22,100	2,865	2,419	2,865	2,674
22,100	22,150	2,873	2,426	2,873	2,681
22,150	22,200	2,880	2,434	2,880	2,689
22,200	22,250	2,888	2,441	2,888	2,696
22,250	22,300	2,895	2,449	2,895	2,704
22,300	22,350	2,903	2,456	2,903	2,711
22,350	22,400	2,910	2,464	2,910	2,719
22,400	22,450	2,918	2,471	2,918	2,726
22,450	22,500	2,925	2,479	2,925	2,734
22,500	22,550	2,933	2,486	2,933	2,741
22,550	22,600	2,940	2,494	2,940	2,749
22,600	22,650	2,948	2,501	2,948	2,756
22,650	22,700	2,955	2,509	2,955	2,764
22,700	22,750	2,963	2,516	2,963	2,771
22,750	22,800	2,970	2,524	2,970	2,779
22,800	22,850	2,978	2,531	2,978	2,786
22,850	22,900	2,985	2,539	2,985	2,794
22,900	22,950	2,993	2,546	2,993	2,801
22,950	23,000	3,000	2,554	3,000	2,809
23,000					
23,000	23,050	3,008	2,561	3,008	2,816
23,050	23,100	3,015	2,569	3,015	2,824
23,100	23,150	3,023	2,576	3,023	2,831
23,150	23,200	3,030	2,584	3,030	2,839
23,200	23,250	3,038	2,591	3,038	2,846
23,250	23,300	3,045	2,599	3,045	2,854
23,300	23,350	3,053	2,606	3,053	2,861
23,350	23,400	3,060	2,614	3,060	2,869
23,400	23,450	3,068	2,621	3,068	2,876
23,450	23,500	3,075	2,629	3,075	2,884
23,500	23,550	3,083	2,636	3,083	2,891
23,550	23,600	3,090	2,644	3,090	2,899
23,600	23,650	3,098	2,651	3,098	2,906
23,650	23,700	3,105	2,659	3,105	2,914
23,700	23,750	3,113	2,666	3,113	2,921
23,750	23,800	3,120	2,674	3,120	2,929
23,800	23,850	3,128	2,681	3,128	2,936
23,850	23,900	3,135	2,689	3,135	2,944
23,900	23,950	3,143	2,696	3,143	2,951
23,950	24,000	3,150	2,704	3,150	2,959
24,000					
24,000	24,050	3,158	2,711	3,158	2,966
24,050	24,100	3,165	2,719	3,165	2,974
24,100	24,150	3,173	2,726	3,173	2,981
24,150	24,200	3,180	2,734	3,180	2,989
24,200	24,250	3,188	2,741	3,188	2,996
24,250	24,300	3,195	2,749	3,195	3,004
24,300	24,350	3,203	2,756	3,203	3,011
24,350	24,400	3,210	2,764	3,210	3,019
24,400	24,450	3,218	2,771	3,218	3,026
24,450	24,500	3,225	2,779	3,225	3,034
24,500	24,550	3,233	2,786	3,233	3,041
24,550	24,600	3,240	2,794	3,240	3,049
24,600	24,650	3,248	2,801	3,248	3,056
24,650	24,700	3,255	2,809	3,255	3,064
24,700	24,750	3,263	2,816	3,263	3,071
24,750	24,800	3,270	2,824	3,270	3,079
24,800	24,850	3,278	2,831	3,278	3,086
24,850	24,900	3,285	2,839	3,285	3,094
24,900	24,950	3,293	2,846	3,293	3,101
24,950	25,000	3,300	2,854	3,300	3,109
25,000					
25,000	25,050	3,308	2,861	3,308	3,116
25,050	25,100	3,315	2,869	3,315	3,124
25,100	25,150	3,323	2,876	3,323	3,131
25,150	25,200	3,330	2,884	3,330	3,139
25,200	25,250	3,338	2,891	3,338	3,146
25,250	25,300	3,345	2,899	3,345	3,154
25,300	25,350	3,353	2,906	3,353	3,161
25,350	25,400	3,360	2,914	3,360	3,169
25,400	25,450	3,368	2,921	3,368	3,176
25,450	25,500	3,375	2,929	3,375	3,184
25,500	25,550	3,383	2,936	3,383	3,191
25,550	25,600	3,390	2,944	3,390	3,199
25,600	25,650	3,398	2,951	3,398	3,206
25,650	25,700	3,405	2,959	3,405	3,214
25,700	25,750	3,413	2,966	3,413	3,221
25,750	25,800	3,420	2,974	3,420	3,229
25,800	25,850	3,428	2,981	3,428	3,236
25,850	25,900	3,435	2,989	3,435	3,244
25,900	25,950	3,443	2,996	3,443	3,251
25,950	26,000	3,450	3,004	3,450	3,259
26,000					
26,000	26,050	3,458	3,011	3,458	3,266
26,050	26,100	3,465	3,019	3,465	3,274
26,100	26,150	3,473	3,026	3,473	3,281
26,150	26,200	3,480	3,034	3,480	3,289
26,200	26,250	3,488	3,041	3,488	3,296
26,250	26,300	3,495	3,049	3,495	3,304
26,300	26,350	3,503	3,056	3,503	3,311
26,350	26,400	3,510	3,064	3,510	3,319
26,400	26,450	3,518	3,071	3,518	3,326
26,450	26,500	3,525	3,079	3,525	3,334
26,500	26,550	3,533	3,086	3,533	3,341
26,550	26,600	3,540	3,094	3,540	3,349
26,600	26,650	3,548	3,101	3,548	3,356
26,650	26,700	3,555	3,109	3,555	3,364
26,700	26,750	3,563	3,116	3,563	3,371
26,750	26,800	3,570	3,124	3,570	3,379
26,800	26,850	3,578	3,131	3,578	3,386
26,850	26,900	3,585	3,139	3,585	3,394
26,900	26,950	3,593	3,146	3,593	3,401
26,950	27,000	3,600	3,154	3,600	3,409
27,000					
27,000	27,050	3,608	3,161	3,608	3,416
27,050	27,100	3,615	3,169	3,615	3,424
27,100	27,150	3,623	3,176	3,623	3,431
27,150	27,200	3,630	3,184	3,630	3,439
27,200	27,250	3,638	3,191	3,638	3,446
27,250	27,300	3,645	3,199	3,645	3,454
27,300	27,350	3,653	3,206	3,653	3,461
27,350	27,400	3,660	3,214	3,660	3,469
27,400	27,450	3,668	3,221	3,668	3,476
27,450	27,500	3,675	3,229	3,675	3,484
27,500	27,550	3,683	3,236	3,683	3,491
27,550	27,600	3,690	3,244	3,690	3,499
27,600	27,650	3,698	3,251	3,698	3,506
27,650	27,700	3,705	3,259	3,705	3,514
27,700	27,750	3,713	3,266	3,713	3,521
27,750	27,800	3,720	3,274	3,720	3,529
27,800	27,850	3,728	3,281	3,728	3,536
27,850	27,900	3,735	3,289	3,735	3,544
27,900	27,950	3,743	3,296	3,743	3,551
27,950	28,000	3,750	3,304	3,750	3,559
28,000					
28,000	28,050	3,758	3,311	3,758	3,566
28,050	28,100	3,765	3,319	3,765	3,574
28,100	28,150	3,773	3,326	3,773	3,581
28,150	28,200	3,780	3,334	3,780	3,589
28,200	28,250	3,788	3,341	3,788	3,596
28,250	28,300	3,795	3,349	3,795	3,604
28,300	28,350	3,803	3,356	3,803	3,611
28,350	28,400	3,810	3,364	3,810	3,619
28,400	28,450	3,818	3,371	3,818	3,626
28,450	28,500	3,825	3,379	3,825	3,634
28,500	28,550	3,833	3,386	3,833	3,641
28,550	28,600	3,840	3,394	3,840	3,649
28,600	28,650	3,848	3,401	3,848	3,656
28,650	28,700	3,855	3,409	3,855	3,664
28,700	28,750	3,863	3,416	3,863	3,671
28,750	28,800	3,870	3,424	3,870	3,679
28,800	28,850	3,878	3,431	3,878	3,686
28,850	28,900	3,885	3,439	3,885	3,694
28,900	28,950	3,893	3,446	3,893	3,701
28,950	29,000	3,900	3,454	3,900	3,709
29,000					
29,000	29,050	3,908	3,461	3,908	3,716
29,050	29,100	3,915	3,469	3,915	3,724
29,100	29,150	3,923	3,476	3,923	3,731
29,150	29,200	3,930	3,484	3,930	3,739
29,200	29,250	3,938	3,491	3,938	3,746
29,250	29,300	3,945	3,499	3,945	3,754
29,300	29,350	3,953	3,506	3,953	3,761
29,350	29,400	3,960	3,514	3,960	3,769
29,400	29,450	3,968	3,521	3,968	3,776
29,450	29,500	3,975	3,529	3,975	3,784
29,500	29,550	3,983	3,536	3,983	3,791
29,550	29,600	3,990	3,544	3,990	3,799
29,600	29,650	3,998	3,551	3,998	3,806
29,650	29,700	4,005	3,559	4,005	3,814
29,700	29,750	4,013	3,566	4,013	3,821
29,750	29,800	4,020	3,574	4,020	3,829
29,800	29,850	4,028	3,581	4,028	3,836
29,850	29,900	4,035	3,589	4,035	3,844
29,900	29,950	4,043	3,596	4,043	3,851
29,950	30,000	4,050	3,604	4,050	3,859

* This column must also be used by a qualifying widow(er).

(Continued)

2013 Tax Table—Continued

If line 43 (taxable income) is— At least	But less than	And you are— Single	Married filing jointly *	Married filing separately	Head of a household
		Your tax is—			
30,000					
30,000	30,050	4,058	3,611	4,058	3,866
30,050	30,100	4,065	3,619	4,065	3,874
30,100	30,150	4,073	3,626	4,073	3,881
30,150	30,200	4,080	3,634	4,080	3,889
30,200	30,250	4,088	3,641	4,088	3,896
30,250	30,300	4,095	3,649	4,095	3,904
30,300	30,350	4,103	3,656	4,103	3,911
30,350	30,400	4,110	3,664	4,110	3,919
30,400	30,450	4,118	3,671	4,118	3,926
30,450	30,500	4,125	3,679	4,125	3,934
30,500	30,550	4,133	3,686	4,133	3,941
30,550	30,600	4,140	3,694	4,140	3,949
30,600	30,650	4,148	3,701	4,148	3,956
30,650	30,700	4,155	3,709	4,155	3,964
30,700	30,750	4,163	3,716	4,163	3,971
30,750	30,800	4,170	3,724	4,170	3,979
30,800	30,850	4,178	3,731	4,178	3,986
30,850	30,900	4,185	3,739	4,185	3,994
30,900	30,950	4,193	3,746	4,193	4,001
30,950	31,000	4,200	3,754	4,200	4,009
31,000					
31,000	31,050	4,208	3,761	4,208	4,016
31,050	31,100	4,215	3,769	4,215	4,024
31,100	31,150	4,223	3,776	4,223	4,031
31,150	31,200	4,230	3,784	4,230	4,039
31,200	31,250	4,238	3,791	4,238	4,046
31,250	31,300	4,245	3,799	4,245	4,054
31,300	31,350	4,253	3,806	4,253	4,061
31,350	31,400	4,260	3,814	4,260	4,069
31,400	31,450	4,268	3,821	4,268	4,076
31,450	31,500	4,275	3,829	4,275	4,084
31,500	31,550	4,283	3,836	4,283	4,091
31,550	31,600	4,290	3,844	4,290	4,099
31,600	31,650	4,298	3,851	4,298	4,106
31,650	31,700	4,305	3,859	4,305	4,114
31,700	31,750	4,313	3,866	4,313	4,121
31,750	31,800	4,320	3,874	4,320	4,129
31,800	31,850	4,328	3,881	4,328	4,136
31,850	31,900	4,335	3,889	4,335	4,144
31,900	31,950	4,343	3,896	4,343	4,151
31,950	32,000	4,350	3,904	4,350	4,159
32,000					
32,000	32,050	4,358	3,911	4,358	4,166
32,050	32,100	4,365	3,919	4,365	4,174
32,100	32,150	4,373	3,926	4,373	4,181
32,150	32,200	4,380	3,934	4,380	4,189
32,200	32,250	4,388	3,941	4,388	4,196
32,250	32,300	4,395	3,949	4,395	4,204
32,300	32,350	4,403	3,956	4,403	4,211
32,350	32,400	4,410	3,964	4,410	4,219
32,400	32,450	4,418	3,971	4,418	4,226
32,450	32,500	4,425	3,979	4,425	4,234
32,500	32,550	4,433	3,986	4,433	4,241
32,550	32,600	4,440	3,994	4,440	4,249
32,600	32,650	4,448	4,001	4,448	4,256
32,650	32,700	4,455	4,009	4,455	4,264
32,700	32,750	4,463	4,016	4,463	4,271
32,750	32,800	4,470	4,024	4,470	4,279
32,800	32,850	4,478	4,031	4,478	4,286
32,850	32,900	4,485	4,039	4,485	4,294
32,900	32,950	4,493	4,046	4,493	4,301
32,950	33,000	4,500	4,054	4,500	4,309
33,000					
33,000	33,050	4,508	4,061	4,508	4,316
33,050	33,100	4,515	4,069	4,515	4,324
33,100	33,150	4,523	4,076	4,523	4,331
33,150	33,200	4,530	4,084	4,530	4,339
33,200	33,250	4,538	4,091	4,538	4,346
33,250	33,300	4,545	4,099	4,545	4,354
33,300	33,350	4,553	4,106	4,553	4,361
33,350	33,400	4,560	4,114	4,560	4,369
33,400	33,450	4,568	4,121	4,568	4,376
33,450	33,500	4,575	4,129	4,575	4,384
33,500	33,550	4,583	4,136	4,583	4,391
33,550	33,600	4,590	4,144	4,590	4,399
33,600	33,650	4,598	4,151	4,598	4,406
33,650	33,700	4,605	4,159	4,605	4,414
33,700	33,750	4,613	4,166	4,613	4,421
33,750	33,800	4,620	4,174	4,620	4,429
33,800	33,850	4,628	4,181	4,628	4,436
33,850	33,900	4,635	4,189	4,635	4,444
33,900	33,950	4,643	4,196	4,643	4,451
33,950	34,000	4,650	4,204	4,650	4,459
34,000					
34,000	34,050	4,658	4,211	4,658	4,466
34,050	34,100	4,665	4,219	4,665	4,474
34,100	34,150	4,673	4,226	4,673	4,481
34,150	34,200	4,680	4,234	4,680	4,489
34,200	34,250	4,688	4,241	4,688	4,496
34,250	34,300	4,695	4,249	4,695	4,504
34,300	34,350	4,703	4,256	4,703	4,511
34,350	34,400	4,710	4,264	4,710	4,519
34,400	34,450	4,718	4,271	4,718	4,526
34,450	34,500	4,725	4,279	4,725	4,534
34,500	34,550	4,733	4,286	4,733	4,541
34,550	34,600	4,740	4,294	4,740	4,549
34,600	34,650	4,748	4,301	4,748	4,556
34,650	34,700	4,755	4,309	4,755	4,564
34,700	34,750	4,763	4,316	4,763	4,571
34,750	34,800	4,770	4,324	4,770	4,579
34,800	34,850	4,778	4,331	4,778	4,586
34,850	34,900	4,785	4,339	4,785	4,594
34,900	34,950	4,793	4,346	4,793	4,601
34,950	35,000	4,800	4,354	4,800	4,609
35,000					
35,000	35,050	4,808	4,361	4,808	4,616
35,050	35,100	4,815	4,369	4,815	4,624
35,100	35,150	4,823	4,376	4,823	4,631
35,150	35,200	4,830	4,384	4,830	4,639
35,200	35,250	4,838	4,391	4,838	4,646
35,250	35,300	4,845	4,399	4,845	4,654
35,300	35,350	4,853	4,406	4,853	4,661
35,350	35,400	4,860	4,414	4,860	4,669
35,400	35,450	4,868	4,421	4,868	4,676
35,450	35,500	4,875	4,429	4,875	4,684
35,500	35,550	4,883	4,436	4,883	4,691
35,550	35,600	4,890	4,444	4,890	4,699
35,600	35,650	4,898	4,451	4,898	4,706
35,650	35,700	4,905	4,459	4,905	4,714
35,700	35,750	4,913	4,466	4,913	4,721
35,750	35,800	4,920	4,474	4,920	4,729
35,800	35,850	4,928	4,481	4,928	4,736
35,850	35,900	4,935	4,489	4,935	4,744
35,900	35,950	4,943	4,496	4,943	4,751
35,950	36,000	4,950	4,504	4,950	4,759
36,000					
36,000	36,050	4,958	4,511	4,958	4,766
36,050	36,100	4,965	4,519	4,965	4,774
36,100	36,150	4,973	4,526	4,973	4,781
36,150	36,200	4,980	4,534	4,980	4,789
36,200	36,250	4,988	4,541	4,988	4,796
36,250	36,300	4,998	4,549	4,998	4,804
36,300	36,350	5,010	4,556	5,010	4,811
36,350	36,400	5,023	4,564	5,023	4,819
36,400	36,450	5,035	4,571	5,035	4,826
36,450	36,500	5,048	4,579	5,048	4,834
36,500	36,550	5,060	4,586	5,060	4,841
36,550	36,600	5,073	4,594	5,073	4,849
36,600	36,650	5,085	4,601	5,085	4,856
36,650	36,700	5,098	4,609	5,098	4,864
36,700	36,750	5,110	4,616	5,110	4,871
36,750	36,800	5,123	4,624	5,123	4,879
36,800	36,850	5,135	4,631	5,135	4,886
36,850	36,900	5,148	4,639	5,148	4,894
36,900	36,950	5,160	4,646	5,160	4,901
36,950	37,000	5,173	4,654	5,173	4,909
37,000					
37,000	37,050	5,185	4,661	5,185	4,916
37,050	37,100	5,198	4,669	5,198	4,924
37,100	37,150	5,210	4,676	5,210	4,931
37,150	37,200	5,223	4,684	5,223	4,939
37,200	37,250	5,235	4,691	5,235	4,946
37,250	37,300	5,248	4,699	5,248	4,954
37,300	37,350	5,260	4,706	5,260	4,961
37,350	37,400	5,273	4,714	5,273	4,969
37,400	37,450	5,285	4,721	5,285	4,976
37,450	37,500	5,298	4,729	5,298	4,984
37,500	37,550	5,310	4,736	5,310	4,991
37,550	37,600	5,323	4,744	5,323	4,999
37,600	37,650	5,335	4,751	5,335	5,006
37,650	37,700	5,348	4,759	5,348	5,014
37,700	37,750	5,360	4,766	5,360	5,021
37,750	37,800	5,373	4,774	5,373	5,029
37,800	37,850	5,385	4,781	5,385	5,036
37,850	37,900	5,398	4,789	5,398	5,044
37,900	37,950	5,410	4,796	5,410	5,051
37,950	38,000	5,423	4,804	5,423	5,059
38,000					
38,000	38,050	5,435	4,811	5,435	5,066
38,050	38,100	5,448	4,819	5,448	5,074
38,100	38,150	5,460	4,826	5,460	5,081
38,150	38,200	5,473	4,834	5,473	5,089
38,200	38,250	5,485	4,841	5,485	5,096
38,250	38,300	5,498	4,849	5,498	5,104
38,300	38,350	5,510	4,856	5,510	5,111
38,350	38,400	5,523	4,864	5,523	5,119
38,400	38,450	5,535	4,871	5,535	5,126
38,450	38,500	5,548	4,879	5,548	5,134
38,500	38,550	5,560	4,886	5,560	5,141
38,550	38,600	5,573	4,894	5,573	5,149
38,600	38,650	5,585	4,901	5,585	5,156
38,650	38,700	5,598	4,909	5,598	5,164
38,700	38,750	5,610	4,916	5,610	5,171
38,750	38,800	5,623	4,924	5,623	5,179
38,800	38,850	5,635	4,931	5,635	5,186
38,850	38,900	5,648	4,939	5,648	5,194
38,900	38,950	5,660	4,946	5,660	5,201
38,950	39,000	5,673	4,954	5,673	5,209

* This column must also be used by a qualifying widow(er).

(Continued)

2013 Tax Table—Continued

If line 43 (taxable income) is— At least	But less than	And you are— Single	Married filing jointly *	Married filing separately	Head of a household
		Your tax is—			
39,000					
39,000	39,050	5,685	4,961	5,685	5,216
39,050	39,100	5,698	4,969	5,698	5,224
39,100	39,150	5,710	4,976	5,710	5,231
39,150	39,200	5,723	4,984	5,723	5,239
39,200	39,250	5,735	4,991	5,735	5,246
39,250	39,300	5,748	4,999	5,748	5,254
39,300	39,350	5,760	5,006	5,760	5,261
39,350	39,400	5,773	5,014	5,773	5,269
39,400	39,450	5,785	5,021	5,785	5,276
39,450	39,500	5,798	5,029	5,798	5,284
39,500	39,550	5,810	5,036	5,810	5,291
39,550	39,600	5,823	5,044	5,823	5,299
39,600	39,650	5,835	5,051	5,835	5,306
39,650	39,700	5,848	5,059	5,848	5,314
39,700	39,750	5,860	5,066	5,860	5,321
39,750	39,800	5,873	5,074	5,873	5,329
39,800	39,850	5,885	5,081	5,885	5,336
39,850	39,900	5,898	5,089	5,898	5,344
39,900	39,950	5,910	5,096	5,910	5,351
39,950	40,000	5,923	5,104	5,923	5,359
40,000					
40,000	40,050	5,935	5,111	5,935	5,366
40,050	40,100	5,948	5,119	5,948	5,374
40,100	40,150	5,960	5,126	5,960	5,381
40,150	40,200	5,973	5,134	5,973	5,389
40,200	40,250	5,985	5,141	5,985	5,396
40,250	40,300	5,998	5,149	5,998	5,404
40,300	40,350	6,010	5,156	6,010	5,411
40,350	40,400	6,023	5,164	6,023	5,419
40,400	40,450	6,035	5,171	6,035	5,426
40,450	40,500	6,048	5,179	6,048	5,434
40,500	40,550	6,060	5,186	6,060	5,441
40,550	40,600	6,073	5,194	6,073	5,449
40,600	40,650	6,085	5,201	6,085	5,456
40,650	40,700	6,098	5,209	6,098	5,464
40,700	40,750	6,110	5,216	6,110	5,471
40,750	40,800	6,123	5,224	6,123	5,479
40,800	40,850	6,135	5,231	6,135	5,486
40,850	40,900	6,148	5,239	6,148	5,494
40,900	40,950	6,160	5,246	6,160	5,501
40,950	41,000	6,173	5,254	6,173	5,509
41,000					
41,000	41,050	6,185	5,261	6,185	5,516
41,050	41,100	6,198	5,269	6,198	5,524
41,100	41,150	6,210	5,276	6,210	5,531
41,150	41,200	6,223	5,284	6,223	5,539
41,200	41,250	6,235	5,291	6,235	5,546
41,250	41,300	6,248	5,299	6,248	5,554
41,300	41,350	6,260	5,306	6,260	5,561
41,350	41,400	6,273	5,314	6,273	5,569
41,400	41,450	6,285	5,321	6,285	5,576
41,450	41,500	6,298	5,329	6,298	5,584
41,500	41,550	6,310	5,336	6,310	5,591
41,550	41,600	6,323	5,344	6,323	5,599
41,600	41,650	6,335	5,351	6,335	5,606
41,650	41,700	6,348	5,359	6,348	5,614
41,700	41,750	6,360	5,366	6,360	5,621
41,750	41,800	6,373	5,374	6,373	5,629
41,800	41,850	6,385	5,381	6,385	5,636
41,850	41,900	6,398	5,389	6,398	5,644
41,900	41,950	6,410	5,396	6,410	5,651
41,950	42,000	6,423	5,404	6,423	5,659
42,000					
42,000	42,050	6,435	5,411	6,435	5,666
42,050	42,100	6,448	5,419	6,448	5,674
42,100	42,150	6,460	5,426	6,460	5,681
42,150	42,200	6,473	5,434	6,473	5,689
42,200	42,250	6,485	5,441	6,485	5,696
42,250	42,300	6,498	5,449	6,498	5,704
42,300	42,350	6,510	5,456	6,510	5,711
42,350	42,400	6,523	5,464	6,523	5,719
42,400	42,450	6,535	5,471	6,535	5,726
42,450	42,500	6,548	5,479	6,548	5,734
42,500	42,550	6,560	5,486	6,560	5,741
42,550	42,600	6,573	5,494	6,573	5,749
42,600	42,650	6,585	5,501	6,585	5,756
42,650	42,700	6,598	5,509	6,598	5,764
42,700	42,750	6,610	5,516	6,610	5,771
42,750	42,800	6,623	5,524	6,623	5,779
42,800	42,850	6,635	5,531	6,635	5,786
42,850	42,900	6,648	5,539	6,648	5,794
42,900	42,950	6,660	5,546	6,660	5,801
42,950	43,000	6,673	5,554	6,673	5,809
43,000					
43,000	43,050	6,685	5,561	6,685	5,816
43,050	43,100	6,698	5,569	6,698	5,824
43,100	43,150	6,710	5,576	6,710	5,831
43,150	43,200	6,723	5,584	6,723	5,839
43,200	43,250	6,735	5,591	6,735	5,846
43,250	43,300	6,748	5,599	6,748	5,854
43,300	43,350	6,760	5,606	6,760	5,861
43,350	43,400	6,773	5,614	6,773	5,869
43,400	43,450	6,785	5,621	6,785	5,876
43,450	43,500	6,798	5,629	6,798	5,884
43,500	43,550	6,810	5,636	6,810	5,891
43,550	43,600	6,823	5,644	6,823	5,899
43,600	43,650	6,835	5,651	6,835	5,906
43,650	43,700	6,848	5,659	6,848	5,914
43,700	43,750	6,860	5,666	6,860	5,921
43,750	43,800	6,873	5,674	6,873	5,929
43,800	43,850	6,885	5,681	6,885	5,936
43,850	43,900	6,898	5,689	6,898	5,944
43,900	43,950	6,910	5,696	6,910	5,951
43,950	44,000	6,923	5,704	6,923	5,959
44,000					
44,000	44,050	6,935	5,711	6,935	5,966
44,050	44,100	6,948	5,719	6,948	5,974
44,100	44,150	6,960	5,726	6,960	5,981
44,150	44,200	6,973	5,734	6,973	5,989
44,200	44,250	6,985	5,741	6,985	5,996
44,250	44,300	6,998	5,749	6,998	6,004
44,300	44,350	7,010	5,756	7,010	6,011
44,350	44,400	7,023	5,764	7,023	6,019
44,400	44,450	7,035	5,771	7,035	6,026
44,450	44,500	7,048	5,779	7,048	6,034
44,500	44,550	7,060	5,786	7,060	6,041
44,550	44,600	7,073	5,794	7,073	6,049
44,600	44,650	7,085	5,801	7,085	6,056
44,650	44,700	7,098	5,809	7,098	6,064
44,700	44,750	7,110	5,816	7,110	6,071
44,750	44,800	7,123	5,824	7,123	6,079
44,800	44,850	7,135	5,831	7,135	6,086
44,850	44,900	7,148	5,839	7,148	6,094
44,900	44,950	7,160	5,846	7,160	6,101
44,950	45,000	7,173	5,854	7,173	6,109
45,000					
45,000	45,050	7,185	5,861	7,185	6,116
45,050	45,100	7,198	5,869	7,198	6,124
45,100	45,150	7,210	5,876	7,210	6,131
45,150	45,200	7,223	5,884	7,223	6,139
45,200	45,250	7,235	5,891	7,235	6,146
45,250	45,300	7,248	5,899	7,248	6,154
45,300	45,350	7,260	5,906	7,260	6,161
45,350	45,400	7,273	5,914	7,273	6,169
45,400	45,450	7,285	5,921	7,285	6,176
45,450	45,500	7,298	5,929	7,298	6,184
45,500	45,550	7,310	5,936	7,310	6,191
45,550	45,600	7,323	5,944	7,323	6,199
45,600	45,650	7,335	5,951	7,335	6,206
45,650	45,700	7,348	5,959	7,348	6,214
45,700	45,750	7,360	5,966	7,360	6,221
45,750	45,800	7,373	5,974	7,373	6,229
45,800	45,850	7,385	5,981	7,385	6,236
45,850	45,900	7,398	5,989	7,398	6,244
45,900	45,950	7,410	5,996	7,410	6,251
45,950	46,000	7,423	6,004	7,423	6,259
46,000					
46,000	46,050	7,435	6,011	7,435	6,266
46,050	46,100	7,448	6,019	7,448	6,274
46,100	46,150	7,460	6,026	7,460	6,281
46,150	46,200	7,473	6,034	7,473	6,289
46,200	46,250	7,485	6,041	7,485	6,296
46,250	46,300	7,498	6,049	7,498	6,304
46,300	46,350	7,510	6,056	7,510	6,311
46,350	46,400	7,523	6,064	7,523	6,319
46,400	46,450	7,535	6,071	7,535	6,326
46,450	46,500	7,548	6,079	7,548	6,334
46,500	46,550	7,560	6,086	7,560	6,341
46,550	46,600	7,573	6,094	7,573	6,349
46,600	46,650	7,585	6,101	7,585	6,356
46,650	46,700	7,598	6,109	7,598	6,364
46,700	46,750	7,610	6,116	7,610	6,371
46,750	46,800	7,623	6,124	7,623	6,379
46,800	46,850	7,635	6,131	7,635	6,386
46,850	46,900	7,648	6,139	7,648	6,394
46,900	46,950	7,660	6,146	7,660	6,401
46,950	47,000	7,673	6,154	7,673	6,409
47,000					
47,000	47,050	7,685	6,161	7,685	6,416
47,050	47,100	7,698	6,169	7,698	6,424
47,100	47,150	7,710	6,176	7,710	6,431
47,150	47,200	7,723	6,184	7,723	6,439
47,200	47,250	7,735	6,191	7,735	6,446
47,250	47,300	7,748	6,199	7,748	6,454
47,300	47,350	7,760	6,206	7,760	6,461
47,350	47,400	7,773	6,214	7,773	6,469
47,400	47,450	7,785	6,221	7,785	6,476
47,450	47,500	7,798	6,229	7,798	6,484
47,500	47,550	7,810	6,236	7,810	6,491
47,550	47,600	7,823	6,244	7,823	6,499
47,600	47,650	7,835	6,251	7,835	6,506
47,650	47,700	7,848	6,259	7,848	6,514
47,700	47,750	7,860	6,266	7,860	6,521
47,750	47,800	7,873	6,274	7,873	6,529
47,800	47,850	7,885	6,281	7,885	6,536
47,850	47,900	7,898	6,289	7,898	6,544
47,900	47,950	7,910	6,296	7,910	6,551
47,950	48,000	7,923	6,304	7,923	6,559

* This column must also be used by a qualifying widow(er).

(Continued)

2013 Tax Table —Continued

If line 43 (taxable income) is—		And you are—			
At least	But less than	Single	Married filing jointly *	Married filing separately	Head of a household
		Your tax is—			
48,000					
48,000	48,050	7,935	6,311	7,935	6,566
48,050	48,100	7,948	6,319	7,948	6,574
48,100	48,150	7,960	6,326	7,960	6,581
48,150	48,200	7,973	6,334	7,973	6,589
48,200	48,250	7,985	6,341	7,985	6,596
48,250	48,300	7,998	6,349	7,998	6,604
48,300	48,350	8,010	6,356	8,010	6,611
48,350	48,400	8,023	6,364	8,023	6,619
48,400	48,450	8,035	6,371	8,035	6,626
48,450	48,500	8,048	6,379	8,048	6,634
48,500	48,550	8,060	6,386	8,060	6,641
48,550	48,600	8,073	6,394	8,073	6,649
48,600	48,650	8,085	6,401	8,085	6,659
48,650	48,700	8,098	6,409	8,098	6,671
48,700	48,750	8,110	6,416	8,110	6,684
48,750	48,800	8,123	6,424	8,123	6,696
48,800	48,850	8,135	6,431	8,135	6,709
48,850	48,900	8,148	6,439	8,148	6,721
48,900	48,950	8,160	6,446	8,160	6,734
48,950	49,000	8,173	6,454	8,173	6,746
49,000					
49,000	49,050	8,185	6,461	8,185	6,759
49,050	49,100	8,198	6,469	8,198	6,771
49,100	49,150	8,210	6,476	8,210	6,784
49,150	49,200	8,223	6,484	8,223	6,796
49,200	49,250	8,235	6,491	8,235	6,809
49,250	49,300	8,248	6,499	8,248	6,821
49,300	49,350	8,260	6,506	8,260	6,834
49,350	49,400	8,273	6,514	8,273	6,846
49,400	49,450	8,285	6,521	8,285	6,859
49,450	49,500	8,298	6,529	8,298	6,871
49,500	49,550	8,310	6,536	8,310	6,884
49,550	49,600	8,323	6,544	8,323	6,896
49,600	49,650	8,335	6,551	8,335	6,909
49,650	49,700	8,348	6,559	8,348	6,921
49,700	49,750	8,360	6,566	8,360	6,934
49,750	49,800	8,373	6,574	8,373	6,946
49,800	49,850	8,385	6,581	8,385	6,959
49,850	49,900	8,398	6,589	8,398	6,971
49,900	49,950	8,410	6,596	8,410	6,984
49,950	50,000	8,423	6,604	8,423	6,996
50,000					
50,000	50,050	8,435	6,611	8,435	7,009
50,050	50,100	8,448	6,619	8,448	7,021
50,100	50,150	8,460	6,626	8,460	7,034
50,150	50,200	8,473	6,634	8,473	7,046
50,200	50,250	8,485	6,641	8,485	7,059
50,250	50,300	8,498	6,649	8,498	7,071
50,300	50,350	8,510	6,656	8,510	7,084
50,350	50,400	8,523	6,664	8,523	7,096
50,400	50,450	8,535	6,671	8,535	7,109
50,450	50,500	8,548	6,679	8,548	7,121
50,500	50,550	8,560	6,686	8,560	7,134
50,550	50,600	8,573	6,694	8,573	7,146
50,600	50,650	8,585	6,701	8,585	7,159
50,650	50,700	8,598	6,709	8,598	7,171
50,700	50,750	8,610	6,716	8,610	7,184
50,750	50,800	8,623	6,724	8,623	7,196
50,800	50,850	8,635	6,731	8,635	7,209
50,850	50,900	8,648	6,739	8,648	7,221
50,900	50,950	8,660	6,746	8,660	7,234
50,950	51,000	8,673	6,754	8,673	7,246
51,000					
51,000	51,050	8,685	6,761	8,685	7,259
51,050	51,100	8,698	6,769	8,698	7,271
51,100	51,150	8,710	6,776	8,710	7,284
51,150	51,200	8,723	6,784	8,723	7,296
51,200	51,250	8,735	6,791	8,735	7,309
51,250	51,300	8,748	6,799	8,748	7,321
51,300	51,350	8,760	6,806	8,760	7,334
51,350	51,400	8,773	6,814	8,773	7,346
51,400	51,450	8,785	6,821	8,785	7,359
51,450	51,500	8,798	6,829	8,798	7,371
51,500	51,550	8,810	6,836	8,810	7,384
51,550	51,600	8,823	6,844	8,823	7,396
51,600	51,650	8,835	6,851	8,835	7,409
51,650	51,700	8,848	6,859	8,848	7,421
51,700	51,750	8,860	6,866	8,860	7,434
51,750	51,800	8,873	6,874	8,873	7,446
51,800	51,850	8,885	6,881	8,885	7,459
51,850	51,900	8,898	6,889	8,898	7,471
51,900	51,950	8,910	6,896	8,910	7,484
51,950	52,000	8,923	6,904	8,923	7,496
52,000					
52,000	52,050	8,935	6,911	8,935	7,509
52,050	52,100	8,948	6,919	8,948	7,521
52,100	52,150	8,960	6,926	8,960	7,534
52,150	52,200	8,973	6,934	8,973	7,546
52,200	52,250	8,985	6,941	8,985	7,559
52,250	52,300	8,998	6,949	8,998	7,571
52,300	52,350	9,010	6,956	9,010	7,584
52,350	52,400	9,023	6,964	9,023	7,596
52,400	52,450	9,035	6,971	9,035	7,609
52,450	52,500	9,048	6,979	9,048	7,621
52,500	52,550	9,060	6,986	9,060	7,634
52,550	52,600	9,073	6,994	9,073	7,646
52,600	52,650	9,085	7,001	9,085	7,659
52,650	52,700	9,098	7,009	9,098	7,671
52,700	52,750	9,110	7,016	9,110	7,684
52,750	52,800	9,123	7,024	9,123	7,696
52,800	52,850	9,135	7,031	9,135	7,709
52,850	52,900	9,148	7,039	9,148	7,721
52,900	52,950	9,160	7,046	9,160	7,734
52,950	53,000	9,173	7,054	9,173	7,746
53,000					
53,000	53,050	9,185	7,061	9,185	7,759
53,050	53,100	9,198	7,069	9,198	7,771
53,100	53,150	9,210	7,076	9,210	7,784
53,150	53,200	9,223	7,084	9,223	7,796
53,200	53,250	9,235	7,091	9,235	7,809
53,250	53,300	9,248	7,099	9,248	7,821
53,300	53,350	9,260	7,106	9,260	7,834
53,350	53,400	9,273	7,114	9,273	7,846
53,400	53,450	9,285	7,121	9,285	7,859
53,450	53,500	9,298	7,129	9,298	7,871
53,500	53,550	9,310	7,136	9,310	7,884
53,550	53,600	9,323	7,144	9,323	7,896
53,600	53,650	9,335	7,151	9,335	7,909
53,650	53,700	9,348	7,159	9,348	7,921
53,700	53,750	9,360	7,166	9,360	7,934
53,750	53,800	9,373	7,174	9,373	7,946
53,800	53,850	9,385	7,181	9,385	7,959
53,850	53,900	9,398	7,189	9,398	7,971
53,900	53,950	9,410	7,196	9,410	7,984
53,950	54,000	9,423	7,204	9,423	7,996
54,000					
54,000	54,050	9,435	7,211	9,435	8,009
54,050	54,100	9,448	7,219	9,448	8,021
54,100	54,150	9,460	7,226	9,460	8,034
54,150	54,200	9,473	7,234	9,473	8,046
54,200	54,250	9,485	7,241	9,485	8,059
54,250	54,300	9,498	7,249	9,498	8,071
54,300	54,350	9,510	7,256	9,510	8,084
54,350	54,400	9,523	7,264	9,523	8,096
54,400	54,450	9,535	7,271	9,535	8,109
54,450	54,500	9,548	7,279	9,548	8,121
54,500	54,550	9,560	7,286	9,560	8,134
54,550	54,600	9,573	7,294	9,573	8,146
54,600	54,650	9,585	7,301	9,585	8,159
54,650	54,700	9,598	7,309	9,598	8,171
54,700	54,750	9,610	7,316	9,610	8,184
54,750	54,800	9,623	7,324	9,623	8,196
54,800	54,850	9,635	7,331	9,635	8,209
54,850	54,900	9,648	7,339	9,648	8,221
54,900	54,950	9,660	7,346	9,660	8,234
54,950	55,000	9,673	7,354	9,673	8,246
55,000					
55,000	55,050	9,685	7,361	9,685	8,259
55,050	55,100	9,698	7,369	9,698	8,271
55,100	55,150	9,710	7,376	9,710	8,284
55,150	55,200	9,723	7,384	9,723	8,296
55,200	55,250	9,735	7,391	9,735	8,309
55,250	55,300	9,748	7,399	9,748	8,321
55,300	55,350	9,760	7,406	9,760	8,334
55,350	55,400	9,773	7,414	9,773	8,346
55,400	55,450	9,785	7,421	9,785	8,359
55,450	55,500	9,798	7,429	9,798	8,371
55,500	55,550	9,810	7,436	9,810	8,384
55,550	55,600	9,823	7,444	9,823	8,396
55,600	55,650	9,835	7,451	9,835	8,409
55,650	55,700	9,848	7,459	9,848	8,421
55,700	55,750	9,860	7,466	9,860	8,434
55,750	55,800	9,873	7,474	9,873	8,446
55,800	55,850	9,885	7,481	9,885	8,459
55,850	55,900	9,898	7,489	9,898	8,471
55,900	55,950	9,910	7,496	9,910	8,484
55,950	56,000	9,923	7,504	9,923	8,496
56,000					
56,000	56,050	9,935	7,511	9,935	8,509
56,050	56,100	9,948	7,519	9,948	8,521
56,100	56,150	9,960	7,526	9,960	8,534
56,150	56,200	9,973	7,534	9,973	8,546
56,200	56,250	9,985	7,541	9,985	8,559
56,250	56,300	9,998	7,549	9,998	8,571
56,300	56,350	10,010	7,556	10,010	8,584
56,350	56,400	10,023	7,564	10,023	8,596
56,400	56,450	10,035	7,571	10,035	8,609
56,450	56,500	10,048	7,579	10,048	8,621
56,500	56,550	10,060	7,586	10,060	8,634
56,550	56,600	10,073	7,594	10,073	8,646
56,600	56,650	10,085	7,601	10,085	8,659
56,650	56,700	10,098	7,609	10,098	8,671
56,700	56,750	10,110	7,616	10,110	8,684
56,750	56,800	10,123	7,624	10,123	8,696
56,800	56,850	10,135	7,631	10,135	8,709
56,850	56,900	10,148	7,639	10,148	8,721
56,900	56,950	10,160	7,646	10,160	8,734
56,950	57,000	10,173	7,654	10,173	8,746

* This column must also be used by a qualifying widow(er).

(Continued)

2013 Tax Table —Continued

If line 43 (taxable income) is—		And you are—			
At least	But less than	Single	Married filing jointly *	Married filing separately	Head of a household
		Your tax is—			
57,000					
57,000	57,050	10,185	7,661	10,185	8,759
57,050	57,100	10,198	7,669	10,198	8,771
57,100	57,150	10,210	7,676	10,210	8,784
57,150	57,200	10,223	7,684	10,223	8,796
57,200	57,250	10,235	7,691	10,235	8,809
57,250	57,300	10,248	7,699	10,248	8,821
57,300	57,350	10,260	7,706	10,260	8,834
57,350	57,400	10,273	7,714	10,273	8,846
57,400	57,450	10,285	7,721	10,285	8,859
57,450	57,500	10,298	7,729	10,298	8,871
57,500	57,550	10,310	7,736	10,310	8,884
57,550	57,600	10,323	7,744	10,323	8,896
57,600	57,650	10,335	7,751	10,335	8,909
57,650	57,700	10,348	7,759	10,348	8,921
57,700	57,750	10,360	7,766	10,360	8,934
57,750	57,800	10,373	7,774	10,373	8,946
57,800	57,850	10,385	7,781	10,385	8,959
57,850	57,900	10,398	7,789	10,398	8,971
57,900	57,950	10,410	7,796	10,410	8,984
57,950	58,000	10,423	7,804	10,423	8,996
58,000					
58,000	58,050	10,435	7,811	10,435	9,009
58,050	58,100	10,448	7,819	10,448	9,021
58,100	58,150	10,460	7,826	10,460	9,034
58,150	58,200	10,473	7,834	10,473	9,046
58,200	58,250	10,485	7,841	10,485	9,059
58,250	58,300	10,498	7,849	10,498	9,071
58,300	58,350	10,510	7,856	10,510	9,084
58,350	58,400	10,523	7,864	10,523	9,096
58,400	58,450	10,535	7,871	10,535	9,109
58,450	58,500	10,548	7,879	10,548	9,121
58,500	58,550	10,560	7,886	10,560	9,134
58,550	58,600	10,573	7,894	10,573	9,146
58,600	58,650	10,585	7,901	10,585	9,159
58,650	58,700	10,598	7,909	10,598	9,171
58,700	58,750	10,610	7,916	10,610	9,184
58,750	58,800	10,623	7,924	10,623	9,196
58,800	58,850	10,635	7,931	10,635	9,209
58,850	58,900	10,648	7,939	10,648	9,221
58,900	58,950	10,660	7,946	10,660	9,234
58,950	59,000	10,673	7,954	10,673	9,246
59,000					
59,000	59,050	10,685	7,961	10,685	9,259
59,050	59,100	10,698	7,969	10,698	9,271
59,100	59,150	10,710	7,976	10,710	9,284
59,150	59,200	10,723	7,984	10,723	9,296
59,200	59,250	10,735	7,991	10,735	9,309
59,250	59,300	10,748	7,999	10,748	9,321
59,300	59,350	10,760	8,006	10,760	9,334
59,350	59,400	10,773	8,014	10,773	9,346
59,400	59,450	10,785	8,021	10,785	9,359
59,450	59,500	10,798	8,029	10,798	9,371
59,500	59,550	10,810	8,036	10,810	9,384
59,550	59,600	10,823	8,044	10,823	9,396
59,600	59,650	10,835	8,051	10,835	9,409
59,650	59,700	10,848	8,059	10,848	9,421
59,700	59,750	10,860	8,066	10,860	9,434
59,750	59,800	10,873	8,074	10,873	9,446
59,800	59,850	10,885	8,081	10,885	9,459
59,850	59,900	10,898	8,089	10,898	9,471
59,900	59,950	10,910	8,096	10,910	9,484
59,950	60,000	10,923	8,104	10,923	9,496
60,000					
60,000	60,050	10,935	8,111	10,935	9,509
60,050	60,100	10,948	8,119	10,948	9,521
60,100	60,150	10,960	8,126	10,960	9,534
60,150	60,200	10,973	8,134	10,973	9,546
60,200	60,250	10,985	8,141	10,985	9,559
60,250	60,300	10,998	8,149	10,998	9,571
60,300	60,350	11,010	8,156	11,010	9,584
60,350	60,400	11,023	8,164	11,023	9,596
60,400	60,450	11,035	8,171	11,035	9,609
60,450	60,500	11,048	8,179	11,048	9,621
60,500	60,550	11,060	8,186	11,060	9,634
60,550	60,600	11,073	8,194	11,073	9,646
60,600	60,650	11,085	8,201	11,085	9,659
60,650	60,700	11,098	8,209	11,098	9,671
60,700	60,750	11,110	8,216	11,110	9,684
60,750	60,800	11,123	8,224	11,123	9,696
60,800	60,850	11,135	8,231	11,135	9,709
60,850	60,900	11,148	8,239	11,148	9,721
60,900	60,950	11,160	8,246	11,160	9,734
60,950	61,000	11,173	8,254	11,173	9,746
61,000					
61,000	61,050	11,185	8,261	11,185	9,759
61,050	61,100	11,198	8,269	11,198	9,771
61,100	61,150	11,210	8,276	11,210	9,784
61,150	61,200	11,223	8,284	11,223	9,796
61,200	61,250	11,235	8,291	11,235	9,809
61,250	61,300	11,248	8,299	11,248	9,821
61,300	61,350	11,260	8,306	11,260	9,834
61,350	61,400	11,273	8,314	11,273	9,846
61,400	61,450	11,285	8,321	11,285	9,859
61,450	61,500	11,298	8,329	11,298	9,871
61,500	61,550	11,310	8,336	11,310	9,884
61,550	61,600	11,323	8,344	11,323	9,896
61,600	61,650	11,335	8,351	11,335	9,909
61,650	61,700	11,348	8,359	11,348	9,921
61,700	61,750	11,360	8,366	11,360	9,934
61,750	61,800	11,373	8,374	11,373	9,946
61,800	61,850	11,385	8,381	11,385	9,959
61,850	61,900	11,398	8,389	11,398	9,971
61,900	61,950	11,410	8,396	11,410	9,984
61,950	62,000	11,423	8,404	11,423	9,996
62,000					
62,000	62,050	11,435	8,411	11,435	10,009
62,050	62,100	11,448	8,419	11,448	10,021
62,100	62,150	11,460	8,426	11,460	10,034
62,150	62,200	11,473	8,434	11,473	10,046
62,200	62,250	11,485	8,441	11,485	10,059
62,250	62,300	11,498	8,449	11,498	10,071
62,300	62,350	11,510	8,456	11,510	10,084
62,350	62,400	11,523	8,464	11,523	10,096
62,400	62,450	11,535	8,471	11,535	10,109
62,450	62,500	11,548	8,479	11,548	10,121
62,500	62,550	11,560	8,486	11,560	10,134
62,550	62,600	11,573	8,494	11,573	10,146
62,600	62,650	11,585	8,501	11,585	10,159
62,650	62,700	11,598	8,509	11,598	10,171
62,700	62,750	11,610	8,516	11,610	10,184
62,750	62,800	11,623	8,524	11,623	10,196
62,800	62,850	11,635	8,531	11,635	10,209
62,850	62,900	11,648	8,539	11,648	10,221
62,900	62,950	11,660	8,546	11,660	10,234
62,950	63,000	11,673	8,554	11,673	10,246
63,000					
63,000	63,050	11,685	8,561	11,685	10,259
63,050	63,100	11,698	8,569	11,698	10,271
63,100	63,150	11,710	8,576	11,710	10,284
63,150	63,200	11,723	8,584	11,723	10,296
63,200	63,250	11,735	8,591	11,735	10,309
63,250	63,300	11,748	8,599	11,748	10,321
63,300	63,350	11,760	8,606	11,760	10,334
63,350	63,400	11,773	8,614	11,773	10,346
63,400	63,450	11,785	8,621	11,785	10,359
63,450	63,500	11,798	8,629	11,798	10,371
63,500	63,550	11,810	8,636	11,810	10,384
63,550	63,600	11,823	8,644	11,823	10,396
63,600	63,650	11,835	8,651	11,835	10,409
63,650	63,700	11,848	8,659	11,848	10,421
63,700	63,750	11,860	8,666	11,860	10,434
63,750	63,800	11,873	8,674	11,873	10,446
63,800	63,850	11,885	8,681	11,885	10,459
63,850	63,900	11,898	8,689	11,898	10,471
63,900	63,950	11,910	8,696	11,910	10,484
63,950	64,000	11,923	8,704	11,923	10,496
64,000					
64,000	64,050	11,935	8,711	11,935	10,509
64,050	64,100	11,948	8,719	11,948	10,521
64,100	64,150	11,960	8,726	11,960	10,534
64,150	64,200	11,973	8,734	11,973	10,546
64,200	64,250	11,985	8,741	11,985	10,559
64,250	64,300	11,998	8,749	11,998	10,571
64,300	64,350	12,010	8,756	12,010	10,584
64,350	64,400	12,023	8,764	12,023	10,596
64,400	64,450	12,035	8,771	12,035	10,609
64,450	64,500	12,048	8,779	12,048	10,621
64,500	64,550	12,060	8,786	12,060	10,634
64,550	64,600	12,073	8,794	12,073	10,646
64,600	64,650	12,085	8,801	12,085	10,659
64,650	64,700	12,098	8,809	12,098	10,671
64,700	64,750	12,110	8,816	12,110	10,684
64,750	64,800	12,123	8,824	12,123	10,696
64,800	64,850	12,135	8,831	12,135	10,709
64,850	64,900	12,148	8,839	12,148	10,721
64,900	64,950	12,160	8,846	12,160	10,734
64,950	65,000	12,173	8,854	12,173	10,746
65,000					
65,000	65,050	12,185	8,861	12,185	10,759
65,050	65,100	12,198	8,869	12,198	10,771
65,100	65,150	12,210	8,876	12,210	10,784
65,150	65,200	12,223	8,884	12,223	10,796
65,200	65,250	12,235	8,891	12,235	10,809
65,250	65,300	12,248	8,899	12,248	10,821
65,300	65,350	12,260	8,906	12,260	10,834
65,350	65,400	12,273	8,914	12,273	10,846
65,400	65,450	12,285	8,921	12,285	10,859
65,450	65,500	12,298	8,929	12,298	10,871
65,500	65,550	12,310	8,936	12,310	10,884
65,550	65,600	12,323	8,944	12,323	10,896
65,600	65,650	12,335	8,951	12,335	10,909
65,650	65,700	12,348	8,959	12,348	10,921
65,700	65,750	12,360	8,966	12,360	10,934
65,750	65,800	12,373	8,974	12,373	10,946
65,800	65,850	12,385	8,981	12,385	10,959
65,850	65,900	12,398	8,989	12,398	10,971
65,900	65,950	12,410	8,996	12,410	10,984
65,950	66,000	12,423	9,004	12,423	10,996

* This column must also be used by a qualifying widow(er).

(Continued)

If line 43 (taxable income) is— At least	But less than	And you are— Single	Married filing jointly *	Married filing separately	Head of a household
		Your tax is—			
66,000					
66,000	66,050	12,435	9,011	12,435	11,009
66,050	66,100	12,448	9,019	12,448	11,021
66,100	66,150	12,460	9,026	12,460	11,034
66,150	66,200	12,473	9,034	12,473	11,046
66,200	66,250	12,485	9,041	12,485	11,059
66,250	66,300	12,498	9,049	12,498	11,071
66,300	66,350	12,510	9,056	12,510	11,084
66,350	66,400	12,523	9,064	12,523	11,096
66,400	66,450	12,535	9,071	12,535	11,109
66,450	66,500	12,548	9,079	12,548	11,121
66,500	66,550	12,560	9,086	12,560	11,134
66,550	66,600	12,573	9,094	12,573	11,146
66,600	66,650	12,585	9,101	12,585	11,159
66,650	66,700	12,598	9,109	12,598	11,171
66,700	66,750	12,610	9,116	12,610	11,184
66,750	66,800	12,623	9,124	12,623	11,196
66,800	66,850	12,635	9,131	12,635	11,209
66,850	66,900	12,648	9,139	12,648	11,221
66,900	66,950	12,660	9,146	12,660	11,234
66,950	67,000	12,673	9,154	12,673	11,246
67,000					
67,000	67,050	12,685	9,161	12,685	11,259
67,050	67,100	12,698	9,169	12,698	11,271
67,100	67,150	12,710	9,176	12,710	11,284
67,150	67,200	12,723	9,184	12,723	11,296
67,200	67,250	12,735	9,191	12,735	11,309
67,250	67,300	12,748	9,199	12,748	11,321
67,300	67,350	12,760	9,206	12,760	11,334
67,350	67,400	12,773	9,214	12,773	11,346
67,400	67,450	12,785	9,221	12,785	11,359
67,450	67,500	12,798	9,229	12,798	11,371
67,500	67,550	12,810	9,236	12,810	11,384
67,550	67,600	12,823	9,244	12,823	11,396
67,600	67,650	12,835	9,251	12,835	11,409
67,650	67,700	12,848	9,259	12,848	11,421
67,700	67,750	12,860	9,266	12,860	11,434
67,750	67,800	12,873	9,274	12,873	11,446
67,800	67,850	12,885	9,281	12,885	11,459
67,850	67,900	12,898	9,289	12,898	11,471
67,900	67,950	12,910	9,296	12,910	11,484
67,950	68,000	12,923	9,304	12,923	11,496
68,000					
68,000	68,050	12,935	9,311	12,935	11,509
68,050	68,100	12,948	9,319	12,948	11,521
68,100	68,150	12,960	9,326	12,960	11,534
68,150	68,200	12,973	9,334	12,973	11,546
68,200	68,250	12,985	9,341	12,985	11,559
68,250	68,300	12,998	9,349	12,998	11,571
68,300	68,350	13,010	9,356	13,010	11,584
68,350	68,400	13,023	9,364	13,023	11,596
68,400	68,450	13,035	9,371	13,035	11,609
68,450	68,500	13,048	9,379	13,048	11,621
68,500	68,550	13,060	9,386	13,060	11,634
68,550	68,600	13,073	9,394	13,073	11,646
68,600	68,650	13,085	9,401	13,085	11,659
68,650	68,700	13,098	9,409	13,098	11,671
68,700	68,750	13,110	9,416	13,110	11,684
68,750	68,800	13,123	9,424	13,123	11,696
68,800	68,850	13,135	9,431	13,135	11,709
68,850	68,900	13,148	9,439	13,148	11,721
68,900	68,950	13,160	9,446	13,160	11,734
68,950	69,000	13,173	9,454	13,173	11,746

If line 43 (taxable income) is— At least	But less than	And you are— Single	Married filing jointly *	Married filing separately	Head of a household
		Your tax is—			
69,000					
69,000	69,050	13,185	9,461	13,185	11,759
69,050	69,100	13,198	9,469	13,198	11,771
69,100	69,150	13,210	9,476	13,210	11,784
69,150	69,200	13,223	9,484	13,223	11,796
69,200	69,250	13,235	9,491	13,235	11,809
69,250	69,300	13,248	9,499	13,248	11,821
69,300	69,350	13,260	9,506	13,260	11,834
69,350	69,400	13,273	9,514	13,273	11,846
69,400	69,450	13,285	9,521	13,285	11,859
69,450	69,500	13,298	9,529	13,298	11,871
69,500	69,550	13,310	9,536	13,310	11,884
69,550	69,600	13,323	9,544	13,323	11,896
69,600	69,650	13,335	9,551	13,335	11,909
69,650	69,700	13,348	9,559	13,348	11,921
69,700	69,750	13,360	9,566	13,360	11,934
69,750	69,800	13,373	9,574	13,373	11,946
69,800	69,850	13,385	9,581	13,385	11,959
69,850	69,900	13,398	9,589	13,398	11,971
69,900	69,950	13,410	9,596	13,410	11,984
69,950	70,000	13,423	9,604	13,423	11,996
70,000					
70,000	70,050	13,435	9,611	13,435	12,009
70,050	70,100	13,448	9,619	13,448	12,021
70,100	70,150	13,460	9,626	13,460	12,034
70,150	70,200	13,473	9,634	13,473	12,046
70,200	70,250	13,485	9,641	13,485	12,059
70,250	70,300	13,498	9,649	13,498	12,071
70,300	70,350	13,510	9,656	13,510	12,084
70,350	70,400	13,523	9,664	13,523	12,096
70,400	70,450	13,535	9,671	13,535	12,109
70,450	70,500	13,548	9,679	13,548	12,121
70,500	70,550	13,560	9,686	13,560	12,134
70,550	70,600	13,573	9,694	13,573	12,146
70,600	70,650	13,585	9,701	13,585	12,159
70,650	70,700	13,598	9,709	13,598	12,171
70,700	70,750	13,610	9,716	13,610	12,184
70,750	70,800	13,623	9,724	13,623	12,196
70,800	70,850	13,635	9,731	13,635	12,209
70,850	70,900	13,648	9,739	13,648	12,221
70,900	70,950	13,660	9,746	13,660	12,234
70,950	71,000	13,673	9,754	13,673	12,246
71,000					
71,000	71,050	13,685	9,761	13,685	12,259
71,050	71,100	13,698	9,769	13,698	12,271
71,100	71,150	13,710	9,776	13,710	12,284
71,150	71,200	13,723	9,784	13,723	12,296
71,200	71,250	13,735	9,791	13,735	12,309
71,250	71,300	13,748	9,799	13,748	12,321
71,300	71,350	13,760	9,806	13,760	12,334
71,350	71,400	13,773	9,814	13,773	12,346
71,400	71,450	13,785	9,821	13,785	12,359
71,450	71,500	13,798	9,829	13,798	12,371
71,500	71,550	13,810	9,836	13,810	12,384
71,550	71,600	13,823	9,844	13,823	12,396
71,600	71,650	13,835	9,851	13,835	12,409
71,650	71,700	13,848	9,859	13,848	12,421
71,700	71,750	13,860	9,866	13,860	12,434
71,750	71,800	13,873	9,874	13,873	12,446
71,800	71,850	13,885	9,881	13,885	12,459
71,850	71,900	13,898	9,889	13,898	12,471
71,900	71,950	13,910	9,896	13,910	12,484
71,950	72,000	13,923	9,904	13,923	12,496

If line 43 (taxable income) is— At least	But less than	And you are— Single	Married filing jointly *	Married filing separately	Head of a household
		Your tax is—			
72,000					
72,000	72,050	13,935	9,911	13,935	12,509
72,050	72,100	13,948	9,919	13,948	12,521
72,100	72,150	13,960	9,926	13,960	12,534
72,150	72,200	13,973	9,934	13,973	12,546
72,200	72,250	13,985	9,941	13,985	12,559
72,250	72,300	13,998	9,949	13,998	12,571
72,300	72,350	14,010	9,956	14,010	12,584
72,350	72,400	14,023	9,964	14,023	12,596
72,400	72,450	14,035	9,971	14,035	12,609
72,450	72,500	14,048	9,979	14,048	12,621
72,500	72,550	14,060	9,989	14,060	12,634
72,550	72,600	14,073	10,001	14,073	12,646
72,600	72,650	14,085	10,014	14,085	12,659
72,650	72,700	14,098	10,026	14,098	12,671
72,700	72,750	14,110	10,039	14,110	12,684
72,750	72,800	14,123	10,051	14,123	12,696
72,800	72,850	14,135	10,064	14,135	12,709
72,850	72,900	14,148	10,076	14,148	12,721
72,900	72,950	14,160	10,089	14,160	12,734
72,950	73,000	14,173	10,101	14,173	12,746
73,000					
73,000	73,050	14,185	10,114	14,185	12,759
73,050	73,100	14,198	10,126	14,198	12,771
73,100	73,150	14,210	10,139	14,210	12,784
73,150	73,200	14,223	10,151	14,223	12,796
73,200	73,250	14,235	10,164	14,236	12,809
73,250	73,300	14,248	10,176	14,250	12,821
73,300	73,350	14,260	10,189	14,264	12,834
73,350	73,400	14,273	10,201	14,278	12,846
73,400	73,450	14,285	10,214	14,292	12,859
73,450	73,500	14,298	10,226	14,306	12,871
73,500	73,550	14,310	10,239	14,320	12,884
73,550	73,600	14,323	10,251	14,334	12,896
73,600	73,650	14,335	10,264	14,348	12,909
73,650	73,700	14,348	10,276	14,362	12,921
73,700	73,750	14,360	10,289	14,376	12,934
73,750	73,800	14,373	10,301	14,390	12,946
73,800	73,850	14,385	10,314	14,404	12,959
73,850	73,900	14,398	10,326	14,418	12,971
73,900	73,950	14,410	10,339	14,432	12,984
73,950	74,000	14,423	10,351	14,446	12,996
74,000					
74,000	74,050	14,435	10,364	14,460	13,009
74,050	74,100	14,448	10,376	14,474	13,021
74,100	74,150	14,460	10,389	14,488	13,034
74,150	74,200	14,473	10,401	14,502	13,046
74,200	74,250	14,485	10,414	14,516	13,059
74,250	74,300	14,498	10,426	14,530	13,071
74,300	74,350	14,510	10,439	14,544	13,084
74,350	74,400	14,523	10,451	14,558	13,096
74,400	74,450	14,535	10,464	14,572	13,109
74,450	74,500	14,548	10,476	14,586	13,121
74,500	74,550	14,560	10,489	14,600	13,134
74,550	74,600	14,573	10,501	14,614	13,146
74,600	74,650	14,585	10,514	14,628	13,159
74,650	74,700	14,598	10,526	14,642	13,171
74,700	74,750	14,610	10,539	14,656	13,184
74,750	74,800	14,623	10,551	14,670	13,196
74,800	74,850	14,635	10,564	14,684	13,209
74,850	74,900	14,648	10,576	14,698	13,221
74,900	74,950	14,660	10,589	14,712	13,234
74,950	75,000	14,673	10,601	14,726	13,246

* This column must also be used by a qualifying widow(er).

(Continued)

2013 Tax Table —Continued

If line 43 (taxable income) is— At least	But less than	And you are— Single	Married filing jointly *	Married filing separately	Head of a household
		Your tax is—			
75,000					
75,000	75,050	14,685	10,614	14,740	13,259
75,050	75,100	14,698	10,626	14,754	13,271
75,100	75,150	14,710	10,639	14,768	13,284
75,150	75,200	14,723	10,651	14,782	13,296
75,200	75,250	14,735	10,664	14,796	13,309
75,250	75,300	14,748	10,676	14,810	13,321
75,300	75,350	14,760	10,689	14,824	13,334
75,350	75,400	14,773	10,701	14,838	13,346
75,400	75,450	14,785	10,714	14,852	13,359
75,450	75,500	14,798	10,726	14,866	13,371
75,500	75,550	14,810	10,739	14,880	13,384
75,550	75,600	14,823	10,751	14,894	13,396
75,600	75,650	14,835	10,764	14,908	13,409
75,650	75,700	14,848	10,776	14,922	13,421
75,700	75,750	14,860	10,789	14,936	13,434
75,750	75,800	14,873	10,801	14,950	13,446
75,800	75,850	14,885	10,814	14,964	13,459
75,850	75,900	14,898	10,826	14,978	13,471
75,900	75,950	14,910	10,839	14,992	13,484
75,950	76,000	14,923	10,851	15,006	13,496
76,000					
76,000	76,050	14,935	10,864	15,020	13,509
76,050	76,100	14,948	10,876	15,034	13,521
76,100	76,150	14,960	10,889	15,048	13,534
76,150	76,200	14,973	10,901	15,062	13,546
76,200	76,250	14,985	10,914	15,076	13,559
76,250	76,300	14,998	10,926	15,090	13,571
76,300	76,350	15,010	10,939	15,104	13,584
76,350	76,400	15,023	10,951	15,118	13,596
76,400	76,450	15,035	10,964	15,132	13,609
76,450	76,500	15,048	10,976	15,146	13,621
76,500	76,550	15,060	10,989	15,160	13,634
76,550	76,600	15,073	11,001	15,174	13,646
76,600	76,650	15,085	11,014	15,188	13,659
76,650	76,700	15,098	11,026	15,202	13,671
76,700	76,750	15,110	11,039	15,216	13,684
76,750	76,800	15,123	11,051	15,230	13,696
76,800	76,850	15,135	11,064	15,244	13,709
76,850	76,900	15,148	11,076	15,258	13,721
76,900	76,950	15,160	11,089	15,272	13,734
76,950	77,000	15,173	11,101	15,286	13,746
77,000					
77,000	77,050	15,185	11,114	15,300	13,759
77,050	77,100	15,198	11,126	15,314	13,771
77,100	77,150	15,210	11,139	15,328	13,784
77,150	77,200	15,223	11,151	15,342	13,796
77,200	77,250	15,235	11,164	15,356	13,809
77,250	77,300	15,248	11,176	15,370	13,821
77,300	77,350	15,260	11,189	15,384	13,834
77,350	77,400	15,273	11,201	15,398	13,846
77,400	77,450	15,285	11,214	15,412	13,859
77,450	77,500	15,298	11,226	15,426	13,871
77,500	77,550	15,310	11,239	15,440	13,884
77,550	77,600	15,323	11,251	15,454	13,896
77,600	77,650	15,335	11,264	15,468	13,909
77,650	77,700	15,348	11,276	15,482	13,921
77,700	77,750	15,360	11,289	15,496	13,934
77,750	77,800	15,373	11,301	15,510	13,946
77,800	77,850	15,385	11,314	15,524	13,959
77,850	77,900	15,398	11,326	15,538	13,971
77,900	77,950	15,410	11,339	15,552	13,984
77,950	78,000	15,423	11,351	15,566	13,996

If line 43 (taxable income) is— At least	But less than	And you are— Single	Married filing jointly *	Married filing separately	Head of a household
		Your tax is—			
78,000					
78,000	78,050	15,435	11,364	15,580	14,009
78,050	78,100	15,448	11,376	15,594	14,021
78,100	78,150	15,460	11,389	15,608	14,034
78,150	78,200	15,473	11,401	15,622	14,046
78,200	78,250	15,485	11,414	15,636	14,059
78,250	78,300	15,498	11,426	15,650	14,071
78,300	78,350	15,510	11,439	15,664	14,084
78,350	78,400	15,523	11,451	15,678	14,096
78,400	78,450	15,535	11,464	15,692	14,109
78,450	78,500	15,548	11,476	15,706	14,121
78,500	78,550	15,560	11,489	15,720	14,134
78,550	78,600	15,573	11,501	15,734	14,146
78,600	78,650	15,585	11,514	15,748	14,159
78,650	78,700	15,598	11,526	15,762	14,171
78,700	78,750	15,610	11,539	15,776	14,184
78,750	78,800	15,623	11,551	15,790	14,196
78,800	78,850	15,635	11,564	15,804	14,209
78,850	78,900	15,648	11,576	15,818	14,221
78,900	78,950	15,660	11,589	15,832	14,234
78,950	79,000	15,673	11,601	15,846	14,246
79,000					
79,000	79,050	15,685	11,614	15,860	14,259
79,050	79,100	15,698	11,626	15,874	14,271
79,100	79,150	15,710	11,639	15,888	14,284
79,150	79,200	15,723	11,651	15,902	14,296
79,200	79,250	15,735	11,664	15,916	14,309
79,250	79,300	15,748	11,676	15,930	14,321
79,300	79,350	15,760	11,689	15,944	14,334
79,350	79,400	15,773	11,701	15,958	14,346
79,400	79,450	15,785	11,714	15,972	14,359
79,450	79,500	15,798	11,726	15,986	14,371
79,500	79,550	15,810	11,739	16,000	14,384
79,550	79,600	15,823	11,751	16,014	14,396
79,600	79,650	15,835	11,764	16,028	14,409
79,650	79,700	15,848	11,776	16,042	14,421
79,700	79,750	15,860	11,789	16,056	14,434
79,750	79,800	15,873	11,801	16,070	14,446
79,800	79,850	15,885	11,814	16,084	14,459
79,850	79,900	15,898	11,826	16,098	14,471
79,900	79,950	15,910	11,839	16,112	14,484
79,950	80,000	15,923	11,851	16,126	14,496
80,000					
80,000	80,050	15,935	11,864	16,140	14,509
80,050	80,100	15,948	11,876	16,154	14,521
80,100	80,150	15,960	11,889	16,168	14,534
80,150	80,200	15,973	11,901	16,182	14,546
80,200	80,250	15,985	11,914	16,196	14,559
80,250	80,300	15,998	11,926	16,210	14,571
80,300	80,350	16,010	11,939	16,224	14,584
80,350	80,400	16,023	11,951	16,238	14,596
80,400	80,450	16,035	11,964	16,252	14,609
80,450	80,500	16,048	11,976	16,266	14,621
80,500	80,550	16,060	11,989	16,280	14,634
80,550	80,600	16,073	12,001	16,294	14,646
80,600	80,650	16,085	12,014	16,308	14,659
80,650	80,700	16,098	12,026	16,322	14,671
80,700	80,750	16,110	12,039	16,336	14,684
80,750	80,800	16,123	12,051	16,350	14,696
80,800	80,850	16,135	12,064	16,364	14,709
80,850	80,900	16,148	12,076	16,378	14,721
80,900	80,950	16,160	12,089	16,392	14,734
80,950	81,000	16,173	12,101	16,406	14,746

If line 43 (taxable income) is— At least	But less than	And you are— Single	Married filing jointly *	Married filing separately	Head of a household
		Your tax is—			
81,000					
81,000	81,050	16,185	12,114	16,420	14,759
81,050	81,100	16,198	12,126	16,434	14,771
81,100	81,150	16,210	12,139	16,448	14,784
81,150	81,200	16,223	12,151	16,462	14,796
81,200	81,250	16,235	12,164	16,476	14,809
81,250	81,300	16,248	12,176	16,490	14,821
81,300	81,350	16,260	12,189	16,504	14,834
81,350	81,400	16,273	12,201	16,518	14,846
81,400	81,450	16,285	12,214	16,532	14,859
81,450	81,500	16,298	12,226	16,546	14,871
81,500	81,550	16,310	12,239	16,560	14,884
81,550	81,600	16,323	12,251	16,574	14,896
81,600	81,650	16,335	12,264	16,588	14,909
81,650	81,700	16,348	12,276	16,602	14,921
81,700	81,750	16,360	12,289	16,616	14,934
81,750	81,800	16,373	12,301	16,630	14,946
81,800	81,850	16,385	12,314	16,644	14,959
81,850	81,900	16,398	12,326	16,658	14,971
81,900	81,950	16,410	12,339	16,672	14,984
81,950	82,000	16,423	12,351	16,686	14,996
82,000					
82,000	82,050	16,435	12,364	16,700	15,009
82,050	82,100	16,448	12,376	16,714	15,021
82,100	82,150	16,460	12,389	16,728	15,034
82,150	82,200	16,473	12,401	16,742	15,046
82,200	82,250	16,485	12,414	16,756	15,059
82,250	82,300	16,498	12,426	16,770	15,071
82,300	82,350	16,510	12,439	16,784	15,084
82,350	82,400	16,523	12,451	16,798	15,096
82,400	82,450	16,535	12,464	16,812	15,109
82,450	82,500	16,548	12,476	16,826	15,121
82,500	82,550	16,560	12,489	16,840	15,134
82,550	82,600	16,573	12,501	16,854	15,146
82,600	82,650	16,585	12,514	16,868	15,159
82,650	82,700	16,598	12,526	16,882	15,171
82,700	82,750	16,610	12,539	16,896	15,184
82,750	82,800	16,623	12,551	16,910	15,196
82,800	82,850	16,635	12,564	16,924	15,209
82,850	82,900	16,648	12,576	16,938	15,221
82,900	82,950	16,660	12,589	16,952	15,234
82,950	83,000	16,673	12,601	16,966	15,246
83,000					
83,000	83,050	16,685	12,614	16,980	15,259
83,050	83,100	16,698	12,626	16,994	15,271
83,100	83,150	16,710	12,639	17,008	15,284
83,150	83,200	16,723	12,651	17,022	15,296
83,200	83,250	16,735	12,664	17,036	15,309
83,250	83,300	16,748	12,676	17,050	15,321
83,300	83,350	16,760	12,689	17,064	15,334
83,350	83,400	16,773	12,701	17,078	15,346
83,400	83,450	16,785	12,714	17,092	15,359
83,450	83,500	16,798	12,726	17,106	15,371
83,500	83,550	16,810	12,739	17,120	15,384
83,550	83,600	16,823	12,751	17,134	15,396
83,600	83,650	16,835	12,764	17,148	15,409
83,650	83,700	16,848	12,776	17,162	15,421
83,700	83,750	16,860	12,789	17,176	15,434
83,750	83,800	16,873	12,801	17,190	15,446
83,800	83,850	16,885	12,814	17,204	15,459
83,850	83,900	16,898	12,826	17,218	15,471
83,900	83,950	16,910	12,839	17,232	15,484
83,950	84,000	16,923	12,851	17,246	15,496

* This column must also be used by a qualifying widow(er).

(Continued)

2013 Tax Table —Continued

If line 43 (taxable income) is— At least	But less than	And you are— Single	Married filing jointly *	Married filing separately	Head of a household
		Your tax is—			
84,000					
84,000	84,050	16,935	12,864	17,260	15,509
84,050	84,100	16,948	12,876	17,274	15,521
84,100	84,150	16,960	12,889	17,288	15,534
84,150	84,200	16,973	12,901	17,302	15,546
84,200	84,250	16,985	12,914	17,316	15,559
84,250	84,300	16,998	12,926	17,330	15,571
84,300	84,350	17,010	12,939	17,344	15,584
84,350	84,400	17,023	12,951	17,358	15,596
84,400	84,450	17,035	12,964	17,372	15,609
84,450	84,500	17,048	12,976	17,386	15,621
84,500	84,550	17,060	12,989	17,400	15,634
84,550	84,600	17,073	13,001	17,414	15,646
84,600	84,650	17,085	13,014	17,428	15,659
84,650	84,700	17,098	13,026	17,442	15,671
84,700	84,750	17,110	13,039	17,456	15,684
84,750	84,800	17,123	13,051	17,470	15,696
84,800	84,850	17,135	13,064	17,484	15,709
84,850	84,900	17,148	13,076	17,498	15,721
84,900	84,950	17,160	13,089	17,512	15,734
84,950	85,000	17,173	13,101	17,526	15,746
85,000					
85,000	85,050	17,185	13,114	17,540	15,759
85,050	85,100	17,198	13,126	17,554	15,771
85,100	85,150	17,210	13,139	17,568	15,784
85,150	85,200	17,223	13,151	17,582	15,796
85,200	85,250	17,235	13,164	17,596	15,809
85,250	85,300	17,248	13,176	17,610	15,821
85,300	85,350	17,260	13,189	17,624	15,834
85,350	85,400	17,273	13,201	17,638	15,846
85,400	85,450	17,285	13,214	17,652	15,859
85,450	85,500	17,298	13,226	17,666	15,871
85,500	85,550	17,310	13,239	17,680	15,884
85,550	85,600	17,323	13,251	17,694	15,896
85,600	85,650	17,335	13,264	17,708	15,909
85,650	85,700	17,348	13,276	17,722	15,921
85,700	85,750	17,360	13,289	17,736	15,934
85,750	85,800	17,373	13,301	17,750	15,946
85,800	85,850	17,385	13,314	17,764	15,959
85,850	85,900	17,398	13,326	17,778	15,971
85,900	85,950	17,410	13,339	17,792	15,984
85,950	86,000	17,423	13,351	17,806	15,996
86,000					
86,000	86,050	17,435	13,364	17,820	16,009
86,050	86,100	17,448	13,376	17,834	16,021
86,100	86,150	17,460	13,389	17,848	16,034
86,150	86,200	17,473	13,401	17,862	16,046
86,200	86,250	17,485	13,414	17,876	16,059
86,250	86,300	17,498	13,426	17,890	16,071
86,300	86,350	17,510	13,439	17,904	16,084
86,350	86,400	17,523	13,451	17,918	16,096
86,400	86,450	17,535	13,464	17,932	16,109
86,450	86,500	17,548	13,476	17,946	16,121
86,500	86,550	17,560	13,489	17,960	16,134
86,550	86,600	17,573	13,501	17,974	16,146
86,600	86,650	17,585	13,514	17,988	16,159
86,650	86,700	17,598	13,526	18,002	16,171
86,700	86,750	17,610	13,539	18,016	16,184
86,750	86,800	17,623	13,551	18,030	16,196
86,800	86,850	17,635	13,564	18,044	16,209
86,850	86,900	17,648	13,576	18,058	16,221
86,900	86,950	17,660	13,589	18,072	16,234
86,950	87,000	17,673	13,601	18,086	16,246
87,000					
87,000	87,050	17,685	13,614	18,100	16,259
87,050	87,100	17,698	13,626	18,114	16,271
87,100	87,150	17,710	13,639	18,128	16,284
87,150	87,200	17,723	13,651	18,142	16,296
87,200	87,250	17,735	13,664	18,156	16,309
87,250	87,300	17,748	13,676	18,170	16,321
87,300	87,350	17,760	13,689	18,184	16,334
87,350	87,400	17,773	13,701	18,198	16,346
87,400	87,450	17,785	13,714	18,212	16,359
87,450	87,500	17,798	13,726	18,226	16,371
87,500	87,550	17,810	13,739	18,240	16,384
87,550	87,600	17,823	13,751	18,254	16,396
87,600	87,650	17,835	13,764	18,268	16,409
87,650	87,700	17,848	13,776	18,282	16,421
87,700	87,750	17,860	13,789	18,296	16,434
87,750	87,800	17,873	13,801	18,310	16,446
87,800	87,850	17,885	13,814	18,324	16,459
87,850	87,900	17,898	13,826	18,338	16,471
87,900	87,950	17,912	13,839	18,352	16,484
87,950	88,000	17,926	13,851	18,366	16,496
88,000					
88,000	88,050	17,940	13,864	18,380	16,509
88,050	88,100	17,954	13,876	18,394	16,521
88,100	88,150	17,968	13,889	18,408	16,534
88,150	88,200	17,982	13,901	18,422	16,546
88,200	88,250	17,996	13,914	18,436	16,559
88,250	88,300	18,010	13,926	18,450	16,571
88,300	88,350	18,024	13,939	18,464	16,584
88,350	88,400	18,038	13,951	18,478	16,596
88,400	88,450	18,052	13,964	18,492	16,609
88,450	88,500	18,066	13,976	18,506	16,621
88,500	88,550	18,080	13,989	18,520	16,634
88,550	88,600	18,094	14,001	18,534	16,646
88,600	88,650	18,108	14,014	18,548	16,659
88,650	88,700	18,122	14,026	18,562	16,671
88,700	88,750	18,136	14,039	18,576	16,684
88,750	88,800	18,150	14,051	18,590	16,696
88,800	88,850	18,164	14,064	18,604	16,709
88,850	88,900	18,178	14,076	18,618	16,721
88,900	88,950	18,192	14,089	18,632	16,734
88,950	89,000	18,206	14,101	18,646	16,746
89,000					
89,000	89,050	18,220	14,114	18,660	16,759
89,050	89,100	18,234	14,126	18,674	16,771
89,100	89,150	18,248	14,139	18,688	16,784
89,150	89,200	18,262	14,151	18,702	16,796
89,200	89,250	18,276	14,164	18,716	16,809
89,250	89,300	18,290	14,176	18,730	16,821
89,300	89,350	18,304	14,189	18,744	16,834
89,350	89,400	18,318	14,201	18,758	16,846
89,400	89,450	18,332	14,214	18,772	16,859
89,450	89,500	18,346	14,226	18,786	16,871
89,500	89,550	18,360	14,239	18,800	16,884
89,550	89,600	18,374	14,251	18,814	16,896
89,600	89,650	18,388	14,264	18,828	16,909
89,650	89,700	18,402	14,276	18,842	16,921
89,700	89,750	18,416	14,289	18,856	16,934
89,750	89,800	18,430	14,301	18,870	16,946
89,800	89,850	18,444	14,314	18,884	16,959
89,850	89,900	18,458	14,326	18,898	16,971
89,900	89,950	18,472	14,339	18,912	16,984
89,950	90,000	18,486	14,351	18,926	16,996
90,000					
90,000	90,050	18,500	14,364	18,940	17,009
90,050	90,100	18,514	14,376	18,954	17,021
90,100	90,150	18,528	14,389	18,968	17,034
90,150	90,200	18,542	14,401	18,982	17,046
90,200	90,250	18,556	14,414	18,996	17,059
90,250	90,300	18,570	14,426	19,010	17,071
90,300	90,350	18,584	14,439	19,024	17,084
90,350	90,400	18,598	14,451	19,038	17,096
90,400	90,450	18,612	14,464	19,052	17,109
90,450	90,500	18,626	14,476	19,066	17,121
90,500	90,550	18,640	14,489	19,080	17,134
90,550	90,600	18,654	14,501	19,094	17,146
90,600	90,650	18,668	14,514	19,108	17,159
90,650	90,700	18,682	14,526	19,122	17,171
90,700	90,750	18,696	14,539	19,136	17,184
90,750	90,800	18,710	14,551	19,150	17,196
90,800	90,850	18,724	14,564	19,164	17,209
90,850	90,900	18,738	14,576	19,178	17,221
90,900	90,950	18,752	14,589	19,192	17,234
90,950	91,000	18,766	14,601	19,206	17,246
91,000					
91,000	91,050	18,780	14,614	19,220	17,259
91,050	91,100	18,794	14,626	19,234	17,271
91,100	91,150	18,808	14,639	19,248	17,284
91,150	91,200	18,822	14,651	19,262	17,296
91,200	91,250	18,836	14,664	19,276	17,309
91,250	91,300	18,850	14,676	19,290	17,321
91,300	91,350	18,864	14,689	19,304	17,334
91,350	91,400	18,878	14,701	19,318	17,346
91,400	91,450	18,892	14,714	19,332	17,359
91,450	91,500	18,906	14,726	19,346	17,371
91,500	91,550	18,920	14,739	19,360	17,384
91,550	91,600	18,934	14,751	19,374	17,396
91,600	91,650	18,948	14,764	19,388	17,409
91,650	91,700	18,962	14,776	19,402	17,421
91,700	91,750	18,976	14,789	19,416	17,434
91,750	91,800	18,990	14,801	19,430	17,446
91,800	91,850	19,004	14,814	19,444	17,459
91,850	91,900	19,018	14,826	19,458	17,471
91,900	91,950	19,032	14,839	19,472	17,484
91,950	92,000	19,046	14,851	19,486	17,496
92,000					
92,000	92,050	19,060	14,864	19,500	17,509
92,050	92,100	19,074	14,876	19,514	17,521
92,100	92,150	19,088	14,889	19,528	17,534
92,150	92,200	19,102	14,901	19,542	17,546
92,200	92,250	19,116	14,914	19,556	17,559
92,250	92,300	19,130	14,926	19,570	17,571
92,300	92,350	19,144	14,939	19,584	17,584
92,350	92,400	19,158	14,951	19,598	17,596
92,400	92,450	19,172	14,964	19,612	17,609
92,450	92,500	19,186	14,976	19,626	17,621
92,500	92,550	19,200	14,989	19,640	17,634
92,550	92,600	19,214	15,001	19,654	17,646
92,600	92,650	19,228	15,014	19,668	17,659
92,650	92,700	19,242	15,026	19,682	17,671
92,700	92,750	19,256	15,039	19,696	17,684
92,750	92,800	19,270	15,051	19,710	17,696
92,800	92,850	19,284	15,064	19,724	17,709
92,850	92,900	19,298	15,076	19,738	17,721
92,900	92,950	19,312	15,089	19,752	17,734
92,950	93,000	19,326	15,101	19,766	17,746

* This column must also be used by a qualifying widow(er).

(Continued)

2013 Tax Table —Continued

If line 43 (taxable income) is— At least	But less than	And you are— Single	Married filing jointly *	Married filing separately	Head of a household
		Your tax is—			
93,000					
93,000	93,050	19,340	15,114	19,780	17,759
93,050	93,100	19,354	15,126	19,794	17,771
93,100	93,150	19,368	15,139	19,808	17,784
93,150	93,200	19,382	15,151	19,822	17,796
93,200	93,250	19,396	15,164	19,836	17,809
93,250	93,300	19,410	15,176	19,850	17,821
93,300	93,350	19,424	15,189	19,864	17,834
93,350	93,400	19,438	15,201	19,878	17,846
93,400	93,450	19,452	15,214	19,892	17,859
93,450	93,500	19,466	15,226	19,906	17,871
93,500	93,550	19,480	15,239	19,920	17,884
93,550	93,600	19,494	15,251	19,934	17,896
93,600	93,650	19,508	15,264	19,948	17,909
93,650	93,700	19,522	15,276	19,962	17,921
93,700	93,750	19,536	15,289	19,976	17,934
93,750	93,800	19,550	15,301	19,990	17,946
93,800	93,850	19,564	15,314	20,004	17,959
93,850	93,900	19,578	15,326	20,018	17,971
93,900	93,950	19,592	15,339	20,032	17,984
93,950	94,000	19,606	15,351	20,046	17,996
94,000					
94,000	94,050	19,620	15,364	20,060	18,009
94,050	94,100	19,634	15,376	20,074	18,021
94,100	94,150	19,648	15,389	20,088	18,034
94,150	94,200	19,662	15,401	20,102	18,046
94,200	94,250	19,676	15,414	20,116	18,059
94,250	94,300	19,690	15,426	20,130	18,071
94,300	94,350	19,704	15,439	20,144	18,084
94,350	94,400	19,718	15,451	20,158	18,096
94,400	94,450	19,732	15,464	20,172	18,109
94,450	94,500	19,746	15,476	20,186	18,121
94,500	94,550	19,760	15,489	20,200	18,134
94,550	94,600	19,774	15,501	20,214	18,146
94,600	94,650	19,788	15,514	20,228	18,159
94,650	94,700	19,802	15,526	20,242	18,171
94,700	94,750	19,816	15,539	20,256	18,184
94,750	94,800	19,830	15,551	20,270	18,196
94,800	94,850	19,844	15,564	20,284	18,209
94,850	94,900	19,858	15,576	20,298	18,221
94,900	94,950	19,872	15,589	20,312	18,234
94,950	95,000	19,886	15,601	20,326	18,246
95,000					
95,000	95,050	19,900	15,614	20,340	18,259
95,050	95,100	19,914	15,626	20,354	18,271
95,100	95,150	19,928	15,639	20,368	18,284
95,150	95,200	19,942	15,651	20,382	18,296
95,200	95,250	19,956	15,664	20,396	18,309
95,250	95,300	19,970	15,676	20,410	18,321
95,300	95,350	19,984	15,689	20,424	18,334
95,350	95,400	19,998	15,701	20,438	18,346
95,400	95,450	20,012	15,714	20,452	18,359
95,450	95,500	20,026	15,726	20,466	18,371
95,500	95,550	20,040	15,739	20,480	18,384
95,550	95,600	20,054	15,751	20,494	18,396
95,600	95,650	20,068	15,764	20,508	18,409
95,650	95,700	20,082	15,776	20,522	18,421
95,700	95,750	20,096	15,789	20,536	18,434
95,750	95,800	20,110	15,801	20,550	18,446
95,800	95,850	20,124	15,814	20,564	18,459
95,850	95,900	20,138	15,826	20,578	18,471
95,900	95,950	20,152	15,839	20,592	18,484
95,950	96,000	20,166	15,851	20,606	18,496
96,000					
96,000	96,050	20,180	15,864	20,620	18,509
96,050	96,100	20,194	15,876	20,634	18,521
96,100	96,150	20,208	15,889	20,648	18,534
96,150	96,200	20,222	15,901	20,662	18,546
96,200	96,250	20,236	15,914	20,676	18,559
96,250	96,300	20,250	15,926	20,690	18,571
96,300	96,350	20,264	15,939	20,704	18,584
96,350	96,400	20,278	15,951	20,718	18,596
96,400	96,450	20,292	15,964	20,732	18,609
96,450	96,500	20,306	15,976	20,746	18,621
96,500	96,550	20,320	15,989	20,760	18,634
96,550	96,600	20,334	16,001	20,774	18,646
96,600	96,650	20,348	16,014	20,788	18,659
96,650	96,700	20,362	16,026	20,802	18,671
96,700	96,750	20,376	16,039	20,816	18,684
96,750	96,800	20,390	16,051	20,830	18,696
96,800	96,850	20,404	16,064	20,844	18,709
96,850	96,900	20,418	16,076	20,858	18,721
96,900	96,950	20,432	16,089	20,872	18,734
96,950	97,000	20,446	16,101	20,886	18,746
97,000					
97,000	97,050	20,460	16,114	20,900	18,759
97,050	97,100	20,474	16,126	20,914	18,771
97,100	97,150	20,488	16,139	20,928	18,784
97,150	97,200	20,502	16,151	20,942	18,796
97,200	97,250	20,516	16,164	20,956	18,809
97,250	97,300	20,530	16,176	20,970	18,821
97,300	97,350	20,544	16,189	20,984	18,834
97,350	97,400	20,558	16,201	20,998	18,846
97,400	97,450	20,572	16,214	21,012	18,859
97,450	97,500	20,586	16,226	21,026	18,871
97,500	97,550	20,600	16,239	21,040	18,884
97,550	97,600	20,614	16,251	21,054	18,896
97,600	97,650	20,628	16,264	21,068	18,909
97,650	97,700	20,642	16,276	21,082	18,921
97,700	97,750	20,656	16,289	21,096	18,934
97,750	97,800	20,670	16,301	21,110	18,946
97,800	97,850	20,684	16,314	21,124	18,959
97,850	97,900	20,698	16,326	21,138	18,971
97,900	97,950	20,712	16,339	21,152	18,984
97,950	98,000	20,726	16,351	21,166	18,996
98,000					
98,000	98,050	20,740	16,364	21,180	19,009
98,050	98,100	20,754	16,376	21,194	19,021
98,100	98,150	20,768	16,389	21,208	19,034
98,150	98,200	20,782	16,401	21,222	19,046
98,200	98,250	20,796	16,414	21,236	19,059
98,250	98,300	20,810	16,426	21,250	19,071
98,300	98,350	20,824	16,439	21,264	19,084
98,350	98,400	20,838	16,451	21,278	19,096
98,400	98,450	20,852	16,464	21,292	19,109
98,450	98,500	20,866	16,476	21,306	19,121
98,500	98,550	20,880	16,489	21,320	19,134
98,550	98,600	20,894	16,501	21,334	19,146
98,600	98,650	20,908	16,514	21,348	19,159
98,650	98,700	20,922	16,526	21,362	19,171
98,700	98,750	20,936	16,539	21,376	19,184
98,750	98,800	20,950	16,551	21,390	19,196
98,800	98,850	20,964	16,564	21,404	19,209
98,850	98,900	20,978	16,576	21,418	19,221
98,900	98,950	20,992	16,589	21,432	19,234
98,950	99,000	21,006	16,601	21,446	19,246
99,000					
99,000	99,050	21,020	16,614	21,460	19,259
99,050	99,100	21,034	16,626	21,474	19,271
99,100	99,150	21,048	16,639	21,488	19,284
99,150	99,200	21,062	16,651	21,502	19,296
99,200	99,250	21,076	16,664	21,516	19,309
99,250	99,300	21,090	16,676	21,530	19,321
99,300	99,350	21,104	16,689	21,544	19,334
99,350	99,400	21,118	16,701	21,558	19,346
99,400	99,450	21,132	16,714	21,572	19,359
99,450	99,500	21,146	16,726	21,586	19,371
99,500	99,550	21,160	16,739	21,600	19,384
99,550	99,600	21,174	16,751	21,614	19,396
99,600	99,650	21,188	16,764	21,628	19,409
99,650	99,700	21,202	16,776	21,642	19,421
99,700	99,750	21,216	16,789	21,656	19,434
99,750	99,800	21,230	16,801	21,670	19,446
99,800	99,850	21,244	16,814	21,684	19,459
99,850	99,900	21,258	16,826	21,698	19,471
99,900	99,950	21,272	16,839	21,712	19,484
99,950	100,000	21,286	16,851	21,726	19,496

$100,000 or over use the Tax Computation Worksheet

* This column must also be used by a qualifying widow(er).

2013 Tax Computation Worksheet—Line 44

 See the instructions for line 44 to see if you must use the worksheet below to figure your tax.

Note. If you are required to use this worksheet to figure the tax on an amount from another form or worksheet, such as the Qualified Dividends and Capital Gain Tax Worksheet, the Schedule D Tax Worksheet, Schedule J, Form 8615, or the Foreign Earned Income Tax Worksheet, enter the amount from that form or worksheet in column (a) of the row that applies to the amount you are looking up. Enter the result on the appropriate line of the form or worksheet that you are completing.

Section A— Use if your filing status is Single. Complete the row below that applies to you.

Taxable income. If line 43 is—	(a) Enter the amount from line 43	(b) Multiplication amount	(c) Multiply (a) by (b)	(d) Subtraction amount	Tax. Subtract (d) from (c). Enter the result here and on Form 1040, line 44
At least $100,000 but not over $183,250	$	× 28% (.28)	$	$ 6,706.75	$
Over $183,250 but not over $398,350	$	× 33% (.33)	$	$ 15,869.25	$
Over $398,350 but not over $400,000	$	× 35% (.35)	$	$ 23,836.25	$
Over $400,000	$	× 39.6% (.396)	$	$ 42,236.25	$

Section B— Use if your filing status is Married filing jointly or Qualifying widow(er). Complete the row below that applies to you.

Taxable income. If line 43 is—	(a) Enter the amount from line 43	(b) Multiplication amount	(c) Multiply (a) by (b)	(d) Subtraction amount	Tax. Subtract (d) from (c). Enter the result here and on Form 1040, line 44
At least $100,000 but not over $146,400	$	× 25% (.25)	$	$ 8,142.50	$
Over $146,400 but not over $223,050	$	× 28% (.28)	$	$ 12,534.50	$
Over $223,050 but not over $398,350	$	× 33% (.33)	$	$ 23,687.00	$
Over $398,350 but not over $450,000	$	× 35% (.35)	$	$ 31,654.00	$
Over $450,000	$	× 39.6% (.396)	$	$ 52,354.00	$

Section C— Use if your filing status is Married filing separately. Complete the row below that applies to you.

Taxable income. If line 43 is—	(a) Enter the amount from line 43	(b) Multiplication amount	(c) Multiply (a) by (b)	(d) Subtraction amount	Tax. Subtract (d) from (c). Enter the result here and on Form 1040, line 44
At least $100,000 but not over $111,525	$	× 28% (.28)	$	$ 6,267.25	$
Over $111,525 but not over $199,175	$	× 33% (.33)	$	$ 11,843.50	$
Over $199,175 but not over $225,000	$	× 35% (.35)	$	$ 15,827.00	$
Over $225,000	$	× 39.6% (.396)	$	$ 26,177.00	$

Section D— Use if your filing status is Head of household. Complete the row below that applies to you.

Taxable income. If line 43 is—	(a) Enter the amount from line 43	(b) Multiplication amount	(c) Multiply (a) by (b)	(d) Subtraction amount	Tax. Subtract (d) from (c). Enter the result here and on Form 1040, line 44
At least $100,000 but not over $125,450	$	× 25% (.25)	$	$ 5,497.50	$
Over $125,450 but not over $203,150	$	× 28% (.28)	$	$ 9,261.00	$
Over $203,150 but not over $398,350	$	× 33% (.33)	$	$ 19,418.50	$
Over $398,350 but not over $425,000	$	× 35% (.35)	$	$ 27,385.50	$
Over $425,000	$	× 39.6% (.396)	$	$ 46,935.50	$

2013 Tax Rate Schedules

TABLE 1 — Section 1(a) — Married Individuals Filing Joint Returns and Surviving Spouses

If Taxable Income Is:	The Tax Is:
Not over $17,850	10% of the taxable income
Over $17,850 but not over $72,500	$1,785 plus 15% of the excess over $17,850
Over $72,500 but not over $146,400	$9,982.50 plus 25% of the excess over $72,500
Over $146,400 but not over $223,050	$28,457.50 plus 28% of the excess over $146,400
Over $223,050 but not over $398,350	$49,919.50 plus 33% of the excess over $223,050
Over $398,350 but not over $450,000	$107,768.50 plus 35% of the excess over $398,350
Over $450,000	$125,846 plus 39.6% of the excess over $450,000

TABLE 2 — Section 1(b) — Heads of Households

If Taxable Income Is:	The Tax Is:
Not over $12,750	10% of the taxable income
Over $12,750 but not over $48,600	$1,275 plus 15% of the excess over $12,750
Over $48,600 but not over $125,450	$6,652.50 plus 25% of the excess over $48,600
Over $125,450 but not over $203,150	$25,865 plus 28% of the excess over $125,450
Over $203,150 but not over $398,350	$47,621 plus 33% of the excess over $203,150
Over $398,350 but not over $425,000	$112,037 plus 35% of the excess over $398,350
Over $425,000	$121,364.50 plus 39.6% of the excess over $425,000

TABLE 3 — Section 1(c) — Unmarried Individuals (other than Surviving Spouses and Heads of Households)

If Taxable Income Is:	The Tax Is:
Not over $8,925	10% of the taxable income
Over $8,925 but not over $36,250	$892.50 plus 15% of the excess over $8,925
Over $36,250 but not over $87,850	$4,991.25 plus 25% of the excess over $36,250
Over $87,850 but not over $183,250	$17,891.25 plus 28% of the excess over $87,850
Over $183,250 but not over $398,350	$44,603.25 plus 33% of the excess over $183,250
Over $398,350 but not over $400,000	$115,586.25 plus 35% of the excess over $398,350
Over $400,000	$116,163.75 plus 39.6% of the excess over $400,000

TABLE 4 — Section 1(d) — Married Individuals Filing Separate Returns

If Taxable Income Is:	The Tax Is:
Not over $8,925	10% of the taxable income
Over $8,925 but not over $36,250	$892.50 plus 15% of the excess over $8,925
Over $36,250 but not over $73,200	$4,991.25 plus 25% of the excess over $36,250
Over $73,200 but not over $111,525	$14,228.75 plus 28% of the excess over $73,200
Over $111,525 but not over $199,175	$24,959.75 plus 33% of the excess over $111,525
Over $199,175 but not over $225,000	$53,884.25 plus 35% of the excess over $199,175
Over $225,000	$62,923 plus 39.6% of the excess over $225,000

TABLE 5 — Section 1(e) — Estates and Trusts

If Taxable Income Is:	The Tax Is:
Not over $2,450	15% of the taxable income
Over $2,450 but not over $5,700	$367.50 plus 25% of the excess over $2,450
Over $5,700 but not over $8,750	$1,180 plus 28% of the excess over $5,700
Over $8,750 but not over $11,950	$2,034 plus 33% of the excess over $8,750
Over $11,950	$3,090 plus 39.6% of the excess over $11,950

NOTES

Q

R

Do you have everything you need for tax season?

CCH Tax Season Resource Checklist

CCH offers a suite of federal tax publications providing quick answers, practical guidance, and in-depth analysis in a full range of options—from guides, practice manuals and CPE courses to journals, newsletters and internet research libraries. Make CCH your source for federal tax return preparation guidance with helpful, time-saving products.

Federal Tax Practitioner's Guide (2014) *Price*: $399.95, Pub. Dec. 2013, 2,376 pages.
 Book #: 10035816-0001; eBook 10024473-0001

The New 3.8% Medicare Tax: In-Depth Analysis & Planning *Price*: $19.99, Pub. Oct. 2012, 60 pages. Book #: 10028633-0001; eBook: #0-1295-500

U.S. Master Tax Guide (2014) *Price:* $93.50 per copy. Pub.: Dec. 2013, 1,008 pages.
 Book #: 10006149-7777; eBook #: 10024523-0001

U.S. Master Depreciation Guide (2014) *Price:* $105.00 per copy. Pub.: Dec. 2013, 1,040 pages.
 Book #: 10009802-0005; eBook #: 10024484-0001

U.S. Master Estate & Gift Tax Guide (2014) *Price:* $109.50 per copy. Pub.: Dec. 2013, 550 pages.
 Book #: 10031732-0004; eBook #: 10024485-0001

CCH Accounting for Income Taxes, 2014 Edition *Price*: $292.95, Pub. June, 2013, 480 pages.
 Book #: 10030139-0004; eBook #: 10024441-0001

Internal Revenue Code (Winter 2014 Edition) *Price*: $138.00, Pub. Feb. 2014, 2 Vols.
 Book #: 10006146-7777; eBook #: 10024487-0001

Income Tax Regulations (Winter 2014 Edition) *Price*: $199.95, Pub. Dec. 2013; 6 Vols.
 Book #:10006147-7777; eBook #: 10027924-0001

State Tax Handbook (2014) *Price:* $99.95 per copy. Pub.: Dec. 2013; 696 pages.
 Book # 10034384-0005; eBook 10024482-0001

Business Tax Answer Book (2014) *Price:* $244.50 per copy. Pub.: Oct. 2013; 760 pages.
 Book # 10029993-0005; eBook 10024528-0001

Tax Planning Strategies (2013-2014) *Price*: $46.25; Pub. Aug. 2013, 196 pages.
 Book #: 10032108-0004; eBook #: 10024450-0001

Taxation of Individual Retirement Accounts (2013) *Price*: $373.00, Pub. April 2013, 1,224 pages. Book #: 10029988-0003; eBook: #10024438-0001

TAXES – The Tax Magazine (2014) Published monthly. *Price:* $435 Print: 1-9551-0001. Also available in electronic format on the CCH research system, Intelliconnect, and also now available as an App for the iPad. Visit the online store at CCHGroup.com or iTunes.

Top Federal Tax Issues for 2014 Course *Price:* $1.00 per copy (CPE grading and administration fee applicable). Pub.: Nov. 2013, 320 pages. Media #: 10024491-0001

To order or for more information on these and other CCH tax and accounting products and services, call 1-800-248-3248 or visit the Store at CCHGroup.com. **Please note:** eBook pricing is the same as the print pricing. Discount is offered if ordering both print and electronic versions.